Introduction to Management Science

A Modeling and Case Studies Approach with Spreadsheets

The McGraw-Hill/Irwin Series
Operations and Decision Sciences

*Available only through McGraw-Hill's PRIMIS Online Assets Library.

Olson and Shi
Introduction to Business Data Mining
First Edition

Orris
Basic Statistics Using Megastat and Excel
First Edition

Siegel
Practical Business Statistics
Fifth Edition

Wilson, Keating, and John Galt Solutions, Inc.
Business Forecasting
Fifth Edition

QUANTITATIVE METHODS AND MANAGEMENT SCIENCE

Hillier and Hillier
Introduction to Management Science: A Modeling and Case Studies Approach with Spreadsheets
Third Edition

Stevenson and Ozgur
Introduction to Management Science with Spreadsheets
First Edition

Kros
Spreadsheet Modeling for Business Decisions
First Edition

Introduction to Management Science

**A Modeling and Case Studies Approach
with Spreadsheets**

Third Edition

Frederick S. Hillier
Stanford University

Mark S. Hillier
University of Washington

Cases developed by
Karl Schmedders
Northwestern University

Molly Stephens
Quinn, Emanuel, Urquhart, Oliver & Hedges LLP

McGraw-Hill
Irwin

Boston   Burr Ridge, IL   Dubuque, IA   New York   San Francisco   St. Louis
Bangkok   Bogotá   Caracas   Kuala Lumpur   Lisbon   London   Madrid   Mexico City
Milan   Montreal   New Delhi   Santiago   Seoul   Singapore   Sydney   Taipei   Toronto

McGraw-Hill
Irwin

INTRODUCTION TO MANAGEMENT SCIENCE: A MODELING AND CASE STUDIES APPROACH WITH SPREADSHEETS

Published by McGraw-Hill/Irwin, a business unit of The McGraw-Hill Companies, Inc., 1221 Avenue of the Americas, New York, NY, 10020. Copyright © 2008, by The McGraw-Hill Companies, Inc. All rights reserved. No part of this publication may be reproduced or distributed in any form or by any means, or stored in a database or retrieval system, without the prior written consent of The McGraw-Hill Companies, Inc., including, but not limited to, in any network or other electronic storage or transmission, or broadcast for distance learning.

Some ancillaries, including electronic and print components, may not be available to customers outside the United States.

This book is printed on acid-free paper.

2 3 4 5 6 7 8 9 0 CCW/CCW 0 9 8

ISBN 978-0-07-312903-7
MHID 0-07-312903-8

Editorial director: *Stewart Mattson*
Executive editor: *Scott Isenberg*
Editorial assistant: *Katie Jones*
Marketing manager: *Sankha Basu*
Project manager: *Jim Labeots*
Production supervisor: *Gina Hangos*
Lead designer: *Matthew Baldwin*
Media project manager: *Matthew Perry*
Cover design: *Studio Montage*
Cover image: *© Getty Images*
Typeface: *10/12 Times New Roman*
Compositor: *Laserwords Private Limited*
Printer: *Courier Westford*

Library of Congress Cataloging-in-Publication Data

Hillier, Frederick S.
    Introduction to management science : a modeling and case strudies approach with spreadsheets / Frederick S. Hillier, Mark S. Hillier ; Cases developed by Karl Schmedders, Molly Stephens.—3rd ed.
        p. cm.—(The McGraw-Hill/Irwin series operations and decision sciences)
    Includes index.
    ISBN-13: 978-0-07-312903-7 (alk. paper)
    ISBN-10: 0-07-312903-8 (alk. paper)
    1. Management science. 2. Operations research. I. Hillier, Mark S. II. Title.
T56.H55 2008
658.4'032—dc22

                                                                2006036715

www.mhhe.com

To our wives—Ann and Christine—for their steadfast support and to the memory of a beloved mentor, Gerald J. Lieberman, who was one of the true giants of our field

Frederick S. Hillier
Mark S. Hillier

About the Authors

Frederick S. Hillier is professor emeritus of operations research at Stanford University. Dr. Hillier is especially known for his classic, award-winning text, *Introduction to Operations Research,* co-authored with the late Gerald J. Lieberman, which has been translated into well over a dozen languages and is currently in its 8th edition. The 6th edition won honorable mention for the 1995 Lanchester Prize (best English-language publication of any kind in the field) and Dr. Hillier also was awarded the 2004 INFORMS Expository Writing Award for the 8th edition. His other books include *The Evaluation of Risky Interrelated Investments, Queueing Tables and Graphs, Introduction to Stochastic Models in Operations Research,* and *Introduction to Mathematical Programming.* He received his BS in industrial engineering and doctorate specializing in operations research and management science from Stanford University. The winner of many awards in high school and college for writing, mathematics, debate, and music, he ranked first in his undergraduate engineering class and was awarded three national fellowships (National Science Foundation, Tau Beta Pi, and Danforth) for graduate study. Dr. Hillier's research has extended into a variety of areas, including integer programming, queueing theory and its application, statistical quality control, and production and operations management. He also has won a major prize for research in capital budgeting. Twice elected a national officer of professional societies, he has served in many important professional and editorial capacities. For example, he served The Institute of Management Sciences as vice president for meetings, chairman of the publications committee, associate editor of *Management Science,* and co-general chairman of an international meeting. He currently is continuing to serve as the founding series editor for the International Series in Operations Research and Management Science for Springer Science + Business Media. He has had visiting appointments at Cornell University, the Graduate School of Industrial Administration of Carnegie-Mellon University, the Technical University of Denmark, the University of Canterbury (New Zealand), and the Judge Institute of Management Studies at the University of Cambridge (England).

Mark S. Hillier, son of Fred Hillier, is associate professor of quantitative methods at the School of Business at the University of Washington. Dr. Hillier received his BS in engineering (plus a concentration in computer science) from Swarthmore College, and he received his MS with distinction in operations research and PhD in industrial engineering and engineering management from Stanford University. As an undergraduate, he won the McCabe Award for ranking first in his engineering class, won election to Phi Beta Kappa based on his work in mathematics, set school records on the men's swim team, and was awarded two national fellowships (National Science Foundation and Tau Beta Pi) for graduate study. During that time, he also developed a comprehensive software tutorial package, *OR Courseware,* for the Hillier-Lieberman textbook, *Introduction to Operations Research.* As a graduate student, he taught a PhD-level seminar in operations management at Stanford and won a national prize for work based on his PhD dissertation. At the University of Washington, he currently teaches courses in management science and spreadsheet modeling. He has won several MBA teaching awards for the core course in management science and his elective course in spreadsheet modeling, as well as a universitywide teaching award for his work in teaching undergraduate classes in operations management. He also has been awarded an appointment to the Evert McCabe Endowed Faculty Fellowship. His research interests include issues in component commonality, inventory, manufacturing, and the design of production systems. A paper by Dr. Hillier on component commonality won an award for best paper of 2000–2001 in *IIE Transactions.*

About the Case Writers

Karl Schmedders is an associate professor with tenure in the Department of Managerial Economics and Decision Sciences at the Kellogg School of Management at Northwestern University, where he teaches quantitative methods for managerial decision making. His research interests include applications of management science in economic theory, general equilibrium theory with incomplete markets, asset pricing, portfolio choice, and computational economics. Dr. Schmedders received his doctorate in operations research from Stanford University, where he taught both undergraduate and graduate classes in management science. Among the classes taught was a case studies course in management science and he subsequently was invited to speak at a conference sponsored by the Institute of Operations Research and Management Sciences (INFORMS) about his successful experience with this course. He received several teaching awards at Stanford, including the university's prestigious Walter J. Gores Teaching Award. He also has received several awards at both the Kellogg School of Management and the WHU Koblenz (a leading business school in Germany).

Molly Stephens is an associate in the Los Angeles office of Quinn, Emanuel, Urquhart, Oliver & Hedges, LLP. She graduated from Stanford with a BS in industrial engineering and an MS in operations research. Ms. Stephens taught public speaking in Stanford's School of Engineering and served as a teaching assistant for a case studies course in management science. As a teaching assistant, she analyzed management science problems encountered in the real world and transformed these into classroom case studies. Her research was rewarded when she won an undergraduate research grant from Stanford to continue her work and was invited to speak at INFORMS to present her conclusions regarding successful classroom case studies. Following graduation, Ms. Stephens worked at Andersen Consulting as a systems integrator, experiencing real cases from the inside, before receiving her JD degree from the University of Texas School of Law.

Preface

We have long been concerned that traditional management science textbooks have not taken the best approach in introducing business students to this exciting field. Our goal when developing this book was to break out of the old mold and present new and innovative ways of teaching management science more effectively. We have been gratified by the favorable response to our efforts. Many reviewers and other users of the first two editions of the book have expressed appreciation for its various distinctive features, as well as for its clear presentation at just the right level for their business students.

Our goal for this third edition has been to build on the strengths of the first two editions. Co-author Mark Hillier has won several schoolwide teaching awards for his spreadsheet modeling and management science courses at the University of Washington while using the first two editions, and this experience has led to many improvements in the current edition. We also incorporated many user comments and suggestions. Throughout this process, we took painstaking care to enhance the quality of the preceding edition while maintaining the distinctive orientation of the book.

This distinctive orientation is one that closely follows the recommendations in the 1996 report of the operating subcommittee of the INFORMS Business School Education Task Force, including the following extract.

> There is clear evidence that there must be a major change in the character of the (introductory management science) course in this environment. There is little patience with courses centered on algorithms. Instead, the demand is for courses that focus on business situations, include prominent non-mathematical issues, use spreadsheets, and involve model formulation and assessment more than model structuring. Such a course requires new teaching materials.

This book is designed to provide the teaching materials for such a course.

In line with the recommendations of this task force, we believe that a modern introductory management science textbook should have three key elements. As summarized in the subtitle of this book, these elements are a *modeling* and *case studies* approach with *spreadsheets.*

SPREADSHEETS

The modern approach to the teaching of management science clearly is to use spreadsheets as a primary medium of instruction. Both business students and managers now live with spreadsheets, so they provide a comfortable and enjoyable learning environment. Modern spreadsheet software, including Microsoft Excel used in this book, now can be used to do real management science. For student-scale models (which include many practical real-world models), spreadsheets are a much better way of implementing management science models than traditional algebraic solvers. This means that the algebraic curtain that was so prevalent in traditional management science courses and textbooks now can be lifted.

However, with the new enthusiasm for spreadsheets, there is a danger of going overboard. Spreadsheets are not the only useful tool for performing management science analyses. Occasional modest use of algebraic and graphical analyses still have their place and we would be doing a disservice to the students by not developing their skills in these areas when appropriate. Furthermore, the book should not be mainly a spreadsheet cookbook that focuses largely on spreadsheet mechanics. Spreadsheets are a means to an end, not an end in themselves.

A MODELING APPROACH

This brings us to the second key feature of the book, a *modeling approach.* Model formulation lies at the heart of management science methodology. Therefore, we heavily emphasize the art of model formulation, the role of a model, and the analysis of model results. We primarily (but not exclusively) use a spreadsheet format rather than algebra for formulating and presenting a model.

Some instructors have many years of experience in teaching modeling in terms of formulating algebraic models (or what the INFORMS Task Force called "model structuring"). Some of these instructors feel that students should do their modeling in this way and then transfer the model to a spreadsheet simply to use the Excel Solver to solve the model. We disagree with this approach. Our experience (and the experience reported by many others) is that most business students find it more natural and comfortable to do their modeling directly in a spreadsheet. Furthermore, by using the best spreadsheet modeling techniques (as presented in this edition), formulating a spreadsheet model tends to be considerably more efficient and transparent than formulating an algebraic model.

Another break from tradition in this book (and several contemporary textbooks) is to virtually ignore the algorithms that are used to solve the models. We feel that there is no good reason why typical business students should learn the details of algorithms executed by computers. Within the time constraints of a one-term management science course, there are far more important lessons to be learned. Therefore, the focus in this book is on what we believe are these far more important lessons. High on this list is the art of modeling managerial problems on a spreadsheet.

Formulating a spreadsheet model of a real problem typically involves much more than designing the spreadsheet and entering the data. Therefore, we work through the process step by step: understand the unstructured problem, verbally develop some structure for the problem, gather the data, express the relationships in quantitative terms, and then lay out the spreadsheet model. The structured approach highlights the typical components of the model (the data, the decisions to be made, the constraints, and the measure of performance) and the different types of spreadsheet cells used for each. Consequently, the emphasis is on the modeling rather than spreadsheet mechanics.

A CASE STUDIES APPROACH

However, all this still would be quite sterile if we simply presented a long series of brief examples with their spreadsheet formulations. This leads to the third key feature of this book—a *case studies* approach. In addition to examples, essentially every chapter includes one or two case studies patterned after actual applications to convey the whole process of applying management science. In a few instances, the entire chapter revolves around a case study. By drawing the student into the story, we have designed each case study to bring that chapter's technique to life in a context that vividly illustrates the relevance of the technique for aiding managerial decision making. This storytelling, case-centered approach should make the material more enjoyable and stimulating while also conveying the practical considerations that are key factors in applying management science.

We have been pleased to have several reviewers of the first two editions express particular appreciation for our case study approach. Even though this approach has received little use in other management science textbooks, we feel that it is a real key to preparing students for the practical application of management science in all its aspects. Some of the reviewers have highlighted the effectiveness of the dialogue/scenario enactment approach used in some of the case studies. Although unconventional, this approach provides a way of demonstrating the process of managerial decision making with the help of management science. It also enables previewing some key concepts in the language of management.

Except for Chapter 1, every chapter also contains full-fledged cases following the problems at the end of the chapter. These cases usually continue to employ a stimulating storytelling approach, so they can be assigned as interesting and challenging projects. Most of these cases were developed jointly by two talented case writers, Karl Schmedders (a faculty member at the Kellogg School of Management at Northwestern University) and Molly Stephens (formerly a management science consultant with Andersen Consulting). The authors also have added some cases, including several shorter ones.

We are, of course, not the first to incorporate any of these key features into a management science textbook. However, we believe that the book currently is unique in the way that it fully incorporates all three key features together.

OTHER SPECIAL FEATURES

We also should mention some additional special features of the book that are continued from the second edition.

- Diverse examples, problems, and cases convey the pervasive relevance of management science.
- A strong managerial perspective.
- Learning objectives at the beginning of each chapter.
- Numerous margin notes that clarify and highlight key points.
- Excel tips interspersed among the margin notes.
- Review questions at the end of each section.
- A glossary at the end of each chapter.
- Partial answers to selected problems in the back of the book.
- Supplementary text material on the CD-ROM (as identified in the table of contents).
- An Excel-based software package (MS Courseware) on the CD-ROM that includes many add-ins, templates, and files (described below).
- Other helpful supplements on both the student's CD-ROM and the instructor's CD-ROM (described later).

SOFTWARE

The second edition provided a comprehensive Excel-based software package called *MS Courseware* on the student's CD-ROM. The most current version of virtually this entire package is being provided again with the current edition.

This package includes Excel files that provide the live spreadsheets for all the various examples and case studies throughout the book. In addition to further investigating the examples and case studies, these spreadsheets can be used by either the student or instructor as templates to formulate and solve similar problems. The package also includes dozens of Excel templates for solving various models in the book.

Another key resource in the MS Courseware is a collection of Excel add-ins that are integrated into the corresponding chapters.

- **Solver Table** for automating sensitivity analysis in optimization problems (used in several chapters, including especially Chapter 5).
- **Premium Solver for Education**, including its powerful Evolutionary Solver for solving difficult optimization problems (featured in Section 8.5).
- **TreePlan** for generating and analyzing decision trees for decision analysis (used throughout Chapter 9).
- **SensIt** for performing sensitivity analysis with probabilistic systems (used mainly in Chapter 9).
- **RiskSim** for performing basic computer simulations (introduced in Chapter 12).
- **Crystal Ball Professional Edition** for performing a variety of computer simulations (used throughout Chapter 13).
- **CB Predictor** (a module of Crystal Ball) for applying various time-series forecasting methods (featured in the supplement to Chapter 10).
- **OptQuest** (a module of Crystal Ball Professional Edition) for combining computer simulation with an advanced optimization technique (featured in the supplement to Chapter 13).

MS Courseware includes additional software as well.

- **Interactive Management Science Modules** for interactively exploring certain management science techniques in depth (including techniques presented in Chapters 1, 2, 5, 10, 11, 12, and 18).
- **Queueing Simulator** for performing computer simulations of queueing systems (used in Chapter 12).

NEW FEATURES IN THIS EDITION

We have made many important enhancements to the third edition.

- **A Major Streamlining of the Book.** The 870 pages of the second edition provided a considerably more comprehensive introduction to management science than could be covered well in the usual one-term course. Therefore, we have very substantially reduced the size of this new edition to better fit the usual course. This was achieved largely by eliminating three chapters that feedback indicated were seldom being used, namely, the chapters on (1) PERT/CPM Models for Project Management (now commonly covered in an operations management course instead), (2) Goal Programming (seldom covered), and (3) Transportation and Assignment Problems (seldom covered in this depth so a far briefer introduction has been added to another chapter). The danger with eliminating any chapter of course is that it may be one of the favorite chapters of some instructor somewhere, so all three of these chapters are still being made available on the CD-ROM. Considerably more streamlining was achieved by eliminating over a dozen relatively unimportant sections in other chapters (but most of this material also is still available on the CD-ROM). In addition, the material in certain other sections (including some managerial dialogues) has been condensed. We think that the net effect of all this streamlining has been to bring a sharper focus on the essentials of management science.

- **A Modest Reorganization.** We have reversed the order of the previous Chapter 3 (The Art of Modeling with Spreadsheets) and Chapter 4 (Linear Programming: Formulation and Applications) so that Chapter 2 (Linear Programming: Basic Concepts) could flow directly into its companion chapter. Because the previous Chapter 6 (Transportation and Assignment Problems) now has been transferred to the CD-ROM, we also have added both a section on transportation problems and a section on assignment problems to the new Chapter 3. Otherwise, the ordering of the chapters remaining in the book is the same as in the second edition.

- **Integration of the New Excel 2007.** The new Excel 2007 represents by far the most major revision of Excel and its user interface in many, many years. Therefore, to avoid being immediately outdated, we delayed the publication of this edition for several months in order to fully integrate Excel 2007. Since some users will continue to use older versions of Excel for awhile, we also point out the differences.

- **A Complete Revision of Integer Programming Material.** The previous Chapter 9 (Integer Programming) has been transformed into the new Chapter 7 (Using Binary Integer Programming to Deal with Yes-or-No Decisions). Previous material on general integer programming has been integrated into the second chapter on linear programming (because the formulations are so similar) so the new chapter can focus solely on binary integer programming and its applications. This new chapter includes new sections on project selection, site selection, crew scheduling, and dealing with setup costs for initiating production. Advanced formulation techniques for binary integer programming presented in the second edition now has been shifted to the CD-ROM.

- **A New Overview of Forecasting Techniques.** Chapter 10 (Forecasting) has a new initial section that presents an overview of forecasting techniques. Since many courses provide only a very brief introduction to forecasting, this section provides the needed textual material for such a course. For courses that cover forecasting in greater depth, this section eases the way into the in-depth coverage in the remainder of the chapter.

- **New Application Vignettes.** Twenty application vignettes have been added throughout the book. These vignettes succinctly describe recent actual applications of management science that had a dramatic impact on their companies by using techniques similar to those currently being covered in the book. To avoid disrupting the flow of textual material while also highlighting the application, these vignettes are enclosed in shaded boxes.

- **New Solved Problems.** One or more solved problems now have been added to every chapter in the book. The solved problems for each chapter are presented just before the Problems section for that chapter and then the complete solutions are spelled out on the CD-ROM.

Since these solved problems are typical of the problems in the Problems section, these solutions will help guide students through their homework.

- **Supplementary Cases from the Ivey School.** The University of Western Ontario Ivey School of Business (the second-largest producer of teaching cases in the world) now has specially selected cases from their case collection that match the chapters in this textbook. These cases are available on the Ivey Web site, www.cases.ivey.uwo.ca/case, in the segment of the CaseMate area designated for this book. These cases supplement the dozens of cases already provided in this book.

- **A New Appendix on Using Microsoft Excel.** We have added a new appendix (Tips for Using Microsoft Excel for Modeling) to highlight some features of Excel that are particularly useful for modeling.

- **A New Appendix on Using the Solver Table.** The Solver Table is used extensively in Chapter 5 and also comes up in certain other chapters. To provide a central reference on the Solver Table, we have added a new appendix that describes how to use this Excel add-in.

CHANGES IN INDIVIDUAL CHAPTERS

Each chapter in the second edition has been carefully examined and revised as needed to update the material and (when appropriate) to streamline the presentation. The more significant changes are mentioned below.

- **Chapter 1 (Introduction).** In addition to deleting one section, the presentation of the break-even analysis example has been revised by moving the spreadsheet modeling in front of the algebraic modeling.

- **Chapter 2 (Linear Programming: Basic Concepts).** In addition to deleting one section, the presentation of the graphical method has been substantially condensed (but with a full presentation available on the CD-ROM).

- **Chapter 3 (Linear Programming: Formulation and Applications).** This chapter has been substantially condensed and reorganized. The category of distribution-network problems has been replaced by the categories of transportation problems and assignment problems. The relatively complicated example on the management of solid wastes has been converted into an end-of-chapter case.

- **Chapter 4 (The Art of Modeling with Spreadsheets).** No major changes except for integrating Excel 2007.

- **Chapter 5 (What-If Analysis for Linear Programming).** In addition to adding an appendix on installing and using the Solver Table, a chapter supplement on reduced costs now is available on the CD-ROM.

- **Chapter 6 (Network Optimization Problems).** The section on minimum spanning-tree problems has been shifted to the CD-ROM as a chapter supplement.

- **Chapter 7 (Using Binary Integer Programming to Deal with Yes-or-No Decisions).** This chapter has been extensively revised as described in the previous section.

- **Chapter 8 (Nonlinear Programming).** We have added a subsection on applying Evolutionary Solver to a traveling salesman problem.

- **Chapter 9 (Decision Analysis).** We have added the expected value of sample information and simplified the treatment of utilities, including the lottery method for determining utilities. We also added two end-of-chapter cases that are less involved than the two cases that already are there.

- **Chapter 10 (Forecasting).** Three sections have been deleted (including the section on time-series forecasting with CB Predictor that has been shifted to the CD-ROM as a chapter supplement), but with an overview of forecasting techniques added as the initial section (as described above).

- **Chapter 11 (Queueing Models).** In addition to deleting one section, the Erlang models have been shifted to the CD-ROM as part of a chapter supplement.

- **Chapter 12 (Computer Simulation: Basic Concepts).** In addition to deleting one section, the section describing the outline of a major computer simulation study has been substantially condensed. The inverse transformation method has been shifted to the CD-ROM as a chapter supplement. One minor addition is the concept of a seed value for pseudo-random numbers.
- **Chapter 13 (Computer Simulation with Crystal Ball).** Crystal Ball has evolved substantially since the publication of the second edition, so many changes were needed to incorporate the current version of Crystal Ball Professional Edition. The organization of the chapter has remained the same with one exception. Because the new substantially updated version of OptQuest will not be available for another several months at the time of this writing, we will update the section on Optimizing with OptQuest later and transfer it to the book's web site as a chapter supplement.

OTHER SUPPLEMENTS

An instructor's CD-ROM is being provided with this edition. This CD-ROM includes complete solutions to all problems and cases, which will be handy for cutting and pasting homework solutions. Also included is a test bank with computest that includes hundreds of multiple-choice and true-false questions. Presentation materials on PowerPoint slides also are provided. These slides include both lecture materials for nearly every chapter and nearly all the figures (including all the spreadsheets) in the book.

The student's CD-ROM bundled with the book provides the entire MS Courseware package. It also includes a tutorial with sample test questions (different from those in the instructor's test bank) for self-testing quizzes on the various chapters.

A Web page will provide updates about the book, including an errata. To access this site, visit **www.mhhe.com/hillier3e.** In addition, the publisher's operations management supersite at **www.mhhe.com/pom/** links to many resources on the Internet that you might find pertinent to this book.

We invite your comments, suggestions, and errata. You can contact either one of us at the e-mail addresses given below. While giving these addresses, let us also assure instructors that we will continue our policy of not providing solutions to problems and cases in the book to anybody (including your students) who contacts us. We hope that you enjoy the book.

Frederick S. Hillier
Stanford University (fhillier@stanford.edu)

Mark S. Hillier
University of Washington (mhillier@u.washington.edu)

September 2006

Acknowledgments

This new edition has benefited greatly from the sage advice of many individuals. To begin, we would like to express our deep appreciation to the following individuals who provided formal reviews of the second edition:

Thomas Barto
Centenary College

Jim Frendewey
Michigan Technological University

Jim Grayson
Augusta State University

David A. Haas
Kutztown University of Pennsylvania

John Hocking
American Intercontinental University

Jeff Keisler
University of Massachusetts–Boston

Larry Meile
Boston College

Susan Palocsay
James Madison University

Madhu Rao
Bowling Green University

Emily Roth
Bentley College

Harvey Singer
School of Management, George Mason University

Minghe Sun
The University of Texas at San Antonio

Jiamin Wang
Long Island University

Dr. Kari A. Wood
Bemidji State University

Jack Yurkiewicz
Pace University–Lubin School of Business

We also are grateful for the valuable input provided by many of our students as well as various other students and instructors who contacted us via e-mail.

This book has continued to be a team effort involving far more than the two coauthors. As a third co-author for the first edition, the late Gerald J. Lieberman provided important initial impetus for this project. We also are indebted to our case writers, Karl Schmedders and Molly Stephens, for their invaluable contributions. Ann Hillier again devoted numerous long days and nights to sitting with a Macintosh, doing word processing and constructing many figures and tables. While caring for two children, Christine Hillier also managed to devote many hours to supporting the preparation of this new edition. They all were vital members of the team.

McGraw-Hill/Irwin's editorial and production staff provided the other key members of the team, including Scott Isenberg (Executive Editor), Robin Reed (Developmental Editor from Carlisle Publishing Services), and Jim Labeots (Project Manager). This book is a much better product because of their guidance and hard work. It has been a real pleasure working with such a thoroughly professional staff.

Brief Contents

Contents

Chapter **One**

Introduction

Learning objectives

After completing this chapter, you should be able to

1. Define the term *management science.*
2. Describe the nature of management science.
3. Explain what a mathematical model is.
4. Use a mathematical model to perform break-even analysis.
5. Use a spreadsheet model to perform break-even analysis.
6. Identify some special features of this book.

Welcome to the field of *management science!* We think that it is a particularly exciting and interesting field. Exciting because management science is having a dramatic impact on the profitability of numerous business firms around the world. Interesting because the methods used to do this are so ingenious. We are looking forward to giving you a guided tour to introduce you to the special features of the field.

Some students approach a course (and textbook) about management science with a certain amount of anxiety and skepticism. The main source of the anxiety is the reputation of the field as being highly mathematical. This reputation then generates skepticism that such a theoretical approach can have much relevance for dealing with practical managerial problems. Most traditional courses (and textbooks) about management science have only reinforced these perceptions by emphasizing the mathematics of the field rather than its practical application.

Rest easy. This is not a traditional management science textbook. We realize that most readers of this book are aspiring to become managers, not mathematicians. Therefore, the emphasis throughout is on conveying what a future manager needs to know about management science. Yes, this means including a little mathematics here and there, because it is a major language of the field. The mathematics you do see will be at the level of high school algebra plus (in the later chapters) basic concepts of elementary probability theory. We think you will be pleasantly surprised by the new appreciation you gain for how useful and intuitive mathematics at this level can be. However, managers do not need to know any of the heavy mathematical theory that underlies the various techniques of management science. Therefore, the use of mathematics plays only a strictly secondary role in the book.

One reason we can deemphasize mathematics is that powerful *spreadsheet packages* now are available for applying management science. Spreadsheets provide a comfortable and familiar environment for formulating and analyzing managerial problems. The spreadsheet package takes care of applying the necessary mathematics automatically in the background with only a minimum of guidance by the user. This has begun to revolutionize the use of management science. In the past, technically trained management scientists were needed to carry out significant management science studies for management. Now spreadsheets are bringing many of the tools and concepts of management science within the reach of managers for conducting their own analyses. Although busy managers will continue to call upon management science teams to conduct major studies for them, they are increasingly becoming direct users themselves through the medium of spreadsheet packages. Therefore, since this book is aimed at future managers (and management consultants), we will emphasize the use of spreadsheets for applying management science.

What does an enlightened future manager need to learn from a management science course?

1. Gain an appreciation for the relevance and power of management science. (Therefore, we will give many examples of *actual applications* of management science and the *impact* they had on the organizations involved.)
2. Learn to recognize when management science can (and cannot) be fruitfully applied. (Therefore, we will emphasize the *kinds of problems* to which the various management science techniques can be applied.)
3. Learn how to apply the major techniques of management science to analyze a variety of managerial problems. (Therefore, we will focus largely on how spreadsheets enable many such applications with no more background in management science than provided by this book.)
4. Develop an understanding of how to interpret the results of a management science study. (Therefore, we will present many *case studies* that illustrate management science studies and how their results depend on the assumptions and data that were used.)

The objectives just described are the key teaching goals of this book.

We begin this process in the next two sections by introducing the nature of management science and the impact that it is having on many organizations. (These themes will continue throughout the remaining chapters as well.) Section 1.3 then points out some of the special features of this book that you can look forward to seeing in the subsequent chapters.

1.1 THE NATURE OF MANAGEMENT SCIENCE

What is the name *management science* (sometimes abbreviated MS) supposed to convey? It does involve *management* and *science* or, more precisely, *the science of management,* but this still is too vague. Here is a more suggestive definition.

> Management science is a *discipline* that attempts to *aid managerial decision making* by applying a *scientific approach* to managerial problems that involve *quantitative factors.*

Now let us see how elaborating upon each of the italicized terms in this definition conveys much more about the nature of management science.

Management Science Is a Discipline

As a discipline, management science is a whole body of knowledge and techniques that are based on a scientific foundation. For example, it is analogous in some ways to the medical field. A medical doctor has been trained in a whole body of knowledge and techniques that are based on the scientific foundations of the medical field. After receiving this training and entering practice, the doctor must diagnose a patient's illness and then choose the appropriate medical procedures to apply to the illness. The patient then makes the final decision on which medical procedures to accept. For less serious cases, the patient may choose not to consult a doctor and instead use his own basic knowledge of medical principles to treat himself. Similarly, a management scientist must receive substantial training (albeit considerably less than for a medical doctor). This training also is in a whole body of knowledge and techniques that are based on the scientific foundations of the discipline. After entering practice, the management scientist must diagnose a managerial problem and then choose the appropriate management science techniques to apply in analyzing the problem. The cognizant manager then makes the final decision as to which conclusions from this analysis to accept. For less extensive managerial problems where management science can be helpful, the manager may choose not to consult a management scientist and instead use his or her own basic knowledge of management science principles to analyze the problem.

Although it has considerably longer roots, the rapid development of the discipline began in the 1940s and 1950s. The initial impetus came early in World War II, when large numbers of scientists were called upon to apply a scientific approach to the management of the war effort for the allies. Another landmark event was the discovery in 1947 by George Dantzig of the *simplex method* for solving linear programming problems. (Linear programming is the subject of several early chapters.) Another factor that gave great impetus to the growth of the discipline was the onslaught of the computer revolution.

The traditional name given to the discipline (and the one that still is widely used today outside of business schools) is **operations research.** This name was applied because the teams of scientists in World War II were doing *research* on how to manage military *operations.* The abbreviation OR also is widely used. This abbreviation often is combined with the one for management science (MS), thereby referring to the discipline as OR/MS.

One major international professional society for the discipline is the *Institute for Operations Research and the Management Sciences* (INFORMS). Headquartered in the United States, with over 10,000 members, this society holds major conferences in the United States each year plus occasional conferences elsewhere. It also publishes several prominent journals, including *Management Science, Operations Research,* and *Interfaces.* (Articles describing actual applications of management science are featured in *Interfaces,* so you will see many references to this journal throughout the book.)

In addition, there now are a few dozen member countries in the *International Federation of Operational Research Societies* (IFORS), with each member country having a national operations research society. Both Europe and Asia also have federations of operations research societies to coordinate holding international conferences and publishing international journals in those continents.

Thus, operations research/management science (OR/MS) is a truly international discipline. (We hereafter will just use the name *management science.*)

operations research
Management science began its rapid development during World War II with the name *operations research.*

Management Science Aids Managerial Decision Making

The key word here is that management science *aids* managerial decision making. Management scientists don't make managerial decisions. Managers do. A management science study only provides an analysis and recommendations, based on the quantitative factors involved in the problem, as input to the cognizant managers. Managers must also take into account various intangible considerations that are outside the realm of management science and then use their best judgment to make the decision. Sometimes managers find that qualitative factors are as important as quantitative factors in making a decision.

A small informal management science study might be conducted by just a single individual, who may be the cognizant manager. However, management science *teams* normally are used for larger studies. (We often will use the term *team* to cover both cases throughout the book.) Such a team often includes some members who are not management scientists but who provide other types of expertise needed for the study. Although a management science team often is entirely *in-house* (employees of the company), part or all of the team may instead be *consultants* who have been hired for just the one study. Consulting firms that partially or entirely specialize in management science currently are a growing industry.

Management Science Uses a Scientific Approach

Management science is based strongly on some scientific fields, including mathematics and computer science. It also draws on the social sciences, especially economics. Since the field is concerned with the practical management of organizations, a management scientist should have solid training in business administration, including its various functional areas, as well.

To a considerable extent, a management science team will attempt to use the *scientific method* in conducting its study. This means that the team will emphasize conducting a *systematic investigation* that includes careful data gathering, developing and testing hypotheses about the problem (typically in the form of a mathematical model), and then applying sound logic in the subsequent analysis.

When conducting this systematic investigation, the management science team typically will follow the (overlapping) steps outlined and described below.

Step 1: Define the problem and gather data. In this step, the team consults with management to clearly identify the problem of concern and ascertain the appropriate objectives for the study. The team then typically spends a surprisingly large amount of time gathering relevant data about the problem with the assistance of other key individuals in the organization. A common frustration is that some key data are either very rough or completely unavailable. This may necessitate installing a new computer-based management information system.

Fortunately, the rapid development of the *information technology (IT)* field in recent years is leading to a dramatic improvement in the quantity and quality of data that may be available to the management science (MS) team. Corporate IT now is often able to provide the computational resources and databases that are needed by the MS team. Thus, the MS team often will collaborate closely with the IT group.

Step 2: Formulate a model (typically a mathematical model) to represent the problem. Models, or approximate representations, are an integral part of everyday life. Common examples include model airplanes, portraits, globes, and so on. Similarly, models play an important role in science and business, as illustrated by models of the atom, models of genetic structure, mathematical equations describing physical laws of motion or chemical reactions, graphs, organization charts, and industrial accounting systems. Such models are invaluable for abstracting the essence of the subject of inquiry, showing interrelationships, and facilitating analysis.

Mathematical models are also approximate representations, but they are expressed in terms of mathematical symbols and expressions. Such laws of physics as $F = ma$ and $E = mc^2$ are familiar examples. Similarly, the mathematical model of a business problem is the system of equations and related mathematical expressions that describes the essence of the problem.

With the emergence of powerful spreadsheet technology, **spreadsheet models** now are widely used to analyze managerial problems. A spreadsheet model lays out the relevant data, measures of performance, interrelationships, and so forth, on a spreadsheet in an organized way that facilitates fruitful analysis of the problem. It also frequently incorporates an underlying mathematical model to assist in the analysis, but the mathematics is kept in the background so the user can concentrate on the analysis.

The *modeling process* is a creative one. When dealing with real managerial problems (as opposed to some cut-and-dried textbook problems), there normally is no single "correct" model but rather a number of alternative ways to approach the problem. The modeling process also is typically an evolutionary process that begins with a simple "verbal model" to define the essence of the problem and then gradually evolves into increasingly more complete mathematical models (perhaps in a spreadsheet format).

We further describe and illustrate such mathematical models in the next section.

Step 3: Develop a computer-based procedure for deriving solutions to the problem from the model. The beauty of a well-designed mathematical model is that it enables the use of mathematical procedures to find good solutions to the problem. These procedures usually are run on a computer because the calculations are too extensive to be done by hand. In some cases, the management science team will need to develop the procedure. In others, a standard software package already will be available for solving the model. When the mathematical model is incorporated into a spreadsheet, the spreadsheet package normally includes a Solver that usually will solve the model.

Step 4: Test the model and refine it as needed. Now that the model can be solved, the team needs to thoroughly check and test the model to make sure that it provides a sufficiently accurate representation of the real problem. A number of questions should be addressed, perhaps with the help of others who are particularly familiar with the problem. Have all the relevant factors and interrelationships in the problem been accurately incorporated into the model? Does the model seem to provide reasonable solutions? When it is applied to a past situation, does the solution improve upon what was actually done? When assumptions about costs and revenues are changed, do the solutions change in a plausible manner?

Step 5: Apply the model to analyze the problem and develop recommendations for management. The management science team now is ready to solve the model, perhaps under a variety of assumptions, in order to analyze the problem. The resulting recommendations then are presented to the managers who must make the decisions about how to deal with the problem.

If the model is to be applied repeatedly to help guide decisions on an ongoing basis, the team might also develop a **decision support system.** This is an interactive computer-based system that aids managerial decision making. The system draws current data from *databases* or *management information systems* and then solves the various versions of the model specified by the manager.

Step 6: Help to implement the team's recommendations that are adopted by management. Once management makes its decisions, the management science team normally is asked to help oversee the implementation of the new procedures. This includes providing some information to the operating management and personnel involved on the rationale for the changes that are being made. The team also makes sure that the new operating system is consistent with its recommendations as they have been modified and approved by management. If successful, the new system may be used for years to come. With this in mind, the team monitors the initial experience with the system and seeks to identify any modifications that should be made in the future.

Management Science Considers Quantitative Factors

Many managerial problems revolve around such quantitative factors as production quantities, revenues, costs, the amounts available of needed resources, and so on. By incorporating these quantitative factors into a *mathematical model* and then applying mathematical procedures to solve the model, management science provides a uniquely powerful way of analyzing such managerial problems. Although management science is concerned with the practical management of organizations, including taking into account relevant qualitative factors, its special contribution lies in this unique ability to deal with the quantitative factors.

The Special Products Company example discussed below will illustrate how management science considers quantitative factors.

Review
Questions

1. When did the rapid development of the management science discipline begin?
2. What is the traditional name given to this discipline that still is widely used outside of business schools?
3. What does a management science study provide to managers to aid their decision making?
4. Upon which scientific fields and social sciences is management science especially based?
5. What is a *decision support system?*
6. What are some common quantitative factors around which many managerial problems revolve?

1.2   AN ILLUSTRATION OF THE MANAGEMENT SCIENCE APPROACH: BREAK-EVEN ANALYSIS

The Special Products Company produces expensive and unusual gifts to be sold in stores that cater to affluent customers who already have everything. The latest new-product proposal to management from the company's Research Department is a limited edition grandfather clock. Management needs to decide whether to introduce this new product and, if so, how many of these grandfather clocks to produce. Before making this decision, a sales forecast will be obtained to estimate how many clocks can be sold. Management wishes to make the decision that will maximize the company's profit.

A cost that remains the same regardless of the production volume is referred to as a *fixed cost,* whereas a cost that varies with the production volume is called a *variable cost.*

If the company goes ahead with this product, a *fixed cost* of $50,000 would be incurred for setting up the production facilities to produce this product. (Note that this cost would *not* be incurred if management decided *not* to introduce the product since the setup then would not be done.) In addition to this fixed cost, there is a production cost that varies with the number of clocks produced. This *variable cost* is $400 per clock produced, which adds up to $400 *times* the number of clocks produced. (The cost for each additional unit produced, $400, is referred to as the *marginal cost.*) Each clock sold would generate a revenue of $900 for the company.

FIGURE 1.1

A spreadsheet formulation of the Special Products Company problem.

	A	B	C	D	E	F
1		**Special Products Co. Break-Even Analysis**				
2						
3			**Data**			**Results**
4		Unit Revenue	$900		Total Revenue	$180,000
5		Fixed Cost	$50,000		Total Fixed Cost	$50,000
6		Marginal Cost	$400		Total Variable Cost	$80,000
7		Sales Forecast	300		Profit (Loss)	$50,000
8						
9		Production Quantity	200			

Range Name	Cell
FixedCost	C5
MarginalCost	C6
ProductionQuantity	C9
Profit	F7
SalesForecast	C7
TotalFixedCost	F5
TotalRevenue	F4
TotalVariableCost	F6
UnitRevenue	C4

	E	F
3		**Results**
4	Total Revenue	=UnitRevenue * MIN(SalesForecast, ProductionQuantity)
5	Total Fixed Cost	=IF(ProductionQuantity > 0, FixedCost, 0)
6	Total Variable Cost	=MarginalCost * ProductionQuantity
7	Profit (Loss)	=TotalRevenue − (TotalFixedCost + TotalVariableCost)

Spreadsheet Modeling of the Problem

You will see throughout this book that spreadsheets provide a very convenient way of using a management science approach for modeling and analyzing a wide variety of managerial problems. This certainly is true for the Special Products Company problem as well, as we now will demonstrate.

Figure 1.1 shows a spreadsheet formulation of this problem after obtaining a sales forecast that indicates 300 grandfather clocks can be sold. The data have been entered into cells C4 to C7. Cell C9 is used to record a trial value for the decision as to how many grandfather clocks to produce. As one of the many possibilities that eventually might be tried, Figure 1.1 shows the specific trial value of 200.

Cells F4 to F7 give the resulting total revenue, total costs, and profit (loss) by using the Excel equations shown under the spreadsheet in Figure 1.1. The Excel equations could have been written using cell references (e.g., F6 = C6*C9). However, the spreadsheet model is made clearer by naming cells (called *range names*). To define a name for a selected cell (or range of cells), click on the name box (on the left of the formula bar above the spreadsheet) and type a name. Alternatively, click on Define Name on the Formulas tab (for Excel 2007) or choose Name\Define from the Insert menu (for earlier versions of Excel) and type a name. These cell names then can be used in other formulas to create an equation that is easy to decipher (e.g., TotalVariableCost = MarginalCost*ProductionQuantity rather than the more cryptic F6 = C6*C9). Note that spaces are not allowed in range names. When a range name has more than one word, we have used capital letters to distinguish the start of each new word (e.g., ProductionQuantity).

The lower left-hand corner of Figure 1.1 lists the names of the quantities in the spreadsheet in alphabetical order and then gives cell references where the quantities are found. Although this isn't particularly necessary for such a small spreadsheet, you should find it helpful for the larger spreadsheets found later in the book.

This same spreadsheet is provided for you live in your MS Courseware on the CD-ROM. (All the spreadsheets in the book are included in your MS Courseware.) As you can see for yourself by bringing up and playing with the spreadsheet, it provides a straightforward way of performing sensitivity analysis on the problem. What happens if the sales forecast should have been considerably lower? What happens if some of the cost and revenue estimates are wrong? Simply enter a variety of new values for these quantities in the spreadsheet and see what happens to the profit shown in cell F7.

Excel Tip: To update formulas throughout the spreadsheet to incorporate a newly defined range name, choose Apply Names from the Define Name menu on the Formulas tab (Excel 2007) or choose Name\Apply from the Insert menu (earlier versions).

Excel Tip: A list of all the defined names and their corresponding cell references can be pasted into a spreadsheet by choosing Paste Names from the Use in Formula menu on the Formulas tab (Excel 2007) or choosing Name\Paste from the Insert menu (earlier versions), and then click on Paste List.

A spreadsheet is a convenient tool for performing sensitivity analysis.

The Excel function MIN(*a, b*) gives the minimum of the numbers in the cells whose addresses are *a* and *b*.

IF(*a, b, c*) is one of the most widely used Excel functions.

The lower right-hand corner of Figure 1.1 introduces two useful Excel functions, the MIN(*a, b*) function and the IF(*a, b, c*) function. The equation for cell F4 uses the MIN(*a, b*) function, which gives the minimum of *a* and *b*. In this case, the estimated number of grandfather clocks that will be sold is the minimum of the sales forecast and the production quantity, so

$$F4 = \text{UnitRevenue*MIN(SalesForecast,ProductionQuantity)}$$

enters the unit revenue (from cell C4) times the minimum of the sales forecast (from C7) and the production quantity (from C9) into cell F4.

Also note that the equation for cell F5 uses the IF(*a, b, c*) function, which does the following: If statement *a* is true, it uses *b;* otherwise, it uses *c*. Therefore,

$$F5 = \text{IF(ProductionQuantity} > 0, \text{FixedCost}, 0)$$

says to enter the fixed cost (C5) into cell F5 if the production quantity (C9) is greater than zero, but otherwise enter 0 (the fixed cost is avoided if production is not initiated).

The spreadsheet in Figure 1.1, along with its equations for the results in column F, constitutes a *spreadsheet model* for the Special Products Company problem. You will see many examples of such spreadsheet models throughout the book.

This particular spreadsheet model is based on an underlying *mathematical model* that uses algebra to spell out the equations in cells F4:F7 and then to derive some additional useful information. Let us take a look at this mathematical model next.

Expressing the Problem Mathematically

The issue facing management is to make the following decision.

Decision to be made: Number of grandfather clocks to produce (if any).

Since this number is not yet known, we introduce an algebraic variable Q to represent this quantity. Thus,

$$Q = \text{Number of grandfather clocks to produce,}$$

where Q is referred to as a **decision variable.** Naturally, the value chosen for Q should not exceed the sales forecast for the number of clocks that can be sold. Choosing a value of 0 for Q would correspond to deciding not to introduce the product, in which case none of the costs or revenues described in the preceding paragraph would be incurred.

The objective is to choose the value of Q that maximizes the company's profit from this new product. The management science approach is to formulate a mathematical model to represent this problem by developing an equation that expresses the profit in terms of the decision variable Q. To get there, it is necessary first to develop equations in terms of Q for the total cost and revenue generated by the grandfather clocks.

If $Q = 0$, no cost is incurred. However, if $Q > 0$, there is both a fixed cost and a variable cost.

$$\text{Fixed cost} = \$50,000 \quad (\text{if } Q > 0)$$
$$\text{Variable cost} = \$400\,Q$$

Therefore, the total cost would be

$$\text{Total cost} = \begin{cases} 0 & \text{if } Q = 0 \\ \$50,000 + \$400Q & \text{if } Q > 0 \end{cases}$$

Since each grandfather clock sold would generate a revenue of $900 for the company, the total revenue from selling Q clocks would be

$$\text{Total revenue} = \$900Q$$

Consequently, the profit from producing and selling Q clocks would be

$$\text{Profit} = \text{Total revenue} - \text{Total cost}$$
$$= \begin{cases} 0 & \text{if } Q = 0 \\ \$900Q - (\$50,000 + \$400Q) & \text{if } Q > 0 \end{cases}$$

Thus, since $\$900Q - \$400Q = \$500Q$

$$\text{Profit} = -\$50,000 + \$500Q \quad \text{if } Q > 0$$

Analysis of the Problem

This last equation shows that the attractiveness of the proposed new product depends greatly on the value of Q, that is, on the number of grandfather clocks that can be produced and sold. A small value of Q means a loss (negative profit) for the company, whereas a sufficiently large value would generate a positive profit for the company. For example, look at the difference between $Q = 20$ and $Q = 200$.

$$\text{Profit} = -\$50,000 + \$500(20) = -\$40,000 \quad \text{if } Q = 20$$
$$\text{Profit} = -\$50,000 + \$500(200) = \$50,000 \quad \text{if } Q = 200$$

Figure 1.2 plots both the company's total cost and total revenue for the various values of Q. Note that the cost line and the revenue line intersect at $Q = 100$. For any value of $Q < 100$, cost exceeds revenue, so the gap between the two lines represents the *loss* to the company. For any $Q > 100$, revenue exceeds cost, so the gap between the two lines now shows positive profit. At $Q = 100$, the profit is 0. Since 100 units is the production and sales volume at which the company would break even on the proposed new product, this volume is referred to as the **break-even point.** This is the point that must be exceeded to make it worthwhile to introduce the product. Therefore, the crucial question is whether the sales forecast for how many clocks can be sold is above or below the break-even point.

Figure 1.2 illustrates the *graphical procedure* for finding the break-even point. Another alternative is to use an *algebraic procedure* to solve for the point. Because the profit is 0 at this point, the procedure consists of solving the following equation for the unknown Q.

$$\text{Profit} = -\$50,000 + \$500Q = 0$$

FIGURE 1.2
Break-even analysis for the Special Products Company shows that the cost line and revenue line intersect at $Q = 100$ clocks, so this is the break-even point for the proposed new product.

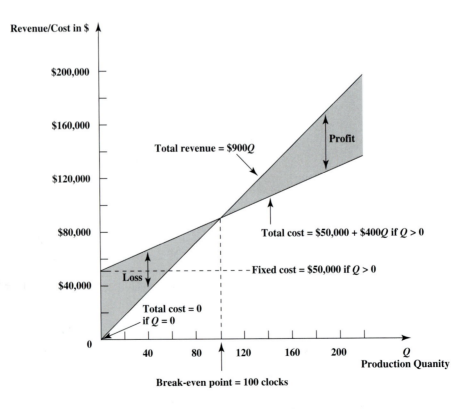

Thus,

$$\$500Q = \$50,000$$

$$Q = \frac{\$50,000}{\$500}$$

$$Q = 100$$

A Complete Mathematical Model for the Problem

The preceding analysis of the problem made use of a basic mathematical model that consisted of the equation for profit expressed in terms of Q. However, implicit in this analysis were some additional factors that can be incorporated into a complete mathematical model for the problem.

Two of these factors concern restrictions on the values of Q that can be considered. One of these is that the number of clocks produced cannot be less than 0. Therefore,

$$Q \geq 0$$

constraints
A *constraint* in a mathematical model is an inequality or equation that expresses some restrictions on the values that can be assigned to the decision variables.

is one of the **constraints** for the complete mathematical model. Another restriction on the value of Q is that it should not exceed the number of clocks that can be sold. A sales forecast has not yet been obtained, so let the symbol s represent this currently unknown value.

s = Sales forecast (not yet available) of the number of grandfather clocks that can be sold

Consequently,

$$Q \leq s$$

parameter
The constants in a mathematical model are referred to as the *parameters* of the model.

is another constraint, where s is a **parameter** of the model whose value has not yet been chosen.

The final factor that should be made explicit in the model is the fact that management's objective is to make the decision that maximizes the company's profit from this new product. Therefore, the complete mathematical model for this problem is to find the value of the decision variable Q so as to

$$\text{Maximize profit} = \begin{cases} 0 & \text{if } Q = 0 \\ -\$50,000 + \$500Q & \text{if } Q > 0 \end{cases}$$

subject to

$$Q \leq s$$
$$Q \geq 0$$

objective function
The *objective function* for a mathematical model is a mathematical expression that gives the measure of performance for the problem in terms of the decision variables.

where the algebraic expression given for Profit is called the **objective function** for the model. The value of Q that solves this model depends on the value that will be assigned to the parameter s (the future forecast of the number of units that can be sold). Because the break-even point is 100, here is how the solution for Q depends on s.

Solution for Mathematical Model

$$\text{Break-even point} = \frac{\text{Fixed cost}}{\text{Unit revenue} - \text{Marginal cost}} = \frac{\$50,000}{\$900 - \$400} = 100$$

If $s \leq 100$, then set $Q = 0$

If $s > 100$, then set $Q = s$

Therefore, the company should introduce the product and produce the number of units that can be sold *only* if this production and sales volume exceeds the break-even point.

Sensitivity Analysis of the Mathematical Model

A mathematical model is intended to be only an approximate representation of the problem. For example, some of the numbers in the model inevitably are only estimates of quantities that cannot be determined precisely at this time.

The above mathematical model is based on four numbers that are only estimates—the fixed cost of $50,000, the marginal cost of $400, the unit revenue of $900, and the sales forecast (after it is obtained). A management science study usually devotes considerable time to investigating what happens to the recommendations of the model if any of the estimates turn out to considerably miss their targets. This is referred to as **sensitivity analysis.**

To assist you in performing sensitivity analysis on this model in a straightforward and enjoyable way, we have provided a *Break-Even Analysis* module in the *Interactive Management Science Modules* at **www.mhhe.com/hillier3e.** (All of the modules in this software package also are included on your CD-ROM.) The default model provided there is the one for the Special Products Company. Therefore, you immediately will see a replica of Figure 1.2. By following the simple directions given there, you can drag either the cost line or the revenue line to change the fixed cost, the marginal cost, or the unit revenue. This immediately enables you to see the effect on the break-even point if any of these cost or revenue numbers should turn out to have values that are somewhat different than their estimates in the model. For example, if the one deviation from the estimates is that the fixed cost turns out to be $75,000 instead of $50,000, then the break-even point becomes 150, as shown in Figure 1.3. We encourage you to try the Break-Even Analysis module to see the effect of other changes as well.

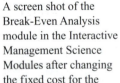
sensitivity analysis
Since estimates can be wrong, *sensitivity analysis* is used to check the effect on the recommendations of a model if the estimates turn out to be wrong.

Incorporating the Break-Even Point into the Spreadsheet Model

A key finding of the above mathematical model is its formula for the break-even point,

$$\text{Break-even point} = \frac{\text{Fixed cost}}{\text{Unit revenue} - \text{Marginal cost}}$$

Therefore, once both the quantities in this formula and the sales forecast have been carefully estimated, the solution for the mathematical model specifies what the production quantity should be.

By contrast, although the spreadsheet in Figure 1.1 enables trying a variety of trial values for the production quantity, it does not directly indicate what the production quantity should be. Figure 1.4 shows how this spreadsheet can be expanded to provide this additional guidance. As indicated by its equation at the bottom of the figure, cell F9 calculates the break-even point by dividing the fixed cost ($50,000) by the net profit per grandfather clock sold ($500), where this net profit is the unit revenue ($900) *minus* the marginal cost ($400). Since the sales forecast of 300 exceeds the break-even point of 100, this forecast has been entered into cell C9.

If desired, the complete mathematical model for break-even analysis can be *fully* incorporated into the spreadsheet by requiring that the model solution for the production quantity be entered into cell C9. This would be done by using the equation

$$C9 = IF(\text{SalesForecast} > \text{BreakEvenPoint}, \text{SalesForecast}, 0)$$

FIGURE 1.3
A screen shot of the Break-Even Analysis module in the Interactive Management Science Modules after changing the fixed cost for the Special Products Company problem from $50,000 to $75,000.

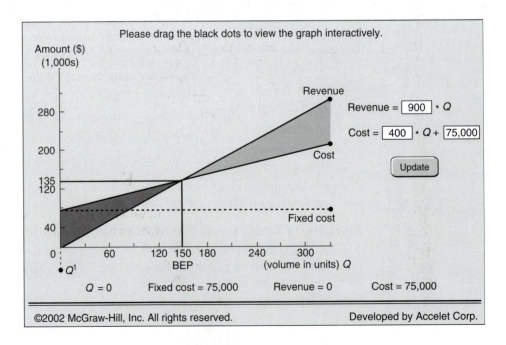

Developed by Accelet Corp.

FIGURE 1.4

An expansion of the spreadsheet in Figure 1.1 that uses the solution for the mathematical model to calculate the break-even point.

	A	B	C	D	E	F
1		**Special Products Co. Break-Even Analysis**				
2						
3			**Data**			**Results**
4		Unit Revenue	$900		Total Revenue	$270,000
5		Fixed Cost	$50,000		Total Fixed Cost	$50,000
6		Marginal Cost	$400		Total Variable Cost	$120,000
7		Sales Forecast	300		Profit (Loss)	$100,000
8						
9		Production Quantity	300		Break-Even Point	100

Range Name	Cell
BreakEvenPoint	F9
FixedCost	C5
MarginalCost	C6
ProductionQuantity	C9
Profit	F7
SalesForecast	C7
TotalFixedCost	F5
TotalRevenue	F4
TotalVariableCost	F6
UnitRevenue	C4

	E	F
3		**Results**
4	Total Revenue	=UnitRevenue * MIN(SalesForecast, ProductionQuantity)
5	Total Fixed Cost	=IF(ProductionQuantity > 0, FixedCost, 0)
6	Total Variable Cost	=MarginalCost * ProductionQuantity
7	Profit (Loss)	=TotalRevenue – (TotalFixedCost + TotalVariableCost)
8		
9	Break-Even Point	=FixedCost/(UnitRevenue – MarginalCost)

However, the disadvantage of introducing this equation is that it would eliminate the possibility of trying other production quantities that might still be of interest. For example, if management does not have much confidence in the sales forecast and wants to minimize the danger of producing more grandfather clocks than can be sold, consideration would be given to production quantities smaller than the forecast. For example, the trial value shown in cell C9 of Figure 1.1 might be chosen instead. As in any application of management science, a mathematical model can provide useful guidance but management needs to make the final decision after considering factors that may not be included in the model.

Review Questions

1. How do the production and sales volume of a new product need to compare to its break-even point to make it worthwhile to introduce the product?
2. What are the factors included in the complete mathematical model for the Special Products Company problem, in addition to an equation for profit?
3. What is the purpose of sensitivity analysis?
4. How can a spreadsheet be used to perform sensitivity analysis?
5. What does the MIN(*a, b*) Excel function do?
6. What does the IF(*a, b, c*) Excel function do?

1.3 SOME SPECIAL FEATURES OF THIS BOOK

The focus of this book is on teaching what an enlightened future manager needs to learn from a management science course. It is not on trying to train technical analysts. This focus has led us to include a number of special features that we hope you enjoy.

One special feature is that the entire book revolves around *modeling* as an aid to managerial decision making. This is what is particularly relevant to a manager. Although they may not use this term, all managers often engage in at least informal modeling (abstracting the essence of a problem to better analyze it), so learning more about the art of modeling is important. Since managers instigate larger management science studies done by others, they also need to be able to recognize the kinds of managerial problems where such a study might be helpful. Thus, a future manager should acquire the ability both to recognize when a management science model might be applicable and to properly interpret the results from analyzing the model. Therefore, rather than spending substantial time in this book on mathematical theory, the mechanics of solution procedures, or the manipulation of spreadsheets, the focus is on the art of model formulation, the role of a model, and the analysis of model results. A wide range of model types is considered.

Another special feature is a heavy emphasis on *case studies* to better convey these ideas in an interesting way in the context of applications. Every subsequent chapter includes at least one case study that introduces and illustrates the application of that chapter's techniques in a realistic setting. In a few instances, the entire chapter revolves around a case study. Although considerably smaller and simpler than most real studies (to maintain clarity), these case studies are patterned after actual applications requiring a major management science study. Consequently, they convey the whole process of such a study, some of the pitfalls involved, and the complementary roles of the management science team and the manager responsible for the decisions to be made.

To complement these case studies, every subsequent chapter also includes major cases at the end. These realistic cases can be used for individual assignments, team projects, or case studies in class. In addition, the University of Western Ontario Ivey School of Business (the second largest producer of teaching cases in the world) also has specially selected cases from its case collection that match the chapters in this textbook. These cases are available on the Ivey Web site, **www.cases.ivey.uwo.ca/case,** in the segment of the CaseMate area designated for this book.

The book also places heavy emphasis on conveying the impressive impact that management science is having on improving the efficiency of numerous organizations around the world. Therefore, you will see many examples of actual applications throughout the book in the form of boxed *application vignettes.* In some cases, these applications resulted in annual savings of millions, tens of millions, or even hundreds of millions of dollars.

In addition, we try to provide you with a broad perspective about the nature of the real world of management science in practice. It is easy to lose sight of this world when cranking through textbook exercises to master the mechanics of a series of techniques. Therefore, we shift some emphasis from mastering these mechanics to seeing the big picture. The case studies, cases, and descriptions of actual applications are part of this effort.

A feature that is new with this edition is the inclusion of one or more *solved problems* for each chapter to help you get started on your homework for that chapter. The statement of each solved problem is given just above the Problems section of the chapter and then the complete solution is given on both the CD-ROM and the Web site for the book.

The last, but certainly not the least, of the special features of this book is the accompanying software. We will describe and illustrate how to use today's premier spreadsheet package, Microsoft Excel, to formulate many management science models in a spreadsheet format. Excel 2007 implements a significant overhaul of the user interface. Where different, the steps required for both Excel 2007 and for earlier versions of Excel will be included. Some of these models can be solved using standard Excel. However, Excel add-ins will be required to solve most of the models considered in this book.

Shrinkwrapped in the back of the book is an extensive collection of software that we collectively refer to as **MS Courseware.** Included within this collection are spreadsheet files, many add-ins for Excel, and a package of Interactive Management Science Modules. Each of these is briefly described below.

MS Courseware includes numerous spreadsheet files for every chapter in this book. Each time a spreadsheet example is presented in the book, a live spreadsheet that shows the formulation and solution for the example also is available in MS Courseware. This provides a convenient reference, or even useful templates, when you set up spreadsheets to solve similar problems. Also, for many models in the book, template spreadsheet files are provided that already include all the equations necessary to solve the model. You simply enter the data for the model and the solution is immediately calculated.

Solver Table is an Excel add-in developed by the authors to automate sensitivity analysis in optimization problems. This add-in will be used in several chapters, including especially Chapter 5. A complete description of how to use Solver Table also is provided in Appendix A. Similarly, Appendix B provides a primer on the use of Excel.

Included with standard Excel is an add-in, called Solver, which is used to solve most of the optimization models considered in the first half of this book. The standard Solver was developed by Frontline Systems, Inc. Frontline Systems also has developed several more powerful Solver packages for Excel. One of these, called Premium Solver for Education, is included within MS Courseware. A primary difference between the standard Solver and Premium Solver is that Premium Solver includes an option called Evolutionary Solver that will solve additional kinds of optimization models discussed in Chapter 8.

Also included within MS Courseware are three Excel add-ins developed by Professor Michael Middleton. TreePlan allows you to build decision trees within Excel, as covered in Chapter 9. SensIt is used to generate a number of charts useful for performing sensitivity analysis. RiskSim is a tool used to perform computer simulation, which is the topic of Chapters 12 and 13.

Decisioneering, Inc., has developed several powerful Excel add-ins that are also included within MS Courseware. Crystal Ball greatly simplifies performing Monte Carlo simulation within Excel, as covered in Chapter 13. OptQuest allows you to perform optimization within a simulation model. Finally, CB Predictor is a tool that will be useful in forecasting, as discussed in the supplement to Chapter 10.

As mentioned in Section 1.2, another learning aid accompanying the book is the package of Interactive Management Science Modules provided at **www.mhhe.com/hillier3e.** This innovative tool includes several modules that enable you to interactively explore several management science techniques in depth. For your convenience, an offline version of this package also is included in your MS Courseware on the CD-ROM.

Given this choice of software, we should point out that Excel is not designed for dealing with the really large management science models that occasionally arise in practice. More powerful software packages that are not based on spreadsheets generally are used to solve such models instead. However, management science teams, not managers, primarily use these sophisticated packages (including using *modeling languages* to help input the large models). Since this book is aimed mainly at future managers rather than future management scientists, we will not have you use these packages.

To alert you to relevant material in MS Courseware, the end of each chapter has a list entitled "Learning Aids for This Chapter in Your MS Courseware."

1.4 Summary

Management science is a discipline area that attempts to aid managerial decision making by applying a scientific approach to managerial problems that involve quantitative factors. The rapid development of this discipline began in the 1940s and 1950s. The onslaught of the computer revolution has since continued to give great impetus to its growth. Further impetus now is being provided by the widespread use of spreadsheet packages, which greatly facilitate the application of management science by managers and others.

A major management science study involves conducting a systematic investigation that includes careful data gathering, developing and testing hypotheses about the problem (typically in the form of a mathematical model), and applying sound logic in the subsequent analysis. The management science team then presents its recommendations to the managers who must make the decisions about how to resolve the problem. Smaller studies might be done by managers themselves with the aid of a spreadsheet package.

A major part of a typical management science study involves incorporating the quantitative factors into a mathematical model (perhaps incorporated into a spreadsheet) and then applying mathematical procedures to solve the model. Such a model uses *decision variables* to represent the quantifiable decisions to be made. An *objective function* expresses the appropriate measure of performance in terms of these decision variables. The *constraints* of the model express the restrictions on the values that can be assigned to the decision variables. The *parameters* of the model are the constants that appear in the objective function and the constraints. An example involving *break-even analysis* was used to illustrate a mathematical model.

Management science has had an impressive impact on improving the efficiency of numerous organizations around the world. In fact, many award-winning applications have resulted in annual savings in the millions, tens of millions, or even hundreds of millions of dollars.

The focus of this book is on emphasizing what an enlightened future manager needs to learn from a management science course. Therefore, the book revolves around modeling as an aid to managerial decision making. Many case studies (within the chapters) and cases (at the end of chapters) are used to better convey these ideas.

Glossary

break-even point   The production and sales volume for a product that must be exceeded to achieve a profit. (Section 1.2), 8

constraint   An inequality or equation in a mathematical model that expresses some restrictions on the values that can be assigned to the decision variables. (Section 1.2), 9

decision support system   An interactive computer-based system that aids managerial decision making. (Section 1.1), 5

decision variable   An algebraic variable that represents a quantifiable decision to be made. (Section 1.2), 7

mathematical model   An approximate representation of, for example, a business problem that is expressed in terms of mathematical symbols and expressions. (Section 1.1), 4

model   An approximate representation of something. (Section 1.1), 4

MS Courseware   The name of the software package that is shrinkwrapped with the book. (Section 1.3), 12

objective function   A mathematical expression in a model that gives the measure of performance for a problem in terms of the decision variables. (Section 1.2), 9

operations research   The traditional name for management science that still is widely used outside of business schools. (Section 1.1), 3

parameter   One of the constants in a mathematical model. (Section 1.2), 9

sensitivity analysis   Analysis of how the recommendations of a model might change if any of the estimates providing the numbers in the model eventually need to be corrected. (Section 1.2), 10

spreadsheet model   An approximate representation of, for example, a business problem that is laid out on a spreadsheet in a way that facilitates analysis of the problem. (Section 1.1), 4

Learning Aids for This Chapter in Your MS Courseware

Chapter 1 Excel Files:

Special Products Co. Example

Interactive Management Science Modules:

Module for Break-Even Analysis

Solved Problem (See the CD-ROM for the Solution)

1.S1. Make or Buy?

Power Notebooks, Inc., plans to manufacture a new line of notebook computers. Management is trying to decide whether to purchase the LCD screens for the computers from an outside supplier or to manufacture the screens in-house. The screens cost $100 each from the outside supplier. To set up the assembly process required to produce the screens in-house would cost $100,000. The company could then produce each screen for $75. The number of notebooks that eventually will be produced (Q) is unknown at this point.

a. Set up a spreadsheet that will display the total cost of both options for any value of Q. Use trial and error with the spreadsheet to determine the range of production volumes for which each alternative is best.

b. Use a graphical procedure to determine the break-even point for Q (i.e., the quantity at which both options yield the same cost).

c. Use an algebraic procedure to determine the break-even point for Q.

Problems

1.1. The manager of a small firm is considering whether to produce a new product that would require leasing some special equipment at a cost of $20,000 per month. In addition to this leasing cost, a production cost of $10 would be incurred for each unit of the product produced. Each unit sold would generate $20 in revenue.

Develop a mathematical expression for the monthly profit that would be generated by this product in terms of the number of units produced and sold per month. Then determine how large this number needs to be each month to make it profitable to produce the product.

1.2. Refer to Problem 1.1. A sales forecast has been obtained that indicates that 4,000 units of the new product could be sold. This forecast is considered to be quite reliable, but there is considerable uncertainty about the accuracy of the estimates given for the leasing cost, the marginal production cost, and the unit revenue.

Use the Break-Even Analysis module in the Interactive Management Science Modules to perform the following sensitivity analysis on these estimates.

a. How large can the leasing cost be before this new product ceases to be profitable?

b. How large can the marginal production cost be before this new product ceases to be profitable?

c. How small can the unit revenue be before this new product ceases to be profitable?

1.3. Management of the Toys R4U Company needs to decide whether to introduce a certain new novelty toy for the upcoming Christmas season, after which it would be discontinued. The total cost required to produce and market this toy would be $500,000 plus $15 per toy produced. The company would receive revenue of $35 for each toy sold.

a. Assuming that every unit of this toy that is produced is sold, write an expression for the profit in terms of the number produced and sold. Then find the break-even point that this number must exceed to make it worthwhile to introduce this toy.

b. Now assume that the number that can be sold might be less than the number produced. Write an expression for the profit in terms of these two numbers.

c. Formulate a spreadsheet that will give the profit in part *b* for any values of the two numbers.

d. Write a mathematical expression for the constraint that the number produced should not exceed the number that can be sold.

1.4. A reliable sales forecast has been obtained indicating that the Special Products Company (see Section 1.2) would be able to sell 300 limited edition grandfather clocks, which appears to be enough to justify introducing this new product. However, management is concerned that this conclusion might change if more accurate estimates were available for the cost of setting up the production facilities, the marginal production cost, and the unit revenue. Therefore, before a final decision is made, management wants sensitivity analysis done on these estimates.

Use the Break-Even Analysis module in the Interactive Management Science Modules to perform the following sensitivity analysis.

a. How large can the cost of setting up the production facilities be before the grandfather clocks cease to be profitable?

b. How large can the marginal production cost be before the grandfather clocks cease to be profitable?

c. How small can the unit revenue be before the grandfather clocks cease to be profitable?

1.5. Reconsider the problem facing the management of the Special Products Company as presented in Section 1.2.

A more detailed investigation now has provided better estimates of the data for the problem. The fixed cost of initiating production of the limited edition grandfather clocks still is estimated to be $50,000, but the new estimate of the marginal cost is $500. The revenue from each grandfather clock sold now is estimated to be $700.

a. Use a graphical procedure to find the new break-even point.

b. Use an algebraic procedure to find the new break-even point.

c. State the mathematical model for this problem with the new data.

d. Incorporate this mathematical model into a spreadsheet with a sales forecast of 300. Use this spreadsheet model to find the new break-even point, and then determine the production quantity and the estimated total profit indicated by the model.

e. Suppose that management fears that the sales forecast may be overly optimistic and so does not want to consider producing more than 200 grandfather clocks. Use the spreadsheet from part *d* to determine what the production quantity should be and the estimated total profit that would result.

1.6. The Best-for-Less Corp. supplies its two retail outlets from its two plants. Plant A will be supplying 30 shipments next month. Plant B has not yet set its production schedule for next month but has the capacity to produce and ship any amount up to a maximum of 50 shipments. Retail outlet 1 has submitted its order for 40 shipments for next month. Retail outlet 2 needs a minimum of 25 shipments next month but would be happy to receive more. The production costs are the same at the two plants but the shipping costs differ. The shipping cost per shipment from each plant to each retail outlet is given next, along with a summary of the other data.

The distribution manager, Jennifer Lopez, now needs to develop a plan for how many shipments to send from each

	Unit Shipping Cost		
	Retail Outlet 1	**Retail Outlet 2**	**Supply**
Plant A	$700	$400	= 30 shipments
Plant B	$800	$600	≤ 50 shipments
Needed	= 40 shipments	≥ 25 shipments	

plant to each of the retail outlets next month. Her objective is to minimize the total shipping cost.

a. Identify the individual decisions that Jennifer needs to make. For each of these decisions, define a decision variable to represent the decision.

b. Write a mathematical expression for the total shipping cost in terms of the decision variables.

c. Write a mathematical expression for each of the constraints on what the values of the decision variables can be.

d. State a complete mathematical model for Jennifer's problem.

e. What do you think Jennifer's shipping plan should be? Explain your reasoning. Then express your shipping plan in terms of the decision variables.

1.7. The Water Sports Company soon will be producing and marketing a new model line of motor boats. The production manager, Michael Jensen, now is facing a *make-or-buy decision* regarding the outboard motor to be installed on each of these boats. Based on the total cost involved, should the motors be produced internally or purchased from a vendor? Producing them internally would require an investment of $1 million in new facilities as well as a production cost of $1,600 for each motor produced. If purchased from a vendor instead, the price would be $2,000 per motor.

Michael has obtained a preliminary forecast from the company's marketing division that 3,000 boats in this model line will be sold.

a. Use spreadsheets to display and analyze Michael's two options. Which option should be chosen?

b. Michael realizes from past experience that preliminary sales forecasts are quite unreliable, so he wants to check on whether his decision might change if a more careful forecast differed significantly from the preliminary forecast. Determine a *break-even point* for the production and sales volume below which the buy option is better and above which the make option is better.

1.8. Reconsider the Special Products Company problem presented in Section 1.2.

Although the company is well qualified to do most of the work in producing the limited edition grandfather clocks, it currently lacks expertise in one key area, namely, constructing the timekeeping mechanism for the clocks. Therefore, management now is considering contracting out this part of the job to another company that has this expertise and already has some of its production facilities set up to do this kind of work. If this were done, the Special Products Company would not incur any fixed cost for initiating production of the clocks but would incur a marginal cost of $650 (including its payment to the other company) while still obtaining revenue of $900 for each clock produced and sold. However, if the company does all the production itself, all the data presented in Section 1.2 still apply. After

obtaining an analysis of the sales potential, management believes that 300 grandfather clocks can be sold.

Management now wants to determine whether the *make option* (do all the production internally) or the *buy option* (contract out the production of the time-keeping mechanism) is better.

a. Use a spreadsheet to display and analyze the buy option. Show the relevant data and financial output, including the total profit that would be obtained by producing and selling 300 grandfather clocks.

b. Figure 1.4 shows the analysis for the make option. Compare these results with those from part *a* to determine which option (make or buy) appears to be better.

c. Another way to compare these two options is to find a *break-even point* for the production and sales volume, below which the buy option is better and above which the make option is better. Begin this process by developing an expression for the *difference* in profit between the make and buy options in terms of the number of grandfather clocks to produce for sale. Thus, this expression should give the *incremental profit* from choosing the make option rather than the buy option, where this incremental profit is 0 if 0 grandfather clocks are produced but otherwise is negative below the break-even point and positive above the break-even point. Using this expression as the objective function, state the overall mathematical model (including constraints) for the problem of determining whether to choose the make option and, if so, how many units of the time-keeping mechanism (one per clock) to produce.

d. Use a graphical procedure to find the break-even point described in part *c*.

e. Use an algebraic procedure to find the break-even point described in part *c*.

f. Use a spreadsheet model to find the break-even point described in part *c*. What is the conclusion about what the company should do?

Chapter **Two**

Linear Programming: Basic Concepts

Learning objectives

After completing this chapter, you should be able to

1. Explain what linear programming is.
2. Identify the three key questions to be addressed in formulating any spreadsheet model.
3. Name and identify the purpose of the four kinds of cells used in linear programming spreadsheet models.
4. Formulate a basic linear programming model in a spreadsheet from a description of the problem.
5. Present the algebraic form of a linear programming model from its formulation on a spreadsheet.
6. Apply the graphical method to solve a two-variable linear programming problem.
7. Use Excel to solve a linear programming spreadsheet model.

The management of any organization regularly must make decisions about how to allocate its resources to various activities to best meet organizational objectives. Linear programming is a powerful problem-solving tool that aids management in making such decisions. It is applicable to both profit-making and not-for-profit organizations, as well as governmental agencies. The resources being allocated to activities can be, for example, money, different kinds of personnel, and different kinds of machinery and equipment. In many cases, a wide variety of resources must be allocated simultaneously. The activities needing these resources might be various production activities (e.g., producing different products), marketing activities (e.g., advertising in different media), financial activities (e.g., making capital investments), or some other activities. Some problems might even involve activities of *all* these types (and perhaps others), because they are competing for the same resources.

You will see as we progress that even this description of the scope of linear programming is not sufficiently broad. Some of its applications go beyond the allocation of resources. However, activities always are involved. Thus, a recurring theme in linear programming is the need to find the *best mix* of activities—which ones to pursue and at what levels.

Like the other management science techniques, linear programming uses a *mathematical model* to represent the problem being studied. The word *linear* in the name refers to the form of the mathematical expressions in this model. *Programming* does not refer to computer programming; rather, it is essentially a synonym for planning. Thus, linear programming means the *planning of activities* represented by a *linear* mathematical model.

Because it comprises a major part of management science, linear programming takes up several chapters of this book. Furthermore, many of the lessons learned about how to apply linear programming also will carry over to the application of other management science techniques.

This chapter focuses on the basic concepts of linear programming.

2.1 A CASE STUDY: THE WYNDOR GLASS CO. PRODUCT-MIX PROBLEM

Jim Baker is excited. The group he heads has really hit the jackpot this time. They have had some notable successes in the past, but he feels that this one will be really special. He can hardly wait for the reaction after his memorandum reaches top management.

Jim has had an excellent track record during his seven years as manager of new product development for the Wyndor Glass Company. Although the company is a small one, it has been experiencing considerable growth largely because of the innovative new products developed by Jim's group. Wyndor's president, John Hill, has often acknowledged publicly the key role that Jim has played in the recent success of the company.

Therefore, John felt considerable confidence six months ago in asking Jim's group to develop the following new products:

- An 8-foot glass door with aluminum framing.
- A 4-foot × 6-foot double-hung, wood-framed window.

Although several other companies already had products meeting these specifications, John felt that Jim would be able to work his usual magic in introducing exciting new features that would establish new industry standards.

Now, Jim can't remove the smile from his face. They have done it.

Background

The Wyndor Glass Co. produces high-quality glass products, including windows and glass doors that feature handcrafting and the finest workmanship. Although the products are expensive, they fill a market niche by providing the highest quality available in the industry for the most discriminating buyers. The company has three plants.

Plant 1 produces aluminum frames and hardware.
Plant 2 produces wood frames.
Plant 3 produces the glass and assembles the windows and doors.

Because of declining sales for certain products, top management has decided to revamp the company's product line. Unprofitable products are being discontinued, releasing production capacity to launch the two new products developed by Jim Baker's group if management approves their release.

The 8-foot glass door requires some of the production capacity in Plants 1 and 3, but not Plant 2. The 4-foot × 6-foot double-hung window needs only Plants 2 and 3.

Management now needs to address two issues:

1. Should the company go ahead with launching these two new products?
2. If so, what should be the *product mix*—the number of units of each produced per week—for the two new products?

Management's Discussion of the Issues

Having received Jim Baker's memorandum describing the two new products, John Hill now has called a meeting to discuss the current issues. In addition to John and Jim, the meeting includes Bill Tasto, vice president for manufacturing, and Ann Lester, vice president for marketing.

Let's eavesdrop on the meeting.

John Hill (president):   Bill, we will want to rev up to start production of these products as soon as we can. About how much production output do you think we can achieve?

Bill Tasto (vice president for manufacturing):   We do have a little available production capacity, because of the products we are discontinuing, but not a lot. We should be able to achieve a production rate of a few units per week for each of these two products.

John: Is that all?

Bill: Yes. These are complicated products requiring careful crafting. And, as I said, we don't have much production capacity available.

Swift & Company is a diversified protein-producing business based in Greeley, Colorado. With annual sales of over $8 billion, beef and related products are by far the largest portion of the company's business.

To improve the company's sales and manufacturing performance, upper management concluded that it needed to achieve three major objectives. One was to enable the company's customer service representatives to talk to their more than 8,000 customers with accurate information about the availability of current and future inventory while considering requested delivery dates and maximum product age upon delivery. A second was to produce an efficient shift-level schedule for each plant over a 28-day horizon. A third was to accurately determine whether a plant can ship a requested order-line-item quantity on the requested date and time given the availability of cattle and constraints on the plant's capacity.

To meet these three challenges, a management science team developed an integrated system of 45 linear programming models based on three model formulations to dynamically schedule its beef-fabrication operations at five plants in real time as it receives orders. The total audited benefits realized in the first year of operation of this system were $12.74 million, including $12 million due to optimizing the product mix. Other benefits include a reduction in orders lost, a reduction in price discounting, and better on-time delivery.

Source: A. Bixby, B. Downs, and M. Self, "A Scheduling and Capable-to-Promise Application for Swift & Company, *Interfaces* 36, no. 1 (January–February 2006), pp. 69–86.

John: Ann, will we be able to sell several of each per week?

Ann Lester (vice president for marketing): Easily.

John: OK, good. I would like to set the launch date for these products in six weeks. Bill and Ann, is that feasible?

Bill: Yes.

Ann: We'll have to scramble to give these products a proper marketing launch that soon. But we can do it.

John: Good. Now there's one more issue to resolve. With this limited production capacity, we need to decide how to split it between the two products. Do we want to produce the same number of both products? Or mostly one of them? Or even just produce as much as we can of one and postpone launching the other one for a little while?

Jim Baker (manager of new product development): It would be dangerous to hold one of the products back and give our competition a chance to scoop us.

Ann: I agree. Furthermore, launching them together has some advantages from a marketing standpoint. Since they share a lot of the same special features, we can combine the advertising for the two products. This is going to make a big splash.

The issue is to find the most profitable mix of the two new products.

John: OK. But which mixture of the two products is going to be most profitable for the company?

Bill: I have a suggestion.

John: What's that?

Bill: A couple times in the past, our Management Science Group has helped us with these same kinds of product-mix decisions, and they've done a good job. They ferret out all the relevant data and then dig into some detailed analysis of the issue. I've found their input very helpful. And this is right down their alley.

John: Yes, you're right. That's a good idea. Let's get our Management Science Group working on this issue. Bill, will you coordinate with them?

The meeting ends.

The Management Science Group Begins Its Work

At the outset, the Management Science Group spends considerable time with Bill Tasto to clarify the general problem and specific issues that management wants addressed. A particular concern is to ascertain the appropriate objective for the problem from management's viewpoint. Bill points out that John Hill posed the issue as determining which mixture of the two products is going to be most profitable for the company.

Therefore, with Bill's concurrence, the group defines the key issue to be addressed as follows.

Question: Which combination of *production rates* (the number of units produced per week) for the two new products would *maximize the total profit* from both of them?

The group also concludes that it should consider *all* possible combinations of production rates of both new products permitted by the available production capacities in the three plants. For example, one alternative (despite Jim Baker's and Ann Lester's objections) is to forgo producing one of the products for now (thereby setting its production rate equal to zero) in order to produce as much as possible of the other product. (We must not neglect the possibility that maximum profit from both products might be attained by producing none of one and as much as possible of the other.)

The Management Science Group next identifies the information it needs to gather to conduct this study:

1. Available production capacity in each of the plants.
2. How much of the production capacity in each plant would be needed by each product.
3. Profitability of each product.

Concrete data are not available for any of these quantities, so estimates have to be made. Estimating these quantities requires enlisting the help of key personnel in other units of the company.

Bill Tasto's staff develops the estimates that involve production capacities. Specifically, the staff estimates that the production facilities in Plant 1 needed for the new kind of doors will be available approximately four hours per week. (The rest of the time Plant 1 will continue with current products.) The production facilities in Plant 2 will be available for the new kind of windows about 12 hours per week. The facilities needed for both products in Plant 3 will be available approximately 18 hours per week.

The amount of each plant's production capacity actually used by each product depends on its production rate. It is estimated that each door will require one hour of production time in Plant 1 and three hours in Plant 3. For each window, about two hours will be needed in Plant 2 and two hours in Plant 3.

By analyzing the cost data and the pricing decision, the Accounting Department estimates the profit from the two products. The projection is that the profit per unit will be $300 for the doors and $500 for the windows.

Table 2.1 summarizes the data now gathered.

The Management Science Group recognizes this as being a classic **product-mix problem.** Therefore, the next step is to develop a *mathematical model*—that is, a *linear programming model*—to represent the problem so that it can be solved mathematically. The next four sections focus on how to develop this model and then how to solve it to find the most profitable mix between the two products, assuming the estimates in Table 2.1 are accurate.

Review Questions

1. What is the market niche being filled by the Wyndor Glass Co.?
2. What were the two issues addressed by management?
3. The Management Science Group was asked to help analyze which of these issues?
4. How did this group define the key issue to be addressed?
5. What information did the group need to gather to conduct its study?

TABLE 2.1
Data for the Wyndor Glass Co. Product-Mix Problem

Plant	Production Time Used for Each Unit Produced		Available per Week
	Doors	Windows	
1	1 hour	0	4 hours
2	0	2 hours	12 hours
3	3 hours	2 hours	18 hours
Unit profit	$300	$500	

2.2 FORMULATING THE WYNDOR PROBLEM ON A SPREADSHEET

Spreadsheets provide a powerful and intuitive tool for displaying and analyzing many management problems. We now will focus on how to do this for the Wyndor problem with the popular spreadsheet package Microsoft Excel.[1]

Formulating a Spreadsheet Model for the Wyndor Problem

Excel Tip: Cell shading and borders can be added either by using the borders button and the fill color button in the Font Group of the Home tab (Excel 2007) or the formatting toolbar (earlier versions).

Excel Tip: See the margin notes in Section 1.2 for tips on adding range names.

These are the three key questions to be addressed in formulating any spreadsheet model.

Some students find it helpful to organize their thoughts by verbally writing out their answers to the three key questions before beginning to formulate the spreadsheet model.

Figure 2.1 displays the Wyndor problem by transferring the data in Table 2.1 onto a spreadsheet. (Columns E and F are being reserved for later entries described below.) We will refer to the cells showing the data as **data cells.** To distinguish the data cells from other cells in the spreadsheet, they are shaded light blue. (In the textbook figures, the light blue shading appears as light gray.) The spreadsheet is made easier to interpret by using range names. The data cells in the Wyndor Glass Co. problem are given the range names UnitProfit (C4:D4), HoursUsedPerUnitProduced (C7:D9), and HoursAvailable (G7:G9). To enter a range name, first select the range of cells, then click in the name box on the left of the formula bar above the spreadsheet and type a name.

Three questions need to be answered to begin the process of using the spreadsheet to formulate a mathematical model (in this case, a **linear programming model**) for the problem.

1. What are the *decisions* to be made?
2. What are the *constraints* on these decisions?
3. What is the overall *measure of performance* for these decisions?

The preceding section described how Wyndor's Management Science Group spent considerable time with Bill Tasto, vice president for manufacturing, to clarify management's view of their problem. These discussions provided the following answers to these questions.

1. The decisions to be made are the *production rates* (number of units produced per week) for the two new products.
2. The constraints on these decisions are that the number of hours of production time used per week by the two products in the respective plants cannot exceed the number of hours available.
3. The overall measure of performance for these decisions is the *total profit* per week from the two products.

Figure 2.2 shows how these answers can be incorporated into the spreadsheet. Based on the first answer, the *production rates* of the two products are placed in cells C12 and D12 to locate them in the columns for these products just under the data cells. Since we don't know yet what these production rates should be, they are just entered as zeroes in Figure 2.2. (Actually, any

FIGURE 2.1
The initial spreadsheet for the Wyndor problem after transferring the data in Table 2.1 into data cells.

	A	B	C	D	E	F	G
1		**Wyndor Glass Co. Product-Mix Problem**					
2							
3			**Doors**	**Windows**			
4		Unit Profit	$300	$500			
5							Hours
6			Hours Used per Unit Produced				Available
7		Plant 1	1	0			4
8		Plant 2	0	2			12
9		Plant 3	3	2			18

[1] Other spreadsheet packages with similar capabilities also are available, and the basic ideas presented here are still applicable.

FIGURE 2.2

The complete spreadsheet for the Wyndor problem with an initial trial solution (both production rates equal to zero) entered into the changing cells (C12 and D12).

	A	B	C	D	E	F	G
1		**Wyndor Glass Co. Product-Mix Problem**					
2							
3			**Doors**	**Windows**			
4		Unit Profit	$300	$500			
5					Hours		Hours
6			Hours Used per Unit Produced		Used		Available
7		Plant 1	1	0	0	≤	4
8		Plant 2	0	2	0	≤	12
9		Plant 3	3	2	0	≤	18
10							
11			**Doors**	**Windows**			**Total Profit**
12		Units Produced	0	0			$0

trial solution can be entered, although *negative* production rates should be excluded since they are impossible.) Later, these numbers will be changed while seeking the best mix of production rates. Therefore, these cells containing the decisions to be made are called **changing cells** (or *adjustable cells*). To highlight the changing cells, they are shaded bright yellow with a light border. (In the textbook figures, the bright yellow appears as gray.) The changing cells are given the range name UnitsProduced (C12:D12).

The changing cells contain the decisions to be made.

Using the second answer, the total number of hours of production time used per week by the two products in the respective plants is entered in cells E7, E8, and E9, just to the right of the corresponding data cells. The total number of production hours depends on the production rates of the two products, so this total is zero when the production rates are zero. With positive production rates, the total number of production hours used per week in a plant is the sum of the production hours used per week by the respective products. The production hours used by a product is the number of hours needed for *each* unit of the product *times* the number of units being produced. Therefore, when positive numbers are entered in cells C12 and D12 for the number of doors and windows to produce per week, the data in cells C7:D9 are used to calculate the total production hours per week as follows:

Production hours in Plant 1 = 1(# of doors) + 0(# of windows)

Production hours in Plant 2 = 0(# of doors) + 2(# of windows)

Production hours in Plant 3 = 3(# of doors) + 2(# of windows)

(The colon in C7:D9 is Excel shorthand for the *range from* C7 *to* D9; that is, the entire block of cells in column C or D and in row 7, 8, or 9.) Consequently, the Excel equations for the three cells in column E are

E7 = C7*C12 + D7*D12

E8 = C8*C12 + D8*D12

E9 = C9*C12 + D9*D12

where each asterisk denotes multiplication. Since each of these cells provides output that depends on the changing cells (C12 and D12), they are called **output cells.**

Output cells show quantities that are calculated from the changing cells.

Notice that each of the equations for the output cells involves the sum of two products. There is a function in Excel called SUMPRODUCT that will sum up the product of each of the individual terms in two different ranges of cells when the two ranges have the same number of rows and the same number of columns. Each product being summed is the product of a term in the first range and the term in the corresponding location in the second range. For example, consider the two ranges, C7:D7 and C12:D12, so that each range has one row and two columns. In this case, SUMPRODUCT (C7:D7, C12:D12) takes each of the individual terms in the range C7:D7, multiplies them by the corresponding term in the range C12:D12, and then sums up these individual products, just as shown in the first equation above. Applying the range

The SUMPRODUCT function is used extensively in linear programming spreadsheet models.

name for UnitsProduced (C12:D12), the formula becomes SUMPRODUCT(C7:D7, Units-Produced). Although optional with such short equations, this function is especially handy as a shortcut for entering longer equations.

The formulas in the output cells E7:E9 are very similar. Rather than typing each of these formulas separately into the three cells, it is quicker (and less prone to typos) to type the formula just once in E7 and then copy the formula down into cells E8 and E9. To do this, first enter the formula =SUMPRODUCT(C7:D7, UnitsProduced) in cell E7. Then select cell E7 and drag the fill handle (the small box on the lower right corner of the cell cursor) down through cells E8 and E9.

When using the fill handle, it is important to understand the difference between relative and absolute references. In the formula in cell E7, the reference to cells C7:D7 is based upon the relative position to the cell containing the formula. In this case, this means the two cells in the same row and immediately to the left. This is known as a **relative reference.** When this formula is copied to new cells using the fill handle, the reference is automatically adjusted to refer to the new cell(s) at the same relative location (the two cells in the same row and immediately to the left). The formula in E8 becomes =SUMPRODUCT(C8:D8, UnitsProduced) and the formula in E9 becomes =SUMPRODUCT(C9:D9, UnitsProduced). This is exactly what we want, since we always want the hours used at a given plant to be based upon the hours used per unit produced at that same plant (the two cells in the same row and immediately to the left).

In contrast, the reference to the UnitsProduced in E7 is called an **absolute reference.** These references do not change when they are filled into other cells but instead always refer to the same absolute cell locations.

To make a relative reference, simply enter the cell address (e.g., C7:D7). References referred to by a range name are treated as absolute references. Another way to make an absolute reference to a range of cells is to put $ signs in front of the letter and number of the cell reference (e.g., $C$12:$D$12). See Appendix B for more details about relative and absolute referencing and copying formulas.

Next, ≤ signs are entered in cells F7, F8, and F9 to indicate that each total value to their left cannot be allowed to exceed the corresponding number in column G. The spreadsheet still will allow you to enter trial solutions that violate the ≤ signs. However, these ≤ signs serve as a reminder that such trial solutions need to be rejected if no changes are made in the numbers in column G.

Finally, since the answer to the third question is that the overall measure of performance is the total profit from the two products, this profit (per week) is entered in cell G12. Much like the numbers in column E, it is the sum of products. Since cells C4 and D4 give the profit from *each* door and window produced, the total profit per week from these products is

$$\text{Profit} = \$300(\text{\# of doors}) + \$500(\text{\# of windows})$$

Hence, the equation for cell G12 is

$$\text{G12} = \text{SUMPRODUCT(C4:D4, C12:D12)}$$

Utilizing range names of TotalProfit (G12), UnitProfit (C4:D4), and UnitsProduced (C12:D12), this equation becomes

$$\text{TotalProfit} = \text{SUMPRODUCT(UnitProfit, UnitsProduced)}$$

This is a good example of the benefit of using range names for making the resulting equation easier to interpret.

TotalProfit (G12) is a special kind of output cell. It is the particular cell that is being targeted to be made as large as possible when making decisions regarding production rates. Therefore, TotalProfit (G12) is referred to as the **target cell** (or *objective cell*). The target cell is shaded orange with a heavy border. (In the textbook figures, the orange appears as gray and is distinguished from the changing cells by its heavy border.)

The bottom of Figure 2.3 summarizes all the formulas that need to be entered in the Hours Used column and in the Total Profit cell. Also shown is a summary of the range names (in alphabetical order) and the corresponding cell addresses.

This completes the formulation of the spreadsheet model for the Wyndor problem.

FIGURE 2.3

The spreadsheet model for the Wyndor problem, including the formulas for the target cell TotalProfit (G12) and the other output cells in column E, where the objective is to maximize the target cell.

	A	B	C	D	E	F	G
1		**Wyndor Glass Co. Product-Mix Problem**					
2							
3			**Doors**	**Windows**			
4		Unit Profit	$300	$500			
5					Hours		Hours
6			Hours Used per Unit Produced		Used		Available
7		Plant 1	1	0	0	≤	4
8		Plant 2	0	2	0	≤	12
9		Plant 3	3	2	0	≤	18
10							
11			**Doors**	**Windows**			**Total Profit**
12		Units Produced	0	0			$0

Range Name	Cell
HoursAvailable	G7:G9
HoursUsed	E7:E9
HoursUsedPerUnitProduced	C7:D9
TotalProfit	G12
UnitProfit	C4:D4
UnitsProduced	C12:D12

	E
5	Hours
6	Used
7	=SUMPRODUCT(C7:D7, UnitsProduced)
8	=SUMPRODUCT(C8:D8, UnitsProduced)
9	=SUMPRODUCT(C9:D9, UnitsProduced)

	G
11	Total Profit
12	=SUMPRODUCT(UnitProfit, UnitsProduced)

With this formulation, it becomes easy to analyze any trial solution for the production rates. Each time production rates are entered in cells C12 and D12, Excel immediately calculates the output cells for hours used and total profit. For example, Figure 2.4 shows the spreadsheet when the production rates are set at four doors per week and three windows per week. Cell G12 shows that this yields a total profit of $2,700 per week. Also note that E7 = G7, E8 < G8, and E9 = G9, so the ≤ signs in column F are all satisfied. Thus, this trial solution is *feasible*. However, it would *not* be feasible to further increase both production rates, since this would cause E7 > G7 and E9 > G9.

Does this trial solution provide the best mix of production rates? Not necessarily. It might be possible to further increase the total profit by simultaneously increasing one production

FIGURE 2.4

The spreadsheet for the Wyndor problem with a new trial solution entered into the changing cells, UnitsProduced (C12:D12).

	A	B	C	D	E	F	G
1		**Wyndor Glass Co. Product-Mix Problem**					
2							
3			**Doors**	**Windows**			
4		Unit Profit	$300	$500			
5					Hours		Hours
6			Hours Used per Unit Produced		Used		Available
7		Plant 1	1	0	4	≤	4
8		Plant 2	0	2	6	≤	12
9		Plant 3	3	2	18	≤	18
10							
11			**Doors**	**Windows**			**Total Profit**
12		Units Produced	4	3			$2,700

rate and decreasing the other. However, it is not necessary to continue using trial and error to explore such possibilities. We shall describe in Section 2.5 how the Excel Solver can be used to quickly find the best (optimal) solution.

This Spreadsheet Model Is a Linear Programming Model

The spreadsheet model displayed in Figure 2.3 is an example of a *linear programming* model. The reason is that it possesses all the following characteristics.

Characteristics of a Linear Programming Model on a Spreadsheet

1. Decisions need to be made on the levels of a number of activities, so *changing cells* are used to display these levels. (The two activities for the Wyndor problem are the production of the two new products, so the changing cells display the number of units produced per week for each of these products.)
2. These activity levels can have any value (including fractional values) that satisfy a number of constraints. (The production rates for Wyndor's new products are restricted only by the constraints on the number of hours of production time available in the three plants.)
3. Each **constraint** describes a restriction on the feasible values for the levels of the activities, where a constraint commonly is displayed by having an output cell on the left, a mathematical sign ($\leq$, $\geq$, or $=$) in the middle, and a data cell on the right. (Wyndor's three constraints involving hours available in the plants are displayed in Figures 2.2–2.4 by having output cells in column E, $\leq$ signs in column F, and data cells in column G.)
4. The decisions on activity levels are to be based on an overall measure of performance, which is entered in the *target cell*. The objective is to either *maximize* the target cell or *minimize* the target cell, depending on the nature of the measure of performance. (Wyndor's overall measure of performance is the total profit per week from the two new products, so this measure has been entered in the target cell G12, where the objective is to maximize this target cell.)
5. The Excel equation for each *output cell* (including the target cell) can be expressed as a SUMPRODUCT function,[2] where each term in the sum is the product of a *data cell* and a *changing cell*. (The bottom of Figure 2.3 shows how a SUMPRODUCT function is used for each output cell for the Wyndor problem.)

Characteristics 2 and 5 are key ones for differentiating a linear programming model from other kinds of mathematical models that can be formulated on a spreadsheet.

Characteristic 2 rules out situations where the activity levels need to have *integer* values. For example, such a situation would arise in the Wyndor problem if the decisions to be made were the *total* numbers of doors and windows to produce (which must be integers) rather than the numbers per week (which can have fractional values since a door or window can be started in one week and completed in the next week). When the activity levels do need to have integer values, a similar kind of model (called an *integer programming* model) is used instead by making a small adjustment on the spreadsheet, as will be illustrated in Section 3.2.

Characteristic 5 prohibits those cases where the Excel equation for an output cell cannot be expressed as a SUMPRODUCT function. To illustrate such a case, suppose that the weekly profit from producing Wyndor's new windows can be *more* than doubled by doubling the production rate because of economies in marketing larger amounts. This would mean that the Excel equation for the target cell would need to be more complicated than a SUMPRODUCT function. Consideration of how to formulate such models will be deferred to Chapter 8.

Summary of the Formulation Procedure

The procedure used to formulate a linear programming model on a spreadsheet for the Wyndor problem can be adapted to many other problems as well. Here is a summary of the steps involved in the procedure.

1. Gather the data for the problem (such as summarized in Table 2.1 for the Wyndor problem).
2. Enter the data into *data cells* on a spreadsheet.

---

[2] There also are some special situations where a SUM function can be used instead because all the numbers that would have gone into the corresponding data cells are 1's.

3. Identify the decisions to be made on the levels of activities and designate *changing cells* for displaying these decisions.
4. Identify the constraints on these decisions and introduce *output cells* as needed to specify these constraints.
5. Choose the overall measure of performance to be entered into the *target cell.*
6. Use a SUMPRODUCT function to enter the appropriate value into each output cell (including the target cell).

This procedure does not spell out the details of how to set up the spreadsheet. There generally are alternative ways of doing this rather than a single "right" way. One of the great strengths of spreadsheets is their flexibility for dealing with a wide variety of problems.

Review Questions

1. What are the three questions that need to be answered to begin the process of formulating a linear programming model on a spreadsheet?
2. What are the roles for the data cells, the changing cells, the output cells, and the target cell when formulating such a model?
3. What is the form of the Excel equation for each output cell (including the target cell) when formulating such a model?

2.3 THE MATHEMATICAL MODEL IN THE SPREADSHEET

A linear programming model can be formulated either as a spreadsheet model or as an algebraic model.

There are two widely used methods for formulating a linear programming model. One is to formulate it directly on a spreadsheet, as described in the preceding section. The other is to use algebra to present the model. The two versions of the model are equivalent. The only difference is whether the language of spreadsheets or the language of algebra is used to describe the model. Both versions have their advantages, and it can be helpful to be bilingual. For example, the two versions lead to different, but complementary, ways of analyzing problems like the Wyndor problem (as discussed in the next two sections). Since this book emphasizes the spreadsheet approach, we will only briefly describe the algebraic approach.

Formulating the Wyndor Model Algebraically

The reasoning for the algebraic approach is similar to that for the spreadsheet approach. In fact, except for making entries on a spreadsheet, the initial steps are just as described in the preceding section for the Wyndor problem.

1. Gather the relevant data (Table 2.1 in Section 2.1).
2. Identify the decisions to be made (the production rates for the two new products).
3. Identify the constraints on these decisions (the production time used in the respective plants cannot exceed the amount available).
4. Identify the overall measure of performance for these decisions (the total profit from the two products).
5. Convert the verbal description of the constraints and measure of performance into quantitative expressions in terms of the data and decisions (see below).

Table 2.1 indicates that the number of hours of production time available per week for the two new products in the respective plants are 4, 12, and 18. Using the data in this table for the number of hours used per door or window produced then leads to the following quantitative expressions for the constraints:

$$\text{Plant 1:} \quad (\text{\# of doors}) \leq 4$$
$$\text{Plant 2:} \quad 2(\text{\# of windows}) \leq 12$$
$$\text{Plant 3:} \quad 3(\text{\# of doors}) + 2(\text{\# of windows}) \leq 18$$

In addition, negative production rates are impossible, so two other constraints on the decisions are

$$(\# \text{ of doors}) \geq 0 \quad (\# \text{ of windows}) \geq 0$$

The overall measure of performance has been identified as the total profit from the two products. Since Table 2.1 gives the unit profits for doors and windows as $300 and $500, respectively, the expression obtained in the preceding section for the total profit per week from these products is

$$\text{Profit} = \$300(\# \text{ of doors}) + \$500(\# \text{ of windows})$$

The objective is to make the decisions (number of doors and number of windows) so as to maximize this profit, subject to satisfying all the constraints identified above.

To state this objective in a compact algebraic model, we introduce algebraic symbols to represent the measure of performance and the decisions. Let

P = Profit (total profit per week from the two products, in dollars)

D = # of doors (number of the special new doors to be produced per week)

W = # of windows (number of the special new windows to be produced per week)

Substituting these symbols into the above expressions for the constraints and the measure of performance (and dropping the dollar signs in the latter expression), the linear programming model for the Wyndor problem now can be written in algebraic form as shown below.

Algebraic Model

Choose the values of D and W so as to maximize

$$P = 300D + 500W$$

subject to satisfying all the following constraints:

$$
\begin{aligned}
D &\leq 4 \\
2W &\leq 12 \\
3D + 2W &\leq 18
\end{aligned}
$$

and

$$D \geq 0 \quad W \geq 0$$

Terminology for Linear Programming Models

Much of the terminology of algebraic models also is sometimes used with spreadsheet models. Here are the key terms for both kinds of models in the context of the Wyndor problem.

1. D and W (or C12 and D12 in Figure 2.3) are the **decision variables.**
2. $300D + 500W$ [or SUMPRODUCT (UnitProfit, UnitsProduced)] is the **objective function.**
3. P (or G12) is the *value of the objective function* (or *objective value* for short).
4. $D \geq 0$ and $W \geq 0$ (or C12 ≥ 0 and D12 ≥ 0) are called the **nonnegativity constraints** (or *nonnegativity conditions*).
5. The other constraints are referred to as **functional constraints** (or *structural constraints*).
6. The **parameters** of the model are the constants in the algebraic model (the numbers in the data cells).
7. *Any* choice of values for the decision variables (regardless of how desirable or undesirable the choice) is called a **solution** for the model.
8. A **feasible solution** is one that satisfies all the constraints, whereas an **infeasible solution** violates at least one constraint.
9. The *best* feasible solution, the one that maximizes P (or G12), is called the **optimal solution.**

Comparisons

Management scientists often use algebraic models, but managers generally prefer spreadsheet models.

So what are the relative advantages of algebraic models and spreadsheet models? An algebraic model provides a very concise and explicit statement of the problem. Sophisticated software packages that can solve huge problems generally are based on algebraic models because of both their compactness and their ease of use in rescaling the size of a problem. Management science practitioners with an extensive mathematical background find algebraic models very useful. For others, however, spreadsheet models are far more intuitive. Many very intelligent people (including many managers and business students) find algebraic models overly abstract. Spreadsheets lift this "algebraic curtain." Both managers and business students training to be managers generally live with spreadsheets, not algebraic models. Therefore, the emphasis throughout this book is on spreadsheet models.

Review Questions

1. When formulating a linear programming model, what are the initial steps that are the same with either a spreadsheet formulation or an algebraic formulation?
2. When formulating a linear programming model algebraically, algebraic symbols need to be introduced to represent which kinds of quantities in the model?
3. What are decision variables for a linear programming model? The objective function? Non-negativity constraints? Functional constraints?
4. What is meant by a feasible solution for the model? An optimal solution?

2.4 THE GRAPHICAL METHOD FOR SOLVING TWO-VARIABLE PROBLEMS

graphical method
The graphical method provides helpful intuition about linear programming.

Linear programming problems having only two decision variables, like the Wyndor problem, can be solved by a **graphical method.**

Although this method cannot be used to solve problems with more than two decision variables (and most linear programming problems have far more than two), it still is well worth learning. The procedure provides geometric intuition about linear programming and what it is trying to achieve. This intuition is helpful in analyzing larger problems that cannot be solved directly by the graphical method.

It is more convenient to apply the graphical method to the *algebraic version* of the linear programming model rather than the spreadsheet version. We shall briefly illustrate the method by using the algebraic model obtained for the Wyndor problem in the preceding section. (A far more detailed description of the graphical method, including its application to the Wyndor problem, is provided in the supplement to this chapter on the CD-ROM.) For this purpose, keep in mind that

D = Production rate for the special new doors (the number in changing cell C12 of the spreadsheet)

W = Production rate for the special new windows (the number in changing cell D12 of the spreadsheet)

The key to the graphical method is the fact that possible solutions can be displayed as points on a two-dimensional graph that has a horizontal axis giving the value of D and a vertical axis giving the value of W. Figure 2.5 shows some sample points.

Notation: Either $(D, W) = (2, 3)$ or just $(2, 3)$ refers to the solution where $D = 2$ and $W = 3$, as well as to the corresponding point in the graph. Similarly, $(D, W) = (4, 6)$ means $D = 4$ and $W = 6$, whereas the origin $(0, 0)$ means $D = 0$ and $W = 0$.

To find the optimal solution (the best feasible solution), we first need to display graphically where the feasible solutions are. To do this, we must consider each constraint, identify the solutions graphically that are permitted by that constraint, and then combine this information to identify the solutions permitted by all the constraints. The solutions permitted by all the constraints are the feasible solutions and the portion of the two-dimensional graph where the feasible solutions lie is referred to as the **feasible region.**

FIGURE 2.5
Graph showing the points
$(D, W) = (2, 3)$ and
$(D, W) = (4, 6)$ for the
Wyndor Glass Co.
product-mix problem.

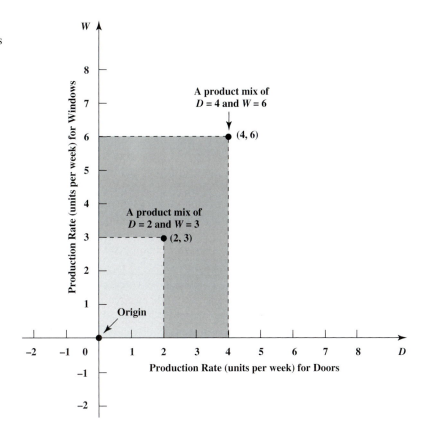

The shaded region in Figure 2.6 shows the feasible region for the Wyndor problem. We now will outline how this feasible region was identified by considering the five constraints one at a time.

FIGURE 2.6
Graph showing how the
feasible region is formed
by the constraint
boundary lines, where the
arrows indicate which side
of each line is permitted
by the corresponding
constraint.

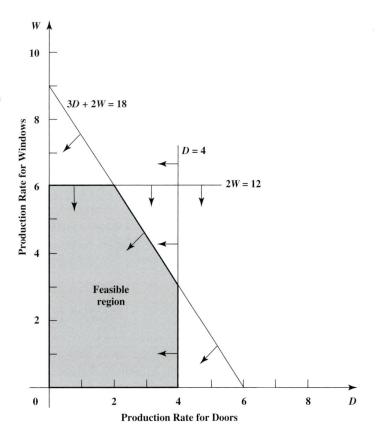

To begin, the constraint $D \geq 0$ implies that consideration must be limited to points that lie on or to the right of the W axis. Similarly, the constraint $W \geq 0$ restricts consideration to the points on or above the D axis.

Next, consider the first functional constraint, $D \leq 4$, which limits the usage of Plant 1 for producing the special new doors to a maximum of four hours per week. The solutions permitted by this constraint are those that lie on, or to the left of, the vertical line that intercepts the D axis at $D = 4$, as indicated by the arrows pointing to the left from this line in Figure 2.6.

The second functional constraint, $2W \leq 12$, has a similar effect, except now the boundary of its permissible region is given by a *horizontal* line with the equation, $2W = 12$ (or $W = 6$), as indicated by the arrows pointing downward from this line in Figure 2.6. The line forming the boundary of what is permitted by a constraint is sometimes referred to as a **constraint boundary line,** and its equation may be called a **constraint boundary equation.** Frequently, a *constraint boundary line* is identified by its equation.

For each of the first two functional constraints, $D \leq 4$ and $2W \leq 12$, note that the equation for the constraint boundary line ($D = 4$ and $2W = 12$, respectively) is obtained by replacing the inequality sign with an equality sign. For *any* constraint with an inequality sign (whether a functional constraint or a nonnegativity constraint), the general rule for obtaining its constraint boundary equation is to substitute an equality sign for the inequality sign.

We now need to consider one more functional constraint, $3D + 2W \leq 18$. Its constraint boundary equation

$$3D + 2W = 18$$

includes both variables, so the boundary line it represents is neither a vertical line nor a horizontal line. Therefore, the boundary line must intercept (cross through) both axes somewhere. But where?

When a constraint boundary line is neither a vertical line nor a horizontal line, the line *intercepts* the D axis at the point on the line where $W = 0$. Similarly, the line *intercepts* the W axis at the point on the line where $D = 0$.

Hence, the constraint boundary line $3D + 2W = 18$ intercepts the D axis at the point where $W = 0$.

When $W = 0$, $3D + 2W = 18$ becomes $3D = 18$
so the intercept with the D axis is at $D = 6$

Similarly, the line intercepts the W axis where $D = 0$.

When $D = 0$, $3D + 2W = 18$ becomes $2W = 18$
so the intercept with the D axis is at $W = 9$

Consequently, the constraint boundary line is the line that passes through these two intercept points, as shown in Figure 2.6.

As indicated by the arrows emanating from this line in Figure 2.6, the solutions permitted by the constraint $3D + 2W \leq 18$ are those that lie on the *origin* side of the constraint boundary line $3D + 2W = 18$. The easiest way to verify this is to check whether the origin itself, $(D, W) = (0, 0)$, satisfies the constraint.[3] If it does, then the permissible region lies on the side of the constraint boundary line where the origin is. Otherwise, it lies on the other side. In this case,

$$3(0) + 2(0) = 0$$

so $(D, W) = (0, 0)$ satisfies

$$3D + 2W \leq 18$$

(In fact, the origin satisfies *any* constraint with a $\leq$ sign and a positive right-hand side.)

A feasible solution for a linear programming problem must satisfy *all* the constraints *simultaneously.* The arrows in Figure 2.6 indicate that the nonnegative solutions permitted by

[3] The one case where using the origin to help determine the permissible region does *not* work is if the constraint boundary line passes through the origin. In this case, any other point *not* lying on this line can be used just like the origin.

feasible region
The points in the feasible region are those that satisfy *every* constraint.

each of these constraints lie on the side of the constraint boundary line where the origin is (or on the line itself). Therefore, the *feasible solutions* are those that lie nearer to the origin than *all three* constraint boundary lines (or on the line nearest the origin).

Having identified the feasible region, the final step is to find which of these feasible solutions is the best one—the *optimal solution*. For the Wyndor problem, the objective happens to be to *maximize* the total profit per week from the two products (denoted by P). Therefore, we want to find the feasible solution (D, W) that makes the value of the objective function

$$P = 300D + 500W$$

as large as possible.

To accomplish this, we need to be able to locate all the points (D, W) on the graph that give a specified value of the objective function. For example, consider a value of $P = 1,500$ for the objective function. Which points (D, W) give $300D + 500W = 1,500$?

This equation is the equation of a *line*. Just as when plotting constraint boundary lines, the location of this line is found by identifying its intercepts with the two axes. When $W = 0$, this equation yields $D = 5$, and similarly, $W = 3$ when $D = 0$, so these are the two intercepts, as shown by the bottom slanting line passing through the feasible region in Figure 2.7.

$P = 1,500$ is just one sample value of the objective function. For any other specified value of P, the points (D, W) that give this value of P also lie on a line called an *objective function line*.

An **objective function line** is a line whose points all have the same value of the objective function.

For the bottom objective function line in Figure 2.7, the points on this line that lie in the feasible region provide alternate ways of achieving an objective function value of $P = 1,500$. Can we do better? Let us try doubling the value of P to $P = 3,000$. The corresponding objective function line

$$300D + 500W = 3,000$$

is shown as the middle line in Figure 2.7. (Ignore the top line for the moment.) Once again, this line includes points in the feasible region, so $P = 3,000$ is achievable.

Let us pause to note two interesting features of these objective function lines for $P = 1,500$ and $P = 3,000$. First, these lines are *parallel*. Second, *doubling* the value of P from 1,500 to 3,000 also *doubles* the value of W at which the line intercepts the W axis from $W = 3$ to $W = 6$. These features are no coincidence, as indicated by the following properties.

FIGURE 2.7
Graph showing three objective function lines for the Wyndor Glass Co. product-mix problem, where the top one passes through the optimal solution.

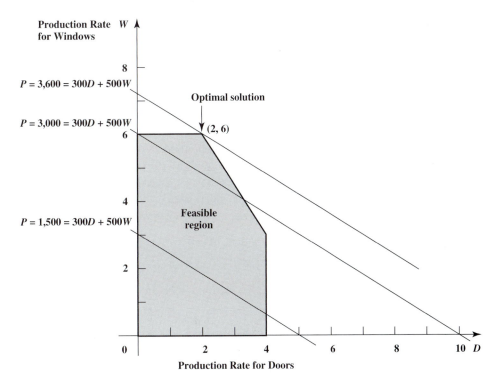

Key Properties of Objective Function Lines: All objective function lines for the same problem are *parallel*. Furthermore, the value of W at which an objective function line intercepts the W axis is *proportional* to the value of P.

These key properties of objective function lines suggest the strategy to follow to find the optimal solution. We already have tried $P = 1,500$ and $P = 3,000$ in Figure 2.7 and found that their objective function lines include points in the feasible region. Increasing P again will generate another parallel objective function line farther from the origin. The objective function line of special interest is the one farthest from the origin that still includes a point in the feasible region. This is the third objective function line in Figure 2.7. The point on this line that is in the feasible region, $(D, W) = (2, 6)$, is the optimal solution since no other feasible solution has a larger value of P.

Optimal Solution

$D = 2$ (Produce 2 special new doors per week)

$W = 6$ (Produce 6 special new windows per week)

These values of D and W can be substituted into the objective function to find the value of P.

$$P = 300D + 500W = 300(2) + 500(6) = 3,600$$

Check out this module in the Interactive Management Science Modules to learn more about the graphical method.

The Interactive Management Science Modules (available at **www.mhhe.com/hillier3e** or in your CD-ROM) includes a module that is designed to help increase your understanding of the graphical method. This module, called *Graphical Linear Programming and Sensitivity Analysis,* enables you to immediately see the constraint boundary lines and objective function lines that result from any linear programming model with two decision variables. You also can see how the objective function lines lead you to the optimal solution. Another key feature of the module is the ease with which you can perform what-if analysis.

Summary of the Graphical Method

The graphical method can be used to solve any linear programming problem having only two decision variables. The method uses the following steps:

1. Draw the constraint boundary line for each functional constraint. Use the origin (or any point not on the line) to determine which side of the line is permitted by the constraint.
2. Find the feasible region by determining where all constraints are satisfied simultaneously.
3. Determine the slope of one objective function line. All other objective function lines will have the same slope.
4. Move a straight edge with this slope through the feasible region in the direction of improving values of the objective function. Stop at the last instant that the straight edge still passes through a point in the feasible region. This line given by the straight edge is the optimal objective function line.
5. A feasible point on the optimal objective function line is an optimal solution.

Review Questions

1. The graphical method can be used to solve linear programming problems with how many decision variables?
2. What do the axes represent when applying the graphical method to the Wyndor problem?
3. What is a constraint boundary line? A constraint boundary equation?
4. What is the easiest way of determining which side of a constraint boundary line is permitted by the constraint?

2.5 USING EXCEL TO SOLVE LINEAR PROGRAMMING PROBLEMS

The graphical method is very useful for gaining geometric intuition about linear programming, but its practical use is severely limited by only being able to solve tiny problems with two decision variables. Another procedure that will solve linear programming problems of any

Excel Tip: If you select cells by clicking on them, they will first appear in the dialogue box with their cell addresses and with dollar signs (e.g., $C$9:$D$9). You can ignore the dollar signs. Solver eventually will replace both the cell addresses and the dollar signs with the corresponding range name (if a range name has been defined for the given cell addresses), but only after either adding a constraint or closing and reopening the Solver dialogue box.

reasonable size is needed. Fortunately, Excel includes a tool called **Solver** that will do this once the spreadsheet model has been formulated as described in Section 2.2. (A more powerful version of Solver, called *Premium Solver for Education* also is available in your MS Courseware.) To access Solver the first time, you need to install it by going to Excel's Add-in menu and adding Solver, after which you will find it in the Tools menu.

Figure 2.3 in Section 2.2 shows the spreadsheet model for the Wyndor problem. The values of the decision variables (the production rates for the two products) are in the *changing cells,* UnitsProduced (C12:D12), and the value of the objective function (the total profit per week from the two products) is in the *target cell,* TotalProfit (G12). To get started, an arbitrary trial solution has been entered by placing zeroes in the changing cells. The Solver will then change these to the optimal values after solving the problem.

This procedure is started by choosing Solver on the Data tab (for Excel 2007) or in the Tools menu (for earlier versions of Excel). The Solver dialogue box is shown in Figure 2.8.

Before the Solver can start its work, it needs to know exactly where each component of the model is located on the spreadsheet. You have the choice of typing the range names, typing in the cell addresses, or clicking on the cells in the spreadsheet. Figure 2.8 shows the result of using the first choice, so TotalProfit (rather than G12) has been entered for the target cell and UnitsProduced (rather than the range C12:D12) has been entered for the changing cells. Since the goal is to maximize the target cell, Max also has been selected.

Next, the cells containing the functional constraints need to be specified. This is done by clicking on the Add button on the Solver dialogue box. This brings up the Add Constraint dialogue box shown in Figure 2.9. The ≤ signs in cells F7, F8, and F9 of Figure 2.3 are a reminder that the cells in HoursUsed (E7:E9) all need to be less than or equal to the corresponding cells in HoursAvailable (G7:G9). These constraints are specified for the Solver by entering HoursUsed (or E7:E9) on the left-hand side of the Add Constraint dialogue box and HoursAvailable (or G7:G9) on the right-hand side. For the sign between these two sides, there is a menu to choose between $<=$, $=$, or $>=$, so $<=$ has been chosen. This choice is needed

FIGURE 2.8

The Solver dialogue box after specifying which cells in Figure 2.3 are the target cell and the changing cells, plus indicating that the target cell is to be maximized.

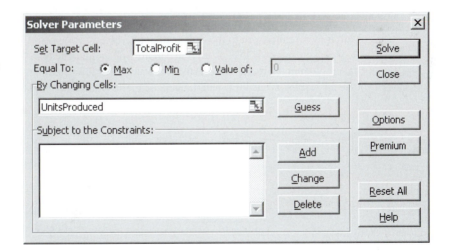

FIGURE 2.9

The Add Constraint dialogue box after specifying that cells E7, E8, and E9 in Figure 2.3 are required to be less than or equal to cells G7, G8, and G9, respectively.

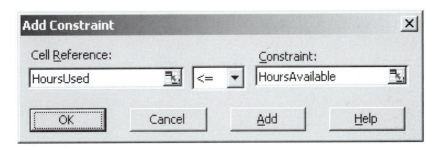

FIGURE 2.10

The Solver dialogue box after specifying the entire model in terms of the spreadsheet.

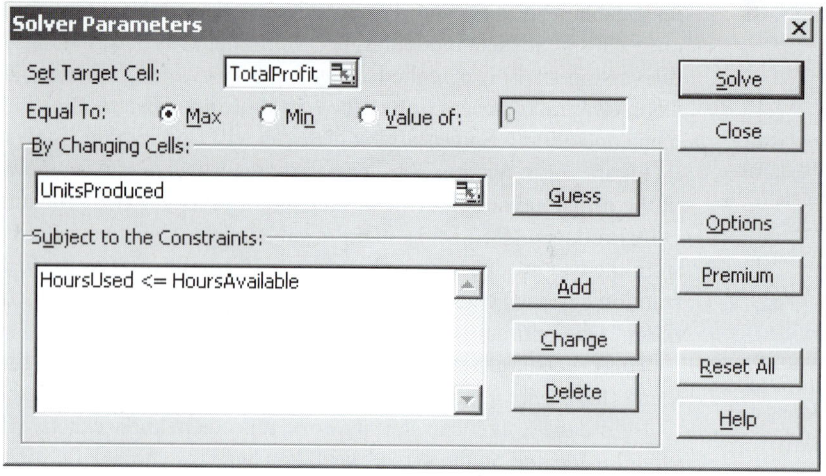

The Add Constraint dialogue box is used to specify all the functional constraints.

even though ≤ signs were previously entered in column F of the spreadsheet because the Solver only uses the constraints that are specified with the Add Constraint dialogue box.

If there were more functional constraints to add, you would click on Add to bring up a new Add Constraint dialogue box. However, since there are no more in this example, the next step is to click on OK to go back to the Solver dialogue box.

The Solver dialogue box now summarizes the complete model (see Figure 2.10) in terms of the spreadsheet in Figure 2.3. However, before asking Solver to solve the model, one more step should be taken. Clicking on the Options button brings up the dialogue box shown in Figure 2.11. This box allows you to specify a number of options about how the problem will be solved. The most important of these are the Assume Linear Model option and the Assume Non-Negative option. Be sure that both options are checked as shown in the figure. This tells Solver that the problem is a *linear* programming problem and that nonnegativity constraints are needed for the changing cells to reject negative production rates. Regarding the other options, accepting the default values shown in the figure usually is fine for small problems. Clicking on the OK button then returns you to the Solver dialogue box.

The Assume Linear Model and Assume Non-Negative options specify that the problem is a linear programming problem with nonnegativity constraints.

Now you are ready to click on Solve in the Solver dialogue box, which will start the solving of the problem in the background. After a few seconds (for a small problem), Solver will then indicate the results. Typically, it will indicate that it has found an optimal solution, as specified in the

FIGURE 2.11

The Solver Options dialogue box after checking the Assume Linear Model and Assume Non-Negative options to indicate that we wish to solve a linear programming model that has nonnegativity constraints.

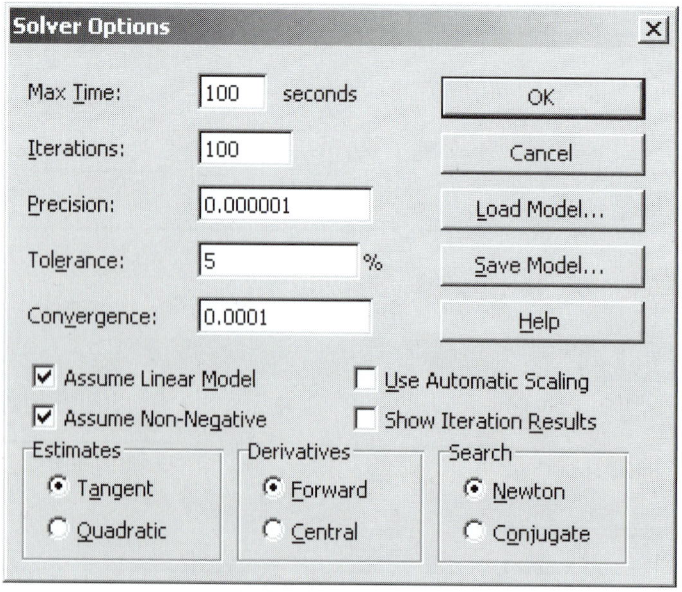

Frontline Systems, the original developer of the standard Solver included with Excel, also has developed Premium versions of Solver that provide additional functionality. One such version (Premium Solver for Education) is available in your MS Courseware. Once it is installed, it is invoked by choosing Premium Solver from the Add-Ins tab (for Excel 2007) or the Tools menu (for earlier versions of Excel). This brings up the dialogue box shown below for a typical example.

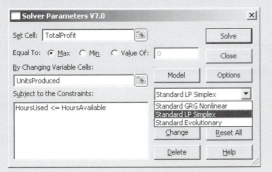

Premium Solver for Education is more robust than the standard Solver in the sense that it sometimes will accurately solve difficult problems where the standard Solver fails. In addition to this advantage, the other key advantage of Premium Solver for Education is that it includes three different search techniques chosen in a dropdown menu. The choices are Standard GRG Nonlinear, Standard LP Simplex, and Standard Evolutionary. The first choice (Standard GRG Nonlinear) is basically identical to using the standard Solver *without* the "Assume Linear Model" option selected. The second choice (Standard Simplex LP) is basically equivalent to using the standard Solver *with* the "Assume Linear Model" option selected. The final choice (Standard Evolutionary) employs the Evolutionary Solver that will be discussed in Chapter 8. This choice is not available with the standard Solver.

Even with the Premium Solver for Education installed, the standard Excel Solver can still be used in the usual way by choosing Solver on the Data tab (for Excel 2007) or the Tools menu (for earlier versions of Excel). We encourage you to install and try the Premium Solver for Education as well.

Solver Tip: The message "Solver could not find a feasible solution" means that there are no solutions that satisfy all the constraints. The message "The Set Cell values do not converge" means that Solver could not find a best solution, because better solutions always are available (e.g., if the constraints do not prevent infinite profit). The message "The conditions for Assume Linear Model are not satisfied" means that the Assume Linear Model checkbox was checked, but the model is not linear.

Solver Results dialogue box shown in Figure 2.12. If the model has no feasible solutions or no optimal solution, the dialogue box will indicate that instead by stating that "Solver could not find a feasible solution" or that "The Set Cell values do not converge." (Section 14.1 will describe how these possibilities can occur.) The dialogue box also presents the option of generating various reports. One of these (the Sensitivity Report) will be discussed in detail in Chapter 5.

After solving the model, the Solver replaces the original numbers in the changing cells with the optimal numbers, as shown in Figure 2.13. Thus, the optimal solution is to produce two doors per week and six windows per week, just as was found by the graphical method in the preceding section. The spreadsheet also indicates the corresponding number in the target cell (a total profit of $3,600 per week), as well as the numbers in the output cells HoursUsed (E7:E9).

At this point, you might want to check what would happen to the optimal solution if any of the numbers in the data cells were to be changed to other possible values. This is easy to do because Solver saves all the addresses for the target cell, changing cells, constraints, and so on when you save the file. All you need to do is make the changes you want in the data cells and then click on Solve in the Solver dialogue box again. (Chapter 5 will focus on this kind of *what-if analysis,* including how to use the Solver's Sensitivity Report to expedite the analysis.)

To assist you with experimenting with these kinds of changes, your MS Courseware includes Excel files for this chapter (as for others) that provide a complete formulation and

---

FIGURE 2.12
The Solver Results dialogue box that indicates that an optimal solution has been found.

solution of the examples here (the Wyndor problem and the one in the next section) in a spreadsheet format. We encourage you to "play" with these examples to see what happens with different data, different solutions, and so forth. You might also find these spreadsheets useful as templates for homework problems.

Review Questions

1. Which dialogue box is used to enter the addresses for the target cell and the changing cells?
2. Which dialogue box is used to specify the functional constraints for the model?
3. With the Solver Options dialogue box, which options normally need to be chosen to solve a linear programming model?

2.6 A MINIMIZATION EXAMPLE—THE PROFIT & GAMBIT CO. ADVERTISING-MIX PROBLEM

The analysis of the Wyndor Glass Co. case study in Sections 2.2 and 2.5 illustrated how to formulate and solve one type of linear programming model on a spreadsheet. The same general approach can be applied to many other problems as well. The great flexibility of linear programming and spreadsheets provides a variety of options for how to adapt the

FIGURE 2.13
The spreadsheet obtained after solving the Wyndor problem.

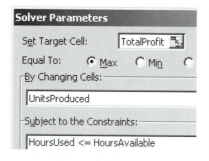

	A	B	C	D	E	F	G
1		**Wyndor Glass Co. Product-Mix Problem**					
2							
3			**Doors**	**Windows**			
4		Unit Profit	$300	$500			
5					Hours		Hours
6			Hours Used per Unit Produced		Used		Available
7		Plant 1	1	0	2	≤	4
8		Plant 2	0	2	12	≤	12
9		Plant 3	3	2	18	≤	18
10							
11			**Doors**	**Windows**			**Total Profit**
12		Units Produced	2	6			$3,600

Solver Parameters

Set Target Cell: TotalProfit
Equal To: ⦿ Max ○ Min
By Changing Cells:
UnitsProduced
Subject to the Constraints:
HoursUsed <= HoursAvailable

Solver Options
☑ Assume Linear Model
☑ Assume Non-Negative

	E
5	Hours
6	Used
7	=SUMPRODUCT(C7:D7, UnitsProduced)
8	=SUMPRODUCT(C8:D8, UnitsProduced)
9	=SUMPRODUCT(C9:D9, UnitsProduced)

	G
11	Total Profit
12	=SUMPRODUCT(UnitProfit, UnitsProduced)

Range Name	Cell
HoursAvailable	G7:G9
HoursUsed	E7:E9
HoursUsedPerUnitProduced	C7:D9
TotalProfit	G12
UnitProfit	C4:D4
UnitsProduced	C12:D12

formulation of the spreadsheet model to fit each new problem. Our next example illustrates some options not used for the Wyndor problem.

Planning an Advertising Campaign

The Profit & Gambit Co. produces cleaning products for home use. This is a highly competitive market, and the company continually struggles to increase its small market share. Management has decided to undertake a major new advertising campaign that will focus on the following three key products:

- A spray prewash stain remover.
- A liquid laundry detergent.
- A powder laundry detergent.

This campaign will use both television and the print media. A commercial has been developed to run on national television that will feature the liquid detergent. The advertisement for the print media will promote all three products and will include cents-off coupons that consumers can use to purchase the products at reduced prices. The general goal is to increase the sales of each of these products (but especially the liquid detergent) over the next year by a significant percentage over the past year. Specifically, management has set the following goals for the campaign:

- Sales of the stain remover should increase by at least 3 percent.
- Sales of the liquid detergent should increase by at least 18 percent.
- Sales of the powder detergent should increase by at least 4 percent.

Table 2.2 shows the estimated increase in sales for each *unit* of advertising in the respective outlets.[4] (A *unit* is a standard block of advertising that Profit & Gambit commonly purchases, but other amounts also are allowed.) The reason for -1 percent for the powder detergent in the Television column is that the TV commercial featuring the new liquid detergent will take away some sales from the powder detergent. The bottom row of the table shows the cost per unit of advertising for each of the two outlets.

Management's objective is to determine how much to advertise in each medium to meet the sales goals at a minimum total cost.

Formulating a Spreadsheet Model for This Problem

The procedure summarized at the end of Section 2.2 can be used to formulate the spreadsheet model for this problem. Each step of the procedure is repeated below, followed by a description of how it is performed here.

1. Gather the data for the problem. This has been done as presented in Table 2.2.
2. Enter the data into *data cells* on a spreadsheet. The top half of Figure 2.14 shows this spreadsheet. The data cells are in columns C and D (rows 4 and 8 to 10), as well as in cells G8:G10. Note how this particular formatting of the spreadsheet has facilitated a direct transfer of the data from Table 2.2.

TABLE 2.2
Data for the Profit & Gambit Co. Advertising-Mix Problem

Product	Increase in Sales per Unit of Advertising		Minimum Required Increase
	Television	Print Media	
Stain remover	0%	1%	3%
Liquid detergent	3	2	18
Powder detergent	−1	4	4
Unit cost	$1 million	$2 million	

[4] A simplifying assumption is being made that each additional unit of advertising in a particular outlet will yield the same increase in sales regardless of how much advertising already is being done. This becomes a poor assumption when the levels of advertising under consideration can reach a saturation level (as in Case 8.1), but is a reasonable approximation for the small levels of advertising being considered in this problem.

FIGURE 2.14

The spreadsheet model for the Profit & Gambit problem, including the formulas for the target cell TotalCost (G14) and the other output cells in column E, as well as the specifications needed to set up the Solver. The changing cells, AdvertisingUnits (C14:D14), show the optimal solution obtained by the Solver.

	A	B	C	D	E	F	G
1		**Profit & Gambit Co. Advertising-Mix Problem**					
2							
3			Television	Print Media			
4		Unit Cost ($millions)	1	2			
5							
6					Increased		Minimum
7			Increase in Sales per Unit of Advertising		Sales		Increase
8		Stain Remover	0%	1%	3%	≥	3%
9		Liquid Detergent	3%	2%	18%	≥	18%
10		Powder Detergent	-1%	4%	8%	≥	4%
11							
12							Total Cost
13			Television	Print Media			($millions)
14		Advertising Units	4	3			10

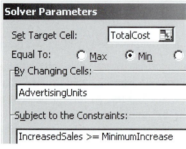

Solver Parameters

Set Target Cell: `TotalCost`

Equal To: ○ Max ● Min ○

By Changing Cells:

`AdvertisingUnits`

Subject to the Constraints:

`IncreasedSales >= MinimumIncrease`

Solver Options

☑ Assume Linear Model

☑ Assume Non-Negative

	E
6	Increased
7	Sales
8	=SUMPRODUCT(C8:D8, AdvertisingUnits)
9	=SUMPRODUCT(C9:D9, AdvertisingUnits)
10	=SUMPRODUCT(C10:D10, AdvertisingUnits)

	G
12	Total Cost
13	($millions)
14	=SUMPRODUCT(UnitCost, AdvertisingUnits)

Range Name	Cells
AdvertisingUnits	C14: D14
IncreasedSales	E8: E10
IncreasedSalesPerUnitAdvertising	C8: D10
MinimumIncrease	G8: G10
TotalCost	G14
UnitCost	C4: D4

3. Identify the decisions to be made on the levels of activities and designate *changing cells* for making these decisions. In this case, the activities of concern are *advertising on television* and *advertising in the print media,* so the *levels* of these activities refer to the *amount* of advertising in these media. Therefore, the decisions to be made are

Decision 1: TV = Number of units of advertising on television

Decision 2: PM = Number of units of advertising in the print media

The two gray cells with light borders in Figure 2.14—C14 and D14—have been designated as the changing cells to hold these numbers:

TV → cell C14   PM → cell D14

with AdvertisingUnits as the range name for these cells. (See the bottom of Figure 2.14 for a list of all the range names.) These are natural locations for the changing cells, since each one is in the column for the corresponding advertising medium. To get started, an arbitrary trial solution (such as all zeroes) is entered into these cells. (Figure 2.14 shows the optimal solution after having already applied the Solver.)

4. Identify the constraints on these decisions and introduce *output cells* as needed to specify these constraints. The three constraints imposed by management are the goals for the increased sales for the respective products, as shown in the rightmost column of Table 2.2. These constraints are

Stain remover:	Total increase in sales ≥ 3%
Liquid detergent:	Total increase in sales ≥ 18%
Powder detergent:	Total increase in sales ≥ 4%

The second and third columns of Table 2.2 indicate that the *total* increases in sales from both forms of advertising are

Total for stain remover	= 1% of PM
Total for liquid detergent	= 3% of TV + 2% of PM
Total for powder detergent	= −1% of TV + 4% of PM

Unlike the Wyndor problem, we need to use ≥ signs for these constraints.

Consequently, since rows 8, 9, and 10 in the spreadsheet are being used to provide information about the three products, cells E8, E9, and E10 are introduced as output cells to show the total increase in sales for the respective products. In addition, ≥ signs have been entered in column F to remind us that the increased sales need to be at least as large as the numbers in column G. (The use of ≥ signs here rather than ≤ signs is one key difference from the spreadsheet model for the Wyndor problem in Figure 2.3.)

Unlike the Wyndor problem, the objective now is to minimize the target cell.

5. Choose the overall measure of performance to be entered into the *target cell*. Management's stated objective is to determine how much to advertise in each medium to meet the sales goals at a *minimum total cost*. Therefore, the *total cost* of the advertising is entered in the target cell TotalCost(G14). G14 is a natural location for this cell since it is in the same row as the changing cells. The bottom row of Table 2.2 indicates that the number going into this cell is

$$\text{Cost} = (\$1 \text{ million}) \text{ TV} + (\$2 \text{ million}) \text{ PM} \rightarrow \text{cell G14}$$

6. Use a SUMPRODUCT function to enter the appropriate value into each output cell (including the target cell). Based on the above expressions for cost and total increases in sales, the SUMPRODUCT functions needed here for the output cells are those shown under the right side of the spreadsheet in Figure 2.14. Note that each of these functions involves the relevant data cells and the changing cells, AdvertisingUnits(C14, D14).

   This spreadsheet model is a linear programming model, since it possesses all the characteristics of such models enumerated in Section 2.2.

Applying the Solver to This Model

The procedure for using the Excel Solver to obtain an optimal solution for this model is basically the same as described in Section 2.5. The key part of the Solver dialogue box is shown below the left-hand side of the spreadsheet in Figure 2.14. In addition to specifying the target cell and changing cells, the constraints that IncreasedSales ≥ MinimumIncrease have been specified in this box by using the Add Constraint dialogue box. Since the objective is to *minimize* total cost, Min also has been selected. (This is in contrast to the choice of Max for the Wyndor problem.)

   The lower left-hand side of Figure 2.14 shows the options selected after clicking on the Options button in the Solver dialogue box. The Assume Linear Model option specifies that the model is a linear programming model. The Assume Non-Negative option specifies that the changing cells need nonnegativity constraints because negative values of advertising levels are not possible alternatives.

   After clicking on Solve in the Solver dialogue box, the optimal solution shown in the changing cells of the spreadsheet in Figure 2.14 is obtained.

An Application Vignette

Samsung Electronics Corp., Ltd. (SEC), is a leading merchant of dynamic and static random access memory devices and other advanced digital integrated circuits. Its site at Kiheung, South Korea (probably the largest semiconductor fabrication site in the world), fabricates more than 300,000 silicon wafers per month and employs over 10,000 people.

Cycle time is the industry's term for the elapsed time from the release of a batch of blank silicon wafers into the fabrication process until completion of the devices that are fabricated on those wafers. Reducing cycle times is an ongoing goal since it both decreases costs and enables offering shorter lead times to potential customers, a real key to maintaining or increasing market share in a very competitive industry.

Three factors present particularly major challenges when striving to reduce cycle times. One is that the product mix changes continually. Another is that the company often needs to make substantial changes in the fab-out schedule inside the target cycle time as it revises forecasts of customer demand. The third is that the machines of a general type are not homogeneous so only a small number of machines are qualified to perform each device step.

A management science team developed a huge linear programming model with tens of thousands of decision variables and functional constraints to cope with these challenges. The objective function involved minimizing backorders and finished-goods inventory.

The ongoing implementation of this model enabled the company to reduce manufacturing cycle times to fabricate dynamic random access memory devices from more than 80 days to less than 30 days. This tremendous improvement and the resulting reduction in both manufacturing costs and sale prices enabled Samsung to capture an additional $200 million in annual sales revenue.

Source: R. C. Leachman, J. Kang, and Y. Lin, "SLIM: Short Cycle Time and Low Inventory in Manufacturing at Samsung Electronics," *Interfaces* 32, no.1 (January–February 2002), pp. 61–77.

Optimal Solution

$C14 = 4$ (Undertake 4 units of advertising on television)

$D14 = 3$ (Undertake 3 units of advertising in the print media)

The target cell indicates that the total cost of this advertising plan would be $10 million.

The Mathematical Model in the Spreadsheet

When performing step 5 of the procedure for formulating a spreadsheet model, the total cost of advertising was determined to be

$$\text{Cost} = \text{TV} + 2\,\text{PM} \quad \text{(in millions of dollars)}$$

where the objective is to choose the values of TV (number of units of advertising on television) and PM (number of units of advertising in the print media) so as to minimize this cost. Step 4 identified three functional constraints:

Stain remover: $\qquad\qquad\qquad\qquad 1\% \text{ of PM} \geq 3\%$

Liquid detergent: $\qquad 3\% \text{ of TV} + 2\% \text{ of PM} \geq 18\%$

Powder detergent: $\quad -1\% \text{ of TV} + 4\% \text{ of PM} \geq 4\%$

Choosing the Assume Non-Negative option with the Solver recognized that TV and PM cannot be negative. Therefore, after dropping the percentage signs from the functional constraints, the complete mathematical model in the spreadsheet can be stated in the following succinct form.

Minimize $\text{Cost} = \text{TV} + 2\,\text{PM}$ (in millions of dollars)

subject to

Stain remover increased sales: $\qquad\qquad \text{PM} \geq 3$

Liquid detergent increased sales: $\quad 3\,\text{TV} + 2\,\text{PM} \geq 18$

Powder detergent increased sales: $\quad -\text{TV} + 4\,\text{PM} \geq 4$

and

$$\text{TV} \geq 0 \qquad \text{PM} \geq 0$$

Implicit in this statement is "Choose the values of TV and PM so as to . . . ." The term "subject to" is shorthand for "Choose these values *subject to* the requirement that the values satisfy all the following constraints."

This model is the *algebraic* version of the *linear programming* model in the spreadsheet. Note how the parameters (constants) of this algebraic model come directly from the numbers in Table 2.2. In fact, the entire model could have been formulated directly from this table.

The differences between this algebraic model and the one obtained for the Wyndor problem in Section 2.3 lead to some interesting changes in how the graphical method is applied to solve the model. To further expand your geometric intuition about linear programming, we briefly describe this application of the graphical method next.

Since this linear programming model has only two decision variables, it can be solved by the graphical method described in Section 2.4. The method needs to be adapted in two ways to fit this particular problem. First, because all the functional constraints now have a $\geq$ sign with a positive right-hand side, after obtaining the constraint boundary lines in the usual way, the arrows indicating which side of each line satisfies that constraint now all point *away* from the origin. Second, the method is adapted to *minimization* by moving the objective function lines in the direction that *reduces* Cost and then stopping at the last instant that an objective function line still passes through a point in the feasible region, where such a point then is an optimal solution. The supplement to this chapter includes a description of how the graphical method is applied to the Profit & Gambit problem in this way.

Review
Questions

1. What kind of product is produced by the Profit & Gambit Co.?
2. Which advertising media are being considered for the three products under consideration?
3. What is management's objective for the problem being addressed?
4. What was the rationale for the placement of the target cell and the changing cells in the spreadsheet model?
5. The algebraic form of the linear programming model for this problem differs from that for the Wyndor Glass Co. problem in which two major ways?

2.7   LINEAR PROGRAMMING FROM A BROADER PERSPECTIVE

Linear programming is an invaluable aid to managerial decision making in all kinds of companies throughout the world. The emergence of powerful spreadsheet packages has helped to further spread the use of this technique. The ease of formulating and solving small linear programming models on a spreadsheet now enables some managers with a very modest background in management science to do this themselves on their own desktop.

Many linear programming studies are major projects involving decisions on the levels of many hundreds or thousands of activities. For such studies, sophisticated software packages that go beyond spreadsheets generally are used for both the formulation and solution processes. These studies normally are conducted by technically trained teams of management scientists, sometimes called operations research analysts, at the instigation of management. Management needs to keep in touch with the management science team to ensure that the study reflects management's objectives and needs. However, management generally does not get involved with the technical details of the study.

Consequently, there is little reason for a manager to know the details of how linear programming models are solved beyond the rudiments of using the Excel Solver. (Even most management science teams will use commercial software packages for solving their models on a computer rather than developing their own software.) Similarly, a manager does not need to know the technical details of how to formulate complex models, how to validate such a model, how to interact with the computer when formulating and solving a large model, how to efficiently perform what-if analysis with such a model, and so forth. Therefore, these technical details are de-emphasized in this book. A student who becomes interested in conducting technical analyses as part of a management science team should plan to take additional, more technically oriented courses in management science.

So what does an enlightened manager need to know about linear programming? A manager needs to have a good intuitive feeling for what linear programming is. One objective of this chapter is to begin to develop that intuition. That's the purpose of studying the graphical method for solving two-variable problems. It is rare to have a *real* linear programming problem with as few as two decision variables. Therefore, the graphical method has essentially no practical value for solving real problems. However, it has great value for conveying the basic notion that linear programming involves pushing up against constraint boundaries and moving objective function values in a favorable direction as far as possible. You also will see in Chapter 14 that this approach provides considerable geometric insight into how to analyze larger models by other methods.

A manager must also have an appreciation for the relevance and power of linear programming to encourage its use where appropriate. For *future* managers using this book, this appreciation is being promoted by describing *real* applications of linear programming and the resulting impact, as well as by including (in miniature form) various realistic examples and case studies that illustrate what can be done.

Certainly a manager must be able to recognize situations where linear programming is applicable. We focus on developing this skill in Chapter 3, where you will learn how to recognize the *identifying features* for each of the major types of linear programming problems (and their mixtures).

In addition, a manager should recognize situations where linear programming should *not* be applied. Chapter 8 will help to develop this skill by examining certain underlying assumptions of linear programming and the circumstances that violate these assumptions. That chapter also describes other approaches that *can* be applied where linear programming should not.

A manager needs to be able to distinguish between competent and shoddy studies using linear programming (or any other management science technique). Therefore, another goal of the upcoming chapters is to demystify the overall process involved in conducting a management science study, all the way from first studying a problem to final implementation of the managerial decisions based on the study. This is one purpose of the case studies throughout the book.

Finally, a manager must understand how to interpret the results of a linear programming study. He or she especially needs to understand what kinds of information can be obtained through *what-if analysis,* as well as the implications of such information for managerial decision making. Chapter 5 focuses on these issues.

Review Questions

1. Does management generally get heavily involved with the technical details of a linear programming study?
2. What is the purpose of studying the graphical method for solving problems with two decision variables when essentially all real linear programming problems have more than two?
3. List the things that an enlightened manager should know about linear programming.

2.8 Summary

Linear programming is a powerful technique for aiding managerial decision making for certain kinds of problems. The basic approach is to formulate a mathematical model called a linear programming model to represent the problem and then to analyze this model. Any linear programming model includes decision variables to represent the decisions to be made, constraints to represent the restrictions on the feasible values of these decision variables, and an objective function that expresses the overall measure of performance for the problem.

Spreadsheets provide a flexible and intuitive way of formulating and solving a linear programming model. The data are entered into data cells. Changing cells display the values of the decision variables, and a target cell shows the value of the objective function. Output cells are used to help specify the constraints. After formulating the model on the spreadsheet and specifying it further with the Solver dialogue box, the Solver is used to quickly find an optimal solution.

The graphical method can be used to solve a linear programming model having just two decision variables. This method provides considerable insight into the nature of linear programming models and optimal solutions.

Glossary

absolute reference A reference to a cell (or a column or a row) with a fixed address, as indicated either by using a range name or by placing a $ sign in front of the letter and number of the cell reference. (Section 2.2), 23

changing cells The cells in the spreadsheet that show the values of the decision variables. (Section 2.2), 22

constraint A restriction on the feasible values of the decision variables. (Sections 2.2 and 2.3), 25

constraint boundary equation The equation for the constraint boundary line. (Section 2.4), 30

constraint boundary line For linear programming problems with two decision variables, the line forming the boundary of the solutions that are permitted by the constraint. (Section 2.4), 30

data cells The cells in the spreadsheet that show the data of the problem. (Section 2.2), 21

decision variable An algebraic variable that represents a decision regarding the level of a particular activity. The value of the decision variable appears in a changing cell on the spreadsheet. (Section 2.3), 27

feasible region The geometric region that consists of all the feasible solutions. (Section 2.4), 28

feasible solution A solution that simultaneously satisfies all the constraints in the linear programming model. (Section 2.3), 27

functional constraint A constraint with a function of the decision variables on the left-hand side. All constraints in a linear programming model that are not nonnegativity constraints are called functional constraints. (Section 2.3), 27

graphical method A method for solving linear programming problems with two decision variables on a two-dimensional graph. (Section 2.4), 28

infeasible solution A solution that violates at least one of the constraints in the linear programming model. (Section 2.3), 27

linear programming model The mathematical model that represents a linear programming problem. (Sections 2.2 and 2.3), 21

nonnegativity constraint A constraint that expresses the restriction that a particular decision variable must be nonnegative (greater than or equal to zero). (Section 2.3), 27

objective function The part of a linear programming model that expresses what needs to be either maximized or minimized, depending on the objective for the problem. The value of the objective function appears in the target cell on the spreadsheet. (Section 2.3), 27

objective function line For a linear programming problem with two decision variables, a line whose points all have the same value of the objective function. (Section 2.4), 31

optimal solution The best feasible solution according to the objective function. (Section 2.3), 27

output cells The cells in the spreadsheet that provide output that depends on the changing cells. These cells frequently are used to help specify constraints. (Section 2.2), 22

parameter The parameters of a linear programming model are the constants (coefficients or right-hand sides) in the functional constraints and the objective function. Each parameter represents a quantity (e.g., the amount available of a resource) that is of importance for the analysis of the problem. (Section 2.3), 27

product-mix problem A type of linear programming problem where the objective is to find the most profitable mix of production levels for the products under consideration. (Section 2.1), 20

relative reference A reference to a cell whose address is based upon its position relative to the cell containing the formula. (Section 2.2), 23

solution Any single assignment of values to the decision variables, regardless of whether the assignment is a good one or even a feasible one. (Section 2.3), 27

Solver The spreadsheet tool that is used to specify the model in the spreadsheet and then to obtain an optimal solution for that model. (Section 2.5), 33

target cell The cell in the spreadsheet that shows the overall measure of performance of the decisions. (Section 2.2), 23

Learning Aids for This Chapter in Your MS Courseware

Chapter 2 Excel Files:

Wyndor Example
Profit & Gambit Example

Interactive Management Science Modules:

Module for Graphical Linear Programming and Sensitivity Analysis

Excel Add-ins:

Premium Solver for Education

Supplement to Chapter 2 on the CD-ROM:

More About the Graphical Method for Linear Programming

Solved Problem (See the CD-ROM for the Solution)

2.S1. Conducting a Marketing Survey

The marketing group for a cell phone manufacturer plans to conduct a telephone survey to determine consumer attitudes toward a new cell phone that is currently under development. In order to have a sufficient sample size to conduct the analysis, they need to contact at least 100 young males (under age 40), 150 older males (over age 40), 120 young females (under age 40), and 200 older females (over age 40). It costs $1 to make a daytime phone call and $1.50 to make an evening phone call (because of higher labor costs). This cost is incurred whether or not anyone answers the phone. The table below shows the likelihood of a given customer type answering each phone call. Assume the survey is conducted with whoever first answers the phone. Also, because of limited evening staffing, at most one-third of phone calls placed can be evening phone calls. How should the marketing group conduct the telephone survey so as to meet the sample size requirements at the lowest possible cost?

Who Answers?	Daytime Calls	Evening Calls
Young male	10%	20%
Older male	15%	30%
Young female	20%	20%
Older female	35%	25%
No answer	20%	5%

Problems

We have inserted the symbol E* (for Excel) to the left of e1ch problem or part where Excel should be used. An asterisk on the problem number indicates that at least a partial answer is given in the back of the book.

2.1   Reconsider the Wyndor Glass Co. case study introduced in Section 2.1. Suppose that the estimates of the unit profits for the two new products now have been revised to $600 for the doors and $300 for the windows.

E*   *a.* Formulate and solve the revised linear programming model for this problem on a spreadsheet.

b. Formulate this same model algebraically.

c. Use the graphical method to solve this revised model.

2.2   Reconsider the Wyndor Glass Co. case study introduced in Section 2.1. Suppose that Bill Tasto (Wyndor's vice president for manufacturing) now has found a way to provide a little additional production time in Plant 2 to the new products.

a. Use the graphical method to find the new optimal solution and the resulting total profit if *one* additional hour per week is provided.

b. Repeat part *a* if *two* additional hours per week are provided instead.

c. Repeat part *a* if *three* additional hours per week are provided instead.

d. Use these results to determine how much each additional hour per week would be worth in terms of increasing the total profit from the two new products.

E*2.3   Use the Excel Solver to do Problem 2.2.

2.4   The following table summarizes the key facts about two products, A and B, and the resources, Q, R, and S, required to produce them.

	Resource Usage per Unit Produced		
Resource	Product A	Product B	Amount of Resource Available
Q	2	1	2
R	1	2	2
S	3	3	4
Profit/unit	$3,000	$2,000	

All the assumptions of linear programming hold.

E*   *a.* Formulate and solve a linear programming model for this problem on a spreadsheet.

b. Formulate this same model algebraically.

2.5*   This is your lucky day. You have just won a $10,000 prize. You are setting aside $4,000 for taxes and partying expenses, but you have decided to invest the other $6,000. Upon hearing this news, two different friends have offered you an opportunity to become a partner in two different entrepreneurial ventures, one planned by each friend. In both cases, this investment would involve expending some of your time next summer as well as putting up cash. Becoming a *full* partner in the first friend's venture would require an investment of $5,000 and 400 hours, and your estimated profit (ignoring the value of your time) would be $4,500. The corresponding figures for the second friend's venture are $4,000 and 500 hours, with an estimated profit to you of $4,500. However, both friends are flexible and would allow you to come in at any *fraction* of a full partnership you would like. If you choose a fraction of a full partnership, all the above figures given for a full partnership (money investment, time investment, and your profit) would be multiplied by this same fraction.

Because you were looking for an interesting summer job anyway (maximum of 600 hours), you have decided to participate in one or both friends' ventures in whichever combination would maximize your total estimated profit. You now need to solve the problem of finding the best combination.

a. Describe the analogy between this problem and the Wyndor Glass Co. problem discussed in Section 2.1. Then construct and fill in a table like Table 2.1 for this problem, identifying both the activities and the resources.

b. Identify verbally the decisions to be made, the constraints on these decisions, and the overall measure of performance for the decisions.

c. Convert these verbal descriptions of the constraints and the measure of performance into quantitative expressions in terms of the data and decisions.

E* d. Formulate a spreadsheet model for this problem. Identify the data cells, the changing cells, and the target cell. Also show the Excel equation for each output cell expressed as a SUMPRODUCT function. Then use the Excel Solver to solve this model.

e. Indicate why this spreadsheet model is a linear programming model.

f. Formulate this same model algebraically.

g. Identify the decision variables, objective function, nonnegativity constraints, functional constraints, and parameters in both the algebraic version and spreadsheet version of the model.

h. Use the graphical method by hand to solve this model. What is your total estimated profit?

i. Use the Graphical Linear Programming and Sensitivity Analysis module in your Interactive Management Science Modules to apply the graphical method to this model.

2.6 You are given the following linear programming model in algebraic form, where x_1 and x_2 are the decision variables and Z is the value of the overall measure of performance.

$$\text{Maximize} \quad Z = x_1 + 2x_2$$

subject to

Constraint on resource 1: $x_1 + x_2 \leq 5$ (amount available)
Constraint on resource 2: $x_1 + 3x_2 \leq 9$ (amount available)

and

$$x_1 \geq 0 \qquad x_2 \geq 0$$

a. Identify the objective function, the functional constraints, and the nonnegativity constraints in this model.

E* b. Incorporate this model into a spreadsheet.

c. Is $(x_1, x_2) = (3, 1)$ a feasible solution?

d. Is $(x_1, x_2) = (1, 3)$ a feasible solution?

E* e. Use the Excel Solver to solve this model.

2.7 You are given the following linear programming model in algebraic form, where x_1 and x_2 are the decision variables and Z is the value of the overall measure of performance.

$$\text{Maximize} \quad Z = 3x_1 + 2x_2$$

subject to

Constraint on resource 1: $3x_1 + x_2 \leq 9$ (amount available)
Constraint on resource 2: $x_1 + 2x_2 \leq 8$ (amount available)

and

$$x_1 \geq 0 \qquad x_2 \geq 0$$

a. Identify the objective function, the functional constraints, and the nonnegativity constraints in this model.

E* b. Incorporate this model into a spreadsheet.

c. Is $(x_1, x_2) = (2, 1)$ a feasible solution?

d. Is $(x_1, x_2) = (2, 3)$ a feasible solution?

e. Is $(x_1, x_2) = (0, 5)$ a feasible solution?

E* f. Use the Excel Solver to solve this model.

2.8 The Whitt Window Company is a company with only three employees that makes two different kinds of handcrafted windows: a wood-framed and an aluminum framed window. They earn $60 profit for each wood-framed window and $30 profit for each aluminum-framed window. Doug makes the wood frames and can make 6 per day. Linda makes the aluminum frames and can make 4 per day. Bob forms and cuts the glass and can make 48 square feet of glass per day. Each wood-framed window uses 6 square feet of glass and each aluminum-framed window uses 8 square feet of glass.

The company wishes to determine how many windows of each type to produce per day to maximize total profit.

a. Describe the analogy between this problem and the Wyndor Glass Co. problem discussed in Section 2.1. Then construct and fill in a table like Table 2.1 for this problem, identifying both the activities and the resources.

b. Identify verbally the decisions to be made, the constraints on these decisions, and the overall measure of performance for the decisions.

c. Convert these verbal descriptions of the constraints and the measure of performance into quantitative expressions in terms of the data and decisions.

E* d. Formulate a spreadsheet model for this problem. Identify the data cells, the changing cells, and the target cell. Also show the Excel equation for each output cell expressed as a SUMPRODUCT function. Then use the Excel Solver to solve this model.

e. Indicate why this spreadsheet model is a linear programming model.

f. Formulate this same model algebraically.

g. Identify the decision variables, objective function, nonnegativity constraints, functional constraints, and parameters in both the algebraic version and spreadsheet version of the model.

h. Use the graphical method to solve this model.

i. A new competitor in town has started making wood-framed windows as well. This may force the company to lower the price it charges and so lower the profit made for each wood-framed window. How would the optimal solution change (if at all) if the profit per wood-framed window decreases from $60 to $40? From $60 to $20?

j. Doug is considering lowering his working hours, which would decrease the number of wood frames he makes per day. How would the optimal solution change if he only makes 5 wood frames per day?

2.9 The Apex Television Company has to decide on the number of 27" and 20" sets to be produced at one of its factories. Market research indicates that at most 40 of the 27" sets and 10 of the 20" sets can be sold per month. The maximum number of work-hours available is 500 per month. A 27" set requires 20 work-hours and a 20" set requires 10 work-hours. Each 27" set sold produces a profit of $120 and each 20" set produces a profit of $80. A wholesaler has agreed to purchase all the television sets produced if the numbers do not exceed the maxima indicated by the market research.

E* a. Formulate and solve a linear programming model for this problem on a spreadsheet.

b. Formulate this same model algebraically.

c. Solve this model by using the Graphical Linear Programming and Sensitivity Analysis module in your Interactive Management Science Modules to apply the graphical method.

2.10 The WorldLight Company produces two light fixtures (products 1 and 2) that require both metal frame parts and electrical components. Management wants to determine how many units of each product to produce so as to maximize profit. For each unit of product 1, one unit of frame parts and two units of electrical components are required. For each unit of product 2, three units of frame parts and two units of electrical components are required. The company has 200 units of frame parts and 300 units of electrical components. Each unit of product 1 gives a profit of $1, and each unit of product 2, up to 60 units, gives a profit of $2. Any excess over 60 units of product 2 brings no profit, so such an excess has been ruled out.

a. Identify verbally the decisions to be made, the constraints on these decisions, and the overall measure of performance for the decisions.

b. Convert these verbal descriptions of the constraints and the measure of performance into quantitative expressions in terms of the data and decisions.

E* c. Formulate and solve a linear programming model for this problem on a spreadsheet.

d. Formulate this same model algebraically.

e. Solve this model by using the Graphical Linear Programming and Sensitivity Analysis module in your Interactive Management Science Modules to apply the graphical method. What is the resulting total profit?

2.11 The Primo Insurance Company is introducing two new product lines: special risk insurance and mortgages. The expected profit is $5 per unit on special risk insurance and $2 per unit on mortgages.

Management wishes to establish sales quotas for the new product lines to maximize total expected profit. The work requirements are as follows:

| | **Work-Hours per Unit** | | **Work-Hours** |
Department	Special Risk	Mortgage	Available
Underwriting	3	2	2,400
Administration	0	1	800
Claims	2	0	1,200

a. Identify verbally the decisions to be made, the constraints on these decisions, and the overall measure of performance for the decisions.

b. Convert these verbal descriptions of the constraints and the measure of performance into quantitative expressions in terms of the data and decisions.

E* c. Formulate and solve a linear programming model for this problem on a spreadsheet.

d. Formulate this same model algebraically.

2.12.* You are given the following linear programming model in algebraic form, with x_1 and x_2 as the decision variables and constraints on the usage of four resources:

Maximize   Profit $= 2x_1 + x_2$

subject to

$$x_2 \leq 10 \quad \text{(resource 1)}$$
$$2x_1 + 5x_2 \leq 60 \quad \text{(resource 2)}$$
$$x_1 + x_2 \leq 18 \quad \text{(resource 3)}$$
$$3x_1 + x_2 \leq 44 \quad \text{(resource 4)}$$

and

$$x_1 \geq 0 \qquad x_2 \geq 0$$

a. Use the graphical method to solve this model.

E* b. Incorporate this model into a spreadsheet and then use the Excel Solver to solve this model.

2.13 Because of your knowledge of management science, your boss has asked you to analyze a product mix problem involving two products and two resources. The model is shown below in algebraic form, where x_1 and x_2 are the production rates for the two products and P is the total profit.

$$\text{Maximize} \quad P = 3x_1 + 2x_2$$

subject to

$$x_1 + x_2 \leq 8 \quad \text{(resource 1)}$$
$$2x_1 + x_2 \leq 10 \quad \text{(resource 2)}$$

and

$$x_1 \geq 0 \quad x_2 \geq 0$$

a. Use the graphical method to solve this model.

E* b. Incorporate this model into a spreadsheet and then use the Excel Solver to solve this model.

2.14 Weenies and Buns is a food processing plant that manufactures hot dogs and hot dog buns. They grind their own flour for the hot dog buns at a maximum rate of 200 pounds per week. Each hot dog bun requires 0.1 pound of flour. They currently have a contract with Pigland, Inc., which specifies that a delivery of 800 pounds of pork product is delivered every Monday. Each hot dog requires 1/4 pound of pork product. All the other ingredients in the hot dogs and hot dog buns are in plentiful supply. Finally, the labor force at Weenies and Buns consists of five employees working full time (40 hours per week each). Each hot dog requires three minutes of labor, and each hot dog bun requires two minutes of labor. Each hot dog yields a profit of $0.20, and each bun yields a profit of $0.10.

Weenies and Buns would like to know how many hot dogs and how many hot dog buns they should produce each week so as to achieve the highest possible profit.

a. Identify verbally the decisions to be made, the constraints on these decisions, and the overall measure of performance for the decisions.

b. Convert these verbal descriptions of the constraints and the measure of performance into quantitative expressions in terms of the data and decisions.

E* c. Formulate and solve a linear programming model for this problem on a spreadsheet.

d. Formulate this same model algebraically.

e. Use the graphical method to solve this model. Decide yourself whether you would prefer to do this by hand or by using the Graphical Linear Programming and Sensitivity Analysis module in your Interactive Management Science Modules.

2.15 The Oak Works is a family-owned business that makes handcrafted dining room tables and chairs. They obtain the oak from a local tree farm, which ships them 2,500 pounds of oak each month. Each table uses 50 pounds of oak while each chair uses 25 pounds of oak. The family builds all the furniture itself and has 480 hours of labor available each month. Each table or chair requires six hours of labor. Each table nets Oak Works $400 in profit, while each chair nets $100 in profit. Since chairs are often sold with the tables, they want to produce *at least* twice as many chairs as tables.

The Oak Works would like to decide how many tables and chairs to produce so as to maximize profit.

a. Formulate and solve a linear programming model for this problem on a spreadsheet.

b. Formulate this same model algebraically.

2.16 Nutri-Jenny is a weight-management center. It produces a wide variety of frozen entrees for consumption by its clients. The entrees are strictly monitored for nutritional content to ensure that the clients are eating a balanced diet. One new entree will be a "beef sirloin tips dinner." It will consist of beef tips and gravy, plus some combination of peas, carrots, and a dinner roll. Nutri-Jenny would like to determine what quantity of each item to include in the entree to meet the nutritional requirements, while costing as little as possible. The nutritional information for each item and its cost are given in the following table.

Item	Calories (per oz.)	Calories from Fat (per oz.)	Vitamin A (IU per oz.)	Vitamin C (mg per oz.)	Protein (gr. per oz.)	Cost (per oz.)
Beef tips	54	19	0	0	8	40¢
Gravy	20	15	0	1	0	35¢
Peas	15	0	15	3	1	15¢
Carrots	8	0	350	1	1	18¢
Dinner roll	40	10	0	0	1	10¢

The nutritional requirements for the entree are as follows: (1) it must have between 280 and 320 calories, (2) calories from fat should be no more than 30 percent of the total number of calories, and (3) it must have at least 600 IUs of vitamin A, 10 milligrams of vitamin C, and 30 grams of protein. Furthermore, for practical reasons, it must include at least 2 ounces of beef, and it must have at least half an ounce of gravy per ounce of beef.

E* a. Formulate and solve a linear programming model for this problem on a spreadsheet.

b. Formulate this same model algebraically.

2.17 Ralph Edmund loves steaks and potatoes. Therefore, he has decided to go on a steady diet of only these two foods (plus some liquids and vitamin supplements) for all his meals. Ralph realizes that this isn't the healthiest diet, so he wants to make sure that he eats the right quantities of the two foods to satisfy some key nutritional requirements. He has obtained the following nutritional and cost information:

	Grams of Ingredient per Serving		
Ingredient	Steak	Potatoes	Daily Requirement (grams)
Carbohydrates	5	15	≥ 50
Protein	20	5	≥ 40
Fat	15	2	≤ 60
Cost per serving	$4	$2	

Ralph wishes to determine the number of daily servings (may be fractional) of steak and potatoes that will meet these requirements at a minimum cost.

a. Identify verbally the decisions to be made, the constraints on these decisions, and the overall measure of performance for the decisions.

b. Convert these verbal descriptions of the constraints and the measure of performance into quantitative expressions in terms of the data and decisions.

c. Formulate and solve a linear programming model for this problem on a spreadsheet.

d. Formulate this same model algebraically.

e. Use the graphical method by hand to solve this model.

f. Use the Graphical Linear Programming and Sensitivity Analysis module in your Interactive Management Science Modules to apply the graphical method to this model.

2.18 Dwight is an elementary school teacher who also raises pigs for supplemental income. He is trying to decide what to feed his pigs. He is considering using a combination of pig feeds available from local suppliers. He would like to feed the pigs at minimum cost while also making sure each pig receives an adequate supply of calories and vitamins. The cost, calorie content, and vitamin content of each feed is given in the table below.

Contents	Feed Type A	Feed Type B
Calories (per pound)	800	1,000
Vitamins (per pound)	140 units	70 units
Cost (per pound)	$0.40	$0.80

Each pig requires at least 8,000 calories per day and at least 700 units of vitamins. A further constraint is that no more than 1/3 of the diet (by weight) can consist of Feed Type A, since it contains an ingredient that is toxic if consumed in too large a quantity.

a. Identify verbally the decisions to be made, the constraints on these decisions, and the overall measure of performance for the decisions.

b. Convert these verbal descriptions of the constraints and the measure of performance into quantitative expressions in terms of the data and decisions.

E* c. Formulate and solve a linear programming model for this problem on a spreadsheet.

d. Formulate this same model algebraically.

2.19 Reconsider the Profit & Gambit Co. problem described in Section 2.6. Suppose that the estimated data given in Table 2.2 now have been changed as shown in the table that accompanies this problem.

E* a. Formulate and solve a linear programming model on a spreadsheet for this revised version of the problem.

b. Formulate this same model algebraically.

c. Use the graphical method to solve this model.

d. What were the key changes in the data that caused your answer for the optimal solution to change from the one for the original version of the problem?

	Increase in Sales per Unit of Advertising		
Product	Television	Print Media	Minimum Required Increase
Stain remover	0%	1.5%	3%
Liquid detergent	3	4	18
Powder detergent	−1	2	4
Unit cost	$1 million	$2 million	

e. Write a paragraph to the management of the Profit & Gambit Co. presenting your conclusions from the above parts. Include the potential effect of further refining the key data in the above table. Also point out the leverage that your results might provide to management in negotiating a decrease in the unit cost for either of the advertising media.

2.20 You are given the following linear programming model in algebraic form, with x_1 and x_2 as the decision variables:

$$\text{Minimize} \qquad \text{Cost} = 40x_1 + 50x_2$$

subject to

$$\text{Constraint 1:} \quad 2x_1 + 3x_2 \geq 30$$
$$\text{Constraint 2:} \quad x_1 + x_2 \geq 12$$
$$\text{Constraint 3:} \quad 2x_1 + x_2 \geq 20$$

and

$$x_1 \geq 0 \qquad x_2 \geq 0$$

a. Use the graphical method to solve this model.

b. How does the optimal solution change if the objective function is changed to Cost $= 40x_1 + 70x_2$?

c. How does the optimal solution change if the third functional constraint is changed to $2x_1 + x_2 \geq 15$?

E* d. Now incorporate the original model into a spreadsheet and use the Excel Solver to solve this model.

E* e. Use Excel to do parts b and c.

2.21 The Learning Center runs a day camp for 6–10 year olds during the summer. Its manager, Elizabeth Reed, is trying to reduce the center's operating costs to avoid having to raise the tuition fee. Elizabeth is currently planning what to feed the children for lunch. She would like to keep costs to a minimum, but also wants to make sure she is meeting the nutritional requirements of the children. She has already decided to go with peanut butter and jelly sandwiches, and some combination of apples, milk, and/or cranberry juice. The nutritional content of each food choice and its cost are given in the table that accompanies this problem.

Food Item	Calories from Fat	Total Calories	Vitamin C (mg)	Fiber (g)	Cost (¢)
Bread (1 slice)	15	80	0	4	6
Peanut butter (1 tbsp)	80	100	0	0	5
Jelly (1 tbsp)	0	70	4	3	8
Apple	0	90	6	10	35
Milk (1 cup)	60	120	2	0	20
Cranberry juice (1 cup)	0	110	80	1	40

The nutritional requirements are as follows. Each child should receive between 300 and 500 calories, but no more than 30 percent of these calories should come from fat. Each child should receive at least 60 milligrams (mg) of vitamin C and at least 10 grams (g) of fiber. To ensure tasty sandwiches, Elizabeth wants each child to have a minimum of 2 slices of bread, 1 tablespoon (tbsp) of peanut butter, and 1 tbsp of jelly, along with at least 1 cup of liquid (milk and/or cranberry juice).

Elizabeth would like to select the food choices that would minimize cost while meeting all these requirements.

E* a. Formulate and solve a linear programming model for this problem on a spreadsheet.

b. Formulate this same model algebraically.

Case 2-1

Auto Assembly

Automobile Alliance, a large automobile manufacturing company, organizes the vehicles it manufactures into three families: a family of trucks, a family of small cars, and a family of midsized and luxury cars. One plant outside Detroit, Michigan, assembles two models from the family of midsized and luxury cars. The first model, the Family Thrillseeker, is a four-door sedan with vinyl seats, plastic interior, standard features, and excellent gas mileage. It is marketed as a smart buy for middle-class families with tight budgets, and each Family Thrillseeker sold generates a modest profit of

$3,600 for the company. The second model, the Classy Cruiser, is a two-door luxury sedan with leather seats, wooden interior, custom features, and navigational capabilities. It is marketed as a privilege of affluence for upper-middle-class families, and each Classy Cruiser sold generates a healthy profit of $5,400 for the company.

Rachel Rosencrantz, the manager of the assembly plant, is currently deciding the production schedule for the next month. Specifically, she must decide how many Family Thrillseekers and how many Classy Cruisers to assemble in the plant to maximize profit for the company. She knows that the plant possesses a capacity of 48,000 labor-hours during the month. She also knows that it takes six labor-hours to assemble one Family Thrillseeker and 10.5 labor-hours to assemble one Classy Cruiser.

Because the plant is simply an assembly plant, the parts required to assemble the two models are not produced at the plant. Instead, they are shipped from other plants around the Michigan area to the assembly plant. For example, tires, steering wheels, windows, seats, and doors all arrive from various supplier plants. For the next month, Rachel knows that she will only be able to obtain 20,000 doors from the door supplier. A recent labor strike forced the shutdown of that particular supplier plant for several days, and that plant will not be able to meet its production schedule for the next month. Both the Family Thrillseeker and the Classy Cruiser use the same door part.

In addition, a recent company forecast of the monthly demands for different automobile models suggests that the demand for the Classy Cruiser is limited to 3,500 cars. There is no limit on the demand for the Family Thrillseeker within the capacity limits of the assembly plant.

a. Formulate and solve a linear programming model to determine the number of Family Thrillseekers and the number of Classy Cruisers that should be assembled.

Before she makes her final production decisions, Rachel plans to explore the following questions independently, except where otherwise indicated.

b. The marketing department knows that it can pursue a targeted $500,000 advertising campaign that will raise the demand for the Classy Cruiser next month by 20 percent. Should the campaign be undertaken?

c. Rachel knows that she can increase next month's plant capacity by using overtime labor. She can increase the plant's labor-hour capacity by 25 percent. With the new assembly plant capacity, how many Family Thrillseekers and how many Classy Cruisers should be assembled?

d. Rachel knows that overtime labor does not come without an extra cost. What is the maximum amount she should be willing to pay for all overtime labor beyond the cost of this labor at regular-time rates? Express your answer as a lump sum.

e. Rachel explores the option of using both the targeted advertising campaign and the overtime labor hours. The advertising campaign raises the demand for the Classy Cruiser by 20 percent, and the overtime labor increases the plant's labor-hour capacity by 25 percent. How many Family Thrillseekers and how many Classy Cruisers should be assembled using the advertising campaign and overtime labor-hours if the profit from each Classy Cruiser sold continues to be 50 percent more than for each Family Thrillseeker sold?

f. Knowing that the advertising campaign costs $500,000 and the maximum usage of overtime labor hours costs $1,600,000 beyond regular time rates, is the solution found in part *e* a wise decision compared to the solution found in part *a*?

g. Automobile Alliance has determined that dealerships are actually heavily discounting the price of the Family Thrillseekers to move them off the lot. Because of a profit-sharing agreement with its dealers, the company is not making a profit of $3,600 on the Family Thrillseeker but instead is making a profit of $2,800. Determine the number of Family Thrillseekers and the number of Classy Cruisers that should be assembled given this new discounted profit.

h. The company has discovered quality problems with the Family Thrillseeker by randomly testing Thrillseekers at the end of the assembly line. Inspectors have discovered that in over 60 percent of the cases, two of the four doors on a Thrillseeker do not seal properly. Because the percentage of defective Thrillseekers determined by the random testing is so high, the floor foreman has decided to perform quality control tests on every Thrillseeker at the end of the line. Because of the added tests, the time it takes to assemble one Family Thrillseeker has increased from 6 hours to 7.5 hours. Determine the number of units of each model that should be assembled given the new assembly time for the Family Thrillseeker.

i. The board of directors of Automobile Alliance wishes to capture a larger share of the luxury sedan market and therefore would like to meet the full demand for Classy Cruisers. They ask Rachel to determine by how much the profit of her assembly plant would decrease as compared to the profit found in part *a*. They then ask her to meet the full demand for Classy Cruisers if the decrease in profit is not more than $2,000,000.

j. Rachel now makes her final decision by combining all the new considerations described in parts *f, g,* and *h*. What are her final decisions on whether to undertake the advertising campaign, whether to use overtime labor, the number of Family Thrillseekers to assemble, and the number of Classy Cruisers to assemble?

Case 2-2

Cutting Cafeteria Costs

A cafeteria at All-State University has one special dish it serves like clockwork every Thursday at noon. This supposedly tasty dish is a casserole that contains sautéed onions, boiled sliced potatoes, green beans, and cream of mushroom soup. Unfortunately, students fail to see the special quality of this dish, and they loathingly refer to it as the Killer Casserole. The students reluctantly eat the casserole, however, because the cafeteria provides only a limited selection of dishes for Thursday's lunch (namely, the casserole).

Maria Gonzalez, the cafeteria manager, is looking to cut costs for the coming year, and she believes that one sure way to cut costs is to buy less expensive and perhaps lower quality ingredients. Because the casserole is a weekly staple of the cafeteria menu, she concludes that if she can cut costs on the ingredients purchased for the casserole, she can significantly reduce overall cafeteria operating costs. She therefore decides to invest time in determining how to minimize the costs of the casserole while maintaining nutritional and taste requirements.

Maria focuses on reducing the costs of the two main ingredients in the casserole, the potatoes and green beans. These two ingredients are responsible for the greatest costs, nutritional content, and taste of the dish.

Maria buys the potatoes and green beans from a wholesaler each week. Potatoes cost $0.40 per pound (lb), and green beans cost $1.00 per lb.

All-State University has established nutritional requirements that each main dish of the cafeteria must meet. Specifically, the dish must contain 180 grams (g) of protein, 80 milligrams (mg) of iron, and 1,050 mg of vitamin C. (There are 454 g in one lb and 1,000 mg in one g.) For simplicity when planning, Maria assumes that only the potatoes and green beans contribute to the nutritional content of the casserole.

Because Maria works at a cutting-edge technological university, she has been exposed to the numerous resources on the World Wide Web. She decides to surf the Web to find the nutritional content of potatoes and green beans. Her research yields the following nutritional information about the two ingredients:

	Potatoes	Green Beans
Protein	1.5 g per 100 g	5.67 g per 10 ounces
Iron	0.3 mg per 100 g	3.402 mg per 10 ounces
Vitamin C	12 mg per 100 g	28.35 mg per 10 ounces

(There are 28.35 g in one ounce.)

Edson Branner, the cafeteria cook who is surprisingly concerned about taste, informs Maria that an edible casserole must contain at least a six-to-five ratio in the weight of potatoes to green beans.

Given the number of students who eat in the cafeteria, Maria knows that she must purchase enough potatoes and green beans to prepare a minimum of 10 kilograms (kg) of casserole each week. (There are 1,000 g in one kg.) Again, for simplicity in planning, she assumes that only the potatoes and green beans determine the amount of casserole that can be prepared. Maria does not establish an upper limit on the amount of casserole to prepare since she knows all leftovers can be served for many days thereafter or can be used creatively in preparing other dishes.

a. Determine the amount of potatoes and green beans Maria should purchase each week for the casserole to minimize the ingredient costs while meeting nutritional, taste, and demand requirements.

Before she makes her final decision, Maria plans to explore the following questions independently, except where otherwise indicated.

b. Maria is not very concerned about the taste of the casserole; she is only concerned about meeting nutritional requirements and cutting costs. She therefore forces Edson to change the recipe to allow only for at least a one-to-two ratio in the weight of potatoes to green beans. Given the new recipe, determine the amount of potatoes and green beans Maria should purchase each week.

c. Maria decides to lower the iron requirement to 65 mg since she determines that the other ingredients, such as the onions and cream of mushroom soup, also provide iron. Determine the amount of potatoes and green beans Maria should purchase each week given this new iron requirement.

d. Maria learns that the wholesaler has a surplus of green beans and is therefore selling the green beans for a lower price of $0.50 per lb. Using the same iron requirement from part c and the new price of green beans, determine the amount of potatoes and green beans Maria should purchase each week.

e. Maria decides that she wants to purchase lima beans instead of green beans since lima beans are less expensive and provide a greater amount of protein and iron than green beans. Maria again wields her absolute power and forces Edson to change the recipe to include lima beans instead of green beans. Maria knows she can purchase lima beans for $0.60 per lb from the wholesaler. She also knows that lima beans contain 22.68 g of protein and 6.804 mg of iron per 10 ounces of lima beans and no vitamin C. Using the new cost and nutritional content of lima beans, determine the amount of potatoes and lima beans Maria should purchase each week to minimize the ingredient costs while meeting nutritional, taste, and demand requirements. The nutritional requirements include the reduced iron requirement from part c.

f. Will Edson be happy with the solution in part e? Why or why not?

g. An All-State student task force meets during Body Awareness Week and determines that All-State University's nutritional requirements for iron are too lax and that those for vitamin C are too stringent. The task force urges the university to adopt a policy that requires each serving of an entrée to contain at least 120 mg of iron and at least 500 mg of vitamin C. Using potatoes and lima beans as the ingredients for the dish and using the new nutritional requirements, determine the amount of potatoes and lima beans Maria should purchase each week.

Case 2-3

Staffing a Call Center

California Children's Hospital has been receiving numerous customer complaints because of its confusing, decentralized appointment and registration process. When customers want to make appointments or register child patients, they must contact the clinic or department they plan to visit. Several problems exist with this current strategy. Parents do not always know the most appropriate clinic or department they must visit to address their children's ailments. They therefore spend a significant amount of time on the phone being transferred from clinic to clinic until they reach the most appropriate clinic for their needs. The hospital also does not publish the phone numbers of all clinics and departments, and parents must therefore invest a large amount of time in detective work to track down the correct phone number. Finally, the various clinics and departments do not communicate with each other. For example, when a doctor schedules a referral with a colleague located in another department or clinic, that department or clinic almost never receives word of the referral. The parent must contact the correct department or clinic and provide the needed referral information.

In efforts to reengineer and improve its appointment and registration process, the children's hospital has decided to centralize the process by establishing one call center devoted exclusively to appointments and registration. The hospital is currently in the middle of the planning stages for the call center. Lenny Davis, the hospital manager, plans to operate the call center from 7 AM to 9 PM during the weekdays.

Several months ago, the hospital hired an ambitious management consulting firm, Creative Chaos Consultants, to forecast the number of calls the call center would receive each hour of the day. Since all appointment and registration-related calls would be received by the call center, the consultants decided that they could forecast the calls at the call center by totaling the number of appointment and registration-related calls received by all clinics and departments. The team members visited all the clinics and departments, where they diligently recorded every call relating to appointments and registration. They then totaled these calls and altered the totals to account for calls missed during data collection. They also altered totals to account for repeat calls that occurred when the same parent called the hospital many times because of the confusion surrounding the decentralized process. Creative Chaos Consultants determined the average number of calls the call center should expect during each hour of a weekday. The following table provides the forecasts.

Work Shift	Average Number of Calls
7 AM to 9 AM	40 calls per hour
9 AM to 11 AM	85 calls per hour
11 AM to 1 PM	70 calls per hour
1 PM to 3 PM	95 calls per hour
3 PM to 5 PM	80 calls per hour
5 PM to 7 PM	35 calls per hour
7 PM to 9 PM	10 calls per hour

After the consultants submitted these forecasts, Lenny became interested in the percentage of calls from Spanish speakers since the hospital services many Spanish patients. Lenny knows that he has to hire some operators who speak Spanish to handle these calls. The consultants performed further data collection and determined that, on average, 20 percent of the calls were from Spanish speakers.

Given these call forecasts, Lenny must now decide how to staff the call center during each two-hour shift of a weekday. During the forecasting project, Creative Chaos Consultants closely observed the operators working at the individual clinics and departments and determined the number of calls operators process per hour. The consultants informed Lenny that an operator is able to process an average of six calls per hour. Lenny also knows that he has both full-time and part-time workers available to staff the call center. A full-time employee works eight hours per day, but because of paperwork that must also be completed, the employee spends only four hours per day on the phone. To balance the schedule, the employee alternates the two-hour shifts between answering phones and completing paperwork. Full-time employees can start their day either by answering phones or by completing paperwork on the first shift. The full-time employees speak either Spanish or English, but none of them are bilingual. Both Spanish-speaking and English-speaking employees are paid $10 per hour for work before 5 PM and $12 per hour for work after 5 PM. The full-time employees can begin work at the beginning of the 7 AM to 9 AM shift, 9 AM to 11 AM shift, 11 AM to 1 PM shift, or 1 PM to 3 PM shift. The part-time employees work for four hours, only answer calls, and only speak English. They can start work at the beginning of the 3 PM to 5 PM shift or the 5 PM to 7 PM shift, and, like the full-time employees, they are paid $10 per hour for work before 5 PM and $12 per hour for work after 5 PM.

For the following analysis, consider only the labor cost for the time employees spend answering phones. The cost for paperwork time is charged to other cost centers.

a. How many Spanish-speaking operators and how many English-speaking operators does the hospital need to staff the call center during each two-hour shift of the day in order to answer all calls? Please provide an integer number since half a human operator makes no sense.

b. Lenny needs to determine how many full-time employees who speak Spanish, full-time employees who speak English, and part-time employees he should hire to begin on each shift. Creative Chaos Consultants advises him that linear programming can be used to do this in such a way as to minimize operating costs while answering all calls. Formulate a linear programming model of this problem.

c. Obtain an optimal solution for the linear programming model formulated in part *b* to guide Lenny's decision.

d. Because many full-time workers do not want to work late into the evening, Lenny can find only one qualified English-speaking operator willing to begin work at 1 pm. Given this new constraint, how many full-time English-speaking operators, full-time Spanish-speaking operators, and part-time operators should Lenny hire for each shift to minimize operating costs while answering all calls?

e. Lenny now has decided to investigate the option of hiring bilingual operators instead of monolingual operators. If all the operators are bilingual, how many operators should be working during each two-hour shift to answer all phone calls? As in part *a*, please provide an integer answer.

f. If all employees are bilingual, how many full-time and part-time employees should Lenny hire to begin on each shift to minimize operating costs while answering all calls? As in

part *b*, formulate a linear programming model to guide Lenny's decision.

g. What is the maximum percentage increase in the hourly wage rate that Lenny can pay bilingual employees over monolingual employees without increasing the total operating costs?

h. What other features of the call center should Lenny explore to improve service or minimize operating costs?

Source: This case is based on an actual project completed by a team of master's students in what is now the Department of Management Science and Engineering at Stanford University.

Chapter **Three**

Linear Programming: Formulation and Applications

Learning objectives

After completing this chapter, you should be able to

1. Recognize various kinds of managerial problems to which linear programming can be applied.
2. Describe the five major categories of linear programming problems, including their identifying features.
3. Formulate a linear programming model from a description of a problem in any of these categories.
4. Describe the difference between resource constraints and benefit constraints, including the difference in how they arise.
5. Describe fixed-requirement constraints and where they arise.
6. Identify the kinds of Excel functions that linear programming spreadsheet models use for the output cells, including the target cell.
7. Identify the four components of any linear programming model and the kind of spreadsheet cells used for each component.
8. Recognize managerial problems that can be formulated and analyzed as linear programming problems.
9. Understand the flexibility that managers have in prescribing key considerations that can be incorporated into a linear programming model.

Linear programming problems come in many guises. And their models take various forms. This diversity can be confusing to both students and managers, making it difficult to recognize when linear programming can be applied to address a managerial problem. Since managers instigate management science studies, the ability to recognize the applicability of linear programming is an important managerial skill. This chapter focuses largely on developing this skill.

The usual textbook approach to trying to teach this skill is to present a series of diverse examples of linear programming applications. The weakness of this approach is that it emphasizes differences rather than the common threads between these applications. Our approach will be to emphasize these common threads—the **identifying features**—that tie together linear programming problems even when they arise in very different contexts. We will describe some broad categories of linear programming problems and the identifying features that characterize them. Then we will use diverse examples, but with the purpose of illustrating and emphasizing the common threads among them.

We will focus on five key categories of linear programming problems: resource-allocation problems, cost–benefit–trade-off problems, mixed problems, transportation problems, and assignment problems. In each case, an important identifying feature is the nature of the restrictions on what decisions can be made, and thus the nature of the resulting functional constraints in the linear programming model. For each category, you will see how the basic data for a problem lead directly to a linear programming model with a certain distinctive form. Thus, model formulation becomes a by-product of proper problem formulation.

The chapter begins with a case study that initially involves a resource-allocation problem. We then return to the case study in Section 3.4, where additional managerial considerations turn the problem into a mixed problem.

Sections 3.2 to 3.6 focus on the five categories of linear programming problems in turn. Section 3.7 then takes a broader look at the formulation of linear programming models from a managerial perspective. This section (along with Section 3.4) highlights the importance of having the model accurately reflect the managerial view of the problem. These (and other) sections also describe the flexibility available to managers for having the model structured to best fit their view of the important considerations.

3.1   A CASE STUDY: THE SUPER GRAIN CORP. ADVERTISING-MIX PROBLEM

Claire Syverson, vice president for marketing of the Super Grain Corporation, is facing a daunting challenge: how to break into an already overly crowded breakfast cereal market in a big way. Fortunately, the company's new breakfast cereal—Crunchy Start—has a lot going for it: Great taste. Nutritious. Crunchy from start to finish. She can recite the litany in her sleep now. It has the makings of a winning promotional campaign.

However, Claire knows that she has to avoid the mistakes she made in her last campaign for a breakfast cereal. That had been her first big assignment since she won this promotion, and what a disaster! She thought she had developed a really good campaign. But somehow it had failed to connect with the most crucial segments of the market—young children and parents of young children. She also has concluded that it was a mistake not to include cents-off coupons in the magazine and newspaper advertising. Oh well. Live and learn.

But she had better get it right this time, especially after the big stumble last time. The company's president, David Sloan, already has impressed on her how important the success of Crunchy Start is to the future of the company. She remembers exactly how David concluded the conversation. "The company's shareholders are not happy. We need to get those earnings headed in the right direction again." Claire had heard this tune before, but she saw in David's eyes how deadly serious he is this time.

Claire often uses spreadsheets to help organize her planning. Her management science course in business school impressed upon her how valuable spreadsheet modeling can be. She regrets that she did not rely more heavily on spreadsheet modeling for the last campaign. That was a mistake that she is determined not to repeat.

Now it is time for Claire to carefully review and formulate the problem in preparation for formulating a spreadsheet model.

The Problem

Claire already has employed a leading advertising firm, Giacomi & Jackowitz, to help design a nationwide promotional campaign that will achieve the largest possible exposure for Crunchy Start. Super Grain will pay this firm a fee based on services performed (not to exceed $1 million) and has allocated an additional $4 million for advertising expenses.

Giacomi & Jackowitz has identified the three most effective advertising media for this product:

Medium 1: Television commercials on Saturday morning programs for children.

Medium 2: Advertisements in food and family-oriented magazines.

Medium 3: Advertisements in Sunday supplements of major newspapers.

TABLE 3.1
Cost and Exposure Data
for the Super Grain
Corp. Advertising-Mix
Problem

Cost Category	Costs		
	Each TV Commercial	Each Magazine Ad	Each Sunday Ad
Ad budget	$300,000	$150,000	$100,000
Planning budget	90,000	30,000	40,000
Expected number of exposures	1,300,000	600,000	500,000

The problem now is to determine which *levels* should be chosen for these *advertising activities* to obtain the most effective *advertising mix*.

To determine the *best mix of activity levels* for this particular advertising problem, it is necessary (as always) to identify the *overall measure of performance* for the problem and then the contribution of each activity toward this measure. An ultimate goal for Super Grain is to maximize its profits, but it is difficult to make a direct connection between advertising exposure and profits. Therefore, as a rough surrogate for profit, Claire decides to use *expected number of exposures* as the overall measure of performance, where each viewing of an advertisement by some individual counts as one exposure.

Giacomi & Jackowitz has made preliminary plans for advertisements in the three media. The firm also has estimated the expected number of exposures for each advertisement in each medium, as given in the bottom row of Table 3.1.

The number of advertisements that can be run in the different media are restricted by both the advertising budget (a limit of $4 million) and the planning budget (a limit of $1 million for the fee to Giacomi & Jackowitz). Another restriction is that there are only five commercial spots available for running different commercials (one commercial per spot) on children's television programs Saturday morning (medium 1) during the time of the promotional campaign. (The other two media have an ample number of spots available.)

Consequently, the three *resources* for this problem are:

Resource 1: Advertising budget ($4 million).
Resource 2: Planning budget ($1 million).
Resource 3: TV commercial spots available (5).

Table 3.1 shows how much of the advertising budget and the planning budget would be used by each advertisement in the respective media.

- The first row gives the cost per advertisement in each medium.
- The second row shows Giacomi & Jackowitz's estimates of its total cost (including overhead and profit) for designing and developing each advertisement for the respective media.[1] (This cost represents the billable fee from Super Grain.)
- The last row then gives the expected number of exposures per advertisement.

Analysis of the Problem

Claire decides to formulate and solve a linear programming model for this problem on a spreadsheet. The formulation procedure summarized at the end of Section 2.2 guides this process. Like any linear programming model, this model will have four components:

1. The data
2. The decisions
3. The constraints
4. The measure of performance

[1] When presenting its estimates in this form, the firm is making two simplifying assumptions. One is that its cost for designing and developing each additional advertisement in a medium is roughly the same as for the first advertisement in that medium. The second is that its cost when working with one medium is unaffected by how much work it is doing (if any) with the other media.

The spreadsheet needs to be formatted to provide the following kinds of cells for these components:

Four kinds of cells are needed for these four components of a spreadsheet model.

Data → data cells

Decisions → changing cells

Constraints → output cells

Measure of performance → target cell

Figure 3.1 shows the spreadsheet model formulated by Claire. Let us see how she did this by considering each of the components of the model individually.

FIGURE 3.1

The spreadsheet model for the Super Grain problem (Section 3.1), including the target cell TotalExposures (H13) and the other output cells BudgetSpent (F8:F9), as well as the specifications needed to set up the Solver. The changing cells NumberOfAds (C13:E13) show the optimal solution obtained by the Solver.

	A	B	C	D	E	F	G	H
1		**Super Grain Corp. Advertising-Mix Problem**						
2								
3			TV Spots	Magazine Ads	SS Ads			
4		Exposures per Ad	1,300	600	500			
5		(thousands)						
6						Budget		Budget
7			Cost per Ad ($thousands)			Spent		Available
8		Ad Budget	300	150	100	4,000	≤	4,000
9		Planning Budget	90	30	40	1,000	≤	1,000
10								
11								Total Exposures
12			TV Spots	Magazine Ads	SS Ads			(thousands)
13		Number of Ads	0	20	10			17,000
14			≤					
15		Max TV Spots	5					

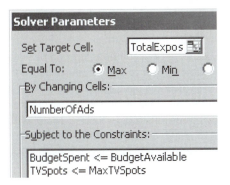

Solver Parameters
Set Target Cell: [TotalExpos]
Equal To: ⊙ Max   ○ Min   ○
By Changing Cells:
[NumberOfAds]
Subject to the Constraints:
BudgetSpent <= BudgetAvailable
TVSpots <= MaxTVSpots

Solver Options
- ☑ Assume Linear Model
- ☑ Assume Non-Negative

	F
6	Budget
7	Spent
8	=SUMPRODUCT(C8:E8,NumberOfAds)
9	=SUMPRODUCT(C9:E9,NumberOfAds)

	H
11	Total Exposures
12	(thousands)
13	=SUMPRODUCT(ExposuresPerAd,NumberOfAds)

Range Name	Cells
BudgetAvailable	H8: H9
BudgetSpent	F8: F9
CostPerAd	C8: E9
ExposuresPerAd	C4: E4
MaxTVSpots	C15
NumberOfAds	C13: E13
TotalExposures	H13
TVSpots	C13

The Data

One important kind of data is the information given earlier about the amounts available of the three resources for the problem (the advertising budget, the planning budget, and the commercial spots available). Table 3.1 provides the other key data for the problem. Using units of thousands of dollars, these data have been transferred directly into data cells in the spreadsheet in Figure 3.1 and given these range names: ExposuresPerAd (C4:E4), CostPerAd (C8:E9), BudgetAvailable (H8:H9), and MaxTVSpots (C15).

The Decisions

The problem has been defined as determining the most effective advertising mix among the three media selected by Giacomi & Jackowitz. Therefore, there are three decisions:

Decision 1:   TV = Number of commercials for separate spots on television.

Decision 2:   M = Number of advertisements in magazines.

Decision 3:   SS = Number of advertisements in Sunday supplements.

The changing cells to hold these numbers have been placed in row 13 in the columns for these media:

$$TV \rightarrow \text{cell C13} \qquad M \rightarrow \text{cell D13} \qquad SS \rightarrow \text{cell E13}$$

These changing cells are collectively referred to by the range name NumberOfAds (C13:E13).

The Constraints

These changing cells need to be nonnegative. In addition, constraints are needed for the three resources. The first two resources are the ad budget and planning budget. The amounts available for these two budgets are shown in the range BudgetAvailable (H8:H9). As suggested by the ≤ signs entered into column G, the corresponding constraints are

Total spending on advertising ≤ 4,000   (Ad budget in $1,000s)

Total cost of planning ≤ 1,000   (Planning budget in $1,000s)

Using the data in columns C, D, and E for the resources, these totals are

Total spending on advertising = 300TV + 150M + 100SS

Total cost of planning   = 90TV + 30M + 40SS

These sums of products on the right-hand side are entered into the output cells BudgetSpent (F8:F9) by using the SUMPRODUCT functions shown in the lower right-hand side of Figure 3.1. Although the ≤ signs entered in column G are only cosmetic (trial solutions still can be entered in the changing cells that violate these inequalities), they will serve as a reminder later to use these same ≤ signs when entering the constraints in the Solver dialogue box.

Excel Tip: Range names may overlap. For instance, we have used NumberOfAds to refer to the whole range of changing cells, C13:E13, and TVSpots to refer to the single cell, C13.

The third resource is TV spots for different commercials. Five such spots are available for purchase. The number of spots used is one of the changing cells (C13). Since this cell will be used in a constraint, we assign the cell its own range name: TVSpots (C13). The maximum number of TV spots available is in the data cell MaxTVSpots (C15). Thus, the required constraint is TVSpots ≤ MaxTVSpots.

The Measure of Performance

Claire Syverson is using *expected number of exposures* as the overall measure of performance, so let

Exposure = Expected number of exposures (in thousands) from all the advertising

The data cells ExposuresPerAd (C4:E4) provide the expected number of exposures (in thousands) per advertisement in the respective media and the changing cells NumberOfAds (C13:E13) give the number of each type of advertisement. Therefore,

$$\text{Exposure} = 1{,}300\text{TV} + 600M + 500\text{SS}$$

$$= \text{SUMPRODUCT (ExposuresPerAd, NumberOfAds)}$$

is the formula that needs to be entered into the target cell, TotalExposures (H13).

Summary of the Formulation

The above analysis of the four components of the model has formulated the following linear programming model (in algebraic form) on the spreadsheet:

$$\text{Maximize} \quad \text{Exposure} = 1{,}300\text{TV} + 600M + 500\text{SS}$$

subject to

Ad spending:	$300\text{TV} + 150M + 100\text{SS} \leq 4{,}000$	
Planning costs:	$90\text{TV} + 30M + 40\text{SS} \leq 1{,}000$	
Number of television spots:	$\text{TV} \qquad\qquad\qquad \leq \quad 5$	

and

$$\text{TV} \geq 0 \quad M \geq 0 \quad \text{SS} \geq 0$$

The difficult work of defining the problem and gathering all the relevant data in Table 3.1 leads directly to this formulation.

Solving the Model

Excel Tip: The Solver dialogue box is used to tell Solver the location on the spreadsheet of several of the elements of the model: the changing cells, the target cell, and the constraints.

To solve the spreadsheet model formulated above, some key information needs to be entered into the Solver dialogue box. The lower left-hand side of Figure 3.1 shows the needed entries: the target cell (TotalExposures), the changing cells (NumberOfAds), the objective of maximizing the target cell, and the constraints BudgetSpent $\leq$ BudgetAvailable and TVSpots $\leq$ MaxTVSpots. In addition, the lower left-hand corner of the figure shows that two Solver options need to be selected: Assume Linear Model (because the model is a linear programming model) and Assume Non-Negative (because negative levels of advertising are impossible). Clicking on the Solve button then tells the Solver to find an optimal solution for the model and display it in the changing cells.

The optimal solution given in row 13 of the spreadsheet provides the following plan for the promotional campaign:

Do not run any television commercials.

Run 20 advertisements in magazines.

Run 10 advertisements in Sunday supplements.

Since TotalExposures (H13) gives the expected number of exposures in thousands, this plan would be expected to provide 17,000,000 exposures.

Evaluation of the Adequacy of the Model

When she chose to use a linear programming model to represent this advertising-mix problem, Claire recognized that this kind of model does not provide a perfect match to this problem. However, a mathematical model is intended to be only an approximate representation of the real problem. Approximations and simplifying assumptions generally are required to have a workable model. All that is really needed is that there be a reasonably high correlation between the prediction of the model and what would actually happen in the real problem. The team now needs to check whether this criterion is satisfied.

Linear programming models allow fractional solutions.

One assumption of linear programming is that *fractional* solutions are allowed. For the current problem, this means that a fractional number (e.g., 3½) of television commercials (or of ads in magazines or Sunday supplements) should be allowed. This is technically true, since a commercial can be aired for less than a normal run, or an ad can be run in just a fraction of the usual magazines or Sunday supplements. However, one defect of the model is that it assumes that Giacomi & Jackowitz's cost for planning and developing a commercial or ad that receives only a fraction of its usual run is only that fraction of its usual cost, even though the actual cost would be the same as for a full run. Fortunately, the optimal solution obtained above was an *integer* solution (0 television commercials, 20 ads in magazines, and 10 ads in Sunday supplements), so the assumption that fractional solutions are allowed was not even needed.

Another key assumption of linear programming is that the appropriate equation for each of the output cells, including the target cell, is one that can be expressed as a SUMPRODUCT of data cells and changing cells (or occasionally just a SUM of changing cells). For the target cell (cell H13) in Figure 3.1, this implies that the expected number of exposures to be obtained from each advertising medium is *proportional* to the number of advertisements in that medium. This proportionality seems true, since each viewing of the advertisements by some individual counts as another exposure. Another implication of using a SUMPRODUCT function is that the expected number of exposures to be obtained from an advertising medium is unaffected by the number of advertisements in the other media. Again, this implication seems valid, since viewings of advertisements in different media count as separate exposures.

Although a SUMPRODUCT function is appropriate for calculating the expected number of exposures, the choice of this number for the overall measure of performance is somewhat questionable. Management's real objective is to maximize the profit generated as a result of the advertising campaign, but this is difficult to measure so *expected number of exposures* was selected to be a surrogate for profit. This would be valid if profit were proportional to the expected number of exposures. However, proportionality is only an approximation in this case because too many exposures for the same individual reach a saturation level where the impact (potential profit) from one more exposure is substantially less than for the first exposure.

To check how reasonable it is to use expected number of exposures as a surrogate for profit, Claire meets with Sid Jackowitz, one of the senior partners of Giacomi & Jackowitz. Sid indicates that the contemplated promotional campaign (20 advertisements in magazines and 10 in Sunday supplements) is a relatively modest one well below saturation levels. Most readers will only notice these ads once or twice, and a second notice is very helpful for reinforcing the first one. Furthermore, the readership of magazines and Sunday supplements is sufficiently different that the interaction of the advertising impact in these two media should be small. Consequently, Claire concludes that using expected number of exposures for the target cell in Figure 3.1 provides a reasonable approximation. (A continuation of this case study in Case 8-1 will delve into the more complicated analysis that is required in order to use profit directly as the measure of performance to be recorded in the target cell instead of making this approximation.)

Next, Claire quizzes Sid about his firm's costs for planning and developing advertisements in these media. Is it reasonable to assume that the cost in a given medium is proportional to the number of advertisements in that medium? Is it reasonable to assume that the cost of developing advertisements in one medium would not be substantially reduced if the firm had just finished developing advertisements in another medium that might have similar themes? Sid acknowledges that there is some carryover in ad planning from one medium to another, especially if both are print media (e.g., magazines and Sunday supplements), but that the carryover is quite limited because of the distinct differences in these media. Furthermore, he feels that the proportionality assumption is quite reasonable for any given medium since the amount of work involved in planning and developing each additional advertisement in the medium is nearly the same as for the first one in the medium. The total fee that Super Grain will pay Giacomi & Jackowitz will eventually be based on a detailed accounting of the amount of work done by the firm. Nevertheless, Sid feels that the cost estimates previously provided by the firm (as entered in cells C9, D9, and E9 in units of thousands of dollars) give a reasonable basis for roughly projecting what the fee will be for any given plan (the entries in the changing cells) for the promotional campaign.

Based on this information, Claire concludes that using a SUMPRODUCT function for cell F9 provides a reasonable approximation. Doing the same for cell F8 is clearly justified. Given her earlier conclusions as well, Claire decides that the linear programming model incorporated into Figure 3.1 (plus any expansions of the model needed later for the detailed planning) is a sufficiently accurate representation of the real advertising-mix problem. It will not be necessary to refine the results from this model by turning next to a more complicated kind of mathematical model (such as those to be described in Chapter 8).

Therefore, Claire sends a memorandum to the company's president, David Sloan, describing a promotional campaign that corresponds to the optimal solution from the linear programming model (no TV commercials, 20 ads in magazines, and 10 ads in Sunday supplements). She also requests a meeting to evaluate this plan and discuss whether some modifications should be made.

We will pick up this story again in Section 3.4.

Review
Questions

1. What is the problem being addressed in this case study?
2. What overall measure of performance is being used?
3. Why is David Sloan concerned about the plan recommended by the linear programming spreadsheet model?
4. What are the assumptions of linear programming that need to be checked to evaluate the adequacy of using a linear programming model to represent the problem under consideration?

3.2   RESOURCE-ALLOCATION PROBLEMS

In the opening paragraph of Chapter 2, we described managerial problems involving the allocation of an organization's resources to its various productive activities. Those were *resource-allocation* problems.

> **Resource-allocation problems** are linear programming problems involving the *allocation of resources to activities*. The *identifying feature* for any such problem is that each functional constraint in the linear programming model is a **resource constraint,** which has the form,

$$\text{Amount of resource used} \leq \text{Amount of resource available}$$

for one of the resources.

The amount of a resource used depends on which activities are undertaken, the levels of those activities, and how heavily those activities need to use the resource. Thus, the resource constraints place limits on the levels of the activities. The objective is to choose the levels of the activities so as to maximize some overall measure of performance (such as total profit) from the activities while satisfying all the resource constraints.

Beginning with the case study and then the familiar Wyndor Glass Co. product-mix problem, we will look at four examples that illustrate the characteristics of resource-allocation problems. These examples also demonstrate how this type of problem can arise in a variety of contexts.

The Super Grain Corp. Advertising-Mix Problem

The linear programming model formulated in Section 3.1 for the Super Grain case study is one example of a resource-allocation problem. The three *activities* under consideration are the advertising in the three types of media chosen by Giacomi & Jackowitz.

Activity 1:   TV commercials.
Activity 2:   Magazine ads.
Activity 3:   Sunday ads.

An initial step in formulating any resource-allocation problem is to identify the activities and the resources.

The decisions being made are the *levels* of these activities, that is, the *number* of TV commercials, magazine ads, and Sunday ads to run.

The *resources* to be allocated to these activities are

Resource 1:   Advertising budget ($4 million).
Resource 2:   Planning budget ($1 million).
Resource 3:   TV spots available for different commercials (5).

where the *amounts available* of these resources are given in parentheses. Thus, this problem has three resource constraints:

Advertising budget used   ≤ $4 million

Planning budget used   ≤ $1 million

TV spots used   ≤ 5

Rows 8–9 and cells C13:C15 in Figure 3.1 show these constraints in a spreadsheet. Cells C8:E9 give the amount of the advertising budget and the planning budget used by *each unit* of each activity, that is, the amount used by one TV spot, one magazine ad, and one Sunday ad, respectively.

Cells C4, D4, and E4 on this spreadsheet give the *contribution per unit of each activity* to the overall measure of performance (expected number of exposures).

Characteristics of Resource-Allocation Problems

For each proposed activity, a decision needs to be made as to how much of the activity to do. In other words, what should the level of the activity be?

Other resource-allocation problems have the same kinds of characteristics as the Super Grain problem. In each case, there are activities where the decisions to be made are the *levels* of these activities. The contribution of each activity to the overall measure of performance is proportional to the level of that activity. Commonly, this measure of performance is the *total profit* from the activities, but occasionally it is something else (as in the Super Grain problem).

Every problem of this type has a resource constraint for each resource. The amounts of the resources used depend on the levels of the activities. For each resource, the amount used by each activity is proportional to the level of that activity.

These three kinds of data are needed for any resource-allocation problem.

The manager or management science team studying a resource allocation problem needs to gather (with considerable help) three kinds of data:

1. The *amount available* of each resource.
2. The amount of each resource needed by each activity. Specifically, for each combination of resource and activity, the *amount of the resource used per unit of the activity* must be estimated.
3. The *contribution per unit of each activity* to the overall measure of performance.

Generally there is considerable work involved in developing these data. A substantial amount of digging and consultation is needed to obtain the best estimates available in a timely fashion. This step is critical. Well-informed estimates are needed to obtain a valid linear programming model for guiding managerial decisions. The dangers involved in inaccurate estimates are one reason why *what-if analysis* (Chapter 5) is such an important part of most linear programming studies.

The Wyndor Glass Co. Product-Mix Problem

The product-mix problem facing the management of the Wyndor Glass Co. in Section 2.1 is to determine the most profitable mix of production rates for the two new products, considering the limited availability of spare production capacity in the company's three plants. This is a resource-allocation problem.

The *activities* under consideration are

Activity 1: Produce the special new doors.
Activity 2: Produce the special new windows.

The decisions being made are the *levels* of these activities, that is, the production rates for the doors and windows. Production rate is being measured as the number of units (doors or windows) produced per week. Management's objective is to maximize the total profit generated by the two new products, so the overall measure of performance is total profit. The contribution of each product to profit is proportional to the production rate for that product.

The *resources* to be allocated to these activities are

Resource 1: Production capacity in Plant 1.
Resource 2: Production capacity in Plant 2.
Resource 3: Production capacity in Plant 3.

Each of the three functional constraints in the linear programming model formulated in Section 2.2 (see rows 7–9 of the spreadsheet in Figure 2.3 or 2.4) is a *resource constraint* for one of these three resources. Column E shows the amount of production capacity used in each plant and column G gives the amount available.

Table 2.1 in Section 2.1 provides the data for the Wyndor problem. You already have seen how the numbers in Table 2.1 become the parameters in the linear programming model in either its spreadsheet formulation (Section 2.2) or its algebraic form (Section 2.3).

The TBA Airlines Problem

TBA Airlines is a small regional company that specializes in short flights in small airplanes. The company has been doing well and management has decided to expand its operations.

The Problem

The basic issue facing management now is whether to purchase more small airplanes to add some new short flights or to start moving into the national market by purchasing some large airplanes for new cross-country flights (or both). Many factors will go into management's final decision, but the most important one is which strategy is likely to be most profitable.

The first row of Table 3.2 shows the estimated net annual profit (inclusive of capital recovery costs) from each type of airplane purchased. The second row gives the purchase cost per airplane and also notes that the total amount of capital available for airplane purchases is $100 million. The third row records the fact that management does not want to purchase more than two small airplanes because of limited possibilities for adding lucrative short flights, whereas they have not specified a maximum number for large airplanes (other than that imposed by the limited capital available).

How many airplanes of each type should be purchased to maximize the total net annual profit?

Formulation

This is a *resource-allocation problem*. The activities under consideration are

    Activity 1:   Purchase small airplanes.
    Activity 2:   Purchase large airplanes.

The decisions to be made are the levels of these activities, that is,

    S = Number of small airplanes to purchase
    L = Number of large airplanes to purchase

The one resource to be allocated to these activities is

    Resource: Investment capital ($100 million).

Thus, there is a single resource constraint:

$$\text{Investment capital spent} \leq \$100 \text{ million}$$

In addition, management has specified one side constraint,

$$\text{Number of small airplanes purchased} \leq 2$$

Figure 3.2 shows the formulation of a spreadsheet model for this problem, where the data in Table 3.2 have been transferred into the data cells—UnitProfit (C4:D4), CapitalPerUnitPurchased (C8:D8). CapitalAvailable (G8), and MaxSmallAirplanes (C14). The resource constraint then appears in cells C8:G8 while C12:C14 shows the side constraint. The objective for this problem is to maximize the total net annual profit, so the equation for the target cell is

TABLE 3.2
Data for the TBA Airlines Problem

	Small Airplane	Large Airplane	Capital Available
Net annual profit per airplane	$1 million	$5 million	
Purchase cost per airplane	$5 million	$50 million	$100 million
Maximum purchase quantity	2	No maximum	

FIGURE 3.2

A spreadsheet model for the TBA Airlines integer programming problem where the changing cells, UnitsProduced (C12:D12), show the optimal airplane purchases obtained by the Solver, and the target cell, TotalProfit (G12), gives the resulting total profit in millions of dollars.

	A	B	C	D	E	F	G
1		**TBA Airlines Airplane Purchasing Problem**					
2							
3			Small Airplane	Large Airplane			
4		Unit Profit ($millions)	1	5			
5							
6					Capital		Capital
7			Capital per Unit Purchased		Spent		Available
8		Capital ($millions)	5	50	100	<=	100
9							
10							Total Profit
11			Small Airplane	Large Airplane			($millions)
12		Number Purchased	0	2			10
13			<=				
14		Maximum Small Airplanes	2				

	E
6	Capital
7	Spent
8	=SUMPRODUCT(CapitalPerUnitPurchased,NumberPurchased)

	G
10	Total Profit
11	($millions)
12	=SUMPRODUCT(UnitProfit,NumberPurchased)

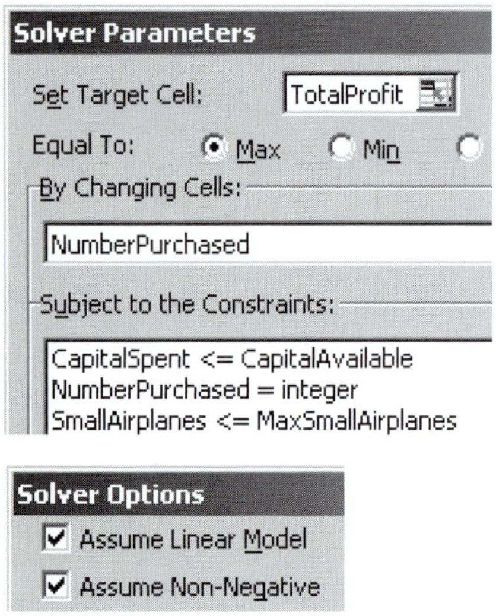

Solver Parameters

Set Target Cell: TotalProfit

Equal To: ● Max ○ Min ○

By Changing Cells:

NumberPurchased

Subject to the Constraints:

CapitalSpent <= CapitalAvailable
NumberPurchased = integer
SmallAirplanes <= MaxSmallAirplanes

Solver Options
☑ Assume Linear Model
☑ Assume Non-Negative

Range Name	Cells
Capital Available	G8
CapitalPerUnitPurchased	C8:D8
CapitalSpent	E8
MaxSmallAirplanes	C14
NumberPurchased	C12:D12
SmallAirplanes	C12
TotalProfit	G12
UnitProfit	C4:D4

TotalProfit (G12) = SUMPRODUCT (UnitProfit, UnitsPurchased)

Since the TBA Airlines problem is a resource-allocation problem, this spreadsheet model has essentially the same form as the Super Grain and Wyndor problems except for one small difference. The changing cells in this case must have *integer* values since it is not feasible for the company to purchase and operate a fraction of an airplane. Therefore, constraints that the changing cells need to be integer are added in the Add Constraint dialogue box. Choose the range of these cells (C12:D12) as the left-hand side and then choose int from the pop-up menu between the left-hand and right-hand side.[2]

[2] On most versions of Excel, Solver will automatically fill in "integer" in the right-hand side of the Add Constraint dialogue box after choosing int from the pop-up menu. Macintosh versions leave the right-hand side of the Add Constraint dialogue box blank and then give an error message if you click OK. Typing "integer" into the right-hand side before clicking OK is a workaround.

These changing cells in Figure 3.2 show the optimal solution, $(S, L) = (0, 2)$, obtained after clicking on the Solve button.

One of the assumptions of linear programming is that the changing cells are allowed to have *any* values, including *fractional* values, that satisfy the functional and nonnegativity constraints. Therefore, technically speaking, the TBA problem is not a linear programming problem because of adding the constraints,

$$\text{UnitsProduced} = \text{Integer}$$

that are displayed at the bottom of the Solver dialogue box in Figure 3.2. Such a problem that fits linear programming except for adding such constraints is called an **integer programming problem.** The method used by Solver to solve integer programming problems is quite different from that for solving linear programming problems. In fact, integer programming problems tend to be much more difficult to solve than linear programming problems so there is considerably more limitation on the size of the problem. However, this doesn't matter to a spreadsheet modeler dealing with small problems. From his or her viewpoint, there is virtually no distinction between linear programming and integer programming problems. They are formulated in exactly the same way. Then, at the very end, a decision needs to be made as to whether any of the changing cells need to be restricted to integer values. If so, those constraints are added as described above. Keep this option in mind as we continue to discuss the formulation of various types of linear programming problems throughout the chapter.

Summary of the Formulation

The above formulation of a model with one resource constraint and one side constraint for the TBA Airlines problem now can be summarized (in algebraic form) as follows.

$$\text{Maximize} \quad \text{Profit} = S + 5L$$

subject to

$$5S + 50L \leq 100$$
$$S \leq 2$$

and

$$S \geq 0 \qquad L \geq 0$$

Capital Budgeting

Financial planning is one of the most important areas of application for resource-allocation problems. The resources being allocated in this area are quite different from those for applications in the *production planning* area (such as the Wyndor Glass Co. product-mix problem), where the resources tend to be *production facilities* of various kinds. For financial planning, the resources tend to be *financial assets* such as cash, securities, accounts receivable, lines of credit, and so forth. Our specific example involves *capital budgeting*, where the resources are amounts of investment capital available at different points in time.

The Problem

The Think-Big Development Co. is a major investor in commercial real-estate development projects. It currently has the opportunity to share in three large construction projects:

Project 1: Construct a high-rise office building.
Project 2: Construct a hotel.
Project 3: Construct a shopping center.

Each project requires each partner to make investments at four different points in time: a down payment now, and additional capital after one, two, and three years. Table 3.3 shows for each project the *total* amount of investment capital required from all the partners at these four points in time. Thus, a partner taking a certain percentage share of a project is obligated to invest that percentage of each of the amounts shown in the table for the project.

TABLE 3.3
Financial Data for the Projects Being Considered for Partial Investment by the Think-Big Development Co.

| Year | Investment Capital Requirements | | |
	Office Building	Hotel	Shopping Center
0	$40 million	$80 million	$90 million
1	60 million	80 million	50 million
2	90 million	80 million	20 million
3	10 million	70 million	60 million
Net present value	$45 million	$70 million	$50 million

All three projects are expected to be very profitable in the long run. So the management of Think-Big wants to invest as much as possible in some or all of them. Management is willing to commit all the company's investment capital currently available, as well as all additional investment capital expected to become available over the next three years. The objective is to determine the *investment mix* that will be most profitable, based on current estimates of profitability.

Since it will be several years before each project begins to generate income, which will continue for many years thereafter, we need to take into account the *time value of money* in evaluating how profitable it might be. This is done by *discounting* future cash outflows (capital invested) and cash inflows (income), and then adding discounted net cash flows, to calculate a project's *net present value.*

Based on current estimates of future cash flows (not included here except for outflows), the estimated net present value for each project is shown in the bottom row of Table 3.3. All the investors, including Think-Big, then will split this net present value in proportion to their share of the total investment.

For each project, *participation shares* are being sold to major investors, such as Think-Big, who become the partners for the project by investing their proportional shares at the four specified points in time. For example, if Think-Big takes a 10 percent share of the office building, it will need to provide $4 million now, and then $6 million, $9 million, and $1 million in 1 year, 2 years, and 3 years, respectively.

The company currently has $25 million available for capital investment. Projections are that another $20 million will become available after one year, $20 million more after two years, and another $15 million after three years. What share should Think-Big take in the respective projects to maximize the total net present value of these investments?

Formulation

This is a *resource-allocation problem.* The activities under consideration are

  Activity 1: Invest in the construction of an office building.

  Activity 2: Invest in the construction of a hotel.

  Activity 3: Invest in the construction of a shopping center.

Thus, the decisions to be made are the levels of these activities, that is, what participation share to take in investing in each of these projects. A participation share can be expressed as either a fraction or a percentage of the entire project, so the entire project is considered to be one "unit" of that activity.

The resources to be allocated to these activities are the funds available at the four investment points. Funds not used at one point are available at the next point. (For simplicity, we will ignore any interest earned on these funds.) Therefore, the *resource constraint* for each point must reflect the cumulative funds to that point.

  Resource 1: Total investment capital available now.

  Resource 2: Cumulative investment capital available by the end of one year.

  Resource 3: Cumulative investment capital available by the end of two years.

  Resource 4: Cumulative investment capital available by the end of three years.

TABLE 3.4
Resource Data for the
Think-Big Development
Co. Investment-Mix
Problem

	Cumulative Investment Capital Required for an Entire Project			
Resource	**Office Building**	**Hotel**	**Shopping Center**	**Amount of Resource Available**
1 (Now)	$ 40 million	$ 80 million	$ 90 million	$25 million
2 (End of year 1)	100 million	160 million	140 million	45 million
3 (End of year 2)	190 million	240 million	160 million	65 million
4 (End of year 3)	200 million	310 million	220 million	80 million

Since the amount of investment capital available is $25 million now, another $20 million in one year, another $20 million in two years, and another $15 million in three years, the amounts available of the resources are the following.

Amount of resource 1 available = $25 million

Amount of resource 2 available = $(25 + 20) million = $45 million

Amount of resource 3 available = $(25 + 20 + 20) million = $65 million

Amount of resource 4 available = $(25 + 20 + 20 + 15) million = $80 million

Table 3.4 shows all the data involving these resources. The rightmost column gives the amounts of resources available calculated above. The middle columns show the *cumulative* amounts of the investment capital requirements listed in Table 3.3. For example, in the Office Building column of Table 3.4, the second number ($100 million) is obtained by adding the first two numbers ($40 million and $60 million) in the Office Building column of Table 3.3.

The Data As with any resource-allocation problem, three kinds of data need to be gathered. One is the amounts available of the resources, as given in the rightmost column of Table 3.4. A second is the amount of each resource needed by each project, which is given in the middle columns of this table. A third is the contribution of each project to the overall measure of performance (net present value), as given in the bottom row of Table 3.3.

The first step in formulating the spreadsheet model is to enter these data into data cells in the spreadsheet. In Figure 3.3, the data cells (and their range names) are NetPresentValue (C5:E5), CapitalRequired (C9:E12), and CapitalAvailable (H9:H12). To save space on the spreadsheet, these numbers are entered in units of millions of dollars.

The Decisions With three activities under consideration, there are three decisions to be made.

Decision 1: OB = Participation share in the office building

Decision 2: H = Participation share in the hotel

Decision 3: SC = Participation share in the shopping center

For example, if Think-Big management were to decide to take a one-tenth participation share (i.e., a 10 percent participation share) in each of these projects, then

OB = 0.1 = 10%

 H = 0.1 = 10%

SC = 0.1 = 10%

However, it may not be desirable to take the same participation share (expressed as either a fraction or a percentage) in each of the projects, so the idea is to choose the best combination of values of OB, H, and SC. In Figure 3.3, the participation shares (expressed as percentages) have been placed in changing cells under the data cells (row 16) in the columns for the three projects, so

$$OB \rightarrow cell\ C16 \qquad H \rightarrow D16 \qquad SC \rightarrow cell\ E16$$

where these cells are collectively referred to by the range name ParticipationShare (C16:E16).

The Constraints The numbers in these changing cells make sense only if they are nonnegative, so the *Assume Non-Negative* option will need to be selected in the Solver dialogue box. In addition, the four resources require resource constraints:

Total invested now	≤ 25	(millions of dollars available)
Total invested within 1 year	≤ 45	(millions of dollars available)
Total invested within 2 years	≤ 65	(millions of dollars available)
Total invested within 3 years	≤ 80	(millions of dollars available)

The data in columns C, D, and E indicate that (in millions of dollars)

Total invested now	$=$	$40\,OB + 80\,H + 90\,SC$
Total invested within 1 year	$=$	$100\,OB + 160\,H + 140\,SC$
Total invested within 2 years	$=$	$190\,OB + 240\,H + 160\,SC$
Total invested within 3 years	$=$	$200\,OB + 310\,H + 220\,SC$

These totals are calculated in the output cells CapitalSpent (F9:F12) using the SUMPRODUCT function, as shown below the spreadsheet in Figure 3.3. Finally, $\leq$ signs are entered into column G to indicate the resource constraints that will need to be entered in the Solver dialogue box.

FIGURE 3.3

The spreadsheet model for the Think-Big problem, including the formulas for the target cell TotalNPV (H16) and the other output cells CapitalSpent (F9:F12), as well as the specifications needed to set up the Solver. The changing cells ParticipationShare (C16:E16) show the optimal solution obtained by the Solver.

	A	B	C	D	E	F	G	H
1		**Think-Big Development Co. Capital Budgeting Program**						
2								
3			Office		Shopping			
4			Building	Hotel	Center			
5		Net Present Value	45	70	50			
6		($millions)				Cumulative		Cumulative
7						Capital		Capital
8			Cumulative Capital Required ($millions)			Spent		Available
9		Now	40	80	90	25	$\leq$	25
10		End of Year 1	100	160	140	44.76	$\leq$	45
11		End of Year 2	190	240	160	60.58	$\leq$	65
12		End of Year 3	200	310	220	80	$\leq$	80
13								
14			Office		Shopping			Total NPV
15			Building	Hotel	Center			($millions)
16		Participation Share	0.00%	16.50%	13.11%			18.11

Range Name	Cells
CapitalAvailable	H9:H12
CapitalRequired	C9:E12
CapitalSpent	F9:F12
ParticipationShare	C16:E16
NetPresentValue	C5:E5
TotalNPV	H16

Solver Parameters
Set Target Cell: TotalNPV
Equal To: ● Max ○ Min
By Changing Cells: ParticipationShare
Subject to the Constraints: CapitalSpent <= CapitalAvailable

Solver Options
☑ Assume Linear Model
☑ Assume Non-Negative

	F
6	Cumulative
7	Capital
8	Spent
9	=SUMPRODUCT(C9:E9,ParticipationShare)
10	=SUMPRODUCT(C10:E10,ParticipationShare)
11	=SUMPRODUCT(C11:E11,ParticipationShare)
12	=SUMPRODUCT C12:E12,ParticipationShare)

	H
14	Total NPV
15	($millions)
16	=SUMPRODUCT(NetPresentValue,ParticipationShare)

The Measure of Performance   The objective is to

$$\text{Maximize}\quad \text{NPV} = \text{total } \textit{net present value} \text{ of the investments}$$

NetPresentValue (C5:E5) shows the net present value of each entire project, while Participation-Share (C16:E16) shows the participation share for each of the projects. Therefore, the total net present value of all the participation shares purchased in all three projects is (in millions of dollars)

$$\begin{aligned} \text{NPV} &= 45\,\text{OB} + 70\,\text{H} + 50\,\text{SC} \\ &= \text{SUMPRODUCT (NetPresentValue, ParticipationShare)} \\ &\rightarrow \text{cell H16} \end{aligned}$$

Summary of the Formulation   This completes the formulation of the linear programming model on the spreadsheet, as summarized below (in algebraic form).

$$\text{Maximize}\qquad \text{NPV} = 45\,\text{OB} + 70\,\text{H} + 50\,\text{SC}$$

subject to

Total invested now:	$40\,\text{OB} + 80\,\text{H} + 90\,\text{SC} \le 25$
Total invested within 1 year:	$100\,\text{OB} + 160\,\text{H} + 140\,\text{SC} \le 45$
Total invested within 2 years:	$190\,\text{OB} + 240\,\text{H} + 160\,\text{SC} \le 65$
Total invested within 3 years:	$200\,\text{OB} + 310\,\text{H} + 220\,\text{SC} \le 80$

and

$$\text{OB} \ge 0 \quad \text{H} \ge 0 \quad \text{SC} \ge 0$$

where all these numbers are in units of millions of dollars.

Note that this model possesses the key *identifying feature* for resource-allocation problems, namely, each functional constraint is a *resource constraint* that has the form

$$\text{Amount of resource used} \le \text{Amount of resource available}$$

Solving the Model   The lower left-hand side of Figure 3.3 shows the entries needed in the Solver dialogue box to specify the model, along with the selection of the usual two options. The spreadsheet shows the resulting optimal solution in row 16, namely,

Invest nothing in the office building.
Invest in 16.50 percent of the hotel.
Invest in 13.11 percent of the shopping center.

TotalNPV (H16) indicates that this investment program would provide a total net present value of \$18.11 million.

This amount actually is only an estimate of what the total net present value would turn out to be, depending on the accuracy of the financial data given in Table 3.3. There is some uncertainty about the construction costs for the three real estate projects, so the actual investment capital requirements for years 1, 2, and 3 may deviate somewhat from the amounts specified in this table. Because of the risk involved in these projects, the net present value for each one also might deviate from the amounts given at the bottom of the table. Chapter 5 describes one approach to analyzing the effect of such deviations. Chapters 12 and 13 will present another technique, called *computer simulation,* for systematically taking future uncertainties into account. Section 13.5 will focus on further analysis of this same example.

Another Look at Resource Constraints

These examples of resource-allocation problems illustrate a variety of resources: financial allocations for advertising and planning purposes, TV commercial spots available for purchase, available production capacities of different plants, the total amount of capital available for investment, and cumulative investment capital available by certain times. However, these illustrations only scratch the surface of the realm of possible resources that need to be allocated to activities in resource-allocation problems. In fact, by interpreting *resource* sufficiently broadly, *any* restriction on the decisions to be made that has the form

$$\text{Amount used} \leq \text{Amount available}$$

can be thought of as a *resource constraint,* where the thing whose amount is being measured is the corresponding "resource." Since *any* functional constraint with a ≤ sign in a linear programming model (including the side constraint in the TBA Airlines example) can be verbalized in this form, any such constraint can be thought of as a resource constraint.

> Hereafter, we will use **resource constraint** to refer to *any* functional constraint with a ≤ sign in a linear programming model. The constant on the right-hand side represents the *amount available* of a resource. Therefore, the left-hand side represents the *amount used* of this resource. In the algebraic form of the constraint, the coefficient (positive or negative) of each decision variable is the *resource usage per unit* of the corresponding activity.

Summary of the Formulation Procedure for Resource-Allocation Problems

The four examples illustrate that the following steps are used for any resource-allocation problem to define the specific problem, gather the relevant data, and then formulate the linear programming model.

1. Since any linear programming problem involves finding the *best mix* of levels of various activities, identify these *activities* for the problem at hand. The decisions to be made are the levels of these activities.
2. From the viewpoint of management, identify an appropriate *overall measure of performance* (commonly *profit,* or a surrogate for profit) for solutions of the problem.
3. For each activity, estimate the *contribution per unit of the activity* to this overall measure of performance.
4. Identify the *resources* that must be allocated to the activities.
5. For each resource, identify the *amount available* and then the *amount used per unit of each activity.*
6. Enter the data gathered in steps 3 and 5 into *data cells* in a spreadsheet. A convenient format is to leave two blank columns between the *activity* columns and the *amount of resource available* column. Figure 3.4 shows a template of the overall format of a spreadsheet model for resource-allocation problems.
7. Designate *changing cells* for displaying the decisions on activity levels.

FIGURE 3.4

A template of a spreadsheet model for pure resource-allocation problems.

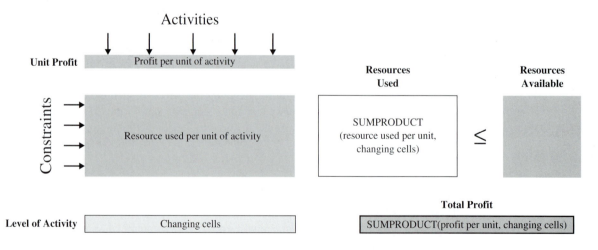

8. For the two blank columns created in step 6, use the left one as a *Totals* column for *output cells* and enter ≤ signs into the right one for all the resources. In the row for each resource, use the SUMPRODUCT function to enter the *total amount used* in the Totals column.

9. Designate a *target cell* for displaying the overall measure of performance. Use a SUMPRODUCT function to enter this measure of performance.

All the functional constraints in this linear programming model in a spreadsheet are *resource constraints,* that is, constraints with a ≤ sign. This is the *identifying feature* that classifies the problem as being a resource-allocation problem.

Review
Questions

1. What is the identifying feature for a resource-allocation problem?
2. What is the form of a resource constraint?
3. What are the three kinds of data that need to be gathered for a resource-allocation problem?
4. Compare the types of activities for the four examples of resource-allocation problems.
5. Compare the types of resources for the four examples of resource-allocation problems.

3.3   COST–BENEFIT–TRADE-OFF PROBLEMS

Cost–benefit–trade-off problems have a form that is very different from resource-allocation problems. The difference arises from *managerial objectives* that are very different for the two kinds of problems.

For resource-allocation problems, limits are set on the use of various resources (including financial resources), and then the objective is to make the most effective use (according to some overall measure of performance) of these given resources.

For cost–benefit–trade-off problems, management takes a more aggressive stance, prescribing what *benefits* must be achieved by the activities under consideration (regardless of the resulting resource usage), and then the objective is to achieve all these benefits with *minimum cost.* By prescribing a *minimum acceptable level* for each kind of benefit, and then minimizing the cost needed to achieve these levels, management hopes to obtain an appropriate *trade-off* between cost and benefits. (You will see in Chapter 5 that *what-if analysis* plays a key role in providing the additional information needed for management to choose the best trade-off between cost and benefits.)

This way of formulating a problem enables management to specify minimum goals for the benefits that need to be achieved by the activities.

> **Cost–benefit–trade-off problems** are linear programming problems where the mix of levels of various activities is chosen to achieve minimum acceptable levels for various benefits at a minimum cost. The *identifying feature* is that each functional constraint is a **benefit constraint,** which has the form

$$\text{Level achieved} \geq \text{Minimum acceptable level}$$

for one of the benefits.

Interpreting *benefit* broadly, we can think of *any* functional constraint with a ≥ sign as a *benefit constraint.* In most cases, the *minimum acceptable level* will be prescribed by management as a policy decision, but occasionally this number will be dictated by other circumstances.

For any cost–benefit–trade-off problem, a major part of the study involves identifying all the activities and benefits that should be considered and then gathering the data relevant to these activities and benefits.

These three kinds of data are needed for any cost–benefit–trade-off problem.

Three kinds of data are needed:

1. The *minimum acceptable level* for each benefit (a managerial policy decision).
2. For each benefit, the *contribution of each activity* to that benefit (per unit of the activity).
3. The *cost* per unit of each activity.

Let's examine two examples of cost–benefit–trade-off problems.

The Profit & Gambit Co. Advertising-Mix Problem

As described in Section 2.6, the Profit & Gambit Co. will be undertaking a major new advertising campaign focusing on three cleaning products. The two kinds of advertising to be used are television and the print media. Management has established minimum goals—the minimum acceptable increase in sales for each product—to be gained by the campaign.

The problem is to determine how much to advertise in each medium to meet all the sales goals at a minimum total cost.

The activities in this cost–benefit–trade-off problem are:

Activity 1:   Advertise on television.

Activity 2:   Advertise in the print media.

The benefits being sought from these activities are:

Benefit 1:   Increased sales for a spray prewash stain remover.

Benefit 2:   Increased sales for a liquid laundry detergent.

Benefit 3:   Increased sales for a powder laundry detergent.

Management wants these increased sales to be at least 3 percent, 18 percent, and 4 percent, respectively. As shown in Section 2.6, each benefit leads to a *benefit constraint* that incorporates the managerial goal for the *minimum acceptable level* of increase in the sales for the corresponding product, namely,

Level of benefit 1 achieved $\geq 3\%$

Level of benefit 2 achieved $\geq 18\%$

Level of benefit 3 achieved $\geq 4\%$

The data for this problem are given in Table 2.2 (Section 2.6). Section 2.6 describes how the linear programming model is formulated directly from the numbers in this table.

This example provides an interesting contrast with the Super Grain Corp. case study in Section 3.1, which led to a formulation as a resource-allocation problem. Both are advertising-mix problems, yet they lead to entirely different linear programming models. They differ because of the differences in the managerial view of the key issues in each case:

- As the vice president for marketing of Super Grain, Claire Syverson focused first on how much to spend on the advertising campaign and then set limits (an advertising budget of $4 million and a planning budget of $1 million) that led to resource constraints.
- The management of Profit & Gambit instead focused on what it wanted the advertising campaign to accomplish and then set goals (minimum required increases in sales) that led to benefit constraints.

From this comparison, we see that it is not the nature of the *application* that determines the classification of the resulting linear programming formulation. Rather, it is the nature of the *restrictions* imposed on the decisions regarding the mix of activity levels. If the restrictions involve *limits* on the usage of resources, that identifies a resource-allocation problem. If the restrictions involve *goals* on the levels of benefits, that characterizes a cost–benefit–trade-off problem. Frequently, the nature of the restrictions arise from the way management frames the problem.

However, we don't want you to get the idea that every linear programming problem falls entirely and neatly into either one type or the other. In the preceding section and this one, we are looking at *pure* resource-allocation problems and *pure* cost–benefit–trade-off problems. Although many *real* problems tend to be either one type or the other, it is fairly common to have *both* resource constraints and benefit constraints, even though one may predominate. Furthermore, we still need to consider additional categories of linear programming problems in the section that follows.

Now, another example of a pure cost–benefit–trade-off problem.

Personnel Scheduling

One of the common applications of cost–benefit–trade-off analysis involves personnel scheduling for a company that provides some kind of service, where the objective is to schedule the work times of the company's employees so as to minimize the cost of providing the level of service specified by management. The following example illustrates how this can be done.

An initial step in formulating any cost–benefit–trade-off problem is to identify the activities and the benefits.

Cost control is essential for survival in the airline industry. Therefore, upper management of United Airlines initiated a management science study to improve the utilization of personnel at the airline's reservations offices and airports by matching work schedules to customer needs more closely. The number of employees needed at each location to provide the required level of service varies greatly during the 24-hour day and might fluctuate considerably from one half hour to the next.

Trying to design the work schedules for all the employees at a given location to meet these service requirements most efficiently is a nightmare of combinatorial considerations. Once an employee arrives, he or she will be there continuously for the entire shift (2 to 10 hours, depending on the employee), *except* for either a meal break or short rest breaks every two hours. Given the *minimum* number of employees needed on duty for *each* half-hour interval over a 24-hour day (this minimum changes from day to day over a seven-day week), *how many* employees of *each shift length* should begin work at *what start time* over *each* 24-hour day of a seven-day week? Fortunately, linear programming thrives on such combinatorial nightmares. The linear programming model for some of the locations scheduled involves over 20,000 decisions!

This application of linear programming was credited with saving United Airlines more than $6 million *annually* in just direct salary and benefit costs. Other benefits included improved customer service and reduced workloads for support staff.

Source: T. J. Holloran and J. E. Bryne, "United Airlines Station Manpower Planning System," *Interfaces* 16, no. 1 (January–February 1986), pp. 39–50.

The Problem

Union Airways is adding more flights to and from its hub airport and so needs to hire additional customer service agents. However, it is not clear just how many more should be hired. Management recognizes the need for cost control while also consistently providing a satisfactory level of service to the company's customers, so a desirable trade-off between these two factors is being sought. Therefore, a management science team is studying how to schedule the agents to provide satisfactory service with the smallest personnel cost.

Based on the new schedule of flights, an analysis has been made of the *minimum* number of customer service agents that need to be on duty at different times of the day to provide a satisfactory level of service. These numbers are shown in the last column of Table 3.5 for the time periods given in the first column. The other entries in this table reflect one of the provisions in the company's current contract with the union that represents the customer service agents. The provision is that each agent works an eight-hour shift. The authorized shifts are

Shift 1: 6:00 AM to 2:00 PM.
Shift 2: 8:00 AM to 4:00 PM.
Shift 3: Noon to 8:00 PM.
Shift 4: 4:00 PM to midnight.
Shift 5: 10:00 PM to 6:00 AM.

TABLE 3.5
Data for the Union Airways Personnel Scheduling Problem

Time Period	Time Periods Covered by Shift					Minimum Number of Agents Needed
	1	2	3	4	5	
6:00 AM to 8:00 AM	✔					48
8:00 AM to 10:00 AM	✔	✔				79
10:00 AM to noon	✔	✔				65
Noon to 2:00 PM	✔	✔	✔			87
2:00 PM to 4:00 PM		✔	✔			64
4:00 PM to 6:00 PM			✔	✔		73
6:00 PM to 8:00 PM			✔	✔		82
8:00 PM to 10:00 PM				✔		43
10:00 PM to midnight				✔	✔	52
Midnight to 6:00 AM					✔	15
Daily cost per agent	$170	$160	$175	$180	$195	

Check marks in the main body of Table 3.5 show the time periods covered by the respective shifts. Because some shifts are less desirable than others, the wages specified in the contract differ by shift. For each shift, the daily compensation (including benefits) for each agent is shown in the bottom row. The problem is to determine how many agents should be assigned to the respective shifts each day to minimize the *total* personnel cost for agents, based on this bottom row, while meeting (or surpassing) the service requirements given in the last column.

Formulation

This problem is, in fact, a pure cost–benefit–trade-off problem. To formulate the problem, we need to identify the *activities* and *benefits* involved.

Activities correspond to shifts.
The *level* of each activity is the number of agents assigned to that shift.
A *unit* of each activity is one agent assigned to that shift.

Thus, the general description of a linear programming problem as finding the *best mix of activity levels* can be expressed for this specific application as finding the *best mix of shift sizes.*

Benefits correspond to time periods.
For each time period, the *benefit* provided by the activities is the service that agents provide customers during that period.
The *level* of a benefit is measured by the number of agents on duty during that time period.

Once again, a careful formulation of the problem, including gathering all the relevant data, leads rather directly to a spreadsheet model. This model is shown in Figure 3.5, and we outline its formulation below.

The Data   As indicated in this figure, all the data in Table 3.5 have been entered directly into the data cells CostPerShift (C5:G5), ShiftWorksTimePeriod (C8:G17), and MinimumNeeded (J8:J17).

The Decisions   Since the activities in this case correspond to the five shifts, the decisions to be made are

S_1 = Number of agents to assign to Shift 1 (starts at 6 AM)
S_2 = Number of agents to assign to Shift 2 (starts at 8 AM)
S_3 = Number of agents to assign to Shift 3 (starts at noon)
S_4 = Number of agents to assign to Shift 4 (starts at 4 PM)
S_5 = Number of agents to assign to Shift 5 (starts at 10 PM)

The changing cells to hold these numbers have been placed in the activity columns in row 21, so

$$S_1 \rightarrow \text{cell C21} \qquad S_2 \rightarrow \text{cell D21} \qquad \ldots \qquad S_5 \rightarrow \text{cell G21}$$

where these cells are collectively referred to by the range name NumberWorking (C21:G21).

The Constraints   These changing cells need to be nonnegative. In addition, we need 10 *benefit constraints,* where each one specifies that the *total* number of agents serving in the corresponding time period listed in column B must be no less than the minimum acceptable number given in column J. Thus, these constraints are

Total number of agents serving 6–8 AM ≥ 48 (min. acceptable)
Total number of agents serving 8–10 AM ≥ 79 (min. acceptable)

.

.

.

Total number of agents serving midnight–6 AM ≥ 15 (min. acceptable)

FIGURE 3.5

The spreadsheet model for the Union Airways problem, including the formulas for the target cell TotalCost (J21) and the other output cells TotalWorking (H8:H17), as well as the specifications needed to set up the Solver. The changing cells NumberWorking (C21:G21) show the optimal solution obtained by the Solver.

	A	B	C	D	E	F	G	H	I	J
1		**Union Airways Personnel Scheduling Problem**								
2										
3			6AM–2PM	8AM–4PM	Noon–8PM	4PM–Midnight	10PM–6AM			
4			Shift	Shift	Shift	Shift	Shift			
5		Cost per Shift	$170	$160	$175	$180	$195			
6								Total		Minimum
7		Time Period			Shift Works Time Period? (1=yes, 0=no)			Working		Needed
8		6AM–8AM	1	0	0	0	0	48	≥	48
9		8AM–10AM	1	1	0	0	0	79	≥	79
10		10AM–12PM	1	1	0	0	0	79	≥	65
11		12PM–2PM	1	1	1	0	0	118	≥	87
12		2PM–4PM	0	1	1	0	0	70	≥	64
13		4PM–6PM	0	0	1	1	0	82	≥	73
14		6PM–8PM	0	0	1	1	0	82	≥	82
15		8PM–10PM	0	0	0	1	0	43	≥	43
16		10PM–12AM	0	0	0	1	1	58	≥	52
17		12AM–6AM	0	0	0	0	1	15	≥	15
18										
19			6AM–2PM	8AM–4PM	Noon–8PM	4PM–Midnight	10PM–6AM			
20			Shift	Shift	Shift	Shift	Shift			Total Cost
21		Number Working	48	31	39	43	15			$30,610

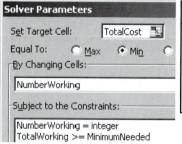

Solver Parameters

Set Target Cell: TotalCost

Equal To: ○ Max ● Min

By Changing Cells:
NumberWorking

Subject to the Constraints:
NumberWorking = integer
TotalWorking >= MinimumNeeded

Solver Options
☑ Assume Linear Model
☑ Assume Non-Negative

Range Name	Cells
CostPerShift	C5:G5
MinimumNeeded	J8:J17
NumberWorking	C21:G21
ShiftWorksTimePeriod	C8:G17
TotalCost	J21
TotalWorking	H8:H17

	H
6	Total
7	Working
8	=SUMPRODUCT(C8:G8,NumberWorking)
9	=SUMPRODUCT(C9:G9,NumberWorking)
10	=SUMPRODUCT(C10:G10,NumberWorking)
11	=SUMPRODUCT(C11:G11,NumberWorking)
12	=SUMPRODUCT(C12:G12,NumberWorking)
13	=SUMPRODUCT(C13:G13,NumberWorking)
14	=SUMPRODUCT(C14:G14,NumberWorking)
15	=SUMPRODUCT(C15:G15,NumberWorking)
16	=SUMPRODUCT(C16:G16,NumberWorking)
17	=SUMPRODUCT(C17:G17,NumberWorking)

	J
20	Total Cost
21	=SUMPRODUCT(CostPerShift,NumberWorking)

Since columns C to G indicate which of the shifts serve each of the time periods, these totals are

Total number of agents serving 6–8 AM	$= S_1$
Total number of agents serving 8–10 AM	$= S_1 + S_2$
.	
.	
.	
Total number of agents serving midnight–6 AM	$= S_5$

These totals are calculated in the output cells TotalWorking (H8:H17) using the SUMPRODUCT functions shown below the spreadsheet in Figure 3.5.

One other type of constraint is that the number of agents assigned to each shift must have an integer value. These constraints for the five shifts should be added in the same way as described for the TBA Airlines problem in Section 3.2. In particular, they are added in the Add Constraint dialogue box by entering Number Working on the left-hand side and then choosing int from the pop-up menu between the left-hand side and the right-hand side. The set of constraints, NumberWorking = integer, then appears in the Solver dialogue box, as shown in Figure 3.5.

The Measure of Performance   The objective is to

$$\text{Minimize} \quad \text{Cost} = \text{Total daily personnel cost for all agents}$$

Since CostPerShift (C5:G5) gives the daily cost per agent on each shift and NumberWorking (C21:G21) gives the number of agents working each shift,

$$\text{Cost} = 170S_1 + 160S_2 + 175S_3 + 180S_4 + 195S_5 \quad \text{(in dollars)}$$
$$= \text{SUMPRODUCT (CostPerShift, NumberWorking)}$$
$$\rightarrow \text{cell J21}$$

Summary of the Formulation   The above steps provide the complete formulation of the linear programming model on a spreadsheet, as summarized below (in algebraic form).

$$\text{Minimize} \quad \text{Cost} = 170S_1 + 160S_2 + 175S_3 + 180S_4 + 195S_5 \quad \text{(in dollars)}$$

subject to

Total agents 6–8 AM:	S_1	≥ 48
Total agents 8–10 AM:	$S_1 + S_2$	≥ 79
.		
.		
.		
Total agents midnight–6 AM:		$S_5 \geq 15$

and

$$S_1 \geq 0 \quad S_2 \geq 0 \quad S_3 \geq 0 \quad S_4 \geq 0 \quad S_5 \geq 0$$

Solving the Model   The Solver now can be applied to this model by making the entries in the Solver dialogue box shown in the lower left-hand corner of Figure 3.5, along with selecting the usual two Solver options indicated in the figure. NumberWorking (C21:G21) in the spreadsheet shows the resulting optimal solution for the number of agents that should be assigned to each shift. TotalCost (J21) indicates that this plan would cost $30,610 per day.

FIGURE 3.6

A template of a spreadsheet model for pure cost–benefit–trade-off problems.

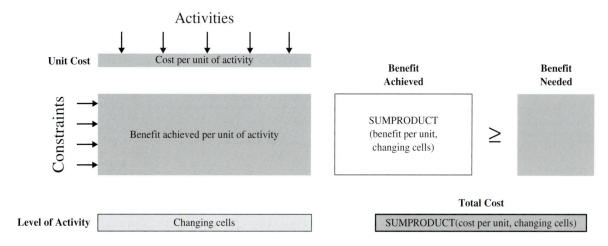

Summary of the Formulation Procedure for Cost–Benefit–Trade-off Problems

The nine steps in formulating any cost–benefit–trade-off problem follow the same pattern as presented at the end of the preceding section for resource-allocation problems, so we will not repeat them here. The main differences are that the overall measure of performance now is the total cost of the activities (or some surrogate of total cost chosen by management) in steps 2 and 3, benefits now replace resources in steps 4 and 5, and ≥ signs now are entered to the right of the output cells for benefits in step 8. Figure 3.6 shows a template of the format of a spreadsheet model for cost–benefit–trade-off problems.

All the functional constraints in the resulting model are *benefit constraints,* that is, constraints with a ≥ sign. This is the *identifying feature* of a pure cost–benefit–trade-off problem.

Review Questions

1. What is the difference in managerial objectives between resource-allocation problems and cost–benefit–trade-off problems?
2. What is the identifying feature of a cost–benefit–trade-off problem?
3. What is the form of a benefit constraint?
4. What are the three kinds of data that need to be gathered for a cost–benefit–trade-off problem?
5. Compare the types of activities for the two examples of cost–benefit–trade-off problems.
6. Compare the types of benefits for the two examples of cost–benefit–trade-off problems.

3.4   MIXED PROBLEMS

Sections 3.2 and 3.3 each described a broad category of linear programming problems—resource-allocation and cost–benefit–trade-off problems. As summarized in Table 3.6, each features one of the first two types of functional constraints shown there. In fact, the *identifying feature* of a *pure* resource-allocation problem is that *all* its functional constraints are *resource constraints.* The *identifying feature* of a *pure* cost–benefit–trade-off problem is that *all* its functional constraints are *benefit constraints.* (Keep in mind that the functional constraints include *all* the constraints of a problem *except* its nonnegativity constraints.)

The bottom row of Table 3.6 shows the last of the three types of functional constraints, namely, **fixed-requirement constraints,** which require that the left-hand side of each such constraint must exactly equal some fixed amount. Thus, since the left-hand side represents the amount provided of some quantity, the form of a fixed-requirement constraint is

$$\text{Amount provided} = \text{Required amount}$$

TABLE 3.6 Types of Functional Constraints

Type	Form*	Typical Interpretation	Main Usage
Resource constraint	LHS ≤ RHS	For some resource, Amount used ≤ Amount available	Resource-allocation problems and mixed problems
Benefit constraint	LHS ≥ RHS	For some benefit, Level achieved ≥ Minimum acceptable level	Cost–benefit–trade-off problems and mixed problems
Fixed-requirement constraint	LHS = RHS	For some quantity, Amount provided = Required amount	Fixed-requirements problems and mixed problems

*LHS = Left-hand side (a SUMPRODUCT function).
RHS = Right-hand side (a constant).

The *identifying feature* of a *pure* **fixed-requirements problem** is that it is a linear programming problem where *all* its functional constraints are fixed-requirement constraints. The next two sections will describe two particularly prominent types of fixed-requirement problems called *transportation problems* and *assignment problems.*

However, before turning to these types of problems, we first will use a continuation of the Super Grain case study from Section 3.1 to illustrate how many linear programming problems fall into another broad category called *mixed problems.*

> Many linear programming problems do not fit completely into any of the previously discussed categories (pure resource-allocation problems, cost–benefit–trade-off problems, and fixed-requirement problems) because the problem's functional constraints include more than one of the types shown in Table 3.6. Such problems are called ***mixed problems.***

Now let us see how a more careful analysis of the Super Grain case study turns this resource-allocation problem into a mixed problem that includes all three types of functional constraints shown in Table 3.6.

Super Grain Management Discusses Its Advertising-Mix Problem

The description of the Super Grain case study in Section 3.1 ends with Clair Syverson (Super Grain's vice president for marketing) sending a memorandum to the company's president, David Sloan, requesting a meeting to evaluate her proposed promotional campaign for the company's new breakfast cereal.

Soon thereafter, Claire Syverson and David Sloan meet to discuss plans for the campaign.

David Sloan (president): Thanks for your memo, Claire. The plan you outline for the promotional campaign looks like a reasonable one. However, I am surprised that it does not make any use of TV commercials. Why is that?

Claire Syverson (vice president for marketing): Well, as I described in my memo, I used a spreadsheet model to see how to maximize the number of exposures from the campaign and this turned out to be the plan that does this. I also was surprised that it did not include TV commercials, but the model indicated that introducing commercials would provide less exposures on a dollar-for-dollar basis than magazine ads and Sunday supplement ads. Don't you think it makes sense to use the plan that maximizes the number of exposures?

David: Not necessarily. Some exposures are a lot less important than others. For example, we know that middle-aged adults are not big consumers of our cereals, so we don't care very much how many of those people see our ads. On the other hand, young children are big consumers. Having TV commercials on the Saturday morning programs for children is our primary method of reaching young children. You know how important it will be to get young children to ask their parents for Crunchy Start. That is our best way of generating first-time sales. Those commercials also get seen by a lot of parents who are watching the programs with their kids. What we need is a commercial that is appealing to both parents and kids, and that gets the kids immediately bugging their parents to go buy Crunchy Start. I think that is a real key to a successful campaign.

Claire: Yes, that makes a lot of sense. In fact, I already have set some goals regarding the number of young children and the number of parents of young children that need to be reached by this promotional campaign.

David: Good. Did you include those goals in your spreadsheet model?

Claire: No, I didn't.

David: Well, I suggest that you incorporate them directly into your model. I suspect that maximizing exposures while also meeting your goals will give us a high impact plan that includes some TV commercials.

Claire: Good idea. I'll try it.

David: Are there any other factors that the plan in your memo doesn't take into account as well as you would like?

Claire: Well, yes, one. The plan doesn't take into account my budget for cents-off coupons in magazines and newspapers.

David: You should be able to add that to your model as well. Why don't you go back and see what happens when you incorporate these additional considerations?

Claire: OK, will do. You seem to have had a lot of experience with spreadsheet modeling.

David: Yes. It is a great tool as long as you maintain some healthy skepticism about what comes out of the model. No model can fully take into account everything that we must consider when dealing with managerial problems. This is especially true the first time or two you run the model. You need to keep asking, what are the missing quantitative considerations that I still should add to the model? Then, after you have made the model as complete as possible and obtained a solution, you still need to use your best managerial judgment to weigh intangible considerations that cannot be incorporated into the model.

Incorporating Additional Managerial Considerations into the Super Grain Model

Therefore, David and Claire conclude that the spreadsheet model needs to be expanded to incorporate some additional considerations. In particular, since the promotional campaign is for a breakfast cereal that should have special appeal to young children, they feel that two audiences should be targeted—*young children* and *parents of young children*. (This is why one of the three advertising media recommended by Giacomi & Jackowitz is commercials on children's television programs Saturday morning.) Consequently, Claire now has set two new goals for the campaign.

Goal 1:   The advertising should be seen by at least five million young children.

Goal 2:   The advertising should be seen by at least five million parents of young children.

In effect, these two goals are *minimum acceptable levels* for two special *benefits* to be achieved by the advertising activities.

Benefit 1:   Promoting the new breakfast cereal to young children.

Benefit 2:   Promoting the new breakfast cereal to parents of young children.

Because of the way the goals have been articulated, the *level* of each of these benefits is measured by the *number of people* in the specified category that are reached by the advertising.

To enable constructing the corresponding *benefit constraints* (as described in Section 3.3), Claire asks Giacomi & Jackowitz to estimate how much each advertisement in each of the media will contribute to each benefit, as measured by the number of people reached in the specified category. These estimates are given in Table 3.7.

It is interesting to observe that management wants special consideration given to these two kinds of benefits even though the original spreadsheet model (Figure 3.1) already takes them into account to some extent. As described in Section 3.1, the *expected number of exposures* is the overall measure of performance to be maximized. This measure counts up all the times

TABLE 3.7 Benefit Data for the Revised Super Grain Corp. Advertising-Mix Problem

Target Category	Number Reached in Target Category (in millions)			
	Each TV Commercial	Each Magazine Ad	Each Sunday Ad	Minimum Acceptable Level
Young children	1.2	0.1	0	5
Parents of young children	0.5	0.2	0.2	5

Benefit constraints are useful for incorporating managerial goals into the model.

that an advertisement is seen by any individual, including all those individuals in the target audiences. However, maximizing this *general* measure of performance does *not* ensure that the two *specific goals* prescribed by management (Claire Syverson) will be achieved. Claire feels that achieving these goals is essential to a successful promotional campaign. Therefore, she complements the general objective with specific benefit constraints that *do* ensure that the goals will be achieved. Having benefit constraints added to incorporate managerial goals into the model is a prerogative of management.

Claire has one more consideration she wants to incorporate into the model. She is a strong believer in the promotional value of *cents-off coupons* (coupons that shoppers can clip from printed advertisements to obtain a refund of a designated amount when purchasing the advertised item). Consequently, she always earmarks a major portion of her annual marketing budget for the redemption of these coupons. She still has $1,490,000 left from this year's allotment for coupon redemptions. Because of the importance of Crunchy Start to the company, she has decided to use this entire remaining allotment in the campaign promoting this cereal.

This *fixed amount* for coupon redemptions is a *fixed requirement* that needs to be expressed as a *fixed-requirement constraint.* As described at the beginning of this section, the form of a fixed-requirement constraint is that, for some type of quantity,

$$\text{Amount provided} = \text{Required amount}$$

In this case, the quantity involved is the amount of money provided for the redemption of cents-off coupons. To specify this constraint in the spreadsheet, we need to estimate how much each advertisement in each of the media will contribute toward fulfilling the required amount for the quantity. Both medium 2 (advertisements in food and family-oriented magazines) and medium 3 (advertisements in Sunday supplements of major newspapers) will feature cents-off coupons. The estimates of the amount of coupon redemption per advertisement in each of these media is given in Table 3.8.

Formulation of the Revised Spreadsheet Model

Figure 3.7 shows one way of formatting the spreadsheet to expand the original spreadsheet model in Figure 3.1 to incorporate the additional managerial considerations. We outline the four components of the revised model below.

The Data

Additional data cells in NumberReachedPerAd (C11:E12), MinimumAcceptable (H11:H12), CouponRedemptionPerAd (C15:E15), and RequiredAmount (H15) give the data in Tables 3.7 and 3.8.

TABLE 3.8 Data for the Fixed-Requirement Constraint for the Revised Super Grain Corp. Advertising-Mix Problem

Requirement	Contribution toward Required Amount			
	Each TV Spot	Each Magazine Ad	Each Sunday Ad	Required Amount
Coupon redemption	0	$40,000	$120,000	$1,490,000

FIGURE 3.7

The spreadsheet model for the revised Super Grain problem, including the formulas for the target cell TotalExposures (H19) and the other output cells in column F, as well as the specifications needed to set up the Solver.
The changing cells NumberOfAds (C19:E19) show the optimal solution obtained by the Solver.

	A	B	C	D	E	F	G	H
1		**Super Grain Corp. Advertising-Mix Problem**						
2								
3			TV Spots	Magazine Ads	SS Ads			
4		Exposures per Ad	1,300	600	500			
5		(thousands)						
6			Cost per Ad ($thousands)			Budget Spent		Budget Available
7		Ad Budget	300	150	100	3,775	≤	4,000
8		Planning Budget	90	30	40	1,000	≤	1,000
9								
10			Number Reached per Ad (millions)			Total Reached		Minimum Acceptable
11		Young Children	1.2	0.1	0	5	≥	5
12		Parents of Young Children	0.5	0.2	0.2	5.85	≥	5
13								
14			TV Spots	Magazine Ads	SS Ads	Total Redeemed		Required Amount
15		Coupon Redemption	0	40	120	1,490	=	1,490
16		per Ad ($thousands)						
17								Total Exposures
18			TV Spots	Magazine Ads	SS Ads			(thousands)
19		Number of Ads	3	14	7.75			16,175
20			≤					
21		Maximum TV Spots	5					

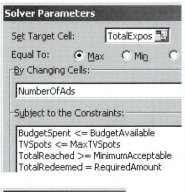

Solver Parameters

Set Target Cell: `TotalExpos`

Equal To: ● Max ○ Min ○

By Changing Cells:

`NumberOfAds`

Subject to the Constraints:

```
BudgetSpent <= BudgetAvailable
TVSpots <= MaxTVSpots
TotalReached >= MinimumAcceptable
TotalRedeemed = RequiredAmount
```

Solver Options

☑ Assume Linear Model
☑ Assume Non-Negative

Range Name	Cells
BudgetAvailable	H7:H8
BudgetSpent	F7:F8
CostPerAd	C7:E8
CouponRedemptionPerAd	C15:E15
ExposuresPerAd	C4:E4
MaxTVSpots	C21
MinimumAcceptable	H11:H12
NumberOfAds	C19:E19
NumberReachedPerAd	C11:E12
RequiredAmount	H15
TotalExposures	H19
TotalReached	F11:F12
TotalRedeemed	F15
TVSpots	C19

	F
6	Budget Spent
7	=SUMPRODUCT(C7:E7,NumberOfAds)
8	=SUMPRODUCT(C8:E8,NumberOfAds)
9	
10	Total Reached
11	=SUMPRODUCT(C11:E11,NumberOfAds)
12	=SUMPRODUCT(C12:E12,NumberOfAds)
13	
14	Total Redeemed
15	=SUMPRODUCT(CouponRedemptionPerAd, NumberOfAds)

	H
17	Total Exposures
18	(thousands)
19	=SUMPRODUCT(ExposuresPerAd,NumberOfAds)

The Decisions

Recall that, as before, the decisions to be made are

TV = Number of commercials on television

M = Number of advertisements in magazines

SS = Number of advertisements in Sunday supplements

The changing cells to hold these numbers continue to be in NumberOfAds (C19:E19).

The Constraints

In addition to the original constraints, we now have two benefit constraints and one fixed-requirement constraint. As specified for us (but not for the Solver) in rows 11 and 12, columns F to H, the benefit constraints are

Total number of young children reached ≥ 5 (goal 1 in millions)

Total number of parents reached ≥ 5 (goal 2 in millions)

Using the data in columns C to E of these rows,

Total number of young children reached $= 1.2TV + 0.1M + 0SS$

$= $ SUMPRODUCT (C11:E11, NumberOfAds)

$\rightarrow$ cell F11

Total number of parents reached $= 0.5TV + 0.2M + 0.2SS$

$= $ SUMPRODUCT (C12:E12, NumberOfAds)

$\rightarrow$ cell F12

These output cells are given the range name TotalReached (F11:F12).

The fixed-requirement constraint indicated in row 15 is that

Total coupon redemption $= 1,490$ (allotment in \$1,000s)

CouponRedemptionPerAd (C15:E15) gives the number of coupons redeemed per ad, so

Total coupon redemption $= 0TV + 40M + 120SS$

$= $ SUMPRODUCT (CouponRedemptionPerAd, NumberOfAds)

$\rightarrow$ cell F15

These same constraints are specified for the Solver in the Solver dialogue box, along with the original constraints, in Figure 3.7.

The Measure of Performance

The measure of performance continues to be

Exposure $= 1,300TV + 600M + 500SS$

$= $ SUMPRODUCT (ExposuresPerAd, NumberOfAds)

$\rightarrow$ cell H19

so H19 is the new address for the target cell.

Summary of the Formulation

The above steps have resulted in formulating the following linear programming model (in algebraic form) on a spreadsheet.

Maximize   Exposure $= 1,300TV + 600M + 500SS$

subject to the following constraints:

1. *Resource constraints:*

$$300TV + 150M + 100SS \leq 4,000 \quad \text{(ad budget in \$1,000s)}$$
$$90TV + 30M + 40SS \leq 1,000 \quad \text{(planning budget in \$1,000s)}$$
$$TV \quad \leq \quad 5 \quad \text{(television spots available)}$$

2. *Benefit constraints:*

$$1.2TV + 0.1M \quad \geq \quad 5 \quad \text{(millions of young children)}$$
$$0.5TV + 0.2M + 0.2SS \geq \quad 5 \quad \text{(millions of parents)}$$

3. *Fixed-requirement constraint:*

$$40M + 120SS = 1,490 \quad \text{(coupon budget in \$1,000s)}$$

4. *Nonnegativity constraints:*

$$TV \geq 0 \quad M \geq 0 \quad SS \geq 0$$

Solving the Model

After making all the entries in the Solver dialogue box shown in Figure 3.7, plus selecting the usual two Solver options, the Solver finds the optimal solution given in row 19. This optimal solution provides the following plan for the promotional campaign:

Run 3 television commercials.

Run 14 advertisements in magazines.

Run 7.75 advertisements in Sunday supplements (so the eighth advertisement would appear in only 75 percent of the newspapers).

Although the expected number of exposures with this plan is only 16,175,000, versus the 17,000,000 with the first plan shown in Figure 3.1, both Claire Syverson and David Sloan feel that the new plan does a much better job of meeting all of management's goals for this campaign. They decide to adopt the new plan.

A model may need to be modified a number of times before it adequately incorporates all the important considerations.

This case study illustrates a common theme in real applications of linear programming—the continuing evolution of the linear programming model. It is common to make later adjustments in the initial version of the model, perhaps even many times, as experience is gained in using the model. Frequently, these adjustments are made to more adequately reflect some important managerial considerations. This may result in a mixed problem because the new functional constraints needed to incorporate the managerial considerations may be of a different type from those in the original model.

Summary of the Formulation Procedure for Mixed Linear Programming Problems

The procedure for formulating mixed problems is similar to those for the other three categories of linear programming problems. However, each of these other categories features just one of the three types of functional constraints (resource constraints, benefit constraints, and fixed-requirement constraints), whereas mixed problems can include all three types. The following summary for mixed problems includes separate steps for dealing with these different types of functional constraints. Also see Figure 3.8 for a template of the format for a spreadsheet model of mixed problems. (This format works well for most mixed problems, including those encountered in this chapter, but more flexibility is occasionally needed, as will be illustrated in the next chapter.)

1. Since any linear programming problem involves finding the *best mix* of levels of various activities, identify these *activities* for the problem at hand. The decisions to be made are the *levels* of these activities.

FIGURE 3.8

A template of a spreadsheet model for mixed problems.

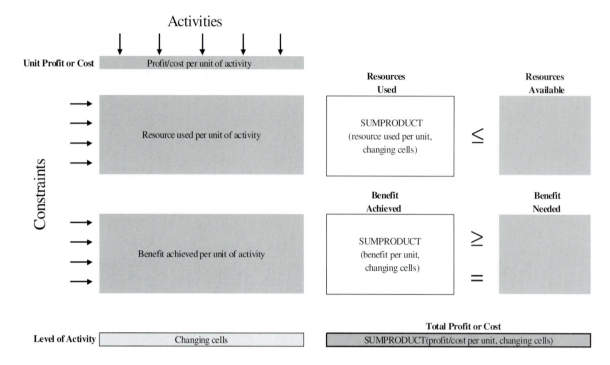

2. From the viewpoint of management, identify an appropriate *overall measure of performance* for solutions of the problem.

3. For each activity, estimate the *contribution per unit* of the activity to this overall measure of performance.

4. Identify any *resources* that must be allocated to the activities (as described in Section 3.2). For each one, identify the *amount available* and then the *amount used per unit of each activity.*

5. Identify any *benefits* to be obtained from the activities (as described in Section 3.3). For each one, identify the *minimum acceptable level* prescribed by management and then the *benefit contribution per unit of each activity.*

6. Identify any *fixed requirements* that, for some type of quantity, the amount provided must equal a required amount (as described in Section 3.4). For each fixed requirement, identify the *required amount* and then the *contribution toward this required amount per unit of each activity.*

7. Enter the data gathered in steps 3–6 into *data cells* in a spreadsheet.

8. Designate *changing cells* for displaying the decisions on activity levels.

9. Use *output cells* to specify the constraints on resources, benefits, and fixed requirements.

10. Designate a *target cell* for displaying the overall measure of performance.

Review Questions

1. What types of functional constraints can appear in a mixed linear programming problem?

2. What managerial goals needed to be incorporated into the expanded linear programming model for the Super Grain Corp. problem?

3. Which categories of functional constraints are included in the new linear programming model?

4. Why did management adopt the new plan even though it provides a smaller expected number of exposures than the original plan recommended by the original linear programming model?

3.5   TRANSPORTATION PROBLEMS

One of the most common applications of linear programming involves optimizing a shipping plan for transporting goods. In a typical application, a company has several plants producing a certain product that needs to be shipped to the company's customers (or perhaps to distribution centers). How much should each plant ship to each customer in order to minimize the total cost? Linear programming can provide the answer. This type of linear programming problem is called a **transportation problem.**

This kind of application normally needs two kinds of functional constraints. One kind specifies that the amount of the product produced at each plant must equal the total amount shipped to customers. The other kind specifies that the total amount received from the plants by each customer must equal the amount ordered. These are *fixed-requirement constraints,* which makes the problem a *fixed-requirements problem.* However, there also are variations of this problem where resource constraints or benefit constraints are needed.

Transportation problems and assignment problems (described in the next section) are such important types of linear programming problems that the entire Chapter 15 on the CD-ROM is devoted to further describing these two related types of problems and providing examples of a wide variety of applications.

We provide below an example of a typical transportation problem.

The Big M Company Transportation Problem

The Big M Company produces a variety of heavy duty machines at two factories. One of its products is a large turret lathe. Orders have been received from three customers to purchase some of these turret lathes next month. These lathes will be shipped individually, and Table 3.9 shows what the cost will be for shipping each lathe from each factory to each customer. This table also shows how many lathes have been ordered by each customer and how many will be produced by each factory. The company's distribution manager now wants to determine how many machines to ship from each factory to each customer to minimize the total shipping cost.

Figure 3.9 depicts the distribution network for this problem. This network ignores the geographical layout of the factories and customers and instead lines up the two factories in one column on the left and the three customers in one column on the right. Each arrow shows one of the shipping lanes through this distribution network.

Formulation of the Problem in Linear Programming Terms

We need to identify the *activities* and *requirements* of this transportation problem to formulate it as a linear programming problem. In this case, two kinds of activities have been mentioned—the *production* of the turret lathes at the two factories and the *shipping* of these lathes along the various shipping lanes. However, we know the specific amounts to be produced at each factory, so no decisions need to be made about the production activities. The decisions to be made concern the levels of the *shipping activities*—how many lathes to ship through each shipping lane. Therefore, we need to focus on the shipping activities for the linear programming formulation.

The *activities* correspond to shipping lanes, depicted by arrows in Figure 3.9.

The *level* of each activity is the number of lathes shipped through the corresponding shipping lane.

TABLE 3.9
Some Data for the Big M Company Distribution-Network Problem

	Shipping Cost for Each Lathe			
To From	Customer 1	Customer 2	Customer 3	Output
Factory 1	$700	$900	$800	12 lathes
Factory 2	800	900	700	15 lathes
Order size	10 lathes	8 lathes	9 lathes	

FIGURE 3.9

The distribution network for the Big M Company problem.

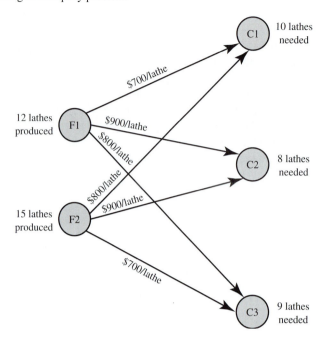

Just as any linear programming problem can be described as finding the best mix of activity levels, this one involves finding the *best mix of shipping amounts* for the various shipping lanes. The decisions to be made are

S_{F1-C1} = Number of lathes shipped from Factory 1 to Customer 1

S_{F1-C2} = Number of lathes shipped from Factory 1 to Customer 2

S_{F1-C3} = Number of lathes shipped from Factory 1 to Customer 3

S_{F2-C1} = Number of lathes shipped from Factory 2 to Customer 1

S_{F2-C2} = Number of lathes shipped from Factory 2 to Customer 2

S_{F2-C3} = Number of lathes shipped from Factory 2 to Customer 3

so six changing cells will be needed in the spreadsheet.

The objective is to

$$\text{Minimize} \quad \text{Cost} = \text{Total cost for shipping the lathes}$$

Using the shipping costs given in Table 3.9,

$$\text{Cost} = 700S_{F1-C1} + 900S_{F1-C2} + 800S_{F1-C3} + 800S_{F2-C1} + 900S_{F2-C2} + 700S_{F2-C3}$$

is the quantity in dollars to be entered into the target cell. (We will use a SUMPRODUCT function to do this a little later.)

The spreadsheet model also will need five constraints involving *fixed requirements.* Both Table 3.9 and Figure 3.9 show these requirements.

Requirement 1:   Factory 1 must ship 12 lathes.

Requirement 2:   Factory 2 must ship 15 lathes.

Requirement 3:   Customer 1 must receive 10 lathes.

Requirement 4:   Customer 2 must receive 8 lathes.

Requirement 5:   Customer 3 must receive 9 lathes.

Thus, there is a specific requirement associated with each of the five locations in the distribution network shown in Figure 3.9.

Proctor & Gamble (P & G) makes and markets over 300 brands of consumer goods worldwide. The company has grown continuously over its long history tracing back to the 1830s. To maintain and accelerate that growth, a major management science study was undertaken to strengthen P & G's global effectiveness. Prior to the study, the company's supply chain consisted of hundreds of suppliers, over 50 product categories, over 60 plants, 15 distribution centers, and over 1,000 customer zones. However, as the company moved toward global brands, management realized that it needed to consolidate plants to reduce manufacturing expenses, improve speed to market, and reduce capital investment. Therefore, the study focused on redesigning the company's production and distribution system for its North American operations. The result was a reduction in the number of North American plants by almost 20 percent, saving over $200 million in pretax costs per year.

A major part of the study revolved around formulating and solving transportation problems for individual product categories. For each option regarding keeping certain plants open, and so forth, solving the corresponding transportation problem for a product category showed what the distribution cost would be for shipping the product category from those plants to the distribution centers and customer zones.

Source: J. D. Camm, T. E. Chorman, F. A. Dill, J. R. Evans, D. J. Sweeney, and G. W. Wegryn, "Blending OR/MS, Judgment, and GIS: Restructuring P & G's Supply Chain," *Interfaces* 27, no. 1 (January–February 1997), pp. 128–142.

All five of these requirements can be expressed in constraint form as

$$\text{Amount provided} = \text{Required amount}$$

For example, Requirement 1 can be expressed algebraically as

$$S_{\text{F1-C1}} + S_{\text{F1-C2}} + S_{\text{F1-C3}} = 12$$

where the left-hand side gives the total number of lathes shipped from Factory 1, and 12 is the required amount to be shipped from Factory 1. Therefore, this constraint restricts $S_{\text{F1-C1}}$, $S_{\text{F1-C2}}$, and $S_{\text{F1-C3}}$ to values that sum to the required amount of 12. In contrast to the $\leq$ form for resource constraints and the $\geq$ form for benefit constraints, the constraints express *fixed requirements* that must hold with equality, so this transportation problem falls into the category of fixed-requirements problems introduced in the preceding section. However, Chapter 15 (on the CD-ROM) gives several examples that illustrate how variants of transportation problems can have resource constraints or benefit constraints as well. Such variations can be incorporated readily into the spreadsheet model.

Formulation of the Spreadsheet Model

Careful *problem* formulation needs to precede *model* formulation.

In preparation for formulating the *model*, the *problem* has been formulated above by identifying the decisions to be made, the constraints on these decisions, and the overall measure of performance, as well as gathering all the important data displayed in Table 3.9. All this information leads to the spreadsheet model shown in Figure 3.10. The data cells include ShippingCost (C5:E6), Output (H11:H12), and OrderSize (C15:E15), incorporating all the data from Table 3.9. The changing cells are UnitsShipped (C11:E12), which give the decisions on the amounts to be shipped through the respective shipping lanes. The output cells are Total-

Here is an example where SUM functions are used for output cells instead of SUMPRODUCT functions.

ShippedOut (F11:F12) and TotalToCustomer (C13:E13), where the SUM functions entered into these cells are shown below the spreadsheet in Figure 3.10. The constraints are that TotalShippedOut is required to equal Output and TotalToCustomer is required to equal OrderSize. These constraints have been specified on the spreadsheet and entered into the Solver dialogue box. The target cell is TotalCost (H15), where its SUMPRODUCT function gives the total shipping cost. The Solver dialogue box specifies that the objective is to minimize this cost. Finally, the figure indicates that the usual two Solver options have been selected to specify that the model is a linear programming model that has nonnegativity constraints.

UnitsShipped (C11:E12) in the spreadsheet in Figure 3.10 shows the result of applying the Solver to obtain an optimal solution for the number of lathes to ship through each shipping lane. TotalCost (H15) indicates that the total shipping cost for this shipping plan is $20,500.

FIGURE 3.10

The spreadsheet model for the Big M Company problem, including the formulas for the target cell TotalCost (H15) and the other output cells TotalShippedOut (F11:F12) and TotalToCustomer (C13:E13), as well as the specifications needed to set up the Solver. The changing cells UnitsShipped (C11:E12) show the optimal solution obtained by the Solver.

	A	B	C	D	E	F	G	H
1		**Big M Company Distribution Problem**						
2								
3		**Shipping Cost**						
4		**(per Lathe)**	Customer 1	Customer 2	Customer 3			
5		Factory 1	$700	$900	$800			
6		Factory 2	$800	$900	$700			
7								
8						Total		
9						Shipped		
10		**Units Shipped**	Customer 1	Customer 2	Customer 3	Out		Output
11		Factory 1	10	2	0	12	=	12
12		Factory 2	0	6	9	15	=	15
13		Total to Customer	10	8	9			
14			=	=	=			**Total Cost**
15		Order Size	10	8	9			$20,500

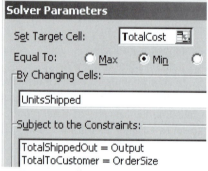

Solver Parameters
Se̲t Target Cell: [TotalCost]
Equal To: ○ Ma̲x ◉ Mi̲n ○
B̲y Changing Cells:
[UnitsShipped]
S̲ubject to the Constraints:
TotalShippedOut = Output
TotalToCustomer = OrderSize

Solver Options
☑ Assume Linear Mo̲del
☑ Assume Non-Negative

Range Name	Cells
OrderSize	C15:E15
Output	H11:H12
ShippingCost	C5:E6
TotalCost	H15
TotalShippedOut	F11:F12
TotalToCustomer	C13:E13
UnitsShipped	C11:E12

	F
8	Total
9	Shipped
10	Out
11	=SUM(C11:E11)
12	=SUM(C12:E12)

	B	C	D	E
13	Total to Customer	=SUM(C11:C12)	=SUM(D11:D12)	=SUM(E11:E12)

	H
14	Total Cost
15	=SUMPRODUCT(ShippingCost,UnitsShipped)

To summarize, here is the algebraic form of the linear programming model that has been formulated in the spreadsheet.

$$\text{Minimize} \quad \text{Cost} = 700S_{F1\text{-}C1} + 900S_{F1\text{-}C2} + 800S_{F1\text{-}C3} + 800S_{F2\text{-}C1} + 900S_{F2\text{-}C2} + 700S_{F2\text{-}C3}$$

subject to the following constraints:

1. *Fixed-requirement constraints:*

$$
\begin{array}{llll}
S_{F1\text{-}C1} + S_{F1\text{-}C2} + S_{F1\text{-}C3} & & = 12 & \text{(Factory 1)} \\
 & S_{F2\text{-}C1} + S_{F2\text{-}C2} + S_{F2\text{-}C3} & = 15 & \text{(Factory 2)} \\
S_{F1\text{-}C1} & + S_{F2\text{-}C1} & = 10 & \text{(Customer 1)} \\
\quad S_{F1\text{-}C2} & \quad + S_{F2\text{-}C2} & = 8 & \text{(Customer 2)} \\
\qquad S_{F1\text{-}C3} & \qquad + S_{F2\text{-}C3} & = 9 & \text{(Customer 3)}
\end{array}
$$

2. *Nonnegativity constraints:*

$$S_{F1\text{-}C1} \geq 0 \quad S_{F1\text{-}C2} \geq 0 \quad S_{F1\text{-}C3} \geq 0 \quad S_{F2\text{-}C1} \geq 0 \quad S_{F2\text{-}C2} \geq 0 \quad S_{F2\text{-}C3} \geq 0$$

1. Why are transportation problems given this name?
2. What is an identifying feature of transportation problems?
3. How does the form of a fixed-requirement constraint differ from that of a resource constraint? A benefit constraint?
4. What are the quantities with fixed requirements in the Big M Company problem?

3.6   ASSIGNMENT PROBLEMS

We now turn to another special type of linear programming problem called **assignment problems.** As the name suggests, this kind of problem involves making *assignments.* Frequently, these are assignments of people to jobs. Thus, many applications of the assignment problem involve aiding managers in matching up their personnel with tasks to be performed. Other applications might instead involve assigning machines, vehicles, or plants to tasks.

Here is a typical example.

An Example: The Sellmore Company Problem

The marketing manager of the Sellmore Company will be holding the company's annual sales conference soon for sales regional managers and personnel. To assist in the administration of the conference, he is hiring four temporary employees (Ann, Ian, Joan, and Sean), where each will handle one of the following four tasks:

1. Word processing of written presentations.
2. Computer graphics for both oral and written presentations.
3. Preparation of conference packets, including copying and organizing written materials.
4. Handling of advance and on-site registrations for the conference.

Decisions need to be made regarding which person to assign to each task.

He now needs to decide which person to assign to each task.

Although each temporary employee has at least the minimal background necessary to perform any of the four tasks, they differ considerably in how efficiently they can handle the different types of work. Table 3.10 shows how many hours each would need for each task. The rightmost column gives the hourly wage based on the background of each employee.

Formulation of a Spreadsheet Model

Using Cost (D15:G18), the objective is to minimize the total cost of the assignments.

Figure 3.11 shows a spreadsheet model for this problem. Table 3.10 is entered at the top. Combining these required times and wages gives the cost (cells D15:G18) for each possible assignment of a temporary employee to a task, using equations shown at the bottom of Figure 3.11. This *cost table* is just the way that any assignment problem is displayed. The objective is to determine which assignments should be made to minimize the sum of the associated costs.

The values of 1 in Supply (J24:J27) indicate that each person (assignee) listed in column C must perform exactly one task. The values of 1 in Demand (D30:G30) indicate that each task must be performed by exactly one person. These requirements then are specified in the constraints given in the Solver dialogue box.

A value of 1 in a changing cell indicates that the corresponding assignment is being made, whereas 0 means that the assignment is not being made.

Each of the changing cells Assignment (D24:G27) is given a value of 1 when the corresponding assignment is being made, and a value of 0 otherwise. Therefore, the Excel equation for the target cell, TotalCost = SUMPRODUCT(Cost, Assignment), gives the total cost for

TABLE 3.10
Data for the Sellmore Co. Problem

Temporary Employee	Required Time per Task (Hours)				Hourly Wage
	Word Processing	Graphics	Packets	Registrations	
Ann	35	41	27	40	$14
Ian	47	45	32	51	12
Joan	39	56	36	43	13
Sean	32	51	25	46	15

FIGURE 3.11

A spreadsheet formulation of the Sellmore Co. problem as an assignment problem, including the target cell TotalCost (J30) and the other output cells Cost (D15:G18), TotalAssignments (H24:H27), and TotalAssigned (D28:G28), as well as the specifications needed to set up the model. The values of 1 in the changing cells Assignment (D24:G27) show the optimal plan obtained by the Solver for assigning the people to the tasks.

	A	B	C	D	E	F	G	H	I	J
1		**Sellmore Co. Assignment Problem**								
2										
3						**Task**				
4		**Required Time**		Word					Hourly	
5		**(Hours)**		Processing	Graphics	Packets	Registrations		Wage	
6			Ann	35	41	27	40		$14	
7		Assignee	Ian	47	45	32	51		$12	
8			Joan	39	56	36	43		$13	
9			Sean	32	51	25	46		$15	
10										
11										
12						**Task**				
13				Word						
14		**Cost**		Processing	Graphics	Packets	Registrations			
15			Ann	$490	$574	$378	$560			
16		Assignee	Ian	$564	$540	$384	$612			
17			Joan	$507	$728	$468	$559			
18			Sean	$480	$765	$375	$690			
19										
20										
21						**Task**				
22		**Assignment**		Word				Total		
23				Processing	Graphics	Packets	Registrations	Assignments		Supply
24			Ann	0	0	1	0	1	=	1
25		Assignee	Ian	0	1	0	0	1	=	1
26			Joan	0	0	0	1	1	=	1
27			Sean	1	0	0	0	1	=	1
28			Total Assigned	1	1	1	1			
29				=	=	=	=			Total Cost
30			Demand	1	1	1	1			$1,957

	B	C	D	E	F	G			H
13			Word					22	Total
14	**Cost**		Processing	Graphics	Packets	Registrations		23	Assignments
15		Ann	=D6*I6	=E6*I6	=F6*I6	=G6*I6		24	=SUM(D24:G24)
16	Assignee	Ian	=D7*I7	=E7*I7	=F7*I7	=G7*I7		25	=SUM(D25:G25)
17		Joan	=D8*I8	=E8*I8	=F8*I8	=G8*I8		26	=SUM(D26:G26)
18		Sean	=D9*I9	=E9*I9	=F9*I9	=G9*I9		27	=SUM(D27:G27)

Solver Parameters

Set Target Cell: TotalCost
Equal To: ○ Max ● Min ○
By Changing Cells:
Assignment
Subject to the Constraints:
TotalAssigned = Demand
TotalAssignments = Supply

Solver Options
☑ Assume Linear Model
☑ Assume Non-Negative

		J
29		Total Cost
30		=SUMPRODUCT(Cost,Assignment)

Range Name	Cells
Assignment	D24:G27
Cost	D15:G18
Demand	D30:G30
HourlyWage	I6:I9
RequiredTime	D6:G9
Supply	J24:J27
TotalAssigned	D28:G28
TotalAssignments	H24:H27
TotalCost	J30

	C	D	E	F	G
28	Total Assigned	=SUM(D24:D27)	=SUM(E24:E27)	=SUM(F24:F27)	=SUM(G24:G27)

Excel Tip: When solving an assignment problem, rounding errors occasionally will cause Excel to return a noninteger value very close to 0 (e.g., 1.23 E-10, meaning 0.000000000123) or very close to 1 (e.g., 0.9999912). To make the spreadsheet cleaner, you may replace these "ugly" representations by their proper value of 0 or 1 in the changing cells.

the assignments being made. The Solver dialogue box specifies that the objective is to minimize this target cell.

The changing cells in Figure 3.11 show the optimal solution obtained after clicking on the Solve button. This solution is

Assign Ann to prepare conference packets.

Assign Ian to do the computer graphics.

Assign Joan to handle registrations.

Assign Sean to do the word processing.

The total cost given in cell J30 is $1,957.

Characteristics of Assignment Problems

Note that all the functional constraints of the Sellmore Co. problem (as shown in cells H24:J27 and D28:G30 of Figure 3.11) are fixed-requirement constraints which require each person to perform exactly one task and require each task to be performed by exactly one person. Thus, like the Big M Company transportation problem, the Sellmore Co. is a fixed-requirements problem. This is a characteristic of all pure assignment problems. However, Chapter 15 (on the CD-ROM) gives some examples of variants of assignment problems where this is not the case.

Like the changing cells Assignment (D24:G27) in Figure 3.11, the changing cells in the spreadsheet model for any pure assignment problem gives a value of 1 when the corresponding assignment is being made, and a value of 0 otherwise. Since the fixed-requirement constraints require only each row or column of changing cells to add up to 1 (which could happen, e.g., if two of the changing cells in the same row or column had a value of 0.5 and the rest 0), this would seem to necessitate adding the constraints that each of the changing cells must be *integer*. After choosing the Solver option, *Assume Non-Negative*, this then would force each of the changing cells to be 0 or 1. However, it turned out to be unnecessary to add the constraints that require the changing cells to have values of 0 or 1 in Figure 3.11 because Solver gave an optimal solution that had only values of 0 or 1 anyway. In fact, a general characteristic of pure assignment problems is that Solver always provides such an optimal solution without needing to add these additional constraints.

Review Questions

1. Why are assignment problems given this name?
2. Pure assignment problems have what type of functional constraints?
3. What is the interpretation of the changing cells in the spreadsheet model of a pure assignment problem?

3.7 MODEL FORMULATION FROM A BROADER PERSPECTIVE

Formulating and analyzing a linear programming model provides information to help managers make their decisions. That means the model must accurately reflect the managerial view of the problem:

Both the measure of performance and the constraints in a model need to reflect the managerial view of the problem.

- The overall *measure of performance* must capture what management wants accomplished.
- When management limits the amounts of resources that will be made available to the activities under consideration, these limitations should be expressed as *resource constraints*.
- When management establishes minimum acceptable levels for benefits to be gained from the activities, these managerial goals should be incorporated into the model as *benefit constraints*.
- If management has fixed requirements for certain quantities, then *fixed-requirement constraints* are needed.

With the help of spreadsheets, some managers now are able to formulate and solve small linear programming models themselves. However, larger linear programming models generally are formulated by *management science teams,* not managers. When this is done, the management science team must thoroughly understand the managerial view of the problem. This requires clear communication with management from the very beginning of the study and maintaining effective communication as new issues requiring managerial guidance are identified. Management needs to clearly convey its view of the problem and the important issues involved. A manager cannot expect to obtain a helpful linear programming study without making clear just what help is wanted.

You will gain a greater appreciation for the importance of clear communication between the management science team and management when you become involved with real applications of linear programming. As is necessary in any textbook, the examples in this chapter are far smaller, simpler, and more clearly spelled out than is typical of real applications. Many real studies require formulating complicated linear programming models involving hundreds or thousands of decisions and constraints. In these cases, there usually are many ambiguities about just what should be incorporated into the model. Strong managerial input and support are vital to the success of a linear programming study for such complex problems.

When dealing with huge real problems, there is no such thing as "the" correct linear programming model for the problem. The model continually evolves throughout the course of the study. Early in the study, various techniques are used to test initial versions of the model to identify the errors and omissions that inevitably occur when constructing such a large model. This testing process is referred to as **model validation.**

Once the basic formulation has been validated, there are many reasonable variations of the model that might be used. Which variation to use depends on such factors as the assumptions about the problem that seem most reasonable, the estimates of the parameters of the model that seem most reliable, and the degree of detail desired in the model.

In large linear programming studies, a good approach is to begin with a relatively simple version of the model and then use the experience gained with this model to evolve toward more elaborate models that more nearly reflect the complexity of the real problem. This process of **model enrichment** continues only as long as the model remains reasonably easy to solve. It must be curtailed when the study's results are needed by management. Managers often need to curb the natural instinct of management science teams to continue adding "bells and whistles" to the model rather than winding up the study in a timely fashion with a less elegant but adequate model.

When managers study the output of the current model, they often detect some undesirable characteristics that point toward needed model enrichments. These enrichments frequently take the form of new *benefit constraints* to satisfy some managerial goals not previously articulated. (Recall that this is what happened in the Super Grain case study.)

Even though many reasonable variations of the model could be used, an *optimal solution* can be solved for only with respect to one specific version of the model at a time. This is why *what-if analysis* is such an important part of a linear programming study. After obtaining an optimal solution with respect to one specific model, management will have many what-if questions:

- What if the estimates of the parameters in the model are incorrect?
- How do the conclusions change if different plausible assumptions are made about the problem?
- What happens when certain managerial options are pursued that are not incorporated into the current model?

Chapter 5 is devoted primarily to describing how what-if analysis addresses these and related issues, as well as how managers use this information.

Because managers *instigate* management science studies, they need to know enough about linear programming models and their formulation to be able to recognize managerial problems to which linear programming can be applied. Furthermore, since managerial input is so important for linear programming studies, managers need to understand the kinds of managerial concerns that can be incorporated into the model. Developing these two skills have been the most important goals of this chapter.

Linear programming studies need strong managerial input and support.

What-if analysis addresses some key questions that remain after formulating and solving a model.

Review
Questions

1. A linear programming model needs to reflect accurately whose view of the problem?
2. Who generally formulates large linear programming models?
3. What line of communication is vital in a linear programming study?
4. What is meant by *model validation?*
5. What is meant by the process of *model enrichment?*
6. Why is what-if analysis an important part of a linear programming study?

3.8 Summary

Functional constraints with a $\leq$ sign are called *resource constraints,* because they require that the *amount used* of some resource must be *less than or equal to* the *amount available* of that resource. The identifying feature of *resource-allocation problems* is that all their functional constraints are resource constraints.

Functional constraints with a $\geq$ sign are called *benefit constraints,* since their form is that the *level achieved* for some benefit must be *greater than or equal to* the *minimum acceptable level* for that benefit. Frequently, benefit constraints express goals prescribed by management. If every functional constraint is a benefit constraint, then the problem is a *cost–benefit–trade-off problem.*

Functional constraints with an = sign are called *fixed-requirement constraints,* because they express the fixed requirement that, for some quantity, the *amount provided* must be *equal to* the *required amount.* The identifying feature of *fixed-requirements problems* is that their functional constraints are fixed-requirement constraints. One prominent type of fixed-requirements problem is transportation problems, which typically involve finding a shipping plan that minimizes the total cost of transporting a product from a number of plants to a number of customers. Another prominent type is assignment problems, which typically involves assigning people to tasks so as to minimize the total cost of performing these tasks.

Linear programming problems that do not fit into any of these three categories are called *mixed problems.*

In many real applications, management science teams formulate and analyze large linear programming models to help guide managerial decision making. Such teams need strong managerial input and support to help ensure that their work really meets management's needs.

Glossary

assignment problem   A type of linear programming problem that typically involves assigning people to tasks so as to minimize the total cost of performing these tasks. (Section 3.6), 89

benefit constraint   A functional constraint with a $\geq$ sign. The left-hand side is interpreted as the level of some benefit that is achieved by the activities under consideration, and the right-hand side is the minimum acceptable level for that benefit. (Section 3.3), 71

cost–benefit–trade-off problem   A type of linear programming problem involving the trade-off between the total cost of the activities under consideration and the benefits to be achieved by these activities. Its identifying feature is that each functional constraint in the linear programming model is a benefit constraint. (Section 3.3), 71

fixed-requirement constraint   A functional constraint with an = sign. The left-hand side represents the amount provided of some type of quantity, and the right-hand side represents the required amount for that quantity. (Section 3.4), 77

fixed-requirements problem   A type of linear programming problem concerned with optimizing how to meet a number of fixed requirements. Its identifying feature is that each functional constraint in its model is a fixed-requirement constraint. (Section 3.4), 78

identifying feature   A feature of a model that identifies the category of linear programming problem it represents. (Chapter introduction), 54

integer programming problem   A variation of a linear programming problem that has the additional restriction that some or all of the decision variables must have integer values. (Section 3.2), 65

mixed problem   Any linear programming problem that includes at least two of the three types of functional constraints (resource constraints, benefit constraints, and fixed-requirement constraints). (Section 3.4), 78

model enrichment   The process of using experience with a model to identify and add important details that will provide a better representation of the real problem. (Section 3.7), 92

model validation The process of checking and testing a model to develop a valid model. (Section 3.7), 92

resource-allocation problem A type of linear programming problem concerned with allocating resources to activities. Its identifying feature is that each functional constraint in its model is a resource constraint. (Section 3.2), 61

resource constraint A functional constraint with a ≤ sign. The left-hand side represents the amount of some resource that is used by the activities under consideration, and the right-hand side represents the amount available of that resource. (Section 3.2), 61

transportation problem A type of linear programming problem that typically involves finding a shipping plan that minimizes the total cost of transporting a product from a number of plants to a number of customers. (Section 3.5), 85

Learning Aids for This Chapter in Your MS Courseware

Chapter 3 Excel Files:

Super Grain Example

TBA Airlines Example

Think-Big Example

Union Airways Example

Big M Example

Revised Super Grain Example

Sellmore Example

An Excel Add-in:

Premium Solver for Education

Solved Problems (See the CD-ROM for the Solutions)

3.S1. Farm Management

Dwight and Hattie have run the family farm for over 30 years. They are currently planning the mix of crops to plant on their 120-acre farm for the upcoming season. The table below gives the labor-hours and fertilizer required per acre, as well as the total expected profit per acre for each of the potential crops under consideration. Dwight, Hattie, and their children can work at most 6,500 total hours during the upcoming season. They have 20 tons of fertilizer available. What mix of crops should be planted to maximize the family's total profit? Formulate and solve a linear programming model in a spreadsheet.

Crop	Labor Required (hours per acre)	Fertilizer Required (tons per acre)	Expected Profit (per acre)
Oats	50	1.5	$500
Wheat	60	2	$600
Corn	105	4	$950

3.S2. Diet Problem

The kitchen manager for Sing Sing prison is trying to decide what to feed its prisoners. She would like to offer some combination of milk, beans, and oranges. The goal is to minimize cost, subject to meeting the minimum nutritional requirements imposed by law. The cost and nutritional content of each food, along with the minimum nutritional requirements, are shown below. What diet should be fed to each prisoner? Formulate and solve a linear programming model in a spreadsheet.

	Milk (gallons)	Navy Beans (cups)	Oranges (large Calif. Valencia)	Minimum Daily Requirement
Niacin (mg)	3.2	4.9	0.8	13.0
Thiamin (mg)	1.12	1.3	0.19	1.5
Vitamin C (mg)	32.0	0.0	93.0	45.0
Cost ($)	2.00	0.20	0.25	

3.S3. Cutting Stock Problem

Decora Accessories manufactures a variety of bathroom accessories, including decorative towel rods and shower curtain rods. Each of the accessories includes a rod made out of stainless steel. However, many different lengths are needed: 12, 18, 24, 40, and 60 inches. Decora purchases 60-inch rods from an outside supplier and then cuts the rods as needed for their products. Each 60-inch rod can be used to make a number of smaller rods. For example, a 60-inch rod could be used to make a 40-inch and an 18-inch rod (with 2 inches of waste), or five 12-inch rods (with no waste). For the next production period, Decora needs twenty-five 12-inch rods, fifty-two 18-inch rods, forty-five 24-inch rods, thirty 40-inch rods, and twelve 60-inch rods. What is the fewest number of 60-inch rods that can be purchased to meet their production needs? Formulate and solve an integer programming model in a spreadsheet.

3.S4. Bidding for Classes

In the MBA program at a prestigious university in the Pacific Northwest, students bid for electives in the second year of their program. Each student has 100 points to bid (total) and must take two electives. There are four electives available: Management Science, Finance, Operations Management, and Marketing. Each class is limited to 5 students. The bids submitted for each of the 10 students are shown in the table below.

Student Bids for Classes

Student	Management Science	Finance	Operations Management	Marketing
George	60	10	10	20
Fred	20	20	40	20
Ann	45	45	5	5
Eric	50	20	5	25
Susan	30	30	30	10
Liz	50	50	0	0
Ed	70	20	10	0
David	25	25	35	15
Tony	35	15	35	15
Jennifer	60	10	10	20

a. Formulate and solve a spreadsheet model to determine an assignment of students to classes so as to maximize the total bid points of the assignments.

b. Does the resulting solution seem like a fair assignment?

c. Which alternative objectives might lead to a fairer assignment?

Problems

We have inserted the symbol E* to the left of each problem (or its parts) where Excel should be used (unless your instructor gives you contrary instructions). An asterisk on the problem number indicates that at least a partial answer is given in the back of the book.

3.1 Reconsider the Super Grain Corp. case study as presented in Section 3.1. The advertising firm, Giacomi & Jackowitz, now has suggested a fourth promising advertising medium—radio commercials—to promote the company's new breakfast cereal, Crunchy Start. Young children are potentially major consumers of this cereal, but parents of young children (the major potential purchasers) often are too busy to do much reading (so may miss the company's advertisements in magazines and Sunday supplements) or even to watch the Saturday morning programs for children where the company's television commercials are aired. However, these parents do tend to listen to the radio during the commute to and from work. Therefore, to better reach these parents, Giacomi & Jackowitz suggests giving consideration to running commercials for Crunchy Start on nationally syndicated radio programs that appeal to young adults during typical commuting hours.

Giacomi & Jackowitz estimates that the cost of developing each new radio commercial would be $50,000, and that the expected number of exposures per commercial would be 900,000. The firm has determined that 10 spots are available for different radio commercials, and each one would cost $200,000 for a normal run.

E* a. Formulate and solve a spreadsheet model for the revised advertising-mix problem that includes this fourth advertising medium. Identify the data cells, the changing cells, and the target cell. Also show the Excel equation for each output cell expressed as a SUMPRODUCT function.

b. Indicate why this spreadsheet model is a linear programming model.

c. Express this model in algebraic form.

3.2* Consider a resource-allocation problem having the following data:

Resource	Resource Usage per Unit of Each Activity		Amount of Resource Available
	1	2	
1	2	1	10
2	3	3	20
3	2	4	20
Contribution per unit	$20	$30	

Contribution per unit = profit per unit of the activity.

E* a. Formulate a linear programming model for this problem on a spreadsheet.

E* b. Use the spreadsheet to check the following solutions: $(x_1, x_2) = (2, 2), (3, 3), (2, 4), (4, 2), (3, 4), (4, 3)$. Which of these solutions are feasible? Which of these feasible solutions has the best value of the objective function?

E* c. Use the Solver to find an optimal solution.
    d. Express this model in algebraic form.
    e. Use the graphical method to solve this model.

3.3 Consider a resource-allocation problem having the following data.

Resource	Resource Usage per Unit of Each Activity			Amount of Resource Available
	1	2	3	
A	30	20	0	500
B	0	10	40	600
C	20	20	30	1,000
Contribution per unit	$50	$40	$70	

Contribution per unit = profit per unit of the activity.

E* a. Formulate and solve a linear programming model for this problem on a spreadsheet.
    b. Express this model in algebraic form.

E*3.4 Consider a resource-allocation problem having the following data:

Resource	Resource Usage per Unit of Each Activity				Amount of Resource Available
	1	2	3	4	
P	3	5	−2	4	400
Q	4	−1	3	2	300
R	6	3	2	−1	400
S	−2	2	5	3	300
Contribution per unit	$11	$9	$8	$9	

Contribution per unit = profit per unit of the activity.

a. Formulate a linear programming model for this problem on a spreadsheet.
b. Make five guesses of your own choosing for the optimal solution. Use the spreadsheet to check each one for feasibility and, if feasible, for the value of the objective function. Which feasible guess has the best objective function value?
c. Use the Solver to find an optimal solution.

3.5* The Omega Manufacturing Company has discontinued the production of a certain unprofitable product line. This act created considerable excess production capacity. Management is considering devoting this excess capacity to one or more of three products, products 1, 2, and 3. The available capacity of the machines that might limit output is summarized in the following table:

Machine Type	Available Time (in Machine-Hours per Week)
Milling machine	500
Lathe	350
Grinder	150

The number of machine-hours required for each unit of the respective products is as follows:

Productivity Coefficient (in Machine-Hours per Unit)

Machine Type	Product 1	Product 2	Product 3
Milling machine	9	3	5
Lathe	5	4	0
Grinder	3	0	2

The Sales Department indicates that the sales potential for products 1 and 2 exceeds the maximum production rate and that the sales potential for product 3 is 20 units per week. The unit profit would be $50, $20, and $25, respectively, for products 1, 2, and 3. The objective is to determine how much of each product Omega should produce to maximize profit.

a. Indicate why this is a resource-allocation problem by identifying both the activities and the limited resources to be allocated to these activities.

b. Identify verbally the decisions to be made, the constraints on these decisions, and the overall measure of performance for the decisions.

c. Convert these verbal descriptions of the constraints and the measure of performance into quantitative expressions in terms of the data and decisions.

E* d. Formulate a spreadsheet model for this problem. Identify the data cells, the changing cells, the target cell, and the other output cells. Also show the Excel equation for each output cell expressed as a SUMPRODUCT function. Then use the Excel Solver to solve the model.

e. Summarize the model in algebraic form.

3.6 Ed Butler is the production manager for the Bilco Corporation, which produces three types of spare parts for automobiles. The manufacture of each part requires processing on each of two machines, with the following processing times (in hours):

| | Part | | |
Machine	A	B	C
1	0.02	0.03	0.05
2	0.05	0.02	0.04

Each machine is available 40 hours per month. Each part manufactured will yield a unit profit as follows:

| | Part | | |
	A	B	C
Profit	$50	$40	$30

Ed wants to determine the mix of spare parts to produce to maximize total profit.

a. Identify both the activities and the resources for this resource-allocation problem.

E* b. Formulate a linear programming model for this problem on a spreadsheet.

E* c. Make three guesses of your own choosing for the optimal solution. Use the spreadsheet to check each one for feasibility and, if feasible, for the value of the objective function. Which feasible guess has the best objective function value?

E* d. Use the Solver to find an optimal solution.

e. Express the model in algebraic form.

E*3.7 Consider the following algebraic formulation of a resource-allocation problem with three resources, where the decisions to be made are the levels of three activities $(A_1, A_2, \text{and } A_3)$.

$$\text{Maximize} \quad \text{Profit} = 20A_1 + 40A_2 + 30A_3$$

subject to

Resource 1: $3A_1 + 5A_2 + 4A_3 \leq 400$ (amount available)

Resource 2: $A_1 + A_2 + A_3 \leq 100$ (amount available)

Resource 3: $A_1 + 3A_2 + 2A_3 \leq 200$ (amount available)

and

$$A_1 \geq 0 \quad A_2 \geq 0 \quad A_3 \geq 0$$

Formulate and solve the spreadsheet model for this problem.

3.8 Consider a cost–benefit–trade-off problem having the following data:

| | Benefit Contribution per Unit of Each Activity | | Minimum Acceptable Level |
Benefit	1	2	
1	5	3	60
2	2	2	30
3	7	9	126
Unit cost	$60	$50	

E* a. Formulate a linear programming model for this problem on a spreadsheet.

E* b. Use the spreadsheet to check the following solutions: $(x_1, x_2) = (7, 7), (7, 8), (8, 7), (8, 8), (8, 9), (9, 8)$. Which of these solutions are feasible? Which of these feasible solutions has the best value of the objective function?

E* c. Use the Solver to find an optimal solution.

d. Express the model in algebraic form.

e. Use the graphical method to solve this model.

E*3.9 Consider a cost–benefit–trade-off problem having the following data:

| | Benefit Contribution per Unit of Each Activity | | | | Minimum Acceptable Level |
Benefit	1	2	3	4	
P	2	−1	4	3	80
Q	1	4	−1	2	60
R	3	5	4	−1	110
Unit cost	$400	$600	$500	$300	

a. Formulate a linear programming model for this problem on a spreadsheet.

b. Make five guesses of your own choosing for the optimal solution. Use the spreadsheet to check each one for feasibility and, if feasible, for the value of the objective function. Which feasible guess has the best objective function value?

c. Use the Solver to find an optimal solution.

3.10* Fred Jonasson manages a family-owned farm. To supplement several food products grown on the farm, Fred

also raises pigs for market. He now wishes to determine the quantities of the available types of feed (corn, tankage, and alfalfa) that should be given to each pig. Since pigs will eat any mix of these feed types, the objective is to determine which mix will meet certain nutritional requirements at a *minimum cost*. The number of units of each type of basic nutritional ingredient contained within a kilogram of each feed type is given in the following table, along with the daily nutritional requirements and feed costs:

Nutritional Ingredient	Kilogram of Corn	Kilogram of Tankage	Kilogram of Alfalfa	Minimum Daily Requirement
Carbohydrates	90	20	40	200
Protein	30	80	60	180
Vitamins	10	20	60	150
Cost (¢)	84	72	60	

E* a. Formulate a linear programming model for this problem on a spreadsheet.

E* b. Use the spreadsheet to check if $(x_1, x_2, x_3) = (1, 2, 2)$ is a feasible solution and, if so, what the daily cost would be for this diet. How many units of each nutritional ingredient would this diet provide daily?

E* c. Take a few minutes to use a trial-and-error approach with the spreadsheet to develop your best guess for the optimal solution. What is the daily cost for your solution?

E* d. Use the Solver to find an optimal solution.

e. Express the model in algebraic form.

3.11 Maureen Laird is the chief financial officer for the Alva Electric Co., a major public utility in the Midwest. The company has scheduled the construction of new hydroelectric plants 5, 10, and 20 years from now to meet the needs of the growing population in the region served by the company. To cover the construction costs, Maureen needs to invest some of the company's money now to meet these future cash flow needs. Maureen may purchase only three kinds of financial assets, each of which costs $1 million per unit. Fractional units may be purchased. The assets produce income 5, 10, and 20 years from now, and that income is needed to cover minimum cash flow requirements in those years, as shown in the following table.

	Income per Unit of Asset			
Year	Asset 1	Asset 2	Asset 3	Minimum Cash Flow Required
5	$2 million	$1 million	$0.5 million	$400 million
10	0.5 million	0.5 million	1 million	100 million
20	0	1.5 million	2 million	300 million

Maureen wishes to determine the mix of investments in these assets that will cover the cash flow requirements while minimizing the total amount invested.

E* a. Formulate a linear programming model for this problem on a spreadsheet.

E* b. Use the spreadsheet to check the possibility of purchasing 100 units of asset 1, 100 units of asset 2, and 200 units of asset 3. How much cash flow would this mix of investments generate 5, 10, and 20 years from now? What would be the total amount invested?

E* c. Take a few minutes to use a trial-and-error approach with the spreadsheet to develop your best guess for the

optimal solution. What is the total amount invested for your solution?

E* d. Use the Solver to find an optimal solution.

e. Summarize the model in algebraic form.

3.12 Web Mercantile sells many household products through an online catalog. The company needs substantial warehouse space for storing its goods. Plans now are being made for leasing warehouse storage space over the next five months. Just how much space will be required in each of these months is known. However, since these space requirements are quite different, it may be most economical to lease only the amount needed each month on a month-by-month basis. On the other hand, the additional cost for leasing space for additional months is much less than for the first month, so it may be less expensive to lease the maximum amount needed for the entire five months. Another option is the intermediate approach of changing the total amount of space leased (by adding a new lease and/or having an old lease expire) at least once but not every month.

The space requirement and the leasing costs for the various leasing periods are as follows:

Month	Required Space (Square Feet)
1	30,000
2	20,000
3	40,000
4	10,000
5	50,000

Leasing Period (Months)	Cost per Sq. Ft. Leased
1	$ 65
2	100
3	135
4	160
5	190

The objective is to minimize the total leasing cost for meeting the space requirements.

a. Indicate why this is a cost–benefit–trade-off problem by identifying both the activities and the benefits being sought from these activities.

b. Identify verbally the decisions to be made, the constraints on these decisions, and the overall measure of performance for the decisions.

c. Convert these verbal descriptions of the constraints and the measure of performance into quantitative expressions in terms of the data and decisions.

E* d. Formulate a spreadsheet model for this problem. Identify the data cells, the changing cells, the target cell, and the other output cells. Also show the Excel equation for each output cell expressed as a SUMPRODUCT function. Then use the Excel Solver to solve the model.

e. Summarize the model in algebraic form.

E*3.13 Consider the following algebraic formulation of a cost–benefit–trade-off problem involving three benefits, where the decisions to be made are the levels of four activities (A_1, A_2, A_3, and A_4):

Minimize   Cost $= 2A_1 + A_2 - A_3 + 3A_4$

subject to

Benefit 1: $3A_1 + 2A_2 - 2A_3 + 5A_4 \geq 80$ (minimum acceptable level)

Benefit 2: $A_1 - A_2 + A_4 \geq 10$ (minimum acceptable level)

Benefit 3: $A_1 + A_2 - A_3 + 2A_4 \geq 30$ (minimum acceptable level)

and

$$A_1 \geq 0 \quad A_2 \geq 0 \quad A_3 \geq 0 \quad A_4 \geq 0$$

Formulate and solve the spreadsheet model for this problem.

3.14 Larry Edison is the Director of the Computer Center for Buckly College. He now needs to schedule the staffing of the center. It is open from 8 AM until midnight. Larry has monitored the usage of the center at various times of the day and determined that the following number of computer consultants are required:

Time of Day	Minimum Number of Consultants Required to Be on Duty
8 AM–noon	6
Noon–4 PM	8
4 PM–8 PM	12
8 PM–midnight	6

Two types of computer consultants can be hired: full-time and part-time. The full-time consultants work for eight consecutive hours in any of the following shifts: morning (8 AM–4 PM), afternoon (noon–8 PM), and evening (4 PM–midnight). Full-time consultants are paid $14 per hour.

Part-time consultants can be hired to work any of the four shifts listed in the table. Part-time consultants are paid $12 per hour.

An additional requirement is that during every time period, there must be at least two full-time consultants on duty for every part-time consultant on duty.

Larry would like to determine how many full-time and part-time consultants should work each shift to meet the above requirements at the minimum possible cost.

a. Which category of linear programming problem does this problem fit? Why?

E* b. Formulate and solve a linear programming model for this problem on a spreadsheet.

c. Summarize the model in algebraic form.

3.15* The Medequip Company produces precision medical diagnostic equipment at two factories. Three medical centers have placed orders for this month's production output. The following table shows what the cost would be for shipping each unit from each factory to each of these customers. Also shown are the number of units that will be produced at each factory and the number of units ordered by each customer.

	Unit Shipping Cost			
From \ **To**	**Customer 1**	**Customer 2**	**Customer 3**	**Output**
Factory 1	$600	$800	$700	400 units
Factory 2	400	900	600	500 units
Order size	300 units	200 units	400 units	

A decision now needs to be made about the shipping plan for how many units to ship from each factory to each customer.

a. Which category of linear programming problem does this problem fit? Why?

E* b. Formulate and solve a linear programming model for this problem on a spreadsheet.

c. Summarize this formulation in algebraic form.

3.16 The Fagersta Steelworks currently is working two mines to obtain its iron ore. This iron ore is shipped to either of two storage facilities. When needed, it then is shipped on to the company's steel plant. The diagram below depicts this distribution network, where M1 and M2 are the two mines, S1 and S2 are the two storage facilities, and P is the steel plant. The diagram also shows the monthly amounts produced at the mines and needed at the plant, as well as the shipping cost and the maximum amount that can be shipped per month through each shipping lane.

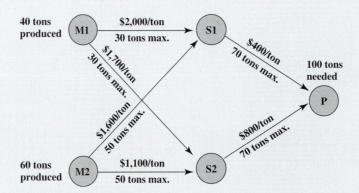

Management now wants to determine the most economical plan for shipping the iron ore from the mines through the distribution network to the steel plant.

a. Identify all the requirements that will need to be expressed in fixed-requirement constraints.

E* b. Formulate and solve a linear programming model for this problem on a spreadsheet.

c. Express this model in algebraic form.

3.17* Al Ferris has $60,000 that he wishes to invest now in order to use the accumulation for purchasing a retirement annuity in five years. After consulting with his financial advisor, he has been offered four types of fixed-income investments, which we will label as investments A, B, C, and D.

Investments A and B are available at the beginning of each of the next five years (call them years 1 to 5). Each dollar invested in A at the beginning of a year returns $1.40 (a profit of $0.40) two years later (in time for immediate reinvestment). Each dollar invested in B at the beginning of a year returns $1.70 three years later.

Investments C and D will each be available at one time in the future. Each dollar invested in C at the beginning of year 2 returns $1.90 at the end of year 5. Each dollar invested in D at the beginning of year 5 returns $1.30 at the end of year 5.

Al wishes to know which investment plan maximizes the amount of money that can be accumulated by the beginning of year 6.

a. For this problem, all its functional constraints can be expressed as fixed-requirement constraints. To do this, let A_t, B_t, C_t, and D_t be the amounts invested in investments A, B, C, and D, respectively, at the beginning of year t for each t where the investment is available and will mature by the end of year 5. Also let R_t be the number of available dollars *not* invested at the beginning of year t (and so available for investment in a later year). Thus, the amount invested at the beginning of year t *plus* R_t must equal the number of dollars available for investment at that time. Write such an equation in terms of the relevant variables above for the beginning of each of the five years to obtain the five fixed-requirement constraints for this problem.

b. Formulate a complete linear programming model for this problem in algebraic form.

E* *c.* Formulate and solve this model on a spreadsheet.

3.18 The Metalco Company desires to blend a new alloy of 40 percent tin, 35 percent zinc, and 25 percent lead from several available alloys having the following properties:

	Alloy				
Property	**1**	**2**	**3**	**4**	**5**
Percentage of tin	60	25	45	20	50
Percentage of zinc	10	15	45	50	40
Percentage of lead	30	60	10	30	10
Cost ($/lb)	22	20	25	24	27

The objective is to determine the proportions of these alloys that should be blended to produce the new alloy at a minimum cost.

a. Identify all the requirements that will need to be expressed in fixed-requirement constraints.

E* *b.* Formulate and solve a linear programming model for this problem on a spreadsheet.

c. Express this model in algebraic form.

3.19 The Weigelt Corporation has three branch plants with excess production capacity. Fortunately, the corporation has a new product ready to begin production, and all three plants have this capability, so some of the excess capacity can be used in this way. This product can be made in three sizes—large, medium, and small—that yield a net unit profit of $420, $360, and $300, respectively. Plants 1, 2, and 3 have the excess capacity to produce 750, 900, and 450 units per day of this product, respectively, regardless of the size or combination of sizes involved.

The amount of available in-process storage space also imposes a limitation on the production rates of the new product. Plants 1, 2, and 3 have 13,000, 12,000, and 5,000 square feet, respectively, of in-process storage space available for a day's production of this product. Each unit of the large, medium, and small sizes produced per day requires 20, 15, and 12 square feet, respectively.

Sales forecasts indicate that if available, 900, 1,200, and 750 units of the large, medium, and small sizes, respectively, would be sold per day.

At each plant, some employees will need to be laid off unless most of the plant's excess production capacity can be used to produce the new product. To avoid layoffs if possible, management has decided that the plants should use the same percentage of their excess capacity to produce the new product.

Management wishes to know how much of each of the sizes should be produced by each of the plants to maximize profit.

E* *a.* Formulate and solve a linear programming model for this mixed problem on a spreadsheet.

b. Express the model in algebraic form.

3.20* A cargo plane has three compartments for storing cargo: front, center, and back. These compartments have capacity limits on both *weight* and *space,* as summarized below:

Compartment	Weight Capacity (Tons)	Space Capacity (Cubic Feet)
Front	12	7,000
Center	18	9,000
Back	10	5,000

Furthermore, the weight of the cargo in the respective compartments must be the same proportion of that compartment's weight capacity to maintain the balance of the airplane.

The following four cargoes have been offered for shipment on an upcoming flight as space is available:

Cargo	Weight (Tons)	Volume (Cubic Feet/Ton)	Profit ($/Ton)
1	20	500	320
2	16	700	400
3	25	600	360
4	13	400	290

Any portion of these cargoes can be accepted. The objective is to determine how much (if any) of each cargo should be accepted and how to distribute each among the compartments to maximize the total profit for the flight.

E* *a.* Formulate and solve a linear programming model for this mixed problem on a spreadsheet.

b. Express the model in algebraic form.

3.21 Comfortable Hands is a company that features a product line of winter gloves for the entire family—men, women, and children. They are trying to decide what mix of these three types of gloves to produce.

Comfortable Hands's manufacturing labor force is unionized. Each full-time employee works a 40-hour week. In addition, by union contract, the number of full-time employees can never drop below 20. Nonunion, part-time workers also can be hired with the following union-imposed restrictions: (1) each part-time worker works 20 hours per week and (2) there must be at least two full-time employees for each part-time employee.

All three types of gloves are made out of the same 100 percent genuine cowhide leather. Comfortable Hands has a long-term contract with a supplier of the leather and receives a 5,000-square-foot shipment of the material each week. The material requirements and labor requirements, along with the *gross profit* per glove sold (not considering labor costs), are given in the following table.

Glove	Material Required (Square Feet)	Labor Required (Minutes)	Gross Profit (per Pair)
Men's	2	30	$ 8
Women's	1.5	45	10
Children's	1	40	6

Each full-time employee earns $13 per hour, while each part-time employee earns $10 per hour. Management wishes to know what mix of each of the three types of gloves to produce per week, as well as how many full-time and part-time workers to employ. They would like to maximize their *net profit*—their gross profit from sales minus their labor costs.

E* a. Formulate and solve a linear programming model for this problem on a spreadsheet.

b. Summarize this formulation in algebraic form.

E*3.22 Oxbridge University maintains a powerful mainframe computer for research use by its faculty, Ph.D. students, and research associates. During all working hours, an operator must be available to operate and maintain the computer, as well as to perform some programming services. Beryl Ingram, the director of the computer facility, oversees the operation.

It is now the beginning of the fall semester and Beryl is confronted with the problem of assigning different working hours to her operators. Because all the operators are currently enrolled in the university, they are available to work only a limited number of hours each day.

There are six operators (four undergraduate students and two graduate students). They all have different wage rates because of differences in their experience with computers and in their programming ability. The following table shows their wage rates, along with the maximum number of hours that each can work each day.

Operators	Wage Rate	Maximum Hours of Availability				
		Mon.	Tue.	Wed.	Thurs.	Fri.
K. C.	$10.00/hour	6	0	6	0	6
D. H.	$10.10/hour	0	6	0	6	0
H. B.	$9.90/hour	4	8	4	0	4
S. C.	$9.80/hour	5	5	5	0	5
K. S.	$10.80/hour	3	0	3	8	0
N. K.	$11.30/hour	0	0	0	6	2

Each operator is guaranteed a certain minimum number of hours per week that will maintain an adequate knowledge of the operation. This level is set arbitrarily at 8 hours per week for the undergraduate students (K. C., D. H., H. B., and S. C.) and 7 hours per week for the graduate students (K. S. and N. K.).

The computer facility is to be open for operation from 8 AM to 10 PM Monday through Friday with exactly one operator on duty during these hours. On Saturdays and Sundays, the computer is to be operated by other staff.

Because of a tight budget, Beryl has to minimize cost. She wishes to determine the number of hours she should assign to each operator on each day. Formulate and solve a spreadsheet model for this problem.

3.23. Slim-Down Manufacturing makes a line of nutritionally complete, weight-reduction beverages. One of its products is a strawberry shake that is designed to be a complete meal. The strawberry shake consists of several ingredients. Some information about each of these ingredients is given next.

Ingredient	Calories from Fat (per tbsp.)	Total Calories (per tbsp.)	Vitamin Content (mg/tbsp.)	Thickeners (mg/tbsp.)	Cost (¢/tbsp.)
Strawberry flavoring	1	50	20	3	10
Cream	75	100	0	8	8
Vitamin supplement	0	0	50	1	25
Artificial sweetener	0	120	0	2	15
Thickening agent	30	80	2	25	6

The nutritional requirements are as follows. The beverage must total between 380 and 420 calories (inclusive). No more than 20 percent of the total calories should come from fat. There must be at least 50 milligrams (mg) of vitamin content. For taste reasons, there must be at least two tablespoons (tbsp.) of strawberry flavoring for each tbsp. of artificial sweetener. Finally, to maintain proper thickness, there must be exactly 15 mg of thickeners in the beverage.

Management would like to select the quantity of each ingredient for the beverage that would minimize cost while meeting the above requirements.

a. Identify the requirements that lead to resource constraints, to benefit constraints, and to fixed-requirement constraints.

E* b. Formulate and solve a linear programming model for this problem on a spreadsheet.

c. Summarize this formulation in algebraic form.

3.24 Joyce and Marvin run a day care for preschoolers. They are trying to decide what to feed the children for lunches. They would like to keep their costs down, but they also need to meet the nutritional requirements of the children. They have already decided to go with peanut butter and jelly sandwiches, and some combination of graham crackers, milk, and orange juice. The nutritional content of each food choice and its cost are given in the table below.

Food Item	Calories from Fat	Total Calories	Vitamin C (mg)	Protein (g)	Cost (¢)
Bread (1 slice)	10	70	0	3	5
Peanut butter (1 tbsp.)	75	100	0	4	4
Strawberry jelly (1 tbsp.)	0	50	3	0	7
Graham cracker (1 cracker)	20	60	0	1	8
Milk (1 cup)	70	150	2	8	15
Juice (1 cup)	0	100	120	1	35

The nutritional requirements are as follows. Each child should receive between 400 and 600 calories. No more than 30 percent of the total calories should come from fat. Each child should consume at least 60 milligrams (mg) of vitamin C and 12 grams (g) of protein. Furthermore, for practical reasons, each child needs exactly 2 slices of bread (to make the sandwich), at least twice as much peanut butter as jelly, and at least 1 cup of liquid (milk and/or juice).

Joyce and Marvin would like to select the food choices for each child that minimize cost while meeting the above requirements.

a. Identify the requirements that lead to resource constraints, to benefit constraints, and to fixed-requirement constraints.

E* b. Formulate and solve a linear programming model for this problem on a spreadsheet.

c. Express the model in algebraic form.

E*3.25 The Cost-Less Corp. supplies its four retail outlets from its four plants. The shipping cost per shipment from each plant to each retail outlet is given below.

	Unit Shipping Cost			
Retail Outlet:	1	2	3	4
Plant				
1	$500	$600	$400	$200
2	200	900	100	300
3	300	400	200	100
4	200	100	300	200

Plants 1, 2, 3, and 4 make 10, 20, 20, and 10 shipments per month, respectively. Retail outlets 1, 2, 3, and 4 need to receive 20, 10, 10, and 20 shipments per month, respectively.

The distribution manager, Randy Smith, now wants to determine the best plan for how many shipments to send from each plant to the respective retail outlets each month. Randy's objective is to minimize the total shipping cost.

Formulate this problem as a transportation problem on a spreadsheet and then use the Excel Solver to obtain an optimal solution.

	Distance to Distribution Center (Miles)			
	1	2	3	4
Plant				
1	800	1,300	400	700
2	1,100	1,400	600	1,000
3	600	1,200	800	900

The freight cost for each shipment is $100 plus 50 cents/mile.

How much should be shipped from each plant to each of the distribution centers to minimize the total shipping cost?

Formulate this problem as a transportation problem on a spreadsheet and then use the Excel Solver to obtain an optimal solution.

	Customer			
	1	2	3	4
Plant				
1	$800	$700	$500	$200
2	500	200	100	300
3	600	400	300	500

Management wishes to know how many units to sell to customers 3 and 4 and how many units to ship from each of the plants to each of the customers to maximize profit. Formulate and solve a spreadsheet model for this problem.

E*3.28 The Move-It Company has two plants building forklift trucks that then are shipped to three distribution centers. The production costs are the same at the two plants, and the cost of shipping each truck is shown below for each combination of plant and distribution center:

	Distribution Center		
	1	2	3
Plant			
A	$800	$700	$400
B	600	800	500

E*3.26 The Childfair Company has three plants producing child push chairs that are to be shipped to four distribution centers. Plants 1, 2, and 3 produce 12, 17, and 11 shipments per month, respectively. Each distribution center needs to receive 10 shipments per month. The distance from each plant to the respective distribution centers is given below:

E*3.27 The Onenote Co. produces a single product at three plants for four customers. The three plants will produce 60, 80, and 40 units, respectively, during the next week. The firm has made a commitment to sell 40 units to customer 1, 60 units to customer 2, and at least 20 units to customer 3. Both customers 3 and 4 also want to buy as many of the remaining units as possible. The net profit associated with shipping a unit from plant i for sale to customer j is given by the following table:

A total of 60 forklift trucks are produced and shipped per week. Each plant can produce and ship any amount up to a maximum of 50 trucks per week, so there is considerable flexibility on how to divide the total production between the two plants so as to reduce shipping costs. However, each distribution center must receive exactly 20 trucks per week.

Management's objective is to determine how many forklift trucks should be produced at each plant, and then what the overall shipping pattern should be to minimize total shipping cost. Formulate and solve a spreadsheet model for this problem.

E*3.29 Redo Problem 3.28 when any distribution center may receive any quantity between 10 and 30 forklift trucks per week in order to further reduce total shipping cost, provided only that the total shipped to all three distribution centers must still equal 60 trucks per week.

E*3.30. Consider the assignment problem having the following cost table:

	Job		
	1	**2**	**3**
Person			
A	$5	$7	$4
B	3	6	5
C	2	3	4

The optimal solution is A-3, B-1, C-2, with a total cost of $10.

Formulate this problem on a spreadsheet and then use the Excel Solver to obtain the optimal solution identified above.

3.31 Four cargo ships will be used for shipping goods from one port to four other ports (labeled 1, 2, 3, 4). Any ship can be used for making any one of these four trips. However, because of differences in the ships and cargoes, the total cost of loading, transporting, and unloading the goods for the different ship–port combinations varies considerably, as shown in the following table:

	Port			
	1	**2**	**3**	**4**
Ship				
1	$500	$400	$600	$700
2	600	600	700	500
3	700	500	700	600
4	500	400	600	600

The objective is to assign the four ships to four different ports in such a way as to minimize the total cost for all four shipments.

a. Describe how this problem fits into the format for an assignment problem.

E* *b.* Formulate and solve this problem on a spreadsheet.

E*3.32 Reconsider Problem 3.28. Now distribution centers 1, 2, and 3 must receive exactly 10, 20, and 30 units per week, respectively. For administrative convenience, management has decided that each distribution center will be supplied totally by a single plant, so that one plant will supply one distribution center and the other plant will supply the other two distribution centers. The choice of these assignments of plants to distribution centers is to be made solely on the basis of minimizing total shipping cost.

Formulate and solve a spreadsheet model for this problem.

3.33 Vincent Cardoza is the owner and manager of a machine shop that does custom order work. This Wednesday afternoon, he has received calls from two customers who would like to place rush orders. One is a trailer hitch company that would like some custom-made heavy-duty tow bars. The other is a mini-car-carrier company that needs some customized stabilizer bars. Both customers would like as many as possible by the end of the week (two working days). Since both products would require the use of the same two machines, Vincent needs to decide and inform the customers this afternoon about how many of each product he will agree to make over the next two days.

Each tow bar requires 3.2 hours on machine 1 and 2 hours on machine 2. Each stabilizer bar requires 2.4 hours on machine 1 and 3 hours on machine 2. Machine 1 will be available for 16 hours over the next two days and machine 2 will be available for 15 hours. The profit for each tow bar produced would be $130 and the profit for each stabilizer bar produced would be $150.

Vincent now wants to determine the mix of these production quantities that will maximize the total profit.

a. Formulate an integer programming model in algebraic form for this problem.

E* *b.* Formulate and solve the model on a spreadsheet.

3.34 Pawtucket University is planning to buy new copier machines for its library. Three members of its Management Science Department are analyzing what to buy. They are considering two different models: Model A, a high-speed copier, and Model B, a lower speed but less expensive copier. Model A can handle 20,000 copies a day and costs $6,000. Model B can handle 10,000 copies a day but only costs $4,000. They would like to have at least six copiers so that they can spread them throughout the library. They also would like to have at least one high-speed copier. Finally, the copiers need to be able to handle a capacity of at least 75,000 copies per day. The objective is to determine the mix of these two copiers that will handle all these requirements at minimum cost.

E* *a.* Formulate and solve a spreadsheet model for this problem.

b. Formulate this same model in algebraic form.

3.35 Northeastern Airlines is considering the purchase of new long-, medium-, and short-range jet passenger airplanes. The purchase price would be $67 million for each long-range plane, $50 million for each medium-range plane, and $35 million for each short-range plane. The board of directors has authorized a maximum commitment of $1.5 billion for these purchases. Regardless of which airplanes are purchased, air travel of all distances is expected to be sufficiently large that these planes would be utilized at essentially maximum capacity. It is estimated that the net annual profit (after capital recovery costs are subtracted) would be $4.2 million per long-range plane, $3 million per medium-range plane, and $2.3 million per short-range plane.

It is predicted that enough trained pilots will be available to the company to crew 30 new airplanes. If only short-range planes were purchased, the maintenance facilities would be able to handle 40 new planes. However, each medium-range plane is equivalent to 1⅓ short-range planes, and each long-range plane is equivalent to 1⅔ short-range planes in terms of their use of the maintenance facilities.

The information given here was obtained by a preliminary analysis of the problem. A more detailed analysis will be conducted subsequently. However, using the preceding data as a first approximation, management wishes to know how many planes of each type should be purchased to maximize profit.

E* *a.* Formulate and solve a spreadsheet model for this problem.

b. Formulate this model in algebraic form.

Case 3-1

Shipping Wood to Market

Alabama Atlantic is a lumber company that has three sources of wood and five markets to be supplied. The annual availability of wood at sources 1, 2, and 3 is 15, 20, and 15 million board feet, respectively. The amount that can be sold annually at markets 1, 2, 3, 4, and 5 is 11, 12, 9, 10, and 8 million board feet, respectively.

In the past, the company has shipped the wood by train. However, because shipping costs have been increasing, the alternative of using ships to make some of the deliveries is being investigated. This alternative would require the company to invest in some ships. Except for these investment costs, the shipping costs in thousands of dollars per million board feet by rail and by water (when feasible) would be the following for each route:

	Unit Cost by Rail ($1,000s) to Market					Unit Cost by Ship ($1,000s) to Market				
Source	1	2	3	4	5	1	2	3	4	5
1	61	72	45	55	66	31	38	24	—	35
2	69	78	60	49	56	36	43	28	24	31
3	59	66	63	61	47	—	33	36	32	26

The capital investment (in thousands of dollars) in ships required for each million board feet to be transported annually by ship along each route is given as follows:

	Unit Investment for Ships ($1,000s) to Market				
Source	1	2	3	4	5
1	275	303	238	—	285
2	293	318	270	250	265
3	—	283	275	268	240

Considering the expected useful life of the ships and the time value of money, the equivalent uniform annual cost of these investments is one-tenth the amount given in the table. The objective is to determine the overall shipping plan that minimizes the total equivalent uniform annual cost (including shipping costs).

You are the head of the management science team that has been assigned the task of determining this shipping plan for each of the following three options.

Option 1: Continue shipping exclusively by rail.

Option 2: Switch to shipping exclusively by water (except where only rail is feasible).

Option 3: Ship by either rail or water, depending on which is less expensive for the particular route.

Present your results for each option. Compare.

Finally, consider the fact that these results are based on current shipping and investment costs, so that the decision on the option to adopt now should take into account management's projection of how these costs are likely to change in the future. For each option, describe a scenario of future cost changes that would justify adopting that option now.

Case 3-2

Capacity Concerns

Bentley Hamilton throws the business section of *The New York Times* onto the conference room table and watches as his associates jolt upright in their overstuffed chairs.

Mr. Hamilton wants to make a point.

He throws the front page of the *The Wall Street Journal* on top of *The New York Times* and watches as his associates widen their eyes once heavy with boredom.

Mr. Hamilton wants to make a big point.

He then throws the front page of the *Financial Times* on top of the newspaper pile and watches as his associates dab the fine beads of sweat off their brows.

Mr. Hamilton wants his point indelibly etched into his associates' minds.

"I have just presented you with three leading financial newspapers carrying today's top business story," Mr. Hamilton declares in a tight, angry voice. "My dear associates, our company is going to hell in a hand basket! Shall I read you the headlines? From *The New York Times,* 'CommuniCorp stock drops to lowest in 52 weeks.' From *The Wall Street Journal,* 'CommuniCorp loses 25 percent of the pager market in only one year.' Oh, and my favorite, from the *Financial Times,* 'CommuniCorp cannot CommuniCate: CommuniCorp stock drops because of internal communications disarray.' How did our company fall into such dire straits?"

Mr. Hamilton throws a transparency showing a line sloping slightly upward onto the overhead projector. "This is a graph of our productivity over the last 12 months. As you can see from the graph, productivity in our pager production facility has increased steadily over the last year. Clearly, productivity is not the cause of our problem."

Mr. Hamilton throws a second transparency showing a line sloping steeply upward onto the overhead projector. "This is a graph of our missed or late orders over the last 12 months." Mr. Hamilton hears an audible gasp from his associates. "As you can see from the graph, our missed or late orders have increased steadily and significantly over the past 12 months. I think this trend explains why we have been losing market share, causing our stock to drop to its lowest level in 52 weeks. We have angered and lost the business of retailers, our customers who depend upon on-time deliveries to meet the demand of consumers."

"Why have we missed our delivery dates when our productivity level should have allowed us to fill all orders?" Mr. Hamilton asks. "I called several departments to ask this question."

"It turns out that we have been producing pagers for the hell of it!" Mr. Hamilton says in disbelief. "The marketing and sales departments do not communicate with the manufacturing department, so manufacturing executives do not know what pagers to produce to fill orders. The manufacturing executives want to keep the plant running, so they produce pagers regardless of whether the pagers have been ordered. Finished pagers are sent to the warehouse, but marketing and sales executives do not know the number and styles of pagers in the warehouse. They try to communicate with warehouse executives to determine if the pagers in inventory can fill the orders, but they rarely receive answers to their questions."

Mr. Hamilton pauses and looks directly at his associates. "Ladies and gentlemen, it seems to me that we have a serious internal communications problem. I intend to correct this problem immediately. I want to begin by installing a companywide computer network to ensure that all departments have access to critical documents and are able to easily communicate with each other through e-mail. Because this intranet will represent a large change from the current communications infrastructure, I expect some bugs in the system and some resistance from employees. I therefore want to phase in the installation of the intranet."

Mr. Hamilton passes the following time line and requirements chart to his associates (IN = intranet).

Month 1	Month 2	Month 3	Month 4	Month 5
IN education	Install IN in sales	Install IN in manufacturing	Install IN in warehouse	Install IN in marketing

Department	Number of Employees
Sales	60
Manufacturing	200
Warehouse	30
Marketing	75

Mr. Hamilton proceeds to explain the time line and requirements chart. "In the first month, I do not want to bring any department onto the intranet; I simply want to disseminate information about it and get buy-in from employees. In the second month, I want to bring the sales department onto the intranet since the sales department receives all critical information from customers. In the third month, I want to bring the manufacturing department onto the

intranet. In the fourth month, I want to install the intranet at the warehouse, and in the fifth and final month, I want to bring the marketing department onto the intranet. The requirements chart under the time line lists the number of employees requiring access to the intranet in each department."

Mr. Hamilton turns to Emily Jones, the head of Corporate Information Management. "I need your help in planning for the installation of the intranet. Specifically, the company needs to purchase servers for the internal network. Employees will connect to company servers and download information to their own desktop computers."

Mr. Hamilton passes Emily the following chart detailing the types of servers available, the number of employees each server supports, and the cost of each server.

Type of Server	Number of Employees Server Supports	Cost of Server
Standard Intel Pentium PC	Up to 30 employees	$ 2,500
Enhanced Intel Pentium PC	Up to 80 employees	5,000
SGI Workstation	Up to 200 employees	10,000
Sun Workstation	Up to 2,000 employees	25,000

"Emily, I need you to decide what servers to purchase and when to purchase them to minimize cost and to ensure that the company possesses enough server capacity to follow the intranet implementation timeline," Mr. Hamilton says. "For example, you may decide to buy one large server during the first month to support all employees, or buy several small servers during the first month to support all employees, or buy one small server each month to support each new group of employees gaining access to the intranet."

"There are several factors that complicate your decision," Mr. Hamilton continues. "Two server manufacturers are willing to offer discounts to CommuniCorp. SGI is willing to give you a discount of 10 percent off each server purchased, but only if you purchase servers in the first or second month. Sun is willing to give you a 25 percent discount off all servers purchased in the first two months. You are also limited in the amount of money you can spend during the first month. CommuniCorp has already allocated much of the budget for the next two months, so you only have a total of $9,500 available to purchase servers in months 1 and 2. Finally, the manufacturing department requires at least one of the three more powerful servers. Have your decision on my desk at the end of the week."

a. Emily first decides to evaluate the number and type of servers to purchase on a month-to-month basis. For each month, formulate a spreadsheet model to determine which servers Emily should purchase in that month to minimize costs in that month and support the new users given your results for the preceding months. How many and which types of servers should she purchase in each month? How much is the total cost of the plan?

b. Emily realizes that she could perhaps achieve savings if she bought a larger server in the initial months to support users in the final months. She therefore decides to evaluate the number and type of servers to purchase over the entire planning period. Formulate a spreadsheet model to determine which servers Emily should purchase in which months to minimize total cost and support all new users. How many and which types of servers should she purchase in each month? How much is the total cost of the plan?

c. Why is the answer using the first method different from that using the second method?

d. Are there other costs for which Emily is not accounting in her problem formulation? If so, what are they?

e. What further concerns might the various departments of CommuniCorp have regarding the intranet?

Case 3-3
Fabrics and Fall Fashions

From the 10th floor of her office building, Katherine Rally watches the swarms of New Yorkers fight their way through the streets infested with yellow cabs and the sidewalks littered with hot dog stands. On this sweltering July day, she pays particular attention to the fashions worn by the various women and wonders what they will choose to wear in the fall. Her thoughts are not simply random musings; they are critical to her work since she owns and manages TrendLines, an elite women's clothing company.

Today is an especially important day because she must meet with Ted Lawson, the production manager, to decide upon next month's production plan for the fall line. Specifically, she must determine the quantity of each clothing item she should produce given the plant's production capacity, limited resources, and demand forecasts. Accurate planning for next month's production is critical to fall sales since the items produced next month will appear in stores during September and women generally buy the majority of the fall fashions when they first appear in September.

She turns back to her sprawling glass desk and looks at the numerous papers covering it. Her eyes roam across the clothing patterns designed almost six months ago, the lists of material requirements for each pattern, and the lists of demand forecasts for each pattern determined by customer surveys at fashion shows. She remembers the hectic and sometimes nightmarish days of designing the fall line and presenting it at fashion shows in New York, Milan, and Paris. Ultimately, she paid her team of six designers a total of $860,000 for their work on her fall line. With the cost of hiring runway models, hair stylists, and make-up artists; sewing and fitting clothes; building the set; choreographing and rehearsing the show; and renting the conference hall, each of the three fashion shows cost her an additional $2,700,000.

She studies the clothing patterns and material requirements. Her fall line consists of both professional and casual fashions. She determined the price for each clothing item by taking into account the quality and cost of material, the cost of labor and machining, the demand for the item, and the prestige of the TrendLines brand name.

The fall professional fashions include:

Clothing Item	Material Requirements	Price	Labor and Machine Cost
Tailored wool slacks	3 yards of wool 2 yards of acetate for lining	$300	$160
Cashmere sweater	1.5 yards of cashmere	450	150
Silk blouse	1.5 yards of silk	180	100
Silk camisole	0.5 yard of silk	120	60
Tailored skirt	2 yards of rayon 1.5 yards of acetate for lining	270	120
Wool blazer	2.5 yards of wool 1.5 yards of acetate for lining	320	140

The fall casual fashions include:

Clothing Item	Material Requirements	Price	Labor and Machine Cost
Velvet pants	3 yards of velvet 2 yards of acetate for lining	$350	$175
Cotton sweater	1.5 yards of cotton	130	60
Cotton miniskirt	0.5 yard of cotton	75	40
Velvet shirt	1.5 yards of velvet	200	160
Button-down blouse	1.5 yards of rayon	120	90

She knows that for the next month, she has ordered 45,000 yards of wool, 28,000 yards of acetate, 9,000 yards of cashmere, 18,000 yards of silk, 30,000 yards of rayon, 20,000 yards of velvet, and 30,000 yards of cotton for production. The prices of the materials are listed below.

Material	Price per Yard
Wool	$ 9.00
Acetate	1.50
Cashmere	60.00
Silk	13.00
Rayon	2.25
Velvet	12.00
Cotton	2.50

Any material that is not used in production can be sent back to the textile wholesaler for a full refund, although scrap material cannot be sent back to the wholesaler.

She knows that the production of both the silk blouse and cotton sweater leaves leftover scraps of material. Specifically, for the production of one silk blouse or one cotton sweater, 2 yards of silk and cotton, respectively, are needed. From these 2 yards, 1.5 yards are used for the silk blouse or the cotton sweater and 0.5 yard is left as scrap material. She does not want to waste the material, so she plans to use the rectangular scrap of silk or cotton to produce a silk camisole or cotton miniskirt, respectively. Therefore, whenever a silk blouse is produced, a silk camisole is also produced. Likewise, whenever a cotton sweater is produced, a cotton miniskirt is also produced. Note that it is possible to produce a silk camisole without producing a silk blouse and a cotton miniskirt without producing a cotton sweater.

The demand forecasts indicate that some items have limited demand. Specifically, because the velvet pants and velvet shirts are fashion fads, TrendLines has forecasted that it can sell only 5,500 pairs of velvet pants and 6,000 velvet shirts. TrendLines does not want to produce more than the forecasted demand because once the pants and shirts go out of style, the company cannot sell them. TrendLines can produce less than the forecasted demand, however, since the company is not required to meet the demand. The cashmere sweater also has limited demand because it is quite expensive, and TrendLines knows it can sell at most 4,000 cashmere sweaters. The silk blouses and camisoles have limited demand because many women think silk is too hard to care for, and TrendLines projects that it can sell at most 12,000 silk blouses and 15,000 silk camisoles.

The demand forecasts also indicate that the wool slacks, tailored skirts, and wool blazers have a great demand because they are basic items needed in every professional wardrobe.

Specifically, the demand is 7,000 pairs of wool slacks and 5,000 wool blazers. Katherine wants to meet at least 60 percent of the demand for these two items to maintain her loyal customer base and not lose business in the future. Although the demand for tailored skirts could not be estimated, Katherine feels she should make at least 2,800 of them.

a. Ted is trying to convince Katherine not to produce any velvet shirts since the demand for this fashion fad is quite low. He argues that this fashion fad alone accounts for $500,000 of the fixed design and other costs. The net contribution (price of clothing item − materials cost − labor cost) from selling the fashion fad should cover these fixed costs. Each velvet shirt generates a net contribution of $22. He argues that given the net contribution, even satisfying the maximum demand will not yield a profit. What do you think of Ted's argument?

b. Formulate and solve a linear programming problem to maximize profit given the production, resource, and demand constraints.

Before she makes her final decision, Katherine plans to explore the following questions independently, except where otherwise indicated.

c. The textile wholesaler informs Katherine that the velvet cannot be sent back because the demand forecasts show that the demand for velvet will decrease in the future. Katherine can therefore get no refund for the velvet. How does this fact change the production plan?

d. What is an intuitive economic explanation for the difference between the solutions found in parts b and c?

e. The sewing staff encounters difficulties sewing the arms and lining into the wool blazer since the blazer pattern has an awkward shape and the heavy wool material is difficult to cut and sew. The increased labor time to sew a wool blazer increases the labor and machine cost for each blazer by $80. Given this new cost, how many of each clothing item should TrendLines produce to maximize profit?

f. The textile wholesaler informs Katherine that since another textile customer canceled his order, she can obtain an extra 10,000 yards of acetate. How many of each clothing item should TrendLines now produce to maximize profit?

g. TrendLines assumes that it can sell every item that was not sold during September and October in a big sale in November at 60 percent of the original price. Therefore, it can sell all items in unlimited quantity during the November sale. (The previously mentioned upper limits on demand only concern the sales during September and October.) What should the new production plan be to maximize profit?

Case 3-4

New Frontiers

Rob Richman, president of AmeriBank, takes off his glasses, rubs his eyes in exhaustion, and squints at the clock in his study. It reads 3 AM. For the last several hours, Rob has been poring over AmeriBank's financial statements from the last three quarters of operation. AmeriBank, a medium-sized bank with branches throughout the United States, is headed for dire economic straits. The bank, which provides transaction, savings, investment, and loan services, has been experiencing a steady decline in its net income over the past year, and trends show that the decline will continue. The bank is simply losing customers to nonbank and foreign bank competitors.

AmeriBank is not alone in its struggle to stay out of the red. From his daily industry readings, Rob knows that many American banks have been suffering significant losses because of increasing competition from nonbank and foreign bank competitors offering services typically in the domain of American banks. Because the nonbank and foreign bank competitors specialize in particular services, they are able to better capture the market for those services by offering less expensive, more efficient, more convenient services. For example, large corporations now turn to foreign banks and commercial paper offerings for loans, and affluent Americans now turn to money-market funds for investment. Banks face the daunting challenge of distinguishing themselves from nonbank and foreign bank competitors.

Rob has concluded that one strategy for distinguishing AmeriBank from its competitors is to improve services that nonbank and foreign bank competitors do not readily provide: transaction services. He has decided that a more convenient transaction method must logically succeed the automatic teller machine, and he believes that electronic banking over the Internet allows this convenient transaction method. Over the Internet, customers are able to perform transactions on their desktop computers either at home or work. The explosion of the Internet means that many potential customers understand and use the World Wide Web. He therefore feels that if AmeriBank offers Web banking (as the practice of Internet banking is commonly called), the bank will attract many new customers.

Before Rob undertakes the project to make Web banking possible, however, he needs to understand the market for Web banking and the services AmeriBank should provide over the Internet. For example, should the bank only allow customers to access account balances and historical transaction information over the Internet, or should the bank develop a strategy to allow customers to make deposits and withdrawals over the Internet? Should the bank try to recapture a portion of the investment market by continuously running stock prices and allowing customers to make stock transactions over the Internet for a minimal fee?

Because AmeriBank is not in the business of performing surveys, Rob has decided to outsource the survey project to a professional survey company. He has opened the project up for bidding by several survey companies and will award the project to the company that is willing to perform the survey for the least cost. Rob provided each survey company with a list of survey requirements to ensure that AmeriBank receives the needed information for planning the Web banking project.

Because different age groups require different services, AmeriBank is interested in surveying four different age groups. The first group encompasses customers who are 18 to 25 years old. The bank assumes that this age group has limited yearly income and performs minimal transactions. The second group encompasses customers who are 26 to 40 years old. This age group has significant sources of income, performs many transactions, requires numerous loans for new houses and cars, and invests in various securities. The third group encompasses customers who are 41 to 50 years old. These customers typically have the same level of income and perform the same number of transactions as the second age group, but the bank assumes that these customers are less likely to use Web banking since they have not become as comfortable with the explosion of computers or the Internet. Finally, the fourth group encompasses customers who are 51 years of age and over. These customers commonly crave security and require continuous information on retirement funds. The bank believes that it is highly unlikely that customers in this age group will use Web banking, but the bank desires to learn the needs of this age group for the future. AmeriBank wants to interview 2,000 customers with at least 20 percent from the first age group, at least 27.5 percent from the second age group, at least 15 percent from the third age group, and at least 15 percent from the fourth age group.

Rob understands that the Internet is a recent phenomenon and that some customers may not have heard of the World Wide Web. He therefore wants to ensure that the survey includes a mix of customers who know the Internet well and those that have less exposure to the Internet. To ensure that AmeriBank obtains the correct mix, he wants to interview at least 15 percent of customers from the Silicon Valley where Internet use is high, at least 35 percent of customers from big cities where Internet use is medium, and at least 20 percent of customers from small towns where Internet use is low.

Sophisticated Surveys is one of three survey companies competing for the project. It has performed an initial analysis of these survey requirements to determine the cost of surveying different populations. The costs per person surveyed are listed in the following table:

| | Age Group | | | |
Region	18 to 25	26 to 40	41 to 50	51 and over
Silicon Valley	$4.75	$6.50	$6.50	$5.00
Big cities	5.25	5.75	6.25	6.25
Small towns	6.50	7.50	7.50	7.25

Sophisticated Surveys explores the following options cumulatively.

a. Formulate a linear programming model to minimize costs while meeting all survey constraints imposed by AmeriBank.

b. If the profit margin for Sophisticated Surveys is 15 percent of cost, what bid will it submit?

c. After submitting its bid, Sophisticated Surveys is informed that it has the lowest cost but that AmeriBank does not like the solution. Specifically, Rob feels that the selected survey population is not representative enough of the banking customer population. Rob wants at least 50 people of each age group surveyed in each region. What is the new bid made by Sophisticated Surveys?

d. Rob feels that Sophisticated Surveys oversampled the 18-to-25-year-old population and the Silicon Valley population. He imposes a new constraint that no more than 600 individuals can be surveyed from the 18-to-25-year-old population and no more than 650 individuals can be surveyed from the Silicon Valley population. What is the new bid?

e. When Sophisticated Surveys calculated the cost of reaching and surveying particular individuals, the company thought that reaching individuals in young populations would be easiest. In a recently completed survey, however, Sophisticated Surveys learned that this assumption was wrong. The new costs for surveying the 18-to-25-year-old population are listed at the top of the next column:

Region	Cost per Person
Silicon Valley	$6.50
Big cities	6.75
Small towns	7.00

Given the new costs, what is the new bid?

f. To ensure the desired sampling of individuals, Rob imposes even stricter requirements. He fixes the exact percentage of people that should be surveyed from each population. The requirements are listed next.

Population	Percentage of People Surveyed
18 to 25	25%
26 to 40	35
41 to 50	20
51 and over	20
Silicon Valley	20
Big cities	50
Small towns	30

By how much would these new requirements increase the cost of surveying for Sophisticated Surveys? Given the 15 percent profit margin, what would Sophisticated Surveys bid?

Case 3-5

Assigning Students to Schools

The Springfield School Board has made the decision to close one of its middle schools (sixth, seventh, and eighth grades) at the end of this school year and reassign all of next year's middle school students to the three remaining middle schools. The school district provides busing for all middle school students who must travel more than approximately a mile, so the school board wants a plan for reassigning the students that will minimize the total busing cost. The annual cost per student for busing from each of the six residential areas of the city to each of the schools is shown in the following table (along with other basic data for next year), where 0 indicates that busing is not needed and a dash indicates an infeasible assignment.

					Busing Cost per Student		
Area	Number of Students	Percentage in 6th Grade	Percentage in 7th Grade	Percentage in 8th Grade	School 1	School 2	School 3
1	450	32	38	30	$300	$ 0	$700
2	600	37	28	35	—	400	500
3	550	30	32	38	600	300	200
4	350	28	40	32	200	500	—
5	500	39	34	27	0	—	400
6	450	34	28	38	500	300	0
				School capacity:	900	1,100	1,000

The school board also has imposed the restriction that each grade must constitute between 30 and 36 percent of each school's population. The above table shows the percentage of each area's middle school population for next year that falls into each of the three grades. The school attendance zone boundaries can be drawn so as to split any given area among more than one school, but assume that the percentages shown in the table will continue to hold for any partial assignment of an area to a school.

You have been hired as a management science consultant to assist the school board in determining how many students in each area should be assigned to each school.

a. Formulate and solve a linear programming model for this problem.

b. What is your resulting recommendation to the school board?

After seeing your recommendation, the school board expresses concern about all the splitting of residential areas among multiple schools. They indicate that they "would like to keep each neighborhood together."

c. Adjust your recommendation as well as you can to enable each area to be assigned to just one school. (Adding this restriction may force you to fudge on some other constraints.) How much does this increase the total busing cost? (This line of analysis will be pursued more rigorously in Case 7-3.)

The school board is considering eliminating some busing to reduce costs. Option 1 is to only eliminate busing for students traveling 1 to 1.5 miles, where the cost per student is given in the table as $200. Option 2 is to also eliminate busing for students traveling 1.5 to 2 miles, where the estimated cost per student is $300.

d. Revise the model from part a to fit Option 1, and solve. Compare these results with those from part b, including the reduction in total busing cost.

e. Repeat part d for Option 2.

The school board now needs to choose among the three alternative busing plans (the current one or Option 1 or Option 2). One important factor is busing costs. However, the school board also wants to place equal weight on a second factor: the inconvenience and safety problems caused by forcing students to travel by foot or bicycle a substantial distance (more than a mile, and especially more than 1.5 miles). Therefore, they want to choose a plan that provides the best trade-off between these two factors.

f. Use your results from parts b, d, and e to summarize the key information related to these two factors that the school board needs to make this decision.

g. Which decision do you think should be made? Why?

Note: This case will be continued in later chapters (Cases 5-4 and 7-3), so we suggest that you save your analysis, including your basic spreadsheet model.

Case 3-6

Reclaiming Solid Wastes

The Save-It Company operates a reclamation center that collects four types of solid waste materials and then treats them so that they can be amalgamated (treating and amalgamating are separate processes) into a salable product. Three different grades of this product can be made, depending on the mix of the materials used. (See the first table.) Although there is some flexibility in the mix for each grade, quality standards specify the minimum or maximum amount of the materials allowed in that product grade. (This minimum or maximum amount is the weight of the material expressed as a percentage of the total weight for that product grade.) For each of the two higher grades, a fixed percentage is specified for one of the materials. These specifications are given in the first table along with the cost of amalgamation and the selling price for each grade.

The reclamation center collects its solid waste materials from some regular sources and so is normally able to maintain a steady rate for treating them. The second table gives the quantities available for collection and treatment each week, as well as the cost of treatment, for each type of material.

The Save-It Co. is solely owned by Green Earth, an organization that is devoted to dealing with environmental issues; Save-It's profits are all used to help support Green Earth's activities. Green Earth has raised contributions and grants, amounting to $30,000 per week, to be used exclusively to cover the entire treatment cost for the solid waste materials. The board of directors of Green Earth has instructed the management of Save-It to divide this money among the materials in such a way that *at least half* of the amount available of each material is actually collected and treated. These additional restrictions are listed in the second table.

Within the restrictions specified in the two tables, management wants to allocate the materials to product grades so as to maximize the total weekly profit (total sales income *minus* total amalgamation cost).

a. Formulate this problem in linear programming terms by identifying all the activities, resources, benefits, and fixed requirements that lurk within it.

Grade	Specification	Amalgamation Cost per Pound	Selling Price per Pound
A	Material 1: Not more than 30% of the total Material 2: Not less than 40% of the total Material 3: Not more than 50% of the total Material 4: Exactly 20% of the total	$3.00	$8.50
B	Material 1: Not more than 50% of the total Material 2: Not less than 10% of the total Material 4: Exactly 10% of the total	2.50	7.00
C	Material 1: Not more than 70% of the total	2.00	5.50

Material	Pounds/Week Available	Treatment Cost per Pound	Additional Restrictions
1	3,000	$3.00	1. For each material, at least half of
2	2,000	6.00	the pounds/week available should
3	4,000	4.00	be collected and treated.
4	1,000	5.00	2. $30,000 per week should be used
			to treat these materials.

b. Formulate and solve a spreadsheet model for this linear programming problem.

c. Express this linear programming model in the spreadsheet in algebraic form.

Case 3-7

Project Pickings

Tazer, a pharmaceutical manufacturing company, entered the pharmaceutical market 12 years ago with the introduction of six new drugs. Five of the six drugs were simply permutations of existing drugs and therefore did not sell very heavily. The sixth drug, however, addressed hypertension and was a huge success. Since Tazer had a patent on the hypertension drug, it experienced no competition, and profits from the hypertension drug alone kept Tazer in business.

During the past 12 years, Tazer continued a moderate amount of research and development, but it never stumbled upon a drug as successful as the hypertension drug. One reason is that the company never had the motivation to invest heavily in innovative research and development. The company was riding the profit wave generated by its hypertension drug and did not feel the need to commit significant resources to finding new drug breakthroughs.

Now Tazer is beginning to fear the pressure of competition. The patent for the hypertension drug expires in five years,[1] and Tazer knows that once the patent expires, generic drug manufacturing companies will swarm into the market like vultures. Historical trends show that generic drugs decrease sales of branded drugs by 75 percent.

Tazer is therefore looking to invest significant amounts of money in research and development this year to begin the search for a new breakthrough drug that will offer the company the same success as the hypertension drug. Tazer believes that if the company begins extensive research and development now, the probability of finding a successful drug shortly after the expiration of the hypertension patent will be high.

As head of research and development at Tazer, you are responsible for choosing potential projects and assigning project directors to lead each of the projects. After researching the needs of the market, analyzing the shortcomings of current drugs, and interviewing numerous scientists concerning the promising areas of medical research, you have decided that your department will pursue five separate projects, which are listed below:

Project Up: Develop a more effective antidepressant that does not cause serious mood swings.

Project Stable: Develop a drug that addresses manic-depression.

Project Choice: Develop a less intrusive birth control method for women.

Project Hope: Develop a vaccine to prevent HIV infection.

Project Release: Develop a more effective drug to lower blood pressure.

For each of the five projects, you are only able to specify the medical ailment the research should address since you do not know what compounds will exist and be effective without research.

You also have five senior scientists to lead the five projects. You know that scientists are very temperamental people and will only work well if they are challenged and motivated by the project. To ensure that the senior scientists are assigned to projects they find motivating, you have established a bidding system for the projects. You have given each of the five scientists 1,000 bid points. They assign bids to each project, giving a higher number of bid points to projects they most prefer to lead.

The following table provides the bids from the five senior scientists for the five individual projects:

Project	Dr. Kvaal	Dr. Zuner	Dr. Tsai	Dr. Mickey	Dr. Rollins
Project Up	100	0	100	267	100
Project Stable	400	200	100	153	33
Project Choice	200	800	100	99	33
Project Hope	200	0	100	451	34
Project Release	100	0	600	30	800

[1] In general, patents protect inventions for 17 years. In 1995, GATT legislation extending the protection given by new pharmaceutical patents to 20 years became effective. The patent for Tazer's hypertension drug was issued prior to the GATT legislation, however. Thus, the patent only protects the drug for 17 years.

You decide to evaluate a variety of scenarios you think are likely.

a. Given the bids, you need to assign one senior scientist to each of the five projects to maximize the preferences of the scientists. What are the assignments?

b. Dr. Rollins is being courted by Harvard Medical School to accept a teaching position. You are fighting desperately to keep her at Tazer, but the prestige of Harvard may lure her away. If this were to happen, the company would give up the project with the least enthusiasm. Which project would not be done?

c. You do not want to sacrifice any project since researching only four projects decreases the probability of finding a breakthrough new drug. You decide that either Dr. Zuner or Dr. Mickey could lead two projects. Under these new conditions with just four senior scientists, which scientists will lead which projects to maximize preferences?

d. After Dr. Zuner was informed that she and Dr. Mickey are being considered for two projects, she decided to change her bids. Dr. Zuner's new bids for each of the projects are the following:

Project Up: 20

Project Stable: 450

Project Choice: 451

Project Hope: 39

Project Release: 40

Under these new conditions with just four senior scientists, which scientists will lead which projects to maximize preferences?

e. Do you support the assignments found in part *d*? Why or why not?

f. Now you again consider all five scientists. You decide, however, that several scientists cannot lead certain projects. In particular, Dr. Mickey does not have experience with research on the immune system, so he cannot lead Project Hope. His family also has a history of manic-depression, and you feel that he

would be too personally involved in Project Stable to serve as an effective project leader. Dr. Mickey therefore cannot lead Project Stable. Dr. Kvaal also does not have experience with research on the immune system and cannot lead Project Hope. In addition, Dr. Kvaal cannot lead Project Release because he does not have experience with research on the cardiovascular system. Finally, Dr. Rollins cannot lead Project Up because her family has a history of depression and you feel she would be too personally involved in the project to serve as an effective leader. Because Dr. Mickey and Dr. Kvaal cannot lead two of the five projects, they each have only 600 bid points. Dr. Rollins has only 800 bid points because she cannot lead one of the five projects. The following table provides the new bids of Dr. Mickey, Dr. Kvaal, and Dr. Rollins:

Project	Dr. Mickey	Dr. Kvaal	Dr. Rollins
Project Up	300	86	Can't lead
Project Stable	Can't lead	343	50
Project Choice	125	171	50
Project Hope	Can't lead	Can't lead	100
Project Release	175	Can't lead	600

Which scientists should lead which projects to maximize preferences?

g. You decide that Project Hope and Project Release are too complex to be led by only one scientist. Therefore, each of these projects will be assigned two scientists as project leaders. You decide to hire two more scientists in order to staff all projects: Dr. Arriaga and Dr. Santos. Because of religious reasons, neither of them want to lead Project Choice and so they assign 0 bid points to this project. The following table lists all projects, scientists, and their bids.

Project	Kvaal	Zuner	Tsai	Mickey	Rollins	Arriaga	Santos
Up	86	0	100	300	Can't lead	250	111
Stable	343	200	100	Can't lead	50	250	1
Choice	171	800	100	125	50	0	0
Hope	Can't lead	0	100	Can't lead	100	250	333
Release	Can't lead	0	600	175	600	250	555

Which scientists should lead which projects to maximize preferences?

h. Do you think it is wise to base your decision in part *g* only on an optimal solution for a variant of an assignment problem?

Chapter **Four**

The Art of Modeling with Spreadsheets

Learning objectives

After completing this chapter, you should be able to

1. Describe the general process for modeling in spreadsheets.
2. Describe some guidelines for building good spreadsheet models.
3. Apply both the general process for modeling in spreadsheets and the guidelines in this chapter to develop your own spreadsheet model from a description of the problem.
4. Identify some deficiencies in a poorly formulated spreadsheet model.
5. Apply a variety of techniques for debugging a spreadsheet model.

Nearly all managers now make extensive use of spreadsheets to analyze business problems. What they are doing is *modeling* with spreadsheets.

Spreadsheet modeling is a major emphasis throughout this book. Section 1.2 in Chapter 1 introduced a spreadsheet model for performing break-even analysis. Section 2.2 in Chapter 2 described how to use spreadsheets to formulate linear programming models. Chapter 3 focused on spreadsheet models for five key categories of linear programming problems: resource-allocation problems, cost–benefit–trade-off problems, mixed problems, transportation problems, and assignment problems. Many kinds of spreadsheet models are discussed in subsequent chapters as well. However, those presentations focus mostly on the characteristics of spreadsheet models that fit the management science techniques (such as linear programming) being covered in those chapters. We devote this chapter instead to the general *process* of building models with spreadsheets.

Modeling in spreadsheets is more an art than a science. There is no systematic procedure that invariably will lead to a single correct spreadsheet model. For example, if two managers were given exactly the same business problem to analyze with a spreadsheet, their spreadsheet models would likely look quite different. There is no one right way of modeling any given problem. However, some models will be better than others.

Although no completely systematic procedure is available for modeling in spreadsheets, there is a general process that should be followed. This process has four major steps: (1) *plan* the spreadsheet model, (2) *build* the model, (3) *test* the model, and (4) *analyze* the model and its results. After introducing a case study in Section 4.1, the next section will describe this plan-build-test-analyze process in some detail and illustrate the process in the context of the case study. Section 4.2 also will discuss some ways of overcoming common stumbling blocks in the modeling process.

Unfortunately, despite its logical approach, there is no guarantee that the plan-build-test-analyze process will lead to a "good" spreadsheet model. A good spreadsheet model is easy to understand, easy to debug, and easy to modify. Section 4.3 presents some guidelines for building such models. This section also uses the case study in Section 4.1 to illustrate the difference between appropriate formulations and poor formulations of a model.

Even with an appropriate formulation, the initial versions of large spreadsheet models commonly will include some small but troublesome errors, such as inaccurate references to cell addresses or typographical errors when entering equations into cells. These errors often can be difficult to track down. Section 4.4 presents some helpful ways to debug a spreadsheet model and root out such errors.

The overriding goal of this chapter is to provide a solid foundation for becoming a successful spreadsheet modeler. However, this chapter by itself will not turn you into a highly skilled modeler. Ultimately, to reach this point you also will need to study various examples of good spreadsheet models in the different areas of management science and then have lots of practice in formulating your own models. This process will continue throughout the remainder of this book.

4.1 A CASE STUDY: THE EVERGLADE GOLDEN YEARS COMPANY CASH FLOW PROBLEM

The Everglade Golden Years Company operates upscale retirement communities in certain parts of southern Florida. The company was founded in 1946 by Alfred Lee, who was in the right place at the right time to enjoy many successful years during the boom in the Florida economy as many wealthy retirees flooded into the area. Today, the company continues to be run by the Lee family, with Alfred's grandson, Sheldon Lee, as the CEO.

The past few years have been difficult ones for Everglade. The demand for retirement community housing has been light and Everglade has been unable to maintain full occupancy. However, this market has picked up recently and the future is looking brighter. Everglade has recently broken ground for the construction of a new retirement community and has more new construction planned over the next 10 years.

> With only $1 million in cash reserves and negative cash flows looming soon, loans will be needed to observe the company policy of maintaining a balance of at least $500,000 at all times.

Julie Lee is the chief financial officer (CFO) at Everglade. She has spent the last week in front of her computer trying to come to grips with the company's imminent cash flow problem. Julie has projected Everglade's net cash flows over the next 10 years as shown in Table 4.1. With less money currently coming in than would be provided by full occupancy and with all the construction costs for the new retirement community, Everglade will have negative cash flow for the next few years. With only $1 million in cash reserves, it appears that Everglade will need to take out some loans in order to meet its financial obligations. Also, to protect against uncertainty, company policy dictates maintaining a balance of at least $500,000 in cash reserves at all times.

The company's bank has offered two types of loans to Everglade. The first is a 10-year loan with interest-only payments made annually and then the entire principal repaid in a single balloon payment after 10 years. The interest rate on this long-term loan is a favorable 7 percent per year. The second option is a series of one-year loans. These loans can be taken out each year as needed, but each must be repaid (with interest) the following year. Each new loan can be used to help repay the loan for the preceding year if needed. The interest rate for these short-term loans currently is projected to be 10 percent per year.

Armed with her cash flow projections and the loan options from the bank, Julie schedules a meeting with the CEO, Sheldon Lee. Their discussion is as follows:

Julie: Well, we really seem to be in a pickle. There is no way to meet our cash flow problems without borrowing money.

Sheldon: I was afraid of that. What are our options?

TABLE 4.1
Projected Net Cash Flows for the Everglade Golden Years Company over the Next Ten Years

Year	Projected Net Cash Flow (millions of dollars)
2007	−8
2008	−2
2009	−4
2010	3
2011	6
2012	3
2013	−4
2014	7
2015	−2
2016	10

Julie: I've talked to the bank, and we can take out a 10-year loan with an interest rate of 7 percent, or a series of one-year loans at a projected rate of 10 percent.

Sheldon: Wow. That 7 percent rate sounds good. Can we just borrow all that we need using the 10-year loan?

Julie: That was my initial reaction as well. However, after looking at the cash flow projections I'm not sure the answer is so clear-cut. While we have negative cash flow for the next few years, the situation looks much brighter down the road. With a 10-year loan, we are obligated to keep the loan and make the interest payments for 10 years. The one-year loans are more flexible. We can borrow the money only in the years we need it. This way we can save on interest payments in the future.

Sheldon: Okay. I can see how the flexibility of the one-year loans could save us some money. Those loans also will look better if interest rates come down in future years.

Julie: Or they could go higher instead. There's no way to predict future interest rates, so we might as well just plan on the basis of the current projection of 10 percent per year.

Sheldon: Yes, you're right. So which do you recommend, a 10-year loan or a series of one-year loans?

Julie: Well, there's actually another option as well. We could consider a combination of the two types of loans. We could borrow some money long-term to get the lower interest rate and borrow some money short-term to retain flexibility.

Sheldon: That sounds complicated. What we want is a plan that will keep us solvent throughout the 10 years and then leave us with as large a cash balance as possible at the end of the 10 years after paying off all the loans. Could you set this up on a spreadsheet to figure out the best plan?

Julie: You bet. I'll try that and get back to you.

Sheldon: Great. Let's plan to meet again next week when you have your report ready.

You'll see in the next two sections how Julie carefully develops her spreadsheet model for this cash flow problem.

> The objective is to develop a financial plan that will keep the company solvent and then maximize the cash balance in 2017, after all the loans are paid off.

Review Questions

1. What is the advantage of the long-term loan for Everglade?
2. What is the advantage of the series of short-term loans for Everglade?
3. What is the objective for the financial plan that needs to be developed?

4.2 OVERVIEW OF THE PROCESS OF MODELING WITH SPREADSHEETS

You will see later that a linear programming model can be incorporated into a spreadsheet to solve this problem. However, you also will see that the format of this spreadsheet model does not fit readily into any of the categories of linear programming models described in Chapter 3. Even the template given in Figure 3.8 that shows the format for a spreadsheet model of *mixed problems* (the broadest category of linear programming problems) does not help in formulating the model for the current problem. The reason is that the Everglade cash flow management problem is an example of a more complicated type of linear programming problem (a *dynamic problem* with many time periods) that requires starting from scratch in carefully formulating the spreadsheet model. Therefore, this example will nicely illustrate the process of modeling with spreadsheets when dealing with complicated problems of any type, including those discussed later in the book that do not fit linear programming.

When presented with a problem like the Everglade problem, the temptation is to jump right in, launch Excel, and start entering a model. Resist this urge. Developing a spreadsheet model without proper planning inevitably leads to a model that is poorly organized and filled with "spaghetti code."

> *Spaghetti code* is a term from computer programming. It refers to computer code that is not logically organized and thus jumps all over the place, so it is jumbled like a plate of spaghetti.

FIGURE 4.1

A flow diagram for the general plan-build-test-analyze process for modeling with spreadsheets.

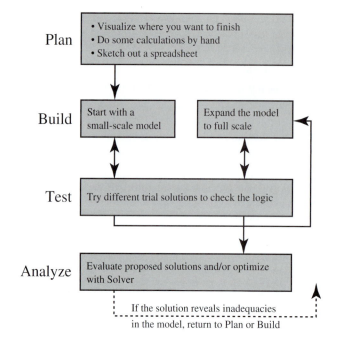

Part of the challenge of planning and developing a spreadsheet model is that there is no standard procedure to follow. It is more an art than a science. However, to provide you with some structure as you begin learning this art, we suggest that you follow the modeling process depicted in Figure 4.1.

As suggested by the figure, the four major steps in this process are to (1) plan, (2) build, (3) test, and (4) analyze the spreadsheet model. The process mainly flows in this order. However, the two-headed arrows between Build and Test indicate a recursive process where testing frequently results in returning to the Build step to fix some problems discovered during the Test step. This back and forth movement between Build and Test may occur several times until the modeler is satisfied with the model. At the same time that this back and forth movement is occurring, the modeler may be involved with further building of the model. One strategy is to begin with a small version of the model to establish its basic logic and then, after testing verifies its accuracy, to expand to a full-scale model. Even after completing the testing and then the analyzing of the model, the process may return to the Build step or even the Plan step if the Analysis step reveals inadequacies in the model.

A modeler might go back and forth between the Build and Test steps several times.

Each of these four major steps may also include some detailed steps. For example, Figure 4.1 lists three detailed steps within the Plan step. Initially, when dealing with a fairly complicated problem, it is helpful to take some time to perform each of these detailed steps manually one at a time. However, as you become more experienced with modeling in spreadsheets, you may find yourself merging some of the detailed steps and quickly performing them mentally. An experienced modeler often is able to do some of these steps mentally, without working them out explicitly on paper. However, if you find yourself getting stuck, it is likely that you are missing a key element from one of the previous detailed steps. You then should go back a step or two and make sure that you have thoroughly completed those preceding steps.

We now describe the various components of the modeling process in the context of the Everglade cash flow problem. At the same time, we also point out some common stumbling blocks encountered while building a spreadsheet model and how these can be overcome.

Plan: Visualize Where You Want to Finish

One common stumbling block in the modeling process occurs right at the very beginning. Given a complicated situation like the one facing Julie at Everglade, sometimes it can be difficult to decide how to even get started. At this point, it can be helpful to think about where you want to end up. For example, what information should Julie provide in her report to Sheldon? What should the "answer" look like when presenting the recommended approach to the problem?

What kinds of numbers need to be included in the recommendation? The answers to these questions can quickly lead you to the heart of the problem and help get the modeling process started.

The question that Julie is addressing is *which loan,* or combination of loans, to use and in *what amounts.* The long-term loan is taken in a single lump sum. Therefore, the "answer" should include a single number indicating how much money to borrow now at the long-term rate. The short-term loan can be taken in any or all of the 10 years, so the "answer" should include 10 numbers indicating how much to borrow at the short-term rate in each given year. These will be the changing cells in the spreadsheet model.

What other numbers should Julie include in her report to Sheldon? The key numbers would be the projected cash balance each year, the amount of the interest payments, and when loan payments are due. These will be output cells in the spreadsheet model.

It is important to distinguish between the numbers that represent decisions (changing cells) and those that represent results (output cells). For instance, it may be tempting to include the cash balances as changing cells. These cells clearly change depending on the decisions made. However, the cash balances are a *result* of how much is borrowed, how much is paid, and all of the other cash flows. They cannot be chosen independently but instead are a function of the other numbers in the spreadsheet. The distinguishing characteristic of changing cells (the loan amounts) is that they do not depend on anything else. They represent the independent decisions being made. They impact the other numbers, but not vice versa.

At this point, you should know what changing cells and output cells are needed.

At this stage in the process, you should have a clear idea of what the answer will look like, including what and how many changing cells are needed, and what kind of results (output cells) should be obtained.

Plan: Do Some Calculations by Hand

When building a model, another common stumbling block can arise when trying to enter a formula in one of the output cells. For example, just how does Julie keep track of the cash balances in the Everglade cash flow problem? What formulas need to be entered? There are a lot of factors that enter into this calculation, so it is easy to get overwhelmed.

If you are getting stuck at this point, it can be a very useful exercise to do some calculations by hand. Just pick some numbers for the changing cells and determine with a calculator or pencil and paper what the results should be. For example, pick some loan amounts for Everglade and then calculate the company's resulting cash balance at the end of the first couple of years. Let's say Everglade takes a long-term loan of $6 million and then adds short-term loans of $2 million in 2007 and $5 million in 2008. How much cash would the company have left at the end of 2007 and at the end of 2008?

These two quantities can be calculated by hand as follows. In 2007, Everglade has some initial money in the bank ($1 million), a negative cash flow from its business operations (−$8 million), and a cash inflow from the long-term and short-term loans ($6 million and $2 million, respectively). Thus, the ending balance for 2007 would be:

Ending balance (2007) =	Starting balance	$1 million
	+ Cash flow (2007)	−$8 million
	+ LT loan (2007)	+ $6 million
	+ ST loan (2007)	+ $2 million
		$1 million

The calculations for the year 2008 are a little more complicated. In addition to the starting balance left over from 2007 ($1 million), negative cash flow from business operations for 2008 (−$2 million), and a new short-term loan for 2008 ($5 million), the company will need to make interest payments on its 2007 loans as well as pay back the short-term loan from 2007. The ending balance for 2008 is therefore:

Ending balance (2008) =	Starting balance (from end of 2007)	$1 million
	+ Cash flow (2008)	−$2 million
	+ ST loan (2008)	+ $5 million
	−LT interest payment	−(7%)($6 million)

$$
\begin{aligned}
-\text{ST interest payment} &\quad -(10\%)(\$2 \text{ million}) \\
-\text{ST loan payback (2007)} &\quad \underline{-\ \$2 \text{ million}} \\
&\quad \$1.38 \text{ million}
\end{aligned}
$$

Doing calculations by hand can help in a couple of ways. First, it can help clarify what formula should be entered for an output cell. For instance, looking at the by-hand calculations above, it appears that the formula for the ending balance for a particular year should be

$$\text{Ending balance} = \text{Starting balance} + \text{Cash flow} + \text{Loans} - \text{Interest payments} - \text{Loan paybacks}$$

Hand calculations can clarify what formulas are needed for the output cells.

It now will be a simple exercise to enter the proper cell references in the formula for the ending balance in the spreadsheet model. Second, hand calculations can help to verify the spreadsheet model. By plugging in a long-term loan of $6 million, along with short-term loans of $2 million in 2007 and $5 million in 2008, into a completed spreadsheet, the ending balances should be the same as calculated above. If they're not, this suggests an error in the spreadsheet model (assuming the hand calculations are correct).

Plan: Sketch Out a Spreadsheet

Any model typically has a large number of different elements that need to be included on the spreadsheet. For the Everglade problem, these would include some data cells (interest rates, starting balance, minimum balances, and cash flows), some changing cells (loan amounts), and a number of output cells (interest payments, loan paybacks, and ending balances). Therefore, a potential stumbling block can arise when trying to organize and lay out the spreadsheet model. Where should all the pieces fit on the spreadsheet? How do you begin putting together the spreadsheet?

Before firing up Excel and blindly entering the various elements, it can be helpful to sketch a layout of the spreadsheet. Is there a logical way to arrange the elements? A little planning at this stage can go a long way toward building a spreadsheet that is well organized. Don't bother with numbers at this point. Simply sketch out blocks on a piece of paper for the various data cells, changing cells, and output cells, and label them. Concentrate on the layout. Should a block of numbers be laid out in a row or a column, or as a two-dimensional table? Are there common row or column headings for different blocks of cells? If so, try to arrange the blocks in consistent rows or columns so they can utilize a single set of headings. Try to arrange the spreadsheet so that it starts with the data at the top and progresses logically toward the target cell at the bottom. This will be easier to understand and follow than if the data cells, changing cells, output cells, and target cell are all scattered throughout the spreadsheet.

Plan where the various blocks of data cells, changing cells, and output cells should go on the spreadsheet by sketching your layout ideas on paper.

A sketch of a potential spreadsheet layout for the Everglade problem is shown in Figure 4.2. The data cells for the interest rates, starting balance, and minimum cash balance are at the top

FIGURE 4.2

Sketch of the spreadsheet for Everglade's cash flow problem.

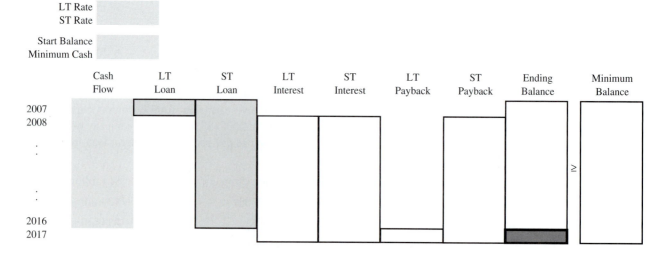

of the spreadsheet. All of the remaining elements in the spreadsheet then follow the same structure. The rows represent the different years (from 2007 through 2017). All the various cash inflows and outflows are then broken out in the columns, starting with the projected cash flow from the business operations (with data for each of the 10 years), continuing with the loan inflows, interest payments, and loan paybacks, and culminating with the ending balance (calculated for each year). The long-term loan is a one-time loan (in 2007), so it is sketched as a single cell. The short-term loan can occur in any of the 10 years (2007 through 2016), so it is sketched as a block of cells. The interest payments start one year after the loans. The long-term loan is paid back 10 years later (2017).

Organizing the elements with a consistent structure, like in Figure 4.2, not only saves having to retype the year labels for each element, but also makes the model easier to understand. Everything that happens in a given year is arranged together in a single row.

It is generally easiest to start sketching the layout with the data. The structure of the rest of the model should then follow the structure of the data cells. For example, once the projected cash flows data are sketched as a vertical column (with each year in a row), then it follows that the other cash flows should be structured the same way.

There is also a logical progression to the spreadsheet. The data for the problem are located at the top and left of the spreadsheet. Then, since the cash flow, loan amounts, interest payments, and loan paybacks are all part of the calculation for the ending balance, the columns are arranged this way, with the ending balance directly to the right of all these other elements. Since Sheldon has indicated that the objective is to maximize the ending balance in 2017, this cell is designated to be the target cell.

Each year, the balance must be greater than the minimum required balance ($500,000). Since this will be a constraint in the model, it is logical to arrange the balance and minimum balance blocks of numbers adjacent to each other in the spreadsheet. You can put the $\geq$ signs on the sketch to remind yourself that these will be constraints.

> The spreadsheet in Figure 4.2 has a logical progression, starting with the data on the top left and then moving through the calculations toward the target cell on the bottom right.

Build: Start with a Small Version of the Spreadsheet

Once you've thought about a logical layout for the spreadsheet, it is finally time to open a new worksheet in Excel and start building the model. If it is a complicated model, you may want to start by building a small, readily manageable version of the model. The idea is to first make sure that you've got the logic of the model worked out correctly for the small version before expanding the model to full scale.

> Work out the logic for a small version of the spreadsheet model before expanding to full size.

For example, in the Everglade problem, we could get started by building a model for just the first two years (2007 and 2008), like the spreadsheet shown in Figure 4.3.

This spreadsheet is set up to follow the layout suggested in the sketch of Figure 4.2. The loan amounts are in columns D and E. Since the interest payments are not due until the following year, the formulas in columns F and G refer to the loan amounts from the preceding year (LTLoan, or D11, for the long-term loan, and E11 for the short-term loan). The loan payments are calculated in columns H and I. Column H is blank because the long-term loan does not need to be repaid until 2017. The short-term loan is repaid one year later, so the formula in cell I12 refers to the short-term loan taken the preceding year (cell E11). The ending balance in 2007 is the starting balance plus the sum of all the various cash flows that occur in 2007 (cells C11:I11). The ending balance in 2008 is the ending balance in 2007 (cell J11) plus the sum of all the various cash flows that occur in 2008 (cells C12:I12). All these formulas are summarized below the spreadsheet in Figure 4.3.

Building a small version of the spreadsheet works very well for spreadsheets that have a time dimension. For example, instead of jumping right into a 10-year planning problem, we can start with the simpler problem of just looking at a couple of years. Once this smaller model is working correctly, you then can expand the model to 10 years.

Even if a spreadsheet model does not have a time dimension, the same concept of starting small can be applied. For example, if certain constraints considerably complicate a problem, start by working on a simpler problem without the difficult constraints. Get the simple model working and then move on to tackle the difficult constraints. If a model has many sets of output cells, you can build up a model piece by piece by working on one set of output cells at a time, making sure each set works correctly before moving on to the next.

Test: Test the Small Version of the Model

If you do start with a small version of the model first, be sure to test this version thoroughly to make sure that all the logic is correct. It is far better to fix a problem early, while the spreadsheet is still a manageable size, rather than later after an error has been propagated throughout a much larger spreadsheet.

Try entering numbers in the changing cells for which you know what the values of the output cells should be.

To test the spreadsheet, try entering values in the changing cells for which you know what the values of the output cells should be, and then see if the spreadsheet gives the results that you expect. For example, in Figure 4.3, if zeroes are entered for the loan amounts, then the interest payments and loan payback quantities also should be zero. If $1 million is borrowed for both the long-term loan and the short-term loan, then the interest payments the following year should be $70,000 and $100,000, respectively. (Recall that the interest rates are 7 percent and 10 percent, respectively.) If Everglade takes out a $6 million long-term loan and a $2 million short-term loan in 2007, plus a $5 million short-term loan in 2008, then the ending balances should be $1 million for 2007 and $1.38 million for 2008 (based on the calculations done earlier by hand). All these tests work correctly for the spreadsheet in Figure 4.3, so we can be fairly certain that it is correct.

If the output cells are not giving the results that you expect, then carefully look through the formulas to see if you can determine and fix the problem. Section 4.4 will give further guidance on some ways to debug a spreadsheet model.

Build: Expand the Model to Full-Scale Size

Once a small version of the spreadsheet has been tested to make sure all the formulas are correct and everything is working properly, the model can be expanded to full-scale size. Excel's fill commands often can be used to quickly copy the formulas into the remainder of the

FIGURE 4.3

A small version (years 2007 and 2008 only) of the spreadsheet for the Everglade cash flow management problem.

	A	B	C	D	E	F	G	H	I	J	K	L
1		**Everglade Cash Flow Management Problem (Years 2007 and 2008)**										
2												
3		LT Rate	7%									
4		ST Rate	10%									
5					(all cash figures in millions of dollars)							
6		Start Balance	1									
7		Minimum Cash	0.5									
8												
9			Cash	LT	ST	LT	ST	LT	ST	Ending		Minimum
10		Year	Flow	Loan	Loan	Interest	Interest	Payback	Payback	Balance		Balance
11		2007	−8	6	2					1.00	≥	0.50
12		2008	−2		5	−0.42	−0.20		−2.00	1.38	≥	0.50

	F	G	H	I	J	K	L
9	LT	ST	LT	ST	Ending		Minimum
10	Interest	Interest	Payback	Payback	Balance		Balance
11					=StartBalance+SUM(C11:I11)	≥	=MinimumCash
12	= −LTRate*LTLoan	= −STRate*E11		= −E11	=J11+SUM(C12:I12)	≥	=MinimumCash

Range Name	Cell
LTLoan	D11
LTRate	C3
MinimumCash	C7
StartBalance	C6
STRate	C4

Excel Tip: A shortcut for filling down or filling across to the right is to select the cell you want to copy, click on the small box in the lower right-hand corner of the selection rectangle, and drag through the cells you want to fill.

model. For Figure 4.3, the formulas in columns F, G, I, J, and L can be copied using the Fill Down command in the Editing Group of the Home tab (for Excel 2007) or in the Edit menu (for earlier versions of Excel) to obtain all the formulas shown in Figure 4.4. For example, selecting cells G12:G21 and choosing Fill Down will take the formula in cell G12 and copy it (after adjusting the cell address in Column E for the formula) into cells G13 through G21.

Before using the fill commands to copy formulas, be sure that the relative and absolute references have been used appropriately. For example, in G12 ($=-$STRate*E11) using a range name for STRate makes this an absolute reference. When copied into cells G13:G21, the short-term loan interest rate used will always be the value in STRate (C4). The reference to E11 (the loan amount from the previous year) is a relative reference. E11 is two cells to the left and one cell up. When the formula is copied from G12 into G13:G21, the reference in each of these cells will continue to be two cells to the left and one cell up. This is exactly what we want, since we always want the interest payment to be based on the short-term loan that was taken one year ago (two cells to the left and one cell up).

Excel Tip: A shortcut for changing a cell reference from relative to absolute is to press the F4 key on a PC or command-T on a Mac.

After using the Fill Down command to copy the formulas in columns F, G, I, J, and L and entering the LT loan payback into cell H21, the complete model appears as shown in Figure 4.4.

Test: Test the Full-Scale Version of the Model

Just as it was important to test the small version of the model, it needs to be tested again after it is expanded to full-scale size. The procedure is the same one followed for testing the small version, including the ideas that will be presented in Section 4.4 for debugging a spreadsheet model.

Analyze: Analyze the Model

Before using the Solver dialogue box to prepare for applying Solver, the spreadsheet in Figure 4.4 is merely an evaluative model for Everglade. It can be used to evaluate any proposed solution, including quickly determining what interest and loan payments will be required and what the resulting balances will be at the end of each year. For example, LTLoan (D11) and STLoan (E11:E20) in Figure 4.4 show one possible plan, which turns out to be unacceptable because EndingBalance (J11:J21) indicates that a negative ending balance would result in four of the years.

To optimize the model, the Solver dialogue box is used as shown in Figure 4.5 to specify the target cell, the changing cells, and the constraints. Everglade management wants to find a combination of loans that will keep the company solvent throughout the next 10 years (2007–2016) and then will leave as large a cash balance as possible in 2017 after paying off all the loans. Therefore, the target cell to be maximized is EndBalance (J21) and the changing cells are the loan amounts LTLoan (D11) and STLoan (E11:E20). To assure that Everglade maintains a minimum balance of at least $500,000 at the end of each year, the constraints for the model are EndingBalance (J11:J21) $\geq$ MinimumBalance (L11:L21).

After running Solver, the optimal solution is shown in Figure 4.5. The changing cells, LTLoan (D11) and STLoan (E11:E20) give the loan amounts in the various years. The target cell EndBalance (J21) indicates that the ending balance in 2017 will be $2.92 million.

Conclusion of the Case Study

The spreadsheet model developed by Everglade's CFO, Julie Lee, is the one shown in Figure 4.5. Her next step is to submit a report to her CEO, Sheldon Lee, that recommends the plan obtained by this model.

Soon thereafter, Sheldon and Julie meet to discuss her report.

Sheldon: Thanks for your report, Julie. Excellent job. Your spreadsheet really lays everything out in a very understandable way.

Julie: Thanks. It took a little while to get the spreadsheet organized properly and to make sure it was operating correctly, but I think the time spent was worthwhile.

Sheldon: Yes, it was. You can't rush those things. But one thing is still bothering me.

Julie: What's that?

Sheldon: It has to do with our forecasts for the company's future cash flows. We have been assuming that the cash flows in the coming years will be the ones shown in column C of

FIGURE 4.4

A complete spreadsheet model for the Everglade cash flow management problem, including the equations entered into the target cell EndBalance (J21) and all the other output cells, to be used before calling on the Excel Solver. The entries in the changing cells, LTLoan (D11) and STLoan (E11:E20), are only a trial solution at this stage.

	A	B	C	D	E	F	G	H	I	J	K	L
1		**Everglade Cash Flow Management Problem**										
2												
3		LT Rate	7%									
4		ST Rate	10%									
5						(all cash figures in millions of dollars)						
6		Start Balance	1									
7		Minimum Cash	0.5									
8												
9			Cash	LT	ST	LT	ST	LT	ST	Ending		Minimum
10		Year	Flow	Loan	Loan	Interest	Interest	Payback	Payback	Balance		Balance
11		2007	−8	6	2					1.00	≥	0.5
12		2008	−2		5	−0.42	−0.20		−2	1.38	≥	0.5
13		2009	−4		0	−0.42	−0.50		−5	−8.54	≥	0.5
14		2010	3		0	−0.42	0		0	−5.96	≥	0.5
15		2011	6		0	−0.42	0		0	−0.38	≥	0.5
16		2012	3		0	−0.42	0		0	2.20	≥	0.5
17		2013	−4		0	−0.42	0		0	−2.22	≥	0.5
18		2014	7		0	−0.42	0		0	4.36	≥	0.5
19		2015	−2		0	−0.42	0		0	1.94	≥	0.5
20		2016	10		0	−0.42	0		0	11.52	≥	0.5
21		2017				−0.42	0	−6	0	5.10	≥	0.5

	F	G	H	I	J	K	L
9	LT	ST	LT	ST	Ending		Minimum
10	Interest	Interest	Payback	Payback	Balance		Balance
11					=StartBalance+SUM(C11:I11)	≥	=MinimumCash
12	=−LTRate*LTLoan	=−STRate*E11		=−E11	=J11+SUM(C12:I12)	≥	=MinimumCash
13	=−LTRate*LTLoan	=−STRate*E12		=−E12	=J12+SUM(C13:I13)	≥	=MinimumCash
14	=−LTRate*LTLoan	=−STRate*E13		=−E13	=J13+SUM(C14:I14)	≥	=MinimumCash
15	=−LTRate*LTLoan	=−STRate*E14		=−E14	=J14+SUM(C15:I15)	≥	=MinimumCash
16	=−LTRate*LTLoan	=−STRate*E15		=−E15	=J15+SUM(C16:I16)	≥	=MinimumCash
17	=−LTRate*LTLoan	=−STRate*E16		=−E16	=J16+SUM(C17:I17)	≥	=MinimumCash
18	=−LTRate*LTLoan	=−STRate*E17		=−E17	=J17+SUM(C18:I18)	≥	=MinimumCash
19	=−LTRate*LTLoan	=−STRate*E18		=−E18	=J18+SUM(C19:I19)	≥	=MinimumCash
20	=−LTRate*LTLoan	=−STRate*E19		=−E19	=J19+SUM(C20:I20)	≥	=MinimumCash
21	=−LTRate*LTLoan	=−STRate*E20	=−LTLoan	=−E20	=J20+SUM(C21:I21)	≥	=MinimumCash

Range Name	Cells
CashFlow	C11:C20
EndBalance	J21
EndingBalance	J11:J21
LTLoan	D11
LTRate	C3
MinimumBalance	L11:L21
MinimumCash	C7
StartBalance	C6
STLoan	E11:E20
STRate	C4

FIGURE 4.5

A complete spreadsheet model for the Everglade cash flow management problem after calling on the Excel Solver to obtain the optimal solution shown in the changing cells, LTLoan (D11) and STLoan (E11:E20). The target cell EndBalance (J21) indicates that the resulting cash balance in 2017 will be $2.92 million if all the data cells prove to be accurate.

	A	B	C	D	E	F	G	H	I	J	K	L
1		**Everglade Cash Flow Management Problem**										
2												
3		LT Rate	7%									
4		ST Rate	10%									
5					(all cash figures in millions of dollars)							
6		Start Balance	1									
7		Minimum Cash	0.5									
8												
9			Cash	LT	ST	LT	ST	LT	ST	Ending		Minimum
10		Year	Flow	Loan	Loan	Interest	Interest	Payback	Payback	Balance		Balance
11		2007	−8	6.65	0.85					0.50	≥	0.50
12		2008	−2		3.40	−0.47	−0.09		−0.85	0.50	≥	0.50
13		2009	−4		8.21	−0.47	−0.34		−3.40	0.50	≥	0.50
14		2010	3		6.49	−0.47	−0.82		−8.21	0.50	≥	0.50
15		2011	6		1.61	−0.47	−0.65		−6.49	0.50	≥	0.50
16		2012	3		0	−0.47	−0.16		−1.61	1.27	≥	0.50
17		2013	−4		3.70	−0.47	0		0	0.50	≥	0.50
18		2014	7		0	−0.47	−0.37		−3.70	2.97	≥	0.50
19		2015	−2		0	−0.47	0		0	0.50	≥	0.50
20		2016	10		0	−0.47	0		0	10.03	≥	0.50
21		2017				−0.47	0	−6.65	0	2.92	≥	0.50

	F	G	H	I	J	K	L
9	LT	ST	LT	ST	Ending		Minimum
10	Interest	Interest	Payback	Payback	Balance		Balance
11					= StartBalance+SUM(C11:I11)	≥	=MinimumCash
12	=−LTRate*LTLoan	=−STRate*E11		=−E11	=J11+SUM(C12:I12)	≥	=MinimumCash
13	=−LTRate*LTLoan	=−STRate*E12		=−E12	=J12+SUM(C13:I13)	≥	=MinimumCash
14	=−LTRate*LTLoan	=−STRate*E13		=−E13	=J13+SUM(C14:I14)	≥	=MinimumCash
15	=−LTRate*LTLoan	=−STRate*E14		=−E14	=J14+SUM(C15:I15)	≥	=MinimumCash
16	=−LTRate*LTLoan	=−STRate*E15		=−E15	=J15+SUM(C16:I16)	≥	=MinimumCash
17	=−LTRate*LTLoan	=−STRate*E16		=−E16	=J16+SUM(C17:I17)	≥	=MinimumCash
18	=−LTRate*LTLoan	=−STRate*E17		=−E17	=J17+SUM(C18:I18)	≥	=MinimumCash
19	=−LTRate*LTLoan	=−STRate*E18		=−E18	=J18+SUM(C19:I19)	≥	=MinimumCash
20	=−LTRate*LTLoan	=−STRate*E19		=−E19	=J19+SUM(C20:I20)	≥	=MinimumCash
21	=−LTRate*LTLoan	=−STRate*E20	=−LTLoan	=−E20	=J20+SUM(C21:I21)	≥	=MinimumCash

Range Name	Cells
CashFlow	C11:C20
EndBalance	J21
EndingBalance	J11:J21
LTLoan	D11
LTRate	C3
MinimumBalance	L11:L21
MinimumCash	C7
StartBalance	C6
STLoan	E11:E20
STRate	C4

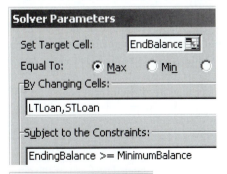

Solver Parameters

Set Target Cell: [EndBalance]

Equal To: ⦿ Max ○ Min ○

By Changing Cells:

[LTLoan,STLoan]

Subject to the Constraints:

[EndingBalance >= MinimumBalance]

Solver Options

☑ Assume Linear Model

☑ Assume Non-Negative

your spreadsheet. Those are good estimates, but we both know that they are only estimates. A lot of changes that we can't foresee now are likely to occur over the next 10 years. When there is a shift in the economy, or when other unexpected developments occur that impact the company, those cash flows can change a lot. How do we know if your recommended plan will still be a good one if those kinds of changes occur?

Julie: A very good question. To answer it, we should do some what-if analysis to see what would happen if those kinds of changes occur. Now that the spreadsheet is set up properly, it will be very easy to do that by simply changing some of the cash flows in column C and seeing what would happen with the current plan. You can try out any change or changes you want and immediately see the effect. Each time you change a future cash flow, you also have the option of trying out changes on short-term loan amounts to see what kind of adjustments would be needed to maintain a balance of at least $500,000 in every year.

OK, are you ready? Shall we do some what-if analysis now?

Sheldon: Let's do.

Fortunately, Julie had set up the spreadsheet properly (providing a data cell for the cash flow in each of the next 10 years) to enable performing what-if analysis immediately by simply trying different numbers in some of these data cells. After spending half an hour trying different numbers, Sheldon and Julie conclude that the plan in Figure 4.5 will be a sound initial financial plan for the next 10 years, even if future cash flows deviate somewhat from current forecasts. If deviations do occur, adjustments will of course need to be made in the short-term loan amounts. At any point, Julie also will have the option of returning to the company's bank to try to arrange another long-term loan for the remainder of the 10 years at a lower interest rate than that offered for short-term loans. If so, essentially the same spreadsheet model as in Figure 4.5 can be used, along with the Excel Solver, to find the optimal adjusted financial plan for the remainder of the 10 years.

A management science technique called *computer simulation* provides another effective way of taking the uncertainty of future cash flows into account. Chapters 12 and 13 will describe this technique and Section 13.4 will be devoted to continuing the analysis of this same case study.

> *Providing a data cell for each piece of data makes it easy to check what would happen if the correct value for a piece of data differs from its initial estimate.*

Review Questions

1. What is a good way to get started with a spreadsheet model if you don't even know where to begin?
2. What are two ways in which doing calculations by hand can help you?
3. Describe a useful way to get started organizing and laying out a spreadsheet.
4. What types of values should be put into the data cells to test the model?
5. What is the difference between an absolute cell reference and a relative cell reference?

4.3   SOME GUIDELINES FOR BUILDING "GOOD" SPREADSHEET MODELS

There are many ways to set up a model on a spreadsheet. While one of the benefits of spreadsheets is the flexibility they offer, this flexibility also can be dangerous. Although Excel provides many features (such as range names, shading, borders, etc.) that allow you to create "good" spreadsheet models that are easy to understand, easy to debug, and easy to modify, it is also easy to create "bad" spreadsheet models that are difficult to understand, difficult to debug, and difficult to modify. The goal of this section is to provide some guidelines that will help you to create "good" spreadsheet models.

Enter the Data First

> *All the data should be laid out on the spreadsheet before beginning to formulate the rest of the spreadsheet model.*

Any spreadsheet model is driven by the data in the spreadsheet. The form of the entire model is built around the structure of the data. Therefore, it is always a good idea to enter and carefully lay out all the data before you begin to set up the rest of the model. The model structure then can conform to the layout of the data as closely as possible.

Welch's, Inc., is the world's largest processor of Concord and Niagara grapes with annual sales surpassing $550 million per year. Such products as Welch's grape jelly and Welch's grape juice have been enjoyed by generations of American consumers.

Every September, growers begin delivering grapes to processing plants that then press the raw grapes into juice. Time must pass before the grape juice is ready for conversion into finished jams, jellies, juices, and concentrates.

Deciding how to use the grape crop is a complex task given changing demand and uncertain crop quality and quantity. Typical decisions include what recipes to use for major product groups, the transfer of grape juice between plants, and the mode of transportation for these transfers.

Because Welch's lacked a formal system for optimizing raw material movement and the recipes used for production, a management science team developed a preliminary linear programming model. This was a large model with 8,000 decision variables that focused on the component level of detail. Small-scale testing proved that the model worked.

To make the model more useful, the team then revised it by aggregating demand by product group rather than by component. This reduced its size to 324 decision variables and 361 functional constraints. The model then was incorporated into a spreadsheet.

The company has run the continually updated version of this spreadsheet model each month since 1994 to provide senior management with information on the optimal logistics plan generated by the Solver. The savings from using and optimizing this model were approximately $150,000 in the first year alone. A major advantage of incorporating the linear programming model into a spreadsheet has been the ease of explaining the model to managers with differing levels of mathematical understanding. This has led to a widespread appreciation of the management science approach for both this application and others.

Source: E. W. Schuster and S. J. Allen, "Raw Material Management at Welch's, Inc.," *Interfaces* 28, no. 5 (September–October 1998), pp. 13–24.

Often, it is easier to set up the rest of the model when the data are already on the spreadsheet. In the Everglade problem (see Figure 4.5), the data for the cash flows have been laid out in the first columns of the spreadsheet (B and C), with the year labels in column B and the data in cells C11:C20. Once the data are in place, the layout for the rest of the model quickly falls into place around the structure of the data. It is only logical to lay out the changing cells and output cells using the same structure, with each of the various cash flows in columns that utilize the same row labels from column B.

Now reconsider the spreadsheet model developed in Section 2.2 for the Wyndor Glass Co. problem. The spreadsheet is repeated here in Figure 4.6. The data for the Hours Used per Unit Produced have been laid out in the center of the spreadsheet in cells C7:D9. The output cells, HoursUsed (E7:E9), then have been placed immediately to the right of these data and to the left of the data on HoursAvailable(G7:G9), where the row labels for these output cells are the same as for all these data. This makes it easy to interpret the three constraints being laid out in rows 7–9 of the spreadsheet model. Next, the changing cells and target cell have been placed together in row 12 below the data, where the column labels for the changing cells are the same as for the columns of data above.

The locations of the data occasionally will need to be shifted somewhat to better accommodate the overall model. However, with this caveat, the model structure generally should conform to the data as closely as possible.

Organize and Clearly Identify the Data

Related data should be grouped together in a convenient format and entered into the spreadsheet with labels that clearly identify the data. For data that are laid out in tabular form, the table should have a heading that provides a general description of the data and then each row and column should have a label that will identify each entry in the table. The units of the data also should be identified. Different types of data should be well separated in the spreadsheet. However, if two tables need to use the same labels for either their rows or columns, then be consistent in making them either rows in both tables or columns in both tables.

Provide labels in the spreadsheet that clearly identify all the data.

In the Wyndor Glass Co. problem (Figure 4.6), the three sets of data have been grouped into tables and clearly labeled Unit Profit, Hours Used per Unit Produced, and Hours Available. The units of the data are identified (dollar signs are included in the unit profit data and hours are indicated in the labels of the time data). Finally, all three data tables make consistent use of rows and columns. Since the Unit Profit data have their product labels (Doors and Windows) in

FIGURE 4.6

The spreadsheet model formulated in Section 2.2 for the Wyndor Glass Co. product-mix problem.

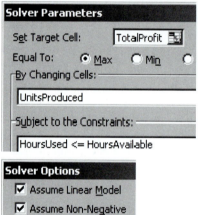

	A	B	C	D	E	F	G
1		**Wyndor Glass Co. Product-Mix Problem**					
2							
3			Doors	Windows			
4		Unit Profit	$300	$500			
5					Hours		Hours
6			Hours Used per Unit Produced		Used		Available
7		Plant 1	1	0	2	≤	4
8		Plant 2	0	2	12	≤	12
9		Plant 3	3	2	18	≤	18
10							
11			Doors	Windows			Total Profit
12		Units Produced	2	6			$3,600

Solver Parameters

Se̲t Target Cell: TotalProfit

Equal To: ⦿ M̲ax   ○ Mi̲n   ○

B̲y Changing Cells:

UnitsProduced

S̲ubject to the Constraints:

HoursUsed <= HoursAvailable

Solver Options

☑ Assume Linear M̲odel

☑ Assume Non-Negative

	E
5	Hours
6	Used
7	=SUMPRODUCT(C7:D7,UnitsProduced)
8	=SUMPRODUCT(C8:D8,UnitsProduced)
9	=SUMPRODUCT(C9:D9,UnitsProduced)

	G
11	Total Profit
12	=SUMPRODUCT(Unit Profit,UnitsProduced)

Range Name	Cells
HoursAvailable	G7:G9
HoursUsed	E7:E9
HoursUsedPerUnitProduced	C7:D9
TotalProfit	G12
UnitProfit	C4:D4
UnitsProduced	C12:D12

columns C and D, the Hours Used per Unit Produced data use this same structure. This structure also is carried through to the changing cells (Units Produced). Similarly, the data for each plant (rows 7–9) are in the rows for both the Hours Used per Unit Produced data *and* the Hours Available data. Keeping the data oriented the same way is not only less confusing, but it also makes it possible to use the SUMPRODUCT function. Recall that the SUMPRODUCT function assumes that the two ranges are exactly the same shape (i.e., the same number of rows *and* columns). If the Unit Profit data and the Units Produced data had not been oriented the same way (e.g., one in a column and the other in a row), it would not have been possible to use the SUMPRODUCT function in the Total Profit calculation.

Similarly, for the Everglade problem (Figure 4.5), the five sets of data have been grouped into cells and tables and clearly labeled ST Rate, LT Rate, Start Balance, Cash Flow, and Minimum Cash. The units of the data are identified (cells F5:I5 specify that all cash figures are in millions of dollars), and all the tables make consistent use of rows and columns (years in the rows).

Enter Each Piece of Data into One Cell Only

Every formula using the same piece of data should refer to the same single data cell.

If a piece of data is needed in more than one formula, then refer to the original data cell rather than repeating the data in additional places. This makes the model much easier to modify. If the value of that piece of data changes, it only needs to be changed in one place. You do not need to search through the entire model to find all the places where the data value appears.

For example, in the Everglade problem (Figure 4.5), there is a company policy of maintaining a cash balance of at least $500,000 at all times. This translates into a constraint for the minimum balance of $500,000 at the end of each year. Rather than entering the minimum cash position of 0.5 (in millions of dollars) into all the cells in column L, it is entered once in MinimumCash (C7) and then referred to by the cells in MinimumBalance (L11:L21). Then, if this policy were to change to, say, a minimum of $200,000 cash, the number would need to be changed in only one place.

Separate Data from Formulas

Formulas should refer to data cells for any needed numbers.

Avoid using numbers directly in formulas. Instead, enter any needed numbers into data cells and then refer to the data cells as needed. For example, in the Everglade problem (Figure 4.5), all the data (the interest rates, starting balance, minimum cash, and projected cash flows) are entered into separate data cells on the spreadsheet. When these numbers are needed to calculate the interest charges (in columns F and G), loan payments (in column H and I), ending balances (column J), and minimum balances (column L), the data cells are referred to rather than entering these numbers directly in the formulas.

Separating the data from the formulas has a couple advantages. First, all the data are visible on the spreadsheet rather than buried in formulas. Seeing all the data makes the model easier to interpret. Second, the model is easier to modify since changing data only requires modifying the corresponding data cells. You don't need to modify any formulas. This proves to be very important when it comes time to perform what-if analysis to see what the effect would be if some of the estimates in the data cells were to take on other plausible values.

Keep It Simple

Make the spreadsheet as easy to interpret as possible.

Avoid the use of powerful Excel functions when simpler functions are available that are easier to interpret. As much as possible, stick to SUMPRODUCT or SUM functions. This makes the model easier to understand and also helps to ensure that the model will be linear. (Linear models are considerably easier to solve than others.) Try to keep formulas short and simple. If a complicated formula is required, break it out into intermediate calculations with subtotals. For example, in the Everglade spreadsheet, each element of the loan payments is broken out explicitly: LT Interest, ST Interest, LT Payback, and ST Payback. Some of these columns could have been combined (e.g., into two columns with LT Payments and ST Payments, or even into one column for all Loan Payments). However, this makes the formulas more complicated and also makes the model harder to test and debug. As laid out, the individual formulas for the loan payments are so simple that their values can be predicted easily without even looking at the formula. This simplifies the testing and debugging of the model.

Use Range Names

Range names make formulas much easier to interpret.

One way to refer to a block of related cells (or even a single cell) in a spreadsheet formula is to use its cell address (e.g., L11:L21 or C3). However, when reading the formula, this requires looking at that part of the spreadsheet to see what kind of information is given there. A better alternative is to assign a descriptive **range name** to the block of cells that immediately identifies what is there. (This is done by selecting the block of cells, clicking on the name box on the left of the formula bar above the spreadsheet, and then typing a name.) This is especially helpful when writing a formula for an output cell. Writing the formula in terms of range names instead of cell addresses makes the formula much easier to interpret. Range names also make the description of the model in the Solver dialogue box much easier to understand.

Figure 4.5 illustrates the use of range names for the Everglade spreadsheet model. For example, consider the formula for long-term interest in cell F12. Since the long-term rate is given in cell C3 and the long-term loan amount is in cell D11, the formula for the long-term interest could have been written as $= -C3*D11$. However, by using the range name LTRate for cell C3 and the range name LTLoan for cell D11, the formula instead becomes $= -LTRate*LTLoan$, which is much easier to interpret at a glance.

On the other hand, be aware that it is easy to get carried away with defining range names. Defining too many range names can be more trouble than it is worth. For example, when related data are grouped together in a table, we recommend giving a range name only for the entire table rather than for the individual rows and columns. In general, we suggest defining range names only for each group of data cells, the changing cells, the target cell, and both sides of each group of constraints (the left-hand side and the right-hand side).

Spaces are not allowed in range names. When a range name has more than one word, we have used capital letters to distinguish the start of each new word in a range name (e.g., MinimumBalance). Another way is to use the underscore character (e.g., Minimum_Balance).

Care also should be taken to assure that it is easy to quickly identify which cells are referred to by a particular range name. Use a name that corresponds exactly to the label on the spreadsheet. For example, in Figure 4.5, columns J and L are labeled Ending Balance and Minimum Balance on the spreadsheet, so we use the range names EndingBalance and MinimumBalance. Using exactly the same name as the label on the spreadsheet makes it quick and easy to find the cells that are referred to by a range name.

When desired, a list of all the range names and their corresponding cell addresses can be pasted directly into the spreadsheet by choosing Paste from the Use in Formula menu on the Formulas tab (for Excel 2007) or Name\Paste from the Insert menu (for earlier versions of Excel), and then clicking Paste List. Such a list (after reformatting) is included below essentially all the spreadsheets displayed in this text.

When modifying an existing model that utilizes range names, care should be taken to assure that the range names continue to refer to the correct range of cells. When inserting a row or column into a spreadsheet model, it is helpful to insert the row or column into the middle of a range rather than at the end. For example, to add another product to a product-mix model with four products, add a column between products 2 and 3 rather than after product 4. This will automatically extend the relevant range names to span across all five columns since these range names will continue to refer to everything between product 1 and product 4, including the newly inserted column for the fifth product. Similarly, deleting a row or column from the middle of a range will contract the span of the relevant range names appropriately. You can double-check the cells that are referred to by a range name by choosing that range name from the name box (on the left of the formula bar above the spreadsheet). This will highlight the cells that are referred to by the chosen range name.

Use Relative and Absolute References to Simplify Copying Formulas

Excel's fill commands provide a quick and reliable way to replicate a formula into multiple cells.

Whenever multiple related formulas will be needed, try to enter the formula just once and then use Excel's fill commands to replicate the formula. Not only is this quicker than retyping the formula, but it is also less prone to error.

We saw a good example of this when discussing the expansion of the model to full-scale size in the preceding section. Starting with the two-year spreadsheet in Figure 4.3, fill commands were used to copy the formulas in columns F, G, I, J, and L for the remaining years to create the full-scale, 10-year spreadsheet in Figure 4.4.

Using relative and absolute references for related formulas not only aids in building a model but also makes it easier to modify an existing model or template. For example, suppose that you have formulated a spreadsheet model for a product-mix problem but now wish to modify the model to add another resource. This requires inserting a row into the spreadsheet. If the output cells are written with proper relative and absolute references, then it is simple to copy the existing formulas into the inserted row.

Use Borders, Shading, and Colors to Distinguish between Cell Types

Make it easy to spot all the cells of the same type.

It is important to be able to easily distinguish between the data cells, changing cells, output cells, and target cell in a spreadsheet. One way to do this is to use different borders and cell shading for each of these different types of cells. In the text, data cells appear lightly shaded, changing cells are shaded a medium amount with a light border, output cells appear with no shading, and the target cell is shaded darkly with a heavy border.

In the spreadsheet files in MS Courseware, data cells are light blue, changing cells are yellow, and the target cell is orange. Obviously, you may use any scheme that you like. The important thing is to be consistent, so that you can quickly recognize the types of cells. Then, when you want to examine the cells of a certain type, the color will immediately guide you there.

Show the Entire Model on the Spreadsheet

The Solver uses a combination of the spreadsheet and the Solver dialogue box to specify the model to be solved. Therefore, it is possible to include certain elements of the model (such as the $\leq$, $=$, or $\geq$ signs and/or the right-hand sides of the constraints) in the Solver dialogue box without displaying them in the spreadsheet. However, we strongly recommend that *every* element of the model be displayed *on the spreadsheet.* Every person using or adapting the model, or referring back to it later, needs to be able to interpret the model. This is much easier to do by viewing the model on the spreadsheet than by trying to decipher it from the Solver dialogue box. Furthermore, a printout of the spreadsheet does not include information from the Solver dialogue box.

In particular, all the elements of a constraint should be displayed on the spreadsheet. For each constraint, three adjacent cells should be used for the total of the left-hand side, the $\leq$, $=$, or $\geq$ sign in the middle, and the right-hand side. (Note in Figure 4.5 that this was done in columns J, K, and L of the spreadsheet for the Everglade problem.) As mentioned earlier, the changing cells and target cell should be highlighted in some manner (e.g., with borders and/or cell shading). A good test is that you should not need to go to the Solver dialogue box to determine any element of the model. You should be able to identify the changing cells, the target cell, and all the constraints in the model just by looking at the spreadsheet.

Display every element of the model on the spreadsheet rather than relying on only the Solver dialogue box to include certain elements.

A Poor Spreadsheet Model

It is certainly possible to set up a linear programming spreadsheet model without utilizing any of these ideas. Figure 4.7 shows an alternative spreadsheet formulation for the Everglade problem that violates nearly every one of these guidelines. This formulation can still be solved using Solver, which in fact yields the same optimal solution as in Figure 4.5. However, the

FIGURE 4.7

A poor formulation of the spreadsheet model for the Everglade cash flow management problem.

	A	B	C	D	E	F
1		**A Poor Formulation of the Everglade Cash Flow Problem**				
2						
3			LT	ST	Ending	
4		Year	Loan	Loan	Balance	
5		2007	6.65	0.85	0.50	
6		2008		3.40	0.50	
7		2009		8.21	0.50	
8		2010		6.49	0.50	
9		2011		1.61	0.50	
10		2012		0	1.27	
11		2013		3.70	0.50	
12		2014		0	2.97	
13		2015		0	0.50	
14		2016		0	10.03	
15		2017			2.92	

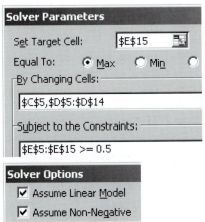

	E
3	Ending
4	Balance
5	=1–8+C5+D5
6	=E5–2+D6–$C$5*(0.07)–D5*(1.1)
7	=E6–4+D7–$C$5*(0.07)–D6*(1.1)
8	=E7+3+D8–$C$5*(0.07)–D7*(1.1)
9	=E8+6+D9–$C$5*(0.07)–D8*(1.1)
10	=E9+3+D10–$C$5*(0.07)–D9*(1.1)
11	=E10–4+D11–$C$5*(0.07)–D10*(1.1)
12	=E11+7+D12–$C$5*(0.07)–D11*(1.1)
13	=E12–2+D13–$C$5*(0.07)–D12*(1.1)
14	=E13+10+D14–$C$5*(0.07)–D13*(1.1)
15	=E14+D15–$C$5*(1.07)–D14*(1.1)

formulation has many problems. It is not clear which cells yield the solution (borders and/or shading are not used to highlight the changing cells and target cell). Without going to the Solver dialogue box, the constraints in the model cannot be identified (the spreadsheet does not show the entire model). The spreadsheet also does not show most of the data. For example, to determine the data used for the projected cash flows, the interest rates, or the starting balance, you need to dig into the formulas in column E (the data are not separate from the formulas). If any of these data change, the actual formulas need to be modified rather than simply changing a number on the spreadsheet. Furthermore, the formulas and the model in the Solver dialogue box are difficult to interpret (range names are not utilized).

Compare Figures 4.5 and 4.7. Applying the guidelines for good spreadsheet models (as is done for Figure 4.5) results in a model that is easier to understand, easier to debug, and easier to modify. This is especially important for models that will have a long life span. If this model is going to be reused months later, the "good" model of Figure 4.5 immediately can be understood, modified, and reapplied as needed, whereas deciphering the spreadsheet model of Figure 4.7 again would be a great challenge.

Review Questions

1. Which part of the model should be entered first on the spreadsheet?
2. Should numbers be included in formulas or entered separately in data cells?
3. How do range names make formulas and the model in the Solver dialogue box easier to interpret? How should range names be chosen?
4. What are some ways to distinguish data cells, changing cells, output cells, and target cells on a spreadsheet?
5. How many cells are needed to completely specify a constraint on a spreadsheet?

4.4 DEBUGGING A SPREADSHEET MODEL

Debugging a spreadsheet model sometimes is as challenging as debugging a computer program.

No matter how carefully it is planned and built, even a moderately complicated model usually will not be error-free the first time it is run. Often the mistakes are immediately obvious and quickly corrected. However, sometimes an error is harder to root out. Following the guidelines in Section 4.3 for developing a good spreadsheet model can make the model *much* easier to debug. Even so, much like debugging a computer program, debugging a spreadsheet model can be a difficult task. This section presents some tips and a variety of Excel features that can make debugging easier.

As a first step in debugging a spreadsheet model, test the model using the principles discussed in the first subsection on testing in Section 4.2. In particular, try different values for the changing cells for which you can predict the correct result in the output cells and see if they calculate as expected. Values of 0 are good ones to try initially because usually it is then obvious what should be in the output cells. Try other simple values, such as all 1s, where the correct results in the output cells are reasonably obvious. For more complicated values, break out a calculator and do some manual calculations to check the various output cells. Include some very large values for the changing cells to ensure that the calculations are behaving reasonably for these extreme cases.

If you have added rows or columns to the spreadsheet, make sure that each of the range names still refers to the correct cells.

If you have defined range names, be sure that they still refer to the correct cells. Sometimes they can become disjointed when you add rows or columns to the spreadsheet. To test the range names, you can either select the various range names in the name box, which will highlight the selected range in the spreadsheet, or paste the entire list of range names and their references into the spreadsheet.

toggle
The toggle feature in Excel is a great way to check the formulas for the output cells.

Carefully study each formula to be sure it is entered correctly. A very useful feature in Excel for checking formulas is the **toggle** to switch back and forth between viewing the formulas in the worksheet and viewing the resulting values in the output cells. By default, Excel shows the values that are calculated by the various output cells in the model. Typing control-~ on a PC (or command-~ on a Mac) switches the current worksheet to instead display the formulas in the output cells, as shown in Figure 4.8. Typing control-~ again switches back to the standard view of displaying the values in the output cells (like Figure 4.5).

FIGURE 4.8

The spreadsheet obtained by toggling the spreadsheet in Figure 4.5 once to replace the values in the output cells by the formulas entered into those cells. Using the toggle feature in Excel once more will restore the view of the spreadsheet shown in Figure 4.5.

	A	B	C	D	E	F	G	H	I	J	K	L
1		Everglade Cash Flow Management Problem										
2												
3		LT Rate	0.07									
4		ST Rate	0.1									
5						(all cash figures in millions of dollars)						
6		Start Balance	1									
7		Minimum Cash	0.5									
8												
9			Cash	LT	ST	LT	ST	LT	ST	Ending		Minimum
10		Year	Flow	Loan	Loan	Interest	Interest	Payback	Payback	Balance		Balance
11		2007	−8	6.64945	0.85054	=−LTRate*LTLoan	=−STRate*E11		=−E11	=StartBalance+SUM(C11:I11)	≥	=MinimumCash
12		2008	−2		3.40105	=−LTRate*LTLoan	=−STRate*E12		=−E12	=J11+SUM(C12:I12)	≥	=MinimumCash
13		2009	−4		8.20662	=−LTRate*LTLoan	=−STRate*E13		=−E13	=J12+SUM(C13:I13)	≥	=MinimumCash
14		2010	3		6.49274	=−LTRate*LTLoan	=−STRate*E14		=−E14	=J13+SUM(C14:I14)	≥	=MinimumCash
15		2011	6		1.60748	=−LTRate*LTLoan	=−STRate*E15		=−E15	=J14+SUM(C15:I15)	≥	=MinimumCash
16		2012	3		0	=−LTRate*LTLoan	=−STRate*E16		=−E16	=J15+SUM(C16:I16)	≥	=MinimumCash
17		2013	−4		3.69915	=−LTRate*LTLoan	=−STRate*E17		=−E17	=J16+SUM(C17:I17)	≥	=MinimumCash
18		2014	7		0	=−LTRate*LTLoan	=−STRate*E18		=−E18	=J17+SUM(C18:I18)	≥	=MinimumCash
19		2015	−2		0	=−LTRate*LTLoan	=−STRate*E19		=−E19	=J18+SUM(C19:I19)	≥	=MinimumCash
20		2016	10		0	=−LTRate*LTLoan	=−STRate*E20		=−E20	=J19+SUM(C20:I20)	≥	=MinimumCash
21		2017				=−LTRate*LTLoan	=−STRate*E20	=−LTLoan		=J20+SUM(C21:I21)	≥	=MinimumCash

Excel Tip: Pressing control-~ on a PC (or command-~ on a Mac) toggles the worksheet between viewing values and viewing formulas in all the output cells.

Another useful set of features built into Excel are the **auditing tools.** The auditing tools are available in the Formula Auditing group of the Formulas Tab (for Excel 2007) or under the Tools\Auditing menu (for earlier versions of Excel).

The auditing tools can be used to graphically display which cells make direct links to a given cell. For example, selecting LTLoan (D11) in Figure 4.5 and then Trace Dependents generates the arrows on the spreadsheet shown in Figure 4.9.

You now can immediately see that LTLoan (D11) is used in the calculation of LT Interest for every year in column F, in the calculation of LTPayback (H21), and in the calculation of the ending balance in 2007 (J11). This can be very illuminating. Think about what output cells LTLoan should impact directly. There should be an arrow to each of these cells. If, for example, LTLoan is missing from any of the formulas in column F, the error will be immediately revealed by the missing arrow. Similarly, if LTLoan is mistakenly entered in any of the short-term loan output cells, this will show up as extra arrows.

Excel's auditing tools enable you to either trace forward or backward to see the linkages between cells.

You also can trace backward to see which cells provide the data for any given cell. These can be displayed graphically by choosing Trace Precedents. For example, choosing Trace Precedents for the ST Interest cell for 2008 (G12) displays the arrows shown in Figure 4.10. These arrows indicate that the ST Interest cell for 2008 (G12) refers to the ST Loan in 2007 (E11) and to STRate (C4).

When you are done, choose Remove Arrows.

Review Questions

1. What is a good first step for debugging a spreadsheet model?
2. How do you toggle between viewing formulas and viewing values in output cells?
3. Which Excel tool can be used to trace the dependents or precedents for a given cell?

FIGURE 4.9

The spreadsheet obtained by using the Excel auditing tools to trace the dependents of the LT Loan value in cell D11 of the spreadsheet in Figure 4.5.

	A	B	C	D	E	F	G	H	I	J	K	L
1		**Everglade Cash Flow Management Problem**										
2												
3		LT Rate	7%									
4		ST Rate	10%									
5						(all cash figures in millions of dollars)						
6		Start Balance	1									
7		Minimum Cash	0.5									
8												
9			Cash	LT	ST	LT	ST	LT	ST	Ending		Minimum
10		Year	Flow	Loan	Loan	Interest	Interest	Payback	Payback	Balance		Balance
11	2007	−8	6.65	0.85						0.50	≥	0.5
12	2008	−2		3.40	−0.47	−0.09		−0.85	0.50	≥	0.5
13	2009	−4		8.21	−0.47	−0.34		−3.40	0.50	≥	0.5
14	2010	3		6.49	−0.47	−0.82		−8.21	0.50	≥	0.5
15	2011	6		1.61	−0.47	−0.65		−6.49	0.50	≥	0.5
16	2012	3		0	0.47	−0.16		−1.61	1.27	≥	0.5
17	2013	−4		3.70	−0.47	0		0	0.50	≥	0.5
18	2014	7		0	−0.47	−0.37		−3.70	2.97	≥	0.5
19	2015	−2		0	−0.47	0		0	0.50	≥	0.5
20	2016	10		0	−0.47	0		0	10.03	≥	0.5
21	2017				−0.47	0	−6.65	0	2.92	≥	0.5

FIGURE 4.10

The spreadsheet obtained by using the Excel auditing tools to trace the precedents of the ST Interest (2008) calculation in cell G12 of the spreadsheet in Figure 4.5.

	A	B	C	D	E	F	G	H	I	J	K	L
1		**Everglade Cash Flow Management Problem**										
2												
3		LT Rate	7%									
4		ST Rate	●10%									
5						(all cash figures in millions of dollars)						
6		Start Balance	1									
7		Minimum Cash	0.5									
8												
9			Cash	LT	ST	LT	ST	LT	ST	Ending		Minimum
10		Year	Flow	Loan	Loan	Interest	Interest	Payback	Payback	Balance		Balance
11		2007	−8	6.65	●0.85					0.50	≥	0.5
12		2008	−2		3.40	−0.47	−0.09		−0.85	0.50	≥	0.5
13		2009	−4		8.21	−0.47	−0.34		−3.40	0.50	≥	0.5
14		2010	3		6.49	−0.47	−0.82		−8.21	0.50	≥	0.5
15		2011	6		1.61	−0.47	−0.65		−6.49	0.50	≥	0.5
16		2012	3		0	−0.47	−0.16		−1.61	1.27	≥	0.5
17		2013	−4		3.70	−0.47	0		0	0.50	≥	0.5
18		2014	7		0	−0.47	−0.37		−3.70	2.97	≥	0.5
19		2015	−2		0	−0.47	0		0	0.50	≥	0.5
20		2016	10		0	−0.47	0		0	10.03	≥	0.5
21		2017				−0.47	0	−6.65	0	2.92	≥	0.5

4.5 Summary

There is a considerable art to modeling well with spreadsheets. This chapter focuses on providing a foundation for learning this art.

The general process of modeling in spreadsheets has four major steps: (1) plan the spreadsheet model, (2) build the model, (3) test the model, and (4) analyze the model and its results. During the planning step, it is helpful to begin by visualizing where you want to finish and then doing some calculations by hand to clarify the needed computations before starting to sketch out a logical layout for the spreadsheet. Then, when you are ready to undertake the building step, it is a good idea to start by building a small, readily manageable version of the model before expanding the model to full-scale size. This enables you to test the small version first to get all the logic straightened out correctly before expanding to a full-scale model and undertaking a final test. After completing all of this, you are ready for the analysis step, which involves applying the model to evaluate proposed solutions and perhaps using Solver to optimize the model.

Using this plan-build-test-analyze process should yield a spreadsheet model, but it doesn't guarantee that you will obtain a good one. Section 4.3 describes in detail the following guidelines for building "good" spreadsheet models:

- Enter the data first.
- Organize and clearly identify the data.
- Enter each piece of data into one cell only.
- Separate data from formulas.
- Keep it simple.
- Use range names.
- Use relative and absolute references to simplify copying formulas.
- Use borders, shading, and colors to distinguish between cell types.
- Show the entire model on the spreadsheet.

Even if all these guidelines are followed, a thorough debugging process may be needed to eliminate the errors that lurk within the initial version of the model. It is important to check whether the output cells are giving correct results for various values of the changing cells. Other items to check include whether range names refer to the appropriate cells and whether formulas have been entered into output cells correctly. Excel provides a number of useful features to aid in the debugging process. One is the ability to toggle the worksheet between viewing the results in the output cells and the formulas entered into those output cells. Several other helpful features are available with Excel's auditing tools.

Glossary

auditing tools   A set of tools provided by Excel to aid in debugging a spreadsheet model. (Section 4.4), 134

range name   A descriptive name given to a block of cells that immediately identifies what is there. (Section 4.3), 129

toggle   The act of switching back and forth between viewing the results in the output cells and viewing the formulas entered into those output cells. (Section 4.4), 132

Learning Aids for This Chapter in Your MS Courseware

Chapter 4 Excel Files:

Everglade Case Study
Wyndor Example

An Excel Add-in:

Premium Solver for Education

Solved Problems (See the CD-ROM for the Solutions)

4.S1. Production and Inventory Planning Model

Surfs Up produces high-end surfboards. Their production facility can produce at most 50 boards per month. A challenge faced by Surfs Up is that their demand is highly seasonal. Demand exceeds production capacity during the warm summer months, but is very low in the winter months. To meet the high demand during the summer, Surfs Up typically produces more surfboards than are needed in the winter months and then carries inventory into the summer months. The production cost of a surfboard is $125. The boards are sold for $200. Because of storage cost and the opportunity cost of capital, each board held in inventory from one month to the next incurs a cost of $5 per board. Since demand is uncertain, Surfs Up would like to maintain an ending inventory (safety stock) of at least 10 boards during the warm months (May–September) and at least 5 boards during the other months (October–April). It is now the start of January and Surfs Up has 5 boards in inventory. The forecast of demand over the next 12 months is shown in the table below. Formulate and solve a linear programming model in a spreadsheet to determine how many surfboards should be produced each month to maximize total profit.

Forecasted Demand

Jan.	Feb.	Mar.	Apr.	May	June	July	Aug.	Sept.	Oct.	Nov.	Dec.
10	14	15	20	45	65	85	85	40	30	15	15

4.S2. Aggregate Planning: Manpower Hiring/Firing/Training

Cool Power produces air-conditioning units for large commercial properties. Because of the low cost and efficiency of its products, the company has been growing from year to year. Also, seasonality in construction and weather conditions create production requirements that vary from month to month. Cool Power currently has 10 fully trained employees working in manufacturing. Each trained employee can work 160 hours per month and is paid a monthly wage of $4,000. New trainees can be hired at the beginning of any month. Because of their lack of initial skills and required training, a new trainee provides only 100 hours of useful labor in the first month, but is still paid a full monthly wage of $4,000. Furthermore, because of required interviewing and training, there is a $2,500 hiring cost for each employee hired. After one month, a trainee is considered fully trained. An employee can be fired at the beginning of any month, but must be paid two weeks of severance pay ($2,000). Over the next 12 months, Cool Power forecasts the labor requirements shown in the table on the next page. Since management anticipates higher requirements next year, Cool Power would like to end the year with at least 12 fully trained employees. How many trainees should be hired and/or workers fired in each month to meet the labor requirements at the minimum possible cost? Formulate and solve a linear programming spreadsheet model.

Labor Requirements (hours)

Jan.	Feb.	Mar.	Apr.	May	June	July	Aug.	Sept.	Oct.	Nov.	Dec.
1,600	2,000	2,000	2,000	2,800	3,200	3,600	3,200	1,600	1,200	800	800

Problems

We have inserted the symbol E* (for Excel) to the left of each problem or part where Excel should be used. An asterisk on the problem number indicates that at least a partial answer is given in the back of the book.

E*4.1.   Consider the Everglade cash flow problem discussed in this chapter. Suppose that extra cash is kept in an interest-bearing savings account. Assume that any cash left at the end of a year earns 3 percent interest the following year. Make any necessary modifications to the spreadsheet and re-solve. (The original spreadsheet for this problem is available on the CD-ROM.)

4.2.*   The Pine Furniture Company makes fine country furniture. The company's current product lines consist of end tables, coffee tables, and dining room tables. The production of each of these tables requires 8, 15, and 80 pounds of pine wood, respectively. The tables are handmade and require one hour, two hours, and four hours, respectively. Each table sold generates $50, $100, and $220 profit, respectively. The company has 3,000 pounds of pine wood and 200 hours of labor available for the coming week's production. The chief operating officer (COO) has asked you to do some spreadsheet modeling with these data to analyze what the product mix should be for the coming week and make a recommendation.

    a. Visualize where you want to finish. What numbers will the COO need? What are the decisions that need to be made? What should the objective be?

    b. Suppose that Pine Furniture were to produce three end tables and three dining room tables. Calculate by hand the amount of pine wood and labor that would be required, as well as the profit generated from sales.

    c. Make a rough sketch of a spreadsheet model, with blocks laid out for the data cells, changing cells, output cells, and target cell.

E*   *d.* Build a spreadsheet model and then solve it.

4.3.   Reboot, Inc., is a manufacturer of hiking boots. Demand for boots is highly seasonal. In particular, the demand in the next year is expected to be 3,000, 4,000, 8,000, and 7,000 pairs of boots in quarters 1, 2, 3, and 4, respectively. With its current production facility, the company can produce at most 6,000 pairs of boots in any quarter. Reboot would like to meet all the expected demand, so it will need to carry inventory to meet demand in the later quarters. Each pair of boots sold generates a profit of $20 per pair. Each pair of boots in inventory at the end of a quarter incurs $8 in storage and capital recovery costs. Reboot has 1,000 pairs of boots in inventory at the start of quarter 1. Reboot's top management has given you the assignment of doing some spreadsheet modeling to analyze what the production schedule should be for the next four quarters and make a recommendation.

    a. Visualize where you want to finish. What numbers will top management need? What are the decisions that need to be made? What should the objective be?

    b. Suppose that Reboot were to produce 5,000 pairs of boots in each of the first two quarters. Calculate by hand the ending inventory, profit from sales, and inventory costs for quarters 1 and 2.

    c. Make a rough sketch of a spreadsheet model, with blocks laid out for the data cells, changing cells, output cells, and target cell.

E*   *d.* Build a spreadsheet model for quarters 1 and 2, and then thoroughly test the model.

E*   *e.* Expand the model to full scale and then solve it.

E*4.4.*   The Fairwinds Development Corporation is considering taking part in one or more of three different development projects—A, B, and C—that are about to be launched. Each project requires a significant investment over the next few years and then would be sold upon completion. The projected cash flows (in millions of dollars) associated with each project are shown in the table below.

Year	Project A	Project B	Project C
1	−4	−8	−10
2	−6	−8	−7
3	−6	−4	−7
4	24	−4	−5
5	0	30	−3
6	0	0	44

Fairwinds has $10 million available now and expects to receive $6 million from other projects by the end of each year (1 through 6) that would be available for the ongoing investments the following year in projects A, B, and C. By acting now, the company may participate in each project either fully, fractionally (with other development partners), or not at all. If Fairwinds participates at less than 100 percent, then all the cash flows associated with that project are reduced proportionally. Company policy requires ending each year with a cash balance of at least $1 million.

    a. Visualize where you want to finish. What numbers are needed? What are the decisions that need to be made? What should the objective be?

    b. Suppose that Fairwinds were to participate in Project A fully and in Project C at 50 percent. Calculate by hand what the ending cash positions would be after year 1 and year 2.

c. Make a rough sketch of a spreadsheet model, with blocks laid out for the data cells, changing cells, output cells, and target cell.

E* *d.* Build a spreadsheet model for years 1 and 2, and then thoroughly test the model.

E* *e.* Expand the model to full scale, and then solve it.

4.5. Refer to the scenario described in Problem 3.12 (Chapter 3), but ignore the instructions given there. Focus instead on using spreadsheet modeling to address Web Mercantile's problem by doing the following.

a. Visualize where you want to finish. What numbers will Web Mercantile require? What are the decisions that need to be made? What should the objective be?

b. Suppose that Web Mercantile were to lease 30,000 square feet for all five months and then 20,000 additional square feet for the last three months. Calculate the total costs by hand.

c. Make a rough sketch of a spreadsheet model, with blocks laid out for the data cells, changing cells, output cells, and target cell.

E* *d.* Build a spreadsheet model for months 1 and 2, and then thoroughly test the model.

E* *e.* Expand the model to full scale, and then solve it.

4.6.* Refer to the scenario described in Problem 3.14 (Chapter 3), but ignore the instructions given there. Focus instead on using spreadsheet modeling to address Larry Edison's problem by doing the following.

a. Visualize where you want to finish. What numbers will Larry require? What are the decisions that need to be made? What should the objective be?

b. Suppose that Larry were to hire three full-time workers for the morning shift, two for the afternoon shift,

and four for the evening shift, as well as three part-time workers for each of the four shifts. Calculate by hand how many workers would be working at each time of the day and what the total cost would be for the entire day.

c. Make a rough sketch of a spreadsheet model, with blocks laid out for the data cells, changing cells, output cells, and target cell.

E* *d.* Build a spreadsheet model and then solve it.

4.7. Refer to the scenario described in Problem 3.17 (Chapter 3), but ignore the instructions given there. Focus instead on using spreadsheet modeling to address Al Ferris's problem by doing the following.

a. Visualize where you want to finish. What numbers will Al require? What are the decisions that need to be made? What should the objective be?

b. Suppose that Al were to invest $20,000 each in investment *A* (year 1), investment *B* (year 2), and investment *C* (year 2). Calculate by hand what the ending cash position would be after each year.

c. Make a rough sketch of a spreadsheet model, with blocks laid out for the data cells, changing cells, output cells, and target cell.

E* *d.* Build a spreadsheet model for years 1 through 3, and then thoroughly test the model.

E* *e.* Expand the model to full scale, and then solve it.

4.8. In contrast to the spreadsheet model for the Wyndor Glass Co. product-mix problem shown in Figure 4.6, the spreadsheet given below is an example of a poorly formulated spreadsheet model for this same problem. Referring to Section 4.3, identify the guidelines violated by the model below. Then, explain how each guideline has been violated and why the model in Figure 4.6 is a better alternative.

E* 4.9. Refer to the spreadsheet file named "Everglade Problem 4.9" contained on the CD-ROM. This file contains a formulation of the Everglade problem considered in this chapter. However, three errors are included in this formulation. Use the ideas presented in Section 4.4 for debugging a spreadsheet model to find the errors. In particular, try different trial values for which you can predict the correct results, use the toggle to examine all the formulas, and use the auditing tools to check precedence and dependence relationships among the various changing cells, data cells, and output cells. Describe the errors found and how you found them.

E*4.10. Refer to the spreadsheet file named "Everglade Problem 4.10" contained on the CD-ROM. This file contains a formulation of the Everglade problem considered in this chapter. However, three errors are included in this formulation. Use the ideas presented in Section 4.4 for debugging a spreadsheet model to find the errors. In particular, try different trial values for which you can predict the correct results, use the toggle to examine all the formulas, and use the auditing tools to check precedence and dependence relationships among the various changing cells, data cells, and output cells. Describe the errors found and how you found them.

Case 4-1

Prudent Provisions for Pensions

Among its many financial products, the Prudent Financial Services Corporation (normally referred to as PFS) manages a well-regarded pension fund that is used by a number of companies to provide pensions for their employees. PFS's management takes pride in the rigorous professional standards used in operating the fund. Since the Enron collapse in late 2001 and the subsequent tightening of federal and state regulations for operating pension funds, PFS has redoubled its efforts to provide prudent management of the fund.

It is now December 2006. The total pension payments that will need to be made by the fund over the next 10 years are shown in the table below.

Year	Pension Payments ($ millions)
2007	8
2008	12
2009	13
2010	14
2011	16
2012	17
2013	20
2014	21
2015	22
2016	24

By using interest as well, PFS currently has enough liquid assets to meet all these pension payments. Therefore, to safeguard the pension fund, PFS would like to make a number of investments whose payouts would match the pension payments over the next 10 years. The only investments that PFS trusts for the pension fund are a money market fund and bonds. The money market fund pays an annual interest rate of 5 percent. The characteristics of each unit of the four bonds under consideration are shown in the table below.

	Current Price	Coupon Rate	Maturity Date	Face Value
Bond 1	$980	4%	Jan. 1, 2008	$1,000
Bond 2	920	2	Jan. 1, 2010	1,000
Bond 3	750	0	Jan. 1, 2012	1,000
Bond 4	800	3	Jan. 1, 2015	1,000

All of these bonds will be available for purchase on January 1, 2007, in as many units as desired. The coupon rate is the percentage of the face value that will be paid in interest on January 1 of each year, starting one year after purchase and continuing until (and including) the maturity date. Thus, these interest payments on January 1 of each year are in time to be used toward the pension payments for that year. Any excess interest payments will be deposited into the money market fund. To be conservative in its financial planning, PFS assumes that all the pension payments for the year occur at the beginning of the year immediately after these interest payments (including a year's interest from the money market fund) are received. The entire face value of a bond also will be received on its maturity date. Since the current price of each bond is less than its face value, the actual yield of the bond exceeds its coupon rate. Bond 3 is a zero-coupon bond, so it pays no interest but instead pays a face value on the maturity date that greatly exceeds the purchase price.

PFS would like to make the smallest possible investment (including any deposit into the money market fund) on January 1, 2007, to cover all its required pension payments through 2016. Some spreadsheet modeling needs to be done to see how to do this.

a. Visualize where you want to finish. What numbers are needed by PFS management? What are the decisions that need to be made? What should the objective be?

b. Suppose that PFS were to invest $28 million in the money market fund and purchase 10,000 units each of bond 1 and bond 2 on January 1, 2007. Calculate by hand the payments received from bonds 1 and 2 on January 1 of 2008 and 2009. Also calculate the resulting balance in the money market fund on January 1 of 2007, 2008, and 2009 after receiving these payments, making the pension payments for the year, and depositing any excess into the money market fund.

c. Make a rough sketch of a spreadsheet model, with blocks laid out for the data cells, changing cells, output cells, and target cell.

d. Build a spreadsheet model for years 2007 through 2009, and then thoroughly test the model.

e. Expand the model to consider all years through 2016, and then solve it.

Chapter **Five**

What-If Analysis for Linear Programming

Learning objectives

After completing this chapter, you should be able to

1. Explain what is meant by *what-if analysis.*
2. Summarize the benefits of what-if analysis.
3. Enumerate the different kinds of changes in the model that can be considered by what-if analysis.
4. Describe how the spreadsheet formulation of the problem can be used to perform any of these kinds of what-if analysis.
5. Use the Solver Table to systematically investigate the effect of changing either one or two data cells to various other trial values.
6. Find how much any single coefficient in the objective function can change without changing the optimal solution.
7. Evaluate simultaneous changes in objective function coefficients to determine whether the changes are small enough that the original optimal solution must still be optimal.
8. Predict how the value in the target cell would change if a small change were to be made in the right-hand side of one or more of the functional constraints.
9. Find how much the right-hand side of a single functional constraint can change before this prediction becomes no longer valid.
10. Evaluate simultaneous changes in right-hand sides to determine whether the changes are small enough that this prediction must still be valid.

Chapters 2 to 4 have described and illustrated how to formulate a linear programming model on a spreadsheet to represent a variety of managerial problems, and then how to use the Solver to find an optimal solution for this model. You might think that this would finish our story about linear programming: Once the manager learns the optimal solution, she would immediately implement this solution and then turn her attention to other matters. However, this is not the case. The enlightened manager demands much more from linear programming, and linear programming has much more to offer her—as you will discover in this chapter.

An optimal solution is only optimal with respect to a particular mathematical model that provides only a rough representation of the real problem. A manager is interested in much more than just finding such a solution. The purpose of a linear programming study is to help guide management's final decision by providing insights into the likely consequences of pursuing various managerial options under a variety of assumptions about future conditions. Most of the important insights are gained while conducting analysis *after* finding an optimal solution for the original version of the basic model. This analysis is commonly referred to as **what-if analysis** because it involves addressing some questions about *what* would happen to the optimal solution *if* different assumptions were made about future conditions. Spreadsheets play a central role in addressing these *what-if questions.*

This chapter focuses on the types of information provided by what-if analysis and why it is valuable to managers. The first section provides an overview. Section 5.2 returns to the Wyndor Glass Co. product-mix case study (Section 2.1) to describe the what-if analysis that is needed in this situation. The subsequent sections then flesh out the picture in the context of this case study.

5.1 THE IMPORTANCE OF WHAT-IF ANALYSIS TO MANAGERS

In real applications, many of the numbers in the model may be only rough estimates.

The examples and problems in the preceding chapters on linear programming have provided the data needed to determine precisely all the numbers that should go into the data cells for the spreadsheet formulation of the linear programming model. (Recall that these numbers are referred to as the **parameters of the model.**) Real applications seldom are this straightforward. Substantial time and effort often are needed to track down the needed data. Even then, it may be possible to develop only rough estimates of the parameters of the model.

For example, in the Wyndor case study, two key parameters of the model are the coefficients in the objective function that represent the unit profits of the two new products. These parameters were estimated to be $300 for the doors and $500 for the windows. However, what these unit profits actually will turn out to be depends on many factors—the costs of raw materials, production, shipping, advertising, and so on, as well as such things as the market reception to the new products and the amount of competition encountered. Some of these factors cannot be estimated with real accuracy until long after the linear programming study has been completed and the new products have been on the market for some time.

Therefore, before Wyndor's management makes a decision on the product mix, it will want to know what the effect would be if the unit profits turn out to differ significantly from the estimates. For example, would the optimal solution change if the unit profit for the doors turned out to be $200 instead of the estimate of $300? How inaccurate can the estimate be in either direction before the optimal solution changes?

Such questions are addressed in Section 5.3 when only one estimate is inaccurate. Section 5.4 will address similar questions when multiple estimates are inaccurate.

What happens to the optimal solution if an error is made in estimating a parameter of the model?

If the optimal solution will remain the same over a wide range of values for a particular coefficient in the objective function, then management will be content with a fairly rough estimate for this coefficient. On the other hand, if even a small error in the estimate would change the optimal solution, then management will want to take special care to refine this estimate. Management sometimes will get involved directly in adjusting such estimates to its satisfaction.

Here then is a summary of the first benefit of what-if analysis:

1. Typically, many of the parameters of a linear programming model are only *estimates* of quantities (e.g., unit profits) that cannot be determined precisely at this time. What-if analysis reveals how close each of these estimates needs to be to avoid obtaining an erroneous optimal solution, and therefore pinpoints the **sensitive parameters** (those parameters where extra care is needed to refine their estimates because even small changes in their values can change the optimal solution).

Several sections describe how what-if analysis provides this benefit for the most important parameters. Sections 5.3 and 5.4 do this for the coefficients in the objective function (these numbers appear in the spreadsheet in the row for the unit contribution of each activity toward the overall measure of performance). Sections 5.5 and 5.6 do the same for the *right-hand sides of the functional constraints* (these are the numbers that typically are in the right-hand column of the spreadsheet just to the right of the ≤, ≥, or = signs).

Businesses operate in a dynamic environment. Even when management is satisfied with the current estimates and implements the corresponding optimal solution, conditions may change later. For example, suppose that Wyndor's management is satisfied with $300 as the estimate of the unit profit for the doors, but increased competition later forces a price reduction that reduces this unit profit. Does this change the optimal product mix? The what-if analysis shown in Section 5.3 immediately indicates in advance which new unit profits would leave the optimal product mix unchanged, which can help guide management in its new pricing decision. Furthermore, if the optimal product mix is unchanged, then there is no need to solve the model again with the new coefficient. Avoiding solving the model again is no big deal for the tiny two-variable Wyndor problem, but it is extremely welcome for real applications that may have hundreds or thousands of constraints and variables. In fact, for such large models, it may not even be practical to re-solve the model repeatedly to consider the many possible changes of interest.

Thus, here is the second benefit of what-if analysis:

2. If conditions change after the study has been completed (a common occurrence), what-if analysis leaves signposts that indicate (without solving the model again) whether a resulting change in a parameter of the model changes the optimal solution.

Again, several subsequent sections describe how what-if analysis does this.

These sections focus on studying how changes in the parameters of a linear programming model affect the optimal solution. This type of what-if analysis commonly is referred to as **sensitivity analysis,** because it involves checking how *sensitive* the optimal solution is to the value of each parameter. Sensitivity analysis is a vital part of what-if analysis.

However, rather than being content with the passive sensitivity analysis approach of checking the effect of parameter estimates being inaccurate, what-if analysis often goes further to take a proactive approach. An analysis may be made of various possible managerial actions that would result in changes to the model.

A prime example of this proactive approach arises when certain parameters of the model represent *managerial policy decisions* rather than quantities that are largely outside the control of management. For example, for the Wyndor product-mix problem, the right-hand sides of the three functional constraints (4, 12, 18) represent the number of hours of production time in the three respective plants being made available per week for the production of the two new products. Management can change these three resource amounts by altering the production levels for the old products in these plants. Therefore, after learning the optimal solution, management will want to know the impact on the profit from the new products if these resource amounts are changed in certain ways. One key question is how much this profit can be increased by increasing the available production time for the new products in just one of the plants. Another is how much this profit can be increased by simultaneously making helpful changes in the available production times in all the plants. If the profit from the new products can be increased enough to more than compensate for the profit lost by decreasing the production levels for certain old products, management probably will want to make the change.

We now can summarize the third benefit of what-if analysis:

3. When certain parameters of the model represent managerial policy decisions, what-if analysis provides valuable guidance to management regarding the impact of altering these policy decisions.

Sections 5.5 and 5.6 will explore this benefit further.

What-if analysis sometimes goes even further in providing helpful guidance to management, such as when analyzing alternate scenarios for how business conditions might evolve. However, this chapter will focus on the three benefits summarized above.

Review Questions

1. What are the *parameters* of a linear programming model?
2. How can inaccuracies arise in the parameters of a model?
3. What does what-if analysis reveal about the parameters of a model that are only estimates?
4. Is it always inappropriate to make only a fairly rough estimate for a parameter of a model? Why?
5. How is it possible for the parameters of a model to be accurate initially and then become inaccurate at a later date?
6. How does what-if analysis help management prepare for changing conditions?
7. What is meant by *sensitivity analysis?*
8. For what kinds of managerial policy decisions does what-if analysis provide guidance?

5.2 CONTINUING THE WYNDOR CASE STUDY

We now return to the case study introduced in Section 2.1 involving the Wyndor Glass Co. product-mix problem.

To review briefly, recall that the company is preparing to introduce two exciting new products:

- An 8-foot glass door with aluminum framing.
- A 4-foot × 6-foot double-hung wood-framed window.

To analyze which mix of the two products would be most profitable, the company's Management Science Group introduced two decision variables:

D = Production rate of this new kind of door

W = Production rate of this new kind of window

where this rate measures the number of units produced per week. Three plants will be involved in the production of these products. Based on managerial decisions regarding how much these plants will continue to be used to produce current products, the number of hours of production time per week being made available in plants 1, 2, and 3 for the new products is 4, 12, and 18, respectively. After obtaining rough estimates that the profit per unit will be $300 for the doors and $500 for the windows, the Management Science Group then formulated the linear programming model shown in Figure 5.1, where the objective is to choose the values of D and W in the changing cells UnitsProduced (C12:D12) so as to maximize the total profit (per week) given in the target cell TotalProfit (G12). Applying the Solver to this model yielded the optimal solution shown on this spreadsheet and summarized as follows.

Optimal Solution

$D = 2$	(Produce 2 doors per week.)
$W = 6$	(Produce 6 windows per week.)
Profit = 3,600	(The estimated total weekly profit is $3,600.)

However, this optimal solution assumes that all the estimates that provide the parameters of the model (as shown in the UnitProfit (C4:D4), HoursUsedPerUnitProduced (C7:D9), and HoursAvailable (G7:G9) data cells) are accurate.

The head of the Management Science Group, Lisa Taylor, now is ready to meet with management to discuss the group's recommendation that the above product mix be used.

Management's Discussion of the Recommended Product Mix

Lisa Taylor (head of Management Science Group):   I asked for this meeting so we could explore what questions the two of you would like us to pursue further. In particular, I am especially concerned that we weren't able to better pin down just what the numbers should be to go into our model. Which estimates do you think are the shakiest?

Bill Tasto (vice president for manufacturing):   Without question, the estimates of the unit profits for the two products. Since the products haven't gone into production yet, all we could do is analyze the data from similar current products and then try to project what the changes would be for these new products. We have some numbers, but they are pretty rough. We would need to do a lot more work to pin down the numbers better.

John Hill (president):   We may need to do that. Lisa, do you have a way of checking how far off one of these estimates can be without changing the optimal product mix?

Lisa: Yes, we do. We can quickly find what we call the *allowable range* for each unit profit. As long as the true value of the unit profit is within this allowable range, and the other unit profit is correct, the optimal product mix will not change. If this range is pretty wide, you don't need to worry about refining the estimate of the unit profit. However, if the range is quite narrow, then it is important to pin down the estimate more closely.

The allowable range for a unit profit indicates how far its estimate can be off without affecting the optimal product mix.

FIGURE 5.1

The spreadsheet model and its optimal solution for the original Wyndor problem before beginning what-if analysis.

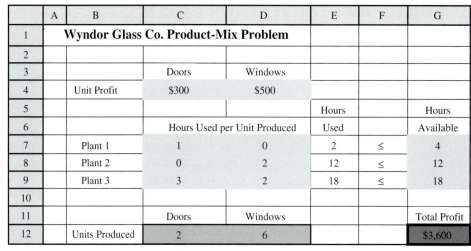

	A	B	C	D	E	F	G
1			**Wyndor Glass Co. Product-Mix Problem**				
2							
3			Doors	Windows			
4		Unit Profit	$300	$500			
5					Hours		Hours
6			Hours Used per Unit Produced		Used		Available
7		Plant 1	1	0	2	≤	4
8		Plant 2	0	2	12	≤	12
9		Plant 3	3	2	18	≤	18
10							
11			Doors	Windows			Total Profit
12		Units Produced	2	6			$3,600

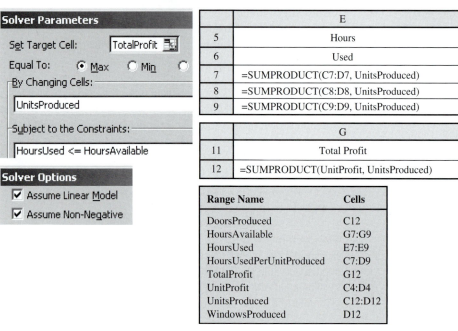

Solver Parameters

Set Target Cell: TotalProfit

Equal To: ⊙ Max ○ Min ○

By Changing Cells:

UnitsProduced

Subject to the Constraints:

HoursUsed <= HoursAvailable

Solver Options

☑ Assume Linear Model
☑ Assume Non-Negative

	E
5	Hours
6	Used
7	=SUMPRODUCT(C7:D7, UnitsProduced)
8	=SUMPRODUCT(C8:D8, UnitsProduced)
9	=SUMPRODUCT(C9:D9, UnitsProduced)

	G
11	Total Profit
12	=SUMPRODUCT(UnitProfit, UnitsProduced)

Range Name	Cells
DoorsProduced	C12
HoursAvailable	G7:G9
HoursUsed	E7:E9
HoursUsedPerUnitProduced	C7:D9
TotalProfit	G12
UnitProfit	C4:D4
UnitsProduced	C12:D12
WindowsProduced	D12

John: What happens if both estimates are off?

Lisa: We can provide a way of checking whether the optimal product mix might change for any new combination of unit profits you think might be the true one.

John: Great. That's what we need. There's also one more thing. Bill gave you the numbers for how many hours of production time we're making available per week in the three plants for these new products. I noticed you used these numbers on your spreadsheet.

Lisa: Yes. They're the right-hand sides of our constraints. Is something wrong with these numbers?

John: No, not at all. I just wanted to let you know that we haven't made a final decision on whether these are the numbers we want to use. We would like your group to provide us with some analysis of what the effect would be if we change any of those numbers. How much more profit could we get from the new products for each additional hour of production time per week we provide in one of the plants? That sort of thing.

Lisa: Yes, we can get that analysis to you right away also.

John: We might also be interested in changing the available production hours for two or three of the plants.

Lisa: No problem. We'll give you information about that as well.

Summary of Management's What-If Questions

Here is a summary of John Hill's what-if questions that Lisa and her group will be addressing in the coming sections.

1. What happens if the estimate of the unit profit of one of Wyndor's new products is inaccurate? (Section 5.3)
2. What happens if the estimates of the unit profits of both of Wyndor's new products are inaccurate? (Section 5.4)
3. What happens if a change is made in the number of hours of production time per week being made available to Wyndor's new products in one of the plants? (Section 5.5)
4. What happens if simultaneous changes are made in the number of hours of production time per week being made available to Wyndor's new products in all the plants? (Section 5.6)

Review
Questions

1. Which estimates of the parameters in the linear programming model for the Wyndor problem are most questionable?
2. Which numbers in this model represent tentative managerial decisions that management might want to change after receiving the Management Science Group's analysis?

5.3   THE EFFECT OF CHANGES IN ONE OBJECTIVE FUNCTION COEFFICIENT

Section 5.1 began by discussing the fact that many of the parameters of a linear programming model typically are only *estimates* of quantities that cannot be determined precisely at the time. What-if analysis (or *sensitivity analysis* in particular) reveals how close each of these estimates needs to be to avoid obtaining an erroneous optimal solution.

We focus in this section on how sensitivity analysis does this when the parameters involved are *coefficients in the objective function.* (Recall that each of these coefficients gives the *unit contribution* of one of the activities toward the overall measure of performance.) In the process, we will address the first of the what-if questions posed by Wyndor management in the preceding section.

Question 1: What happens if the estimate of the unit profit of one of Wyndor's new products is inaccurate?

To start this process, first consider the question of what happens if the estimate of $300 for the unit profit for Wyndor's new kind of door is inaccurate. To address this question, let

P_D = Unit profit for the new kind of door

= Cell C4 in the spreadsheet (see Figure 5.1)

Although $P_D = \$300$ in the current version of Wyndor's linear programming model, we now want to explore how much larger or how much smaller P_D can be and still have $(D, W) = (2, 6)$ as the optimal solution. In other words, how much can the estimate of $300 for the unit profit for these doors be off before the model will give an erroneous optimal solution?

Using the Spreadsheet to Do Sensitivity Analysis

One of the great strengths of a spreadsheet is the ease with which it can be used interactively to perform various kinds of what-if analysis, including the sensitivity analysis being considered in this section. Once the Solver has been set up to obtain an optimal solution, you can immediately find out what would happen if one of the parameters of the model were to be changed to some other value. All you have to do is make this change on the spreadsheet and then click on the Solve button again.

To illustrate, Figure 5.2 shows what would happen if the unit profit for doors were to be decreased from $P_D = \$300$ to $P_D = \$200$. Comparing with Figure 5.1, there is no change at all in the optimal solution. In fact, the *only* changes in the new spreadsheet are the new value

Click on the Solve button again and the spreadsheet immediately reveals the effect of changing any values in the data cells.

FIGURE 5.2

The revised Wyndor problem where the estimate of the unit profit for doors has been decreased from $P_D =$ $300 to $P_D =$ $200, but no change occurs in the optimal solution.

	A	B	C	D	E	F	G
1		**Wyndor Glass Co. Product-Mix Problem**					
2							
3			Doors	Windows			
4		Unit Profit	$200	$500			
5					Hours		Hours
6			Hours Used per Unit Produced		Used		Available
7		Plant 1	1	0	2	≤	4
8		Plant 2	0	2	12	≤	12
9		Plant 3	3	2	18	≤	18
10							
11			Doors	Windows			Total Profit
12		Units Produced	2	6			$3,400

FIGURE 5.3

The revised Wyndor problem where the estimate of the unit profit for doors has been increased from $P_D =$ $300 to $P_D =$ $500, but no change occurs in the optimal solution.

	A	B	C	D	E	F	G
1		**Wyndor Glass Co. Product-Mix Problem**					
2							
3			Doors	Windows			
4		Unit Profit	$500	$500			
5					Hours		Hours
6			Hours Used per Unit Produced		Used		Available
7		Plant 1	1	0	2	≤	4
8		Plant 2	0	2	12	≤	12
9		Plant 3	3	2	18	≤	18
10							
11			Doors	Windows			Total Profit
12		Units Produced	2	6			$4,000

of P_D in cell C4 and a decrease of $200 in the total profit shown in cell G12 (because each of the two doors produced per week provides $100 less profit). Because the optimal solution does not change, we now know that the original estimate of $P_D =$ $300 can be considerably *too high* without invalidating the model's optimal solution.

But what happens if this estimate is *too low* instead? Figure 5.3 shows what would happen if P_D were to be increased to $P_D =$ $500. Again, there is no change in the optimal solution.

Because the original value of $P_D =$ $300 can be changed considerably in either direction without changing the optimal solution, P_D is said to be *not a sensitive parameter.* It is not necessary to pin down this estimate with great accuracy to have confidence that the model is providing the correct optimal solution.

This may be all the information that is needed about P_D. However, if there is a good possibility that the true value of P_D will turn out to be outside this broad range from $200 to $500, further investigation would be desirable. How much higher or lower can P_D be before the optimal solution would change?

Figure 5.4 demonstrates that the optimal solution would indeed change if P_D were increased all the way up to $P_D =$ $1,000. Thus, we now know that this change occurs somewhere between $500 and $1,000 during the process of increasing P_D.

Using the Solver Table to Do Sensitivity Analysis Systematically

To pin down just when the optimal solution will change, we could continue selecting new values of P_D at random. However, a better approach is to systematically consider a range of values of P_D. An Excel add-in developed by the authors, called the *Solver Table,* is designed to

FIGURE 5.4

The revised Wyndor problem where the estimate of the unit profit for doors has been increased from $P_D =$ $300 to $P_D =$ $1,000, which results in a change in the optimal solution.

	A	B	C	D	E	F	G
1		**Wyndor Glass Co. Product-Mix Problem**					
2							
3			Doors	Windows			
4		Unit Profit	$1,000	$500			
5					Hours		Hours
6			Hours Used per Unit Produced		Used		Available
7		Plant 1	1	0	4	≤	4
8		Plant 2	0	2	6	≤	12
9		Plant 3	3	2	18	≤	18
10							
11			Doors	Windows			Total Profit
12		Units Produced	4	3			$5.500

perform just this sort of analysis. It is available to you in your MS Courseware. Complete instructions for using the Solver Table are given in Appendix A.

The Solver Table re-solves the problem for a whole range of values of a data cell.

The Solver Table is used to show the results in the changing cells and/or certain output cells for various trial values in a data cell. For each trial value in the data cell, Solver is called on to re-solve the problem.

To use the Solver Table, first expand the original spreadsheet (Figure 5.1) to make a table with headings as shown in Figure 5.5. In the first column of the table (cells B19:B28), list the trial values for the data cell (the unit profit for doors), except leave the first row (cell B18) blank. The headings of the next columns specify which output will be evaluated. For each of these columns, use the first row of the table (cells C18:E18) to write an equation that refers to the relevant changing cell or output cell. In this case, the cells of interest are DoorsProduced (C12), WindowsProduced (D12), and TotalProfit (G12), so the equations for C18:E18 are those shown in Figure 5.5.

Excel Tip: When filling in the first column of a Solver Table with the trial values for the data cell of interest, skip the first row to leave room in the other columns for the equations referring to the changing cells and/or output cells of interest.

Next, select the entire table by clicking and dragging from cells B18 through E28, and then choose the Solver Table from the Add-Ins tab (for Excel 2007) or Tools menu (for earlier versions of Excel). In the Solver Table dialogue box (as shown at the bottom of Figure 5.5), indicate the column input cell (C4), which refers to the data cell that is being changed in the first column of the table. Nothing is entered for the row input cell because no row is being used to list the trial values of a data cell in this case.

The Solver Table shown in Figure 5.6 is then generated automatically by clicking on the OK button. For each trial value listed in the first column of the table for the data cell of interest, Excel re-solves the problem using Solver and then fills in the corresponding values in the other columns of the table. (The numbers in the first row of the table come from the original solution in the spreadsheet before changing the original value in the data cell.)

The table reveals that the optimal solution remains the same all the way from $P_D =$ $100 (and perhaps lower) to $P_D =$ $700, but that a change occurs somewhere between $700 and $800. We next could systematically consider values of P_D between $700 and $800 to determine more closely where the optimal solution changes. However, here is a shortcut. The range of values of P_D over which $(D, W) = (2, 6)$ remains as the optimal solution is referred to as the **allowable range for an objective function coefficient,** or just the **allowable range** for short. Upon request, the Excel Solver will provide a report called the *sensitivity report* that, after a couple of simple calculations, reveals exactly what this allowable range is.

The allowable range for a coefficient in the objective function is the range of values for this coefficient over which the optimal solution for the original model remains optimal.

Using the Sensitivity Report to Find the Allowable Range

As was shown in Figure 2.12, when the Solver gives the message that it has found a solution, it also gives on the right a list of three reports that can be provided. By selecting the second one (labeled Sensitivity), you will obtain the sensitivity report.

FIGURE 5.5

Expansion of the spreadsheet in Figure 5.1 to prepare for using the Solver Table to show the effect of systematically varying the estimate of the unit profit for doors in the Wyndor problem.

	A	B	C	D	E	F	G
1		**Wyndor Glass Co. Product-Mix Problem**					
2							
3			Doors	Windows			
4		Unit Profit	$300	$500			
5					Hours		Hours
6			Hours Used per Unit Produced		Used		Available
7		Plant 1	1	0	2	≤	4
8		Plant 2	0	2	12	≤	12
9		Plant 3	3	2	18	≤	18
10							
11			Doors	Windows			Total Profit
12		Units Produced	2	6			$3,600
13							
14							Select
15							these cells
16		Unit Profit	Optimal Units Produced		Total		(B18:E28)
17		for Doors	Doors	Windows	Profit		before
18			2	6	$3,600		choosing
19		$100					the Solver
20		$200					Table.
21		$300					
22		$400					
23		$500					
24		$600					
25		$700					
26		$800					
27		$900					
28		$1,000					

	C	D	E
16	Optimal Units Produced		Total
17	Doors	Windows	Profit
18	=DoorsProduced	=WindowsProduced	=TotalProfit

Range Name	Cells
DoorsProduced	C12
TotalProfit	G12
WindowsProduced	D12

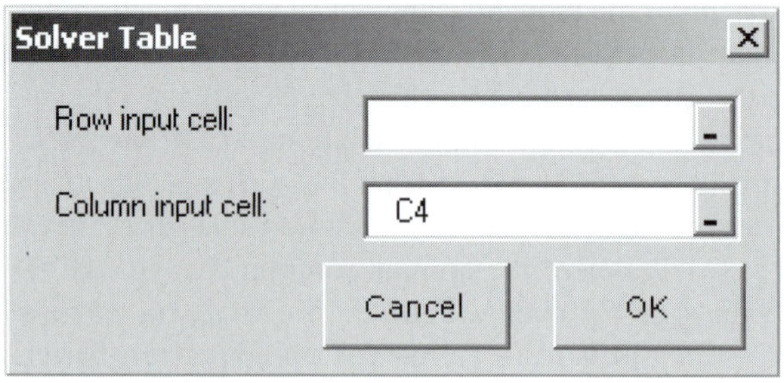

Solver Table   ☒

Row input cell: [   ]   ▪

Column input cell: [C4   ]   ▪

[Cancel]   [OK]

The sensitivity report generated by the Excel Solver reveals the allowable range for each coefficient in the objective function.

Figure 5.7 shows the relevant part of this report for the Wyndor problem. The Final Value column indicates the optimal solution. The next column gives the *reduced costs,* which can provide some useful information when any of the changing cells equal zero in the optimal solution, which is not the case here. (For a zero-valued changing cell, the corresponding reduced cost can be used to determine what the effect would be of either increasing that changing cell or making a change in its coefficient in the objective function. Because of the

FIGURE 5.6

An application of the Solver Table that shows the effect of systematically varying the estimate of the unit profit for doors in the Wyndor problem.

	B	C	D	E
16	Unit Profit	Optimal Units Produced		Total
17	for Doors	Doors	Windows	Profit
18		2	6	$3,600
19	$100	2	6	$3,200
20	$200	2	6	$3,400
21	$300	2	6	$3,600
22	$400	2	6	$3,800
23	$500	2	6	$4,000
24	$600	2	6	$4,200
25	$700	2	6	$4,400
26	$800	4	3	$4,700
27	$900	4	3	$5,100
28	$1,000	4	3	$5,500

FIGURE 5.7

Part of the sensitivity report generated by the Excel Solver for the original Wyndor problem (Figure 5.1), where the last three columns enable identifying the allowable ranges for the unit profits for doors and windows.

Adjustable Cells

Cell	Name	Final Value	Reduced Cost	Objective Coefficient	Allowable Increase	Allowable Decrease
$C$12	DoorsProduced	2	0	300	450	300
$D$12	WindowsProduced	6	0	500	1E+30	300

relatively technical nature of these interpretations of reduced costs, we will not discuss them further here, but will provide a full explanation in the supplement to this chapter on the CD-ROM.) The next three columns provide the information needed to identify the *allowable range* for each coefficient in the objective function. The Objective Coefficient column gives the current value of each coefficient, and then the next two columns give the *allowable increase* and the *allowable decrease* from this value to remain within the allowable range.

For example, consider P_D, the coefficient of D in the objective function. Since D is the production rate for these special doors, the Doors row in the table provides the following information (without the dollar sign) about P_D:

Current value of P_D: 300

Allowable increase in P_D: 450   So $P_D \leq 300 + 450 = 750$

Allowable decrease in P_D: 300   So $P_D \geq 300 - 300 = 0$

Allowable range for P_D: $0 \leq P_D \leq 750$

Therefore, if P_D is changed from its current value (without making any other change in the model), the current solution $(D, W) = (2, 6)$ will remain optimal so long as the new value of P_D is within this allowable range.

Figure 5.8 provides graphical insight into this allowable range. For the original value of $P_D = 300$, the solid line in the figure shows the slope of the objective function line passing through (2, 6). At the lower end of the allowable range, when $P_D = 0$, the objective function line that passes through (2, 6) now is line B in the figure, so every point on the line segment between (0, 6) and (2, 6) is an optimal solution. For any value of $P_D <$ 0, the objective function line will have rotated even further so that (0, 6) becomes the only optimal solution. At the upper end of the allowable range, when $P_D = 750$, the objective function line that passes through (2, 6) becomes line C, so every point on the line segment between (2, 6) and (4, 3) becomes an optimal solution. For any value of P_D > 750, the objective function line is even steeper than line C, so (4, 3) becomes the only optimal solution.

FIGURE 5.8

The two dashed lines that pass through solid constraint boundary lines are the objective function lines when P_D (the unit profit for doors) is at an endpoint of its allowable range, $0 \leq P_D \leq 750$, since either line or any objective function line in between still yields $(D, W) = (2, 6)$ as an optimal solution for the Wyndor problem.

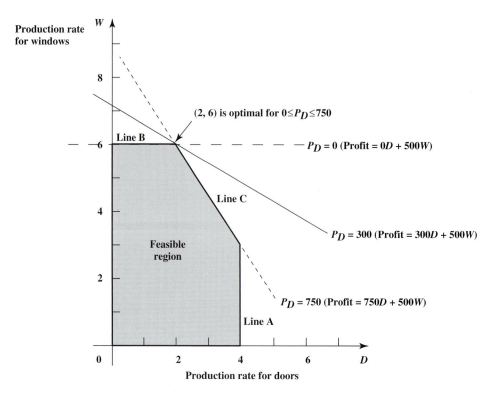

Check out this module in the Interactive Management Science Modules to gain graphical insight into the allowable range.

The module called *Graphical Linear Programming and Sensitivity Analysis* in the Interactive Management Science Modules (available at **www.mhhe.com/hillier3e/** or in your CD-ROM) is designed to help you perform this kind of graphical analysis. After you enter the model for the original Wyndor problem, the module provides you with the graph shown in Figure 5.8 (without the dashed lines). You then can simply drag one end of the objective function line up or down to see how far you can increase or decrease P_D before $(D, W) = (2, 6)$ will no longer be optimal.

Conclusion: The allowable range for P_D is $0 \leq P_D \leq 750$, because $(D, W) = (2, 6)$ remains optimal over this range but not beyond. (When $P_D = 0$ or $P_D = 750$, there are multiple optimal solutions, but $(D, W) = (2, 6)$ still is one of them.) With the range this wide around the original estimate of \$300 ($P_D = 300$) for the unit profit for doors, we can be quite confident of obtaining the correct optimal solution for the true unit profit even though the discussion in Section 5.2 indicates that this estimate is fairly rough.

The sensitivity report also can be used to find the allowable range for the unit profit for Wyndor's other new product. In particular, let

P_W = Unit profit for Wyndor's new kind of window

= Cell D4 in the spreadsheet

Referring to the Windows row of the sensitivity report (Figure 5.7), this row indicates that the allowable decrease in P_W is 300 (so $P_W \geq 500 - 300 = 200$) and the allowable increase is 1E+30. What is meant by 1E+30? This is shorthand in Excel for 10^{30} (1 with 30 zeroes after it). This tremendously huge number is used by Excel to represent *infinity*. Therefore, the allowable range of P_W is obtained from the sensitivity report as follows:

Current value of P_W:	500	
Allowable increase in P_W:	Unlimited	So P_W has no upper limit
Allowable decrease in P_W:	300	So $P_W \geq 500 - 300 = 200$
Allowable range:	$P_W \geq 200$	

The allowable range is quite wide for both objective function coefficients. Thus, even though P_D = \$300 and P_W = \$500 were only rough estimates of the true unit profit for the doors and windows, respectively, we can still be confident that we have obtained the correct optimal solution.

We are not always so lucky. For some linear programming problems, even a small change in the value of certain coefficients in the objective function can change the optimal solution. Such coefficients are referred to as *sensitive parameters*. The sensitivity report will immediately indicate which of the objective function coefficients (if any) are sensitive parameters. These are parameters that have a small allowable increase and/or a small allowable decrease. Hence, extra care should be taken to refine these estimates.

Once this has been done and the final version of the model has been solved, the allowable ranges continue to serve an important purpose. As indicated in Section 5.1, the second benefit of what-if analysis is that if conditions change after the study has been completed (a common occurrence), what-if analysis leaves signposts that indicate (without solving the model again) whether a resulting change in a parameter of the model changes the optimal solution. Thus, if weeks, months, or even years later, the unit profit for one of Wyndor's new products changes substantially, its allowable range indicates immediately whether the old optimal product mix still is the appropriate one to use. Being able to draw an affirmative conclusion without reconstructing and solving the revised model is extremely helpful for any linear programming problem, but especially so when the model is a large one.

> A parameter is considered sensitive if even a small change in its value can change the optimal solution.

Review Questions

1. What is meant by the *allowable range* for a coefficient in the objective function?
2. What is the significance if the true value for a coefficient in the objective function turns out to be so different from its estimate that it lies outside its allowable range?
3. In Excel's sensitivity report, what is the interpretation of the Objective Coefficient column? The Allowable Increase column? The Allowable Decrease column?

5.4 THE EFFECT OF SIMULTANEOUS CHANGES IN OBJECTIVE FUNCTION COEFFICIENTS

The coefficients in the objective function typically represent quantities (e.g., unit profits) that can only be estimated because of considerable uncertainty about what their true values will turn out to be. The allowable ranges described in the preceding section deal with this uncertainty by focusing on just one coefficient at a time. In effect, the allowable range for a particular coefficient assumes that the original estimates for all the other coefficients are completely accurate so that this coefficient is the only one whose true value may differ from its original estimate.

In actuality, the estimates for *all* the coefficients (or at least more than one of them) may be inaccurate simultaneously. The crucial question is whether this is likely to result in obtaining the wrong optimal solution. If so, greater care should be taken to refine these estimates as much as possible, at least for the more crucial coefficients. On the other hand, if what-if analysis reveals that the anticipated errors in estimating the coefficients are unlikely to affect the optimal solution, then management can be reassured that the current linear programming model and its results are providing appropriate guidance.

This section focuses on how to determine, without solving the problem again, whether the optimal solution might change if certain changes occur simultaneously in the coefficients of the objective function (due to their true values differing from their estimates). In the process, we will address the second of Wyndor management's what-if questions.

> **Question 2:** What happens if the estimates of the unit profits of both of Wyndor's new products are inaccurate?

Using the Spreadsheet for This Analysis

Once again, the quickest and easiest way to address this kind of question is to simply try out different estimates on the spreadsheet formulation of the model and see what happens each time when clicking on the Solve button.

The Pacific Lumber Company (PALCO) is a large timber-holding company with headquarters in Scotia, California. The company has over 200,000 acres of highly productive forest lands that support five mills located in Humboldt County in northern California. The lands include some of the most spectacular redwood groves in the world that have been given or sold at low cost to be preserved as parks. PALCO manages the remaining lands intensively for sustained timber production, subject to strong forest practice laws. Since PALCO's forests are home to many species of wildlife, including endangered species such as spotted owls and marbled murrelets, the provisions of the federal Endangered Species Act also need to be carefully observed.

To obtain a sustained yield plan for the entire landholding, PALCO management contracted with a team of management science consultants to develop a 120-year, 12-period, long-term forest ecosystem management plan. The management science team performed this task by formulating and applying a linear programming model to optimize the company's overall timberland operations and profitability after satisfying the various constraints. The model was a huge one with approximately 8,500 functional constraints and 353,000 decision variables.

A major challenge in applying the linear programming model was the many uncertainties in estimating what the parameters of the model should be. The major factors causing these uncertainties were the continuing fluctuations in market supply and demand, logging costs, and environmental regulations. Therefore, the management science team made extensive use of detailed sensitivity analysis. The resulting sustained yield plan increased the company's present net worth by over $398 million while also generating a better mix of wildlife habitat acres.

Source: L. R. Fletcher, H. Alden, S. P. Holmen, D. P. Angelis, and M. J. Etzenhouser, "Long-Term Forest Ecosystem Planning at Pacific Lumber," *Interfaces* 29, no. 1 (January–February 1999), pp. 90–112.

In this case, the optimal product mix indicated by the model is heavily weighted toward producing the windows (6 per week) rather than the doors (only 2 per week). Since there is equal enthusiasm for both new products, management is concerned about this imbalance. Therefore, management has raised a what-if question. What would happen if the estimate of the unit profit for the doors ($300) were too low and the corresponding estimate for the windows ($500) were too high? The estimates could easily be off in these directions (as could be checked with considerable additional investigation). If this were the case, would this lead to a more balanced product mix being the most profitable one?

This question can be answered in a matter of seconds simply by substituting new estimates of the unit profits in the original spreadsheet in Figure 5.1 and clicking on the Solve button. Figure 5.9 shows that new estimates of $450 for doors and $400 for windows causes no change at all in the solution for the optimal product mix. (The total profit does change, but this occurs only because of the changes in the unit profits.) Would even larger changes in the estimates of unit profits finally lead to a change in the optimal product mix? Figure 5.10 shows that this does happen, yielding a relatively balanced product mix of $(D, W) = (4, 3)$, when estimates of $600 for doors and $300 for windows are used.

FIGURE 5.9

The revised Wyndor problem where the estimates of the unit profits for doors and windows have been changed to $P_D = \$450$ and $P_W = \$400$, respectively, but no change occurs in the optimal solution.

	A	B	C	D	E	F	G
1		**Wyndor Glass Co. Product-Mix Problem**					
2							
3			Doors	Windows			
4		Unit Profit	$450	$400			
5					Hours		Hours
6			Hours Used per Unit Produced		Used		Available
7		Plant 1	1	0	2	≤	4
8		Plant 2	0	2	12	≤	12
9		Plant 3	3	2	18	≤	18
10							
11			Doors	Windows			Total Profit
12		Units Produced	2	6			$3,300

FIGURE 5.10

The revised Wyndor problem where the estimates of the unit profits for doors and windows have been changed to $600 and $300, respectively, which results in a change in the optimal solution.

	A	B	C	D	E	F	G
1		**Wyndor Glass Co. Product-Mix Problem**					
2							
3			Doors	Windows			
4		Unit Profit	$600	$300			
5					Hours		Hours
6			Hours Used per Unit Produced		Used		Available
7		Plant 1	1	0	4	≤	4
8		Plant 2	0	2	6	≤	12
9		Plant 3	3	2	18	≤	18
10							
11			Doors	Windows			Total Profit
12		Units Produced	4	3			$3,300

Using Two-Dimensional Solver Tables for This Analysis

A *two-way* Solver Table provides a way of systematically investigating the effect if the estimates of both unit profits are inaccurate. This kind of Solver Table shows the results in a single output cell for various trial values in two data cells. Therefore, it can be used to show how TotalProfit (G12) in Figure 5.1 varies over a range of trial values in the two data cells, Unit-Profit (C4:D4). For each pair of trial values in these data cells, Solver is called on to re-solve the problem.

To create a two-way Solver Table for the Wyndor problem, expand the original spreadsheet (Figure 5.1) to make a table with column and row headings as shown in rows 16–21 of the spreadsheet in Figure 5.11. In the upper left-hand corner of the table (C17), write an equation that refers to the target cell (=TotalProfit). In the first column of the table (column C, below the equation in cell C17), insert various trial values for the first data cell of interest (the unit profit for doors). In the first row of the table (row 17, to the right of the equation in cell C17), insert various trial values for the second data cell of interest (the unit profit for windows).

Next, select the entire table (C17:H21) and choose Solver Table from the Add-Ins tab (for Excel 2007) or Tools menu (for earlier versions of Excel). In the Solver Table dialogue box (shown at the bottom of Figure 5.11), indicate which data cells are being changed simultaneously. The column input cell C4 refers to the data cell whose various trial values are listed in the first column of the table (C18:C21), while the row input cell refers to the data cell whose various trial values are listed in the first row of the table (D17:H17).

The Solver Table shown in Figure 5.12 is then generated automatically by clicking on the OK button. For each pair of trial values for the two data cells, Excel re-solves the problem using Solver and then fills in the total profit in the corresponding spot in the table. (The number in C17 comes from the target cell in the original spreadsheet before the original values in the two data cells have been changed.)

Unlike a one-way Solver Table that can show the results of *multiple* changing cells and/or output cells for various trial values of a single data cell, a two-way Solver Table is limited to showing the results in a *single* cell for each pair of trial values in the two data cells of interest. However, there is a trick using the & symbol that enables the Solver Table to show the results from multiple changing cells and/or output cells within a single cell of the table. We utilize this trick in the Solver Table shown in Figure 5.13 to show the results for *both* changing cells DoorsProduced (C12) and WindowsProduced (D12) for each pair of trial values for Unit-Profit (C4:D4). The key formula is in cell C25:

$$C25 = \text{"(" \& DoorsProduced \& ", " \& WindowsProduced \& ")"}$$

The & character tells Excel to concatenate, so the result will be a left parenthesis, followed by the value in DoorsProduced (C12), then a comma and the contents in WindowsProduced

Unlike a one-way Solver Table (as in Figure 5.6) which shows results for trial values in a single data cell, a two-way Solver Table shows results for trial values in two data cells.

Although a two-way Solver Table is limited to showing results in a single cell of the table for each combination of trial values in two data cells, the & symbol can be used to show results from multiple cells of the original spreadsheet in this single cell.

FIGURE 5.11

Expansion of the spreadsheet in Figure 5.1 to prepare for using a two-dimensional Solver Table to show the effect on total profit of systematically varying the estimates of the unit profits of doors and windows for the Wyndor problem.

	A	B	C	D	E	F	G	H	I
1		**Wyndor Glass Co. Product-Mix Problem**							
2									
3			Doors	Windows					
4		Unit Profit	$300	$500					
5					Hours		Hours		
6			Hours Used per Unit		Used		Available		
7		Plant 1	1	0	2	≤	4		
8		Plant 2	0	2	12	≤	12		
9		Plant 3	3	2	18	≤	18		Select these cells (C17:H21) before choosing the Solver Table.
10									
11			Doors	Windows			Total Profit		
12		Units Produced	2	6			$3,600		
13									
14									
15									
16		**Total Profit**			Unit Profit for Windows				
17			$3,600	$100	$200	$300	$400	$500	
18			$300						
19		Unit Profit	$400						
20		for Doors	$500						
21			$600						

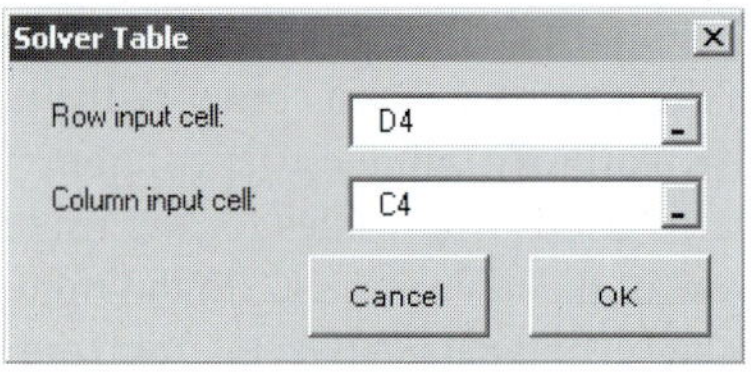 Solver Table	
Row input cell:	D4
Column input cell:	C4
	Cancel OK

	C
17	= TotalProfit

Range Name	Cell
TotalProfit	G12

FIGURE 5.12

A two-dimensional application of the Solver Table that shows the effect on total profit of systematically varying the estimates of the unit profits of doors and windows for the Wyndor problem.

	B	C	D	E	F	G	H
16	**Total Profit**			Unit Profit for Windows			
17		$3,600	$100	$200	$300	$400	$500
18		$300	$1,500	$1,800	$2,400	$3,000	$3,600
19	Unit Profit	$400	$1,900	$2,200	$2,600	$3,200	$3,800
20	for Doors	$500	$2,300	$2,600	$2,900	$3,400	$4,000
21		$600	$2,700	$3,000	$3,300	$3,600	$4,200

Excel Tip: Any text that you would like a formula to display (such as the parentheses and commas in the formula in C25 of Figure 5.13) must be enclosed within quotation marks.

(D12), and finally a right parenthesis. If DoorsProduced = 2 and WindowsProduced = 6, the result is (2, 6). Thus, the results from *both* changing cells are displayed within a *single* cell of the table.

After the usual preliminaries in entering the information shown in rows 24–25 and columns B–C of Figure 5.13, along with the formula in C25, clicking on the OK button automatically generates the entire Solver Table. Cells D26:H29 show the optimal solution for the various combinations of trial values for the unit profits of the doors and windows. The upper right-hand corner (cell H26) of this Solver Table gives the optimal solution of (*D, W*) = (2, 6) when using the original unit-profit estimates of $300 for doors and $500 for windows. Moving down from this cell corresponds to increasing this estimate for doors, while moving to the left amounts to decreasing the estimate for windows. (The cells when moving up or to the right of H26 are not shown because these changes would only increase the attractiveness of

FIGURE 5.13

A two-dimensional application of the Solver Table that shows the effect on the optimal solution of systematically varying the estimates of the unit profits of doors and windows for the Wyndor problem.

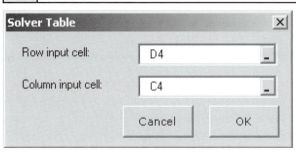

	B	C	D	E	F	G	H
24	**Units Produced (Doors, Windows)**			Unit Profit for Windows			
25		(2,6)	$100	$200	$300	$400	$500
26		$300	(4,3)	(4,3)	(2,6)	(2,6)	(2,6)
27	Unit Profit	$400	(4,3)	(4,3)	(2,6)	(2,6)	(2,6)
28	for Doors	$500	(4,3)	(4,3)	(4,3)	(2,6)	(2,6)
29		$600	(4,3)	(4,3)	(4,3)	(4,3)	(2,6)

	C
25	= "(" & DoorsProduced & "," & WindowsProduced & ")"

Range Name	Cell
DoorsProduced	C12
WindowsProduced	D12

Solver Table

Row input cell: D4

Column input cell: C4

Cancel   OK

$(D, W) = (2, 6)$ as the optimal solution.) Note that $(D, W) = (2, 6)$ continues to be the optimal solution for all the cells near H18. This indicates that the original estimates of unit profit would need to be very inaccurate indeed before the optimal product mix would change. Although the estimates are fairly rough, management is confident that they are not that inaccurate. Therefore, there is no need to expend the considerable effort that would be needed to refine the estimates.

At this point, it continues to appear that $(D, W) = (2, 6)$ is the best product mix for initiating the production of the two new products (although additional what-if questions remain to be addressed in subsequent sections). However, we also now know from Figure 5.13 that as conditions change in the future, if the unit profits for both products change enough, it may be advisable to change the product mix later. We still need to leave clear signposts behind to signal when a future change in the product mix should be considered, as described next.

What-if analysis shows that there is no need to refine Wyndor's estimates of the unit profits for doors and windows.

Gleaning Additional Information from the Sensitivity Report

The preceding section described how the data in the sensitivity report enable finding the allowable range for an individual coefficient in the objective function when that coefficient is the only one that changes from its original value. These same data (the allowable increase and allowable decrease in each coefficient) also can be used to analyze the effect of *simultaneous* changes in these coefficients. Here is how.

A sum ≤ 100 percent guarantees that the original optimal solution is still optimal.

> *The 100 Percent Rule for Simultaneous Changes in Objective Function Coefficients:* If simultaneous changes are made in the coefficients of the objective function, calculate for each change the percentage of the allowable change (increase or decrease) for that coefficient to remain within its allowable range. If the *sum* of the percentage changes does *not* exceed 100 percent, the original optimal solution definitely will still be optimal. (If the sum *does* exceed 100 percent, then we cannot be sure.)

This rule does not spell out what happens if the sum of the percentage changes *does* exceed 100 percent. The consequence depends on the directions of the changes in the coefficients. Exceeding 100 percent may or may not change the optimal solution, but so long as 100 percent is not exceeded, the original optimal solution *definitely* will still be optimal.

Keep in mind that we can safely use the entire allowable increase or decrease in a single objective function coefficient only if none of the other coefficients have changed at all. With simultaneous changes in the coefficients, we focus on the *percentage* of the allowable increase or decrease that is being used for each coefficient.

To illustrate, consider the Wyndor problem again, along with the information provided by the sensitivity report in Figure 5.7. Suppose conditions have changed after the initial study, and the unit profit for doors (P_D) has increased from $300 to $450 while the unit profit for windows (P_W) has decreased from $500 to $400. The calculations for the 100 percent rule then are

P_D: $300 → $450

$$\text{Percentage of allowable increase} = 100\left(\frac{450 - 300}{450}\right)\% = 33\tfrac{1}{3}\%$$

P_W: $500 → $400

$$\text{Percentage of allowable decrease} = 100\left(\frac{500 - 400}{300}\right)\% = 33\tfrac{1}{3}\%$$

$$\text{Sum} = \overline{66\tfrac{2}{3}\%}$$

Since the sum of the percentages does not exceed 100 percent, the original optimal solution $(D, W) = (2, 6)$ definitely is still optimal, just as we found earlier in Figure 5.9.

Now suppose conditions have changed even further, so P_D has increased from $300 to $600 while P_W has decreased from $500 to $300. The calculations for the 100 percent rule now are

P_D: $300 → $600

$$\text{Percentage of allowable increase} = 100\left(\frac{600 - 300}{450}\right)\% = 66\tfrac{2}{3}\%$$

P_W: $500 → $300

$$\text{Percentage of allowable decrease} = 100\left(\frac{500 - 300}{300}\right)\% = 66\tfrac{2}{3}\%$$

$$\text{Sum} = \overline{133\tfrac{1}{3}\%}$$

Since the sum of the percentages now exceeds 100 percent, the 100 percent rule says that we can no longer guarantee that $(D, W) = (2, 6)$ is still optimal. In fact, we found earlier in both Figures 5.10 and 5.13 that the optimal solution has changed to $(D, W) = (4, 3)$.

These results suggest how to find just where the optimal solution changes while P_D is being increased and P_W is being decreased in this way. Since 100 percent is midway between 66⅔ percent and 133⅓ percent, the sum of the percentage changes will equal 100 percent when the values of P_D and P_W are midway between their values in the above cases. In particular, P_D = $525 is midway between $450 and $600 and P_W = $350 is midway between $400 and $300. The corresponding calculations for the 100 percent rule are

P_D: $300 → $525

$$\text{Percentage of allowable increase} = 100\left(\frac{525 - 300}{450}\right)\% = 50\%$$

P_W: $500 → $350

$$\text{Percentage of allowable decrease} = 100\left(\frac{500 - 350}{300}\right)\% = 50\%$$

$$\text{Sum} = \overline{100\%}$$

Although the sum of the percentages equals 100 percent, the fact that it does not *exceed* 100 percent guarantees that $(D, W) = (2, 6)$ is still optimal. Figure 5.14 shows graphically that *both* (2, 6) and (4, 3) are now optimal, as well as all the points on the line segment connecting these two points. However, if P_D and P_W were to be changed any further from their original

FIGURE 5.14

When the estimates of the unit profits for doors and windows change to $P_D = \$525$ and $P_W = \$350$, which lies at the edge of what is allowed by the 100 percent rule, the graphical method shows that $(D, W) = (2, 6)$ still is an optimal solution, but now every other point on the line segment between this solution and $(4, 3)$ also is optimal.

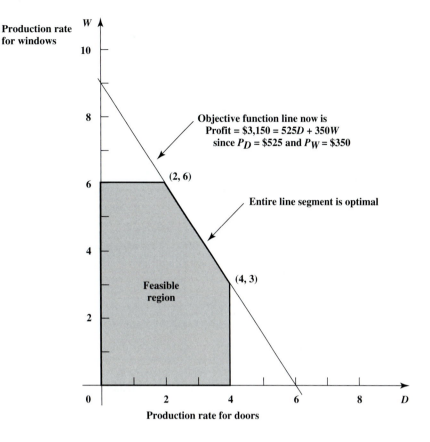

values (so that the sum of the percentages exceeds 100 percent), the objective function line would be rotated so far toward the vertical that $(D, W) = (4, 3)$ would become the only optimal solution.

At the same time, keep in mind that having the sum of the percentages of allowable changes exceed 100 percent does not automatically mean that the optimal solution will change. For example, suppose that the estimates of both unit profits are halved. The resulting calculations for the 100 percent rule are

Here is an example where the original optimal solution is still optimal even though the sum exceeds 100 percent.

P_D: $\$300 \rightarrow \$150$

$$\text{Percentage of allowable decrease} = 100\left(\frac{300 - 150}{300}\right)\% = 50\%$$

P_W: $\$500 \rightarrow \$250$

$$\text{Percentage of allowable decrease} = 100\left(\frac{500 - 250}{300}\right)\% = 83\%$$

$$\text{Sum} = \overline{133\%}$$

Even though this sum exceeds 100 percent, Figure 5.15 shows that the original optimal solution is still optimal. In fact, the objective function line has the same slope as the original objective function line (the solid line in Figure 5.8). This happens whenever *proportional changes* are made to all the unit profits, which will automatically lead to the same optimal solution.

Comparisons

You now have seen three approaches to investigating what happens if simultaneous changes occur in the coefficients of the objective function: (1) try out changes directly on a spreadsheet, (2) use a two-way Solver Table, and (3) apply the 100 percent rule.

FIGURE 5.15

When the estimates of the unit profits for doors and windows change to $P_D =$ $150 and $P_W =$ $250 (half their original values), the graphical method shows that the optimal solution still is $(D, W) = (2, 6)$, even though the 100 percent rule says that the optimal solution might change.

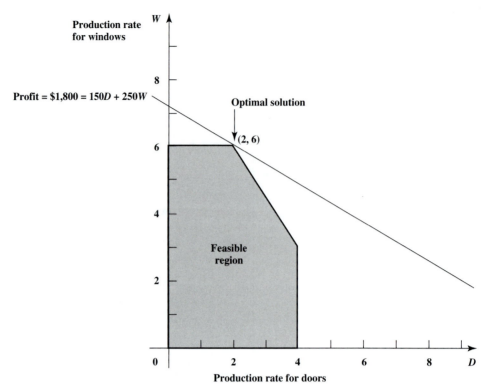

The spreadsheet approach is a good place to start, especially for less experienced modelers, because it is simple and quick. If you are only interested in checking one specific set of changes in the coefficients, you can immediately see what happens after making the changes in the spreadsheet.

More often, there will be numerous possibilities for what the true values of the coefficients will turn out to be, because of uncertainty in the original estimates of these coefficients. The Solver Table is useful for systematically checking a variety of possible changes in one or two objective function coefficients. Trying out representative possibilities on the spreadsheet may provide all the insight that is needed. Perhaps the optimal solution for the original model will remain optimal over nearly all these possibilities, so this solution can be confidently used. Or perhaps it will become clear that the original estimates need to be refined before selecting a solution.

When the spreadsheet approach and/or Solver Table does not provide a clear conclusion, the 100 percent rule can usefully complement this approach in the following ways:

- The 100 percent rule can be used to determine just how large the changes in the objective function coefficients need to be before the original optimal solution may no longer be optimal.
- When the model has a large number of decision variables (as is common for real problems), it may become impractical to use the spreadsheet approach to systematically try out a variety of simultaneous changes in many or all of the coefficients in the objective function because of the huge number of representative possibilities. The Solver Table can only be used to systematically check possible changes in—at most—two coefficients at a time. However, by dividing each coefficient's allowable increase or allowable decrease by the number of decision variables, the 100 percent rule immediately indicates how much each coefficient can be safely changed without invalidating the current optimal solution.
- After completing the study, if conditions change in the future that cause some or all of the coefficients in the objective function to change, the 100 percent rule quickly indicates whether the original optimal solution must remain optimal. If the answer is affirmative, there is no need to take all the time that may be required to reconstruct the (revised) spreadsheet model. The time saved can be very substantial for large models.

Review
Questions

1. In the 100 percent rule for simultaneous changes in objective function coefficients, what are the percentage changes that are being considered?
2. In this 100 percent rule, if the sum of the percentage changes does not exceed 100 percent, what does this say about the original optimal solution?
3. In this 100 percent rule, if the sum of the percentage changes exceeds 100 percent, does this mean that the original optimal solution is no longer optimal?

5.5 THE EFFECT OF SINGLE CHANGES IN A CONSTRAINT

We now turn our focus from the coefficients in the objective function to the effect of changing the functional constraints. The changes might occur either in the coefficients on the left-hand sides of the constraints or in the values of the right-hand sides.

We might be interested in the effect of such changes for the same reason we are interested in this effect for objective function coefficients, namely, that these parameters of the model are only *estimates* of quantities that cannot be determined precisely at this time so we want to determine the effect if these estimates are inaccurate.

However, a more common reason for this interest is the one discussed at the end of Section 5.1, namely, that the right-hand sides of the functional constraints may well represent *managerial policy decisions* rather than quantities that are largely outside the control of management. Therefore, after the model has been solved, management will want to analyze the effect of altering these policy decisions in a variety of ways to see if these decisions can be improved. What-if analysis provides valuable guidance to management in determining the effect of altering these policy decisions. (Recall that this was cited as the third benefit of what-if analysis in Section 5.1.)

This section describes how to perform what-if analysis when making changes in just one spot (a coefficient or a right-hand side) of a single constraint. The next section then will deal with simultaneous changes in the constraints.

The procedure for determining the effect if a single change is made in a constraint is the same regardless of whether the change is in a coefficient on the left-hand side or in the value on the right-hand side. (The one exception is that the Excel sensitivity report provides information about changes in the right-hand side but does not do so for the left-hand side.) Therefore, we will illustrate the procedure by making changes in a right-hand side.

In particular, we return to the Wyndor case study to address the third what-if question posed by Wyndor management in Section 5.2.

> **Question 3:** What happens if a change is made in the number of hours of production time per week being made available to Wyndor's new products in one of the plants?

The number of hours available in each plant is the value of the right-hand side for the corresponding constraint, so we want to investigate the effect of changing this right-hand side for one of the plants. With the original optimal solution, $(D, W) = (2, 6)$, only 2 of the 4 available hours in plant 1 are used, so changing this number of available hours (barring a large decrease) would have no effect on either the optimal solution or the resulting total profit from the two new products. However, it is unclear what would happen if the number of available hours in either plant 2 or plant 3 were to be changed. Let's start with plant 2.

Using the Spreadsheet for This Analysis

Referring back to Section 5.2, Figure 5.1 shows the spreadsheet model for the original Wyndor problem before beginning what-if analysis. The optimal solution is $(D, W) = (2, 6)$ with a total profit of $3,600 per week from the two new products. Cell G8 shows that 12 hours of production time per week are being made available for the new products in plant 2.

To see what happens if a specific change is made in this number of hours, all you need to do is substitute the new number in cell G8 and click on the Solve button again. For example, Figure 5.16 shows the result if the number of hours is increased from 12 to 13. The corresponding optimal solution in C12:D12 gives a total profit of $3,750. Thus, the resulting change in profit would be

$$\text{Incremental profit} = \$3,750 - \$3,600$$

$$= \$150$$

When the right-hand sides represent managerial policy decisions, what-if analysis provides guidance regarding the effect of altering these decisions.

FIGURE 5.16

The revised Wyndor problem where the hours available in plant 2 per week have been increased from 12 (as in Figure 5.1) to 13, which results in an increase of $150 in the total profit per week from the two new products.

	A	B	C	D	E	F	G
1		**Wyndor Glass Co. Product-Mix Problem**					
2							
3			Doors	Windows			
4		Unit Profit	$300	$500			
5					Hours		Hours
6			Hours Used per Unit Produced		Used		Available
7		Plant 1	1	0	1.66667	≤	4
8		Plant 2	0	2	13	≤	13
9		Plant 3	3	2	18	≤	18
10							
11			Doors	Windows			Total Profit
12		Units Produced	1.667	6.5			$3,750

FIGURE 5.17

A further revision of the Wyndor problem in Figure 5.16 to further increase the hours available in plant 2 from 13 to 18, which results in a further increase in total profit of $750 (which is the $150 per hour added in plant 2).

	A	B	C	D	E	F	G
1		**Wyndor Glass Co. Product-Mix Problem**					
2							
3			Doors	Windows			
4		Unit Profit	$300	$500			
5					Hours		Hours
6			Hours Used per Unit Produced		Used		Available
7		Plant 1	1	0	0	≤	4
8		Plant 2	0	2	18	≤	18
9		Plant 3	3	2	18	≤	18
10							
11			Doors	Windows			Total Profit
12		Units Produced	0	9			$4,500

Since this increase in profit is obtained by adding just one more hour in plant 2, it would be interesting to see the effect of adding several more hours. Figure 5.17 shows the effect of adding five more hours. Comparing Figure 5.17 to Figure 5.16, the additional profit from providing five more hours would be

So far, each additional hour provided in plant 2 adds $150 to profit.

$$\text{Incremental profit} = \$4,500 - \$3,750$$
$$= \$750 \text{ from adding 5 hours}$$
$$= \$150 \text{ per hour added}$$

Would adding even more hours increase profit even further? Figure 5.18 shows what would happen if a total of 20 hours per week were made available to the new products in plant 2. Both the optimal solution and the total profit are the same as in Figure 5.17, so increasing from 18 to 20 hours would not help. (The reason is that the 18 hours available in plant 3 prevent producing more than 9 windows per week, so only 18 hours can be used in plant 2.) Thus, it appears that 18 hours is the maximum that should be considered for plant 2.

Now management needs to consider the trade-off between adding production time for the new products and decreasing it for other products.

However, the fact that the total profit from the two new products can be increased substantially by increasing the number of hours per week made available to the new products from 12 to 18 does not mean that these additional hours should be provided automatically. The production time made available for these two new products can be increased only if it is decreased for other products. Therefore, management will need to assess the disadvantages of decreasing the production time for any other products (including both lost profit and less tangible disadvantages)

FIGURE 5.18

A further revision of the Wyndor problem in Figure 5.17 to further increase the hours available in plant 2 from 18 to 20, which results in no change in total profit because the optimal solution cannot make use of these additional hours.

	A	B	C	D	E	F	G
1		**Wyndor Glass Co. Product-Mix Problem**					
2							
3			Doors	Windows			
4		Unit Profit	$300	$500			
5					Hours		Hours
6			Hours Used per Unit Produced		Used		Available
7		Plant 1	1	0	0	≤	4
8		Plant 2	0	2	18	≤	20
9		Plant 3	3	2	18	≤	18
10							
11			Doors	Windows			Total Profit
12		Units Produced	0	9			$4,500

before deciding whether to increase the production time for the new products. This analysis also might lead to *decreasing* the production time made available to the two new products in one or more of the plants.

Using the Solver Table for This Analysis

Complete instructions for using the Solver Table are given in Appendix A.

A Solver Table can be used to systematically determine the effect of making various changes in one of the parameters in a constraint. In Figure 5.19, we use the Solver Table to show how the changing cells and total profit change as the number of available hours in plant 2 range between 4 and 20. The trial values considered for this number are listed in the first column of the table (B19:B35). The output cells of interest are the DoorsProduced (C12), WindowsProduced (D12), and TotalProfit (G12), so equations referring to these cells are entered in the first row of the table (C18:E18). Running the Solver Table (with the column input cell as G8, the hours available in plant 2) then fills in the values in the body of the table (C19:E35). We also have calculated in column F the incremental profit, that is, the additional profit that was obtained by adding the last hour to the time available in plant 2.

An interesting pattern is apparent in the incremental profit column. Starting at 12 hours available at plant 2 (the current allotment), each additional hour allocated yields an additional $150 in profit (up to 18 hours). Similarly, if hours are taken away from plant 2, each hour lost causes a loss of $150 profit (down to six hours). This rate of change in the profit for increases or decreases in the right-hand side of a constraint is known as the *shadow price*.

In general, the shadow price for a constraint reveals the rate at which the target cell can be increased by increasing the right-hand side of that constraint. This remains valid as long as the right-hand side is within its allowable range.

> Given an optimal solution and the corresponding value of the objective function for a linear programming model, the **shadow price** for a functional constraint is the *rate* at which the value of the objective function can be increased by increasing the right-hand side of the constraint by a small amount.

However, the shadow price of $150 for the plant 2 constraint is valid only within a range of values near 12 (in particular, between 6 hours and 18 hours). If the number of available hours is increased beyond 18 hours, then the incremental profit drops to zero. If the available hours are reduced below six hours, then profit drops at a faster rate of $250 per hour. Therefore, letting RHS denote the value of the right-hand side, the shadow price of $150 is valid for

In contrast to the allowable ranges for objective function coefficients described in Section 5.3, this allowable range focuses on a right-hand side and the corresponding shadow price.

$$6 \leq RHS \leq 18$$

This range is known as the **allowable range for the right-hand side** (or just **allowable range** for short).

> The **allowable range for the right-hand side** of a functional constraint is the range of values for this right-hand side over which this constraint's shadow price remains valid.

FIGURE 5.19
An application of the Solver Table that shows the effect of varying the number of hours of production time being made available per week in plant 2 for Wyndor's new products.

	A	B	C	D	E	F	G
1		**Wyndor Glass Co. Product-Mix Problem**					
2							
3			Doors	Windows			
4		Unit Profit	$300	$500			
5					Hours		Hours
6			Hours Used per Unit Produced		Used		Available
7		Plant 1	1	0	2	≤	4
8		Plant 2	0	2	12	≤	12
9		Plant 3	3	2	18	≤	18
10							
11			Doors	Windows			Total Profit
12		Units Produced	2	6			$3,600
13							
14							
15							
16		Time Available in	Optimal Units Produced		Total	Incremental	
17		Plant 2 (hours)	Doors	Windows	Profit	Profit	
18			2	6	$3,600		
19		4	4	2	$2,200		
20		5	4	2.5	$2,450	$250	
21		6	4	3	$2,700	$250	
22		7	3.667	3.5	$2,850	$150	
23		8	3.333	4	$3,000	$150	
24		9	3	4.5	$3,150	$150	
25		10	2.667	5	$3,300	$150	
26		11	2.333	5.5	$3,450	$150	
27		12	2	6	$3,600	$150	
28		13	1.667	6.5	$3,750	$150	
29		14	1.333	7	$3,900	$150	
30		15	1	7.5	$4,050	$150	
31		16	0.667	8	$4,200	$150	
32		17	0.333	8.5	$4,350	$150	
33		18	0	9	$4,500	$150	
34		19	0	9	$4,500	$0	
35		20	0	9	$4,500	$0	

Select these cells (B18:E35) before choosing the Solver Table.

	C	D	E
16	Optimal Units Produced		Total
17	Doors	Windows	Profit
18	=DoorsProduced	=WindowsProduced	=TotalProfit

	F
16	Incremental
17	Profit
18	
19	
20	=E20-E19
21	=E21-E20
22	=E22-E21
23	=E23-E22

Solver Table

Row input cell:

Column input cell: G8

Cancel   OK

Range Name	Cell
DoorsProduced	C12
TotalProfit	G12
WindowsProduced	D12

Using the Sensitivity Report to Obtain the Key Information

As illustrated above, it is straightforward to use the Solver Table to calculate the *shadow price* for a functional constraint, as well as to find (or at least closely approximate) the *allowable range* for the right-hand side of this constraint over which the shadow price remains valid. However, this same information also can be obtained immediately from Solver's sensitivity report for all the functional constraints. Figure 5.20 shows the full sensitivity report provided by the Solver for the original Wyndor problem after obtaining the optimal solution given in Figure 5.1. The top half is the part already shown in Figure 5.7 for finding allowable ranges for the objective function coefficients. The bottom half focuses on the functional constraints, including providing the shadow prices for these constraints in the fourth column. The first three columns remind us that (1) the output cells for these constraints in Figure 5.1 are cells E7 to E9, (2) these cells give the number of production hours used per week in the three plants, and (3) the final values in these cells are 2, 12, and 18 (as shown in column E of Figure 5.1). (We will discuss the last three columns a little later.)

The shadow price given in the fourth column for each constraint tells us how much the value of the objective function [target cell (G12) in Figure 5.1] would increase if the right-hand side of that constraint (cell G7, G8, or G9) were to be increased by 1. Conversely, it also tells us how much the value of the objective function would *decrease* if the right-hand side were to be decreased by 1. The shadow price for the plant 1 constraint is 0, because this plant already is using less hours (2) than are available (4) so there would be no benefit to making an additional hour available. However, plants 2 and 3 are using all the hours available to them for the two new products (with the product mix given by the changing cells). Thus, it is not surprising that the shadow prices indicate that the target cell would increase if the hours available in either plant 2 or plant 3 were to be increased.

The shadow prices reveal the relationship between profit and the amount of production time made available in the plants.

To express this information in the language of management, the value of the objective function for this problem [target cell (G12) in Figure 5.1] represents the *total profit* in dollars per week from the two new products under consideration. The right-hand side of each functional constraint represents the number of hours of production time being made available per week for these products in the plant that corresponds to this constraint. Therefore, the shadow price for a functional constraint informs management as to how much the total profit from the two new products could be increased for each additional hour of production time made available to these products per week in the corresponding plant. Conversely, the shadow price indicates how much this profit would decrease for each reduction of an hour of production time in that plant. This interpretation of the shadow price remains valid as long as the change in the number of hours of production time is not very large.

Here is how to find the allowable ranges for the right-hand sides from the sensitivity report.

Specifically, this interpretation of the shadow price remains valid as long as the number of hours of production time remains within its *allowable range*. The Solver's sensitivity report provides all the data needed to identify the allowable range of each functional constraint. Refer back to the bottom of this report given in Figure 5.20. The final three columns enable

FIGURE 5.20

The complete sensitivity report generated by the Excel Solver for the original Wyndor problem as formulated in Figure 5.1.

Adjustable Cells

Cell	Name	Final Value	Reduced Cost	Objective Coefficient	Allowable Increase	Allowable Decrease
$C$12	DoorsProduced	2	0	300	450	300
$D$12	WindowsProduced	6	0	500	1E+30	300

Constraints

Cell	Name	Final Value	Shadow Price	Constraint R. H. Side	Allowable Increase	Allowable Decrease
$E$7	Plant 1 Used	2	0	4	1E+30	2
$E$8	Plant 2 Used	12	150	12	6	6
$E$9	Plant 3 Used	18	100	18	6	6

calculating this range. The "Constraint R. H. Side" column indicates the original value of the right-hand side before any change is made. Adding the number in the "Allowable Increase" column to this original value then gives the upper endpoint of the allowable range. Similarly, subtracting the number in the "Allowable Decrease" column from this original value gives the lower endpoint. Using the fact that 1E+30 represents infinity (∞), these calculations of the allowable ranges are shown below, where a subscript has been added to each RHS to identify the constraint involved.

Plant 1 constraint: $4 - 2 \leq RHS_1 \leq 4 + \infty$, so $2 \leq RHS_1$ (no upper limit)

Plant 2 constraint: $12 - 6 \leq RHS_2 \leq 12 + 6$, so $6 \leq RHS_2 \leq 18$

Plant 3 constraint: $18 - 6 \leq RHS_3 \leq 18 + 6$, so $12 \leq RHS_3 \leq 24$

In the case of the plant 2 constraint, Figure 5.21 provides graphical insight into why $6 \leq RHS \leq 18$ is the range of validity for the shadow price. The optimal solution for the original problem, $(D, W) = (2, 6)$, lies at the intersection of line B and line C. The equation for line B is $2W = 12$ because this is the constraint boundary line for the plant 2 constraint ($2W \leq 12$). However, if the value of this right-hand side ($RHS_2 = 12$) is changed, line B will either shift upward (for a larger value of RHS_2) or downward (for a smaller value of RHS_2). As line B shifts, the boundary of the feasible region shifts accordingly and the optimal solution continues to lie at the intersection of the shifted line B and line C—provided the shift in line B is not so large that this intersection is no longer feasible. Each time RHS_2 is increased (or decreased) by 1, this intersection shifts enough to increase (or decrease) Profit by the amount of the shadow price ($150). Figure 5.21 indicates that this intersection remains feasible (and so optimal) as RHS_2 increases from 12 to 18, because the feasible region expands upward as line B shifts upward. However, for values of RHS_2 larger than 18, this intersection is no longer feasible because it gives a negative value of D (the production rate for doors). Thus, each increase of 1 above 18 no longer increases Profit by the amount of the shadow price. Similarly, as RHS_2 decreases from 12 to 6, this intersection remains feasible (and so optimal) as line B shifts down

FIGURE 5.21

A graphical interpretation of the allowable range, $6 \leq RHS_2 \leq 18$, for the right-hand side of Wyndor's plant 2 constraint.

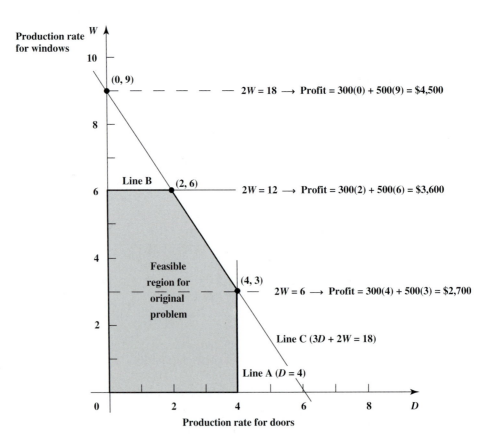

accordingly. However, for values of RHS$_2$ less than 6, this intersection is no longer feasible because it violates the plant 1 constraint ($D \leq 4$) whose boundary line is line A. Hence, each decrease of 1 below 6 no longer decreases Profit by the amount of the shadow price. Consequently, $6 \leq \text{RHS} \leq 18$ is the allowable range over which the shadow price is valid.

Summary

Recall again that the right-hand side of each functional constraint represents the number of hours of production time per week in the corresponding plant that is being made available to the two new products. The *shadow price* for each constraint reveals how much the total profit from these new products would increase for each additional hour of production time made available in the corresponding plant for these products. This interpretation of the shadow price remains valid as long as the number of hours remains within its *allowable range.* Therefore, each shadow price can be applied by management to evaluate a change in its original decision regarding the number of hours as long as the new number is within the corresponding allowable range. This evaluation also would need to take into account how the change in the number of hours made available to the new products would impact the production rates and profits for the company's other products.

Review
Questions

1. Why might it be of interest to investigate the effect of making changes in a functional constraint?
2. Why might it be possible to alter the right-hand side of a functional constraint?
3. What is meant by a *shadow price?*
4. How can a shadow price be found by using the spreadsheet? By using the Solver Table? By using Solver's sensitivity report?
5. Why are shadow prices of interest to managers?
6. Can shadow prices be used to determine the effect of *decreasing* rather than increasing the right-hand side of a functional constraint?
7. What does a shadow price of 0 tell a manager?
8. Which columns of the Solver's sensitivity report are used to find the allowable range for the right-hand side of a functional constraint?
9. Why are these allowable ranges of interest to managers?

5.6 THE EFFECT OF SIMULTANEOUS CHANGES IN THE CONSTRAINTS

The preceding section described how to perform what-if analysis to investigate the effect of changes in a single spot of a constraint. We now turn our consideration to the effect of simultaneous changes in the constraints.

The need to consider these simultaneous changes arises frequently. There may be considerable uncertainty about the estimates for a number of the parameters in the functional constraints, so questions will arise as to the effect if the true values of the parameters simultaneously deviate significantly from the estimates. Since the right-hand sides of the constraints often represent managerial policy decisions, questions will arise about what would happen if some of these decisions were to be changed. These decisions frequently are interrelated and so need to be considered simultaneously.

Managerial policy decisions involving right-hand sides frequently are interrelated, so changes in these decisions should be considered simultaneously.

We outline next how the usual three methods for performing what-if analysis can be applied to considering simultaneous changes in the constraints. The third one (using Solver's sensitivity report) is only helpful for changing right-hand sides. For the first two (using the spreadsheet and using the Solver Table), the procedure is the same regardless of whether the changes are in the coefficients on the left-hand sides or in the right-hand sides of the constraints (or both). Since changing the right-hand sides is the more important case, we will focus on this case.

In particular, we now will deal with the last of Wyndor management's what-if questions.

Question 4: What happens if simultaneous changes are made in the number of hours of production time per week being made available to Wyndor's new products in all the plants?

In particular, after seeing that the plant 2 constraint has the largest shadow price (150), versus a shadow price of 100 for the plant 3 constraint, management now is interested in exploring a specific type of simultaneous change in these production hours. By shifting the production of one of the company's current products from plant 2 to plant 3, it is possible to increase the number of production hours available to the new products in plant 2 by decreasing the number of production hours available in plant 3 by the same amount. Management wonders what would happen if these simultaneous changes in production hours were made.

Using the Spreadsheet for This Analysis

According to the shadow prices, the effect of shifting one hour of production time per week from plant 3 to plant 2 would be as follows.

RHS$_2$: 12 → 13   Change in total profit =   Shadow price = $150
RHS$_3$: 18 → 17   Change in total profit = − Shadow price = $\underline{-100}$
                              Net increase in total profit = $50

We now are checking to see whether the shadow prices remain valid for evaluating such large simultaneous changes in the right-hand sides.

However, we don't know if these shadow prices remain valid if *both* right-hand sides are changed by this amount.

A quick way to check this is to substitute the new right-hand sides into the original spreadsheet in Figure 5.1 and click on the Solve button again. The resulting spreadsheet in Figure 5.22 shows that the net increase in total profit (from $3,600 to $3,650) is indeed $50, so the shadow prices are valid for these particular simultaneous changes in right-hand sides.

How long will these shadow prices remain valid if we continue shifting production hours from plant 3 to plant 2? We could continue checking this by substituting other combinations of right-hand sides into the spreadsheet and re-solving each time. However, a more systematic way of doing this is to use the Solver Table as described below.

Using the Solver Table for This Analysis

Complete instructions for using the Solver Table are given in Appendix A.

Since it can become tedious, or even impractical, to use the spreadsheet to investigate a large number of simultaneous changes in the right-hand sides, let us see how a Solver Table (provided in your MS Courseware) can be used to do this analysis more systematically.

We could use a two-way Solver Table to investigate how the profit and optimal production rates vary for different combinations of the number of hours available in plant 2 and plant 3. However, in this case we aren't interested in *all* combinations of hours in the two plants, but rather only those combinations that involve a simple *shifting* of available hours from plant 3 to plant 2. For this analysis, we will see that a one-way Solver Table is sufficient.

FIGURE 5.22
The revised Wyndor problem where column G in Figure 5.1 has been changed by shifting one of the hours available in plant 3 to plant 2 and then re-solving.

	A	B	C	D	E	F	G
1		**Wyndor Glass Co. Product-Mix Problem**					
2							
3			Doors	Windows			
4		Unit Profit	$300	$500			
5					Hours		Hours
6			Hours Used per Unit Produced		Used		Available
7		Plant 1	1	0	1.33333	≤	4
8		Plant 2	0	2	13	≤	13
9		Plant 3	3	2	17	≤	17
10							
11			Doors	Windows			Total Profit
12		Units Produced	1.333	6.5			$3,650

For each hour reduced in plant 3, an additional hour is made available in plant 2. Thus, the number of available hours in plant 2 is a function of the number of available hours in plant 3. In particular, since there are 30 total hours available at the two plants ($RHS_2 + RHS_3 = 30$), the number of available hours in plant 2 (RHS_2) is

$$RHS_2 = 30 - RHS_3$$

By entering a formula into one data cell in terms of another one, the one-way Solver Table is able to investigate interrelated trial values in both data cells.

Figure 5.23 shows the Wyndor Glass Co. spreadsheet with the data cell for the number of available hours in plant 2 replaced by the above formula. Because of this formula, whenever the number of available hours in plant 3 is reduced, the number of available hours in plant 2 will automatically increase by the same amount. Now a one-way Solver Table can be used to investigate various numbers of available hours in plant 3 (with the corresponding automatic adjustment made to the available hours at plant 2). The trial values for the number of hours available in plant 3 are shown in the Solver Table at the bottom of the spreadsheet in Figure 5.23 (C20:C26). We are interested in the output cells DoorsProduced (C12), WindowsProduced (D12), and TotalProfit (G12), so equations referring to these cells are entered in the first row of the table (D19:F19). Running the Solver Table (with the column input cell as G9, the hours available in plant 3) then fills in the values in the body of the table (D20:F26). We have calculated the incremental profit (in column G) for each hour shifted from plant 3 to plant 2.

Again there is a pattern to the incremental profit. For each hour shifted from plant 3 to plant 2 (up to 3 hours), an additional profit of $50 is achieved. However, if more than 3 hours are shifted, the incremental profit becomes $-$250. Thus, it appears worthwhile to shift up to 3 available hours from plant 3 to plant 2, but no more.

Although a one-way Solver Table is limited to enumerating trial values for only one data cell, you have just seen how such a Solver Table still can systematically investigate a large number of simultaneous changes in two data cells by entering a formula for the second data cell in terms of the first one. The two data cells considered above happened to be right-hand sides of constraints, but either or both could have been coefficients on the left-hand side instead. It is even possible to enter formulas for multiple data cells in terms of the one whose trial values are being enumerated. Furthermore, by using the two-way Solver Table, trial values can be enumerated simultaneously for two data cells, with the possibility of entering formulas for additional data cells in terms of these two.

Gleaning Additional Information from the Sensitivity Report

Despite the versatility of the Solver Table, it cannot handle a number of important cases. The most important one is where management wants to explore various possibilities for changing its policy decisions that correspond to changing several right-hand sides simultaneously in a variety of ways. Although the spreadsheet can be used to see the effect of any combination of simultaneous changes, it can take an exorbitant amount of time to systematically investigate a large number of simultaneous changes in right-hand sides in this way. Fortunately, Solver's sensitivity report provides valuable information for guiding such an investigation. In particular, there is a *100 percent rule* (analogous to the one presented in Section 5.4) that uses this information to conduct this kind of investigation.

Recall that the 100 percent rule described in Section 5.4 is used to investigate simultaneous changes in *objective function coefficients*. The new 100 percent rule presented next investigates simultaneous changes in *right-hand sides* in a similar way.

The data needed to apply the new 100 percent rule for the Wyndor problem are given by the last three columns in the bottom part of the sensitivity report in Figure 5.20. Keep in mind that we can safely use the entire allowable decrease or increase from the current value of a right-hand side only if none of the other right-hand sides are changed at all. With simultaneous changes in the right-hand sides, we focus for each change on the *percentage* of the allowable decrease or increase that is being used. As detailed below, the 100 percent rule basically says that we can safely make the simultaneous changes only if the *sum* of these percentages does not exceed 100 percent.

FIGURE 5.23

By inserting a formula into cell G8 that keeps the total number of hours available in plant 2 and plant 3 equal to 30, this one-dimensional application of the Solver Table shows the effect of shifting more and more of the hours available from plant 3 to plant 2.

	A	B	C	D	E	F	G	H
1		**Wyndor Glass Co. Product-Mix Problem**						
2								
3			Doors	Windows				
4		Unit Profit	$300	$500				
5					Hours		Hours	
6			Hours Used per Unit Produced		Used		Available	
7		Plant 1	1	0	2	≤	4	Total (Plants 2 & 3)
8		Plant 2	0	2	12	≤	12	30
9		Plant 3	3	2	18	≤	18	
10								
11			Doors	Windows			Total Profit	
12		Units Produced	2	6			$3,600	
13								
14								
15								
16								
17		Time Available in	Time Available in	Optimal Units Produced		Total	Incremental	
18		Plant 2 (hours)	Plant 3 (hours)	Doors	Windows	Profit	Profit	
19				2	6	$3,600		Select these cells (C19:F26), before choosing the Solver Table.
20		12	18	2	6	$3,600		
21		13	17	1.333	6.5	$3,650	$50	
22		14	16	0.667	7	$3,700	$50	
23		15	15	0	7.5	$3,750	$50	
24		16	14	0	7	$3,500	-$250	
25		17	13	0	6.5	$3,250	-$250	
26		18	12	0	6	$3,000	-$250	

Solver Table

Row input cell: [ ]
Column input cell: [G9]
Cancel   OK

Range Name	Cells
DoorsProduced	C12
TotalProfit	G12
WindowsProduced	D12

	G	H
5	Hours	
6	Available	
7	4	Total (Plants 2 & 3)
8	=H8-G9	30
9	18	

	B	C	D	E	F	G
17	Time Available in	Time Available in	Optimal Units Produced		Total	Incremental
18	Plant 2 (hours)	Plant 3 (hours)	Doors	Windows	Profit	Profit
19			=DoorsProduced	=WindowsProduced	=TotalProfit	
20	=$H$8-C20	18	2	6	$3,600	
21	=$H$8-C21	17	1.333	6.5	$3,650	=F21-F20
22	=$H$8-C22	16	0.667	7	$3,700	=F22-F21
23	=$H$8-C23	15	0	7.5	$3,750	=F23-F22
24	=$H$8-C24	14	0	7	$3,500	=F24-F23
25	=$H$8-C25	13	0	6.5	$3,250	=F25-F24
26	=$H$8-C26	12	0	6	$3,000	=F26-F25

This 100 percent rule reveals whether the simultaneous changes in the right-hand sides are small enough to guarantee that the shadow prices are still valid.

The 100 Percent Rule for Simultaneous Changes in Right-Hand Sides: The shadow prices remain valid for predicting the effect of simultaneously changing the right-hand sides of some of the functional constraints as long as the changes are not too large. To check whether the changes are small enough, calculate for each change the percentage of the allowable change (decrease or increase) for that right-hand side to remain within its allowable range. If the *sum* of the percentage changes does *not* exceed 100 percent, the shadow prices definitely will still be valid. (If the sum *does* exceed 100 percent, then we cannot be sure.)

To illustrate this rule, consider again the simultaneous changes (shifting one hour of production time per week from plant 3 to plant 2) that led to Figure 5.22. The calculations for the 100 percent rule in this case are

RHS_2: $12 \to 13$

$$\text{Percentage of allowable increase} = 100\left(\frac{13-12}{6}\right) = 16\tfrac{2}{3}\%$$

RHS_3: $18 \to 17$

$$\text{Percentage of allowable decrease} = 100\left(\frac{18-17}{6}\right) = 16\tfrac{2}{3}\%$$

$$\text{Sum} = \overline{33\tfrac{1}{3}\%}$$

Since the sum of 33⅓ percent is less than 100 percent, the shadow prices definitely are valid for predicting the effect of these changes, as was illustrated with Figure 5.22.

The fact that 33⅓ percent is one-third of 100 percent suggests that the changes can be three times as large as above without invalidating the shadow prices. To check this, let us apply the 100 percent rule with these larger changes.

RHS_2: $12 \to 15$

$$\text{Percentage of allowable increase} = \left(\frac{15-12}{6}\right)\% = 50\%$$

RHS_3: $18 \to 15$

$$\text{Percentage of allowable decrease} = \left(\frac{18-15}{6}\right)\% = 50\%$$

$$\text{Sum} = \overline{100\%}$$

Because the sum does *not exceed* 100 percent, the shadow prices are still valid, but these are the largest changes in the right-hand sides that can provide this guarantee. In fact, Figure 5.23 demonstrated that the shadow prices become invalid for larger changes.

Review Questions

1. Why might it be of interest to investigate the effect of making simultaneous changes in the functional constraints?
2. How can the spreadsheet be used to investigate simultaneous changes in the functional constraints?
3. What are the capabilities of the Solver Table for investigating simultaneous changes in the functional constraints?
4. Why might a manager be interested in considering simultaneous changes in right-hand sides?
5. What is the 100 percent rule for simultaneous changes in right-hand sides?
6. What are the data needed to apply the 100 percent rule for simultaneous changes in right-hand sides?
7. What is guaranteed if the sum of the percentages of allowable changes in the right-hand sides does not exceed 100 percent?
8. What is the conclusion if the sum of the percentages of allowable changes in the right-hand sides does exceed 100 percent?

5.7 Summary

What-if analysis is analysis done *after* finding an optimal solution for the original version of the basic model. This analysis provides important insights to help guide managerial decision making. This chapter describes how this is done when the basic model is a linear programming model. The spreadsheet for the model, the Solver Table provided in your MS Courseware, and the sensitivity report generated by the Excel Solver all play a central role in this process.

The coefficients in the objective function typically represent quantities that can only be roughly estimated when the model is formulated. Will the optimal solution obtained from the model be the correct one if the true value of one of these coefficients is significantly different from the estimate used in the model? The spreadsheet can be used to quickly check specific changes in the coefficient. The Solver Table enables the systematic investigation of many trial values for this coefficient. For a broader investigation, the *allowable range* for each coefficient identifies the interval within which the true value must lie in order for this solution to still be the correct optimal solution. These ranges are easily calculated from the data in the sensitivity report provided by the Excel Solver.

What happens if there are significant inaccuracies in the estimates of two or more coefficients in the objective function? Specific simultaneous changes can be checked with the spreadsheet. A two-way Solver Table can systematically investigate various simultaneous changes in two coefficients. To go further, the *100 percent rule for simultaneous changes in objective function coefficients* provides a convenient way of checking whole ranges of simultaneous changes, again by using the data in the Solver's sensitivity report.

What-if analysis usually extends to considering the effect of changes in the functional constraints as well. Occasionally, changes in the coefficients of these constraints will be considered because of the uncertainty in their original estimates. More frequently, the changes considered will be in the right-hand sides of the constraints. The right-hand sides frequently represent managerial policy decisions. In such cases, *shadow prices* provide valuable guidance to management about the potential effects of altering these policy decisions. The shadow price for each constraint is easily found by using the spreadsheet, the Solver Table, or the sensitivity report.

Shadow price analysis can be validly applied to investigate possible changes in right-hand sides as long as these changes are not too large. The *allowable range* for each right-hand side indicates just how far it can be changed, assuming no other changes are made. If, in fact, other changes are made as well, the *100 percent rule for simultaneous changes in right-hand sides* enables checking whether the changes definitely are not too large. The Solver's sensitivity report provides the key information needed to find each allowable range or to apply this 100 percent rule. Both the spreadsheet and the Solver Table also can sometimes be used to help investigate these simultaneous changes.

Glossary

allowable range for an objective function coefficient The range of values for a particular coefficient in the objective function over which the optimal solution for the original model remains optimal. (Section 5.3), 147

allowable range for the right-hand side The range of values for the right-hand side of a functional constraint over which this constraint's shadow price remains valid. (Section 5.5), 161

parameters of the model The parameters of a linear programming model are the constants (coefficients or right-hand sides) in the functional constraints and the objective function. (Section 5.1), 141

sensitive parameter A parameter is considered sensitive if even a small change in its value can change the optimal solution. (Section 5.1), 141

sensitivity analysis The part of what-if analysis that focuses on individual parameters of the model. It involves checking how sensitive the optimal solution is to the value of each parameter. (Section 5.1), 142

shadow price The shadow price for a functional constraint is the rate at which the optimal value of the objective function can be increased by increasing the right-hand side of the constraint by a small amount. (Section 5.5), 161

what-if analysis Analysis that addresses questions about what would happen to the optimal solution if different assumptions were made about future conditions. (Chapter introduction), 140

Learning Aids for This Chapter in Your MS Courseware

Chapter 5 Excel Files:

Wyndor Example

Profit & Gambit Example

Excel Add-ins:

Premium Solver for Education

Solver Table

Interactive Management Science Modules:

Module for Graphical Linear Programming and Sensitivity Analysis

Supplement to Chapter 5 on the CD-ROM:

Reduced Costs

Solved Problem (See the CD-ROM for the Solution)

5.S1. Sensitivity Analysis at Stickley Furniture

Stickley Furniture is a manufacturer of fine hand-crafted furniture. During the next production period, management is considering producing dining room tables, dining room chairs, and/or bookcases. The time required for each item

to go through the two stages of production (assembly and finishing), the amount of wood required (fine cherry wood), and the corresponding unit profits are given in the following table, along with the amount of each resource available in the upcoming production period.

	Tables	Chairs	Bookcases	Available
Assembly (minutes)	80	40	50	8,100
Finishing (minutes)	30	20	30	4,500
Wood (pounds)	80	10	50	9,000
Unit profit	$360	$125	$300	

After formulating a linear programming model to determine the production levels that would maximize profit, the solved model

and the corresponding sensitivity report are shown below.

	B	C	D	E	F	G	H
3		Tables	Chairs	Bookcases			
4	Unit Profit	$360	$125	$300			
5							
6		Resources Required per Unit			Used		Available
7	Assembly (minutes)	80	40	50	8,100	<=	8,100
8	Finishing (minutes)	30	20	30	4,500	<=	4,500
9	Woods (pounds)	80	10	50	8,100	<=	9,000
10							
11		Tables	Chairs	Bookcases			Total Profit
12	Production	20	0	130			$46,200

Adjustable Cells

Cell	Name	Final Value	Reduced Cost	Objective Coefficient	Allowable Increase	Allowable Decrease
$C$12	Production Tables	20	0	360	120	60
$D$12	Production Chairs	0	-88.333	125	88.333	1E+30
$E$12	Production Bookcases	130	0	300	60	75

Constraints

Cell	Name	Final Value	Shadow Price	Constraint R. H. Side	Allowable Increase	Allowable Decrease
$F$7	Assembly (minutes) Used	8,100	2	8,100	900	600
$F$8	Finishing (minutes) Used	4,500	6.67	4,500	360	1,462.5
$F$9	Wood (pounds) Used	8,100	0	9,000	1E+30	900

a. Suppose the profit per table increases by $100. Will this change the optimal production quantities? What can be said about the change in total profit?

b. Suppose the profit per chair increases by $100. Will this change the optimal production quantities? What can be said about the change in total profit?

c. Suppose the profit per table increases by $90 and the profit per bookcase decreases by $50. Will this change the optimal production quantities? What can be said about the change in total profit?

d. Suppose a worker in the assembly department calls in sick, so eight fewer hours now are available in the assembly department. How much would this affect total profit? Would it change the optimal production quantities?

e. Explain why the shadow price for the wood constraint is zero.

f. A new worker has been hired who is trained to do both assembly and finishing. She will split her time between the two areas, so there now are four additional hours available in both assembly and finishing. How much would this affect total profit? Would this change the optimal production quantities?

g. Based on the sensitivity report, is it wise to have the new worker in part *f* split her time equally

between assembly and finishing, or would some other plan be better?

h. Use the Solver Table to determine how the optimal production quantities and total profit will change depending on how the new worker in part *f* allocates her time between assembly and finishing. In particular, assume 0, 1, 2, . . . , or 8 hours are added to assembly, with a corresponding 8, 7, 6, . . . , or 0 hours added to finishing. (The original spreadsheet is contained on the CD included with the textbook.)

Problems

We have inserted the symbol E* to the left of each problem (or its parts) where Excel should be used (unless your instructor gives you contrary instructions). An asterisk on the problem number indicates that at least a partial answer is given in the back of the book.

5.1.* One of the products of the G.A. Tanner Company is a special kind of toy that provides an estimated unit profit of $3. Because of a large demand for this toy, management would like to increase its production rate from the current level of 1,000 per day. However, a limited supply of two subassemblies (A and B) from vendors makes this difficult. Each toy requires two subassemblies of type A, but the vendor providing these subassemblies would only be able to increase its supply rate from the current 2,000 per day to a maximum of 3,000 per day. Each toy requires only one subassembly of type B, but the vendor providing these subassemblies

would be unable to increase its supply rate above the current level of 1,000 per day.

Because no other vendors currently are available to provide these subassemblies, management is considering initiating a new production process internally that would simultaneously produce an equal number of subassemblies of the two types to supplement the supply from the two vendors. It is estimated that the company's cost for producing one subassembly of each type would be $2.50 more than the cost of purchasing these subassemblies from the two vendors. Management wants to determine both the production rate of the toy and the production rate of each pair of subassemblies (one A and one B) that would maximize the total profit.

Viewing this problem as a resource-allocation problem, one of the company's managers has organized its data as follows:

| | Resource Usage per Unit of Each Activity | | |
Resource	Produce Toys	Produce Subassemblies	Amount of Resource Available
Subassembly A	2	−1	3,000
Subassembly B	1	−1	1,000
Unit profit	$3	−$2.50	

E* a. Formulate and solve a spreadsheet model for this problem.

E* b. Since the stated unit profits for the two activities are only estimates, management wants to know how much each of these estimates can be off before the optimal solution would change. Begin exploring this question for the first activity (producing toys) by using the spreadsheet and Solver to manually generate a table that gives the optimal solution and total profit as the unit profit for this activity increases in 50¢ increments from $2.00 to $4.00. What conclusion can be drawn about how much the estimate of

this unit profit can differ in each direction from its original value of $3.00 before the optimal solution would change?

E* c. Repeat part *b* for the second activity (producing subassemblies) by generating a table as the unit profit for this activity increases in 50¢ increments from −$3.50 to −$1.50 (with the unit profit for the first activity fixed at $3).

E* d. Use the Solver Table to systematically generate all the data requested in parts *b* and *c*, except use 25¢ increments instead of 50¢ increments. Use these data to refine your conclusions in parts *b* and *c*.

E*   e. Use Excel's sensitivity report to find the allowable range for the unit profit of each activity.

E*   f. Use a two-dimensional Solver Table to systematically generate the total profit as the unit profits of the two activities are changed simultaneously as described in parts b and c.

g. Use the information provided by Excel's sensitivity report to describe how far the unit profits of the two activities can change simultaneously before the optimal solution might change.

5.2. Consider a resource-allocation problem having the following data:

	Resource Usage per Unit of Each Activity		
Resource	1	2	Amount of Resource Available
1	1	2	10
2	1	3	12
Unit profit	$2	$5	

The objective is to determine the number of units of each activity to undertake so as to maximize the total profit.

While doing what-if analysis, you learn that the estimates of the unit profits are accurate only to within ± 50 percent. In other words, the ranges of *likely values* for these unit profits are $1 to $3 for activity 1 and $2.50 to $7.50 for activity 2.

E*   a. Formulate a spreadsheet model for this problem based on the original estimates of the unit profits. Then use the Solver to find an optimal solution and to generate the sensitivity report.

E*   b. Use the spreadsheet and Solver to check whether this optimal solution remains optimal if the unit profit for activity 1 changes from $2 to $1. From $2 to $3.

E*   c. Also check whether the optimal solution remains optimal if the unit profit for activity 1 still is $2 but the unit profit for activity 2 changes from $5 to $2.50. From $5 to $7.50.

E*   d. Use the Solver Table to systematically generate the optimal solution and total profit as the unit profit of activity 1 increases in 20¢ increments from $1 to $3 (without changing the unit profit of activity 2). Then do the same as the unit profit of activity 2 increases in 50¢ increments from $2.50 to $7.50 (without changing the unit profit of activity 1). Use these results to estimate the allowable range for the unit profit of each activity.

e. Use the Graphical Linear Programming and Sensitivity Analysis module in your Interactive Management Science Modules to estimate the allowable range for the unit profit of each activity.

E*   f. Use the sensitivity report to find the allowable range for the unit profit of each activity. Then use these ranges to check your results in parts b–e.

E*   g. Use a two-dimensional Solver Table to systematically generate the optimal solution as the unit profits of the two activities are changed simultaneously as described in part d.

h. Use the Graphical Linear Programming and Sensitivity Analysis module to interpret the results in part g graphically.

E*5.3. Consider the Big M Co. problem presented in Section 3.5, including the spreadsheet in Figure 3.10 showing its formulation and optimal solution.

There is some uncertainty about what the unit costs will be for shipping through the various shipping lanes. Therefore, before adopting the optimal solution in Figure 3.10, management wants additional information about the effect of inaccuracies in estimating these unit costs.

Use the Excel Solver to generate the sensitivity report preparatory to addressing the following questions.

a. Which of the unit shipping costs given in Table 3.9 has the smallest margin for error without invalidating the optimal solution given in Figure 3.10? Where should the greatest effort be placed in estimating the unit shipping costs?

b. What is the allowable range for each of the unit shipping costs?

c. How should the allowable range be interpreted to management?

d. If the estimates change for more than one of the unit shipping costs, how can you use the sensitivity report to determine whether the optimal solution might change?

E*5.4.* Consider the Union Airways problem presented in Section 3.3, including the spreadsheet in Figure 3.5 showing its formulation and optimal solution.

Management is about to begin negotiations on a new contract with the union that represents the company's customer service agents. This might result in some small changes in the daily costs per agent given in Table 3.5 for the various shifts. Several possible changes listed below are being considered separately. In each case, management would like to know whether the change might result in the solution in Figure 3.5 no longer being optimal. Answer this question in parts a to e by using the spreadsheet and Solver directly. If the optimal solution changes, record the new solution.

a. The daily cost per agent for shift 2 changes from $160 to $165.

b. The daily cost per agent for shift 4 changes from $180 to $170.

c. The changes in parts a and b both occur.

d. The daily cost per agent increases by $4 for shifts 2, 4, and 5, but decreases by $4 for shifts 1 and 3.

e. The daily cost per agent increases by 2 percent for each shift.

f. Use the Solver to generate the sensitivity report for this problem. Suppose that the above changes are being considered later without having the spreadsheet model immediately available on a computer. Show in each case how the sensitivity report can be used to check whether the original optimal solution must still be optimal.

g. For each of the five shifts in turn, use the Solver Table to systematically generate the optimal solution and total cost when the only change is that the daily cost per agent on that shift increases in $3 increments from $15 less than the current cost up to $15 more than the current cost.

E*5.5. Consider the Think-Big Development Co. problem presented in Section 3.2, including the spreadsheet in Figure 3.3 showing its formulation and optimal solution. In parts *a–g*, use the spreadsheet and Solver to check whether the optimal solution would change and, if so, what the new optimal solution would be, if the estimates in Table 3.3 of the net present values of the projects were to be changed in each of the following ways. (Consider each part by itself.)

a. The net present value of project 1 (a high-rise office building) increases by $200,000.

b. The net present value of project 2 (a hotel) increases by $200,000.

c. The net present value of project 1 decreases by $5 million.

d. The net present value of project 3 (a shopping center) decreases by $200,000.

e. All three changes in parts *b*, *c*, and *d* occur simultaneously.

f. The net present values of projects 1, 2, and 3 change to $46 million, $69 million, and $49 million, respectively.

g. The net present values of projects 1, 2, and 3 change to $54 million, $84 million, and $60 million, respectively.

h. Use the Solver to generate the sensitivity report for this problem. For each of the above parts, suppose that the change occurs later without having the spreadsheet model immediately available on a computer. Show in each case how the sensitivity report can be used to check whether the original optimal solution must still be optimal.

i. For each of the three projects in turn, use the Solver Table to systematically generate the optimal solution

and the total net present value when the only change is that the net present value of that project increases in $1 million increments from $5 million less than the current value up to $5 million more than the current value.

5.6. Ken and Larry, Inc., supplies its ice cream parlors with three flavors of ice cream: chocolate, vanilla, and banana. Due to extremely hot weather and a high demand for its products, the company has run short of its supply of ingredients: milk, sugar, and cream. Hence, they will not be able to fill all the orders received from their retail outlets, the ice cream parlors. Due to these circumstances, the company has decided to choose the amount of each flavor to produce that will maximize total profit, given the constraints on the supply of the basic ingredients.

The chocolate, vanilla, and banana flavors generate, respectively, $1.00, $0.90, and $0.95 of profit per gallon sold. The company has only 200 gallons of milk, 150 pounds of sugar, and 60 gallons of cream left in its inventory. The linear programming formulation for this problem is shown below in algebraic form.

Let

C = Gallons of chocolate ice cream produced

V = Gallons of vanilla ice cream produced

B = Gallons of banana ice cream produced

Maximize   Profit = $1.00C + 0.90V + 0.95B$

subject to

Milk: $0.45C + 0.50V + 0.40B \leq 200$ gallons

Sugar: $0.50C + 0.40V + 0.40B \leq 150$ pounds

Cream: $0.10C + 0.15V + 0.20B \leq 60$ gallons

and

$C \geq 0 \quad V \geq 0 \quad B \geq 0$

This problem was solved using the Excel Solver. The spreadsheet (already solved) and the sensitivity report are shown below. (Note: The numbers in the sensitivity report for the milk constraint are missing on purpose, since you will be asked to fill in these numbers in part *f*.)

	A	B	C	D	E	F	G
1		Chocolate	Vanilla	Banana			
2	Unit Profit	$1.00	$0.90	$0.95			
3							
4	Resource	Resources Used per Gallon Produced			Used		Available
5	Milk	0.45	0.5	0.4	180	≤	200
6	Sugar	0.5	0.4	0.4	150	≤	150
7	Cream	0.1	0.15	0.2	60	≤	60
8							
9		Chocolate	Vanilla	Banana			Total Profit
10	Gallons Produced	0	300	75			$341.25

Adjustable Cells

Cell	Name	Final Value	Reduced Cost	Objective Coefficient	Allowable Increase	Allowable Decrease
$B$10	Gallons Produced Chocolate	0	−0.0375	1	0.0375	1E+30
$C$10	Gallons Produced Vanilla	300	0	0.9	0.05	0.0125
$D$10	Gallons Produced Banana	75	0	0.95	0.0214	0.05

Constraints

Cell	Name	Final Value	Shadow Price	Constraint R. H. Side	Allowable Increase	Allowable Decrease
$E$5	Milk Used					
$E$6	Sugar Used	150	1.875	150	10	30
$E$7	Cream Used	60	1	60	15	3.75

For each of the following parts, answer the question as specifically and completely as possible without solving the problem again with the Excel Solver. Note: Each part is independent (i.e., any change made to the model in one part does not apply to any other parts).

a. What is the optimal solution and total profit?

b. Suppose the profit per gallon of banana changes to $1.00. Will the optimal solution change and what can be said about the effect on total profit?

c. Suppose the profit per gallon of banana changes to 92¢. Will the optimal solution change and what can be said about the effect on total profit?

d. Suppose the company discovers that three gallons of cream have gone sour and so must be thrown out. Will the optimal solution change and what can be said about the effect on total profit?

e. Suppose the company has the opportunity to buy an additional 15 pounds of sugar at a total cost of $15. Should it do so? Explain.

f. Fill in all the sensitivity report information for the milk constraint, given just the optimal solution for the problem. Explain how you were able to deduce each number.

5.7. David, LaDeana, and Lydia are the sole partners and workers in a company that produces fine clocks. David and LaDeana are each available to work a maximum of 40 hours per week at the company, while Lydia is available to work a maximum of 20 hours per week.

The company makes two different types of clocks: a grandfather clock and a wall clock. To make a clock, David (a mechanical engineer) assembles the inside mechanical parts of the clock while LaDeana (a wood-worker) produces the hand-carved wood casings. Lydia is responsible for taking orders and shipping the clocks. The amount of time required for each of these tasks is shown next.

	Time Required	
Task	Grandfather Clock	Wall Clock
Assemble clock mechanism	6 hours	4 hours
Carve wood casing	8 hours	4 hours
Shipping	3 hours	3 hours

Each grandfather clock built and shipped yields a profit of $300, while each wall clock yields a profit of $200.

The three partners now want to determine how many clocks of each type should be produced per week to maximize the total profit.

a. Formulate a linear programming model in algebraic form for this problem.

b. Use the Graphical Linear Programming and Sensitivity Analysis module in your Interactive Management Science Modules to solve the model. Then use this module to check if the optimal solution would change if the unit profit for grandfather clocks were changed from $300 to $375 (with no other changes

in the model). Then check if the optimal solution would change if, in addition to this change in the unit profit for grandfather clocks, the estimated unit profit for wall clocks also changed from $200 to $175.

E* c. Formulate and solve the original version of this model on a spreadsheet.

E* d. Use the Excel Solver to check the effect of the changes specified in part b.

E* e. Use the Solver Table to systematically generate the optimal solution and total profit as the unit profit for grandfather clocks is increased in $20 increments from $150 to $450 (with no change in the unit profit for wall clocks). Then do the same as the unit profit for wall clocks is increased in $20 increments from $50 to $350 (with no change in the unit profit for grandfather clocks). Use this information to estimate the allowable range for the unit profit of each type of clock.

E* f. Use a two-dimensional Solver Table to systematically generate the optimal solution (similar to Figure 5.13) as the unit profits for the two types of clocks are changed simultaneously as specified in part *e*, except use $50 increments instead of $20 increments.

E* g. For each of the three partners in turn, use the Excel Solver to determine the effect on the optimal solution and the total profit if that partner alone were to increase his or her maximum number of work hours available per week by 5 hours.

E* h. Use the Solver Table to systematically generate the optimal solution and the total profit when the only change is that David's maximum number of hours available to work per week changes to each of the following values: 35, 37, 39, 41, 43, 45. Then do the same when the only change is that LaDeana's maximum number of hours available to work per week changes in the same way. Then do the same when the only change is that Lydia's maximum number of hours available to work per week changes to each of the following values: 15, 17, 19, 21, 23, 25.

E* i. Generate the Excel sensitivity report and use it to determine the allowable range for the unit profit for each type of clock and the allowable range for the maximum number of hours each partner is available to work per week.

j. To increase the total profit, the three partners have agreed that one of them will slightly increase the maximum number of hours available to work per week. The choice of which one will be based on which one would increase the total profit the most. Use the sensitivity report to make this choice. (Assume no change in the original estimates of the unit profits.)

k. Explain why one of the shadow prices is equal to zero.

l. Can the shadow prices in the sensitivity report be validly used to determine the effect if Lydia were to change her maximum number of hours available to work per week from 20 to 25? If so, what would be the increase in the total profit?

m. Repeat part *l* if, in addition to the change for Lydia, David also were to change his maximum number of hours available to work per week from 40 to 35.

n. Use graphical analysis to verify your answer in part *m*.

E*5.8.* Reconsider Problem 5.1. After further negotiations with each vendor, management of the G.A. Tanner Company has learned that either of them would be willing to consider increasing their supply of their respective subassemblies over the previously stated maxima (3,000

subassemblies of type A per day and 1,000 of type B per day) if the company would pay a small premium over the regular price for the extra subassemblies. The size of the premium for each type of subassembly remains to be negotiated. The demand for the toy being produced is sufficiently high that 2,500 per day could be sold if the supply of subassemblies could be increased enough to support this production rate. Assume that the original estimates of unit profits given in Problem 5.1 are accurate.

a. Formulate and solve a spreadsheet model for this problem with the original maximum supply levels and the additional constraint that no more than 2,500 toys should be produced per day.

b. Without considering the premium, use the spreadsheet and Solver to determine the shadow price for the subassembly A constraint by solving the model again after increasing the maximum supply by one. Use this shadow price to determine the maximum premium that the company should be willing to pay for each subassembly of this type.

c. Repeat part *b* for the subassembly B constraint.

d. Estimate how much the maximum supply of subassemblies of type A could be increased before the shadow price (and the corresponding premium) found in part *b* would no longer be valid by using the Solver Table to generate the optimal solution and total profit (excluding the premium) as the maximum supply increases in increments of 100 from 3,000 to 4,000.

e. Repeat part *d* for subassemblies of type B by using the Solver Table as the maximum supply increases in increments of 100 from 1,000 to 2,000.

f. Use the Solver's sensitivity report to determine the shadow price for each of the subassembly constraints and the allowable range for the right-hand side of each of these constraints.

E*5.9. Reconsider the model given in Problem 5.2. While doing what-if analysis, you learn that the estimates of the right-hand sides of the two functional constraints are accurate only to within ± 50 percent. In other words, the ranges of *likely values* for these parameters are 5 to 15 for the first right-hand side and 6 to 18 for the second right-hand side.

a. After solving the original spreadsheet model, determine the shadow price for the first functional constraint by increasing its right-hand side by one and solving again.

b. Use the Solver Table to generate the optimal solution and total profit as the right-hand side of the first functional constraint is incremented by 1 from 5 to 15. Use this table to estimate the allowable range for this right-hand side, that is, the range over which the shadow price obtained in part *a* is valid.

c. Repeat part *a* for the second functional constraint.

d. Repeat part *b* for the second functional constraint where its right-hand side is incremented by 1 from 6 to 18.

e. Use the Solver's sensitivity report to determine the shadow price for each functional constraint and the allowable range for the right-hand side of each of these constraints.

5.10. Consider a resource-allocation problem having the following data:

Resource	Resource Usage per Unit of Each Activity		Amount of Resource Available
	1	2	
1	1	3	8
2	1	1	4
Unit profit	$1	$2	

The objective is to determine the number of units of each activity to undertake so as to maximize the total profit.

a. Use the graphical method to solve this model.

b. Use graphical analysis to determine the shadow price for each of these resources by solving again after increasing the amount of the resource available by one.

E* c. Use the spreadsheet model and the Solver instead to do parts a and b.

E* d. For each resource in turn, use the Solver Table to systematically generate the optimal solution and the total profit when the only change is that the amount of that resource available increases in increments of 1 from 4 less than the original value up to 6 more than the original value. Use these results to estimate the allowable range for the amount available for each resource.

E* e. Use the Solver's sensitivity report to obtain the shadow prices. Also use this report to find the range for the amount of each resource available over which the corresponding shadow price remains valid.

f. Describe why these shadow prices are useful when management has the flexibility to change the amounts of the resources being made available.

5.11. Follow the instructions of Problem 5.10 for a resource-allocation problem that again has the objective of maximizing total profit and that has the following data:

Resource	Resource Usage per Unit of Each Activity		Amount of Resource Available
	1	2	
1	1	0	4
2	1	3	15
3	2	1	10
Unit profit	$3	$2	

E*5.12.* Consider the Super Grain Corp. case study as presented in Section 3.1, including the spreadsheet in Figure 3.1 showing its formulation and optimal solution. Use the Excel Solver to generate the sensitivity report. Then use this report to independently address each of the following questions.

a. How much could the total expected number of exposures be increased for each additional $1,000 added to the advertising budget?

b. Your answer in part a would remain valid for how large of an increase in the advertising budget?

c. How much could the total expected number of exposures be increased for each additional $1,000 added to the planning budget?

d. Your answer in part c would remain valid for how large of an increase in the planning budget?

e. Would your answers in parts a and c definitely remain valid if both the advertising budget and planning budget were increased by $100,000 each?

f. If only $100,000 can be added to either the advertising budget or the planning budget, where should it be added to do the most good?

g. If $100,000 must be removed from either the advertising budget or the planning budget, from which budget should it be removed to do the least harm?

E*5.13. Follow the instructions of Problem 5.12 for the continuation of the Super Grain Corp. case study as presented in Section 3.4 including the spreadsheet in Figure 3.7 showing its formulation and optimal solution.

E*5.14. Consider the Union Airways problem presented in Section 3.3, including the spreadsheet in Figure 3.5 showing its formulation and optimal solution.

Management now is considering increasing the level of service provided to customers by increasing one or more of the numbers in the rightmost column of Table 3.5 for the minimum number of agents needed in the various time periods. To guide them in making this decision, they would like to know what impact this change would have on total cost.

Use the Excel Solver to generate the sensitivity report in preparation for addressing the following questions.

a. Which of the numbers in the rightmost column of Table 3.5 can be increased without increasing total cost? In each case, indicate how much it can be increased (if it is the only one being changed) without increasing total cost.

b. For each of the other numbers, how much would the total cost increase per increase of 1 in the number? For each answer, indicate how much the number can be increased (if it is the only one being changed) before the answer is no longer valid.

c. Do your answers in part b definitely remain valid if all the numbers considered in part b are simultaneously increased by 1?

d. Do your answers in part b definitely remain valid if all 10 numbers are simultaneously increased by 1?

e. How far can all 10 numbers be simultaneously increased by the same amount before your answers in part b may no longer be valid?

Case 5-1

Selling Soap

Reconsider the Profit & Gambit Co. advertising-mix problem presented in Section 2.6. Recall that a major advertising campaign is being planned that will focus on three key products: a stain remover, a liquid detergent, and a powder detergent. Management has made the following policy decisions about what needs to be achieved by this campaign.

- Sales of the stain remover should increase by at least 3 percent.
- Sales of the liquid detergent should increase by at least 18 percent.
- Sales of the powder detergent should increase by at least 4 percent.

The spreadsheet in Figure 2.14 shows the linear programming model that was formulated for this problem. The minimum required increases in the sales of the three products are given in the data cells MinimumIncrease (G8:G10). The changing cells Advertising Units (C14:D14) indicate that an optimal solution for the model is to undertake four units of advertising on television and three units of advertising in the print media. The target cell TotalCost (G14) shows that the total cost for this advertising campaign would be $10 million.

After receiving this information, Profit & Gambit management now wants to analyze the trade-off between the total advertising cost and the resulting benefits achieved by increasing the sales of the three products. Therefore, a management science team (you) has been given the assignment of developing the information that management will need to analyze this trade-off and decide whether it should change any of its policy decisions regarding the required minimum increases in the sales of the three products. In particular, management needs some detailed information about how the total advertising cost would change if it were to change any or all of these policy decisions.

a. For each of the three products in turn, use graphical analysis to determine how much the total advertising cost would

change if the required minimum increase in the sales of that product were to be increased by 1 percent (without changing the required minimum increases for the other two products).

b. Use the spreadsheet shown in Figure 2.14 (available on the CD-ROM) to obtain the information requested in part *a.*

c. For each of the three products in turn, use the Solver Table (available on the CD-ROM) to determine how the optimal solution for the model and the resulting total advertising cost would change if the required minimum increase in the sales of that product were to be systematically varied over a range of values (without changing the required minimum increases for the other two products). In each case, start the range of values at 0 percent and increase by 1 percent increments up to double the original minimum required increase.

d. Use the Solver to generate the sensitivity report and indicate how the report is able to provide the information requested in part *a.* Also use the report to obtain the allowable range for the required minimum increase in the sales of each product. Interpret how each of these allowable ranges relates to the results obtained in part *c.*

e. Suppose that all the original numbers in MinimumIncrease (G8:G10) were to be increased simultaneously by the same amount. How large can this amount be before the shadow prices provided by the sensitivity report may no longer be valid?

f. Below is the beginning of a memorandum from the management science team to Profit & Gambit management that is intended to provide management with the information it needs to perform its trade-off analysis. Write the rest of this memorandum based on a summary of the results obtained in the preceding parts. Present your information in clear, simple terms that use the language of management. Avoid technical terms such as shadow prices, allowable ranges, and so forth.

MEMORANDUM

To: Profit & Gambit management
From: The Management Science Team
Subject: The trade-off between advertising expenditures and increased sales

As instructed, we have been continuing our analysis of the plans for the major new advertising campaign that will focus on our spray prewash stain remover, our liquid formulation laundry detergent, and our powder laundry detergent.

Our recent report presented our preliminary conclusions on how much advertising to do in the different media to meet the sales goals at a minimum total cost:

Allocate $4 million to advertising on television.

Allocate $6 million to advertising in the print media.

Total advertising cost: $10 million.

(concluded)

We estimate that the resulting increases in sales will be

Stain remover:	3 percent increase in sales
Liquid detergent:	18 percent increase in sales
Powder detergent:	8 percent increase in sales.

You had specified that these increases should be at least 3 percent, 18 percent, and 4 percent, respectively, so we have met the minimum levels for the first two products and substantially exceeded it for the third.

However, you also indicated that your decisions on these minimum required increases in sales (3 percent, 18 percent, and 4 percent) had been tentative ones. Now that we have more specific information on what the advertising costs and the resulting increases in sales will be, you plan to reevaluate these decisions to see if small changes might improve the trade-off between advertising cost and increased sales.

To assist you in reevaluating your decisions, we now have analyzed this trade-off for each of the three products. Our best estimates are the following.

Case 5-2

Controlling Air Pollution

The Nori & Leets Co. is one of the major producers of steel in its part of the world. It is located in the city of Steeltown and is the only large employer there. Steeltown has grown and prospered along with the company, which now employs nearly 50,000 residents. Therefore, the attitude of the townspeople always has been, "What's good for Nori & Leets is good for the town." However, this attitude is now changing; uncontrolled air pollution from the company's furnaces is ruining the appearance of the city and endangering the health of its residents.

A recent stockholders' revolt resulted in the election of a new enlightened board of directors for the company. These directors are determined to follow socially responsible policies, and they have been discussing with Steeltown city officials and citizens' groups what to do about the air pollution problem. Together they have worked out stringent air quality standards for the Steeltown airshed.

The three main types of pollutants in this airshed are particulate matter, sulfur oxides, and hydrocarbons. The new standards require that the company reduce its annual emission of these pollutants by the amounts shown in the following table.

Pollutant	Required Reduction in Annual Emission Rate (million pounds)
Particulates	60
Sulfur oxides	150
Hydrocarbons	125

The board of directors has instructed management to have the engineering staff determine how to achieve these reductions in the most economical way.

The steelworks have two primary sources of pollution, namely, the blast furnaces for making pig iron and the open-hearth furnaces for changing iron into steel. In both cases, the engineers have decided that the most effective abatement methods are (1) increasing the height of the smokestacks,[1] (2) using filter devices (including gas traps) in the smokestacks, and (3) including cleaner, high-grade materials among the fuels for the furnaces. Each of these methods has a technological limit on how heavily it can be used (e.g., a maximum feasible increase in the height of the smokestacks), but there also is considerable flexibility for using the method at a fraction of its technological limit.

The next table shows how much emissions (in millions of pounds per year) can be eliminated from each type of furnace by fully using any abatement method to its technological limit.

For purposes of analysis, it is assumed that each method also can be less fully used to achieve any fraction of the abatement capacities shown in this table. Furthermore, the fractions can be different for blast furnaces and open-hearth furnaces. For either type of furnace, the emission reduction achieved by each method is not substantially affected by whether or not the other methods also are used.

After these data were developed, it became clear that no single method by itself could achieve all the required reductions. On the other hand, combining all three methods at full capacity on both types of furnaces (which would be prohibitively expensive if the company's products are to remain competitively

---

[1] Subsequent to this study, this particular abatement method has become a controversial one. Because its effect is to reduce ground-level pollution by spreading emissions over a greater distance, environmental groups contend that this creates more acid rain by keeping sulfur oxides in the air longer. Consequently, the U.S. Environmental Protection Agency adopted new rules to remove incentives for using tall smokestacks.

Reduction in Emission Rate from the Maximum Feasible Use of an Abatement Method

Pollutant	Taller Smokestacks		Filters		Better Fuels	
	Blast Furnaces	Open-Hearth Furnaces	Blast Furnaces	Open-Hearth Furnaces	Blast Furnaces	Open-Hearth Furnaces
Particulates	12	9	25	20	17	13
Sulfur oxides	35	42	18	31	56	49
Hydrocarbons	37	53	28	24	29	20

priced) is much more than adequate. Therefore, the engineers concluded that they would have to use some combination of the methods, perhaps with fractional capacities, based on their relative costs. Furthermore, because of the differences between the blast and the open-hearth furnaces, the two types probably should not use the same combination.

An analysis was conducted to estimate the total annual cost that would be incurred by each abatement method. A method's annual cost includes increased operating and maintenance expenses, as well as reduced revenue due to any loss in the efficiency of the production process caused by using the method. The other major cost is the start-up cost (the initial capital outlay) required to install the method. To make this one-time cost commensurable with the ongoing annual costs, the time value of money was used to calculate the annual expenditure that would be equivalent in value to this start-up cost.

This analysis led to the total annual cost estimates given in the following table for using the methods at their full abatement capacities.

Total Annual Cost from the Maximum Feasible Use of an Abatement Method

Abatement Method	Blast Furnaces	Open-Hearth Furnaces
Taller smokestacks	$8 million	$10 million
Filters	7 million	6 million
Better fuels	11 million	9 million

It also was determined that the cost of a method being used at a lower level is roughly proportional to the fraction of the abatement capacity (given in the preceding table) that is achieved. Thus, for any given fraction achieved, the total annual cost would be roughly that fraction of the corresponding quantity in the cost table.

The stage now is set to develop the general framework of the company's plan for pollution abatement. This plan needs to specify which types of abatement methods will be used and at what fractions of their abatement capacities for (1) the blast furnaces and (2) the open-hearth furnaces.

You have been asked to head a management science team to analyze this problem. Management wants you to begin by determining which plan would minimize the total annual cost of achieving the required reductions in annual emission rates for the three pollutants.

a. Identify verbally the components of a linear programming model for this problem.

b. Display the model on a spreadsheet.

c. Obtain an optimal solution and generate the sensitivity report.

Management now wants to conduct some what-if analysis with your help. Since the company does not have much prior experience with the pollution abatement methods under consideration, the cost estimates given in the third table are fairly rough, and each one could easily be off by as much as 10 percent in either direction. There also is some uncertainty about the values given in the second table, but less so than for the third table. By contrast, the values in the first table are policy standards and so are prescribed constants.

However, there still is considerable debate about where to set these policy standards on the required reductions in the emission rates of the various pollutants. The numbers in the first table actually are preliminary values tentatively agreed upon before learning what the total cost would be to meet these standards. Both the city and company officials agree that the final decision on these policy standards should be based on the *trade-off* between costs and benefits. With this in mind, the city has concluded that each 10 percent increase in the policy standards over the current values (all the numbers in the first table) would be worth $3.5 million to the city. Therefore, the city has agreed to reduce the company's tax payments to the city by $3.5 million for *each* 10 percent increase in the policy standards (up to 50 percent) that is accepted by the company.

Finally, there has been some debate about the *relative* values of the policy standards for the three pollutants. As indicated in the first table, the required reduction for particulates now is less than half of that for either sulfur oxides or hydrocarbons. Some have argued for decreasing this disparity. Others contend that an even greater disparity is justified because sulfur oxides and hydrocarbons cause considerably more damage than particulates. Agreement has been reached that this issue will be reexamined after information is obtained about which trade-offs in policy standards (increasing one while decreasing another) are available without increasing the total cost.

d. Identify the parameters of the linear programming model that should be classified as *sensitive parameters*. Make a resulting recommendation about which parameters should be estimated more closely, if possible.

e. Analyze the effect of an inaccuracy in estimating each cost parameter given in the third table. If the true value were 10 percent less than the estimated value, would this change the optimal solution? Would it change if the true value were 10 percent more than the estimated value? Make a resulting recommendation about where to focus further work in estimating the cost parameters more closely.

f. For each pollutant, specify the rate at which the total cost of an optimal solution would change with any small change in the required reduction in the annual emission rate of the pollutant. Also specify how much this required reduction can be changed (up or down) without affecting the rate of change in the total cost.

g. For each unit change in the policy standard for particulates given in the first table, determine the change in the opposite direction for sulfur oxides that would keep the total cost of an optimal solution unchanged. Repeat this for hydrocarbons instead of sulfur oxides. Then do it for a simultaneous and equal change for both sulfur oxides and hydrocarbons in the opposite direction from particulates.

h. Letting θ denote the percentage increase in all the policy standards given in the first table, use the Solver Table to

systematically find an optimal solution and the total cost for the revised linear programming problem for each $\theta = 10, 20, 30, 40, 50$. Considering the tax incentive offered by the city, use these results to determine which value of θ (including the option of $\theta = 0$) should be chosen by the company to minimize its total cost of both pollution abatement and taxes.

i. For the value of θ chosen in part *h,* generate the sensitivity report and repeat parts *f* and *g* so that the decision makers can make a final decision on the relative values of the policy standards for the three pollutants.

Case 5-3
Farm Management

The Ploughman family owns and operates a 640-acre farm that has been in the family for several generations. The Ploughmans always have had to work hard to make a decent living from the farm and have had to endure some occasional difficult years. Stories about earlier generations overcoming hardships due to droughts, floods, and so forth, are an important part of the family history. However, the Ploughmans enjoy their self-reliant lifestyle and gain considerable satisfaction from continuing the family tradition of successfully living off the land during an era when many family farms are being abandoned or taken over by large agricultural corporations.

John Ploughman is the current manager of the farm, while his wife Eunice runs the house and manages the farm's finances. John's father, Grandpa Ploughman, lives with them and still puts in many hours working on the farm. John and Eunice's older children, Frank, Phyllis, and Carl, also are given heavy chores before and after school.

The entire family can produce a total of 4,000 person-hours' worth of labor during the winter and spring months and 4,500 person-hours during the summer and fall. If any of these person-hours are not needed, Frank, Phyllis, and Carl will use them to work on a neighboring farm for $5/hour during the winter and spring months and $5.50/hour during the summer and fall.

The farm supports two types of livestock, dairy cows and laying hens, as well as three crops: soybeans, corn, and wheat. (All three are cash crops, but the corn also is a feed crop for the cows and the wheat also is used for chicken feed.) The crops are harvested during

the late summer and fall. During the winter months, John, Eunice, and Grandpa make a decision about the mix of livestock and crops for the coming year.

Currently, the family has just completed a particularly successful harvest that has provided an investment fund of $20,000 that can be used to purchase more livestock. (Other money is available for ongoing expenses, including the next planting of crops.) The family currently has 30 cows valued at $35,000 and 2,000 hens valued at $5,000. They wish to keep all this livestock and perhaps purchase more. Each new cow would cost $1,500, and each new hen would cost $3.

Over a year's time, the value of a herd of cows will decrease by about 10 percent and the value of a flock of hens will decrease by about 25 percent due to aging.

Each cow will require two acres of land for grazing and 10 person-hours of work per month, while producing a net annual cash income of $850 for the family. The corresponding figures for each hen are no significant acreage, 0.05 person-hours per month, and an annual net cash income of $4.25. The chicken house can accommodate a maximum of 5,000 hens, and the size of the barn limits the herd to a maximum of 42 cows.

For each acre planted in each of the three crops, the following table gives the number of person-hours of work that will be required during the first and second halves of the year, as well as a rough estimate of the crop's net value (in either income or savings in purchasing feed for the livestock).

Data per Acre Planted

	Soybeans	Corn	Wheat
Winter and spring, person-hours	1.0	0.9	0.6
Summer and fall, person-hours	1.4	1.2	0.7
Net value	$70	$60	$40

To provide much of the feed for the livestock, John wants to plant at least one acre of corn for each cow in the coming year's herd and at least 0.05 acre of wheat for each hen in the coming year's flock.

John, Eunice, and Grandpa now are discussing how much acreage should be planted in each of the crops and how many cows and hens to have for the coming year. Their objective is to

maximize the family's monetary worth at the end of the coming year (the *sum* of the net income from the livestock for the coming year *plus* the net value of the crops for the coming year *plus* what remains from the investment fund *plus* the value of the livestock at the end of the coming year *plus* income from working on a neighboring farm *minus* living expenses of $40,000 for the year).

a. Identify verbally the components of a linear programming model for this problem.

b. Display the model on a spreadsheet.

c. Obtain an optimal solution and generate the sensitivity report. What does the model predict regarding the family's monetary worth at the end of the coming year?

d. Find the allowable range for the net value per acre planted for each of the three crops.

The above estimates of the net value per acre planted in each of the three crops assumes good weather conditions. Adverse weather conditions would harm the crops and greatly reduce the resulting value. The scenarios particularly feared by the family are a drought, a flood, an early frost, *both* a drought and an early frost, and *both* a flood and an early frost. The estimated net values for the year under these scenarios are shown next.

Scenario	Net Value per Acre Planted		
	Soybeans	Corn	Wheat
Drought	−$10	−$15	0
Flood	15	20	$10
Early frost	50	40	30
Drought and early frost	−15	−20	−10
Flood and early frost	10	10	5

e. Find an optimal solution under each scenario after making the necessary adjustments to the linear programming model formulated in part *b*. In each case, what is the prediction regarding the family's monetary worth at the end of the year?

f. For the optimal solution obtained under each of the six scenarios (including the good weather scenario considered in parts *a–d*), calculate what the family's monetary worth would be at the end of the year if each of the other five scenarios occurs instead. In your judgment, which solution provides the best balance between yielding a large monetary worth under good weather conditions and avoiding an overly small monetary worth under adverse weather conditions?

Grandpa has researched what the weather conditions were in past years as far back as weather records have been kept and obtained the following data.

Scenario	Frequency
Good weather	40%
Drought	20
Flood	10
Early frost	15
Drought and early frost	10
Flood and early frost	5

With these data, the family has decided to use the following approach to making its planting and livestock decisions. Rather than the optimistic approach of assuming that good weather conditions will prevail (as done in parts *a–d*), the *average* net value under all weather conditions will be used for each crop (weighting the net values under the various scenarios by the frequencies in the above table).

g. Modify the linear programming model formulated in part *b* to fit this new approach.

h. Repeat part *c* for this modified model.

i. Use a shadow price obtained in part *h* to analyze whether it would be worthwhile for the family to obtain a bank loan with a 10 percent interest rate to purchase more livestock now beyond what can be obtained with the $20,000 from the investment fund.

j. For each of the three crops, use the sensitivity report obtained in part *h* to identify how much latitude for error is available in estimating the net value per acre planted for that crop without changing the optimal solution. Which two net values need to be estimated most carefully? If both estimates are incorrect simultaneously, how close do the estimates need to be to guarantee that the optimal solution will not change? Use a two-dimensional Solver Table to systematically generate the optimal monetary worth as these two net values are varied simultaneously over ranges that go up to twice as far from the estimates as needed to guarantee that the optimal solution will not change.

This problem illustrates a kind of situation that is frequently faced by various kinds of organizations. To describe the situation in general terms, an organization faces an uncertain future where any one of a number of scenarios may unfold. Which one will occur depends on conditions that are outside the control of the organization. The organization needs to choose the levels of various activities, but the unit contribution of each activity to the overall measure of performance is greatly affected by which scenario unfolds. Under these circumstances, what is the best mix of activities?

k. Think about specific situations outside of farm management that fit this description. Describe one.

Case 5-4

Assigning Students to Schools (Revisited)

Reconsider Case 3-5. The Springfield School Board still has the policy of providing busing for all middle school students who must travel more than approximately a mile. Another current policy is to allow splitting residential areas among multiple schools if this will reduce the total busing cost. (This latter policy will be reversed in Case 7-3.) However, before adopting a busing plan based on part *a* of Case 3-5, the school board now wants to conduct some what-if analysis.

a. If you have not already done so for part *a* of Case 3-5, formulate and solve a linear programming model for this problem on a spreadsheet.

b. Use the Solver to generate the sensitivity report.

One concern of the school board is the ongoing road construction in area 6. These construction projects have been delaying traffic considerably and are likely to affect the cost of busing students from area 6, perhaps increasing costs as much as 10 percent.

c. Use the sensitivity report to check how much the busing cost from area 6 to school 1 can increase (assuming no change in the costs for the other schools) before the current optimal solution would no longer be optimal. If the allowable increase is less than 10 percent, use the Solver to find the new optimal solution with a 10 percent increase.

d. Repeat part *c* for school 2 (assuming no change in the costs for the other schools).

e. Now assume that the busing cost from area 6 would increase by the same percentage for all the schools. Use the sensitivity report to determine how large this percentage can be before the current optimal solution might no longer be optimal. If the allowable increase is less than 10 percent, use the Solver to find the new optimal solution with a 10 percent increase.

The school board has the option of adding portable classrooms to increase the capacity of one or more of the middle schools for a few years. However, this is a costly move that the board would only consider if it would significantly decrease busing costs. Each portable classroom holds 20 students and has a leasing cost of $2,500 per year. To analyze this option, the school board decides to assume that the road construction in area 6 will wind down without significantly increasing the busing costs from that area.

f. For each school, use the corresponding shadow price from the sensitivity report to determine whether it would be worthwhile to add any portable classrooms.

g. For each school where it is worthwhile to add any portable classrooms, use the sensitivity report to determine how many could be added before the shadow price would no longer be valid (assuming this is the only school receiving portable classrooms).

h. If it would be worthwhile to add portable classrooms to more than one school, use the sensitivity report to determine the combinations of the number to add for which the shadow prices definitely would still be valid. Then use the shadow prices to determine which of these combinations is best in terms of minimizing the total cost of busing students and leasing portable classrooms. Use the Solver for finding the corresponding optimal solution for assigning students to schools.

i. If part *h* was applicable, modify the best combination of portable classrooms found there by adding one more to the school with the most favorable shadow price. Use the Solver to find the corresponding optimal solution for assigning students to schools and to generate the corresponding sensitivity report. Use this information to assess whether the plan developed in part *h* is the best one available for minimizing the total cost of busing students and leasing portables. If not, find the best plan.

Chapter **Six**

Network Optimization Problems

Learning objectives

After completing this chapter, you should be able to

1. Formulate network models for various types of network optimization problems.
2. Describe the characteristics of minimum-cost flow problems, maximum flow problems, and shortest path problems.
3. Identify some areas of application for these types of problems.
4. Identify several categories of network optimization problems that are special types of minimum-cost flow problems.
5. Formulate and solve a spreadsheet model for a minimum-cost flow problem, a maximum flow problem, or a shortest path problem from a description of the problem.

Networks arise in numerous settings and in a variety of guises. Transportation, electrical, and communication networks pervade our daily lives. Network representations also are widely used for problems in such diverse areas as production, distribution, project planning, facilities location, resource management, and financial planning—to name just a few examples. In fact, a network representation provides such a powerful visual and conceptual aid for portraying the relationships between the components of systems that it is used in virtually every field of scientific, social, and economic endeavor.

One of the most exciting developments in management science in recent years has been the unusually rapid advance in both the methodology and application of network optimization problems. A number of algorithmic breakthroughs have had a major impact, as have ideas from computer science concerning data structures and efficient data manipulation. Consequently, algorithms and software now are available and are being used to solve huge problems on a routine basis that would have been completely intractable a couple of decades ago.

This chapter presents the network optimization problems that have been particularly helpful in dealing with managerial issues. We focus on the nature of these problems and their applications rather than on the technical details and the algorithms used to solve the problems.

You already have seen some examples of network optimization problems in Chapter 3. In particular, transportation problems (described in Section 3.5) have a network representation, as illustrated in Figure 3.9, and assignment problems (Section 3.6) have a similar network representation (as described in Chapter 15 on the CD-ROM). Therefore, both transportation problems and assignment problems are simple types of network optimization problems.

Like transportation problems and assignment problems, many other network optimization problems (including all the types considered in this chapter) also are special types of *linear programming* problems. Consequently, after formulating a spreadsheet model for these problems, they can be readily solved by the Excel Solver.

Section 6.1 discusses an especially important type of network optimization problem called a *minimum-cost flow problem.* A typical application involves minimizing the cost of shipping goods through a distribution network.

Section 6.3 presents *maximum flow problems,* which are concerned with such issues as how to maximize the flow of goods through a distribution network. Section 6.2 lays the groundwork by introducing a case study of a maximum flow problem.

Section 6.4 considers *shortest path problems.* In their simplest form, the objective is to find the shortest route between two locations.

A supplement to this chapter on the CD-ROM discusses *minimum spanning-tree problems,* which are concerned with minimizing the cost of providing connections between all users of a system. This is the only network optimization problem considered in this book that is not, in fact, a special type of linear programming problem.

6.1 MINIMUM-COST FLOW PROBLEMS

Before describing the general characteristics of minimum-cost flow problems, let us first look at a typical example.

An Example: The Distribution Unlimited Co. Problem

The Distribution Unlimited Co. has two factories producing a product that needs to be shipped to two warehouses. Here are some details.

Factory 1 is producing 80 units.

Factory 2 is producing 70 units.

Warehouse 1 needs 60 units.

Warehouse 2 needs 90 units.

(Each unit corresponds to a full truckload of the product.)

Figure 6.1 shows the distribution network available for shipping this product, where F1 and F2 are the two factories, W1 and W2 are the two warehouses, and DC is a distribution center. The arrows show feasible shipping lanes. In particular, there is a rail link from factory 1 to warehouse 1 and another from factory 2 to warehouse 2. (Any amounts can be shipped along these rail links.) In addition, independent truckers are available to ship up to 50 units from each factory to the distribution center, and then to ship up to 50 units from the distribution center to each warehouse. (Whatever is shipped to the distribution center must subsequently be shipped on to the warehouses.) Management's objective is to determine the shipping plan (how many units to ship along each shipping lane) that will minimize the total shipping cost.

The objective is to minimize the total shipping cost through the distribution network.

The shipping costs differ considerably among these shipping lanes. The cost per unit shipped through each lane is shown above the corresponding arrow in the *network* in Figure 6.2.

To make the network less crowded, the problem usually is presented even more compactly, as shown in Figure 6.3. The number in square brackets next to the location of each facility

FIGURE 6.1

The distribution network for the Distribution Unlimited Co. problem, where each feasible shipping lane is represented by an arrow.

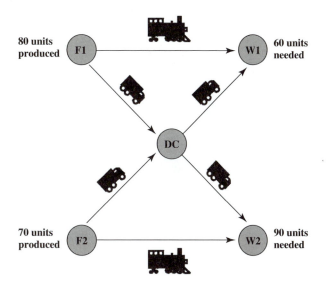

FIGURE 6.2

The data for the distribution network for the Distribution Unlimited Co. problem.

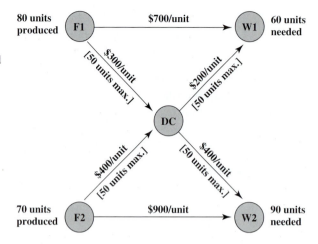

indicates the net number of units (outflow minus inflow) generated there. Thus, the number of units terminating at each warehouse is shown as a negative number. The number at the distribution center is 0 since the number of units leaving *minus* the number of units arriving must equal 0. The number on top of each arrow shows the unit shipping cost along that shipping lane. Any number in square brackets underneath an arrow gives the maximum number of units that can be shipped along that shipping lane. (The absence of a number in square brackets underneath an arrow implies that there is no limit on the shipping amount there.) This network provides a complete representation of the problem, including all the necessary data, so it constitutes a *network model* for this minimum-cost flow problem.

Figure 6.3 illustrates how a minimum-cost flow problem can be completely depicted by a network.

Since this is such a tiny problem, you probably can see what the optimal solution must be. (Try it.) This solution is shown in Figure 6.4, where the shipping amount along each shipping lane is given in parentheses. (To avoid confusion, we delete the unit shipping costs and shipping capacities in this figure.) Combining these shipping amounts with the unit shipping costs given in Figures 6.2 and 6.3, the total shipping cost for this solution is

$$\text{Total shipping cost} = 30(\$700) + 50(\$300) + 50(\$400) + 50(\$200)$$
$$+ 50(\$400) + 20(\$900)$$
$$= \$104,000$$

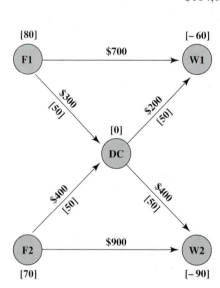

FIGURE 6.3

A network model for the Distribution Unlimited Co. problem as a minimum-cost flow problem.

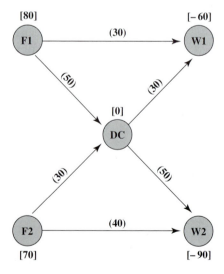

FIGURE 6.4

The optimal solution for the Distribution Unlimited Co. problem, where the shipping amounts are shown in parentheses over the arrows.

An especially challenging problem encountered daily by any major airline company is how to compensate effectively for disruptions in the airline's flight schedules. Bad weather can disrupt flight arrivals and departures. So can mechanical problems. Each delay or cancellation involving a particular airplane can then cause subsequent delays or cancellations because that airplane is not available on time for its next scheduled flights.

An airline has two primary ways of compensating for delays or cancellations. One is to swap aircraft so that an airplane scheduled for a later flight can take the place of the delayed or canceled airplane. The other is to use a spare airplane (often after flying it in) to replace the delayed or canceled airplane. However, it is a real challenge to quickly make good decisions of these types when a considerable number of delays or cancellations occur throughout the day.

In recent years, United Airlines has led the way in applying management science to this problem. This is done by formulating and solving the problem as a minimum-cost flow problem where each node in the network represents an airport and each arc represents the route of a flight. The objective of the model then is to keep the airplanes flowing through the network in a way that minimizes the cost incurred by having delays or cancellations. When a status monitor subsystem alerts an operations controller of impending delays or cancellations, the controller provides the necessary input into the model and then solves it in order to provide the updated operating plan in a matter of minutes. This application of the minimum-cost flow problem has resulted in reducing passenger delays by about 50 percent.

Source: A. Rakshit, N. Krishnamurthy, and G. Yu, "System Operations Advisor: A Real-Time Decision Support System for Managing Airline Operations at United Airlines," *Interfaces* 26, no. 2 (March–April 1996), pp. 50–58.

General Characteristics

This example possesses all the general characteristics of any minimum-cost flow problem. Before summarizing these characteristics, here is the terminology you will need.

Terminology

1. The model for any minimum-cost flow problem is represented by a *network* with flow passing through it.
2. The circles in the network are called **nodes.**

> A supply node has net flow going out whereas a demand node has net flow coming in.

3. Each node where the net amount of flow generated (outflow minus inflow) is a fixed *positive* number is a **supply node.** (Thus, F1 and F2 are the supply nodes in Figure 6.3.)
4. Each node where the net amount of flow generated is a fixed *negative* number is a **demand node.** (Consequently, W1 and W2 are the demand nodes in the example.)
5. Any node where the net amount of flow generated is fixed at *zero* is a **transshipment node.** (Thus, DC is the transshipment node in the example.) Having the amount of flow out of the node equal the amount of flow into the node is referred to as **conservation of flow.**
6. The arrows in the network are called **arcs.**
7. The maximum amount of flow allowed through an arc is referred to as the **capacity** of that arc.

Using this terminology, the general characteristics of minimum-cost flow problems (the model for this type of problem) can be described in terms of the following assumptions.

Assumptions of a Minimum-Cost Flow Problem

1. *At least one* of the nodes is a *supply node.*
2. *At least one* of the other nodes is a *demand node.*
3. All the remaining nodes are *transshipment nodes.*

> Since the arrowhead on an arc indicates the direction in which flow is allowed, a pair of arcs pointing in opposite directions is used if flow can occur in both directions.

4. Flow through an arc is only allowed in the direction indicated by the arrowhead, where the maximum amount of flow is given by the *capacity* of that arc. (If flow can occur in both directions, this would be represented by a pair of arcs pointing in opposite directions.)
5. The network has enough arcs with sufficient capacity to enable all the flow generated at the *supply nodes* to reach all the *demand nodes.*

6. The cost of the flow through each arc is *proportional* to the amount of that flow, where the cost per unit flow is known.

7. The objective is to minimize the total cost of sending the available supply through the network to satisfy the given demand. (An alternative objective is to maximize the total profit from doing this.)

The objective is to minimize the total cost of supplying the demand nodes.

A *solution* for this kind of problem needs to specify how much flow is going through each arc. To be a *feasible* solution, the amount of flow through each arc cannot exceed the capacity of that arc and the net amount of flow generated at each node must equal the specified amount for that node. The following property indicates when the problem will have feasible solutions.

> **The Feasible Solutions Property:** Under the above assumptions, a minimum-cost flow problem will have feasible solutions if and only if the sum of the supplies from its supply nodes *equals* the sum of the demands at its demand nodes.

Note that this property holds for the Distribution Unlimited Co. problem, because the sum of its supplies is $80 + 70 = 150$ and the sum of its demands is $60 + 90 = 150$.

For many applications of minimum-cost flow problems, management desires a solution with *integer* values for all the flow quantities (e.g., integer numbers of *full* truckloads along each shipping lane). The model does not include any constraints that require this for feasible solutions. Fortunately, such constraints are not needed because of the following property.

> **Integer Solutions Property:** As long as all its supplies, demands, and arc capacities have integer values, any minimum-cost flow problem with feasible solutions is guaranteed to have an optimal solution with integer values for all its flow quantities.

See in Figure 6.2 that this property holds for the Distribution Unlimited Co. problem. All the supplies (80 and 70), demands (60 and 90), and arc capacities (50) have integer values. Therefore, all the flow quantities in the optimal solution given in Figure 6.4 (30 three times, 50 two times, and 40) have integer values. This ensures that only full truckloads will be shipped into and out of the distribution center. (Remember that each unit corresponds to a full truckload of the product.)

Now let us see how to obtain an optimal solution for the Distribution Unlimited Co. problem by formulating a spreadsheet model and then applying the Excel Solver.

Using Excel to Formulate and Solve Minimum-Cost Flow Problems

Figure 6.5 shows a spreadsheet model that is based directly on the network representation of the problem in Figure 6.3. The arcs are listed in columns B and C, along with their capacities (unless unlimited) in column F and their costs per unit flow in column G. The changing cells Ship (D4:D9) show the flow amounts through these arcs and the target cell TotalCost (D11) provides the total cost of this flow by using the equation

$$D11 = \text{SUMPRODUCT(Ship,UnitCost)}$$

Capacity constraints like these are needed in any minimum-cost flow problem that has any arcs with limited capacity.

The first set of constraints in the Solver dialogue box, D5:D8 ≤ Capacity (F5:F8), ensures that the arc capacities are not exceeded.

Similarly, Column I lists the nodes, column J calculates the actual net flow generated at each node (given the flows in the changing cells), and column L specifies the net amount of flow that needs to be generated at each node. Thus, the second set of constraints in the Solver dialogue box is NetFlow (J4:J8) = SupplyDemand (L4:L8), requiring that the actual net amount of flow generated at each node must equal the specified amount.

Any minimum-cost flow problem needs net flow constraints like this for every node.

Excel Tip: SUMIF(A, B, C) adds up each entry in the range C for which the corresponding entry in range A equals B. This function is especially useful in network problems for calculating the net flow generated at a node.

The equations entered into NetFlow (J4:J8) use the difference of two SUMIF functions to calculate the net flow (outflow minus inflow) generated at each node. In each case, the first SUMIF function calculates the flow leaving the node and the second one calculates the flow entering the node. For example, consider the F1 node (I4). SUMIF(From,I4,Ship) sums each individual entry in Ship (D4:D9) if that entry is in a row where the entry in From (B4:B9) is the same as in I4. Since I4 = F1 and the only rows that have F1 in the From column are rows 4 and 5, the sum in the Ship column is only over these same rows, so this sum is D4 + D5. Similarly, SUMIF(To,I4,Ship) sums each individual entry in Ship (D4:D9) if that entry is in a

FIGURE 6.5

A spreadsheet model for the Distribution Unlimited Co. minimum-cost flow problem, including the target cell TotalCost (D11) and the other output cells NetFlow (J4:J8), as well as the equations entered into these cells and the other specifications needed to set up the model. The changing cells Ship (D4:D9) show the optimal shipping quantities through the distribution network obtained by the Solver.

	A	B	C	D	E	F	G	H	I	J	K	L
1		**Distribution Unlimited Co. Minimum Cost Flow Problem**										
2												
3		**From**	**To**	**Ship**		**Capacity**	**Unit Cost**		**Nodes**	**Net Flow**		**Supply/Demand**
4		F1	W1	30			$700		F1	80	=	80
5		F1	DC	50	≤	50	$300		F2	70	=	70
6		DC	W1	30	≤	50	$200		DC	0	=	0
7		DC	W2	50	≤	50	$400		W1	-60	=	-60
8		F2	DC	30	≤	50	$400		W2	-90	=	-90
9		F2	W2	40			$900					
10												
11			**Total Cost**	$110,000								

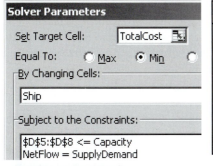

Range Name	Cells
Capacity	F5:F8
From	B4:B9
NetFlow	J4:J8
Nodes	I4:I8
Ship	D4:D9
SupplyDemand	L4:L8
To	C4:C9
TotalCost	D11
UnitCost	G4:G9

	J
3	**Net Flow**
4	=SUMIF(From,I4,Ship)-SUMIF(To,I4,Ship)
5	=SUMIF(From,I5,Ship)-SUMIF(To,I5,Ship)
6	=SUMIF(From,I6,Ship)-SUMIF(To,I6,Ship)
7	=SUMIF(From,I7,Ship)-SUMIF(To,I7,Ship)
8	=SUMIF(From,I8,Ship)-SUMIF(To,I8,Ship)

	C	D
11	**Total Cost**	=SUMPRODUCT(Ship,UnitCost)

Solver Parameters

Set Target Cell: TotalCost

Equal To: ○ Max ● Min ○

By Changing Cells:

Ship

Subject to the Constraints:

$D$5:$D$8 <= Capacity
NetFlow = SupplyDemand

Solver Options

☑ Assume Linear Model
☑ Assume Non-Negative

row where the entry in To (C4:C9) is the same as in I4. However, F1 never appears in the To column, so this sum is 0. Therefore, the overall equation for J4 yields J4 = D4 + D5 = 30 + 50 = 80, which is the net flow generated at the F1 node.

While it appears more complicated to use the SUMIF function rather than just entering J4 = D4 + D5, J5 = D8 + D9, J6 = D6 + D7 − D5 − D8, and so on, it is actually simpler. The SUMIF formula only needs to be entered once (in cell J4). It can then be copied down into the remaining cells in NetFlow (J5:J8). For a problem with many nodes, this is much quicker and (perhaps more significantly) less prone to error. In a large problem, it is all too easy to miss an arc when determining which cells in the Ship column to add and subtract to calculate the net flow for a given node.

The first Solver option selected (Assume Linear Model) acknowledges that this is still a linear programming problem (in a streamlined form). The second option (Assume Non-Negative) specifies that the flow amounts cannot be negative.

Clicking on the Solve button gives the optimal solution shown in Ship (D4:D9). This is the same solution as displayed in Figure 6.4.

Solving Large Minimum-Cost Flow Problems More Efficiently

Because minimum-cost flow problems are a special type of linear programming problem, and the *simplex method* can solve any linear programming problem, it also can solve any minimum-cost flow problem in the standard way. For example, the Excel Solver uses the simplex method to solve this type (or any other type) of linear programming problem. This works fine for small problems, like the Distribution Unlimited Co. problem, and for considerably larger ones as well. Therefore, the approach illustrated in Figure 6.5 will serve you well for any minimum-cost flow problem encountered in this book and for many that you will encounter subsequently.

However, we should mention that a different approach is sometimes needed in practice to solve really big problems. Because of the special form of minimum-cost flow problems, it is possible to greatly *streamline* the simplex method to solve them far more quickly. In particular, rather than going through all the algebra of the simplex method, it is possible to execute the same steps far more quickly by working directly with the network for the problem.

This streamlined version of the simplex method is called the **network simplex method.** The network simplex method can solve some huge problems that are much too large for the simplex method.

The network simplex method can solve much larger minimum-cost flow problems (sometimes with millions of nodes and arcs) than can the simplex method used by the Excel Solver.

Like the simplex method, the network simplex method not only finds an optimal solution but also can be a valuable aid to managers in conducting the kinds of what-if analyses described in Chapter 5.

Many companies now use the network simplex method to solve their minimum-cost flow problems. Some of these problems are huge, with many tens of thousands of nodes and arcs. Occasionally, the number of arcs will even be far larger, perhaps into the millions.

Although the Excel Solver does not, other commercial software packages for linear programming commonly include the network simplex method.

An important advance in recent years has been the development of excellent *graphical interfaces* for modeling minimum-cost flow problems. These interfaces make the design of the model and the interpretation of the output of the network simplex method completely visual and intuitive with no mathematics involved. This is very helpful for managerial decision making.

Some Applications

Probably the most important kind of application of minimum-cost flow problems is to the operation of a distribution network, such as the one depicted in Figures 6.1–6.4 for the Distribution Unlimited Co. problem. As summarized in the first row of Table 6.1, this kind of application always involves determining a plan for shipping goods from their *sources* (factories, etc.) to *intermediate storage facilities* (as needed) and then on to the *customers.*

For some applications of minimum-cost flow problems, all the transshipment nodes are *processing facilities* rather than intermediate storage facilities. This is the case for *solid waste management,* as indicated in Table 6.1. Here, the flow of materials through the network begins at the sources of the solid waste, then goes to the facilities for processing these waste materials into a form suitable for landfill, and then sends them on to the various landfill locations. However, the objective still is to determine the flow plan that minimizes the total cost, where the cost now is for both shipping and processing.

In other applications, the *demand nodes* might be processing facilities. For example, in the third row of Table 6.1, the objective is to find the minimum-cost plan for obtaining supplies from various possible vendors, storing these goods in warehouses (as needed), and then shipping the supplies to the company's processing facilities (factories, etc.).

The next kind of application in Table 6.1 (coordinating product mixes at plants) illustrates that arcs can represent something other than a shipping lane for a physical flow of materials.

TABLE 6.1 Typical Kinds of Applications of Minimum-Cost Flow Problems

Kind of Application	Supply Nodes	Transshipment Nodes	Demand Nodes
Operation of a distribution network	Sources of goods	Intermediate storage facilities	Customers
Solid waste management	Sources of solid waste	Processing facilities	Landfill locations
Operation of a supply network	Vendors	Intermediate warehouses	Processing facilities
Coordinating product mixes at plants	Plants	Production of a specific product	Market for a specific product
Cash flow management	Sources of cash at a specific time	Short-term investment options	Needs for cash at a specific time

This application involves a company with several plants (the supply nodes) that can produce the same products but at different costs. Each arc from a supply node represents the production of one of the possible products at that plant, where this arc leads to the transshipment node that corresponds to this product. Thus, this transshipment node has an arc coming in from each plant capable of producing this product, and then the arcs leading out of this node go to the respective customers (the demand nodes) for this product. The objective is to determine how to divide each plant's production capacity among the products so as to minimize the total cost of meeting the demand for the various products.

The last application in Table 6.1 (cash flow management) illustrates that different nodes can represent some event that occurs at different times. In this case, each supply node represents a specific time (or time period) when some cash will become available to the company (through maturing accounts, notes receivable, sales of securities, borrowing, etc.). The supply at each of these nodes is the amount of cash that will become available then. Similarly, each demand node represents a specific time (or time period) when the company will need to draw on its cash reserves. The demand at each such node is the amount of cash that will be needed then. The objective is to maximize the company's income from investing the cash between each time it becomes available and when it will be used. Therefore, each transshipment node represents the choice of a specific short-term investment option (e.g., purchasing a certificate of deposit from a bank) over a specific time interval. The resulting network will have a succession of flows representing a schedule for cash becoming available, being invested, and then being used after the maturing of the investment.

Special Types of Minimum-Cost Flow Problems

There are five important categories of network problems that turn out to be special types of minimum-cost flow problems.

One is the *transportation problems* discussed in section 3.5. Figure 3.9 shows the network representation of a typical transportation problem. In our current terminology, the sources and destinations of a transportation problem are the supply nodes and demand nodes, respectively. Thus, a transportation problem is just a minimum-cost flow problem without any transshipment nodes and without any capacity constraints on the arcs (all of which go directly from a supply node to a demand node).

A second category is the *assignment problems* discussed in Section 3.6. Recall that this kind of problem involves assigning a group of people (or other operational units) to a group of tasks where each person is to perform a single task. An assignment problem can be viewed as a special type of transportation problem whose sources are the assignees and whose destinations are the tasks. This then makes the assignment problem also a special type of minimum-cost flow problem with the characteristics described in the preceding paragraph. In addition, each person is a supply node with a supply of 1 and each task is a demand node with a demand of 1.

A transshipment problem is just a minimum-cost flow problem that has unlimited capacities for all its arcs.

A third special type of minimum-cost flow problem is **transshipment problems.** This kind of problem is just like a transportation problem except for the additional feature that the shipments from the sources (supply nodes) to the destinations (demand nodes) might also pass through intermediate transfer points (transshipment nodes) such as distribution centers. Like a transportation problem, there are no capacity constraints on the arcs. Consequently, any minimum-cost flow problem where each arc can carry any desired amount of flow is a transshipment problem. For example, if the data in Figure 6.2 were altered so that any amounts (within the ranges of the supplies and demands) could be shipped into and out of the distribution center, the Distribution Unlimited Co. would become just a transshipment problem.[1]

Because of their close relationship to a general minimum-cost flow problem, we will not discuss transshipment problems further.

The other two important special types of minimum-cost flow problems are *maximum flow problems* and *shortest path problems,* which will be described in Sections 6.3 and 6.4 after presenting a case study of a maximum flow problem in the next section.

---

[1] Be aware that a minimum-cost flow problem that does have capacity constraints on the arcs is sometimes referred to as a *capacitated transshipment problem.* We will not use this terminology.

The network simplex method can be used to solve huge problems of any of these five special types.

In case you are wondering why we are bothering to point out that these five kinds of problems are special types of minimum-cost flow problems, here is one very important reason. It means that the *network simplex method* can be used to solve large problems of any of these types that might be difficult or impossible for the simplex method to solve. It is true that other efficient *special-purpose algorithms* also are available for each of these kinds of problems. However, recent implementations of the network simplex method have become so powerful that it now provides an excellent alternative to these other algorithms in most cases. This is especially valuable when the available software package includes the network simplex method but not another relevant special-purpose algorithm. Furthermore, even after finding an optimal solution, the network simplex method can continue to be helpful in aiding managerial what-if sessions along the lines discussed in Chapter 5.

Review *Questions*

1. Name and describe the three kinds of nodes in a minimum-cost flow problem.
2. What is meant by the *capacity* of an arc?
3. What is the usual objective for a minimum-cost flow problem?
4. What property is necessary for a minimum-cost flow problem to have feasible solutions?
5. What is the integer solutions property for minimum-cost flow problems?
6. What is the name of the streamlined version of the simplex method that is designed to solve minimum-cost flow problems very efficiently?
7. What are a few typical kinds of applications of minimum-cost flow problems?
8. Name five important categories of network optimization problems that turn out to be special types of minimum-cost flow problems.

6.2 A CASE STUDY: THE BMZ CO. MAXIMUM FLOW PROBLEM

What a day! First being called into his boss's office and then receiving an urgent telephone call from the company president himself. Fortunately, he was able to reassure them that he has the situation under control.

Although his official title is Supply Chain Manager for the BMZ Company, Karl Schmidt often tells his friends that he really is the company's *crisis manager*. One crisis after another. The supplies needed to keep the production lines going haven't arrived yet. Or the supplies have arrived but are unusable because they are the wrong size. Or an urgent shipment to a key customer has been delayed. This current crisis is typical. One of the company's most important distribution centers—the one in Los Angeles—urgently needs an increased flow of shipments from the company.

Karl was chosen for this key position because he is considered a rising young star. Having just received his MBA degree from a top American business school four years ago, he is the youngest member of upper-level management in the entire company. His business school training in the latest management science techniques has proven invaluable in improving supply chain management throughout the company. The crises still occur, but the frequent chaos of past years has been eliminated.

Karl has a plan for dealing with the current crisis. This will mean calling on management science once again.

Background

The BMZ Company is a European manufacturer of luxury automobiles. Although its cars sell well in all the developed countries, its exports to the United States are particularly important to the company.

BMZ has a well-deserved reputation for providing excellent service. One key to maintaining this reputation is having a plentiful supply of automobile replacement parts readily available to the company's numerous dealerships and authorized repair shops. These parts are mainly stored in the company's distribution centers and then delivered promptly when needed. One of Karl Schmidt's top priorities is avoiding shortages at these distribution centers.

The company has several distribution centers in the United States. However, the closest one to the Los Angeles center is over 1,000 miles away in Seattle. Since BMZ cars are becoming especially popular in California, it is particularly important to keep the Los Angeles center well supplied. Therefore, the fact that supplies there are currently dwindling is a matter of real concern to BMZ top management—as Karl learned forcefully today.

Most of the automobile replacement parts are produced at the company's main factory in Stuttgart, Germany, along with the production of new cars. It is this factory that has been supplying the Los Angeles center with spare parts. Some of these parts are bulky, and very large numbers of certain parts are needed, so the total volume of the supplies has been relatively massive—over 300,000 cubic feet of goods arriving monthly. Now a much larger amount will be needed over the next month to replenish the dwindling inventory.

The Problem

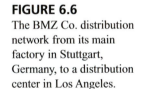
The problem is to maximize the flow of automobile replacement parts from the factory in Stuttgart, Germany, to the distribution center in Los Angeles.

Karl needs to execute a plan quickly for shipping as much as possible from the main factory to the distribution center in Los Angeles over the next month. He already has recognized that this is a *maximum flow problem*—a problem of maximizing the flow of replacement parts from the factory to this distribution center.

The factory is producing far more than can be shipped to this one distribution center. Therefore, the limiting factor on how much can be shipped is the limited capacity of the company's distribution network.

This distribution network is depicted in Figure 6.6, where the nodes labeled ST and LA are the factory in Stuttgart and the distribution center in Los Angeles, respectively. There is a rail head at the factory, so shipments first go by rail to one of three European ports: Rotterdam (node RO), Bordeaux (node BO), and Lisbon (node LI). They then go by ship to ports in the United States, either New York (node NY) or New Orleans (node NO). Finally, they are shipped by truck from these ports to the distribution center in Los Angeles.

The organizations operating these railroads, ships, and trucks are independently owned companies that ship goods for numerous firms. Because of prior commitments to their regular customers, these companies are unable to drastically increase the allocation of space to any single customer on short notice. Therefore, the BMZ Co. is only able to secure a limited amount of shipping space along each shipping lane over the next month. The amounts available are given in Figure 6.6, using units of *hundreds of cubic meters*. (Since each unit of 100 cubic meters is a little over 3,500 cubic feet, these are large volumes of goods that need to be moved.)

FIGURE 6.6

The BMZ Co. distribution network from its main factory in Stuttgart, Germany, to a distribution center in Los Angeles.

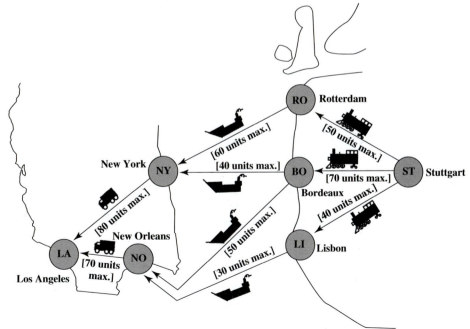

FIGURE 6.7

A network model for the BMZ Co. problem as a maximum flow problem, where the number in square brackets below each arc is the capacity of that arc.

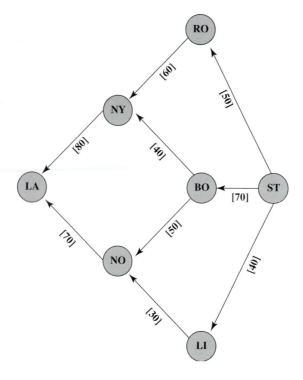

Model Formulation

Figure 6.7 shows the *network model* for this maximum flow problem. Rather than showing the geographical layout of the distribution network, this network simply lines up the nodes (representing the cities) in evenly spaced columns. The arcs represent the shipping lanes, where the capacity of each arc (given in square brackets under the arc) is the amount of shipping space available along that shipping lane. The objective is to determine how much flow to send through each arc (how many units to ship through each shipping lane) to maximize the total number of units flowing from the factory in Stuttgart to the distribution center in Los Angeles.

Figure 6.8 shows the corresponding spreadsheet model for this problem when using the format introduced in Figure 6.5. The main difference from the model in Figure 6.5 is the change in the objective. Since we are no longer minimizing the total cost of the flow through the network, column G in Figure 6.5 can be deleted in Figure 6.8. The target cell MaxFlow (D14) in Figure 6.8 now needs to give the total number of units flowing from Stuttgart to Los Angeles. Thus, the equations at the bottom of the figure include D14 = I4, where I4 gives the net flow leaving Stuttgart to go to Los Angeles. As in Figure 6.5, the equations in Figure 6.8 entered into NetFlow (I4:I10) again use the difference of two SUMIF functions to calculate the net flow generated at each node. Since the objective is to maximize the flow shown in MaxFlow (D14), the Solver dialogue box specifies that this target cell is to be maximized. After clicking on the Solve button, the optimal solution shown in the changing cells Ship (D4:D12) is obtained for the amount that BMZ should ship through each shipping lane.

In contrast to the spreadsheet model in Figure 6.5, which *minimizes* TotalCost (D11), the spreadsheet model in Figure 6.8 *maximizes* the target cell MaxFlow (D14).

However, Karl is not completely satisfied with this solution. He has an idea for doing even better. This will require formulating and solving another maximum flow problem. (This story continues in the middle of the next section.)

Review Questions

1. What is the current crisis facing the BMZ Co.?
2. When formulating this problem in network terms, what is flowing through BMZ's distribution network? From where to where?
3. What is the objective of the resulting maximum flow problem?

FIGURE 6.8

A spreadsheet model for the BMZ Co. maximum flow problem, including the equations entered into the target cell MaxFlow (D14) and the other output cells NetFlow (I4:I10), as well as the other specifications needed to set up the model. The changing cells Ship (D4:D12) show the optimal shipping quantities through the distribution network obtained by the Solver.

	A	B	C	D	E	F	G	H	I	J	K
1		**BMZ Co. Maximum Flow Problem**									
2											
3		**From**	**To**	**Ship**		**Capacity**		**Nodes**	**Net Flow**		**Supply/Demand**
4		Stuttgart	Rotterdam	50	≤	50		Stuttgart	150		
5		Stuttgart	Bordeaux	70	≤	70		Rotterdam	0	=	0
6		Stuttgart	Lisbon	30	≤	40		Bordeaux	0	=	0
7		Rotterdam	New York	50	≤	60		Lisbon	0	=	0
8		Bordeaux	New York	30	≤	40		New York	0	=	0
9		Bordeaux	New Orleans	40	≤	50		New Orleans	0	=	0
10		Lisbon	New Orleans	30	≤	30		Los Angeles	-150		
11		New York	Los Angeles	80	≤	80					
12		New Orleans	Los Angeles	70	≤	70					
13											
14			**Maximum Flow**	150							

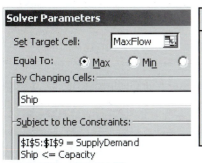

Range Name	Cells
Capacity	F4:F12
From	B4:B12
MaxFlow	D14
NetFlow	I4:I10
Nodes	H4:H10
Ship	D4:D12
SupplyDemand	K5:K9
To	C4:C12

	I
3	**Net Flow**
4	=SUMIF(From,H4,Ship)-SUMIF(To,H4,Ship)
5	=SUMIF(From,H5,Ship)-SUMIF(To,H5,Ship)
6	=SUMIF(From,H6,Ship)-SUMIF(To,H6,Ship)
7	=SUMIF(From,H7,Ship)-SUMIF(To,H7,Ship)
8	=SUMIF(From,H8,Ship)-SUMIF(To,H8,Ship)
9	=SUMIF(From,H9,Ship)-SUMIF(To,H9,Ship)
10	=SUMIF(From,H10,Ship)-SUMIF(To,H10,Ship)

	C	D
14	**Maximum Flow**	=I4

6.3   MAXIMUM FLOW PROBLEMS

Like a minimum-cost flow problem, a maximum flow problem is concerned with *flow through a network.* However, the objective now is different. Rather than minimizing the cost of the flow, the objective now is to find a flow plan that maximizes the amount flowing through the network. This is how Karl Schmidt was able to find a flow plan that maximizes the number of units of automobile replacement parts flowing through BMZ's distribution network from its factory in Stuttgart to the distribution center in Los Angeles.

General Characteristics

Except for the difference in objective (maximize flow versus minimize cost), the characteristics of the maximum flow problem are quite similar to those for the minimum-cost flow problem. However, there are some minor differences, as we will discuss after summarizing the assumptions.

Assumptions of a Maximum Flow Problem

1. All flow through the network originates at one node, called the **source,** and terminates at one other node, called the **sink.** (The source and sink in the BMZ problem are the factory and the distribution center, respectively.)

2. All the remaining nodes are *transshipment nodes.* (These are nodes RO, BO, LI, NY, and NO in the BMZ problem.)

3. Flow through an arc is only allowed in the direction indicated by the arrowhead, where the maximum amount of flow is given by the *capacity* of that arc. At the *source,* all arcs point away from the node. At the *sink,* all arcs point into the node.

4. The objective is to maximize the total amount of flow from the source to the sink. This amount is measured in either of two equivalent ways, namely, either the amount *leaving the source* or the amount *entering the sink.* (Cells D14 and I4 in Figure 6.8 use the amount leaving the source.)

The objective is to find a flow plan that maximizes the flow from the source to the sink.

The source and sink of a maximum flow problem are analogous to the supply nodes and demand nodes of a minimum-cost flow problem. These are the only nodes in both problems that do not have conservation of flow (flow out equals flow in). Like the supply nodes, the source *generates flow.* Like the demand nodes, the sink *absorbs flow.*

However, there are two differences between these nodes in a minimum-cost flow problem and the corresponding nodes in a maximum flow problem.

One difference is that, whereas supply nodes have fixed supplies and demand nodes have fixed demands, the source and sink do not. The reason is that the objective is to maximize the flow leaving the source and entering the sink rather than fixing this amount.

Although a maximum flow problem has only a single source and a single sink, variants with multiple sources and sinks also can be solved, as illustrated below.

The second difference is that, whereas the number of supply nodes and the number of demand nodes in a minimum-cost flow problem may be *more than one,* there can be *only one* source and *only one* sink in a maximum flow problem. However, variants of maximum flow problems that have multiple sources and sinks can still be solved by the Excel Solver, as you now will see illustrated by the BMZ case study introduced in the preceding section.

Continuing the Case Study with Multiple Supply Points and Multiple Demand Points

Here is Karl Schmidt's idea for how to improve upon the flow plan obtained at the end of Section 6.2 (as given in column D of Figure 6.8).

The company has a second, smaller factory in Berlin, north of its Stuttgart factory, for producing automobile parts. Although this factory normally is used to help supply distribution centers in northern Europe, Canada, and the northern United States (including one in Seattle), it also is able to ship to the distribution center in Los Angeles. Furthermore, the distribution center in Seattle has the capability of supplying parts to the customers of the distribution center in Los Angeles when shortages occur at the latter center.

In this light, Karl now has developed a better plan for addressing the current inventory shortages in Los Angeles. Rather than simply maximizing shipments from the Stuttgart factory to Los Angeles, he has decided to maximize shipments from both factories to the distribution centers in both Los Angeles and Seattle.

Figure 6.9 shows the network model representing the expanded distribution network that encompasses both factories and both distribution centers. In addition to the nodes shown in Figures 6.6 and 6.7, node BE is the second, smaller factory in Berlin; nodes HA and BN are additional ports used by this factory in Hamburg and Boston, respectively; and node SE is the distribution center in Seattle. As before, the arcs represent the shipping lanes, where the number in square brackets below each arc is the capacity of that arc, that is, the maximum number of units that can be shipped through that shipping lane over the next month.

The corresponding spreadsheet model is displayed in Figure 6.10. The format is the same as in Figure 6.8. However, the target cell MaxFlow (D21) now gives the total flow from Stuttgart and Berlin, so D21 = I4 + I5 (as shown by the equation for this target cell given at the bottom of the figure).

The changing cells Ship (D4:D19) in this figure show the optimal solution obtained for the number of units to ship through each shipping lane over the next month. Comparing this solution with the one in Figure 6.8 shows the impact of Karl Schmidt's decision to expand the distribution network to include the second factory and the distribution center in Seattle. As indicated in column I of the two figures, the number of units going to Los Angeles directly has been increased from 150 to 160, in addition to the 60 units going to Seattle as a backup for the inventory shortage in Los Angeles. This plan solved the crisis in Los Angeles and won Karl commendations from top management.

FIGURE 6.9

A network model for the expanded BMZ Co. problem as a variant of a maximum flow problem, where the number in square brackets below each arc is the capacity of that arc.

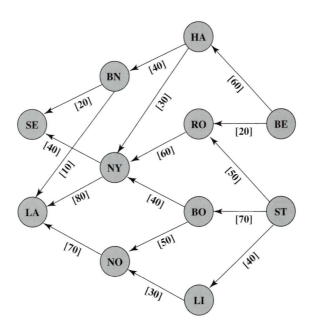

Some Applications

The applications of maximum flow problems and their variants are somewhat similar to those for minimum-cost flow problems described in the preceding section when management's objective is to *maximize flow* rather than to *minimize cost*. Here are some typical kinds of applications.

1. Maximize the flow through a distribution network, as for the BMZ Co. problem.
2. Maximize the flow through a company's supply network from its vendors to its processing facilities.
3. Maximize the flow of oil through a system of pipelines.
4. Maximize the flow of water through a system of aqueducts.
5. Maximize the flow of vehicles through a transportation network.

Solving Very Large Problems

The expanded BMZ network in Figure 6.9 has 11 nodes and 16 arcs. However, the networks for most real applications are considerably larger, and occasionally vastly larger. As the number of nodes and arcs grows into the hundreds or thousands, the formulation and solution approach illustrated in Figures 6.8 and 6.10 quickly becomes impractical.

Fortunately, management scientists have other techniques available for formulating and solving huge problems with many tens of thousands of nodes and arcs. One technique is to reformulate a variant of a maximum flow problem so that an extremely efficient special-purpose algorithm for maximum flow problems still can be applied. Another is to reformulate the problem to fit the format for a minimum-cost flow problem so that the network simplex method can be applied. These special algorithms are available in some software packages, but not in the Excel Solver. Thus, if you should ever encounter a maximum flow problem or a variant that is beyond the scope of the Excel Solver (which won't happen in this book), rest assured that it probably can be formulated and solved in another way.

Review
Questions

1. How does the objective of a maximum flow problem differ from that for a minimum-cost flow problem?
2. What are the *source* and the *sink* for a maximum flow problem? For each, in what direction do all their arcs point?
3. What are the two equivalent ways in which the total amount of flow from the source to the sink can be measured?
4. The source and sink of a maximum flow problem are different from the supply nodes and demand nodes of a minimum-cost flow problem in what two ways?
5. What are a few typical kinds of applications of maximum flow problems?

FIGURE 6.10

A spreadsheet model for the expanded BMZ Co. problem as a variant of a maximum flow problem with sources in both Stuttgart and Berlin and sinks in both Los Angeles and Seattle. Using the target cell MaxFlow (D21) to maximize the total flow from the two sources to the two sinks, the Solver yields the optimal shipping plan shown in the changing cells Ship (D4:D19).

	A	B	C	D	E	F	G	H	I	J	K
1		**BMZ Co. Expanded Maximum Flow Problem**									
2											
3		**From**	**To**	**Ship**		**Capacity**		**Nodes**	**Net Flow**		**Supply/Demand**
4		Stuttgart	Rotterdam	40	≤	50		Stuttgart	140		
5		Stuttgart	Bordeaux	70	≤	70		Berlin	80		
6		Stuttgart	Lisbon	30	≤	40		Hamburg	0	=	0
7		Berlin	Rotterdam	20	≤	20		Rotterdam	0	=	0
8		Berlin	Hamburg	60	≤	60		Bordeaux	0	=	0
9		Rotterdam	New York	60	≤	60		Lisbon	0	=	0
10		Bordeaux	New York	30	≤	40		Boston	0	=	0
11		Bordeaux	New Orleans	40	≤	50		New York	0	=	0
12		Lisbon	New Orleans	30	≤	30		New Orleans	0	=	0
13		Hamburg	New York	30	≤	30		Los Angeles	-160		
14		Hamburg	Boston	30	≤	40		Seattle	-60		
15		New Orleans	Los Angeles	70	≤	70					
16		New York	Los Angeles	80	≤	80					
17		New York	Seattle	40	≤	40					
18		Boston	Los Angeles	10	≤	10					
19		Boston	Seattle	20	≤	20					
20											
21			**Maximum Flow**	220							

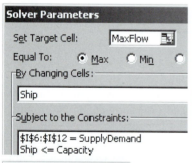

Range Name	Cells
Capacity	F4:F19
From	B4:B19
MaxFlow	D21
NetFlow	I4:I14
Nodes	H4:H14
Ship	D4:D19
SupplyDemand	K6:K12
To	C4:C19

	I
3	**Net Flow**
4	=SUMIF(From,H4,Ship)-SUMIF(To,H4,Ship)
5	=SUMIF(From,H5,Ship)-SUMIF(To,H5,Ship)
6	=SUMIF(From,H6,Ship)-SUMIF(To,H6,Ship)
7	=SUMIF(From,H7,Ship)-SUMIF(To,H7,Ship)
8	=SUMIF(From,H8,Ship)-SUMIF(To,H8,Ship)
9	=SUMIF(From,H9,Ship)-SUMIF(To,H9,Ship)
10	=SUMIF(From,H10,Ship)-SUMIF(To,H10,Ship)
11	=SUMIF(From,H11,Ship)-SUMIF(To,H11,Ship)
12	=SUMIF(From,H12,Ship)-SUMIF(To,H12,Ship)
13	=SUMIF(From,H13,Ship)-SUMIF(To,H13,Ship)
14	=SUMIF(From,H14,Ship)-SUMIF(To,H14,Ship)

	C	D
21	**Maximum Flow**	=I4+I5

6.4 SHORTEST PATH PROBLEMS

The most common applications of shortest path problems are for what the name suggests—finding the *shortest path* between two points. Here is an example.

An Example: The Littletown Fire Department Problem

Littletown is a small town in a rural area. Its fire department serves a relatively large geographical area that includes many farming communities. Since there are numerous roads

FIGURE 6.11

The road system between the Littletown Fire Station and a certain farming community, where A, B, . . . , H are junctions and the number next to each road shows its distance in miles.

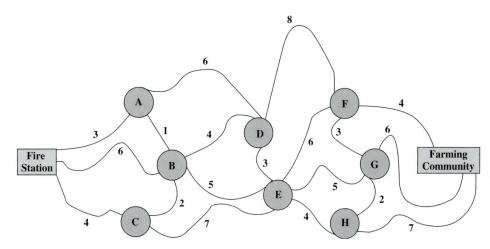

The objective is to find the shortest route from the fire station to the farming community.

throughout the area, many possible routes may be available for traveling to any given farming community from the fire station. Since time is of the essence in reaching a fire, the fire chief wishes to determine in advance the *shortest path* from the fire station to each of the farming communities.

Figure 6.11 shows the road system connecting the fire station to one of the farming communities, including the mileage along each road. Can you find which route from the fire station to the farming community minimizes the total number of miles?

Model Formulation for the Littletown Problem

Figure 6.12 gives the network representation of this problem, which ignores the geographical layout and the curves in the roads. This network model is the usual way of representing a shortest path problem. The junctions now are nodes of the network, where the fire station and farming community are two additional nodes labeled as O (for *origin*) and T (for *destination*), respectively. Since travel (flow) can go in either direction between the nodes, the lines connecting the nodes now are referred to as **links**[2] instead of *arcs.* A link between a pair of nodes allows travel in either direction, whereas an arc allows travel in only the direction indicated by an arrowhead, so the lines in Figure 6.12 need to be links instead of arcs. (Notice that the links do not have an arrowhead at either end.)

Have you found the shortest path from the origin to the destination yet? (Try it now before reading further.) It is

$$O \rightarrow A \rightarrow B \rightarrow E \rightarrow F \rightarrow T$$

with a total distance of 19 miles.

This problem (like any shortest path problem) can be thought of as a special kind of minimum-cost flow problem (Section 6.1) where the *miles traveled* now are interpreted to be the *cost* of flow through the network. A trip from the fire station to the farming community is interpreted to be a flow of 1 on the chosen path through the network, so minimizing the cost of this flow is equivalent to minimizing the number of miles traveled. The fire station is considered to be the one

In a shortest path problem, travel goes from the origin to the destination through a series of links (such as roads) that connect pairs of nodes (junctions) in the network.

FIGURE 6.12

The network representation of Figure 6.11 as a shortest path problem.

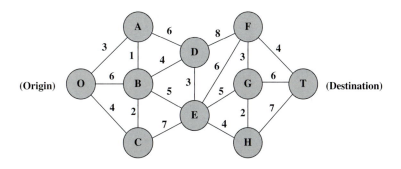

[2] Another name sometimes used is *undirected arc,* but we will not use this terminology.

An Application Vignette

Incorporated in 1881, Canadian Pacific Railway (CPR) was North America's first transcontinental railway. CPR transports rail freight over a 14,000-mile network extending from Montreal to Vancouver and throughout the U.S. Northwest and Midwest. Alliances with other carriers extend CPR's market reach into the major business centers of Mexico as well.

Every day CPR receives approximately 7,000 new shipments from its customers going to destinations across North America and for export. It must route and move these shipments in railcars over the network of track, where a railcar may be switched a number of times from one locomotive engine to another before reaching its destination. CPR must coordinate the shipments with its operational plans for 1,600 locomotives, 65,000 railcars, over 5,000 train crew members, and 250 train yards.

CPR management turned to a management science consulting firm, MultiModal Applied Systems, to work with CPR employees in developing a management science approach to this problem. A variety of management science techniques were used to create a new operating strategy. However, the foundation of the approach was to represent the flow of blocks of railcars as flow through a network where each node corresponds to both a location and a point in time. This representation then enabled the application of network optimization techniques. For example, numerous shortest path problems are solved each day as part of the overall approach.

This application of management science is saving CPR roughly US$100 million per year. Labor productivity, locomotive productivity, fuel consumption, and railcar velocity have improved very substantially. In addition, CPR now provides its customers with reliable delivery times and has received many awards for its improvement in service.

Source: P. Ireland, R. Case, J. Fallis, C. Van Dyke, J. Kuehn, and M. Meketon, "The Canadian Pacific Railway Transforms Operations by Using Models to Develop Its Operating Plans," *Interfaces* 34, no. 1 (January–February 2004), pp. 5–14.

supply node, with a supply of 1 to represent the start of this trip. The farming community is the one demand node, with a demand of 1 to represent the completion of this trip. All the other nodes in Figure 6.12 are transshipment nodes, so the net flow generated at each is 0.

> This spreadsheet model is like one for a minimum-cost flow problem with no arc capacity constraints except that distances replace unit costs and travel on a chosen path is interpreted as a flow of 1 through this path.

Figure 6.13 shows the spreadsheet model that results from this interpretation. The format is basically the same as for the minimum-cost flow problem formulated in Figure 6.5, except now there are no arc capacity constraints and the unit cost column is replaced by a column of distances in miles. The flow quantities given by the changing cells OnRoute (D4:D27) are 1 for each arc that is on the chosen path from the fire station to the farming community and 0 otherwise. The target cell TotalDistance (D29) gives the total distance of this path in miles. (See the equation for this cell at the bottom of the figure.) Columns B and C together list all the vertical links in Figure 6.12 twice, once as a downward arc and once as an upward arc, since either direction might be on the chosen path. The other links are only listed as left-to-right arcs, since this is the only direction of interest for choosing a shortest path from the origin to the destination.

Column K shows the net flow that needs to be generated at each of the nodes. Using the equations at the bottom of the figure, each column I cell then calculates the *actual* net flow at that node by adding the flow out and subtracting the flow in. The corresponding constraints, Nodes (H4:H13) = SupplyDemand (K4:K13), are specified in the Solver dialogue box.

The solution shown in OnRoute (D4:D27) is the optimal solution obtained after clicking on the Solve button. It is exactly the same as the shortest path given earlier.

Just as for minimum-cost flow problems and maximum flow problems, special algorithms are available for solving large shortest path problems very efficiently, but these algorithms are not included in the Excel Solver. Using a spreadsheet formulation and the Solver is fine for problems of the size of the Littletown problem and somewhat larger, but you should be aware that vastly larger problems can still be solved by other means.

General Characteristics

Except for more complicated variations beyond the scope of this book, all shortest path problems share the characteristics illustrated by the Littletown problem. Here are the basic assumptions.

Assumptions of a Shortest Path Problem

1. You need to choose a path through the network that starts at a certain node, called the **origin,** and ends at another certain node, called the **destination.**

FIGURE 6.13

A spreadsheet model for the Littletown Fire Department shortest path problem, including the equations entered into the target cell TotalDistance (D29) and the other output cells SupplyDemand (K4:K13). The values of 1 in the changing cells OnRoute (D4:D27) reveal the optimal solution obtained by the Solver for the shortest path (19 miles) from the fire station to the farming community.

	A	B	C	D	E	F	G	H	I	J	K
1		**Littletown Fire Department Shortest Path Problem**									
2											
3		**From**	**To**	**On Route**		**Distance**		**Nodes**	**Net Flow**		**Supply/Demand**
4		Fire St.	A	1		3		Fire St.	1	=	1
5		Fire St.	B	0		6		A	0	=	0
6		Fire St.	C	0		4		B	0	=	0
7		A	B	1		1		C	0	=	0
8		A	D	0		6		D	0	=	0
9		B	A	0		1		E	0	=	0
10		B	C	0		2		F	0	=	0
11		B	D	0		4		G	0	=	0
12		B	E	1		5		H	0	=	0
13		C	B	0		2		Farm Com.	-1	=	-1
14		C	E	0		7					
15		D	E	0		3					
16		D	F	0		8					
17		E	D	0		3					
18		E	F	1		6					
19		E	G	0		5					
20		E	H	0		4					
21		F	G	0		3					
22		F	Farm Com.	1		4					
23		G	F	0		3					
24		G	H	0		2					
25		G	Farm Com.	0		6					
26		H	G	0		2					
27		H	Farm Com.	0		7					
28											
29			**Total Distance**	19							

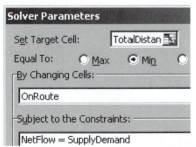

Solver Parameters

Set Target Cell: TotalDistan

Equal To: ○ Max ● Min ○

By Changing Cells:

OnRoute

Subject to the Constraints:

NetFlow = SupplyDemand

Solver Options

☑ Assume Linear Model
☑ Assume Non-Negative

Range Name	Cells
Distance	F4:F27
From	B4:B27
NetFlow	I4:I13
Nodes	H4:H13
OnRoute	D4:D27
SupplyDemand	K4:K13
To	C4:C27
TotalDistance	D29

	I
3	**Net Flow**
4	=SUMIF(From,H4,OnRoute)-SUMIF(To,H4,OnRoute)
5	=SUMIF(From,H5,OnRoute)-SUMIF(To,H5,OnRoute)
6	=SUMIF(From,H6,OnRoute)-SUMIF(To,H6,OnRoute)
7	=SUMIF(From,H7,OnRoute)-SUMIF(To,H7,OnRoute)
8	=SUMIF(From,H8,OnRoute)-SUMIF(To,H8,OnRoute)
9	=SUMIF(From,H9,OnRoute)-SUMIF(To,H9,OnRoute)
10	=SUMIF(From,H10,OnRoute)-SUMIF(To,H10,OnRoute)
11	=SUMIF(From,H11,OnRoute)-SUMIF(To,H11,OnRoute)
12	=SUMIF(From,H12,OnRoute)-SUMIF(To,H12,OnRoute)
13	=SUMIF(From,H13,OnRoute)-SUMIF(To,H13,OnRoute)

	C	D
29	**Total Distance**	=SUMPRODUCT(OnRoute,Distance)

2. The lines connecting certain pairs of nodes commonly are *links* (which allow travel in either direction), although arcs (which only permit travel in one direction) also are allowed.

3. Associated with each link (or arc) is a nonnegative number called its **length.** (Be aware that the drawing of each link in the network typically makes no effort to show its true length other than giving the correct number next to the link.)

4. The objective is to find the shortest path (the path with the minimum total length) from the origin to the destination.

The objective is to find the shortest path from the origin to the destination.

Some Applications

Not all applications of shortest path problems involve minimizing the distance traveled from the origin to the destination. In fact, they might not even involve travel at all. The links (or arcs) might instead represent activities of some other kind, so choosing a path through the network corresponds to selecting the best sequence of activities. The numbers giving the "lengths" of the links might then be, for example, the costs of the activities, in which case the objective would be to determine which sequence of activities minimizes the total cost.

Here are three categories of applications.

1. Minimize the total *distance* traveled, as in the Littletown example.
2. Minimize the total *cost* of a sequence of activities, as in the example that follows in the subsection below.
3. Minimize the total *time* of a sequence of activities, as in the example involving the Quick Company at the end of this section.

An Example of Minimizing Total Cost

Sarah has just graduated from high school. As a graduation present, her parents have given her a car fund of $21,000 to help purchase and maintain a certain three-year-old used car for college. Since operating and maintenance costs go up rapidly as the car ages, Sarah's parents tell her that she will be welcome to trade in her car on another three-year-old car one or more times during the next three summers if she determines that this would minimize her total net cost. They also inform her that they will give her a new car in four years as a college graduation present, so she should definitely plan to trade in her car then. (These are pretty nice parents!)

Sarah needs a schedule for trading in her car that will minimize her total net cost.

Table 6.2 gives the relevant data for *each* time Sarah purchases a three-year-old car. For example, if she trades in her car after two years, the next car will be in ownership year 1 during her junior year, and so forth.

When should Sarah trade in her car (if at all) during the next three summers to minimize her total net cost of purchasing, operating, and maintaining the car(s) over her four years of college?

Figure 6.14 shows the network formulation of this problem as a shortest path problem. Nodes 1, 2, 3, and 4 are the end of Sarah's first, second, third, and fourth years of college, respectively. Node 0 is now, before starting college. Each arc from one node to a second node corresponds to the activity of purchasing a car at the time indicated by the first of these two nodes and then trading it in at the time indicated by the second node. Sarah begins by purchasing a car now, and she ends by trading in a car at the end of year 4, so node 0 is the *origin* and node 4 is the *destination.*

The number of arcs on the path chosen from the origin to the destination indicates how many times Sarah will purchase and trade in a car. For example, consider the path

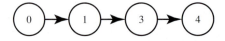

TABLE 6.2
Sarah's Data Each Time She Purchases a Three-Year-Old Car

Purchase Price	Operating and Maintenance Costs for Ownership Year				Trade-in Value at End of Ownership Year			
	1	2	3	4	1	2	3	4
$12,000	$2,000	$3,000	$4,500	$6,500	$8,500	$6,500	$4,500	$3,000

FIGURE 6.14

Formulation of the problem of when Sarah should trade in her car as a shortest path problem. The node labels measure the number of years from now. Each arc represents purchasing a car and then trading it in later.

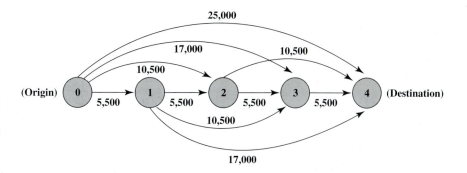

This corresponds to purchasing a car now, then trading it in at the end of year 1 to purchase a second car, then trading in the second car at the end of year 3 to purchase a third car, and then trading in this third car at the end of year 4.

Since Sarah wants to minimize her total net cost from now (node 0) to the end of year 4 (node 4), each arc length needs to measure the net cost of that arc's cycle of purchasing, maintaining, and trading in a car. Therefore,

Arc length = Purchase price + Operating and maintenance costs − Trade-in value

For example, consider the arc from node 1 to node 3. This arc corresponds to purchasing a car at the end of year 1, operating and maintaining it during ownership years 1 and 2, and then trading it in at the end of ownership year 2. Consequently,

$$\text{Length of arc from } ① \text{ to } ③ = 12{,}000 + 2{,}000 + 3{,}000 - 6{,}500$$
$$= 10{,}500 \quad \text{(in dollars)}$$

The sum of the arc lengths on any path through this network gives the total net cost of the corresponding plan for trading in cars.

The arc lengths calculated in this way are shown next to the arcs in Figure 6.14. Adding up the lengths of the arcs on any path from node 0 to node 4 then gives the total net cost for that particular plan for trading in cars over the next four years. Therefore, finding the shortest path from the origin to the destination identifies the plan that will minimize Sarah's total net cost.

The target cell now is TotalCost instead of TotalDistance.

Figure 6.15 shows the corresponding spreadsheet model, formulated in just the same way as for Figure 6.13 except that distances are now costs. Thus, the target cell TotalCost (D23) now gives the total cost that is to be minimized. The changing cells OnRoute (D12:D21) in the figure display the optimal solution obtained after having clicked on the Solve button. Since values of 1 indicate the path being followed, the shortest path turns out to be

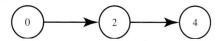

Trade in the first car at the end of year 2.
Trade in the second car at the end of year 4.

The length of this path is 10,500 + 10,500 = 21,000, so Sarah's total net cost is $21,000, as given by the target cell. Recall that this is exactly the amount in Sarah's car fund provided by her parents. (These are *really* nice parents!)

An Example of Minimizing Total Time

The Quick Company has learned that a competitor is planning to come out with a new kind of product with great sales potential. Quick has been working on a similar product that had been scheduled to come to market in 20 months. However, research is nearly complete and Quick's management now wishes to rush the product out to meet the competition.

There are four nonoverlapping phases left to be accomplished, including the remaining research (the first phase) that currently is being conducted at a normal pace. However, each phase can instead be conducted at a priority or crash level to expedite completion. These are

FIGURE 6.15

A spreadsheet model that formulates Sarah's problem as a shortest path problem where the objective is to minimize the total cost instead of the total distance. The bottom of the figure shows the equations entered in the target cell TotalCost (D23) and the other output cells Cost (E12:E21) and NetFlow (H12:H16). After applying the Solver, the values of 1 in the changing cells OnRoute (D12:D21) identify the shortest (least expensive) path for scheduling trade-ins.

	A	B	C	D	E	F	G	H	I	J
1		**Sarah's Car Purchasing Problem**								
2										
3			Operating & Maint. Cost	Trade-in Value at End of Year	Purchase Price					
4										
5		Year 1	$2,000	$8,500	$12,000					
6		Year 2	$3,000	$6,500						
7		Year 3	$4,500	$4,500						
8		Year 4	$6,500	$3,000						
9										
10										
11		**From**	**To**	**On Route**	**Cost**		**Nodes**	**Net Flow**		**Supply/Demand**
12		Year 0	Year 1	0	$5,500		Year 0	1	=	1
13		Year 0	Year 2	1	$10,500		Year 1	0	=	0
14		Year 0	Year 3	0	$17,000		Year 2	0	=	0
15		Year 0	Year 4	0	$25,000		Year 3	0	=	0
16		Year 1	Year 2	0	$5,500		Year 4	-1	=	-1
17		Year 1	Year 3	0	$10,500					
18		Year 1	Year 4	0	$17,000					
19		Year 2	Year 3	0	$5,500					
20		Year 2	Year 4	1	$10,500					
21		Year 3	Year 4	0	$5,500					
22										
23			**Total Cost**	$21,000						

Range Name	Cells
Cost	E12:E21
From	B12:B21
NetFlow	H12:H16
Nodes	G12:G16
OnRoute	D12:D21
OpMaint1	C5
OpMaint2	C6
OpMaint3	C7
OpMaint4	C8
PurchasePrice	E5
SupplyDemand	J12:J16
To	C12:C21
TotalCost	D23
TradeIn1	D5
TradeIn2	D6
TradeIn3	D7
TradeIn4	D8

	E
11	**Cost**
12	=PurchasePrice+OpMaint1-TradeIn1
13	=PurchasePrice+OpMaint1+OpMaint2-TradeIn2
14	=PurchasePrice+OpMaint1+OpMaint2+OpMaint3-TradeIn3
15	=PurchasePrice+OpMaint1+OpMaint2+OpMaint3+OpMaint4-TradeIn4
16	=PurchasePrice+OpMaint1-TradeIn1
17	=PurchasePrice+OpMaint1+OpMaint2-TradeIn2
18	=PurchasePrice+OpMaint1+OpMaint2+OpMaint3-TradeIn3
19	=PurchasePrice+OpMaint1-TradeIn1
20	=PurchasePrice+OpMaint1+OpMaint2-TradeIn2
21	=PurchasePrice+OpMaint1-TradeIn1

	H
11	**Net Flow**
12	=SUMIF(From,G12,OnRoute)-SUMIF(To,G12,OnRoute)
13	=SUMIF(From,G13,OnRoute)-SUMIF(To,G13,OnRoute)
14	=SUMIF(From,G14,OnRoute)-SUMIF(To,G14,OnRoute)
15	=SUMIF(From,G15,OnRoute)-SUMIF(To,G15,OnRoute)
16	=SUMIF(From,G16,OnRoute)-SUMIF(To,G16,OnRoute)

	C	D
23	**Total Cost**	=SUMPRODUCT(OnRoute,Cost)

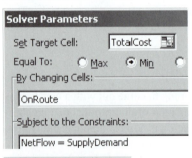

Solver Parameters

Set Target Cell: TotalCost

Equal To: ○ Max ● Min

By Changing Cells:

OnRoute

Subject to the Constraints:

NetFlow = SupplyDemand

Solver Options

☑ Assume Linear Model
☑ Assume Non-Negative

the only levels that will be considered for the last three phases, whereas both the normal level and these two levels will be considered for the first phase. The times required at these levels are shown in Table 6.3.

Management now has allocated $30 million for these four phases. The cost of each phase at the levels under consideration is shown in Table 6.4.

Management wishes to determine at which level to conduct each of the four phases to minimize the total time until the product can be marketed, subject to the budget restriction of $30 million.

Figure 6.16 shows the network formulation of this problem as a shortest path problem. Each node indicates the situation at that point in time. Except for the destination, a node is identified by two numbers:

1. The number of phases completed.
2. The number of millions of dollars left for the remaining phases.

> The objective is to minimize the total time for the project.

The origin is *now*, when 0 phases have been completed and the entire budget of $30 million is left. Each arc represents the choice of a particular level of effort (identified in parentheses below the arc) for that phase. The *time* (in months) required to perform the phase with this level of effort then is the *length* of the arc (shown above the arc). Time is chosen as the measure of arc length because the objective is to minimize the total time for all four phases. Summing the arc lengths for any particular path through the network gives the total time for the plan corresponding to that path. Therefore, the shortest path through the network identifies the plan that minimizes total time.

> The sum of the arc lengths on any path through this network gives the total time of the corresponding plan for preparing the new product.

All four phases have been completed as soon as any one of the four nodes with a first label of 4 has been reached. So why doesn't the network just end with these four nodes rather than

---

TABLE 6.3
Time Required for the Phases of Preparing Quick Co.'s New Product

Level	Remaining Research	Development	Design of Manufacturing System	Initiate Production and Distribution
Normal	5 months	—	—	—
Priority	4 months	3 months	5 months	2 months
Crash	2 months	2 months	3 months	1 month

TABLE 6.4
Cost for the Phases of Preparing Quick Co.'s New Product

Level	Remaining Research	Development	Design of Manufacturing System	Initiate Production and Distribution
Normal	$3 million	—	—	—
Priority	6 million	$6 million	$ 9 million	$3 million
Crash	9 million	9 million	12 million	6 million

FIGURE 6.16
Formulation of the Quick Co. problem as a shortest path problem. Except for the dummy destination, the arc labels indicate, first, the number of phases completed and, second, the amount of money left (in millions of dollars) for the remaining phases. Each arc length gives the time (in months) to perform that phase.

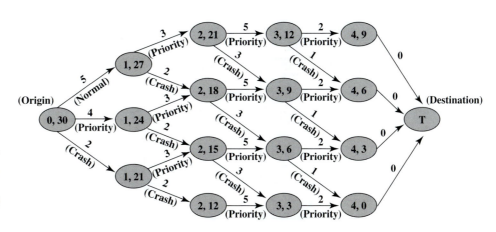

having an arc coming out of each one? The reason is that a shortest path problem is required to have only a single destination. Consequently, a dummy destination is added at the right-hand side.

> When real travel through a network can end at more than one node, an arc with length 0 is inserted from each of these nodes to a **dummy destination** so that the network will have just a single destination.

Since each of the arcs into the dummy destination has length 0, this addition to the network does not affect the total length of a path from the origin to its ending point.

The target cell now is TotalTime instead of TotalDistance.

Figure 6.17 displays the spreadsheet model for this problem. Once again, the format is the same as in Figures 6.13 and 6.15, except now the quantity of concern in column F and the target cell TotalTime (D32) is time rather than distance or cost. Since the Solve button has

FIGURE 6.17

A spreadsheet model that formulates the Quick Co. problem as a shortest path problem where the objective is to minimize the total time instead of the total distance, so the target cell is TotalTime (D32). The other output cells are NetFlow (I4:I20). The values of 1 in the changing cells OnRoute (D4:D30) reveal the shortest (quickest) path obtained by the Solver.

	A	B	C	D	E	F	G	H	I	J	K
1		**Quick Co. Product Development Scheduling Problem**									
2											
3		**From**	**To**	**On Route**		**Time**		**Nodes**	**Net Flow**		**Supply/Demand**
4		(0, 30)	(1, 27)	0		5		(0, 30)	1	=	1
5		(0, 30)	(1, 24)	0		4		(1, 27)	0	=	0
6		(0, 30)	(1, 21)	1		2		(1, 24)	0	=	0
7		(1, 27)	(2, 21)	0		3		(1, 21)	0	=	0
8		(1, 27)	(2, 18)	0		2		(2, 21)	0	=	0
9		(1, 24)	(2, 18)	0		3		(2, 18)	0	=	0
10		(1, 24)	(2, 15)	0		2		(2, 15)	0	=	0
11		(1, 21)	(2, 15)	1		3		(2, 12)	0	=	0
12		(1, 21)	(2, 12)	0		2		(3, 12)	0	=	0
13		(2, 21)	(3, 12)	0		5		(3, 9)	0	=	0
14		(2, 21)	(3, 9)	0		3		(3, 6)	0	=	0
15		(2, 18)	(3, 9)	0		5		(3, 3)	0	=	0
16		(2, 18)	(3, 6)	0		3		(4, 9)	0	=	0
17		(2, 15)	(3, 6)	0		5		(4, 6)	0	=	0
18		(2, 15)	(3, 3)	1		3		(4, 3)	0	=	0
19		(2, 12)	(3, 3)	0		5		(4, 0)	0	=	0
20		(3, 12)	(4, 9)	0		2		(T)	-1	=	-1
21		(3, 12)	(4, 6)	0		1					
22		(3, 9)	(4, 6)	0		2					
23		(3, 9)	(4, 3)	0		1					
24		(3, 6)	(4, 3)	0		2					
25		(3, 6)	(4, 0)	0		1					
26		(3, 3)	(4, 0)	1		2					
27		(4, 9)	(T)	0		0					
28		(4, 6)	(T)	0		0					
29		(4, 3)	(T)	0		0					
30		(4, 0)	(T)	1		0					
31											
32			**Total Time**	10							

(continued)

FIGURE 6.17   *(continued)*

Range Name	Cells
From	B4:B30
NetFlow	I4:I20
Nodes	H4:H20
OnRoute	D4:D30
SupplyDemand	K4:K20
Time	F4:F30
To	C4:C30
TotalTime	D32

Solver Parameters

Set Target Cell: [TotalTime]

Equal To: ○ Max   ● Min   ○

By Changing Cells:

[OnRoute]

Subject to the Constraints:

[NetFlow = SupplyDemand]

Solver Options

☑ Assume Linear Model
☑ Assume Non-Negative

	I
3	**Net Flow**
4	=SUMIF(From,H4,OnRoute)-SUMIF(To,H4,OnRoute)
5	=SUMIF(From,H5,OnRoute)-SUMIF(To,H5,OnRoute)
6	=SUMIF(From,H6,OnRoute)-SUMIF(To,H6,OnRoute)
7	=SUMIF(From,H7, OnRoute)-SUMIF(To,H7,OnRoute)
8	=SUMIF(From,H8,OnRoute)-SUMIF(To,H8,OnRoute)
9	=SUMIF(From,H9,OnRoute)-SUMIF(To,H9,OnRoute)
10	=SUMIF(From,H10,OnRoute)-SUMIF(To,H10,OnRoute)
11	=SUMIF(From,H11,OnRoute)-SUMIF(To,H11,OnRoute)
12	=SUMIF(From,H12,OnRoute)-SUMIF(To,H12,OnRoute)
13	=SUMIF(From,H13,OnRoute)-SUMIF(To,H13,OnRoute)
14	=SUMIF(From,H14,OnRoute)-SUMIF(To,H14,OnRoute)
15	=SUMIF(From,H15,OnRoute)-SUMIF(To,H15,OnRoute)
16	=SUMIF(From,H16,OnRoute)-SUMIF(To,H16,OnRoute)
17	=SUMIF(From,H17,OnRoute)-SUMIF(To,H17,OnRoute)
18	=SUMIF(From,H18,OnRoute)-SUMIF(To,H18,OnRoute)
19	=SUMIF(From,H19,OnRoute)-SUMIF(To,H19,OnRoute)
20	=SUMIF(From,H20,OnRoute)-SUMIF(To,H20,OnRoute)

	C	D
32	**Total Time**	=SUMPRODUCT(OnRoute,Time)

TABLE 6.5
The Optimal Solution Obtained by the Excel Solver for Quick Co.'s Shortest Path Problem

Phase	Level	Time	Cost
Remaining research	Crash	2 months	$ 9 million
Development	Priority	3 months	6 million
Design of manufacturing system	Crash	3 months	12 million
Initiate production and distribution	Priority	2 months	3 million
Total		10 months	$30 million

already been clicked, the changing cells OnRoute (D4:D30) indicate which arcs lie on the path that minimizes the total time. Thus, the shortest path is

with a total length of 2 + 3 + 3 + 2 + 0 = 10 months, as given by TotalTime (D32). The resulting plan for the four phases is shown in Table 6.5. Although this plan does consume the entire budget of $30 million, it reduces the time until the product can be brought to market from the originally planned 20 months down to just 10 months.

Given this information, Quick's management now must decide whether this plan provides the best trade-off between time and cost. What would be the effect on total time of spending a few million more dollars? What would be the effect of reducing the spending somewhat instead? It is easy to provide management with this information as well by quickly solving some shortest path problems that correspond to budgets different from $30 million. The ultimate decision regarding which plan provides the best time–cost trade-off then is a judgment decision that only management can make.

Review Questions

1. What are the origin and the destination in the Littletown Fire Department example?
2. What is the distinction between an arc and a link?
3. What are the supply node and the demand node when a shortest path problem is interpreted as a minimum-cost flow problem? With what supply and demand?
4. What are three measures of the length of a link (or arc) that lead to three categories of applications of shortest path problems?
5. What is the objective for Sarah's shortest path problem?
6. When does a dummy destination need to be added to the formulation of a shortest path problem?
7. What kind of trade-off does the management of the Quick Co. need to consider in making its final decision about how to expedite its new product to market?

6.5 Summary

Networks of some type arise in a wide variety of contexts. Network representations are very useful for portraying the relationships and connections between the components of systems. Each component is represented by a point in the network called a *node,* and then the connections between components (nodes) are represented by lines called *arcs* (for one-way travel) or *links* (for two-way travel).

Frequently, a flow of some type must be sent through a network, so a decision needs to be made about the best way to do this. The kinds of network optimization models introduced in this chapter provide a powerful tool for making such decisions.

The model for minimum-cost flow problems plays a central role among these network optimization models, both because it is so broadly applicable and because it can be readily solved. The Excel Solver solves spreadsheet formulations of reasonable size, and the network simplex method can be used to solve larger problems, including huge problems with tens of thousands of nodes and arcs. A minimum-cost flow problem typically is concerned with optimizing the flow of goods through a network from their points of origin (the *supply nodes*) to where they are needed (the *demand nodes*). The objective is to minimize the total cost of sending the available supply through the network to satisfy the given demand. One typical application (among several) is to optimize the operation of a distribution network.

Special types of minimum-cost flow problems include transportation problems and assignment problems (discussed in Chapter 3) as well as two prominent types introduced in this chapter: maximum flow problems and shortest path problems.

Given the limited capacities of the arcs in the network, the objective of a maximum flow problem is to maximize the total amount of flow from a particular point of origin (the *source*) to a particular terminal point (the *sink*). For example, this might involve maximizing the flow of goods through a company's supply network from its vendors to its processing facilities.

A shortest path problem also has a beginning point (the *origin*) and an ending point (the *destination*), but now the objective is to find a path from the origin to the destination that has the minimum total *length.* For some applications, length refers to distance, so the objective is to minimize the total distance traveled. However, some applications instead involve minimizing either the total cost or the total time of a sequence of activities.

Glossary

arc A channel through which flow may occur from one node to another, shown as an arrow between the nodes pointing in the direction in which flow is allowed. (Section 6.1), 187

capacity of an arc The maximum amount of flow allowed through the arc. (Section 6.1), 187

conservation of flow Having the amount of flow out of a node equal the amount of flow into that node. (Section 6.1), 187

demand node A node where the net amount of flow generated (outflow minus inflow) is a fixed negative number, so that flow is absorbed there. (Section 6.1), 187

destination The node at which travel through the network is assumed to end for a shortest path problem. (Section 6.4), 200

dummy destination A fictitious destination introduced into the formulation of a shortest path problem with multiple possible termination points to satisfy the requirement that there be just a single destination. (Section 6.4), 206

length of a link or arc The number (typically a distance, a cost, or a time) associated with including the link or arc in the selected path for a shortest path problem. (Section 6.4), 202

link A channel through which flow may occur in either direction between a pair of nodes, shown as a line between the nodes. (Section 6.4), 199

network simplex method A streamlined version of the simplex method for solving minimum-cost flow problems very efficiently. (Section 6.1), 190

node   A junction point of a network, shown as a labeled circle. (Section 6.1), 187

origin   The node at which travel through the network is assumed to start for a shortest path problem. (Section 6.4), 200

sink   The node for a maximum flow problem at which all flow through the network terminates. (Section 6.3), 195

source   The node for a maximum flow problem at which all flow through the network originates. (Section 6.3), 195

supply node   A node where the net amount of flow generated (outflow minus inflow) is a fixed positive number. (Section 6.1), 187

transshipment node   A node where the amount of flow out equals the amount of flow in. (Section 6.1), 187

transshipment problem   A special type of minimum-cost flow problem where there are no capacity constraints on the arcs. (Section 6.1), 191

Learning Aids for This Chapter in Your MS Courseware

Chapter 6 Excel Files:

Distribution Unlimited Example
BMZ Example
Expanded BMZ Example
Littletown Fire Department Example
Sarah Example

Quick Example

An Excel Add-in:

Premium Solver for Education

Supplement to Chapter 6 on the CD-ROM:

Minimum Spanning-Tree Problems

Solved Problem (See the CD-ROM for the Solution)

6.S1. Distribution at Heart Beats

Heart Beats is a manufacturer of medical equipment. The company's primary product is a device used to monitor the heart during medical procedures. This device is produced in two factories and shipped to two warehouses. The product is then shipped on demand to four third-party wholesalers. All shipping is done by truck. The product distribution network is shown below. The annual production capacity at factories 1 and 2

is 400 and 250, respectively. The annual demand at wholesalers 1, 2, 3, and 4 is 200, 100, 150, and 200, respectively. The cost of shipping one unit in each shipping lane is shown on the arcs. Because of limited truck capacity, at most 250 units can be shipped from factory 1 to warehouse 1 each year. Formulate and solve a network optimization model in a spreadsheet to determine how to distribute the product at the lowest possible annual cost.

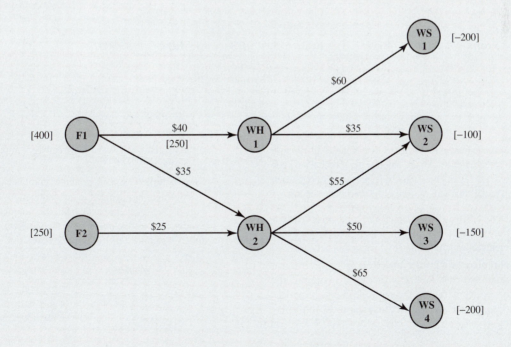

Problems

We have inserted the symbol E* to the left of each problem (or its parts) where Excel should be used (unless your instructor gives you contrary instructions). An asterisk on the problem number indicates that at least a partial answer is given in the back of the book.

6.1.* Consider the transportation problem having the following data.

	\multicolumn{3}{c}{Destination}		
	1	2	3	Supply
Source				
1	6	7	4	40
2	5	8	6	60
Demand	30	40	30	

a. Draw a network that depicts the company's distribution network. Identify the supply nodes, transshipment nodes, and demand nodes in this network.

b. Formulate a network model for this problem as a minimum-cost flow problem by inserting all the necessary data into the network drawn in part *a*. (Use the format depicted in Figure 6.3 to display these data.)

a. Formulate a network model for this problem as a minimum-cost flow problem by drawing a network similar to Figure 6.3.

E* b. Formulate and solve a spreadsheet model for this problem.

6.2 The Makonsel Company is a fully integrated company that both produces goods and sells them at its retail outlets. After production, the goods are stored in the company's two warehouses until needed by the retail outlets. Trucks are used to transport the goods from the two plants to the warehouses, and then from the warehouses to the three retail outlets.

Using units of full truckloads, the following table shows each plant's monthly output, its shipping cost per truckload sent to each warehouse, and the maximum amount that it can ship per month to each warehouse.

To \ From	Unit Shipping Cost		Shipping Capacity		
	Warehouse 1	Warehouse 2	Warehouse 1	Warehouse 2	Output
Plant 1	$425	$560	125	150	200
Plant 2	510	600	175	200	300

For each retail outlet (RO), the next table shows its monthly demand, its shipping cost per truckload from each warehouse, and the maximum amount that can be shipped per month from each warehouse.

To \ From	Unit Shipping Cost			Shipping Capacity		
	RO1	RO2	RO3	RO1	RO2	RO3
Warehouse 1	$470	$505	$490	100	150	100
Warehouse 2	390	410	440	125	150	75
Demand	150	200	150	150	200	150

Management now wants to determine a distribution plan (number of truckloads shipped per month from each plant to each warehouse and from each warehouse to each retail outlet) that will minimize the total shipping cost.

E* c. Formulate and solve a spreadsheet model for this problem.

6.3. The Audiofile Company produces boomboxes. However, management has decided to subcontract out the production of the speakers needed for the boomboxes. Three vendors are available to supply the speakers. Their price for each shipment of 1,000 speakers is shown below.

Vendor	Price
1	$22,500
2	22,700
3	22,300

Each shipment would go to one of the company's two warehouses. In addition to the price for each shipment, each vendor would charge a shipping cost for which it has its own formula based on the mileage to the warehouse. These formulas and the mileage data are shown below.

Vendor	Charge per Shipment	Warehouse 1	Warehouse 2
1	$300 + 40¢/mile	1,600 miles	400 miles
2	$200 + 50¢/mile	500 miles	600 miles
3	$500 + 20¢/mile	2,000 miles	1,000 miles

Whenever one of the company's two factories needs a shipment of speakers to assemble into the boomboxes, the company hires a trucker to bring the shipment in from one of the warehouses. The cost per shipment is given below, along with the number of shipments needed per month at each factory.

	Unit Shipping Cost	
	Factory 1	Factory 2
Warehouse 1	$200	$700
Warehouse 2	400	500
Monthly demand	10	6

Each vendor is able to supply as many as 10 shipments per month. However, because of shipping limitations, each vendor is only able to send a maximum of six shipments per month to each warehouse. Similarly, each warehouse is only able to send a maximum of six shipments per month to each factory.

Management now wants to develop a plan for each month regarding how many shipments (if any) to order from each vendor, how many of those shipments should go to each warehouse, and then how many shipments each warehouse should send to each factory. The objective is to minimize the sum of the purchase costs (including the shipping charge) and the shipping costs from the warehouses to the factories.

a. Draw a network that depicts the company's supply network. Identify the supply nodes, transshipment nodes, and demand nodes in this network.

b. This problem is only a *variant* of a minimum-cost flow problem because the supply from each vendor is a *maximum* of 10 rather than a fixed amount of 10. However, it can be converted to a full-fledged minimum-cost flow problem by adding a dummy demand node that receives (at zero cost) all the unused supply capacity at the vendors. Formulate a network model for this minimum-cost flow problem by inserting all the necessary data into the network drawn in part *a* supplemented by this dummy demand node. (Use the format depicted in Figure 6.3 to display these data.)

E*   c. Formulate and solve a spreadsheet model for the company's problem.

6.4.*   Consider Figure 6.9 (in Section 6.3), which depicts the BMZ Co. distribution network from its factories in Stuttgart and Berlin to the distribution centers in both Los Angeles and Seattle. This figure also gives in brackets the maximum amount that can be shipped through each shipping lane.

In the weeks following the crisis described in Section 6.2, the distribution center in Los Angeles has successfully replenished its inventory. Therefore, Karl Schmidt (the supply chain manager for the BMZ Co.) has concluded that it will be sufficient hereafter to ship 130 units per month to Los Angeles and 50 units per month to Seattle. (One unit is a hundred cubic meters of automobile replacement parts.) The Stuttgart factory (node ST in the figure) will allocate 130 units per month and the Berlin factory (node BE) will allocate 50 units per month out of their total production to cover these shipments. However, rather than resuming the past practice of supplying the Los Angeles distribution center from only the Stuttgart factory and supplying the Seattle distribution center from only the Berlin factory, Karl has decided to allow either factory to supply either distribution center. He feels that this additional flexibility is likely to reduce the total shipping cost.

The following table gives the shipping cost per unit through each of these shipping lanes.

	Unit Shipping Cost to Node								
To From	LI	BO	RO	HA	NO	NY	BN	LA	SE
Node									
ST	$3,200	$2,500	$2,900	—	—	—	—	—	—
BE	—	—	$2,400	$2,000	—	—	—	—	—
LI	—	—	—	—	$6,100	—	—	—	—
BO	—	—	—	—	$6,800	$5,400	—	—	—
RO	—	—	—	—	—	$5,900	—	—	—
HA	—	—	—	—	—	$6,300	$5,700	—	—
NO	—	—	—	—	—	—	—	$3,100	—
NY	—	—	—	—	—	—	—	$4,200	$4,000
BN	—	—	—	—	—	—	—	$3,400	$3,000

Karl wants to determine the shipping plan that will minimize the total shipping cost.

a. Formulate a network model for this problem as a minimum-cost flow problem by inserting all the necessary data into the distribution network shown in Figure 6.9. (Use the format depicted in Figure 6.3 to display these data.)

E* b. Formulate and solve a spreadsheet model for this problem.

c. What is the total shipping cost for this optimal solution?

6.5. Reconsider Problem 6.4. Suppose now that, for administrative convenience, management has decided that all 130 units per month needed at the distribution center in Los Angeles must come from the Stuttgart factory (node ST) and all 50 units per month needed at the distribution center in Seattle must come from the Berlin factory (node BE). For each of these distribution centers, Karl Schmidt wants to determine the shipping plan that will minimize the total shipping cost.

a. For the distribution center in Los Angeles, formulate a network model for this problem as a minimum-cost flow problem by inserting all the necessary data into the distribution network shown in Figure 6.6. (Use the format depicted in Figure 6.3 to display these data.)

E* b. Formulate and solve a spreadsheet model for the problem formulated in part a.

c. For the distribution center in Seattle, draw its distribution network emanating from the Berlin factory at node BE.

d. Repeat part a for the distribution center in Seattle by using the network drawn in part c.

E* e. Formulate and solve a spreadsheet model for the problem formulated in part d.

f. Add the total shipping costs obtained in parts b and e. Compare this sum with the total shipping cost obtained in part c of Problem 6.4 (as given in the back of the book).

6.6. Consider the maximum flow problem formulated in Figures 6.7 and 6.8 for the BMZ case study. Redraw Figure 6.7 and insert the optimal shipping quantities

(cells D4:D12 in Figure 6.8) in parentheses above the respective arcs. Examine the capacities of these arcs. Explain why these arc capacities ensure that the shipping quantities in parentheses must be an optimal solution because the maximum flow cannot exceed 150.

E*6.7. Formulate and solve a spreadsheet model for the maximum flow problem shown below, where node A is the source, node F is the sink, and the arc capacities are the numbers in square brackets shown next to the arcs.

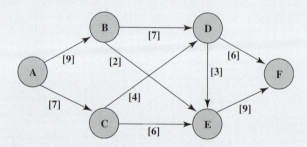

6.8. The diagram depicts a system of aqueducts that originate at three rivers (nodes R1, R2, and R3) and terminate at a major city (node T), where the other nodes are junction points in the system.

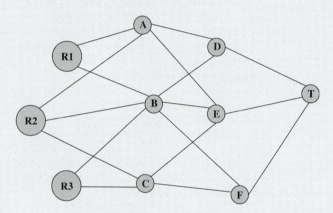

Using units of thousands of acre feet, the following tables show the maximum amount of water that can be pumped through each aqueduct per day.

To From	A	B	C
R1	75	65	—
R2	40	50	60
R3	—	80	70

To From	D	E	F
A	60	45	—
B	70	55	45
C	—	70	90

To From	T
D	120
E	190
F	130

The city water manager wants to determine a flow plan that will maximize the flow of water to the city.

a. Formulate this problem as a maximum flow problem by identifying a source, a sink, and the transshipment nodes, and then drawing the complete network that shows the capacity of each arc.

E* b. Formulate and solve a spreadsheet model for this problem.

6.9. The Texago Corporation has four oil fields, four refineries, and four distribution centers in the locations

identified in the next tables. A major strike involving the transportation industries now has sharply curtailed Texago's capacity to ship oil from the four oil fields to the four refineries and to ship petroleum products from the refineries to the distribution centers. Using units of thousands of barrels of crude oil (and its equivalent in refined products), the following tables show the maximum number of units that can be shipped per day from each oil field to each refinery and from each refinery to each distribution center.

Oil Field	Refinery			
	New Orleans	**Charleston**	**Seattle**	**St. Louis**
Texas	11	7	2	8
California	5	4	8	7
Alaska	7	3	12	6
Middle East	8	9	4	15

Refinery	Distribution Center			
	Pittsburgh	**Atlanta**	**Kansas City**	**San Francisco**
New Orleans	5	9	6	4
Charleston	8	7	9	5
Seattle	4	6	7	8
St. Louis	12	11	9	7

The Texago management now wants to determine a plan for how many units to ship from each oil field to each refinery and from each refinery to each distribution center that will maximize the total number of units reaching the distribution centers.

a. Draw a rough map that shows the location of Texago's oil fields, refineries, and distribution centers. Add arrows to show the flow of crude oil and then petroleum products through this distribution network.

b. Redraw this distribution network by lining up all the nodes representing oil fields in one column, all the nodes representing refineries in a second column, and all the nodes representing distribution centers in a third column. Then add arcs to show the possible flow.

c. Use the distribution network from part *b* to formulate a network model for Texago's problem as a variant of a maximum flow problem.

E* d. Formulate and solve a spreadsheet model for this problem.

E*6.10. Reconsider the Littletown Fire Department problem presented in Section 6.4 and depicted in Figure 6.11. Due to maintenance work on the one-mile road between nodes A and B, a detour currently must be taken that extends the trip between these nodes to four miles.

Formulate and solve a spreadsheet model for this revised problem to find the new shortest path from the fire station to the farming community.

6.11. You need to take a trip by car to another town that you have never visited before. Therefore, you are studying a map to determine the shortest route to your destination. Depending on which route you choose, there are five other towns (call them A, B, C, D, E) through which you might pass on the way. The map shows the mileage along each road that directly connects two towns without any intervening towns. These numbers are summarized in the following table, where a dash indicates that there is no road directly connecting these two towns without going through any other towns.

Town	Miles between Adjacent Towns					
	A	**B**	**C**	**D**	**E**	**Destination**
Origin	40	60	50	—	—	—
A		10	—	70	—	—
B			20	55	40	—
C				—	50	—
D					10	60
E						80

a. Formulate a network model for this problem as a shortest path problem by drawing a network where nodes represent towns, links represent roads, and numbers indicate the length of each link in miles.

E* b. Formulate and solve a spreadsheet model for this problem.

c. Use part *b* to identify your shortest route.

d. If each number in the table represented your *cost* (in dollars) for driving your car from one town to the next, would the answer in part *c* now give your minimum-cost route?

e. If each number in the table represented your *time* (in minutes) for driving your car from one town to the next, would the answer in part *c* now give your minimum-time route?

6.12.* At a small but growing airport, the local airline company is purchasing a new tractor for a tractor-trailer train to bring luggage to and from the airplanes. A new mechanized luggage system will be installed in three years, so the tractor will not be needed after that. However, because it will receive heavy use, so that the running and maintenance costs will increase rapidly as it ages, it may still be more economical to replace the tractor after one or two years. The following table gives the total net discounted cost associated with purchasing a tractor (purchase price minus trade-in allowance, plus running and maintenance costs) at the end of year *i* and trading it in at the end of year *j* (where year 0 is now).

	j		
	1	**2**	**3**
i			
0	$8,000	$18,000	$31,000
1		10,000	21,000
2			12,000

Management wishes to determine at what times (if any) the tractor should be replaced to minimize the total cost for the tractor(s) over three years.

    a. Formulate a network model for this problem as a shortest path problem.

E*   b. Formulate and solve a spreadsheet model for this problem.

6.13. One of Speedy Airlines's flights is about to take off from Seattle for a nonstop flight to London. There is some flexibility in choosing the precise route to be taken, depending upon weather conditions. The following network depicts the possible routes under consideration, where SE and LN are Seattle and London, respectively, and the other nodes represent various intermediate locations.

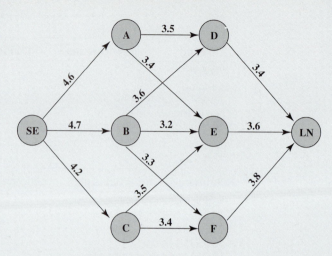

The winds along each arc greatly affect the flying time (and so the fuel consumption). Based on current meteorological reports, the flying times (in hours) for this particular flight are shown next to the arcs. Because the fuel consumed is so expensive, the management of Speedy Airlines has established a policy of choosing the route that minimizes the total flight time.

    a. What plays the role of distances in interpreting this problem to be a shortest path problem?

E*   *b.* Formulate and solve a spreadsheet model for this problem.

Case 6-1

Aiding Allies

Commander Votachev steps into the cold October night and deeply inhales the smoke from his cigarette, savoring its warmth. He surveys the destruction surrounding him—shattered windows, burning buildings, torn roads—and smiles. His two years of work training revolutionaries east of the Ural Mountains has proven successful; his troops now occupy seven strategically important cities in the Russian Federation: Kazan, Perm, Yekaterinburg, Ufa, Samara, Saratov, and Orenburg. His siege is not yet over, however. He looks to the west. Given the political and economic confusion in the Russian Federation at this time, he knows that his troops will be able to conquer Saint Petersburg and Moscow shortly. Commander Votachev will then be able to rule with the wisdom and control exhibited by his communist predecessors Lenin and Stalin.

Across the Pacific Ocean, a meeting of the top security and foreign policy advisors of the United States is in progress at the White House. The president has recently been briefed about the communist revolution masterminded by Commander Votachev and is determining a plan of action. The president reflects upon a

similar October long ago in 1917, and he fears the possibility of a new age of radical Communist rule accompanied by chaos, bloodshed, escalating tensions, and possibly nuclear war. He therefore decides that the United States needs to respond and to respond quickly. Moscow has requested assistance from the United States military, and the president plans to send troops and supplies immediately.

The president turns to General Lankletter and asks him to describe the preparations being taken in the United States to send the necessary troops and supplies to the Russian Federation.

General Lankletter informs the president that along with troops, weapons, ammunition, fuel, and supplies, aircraft, ships, and vehicles are being assembled at two port cities with airfields: Boston and Jacksonville. The aircraft and ships will transfer all troops and cargo across the Atlantic Ocean to the Eurasian continent. The general hands the president a list of the types of aircraft, ships, and vehicles being assembled along with a description of each type. The list is shown next.

Transportation Type	Name	Capacity	Speed
Aircraft	C-141 Starlifter	150 tons	400 miles per hour
Ship	Transport	240 tons	35 miles per hour
Vehicle	Palletized Load System Truck	16,000 kilograms	60 miles per hour

All aircraft, ships, and vehicles are able to carry both troops and cargo. Once an aircraft or ship arrives in Europe, it stays there to support the armed forces.

The president then turns to Tabitha Neal, who has been negotiating with the NATO countries for the last several hours to use their ports and airfields as stops to refuel and resupply before heading to the Russian Federation. She informs the president that the following ports and airfields in the NATO countries will be made available to the U.S. military.

Ports	Airfields
Napoli	London
Hamburg	Berlin
Rotterdam	Istanbul

The president stands and walks to the map of the world projected on a large screen in the middle of the room. He maps the progress of troops and cargo from the United States to three strategic cities in the Russian Federation that have not yet been seized by Commander Votachev. The three cities are Saint Petersburg, Moscow, and Rostov. He explains that the troops and cargo will be used both to defend the Russian cities and to launch a counter attack against Votachev to recapture the cities he currently occupies. (The map is shown at the end of the case.)

The president also explains that all Starlifters and transports leave Boston or Jacksonville. All transports that have traveled across the Atlantic must dock at one of the NATO ports to unload. Palletized load system trucks brought over in the transports will then carry all troops and materials unloaded from the ships at the NATO ports to the three strategic Russian cities not yet seized by Votachev. All Starlifters that have traveled across the Atlantic must land at one of the NATO airfields for refueling. The planes will then carry all troops and cargo from the NATO airfields to the three Russian cities.

a. Draw a network showing the different routes troops and supplies may take to reach the Russian Federation from the United States.

b. Moscow and Washington do not know when Commander Votachev will launch his next attack. Leaders from the two countries therefore have agreed that troops should reach each of the three strategic Russian cities as quickly as possible. The president has determined that the situation is so dire that cost is no object—as many Starlifters, transports, and trucks as are necessary will be used to transfer troops and cargo from the United States to Saint Petersburg, Moscow, and Rostov. Therefore, no limitations exist on the number of troops and amount of cargo that can be transferred between any cities.

The president has been given the following information about the length of the available routes between cities.

From	To	(Kilometers)
Boston	Berlin	7,250 km
Boston	Hamburg	8,250
Boston	Istanbul	8,300
Boston	London	6,200
Boston	Rotterdam	6,900
Boston	Napoli	7,950
Jacksonville	Berlin	9,200
Jacksonville	Hamburg	9,800
Jacksonville	Istanbul	10,100
Jacksonville	London	7,900
Jacksonville	Rotterdam	8,900
Jacksonville	Napoli	9,400
Berlin	Saint Petersburg	1,280
Hamburg	Saint Petersburg	1,880
Istanbul	Saint Petersburg	2,040
London	Saint Petersburg	1,980
Rotterdam	Saint Petersburg	2,200
Napoli	Saint Petersburg	2,970
Berlin	Moscow	1,600
Hamburg	Moscow	2,120
Istanbul	Moscow	1,700
London	Moscow	2,300
Rotterdam	Moscow	2,450
Napoli	Moscow	2,890
Berlin	Rostov	1,730
Hamburg	Rostov	2,470
Istanbul	Rostov	990
London	Rostov	2,860
Rotterdam	Rostov	2,760
Napoli	Rostov	2,800

Given the distance and the speed of the transportation used between each pair of cities, how can the president most quickly move troops from the United States to each of the three strategic Russian cities? Highlight the path(s) on the network. How long will it take troops and supplies to reach Saint Petersburg? Moscow? Rostov?

c. The president encounters only one problem with his first plan: he has to sell the military deployment to Congress. Under the War Powers Act, the president is required to consult with Congress before introducing troops into hostilities or situations where hostilities will occur. If Congress does not give authorization to the president for such use of troops, the president must withdraw troops after 60 days. Congress also has the power to decrease the 60-day time period by passing a concurrent resolution.

The president knows that Congress will not authorize significant spending for another country's war, especially when voters have paid so much attention to decreasing the national debt. He therefore decides that he needs to find a way to get the needed troops and supplies to Saint Petersburg, Moscow, and Rostov at the minimum cost.

Each Russian city has contacted Washington to communicate the number of troops and supplies the city needs at a minimum for reinforcement. After analyzing the requests, General Lankletter has converted the requests from numbers of troops, gallons of gasoline, and so on, to tons of cargo for easier planning. The requirements are listed below.

City	Requirements
Saint Petersburg	320,000 tons
Moscow	440,000 tons
Rostov	240,000 tons

Both in Boston and Jacksonville, there are 500,000 tons of the necessary cargo available. When the United States decides to send a plane, ship, or truck between two cities, several costs occur: fuel costs, labor costs, maintenance costs, and appropriate port or airfield taxes and tariffs. These costs are listed next.

From	To	Cost
Boston	Berlin	$50,000 per Starlifter
Boston	Hamburg	$30,000 per transport
Boston	Istanbul	$55,000 per Starlifter
Boston	London	$45,000 per Starlifter
Boston	Rotterdam	$30,000 per transport
Boston	Napoli	$32,000 per transport
Jacksonville	Berlin	$57,000 per Starlifter
Jacksonville	Hamburg	$48,000 per transport
Jacksonville	Istanbul	$61,000 per Starlifter
Jacksonville	London	$49,000 per Starlifter
Jacksonville	Rotterdam	$44,000 per transport
Jacksonville	Napoli	$56,000 per transport
Berlin	Saint Petersburg	$24,000 per Starlifter
Hamburg	Saint Petersburg	$3,000 per truck
Istanbul	Saint Petersburg	$28,000 per Starlifter
London	Saint Petersburg	$22,000 per Starlifter
Rotterdam	Saint Petersburg	$3,000 per truck
Napoli	Saint Petersburg	$5,000 per truck
Berlin	Moscow	$22,000 per Starlifter
Hamburg	Moscow	$4,000 per truck
Istanbul	Moscow	$25,000 per Starlifter
London	Moscow	$19,000 per Starlifter
Rotterdam	Moscow	$5,000 per truck
Napoli	Moscow	$5,000 per truck
Berlin	Rostov	$23,000 per Starlifter
Hamburg	Rostov	$7,000 per truck
Istanbul	Rostov	$2,000 per Starlifter
London	Rostov	$4,000 per Starlifter
Rotterdam	Rostov	$8,000 per truck
Napoli	Rostov	$9,000 per truck

The president faces a number of restrictions when trying to satisfy the requirements. Early winter weather in northern Russia has brought a deep freeze with much snow. Therefore, General Lankletter is opposed to sending truck convoys in the area. He convinces the president to supply Saint Petersburg

only through the air. Moreover, the truck routes into Rostov are quite limited, so that from each port, at most 2,500 trucks can be sent to Rostov. The Ukrainian government is very sensitive about American airplanes flying through its air space. It restricts the U.S. military to at most 200 flights from Berlin to Rostov and to at most 200 flights from London to Rostov. (The U.S. military does not want to fly around the Ukraine and is thus restricted by the Ukrainian limitations.)

How does the president satisfy each Russian city's military requirements at minimum cost? Highlight the path to be used between the United States and the Russian Federation on the network.

d. Once the president releases the number of planes, ships, and trucks that will travel between the United States and the Russian Federation, Tabitha Neal contacts each of the American cities and NATO countries to indicate the number of planes to expect at the airfields, the number of ships to expect at the docks, and the number of trucks to expect traveling across the roads. Unfortunately, Tabitha learns that several additional restrictions exist that cannot be immediately eliminated. Because of airfield congestion and unalterable flight schedules, only a limited number of planes may be sent between any two cities. These plane limitations are given below.

From	To	Maximum Number of Airplanes
Boston	Berlin	300
Boston	Istanbul	500
Boston	London	500
Jacksonville	Berlin	500
Jacksonville	Istanbul	700
Jacksonville	London	600
Berlin	Saint Petersburg	500
Istanbul	Saint Petersburg	0
London	Saint Petersburg	1,000
Berlin	Moscow	300
Istanbul	Moscow	100
London	Moscow	200
Berlin	Rostov	0
Istanbul	Rostov	900
London	Rostov	100

In addition, because some countries fear that citizens will become alarmed if too many military trucks travel the public highways, they object to a large number of trucks traveling through their countries. These objections mean that a limited number of trucks are able to travel between certain ports and Russian cities. These limitations are listed below.

From	To	Maximum Number of Trucks
Rotterdam	Moscow	600
Rotterdam	Rostov	750
Hamburg	Moscow	700
Hamburg	Rostov	500
Napoli	Moscow	1,500
Napoli	Rostov	1,400

Tabitha learns that all shipping lanes have no capacity limits due to the American control of the Atlantic Ocean.

The president realizes that due to all the restrictions, he will not be able to satisfy all the reinforcement requirements of the three Russian cities. He decides to disregard the cost issue and instead to maximize the total amount of cargo he can get to the Russian cities. How does the president maximize the total amount of cargo that reaches the Russian Federation? Highlight the path(s) used between the United States and the Russian Federation on the network.

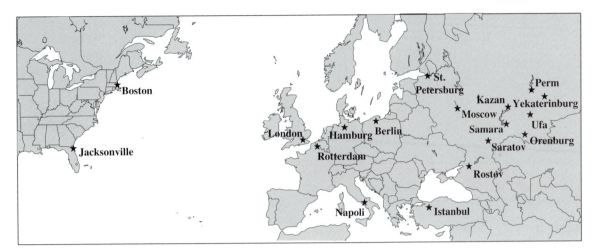

Case 6-2

Money in Motion

Jake Nguyen runs a nervous hand through his once finely combed hair. He loosens his once perfectly knotted silk tie. And he rubs his sweaty hands across his once immaculately pressed trousers. Today has certainly not been a good day.

Over the past few months, Jake had heard whispers circulating from Wall Street—whispers from the lips of investment bankers and stockbrokers famous for their outspokenness. They had whispered about a coming Japanese economic collapse—whispered because they had believed that publicly vocalizing their fears would hasten the collapse.

And, today, their very fears have come true. Jake and his colleagues gather around a small television dedicated exclusively to the Bloomberg channel. Jake stares in disbelief as he listens to the horrors taking place in the Japanese market. And the Japanese market is taking the financial markets in all other East Asian countries with it on its tailspin. He goes numb. As manager of Asian foreign investment for Grant Hill Associates, a small West Coast investment boutique specializing in currency trading, Jake bears personal responsibility for any negative impacts of the collapse. And Grant Hill Associates will experience negative impacts.

Jake had not heeded the whispered warnings of a Japanese collapse. Instead, he had greatly increased the stake Grant Hill Associates held in the Japanese market. Because the Japanese market had performed better than expected over the past year, Jake had increased investments in Japan from $2.5 million to $15 million only one month ago. At that time, one dollar was worth 80 yen.

No longer. Jake realizes that today's devaluation of the yen means that one dollar is worth 125 yen. He will be able to liquidate these investments without any loss in yen, but now the dollar loss when converting back into U.S. currency would be huge. He takes a deep breath, closes his eyes, and mentally prepares himself for serious damage control.

Jake's meditation is interrupted by a booming voice calling for him from a large, corner office. Grant Hill, the president of Grant Hill Associates, yells, "Nguyen, get the hell in here!"

Jake jumps and looks reluctantly toward the corner office hiding the furious Grant Hill. He smooths his hair, tightens his tie, and walks briskly into the office.

Grant Hill meets Jake's eyes upon his entrance and continues yelling, "I don't want one word out of you, Nguyen! No excuses; just fix this debacle! Get all of our money out of Japan! My gut tells me this is only the beginning! Get the money into safe U.S. bonds! NOW! And don't forget to get our cash positions out of Indonesia and Malaysia ASAP with it!"

Jake has enough common sense to say nothing. He nods his head, turns on his heels, and practically runs out of the office.

Safely back at his desk, Jake begins formulating a plan to move the investments out of Japan, Indonesia, and Malaysia. His experiences investing in foreign markets have taught him that when playing with millions of dollars, *how* he gets money out of a foreign market is almost as important as *when* he gets money out of the market. The banking partners of Grant Hill Associates charge different transaction fees for converting one currency into another one and wiring large sums of money around the globe.

And now, to make matters worse, the governments in East Asia have imposed very tight limits on the amount of money an individual or a company can exchange from the domestic currency into a particular foreign currency and withdraw it from the country. The goal of this dramatic measure is to reduce the outflow of foreign investments out of those countries to prevent a complete collapse of the economies in the region. Because of Grant Hill Associates's cash holdings of 10.5 billion Indonesian rupiahs and 28 million Malaysian ringgits, along with the holdings in yen, it is not clear how these holdings should be converted back into dollars.

Jake wants to find the most cost-effective method to convert these holdings into dollars. On his company's website, he always can find on-the-minute exchange rates for most currencies in the world (see Table 1).

TABLE 1
Currency Exchange Rates

From \ To	Yen	Rupiah	Ringgit	U.S. Dollar	Canadian Dollar	Euro	Pound	Peso
Japanese yen	1	50	0.04	0.008	0.01	0.0064	0.0048	0.0768
Indonesian rupiah		1	0.0008	0.00016	0.0002	0.000128	0.000096	0.001536
Malaysian ringgit			1	0.2	0.25	0.16	0.12	1.92
U.S. dollar				1	1.25	0.8	0.6	9.6
Canadian dollar					1	0.64	0.48	7.68
European euro						1	0.75	12
English pound							1	16
Mexican peso								1

The table states that, for example, 1 Japanese yen equals 0.008 U.S. dollars. By making a few phone calls, he discovers the transaction costs his company must pay for large currency transactions during these critical times (see Table 2).

TABLE 2
Transaction Cost (Percent)

From \ To	Yen	Rupiah	Ringgit	U.S. Dollar	Canadian Dollar	Euro	Pound	Peso
Yen	—	0.5	0.5	0.4	0.4	0.4	0.25	0.5
Rupiah		—	0.7	0.5	0.3	0.3	0.75	0.75
Ringgit			—	0.7	0.7	0.4	0.45	0.5
U.S. dollar				—	0.05	0.1	0.1	0.1
Canadian dollar					—	0.2	0.1	0.1
Euro						—	0.05	0.5
Pound							—	0.5
Peso								—

Jake notes that exchanging one currency for another one results in the same transaction cost as a reverse conversion. Finally, Jake finds out the maximum amounts of domestic currencies his company is allowed to convert into other currencies in Japan, Indonesia, and Malaysia (see Table 3).

TABLE 3
Transaction Limits in Equivalent of 1,000 Dollars

From \ To	Yen	Rupiah	Ringgit	U.S. Dollar	Canadian Dollar	Euro	Pound	Peso
Yen	—	5,000	5,000	2,000	2,000	2,000	2,000	4,000
Rupiah	5,000	—	2,000	200	200	1,000	500	200
Ringgit	3,000	4,500	—	1,500	1,500	2,500	1,000	1,000

a. Formulate Jake's problem as a minimum-cost flow problem, and draw the network for his problem. Identify the supply and demand nodes for the network.

b. Which currency transactions must Jake perform to convert the investments from yens, rupiahs, and ringgits into U.S. dollars to ensure that Grant Hill Associates has the maximum dollar amount after all transactions have occurred? How much money does Jake have to invest in U.S. bonds?

c. The World Trade Organization forbids transaction limits because they promote protectionism. If no transaction limits exist, what method should Jake use to convert the Asian holdings from the respective currencies into dollars?

d. In response to the World Trade Organization's mandate forbidding transaction limits, the Indonesian government introduces a new tax to protect its currency that leads to a 500 percent increase in transaction costs for transactions of rupiahs. Given these new transaction costs but no transaction limits, what currency transactions should Jake perform to convert the Asian holdings from the respective currencies into dollars?

e. Jake realizes that his analysis is incomplete because he has not included all aspects that might influence his planned currency exchanges. Describe other factors that Jake should examine before he makes his final decision.

Chapter **Seven**

Using Binary Integer Programming to Deal with Yes-or-No Decisions

Learning objectives

After completing this chapter, you should be able to

1. Describe how binary decision variables are used to represent yes-or-no decisions.
2. Use binary decision variables to formulate constraints for mutually exclusive alternatives and contingent decisions.
3. Formulate a binary integer programming model for the selection of projects.
4. Formulate a binary integer programming model for the selection of sites for facilities.
5. Formulate a binary integer programming model for crew scheduling in the travel industry.
6. Formulate other basic binary integer programming models from a description of the problems.
7. Use mixed binary integer programming to deal with setup costs for initiating the production of a product.

The preceding chapters have considered various kinds of problems where decisions need to be made about *how much to do* of various activities. Thus, the decision variables in the resulting model represent the *level* of the corresponding activities.

We turn now to a common type of problem where, instead of *how-much decisions,* the decisions to be made are **yes-or-no decisions.** A yes-or-no decision arises when a particular option is being considered and the only possible choices are yes, go ahead with this option, or no, decline this option.

The natural choice of a decision variable for a yes-or-no decision is a *binary variable.* **Binary variables** are variables whose only possible values are 0 and 1. Thus, when representing a yes-or-no decision, a **binary decision variable** is assigned a value of 1 for choosing yes and a value of 0 for choosing no.

Models that fit linear programming except that they use binary decision variables are called **binary integer programming (BIP)** models. (We hereafter will use the **BIP** abbreviation.) A **pure BIP** model is one where all the variables are binary variables, whereas a **mixed BIP** model is one where only some of the variables are binary variables.

BIP problems arise with considerable frequency in a wide variety of applications. To illustrate this, we begin with a case study and then present some more examples in the subsequent sections. One of the supplements to this chapter on the CD-ROM also provides additional formulation examples for BIP problems.

You will see throughout this chapter that BIP problems can be formulated on a spreadsheet just as readily as linear programming problems. The Excel Solver also can solve BIP problems of modest size. You normally will have no problem solving the small BIP problems found in this book, but Solver may fail on somewhat larger problems. To provide some perspective on this issue, we include another supplement on the CD-ROM that is entitled Some Perspectives on Solving Binary Integer Programming Problems. The algorithms available for solving BIP problems (including the one used by the Excel Solver) are not nearly as efficient as those for linear programming, so this supplement discusses some of the difficulties and pitfalls involved in solving large BIP problems. One option with any large problem that fits linear programming except that it has decision variables that are restricted to integer values (but not necessarily just 0 and 1) is to ignore the integer constraints and then to round the solution obtained to integer values. This is a reasonable option in some cases but not in others. The supplement emphasizes that this is a particularly dangerous shortcut with BIP problems.

7.1   A CASE STUDY: THE CALIFORNIA MANUFACTURING CO. PROBLEM

"OK, Steve here is the situation. With our growing business, we are strongly considering building a new factory. Maybe even two. The factory needs to be close to a large, skilled labor force, so we are looking at Los Angeles and San Francisco as the potential sites. We also are considering building one new warehouse. Not more than one. This warehouse would make sense in saving shipping costs only if it is in the same city as the new factory. Either Los Angeles or San Francisco. If we decide not to build a new factory at all, we definitely don't want the warehouse either. Is this clear, so far?"

"Yes, Armando, I understand," Steve Chan responds. "What are your criteria for making these decisions?"

"Well, all the other members of top management have joined me in addressing this issue," Armando Ortega replies. "We have concluded that these two potential sites are very comparable on nonfinancial grounds. Therefore, we feel that these decisions should be based mainly on financial considerations. We have $10 million of capital available for this expansion and we want it to go as far as possible in improving our bottom line. Which feasible combination of investments in factories and warehouses in which locations will be most profitable for the company in the long run? In your language, we want to maximize the total net present value of these investments."

"That's very clear. It sounds like a classical management science problem."

What is the most profitable combination of investments?

"That's why I called you in, Steve. I would like you to conduct a quick management science study to determine the most profitable combination of investments. I also would like you to take a look at the amount of capital being made available and its effect on how much profit we can get from these investments. The decision to make $10 million available is only a tentative one. That amount is stretching us, because we now are investigating some other interesting project proposals that would require quite a bit of capital, so we would prefer to use less than $10 million on these particular investments if the last few million don't buy us much. On the other hand, this expansion into either Los Angeles or San Francisco, or maybe both of these key cities, is our number one priority. It will have a real positive impact on the future of this company. So we are willing to go out and raise some more capital if it would give us a lot of bang for the buck. Therefore, we would like you to do some what-if analysis to tell us what the effect would be if we were to change the amount of capital being made available to anything between $5 million and $15 million."

"Sure, Armando, we do that kind of what-if analysis all the time. We refer to it as sensitivity analysis because it involves checking how sensitive the outcome is to the amount of capital being made available."

"Good. Now, Steve, I need your input within the next couple weeks. Can you do it?"

"Well, Armando, as usual, the one question is whether we can gather all the necessary data that quickly. We'll need to get good estimates of the net present value of each of the possible investments. I'll need a lot of help in digging out that information."

"I thought you would say that. I already have my staff working hard on developing those estimates. I can get you together with them this afternoon."

"Great. I'll get right on it."

An Application Vignette

With headquarters in Houston, Texas, Waste Management, Inc. (a Fortune 100 company), is the leading provider of comprehensive waste-management services in North America. Its network of operations includes 293 active landfill disposal sites, 16 waste-to-energy plants, 72 landfill gas-to-energy facilities, 146 recycling plants, 346 transfer stations, and 435 collection operations (depots) to provide services to nearly 20 million residential customers and 2 million commercial customers throughout the United States and Canada.

The company's collection-and-transfer vehicles need to follow nearly 20,000 daily routes. With an annual operating cost of nearly $120,000 per vehicle, management wanted to have a comprehensive route-management system that would make every route as profitable and efficient as possible. Therefore, a management science team that included a number of consultants was formed to attack this problem.

The heart of the route-management system developed by this team is a huge mixed BIP model that optimizes the routes assigned to the respective collection-and-transfer vehicles. Although the objective function takes several factors into account, the primary goal is the minimization of total travel time. The main decision variables are binary variables that equal 1 if the route assigned to a particular vehicle includes a particular possible leg and that equal 0 otherwise. A geographical information system (GIS) provides the data about the distance and time required to go between any two points. All of this is imbedded within a Web-based Java application that is integrated with the company's other systems.

It is estimated that the recent implementation of this comprehensive route-management system will increase the company's cash flow by $648 million over a five-year period, largely because of savings of $498 million in operational expenses over this same period. It also is providing better customer service.

Source: S. Sahoo, S. Kim, B.-I. Kim, B. Krass, and A. Popov, Jr., "Routing Optimization for Waste Management," *Interfaces* 35, no. 1 (January–February 2005), pp. 24–36.

As president of the California Manufacturing Company, Armando Ortega has had many similar conversations in the past with Steve Chan, the company's top management scientist. Armando is confident that Steve will come through for him again.

Background

The California Manufacturing Company is a diversified company with several factories and warehouses throughout California, but none yet in Los Angeles or San Francisco. Because the company is enjoying increasing sales and earnings, management feels that the time may be ripe to expand into one or both of those prime locations. A basic issue is whether to build a new factory in either Los Angeles or San Francisco, or perhaps even in both cities. Management also is considering building at most one new warehouse, but will restrict the choice of location to a city where a new factory is being built.

The decisions to be made are listed in the second column of Table 7.1 in the form of yes-or-no questions. In each case, giving an answer of yes to the question corresponds to the decision to make the investment to build the indicated facility (a factory or a warehouse) in the indicated location (Los Angeles or San Francisco). The capital required for the investment is given in the rightmost column, where management has made the tentative decision that the total amount of capital being made available for all the investments is $10 million. (Note that this amount is inadequate for some of the combinations of investments.) The fourth column shows the estimated *net present value* (net long-run profit considering the time value of money) if the corresponding investment is made. (The net present value is 0 if the investment is not made.) Much of the work of Steve Chan's management science study (with substantial help from the president's staff) goes into developing these estimates of the net present values.

TABLE 7.1
Data for the California Manufacturing Co. Problem

Decision Number	Yes-or-No Question	Decision Variable	Net Present Value (Millions)	Capital Required (Millions)
1	Build a factory in Los Angeles?	x_1	$8	$6
2	Build a factory in San Francisco?	x_2	5	3
3	Build a warehouse in Los Angeles?	x_3	6	5
4	Build a warehouse in San Francisco?	x_4	4	2
			Capital available: $10 million	

TABLE 7.2 Binary Decision Variables for the California Manufacturing Co. Problem

Decision Number	Decision Variable	Possible Value	Interpretation of a Value of 1	Interpretation of a Value of 0
1	x_1	0 or 1	Build a factory in Los Angeles	Do not build this factory
2	x_2	0 or 1	Build a factory in San Francisco	Do not build this factory
3	x_3	0 or 1	Build a warehouse in Los Angeles	Do not build this warehouse
4	x_4	0 or 1	Build a warehouse in San Francisco	Do not build this warehouse

As specified by the company's president, Armando Ortega, the objective now is to find the feasible combination of investments that maximizes the total net present value.

Introducing Binary Decision Variables for the Yes-or-No Decisions

As summarized in the second column of Table 7.1, the problem facing management is to make four interrelated *yes-or-no decisions*. To formulate a mathematical model for this problem, Steve Chan needs to introduce a decision variable for each of these decisions. Since each decision has just two alternatives, choose yes or choose no, the corresponding decision variable only needs to have two values (one for each alternative). Therefore, Steve uses a *binary variable,* whose only possible values are 0 and 1, where 1 corresponds to the decision to choose yes and 0 corresponds to choosing no.

These decision variables are shown in the second column of Table 7.2. The final two columns give the interpretation of a value of 1 and 0, respectively.

Dealing with Interrelationships between the Decisions

Recall that management wants no more than one new warehouse to be built. In terms of the corresponding decision variables, x_3 and x_4, this means that no more than one of these variables is allowed to have the value 1. Therefore, these variables must satisfy the constraint

$$x_3 + x_4 \leq 1$$

as part of the mathematical model for the problem.

These two alternatives (build a warehouse in Los Angeles or build a warehouse in San Francisco) are referred to as **mutually exclusive alternatives** because choosing one of these alternatives excludes choosing the other. Groups of two or more mutually exclusive alternatives arise commonly in BIP problems. For each such group where at most one of the alternatives can be chosen, the constraint on the corresponding binary decision variables has the form shown above, namely, the sum of these variables must be *less than or equal to* 1. For some groups of mutually exclusive alternatives, management will exclude the possibility of choosing *none* of the alternatives, in which case the constraint will set the sum of the corresponding binary decision variables *equal* to 1.

The California Manufacturing Co. problem also has another important kind of restriction. Management will allow a warehouse to be built in a particular city only if a factory also is being built in that city. For example, consider the situation for Los Angeles (LA).

> If decide no, do not build a factory in LA (i.e., if choose $x_1 = 0$),
>   then cannot build a warehouse in LA (i.e., must choose $x_3 = 0$).

> If decide yes, do build a factory in LA (i.e., if choose $x_1 = 1$),
>   then can either build a warehouse in LA or not (i.e., can choose either $x_3 = 1$ or 0).

With a group of mutually exclusive alternatives, only one of the corresponding binary decision variables can equal 1.

How can these interrelationships between the factory and warehouse decisions for LA be expressed in a constraint for a mathematical model? The key is to note that, for either value of x_1, the permissible value or values of x_3 are less than or equal to x_1. Since x_1 and x_3 are binary variables, the constraint

$$x_3 \leq x_1$$

forces x_3 to take on a permissible value given the value of x_1.

Exactly the same reasoning leads to

$$x_4 \leq x_2$$

as the corresponding constraint for San Francisco. Just as for Los Angeles, this constraint forces having no warehouse in San Francisco ($x_4 = 0$) if a factory will not be built there ($x_2 = 0$), whereas going ahead with the factory there ($x_2 = 1$) leaves open the decision to build the warehouse there ($x_4 = 0$ or 1).

For either city, the warehouse decision is referred to as a **contingent decision,** because the decision depends on a prior decision regarding whether to build a factory there. In general, one yes-or-no decision is said to be contingent on another yes-or-no decision if it is allowed to be yes *only if* the other is yes. As above, the mathematical constraint expressing this relationship requires that the binary variable for the former decision must be less than or equal to the binary variable for the latter decision.

The rightmost column of Table 7.1 reveals one more interrelationship between the four decisions, namely, that the amount of capital expended on the four facilities under consideration cannot exceed the amount available ($10 million). Therefore, the model needs to include a constraint that requires

Capital expended $\leq$ $10 million

How can the amount of capital expended be expressed in terms of the four binary decision variables? To start this process, consider the first yes-or-no decision (build a factory in Los Angeles?). Combining the information in the rightmost column of Table 7.1 and the first row of Table 7.2,

$$\text{Capital expended on factory in Los Angeles} = \begin{cases} \$6 \text{ million} & \text{if } x_1 = 1 \\ 0 & \text{if } x_1 = 0 \end{cases}$$

$$= \$6 \text{ million } times \; x_1$$

By the same reasoning, the amount of capital expended on the other three investment opportunities (in units of millions of dollars) is $3x_2$, $5x_3$, and $2x_4$, respectively. Consequently,

$$\text{Capital expended} = 6x_1 + 3x_2 + 5x_3 + 2x_4 \quad \text{(in millions of dollars)}$$

Therefore, the constraint becomes

$$6x_1 + 3x_2 + 5x_3 + 2x_4 \leq 10$$

The BIP Model

As indicated by Armando Ortega in his conversation with Steve Chan, management's objective is to find the feasible combination of investments that *maximizes* the total net present value of these investments. Thus, the value of the objective function should be

NPV = Total net present value

If the investment is made to build a particular facility (so that the corresponding decision variable has a value of 1), the estimated net present value from that investment is given in the fourth column of Table 7.1. If the investment is not made (so the decision variable equals 0), the net present value is 0. Therefore, continuing to use units of millions of dollars,

$$\text{NPV} = 8x_1 + 5x_2 + 6x_3 + 4x_4$$

is the quantity to enter into the target cell to be maximized.

Incorporating the constraints developed in the preceding subsection, the complete BIP model then is shown in Figure 7.1. The format is basically the same as for linear programming models. The one key difference arises when using the Solver dialogue box. Each of the decision variables (cells C18:D18 and C16:D16) is constrained to be binary. This is accomplished in the Add Constraint dialogue box by choosing each range of variables as the left-hand side and then choosing bin from the pop-up menu. The other constraints shown in the Solver dialogue box (see the lower left-hand side of Figure 7.1) have been made quite

One yes-or-no decision is contingent on another yes-or-no decision if the first one is allowed to be yes only if the other one is yes.

Excel Tip: Beware that rounding errors can occur with Excel. Therefore, even when you add a constraint that a changing cell has to be binary, Excel occasionally will return a noninteger value very close to an integer (e.g., 1.23E-10, meaning 0.000000000123). When this happens, you then can replace the noninteger value with the proper integer value.

Excel Tip: To speed up solving very large BIP problems, the Tolerance setting in the Solver options (either 0.05 percent or 5 percent by default) causes Solver to stop when it finds a feasible solution whose objective function value is within the Tolerance of being optimal. For all the problems in this book, you should reset the Tolerance to 0 to guarantee finding an optimal solution.

FIGURE 7.1

A spreadsheet formulation of the BIP model for the California Manufacturing Co. case study where the changing cells BuildFactory? (C18:D18) and BuildWarehouse? (C16:D16) give the optimal solution obtained by using the Excel Solver.

	A	B	C	D	E	F	G
1		California Manufacturing Co. Facility Location Problem					
2							
3		NPV ($millions)	LA	SF			
4		Warehouse	6	4			
5							
6		Factory	8	5			
7							
8		Capital Required					
9		($millions)	LA	SF			
10		Warehouse	5	2	Capital		Capital
11					Spent		Available
12		Factory	6	3	9	≤	10
13							
14					Total		Maximum
15		Build?	LA	SF	Warehouses		Warehouses
16		Warehouse	0	0	0	≤	1
17			≤	≤			
18		Factory	1	1			
19							
20		Total NPV ($millions)	$13				

Solver Parameters

Set Target Cell: TotalNPV

Equal To: ● Max ○ Min ○

By Changing Cells:

BuildWarehouse?,BuildFactory?

Subject to the Constraints:

BuildFactory? = binary
BuildWarehouse? <= BuildFactory?
BuildWarehouse? = binary
CapitalSpent <= CapitalAvailable
TotalWarehouses <= MaxWarehouses

Solver Options

☑ Assume Linear Model
☑ Assume Non-Negative

	E
10	Capital
11	Spent
12	= SUMPRODUCT(CapitalRequired,Build?)
13	
14	Total
15	Warehouses
16	= SUM(BuildWarehouse?)

Range Name	Cells
Build?	C16:D18
BuildWarehouse?	C16:D16
BuildFactory?	C18:D18
CapitalAvailable	G12
CapitalRequired	C10:D12
CapitalSpent	E12
MaxWarehouses	G16
NPV	C4:D6
TotalNPV	D20
TotalWarehouses	E16

	C	D
20	Total NPV ($millions)	=SUMPRODUCT(NPV,Build?)

Note how helpful the range names are for interpreting this BIP spreadsheet model.

intuitive by using the suggestive range names given in the lower right-hand side of the figure. For convenience, the equations entered into the output cells in E12 and D20 use a SUMPRODUCT function that includes C17:D17 and either C11:D11 or C5:D5 because the blanks or ≤ signs in these rows are interpreted as zeroes by the Solver.

The Excel Solver gives the optimal solution shown in C18:D18 and C16:D16 of the spreadsheet, namely, build factories in *both* Los Angeles and San Francisco, but do not build any warehouses. The target cell (D20) indicates that the total net present value from building these two factories is estimated to be $13 million.

Performing Sensitivity Analysis

Now that Steve Chan has used the BIP model to determine what should be done when the amount of capital being made available to these investments is $10 million, his next task is to perform sensitivity analysis on this amount. Recall that Armando Ortega wants him to determine what the effect would be if this amount were changed to anything else between $5 million and $15 million.

In Chapter 5, we described three different methods of performing sensitivity analysis on a linear programming spreadsheet model when there is a change in a constraint: using trial and error with the spreadsheet, applying the Solver Table, or referring to the Excel sensitivity report. The first two of these can be used on integer programming problems in exactly the same way as for linear programming problems. The third method, however, does not work. The sensitivity report is not available for integer programming problems (choosing it results in an error message). This is because the concept of a shadow price and allowable range no longer applies. In contrast to linear programming, the objective function values for an integer programming problem do not change in a predictable manner when the right-hand side of a constraint is changed.

It is straightforward to determine the impact of changing the amount of available capital by trial and error. Simply try different values in the data cell CapitalAvailable (G12) and click Solve in the Solver. However, a more systematic way to perform this analysis is to use an Excel add-in in your MS Courseware called the *Solver Table*. The Solver Table works for integer programming models in exactly the same way as it does for linear programming models (as described in Section 5.3 in the subsection entitled *Using the Solver Table to Do Sensitivity Analysis Systematically*). Appendix A describes the use of the Solver Table in detail.

After expanding the original spreadsheet (Figure 7.1) to make room, the Solver Table has been used to generate the results shown in Figure 7.2 by executing the series of steps outlined in Section 5.3 and Appendix A. Note how Figure 7.2 shows the effect on the optimal solution and the resulting total net present value of varying the amount of capital being made available.

Sensitivity analysis also could be performed on any of the other data cells—NPV (C4:D6), CapitalRequired (C10:D12), and MaxWarehouses (G16)—in a similar way with the Solver Table (or by using trial and error with the spreadsheet). However, a careful job was done in developing good estimates of the net present value of each of the possible investments, and there is little uncertainty in the values entered in the other data cells, so Steve Chan decides that further sensitivity analysis is not needed.

Management's Conclusion

Steve Chan's report is delivered to Armando Ortega within the two-week deadline. The report recommends the plan presented in Figure 7.1 (build a factory in both Los Angeles and San Francisco but no warehouses) if management decides to stick with its tentative decision to make $10 million of capital available for these investments. One advantage of this plan is that it only uses $9 million of this capital, which frees up $1 million of capital for other project proposals currently being investigated. The report also highlights the results shown in Figure 7.2 while emphasizing two points. One is that a heavy penalty would be paid (a reduction in the total net present value from $13 million to $9 million) if the amount of capital being made available were to be reduced below $9 million. The other is that *increasing* the amount of capital being made available by just $1 million (from $10 million to $11 million) would enable a substantial increase of $4 million in the total net present value (from $13 million to $17 million). However, a much larger further increase in the amount of capital being made available (from $11 million to $14 million) would be needed to enable a considerably smaller further increase in the total net present value (from $17 million to $19 million).

Armando Ortega deliberates with other members of top management before making a decision. It is quickly concluded that increasing the amount of capital being made available all the way up to $14 million would be stretching the company's financial resources too dangerously to justify the relatively small payoff. However, there is considerable discussion of the pros and cons of the two options of using either $9 million or $11 million of capital. Because

The Excel sensitivity report is *not* available for integer programming problems.

Trial-and-error and/or the Solver Table can be used to perform sensitivity analysis for integer programming problems. See Section 5.3 and Appendix A for more details on using the Solver Table.

FIGURE 7.2

An application of the Solver Table that shows the effect on the optimal solution and the resulting total net present value of systematically varying the amount of capital being made available for these investments.

	B	C	D	E	F	G	H
23	Capital Available	Warehouse	Warehouse	Factory	Factory	Total NPV	
24	($millions)	in LA?	in SF?	in LA?	in SF?	($millions)	
25		0	0	1	1	13	
26	5	0	1	0	1	9	
27	6	0	1	0	1	9	
28	7	0	1	0	1	9	
29	8	0	1	0	1	9	
30	9	0	0	1	1	13	
31	10	0	0	1	1	13	
32	11	0	1	1	1	17	
33	12	0	1	1	1	17	
34	13	0	1	1	1	17	
35	14	1	0	1	1	19	
36	15	1	0	1	1	19	

Select the entire table (B25:G36), before choosing Solver Table from the Tools menu.

	B	C	D	E	F	G
23	Capital Available	Warehouse	Warehouse	Factory	Factory	Total NPV
24	($millions)	in LA?	in SF?	in LA?	in SF?	($millions)
25		=C16	=D16	=C18	=D18	=TotalNPV

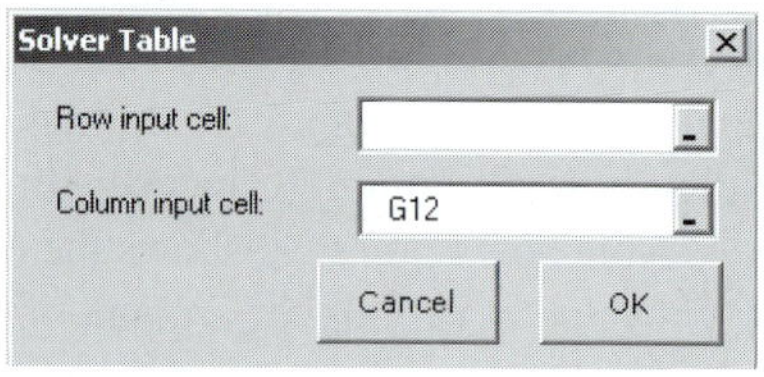

Solver Table [x]

Row input cell: [   ] [▾]

Column input cell: [G12] [▾]

[Cancel]　[OK]

Range Name	Cell
TotalNPV	D20

of the large payoff from the latter option (an additional $4 million in total net present value), management finally decides to adopt the plan presented in row 32 of Figure 7.2. Thus, the company will build new factories in both Los Angeles and San Francisco as well as a new warehouse in San Francisco, with an estimated total net present value of $17 million. However, because of the large capital requirements of this plan, management also decides to defer building the warehouse until the two factories are completed so that their profits can help finance the construction of the warehouse.

Review Questions

1. What are the four interrelated decisions that need to be made by the management of the California Manufacturing Co.?
2. Why are binary decision variables appropriate to represent these decisions?
3. What is the objective specified by management for this problem?
4. What are the mutually exclusive alternatives in this problem? What is the form of the resulting constraint in the BIP model?
5. What are the contingent decisions in this problem? For each one, what is the form of the resulting constraint in the BIP model?
6. What is the tentative managerial decision on which sensitivity analysis needs to be performed?

7.2　USING BIP FOR PROJECT SELECTION: THE TAZER CORP. PROBLEM

The California Manufacturing Co. case study focused on four proposed projects: (1) build a factory in Los Angeles, (2) build a factory in San Francisco, (3) build a warehouse in Los Angeles, and (4) build a warehouse in San Francisco. Management needed to make yes-or-no

TABLE 7.3
Data for the Tazer Project Selection Problem

	Project				
	1 (Up)	**2 (Stable)**	**3 (Choice)**	**4 (Hope)**	**5 (Release)**
R&D investment ($million)	400	300	600	500	200
Success rate	50%	35%	35%	20%	45%
Revenue if successful ($million)	1,400	1,200	2,200	3,000	600
Expected profit ($million)	300	120	170	100	70

decisions on which of these projects to select. This is typical of many applications of BIP. However, the nature of the projects may vary considerably from one application to the next. Instead of the proposed construction projects in the case study, our next example involves the selection of research and development projects.

This example is adapted from both Case 3-7 and its continuation in the supplement to Chapter 13, but all the relevant information is repeated below.

The Tazer Corp. Problem

Tazer Corp., a pharmaceutical manufacturing company, is beginning the search for a new breakthrough drug. The following five potential research and development projects have been identified for attempting to develop such a drug.

> **Project Up:** Develop a more effective antidepressant that does not cause serious mood swings.
>
> **Project Stable:** Develop a drug that addresses manic depression.
>
> **Project Choice:** Develop a less intrusive birth control method for women.
>
> **Project Hope:** Develop a vaccine to prevent HIV infection.
>
> **Project Release:** Develop a more effective drug to lower blood pressure.

In contrast to Case 3-7, Tazer management now has concluded that the company cannot devote enough money to research and development to undertake all of these projects. Only $1.2 billion is available, which will be enough for only two or three of the projects. The first row of Table 7.3 shows the amount needed (in millions of dollars) for each of these projects. The second row estimates each project's probability of being successful. If a project is successful, it is estimated that the resulting drug would generate the revenue shown in the third row. Thus, the *expected revenue* (in the statistical sense) from a potential drug is the product of its numbers in the second and third rows, whereas its *expected profit* is this expected revenue minus the investment given in the first row. These expected profits are shown in the bottom row of Table 7.3.

Tazer management now wants to determine which of these projects should be undertaken to maximize their expected total profit.

The objective is to choose the projects that will maximize the expected profit while satisfying the budget constraint.

Formulation with Binary Variables

Because the decision for each of the five proposed research and development projects is a yes-or-no decision, the corresponding decision variables are binary variables. Thus, the decision variable for each project has the following interpretation.

$$\text{Decision Variable} = \begin{cases} 1, & \text{if approve the project} \\ 0, & \text{if reject the project} \end{cases}$$

Let x_1, x_2, x_3, x_4, and x_5 denote the decision variables for the respective projects in the order in which they are listed in Table 7.3.

If a project is rejected, there is neither any profit nor any loss, whereas the expected profit if a project is approved is given in the bottom row of Table 7.3. Using units of millions of dollars, the expected total profit is

$$P = 300x_1 + 120x_2 + 170x_3 + 100x_4 + 70x_5$$

The objective is to select the projects to approve that will maximize this expected total profit while satisfying the budget constraint.

Other than requiring the decision variables to be binary, the budget constraint limiting the total investment to no more than $1.2 billion is the only constraint that has been imposed by Tazer management on the selection of these research and development projects. Referring to the first row of Table 7.3, this constraint can be expressed in terms of the decision variables as

$$400x_1 + 300x_2 + 600x_3 + 500x_4 + 200x_5 \leq 1,200$$

With this background, the stage now is set for formulating a BIP spreadsheet model for this problem.

A BIP Spreadsheet Model for the Tazer Problem

Figure 7.3 shows a BIP spreadsheet model for this problem. The data in Table 7.3 have been transferred into cells C5:G8. The changing cells are DoProject? (C10:G10) and the target cell is TotalExpectedProfit (H8). The one functional constraint is depicted in cells H5:J5. The Add Constraint dialogue box has been used to officially enter both this constraint and the DoProject? = binary constraints into the model, as shown in the Solver dialogue box.

FIGURE 7.3

A spreadsheet formulation of the BIP model for the Tazer Corp. project selection problem where the changing cells DoProject? (C10:G10) give the optimal solution obtained by the Excel Solver.

	A	B	C	D	E	F	G	H	I	J
1		**Tazer Corp. Project Selection Problem**								
2										
3										
4			Up	Stable	Choice	Hope	Release	Total		Budget
5		R&D Investment ($million)	400	300	600	500	200	1,200	<=	1,200
6		Success Rate	50%	35%	35%	20%	45%			
7		Revenue If Successful ($million)	1,400	1,200	2,200	3,000	600			
8		Expected Profit ($million)	300	120	170	100	70	540		
9										
10		Do Project?	1	0	1	0	1			

	B	C	D	E	F	G
8	Expected Profit ($million)	=C7*C6-C5	=D7*D6-D5	=E7*E6-E5	=F7*F6-F5	=G7*G6-G5

Range Name	Cells
Budget	J5
DoProject?	C10:G10
ExpectedProfit	C8:G8
RandDInvestment	C5:G5
Revenue	C7:G7
SuccessRate	C6:G6
TotalExpectedProfit	H8
TotalRandD	H5

	H
4	Total
5	=SUMPRODUCT(RandDInvestment,DoProject?)
6	
7	
8	=SUMPRODUCT(ExpectedProfit,DoProject?)

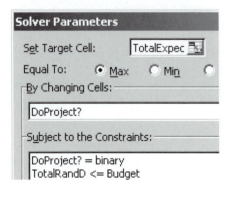

Solver Parameters

Set Target Cell: [TotalExpec]

Equal To: ⦿ Max   ○ Min   ○

By Changing Cells:

[DoProject?]

Subject to the Constraints:

DoProject? = binary
TotalRandD <= Budget

Solver Options

☑ Assume Linear Model
☑ Assume Non-Negative

The changing cells DoProject? (C10:G10) in Figure 7.3 show the optimal solution that has been obtained by the Excel Solver, namely,

Choose Project Up, Project Choice, and Project Release.

The target cell indicates that the resulting total expected profit is $540 million.

Review
Questions

1. How are binary variables used to represent managerial decisions on which projects from a group of proposed projects should be selected for approval?
2. What types of projects are under consideration in the Tazer Corp. problem?
3. What is the objective for this problem?

7.3 USING BIP FOR THE SELECTION OF SITES FOR EMERGENCY SERVICES FACILITIES: THE CALIENTE CITY PROBLEM

Although the problem encountered in the California Manufacturing Co. case study can be described as a *project selection* problem (as was done at the beginning of the preceding section), it could just as well have been called a *site selection* problem. Recall that the company's management needed to select a site (Los Angeles or San Francisco) for its new factory as well as for its possible new warehouse. For either of the possible sites for the new factory (or the warehouse), there is a *yes-or-no decision* for whether that site should be selected, so it becomes natural to represent each such decision by a binary decision variable.

Various kinds of site selection problems are one of the most common types of applications of BIP. The kinds of facilities for which sites need to be selected can be of any type. In some cases, several sites are to be selected for several facilities of a particular type, whereas only a single site is to be selected in other cases.

We will focus here on the selection of sites for emergency services facilities. These facilities might be fire stations, police stations, ambulance centers, and so forth. In any of these cases, the overriding concern commonly is to provide facilities close enough to each part of the area being served that the response time to an emergency anywhere in the area will be sufficiently small. The form of the BIP model then will be basically the same regardless of the specific type of emergency services being considered.

To illustrate, let us consider an example where sites are being selected for fire stations. For simplicity, this example will divide the area being served into only eight tracts instead of the many dozens or hundreds that would be typical in real applications.

The Caliente City Problem

Caliente City is located in a particularly warm and arid part of the United States, so it is especially prone to the occurrence of fires. The city has become a popular place for senior citizens to move to after retirement, so it has been growing rapidly and spreading well beyond its original borders. However, the city still has only one fire station, located in the congested center of the original town site. The result has been some long delays in fire trucks reaching fires in the outer parts of the city, causing much more damage than would have occurred with a prompt response. The city's residents are very unhappy about this, so the city council has directed the city manager to develop a plan for locating multiple fire stations throughout the city that would greatly reduce the response time to any fire. In particular, the city council has adopted the following policy about the maximum acceptable response time for fire trucks to reach a fire anywhere in the city after being notified about the fire.

Response time ≤ 10 minutes

Having had a management science course in college, the city manager recognizes that BIP provides her with a powerful tool for analyzing this problem. To get started, she divides the city into eight tracts and then gathers data on the estimated response time for a fire in each

TABLE 7.4 Response Time and Cost Data for the Caliente City Problem

| | | \multicolumn{8}{c}{Fire Station in Tract} | | | | | | | |
		1	**2**	**3**	**4**	**5**	**6**	**7**	**8**
Response times (minutes) for a fire in tract	1	2	8	18	9	23	22	16	28
	2	9	3	10	12	16	14	21	25
	3	17	8	4	20	21	8	22	17
	4	10	13	19	2	18	21	6	12
	5	21	12	16	13	5	11	9	12
	6	25	15	7	21	15	3	14	8
	7	14	22	18	7	13	15	2	9
	8	30	24	15	14	17	9	8	3
Cost of station ($thousands)		350	250	450	300	50	400	300	200

tract from a potential fire station in each of the eight tracts. These data are shown in Table 7.4. For example, if a decision were to be made to locate a fire station in tract 1 and if that fire station were to be used to respond to a fire in any of the tracts, the second column of Table 7.4 shows what the (estimated) response time would be. (Since the response time would exceed 10 minutes for a fire in tracts 3, 5, 6, 7, or 8, a fire station actually would need to be located nearer to each of these tracts to satisfy the city council's new policy.) The bottom row of Table 7.4 shows what the cost would be of acquiring the land and constructing a fire station in any of the eight tracts. (The cost is far less for tract 5 because the current fire station already is there so only a modest renovation is needed.)

> The objective is to minimize the total cost of ensuring a response time of no more than 10 minutes.

The objective now is to determine which tracts should receive a fire station to minimize the total cost of the stations while ensuring that each tract has at least one station close enough to respond to a fire in no more than 10 minutes.

Formulation with Binary Variables

For each of the eight tracts, there is a yes-or-no decision as to whether that tract should receive a fire station. Therefore, we let $x_1, x_2, \ldots, x_8$ denote the corresponding binary decision variables, where

$$x_j = \begin{cases} 1, & \text{if tract } j \text{ is selected to receive a fire station} \\ 0, & \text{if not} \end{cases}$$

for $j = 1, 2, \ldots, 8$.

Since the objective is to minimize the total cost of the fire stations that will satisfy the city council's new policy on response times, the total cost needs to be expressed in terms of these decision variables. Using units of thousands of dollars while referring to the bottom row of Table 7.4, the total cost is

$$C = 350x_1 + 250x_2 + 450x_3 + 300x_4 + 50x_5 + 400x_6 + 300x_7 + 200x_8$$

We also need to formulate constraints in terms of these decision variables that will ensure that no response times exceed 10 minutes. For example, consider tract 1. When a fire occurs there, the row for tract 1 in Table 7.4 indicates that the only tracts close enough that a fire station would provide a response time not exceeding 10 minutes are tract 1 itself, tract 2, and tract 4. Thus, at least one of these three tracts needs to have a fire station. This requirement is expressed in the constraint

> This constraint ensures that the response time for a fire in tract 1 will be no more than 10 minutes.

$$x_1 + x_2 + x_4 \geq 1$$

Incidentally, this type of constraint (a sum of certain binary variables ≥ 1) is called a **set covering constraint** because it is requiring that a certain *set* (a set of potential sites for fire stations in this case) will be *covered* in the sense that at least one member of the set will be included in the solution.

Applying the above reasoning for tract 1 to all the tracts leads to the following constraints.

Tract 1:	x_1	$+x_2$		$+x_4$			≥ 1
Tract 2:	x_1	$+x_2$	$+x_3$				≥ 1
Tract 3:		x_2	$+x_3$		$+x_6$		≥ 1
Tract 4:	x_1			$+x_4$		$+x_7$	≥ 1
Tract 5:					$+x_5$	$+x_7$	≥ 1
Tract 6:			x_3		$+x_6$	$+x_8$	≥ 1
Tract 7:				x_4		$+x_7$ $+x_8$	≥ 1
Tract 8:					x_6	$+x_7$ $+x_8$	≥ 1

These *set covering constraints* (along with requiring the variables to be binary) are all that is needed to ensure that each tract has at least one fire station close enough to respond to a fire in no more than 10 minutes.

This type of BIP model (minimizing total cost where all the functional constraints are set covering constraints) is called a **set covering problem.** Such problems arise fairly frequently. In fact, you will see another example of a set covering problem in Section 7.4.

Having identified the nature of the constraints for the Caliente City problem, it now is fairly straightforward to formulate its BIP spreadsheet model.

A BIP Spreadsheet Model for the Caliente City Problem

Figure 7.4 shows a BIP spreadsheet model for this problem. The data cells ResponseTime (D5:K12) show all the response times given in Table 7.4 and CostOfStation (D14:K14) provides the cost data from the bottom row of this table. There is a yes-or-no decision for each tract as to whether a fire station should be located there, so the changing cells are StationInTract? (D29:K29). The objective is to minimize total cost, so the target cell is TotalCost (N29). The set covering constraints are displayed in cells L17:N24. The Add Constraint dialogue box has been used to officially enter both these constraints and the StationInTract? = binary constraints into the model, as can be seen in the Solver dialogue box.

After clicking on Solve in the Solver dialogue box, the optimal solution shown in the changing cells StationInTract? (D29:K29) in Figure 7.4 is obtained, namely,

Select tracts 2, 7, and 8 as the sites for fire stations.

The target cell TotalCost (N29) indicates that the resulting total cost is $750,000.

Review Questions

1. How are binary variables used to represent managerial decisions regarding which site or sites should be selected for new facilities?
2. What are some types of emergency services facilities for which sites may need to be selected?
3. What was the objective for the Caliente City problem?
4. What is a set covering constraint and what is a set covering problem?

7.4   USING BIP FOR CREW SCHEDULING: THE SOUTHWESTERN AIRWAYS PROBLEM

Throughout the travel industry (airlines, rail travel, cruise ships, tour companies, etc.), one of the most challenging problems in maintaining an efficient operation is the scheduling of its crews who serve customers during their travels. Given many feasible overlapping sequences of trips for a crew, to which ones should a crew be assigned so as to cover all the trips at a minimum cost? Thus, for each feasible sequence of trips, there is a *yes-or-no decision* as to whether a crew should be assigned to that sequence, so a binary decision variable can be used to represent that decision.

FIGURE 7.4

A spreadsheet formulation of the BIP model for the Caliente City site selection problem where the changing cells StationInTract? (D29:K29) show the optimal solution obtained by the Excel Solver.

	A	B	C	D	E	F	G	H	I	J	K	L	M	N
1		**Caliente City Fire Station Location Problem**												
2														
3						Fire Station in Tract								
4				1	2	3	4	5	6	7	8			
5			1	2	8	18	9	23	22	16	28			
6		Response	2	9	3	10	12	16	14	21	25			
7		Times	3	17	8	4	20	21	8	22	17			
8		(minutes)	4	10	13	19	2	18	21	6	12			
9		for a Fire	5	21	12	16	13	5	11	9	12			
10		in Tract	6	25	15	7	21	15	3	14	8			
11			7	14	22	18	7	13	15	2	9			
12			8	30	24	15	14	17	9	8	3			
13														
14		Cost of Station		350	250	450	300	50	400	300	200			
15		($thousands)										Number		
16												Covering		
17			1	1	1	0	1	0	0	0	0	1	>=	1
18		Response	2	1	1	1	0	0	0	0	0	1	>=	1
19		Time	3	0	1	1	0	0	1	0	0	1	>=	1
20		<=	4	1	0	0	1	0	0	1	0	1	>=	1
21		10	5	0	0	0	0	1	0	1	0	1	>=	1
22		Minutes?	6	0	0	1	0	0	1	0	1	1	>=	1
23			7	0	0	0	1	0	0	1	1	2	>=	1
24			8	0	0	0	0	0	1	1	1	2	>=	1
25														
26														Total
27						Fire Station in Tract								Cost
28				1	2	3	4	5	6	7	8			($thousands)
29		Station in Tract?		0	1	0	0	0	0	1	1			750

	J	K	L
15			Number
16			Covering
17	=IF(J5<=MaxResponseTime,1,0)	=IF(K5<=MaxResponseTime,1,0)	=SUMPRODUCT(D17:K17,StationInTract?)
18	=IF(J6<=MaxResponseTime,1,0)	=IF(K6<=MaxResponseTime,1,0)	=SUMPRODUCT(D18:K18,StationInTract?)
19	=IF(J7<=MaxResponseTime,1,0)	=IF(K7<=MaxResponseTime,1,0)	=SUMPRODUCT(D19:K19,StationInTract?)

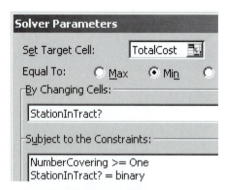

Solver Parameters

Set Target Cell: TotalCost

Equal To: ○ Max ● Min ○

By Changing Cells:

StationInTract?

Subject to the Constraints:

NumberCovering >= One
StationInTract? = binary

Solver Options

☑ Assume Linear Model

☑ Assume Non-Negative

Range Name	Cells
CostOfStation	D14:K14
MaxResponseTime	B21
NumberCovering	L17:L24
One	N17:N24
ResponseTime	D5:K12
StationInTract?	D29:K29
TotalCost	N29

	N
26	Total
27	Cost
28	($thousands)
29	=SUMPRODUCT(CostOfStation,StationInTract?)

An Application Vignette

Commercial airlines must solve two difficult scheduling problems to ensure that aircrews are available for all scheduled flights. One, called the tours-of-duty planning problem, involves constructing sequences of flights with interspersed rest periods that will comprise tours of duty over perhaps many days for individual crews. The second one, called the rostering problem, involves allocating these tours of duty to individual crew members. Management seeks minimum-cost or maximum-productivity solutions for these problems that also satisfy labor agreements and consider the preferences of crew members.

Many major airlines around the world have achieved impressive savings in recent years by using BIP models to obtain optimal solutions for these problems. One of these airlines is Air New Zealand, which is the largest national and international airline based in New Zealand. It employs over 2,000 crew members and operates flights to Australia, Asia, North America, and Europe, as well as between the major centers within New Zealand.

The BIP models used by Air New Zealand typically have hundreds of functional constraints and many thousands of binary variables, where advanced techniques are used to solve these models. A conservative estimate of the savings resulting from the use of these models is US$6.7 million per year, which accounted for 11 percent of the company's operating profit in one recent year. There also are many intangible benefits, including quick implementations, efficiently accommodating late schedule changes, and improved passenger service.

Source: E. R. Butchers, P. R. Day, A. P. Goldie, S. Miller, J. A. Meyer, D. M. Ryan, A. C. Scott, and C. A. Wallace, "Optimized Crew Scheduling at Air New Zealand," *Interfaces* 31, no. 1 (January–February 2001), pp. 30–56.

For many years, airline companies have been using BIP models to determine how to do its crew scheduling in the most cost-efficient way. Some airlines have saved many millions of dollars annually through this application of BIP. Consequently, other segments of the travel industry now are also using management science in this way.

To illustrate the approach, consider the following miniature example of airline crew scheduling.

The Southwestern Airways Problem

Southwestern Airways needs to assign its crews to cover all its upcoming flights. We will focus on the problem of assigning three crews based in San Francisco (SFO) to the 11 flights shown in Figure 7.5. These same flights are listed in the first column of Table 7.5. The other 12 columns show the 12 feasible sequences of flights for a crew. (The numbers in each column indicate the order of the flights.) At most, three of the sequences need to be chosen (one per crew) in such a way that every flight is covered. (It is permissible to have more than one crew on a flight, where the extra crews would fly as passengers, but union contracts require that the extra crews still be paid for their time as if they were working.) The cost of assigning a crew to a particular sequence of flights is given (in thousands of dollars) in the bottom row of the table. The objective is to minimize the total cost of the crew assignments that cover all the flights.

FIGURE 7.5

The arrows show the 11 Southwestern Airways flights that need to be covered by the three crews based in San Francisco.

233

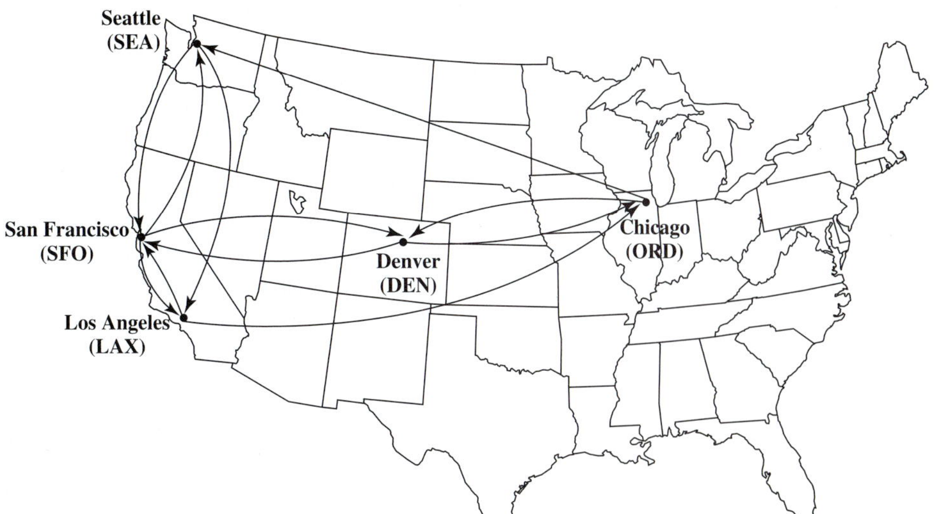

TABLE 7.5 Data for the Southwestern Airways Problem

Flight	Feasible Sequence of Flights											
	1	2	3	4	5	6	7	8	9	10	11	12
1. San Francisco to Los Angeles (SFO–LAX)	1			1			1			1		
2. San Francisco to Denver (SFO–DEN)		1			1			1			1	
3. San Francisco to Seattle (SFO–SEA)			1			1			1			1
4. Los Angeles to Chicago (LAX–ORD)				2			2		3	2		3
5. Los Angeles to San Francisco (LAX–SFO)	2				3					5	5	
6. Chicago to Denver (ORD–DEN)				3	3				4			
7. Chicago to Seattle (ORD–SEA)							3	3		3	3	4
8. Denver to San Francisco (DEN–SFO)		2		4	4				5			
9. Denver to Chicago (DEN–ORD)					2			2			2	
10. Seattle to San Francisco (SEA–SFO)			2				4	4				5
11. Seattle to Los Angeles (SEA–LAX)						2			2	4	4	2
Cost, $1,000s	2	3	4	6	7	5	7	8	9	9	8	9

Formulation with Binary Variables

With 12 feasible sequences of flights, we have 12 yes-or-no decisions:

$$\text{Should sequence } j \text{ be assigned to a crew?} \quad (j = 1, 2, \ldots, 12)$$

Therefore, we use 12 binary variables to represent these respective decisions:

$$x_j = \begin{cases} 1, & \text{if sequence } j \text{ is assigned to a crew} \\ 0, & \text{otherwise} \end{cases}$$

Since the objective is to minimize the total cost of the three crew assignments, we now need to express the total cost in terms of these binary decision variables. Referring to the bottom row of Table 7.5, this total cost (in units of thousands of dollars) is

$$C = 2x_1 + 3x_2 + 4x_3 + 6x_4 + 7x_5 + 5x_6 + 7x_7 + 8x_8 + 9x_9 + 9x_{10} + 8x_{11} + 9x_{12}$$

With only three crews available to cover the flights, we also need the constraint

$$x_1 + x_2 + \cdots + x_{12} \le 3$$

The most interesting part of this formulation is the nature of each constraint that ensures that a corresponding flight is covered. For example, consider the last flight in Table 7.5 (Seattle to Los Angeles). Five sequences (namely, sequences 6, 9, 10, 11, and 12) include this flight. Therefore, at least one of these five sequences must be chosen. The resulting constraint is

$$x_6 + x_9 + x_{10} + x_{11} + x_{12} \ge 1$$

For each of the 11 flights, the constraint that ensures that the flight is covered is constructed in the same way from Table 7.5 by requiring that at least one of the flight sequences that includes that flight is assigned to a crew. Thus, 11 constraints of the following form are needed.

Flight 1: $x_1 + x_4 + x_7 + x_{10} \geq 1$

Flight 2: $x_2 + x_5 + x_8 + x_{11} \geq 1$

.

.

.

Flight 11: $x_6 + x_9 + x_{10} + x_{11} + x_{12} \geq 1$

Note that these constraints have the same form as the constraints for the Caliente City problem in Section 7.3 (a sum of certain binary variables ≥ 1), so these too are *set covering constraints*. Therefore, this crew scheduling problem is another example of a *set covering problem* (where this particular set covering problem also includes the side constraint that $x_1 + x_2 + \cdots + x_{12} \leq 3$).

Having identified the nature of the constraints, the stage now is set for formulating a BIP spreadsheet model for this problem.

A BIP Spreadsheet Model for the Southwestern Airways Problem

Figure 7.6 shows a spreadsheet formulation of the complete BIP model for this problem. The changing cells FlySequence? (C22:N22) contain the values of the 12 binary decision variables. The data in IncludesSegment? (C8:N18) and Cost (C5:N5) come directly from Table 7.5. The last three columns of the spreadsheet are used to show the set covering constraints, Total $\geq$ AtLeastOne, and the side constraint, TotalSequences $\leq$ NumberOfCrews. The Add Constraint dialogue box has been used to officially enter both these constraints and the constraints, FlySequence? = binary, into the model, as shown in the Solver dialogue box.

The Excel Solver provides the optimal solution shown in FlySequence? (C22:N22). In terms of the x_j variables, this solution is

$x_3 = 1$ (assign sequence 3 to a crew)

$x_4 = 1$ (assign sequence 4 to a crew)

$x_{11} = 1$ (assign sequence 11 to a crew)

and all other $x_j = 0$, for a total cost of \$18,000 as given by TotalCost (Q24). (Another optimal solution is $x_1 = 1$, $x_5 = 1$, $x_{12} = 1$, and all other $x_j = 0$.)

We should point out that this BIP model is a tiny one compared to the ones typically used in actual practice. Airline crew scheduling problems involving thousands of possible flight sequences now are being solved by using models similar to the one shown above but with thousands of binary variables rather than just a dozen.

Review Questions

1. What is the crew scheduling problem that is encountered by companies in the travel industry?
2. What are the yes-or-no decisions that need to be made when addressing a crew scheduling problem?
3. For the Southwestern Airways problem, there is a constraint for each flight to ensure that this flight is covered by a crew. Describe the mathematical form of this constraint. Then explain in words what this constraint is saying.

7.5 USING MIXED BIP TO DEAL WITH SETUP COSTS FOR INITIATING PRODUCTION: THE REVISED WYNDOR PROBLEM

All of the examples considered thus far in this chapter have been *pure BIP problems* (problems where all the decision variables are binary variables). However, *mixed BIP problems* (problems where only some of the decision variables are binary variables) also arise quite frequently because only some of the decisions to be made are yes-or-no decisions and the rest are how-much decisions.

FIGURE 7.6

A spreadsheet formulation of the BIP model for the Southwestern Airways crew scheduling problem, where FlySequence (C22:N22) shows the optimal solution obtained by the Excel Solver. The list of flight sequences under consideration is given in cells A25:D37.

	A	B	C	D	E	F	G	H	I	J	K	L	M	N	O	P	Q
1		**Southwestern Airways Crew Scheduling Problem**															
2																	
3								Flight Sequence									
4			1	2	3	4	5	6	7	8	9	10	11	12			
5		Cost ($thousands)	2	3	4	6	7	5	7	8	9	9	8	9			At
6																	Least
7		**Includes Segment?**													Total		One
8		SFO–LAX	1	0	0	1	0	0	1	0	0	1	0	0	1	≥	1
9		SFO–DEN	0	1	0	0	1	0	0	1	0	0	1	0	1	≥	1
10		SFO–SEA	0	0	1	0	0	1	0	0	1	0	0	1	1	≥	1
11		LAX–ORD	0	0	0	1	0	0	1	0	1	1	0	1	1	≥	1
12		LAX–SFO	1	0	0	0	0	1	0	0	0	1	1	0	1	≥	1
13		ORD–DEN	0	0	0	1	1	0	0	0	1	0	0	0	1	≥	1
14		ORD–SEA	0	0	0	0	0	0	1	1	0	1	1	1	1	≥	1
15		DEN–SFO	0	1	0	1	1	0	0	0	1	0	0	0	1	≥	1
16		DEN–ORD	0	0	0	0	1	0	0	1	0	0	1	0	1	≥	1
17		SEA–SFO	0	0	1	0	0	0	1	1	0	0	0	1	1	≥	1
18		SEA–LAX	0	0	0	0	0	1	0	0	1	1	1	1	1	≥	1
19																	
20															Total		Number
21			1	2	3	4	5	6	7	8	9	10	11	12	Sequences		of Crews
22		Fly Sequence?	0	0	1	1	0	0	0	0	0	0	1	0	3	≤	3
23																	
24															Total Cost ($thousands)		18

25	**Flight Sequence Key**	
26	1	SFO-LAX
27	2	SFO-DEN-SFO
28	3	SFO-SEA-SFO
29	4	SFO-LAX-ORD-DEN-SFO
30	5	SFO-DEN-ORD-DEN-SFO
31	6	SFO-SEA-LAX-SFO
32	7	SFO-LAX-ORD-SEA-SFO
33	8	SFO-DEN-ORD-SEA-SFO
34	9	SFO-SEA-LAX-ORD-DEN-SFO
35	10	SFO-LAX-ORD-SEA-LAX-SFO
36	11	SFO-DEN-ORD-SEA-LAX-SFO
37	12	SFO-SEA-LAX-ORD-SEA-SFO

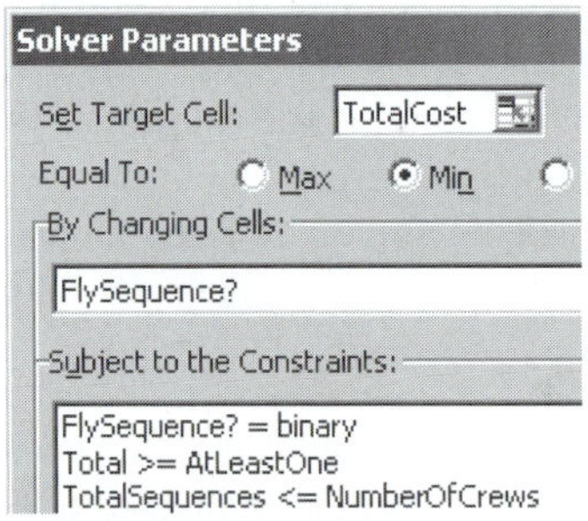

Solver Parameters

Set Target Cell: TotalCost

Equal To: ○ Max ● Min

By Changing Cells:

FlySequence?

Subject to the Constraints:

FlySequence? = binary
Total >= AtLeastOne
TotalSequences <= NumberOfCrews

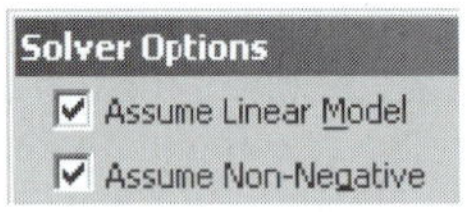

Solver Options

☑ Assume Linear Model
☑ Assume Non-Negative

Range Name	Cells
AtLeastOne	Q8:Q18
Cost	C5:N5
FlySequence?	C22:N22
IncludesSegment?	C8:N18
NumberOfCrews	Q22
Total	O8:O18
TotalCost	Q24
TotalSequences	O22

	O
7	Total
8	=SUMPRODUCT(C8:N8,FlySequence?)
9	=SUMPRODUCT(C9:N9,FlySequence?)
10	=SUMPRODUCT(C10:N10,FlySequence?)
11	=SUMPRODUCT(C11:N11,FlySequence?)
12	=SUMPRODUCT(C12:N12,FlySequence?)
13	=SUMPRODUCT(C13:N13,FlySequence?)
14	=SUMPRODUCT(C14:N14,FlySequence?)
15	=SUMPRODUCT(C15:N15,FlySequence?)
16	=SUMPRODUCT(C16:N16,FlySequence?)
17	=SUMPRODUCT(C17:N17,FlySequence?)
18	=SUMPRODUCT(C18:N18,FlySequence?)
19	
20	Total
21	Sequences
22	=SUM(FlySequence?)

	P	Q
24	Total Cost ($thousands)	=SUMPRODUCT(Cost,FlySequence?)

TABLE 7.6
Net Profit ($) for the
Revised Wyndor
Problem

Number of Units Produced	Net Profit ($)	
	Doors	**Windows**
0	0 (300) − 0 = 0	0 (500) − 0 = 0
1	1 (300) − 700 = −400	1 (500) − 1,300 = −800
2	2 (300) − 700 = −100	2 (500) − 1,300 = −300
3	3 (300) − 700 = 200	3 (500) − 1,300 = 200
4	4 (300) − 700 = 500	4 (500) − 1,300 = 700
5	Not feasible	5 (500) − 1,300 = 1,200
6	Not feasible	6 (500) − 1,300 = 1,700

One important example of this type is the *product-mix problem* introduced in Chapter 2, but now with the added complication that a setup cost must be incurred to initiate the production of each product. Therefore, in addition to the *how-much decisions* of how much to produce of each product, there also is a prior yes-or-no decision for each product of whether to perform a setup to enable initiating its production.

To illustrate this type of problem, we will consider a revised version of the Wyndor Glass Co. product-mix problem that was described in Section 2.1 and analyzed throughout most of Chapter 2.

The Revised Wyndor Problem

Suppose now that the Wyndor Glass Co. will only devote one week each month to the production of the special doors and windows described in Section 2.1, so the question now is *how many* doors and windows to produce during each of these week-long production runs. Each time Wyndor's plants convert from the production of other products to the production of these doors and windows for a week, the following setup costs would be incurred to initiate this production.

Setup cost to produce doors = $700

Setup cost to produce windows = $1,300

Otherwise, all the original data given in Table 2.2 still apply, including a unit profit of $300 for doors and $500 for windows when disregarding these setup costs.

Table 7.6 shows the resulting net profit from producing any feasible quantity for either product. Note that the large setup cost for either product makes it unprofitable to produce less than three units of that product.

The dots in Figure 7.7 show the feasible solutions for this problem. By adding the appropriate entries in Table 7.6, the figure also shows the calculation of the total net profit P for each of the corner points. The optimal solution turns out to be

$$(D, W) = (0, 6) \quad \text{with} \quad P = 1,700$$

By contrast, the original solution

$$(D, W) = (2, 6) \quad \text{with} \quad P = 1,600$$

now gives a smaller value of P. The reason that this original solution (which gave $P = 3,600$ for the original problem) is no longer optimal is that the setup costs reduce the total net profit so much:

$$P = 3,600 − 700 − 1,300 = 1,600$$

Therefore, the graphical method for linear programming can no longer be used to find the optimal solution for this new problem with setup costs.

How can we formulate a model for this problem so that it fits a standard kind of model that can be solved by the Excel Solver? Table 7.6 shows that the net profit for either product is no longer *directly proportional* to the number of units produced. Therefore, as it stands, the problem no longer fits either linear programming or BIP. Before, for the original problem without

FIGURE 7.7

The dots are the feasible solutions for the revised Wyndor problem. Also shown is the calculation of the total net profit P (in dollars) for each corner point from the net profits given in Table 7.6.

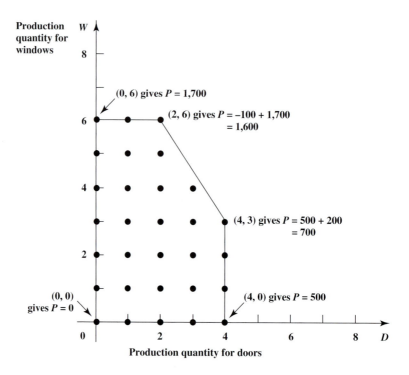

setup costs, the objective function was simply $P = 300D + 500W$. Now we need to subtract from this expression each setup cost *if* the corresponding product will be produced, but we should not subtract the setup cost if the product will not be produced. This is where *binary variables* come to the rescue.

Formulation with Binary Variables

For each product, there is a *yes-or-no decision* regarding whether to perform the setup that would enable initiating the production of the product, so the setup cost is incurred only if the decision is *yes*. Therefore, we can introduce a *binary variable* for each setup cost and associate each value of the binary variable with one of the two possibilities for the setup cost. In particular, let

These binary variables enable subtracting each setup cost only if the setup is performed.

$$y_1 = \begin{cases} 1, & \text{if perform the setup to produce doors} \\ 0, & \text{if not} \end{cases}$$

$$y_2 = \begin{cases} 1, & \text{if perform the setup to produce windows} \\ 0, & \text{if not} \end{cases}$$

Therefore, the objective function now can be written as

$$P = 300D + 500W - 700y_1 - 1{,}300y_2$$

which fits the format for mixed BIP.

Since a setup is required to produce the corresponding product, these binary variables can be related directly to the production quantities as follows.

$$y_1 = \begin{cases} 1, & \text{if } D > 0 \text{ can hold (can produce doors)} \\ 0, & \text{if } D = 0 \text{ must hold (cannot produce doors)} \end{cases}$$

$$y_2 = \begin{cases} 1, & \text{if } W > 0 \text{ can hold (can produce windows)} \\ 0, & \text{if } W = 0 \text{ must hold (cannot produce windows)} \end{cases}$$

We need to include constraints in the model that will ensure that these relationships will hold. (An algorithm solving the model only recognizes the objective function and the constraints, not the definitions of the variables.)

So what are the constraints of the model? We still need all the constraints of the original model. We also need constraints that D and W are integers, and that y_1 and y_2 are binary. In addition, we need some ordinary linear programming constraints that will ensure the following relationships:

If $y_1 = 0$,   then $D = 0$.

If $y_2 = 0$,   then $W = 0$.

(If $y_1 = 1$ or $y_2 = 1$, no restrictions are placed on D or W other than those already imposed by the other constraints.)

It is possible with Excel to use the IF function to represent this relationship between y_1 and D and between y_2 and W.[1] Unfortunately, the IF function does not fit into a linear programming (or BIP) format. Consequently, the Excel Solver has difficulty solving spreadsheet models that use this function. This is why another formulation with ordinary linear programming constraints is needed instead to express these relationships.

Since the other constraints impose bounds on D and W of $0 \le D \le 4$ and $0 \le W \le 6$, here are some ordinary linear programming constraints that ensure these relationships.

$$D \le 4y_1$$
$$W \le 6y_2$$

These constraints force the model to refuse production if the corresponding setup is not performed.

Note that setting $y_1 = 0$ gives $D \le 0$, which forces the nonnegative D to be $D = 0$, whereas setting $y_1 = 1$ gives $D \le 4$, which allows all the values of D already allowed by the other constraints. Then check that the same conclusions apply for W when setting $y_2 = 0$ and $y_2 = 1$.

It was not necessary to choose 4 and 6 for the respective coefficients of y_1 and y_2 in these two constraints. Any coefficients *larger* than 4 and 6 would have the same effect. You just need to avoid *smaller* coefficients, since this would impose undesired restrictions on D and W when $y_1 = 1$ and $y_2 = 1$.

On larger problems, it is sometimes difficult to determine the smallest acceptable coefficients for these binary variables. Therefore, it is common to formulate the model by just using a reasonably large number (say, 99 in this case) that is safely larger than the smallest acceptable coefficient.

With this background, we now are ready to formulate a mixed BIP spreadsheet model for this problem that uses the number 99 in these constraints.

A Mixed BIP Spreadsheet Model for the Revised Wyndor Problem

Figure 7.8 shows one way of formulating this model. The format for the first 14 rows is the same as for the original Wyndor problem, so the difference arises in rows 15–17 of the spreadsheet. The values of the binary variables, y_1 and y_2, appear in the new changing cells, Setup? (C17:D17). The bottom of the figure identifies the equations entered into the output cells in row 16, C16 = 99*C17 and D16 = 99*D17. Consequently, the constraints, UnitsProduced (C14:D14) $\le$ OnlyIfSetup (C16:D16), impose the relationships that $D \le 99y_1$ and $W \le 99y_2$.

The changing cells in this spreadsheet show the optimal solution obtained after applying the Excel Solver. Thus, this solution is to not produce any doors ($y_1 = 0$ and $D = 0$) but to perform the setup to enable producing 6 windows ($y_2 = 1$ and $W = 6$) to obtain a net profit of $1,700.

Note that this optimal solution does indeed satisfy the requirements that $D = 0$ must hold when $y_1 = 0$ and that $W > 0$ can hold when $y_2 = 1$. The constraints do permit performing a setup to produce a product and then not producing any units ($y_1 = 1$ with $D = 0$ or $y_2 = 1$ with $W = 0$), but the objective function causes an optimal solution automatically to avoid this foolish option of incurring the setup cost for no purpose.

---

[1] This is not straightforward since, for example, in the case where y_1 is not equal to 0 in the IF function, D needs to be set equal to a cell that is constrained to equal the changing cell holding the value of D.

FIGURE 7.8

A spreadsheet model for the revised Wyndor problem, where the Excel Solver gives the optimal solution shown in the changing cells, UnitsProduced (C14:D14) and Setup? (C17:D17).

	A	B	C	D	E	F	G	H
1		**Wyndor Glass Co. Product-Mix with Setup Costs**						
2								
3			Doors	Windows				
4		Unit Profit	$300	$500				
5		Setup Cost	$700	$1,300				
6								
7					Hours		Hours	
8			Hours Used per Unit Produced		Used		Available	
9		Plant 1	1	0	0	≤	4	
10		Plant 2	0	2	12	≤	12	
11		Plant 3	3	2	12	≤	18	
12								
13			Doors	Windows				
14		Units Prod'd	0	6				
15			≤	≤			Production Profit	$3,000
16		Only If Setup	0	99			−Total Setup Cost	$1,300
17		Setup?	0	1			Total Profit	$1,700

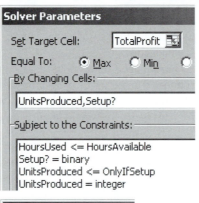

Solver Parameters

Set Target Cell: TotalProfit

Equal To: ○ Max ○ Min ○

By Changing Cells:

UnitsProduced,Setup?

Subject to the Constraints:

HoursUsed <= HoursAvailable
Setup? = binary
UnitsProduced <= OnlyIfSetup
UnitsProduced = integer

Solver Options

☑ Assume Linear Model
☑ Assume Non-Negative

Range Name	Cells
HoursAvailable	G9:G11
HoursUsed	E9:E11
HoursUsedPerUnitProduced	C9:D11
OnlyIfSetup	C16:D16
ProductionProfit	H15
Setup?	C17:D17
SetupCost	C5:D5
TotalProfit	H17
TotalSetupCost	H16
UnitProfit	C4:D4
UnitsProduced	C14:D14

	E
7	Hours
8	Used
9	=SUMPRODUCT(C9:D9,UnitsProduced)
10	=SUMPRODUCT(C10:D10,UnitsProduced)
11	=SUMPRODUCT(C11:D11,UnitsProduced)

	B	C	D
16	Only If Setup	=99*C17	=99*D17

	G	H
15	Production Profit	=SUMPRODUCT(UnitProfit,UnitsProduced)
16	−Total Setup Cost	=SUMPRODUCT(SetupCost,Setup?)
17	Total Profit	=ProductionProfit − TotalSetupCost

Review Questions

1. How does a mixed BIP problem differ from a pure BIP problem?
2. Why is a linear programming formulation no longer valid for a product-mix problem when there are setup costs for initiating production?
3. How can a binary variable be defined in terms of whether a setup is performed to initiate the production of a certain product?
4. What caused the optimal solution for the revised Wyndor problem to differ from that for the original Wyndor problem?

7.6 Summary

Managers frequently must make yes-or-no decisions, where the only two possible choices are yes, go ahead with a particular option, or no, decline this option. A binary integer programming (BIP) model considers many options simultaneously, with a binary decision variable for each option. Mixed BIP models include some continuous decision variables as well.

The California Manufacturing Co. case study involves yes-or-no decisions on whether a new factory should be built in certain cities and then whether a new warehouse also should be built in certain cities. This case study also introduced the modeling of mutually exclusive alternatives and contingent decisions, as well as the performance of sensitivity analysis for BIP models.

Many companies have saved millions of dollars by formulating and solving BIP models for a wide variety of applications. We have described and illustrated some of the most important types, including the selection of projects (e.g., research and development projects), the selection of sites for facilities (e.g., emergency services facilities such as fire stations), and crew scheduling in the travel industry (e.g., airlines). We also have discussed how to use mixed BIP to deal with setup costs for initiating production when addressing product-mix problems.

Glossary

binary decision variable A binary variable that represents a yes-or-no decision by assigning a value of 1 for choosing yes and a value of 0 for choosing no. (Introduction), 219

binary integer programming A type of problem or model that fits linear programming except that it uses binary decision variables. (Introduction), 219

binary variable A variable whose only possible values are 0 and 1. (Introduction), 219

BIP Abbreviation for binary integer programming. (Introduction), 219

contingent decision A yes-or-no decision is a contingent decision if it can be yes only if a certain other yes-or-no decision is yes. (Section 7.1), 223

mixed BIP problem A BIP problem where only some of the variables are restricted to be binary variables. (Introduction), 219

mutually exclusive alternatives A group of alternatives where choosing any one alternative excludes choosing any of the others. (Section 7.1), 222

pure BIP problem A BIP problem where all the variables are restricted to be binary variables. (Introduction), 219

set covering constraint A constraint that requires the sum of certain binary variables to be greater than or equal to 1. (Section 7.3), 230

set covering problem A type of BIP model where the objective is to minimize some quantity such as total cost and all the functional constraints are set covering constraints. (Section 7.3), 231

yes-or-no decision A decision whose only possible choices are (1) yes, go ahead with a certain option, or (2) no, decline this option. (Introduction), 219

Learning Aids for This Chapter in Your MS Courseware

Chapter 7 Excel Files:

California Mfg. Case Study

Tazer Corp. example

Caliente City example

Southwestern Airways Example

Revised Wyndor example

Excel Add-ins:

Premium Solver for Education

Solver Table

Supplements to This Chapter on the CD-ROM:

Advanced Formulation Techniques for Binary Integer Programming

Some Perspectives on Solving Binary Integer Programming Problems

Solved Problems (See the CD-ROM for the Solutions)

7.S1. Capital Budgeting with Contingency Constraints

A company is planning its capital budget over the next several years. There are eight potential projects under consideration. A calculation has been made of the expected net present value of each project, along with the cash outflow that would be required over the next four years. These data, along with the cash that is available each year, are shown in the next table. There also are the following contingency constraints: (a) at least one of project 1, 2, or 3 must be done, (b) projects 6 and 7 cannot both be done, and (c) project 5 can only be done if project 6 is done. Formulate and solve a BIP model in a spreadsheet to determine which projects should be pursued to maximize the total expected net present value.

| | Cash Outflow Required ($million) | | | | | | | | Cash |
| | Project | | | | | | | | Available |
	1	2	3	4	5	6	7	8	($million)
Year 1	1	3	0	3	3	7	2	5	20
Year 2	2	2	2	2	2	3	3	4	20
Year 3	2	3	4	2	3	3	6	2	20
Year 4	2	1	0	5	4	2	1	2	20
NPV ($mil)	10	12	11	15	24	17	16	18	

7.S2. Locating Search and Rescue Teams

The Washington State legislature is trying to decide on locations at which to base search-and-rescue teams. The teams are expensive, so the legislature would like as few as possible while still providing the desired level of service. In particular, since response time is critical, the legislature would like every county to either have a team located in that county or in an adjacent county. Formulate and solve a BIP model in a spreadsheet to determine where the teams should be located.

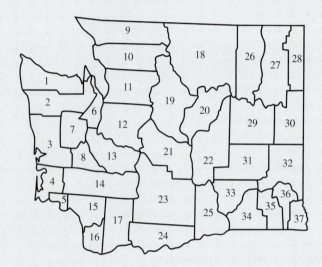

Counties

1. Clallum	19. Chelan
2. Jefferson	20. Douglas
3. Grays Harbor	21. Kittitas
4. Pacific	22. Grant
5. Wahkiakum	23. Yakima
6. Kitsap	24. Klickitat
7. Mason	25. Benton
8. Thurston	26. Ferry
9. Whatcom	27. Stevens
10. Skagit	28. Pend Oreille
11. Snohomish	29. Lincoln
12. King	30. Spokane
13. Pierce	31. Adams
14. Lewis	32. Whitman
15. Cowlitz	33. Franklin
16. Clark	34. Walla Walla
17. Skamania	35. Columbia
18. Okanogan	36. Garfield
	37. Asotin

7.S3. Warehouse Site Selection

Consider a small company that produces a single product in two plants and serves customers in five different regions.

The company has been using a make-to-order policy of producing the product only in the quantities needed to fill the orders that have come in from the various regions. However, because of the problems caused by the sporadic production schedule, management has decided to smooth out the production rate and ship the product to one or more storage warehouses, which then will use inventory to fill the incoming regional orders. Management now needs to decide where to locate the company's new warehouse(s). There are three locations under consideration. For each location, there is a fixed monthly cost associated with leasing and operating the warehouse there. Furthermore, each potential warehouse location has a maximum capacity for monthly shipments restricted primarily by the number of trucking docks at the site. The product costs $400 to produce at plant 1 and $300 to

produce at plant 2. The shipping cost from each plant to each potential warehouse location is shown in the first table below. The fixed leasing and operating cost (if open), the shipping costs, and the capacity (maximum monthly shipments) of each potential warehouse location are shown in the second table below. The monthly demand in each of the customer regions is expected to be 200, 225, 100, 150, and 175 units, respectively. Formulate and solve a BIP model in a spreadsheet to determine which warehouse(s) should be used and how the product should be distributed from plant to warehouse(s) to customer.

Shipping Costs and Capacity of the Plants

| | Shipping Cost (per unit) | | | Capacity |
	WH 1	WH 2	WH 3	(units/month)
Plant 1	$25	$50	$75	500
Plant 2	$50	$75	$25	400

Fixed Cost, Shipping Costs, and Capacity of the Warehouses

	Fixed Cost (per month)	Shipping Cost (per unit)					Capacity (units/month)
		Region 1	Region 2	Region 3	Region 4	Region 5	
WH 1	$50,000	$30	$70	$75	$55	$40	700
WH 2	$30,000	$55	$30	$45	$45	$70	500
WH 3	$70,000	$70	$30	$50	$60	$55	1,000

Problems

To the left of the problems (or their parts), we have inserted an E* whenever Excel should be used (unless your instructor gives you contrary instructions). An asterisk on the problem number indicates that at least a partial answer is given in the back of the book.

7.1.   Reconsider the California Manufacturing Co. case study presented in Section 7.1. The mayor of San Diego now has contacted the company's president, Armando Ortega, to try to persuade him to build a factory and perhaps a warehouse in that city. With the tax incentives being offered the company, Armando's staff estimates that the net present value of building a factory in San Diego would be $7 million and the amount of capital required to do this would be $4 million. The net present value of building a warehouse there would be $5 million and the capital required would be $3 million. (This option will only be considered if a factory also is being built there.)

Armando has asked Steve Chan to revise his previous management science study to incorporate these new alternatives into the overall problem. The objective still is to find the feasible combination of investments that maximizes the total net present value, given that the amount of capital available for these investments is $10 million.

a. Formulate a BIP model in algebraic form for this problem.

E*   *b.* Formulate and solve this model on a spreadsheet.

7.2.*   A young couple, Eve and Steven, want to divide their main household chores (marketing, cooking, dishwashing, and laundering) between them so that each has two tasks but the total time they spend on household duties is kept to a minimum. Their efficiencies on these tasks differ, where the time each would need to perform the task is given by the following table:

	Time Needed per Week (Hours)			
	Marketing	Cooking	Dish Washing	Laundry
Eve	4.5	7.8	3.6	2.9
Steven	4.9	7.2	4.3	3.1

a. Formulate a BIP model in algebraic form for this problem.

E*   *b.* Formulate and solve this model on a spreadsheet.

7.3.   A real-estate development firm, Peterson and Johnson, is considering five possible development projects.

Using units of millions of dollars, the following table shows the estimated long-run profit (net present value) that each project would generate, as well as the amount of investment required to undertake the project.

	Development Project				
	1	2	3	4	5
Estimated profit (millions)	$1	$ 1.8	$ 1.6	$0.8	$1.4
Capital required (millions)	6	12	10	4	8

The owners of the firm, Dave Peterson and Ron Johnson, have raised $20 million of investment capital for these projects. Dave and Ron now want to select the combination of projects that will maximize their total estimated long-run profit (net present value) without investing more than $20 million.

a. Formulate a BIP model in algebraic form for this problem.

E*   *b.* Formulate and solve this model on a spreadsheet.

E*   *c.* Perform sensitivity analysis on the amount of investment capital made available for the development

projects by using the Solver Table to solve the model with the following amounts of investment capital (in millions of dollars): 16, 18, 20, 22, 24, 26, 28, and 30. Include both the changing cells and the target cell as output cells in the Solver Table.

E*7.4. The board of directors of General Wheels Co. is considering seven large capital investments. Each investment can be made only once. These investments differ in the estimated long-run profit (net present value) that they will generate as well as in the amount of capital required, as shown by the following table:

Investment Opportunity	Estimated Profit (millions)	Capital Required (millions)
1	$17	$43
2	10	28
3	15	34
4	19	48
5	7	17
6	13	32
7	9	23

The total amount of capital available for these investments is $100 million. Investment opportunities 1 and 2 are mutually exclusive, and so are 3 and 4. Furthermore, neither 3 nor 4 can be undertaken unless one of the first two opportunities is undertaken. There are no such restrictions on investment opportunities 5, 6, and 7. The objective is to select the combination of capital investments that will maximize the total estimated long-run profit (net present value).

a. Formulate and solve a BIP model on a spreadsheet for this problem.

b. Perform sensitivity analysis on the amount of capital made available for the investment opportunities by using the Solver Table to solve the model with the following amounts of capital (in millions of dollars): 80, 90, 100, 110, . . . , and 200. Include both the changing cells and the target cell as output cells in the Solver Table.

E*7.5 The Fly-Right Airplane Company builds small jet airplanes to sell to corporations for use by their executives. To meet the needs of these executives, the company's customers sometimes order a custom design of the airplanes

being purchased. When this occurs, a substantial start-up cost is incurred to initiate the production of these airplanes.

Fly-Right has recently received purchase requests from three customers with short deadlines. However, because the company's production facilities already are almost completely tied up filling previous orders, it will not be able to accept all three orders. Therefore, a decision now needs to be made on the number of airplanes the company will agree to produce (if any) for each of the three customers.

The relevant data are given in the table below. The first row gives the start-up cost required to initiate the production of the airplanes for each customer. Once production is under way, the marginal net revenue (which is the purchase price minus the marginal production cost) from each airplane produced is shown in the second row. The third row gives the percentage of the available production capacity that would be used for each airplane produced. The last row indicates the maximum number of airplanes requested by each customer (but less will be accepted).

	Customer 1	Customer 2	Customer 3
Start-up cost	$3 million	$2 million	0
Marginal net revenue	$2 million	$3 million	$0.8 million
Capacity used per plane	20%	40%	20%
Maximum order	3 planes	2 planes	5 planes

Fly-Right now wants to determine how many airplanes to produce for each customer (if any) to maximize the company's total profit (total net revenue minus start-up costs). Formulate and solve a spreadsheet model with both integer variables and binary variables for this problem.

E*7.6. Consider the following special type of shortest path problem (discussed in Section 6.4) where the nodes are in columns and the only paths considered always move forward one column at a time.

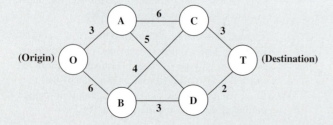

The numbers along the links represent distances (in miles), and the objective is to find the shortest path from the origin to the destination.

This problem also can be formulated as a BIP model involving both mutually exclusive alternatives and contingent decisions. Formulate and solve this BIP model on a spreadsheet. Identify the constraints for (1) mutually exclusive alternatives and (2) contingent decisions.

7.7 Speedy Delivery provides two-day delivery service of large parcels across the United States. Each morning at each collection center, the parcels that have arrived overnight are loaded onto several trucks for delivery throughout the area. Since the competitive battlefield in this business is speed of delivery, the parcels are divided among the trucks according to their geographical destinations to minimize the average time needed to make the deliveries.

On this particular morning, the dispatcher for the Blue River Valley Collection Center, Sharon Lofton, is hard at work. Her three drivers will be arriving in less than an hour to make the day's deliveries. There are nine parcels to be delivered, all at locations many miles apart. As usual, Sharon has loaded these locations into her computer. She is using her company's special software package, a decision support system called Dispatcher.

The first thing Dispatcher does is use these locations to generate a considerable number of attractive possible routes for the individual delivery trucks. These routes are shown in the following table (where the numbers in each column indicate the order of the deliveries), along with the estimated time required to traverse the route.

Delivery Location	Attractive Possible Route									
	1	2	3	4	5	6	7	8	9	10
A	1				1				1	
B		2		1		2			2	2
C			3	3			3		3	
D	2					1		1		
E			2	2		3				
F		1			2					
G	3						1	2		3
H				1	3					1
I		3		4			2			
Time (in hours)	6	4	7	5	4	6	5	3	7	6

Dispatcher is an interactive system that shows these routes to Sharon for her approval or modification. (For example, the computer may not know that flooding has made a particular route infeasible.) After Sharon approves these routes as attractive possibilities with reasonable time estimates, Dispatcher next formulates and solves a BIP model for selecting three routes that minimize their total time while including each delivery location on exactly one route.

E*   a. Using the data in the table, demonstrate how Dispatcher can formulate and solve this BIP model on a spreadsheet.

   b. Describe how the problem addressed in part a is analogous to the crew scheduling problem described in Section 7.4.

E*7.8.   An increasing number of Americans are moving to a warmer climate when they retire. To take advantage of this trend, Sunny Skies Unlimited is undertaking a major real-estate development project. The project is to develop a completely new retirement community (to be

called Pilgrim Haven) that will cover several square miles. One of the decisions to be made is where to locate the two paramedic stations that have been allocated to the community to respond to medical emergencies. For planning purposes, Pilgrim Haven has been divided into five tracts, with no more than one paramedic station to be located in any given tract. Each station is to respond to *all* the medical emergencies that occur in the tract in which it is located as well as in the other tracts that are assigned to this station. Thus, the decisions to be made consist of (1) the tracts to receive a paramedic station and (2) the assignment of each of the other tracts to one of the paramedic stations. The objective is to minimize the overall average of the *response times* to medical emergencies.

The following table gives the average response time to a medical emergency in each tract (the columns) if that tract is served by a station in a given tract (the rows). The bottom row gives the forecasted average number of medical emergencies that will occur in each of the tracts per day.

Assigned Station Located in Tract	Response Times (Minutes) to a Medical Emergency in Tract				
	1	2	3	4	5
1	5	12	30	20	15
2	20	4	15	10	25
3	15	20	6	15	12
4	25	15	25	4	10
5	10	25	15	12	5
Average frequency of medical emergencies per day	2	1	3	1	3

Formulate and solve a BIP model on a spreadsheet for this problem. Identify any constraints that correspond to mutually exclusive alternatives or contingent decisions.

7.9. Reconsider Problem 7.8. The management of Sunny Skies Unlimited now has decided that the decision regarding the locations of the paramedic stations should be based mainly on costs.

The cost of locating a paramedic station in a tract is $200,000 for tract 1, $250,000 for tract 2, $400,000 for tract 3, $300,000 for tract 4, and $500,000 for tract 5. Management's objective now is to determine which tracts should receive a station to minimize the total cost of stations while ensuring that each tract has at least one station close enough to respond to a medical emergency in no more than 15 minutes (on the average). In contrast to the original problem, note that the total number of paramedic stations is no longer fixed. Furthermore, if a tract without a station has more than one station within 15 minutes, it is no longer necessary to assign this tract to just one of these stations.

a. Formulate the algebraic form of a pure BIP model with five binary variables for this problem.

E* *b.* Display and solve this model on a spreadsheet.

7.10. Reconsider the Southwestern Airways crew scheduling problem presented in Section 7.4. Because of a blizzard in the Chicago area, all the flights into and out of Chicago (including flights 4, 6, 7, and 9 in Table 7.5) have been canceled for the time being, so a new crew scheduling plan needs to be developed to cover the seven remaining flights in Table 7.5.

The 12 feasible sequences of flights still are the ones shown in Table 7.5 after deleting the canceled flights. When flights into and out of Chicago had originally been part of a sequence, a crew now would fly as passengers on a Southwestern Airways flight to the next city in the sequence to cover the remaining flights in the sequence. For example, flight sequence 4 now would be San Francisco to Los Angeles to Denver to San Francisco, where a crew would fly as passengers on a flight from Los Angeles to Denver (not shown in the table) to enable serving as the crew from Denver to San Francisco. (Since the original sequence 5 included a round-trip from Denver to Chicago and back, a crew assigned to this sequence now would simply lay over in Denver to await the flight from Denver to San Francisco.) The cost of assigning a crew to any sequence still would be the same as shown in the bottom row of Table 7.5.

The objective still is to minimize the total cost of the crew assignments that cover all the flights. The fact that only 7 flights now need to be covered instead of 11 increases the chance that fewer than three crews will need to be assigned to a flight sequence this time. (The flights where these crews fly as passengers do not need to be covered since they already are assigned to crews that are not based in San Francisco.)

a. Formulate a BIP model in algebraic form for this problem.

E* *b.* Formulate and solve this problem on a spreadsheet.

7.11. Yakima Construction Corporation (YCC) is considering a number of different development projects. The cash outflows that would be required to complete each project are indicated in the table below, along with the expected net present value of each project (all values in millions of dollars).

	Project 1	Project 2	Project 3	Project 4	Project 5
Year 1	$ 8	$10	$12	$4	$14
Year 2	6	8	6	3	6
Year 3	3	7	6	2	5
Year 4	0	5	6	0	7
NPV	$12	$15	$20	$9	$23

Each project must be done in full (with the corresponding cash flows for all four years) or not done at all. Furthermore, there are the following additional considerations. Project 1 cannot be done unless project 2 is also undertaken, and projects 3 and 4 would compete with each other, so they should not both be chosen. YCC expects to have the following cash available to invest in these projects: $40 million for year 1, $25 million for year 2, $16 million for year 3, and $12 million for year 4. Any available money not spent in a given year is then available to spend the following year. YCC's policy is to choose their projects so as to maximize their total expected NPV.

a. Formulate a BIP model in algebraic form for this problem.

E* *b.* Formulate and solve this model on a spreadsheet.

7.12. An electrical utility needs to generate 6,500 megawatts of electricity today. It has five generators. If any electricity is generated by a given generator, that generator must be started up and a fixed start-up cost is incurred. There is an additional cost for each megawatt generated by a generator. These costs, as well as the maximum capacity of each generator, are shown in the following table. The objective is to determine the minimum cost plan that meets the electrical needs for today.

	Generator				
	A	**B**	**C**	**D**	**E**
Fixed start-up cost	$3,000	$2,000	$2,500	$1,500	$1,000
Cost per megawatt generated	$5	$4	$6	$6	$7
Maximum capacity (MW)	2,100	1,800	2,500	1,500	3,000

a. Formulate a BIP model in algebraic form for this problem.

E* *b.* Formulate and solve this model on a spreadsheet.

7.13. The school board for the Bellevue School District has made the decision to purchase 1,350 additional Macintosh computers for computer laboratories in all its schools. Based on past experience, the school board also has directed that these computers should be purchased from some combination of three companies—Educomp, Macwin, and McElectronics. In all three cases, the companies charge a discounted variable cost per computer and a fixed delivery and installation cost for these large sales to school districts. The table below shows these charges as well as the capacity (the maximum number of computers that can be sold from the limited inventory) for each of the companies.

	Educomp	**Macwin**	**McElectronics**
Capacity	700	700	1,000
Fixed cost	$45,000	$35,000	$50,000
Variable cost	$750	$775	$700

The school board wants to determine the minimum-cost plan for meeting its computer needs.

a. Formulate a BIP model in algebraic form for this problem.

E* *b.* Formulate and solve this model on a spreadsheet.

E* *c.* Now suppose that Macwin has not submitted its final bid yet, so the per computer cost is not known with certainty. Generate a Solver Table to show the optimal order quantities and total cost of the optimal solution when the cost per computer for Macwin is $680, $690, $700, $710, . . . , $790, or $800.

E*7.14. Noble Amazon sells books online. Management is trying to determine the best sites for the company's warehouses. Five potential sites are under consideration. Most of the sales come from customers in the United States. The average weekly demand from each region of the country, the average shipping cost from each warehouse site to each region of the country, the fixed cost per week of each warehouse if it is operated, and the maximum capacity of each warehouse (if it is operated) are shown in the table below. Formulate and solve a mixed BIP model in a spreadsheet to determine which warehouse sites Noble Amazon should operate and how books should be distributed from each warehouse to each region of the country to minimize total cost.

	Average Shipping Cost ($/book)					Fixed Cost	Warehouse Capacity
Warehouse Site	**Northwest**	**Southwest**	**Midwest**	**Southeast**	**Northeast**	**(per week)**	**(books/week)**
Spokane, WA	$2.40	$3.50	$4.80	$6.80	$5.75	$40,000	20,000
Reno, NV	$3.25	$2.30	$3.40	$5.25	$6.00	$30,000	20,000
Omaha, NE	$4.05	$3.25	$2.85	$4.30	$4.75	$25,000	15,000
Harrisburg, PA	$5.25	$6.05	$4.30	$3.25	$2.75	$40,000	25,000
Jacksonville, FL	$6.95	$5.85	$4.80	$2.10	$3.50	$30,000	15,000
Customer demand (per week)	8,000	12,000	9,000	14,000	17,000		

E*7.15. Aberdeen Computer Corp. (ACC) is located in Aberdeen, Washington. The company has developed the WebSurfer, a low-cost e-mail and Web-surfing appliance. This product is manufactured at four plants, located in Atlanta, Kansas City, Aberdeen, and Austin. After production, the WebSurfers are shipped to three warehouses, located in Nashville, San Jose, and Houston. ACC sells the WebSurfers through the retail channel. In particular, five different retailers currently sell the WebSurfer—Sears, Circuit City, Fry's, Comp USA, and Office Max. ACC makes weekly shipments to the main warehouses of these five retailers. The shipping cost from each plant to each warehouse, along with the production cost and weekly production capacity at each plant, are given in the table below.

	Shipping Cost ($/unit)			Production Cost ($/unit)	Capacity (units/week)
Plant	**Nashville**	**San Jose**	**Houston**		
Atlanta	$30	$40	$50	$208	200
Kansas City	$25	$45	$40	$214	300
Aberdeen	$45	$30	$55	$215	300
Austin	$30	$50	$30	$210	400

The shipping cost from each warehouse to each customer, the variable cost (cost per unit moved through the warehouse), the capacity (maximum number of units that can be moved through the warehouse per week) for each warehouse, and the weekly demand for each customer are given in the table below.

	Shipping Cost ($/unit)					Variable Cost ($/unit)	Capacity (units/week)
Warehouse	**Sears**	**Circuit City**	**Fry's**	**Comp USA**	**Office Max**		
Nashville	$40	$45	$30	$25	$20	$4	300
San Jose	$15	$50	$25	$15	$40	$5	500
Houston	$50	$35	$15	$40	$50	$5	500
Customer demand (per week)	100	50	75	300	150		

a. Formulate and solve a linear programming model in a spreadsheet to determine the plan for weekly production and distribution of the WebSurfer from the various plants, through the warehouses, to the customers that will minimize total costs.

b. Now suppose that ACC is considering saving money by closing some of its production facilities and/or warehouses. Suppose there is a fixed cost to operate each plant and each warehouse as indicated in the tables to the right. Add binary variables to your model in part *a* to incorporate the decision of which plants and warehouses to keep open so as to minimize total cost (including the fixed costs for any plant or warehouse that is operated).

Plant	Fixed Cost ($/week)
Atlanta	$8,000
Kansas City	$9,000
Aberdeen	$9,000
Austin	$10,000

Warehouse	Fixed Cost ($/week)
Nashville	$4,000
San Jose	$5,000
Houston	$5,000

Case 7-1

Assigning Art

It had been a dream come true for Ash Briggs, a struggling artist living in the San Francisco Bay area. He had made a trip to the corner grocery store late one Friday afternoon to buy some milk, and, on impulse, he had also purchased a California lottery ticket. One week later, he was a multimillionaire.

Ash did not want to squander his winnings on materialistic, trivial items. Instead he wanted to use his money to support his true passion: art. Ash knew all too well the difficulties of gaining recognition as an artist in this post-industrial, technological society where artistic appreciation is rare and financial support even rarer. He therefore decided to use the money to fund an exhibit of up-and-coming modern artists at the San Francisco Museum of Modern Art.

Ash approached the museum directors with his idea, and the directors became excited immediately after he informed them that he would fund the entire exhibit in addition to donating $1 million to the museum. Celeste McKenzie, a museum director, was assigned to work with Ash in planning the exhibit. The exhibit was slated to open one year from the time Ash met with the directors, and the exhibit pieces would remain on display for two months.

Ash began the project by combing the modern art community for potential artists and pieces. He presented a list (see next page) of artists, their pieces, and the price of displaying each piece[2] to Celeste.

Ash possesses certain requirements for the exhibit. He believes the majority of Americans lack adequate knowledge of art and artistic styles, and he wants the exhibit to educate Americans. Ash wants visitors to become aware of the collage as an art form, but he believes collages require little talent. He therefore decides to include only one collage. Additionally, Ash wants viewers to compare the delicate lines in a three-dimensional wire mesh sculpture to the delicate lines in a two-dimensional computer-generated drawing. He therefore wants at least one wire-mesh sculpture displayed if a computer-generated drawing is displayed. Alternatively, he wants at least one computer-generated drawing displayed if a wire-mesh sculpture is displayed. Furthermore, Ash wants to expose viewers to all painting styles, but he wants to limit the number of paintings displayed to achieve a balance in the exhibit between paintings and other art forms. He therefore decides to include at least one photo-realistic painting, at least one cubist painting, at least one expressionist painting, at least one watercolor painting, and at least one oil painting. At the same time, he wants the number of paintings to be no greater than twice the number of other art forms.

Ash wants all his own paintings included in the exhibit since he is sponsoring the exhibit and since his paintings celebrate the San Francisco Bay area, the home of the exhibit.

Ash possesses personal biases for and against some artists. Ash is currently having a steamy affair with Candy Tate, and he wants both of her paintings displayed. Ash counts both David

[2] The display price includes the cost of paying the artist for loaning the piece to the museum, transporting the piece to San Francisco, constructing the display for the piece, insuring the piece while it is on display, and transporting the piece back to its origin.

Lyman and Rick Rawls as his best friends, and he does not want to play favorites among these two artists. He therefore decides to display as many pieces from David Lyman as from Rick Rawls and to display at least one piece from each of them. Although Ziggy Lite is very popular within art circles, Ash believes Ziggy makes a mockery of art. Ash will therefore only accept one display piece from Ziggy, if any at all.

Celeste also possesses her own agenda for the exhibit. As a museum director, she is interested in representing a diverse population of artists, appealing to a wide audience, and creating a politically correct exhibit. To advance feminism, she decides to include at least one piece from a female artist for every two pieces included from a male artist. To advance environmentalism, she decides to include either one or both of the pieces "Aging Earth" and "Wasted Resources." To advance Native American rights, she decides to include at least one piece by Bear Canton. To advance science, she decides to include at least one of the following pieces: "Chaos Reigns?," "Who Has Control?," "Beyond," and "Pioneers."

Celeste also understands that space is limited at the museum. The museum only has enough floor space for four sculptures and enough wall space for 20 paintings, collages, and drawings.

Finally, Celeste decides that if "Narcissism" is displayed, "Reflection" should also be displayed since "Reflection" also suggests narcissism.

Please explore the following questions independently except where otherwise indicated.

a. Ash decides to allocate $4 million to fund the exhibit. Given the pieces available and the specific requirements from Ash and Celeste, formulate and solve a binary integer programming problem to maximize the number of pieces displayed in the exhibit without exceeding the budget. How many pieces are displayed? Which pieces are displayed?

b. To ensure that the exhibit draws the attention of the public, Celeste decides that it must include at least 20 pieces. Formulate and solve a binary integer programming problem to minimize the cost of the exhibit while displaying at least 20 pieces and meeting the requirements set by Ash and Celeste. How much does the exhibit cost? Which pieces are displayed?

Artist	Piece	Description of Piece	Price
Colin Zweibell	"Perfection"	A wire-mesh sculpture of the human body	$300,000
	"Burden"	A wire-mesh sculpture of a mule	250,000
	"The Great Equalizer"	A wire-mesh sculpture of a gun	125,000
Rita Losky	"Chaos Reigns"	A series of computer-generated drawings	400,000
	"Who Has Control?"	A computer-generated drawing intermeshed with lines of computer code	500,000
	"Domestication"	A pen-and-ink drawing of a house	400,000
	"Innocence"	A pen-and-ink drawing of a child	550,000
Norm Marson	"Aging Earth"	A sculpture of trash covering a larger globe	700,000
	"Wasted Resources"	A collage of various packaging materials	575,000
Candy Tate	"Serenity"	An all-blue watercolor painting	200,000
	"Calm before the Storm"	A painting with an all-blue watercolor background and a black watercolor center	225,000
Robert Bayer	"Void"	An all-black oil painting	150,000
	"Sun"	An all-yellow oil painting	150,000
David Lyman	"Storefront Window"	A photo-realistic painting of a jewelry store display window	850,000
	"Harley"	A photo-realistic painting of a Harley-Davidson motorcycle	750,000
Angie Oldman	"Consumerism"	A collage of magazine advertisements	400,000
	"Reflection"	A mirror (considered a sculpture)	175,000
	"Trojan Victory"	A wooden sculpture of a condom	450,000
Rick Rawls	"Rick"	A photo-realistic self-portrait (painting)	500,000
	"Rick II"	A cubist self-portrait (painting)	500,000
	"Rick III"	An expressionist self-portrait (painting)	500,000
Bill Reynolds	"Beyond"	A science fiction oil painting depicting Mars colonization	650,000
	"Pioneers"	An oil painting of three astronauts aboard the space shuttle	650,000
Bear Canton	"Wisdom"	A pen-and-ink drawing of an Apache chieftain	250,000
	"Superior Powers"	A pen-and-ink drawing of a traditional Native American rain dance	350,000
	"Living Land"	An oil painting of the Grand Canyon	450,000
Helen Row	"Study of a Violin"	A cubist painting of a violin	400,000
	"Study of a Fruit Bowl"	A cubist painting of a bowl of fruit	400,000
Ziggy Lite	"My Namesake"	A collage of Ziggy cartoons	300,000
	"Narcissism"	A collage of photographs of Ziggy Lite	300,000
Ash Briggs	"All That Glitters"	A watercolor painting of the Golden Gate Bridge	50,000[*]
	"The Rock"	A watercolor painting of Alcatraz	50,000[*]
	"Winding Road"	A watercolor painting of Lombard Street	50,000[*]
	"Dreams Come True"	A watercolor painting of the San Francisco Museum of Modern Art	50,000[*]

[*]Ash does not require personal compensation, and the cost for moving his pieces to the museum from his home in San Francisco is minimal. The cost of displaying his pieces therefore only includes the cost of constructing the display and insuring the pieces.

c. An influential patron of Rita Losky's work who chairs the museum's board of directors learns that Celeste requires at least 20 pieces in the exhibit. He offers to pay the minimum amount required on top of Ash's $4 million to ensure that exactly 20 pieces are displayed in the exhibit and that all of Rita's pieces are displayed. How much does the patron have to pay? Which pieces are displayed?

Case 7-2

Stocking Sets

Daniel Holbrook, an expediter at the local warehouse for Furniture City, sighed as he moved boxes and boxes of inventory to the side to reach the shelf where the particular item he needed was located. He dropped to his hands and knees and squinted at the inventory numbers lining the bottom row of the shelf. He did not find the number he needed. He worked his way up the shelf until he found the number matching the number on the order slip. Just his luck! The item was on the top row of the shelf! Daniel walked back through the warehouse to find a ladder, stumbling over boxes of inventory littering his path. When he finally climbed the ladder to reach the top shelf, his face crinkled in frustration. Not again! The item he needed was not in stock! All he saw above the inventory number was an empty space covered with dust!

Daniel trudged back through the warehouse to make the dreaded phone call. He dialed the number of Brenda Sims, the saleswoman on the kitchen showroom floor of Furniture City, and informed her that the particular light fixture the customer had requested was not in stock. He then asked her if she wanted him to look for the rest of the items in the kitchen set. Brenda told him that she would talk to the customer and call him back.

Brenda hung up the phone and frowned. Mr. Davidson, her customer, would not be happy. Ordering and receiving the correct light fixture from the regional warehouse would take at least two weeks.

Brenda then paused to reflect upon business during the last month and realized that over 80 percent of the orders for kitchen sets could not be filled because items needed to complete the sets were not in stock at the local warehouse. She also realized that Furniture City was losing customer goodwill and business because of stockouts. The furniture megastore was gaining a reputation for slow service and delayed deliveries, causing customers to turn to small competitors that sold furniture directly from the showroom floor.

Brenda decided to investigate the inventory situation at the local warehouse. She walked the short distance to the building next door and gasped when she stepped inside the warehouse. What she saw could only be described as chaos. Spaces allocated for some items were overflowing into the aisles of the warehouse while other spaces were completely bare. She walked over to one of the spaces overflowing with inventory to determine what item was overstocked. She could not believe her eyes! The warehouse had at least 30 rolls of pea-green wallpaper! No customer had ordered pea-green wallpaper since 1973!

Brenda marched over to Daniel demanding an explanation. Daniel said that the warehouse had been in such a chaotic state since his arrival one year ago. He said the inventory problems occurred because management had a policy of stocking every furniture item on the showroom floor in the local warehouse. Management only replenished inventory every three months, and when inventory was replenished, management ordered every item regardless of whether it had been sold. Daniel also said that he had tried to make management aware of the problems with overstocking unpopular items and understocking popular items, but management would not listen to him because he was simply an expediter.

Brenda understood that Furniture City required a new inventory policy. Not only was the megastore losing money by making customers unhappy with delivery delays, but it was also losing money by wasting warehouse space. By changing the inventory policy to stock only popular items and replenish them immediately when sold, Furniture City would ensure that the majority of customers would receive their furniture immediately and that the valuable warehouse space would be utilized effectively.

Brenda needed to sell her inventory policy to management. Using her extensive sales experience, she decided that the most effective sales strategy would be to use her kitchen department as a model for the new inventory policy. She would identify all kitchen sets comprising 85 percent of customer orders. Given the fixed amount of warehouse space allocated to the kitchen department, she would identify the items Furniture City should stock to satisfy the greatest number of customer orders. She would then calculate the revenue from satisfying customer orders under the new inventory policy, using the bottom line to persuade management to accept her policy.

Brenda analyzed her records over the past three years and determined that 20 kitchen sets were responsible for 85 percent of the customer orders. These 20 kitchen sets were composed of up to eight features in a variety of styles. Brenda listed each feature and its popular styles.

Brenda then created a table (given on page 252) showing the 20 kitchen sets and the particular features composing each set. To simplify the table, she used the codes shown in parentheses below to represent the particular feature and style. For example, kitchen set 1 consists of floor tile T2, wallpaper W2, light fixture L4, cabinet C2, countertop O2, dishwasher D2, sink S2, and range R2. Notice that sets 14 through 20 do not contain dishwashers.

Floor Tile	Wallpaper	Light Fixtures	Cabinets
(T1) White textured tile	(W1) Plain ivory paper	(L1) One large rectangular frosted fixture	(C1) Light solid wood cabinets
(T2) Ivory textured tile	(W2) Ivory paper with dark brown pinstripes	(L2) Three small square frosted fixtures	(C2) Dark solid wood cabinets
(T3) White checkered tile with blue trim	(W3) Blue paper with marble texture	(L3) One large oval frosted fixture	(C3) Light-wood cabinets with glass doors
(T4) White checkered tile with light yellow trim	(W4) Light yellow paper with marble texture	(L4) Three small frosted globe fixtures	(C4) Dark-wood cabinets with glass doors

Countertops	Dishwashers	Sinks	Ranges
(O1) Plain light-wood countertops	(D1) White energy-saving dishwasher	(S1) Sink with separate hot and cold water taps	(R1) White electric oven
(O2) Stained light-wood countertops	(D2) Ivory energy-saving dishwasher	(S2) Divided sink with separate hot and cold water taps and garbage disposal	(R2) Ivory electric oven
(O3) White lacquer-coated countertops		(S3) Sink with one hot and cold water tap	(R3) White gas oven
(O4) Ivory lacquer-coated countertops		(S4) Divided sink with one hot and cold water tap and garbage disposal	(R4) Ivory gas oven

Brenda knew she had only a limited amount of warehouse space allocated to the kitchen department. The warehouse could hold 50 square feet of tile and 12 rolls of wallpaper in the inventory bins. The inventory shelves could hold two light fixtures, two cabinets, three countertops, and two sinks. Dishwashers and ranges are similar in size, so Furniture City stored them in similar locations. The warehouse floor could hold a total of four dishwashers and ranges.

Every kitchen set always includes exactly 20 square feet of tile and exactly five rolls of wallpaper. Therefore, 20 square feet of a particular style of tile and five rolls of a particular style of wallpaper are required for the styles to be in stock.

a. Formulate and solve a binary integer programming problem to maximize the total number of kitchen sets (and thus the number of customer orders) Furniture City stocks in the local warehouse. Assume that when a customer orders a kitchen set, all the particular items composing that kitchen set are replenished at the local warehouse immediately.

b. How many of each feature and style should Furniture City stock in the local warehouse? How many different kitchen sets are in stock?

c. Furniture City decides to discontinue carrying nursery sets, and the warehouse space previously allocated to the nursery department is divided between the existing departments at Furniture City. The kitchen department receives enough additional space to allow it to stock both styles of dishwashers and three of the four styles of ranges. How does the optimal inventory policy for the kitchen department change with this additional warehouse space?

d. Brenda convinces management that the kitchen department should serve as a testing ground for future inventory policies. To provide adequate space for testing, management decides to allocate all the space freed by the nursery department to the kitchen department. The extra space means that the kitchen department can store not only the dishwashers and ranges from part c, but also all sinks, all countertops, three of the four light fixtures, and three of the four cabinets. How much does the additional space help?

e. How would the inventory policy be affected if the items composing a kitchen set could not be replenished immediately? Under what conditions is the assumption of immediate replenishment nevertheless justified?

Case 7-3

Assigning Students to Schools (Revisited)

Reconsider Case 3-5. The Springfield School Board now has made the decision to prohibit the splitting of residential areas among multiple schools. Thus, each of the six areas must be assigned to a single school.

a. Formulate and solve a BIP model for this problem under the current policy of providing busing for all middle school students who must travel more than approximately a mile.

b. Referring to part c of Case 3-5, determine how much the total busing cost increases because of the decision to prohibit the splitting of residential areas among multiple schools.

c, d, e, f. Repeat parts d, e, f, g of Case 3-5 under the new school board decision to prohibit splitting of residential areas among multiple schools.

	T1	T2	T3	T4	W1	W2	W3	W4	L1	L2	L3	L4	C1	C2	C3	C4	O1	O2	O3	O4	D1	D2	S1	S2	S3	S4	R1	R2	R3	R4
Set 1		×				×						×		×						×		×		×				×		
Set 2		×														×				×		×				×		×		
Set 3	×				×				×				×				×				×		×		×				×	
Set 4			×				×			×					×			×	×		×						×			
Set 5				×			×	×			×		×			×				×	×	×		×			×			
Set 6		×				×			×	×													×		×					×
Set 7	×						×					×			×						×	×			×		×			
Set 8		×			×					×							×	×				×		×						×
Set 9		×			×						×		×		×				×									×		
Set 10	×				×				×												×		×			×			×	
Set 11		×	×			×			×				×		×		×	×			×	×							×	
Set 12											×			×										×		×		×		
Set 13								×			×				×		×				×		×		×				×	
Set 14				×				×	×			×							×					×						
Set 15				×			×					×	×				×										×		×	
Set 16			×				×						×						×											
Set 17	×							×		×	×				×				×					×		×	×		×	
Set 18		×					×	×				×		×						×			×					×		
Set 19		×							×				×			×		×		×										×
Set 20		×					×																							×

Chapter **Eight**

Nonlinear Programming

Learning objectives

After completing this chapter, you should be able to

1. Describe how a nonlinear programming model differs from a linear programming model.
2. Recognize when a nonlinear programming model is needed to represent a problem.
3. Formulate a nonlinear programming model from a description of the problem.
4. Construct nonlinear formulas needed for nonlinear programming models.
5. Distinguish between nonlinear programming problems that should be easy to solve and those that may be difficult (if not impossible) to solve.
6. Use the Excel Solver to solve simple types of nonlinear programming problems.
7. Combine the Excel Solver with the Solver Table to attempt to solve some more difficult nonlinear programming problems.
8. Use Evolutionary Solver to attempt to solve some difficult nonlinear programming problems.
9. Recognize when the separable programming technique is applicable to enable using linear programming with a nonlinear objective function.
10. Apply the separable programming technique when applicable.

The previous chapters have introduced you to a wide variety of management science models, including various types of linear programming and integer programming models. However, one characteristic shared by all these linear programming and integer programming models is that they all are *linear models,* that is, models where all the functions (mathematical relationships) involved are linear.

When formulating a linear model in a spreadsheet, this means that the Excel functions being used to express the formulas in output cells include only sums (e.g., C1 + C2, or SUM(C1:C2), or C1 − C2) or products of a number (or data cell) and a changing cell (e.g., 2*C4 or the SUMPRODUCT of data cells with changing cells). If any output cell includes the multiplication or division of changing cells (e.g., C4*C5 or C3/C6 or C4^2) or uses almost any Excel function other than SUM or SUMPRODUCT (such as ROUND, ABS, IF, MAX, MIN, SQRT, etc.), then the resulting model will typically not be linear.

A formula automatically becomes nonlinear if it ever multiplies or divides a changing cell by another changing cell or if it assigns an exponent (other than 1) to any changing cell.

Table 8.1 gives various examples of formulas that could be entered into output cells when the data cells are in column D and the changing cells are in column C. The formulas on the left are all linear while those on the right are not. The first four examples in each column are quite similar. Can you see why the formulas on the left are linear while those on the right are not? The key to seeing this distinction is that a linear formula permits any calculations that involve only the data cells but restricts each changing cell to having only the most basic arithmetic operations: addition or subtraction and multiplication or division by a constant.

Despite the versatility of linear models, managers occasionally encounter problems where such a model does not quite fit because at least one of the formulas that needs to be entered into output cells is not linear. In most cases, this occurs because the formula for the target cell needs to be nonlinear, and this is the case that we will focus on in this chapter. If the model is a linear programming model except for having at least one nonlinear formula for an output cell (such as the target cell), then it is called a *nonlinear programming* model.

TABLE 8.1

Examples of Linear and Nonlinear Formulas in a Spreadsheet When the Data Cells Are in Column D and the Changing Cells Are in Column C

Linear Formulas	Nonlinear Formulas
SUMPRODUCT(D4:D6, C4:C6)	SUMPRODUCT(C4:C6, C1:C3)
[(D1 + D2)/D3]* C4	[(C1 + C2)/C3]* D4
IF(D2 > = 2, 2*C3, 3*C4)	IF(C2 > = 2, 2*C3, 3*C4)
SUMIF(D1:D6, 4, C1:C6)	SUMIF(C1:C6, 4, D1:D6)
SUM(D4:D6)	ROUND(C1)
2*C1 + 3*C4 + C6	MAX(C1, 0)
C1 + C2 + C3	MIN(C1, C2)
	ABS(C1)
	SQRT(C1)
	C1* C2
	C1 / C2
	C1 ^ 2

Note: Data cells are in D1:D6; changing cells are in C1:C6.

Formulating and solving nonlinear programming models often is considerably more challenging than formulating and solving linear programming models. However, these challenges frequently can be overcome, sometimes in relatively straightforward ways. Rest easy. This chapter focuses on the relatively straightforward types of nonlinear programming which require only reasonably routine spreadsheet modeling and the application of the Excel Solver (in some cases) or the Premium Solver (in other cases). This is all a manager (or future manager) needs to know about nonlinear programming. A management science specialist should be called on to deal with more difficult types of nonlinear programming.

Because of the close relationship between linear and nonlinear programming, it is sometimes unclear which technique should be used to analyze a managerial problem. This occurs for problems where the appropriate formula for the target cell is nonlinear but is reasonably close to being linear. In this case, one alternative is to use a linear approximation for the formula so that linear programming can be applied. The advantage is greater ease of formulating and solving the model. Since a model is intended to be only an idealized representation of the real problem, this alternative is reasonable if the linear approximation is a good one. However, the major advantage of using nonlinear programming instead is the greater precision it provides in seeking the best solution for the real problem. When the appropriate nonlinear programming model is not an overly difficult one to formulate and solve, it makes good sense to use this model. If desired, a linear programming model still can be used to perform some quick preliminary analysis, including some what-if analysis, but the greater precision of nonlinear programming should not be foregone lightly for the final analysis.

Nonlinear programming often provides greater precision than linear programming for analyzing managerial problems.

Section 8.1 discusses the challenges encountered when using nonlinear programming. Fortunately, there are some "easy" types of nonlinear programming problems that arise fairly frequently. Two such types are presented in Sections 8.2 and 8.3. Section 8.4 then describes how some "difficult" nonlinear programming problems still can be solved by applying the Excel Solver (or Premium Solver) multiple times with different starting solutions. However, the Excel Solver is unable to solve some other nonlinear programming problems. Therefore, Premium Solver provides an additional procedure called *Evolutionary Solver* for coping with such problems. Evolutionary Solver is described in Section 8.5.

8.1 THE CHALLENGES OF NONLINEAR PROGRAMMING

In almost every respect, a nonlinear programming model is indistinguishable from a linear programming model. In both cases, decisions need to be made regarding the levels of a number of activities, where these activity levels can have any value (including a fractional value) that satisfies a number of constraints. The decisions regarding activity levels are to be based on an overall measure of performance. When the model is formulated in a spreadsheet, the changing cells display the activity levels, output cells help to represent the constraints, and the target cell shows the overall measure of performance.

A nonlinear programming model has the same appearance as a linear programming model except for having a nonlinear formula in at least one output cell (commonly the target cell).

The only way to distinguish a nonlinear programming model from a linear programming model is to examine the formulas entered into the output cells. It is a nonlinear programming model if one or more of these formulas is nonlinear instead of linear. In many applications such a model has only one nonlinear formula and it is the one entered into the target cell. (This is the case we focus on in this chapter.)

Despite such a small difference in the *appearance* of the two kinds of models, their *application* differs in three major ways.

- Nonlinear programming is used to model *nonproportional relationships* between activity levels and the overall measure of performance, whereas linear programming assumes a proportional relationship.

- Constructing the nonlinear formula(s) needed for a nonlinear programming model is considerably more difficult than developing the linear formulas used in linear programming.

- Solving a nonlinear programming model is often much more difficult (if it is possible at all) than solving a linear programming model.

As these comparisons indicate, using nonlinear programming instead of linear programming raises some new challenges. Let us examine these challenges a little more closely.

The Challenge of Nonproportional Relationships

When either a linear programming model or a nonlinear programming model is formulated in a spreadsheet, the target cell needs to show the overall measure of performance that results from the activity levels that are displayed in the changing cells. However, nonlinear programming uses a more complicated relationship between the activity levels and the overall measure of performance than does linear programming.

In the case of linear programming, this relationship is assumed to be a particularly simple one. To illustrate, consider again the Wyndor Glass Co. problem introduced in Section 2.1 and formulated in Section 2.2. The activities for this problem are the production of the special new doors and the special new windows, where the levels of these activities are

D = Number of doors to be produced per week

W = Number of windows to be produced per week

The overall measure of performance is the total weekly profit obtained from the production and sale of these doors and windows. The unit profit has been estimated to be $300 for each door and $500 for each window. The graphs in Figure 8.1 show the resulting relationship between the level of each activity (D and W) and the contribution of that activity to the overall measure of performance. The straight line in each graph shows a **proportional relationship**

FIGURE 8.1

Profit graphs for the Wyndor Glass Co. that show the weekly profit from each product versus the production rate for that product.

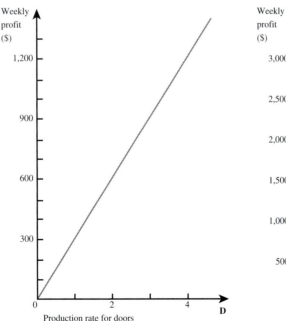

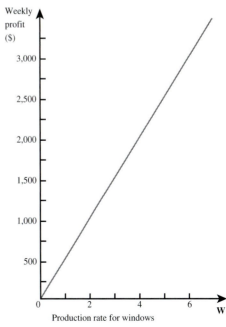

because the weekly profit from each product is *proportional* to the production rate for that product. These straight lines also indicate that the objective function

$$\text{Profit} = \$300D + \$500W$$

is *linear*. The fact that this formula being entered into the target cell is linear helps to make the overall model a linear programming model.

As illustrated by the Wyndor Glass Co. problem, *every* linear programming problem assumes a proportional relationship between each activity and the overall measure of performance. This key assumption can be summarized as follows.

> **Proportionality Assumption of Linear Programming:** The contribution of each activity to the value of the objective function is *proportional* to the level of the activity.[1] In other words, the term in the objective function involving this activity consists of a coefficient times a decision variable, where the coefficient is the contribution per unit of this activity and the decision variable is the level of this activity. (For example, for each product in the Wyndor Glass Co. problem, the coefficient is the product's unit profit and the decision variable is the production rate for the product.)

Nonlinear programming problems arise when this assumption is violated. This occurs whenever any activity has a **nonproportional relationship** with the overall measure of performance because the contribution of the activity to this measure of performance is *not proportional* to the level of the activity.

Figure 8.2 shows four examples of different types of nonproportional relationships. (For definiteness, these graphs assume that the overall measure of performance is profit, but any other measure to be maximized also could be used.)

Nonlinear programming problems arise when the proportionality assumption of linear programming is violated.

FIGURE 8.2
Examples of profit graphs with nonproportional relationships:
(a) decreasing marginal returns; *(b)* piecewise linear with decreasing marginal returns;
(c) decreasing marginal returns except for discontinuities; and
(d) increasing marginal returns.

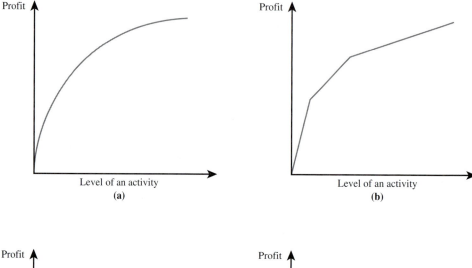

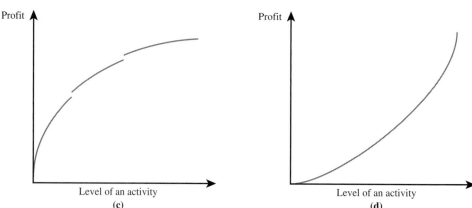

---

[1] The same assumption also is made about the contribution of each activity to the left-hand side of each functional constraint, but we are focusing in this chapter on how to deal with a lack of proportionality in the objective function.

The first of these examples, shown in Figure 8.2(a), illustrates a profit graph with *decreasing marginal returns.*

> Consider any activity where a graph of its profit versus the level of the activity is plotted. Suppose that the *slope* (steepness) of the graph never increases but sometimes decreases as the level of the activity increases. Then the activity is said to have **decreasing marginal returns.**

Similarly, in problems where the objective is to minimize the total cost of the activities, an activity is said to have decreasing marginal returns if the slope of its *cost graph* never decreases but sometimes *increases* as the level of the activity increases.[2]

Since frequently it is difficult to continue increasing profit at the same rate as the level of an activity keeps getting pushed higher and higher, activities with decreasing marginal returns are fairly common. For example, it may be necessary to lower the price of a product to increase its sales. Alternatively, if the price is held constant, the marketing costs may need to go up more than proportionally to attain increases in the level of sales. (The next section begins with an example in which marketing costs behave in this way.) Decreasing marginal returns also occur when less efficient facilities and personnel need to be used to increase the level of an activity.

Figure 8.2(b) illustrates a profit graph that is **piecewise linear** because it consists of a sequence of connected line segments. As the level of the activity increases, the slope of the profit graph remains the same within each line segment but then decreases at the kink where the next line segment begins. Since the slope never increases as the level of the activity increases but does decrease at the kinks, this profit graph also fits the definition of having decreasing marginal returns. This kind of graph might occur, for example, because overtime needs to be used to increase the level of the activity beyond the first kink, and then even more expensive weekend overtime is needed to increase the level beyond the second kink.

Figure 8.2(c) provides an example of a nonproportional relationship that does not quite have decreasing marginal returns. The reason it does not is that there are spots called **discontinuities** where the profit graph is disconnected because it suddenly jumps up or down. Such discontinuities could occur, for example, because quantity discounts for purchasing a component of a product become available when the production level for the product rises above certain thresholds.

Having activities with decreasing marginal returns is not the only way in which the proportionality assumption can be violated. For example, another way is to have activities with *increasing* marginal returns, as illustrated by Figure 8.2(d). In this case, the slope of the profit graph never decreases but sometimes *increases* as the level of the activity increases. (Similarly, a *cost graph* exhibits increasing marginal returns if its slope never increases but sometimes *decreases* as the level of the activity increases.) This can occur because of the greater efficiencies sometimes achieved at higher levels of an activity.

Profit graphs are used when the overall objective is to maximize the total profit from all the activities. However, *cost graphs* are needed instead when the overall objective is to *minimize* the total cost of all the activities. An activity can violate the proportionality assumption in the same ways that are illustrated in Figure 8.2 if its cost graph has any of the shapes shown in Figure 8.3. For each case, note how this cost graph bends in the opposite way from the corresponding profit graph in Figure 8.2. Thus, an increasing slope in the cost graph reflects decreasing marginal returns, whereas a decreasing slope reflects increasing marginal returns. (The same conclusion applies to graphs where the objective is to *minimize* some overall measure of performance other than total cost.)

Figures 8.2 and 8.3 illustrate only some of the possible nonproportional relationships. For example, an activity might have *neither* decreasing marginal returns nor increasing marginal returns because the slope of its graph sometimes decreases and sometimes increases as the level of the activity increases.

In addition, sometimes there are interactions between activities that cause (or help to cause) the objective function to be nonlinear. To illustrate, consider the Wyndor Glass Co. problem again. Suppose now that a major advertising campaign will be required to market

Many activities have decreasing marginal returns.

An activity has increasing marginal returns if its efficiency increases as the level of the activity is increased.

---

[2] Using mathematical terminology, a profit graph with decreasing marginal returns is said to be a *concave function,* whereas a cost graph with decreasing marginal returns is said to be a *convex function.* We are using the more suggestive economic term, decreasing marginal returns, to cover both cases (including for functions of multiple decision variables).

FIGURE 8.3

Examples of cost graphs with nonproportional relationships: (*a*) decreasing marginal returns; (*b*) piecewise linear with decreasing marginal returns; (*c*) decreasing marginal returns except for discontinuities; and (*d*) increasing marginal returns. Each cost graph bends in the opposite way from the corresponding profit graph in Figure 8.2.

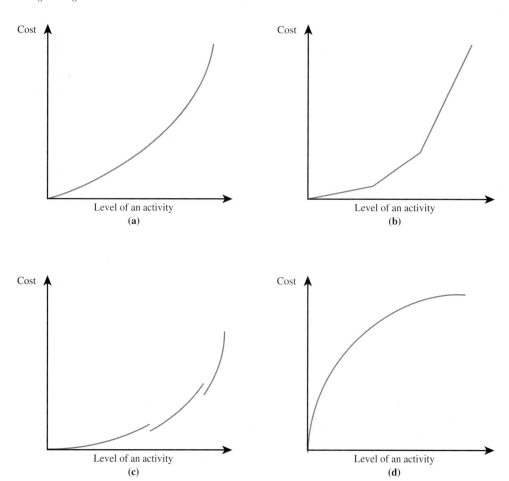

either new product if it is produced by itself, but that the same single campaign can be used to effectively promote both products if both are produced. Because a major cost is saved for the second product, their joint profit is somewhat more than the sum of their individual profits when each is produced by itself. In particular, the appropriate objective function is, say,

$$\text{Profit} = \$300D + \$500W + \$100DW$$

where *DW* denotes the *product* of *D* and *W*. Because of the cross-product term, $\$100DW$, this objective function is nonlinear even though, when either *D* or *W* is fixed at some value, the proportionality assumption still holds for the other product.

When there are interactions between activities, the total profit from all the activities sometimes will still have decreasing marginal returns. (The common technical term for this is that the objective function is *concave.*) The intuitive interpretation of decreasing marginal returns (a profit graph that never bends up but sometimes bends down) continues to apply here. We will not bother with the complex technical definition that is needed in this case.

> Even when the proportionality assumption is satisfied, interactions between activities still can lead to a nonlinear programming model.

The Challenge of Constructing Nonlinear Formulas

For a linear programming model, it is relatively simple to construct the formula that needs to be entered into the target cell by using a SUMPRODUCT function. For example, when the target cell gives the total profit from all the activities (as for the Wyndor Glass Co. problem), each product being summed is simply the product of the unit profit for an activity (as given in a data cell) and the level of that activity (as given in a changing cell).

Considerably more work is needed for a nonlinear programming problem. Even when there are no interactions between activities, it is necessary to construct a nonlinear formula for each activity that represents the contribution of that activity to the objective function that needs to be entered into the target cell. For example, when the objective is to maximize total profit, the nonlinear formula for each activity needs to correspond to the profit graph for that activity.

FIGURE 8.4

An example of an activity for which prior data are available on the profit versus the level of the activity, so Excel's curve fitting method can be applied.

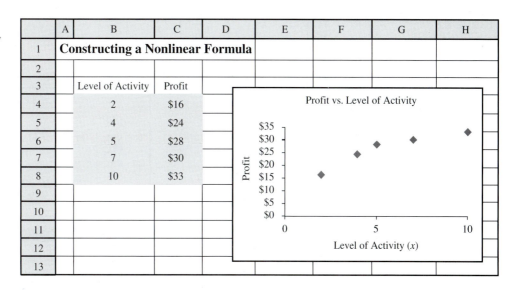

	A	B	C	D	E	F	G	H
1		**Constructing a Nonlinear Formula**						
2								
3		Level of Activity	Profit					
4		2	$16					
5		4	$24					
6		5	$28					
7		7	$30					
8		10	$33					
9								
10								
11								
12								
13								

FIGURE 8.5

The Format Trendline dialogue box that is used to perform the curve fitting method in Excel. For this example, the Polynomial of Order 2 option (a quadratic equation) is chosen for the type of regression. The option to display the equation on the chart is selected.

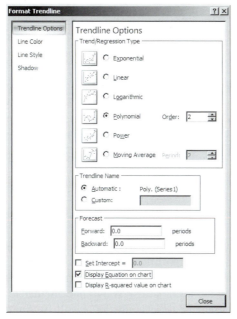

One useful method for fitting a nonlinear formula to a graph begins by assuming a general form for the formula. For a profit graph with decreasing marginal returns, it is common to assume a quadratic form, such as

This quadratic form for a profit graph (or a cost graph) is widely used.

$$\text{Profit from an activity} = a x^2 + b x + c$$

where x is the level of the activity and a is a *negative* constant. Another possibility is to assume a logarithmic form, like

$$\text{Profit from an activity} = a \ln(x) + b$$

where $\ln(x)$ is called the natural logarithm of x.

In either case, the next step is to find the appropriate values of the parameters (e.g., *a, b,* and *c*). Excel has a built-in **curve fitting method** to find the values of the parameters that best fit the data. For example, suppose that prior data (or at least estimates) are available on the profit that would be achieved at several levels of the activity, as shown in the spreadsheet in Figure 8.4.

The first step in applying the curve fitting method in Excel is to graph the profit data (profit versus level of the activity), using an X–Y scatter chart. Next, select the graph by clicking on it and then choose "More Trendline Options" from the Trendline menu on the Chart Tools Layout tab (for Excel 2007) or "Add Trendline" from the Chart menu (for earlier versions of Excel). This brings up the dialogue box shown in Figure 8.5. (The dialogue box

FIGURE 8.6

The quadratic equation found by Excel that most closely matches the profit versus level of activity data for the example introduced in Figure 8.4.

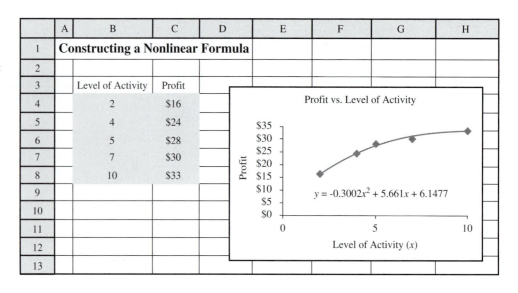

	A	B	C	D	E	F	G	H
1		**Constructing a Nonlinear Formula**						
2								
3		Level of Activity	Profit					
4		2	$16					
5		4	$24					
6		5	$28					
7		7	$30					
8		10	$33					
9								
10								
11								
12								
13								

The order of a polynomial is the highest exponent used in the polynomial. For a quadratic equation, the order is 2.

has a different layout for Excel versions earlier than 2007.) Use this dialogue box to choose the *form* of the equation that you want Excel to fit to the data. For example, to fit a quadratic equation to the data, choose Polynomial with Order 2.

Next choose the option to "Display equation on chart" and click on OK. (For Excel versions earlier than 2007, this option is available by first clicking the Options tab.) Excel then chooses the parameters for the equation of the chosen form that most closely fits the graphed data. For example, the quadratic equation that most closely matches the data in Figure 8.4 is

$$\text{Profit} = -0.3002\, x^2 + 5.661\, x + 6.1477$$

This equation is shown and plotted directly on the graph of profit versus activity level, as shown in Figure 8.6.

The quadratic form provides at least a reasonable approximation for many profit graphs, so it is used often. However, it is prudent to check whether the approximation actually is a reasonable one for any particular activity. This is done by estimating the profit that would be obtained by the activity at several different levels in addition to the data being used by the curve fitting method, and then checking whether the profit at these other levels is reasonably close to what is given by the formula. If it is not, one alternative is to collect more data and reapply the curve fitting method to seek a better overall fit. Another alternative is to adopt a different form for the formula (e.g., logarithmic) and then to apply the corresponding curve fitting method.

The Challenge of Solving Nonlinear Programming Models

It is easy to solve linear programming models with either the Excel Solver or a variety of other software packages. Very large problems are solved routinely every day. In fact, the most advanced software packages now are successfully solving amazingly huge problems. Furthermore, the solution obtained is guaranteed to be optimal.

Despite excellent progress in recent years, life is not nearly this good when dealing with nonlinear programming models. They often are much more difficult to solve than linear programming models. Furthermore, even when a solution is obtained, it sometimes cannot be guaranteed to be optimal.

Although some nonlinear programming models can be very difficult to solve, those that have decreasing marginal returns generally are relatively easy.

Fortunately, some types of nonlinear programming models are relatively easy to solve. Cases (*a*) and (*b*) in Figure 8.2 (when maximizing) or in Figure 8.3 (when minimizing) are examples of "easy" types of nonlinear programming models, namely, types where the activities have decreasing marginal returns. As long as all the activities fit either case (except for any that still satisfy the proportionality assumption), formulating the model in a spreadsheet is not especially difficult and the Excel Solver can readily solve the model if it is not unusually large. The next section focuses on case (*a*) and Section 8.3 considers case (*b*).

FIGURE 8.7

An example of a complicated nonlinear programming model where the Excel Solver obtains three different final solutions when it starts with three different initial solutions.

	A	B	C	D	E
1	Solver Solution				
2	(Starting with $x = 0$)				
3					
4					Maximum
5		$x =$	0.371	$\leq$	5
6					
7		Profit = $0.5x^5 - 6x^4 + 24.5x^3 - 39x^2 + 20x$			
8		=	$3.19		

	A	B	C	D	E
1	Solver Solution				
2	(Starting with $x = 3$)				
3					
4					Maximum
5		$x =$	3.126	$\leq$	5
6					
7		Profit = $0.5x^5 - 6x^4 + 24.5x^3 - 39x^2 + 20x$			
8		=	$6.13		

	A	B	C	D	E
1	Solver Solution				
2	(Starting with $x = 4.7$)				
3					
4					Maximum
5		$x =$	5.000	$\leq$	5
6					
7		Profit = $0.5x^5 - 6x^4 + 24.5x^3 - 39x^2 + 20x$			
8		=	$0.00		

	B	C
7	Profit =	Profit = $0.5x^5 - 6x^4 + 24.5x^3 - 39x^2 + 20x$
8	=	=0.5* x^5-6*x^4+24.5*x^3-39*x^2+20*x

Range Name	Cell
Maximum	E5
x	C5
Profit	C8

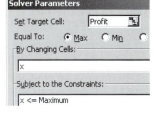

Solver Parameters

Set Target Cell: Profit

Equal To: ⦿ Max ○ Min ○

By Changing Cells:

x

Subject to the Constraints:

x <= Maximum

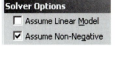

Solver Options

☐ Assume Linear Model

☑ Assume Non-Negative

Unfortunately, other types of nonlinear programming tend to be more difficult. For example, even though case (*c*) in Figures 8.2 and 8.3 has decreasing marginal returns except at the discontinuities in the graph, the presence of such discontinuities for any of the activities makes it uncertain that the Excel Solver will successfully solve the model. Having increasing marginal returns, as in case (*d*), also can create serious complications.

Far more complicated nonlinear programming models can be constructed than any of those suggested by Figures 8.2 and 8.3. For example, consider the following model in algebraic form.

$$\text{Maximize} \quad \text{Profit} = 0.5x^5 - 6x^4 + 24.5x^3 - 39x^2 + 20x$$

subject to

$$x \leq 5$$

$$x \geq 0$$

In this case, there is only a single activity, where x represents the level of this activity. Furthermore, there is only a single functional constraint ($x \leq 5$) in addition to the nonnegativity constraint. Nevertheless, Figure 8.7 demonstrates what a difficult time the Excel Solver has in attempting to cope with this problem. The model is straightforward to formulate in a spreadsheet, with x (C5) as the changing cell and Profit (C8) as the target cell. (Note that the Solver option, Assume Linear Model, is *not* chosen in this case because this is not a linear programming model.) When $x = 0$ is entered as the initial value in the changing cell, the left spreadsheet in Figure 8.7 shows that Solver then indicates that $x = 0.371$ is the optimal solution with Profit = $3.19. However, if $x = 3$ is entered as the initial value instead, as in the middle spreadsheet in Figure 8.7, Solver obtains $x = 3.126$ as the optimal solution with Profit = $6.13. Trying still another initial value of $x = 4.7$ in the right spreadsheet, Solver now indicates an optimal solution of $x = 5$ with Profit $0. What is going on here?

Plotting the profit graph for such a complicated objective function is a difficult task, but doing so in Figure 8.8 does help to explain Solver's difficulties with this problem. Starting at $x = 0$, the profit graph does indeed climb to a peak at $x = 0.371$, as reported in the left spreadsheet of Figure 8.7. Starting at $x = 3$ instead, the graph climbs to a peak at $x = 3.126$, which is the solution found in the middle spreadsheet. Using the right spreadsheet's starting solution of $x = 4.7$, the graph climbs until it reaches the boundary imposed by the $x \leq 5$ constraint, so $x = 5$ is the peak in that direction. These three peaks are referred to as the **local maxima**

FIGURE 8.8

The profit graph for the example considered in Figure 8.7.

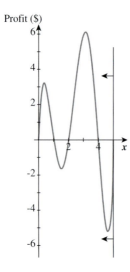

Profit ($)

When maximizing, the standard Excel Solver only climbs to a local maximum and stops. This local maximum may or may not be the global maximum.

A nonlinear programming problem needs to have decreasing marginal returns to guarantee that the solution obtained by the Excel Solver actually is optimal.

(or *local optima*) because each one is a maximum of the graph within a local neighborhood of that point. However, only the largest of these local maxima is the **global maximum,** that is, the highest point on the entire graph. Thus, the middle spreadsheet in Figure 8.7 did succeed in finding the optimal solution at $x = 3.126$ with Profit = \$6.13.

The algorithm used by the Excel Solver to solve nonlinear programming problems can be thought of as a mountain climbing procedure. It starts at the initial solution entered into the changing cells and then begins climbing that mountain until it reaches the peak (or is blocked from climbing further by reaching the boundary imposed by the constraints). The procedure terminates when it reaches this peak (or boundary) and reports this solution. It has no way of detecting whether there is a taller mountain somewhere else on the profit graph.

When the target cell is to be minimized instead of maximized, this algorithm reverses direction and climbs down until it reaches the lowest point in that valley (or is blocked by a boundary). Once again, it has no way of detecting whether there is a lower valley somewhere else on the cost graph.

The reason that having decreasing marginal returns for all the activities (except any with a proportional relationship) is an easy type of nonlinear programming problem is that the profit graph (when maximizing) has only one mountain. Therefore, a local maximum at the peak of the mountain (or a boundary) also is a global maximum, so the solution obtained by the Excel Solver is guaranteed to be optimal. For example, the profit graph based on a quadratic form in Figure 8.6 has decreasing marginal returns, so it has only a single mountain and its peak (which happens to be at $x = 9.43$) is the global maximum. Similarly, when minimizing a cost graph with decreasing marginal returns, there is only one valley so the local minimum at the bottom (or a boundary) also is a global minimum.

Figure 8.7 suggests that one way of dealing with more difficult problems that may have multiple local optima is to apply the Excel Solver repeatedly with a variety of starting solutions and then adopt the best of the final solutions obtained. Although this will not guarantee finding a globally optimal solution, it often will provide a good chance of finding at least a very good solution. Therefore, this is a reasonable approach for some relatively small problems, particularly when a systematic procedure is used to provide a comprehensive cross-section of starting solutions. Solver Table in your MS Courseware is a useful tool for systematically providing starting solutions when only one or two decision variables are being changed simultaneously. Section 8.4 describes this kind of approach to problems that may have multiple local optima.

However, this kind of approach is not very practical for problems with a large number of decision variables, since a huge number of starting solutions would be required to provide a comprehensive cross-section for such problems. What is needed is an algorithm that occasionally will "jump" from the current mountain to another more promising mountain on the profit graph so that the algorithm is likely to eventually reach the tallest mountain on its own regardless of which starting solution is entered into the changing cells. Premium Solver (available in your MS Courseware) provides such an algorithm called *Evolutionary Solver.* Although Evolutionary Solver has its limitations as well, it provides an excellent complement to the Excel Solver for attempting to cope with many nonlinear programming problems. Evolutionary Solver and its use are described in Section 8.5.

Review
Questions

1. What are the features of linear programming models that are shared by nonlinear programming models?
2. How does the appearance of a nonlinear programming model differ from that of a linear programming model?
3. In what three major ways does the application of nonlinear programming models differ from that of linear programming models?
4. What is the proportionality assumption of linear programming that is violated by nonlinear programming problems?
5. When an activity has decreasing marginal returns, how does the slope of its profit graph behave?
6. What could cause the profit graph of an activity to be piecewise linear with decreasing marginal returns?
7. What is a common assumption about the form of the formula for the profit of an activity when applying a curve fitting method?
8. What are the types of nonlinear programming models that are relatively easy to solve?
9. When it is given a starting solution, how does the Excel Solver then proceed to attempt to solve a maximization problem with multiple local maxima?
10. What can be done to give the Excel Solver a better chance of obtaining an optimal solution (or at least a very good solution) for a maximization problem with multiple local maxima?

8.2 NONLINEAR PROGRAMMING WITH DECREASING MARGINAL RETURNS

In this section, we will focus on nonlinear programming problems having the following characteristics.

1. The same constraints as for a linear programming model.
2. A nonlinear objective function.
3. Each activity that violates the proportionality assumption of linear programming has *decreasing marginal returns* (as defined in the preceding section and illustrated in Figures 8.2[a] and 8.3[a]).

The Excel Solver can readily solve such problems because the solution it obtains is guaranteed to be optimal for this type of problem.

This is a particularly simple type of nonlinear programming problem. The Excel Solver can readily solve such problems if they are not unusually large.

For some problems of this type, the objective function will include cross-product terms involving the product of two or more decision variables. In this case, whenever all but one of the decision variables are fixed at particular values, the effect on the value of the objective function of increasing the one decision variable must still satisfy either proportionality or decreasing marginal returns for the third characteristic to hold. (The precise mathematical description of the third characteristic is that an objective function being maximized is required to be *concave* whereas an objective function being minimized is required to be *convex*.)

As discussed in the preceding section, it is fairly common for an activity to provide less and less return as the level of the activity is increased, so the activity has decreasing marginal returns. Consequently, nonlinear programming problems with decreasing marginal returns arise fairly frequently. We will go through two examples in some detail to illustrate how this happens and then describe how to formulate and solve such a problem.

In some cases, when the nonlinear objective function is reasonably close to being linear, a linear programming model will be used as an approximation to perform the preliminary analysis and then a more precise nonlinear programming model will be used to do the detailed

FIGURE 8.9

The spreadsheet model that was formulated in Section 2.2 for the original Wyndor problem introduced in Section 2.1.

	A	B	C	D	E	F	G
1		**Wyndor Glass Co. Product-Mix Problem**					
2							
3			Doors	Windows			
4		Unit Profit	$300	$500			
5					Hours		Hours
6			Hours Used per Unit Produced		Used		Available
7		Plant 1	1	0	2	≤	4
8		Plant 2	0	2	12	≤	12
9		Plant 3	3	2	18	≤	18
10							
11			Doors	Windows			Total Profit
12		Units Produced	2	6			$3,600

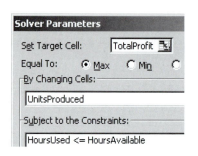

Solver Parameters

Set Target Cell: TotalProfit

Equal To: ⦿ Max ○ Min ○

By Changing Cells:

UnitsProduced

Subject to the Constraints:

HoursUsed <= HoursAvailable

	E
5	Hours
6	Used
7	=SUMPRODUCT(C7:D7,UnitsProduced)
8	=SUMPRODUCT(C8:D8,UnitsProduced)
9	=SUMPRODUCT(C9:D9,UnitsProduced)

	G
11	Total Profit
12	=SUMPRODUCT(UnitProfit,UnitsProduced)

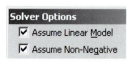

Solver Options

☑ Assume Linear Model
☑ Assume Non-Negative

Range Name	Cells
HoursAvailable	G7:G9
HoursUsed	E7:E9
HoursUsedPerUnitProduced	C7:D9
TotalProfit	G12
UnitProfit	C4:D4
UnitsProduced	C12:D12

analysis. This is what is happening below as the story of the Wyndor Glass Co. case study continues to unfold.

Continuation of the Wyndor Glass Co. Case Study

As described in Section 2.1, the Wyndor Glass Co. produces high-quality glass products, where different parts of the production are performed in three plants. It now is launching two new products (a special kind of door and a special kind of window), where the anticipated profit has been estimated to be $300 per door and $500 per window. Section 2.2 discusses how these estimates of the unit profits, along with information regarding constraints, have led to the formulation of a linear programming model whose objective function to be maximized is Profit = $300D + $500W$, where D and W are the number of doors and windows to be produced per week, respectively.

To refresh your memory, Figure 8.9 shows the spreadsheet model that was formulated in Section 2.2 for this problem. Having clicked on the Solve button, the changing cells Units-Produced (C12:D12) give the optimal solution, $(D, W) = (2, 6)$, and the target cell TotalProfit (G12) indicates that this will yield a weekly profit of $3,600, according to the model.

This model assumes that the profit from either of these new products would be *proportional* to the production rate for the product. However, this is a questionable assumption. Therefore, before making a final decision on the production rates, Wyndor management wants a more precise analysis to be done, as described in the following conversation between two members of management.

John Hill (Wyndor president): How are your marketing plans coming along for the launch of our two new products, Ann? Will it be very expensive?

Ann Lester (Wyndor vice president for marketing): That depends on what sales volume we need to generate. Our market research indicates that we would be able to sell small numbers of the new doors and windows with virtually no advertising. However, it also tells us that we would need an extensive advertising campaign if we produce close to what our plants can handle. Has a final decision been made yet on the production rates?

John: No, it hasn't. In fact, that's why I asked you to come see me. We would like to ask for your help.

Ann: Sure. What can I do?

John: Well, basically what we want is your updated input on what the marketing costs per week would need to be to sell each product if the production rate were to be set at each of several alternative values.

Ann: Sure, I can do that. When they started their analysis before, I was asked to estimate the marketing cost per door and per window. I told them $75 per door and $200 per window. Those looked like good estimates at the time.

John: Yes. Those cost estimates were factored in when they developed their estimated profits of $300 per door and $500 per window. Do your cost estimates still look pretty close?

Ann: No, not really. I don't think it makes sense any more to figure our marketing costs on a per door or per window basis. As I was saying before, our costs would be very small with low production rates, but would need to be very substantial with high production rates. Therefore, figuring $75 per door and $200 per window is much too large with low production rates, about right at medium production rates, and much too small at high production rates.

John: Yes, that's what I suspected. That's why we want you to forget about doing it now on a per door or per window basis and instead estimate your weekly marketing costs for each product if the production rate were to be set at each of several alternative values. This will enable the Management Science Group to perform a more precise analysis of what the production rates should be.

Ann: That makes sense. I'll pull these new estimates together right away.

> A linear formula is no longer adequate for estimating the marketing costs.

After receiving these estimates, the Management Science Group plotted the weekly marketing cost for each product versus the production rate of the product. Each of these plots showed that the marketing cost increases roughly with the *square* of the production rate as this rate is increased. Therefore, a *quadratic form* was assumed to apply Excel's curve fitting procedure to each of these plots.

This curve fitting procedure estimated that the weekly marketing costs required to sustain a production rate of D doors per week would be roughly

$$\text{Marketing cost for doors} = \$25D^2$$

for any fractional or integer value of D permitted by the production constraints. Excluding marketing costs, the gross profit per door sold is about $375. Therefore, the weekly net profit would be roughly

$$\text{Net profit for doors} = \$375D - \$25D^2$$

> The new estimates of marketing costs cause both the doors and windows to have decreasing marginal returns.

The corresponding estimates per week for windows are

$$\text{Marketing cost for windows} = \$66\tfrac{2}{3}W^2$$
$$\text{Gross profit for windows} = \$700W$$
$$\text{Net profit for windows} = \$700W - \$66\tfrac{2}{3}W^2$$

FIGURE 8.10

The smooth curves are the profit graphs for Wyndor's doors and windows for the version of its problem where nonlinear marketing costs must be considered.

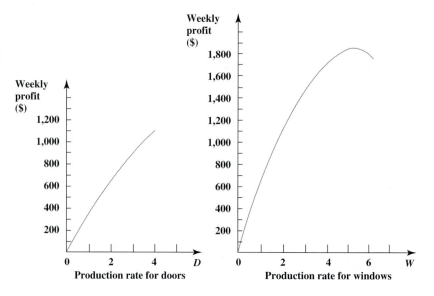

Figure 8.10 shows the resulting profit graphs for both products. Note that both curves show decreasing marginal returns, where this becomes particularly pronounced for larger values of *W*.

Combining the net profit for doors and for windows, the new objective function to be maximized for this problem is

$$\text{Profit} = \$375D - \$25D^2 + \$700W - \$66\tfrac{2}{3}W^2$$

subject to the same constraints as before. Because the terms involving D^2 and W^2 have exponents different from 1 for these decision variables, this objective function is a *nonlinear* function. Therefore, the overall problem is a *nonlinear programming* problem. Furthermore, because this objective function has a *quadratic form* (and the problem has all three characteristics listed at the beginning of this section), the overall problem is a special type of nonlinear programming problem called a **quadratic programming** problem. This is a common type of nonlinear programming problem and also a particularly convenient type to formulate and solve. Special algorithms have been developed just to solve quadratic programming problems very efficiently, so commercial management science software packages often include such an algorithm to enable solving huge problems of this type. (However, the Excel Solver only uses a general algorithm for solving any nonlinear programming problem with decreasing marginal returns.)

> A quadratic programming problem has linear constraints and an objective function that has both a quadratic form and decreasing marginal returns.

A Spreadsheet Formulation

Figure 8.11 shows the formulation of a spreadsheet model for this problem. It is interesting to compare this model with the one for the original Wyndor problem in Figure 8.9. At first glance, they appear to be nearly the same. A closer examination reveals four significant differences.

First, the unit profits in row 4 of Figure 8.9 have been replaced here by the *gross* unit profits, which exclude the marketing costs.

Second, to take the marketing costs into account in calculating the target cell TotalProfit (H16), the spreadsheet in Figure 8.11 has added several output cells: GrossProfitFromSales (H12), MarketingCost (C14:D14), and TotalMarketingCost (H14).

Third, a fundamental difference lies in the equations entered into certain output cells. In Figure 8.9, the formula for TotalProfit (G12) is expressed in terms of the SUMPRODUCT function that is characteristic of linear programming when each product is the product of a data cell and a changing cell. In Figure 8.11, something else is needed for calculating the marketing cost portion of total profit because that portion of the objective function is nonlinear. For example, consider the term involving D^2 in the objective function. Because the value of *D* appears in DoorsProduced

FIGURE 8.11

A spreadsheet model for the Wyndor nonlinear programming problem with nonlinear marketing costs, where the changing cells UnitsProduced (C12:D12) show the optimal production rates and the target cell TotalProfit (H16) gives the resulting total profit per week.

	A	B	C	D	E	F	G	H
1		**Wyndor Problem with Nonlinear Marketing Costs**						
2								
3			Doors	Windows				
4		Unit Profit (Gross)	$375	$700				
5					Hours		Hours	
6			Hours Used per Unit Produced		Used		Available	
7		Plant 1	1	0	3.214	≤	4	
8		Plant 2	0	2	8.357	≤	12	
9		Plant 3	3	2	18	≤	18	
10								
11			Doors	Windows				
12		Units Produced	3.214	4.179			Gross Profit from Sales	$4,130
13								
14		Marketing Cost	$258	$1,164			Total Marketing Cost	$1,422
15								
16							Total Profit	$2,708

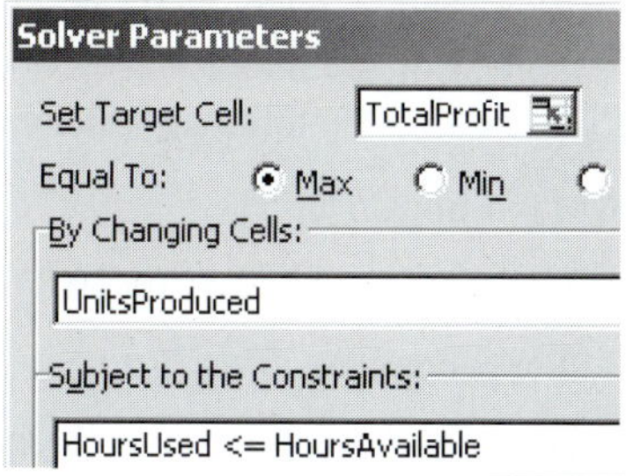

Solver Parameters

Set Target Cell: TotalProfit
Equal To: ⦿ Max ○ Min ○
By Changing Cells:
UnitsProduced
Subject to the Constraints:
HoursUsed <= HoursAvailable

	E
5	Hours
6	Used
7	=SUMPRODUCT(C7:D7,UnitsProduced)
8	=SUMPRODUCT(C8:D8,UnitsProduced)
9	=SUMPRODUCT(C9:D9,UnitsProduced)

	G	H
12	Gross Profit from Sales	=SUMPRODUCT(UnitProfit,UnitsProduced)
13		
14	Total Marketing Cost	=SUM(MarketingCost)
15		
16	Total Profit	=GrossProfitFromSales−TotalMarketingCost

	B	C	D
14	Marketing Cost	=25*(DoorsProduced^2)	=66.667*(WindowsProduced^2)

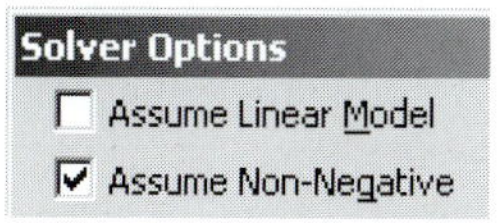

Solver Options
☐ Assume Linear Model
☑ Assume Non-Negative

Range Name	Cells
DoorsProduced	C12
GrossProfitFromSales	H12
HoursAvailable	G7:G9
HoursUsed	E7:E9
HoursUsedPerUnitProduced	C7:D9
MarketingCost	C14:D14
TotalMarketingCost	H14
TotalProfit	H16
UnitProfit	C4:D4
UnitsProduced	C12:D12
WindowsProduced	D12

FIGURE 8.12

Graphical display of the nonlinear programming formulation of the Wyndor problem with nonlinear marketing costs. The curves are objective function curves for some sample values of Profit and the one (Profit = $2,708) that passes through the optimal solution, $(D, W) = (3\frac{3}{14}, 4\frac{5}{28})$

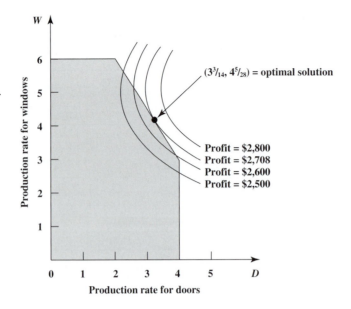

Excel Tip: When a changing cell needs to be raised to some power in a formula, the symbol ^ is placed between the changing cell and the exponent.

(C12), Excel expresses D^2 as DoorsProduced^2, where the symbol ^ indicates that the number following this symbol (2) is the exponent of the number in DoorsProduced (C12). The same approach is used for expressing W^2. Therefore, the formula for total marketing cost is

$$\text{Total Marketing Cost} = \text{SUM(MarketingCost)}$$
$$= 25 * (\text{DoorsProduced}^2) + 66.667 * (\text{WindowsProduced}^2)$$

The formula for the target cell then becomes

$$\text{TotalProfit (H16)} = \text{GrossProfitFromSales (H12)} - \text{TotalMarketingCost (H14)}$$

The fourth difference arises in the selection of the Solver options at the bottom of Figures 8.9 and 8.11. In contrast to Figure 8.9, note that the Assume Linear Model option is *not* selected in Figure 8.11, because the model is not a linear programming model.

Before solving any nonlinear programming model, you should click on the Option button and make sure that the Assume Linear Model option has not been selected.

For this particular model, clicking on the Solve button provides the optimal solution shown in UnitsProduced (C12:D12), namely,

$$D = 3.214 \quad \text{(produce an average of 3.214 doors per week)}$$
$$W = 4.179 \quad \text{(produce an average of 4.179 windows per week)}$$

where TotalProfit (H16) shows a resulting weekly profit of $2,708. These strange values of D and W certainly are not intuitive. Figure 8.12 conveys some graphical intuition into why this answer was obtained. The feasible region is the same as for the original Wyndor problem in Chapter 2. However, instead of having objective function *lines* with which to search for an optimal solution, plotting the points that give any constant value for our nonlinear objective function now gives an objective function *curve* instead. Thus, when using the objective function to calculate Profit for various feasible and infeasible values of (D, W), each of the four curves in the figure shows all the values of (D, W) that give the fixed value of Profit indicated for that curve. (Plotting these points is a tedious and difficult process, so we will not bother with the details of how it is done.) The figure shows that increasing Profit moves the objective function curve to the right. The largest value of Profit such that the objective function curve still passes through any points in the feasible region is Profit = $2,708. Therefore, using fractions, the one feasible point that the Profit = $2,708 curve passes through,

$$(D, W) = (3\tfrac{3}{14}, 4\tfrac{5}{28})$$

is the optimal solution.

Since these are not particularly convenient fractions with which to plan production schedules, they should be adjusted slightly. The curve for Profit = $2,708 in Figure 8.12 indicates that any point on the slanting line at the boundary of the feasible region that is close to the optimal solution will provide a weekly profit very close to $2,708. For example,

$$(D, W) = (3\tfrac{1}{3}, 4)$$

gives a weekly profit of $2,706, so management prefers this more convenient production schedule.

By contrast, consider the linear programming solution in Figure 8.9, $(D, W) = (2, 6)$, that does not take the nonlinearities in the marketing costs into account. When using the current objective function that incorporates these nonlinearities, $(D, W) = (2, 6)$ provides a weekly profit of only $2,450. This illustrates the kind of improvement that can be obtained by replacing an approximate linear programming model by a more precise nonlinear programming model.

Applying Nonlinear Programming to Portfolio Selection

It now is common practice for professional managers of large stock portfolios to use computer models based partially on nonlinear programming to guide them. Because investors are concerned about both the *expected return* (gain) and the *risk* associated with their investments, nonlinear programming is used to determine a portfolio that, under certain assumptions, provides an optimal trade-off between these two factors. This approach is based largely on path-breaking research done by Harry Markowitz and William Sharpe that helped them win the 1990 Nobel Prize in economics.

One way of formulating their approach is as a nonlinear version of the *cost–benefit trade-off problems* discussed in Section 3.3. In this case, the cost involved is the risk associated with the investments. The benefit is the expected return from the portfolio of investments. Therefore, the general form of the model is

This model focuses on the trade-off between risk and expected return from the portfolio of investments.

$$\text{Minimize} \quad \text{Risk}$$

subject to

$$\text{Expected return} \geq \text{Minimum acceptable level}$$

The measure of risk used here is a basic quantity from probability theory called the *variance* of the return. Using standard formulas from probability theory, the objective function then can be expressed as a nonlinear function of the decision variables (the fractions of the total investment to invest in the respective stocks) that yields *decreasing marginal returns* for the stocks. By adding the constraint on expected return, as well as nonnegativity constraints and a constraint that the fractions of the total investment invested in the respective stocks sum to 1, we thereby obtain a simple type of nonlinear programming model for optimizing the selection of the portfolio.

To illustrate the approach, we now will focus on a small numerical example where just three stocks (securities) are being considered for inclusion in the portfolio. Thus, the decision variables are

$$S_1 = \text{Fraction of total investment invested in stock 1}$$
$$S_2 = \text{Fraction of total investment invested in stock 2}$$
$$S_3 = \text{Fraction of total investment invested in stock 3}$$

Since these fractions need to sum to 1,

$$S_1 + S_2 + S_3 = 1$$

will be included as one of the constraints of the model.

Table 8.2 gives the needed data for these three stocks. The second column provides the expected return for each of these stocks, so the expected return for the overall portfolio is

$$\text{Expected return} = (21S_1 + 30S_2 + 8S_3)\%$$

The Bank Hapoalim Group is Israel's largest banking group, providing services within Israel through a network of 327 branches, 9 regional business centers, and various domestic subsidiaries. It also operates worldwide through 37 branches, offices, and subsidiaries in major financial centers in North and South America and Europe.

A major part of Bank Hapoalim's business involves providing investment advisors for its customers. To stay ahead of its competitors, management embarked on a restructuring program to provide these investment advisors with state-of-the-art methodology and technology. A management science team was formed to do this.

The team concluded that it needed to develop a flexible decision-support system for the investment advisors that could be tailored to meet the diverse needs of every customer. Each customer would be asked to provide extensive information about his or her needs, including choosing among various alternatives regarding his or her investment objectives, investment horizon, choice of an index to strive to exceed, preference with regard to liquidity and currency, and so forth. A series of questions also would be asked to ascertain the customer's risk-taking classification.

The natural choice of the model to drive the resulting decision-support system (called the *Opti-Money System*) was the classical nonlinear programming model for portfolio selection described in this section of the book, with modifications to incorporate all the information about the needs of the individual customer. This model generates an optimal weighting of 60 possible asset classes of equities and bonds in the portfolio, and the investment advisor then works with the customer to choose the specific equities and bonds within these classes.

In one recent year, the bank's investment advisors held some 133,000 consultation sessions with 63,000 customers while using this decision-support system. The annual earnings over benchmarks to customers who follow the investment advice provided by the system total approximately US$244 million, while adding more than US$31 million to the bank's annual income.

Source: M. Avriel, H. Pri-Zan, R. Meiri, and A. Peretz, "Opti-Money at Bank Hapoalim: A Model-Based Investment Decision-Support System for Individual Customers," *Interfaces* 34, no. 1 (January–February 2004), pp. 39–50.

The investor's current choice of the minimum acceptable level for this quantity is

$$\text{Minimum acceptable expected return} = 18\%$$

Since the expected returns of stocks 1 and 2 exceed 18%, this minimum acceptable level will be achieved if these stocks comprise a sufficiently large portion of the portfolio.

However, stocks 1 and 2 are much riskier than stock 3. There is no certainty that the expected returns shown in Table 8.2 actually will be achieved, but there is much more uncertainty for stocks 1 and 2 than for stock 3. Each stock has an underlying *probability distribution* of what its return will turn out to be. In each case, the *standard deviation* (i.e., the square root of the variance) of this distribution provides a measure of how spread out this distribution is, since there is roughly a two-thirds probability that the return will turn out to be within one standard deviation of the expected return. This measure of the risk of a stock is given in the third column of Table 8.2.

The challenge is to find the right balance between the high return but high risk from stocks 1 and 2 and the low risk but low return from stock 3.

However, the risk for the portfolio cannot be obtained solely from the third column, since this column only gives the risk for each individual stock considered in isolation. The risk for the portfolio also is affected by whether the particular stocks tend to move up and down together (increased risk) or tend to move in opposite directions (decreased risk). In the rightmost column of Table 8.2, the *positive* joint risk for stocks 1 and 2 indicates that these two stocks have some tendency to move in the same direction. However, the *negative* joint risk for the other two pairs of stocks shows that stock 3 tends to go up when either stock 1 or 2 goes down, and vice versa. (In the terminology of probability theory, the joint risk for *each* of two stocks is the *covariance* of their returns, as given in the rightmost column of Table 8.2, so the total joint risk for two stocks is two times this covariance.)

The data in Table 8.2 typically are obtained by taking samples of the returns of the stocks from a number of previous years and then calculating the averages, standard deviations, and covariances for these samples. Adjustments in the resulting estimate of at least the expected

TABLE 8.2
Data for the Stocks of the Portfolio Selection Example

Stock	Expected Return	Risk (Standard Deviation)	Pair of Stocks	Joint Risk per Stock (Covariance)
1	21%	25%	1 and 2	0.040
2	30	45	1 and 3	−0.005

return of a stock also may be made if it appears that the current prospects for the stock are somewhat different than in previous years. Using the formula from probability theory for calculating the overall variance from individual variances and covariances, the risk for the entire portfolio is

$$\text{Risk} = (0.25S_1)^2 + (0.45S_2)^2 + (0.05S_3)^2 + 2(0.04)S_1S_2 + 2(-0.005)S_1S_3 + 2(-0.01)S_2S_3$$

Therefore, the algebraic form of the nonlinear programming model for this example is

$$\text{Minimize} \quad \text{Risk} = (0.25S_1)^2 + (0.45S_2)^2 + (0.05S_3)^2 + 2(0.04)S_1S_2$$
$$+ 2(-0.005)S_1S_3 + 2(-0.01)S_2S_3$$

subject to

$$21S_1 + 30S_2 + 8S_3 \geq 18$$
$$S_1 + S_2 + S_3 = 1$$

and

$$S_1 \geq 0 \quad S_2 \geq 0 \quad S_3 \geq 0$$

This kind of quadratic programming model is widely used by portfolio managers.

Fortunately, the objective function for this model has decreasing marginal returns. (This is not obvious, but it has been verified that Risk, measured by the variance of the return for the entire portfolio, *always* has decreasing marginal returns for any portfolio.) Furthermore, this is a *quadratic programming* model since the objective function is quadratic (terms consisting of a coefficient times the product of two variables are allowed in a quadratic function) and the model has all three characteristics listed at the beginning of this section. Therefore, this is a particularly simple type of nonlinear programming model to solve.

Figure 8.13 shows the corresponding spreadsheet model after having applied the Solver. For ease of interpretation, the changing cells Portfolio (C14:E14) give the values of S_1, S_2, and S_3 as percentages rather than fractions. These cells indicate that the optimal solution is

FIGURE 8.13

A spreadsheet model for the portfolio selection example of nonlinear programming, where the changing cells Portfolio (C14:E14) give the optimal portfolio and the target cell Variance (C21) shows the resulting risk.

	A	B	C	D	E	F	G	H
1		**Portfolio Selection Problem (Nonlinear Programming)**						
2								
3			Stock 1	Stock 2	Stock 3			
4		**Expected Return**	21%	30%	8%			
5								
6		**Risk (Stand. Dev.)**	25%	45%	5%			
7								
8		**Joint Risk (Covar.)**	Stock 1	Stock 2	Stock 3			
9		Stock 1		0.040	-0.005			
10		Stock 2			-0.010			
11		Stock 3						
12								
13			Stock 1	Stock 2	Stock 3	**Total**		
14		**Portfolio**	40.2%	21.7%	38.1%	100%	=	100%
15								
16					**Minimum**			
17					**Expected**			
18			**Portfolio**		**Return**			
19		**Expected Return**	18%	≥	18%			
20								
21		**Risk (Variance)**	0.0238					
22								
23		**Risk (Stand. Dev.)**	15.4%					

Range Name	Cells
Covar12	D9
Covar13	E9
Covar23	E10
Covariance	C9:E11
ExpectedReturn	C19
MinExpectedReturn	E19
OneHundredPercent	H14
Portfolio	C14:E14
SD1	C6
SD2	D6
SD3	E6
StandDev	C23
Stock1	C14
Stock2	D14
Stock3	E14
StockExpectedReturn	C4:E4
StockStandDev	C6:E6
Total	F14
Variance	C21

	F
13	**Total**
14	=SUM(Portfolio)

Solver Parameters

Set Target Cell: Variance

Equal To: ○ Max ● Min

By Changing Cells:
Portfolio

Subject to the Constraints:
ExpectedReturn >= MinExpectedReturn
Total = OneHundredPercent

Solver Options
☐ Assume Linear Model
☑ Assume Non-Negative

	B	C
19	**Expected Return**	=SUMPRODUCT(StockExpectedReturn,Portfolio)
20		
21	**Risk (Variance)**	=((SD1*Stock1)^2)+((SD2*Stock2)^2)+((SD3*Stock3)^2)+2*Covar12*Stock1*Stock2+2*Covar13*Stock1*Stock3+2*Covar23*Stock2*Stock3
22		
23	**Risk (Stand. Dev.)**	=SQRT(Variance)

$S_1 = 40.2\%$: Allocate 40.2% of the portfolio to stock 1
$S_2 = 21.7\%$: Allocate 21.7% of the portfolio to stock 2
$S_3 = 38.1\%$: Allocate 38.1% of the portfolio to stock 3

Thus, despite its relatively low return, including a substantial amount of stock 3 in the portfolio is worthwhile to counteract the high risk associated with stocks 1 and 2. ExpectedReturn (C19) indicates that this portfolio still achieves an expected return of 18 percent, which equals the minimum acceptable level. The target cell Variance (C21) gives the risk for the portfolio, namely, the variance of the return for the entire portfolio, as 0.0238. To help interpret this quantity, StandDev (C23) calculates the corresponding standard deviation of the return for the portfolio as

> There is a good chance that the return for the portfolio will not deviate from the expected return by more than the standard deviation of the return.

$\sqrt{0.0238} = 0.154 = 15.4\%$. The fact that this standard deviation is less than the expected return is encouraging, because this indicates that it is fairly unlikely that the actual return that eventually is achieved by the portfolio will turn out to be negative. The standard deviation is this small, despite the much larger standard deviations of the returns for stocks 1 and 2 given in StockStandDev (C6:E6), because of the very small standard deviation for stock 3 and the negative values in Covar13 (E9) and Covar23 (E10).

This is an example of a cost–benefit trade-off problem since it involves finding the best trade-off between cost (risk) and a benefit (expected return). Except for the form of the objective function, it is analogous to the cost–benefit trade-off problems discussed in Section 3.3. As discussed further in Chapter 5, analysis of such a problem seldom ends with finding an optimal solution for the original version of the model. The minimum acceptable level stated in the model for the benefit (or benefits) involved is a tentative policy decision. After learning the resulting cost, further analysis is needed to find the best trade-off between costs and benefits. This analysis involves varying the minimum acceptable level for the benefit and seeing what the effect is on the cost. If a lot more benefit can be obtained for relatively little cost, this

> An investor needs the kind of table and graph shown in Figure 8.14 to decide on which portfolio provides the best trade-off between expected return and risk.

probably should be done. On the other hand, if decreasing the benefit a little would save a lot of cost, the minimum acceptable level probably should be decreased.

One way of applying this approach to the current example is to use the Solver Table (in your MS Courseware) as described in Chapter 5 and Appendix A to generate a table that gives the expected return and risk provided by an optimal solution for the model for a range of values of the minimum acceptable expected return. Figure 8.14 shows such a table. In the parlance of the world of finance, the pairs of values in columns F and G are referred to as points on the *efficient frontier.* In fact, the right-hand side of Figure 8.14 shows a plot of this efficient frontier. After examining enough such points, the investor then can make a personal decision about which one provides the best trade-off between expected return and risk.

Review Questions

1. What are the three characteristics of a simple type of nonlinear programming problem that can be readily solved by the Excel Solver?
2. For this simple type of nonlinear programming problem, how does the graphical display for a two-variable problem differ from that for a two-variable linear programming problem?
3. What additional characteristic must this type of nonlinear programming problem have in order to be a quadratic programming problem?
4. When applying nonlinear programming to portfolio selection, a trade-off is being sought between which two factors?

8.3 SEPARABLE PROGRAMMING

Section 8.1 described several types of nonproportional relationships between an activity and the overall measure of performance for a problem. One such relationship is *decreasing marginal returns* and Section 8.2 has just focused on nonlinear programming problems where this type of relationship holds for all the activities. We now turn our attention to a related kind of nonproportional relationship where the activities again have decreasing marginal returns. However, the difference is that the profit or cost graph for each activity now is *piecewise linear*

FIGURE 8.14

An application of the Solver Table that shows the trade-off between expected return and risk when the model of Figure 8.13 is altered by varying the minimum acceptable expected return.

Solver Table for Portfolio Selection Problem

	Minimum Expected Return	Stock 1	Stock 2	Stock 3	Risk (St. Dev.)	Expected Return
		40.20%	21.70%	38.10%	15.40%	18.00%
	8%	7.10%	3.70%	89.10%	3.90%	9.70%
	10%	8.10%	4.30%	87.60%	3.90%	10.00%
	12%	16.20%	8.60%	75.20%	5.60%	12.00%
	14%	24.20%	13.00%	62.80%	8.60%	14.00%
	16%	32.20%	17.30%	50.50%	12.00%	16.00%
	18%	40.20%	21.70%	38.10%	15.40%	18.00%
	20%	48.20%	26.10%	25.70%	18.90%	20.00%
	22%	56.20%	30.40%	13.40%	22.50%	22.00%
	24%	64.20%	34.80%	1.00%	26.10%	24.00%
	26%	44.40%	55.60%	0.00%	30.80%	26.00%
	28%	22.20%	77.80%	0.00%	37.30%	28.00%
	30%	0.00%	100.00%	0.00%	45.00%	30.00%

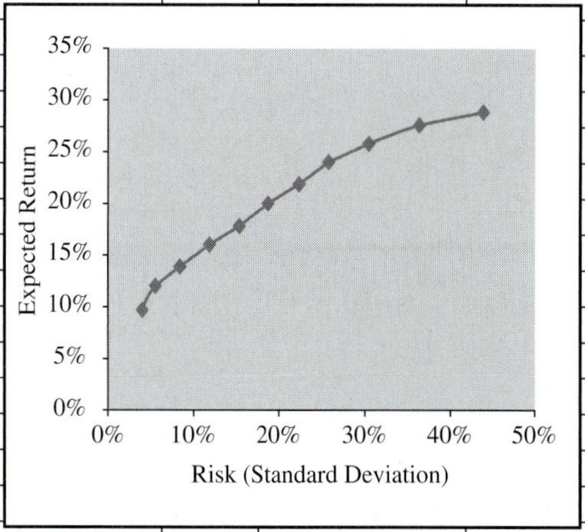

	C	D	E	F	G
28				Risk	Expected
29	Stock 1	Stock 2	Stock 3	(St. Dev.)	Return
30	=Stock1	=Stock2	=Stock3	=StandDev	=ExpectedReturn

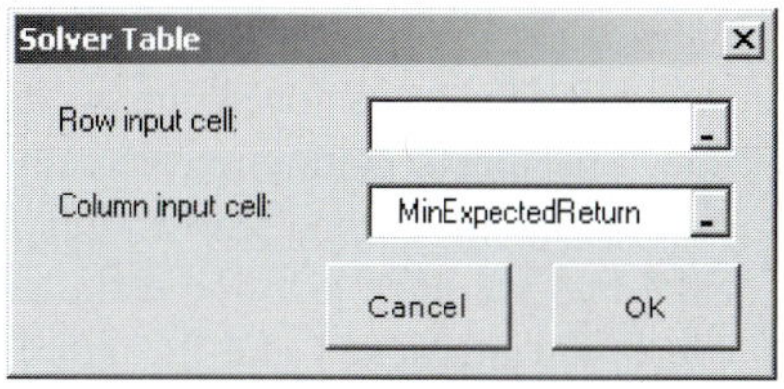

Solver Table
Row input cell:
Column input cell: MinExpectedReturn
Cancel   OK

Range Name	Cells
ExpectedReturn	C19
MinExpectedReturn	E19
StandDev	C23
Stock1	C14
Stock2	D14
Stock3	E14

For nonlinear programming problems with decreasing marginal returns where the profit or cost graphs also are piecewise linear, the separable programming technique converts the problem into an equivalent linear programming problem.

because it consists of a sequence of connected line segments. Figure 8.2(b) in Section 8.1 illustrated such a profit graph (or the graph for any other measure of performance to be maximized) and Figure 8.3(c) did the same for a cost graph (or any related graph with minimization).

There is a special technique called *separable programming* that is designed to deal with this kind of nonlinear programming problem. Thus, the total profit (or cost) is simply the sum of the profits (or costs) obtained directly from these piecewise linear profit (or cost) graphs for the individual activities. (No cross-product terms are allowed and each graph must have decreasing marginal returns.) Because of the line segments in each profit or cost graph, this technique converts the formulation of the model into a *linear programming* model. This enables solving the model extremely efficiently and then applying the powerful tools of what-if analysis for linear programming.

The next episode in the saga of the Wyndor Glass Co. problem illustrates this technique.

The Wyndor Glass Co. Problem When Overtime Is Needed

The company now is ready to begin production of its special new doors and windows, based on the planning described in Chapter 2, Chapter 5, and Section 8.2. Because of the nonlinear marketing costs discussed in Section 8.2, the current plan is to use production rates of

$$(D, W) = (3\tfrac{1}{3}, 4)$$

where D and W are the number of doors and windows to be produced per week, respectively.

However, there now is a new development that might alter this production plan for the first four months.

In particular, the company has accepted a special order for hand-crafted goods to be made in plants 1 and 2 throughout the next four months. Filling this order will require borrowing

TABLE 8.3
Data for the Original Wyndor Problem When Overtime Is Needed

	Maximum Weekly Production			Profit per Unit Produced	
Product	**Regular Time**	**Overtime**	**Total**	**Regular Time**	**Overtime**
Doors	3	1	4	$300	$200
Windows	3	3	6	500	100
		(and $3D + 2W \leq 18$)			

certain employees from the work crews for the regular products, so the remaining workers will need to work overtime to utilize the full production capacity of each plant's machinery and equipment for these products.

Without worrying about the new estimates of nonlinear marketing costs yet, how should the original Wyndor model be modified to consider overtime?

Because of this new development, management has asked the Management Science Group to quickly update its model and check whether the current production plan still would be the most profitable one to use during the first four months. To get a quick handle on the problem, the group decides to ignore the nonlinearities in the marketing costs for now and simply modify the original spreadsheet model shown in Figure 8.9 (in the preceding section) to take overtime into account.

The constraints in this original model, HoursUsed (E7:E9) ≤ HoursAvailable (G7:G9), are still valid, where overtime would be used to fill some of the hours of production time available in plants 1 and 2 as given by cells G7 and G8. However, the objective function no longer is valid because the additional cost of using overtime work reduces the profit obtained from each unit of product produced in this way.

For the portion of the work done in plants 1 and 2, Table 8.3 shows the maximum number of units of each product that can be produced per week on regular time and on overtime. Plant 3 does not need to use overtime, so its unchanged constraint is given in parentheses at the bottom. The fourth column is the sum of the second and third columns, where these sums are implied by the original constraints for plants 1 and 2 ($D \leq 4$ and $2W \leq 12$, so $W \leq 6$). The final two columns give the estimated profit for each unit produced on regular time and on overtime (in plants 1 and 2), based on the original estimates of marketing costs rather than those developed in Section 8.2.

Figure 8.15 plots the weekly profit from each product versus its production rate. Note that the *slope* (steepness) of each profit graph decreases when the production rate is increased sufficiently to require overtime, because the profit per unit produced shown in Table 8.3 is less on overtime than on regular time. Thus, these two products have *decreasing marginal returns*.

Management had considered hiring some temporary workers to avoid the extra expense of using overtime. However, this would mean incurring some training costs, as well as inefficiencies from using inexperienced workers. Therefore, because this is a temporary situation

FIGURE 8.15
Profit graphs for the Wyndor Glass Co. that show the total weekly profit from each product versus the production rate for that product when overtime is needed to exceed a production rate of three units per week. At this point, these profit graphs are based on the original estimates of marketing costs rather than the estimates of nonlinear marketing costs developed in Section 8.2.

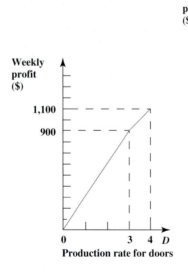

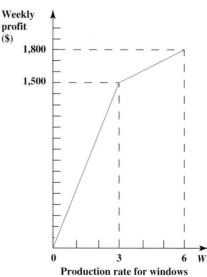

The model needs to
provide a solution that
uses overtime for a
product only if all
available regular time for
that product has been fully
utilized.

where regular production can resume in four months, management has decided to go ahead and use overtime.

However, management does insist that the work crew for each product be fully utilized on regular time before any overtime is used. Furthermore, it feels that the current plans for the production rates should be changed temporarily if this would improve overall profitability.

Applying Separable Programming to This Problem

Since each profit graph in Figure 8.15 is not a straight line, the profit from each product is *not* proportional to its production rate. Consequently, the proportionality assumption of linear programming (discussed in Section 8.1) is violated. However, each profit graph does consist of *two* straight lines (line segments) that are connected together at the point where the slope changes. Thus, within each line segment, the profit graph looks like the proportionality assumption still holds. This suggests the following key idea.

The key idea is to have a
separate decision variable
for each line segment in a
profit graph (or cost graph).

> **The Separable Programming Technique:** For each activity that violates the proportionality assumption, separate its profit graph into parts, with a line segment in each part. Then, instead of using a single decision variable to represent the level of each such activity, introduce a separate new decision variable for each line segment on that activity's profit graph. Since the proportionality assumption holds for these new decision variables, formulate a linear programming model in terms of these variables.

For the Wyndor problem, these new decision variables are

D_R = Number of doors produced per week on regular time

D_O = Number of doors produced per week on overtime

W_R = Number of windows produced per week on regular time

W_O = Number of windows produced per week on overtime

The unit profits associated with these variables are given in the final two columns of Table 8.3, so these numbers become the coefficients in the objective function. The second and third columns give the maximum values of these variables, so corresponding constraints are introduced into the model. The three functional constraints in the model for the original Wyndor problem also need to hold, but with D replaced by ($D_R + D_O$) and W replaced by ($W_R + W_O$).

We now have formulated a
linear programming model
to fit what was originally a
nonlinear programming
problem.

The resulting spreadsheet model is shown in Figure 8.16. The changing cells UnitsProduced (C14:D15) include separate cells for each of the four decision variables. The new constraints, UnitsProduced (C14:D15) $\leq$ Maximum (F14:G15), enforce the upper bounds on these decision variables indicated by the second and third columns of Table 8.3. The new output cells TotalProduced (C16:D16) sum the production quantities on regular time and overtime for each of the products. This then enables calculating the hours used with the equation, HoursUsed (E8:E10) = SUMPRODUCT (HoursUsedPerUnitProduced, TotalProduced). Otherwise, the model is basically the same as the original linear programming model in Figure 8.9. Note that the Assume Linear Model option has been selected because the new model also has been formulated to become a linear programming model. The proportionality assumption now is satisfied for the new decision variables. Therefore, the model can be solved very efficiently. This ability to reformulate the original model to make it fit linear programming is what makes separable programming a valuable technique.

However, there is one important factor that is not taken into account explicitly in this formulation. Recall that management insists that regular time production be fully utilized before using any overtime on each product. There are no constraints in the model that enforce this restriction. Consequently, it actually is feasible in the model to have $D_O > 0$ when $D_R < 3$, or to have $W_O > 0$ when $W_R < 3$.

Fortunately, even though such a solution is feasible in the model, it cannot be optimal. The reason is that the activities (producing the two products) have *decreasing marginal returns,* since the unit profit on overtime is less than on regular time for each product. Therefore, to maximize the total profit, an optimal solution automatically will use up all regular time for a product before starting on overtime.

FIGURE 8.16

A spreadsheet model for the Wyndor separable programming problem when overtime is needed, where the changing cells UnitsProduced (C14:D15) give the optimal production rates obtained by the Solver and the target cell TotalProfit (D18) shows the resulting total profit per week. This model is based on the profit graphs in Figure 8.15 and so does not incorporate the nonlinear marketing costs developed in Section 8.2.

	A	B	C	D	E	F	G
1		**Wyndor Problem with Overtime (Separable Programming)**					
2							
3		**Unit Profit**	Doors	Windows			
4		Regular	$300	$500			
5		Overtime	$200	$100			
6					Hours		Hours
7			Hours Used per Unit Produced		Used		Available
8		Plant 1	1	0	4	≤	4
9		Plant 2	0	2	6	≤	12
10		Plant 3	3	2	18	≤	18
11							
12			**Units Produced**			**Maximum**	
13			Doors	Windows		Doors	Windows
14		Regular	3	3	≤	3	3
15		Overtime	1	0	≤	1	3
16		Total Produced	4	3			
17							
18			Total Profit	$2,600			

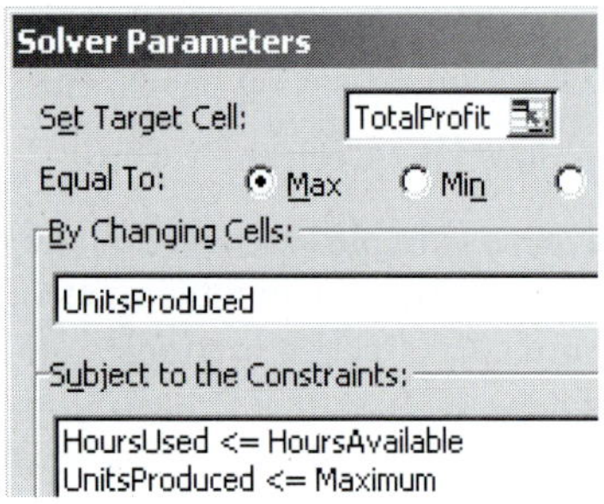

Solver Parameters

Set Target Cell: [TotalProfit]

Equal To: ● Max ○ Min ○

By Changing Cells:

[UnitsProduced]

Subject to the Constraints:

HoursUsed <= HoursAvailable
UnitsProduced <= Maximum

	E
6	Hours
7	Used
8	=SUMPRODUCT(C8:D8,TotalProduced)
9	=SUMPRODUCT(C9:D9,TotalProduced)
10	=SUMPRODUCT(C10:D10,TotalProduced)

	B	C	D
16	Total Produced	=SUM(C14:C15)	=SUM(D14:D15)

	C	D
18	Total Profit	=SUMPRODUCT(UnitProfit,UnitsProduced)

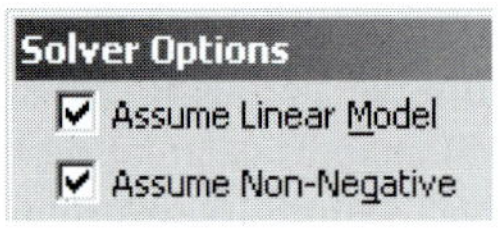

Solver Options

☑ Assume Linear Model
☑ Assume Non-Negative

Range Name	Cells
HoursAvailable	G8:G10
HoursUsed	E8:E10
HoursUsedPerUnitProduced	C8:D10
Maximum	F14:G15
TotalProduced	C16:D16
TotalProfit	D18
UnitProfit	C4:D5
UnitsProduced	C14:D15

Decreasing marginal returns are needed to use the separable programming technique.

The key is to have decreasing marginal returns. Without it, the linear programming model with this approach may not provide a legitimate optimal solution. This is the reason that separable programming is only applicable when the activities have decreasing marginal returns (except for those activities that satisfy the proportionality assumption).

Figure 8.16 shows the changing cells UnitsProduced (C14:D15) after using the Excel Solver to obtain an optimal solution. This optimal solution is

$D_R = 3, D_O = 1$:   Produce 4 doors per week

$W_R = 3, W_O = 0$:   Produce 3 windows per week

FIGURE 8.17
The solid curve shows a profit graph for an activity whose marginal return decreases on a continuous basis. The dashed-line segments display the kind of approximation used by separable programming.

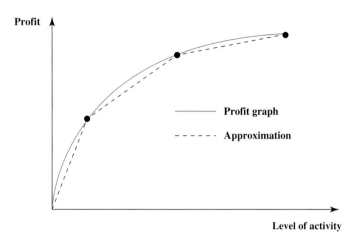

for a total profit of $2,600 per week given by the target cell TotalProfit (D18). This compares with a total profit of $2,567 per week for the previous plan (produce 3⅓ doors and 4 windows per week) that had been adopted before the need to use overtime arose.

Applying Separable Programming with Smooth Profit Graphs

In some applications of separable programming, the profit graphs will be *curves* rather than a series of line segments. This occurs when the marginal return from an activity decreases on a continuous basis rather than just at certain points.

For example, the solid curve in Figure 8.17 shows such a profit graph for an activity. To apply separable programming, this curve can then be approximated by a series of line segments, such as the dashed-line segments in the figure. By introducing a new decision variable for each of the line segments (and repeating this for other activities with such profit graphs), the approach just illustrated by the Wyndor example can again be used to convert the overall problem into a linear programming problem.

This is not the only way to solve problems where the activities have profit graphs with shapes similar to the one shown in Figure 8.17. Section 8.2 discusses problems of just this same type. The Excel Solver can readily solve such problems by using a nonlinear programming model that employs the formulas for the profit graphs. The advantage is that no approximation is needed, whereas separable programming uses the kind of approximation illustrated in Figure 8.17.

However, the separable programming approach also has certain advantages. One is that converting the problem into a linear programming problem tends to make it quicker to solve, which can be very helpful for large problems. Another advantage is that a linear programming formulation makes available Solver's Sensitivity Report, which is a great aid to what-if analysis, whereas the sensitivity information provided when using a nonlinear programming model is not nearly as useful. A third important advantage is that the separable programming approach only requires estimating the profit from each activity at a few points, such as the dots in Figure 8.17. Therefore, it is not necessary to use a curve fitting method to estimate the formula for the profit graph, where this estimation would have introduced an approximation into the process.

The end of the Wyndor story (below) illustrates the application of both approaches.

The approximation in Figure 8.17 only requires estimating the profit at the three dots rather than estimating a formula for the entire profit graph.

The Wyndor Problem with Both Overtime Costs and Nonlinear Marketing Costs

The spreadsheet model in Figure 8.16 provides a good quick estimate of approximately what the production rates should be for the new products over the next four months. This is useful for planning purposes, but the model is a somewhat rough one because it does not take into account the new estimates of nonlinear marketing costs that were developed in Section 8.2. Therefore, the next step for Wyndor's Management Science Group is to enhance the model by incorporating these new estimates.

TABLE 8.4
Data for the Wyndor
Problem with Both
Overtime Costs and
Nonlinear Marketing
Costs

	Maximum Weekly Production			Gross Unit Profit		
Product	**Regular Time**	**Overtime**	**Total**	**Regular Time**	**Overtime**	**Marketing Costs**
Doors	3	1	4	$375	$275	$25D^2$
Windows	3	3	6	700	300	$66\frac{2}{3}W^2$

TABLE 8.5
Calculations of
Wyndor's Weekly Profit
from Producing D Doors
per Week

D	Gross Profit	Marketing Costs	Profit	Incremental Profit
0	0	0	0	—
1	$ 375	$ 25	$ 350	$350
2	750	100	650	300
3	1,125	225	900	250
4	1,400	400	1,000	100

TABLE 8.6
Calculations of
Wyndor's Weekly Profit
from Producing W
Windows per Week

W	Gross Profit	Marketing Costs	Profit	Incremental Profit
0	0	0	0	—
1	$ 700	$ 66⅔	$ 633⅓	$ 633⅓
2	1,400	266⅔	1,133⅓	500
3	2,100	600	1,500	366⅔
4	2,400	1,066⅔	1,333⅓	− 166⅔
5	2,700	1,666⅔	1,033⅓	− 300
6	3,000	2,400	600	− 433⅓

Recall that Ann Lester, Wyndor's vice president for marketing, now is estimating that the marketing costs will need to be $25D^2$ and $66\frac{2}{3}W^2$ to sustain sales of D doors and W windows per week. These costs then would need to be subtracted from the gross profit for each product (the profit excluding marketing costs) to obtain that product's profit. Since the original estimates of marketing costs had been $75 per door and $200 per window when estimating the unit profits given in Table 8.3, the group now needs to use the data shown in Table 8.4.

Based on these data, the fourth column of Table 8.5 shows the weekly profit that would be obtained by producing D doors per week for various values of D. This profit is calculated by subtracting the marketing costs in the third column from the gross profit in the second column. The rightmost column gives the incremental profit from the last increase of 1 in the value of D. Thus, the incremental profit is calculated by taking the profit in the same row and subtracting the profit in the preceding row. Note the large drop in the incremental profit at $D = 4$ because overtime must be used to increase D above 3.

Table 8.6 provides the corresponding calculations for windows. In this case, the incremental profit at $W = 4$, $W = 5$, and $W = 6$ actually is negative because of the large extra costs of the overtime that is needed to increase W above 3.

The solid curves in Figure 8.18 show the entire profit graphs for the doors and windows. The slope of each graph always is decreasing as the production rate increases, so both activities have decreasing marginal returns. This decrease in the slope is almost imperceptible at small production rates and then becomes more pronounced at larger rates. There also is a kink in each graph at $D = 3$ or $W = 3$ because overtime is required to increase the production rate further.

It is very reasonable to use separable programming when the piecewise linear graphs approximate the actual profit graphs this closely.

The Management Science Group now wants to use separable programming to determine what the production rates should be to maximize total profit. For this purpose, the group uses the dashed-line segments in Figure 8.18 to obtain piecewise linear graphs that closely approximate the actual profit graphs. The one place where the approximation is not really close is when the profit graph for windows goes from $1,500, at $W = 3$, to $600, at $W = 6$ (an average decrease of $300 per unit of W). Since the profit decreases when W is increased

FIGURE 8.18

The solid curves show the profit graphs for Wyndor's doors and windows when both overtime costs and nonlinear marketing costs are incorporated into the problem. The dashed-line segments display the approximation used by the separable programming model in Figure 8.19.

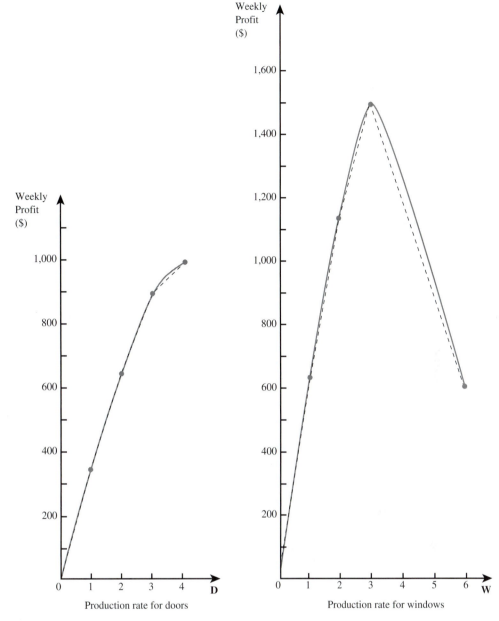

Separable programming calculates unit profits for different parts of a profit graph by using the slopes of the line segments in the piecewise linear approximation of the profit graph.

above $W = 3$, it seems undesirable to increase W this much. Therefore, a particularly close approximation is not needed in this part of the graph, so only a single line segment is used between $W = 3$ and $W = 6$.

Figure 8.19 shows the separable programming spreadsheet model that is based on the piecewise linear profit graphs in Figure 8.18. This model is very similar to the separable programming spreadsheet model in Figure 8.16 that does not incorporate the new estimates of nonlinear marketing costs. The latter model is based on the piecewise linear profit graphs in Figure 8.15, each of which has only two line segments. Therefore, each of the sets of cells, UnitProfit (C4:D5) and UnitsProduced (C14:D15), has only two rows. Because each of the piecewise linear profit graphs in Figure 8.18 has four line segments, each of the corresponding sets of cells in Figure 8.19, UnitProfit (C4:D7) and UnitsProduced (C17:D20), has four rows. The numbers in UnitProfit (C4:D7) are the slopes of the corresponding line segments in Figure 8.18. These slopes come directly from the incremental profits given in Tables 8.5 and 8.6, except for cell D7. This cell is based on the line segment from $W = 3$ to $W = 6$ in Figure 8.18,

FIGURE 8.19

A spreadsheet model for the Wyndor separable programming problem when overtime is needed and nonlinear marketing costs also are incorporated into the problem. By summing the columns of the changing cells UnitsProduced (C17:D20), TotalProduced (C21:D21) gives the optimal production rates obtained by the Solver. Due to rounding error, the target cell TotalProfit (D23) shows a resulting weekly profit of $2,501 rather than the correct amount of $2,500.

	A	B	C	D	E	F	G
1		**Wyndor with Overtime and Marketing Costs (Separable)**					
2							
3		**Unit Profit**	Doors	Windows			
4		Regular (0–1)	$350.00	$633.33			
5		Regular (1–2)	$300.00	$500.00			
6		Regular (2–3)	$250.00	$367.67			
7		Overtime	$100.00	-$300.00			
8							
9					Hours		Hours
10			Hours Used per Unit Produced		Used		Available
11		Plant 1	1	0	4	≤	4
12		Plant 2	0	2	6	≤	12
13		Plant 3	3	2	18	≤	18
14							
15			**Units Produced**			**Maximum**	
16			Doors	Windows		Doors	Windows
17		Regular (0–1)	1	1	≤	1	1
18		Regular (1–2)	1	1	≤	1	1
19		Regular (2–3)	1	1	≤	1	1
20		Overtime	1	0	≤	1	3
21		Total Produced	4	3			
22							
23			Total Profit	$2,501			

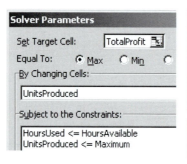

Solver Parameters

Set Target Cell: TotalProfit

Equal To: ◉ Max ○ Min ○

By Changing Cells:

UnitsProduced

Subject to the Constraints:

HoursUsed <= HoursAvailable
UnitsProduced <= Maximum

	E
9	Hours
10	Used
11	=SUMPRODUCT(C11:D11,TotalProduced)
12	=SUMPRODUCT(C12:D12,TotalProduced)
13	=SUMPRODUCT(C13:D13,TotalProduced)

	B	C	D
21	Total Produced	=SUM(C17:C20)	=SUM(D17:D20)

	C	D
23	Total Profit	=SUMPRODUCT(UnitProfit,UnitsProduced)

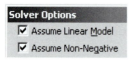

Solver Options

☑ Assume Linear Model
☑ Assume Non-Negative

Range Name	Cells
HoursAvailable	G11:G13
HoursUsed	E11:E13
HoursUsedPerUnitProduced	C11:D13
Maximum	F17:G20
TotalProduced	C21:D21
TotalProfit	D23
UnitProfit	C4:D7
UnitsProduced	C17:D20

which has a slope of −$300 since the profit is decreasing at the rate of $300 per unit increase in W. This slope of −$300 is the average of the last three incremental profits in Table 8.6. All the other line segments in Figure 8.18 run over only one unit of D or W, so the slope of each of these line segments equals the corresponding incremental profit in Table 8.5 or 8.6.

The changing cells in Figure 8.19, UnitsProduced (C17:D20), give the optimal solution obtained by Solver. TotalProduced (C21:D21), which = SUM(UnitsProduced), gives the corresponding total production rates, namely,

$D = 4$:   Produce 4 doors per week, including 1 on overtime

$W = 3$:   Produce 3 windows per week

The target cell TotalProfit (D23) indicates that the resulting weekly profit would be \$2,501. (Solver actually is incurring round-off error here since the correct weekly profit is \$2,500.)

Figures 8.19 and 8.20 provide a comparison between a separable programming model and the kind of nonlinear programming model discussed in Section 8.2.

To check these results, the Management Science Group also formulates and runs the corresponding nonlinear programming model that employs the formulas for the smooth profit graphs in Figure 8.18. This spreadsheet model is shown in Figure 8.20. It is nearly the same as the one in Figure 8.11 that does not include overtime costs. The one difference is that the single row for UnitProfit (C4:D4) and for UnitsProduced (C12:D12) in Figure 8.11 now is split into two rows each, (C4:D5) and (C15:D16), to differentiate between regular time and overtime. Because of the kink in the profit graphs at $D = 3$ and $W = 3$, the pairs of rows are needed to provide separate formulas for the two parts of each profit graph on either side of the kink. TotalProduced (C17:D17) provides the same optimal solution, $(D, W) = (4, 3)$, as the separable programming model in Figure 8.19, with a total profit of \$2,500.

Based on these results, Wyndor management now adopts production rates of $(D, W) = (4, 3)$ for the next four months while overtime is needed. Following that period, the plan is to switch to $(D, W) = (3\frac{1}{3}, 4)$ because of the results obtained in Section 8.2.

Here is one key lesson from the Wyndor case study.

This completes the Wyndor case study. One key lesson is that a management science study may involve developing more than just a single model to represent a problem. As the study goes on and additional relevant considerations come to light, the original model may evolve through a series of enhancements into a rather different kind of model. For example, what started as a linear programming model may end up needing to be a nonlinear programming model.

Review Questions

1. For each activity that violates the proportionality assumption, what must be the shape of its profit graph (or at least an approximation of the profit graph) in order to apply separable programming?

2. What kind of mathematical model is eventually formulated when applying the separable programming technique?

3. For problems where the activities have profit graphs with shapes similar to the one shown in Figure 8.17, what are some advantages of using the kind of approximation displayed in this figure to enable applying separable programming?

4. For these same problems, what is an advantage of instead using a nonlinear programming model that directly employs the formulas for the profit graphs?

8.4   DIFFICULT NONLINEAR PROGRAMMING PROBLEMS

We saw in Section 8.2 that even if a model has a nonlinear objective function, so long as the model has certain properties (e.g., linear constraints and maximizing an objective function with decreasing marginal returns), the Solver can easily find an optimal solution. Furthermore, we saw in Section 8.3 that in some cases separable programming can be used to model (or approximate) a nonlinear problem in such a way that *linear* programming can be used to efficiently find an optimal solution.

The standard Solver often has difficulty solving nonlinear programming models if the constraints are nonlinear or if the profit graphs for any activities are either not smooth or have increasing marginal returns.

However, nonlinear programming problems come in many guises and forms. For example, for problems where the objective is to maximize total profit, some might have *increasing* marginal returns for the profit from certain activities. Some might have nonlinear functions in the constraints. Some might have profit graphs with several disconnected curves. These other kinds of nonlinear programming problems often are much more difficult, if not impossible, to solve. The reason is that there may be many locally optimal solutions that are not globally

FIGURE 8.20

A spreadsheet model for the Wyndor nonlinear programming problem when overtime is needed and nonlinear marketing costs also are incorporated into the problem. TotalProduced (C17:D17) gives the optimal production rates obtained by the Solver and the target cell TotalProfit (H20) shows the resulting weekly profit. Note that this nonlinear programming formulation gives the same results (except for rounding error) as the separable programming formulation in Figure 8.19.

	A	B	C	D	E	F	G	H
1		**Wyndor With Overtime and Marketing Costs (Nonlinear Programming)**						
2								
3		**Unit Profit (Gross)**	Doors	Windows				
4		Regular	$375	$700				
5		Overtime	$275	$300				
6								
7					Hours		Hours	
8			Hours Used per Unit Produced		Used		Available	
9		Plant 1	1	0	4	≤	4	
10		Plant 2	0	2	6	≤	12	
11		Plant 3	3	2	18	≤	18	
12								
13						**Maximum**		
14		**Units Produced**	Doors	Windows		Doors	Windows	
15		Regular	3	3	≤	3	3	
16		Overtime	1	0	≤	1	3	
17		Total Produced	4	3				
18							Gross Profit from Sales	$3,500
19		Marketing Cost	$400	$600			Total Marketing Cost	$1,000
20							Total Profit	$2,500

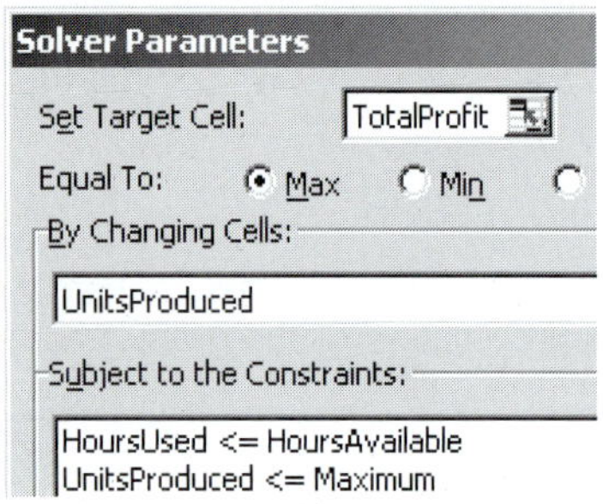

Solver Parameters

Set Target Cell: TotalProfit

Equal To: ⦿ Max ○ Min ○

By Changing Cells:

UnitsProduced

Subject to the Constraints:

HoursUsed <= HoursAvailable
UnitsProduced <= Maximum

Solver Options

☐ Assume Linear Model
☑ Assume Non-Negative

Range Name	Cells
DoorsProduced	C17
GrossProfitFromSales	H18
HoursAvailable	G9:G11
HoursUsed	E9:E11
HoursUsedPerUnitProduced	C9:D11
MarketingCost	C19:D19
Maximum	F15:G16
TotalMarketingCost	H19
TotalProduced	C17:D17
TotalProfit	H20
UnitProfit	C4:D5
UnitsProduced	C15:D16
WindowsProduced	D17

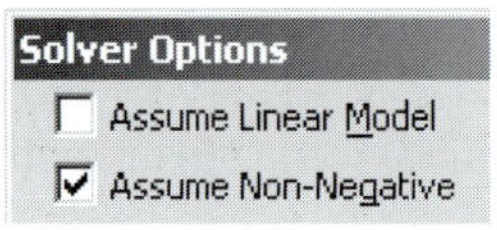

	E
7	Hours
8	Used
9	=SUMPRODUCT(C9:D9,TotalProduced)
10	=SUMPRODUCT(C10:D10,TotalProduced)
11	=SUMPRODUCT(C11:D11,TotalProduced)

	B	C	D
17	Total Produced	=SUM(C15:C16)	=SUM(D15:D16)
18			
19	Marketing Cost	=25*(DoorsProduced^2)	=66.667*(WindowsProduced^2)

	G	H
18	Gross Profit from Sales	=SUMPRODUCT(UnitProfit,UnitsProduced)
19	Total Marketing Cost	=SUM(MarketingCost)
20	Total Profit	=GrossProfitFromSales–TotalMarketingCost

optimal. We saw in Figures 8.7 and 8.8 how the Solver can get stuck at these locally optimal solutions without ever finding the globally optimal solution.

One approach for attempting to solve problems that may have multiple local optima is to run the Solver many times, each time starting with a different initial solution entered into the changing cells on the spreadsheet. For each run, Solver will start its search at the given initial solution (the starting point) and move in a direction that improves the objective function until it finds a local optimum. By trying many starting points, the goal is to find most or all of the local optima. We then pick the best solution found from all the trials. At a minimum, we are likely to end up with a solution that is better than if we just take the first local optimum that Solver finds. With luck, one of the starting points will yield the globally optimal solution.

For example, consider the model in Figure 8.7 with the corresponding profit graph in Figure 8.8. For any starting point x less than 1.5, the objective function increases by moving toward the local maximum at $x = 0.371$ (Profit = \$3.19). Thus, for any starting point x less than 1.5 (including the starting point $x = 0$ tried in the leftmost spreadsheet in Figure 8.7), Solver's search will move toward and eventually converge to this local maximum. Similarly, for any starting point x between 1.5 and 4.6 (such as $x = 3$ tried in the center spreadsheet in Figure 8.7), Solver will converge to the local (and global) maximum at $x = 3.126$ (Profit = \$6.13). Finally, for any starting point x greater than 4.6 (such as $x = 4.7$ tried in the rightmost spreadsheet in Figure 8.7), Solver will converge to the local maximum at $x = 5$ (Profit = \$0). By trying several starting points, three different local optima are found. The best of these local optima is $x = 3.126$ with a corresponding profit of \$6.13.

If there are only one or two changing cells, this approach can be done more systematically by using the Solver Table add-in that is provided in your MS Courseware. To demonstrate, we will continue to use the spreadsheet model shown in Figure 8.7. Figure 8.21 displays how Solver Table is used to try six different starting points (0, 1, 2, 3, 4, and 5) for this model by executing the following steps. In the first row of the table, enter formulas that refer to the changing cell, x (C5), and the target cell, Profit (C8). The different starting points are entered in the first column of the table (G8:G13). Then, select the entire table (G7:I13) and choose the Solver Table from the Add-Ins tab (for Excel 2007) or the Tools menu (for earlier versions of Excel). The column input cell entered in the Solver Table dialogue box is the changing cell, x (C5), since this is where we want the different starting points in the first column of the table

If there are multiple local optima, running Solver many times with different starting points can sometimes find the global optimum.

FIGURE 8.21

An application of the Solver Table (an Excel add-in provided in your MS Courseware) to the example considered in Figures 8.7 and 8.8.

	A	B	C	D	E	F	G	H	I	J
1		**Using Solver Table to Try Different Starting Points**								
2										
3										
4					Maximum		Starting			
5		$x =$	3.126	$\leq$	5		Point	Solution		
6							x	x^*	Profit	
7		Profit $=0.5x^5-6x^4+24.5x^3-39x^2+20x$						3.126	\$6.13	Select the
8		=	\$6.13				0	0.371	\$3.19	entire table
9							1	0.371	\$3.19	(G7:I13),
10							2	3.126	\$6.13	before
11							3	3.126	\$6.13	choosing
12							4	3.126	\$6.13	Solver Table
13							5	5.000	\$0.00	from the Tools menu.

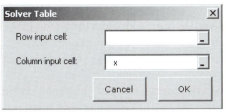

	H	I
5	Solution	
6	x^*	Profit
7	$=x$	$=$Profit

Range Name	Cell
x	C5
Profit	C8

The Solver Table can be used to systematically re-solve a small nonlinear programming model with many different starting points.

to be entered. (No row input cell is entered in this dialogue box since only a column is being used to list the starting points.) Clicking OK then causes the Solver Table to re-solve the problem for all these starting points in the first column and fill in the corresponding results (the local maximum for *x* and Profit referred to in the first row) in the other columns of the table.

This example has only one changing cell. However, the Solver Table also can be used to try multiple starting points for problems with two changing cells. This is done by using the first row and first column of the table to specify different starting points for the two changing cells. Enter an equation referring to the target cell in the upper left-hand corner of the table. Select the entire table and choose Solver Table from the Add-Ins tab or Tools menu, with the two changing cells selected as the column input cell and row input cell. The Solver Table then re-solves the problem for each combination of starting points of the two changing cells and fills in the body of the table with the objective function value of the solution that is found (a local optimum) for each of these combinations. (See Section 5.4 and Appendix A for more details about setting up a two-dimensional Solver Table.)

For problems with more than two changing cells, this same approach still can be used to try multiple starting points for any two of the changing cells at a time. However, this becomes a very cumbersome way of trying a broad range of starting points for all the changing cells when there are more than three or four of these cells.

This approach has some major limitations.

Unfortunately, there is no guarantee in general of finding a globally optimal solution, no matter how many different starting points are tried. Also, if the profit graphs are not smooth (e.g., if they have discontinuities or kinks), as is typically the case if functions like IF, ABS, MAX, or ROUND are used, then Solver may not even be able to find local optima. Fortunately, there is another approach available to attempt to solve these difficult nonlinear problems. We explore this new approach in the next section.

Review Questions

1. The Solver has difficulty solving nonlinear programming problems with certain properties. List three of these properties.
2. What is a method for attempting to solve problems with multiple locally optimal solutions?

8.5 EVOLUTIONARY SOLVER AND GENETIC ALGORITHMS

The installer for Premium Solver is available in your MS Courseware.

Frontline Systems, the original developer of the standard Solver that Microsoft includes with Excel, has developed Premium versions of Solver. One version of Premium Solver (Premium Solver for Education) is available in your MS Courseware (but not included with standard Excel). Every version of Premium Solver, including this one, adds a new search procedure called **Evolutionary Solver** to the set of tools available in Solver. Evolutionary Solver uses an entirely different approach than the standard Solver to search for an optimal solution for a model. The philosophy of Evolutionary Solver is based on genetics, evolution, and the survival of the fittest. Hence, this type of algorithm is sometimes called a **genetic algorithm.**

Evolutionary Solver uses the principles of genetics, evolution, and the survival of the fittest.

The standard Solver starts with a single solution, (the starting point) and then moves in directions that will improve this solution. At any point in time, standard Solver is only keeping track of a single solution (the best one found so far). In contrast, Evolutionary Solver begins by randomly generating a large set of candidate solutions, called the **population.** Throughout the solution process, Evolutionary Solver keeps track of the whole population of candidate solutions. Much like trying different starting points with the standard Solver, this attention to many candidate solutions can help avoid being trapped at a local optimum.

Each pair of parents creates offspring that resemble the parents.

After generating the population, Evolutionary Solver next creates a new **generation** of the population. The existing population of candidate solutions is paired off to create "offspring" for the next generation. Borrowing from the principles of genetics, the offspring combine some elements from each parent. For example, an offspring could combine some of the changing cell values from one parent and some from the other, while other changing cells might be averaged between the two parents.

Among the population of solutions in any generation, some solutions will be good (or "fit") and some will be bad (or "unfit"). The level of fitness is determined by evaluating the

Only the fit parents are allowed to create many offspring.

objective function at each of the candidate solutions in the population. A penalty is subtracted for any solution that does not satisfy one or more of the constraints. Then, borrowing from the principles of evolution and the survival of the fittest, the "fit" members of the population are allowed to reproduce frequently (create many offspring), while the "unfit" members are not allowed to reproduce. In this way, the population eventually evolves to become more and more fit.

Random mutations occasionally occur in the offspring.

Another key feature of genetic algorithms is **mutation.** Like gene mutation in biology, Evolutionary Solver will occasionally make a random change in a member of the population. For example, the value of one changing cell might be replaced with a new random value. This mutation can create offspring that are far removed from the rest of the population. This is important, since it can help the algorithm get unstuck if it is getting trapped near a local optimum.

Evolutionary Solver keeps creating new generations of solutions until there have been no improvements in several consecutive generations. The algorithm then terminates and the best solution found so far is reported.

Now let us look at an example where Evolutionary Solver is needed to solve the problem.

Selecting a Portfolio to Beat the Market

In Section 8.2, we developed a model for finding a portfolio of stocks that minimizes the risk (variance of the return from the portfolio) subject to achieving at least some desired minimum expected return. The standard Solver could be used for that problem because the constraints were linear and the objective function was smooth and had decreasing marginal returns.

Now consider another common goal of portfolio managers—to beat the market. Figure 8.22 shows a spreadsheet model for pursuing this goal when choosing a portfolio from five large stocks traded on the New York Stock Exchange (NYSE): Disney (DIS), Boeing (BA), General Electric (GE), Procter & Gamble (PG), and McDonald's (MCD). The quarterly performance (return) of each of these stocks over a six-year period (2000–2005) is shown in StockData (D4:H27). The performance of the market as a whole, as measured by the NYSE Composite Index, is shown in column K.

The objective is to find the portfolio that beat the market most frequently.

If we assume that past performance is somewhat of an indicator of the future, then picking a portfolio that beat the market most often during these six years might yield a portfolio that will more than likely beat the market in the future. Thus, the model in Figure 8.22 uses the objective of choosing the portfolio that beat the market for the largest number of quarters during this period.

The changing cells in this model are Portfolio (D31:H31), representing the percentage of the portfolio to invest in each individual stock. The return of the given portfolio for each quarter is calculated in column I. Column J then compares the return of the portfolio to the return of the market and determines whether the portfolio beat the market using the IF functions shown below the spreadsheet in Figure 8.22. The number of quarters in which the portfolio beat the market is then calculated in the target cell, NumberBeatingTheMarket (J36). As seen in the figure, a portfolio that was evenly split among the five stocks (20 percent in each) would have beaten the market in 15 of the 24 quarters during this six-year period.

The standard Solver can't handle this kind of problem.

The standard Solver would have little to no chance of solving this model. The objective function is not smooth since changes in the Portfolio can cause instantaneous (nonsmooth) jumps in the target cell (the number of quarters that the portfolio beats the market). However, the target cell remains constant for small changes in the changing cells until the change is significant enough to cause a quarter in column J to switch from Yes to No (or No to Yes). An unfortunate consequence of this is that nearly every solution is a local maximum, since very small changes in the portfolio will lead to no improvement in the target cell. Thus, Solver typically will stop its search immediately and report the initial solution as a local maximum. Since the standard Solver cannot solve this model, we will try the Evolutionary Solver.

Applying Evolutionary Solver to Portfolio Selection to Beat the Market

Installing the Premium Solver available in your MS Courseware adds the Premium Solver option to the Add-Ins tab (for Excel 2007) or the Tools menu (for earlier versions of Excel).

FIGURE 8.22

A spreadsheet model (prior to using the Premium Solver dialogue box) for selecting a portfolio that beat the market most frequently in recent quarters. A starting solution has been entered in the changing cells Portfolio (D31:H31). The target cell is NumberBeatingTheMarket (J36).

	A	B	C	D	E	F	G	H	I	J	K
1	**Beating the Market (Evolutionary Solver)**										
2										Beat	Market
3		Quarter	Year	DIS	BA	GE	PG	MCD	Return	Market?	(NYSE)
4		Q4	2005	0.38%	3.77%	4.85%	−2.15%	2.74%	1.92%	Yes	1.59%
5		Q3	2005	−4.17%	3.34%	−2.21%	13.29%	20.71%	6.19%	Yes	5.75%
6		Q2	2005	−12.35%	13.36%	−3.31%	0.04%	−10.88%	−2.63%	No	0.70%
7		Q1	2005	3.34%	13.45%	−0.57%	−3.33%	−2.90%	2.00%	Yes	−1.14%
8		Q4	2004	24.37%	0.67%	9.32%	2.26%	16.50%	10.62%	Yes	10.35%
9		Q3	2004	−11.52%	1.45%	4.26%	−0.13%	7.84%	0.38%	Yes	−0.50%
10		Q2	2004	2.00%	24.99%	6.80%	4.31%	−9.02%	5.81%	Yes	0.06%
11		Q1	2004	7.12%	−2.17%	−0.89%	5.49%	15.07%	4.93%	Yes	2.09%
12		Q4	2003	16.79%	23.28%	4.61%	8.12%	7.13%	11.99%	No	14.53%
13		Q3	2003	2.08%	0.55%	4.60%	4.64%	6.70%	3.71%	Yes	2.52%
14		Q2	2003	16.09%	37.76%	13.17%	0.60%	52.55%	24.03%	Yes	16.38%
15		Q1	2003	4.36%	−23.61%	5.59%	4.11%	−10.05%	−3.92%	Yes	−5.40%
16		Q4	2002	9.02%	−2.84%	−0.49%	−3.42%	−7.70%	−1.09%	No	6.16%
17		Q3	2002	−19.86%	−23.80%	−14.56%	0.61%	−37.92%	−19.11%	No	−16.44%
18		Q2	2002	−18.15%	−6.39%	−21.84%	0.32%	2.51%	−8.71%	Yes	−11.22%
19		Q1	2002	11.42%	24.95%	−6.24%	14.39%	4.85%	9.87%	Yes	1.80%
20		Q4	2001	12.44%	16.34%	8.23%	9.29%	−1.51%	8.96%	Yes	8.45%
21		Q3	2001	−35.55%	−39.57%	−23.50%	14.73%	0.28%	−16.72%	No	−12.53%
22		Q2	2001	1.03%	0.08%	17.06%	2.54%	1.91%	4.52%	Yes	4.38%
23		Q1	2001	−1.20%	−15.34%	−12.37%	−19.82%	−21.90%	−14.13%	No	−9.32%
24		Q4	2000	−23.81%	2.55%	−16.81%	17.65%	13.37%	−1.41%	No	−0.93%
25		Q3	2000	−1.45%	54.71%	9.62%	18.77%	−8.36%	14.66%	Yes	3.13%
26		Q2	2000	−5.91%	11.00%	2.16%	0.48%	−11.87%	−0.83%	No	−0.74%
27		Q1	2000	41.04%	−8.47%	0.87%	−48.07%	−7.29%	−4.38%	No	−0.40%
28											
29				0%	0%	0%	0%	0%			
30				<=	<=	<=	<=	<=	Sum		
31			Portfolio	20.0%	20.0%	20.0%	20.0%	20.0%	100%	=	100%
32				<=	<=	<=	<=	<=			
33				100%	100%	100%	100%	100%			
34										Number of Quarters	
35										Beating the Market	
36										15	

Range Name	Cells
BeatMarket?	J4:J27
Market	K4:K27
NumberBeatingTheMarket	J36
OneHundredPercent	D33:H33
OneHundredPercent2	K31
Portfolio	D31:H31
Return	I4:I27
StockData	D4:H27
Sum	I31
ZeroPercent	D29:H29

	I	J
2		Beat
3	Return	Market?
4	=SUMPRODUCT(Portfolio,D4:H4)	=IF(Return>Market,"Yes","No")
5	=SUMPRODUCT(Portfolio,D5:H5)	=IF(Return>Market,"Yes","No")
6	=SUMPRODUCT(Portfolio,D6:H6)	=IF(Return>Market,"Yes","No")
7	=SUMPRODUCT(Portfolio,D7:H7)	=IF(Return>Market,"Yes","No")
8	:	:
9	:	:

	I
30	Sum
31	=SUM(Portfolio)

	J
34	Number of Quarters
35	Beating the Market
36	=COUNTIF(BeatMarket?,"Yes")

Premium Solver includes Evolutionary Solver, but the standard Solver does not.

Choosing this option yields the Premium Solver dialogue box shown in Figure 8.23. This dialogue box has a dropdown menu that gives a choice of which algorithm to employ. The choices are Standard GRG Nonlinear, Standard Simplex LP, and Standard Evolutionary. The first choice (GRG Nonlinear) is identical to using standard Solver *without* the "Assume Linear Model" option selected. The second choice (Simplex LP) is equivalent to using standard Solver *with* the "Assume Linear Model" option selected. The final choice (Evolutionary) employs the Evolutionary Solver that is needed for the problem considered in Figure 8.22. A major benefit of using Premium Solver instead of the standard Solver that comes with Excel is the addition of this Evolutionary Solver option. (Certain versions of Premium Solver also are faster and able to solve larger problems than the standard Solver, but Premium Solver for Education provided in your MS Courseware does not have this advantage.)

FIGURE 8.23

The Premium Solver dialogue box that is used to complete the spreadsheet model introduced in Figure 8.22. Selecting Standard Evolutionary from the dropdown menu specifies that Evolutionary Solver will be used to solve the problem.

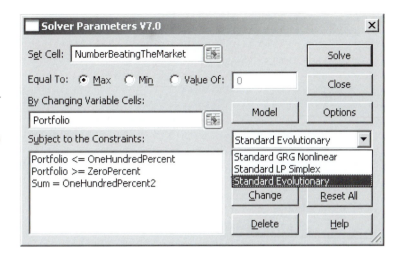

FIGURE 8.24

This Evolutionary Solver Options dialogue box for Premium Solver provides several parameters for Evolutionary Solver. The default values shown here are reasonable choices for most small applications.

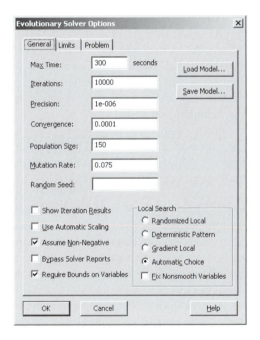

As shown in Figure 8.23, the Premium Solver dialogue box needs to specify the target cell (NumberBeatingTheMarket, or J36) and changing cells (Portfolio, or D31:H31). It also must include the constraints that (1) the portfolio needs to sum to 100 percent and (2) each individual stock must represent between 0 and 100 percent of the portfolio.

Clicking the Options button in the Premium Solver dialogue box yields the Evolutionary Solver Options dialogue box shown in Figure 8.24. This allows changing various parameters of the search, such as the maximum time to allow the search to continue, the size of the population, and the mutation rate. The default values for the parameters displayed in Figure 8.24 are reasonable ones for most small applications. However, feel free to experiment with these parameters. For example, increasing the population size or mutation rate may help with searches that are getting stuck.

Use the Require Bounds on Variables option whenever possible.

The Require Bounds on Variables option is selected by default. This forces all changing cells to be constrained with lower and upper limits. We strongly recommend that you use this option to place bounds on the changing cells whenever possible. This greatly narrows the area over which Evolutionary Solver needs to search and can increase the chances of finding a good solution.

FIGURE 8.25
The Limits tab of the
Evolutionary Solver
Options dialogue box
provides additional
control over when the
search conducted by
Evolutionary Solver
should be terminated.

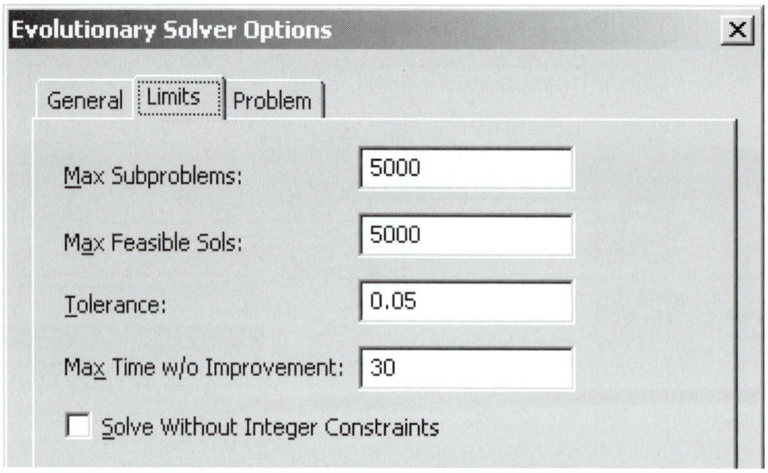

Clicking on the Limits tab in the Evolutionary Solver Options dialogue box yields the dialogue box in Figure 8.25. This dialogue box gives additional control over when to terminate the search. Entering large values in Max Subproblems and Max Feasible Sols will allow the search to continue for a long time. A tolerance value of 0.05 and Max Time w/o Improvement of 30 means Evolutionary Solver will continue the search until it has not improved the solution by more than 5 percent within the last 30 seconds. Decreasing the tolerance and/or increasing the Max Time w/o Improvement generally will allow for longer search time.

This solution found by Evolutionary Solver is not guaranteed to be optimal, but it probably is at least close to optimal.

Clicking Solve in the Premium Solver dialogue box then causes Evolutionary Solver to begin its search. Within a minute or so, the solution shown in Figure 8.26 was found. This represents a portfolio that beat the market in 19 of the 24 quarters over this six-year period. Is this solution optimal? Perhaps not. Unfortunately, there is no way to guarantee that we have found an optimal solution. However, it likely is a good solution (close to optimal).

Applying Evolutionary Solver to a Traveling Salesman Problem

Becky Thomas has just completed her MBA degree from the University of Washington Business School in Seattle and would like to celebrate during the summer with a driving tour of the United States, including visits to see a major league baseball game in every American League city. She would then return home to Seattle to start a job in the fall. She would like to plan her route to minimize the travel distance.

This is an example of a well-known problem in management science called the *traveling-salesman problem*. In the generic version of this problem, a salesperson needs to plan a sales trip to a certain set of cities in some order. Starting from a given location (home) and then returning home at the end, the objective is to find the route that minimizes the total travel distance (or time).

Figure 8.27 displays a map of the United States showing each of the 14 American League cities. Becky will start and end her tour in Seattle. After listing the cities to be visited in alphabetical order, each city has been labeled by both a number (an integer between 1 and 13) and a letter code, as given in cells B6:C18 and E3:Q4 of Figure 8.28. The data cells are Distance (D5:Q18), giving the travel distance between each pair of cities. A decision needs to be made about the order in which to visit the other cities before returning to Seattle. Therefore, the respective changing cells Route (D22:P22) indicate which city (referenced by its number label) is visited at each stage of the route. In other words, the first city visited after Seattle will have its number label in D22, the second in E22, and so on. The spreadsheet in Figure 8.28 shows the route if the cities are visited in alphabetical order (Anaheim 1, Baltimore 2, Boston 3, etc.). The total distance of this route is 18,962 miles.

INDEX(Range, i) returns the ith element in Range, where Range is a block of cells. INDEX (Range, a, b) returns the element in row a and column b of Range.

Row 23 displays the letter code for each city based upon the number label in row 22, using the INDEX function of Excel. Row 24 uses the INDEX function to look up the distance to travel to each city from the preceding city in the route. The target cell TotalMilesTraveled (Q26) adds up the total miles driven in the route.

FIGURE 8.26

After clicking the Solve button in the Premium Solver dialogue box, Evolutionary Solver found the solution shown in the changing cells Portfolio (D31:H31) for the model formulated in Figures 8.22 and 8.23. The target cell NumberBeating TheMarket (J36) indicates that this portfolio beat the market in 19 of these 24 quarters. Clicking Solve again probably would lead to at least a slightly different solution for the portfolio.

	A	B	C	D	E	F	G	H	I	J	K
1		**Beating the Market (Evolutionary Solver)**									
2										Beat	Market
3		Quarter	Year	DIS	BA	GE	PG	MCD	Return	Market?	(NYSE)
4		Q4	2005	0.38%	3.77%	4.85%	−2.15%	2.74%	1.78%	Yes	1.59%
5		Q3	2005	−4.17%	3.34%	−2.21%	13.29%	20.71%	7.26%	Yes	5.75%
6		Q2	2005	−12.35%	13.36%	−3.31%	0.04%	−10.88%	0.88%	Yes	0.70%
7		Q1	2005	3.34%	13.45%	−0.57%	−3.33%	−2.90%	1.80%	Yes	−1.14%
8		Q4	2004	24.37%	0.67%	9.32%	2.26%	16.50%	5.96%	No	10.35%
9		Q3	2004	−11.52%	1.45%	4.26%	−0.13%	7.84%	2.05%	Yes	−0.50%
10		Q2	2004	2.00%	24.99%	6.80%	4.31%	−9.02%	8.46%	Yes	0.06%
11		Q1	2004	7.12%	−2.17%	−0.89%	5.49%	15.07%	3.13%	Yes	2.09%
12		Q4	2003	16.79%	23.28%	4.61%	8.12%	7.13%	11.11%	No	14.53%
13		Q3	2003	2.08%	0.55%	4.60%	4.64%	6.70%	3.79%	Yes	2.52%
14		Q2	2003	16.09%	37.76%	13.17%	0.60%	52.55%	19.73%	Yes	16.38%
15		Q1	2003	4.36%	−23.61%	5.59%	4.11%	−10.05%	−4.12%	Yes	−5.40%
16		Q4	2002	9.02%	−2.84%	−0.49%	−3.42%	−7.70%	−2.71%	No	6.16%
17		Q3	2002	−19.86%	−23.80%	−14.56%	0.61%	−37.92%	−14.53%	Yes	−16.44%
18		Q2	2002	−18.15%	−6.39%	−21.84%	0.32%	2.51%	−7.27%	Yes	−11.22%
19		Q1	2002	11.42%	24.95%	−6.24%	14.39%	4.85%	10.51%	Yes	1.80%
20		Q4	2001	12.44%	16.34%	8.23%	9.29%	−1.51%	9.57%	Yes	8.45%
21		Q3	2001	−35.55%	−39.57%	−23.50%	14.73%	0.28%	−11.69%	Yes	−12.53%
22		Q2	2001	1.03%	0.08%	17.06%	2.54%	1.91%	5.54%	Yes	4.38%
23		Q1	2001	−1.20%	−15.34%	−12.37%	−19.82%	−21.90%	−16.55%	No	−9.32%
24		Q4	2000	−23.81%	2.55%	−16.81%	17.65%	13.37%	3.44%	Yes	−0.93%
25		Q3	2000	−1.45%	54.71%	9.62%	18.77%	−8.36%	21.62%	Yes	3.13%
26		Q2	2000	−5.91%	11.00%	2.16%	0.48%	−11.87%	1.89%	Yes	−0.74%
27		Q1	2000	41.04%	−8.47%	0.87%	−48.07%	−7.29%	−18.41%	No	−0.40%
28											
29				0%	0%	0%	0%	0%			
30				<=	<=	<=	<=	<=	Sum		
31			Portfolio	2.6%	25.0%	25.7%	34.8%	12.0%	100%	=	100%
32				<=	<=	<=	<=	<=			
33				100%	100%	100%	100%	100%			
34									Number of Quarters		
35									Beating the Market		
36									19		

FIGURE 8.27

A map of the United States showing the 14 cities (including Toronto, Canada) with American League ballparks.

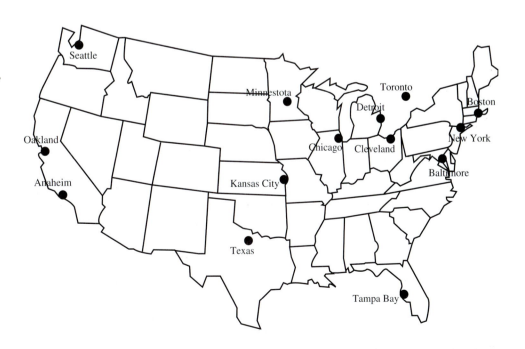

FIGURE 8.28

A spreadsheet model for determining the minimum-distance route from Seattle to the other 13 American League cities and back to Seattle. The changing cells are Route (D22:P22) and the target cell is TotalMilesTraveled (Q26).

	A	B	C	D	E	F	G	H	I	J	K	L	M	N	O	P	Q
1		**Tour of the American League Ballparks**															
2																	
3		Distance			1	2	3	4	5	6	7	8	9	10	11	12	13
4		(miles)		SEA	ANA	BAL	BOS	CHI	CLE	DET	KC	MIN	NY	OAK	TB	TEX	TOR
5			SEA	0	1134	2708	3016	2052	2391	2327	1858	1653	2841	810	3077	2131	2564
6		1	ANA	1134	0	2647	3017	2048	2382	2288	1577	1857	2794	387	2490	1399	2523
7		2	BAL	2708	2647	0	427	717	358	514	1070	1113	199	2623	950	1357	457
8		3	BOS	3016	3017	427	0	994	657	799	1435	1390	222	3128	1293	1753	609
9		4	CHI	2052	2048	717	994	0	348	279	542	410	809	2173	1160	921	515
10		5	CLE	2391	2382	358	657	348	0	172	819	758	471	2483	1108	1189	296
11		6	DET	2327	2288	514	799	279	172	0	769	685	649	2399	1184	1156	240
12		7	KC	1858	1577	1070	1435	542	819	769	0	443	1233	1861	1171	505	1006
13		8	MIN	1653	1857	1113	1390	410	758	685	443	0	1217	1979	1573	949	906
14		9	NY	2841	2794	199	222	809	471	649	1233	1217	0	2930	1150	1559	516
15		10	OAK	810	387	2623	3128	2173	2483	2399	1861	1979	2930	0	2823	1752	2627
16		11	TB	3077	2490	950	1293	1160	1108	1184	1171	1573	1150	2823	0	1079	1348
17		12	TEX	2131	1399	1357	1753	921	1189	1156	505	949	1559	1752	1079	0	1435
18		13	TOR	2564	2523	457	609	515	296	240	1006	906	516	2627	1348	1435	0
19																	
20																	
21		Tour	Start	1st	2nd	3rd	4th	5th	6th	7th	8th	9th	10th	11th	12th	13th	End
22		Route		1	2	3	4	5	6	7	8	9	10	11	12	13	
23		City	SEA	ANA	BAL	BOS	CHI	CLE	DET	KC	MIN	NY	OAK	TB	TEX	TOR	SEA
24		Miles Traveled		1134	2647	427	994	348	172	769	443	1217	2930	2823	1079	1435	2564
25																	
26																Total Miles Traveled	18,982

	B	C	D	E	P	Q
23	City	SEA	=INDEX($C$6:$C$18,D22)	=INDEX($C$6:$C$18,E22)	=INDEX($C$6:$C$18,P22)	SEA
24	Miles Traveled		=INDEX(D6:D18,D22)	=INDEX($E$6:$Q$18,D22,E22)	=INDEX($E$6:$Q$18,O22,P22)	=INDEX(D6:D18,P22)

	P	Q
26	Total Miles Traveled	=SUM(D24:Q24)

FIGURE 8.29

The Add Constraint dialogue box showing the alldifferent constraint.

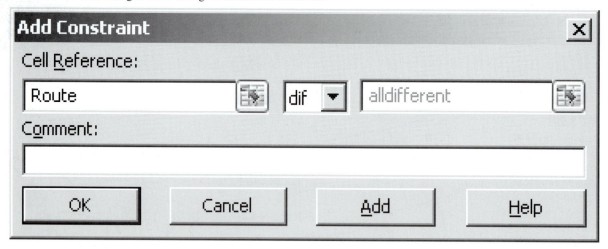

Because each city needs to be visited exactly once, the one constraint needed in this model is that the changing cells all must be *unique* integers from 1 to 13. This constraint would be very difficult to enforce with the standard Solver. Fortunately, the Premium Solver includes a new type of constraint, called *alldifferent,* that does just what we need. When *n* changing cells are choosing integers from 1 to *n,* constraining these changing cells to be *alldifferent* forces them to be unique integers from 1 to *n.* To implement the *alldifferent* constraint with Premium Solver, press the Add button in Solver to bring up the Add Constraint dialogue box. Select the changing cells (Route) for the left-hand side of the dialogue box and then choose *dif* in the pull-down menu in the center of the dialogue box, as shown in Figure 8.29.

The resulting model is not linear because of the INDEX function used to calculate distances and the *alldifferent* constraint. However, the Evolutionary Solver can be used to try to

FIGURE 8.30

After adding the alldifferent constraint, Route (D22:P22) and C23:Q23 show the route from Seattle to the other 13 American League cities and back to Seattle that has been obtained by Evolutionary Solver.

	A	B	C	D	E	F	G	H	I	J	K	L	M	N	O	P	Q
1		Tour of the American League Ballparks															
2																	
3		Distance			1	2	3	4	5	6	7	8	9	10	11	12	13
4		(miles)		SEA	ANA	BAL	BOS	CHI	CLE	DET	KC	MIN	NY	OAK	TB	TEX	TOR
5			SEA	0	1134	2708	3016	2052	2391	2327	1858	1653	2841	810	3077	2131	2564
6		1	ANA	1134	0	2647	3017	2048	2382	2288	1577	1857	2794	387	2490	1399	2523
7		2	BAL	2708	2647	0	427	717	358	514	1070	1113	199	2623	950	1357	457
8		3	BOS	3016	3017	427	0	994	657	799	1435	1390	222	3128	1293	1753	609
9		4	CHI	2052	2048	717	994	0	348	279	542	410	809	2173	1160	921	515
10		5	CLE	2391	2382	358	657	348	0	172	819	758	471	2483	1108	1189	296
11		6	DET	2327	2288	514	799	279	172	0	769	685	649	2399	1184	1156	240
12		7	KC	1858	1577	1070	1435	542	819	769	0	443	1233	1861	1171	505	1006
13		8	MIN	1653	1857	1113	1390	410	758	685	443	0	1217	1979	1573	949	906
14		9	NY	2841	2794	199	222	809	471	649	1233	1217	0	2930	1150	1559	516
15		10	OAK	810	387	2623	3128	2173	2483	2399	1861	1979	2930	0	2823	1752	2627
16		11	TB	3077	2490	950	1293	1160	1108	1184	1171	1573	1150	2823	0	1079	1348
17		12	TEX	2131	1399	1357	1753	921	1189	1156	505	949	1559	1752	1079	0	1435
18		13	TOR	2564	2523	457	609	515	296	240	1006	906	516	2627	1348	1435	0
19																	
20																	
21		Tour	Start	1st	2nd	3rd	4th	5th	6th	7th	8th	9th	10th	11th	12th	13th	End
22		Route		10	1	12	11	2	9	3	13	5	6	4	7	8	
23		City	SEA	OAK	ANA	TEX	TB	BAL	NY	BOS	TOR	CLE	DET	CHI	KC	MIN	SEA
24		Miles Traveled		810	387	1399	1079	950	199	222	609	296	172	279	542	443	1653
25																	
26																Total Miles Traveled	9,040

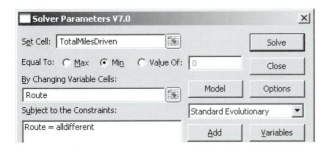

Range Name	Cells
CityName	C5:C18
Distance	D5:Q18
MilesTraveled	D24:Q24
Route	D22:P22
TotalMilesTraveled	Q26

find a good route. After solving with the Evolutionary Solver, the resulting solution is shown in both D22:P22 and D23:P23 in Figure 8.30. This route is much improved over the one shown in Figure 8.28, with a total distance of 9,040 miles instead of 18,962 miles. In this case, Evolutionary Solver has succeeded in finding the optimal solution.

Advantages and Disadvantages of Evolutionary Solver

Evolutionary Solver can handle problems with complicated objective functions and many local optima.

Evolutionary Solver has two significant advantages over the standard Solver for solving difficult nonlinear programming problems. First, the complexity of the objective function does not impact Evolutionary Solver. As long as the function can be evaluated for a given candidate solution (in order to determine the level of fitness), it does not matter if the function has kinks or discontinuities or many local optima. Second, by evaluating whole populations of candidate solutions that aren't necessarily in the same neighborhood as the current best solution, Evolutionary Solver keeps from getting trapped at a local optimum. Furthermore, even if the whole population eventually evolves toward a solution that is only locally optimal, mutation allows for the possibility of getting unstuck. In fact, because of the random mutations, Evolutionary Solver is guaranteed to eventually find an optimal solution for any optimization problem if it runs forever, but this is impractical of course.

However, Evolutionary Solver also has several limitations.

On the other hand, it must be pointed out that Evolutionary Solver is not a panacea. First, it can take *much* longer than the standard Solver to find a final solution. With certain choices of limit options, the search for better solutions can continue for hours or even days. Second, Evolutionary Solver does not perform well on models that have many constraints. For instance, it would not perform very well on many of the models considered in Chapters 2–6, even though the standard Solver can solve these models almost instantaneously. Third, Evolutionary Solver is a random process. Running Evolutionary Solver again on the same model usually will yield a different final solution. Finally, the best solution found typically is not optimal (although it may be very close). Evolutionary Solver is not an optimizer in the same sense that the standard Solver is. It does not continuously move toward better solutions until it reaches a local optimum. Rather it is more like an intelligent search engine, trying out different random solutions. Thus, while it is quite likely to end up with a solution that is very close to optimal, it almost never returns the exact optimal solution on most types of nonlinear programming problems. (However, its chances of finding an optimal solution are much better on problems like the beat-the-market example where the target cell only takes on integer values.) Consequently, it often can be beneficial to run the standard Solver (GRG Nonlinear) after the Evolutionary Solver, starting with the final solution obtained by the Evolutionary Solver, to see if this solution can be improved by searching around its neighborhood.

Review Questions

1. Why is the algorithm used by Evolutionary Solver called a genetic algorithm?
2. What criterion does Evolutionary Solver use to choose which members of a generation are fit and which are unfit?
3. How does mutation help Evolutionary Solver?
4. What is the advantage of Premium Solver for Education over the standard Solver packaged with Excel?
5. What are two advantages that Evolutionary Solver has over the standard Solver for solving difficult nonlinear programming problems?
6. What are three disadvantages of Evolutionary Solver compared to the standard Solver?

8.6 Summary

A nonlinear programming model has the same characteristics as a linear programming model with one key exception. All the mathematical expressions (including the objective function) are linear in a linear programming model, but at least one of these expressions (often just the objective function) is nonlinear in a nonlinear programming model. When formulating the model in a spreadsheet, this means that the model becomes a nonlinear programming model if a nonlinear formula needs to be entered into the target cell (and perhaps into some other output cells). A nonlinear formula is needed for the target cell whenever there is a nonproportional relationship between the level of any of the activities and the overall measure of performance for the problem. This kind of relationship violates the proportionality assumption of linear programming.

Formulating and solving a nonlinear programming model tends to be more difficult than formulating and solving a linear programming model. For example, some nonlinear programming models have a number of locally optimal solutions where only one of these solutions is globally optimal and most of the others are greatly inferior. Unfortunately, after a starting solution is entered into the spreadsheet, the standard Excel Solver will find only one of these locally optimal solutions, with no indication of whether this is the one that also is globally optimal or perhaps one that is far from optimal. Which locally optimal solution is found depends on the choice of the starting solution.

However, when a nonlinear programming model has decreasing marginal returns, it generally is easy to solve. For this type of problem, a locally optimal solution automatically is also a globally optimal solution. Therefore, the solution found by the Excel Solver is guaranteed to be the best solution for the model (or at least one of those tied for being the best).

Some nonlinear programming problems with decreasing marginal returns can be solved in an even easier way. This occurs when the profit graphs (or cost graphs) for the activities are piecewise linear (or at least can be closely approximated by piecewise linear graphs). In this case, the separable programming technique can be applied to convert the problem into a linear programming problem, which is the easiest type of problem for the Excel Solver.

For more difficult nonlinear programming problems that might have a number of locally optimal solutions, one approach is to run the Solver many times, each time starting with a different initial solution entered into the changing cells on the spreadsheet. If there are only one or two changing cells, this approach can be done systematically by using the Solver Table add-in that is provided in your MS Courseware.

However, this method of dealing with difficult problems has two major limitations. First, it is impractical for problems with more than a few changing cells. Second, it does not work for problems with such complicated objective functions that the Solver is not even able to find local optima. If such problems don't have many constraints, another search procedure called Evolutionary Solver is likely to perform well. Using concepts from genetics, evolution, and the survival of the fittest, this procedure is able to gradually move toward the best of the local optima. Given enough search time (which may be a very long time), it frequently succeeds in finding a solution that is very close to optimal.

Glossary

curve fitting method   A method for using the known values in a profit or cost graph to find the equation for the graph that best fits these data. (Section 8.1), 259

decreasing marginal returns   An activity with a profit graph has decreasing marginal returns if the slope (steepness) of this profit graph never increases but sometimes decreases as the level of the activity increases. (Section 8.1), 257

discontinuity   A spot in a graph where it is disconnected because it suddenly jumps up or down. (Section 8.1), 257

Evolutionary Solver   A search procedure provided in Premium Solver that uses concepts from genetics, evolution, and the survival of the fittest. (Section 8.5), 284

generation   A new set of candidate solutions that is created by Evolutionary Solver by pairing off members of the existing population of candidate solutions to create "offspring" for the next generation. (Section 8.5), 284

genetic algorithm   A type of algorithm that uses concepts from genetics. (Section 8.5), 284

global maximum   The highest point on an entire graph. (Section 8.1), 262

local maximum   A point at which a graph reaches its maximum within a local neighborhood of that point. (Section 8.1), 261

mutation   Similar to gene mutation in biology, this is a random change that Evolutionary Solver

occasionally makes in a member of the current population. (Section 8.5), 285

nonproportional relationship   An activity has a nonproportional relationship with the overall measure of performance for a problem if the contribution of the activity to this measure is *not* proportional to the level of the activity. (Section 8.1), 256

piecewise linear   A graph is piecewise linear if it consists of a sequence of connected line segments. (Section 8.1), 257

population   The large set of candidate solutions that is randomly generated by Evolutionary Solver. (Section 8.5), 284

proportional relationship   An activity has a proportional relationship with the overall measure of performance for a problem if the contribution of the activity to this measure is proportional to the level of the activity. (Section 8.1), 255

proportionality assumption   A basic assumption of linear programming that requires the contribution of each activity to the value of the objective function to be proportional to the level of that activity. (Section 8.1), 256

quadratic programming   A special type of nonlinear programming where the objective function has both a quadratic form and decreasing marginal returns and all the constraints are linear. (Section 8.2), 266

Learning Aids for This Chapter in Your MS Courseware

Chapter 8 Excel Files:

Constructing a Nonlinear Formula

An Example with Multiple Local Maxima

Original Wyndor Problem

Wyndor Problem with Nonlinear Marketing Costs

Portfolio Selection Example

Wyndor Problem with Overtime

Wyndor Problem with Overtime and Marketing Costs (Separable Programming)

Wyndor Problem with Overtime and Marketing Costs (Nonlinear Programming)

Beating the Market Example

Tour of American League Ballparks

Excel Add-ins:

Premium Solver for Education

Solver Table

Solved Problem (See the CD-ROM for the Solution)

8.S1. Airline Ticket Pricing Model

Business travelers tend to be less price sensitive than leisure travelers. Knowing this, airlines have discovered that extra profit can be generated by using separate pricing for these two types of customers. For example, airlines often charge more for a midweek flight (mostly business travelers) than for travel that includes a Saturday night stay (mostly leisure travelers).

Suppose an airline has estimated demand versus price for midweek travel (mostly business travelers) and for travel that includes a Saturday night stay (mostly leisure travelers) as shown in the table below. This flight is served by a Boeing 777 with capacity for 300 travelers. The fixed cost of operating the flight is $30,000. The variable cost per passenger (for food and fuel) is $30.

	Demand		
Price	Midweek	Saturday Night Stay	Total
$200	150	465	615
$300	105	210	315
$400	82	127	209
$500	63	82	145
$600	49	60	109
$700	35	45	80
$800	27	37	64

a. One function that can used to estimate demand (D) as a function of price (P) is a *linear* demand function, where $D = a - bP$. For positive values of a and b, this will give lower demand when the price is higher. However, a *nonlinear* demand function usually can provide a better fit to the data. For example, one such function is a constant elasticity demand function, where $D = aP^b$. For positive values of a and negative values of b, this also will give lower demand when the price is higher. Graph the above data and use the *Add Trendline* feature of Excel to find the constant elasticity demand function that best fits the data in the above table for midweek demand, Saturday night stay demand, and total demand.

b. For this part, assume that the airline charges a single price to all customers. Using the demand function for total demand determined in part *a,* formulate and solve a nonlinear programming model in a spreadsheet to determine what the price should be so as to achieve the highest profit for the airline.

c. Now assume that the airline charges separate prices for midweek and Saturday night stay tickets. Using the two demand functions for midweek and Saturday night stay tickets determined in part *a,* formulate and solve a nonlinear programming spreadsheet model to determine what the prices of the two types of tickets should be so as to maximize the profit for the airline.

d. How much extra profit can the airline achieve by charging higher prices for midweek tickets than for Saturday night stay tickets?

Problems

To the left of each of the following problems (or their parts), we have inserted an E* whenever Excel should be used (unless your instructor gives you contrary instructions). An asterisk on the problem number indicates that at least a partial answer is given in the back of the book.

8.1.   The J. P. Atkins Company will soon be introducing a new product. Estimates have been made of the monthly profit that would be generated by this product for each of four alternative values of the monthly production rate, as shown below.

Production Rate	Profit
200	$ 9,500
500	22,500
800	34,000
1,000	40,000

a. Draw a profit graph for this product by plotting the profits for the four production rates and then drawing a smooth curve through the four points by hand. (Start the graph with a profit of 0 at a production rate of 0.)

b. Does the proportionality assumption of linear programming seem to be satisfied reasonably well for this product?

c. To the extent that profit is not strictly proportional to the production rate, does this product have decreasing marginal returns, increasing marginal returns, or neither?

E*   *d.* Use Excel's curve fitting method to (1) obtain a nonlinear formula with a quadratic form for the profit graph and then (2) construct the graph.

8.2.   Consider the following three cases for how the profit from an activity varies with the level of the activity.

	Profit ($)		
Level of Activity	**Case 1**	**Case 2**	**Case 3**
0	0	0	0
1	9	6	5
2	16	14	6
3	21	24	3
4	24	36	4
5	25	50	7

a. For each case, draw the profit graph by plotting the profits for the various levels of the activity and then drawing a smooth curve through the points by hand.

b. For each case, indicate whether the activity has decreasing marginal returns, increasing marginal returns, or neither.

c. How would your answers in part *b* change if the graphs plotted in part *a* were cost graphs instead of profit graphs?

E*   d. For each case, use Excel's curve fitting method to (1) obtain a nonlinear formula with a quadratic form for the profit graph and then (2) construct the graph. For any case where the activity has neither decreasing marginal returns nor increasing marginal returns, comment on how good a fit is provided by using a quadratic form.

8.3.   The Chiplet Corporation is about to launch the production and marketing of a new microchip that is more powerful than anything that is currently on the market. Not surprisingly, the profitability of this microchip will depend greatly on its reception in this highly competitive and fast-moving market. If the sales are fairly low, the company will still be able to make a respectable profit because it will have enough available production capacity to produce the microchip with its current facilities. However, if sales are somewhat higher, the company will need to expand its production facilities, which will have the effect of depressing the profit from the microchip if sales only reach a moderate level. (Fully meeting this demand would still be worthwhile because one of top management's prime goals is to continue increasing the company's market share as it points toward future generations of microchips already under development.) Fortunately, if sales reach a relatively high level, the profit from the microchip will become very substantial. The following table shows the estimated profit for various levels of sales over the short lifetime of this microchip.

Sales	Profit (millions of dollars)
0	0
100,000	15
200,000	18
300,000	13
400,000	4
500,000	1
600,000	6
700,000	30
800,000	70

a. Draw a profit graph for this microchip by plotting the profits for the various sales levels and then drawing a smooth curve that passes through (or very near) these points.

b. Does the microchip have decreasing marginal returns, increasing marginal returns, or neither?

E*   c. Use Excel's curve fitting method to (1) obtain a nonlinear formula with a quadratic form (a polynomial of order 2) for the profit graph and then (2) construct the graph.

E*   d. Repeat part *c* when using the Excel option of a polynomial of order 3 instead of order 2.

e. Which of the Excel options used in parts *c* and *d* does a better job of fitting the profit graph to the data?

8.4.   The following table shows the estimated daily profit from a new product for several of the alternative choices for the production rate.

Production Rate (R)	Profit per Day (P)
0	0
1	$ 95
2	184
3	255
4	320

Because the profit goes up less than proportionally with the production rate (decreasing marginal returns), the management science team analyzing what this production rate (and the production rates of some other products) should be has decided to approximate the profit (P) by a simple *nonlinear function* of the production rate R.

a. One such approximation is $P = \$100R - \$5R^2$. How closely does this nonlinear function approximate the five values of P given in the table?

b. Repeat part *a* for the approximation, $P = \$104R - \$6R^2$.

c. Which of these two nonlinear functions provides the better fit to all the data?

E*   d. Use Excel's curve fitting method to (1) obtain a nonlinear formula with a quadratic form for the profit graph and then (2) construct the graph.

E*8.5.   Reconsider the portfolio selection example, including its spreadsheet model in Figure 8.13, given in Section 8.2. Note in Table 8.2 that stock 2 has the highest expected return and stock 3 has by far the lowest. Nevertheless, the changing cells Portfolio (C14:E14) provide an optimal solution that calls for purchasing far more of stock 3 than of stock 2. Although purchasing so much of stock 3 greatly reduces the risk of the portfolio, an aggressive investor may be unwilling to own so much of a stock with such a low expected return.

For the sake of such an investor, add a constraint to the model that specifies that the percentage of stock 3 in the portfolio cannot exceed the amount specified by the investor. Then compare the expected return and risk (standard deviation of the return) of the optimal portfolio with that in Figure 8.13 when the upper bound on the percentage of stock 3 allowed in the portfolio is set at the following values.

a. 20%

b. 0%

c. Use the Solver Table to systematically try all the percentages at 5% intervals from 0% to 50%.

8.6.* A stockbroker, Richard Smith, has just received a call from his most important client, Ann Hardy. Ann has $50,000 to invest and wants to use it to purchase two stocks. Stock 1 is a solid blue-chip security with a respectable growth potential and little risk involved. Stock 2 is much more speculative. It is being touted in two investment newsletters as having outstanding growth potential, but also is considered very risky. Ann would like a large return on her investment, but also has considerable aversion to risk. Therefore, she has instructed Richard to analyze what mix of investments in the two stocks would be appropriate for her. She also informs him that her plan is to hold the stock being purchased now for three years before selling it.

After doing some research on the historical performances of the two stocks and on the current prospects for the companies involved, Richard is able to make the following estimates. If the entire $50,000 were to be invested in stock 1 now, the profit when sold in three years would have an expected value of $12,500 and a standard deviation of $5,000. If the entire $50,000 were to be invested in stock 2 now, the profit when sold in three years would have an expected value of $20,000 and a standard deviation of $30,000. The two stocks behave independently in different sectors of the market so Richard's calculation from historical data is that the covariance of the profits from the two stocks is 0.

Richard now is ready to use a spreadsheet model to determine how to allocate the $50,000 to the two stocks so as to minimize Ann's risk while providing an expected profit that is at least as large as her minimum acceptable value. He asks Ann to decide what her minimum acceptable value is.

a. Without yet assigning a specific numerical value to the minimum acceptable expected profit, formulate a quadratic programming model in algebraic form for this problem.

E* b. Display this model on a spreadsheet.

E* c. Solve this model for four cases: Minimum acceptable expected profit = $13,000, $15,000, $17,000, and $19,000.

d. Ann was a statistics major in college and so understands well that the *expected return* and *risk* in this model represent estimates of the *mean* and *standard deviation* of the probability distribution of the profit from the corresponding portfolio. Ann uses the notation μ and σ for the mean and standard deviation. She recalls that, for typical probability distributions, the probability is fairly high (about 0.8 or 0.9) that the return will exceed $\mu - \sigma$, and the probability is extremely high (often close to 0.999) that the profit will exceed $\mu - 3\sigma$. Calculate $\mu - \sigma$ and $\mu - 3\sigma$ for the four portfolios obtained in part c. Which portfolio will give Ann the highest μ among those that also give $\mu - \sigma \geq 0$?

8.7. Reconsider the portfolio selection example given in Section 8.2. A fourth stock (stock 4) now has been found that gives a good balance between expected return and risk. Using the same units as in Table 8.2, its expected return is 17% and its risk is 18%. Its joint risk per stock with stocks 1, 2, and 3 is -0.015, -0.025, and 0.003, respectively.

a. Still using a minimum acceptable expected return of 18%, formulate the revised quadratic programming model in algebraic form for this problem.

E* b. Display and solve this model on a spreadsheet.

E* c. Develop a revision of the Solver Table shown in Figure 8.14 for this revised problem.

8.8. The management of the Albert Hanson Company is trying to determine the best product mix for two new products. Because these products would share the same production facilities, the total number of units produced of the two products combined cannot exceed two per hour. Because of uncertainty about how well these products will sell, the profit from producing each product provides decreasing marginal returns as the production rate is increased. In particular, with a production rate of R_1 units per hour, it is estimated that product 1 would provide a profit per hour of $200R_1 - 100R_1^2$. If the production rate of product 2 is R_2 units per hour, its estimated profit per hour would be $300R_2 - 100R_2^2$.

a. Formulate a quadratic programming model in algebraic form for determining the product mix that maximizes the total profit per hour.

E* b. Formulate and solve this model on a spreadsheet.

8.9. The B. J. Jensen Company specializes in the production of power saws and power drills for home use. Sales are relatively stable throughout the year except for a jump upward during the Christmas season. Since the production work requires considerable work and experience, the company maintains a stable employment level and then uses overtime to increase production in November. The workers also welcome this opportunity to earn extra money for the holidays.

B. J. Jensen, Jr., the current president of the company, is overseeing the production plans being made for the upcoming November. He has obtained the following data.

	Maximum Monthly Production*		Profit per Unit Produced	
	Regular Time	Overtime	Regular Time	Overtime
Power saws	3,000	2,000	$150	$50
Power drills	5,000	3,000	100	75

* Assuming adequate supplies of materials from the company's vendors.

However, Mr. Jensen now has learned that, in addition to the limited number of labor hours available, two other factors will limit the production levels that can be achieved this November. One is that the company's vendor for power supply units will only be able to provide 10,000 of these units for November (2,000 more than his usual monthly shipment). Each power saw and each power drill requires one of these units. Second, the vendor who supplies a key part for the gear assemblies will only be able to provide 15,000 for November (4,000 more than for other months). Each power saw requires two of these parts and each power drill requires one.

Mr. Jensen now wants to determine how many power saws and how many power drills to produce in November to maximize the company's total profit.

a. Draw the profit graph for each of these two products.

E* b. Use separable programming to formulate a linear programming model on a spreadsheet for this problem. Then solve the model. What does this say about how many power saws and how many power drills to produce in November?

8.10.* The Dorwyn Company has two new products (special kinds of doors and windows) that will compete with the two new products for the Wyndor Glass Co. (described in Section 2.1). Using units of hundreds of dollars for the objective function, the linear programming model in algebraic form shown below has been formulated to determine the most profitable product mix.

$$\text{Maximize} \quad \text{Profit} = 4D + 6W$$

subject to

$$D + 3W \le 8$$
$$5D + 2W \le 14$$

and

$$D \ge 0 \quad W \ge 0$$

However, because of the strong competition from Wyndor, Dorwyn management now realizes that the company will need to make a strong marketing effort to generate substantial sales of these products. In particular, it is estimated that achieving a production and sales rate of D doors per week will require weekly marketing costs of D^3 hundred dollars (so $100 for $D = 1$, $800 for $D = 2$, $2,700 for $D = 3$, etc.). The corresponding marketing costs for windows are estimated to be $2W^2$ hundred dollars. Thus, the objective function in the model should be

$$\text{Profit} = 4D + 6W - D^3 - 2W^2$$

Dorwyn management now would like to use the revised model to determine the most profitable product mix.

E* a. Formulate and solve this nonlinear programming model on a spreadsheet.

b. Construct tables to show the profit data for each product when the production rate is 0, 1, 2, 3.

c. Draw a figure that plots the weekly profit points for each product when the production rate is 0, 1, 2, 3. Connect the pairs of consecutive points with (dashed) line segments.

E* d. Use separable programming based on this figure to formulate an approximate linear programming model on a spreadsheet for this problem. Then solve the model. What does this say to Dorwyn management about which product mix to use?

e. Compare the solution based on a separable programming approximation in part *d* with the solution obtained in part *a* for the exact nonlinear programming model.

8.11. The MFG Corporation is planning to produce and market three different products. Let x_1, x_2, and x_3 denote the number of units of the three respective products to be produced. The preliminary estimates of their potential profitability are as follows.

For the first 15 units produced of product 1, the unit profit would be approximately $360. The unit profit would be only $30 for any additional units of product 1. For the first 20 units produced of product 2, the unit profit is estimated at $240. The unit profit would be $120 for each of the next 20 units and $90 for any additional units. For the first 10 units of product 3, the unit profit would be $450. The unit profit would be $300 for each of the next 5 units and $180 for any additional units.

Certain limitations on the use of needed resources impose the following constraints on the production of the three products:

$$x_1 + x_2 + x_3 \le 60$$
$$3x_1 + 2x_2 \qquad \le 200$$
$$x_1 \qquad + 2x_3 \le 70$$

Management wants to know what values of x_1, x_2, and x_3 should be chosen to maximize the total profit.

a. Plot the profit graph for each of the three products.

E* b. Use separable programming to formulate a linear programming model on a spreadsheet for this problem. Then solve the model. What is the resulting recommendation to management about the values of $x_1, x_2,$ and x_3 to use?

8.12. Suppose that separable programming has been applied to a certain problem (the "original problem") to convert it to the following equivalent linear programming model in algebraic form:

Maximize   Profit $= 5x_{11} + 4x_{12} + 2x_{13} + 4x_{21} + x_{22}$

subject to

$$3x_{11} + 3x_{12} + 3x_{13} + 2x_{21} + 2x_{22} \leq 25$$
$$2x_{11} + 2x_{12} + 2x_{13} - x_{21} - x_{22} \leq 10$$

and

$$0 \leq x_{11} \leq 2 \quad 0 \leq x_{21} \leq 3$$
$$0 \leq x_{12} \leq 3 \quad 0 \leq x_{22} \leq 1$$
$$0 \leq x_{13}$$

What was the mathematical model for the original problem? Answer this by plotting the profit graph for each of the original activities and then writing the constraints for the original problem in terms of the original decision variables.

8.13. Jim Matthews, vice president for marketing of the J. R. Nickel Company, is planning advertising campaigns for two unrelated products. These two campaigns need to use some of the same resources. Therefore, Jim knows that his decisions on the levels of the two campaigns need to be made jointly after considering these resource constraints. In particular, letting x_1 and x_2 denote the levels of campaigns 1 and 2, respectively, these constraints are $4x_1 + x_2 \leq 20$ and $x_1 + 4x_2 \leq 20$.

In facing these decisions, Jim is well aware that there is a point of diminishing returns when raising the level of an advertising campaign too far. At that point, the cost of additional advertising becomes larger than the increase in net revenue (excluding advertising costs) generated by the advertising. After careful analysis, he and his staff estimate that the net profit from the first product (including advertising costs) when conducting the first campaign at level x_1 would be $3x_1 - (x_1 - 1)^2$ in millions of dollars. The corresponding estimate for the second product is $3x_2 - (x_2 - 2)^2$.

Letting P be total net profit, this analysis led to the following nonlinear programming model for determining the levels of the two advertising campaigns:

Maximize $P = 3x_1 - (x_1 - 1)^2 + 3x_2 - (x_2 - 2)^2$

subject to

$$4x_1 + x_2 \leq 20$$
$$x_1 + 4x_2 \leq 20$$

and

$$x_1 \geq 0 \quad x_2 \geq 0$$

a. Construct tables to show the profit data for each product when the level of its advertising campaign

is $x_1 = 0, 1, 2, 2.5, 3, 4, 5$ (for the first product) or $x_2 = 0, 1, 2, 3, 3.5, 4, 5$ (for the second product).

b. Use these profit data to draw rough-hand a smooth profit graph for each product. (Note that these profit graphs start at negative values when $x_1 = 0$ or $x_2 = 0$ because the products would lose money if there is no advertising to support them.)

c. On the profit graph for the first product, draw an approximation of this profit graph by inserting a dashed-line segment between the profit at $x_1 = 0$ and $x_1 = 2$, between the profit at $x_1 = 2$ and $x_1 = 4$, and between the profit at $x_1 = 4$ and $x_1 = 5$. Then do the same on the profit graph for the second product with $x_2 = 0, 2, 4, 5$.

E* d. Use separable programming with the approximation of the profit graphs obtained in part c to formulate an approximate linear programming model on a spreadsheet for Jim Matthews's problem. Then solve this model. What does this solution say the levels of the advertising campaigns should be? What would the total net profit from the two products be?

E* e. Repeat parts c and d except using $x_1 = 0, 2, 2.5, 3, 5$ and $x_2 = 0, 3, 3.5, 4, 5$ for the approximations of the profit graphs in part c. (These particular approximations actually lead to the exact optimal solution for Jim Matthews's problem.)

E* f. Use Excel and its Solver to formulate and solve the original nonlinear programming model directly. Compare with the answers obtained after completing part e.

g. Use calculus to find the value of x_1 that maximizes $3x_1 - (x_1 - 1)^2$, the net profit from the first product. Also use calculus to find the value of x_2 that maximizes $3x_2 - (x_2 - 2)^2$, the net profit from the second product. Show that these values satisfy the constraints for the nonlinear programming model. Then compare these values with the answers obtained in parts e and f.

E*8.14. Consider the following nonlinear programming problem.

Maximize   Profit $= x^5 - 13x^4 + 59x^3 - 107x^2 + 61x$

subject to

$$0 \leq x \leq 5$$

a. Formulate this problem in a spreadsheet and then use the Solver Table to solve this problem with the following starting points: $x = 0, 1, 2, 3, 4,$ and 5. Include the value of x and the profit as output cells in the Solver Table.

b. Use Evolutionary Solver to solve this problem.

E*8.15. Consider the following nonlinear programming problem.

Maximize   Profit $= 100x^6 - 1{,}359x^5 + 6{,}836x^4 - 15{,}670x^3 + 15{,}870x^2 - 5{,}095x$

subject to

$$0 \leq x \leq 5$$

a. Formulate this problem in a spreadsheet and then use the Solver Table to solve this problem with the following starting points: $x = 0, 1, 2, 3, 4,$ and 5. Include the value of x and the profit as output cells in the Solver Table.

b. Use Evolutionary Solver to solve this problem.

E*8.16. Because of population growth, the state of Washington has been given an additional seat in the House of Representatives, making a total of ten. The state legislature, which is currently controlled by the Republicans, needs to develop a plan for redistricting the state. There are 18 major cities in the state of Washington that need to be assigned to 1 of the 10 congressional districts. The table below gives the numbers of registered Democrats and registered Republicans in each city. Each district must contain between 150,000 and 350,000 of these registered voters. Use Evolutionary Solver to assign each city to 1 of the 10 congressional districts in order to maximize the number of districts that have more registered Republicans than registered Democrats. (Hint: Use the SUMIF function.)

City	Democrat (Thousands)	Republican (Thousands)
1	152	62
2	81	59
3	75	83
4	34	52
5	62	87
6	38	87
7	48	69
8	74	49
9	98	62
10	66	72
11	83	75
12	86	82
13	72	83
14	28	53
15	112	98
16	45	82
17	93	68
18	72	98

8.17. Reconsider the portfolio optimization problem considered in Section 8.5, where the goal was to select the portfolio that beat the market for the largest number of quarters over the last six years.

E*   *a.* Using the naive solution (20 percent in each stock) as a starting point, apply Evolutionary Solver to optimize the portfolio again when considering the data for the first three years only (Q1 2000 through Q4 2002).

b. For how many quarters does this same portfolio beat the market for the next three years (Q1 2003 through Q4 2005)?

c. Comment on the results from parts *a* and *b.*

E*8.18. Reconsider the portfolio optimization problem considered in Section 8.5, where the goal was to select the portfolio that beat the market for the largest number of quarters over the last six years.

a. Use Evolutionary Solver to instead find a portfolio that did not lose money in the largest number of quarters.

b. Use Evolutionary Solver to instead find a portfolio that yielded a return of at least 10 percent for the largest number of quarters.

8.19. Reconsider the Wyndor Glass Co. problem introduced in Section 2.1.

E*   *a.* Solve this problem using the standard Solver.

E*   *b.* Starting with an initial solution of producing 0 doors and 0 windows, solve this problem using Evolutionary Solver.

c. Comment on the performance of the two approaches.

Case 8-1

Continuation of the Super Grain Case Study

Reconsider the Super Grain case study introduced in Section 3.1 and continued in Section 3.4. Recall that Claire Syverson, vice president for marketing of The Super Grain Corporation, is planning an advertising campaign for the company's new breakfast cereal (Crunchy Start) with the help of a leading advertising firm, Giacomi & Jackowitz. The campaign will use three advertising media: television commercials on Saturday morning programs for children, advertisements in food- and family-oriented magazines, and advertisements in Sunday supplements of major newspapers. The problem being addressed is to determine the best mix of these advertising media.

The spreadsheet in Figure 3.7 shows the revised linear programming model that was used to address this problem. This model includes constraints on advertising expenditures, planning

expenditures, and the use of cents-off coupons, as well as on managerial goals involving the numbers of young children and their parents that should be reached by the advertising. The changing cells NumberOfAds (C19:E19) show the optimal number of advertisements to place in each of the three media according to this model. The target cell TotalExposures (H19) gives an estimate of the resulting total number of exposures, where each viewing of an advertisement by some individual counts as one exposure.

The ultimate goal of the advertising campaign is to maximize the company's profits that are attained because of the resulting sales. However, it is difficult to make a direct connection between advertising exposure and profits. Therefore, the total number of exposures was chosen to be a rough surrogate for profit. This is why the target cell in Figure 3.7 (and in Figure 3.1) gives the total number of exposures instead of the total profit.

Claire is uneasy with having done this. She realizes that her assumption—that the total profit from the introduction of Crunchy Start is proportional to the total number of exposures from the advertising campaign—is only a rough approximation. The most important reason is that running too many advertisements in an advertising medium reaches a saturation level, where the impact of one more advertisement is substantially less than that for the first advertisement in that medium. Nevertheless, when the target cell gives the total number of exposures, having an individual see the advertisement one more time after being saturated counts the same (one more exposure) as seeing the advertisement for the first time.

To check the results in Figure 3.7, Claire decides to try using profit directly as the measure of performance to be recorded in the target cell. She carefully defines profit as the total profit obtained from first-time sales of Crunchy Start that occur because of the advertising campaign. Excluded from consideration are profits from impulse purchases of Crunchy Start by customers who have seen no advertisements but are attracted to this new cereal with its shiny box trumpeting its virtues sitting on a store shelf, since these sales have no relevance for evaluating the advertising campaign. Repeat purchases of Crunchy Start also are excluded from consideration because these depend mainly on the reaction to the cereal from the first purchase instead of the advertising campaign.

Claire asks Sid Jackowitz, one of the senior partners of Giacomi & Jackowitz, to develop estimates of the number of first-time purchases of Crunchy Start that should result from various numbers of advertisements in each medium. His estimates are shown in the following tables.

Number of TV Spots	Number of Sales	Number of Magazine Ads	Number of Sales	Number of Ads in Sunday Supplements	Number of Sales
1	1,000,000	5	700,000	2	1,200,000
2	1,750,000	10	1,200,000	4	2,200,000
3	2,450,000	15	1,550,000	6	3,000,000
4	2,800,000	20	1,800,000	8	3,500,000
5	3,000,000	25	2,000,000	10	3,750,000

Sid also reports that it is reasonable to assume that sales resulting from advertising in one of the media are not substantially affected by the amount of advertising in the other media since the audiences for the different media are somewhat different.

It is estimated that the company's gross profits from Crunchy Start will be 75¢ per sale. However, this gross profit excludes the advertising costs and planning costs for the advertising campaign. Therefore, Claire wants to include these costs in her definition of the total profit that should be considered for determining the best advertising mix.

a. For each of the three advertising media, draw a graph of the number of sales versus the number of advertisements by plotting the sales for the five points provided by Sid Jackowitz and then drawing a smooth curve through (or very near) these points. (Fractional advertisements are allowed by using only a portion of the available outlets.)

b. For each of the advertising media, use Excel's curve fitting method to (1) obtain a nonlinear formula for the sales graph and then (2) construct the graph. In each case, try three Excel

options for the form of the graph—a polynomial of order 2 (the quadratic form), a polynomial of order 3, and the logarithmic form—and then choose the option that you feel provides the best fit.

c. Using your results from part *b*, write an expression for the total profit (as defined by Claire) in terms of the number of advertisements of each type.

d. Using your result from part *c*, revise the spreadsheet model in Figure 3.7 (available on the CD-ROM) so that it maximizes total profit instead of the total number of exposures, and then solve.

e. Use the sales tables provided by Sid Jackowitz to apply separable programming to this problem when maximizing total profit.

f. Compare your results in parts *d* and *e* with those in Figure 3.7 and then give your recommendation (with a brief explanation) for the best advertising mix. Do you feel it was worthwhile to introduce a nonlinear profit function into the model in order to refine the linear programming model used in Figure 3.7?

Case 8-2

Savvy Stock Selection

Ever since the day she took her first economics class in high school, Lydia wondered about the financial practices of her parents. They worked very hard to earn enough money to live a comfortable middle-class life, but they never made their money work for them. They simply deposited their hard-earned paychecks in savings accounts earning a nominal amount of interest. (Fortunately, there always was enough money available when it came time to pay her college bills.) She promised herself that when she became an adult, she would not follow the same financially conservative practices as her parents.

And Lydia kept this promise. She took every available finance course in her business program at college. Having landed a coveted job on Wall Street upon graduation, she now begins every morning by watching the CNN financial reports. She plays investment games on the World Wide Web, finding portfolios that maximize her return while minimizing her risk. And she reads *The Wall Street Journal* and *Financial Times*.

Lydia also reads the investment advice columns of the financial magazines. She decides to follow the current advice given by her two favorite columnists. In his monthly column, editor Jonathan Taylor recommends three stocks that he believes will rise far above market average. In addition, the well-known mutual fund guru Donna Carter advocates the purchase of three more stocks that she thinks will outperform the market over the next year.

Bigbell (ticker symbol on the stock exchange: BB), one of the nation's largest telecommunications companies, trades at a price-earnings ratio well below market average. Huge investments over the last eight months have depressed earnings considerably. However, with its new cutting-edge technology, the company is expected to significantly raise its profit margins. Taylor predicts that the stock will rise from its current price of $60 per share to $72 per share within the next year.

Lotsofplace (LOP) is one of the leading hard drive manufacturers in the world. The industry recently underwent major consolidation, as fierce price wars over the last few years were followed by many competitors going bankrupt or being bought by Lotsofplace and its competitors. Due to reduced competition in the hard drive market, revenues and earnings are expected to rise considerably over the next year. Taylor predicts a one-year increase of 42 percent in the stock of Lotsofplace from the current price of $127 per share.

Internetlife (ILI) has survived the many ups and downs of Internet companies. With the next Internet frenzy just around the corner, Taylor expects a doubling of this company's stock price from $4 to $8 within a year.

Healthtomorrow (HEAL) is a leading biotechnology company that is about to get approval for several new drugs from the Food and Drug Administration, which will help earnings to grow 20 percent over the next few years. In particular, a new drug to significantly reduce the risk of heart attacks is supposed to reap huge profits. Also, due to several new great-tasting medications for children, the company has been able to build an excellent image in the media. This public relations coup will surely have a positive effect on the sale of its over-the-counter medications. Carter is convinced that the stock will rise from $50 to $75 per share within a year.

Quicky (QUI) is a fast-food chain that has been vastly expanding its network of restaurants all over the United States. Carter has followed this company closely since it went public some 15 years ago when it had only a few dozen restaurants on the West Coast of the United States. Since then the company has expanded, and it now has restaurants in every state. Due to its emphasis on healthy foods, it is capturing a growing market share. Carter believes that the stock will continue to perform well above market average for an increase of 46 percent in one year from its current stock price of $150.

Automobile Alliance (AUA) is a leading car manufacturer from the Detroit area that just recently introduced two new models. These models show very strong initial sales, and therefore the company's stock is predicted to rise from $20 to $26 over the next year.

On the World Wide Web, Lydia found data about the risk involved in the stocks of these companies. The historical variances of return of the six stocks and their covariances are shown in the following table.

Company	BB	LOP	ILI	HEAL	QUI	AUA
Variance	0.032	0.1	0.333	0.125	0.065	0.08

Covariances	LOP	ILI	HEAL	QUI	AUA
BB	0.005	0.03	−0.031	−0.027	0.01
LOP		0.085	−0.07	−0.05	0.02
ILI			−0.11	−0.02	0.042
HEAL				0.05	−0.06
QUI					−0.02

a. At first, Lydia wants to ignore the risk of all the investments. Given this strategy, what is her optimal investment portfolio; that is, what fraction of her money should she invest in each of the six different stocks? What is the total risk of her portfolio?

b. Lydia decides that she doesn't want to invest more than 40 percent in any individual stock. While still ignoring risk, what is her new optimal investment portfolio? What is the total risk of her new portfolio?

c. Now Lydia wants to take into account the risk of her investment opportunities. For use in the following parts, formulate a quadratic programming model that will minimize her risk (measured by the variance of the return from her portfolio) while ensuring that her expected return is at least as large as her choice of a minimum acceptable value.

d. Lydia wants to ensure that she receives an expected return of at least 35 percent. She wants to reach this goal at minimum risk. What investment portfolio allows her to do that?

e. What is the minimum risk Lydia can achieve if she wants an expected return of at least 25 percent? Of at least 40 percent?

f. Do you see any problems or disadvantages with Lydia's approach to her investment strategy?

Case 8-3

International Investments

Charles Rosen relaxes in a plush, overstuffed recliner by the fire, enjoying the final vestiges of his week-long winter vacation. As a financial analyst working for a large investment firm in Germany, Charles has very few occasions to enjoy these private moments since he is generally catching red-eye flights around the world to evaluate various investment opportunities. Charles pats the loyal golden retriever lying at his feet and takes a swig of brandy, enjoying the warmth of the liquid. He sighs and realizes that he must begin attending to his own financial matters while he still has the time during the holiday. He opens a folder placed conspicuously on the top of a large stack of papers. The folder contains information about an investment Charles made when he graduated from college four years ago . . .

Charles remembers his graduation day fondly. He obtained a degree in business administration and was full of investment ideas that were born while he had been daydreaming in his numerous finance classes. Charles maintained a well-paying job throughout college, and he was able to save a large portion of the college fund that his parents had invested for him.

Upon graduation, Charles decided that he should transfer the college funds to a more lucrative investment opportunity. Since he had signed on to work in Germany, he evaluated investment opportunities in that country. Ultimately, he decided to invest 30,000 German marks (DM) in so-called B bonds that would mature in seven years. Charles purchased the bonds just four years ago last week (in early January of what will be called the "first year" in this discussion). He considered the bonds an excellent investment opportunity since they offered high interest rates (see Table 1) that would rise over the subsequent seven years and because he could sell the bonds whenever he wanted after the first year. He calculated the amount that he would be paid if he sold bonds originally worth DM 100 on the last day of any of the seven years (see Table 2). The amount paid included the principal plus the interest. For example, if he sold bonds originally worth DM 100 on December 31 of the sixth year, he would be paid DM 163.51 (the principal is DM 100 and the interest is DM 63.51).

TABLE 1
Interest Rates over the Seven Years

Year	Interest Rate	Annual Percentage Yield
1	7.50%	7.50%
2	8.50	8.00
3	8.50	8.17
4	8.75	8.31
5	9.00	8.45
6	9.00	8.54
7	9.00	8.61

TABLE 2
Total Return on 100 DM

Year	DM
1	107.50
2	116.64
3	126.55
4	137.62
5	150.01
6	163.51
7	178.23

Charles did not sell any of the bonds during the first four years. Last year, however, the German federal government introduced a capital gains tax on interest income. The German government designated that the first DM 6,100 a single individual earns in interest per year would be tax-free. Any interest income beyond DM 6,100 would be taxed at a rate of 30 percent. For example, if Charles earned interest income of DM 10,100, he would be required to pay 30 percent of DM 4,000 (DM 10,100 − DM 6,100) in taxes, or DM 1,200. His after-tax income would therefore be DM 8,900.

Because of the new tax implemented last year, Charles has decided to reevaluate the investment. He knows that the new tax affects his potential return on the B bonds, but he also knows that most likely a strategy exists for maximizing his return on the bonds. He might be able to decrease the tax he has to pay on interest income by selling portions of his bonds in different years.

Charles considers his strategy viable because the government requires investors to pay taxes on interest income only when they sell their B bonds. For example, if Charles were to sell one-third of his B bonds on December 31 of the sixth year, he would have to pay taxes on the interest income of DM (6,351 − 6,100).

Charles asks himself several questions. Should he keep all the bonds until the end of the seventh year? If so, he would earn 0.7823 times DM 30,000 in interest income, but he would have to pay very substantial taxes for that year. Considering these tax payments, Charles wonders if he should sell a portion of the bonds at the end of this year (the fifth year) and at the end of next year.

If Charles sells his bonds, his alternative investment opportunities are limited. He could purchase a certificate of deposit (CD) paying 4.0 percent interest, so he investigates this alternative. He meets with an investment advisor from the local branch of a bank, and the advisor tells him to keep the B bonds until the end of the seventh year. She argues that even if he had to pay 30 percent in taxes on the 9.00 percent rate of interest that the B bonds would be paying in their last year (see Table 1), this strategy would still result in a net rate of 6.30 percent interest, which is much better than the 4.0 percent interest he could obtain on a CD.

Charles concludes that he will make all his transactions on December 31, regardless of the year. Also, since he intends to attend business school in the United States in the fall of the seventh year and plans to pay his tuition for his second, third, and fourth semester with his investment, he does not plan to keep his money in Germany beyond December 31 of the seventh year.

(For the first three parts, assume that if Charles sells a portion of his bonds, he will put the money under his mattress earning zero percent interest. For the subsequent parts, assume that he could invest the proceeds of the bonds in the certificate of deposit.)

a. Formulate a separable programming model to be used in the following parts.

b. What is the optimal investment strategy for Charles?

c. What is fundamentally wrong with the advice Charles got from the investment advisor at the bank?

d. Now that Charles is considering investing in the certificate of deposit, what is his optimal investment strategy?

e. What would his optimal investment strategy for the fifth, sixth, and seventh years have been if he had originally invested DM 50,000?

f. Charles and his fiancée have been planning to get married after his first year in business school. However, Charles learns that for married couples, the tax-free amount of interest earnings each year is DM 12,200. How much money could Charles save on his DM 30,000 investment by getting married this year (the fifth year for his investment)?

g. Due to a recession in Germany, interest rates are low and are expected to remain low. However, since the American economy is booming, interest rates are expected to rise in the United States. A rise in interest rates would lead to a rise of the dollar in comparison to the mark. Analysts at Charles's investment bank expect the dollar to remain at the current exchange rate of DM 1.50 per dollar for the fifth year and then to rise to DM 1.80 per dollar by the end of the seventh year. Therefore, Charles is considering investing at the beginning of the sixth year in a two-year American municipal bond paying 3.6 percent tax-exempt interest to help pay tuition. How much money should he plan to convert into dollars by selling B bonds for this investment?

Chapter **Nine**

Decision Analysis

Learning objectives

After completing this chapter, you should be able to

1. Identify the kind of decision-making environment for which decision analysis is needed.
2. Describe the logical way in which decision analysis organizes a problem.
3. Formulate a payoff table from a description of the problem.
4. Describe and evaluate several alternative criteria for making a decision based on a payoff table.
5. Apply Bayes' decision rule to solve a decision analysis problem.
6. Formulate and solve a decision tree for dealing with a sequence of decisions.
7. Use TreePlan to construct and solve a decision tree.
8. Perform sensitivity analysis with Bayes' decision rule.
9. Determine whether it is worthwhile to obtain more information before making a decision.
10. Use new information to update the probabilities of the states of nature.
11. Use SensIt to perform sensitivity analysis when dealing with a sequence of decisions.
12. Use utilities to better reflect the values of payoffs.
13. Describe some common features in the practical application of decision analysis.

The previous chapters have focused mainly on managerial decision making when the consequences of alternative decisions are known with a reasonable degree of certainty. This decision-making environment enabled formulating helpful mathematical models (linear programming, integer programming, etc.) with objective functions that specify the estimated consequences of any combination of decisions. Although these consequences usually cannot be predicted with complete certainty, they could at least be estimated with enough accuracy to justify using such models (along with sensitivity analysis, etc.).

However, managers often must make decisions in environments that are fraught with much more uncertainty. Here are a few examples.

1. A manufacturer introducing a new product into the marketplace. What will be the reaction of potential customers? How much should be produced? Should the product be test marketed in a small region before deciding upon full distribution? How much advertising is needed to launch the product successfully?
2. A financial firm investing in securities. Which are the market sectors and individual securities with the best prospects? Where is the economy headed? How about interest rates? How should these factors affect the investment decisions?
3. A government contractor bidding on a new contract. What will be the actual costs of the project? Which other companies might be bidding? What are their likely bids?
4. An agricultural firm selecting the mix of crops and livestock for the upcoming season. What will be the weather conditions? Where are prices headed? What will costs be?
5. An oil company deciding whether to drill for oil in a particular location. How likely is there to be oil in that location? How much? How deep will they need to drill? Should geologists investigate the site further before drilling?

This is the kind of decision making in the face of great uncertainty that *decision analysis* is designed to address. Decision analysis provides a framework and methodology for rational decision making when the outcomes are uncertain.

The first section introduces a case study that will be carried throughout the chapter to illustrate the various phases involved in applying decision analysis. Section 9.2 focuses on choosing an appropriate decision criterion. The next section describes how decision trees can be used to structure and analyze a decision analysis problem. Section 9.4 discusses how sensitivity analysis can be performed efficiently with the help of decision trees. The subsequent three sections deal with whether it would be worthwhile to obtain more information and, if so, how to use this information for making a sequence of decisions. Section 9.8 introduces a useful Excel add-in called SensIt for performing sensitivity analysis even when a sequence of decisions needs to be made. Section 9.9 then describes how to analyze the problem while calibrating the possible outcomes to reflect their true value to the decision maker. Finally, Section 9.10 discusses the practical application of decision analysis.

9.1 A CASE STUDY: THE GOFERBROKE COMPANY PROBLEM

Max Flyer is the founder and sole owner of the Goferbroke Company, which develops oil wells in unproven territory. Max's friends refer to him affectionately as a wildcatter. However, he prefers to think of himself as an entrepreneur. He has poured his life's savings into the company in the hope of making it big with a large strike of oil.

Now his chance possibly has come. His company has purchased various tracts of land that larger oil companies have spurned as unpromising even though they are near some large oil fields. Now Max has received an exciting report about one of these tracts. A consulting geologist has just informed Max that he believes there is one chance in four of oil there.

Max has learned from bitter experience to be skeptical about the chances of oil reported by consulting geologists. Drilling for oil on this tract would require an investment of about $100,000. If the land turns out to be dry (no oil), the entire investment would be lost. Since his company does not have much capital left, this loss would be quite serious.

On the other hand, if the tract does contain oil, the consulting geologist estimates that there would be enough there to generate a net revenue of approximately $800,000, leaving an approximate profit of

$$\text{Profit if find oil} = \text{Revenue if find oil} - \text{Drilling cost}$$
$$= \$800,000 - \$100,000$$
$$= \$700,000$$

Although this wouldn't be quite the big strike for which Max has been waiting, it would provide a very welcome infusion of capital into the company to keep it going until he hopefully can hit the really big gusher.

There is another option. Another oil company has gotten wind of the consulting geologist's report and so has offered to purchase the tract of land from Max for $90,000. This is very tempting. This too would provide a welcome infusion of capital into the company, but without incurring the large risk of a very substantial loss of $100,000.

Table 9.1 summarizes the decision alternatives and prospective payoffs that face Max.

So Max is in a quandary about what to do. Fortunately, help is at hand. Max's daughter Jennifer has recently earned her degree from a fine business school and now has come to work for her proud dad. He asks her to apply her business training to help him analyze the problem.

Should Max sell the land instead of drilling for oil there?

TABLE 9.1
Prospective Profits for the Goferbroke Company

Alternative	Profit Oil	Profit Dry
Drill for oil	$700,000	−$100,000
Sell the land	90,000	90,000
Chance of status	1 in 4	3 in 4

Having studied management science in college, she recommends applying decision analysis. Having paid for her fine education, he agrees to give it a try.

Jennifer begins by interviewing her dad about the problem.

Jennifer: How much faith do you put in the consulting geologist's assessment that there is one chance in four of oil on this tract?

Max: Not too much. These guys sometimes seem to pull numbers out of the air. He has convinced me that there is some chance of oil there. But it could just as well be one chance in three, or one chance in five. They don't really know.

Jennifer: Is there a way of getting more information to pin these odds down better? This is an important option with the decision analysis approach.

Max: Yes. We could arrange for a detailed seismic survey of the land. That would pin down the odds somewhat better. But you don't really find out until you drill. Furthermore, these seismic surveys cost you an arm and a leg. I got a quote for this tract. 30,000 bucks! Then it might say oil is likely, so we drill and we might not find anything. Then I'm out another 100,000 bucks! Losing $130,000 would almost put us out of business.

Jennifer: OK. Let's put the seismic survey on the back burner for now. Here is another key consideration. It sounds like we need to go beyond dollars and cents to look at the consequences of the possible outcomes. Losing $130,000 would hurt a lot more than gaining $130,000 would help.

Max: That's for sure!

Jennifer: Well, decision analysis has a way of taking this into account by using what are called utilities. The **utility** of an outcome measures the true value to you of that outcome rather than just the monetary value.

Max: Sounds good.

Jennifer: Now this is what I suggest we do. We'll start out simple, without considering the option of the seismic survey and without getting into utilities. I'll introduce you to how decision analysis organizes our problem and to the options it provides for the criterion to use for making your decision. You'll be able to choose the criterion that feels right to you. Then we'll look at whether it might be worthwhile to do the seismic survey and, if so, how to best use its information. After that, we'll get into the nitty gritty of carefully analyzing the problem, including incorporating utilities. I think when we finish the process and you make your decision, you'll feel quite comfortable that you are making the best one.

Max: Good. Let's get started.

Here is the tutorial that Jennifer provided her dad about the logical way in which decision analysis organizes a problem.

The utility of an outcome measures the true value to the decision maker of that outcome.

Decision Analysis Terminology

Decision analysis has a few special terms.

The **decision maker** is the individual or group responsible for making the decision (or sequence of decisions) under consideration. For the Goferbroke Co. problem, the decision maker is Max. Jennifer (the management scientist) can help perform the analyses, but the objective is to assist the decision maker in identifying the best possible decision from the decision maker's perspective.

The **alternatives** are the options for the decision to be made by the decision maker. Max's alternatives at this point are to drill for oil or to sell the tract of land.

The outcome of the decision to be made will be affected by random factors that are outside the control of the decision maker. These random factors determine the situation that will be found when the decision is executed. Each of these possible situations is referred to as a possible **state of nature.** For the Goferbroke Co. problem, the possible states of nature are that the tract contains oil or that it is dry (no oil).

The decision maker generally will have some information about the relative likelihood of the possible states of nature. This information may be in the form of just subjective estimates based on the experience or intuition of an individual, or there may be some degree of hard evidence

TABLE 9.2
Prior Probabilities for the First Goferbroke Co. Problem

State of Nature	Prior Probability
The tract of land contains oil	0.25
The tract of land is dry (no oil)	0.75

TABLE 9.3
Payoff Table (Profit in $1,000s) for the First Goferbroke Co. Problem

	State of Nature	
Alternative	**Oil**	**Dry**
Drill for oil	700	−100
Sell the land	90	90
Prior probability	0.25	0.75

involved (such as is contained in the consulting geologist's report). When these estimates are expressed in the form of probabilities, they are referred to as the **prior probabilities** of the respective states of nature. For the Goferbroke Co. problem, the consulting geologist has provided the prior probabilities given in Table 9.2. Although these are unlikely to be the true probabilities based on more information (such as through a seismic survey), they are the best available estimates of the probabilities *prior* to obtaining more information. (Later in the chapter, we will analyze whether it would be worthwhile to conduct a seismic survey, so the current problem of what to do without a seismic survey will be referred to hereafter as the *first* Goferbroke Co. problem.)

Each combination of a decision alternative and a state of nature results in some outcome. The **payoff** is a quantitative measure of the value to the decision maker of the consequences of the outcome. In most cases, the payoff is expressed as a monetary value, such as the profit. As indicated in Table 9.1, the payoff for the Goferbroke Co. at this stage is profit. (In Section 9.9, the company's payoffs will be reexpressed in terms of utilities.)

The Payoff Table

When formulating the problem, it is important to identify *all* the relevant decision alternatives and the possible states of nature. After identifying the appropriate measure for the *payoff* from the perspective of the decision maker, the next step is to estimate the payoff for each combination of a decision alternative and a state of nature. These payoffs then are displayed in a **payoff table**.

Table 9.3 shows the payoff table for the first Goferbroke Co. problem. The payoffs are given in units of thousands of dollars of profit. Note that the bottom row also shows the prior probabilities of the states of nature, as given earlier in Table 9.2.

Review Questions

1. What are the decision alternatives being considered by Max?
2. What is the consulting geologist's assessment of the chances of oil on the tract of land?
3. How much faith does Max put in the consulting geologist's assessment of the chances of oil?
4. What option is available for obtaining more information about the chances of oil?
5. What is meant by the possible *states of nature*?
6. What is meant by *prior probabilities*?
7. What do the *payoffs* represent in a payoff table?

9.2 DECISION CRITERIA

Given the payoff table for the first Goferbroke Co. problem shown in Table 9.3, what criterion should be used in deciding whether to drill for oil or sell the land? There is no single correct answer for this question that is appropriate for every decision maker. The choice of a decision criterion depends considerably on the decision maker's own temperament and attitude toward decision making, as well as the circumstances of the decision to be made. Ultimately, Max Flyer, as the owner of the Goferbroke Co., needs to decide which decision criterion is most appropriate for this situation from his personal viewpoint.

There is no single decision criterion that is best for every situation.

Over a period of many decades (and even centuries), a considerable number of criteria have been suggested for how to make a decision when given the kind of information provided by a payoff table. All these criteria consider the payoffs in some way and some also take into account the prior probabilities of the states of nature, but other criteria do not use probabilities in any way. Each criterion has some rationale as well as some drawbacks. However, in recent decades, a substantial majority of management scientists has concluded that one of these criteria (Bayes' decision rule) is a particularly appropriate criterion for most decision makers in most situations. Therefore, after describing and discussing Bayes' decision rule in this section, the rest of the chapter will focus on how to apply this particular criterion in a variety of contexts.

> Bayes' decision rule is the recommended decision criterion for most situations.

However, before turning to Bayes' decision rule, we briefly introduce three alternative decision criteria below. All of these alternative criteria are particularly simple and intuitive. At the same time, each criterion is quite superficial in the sense that it focuses on only one piece of information provided by the payoff table and ignores the rest (including the pieces considered by the other two criteria). Nevertheless, many individuals informally apply one or more of these criteria at various times in their lives. The first two make no use of prior probabilities, which can be quite reasonable when it is difficult or impossible to obtain relatively reliable values for these probabilities. Bayes' decision rule is quite different from these alternative criteria in that it makes full use of all the information in the payoff table by applying a more structured approach to decision making.

The CD-ROM includes a supplement entitled *Decision Criteria* that provides a much more detailed discussion and critique of these three alternative decision criteria as well as three others that are somewhat more complicated.

Decision Making without Probabilities: The Maximax Criterion

The **maximax criterion** is the decision criterion for the eternal optimist. It says to focus only on the *best* that can happen to us. Here is how this criterion works:

1. Identify the *maximum payoff* from any state of nature for each decision alternative.
2. Find the *maximum* of these maximum payoffs and choose the corresponding decision alternative.

> The maximax criterion always chooses the decision alternative that can give the largest possible payoff.

The rationale for this criterion is that it gives an opportunity for the best possible outcome (the largest payoff in the entire payoff table) to occur. All that is needed is for the right state of nature to occur, which the eternal optimist believes is likely.

Table 9.4 shows the application of this criterion to the first Goferbroke problem. It begins with the payoff table (Table 9.3) without the prior probabilities (since these probabilities are ignored by this criterion). An extra column on the right then shows the maximum payoff for each decision alternative. Since the maximum of these maxima (700) must be the largest payoff in the entire payoff table, the corresponding decision alternative (drill for oil) is selected by this criterion.

> This criterion ignores the prior probabilities.

The biggest drawback of this criterion is that it completely ignores the prior probabilities. For example, it always would say that Goferbroke should drill for oil even if the chance of finding oil were minuscule. Another drawback is that it ignores all the payoffs except the largest one. For example, it again would say that Goferbroke should drill for oil even if the payoff from selling the land were 699 ($699,000).

Decision Making without Probabilities: The Maximin Criterion

The **maximin criterion** is the criterion for the total pessimist. In contrast to the maximax criterion, it says to focus only on the *worst* that can happen to us. Here is how this criterion works:

1. Identify the *minimum payoff* from any state of nature for each decision alternative.
2. Find the *maximum* of these minimum payoffs and choose the corresponding decision alternative.

> The maximin criterion always chooses the decision alternative that provides the best guarantee for its minimum possible payoff.

TABLE 9.4
Application of the Maximax Criterion to the First Goferbroke Co. Problem

	State of Nature		
Alternative	**Oil**	**Dry**	**Maximum in Row**
Drill for oil	700	−100	700 ← Maximax
Sell the land	90	90	90

TABLE 9.5
Application of the Maximin Criterion to the First Goferbroke Co. Problem

	State of Nature		
Alternative	**Oil**	**Dry**	**Minimum in Row**
Drill for oil	700	−100	−100
Sell the land	90	90	90 ← Maximin

The rationale for this criterion is that it provides the best possible protection against being unlucky. Even if each possible choice of a decision alternative were to lead to its worst state of nature occurring, which the total pessimist thinks is likely, the choice indicated by this criterion gives the best possible payoff under these circumstances.

The application of this criterion to the first Goferbroke problem is shown in Table 9.5. The basic difference from Table 9.4 is that the numbers in the right-hand column now are the *minimum* rather than the maximum in each row. Since 90 is the maximum of these two numbers, the alternative to be chosen is to sell the land.

The drawbacks of this criterion are similar to those for the maximax criterion. Because it completely ignores prior probabilities, it always would say that Goferbroke should sell the land even if it were almost certain to find oil if it drilled. Because it ignores all the payoffs except the maximin payoff, it again would say that Goferbroke should sell the land even if the payoff from drilling successfully for oil were 10,000 ($10 million).

This criterion also ignores the prior probabilities.

Decision Making with Probabilities: The Maximum Likelihood Criterion

The **maximum likelihood criterion** says to focus on the *most likely* state of nature as follows.

1. Identify the state of nature with the largest prior probability.
2. Choose the decision alternative that has the largest payoff for this state of nature.

The maximum likelihood criterion assumes that the most likely state of nature will occur and chooses accordingly.

The rationale for this criterion is that by basing our decision on the assumption that the most likely state of nature will occur, we are giving ourselves a better chance of a favorable outcome than by assuming any other state of nature.

Table 9.6 shows the application of this criterion to the first Goferbroke Co. problem. This table is identical to the payoff table given in Table 9.3 except for also showing step 1 (select the *dry* state of nature) and step 2 (select the *sell the land* alternative) of the criterion. Since dry is the state of nature with the larger prior probability, we only consider the payoffs in its column (−100 and 90). The larger of these two payoffs is 90, so we choose the corresponding alternative, sell the land.

This criterion ignores all the payoffs except for the most likely state of nature.

This criterion has a number of drawbacks. One is that with a considerable number of states of nature, the most likely state can have a fairly low prior probability, in which case it would make little sense to base the decision solely on this one state. Another more serious drawback is that it completely ignores all the payoffs (including any extremely large payoffs and any disastrous payoffs) throughout the payoff table except those for the single most likely state of nature. For example, no matter how large the payoff for finding oil, it automatically would say that Goferbroke should sell that land instead of drilling for oil whenever the dry state has a little larger prior probability than the oil state.

TABLE 9.6
Application of the Maximum Likelihood Criterion to the First Goferbroke Co. Problem

	State of Nature		
Alternative	**Oil**	**Dry**	
Drill for oil	700	−100	
Sell the land	90	90	Step 2: ← Maximum
Prior probability	0.25	0.75	

Step 1: Maximum

Decision Making with Probabilities: Bayes' Decision Rule

Bayes' decision rule directly uses the *prior probabilities* of the possible states of nature as summarized below.

1. For each decision alternative, calculate the *weighted average* of its payoffs by multiplying each payoff by the prior probability of the corresponding state of nature and then summing these products. Using statistical terminology, refer to this weighted average as the **expected payoff (EP)** for this decision alternative.

2. Bayes' decision rule says to choose the alternative with the *largest* expected payoff.

The spreadsheet in Figure 9.1 shows the application of this criterion to the first Goferbroke Co. problem. Columns B, C, and D display the payoff table first given in Table 9.3. Cells F5 and F6 then execute step 1 of the procedure by using the equations entered into these cells, namely,

F5 = SUMPRODUCT(PriorProbability, DrillPayoff)

F6 = SUMPRODUCT(PriorProbability, SellPayoff)

Since expected payoff = 100 for the drill alternative (cell F5), versus a smaller value of expected payoff = 90 for the sell the land alternative (cell F6), this criterion says to drill for oil.

Like all the others, this criterion cannot guarantee that the selected alternative will turn out to have been the best one after learning the true state of nature. However, it does provide another guarantee described below.

On the average, Bayes' decision rule provides larger payoffs in the long run than any other criterion.

The expected payoff for a particular decision alternative can be interpreted as what the *average* payoff would become if the same situation were to be repeated numerous times. Therefore, *on the average,* repeatedly using Bayes' decision rule to make decisions will lead to larger payoffs in the long run than any other criterion (assuming the prior probabilities are valid).

Thus, if the Goferbroke Co. owned many tracts of land with this same payoff table, drilling for oil on all of them would provide an average payoff of about 100 ($100,000), versus only 90 ($90,000) for selling. As the following calculations indicate, this is the average payoff from drilling that results from having oil in an average of one tract out of every four (as indicated by the prior probabilities).

FIGURE 9.1

This spreadsheet shows the application of Bayes' decision rule to the first Goferbroke Co. problem, where a comparison of the expected payoffs in cells F5:F6 indicates that the Drill alternative should be chosen because it has the largest expected payoff.

	A	B	C	D	E	F
1		**Bayes' Decision Rule for the Goferbroke Co.**				
2						
3		**Payoff Table**	**State of Nature**			Expected
4		Alternative	Oil	Dry		Payoff
5		Drill	700	−100		100
6		Sell	90	90		90
7						
8		Prior Probability	0.25	0.75		

Range Name	Cells
DrillPayoff	C5:D5
ExpectedPayoff	F5:F6
PriorProbability	C8:D8
SellPayoff	C6:D6

	F
3	Expected
4	Payoff
5	=SUMPRODUCT(PriorProbability,DrillPayoff)
6	=SUMPRODUCT(PriorProbability,SellPayoff)

$$\text{Oil found in one tract:} \quad \text{Payoff} = 700$$

$$\text{Three tracts are dry: Payoff} = 3(-100) = -300$$

$$\text{Total payoff} = 400$$

$$\text{Average payoff} = \frac{400}{4} = 100$$

However, achieving this average payoff might require going through a long stretch of dry tracts until the "law of averages" can prevail to reach 25 percent of the tracts having oil. Surviving a long stretch of bad luck may not be feasible if the company does not have adequate financing.

This criterion also has its share of critics. Here are the main criticisms.

1. There usually is considerable uncertainty involved in assigning values to prior probabilities, so treating these values as true probabilities will not reveal the true range of possible outcomes. (Section 9.4 discusses how *sensitivity analysis* can address this concern.)

2. Prior probabilities inherently are at least largely subjective in nature, whereas sound decision making should be based on objective data and procedures. (Section 9.6 describes how new information sometimes can be obtained to improve prior probabilities and make them more objective.)

3. By focusing on average outcomes, expected (monetary) payoffs ignore the effect that the amount of variability in the possible outcomes should have on the decision making. For example, since Goferbroke does not have the financing to sustain a large loss, selling the land to assure a payoff of 90 ($90,000) may be preferable to an expected payoff of 100 ($100,000) from drilling. Selling would avoid the risk of a large loss from drilling when the land is dry. (Section 9.9 will discuss how utilities can be used to better reflect the value of payoffs.)

By considering only expected payoffs, Bayes' decision rule fails to give special consideration to the possibility of disastrously large losses.

So why is this criterion commonly referred to as Bayes' decision rule? The reason is that it is often credited to the Reverend Thomas Bayes, a nonconforming 18th century English minister who won renown as a philosopher and mathematician, although the same basic idea has even longer roots in the field of economics. (Yes, some management science techniques have *very* long roots!) Bayes' philosophy of decision making still is very influential today, and some management scientists even refer to themselves as Bayesians because of their devotion to this philosophy.

Because of its popularity, the rest of the chapter focuses on procedures that are based on this criterion.

Max's Reaction

Max: So where does this leave us?

Jennifer: Well, now you need to decide which criterion seems most appropriate to you in this situation.

Max: Well, I can't say that I am very excited about any of the criteria. But it sounded like this one is a popular one.

Jennifer: Yes, it is.

Max: Why?

Jennifer: Really, two reasons. First, this is the criterion that uses all the available information. The prior probabilities may not be as accurate as we would like, but they do give us valuable information about roughly how likely each of the possible states of nature is. Many management scientists feel that using this key information should lead to better decisions.

Bayes' decision rule uses all the information provided by the payoff table.

Max: I'm not ready to accept that yet. But what is the second reason?

Jennifer: Remember that this is the criterion that focuses on what the average payoff would be if the same situation were repeated numerous times. We called this the expected payoff. Consistently selecting the decision alternative that provides the best expected payoff would provide the most payoff to the company in the long run. Doing what is best in the long run seems like rational decision making for a manager.

Review Questions

1. How does the maximax criterion select a decision alternative? What kind of person might find this criterion appealing?
2. What are some criticisms of the maximax criterion?
3. How does the maximin criterion select a decision alternative? What kind of person might find this criterion appealing?
4. What are some criticisms of the maximin criterion?
5. Which state of nature does the maximum likelihood criterion focus on?
6. What are some criticisms of the maximum likelihood criterion?
7. How does Bayes' decision rule select a decision alternative?
8. How is the expected payoff for a decision alternative calculated?
9. What are some criticisms of Bayes' decision rule?

9.3 DECISION TREES

The spreadsheet in Figure 9.1 illustrates one useful way of performing decision analysis with Bayes' decision rule. Another enlightening way to apply this decision rule is to use a **decision tree** to display and analyze the problem graphically. The decision tree for the first Goferbroke Co. problem is shown in Figure 9.2. Starting on the left side and moving to the right side shows the progression of events. First, a decision is made as to whether to drill for oil or sell the land. If the decision is to drill, the next event is to learn whether the state of nature is that the land contains oil or is dry. Finally, the payoff is obtained that results from these events.

FIGURE 9.2

The decision tree for the first Goferbroke Co. problem as presented in Table 9.3.

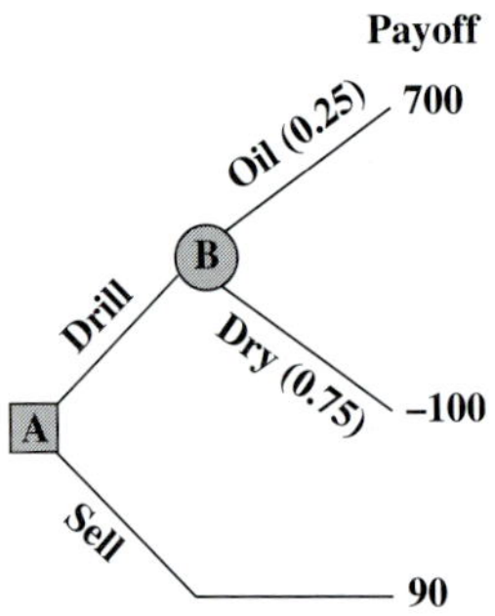

In the terminology of decision trees, the junction points are called **nodes** (or forks) and the lines emanating from the nodes are referred to as **branches.** A distinction is then made between the following two types of nodes.

> A **decision node,** represented by a *square,* indicates that a decision needs to be made at that point in the process. An **event node** (or chance node), represented by a *circle,* indicates that a random event occurs at that point.

Thus, node A in Figure 9.2 is a decision node since the decision on whether to drill or sell occurs there. Node B is an event node since a random event, the occurrence of one of the possible states of nature, takes place there. Each of the two branches emanating from this node corresponds to one of the possible random events, where the number in parentheses along the branch gives the probability that this event will occur.

A decision tree can be very helpful for visualizing and analyzing a problem. When the problem is as small as the one in Figure 9.2, using the decision tree in the analysis process is optional. However, one nice feature of decision trees is that they also can be used for more complicated problems where a sequence of decisions needs to be made. You will see this illustrated for the full Goferbroke Co. problem in Sections 9.7 and 9.9 when a decision on whether to conduct a seismic survey is made before deciding whether to drill or sell.

Spreadsheet Software for Decision Trees

Excel Tip: The TreePlan add-in can be installed either by simply opening the TreePlan file in MS Courseware or by using the installer included in MS Courseware.

We will describe and illustrate how to use TreePlan, an Excel add-in developed by Professor Michael Middleton for constructing and analyzing decision trees on a spreadsheet. The academic version is available to you as shareware in your MS Courseware. (If you want to continue to use it after this course, you will need to register and pay the shareware fee.) Like any Excel add-in, this add-in needs to be installed before it will show up in Excel.

TreePlan Tip: To change the type of a node, or to add or remove branches, click on the cell containing the node and choose Decision Tree from the Add-Ins tab or Tools menu.

To begin creating a decision tree using TreePlan, select Decision Tree from the Add-Ins tab (for Excel 2007) or Tools menu (for earlier versions of Excel) and click on New Tree. This creates the default decision tree shown in Figure 9.3 with a single (square) decision node with two branches. It so happens that this is exactly what is needed for the first node in the Goferbroke problem (this node corresponds to node A in Figure 9.2). However, even if something else were needed, it is easy to make changes to a node in TreePlan. Simply select the cell containing the node (B5 in Figure 9.3) and choose Decision Tree from the Add-Ins tab or Tools menu. This brings up a dialogue box that allows you to change the type of node (e.g., from a decision node to an event node) or add more branches.

By default, the labels for the decisions (cells D2 and D7 in Figure 9.3) are "Decision 1," "Decision 2," etc. These labels are changed by clicking on them and typing a new label. In Figure 9.3, these labels have already been changed to "Drill" and "Sell," respectively.

If the decision is to drill, the next event is to learn whether or not the land contains oil. To create an event node, click on the cell containing the terminal node at the end of the drill branch, just to the right of the vertical line (cell F3 in Figure 9.3), and choose Decision Tree from the Add-Ins tab or Tools menu. This brings up the TreePlan (Education) Terminal dialogue box shown in Figure 9.4. Choose the "Change to event node" option on the left and select the two branches option on the right, and then click OK. This results in the decision tree

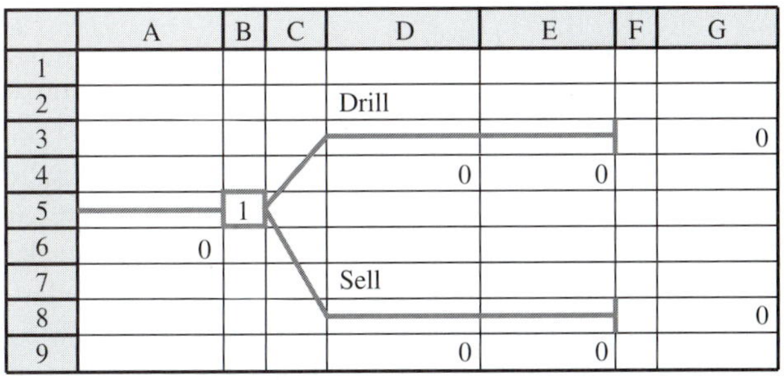

FIGURE 9.3

The default decision tree created by TreePlan by selecting Decision Tree from the Add-Ins tab or Tools menu, clicking on New Tree, and then entering the Drill and Sell labels for the two decision alternatives.

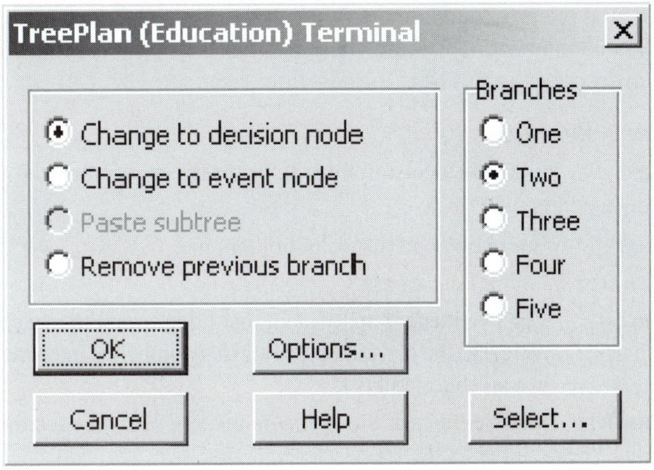

	A	B	C	D	E	F	G
1							
2				Drill			
3							0
4					0	0	
5			1				
6		0					
7				Sell			
8							0
9					0	0	

FIGURE 9.4

The TreePlan dialogue box that is used for making various kinds of changes in the decision tree.

TreePlan (Education) Terminal

- (•) Change to decision node
- ( ) Change to event node
- ( ) Paste subtree
- ( ) Remove previous branch

Branches
- ( ) One
- (•) Two
- ( ) Three
- ( ) Four
- ( ) Five

OK   Options...

Cancel   Help   Select...

FIGURE 9.5

The decision tree constructed and solved by TreePlan for the first Goferbroke Co. problem as presented in Table 9.3, where the 1 in cell B9 indicates that the top branch (the Drill alternative) should be chosen.

	A	B	C	D	E	F	G	H	I	J	K
1								0.25			
2								Oil			
3											700
4				Drill				800	700		
5											
6				-100	100			0.75			
7								Dry			
8											-100
9		1						0	-100		
10	100										
11											
12				Sell							
13											90
14				90	90						

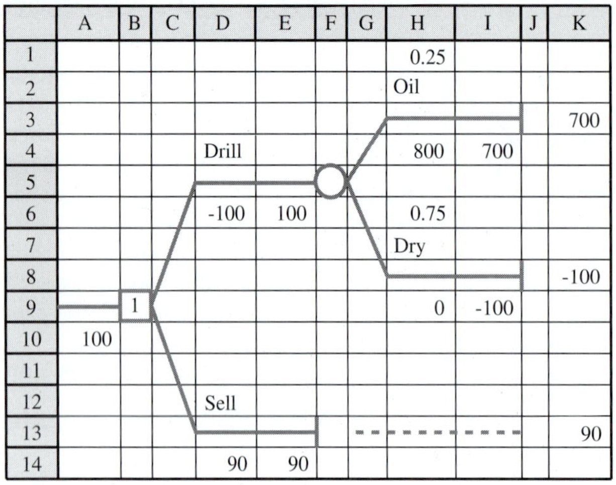

TreePlan Tip: To create a new node at the end of a tree, select the cell containing the terminal node and choose Decision Tree from the Add-Ins tab or Tools menu. This enables you to change the terminal node into either a decision node or an event node with the desired number of branches (between 1 and 5).

with the nodes and branches shown in Figure 9.5 (after replacing the default labels "Event 1" and "Event 2" with "Oil" and "Dry," respectively).

Initially, each branch would show a default value of 0 for the net cash flow being generated there (the numbers appear below the branch labels: D6, D14, H4, and H9 in Figure 9.5). Also, each of the two branches leading from the event node would display default values of 0.5 for their prior probabilities (the probabilities are just above the corresponding labels: H1 and H6 in Figure 9.5). Therefore, you next should click on these default values and replace them with the correct numbers, namely,

$$D6 = -100 \quad \text{(the cost of drilling is \$100,000)}$$
$$D14 = 90 \quad \text{(the profit from selling is \$90,000)}$$
$$H1 = 0.25 \quad \text{(the prior probability of oil is 0.25)}$$
$$H4 = 800 \quad \text{(the net revenue after finding oil is \$800,000)}$$
$$H6 = 0.75 \quad \text{(the prior probability of dry is 0.75)}$$
$$H9 = 0 \quad \text{(the net revenue after finding dry is 0)}$$

as shown in the figure.

At each stage in constructing a decision tree, TreePlan automatically solves for the optimal policy with the current tree when using *Bayes' decision rule*. The number inside each decision node indicates which branch should be chosen (assuming the branches emanating from that node are numbered consecutively from top to bottom). Thus, for the final decision tree in Figure 9.5, the number 1 in cell B9 specifies that the first branch (the Drill alternative) should be chosen. The number on both sides of each terminal node is the payoff if that node is reached. The number 100 in cells A10 and E6 is the *expected payoff* (the measure of performance for Bayes' decision rule) at those stages in the process.

TreePlan always identifies the optimal policy for the current decision tree according to Bayes' decision rule.

This description of TreePlan may seem somewhat complicated. However, we think that you will find the procedure quite intuitive when you execute it on a computer. If you spend considerable time with TreePlan, you also will find that it has many helpful features that haven't been described in this brief introduction.

Max's Reaction

Max: I like this decision tree thing. It puts everything into perspective.

Jennifer: Good.

Max: But one thing still really bothers me.

Jennifer: I think I can guess.

Max: Yes. I've made it pretty plain that I don't want to make my decision based on believing the consulting geologist's numbers. One chance in four of oil. Hah! It's just an educated guess.

Jennifer: Well, let me ask this. What is the key factor in deciding whether to drill for oil or sell the land?

Max:	How likely it is that there is oil there.
Jennifer:	Doesn't the consulting geologist help in determining this?
Max:	Definitely. I hardly ever drill without his input.
Jennifer:	So shouldn't your criterion for deciding whether to drill be based directly on this input?
Max:	Yes, it should.
Jennifer:	But then I don't understand why you keep objecting to using the consulting geologist's numbers.
Max:	I'm not objecting to using his input. This input is vital to my decision. What I object to is using his numbers, one chance in four of oil, as being the gospel truth. That is what this Bayes' decision rule seems to do. We both saw what a close decision this was, 100 versus 90. What happens if his numbers are off some, as they probably are? This is too important a decision to be based on some numbers that are largely pulled out of the air.
Jennifer:	OK, I see. Now he says that there is one chance in four of oil, a 25 percent chance. Do you think that is the right ballpark at least? If not 25 percent, how much lower might it be? Or how much higher?
Max:	I usually add and subtract 10 percent from whatever the consulting geologist says. So I suppose the chance of oil is likely to be somewhere between 15 percent and 35 percent.
Jennifer:	Good. Now we're getting somewhere. I think I know exactly what we should do next.
Max:	What's that?
Jennifer:	There is a management science technique that is designed for just this kind of situation. It is called *sensitivity analysis.* It will allow us to investigate what happens if the consulting geologist's numbers are off.
Max:	Great! Let's do it.

Review Questions

1. What is a *decision tree?*
2. What is a *decision node* in a decision tree? An *event node?*
3. What symbols are used to represent decision nodes and event nodes?

9.4 SENSITIVITY ANALYSIS WITH DECISION TREES

Sensitivity analysis commonly is used with various applications of management science to study the effect if some of the numbers included in the mathematical model are not correct. In this case, the mathematical model is represented by the decision tree shown in Figure 9.5. The numbers in this tree that are most questionable are the prior probabilities in cells H1 and H6, so we will initially focus the sensitivity analysis on these numbers.

It is helpful to start this process by consolidating the data and results on the spreadsheet below the decision tree, as in Figure 9.6. As indicated by the formulas at the bottom of the figure, the cells giving the results make reference to the corresponding output cells on the decision tree. Similarly, the data cells on the decision tree now reference the corresponding data cells below the tree. Consequently, the user can experiment with various alternative values in the data cells below and the results will simultaneously change in both the decision tree and the results section below the tree to reflect the new data.

Consolidating the data and results offers a couple of advantages. First, it assures that each piece of data is in only one place. Each time that piece of data is needed in the decision tree, a reference is made to the single data cell below. This greatly simplifies sensitivity analysis. To change a piece of data, it needs to be changed in only one place rather than searching through the entire tree to find and change all occurrences of that piece of data.[1] A second advantage of

Excel Tip: Consolidating the data and results on the spreadsheet makes it easier to do sensitivity analysis and also makes the model and results easier to interpret.

[1] In this very simple decision tree, this advantage does not become evident since each piece of data is only used once in the tree anyway. However, in later sections, when the possibility of seismic testing is considered, some data will be repeated many times in the tree and this advantage will become more clear.

FIGURE 9.6

In preparation for performing sensitivity analysis on the first Goferbroke Co. problem, the data and results have been consolidated on the spreadsheet below the decision tree.

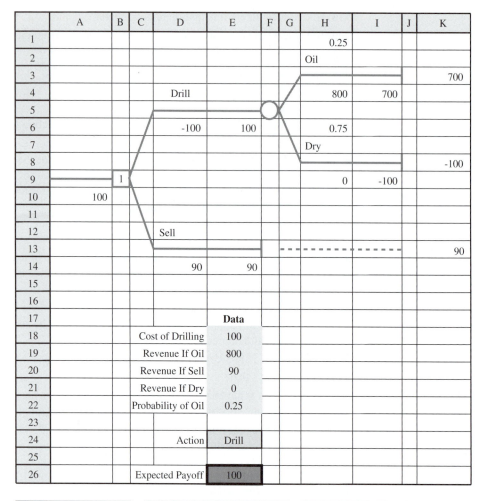

consolidating the data and results is that it makes it easy for *anyone* to interpret the model. It is not necessary to understand TreePlan or how to read a decision tree in order to see what data were used in the model or what the suggested plan of action and expected payoff are.

The sum of the two prior probabilities must equal one, so increasing one of these probabilities automatically decreases the other one by the same amount, and vice versa. This is enforced on the decision tree in Figure 9.6 by the equation in cell H6—the probability of a dry site = H6 = 1 − ProbabilityOfOil (E22). Max has concluded that the true chances of having oil on the tract of land are likely to lie somewhere between 15 and 35 percent. In other words, the true prior probability of having oil is likely to be in the range from 0.15 to 0.35, so the corresponding prior probability of the land being dry would range from 0.85 to 0.65.

We can begin sensitivity analysis by simply trying different trial values for the prior probability of oil. This is done in Figure 9.7, first with this probability at the lower end of the range (0.15) and next with this probability at the upper end (0.35). When the prior probability of oil is only 0.15, the decision swings over to selling the land by a wide margin (an expected payoff of 90 versus only 20 for drilling). However, when this probability is 0.35, the decision is to drill by a wide margin (expected payoff = 180 versus only 90 for selling). Thus, the decision is very *sensitive* to the prior probability of oil. This sensitivity analysis has revealed that it is important to do more, if possible, to pin down just what the true value of the probability of oil is.

Using Data Tables to Do Sensitivity Analysis Systematically

To pin down just where the suggested course of action changes, we could continue selecting new trial values of the prior probability of oil at random. However, a better approach is to systematically consider a range of values. A feature built into Excel, called data tables, is designed to perform just this sort of analysis. Data tables are used to show the results of certain output cells for various trial values of a data cell. Data tables work in the same way as the Solver Table, which was used to do sensitivity analysis for linear programming problems in Chapter 5. The only difference is that a data table does not make use of the Solver to re-solve the problem for each trial value of the data cell. (The Solver is not needed in decision analysis problems.)

To use data tables, first make a table on the spreadsheet with headings as shown in columns I, J, and K in Figure 9.8. In the first column of the table (I19:I29), list the trial values for the data cell (the prior probability of oil), except leave the first row blank. The headings of the next columns specify which output will be evaluated. For each of these columns, use the first row of the table (cells J18:K18) to write an equation that refers to the relevant output cell. In this case, the cells of interest are Action (E24) and ExpectedPayoff (E26), so the equations for J18:K18 are those shown below the spreadsheet in Figure 9.8.

Next, select the entire table (I18:K29) and then choose Data Table from the What-If Analysis menu of the Data tab (for Excel 2007) or Table from the Data menu (for earlier versions of Excel). In the Table dialogue box (as shown at the bottom left of Figure 9.8), indicate the column input cell (E22), which refers to the data cell that is being changed in the first column of the table. Nothing is entered for the row input cell because no row is being used to list the trial values of a data cell in this case.

Clicking OK then generates the data table shown in Figure 9.9. For each trial value for the data cell listed in the first column of the table, the corresponding output cell values are calculated and displayed in the other columns of the table. (The entries in the first row of the table come from the original solution in the spreadsheet.)

Figure 9.9 reveals that the best course of action switches from Sell to Drill for a prior probability of oil somewhere between 0.23 and 0.25. Trial and error (or algebra) can be used to pin this number down more precisely. It turns out to be 0.2375.

For a problem with more than two possible states of nature, the most straightforward approach is to focus the sensitivity analysis on only two states at a time as described above. This again would involve investigating what happens when the prior probability of one state increases as the prior probability of the other state decreases by the same amount, holding fixed the prior probabilities of the remaining states. This procedure then can be repeated for as many other pairs of states as desired.

Max's Reaction

Max: That data table paints a pretty clear picture. I think I'm getting a much better handle on the problem.

Jennifer: Good.

Max: Less than a 23¾ percent chance of oil, I should sell. If it's more, I should drill. It confirms what I suspected all along. This is a close decision, and it all boils down to picking the right number for the chances of oil. I sure wish I had more to go on than the consulting geologist's numbers.

Jennifer: You talked earlier about the possibility of paying $30,000 to get a detailed seismic survey of the land.

A data table displays the results of selected output cells for various trial values of a data cell.

FIGURE 9.7
Performing sensitivity analysis for the first Goferbroke Co. problem by trying alternative values (0.15 and 0.35) of the prior probability of oil.

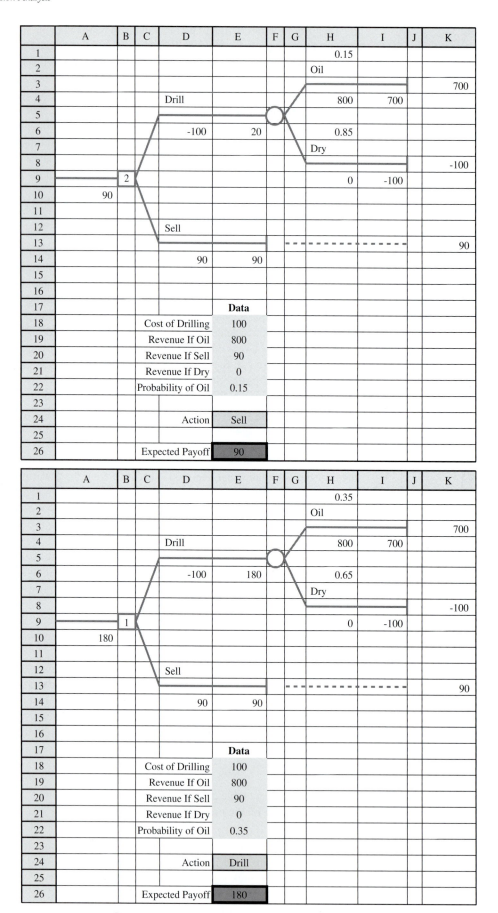

FIGURE 9.8

Expansion of the spreadsheet in Figure 9.6 to prepare for generating a data table, where the choice of E22 for the column input cell in the Table dialogue box indicates that this is the data cell that is being changed in the first column of the data table.

	A	B	C	D	E	F	G	H	I	J	K	L	M
16									Probability		Expected		
17					**Data**				of Oil	Action	Payoff		
18			Cost of Drilling		100					Drill	100		Select these
19			Revenue If Oil		800				0.15			←	cells (I18:K29), before choosing Table from the Data menu.
20			Revenue If Sell		90				0.17				
21			Revenue If Dry		0				0.19				
22			Probability of Oil		0.25				0.21				
23									0.23				
24				Action	Drill				0.25				
25									0.27				
26			Expected Payoff		100				0.29				
27									0.31				
28									0.33				
29									0.35				

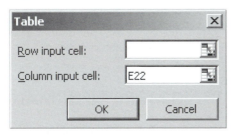

Table

Row input cell: [ ]

Column input cell: [E22]

OK   Cancel

	J	K
16		Expected
17	Action	Payoff
18	=Action	=ExpectedPayoff

Range Name	Cell
Action	E24
ExpectedPayoff	E26

FIGURE 9.9

After the preparation displayed in Figure 9.8, clicking OK generates this data table that shows the optimal action and expected payoff for various trial values of the prior probability of oil.

	I	J	K
16	Probability		Expected
17	of Oil	Action	Payoff
18		Drill	100
19	0.15	Sell	90
20	0.17	Sell	90
21	0.19	Sell	90
22	0.21	Sell	90
23	0.23	Sell	90
24	0.25	Drill	100
25	0.27	Drill	116
26	0.29	Drill	132
27	0.31	Drill	148
28	0.33	Drill	164
29	0.35	Drill	180

The next section describes how to find and use the expected value of perfect information.

Max: Yes, I might have to do that. But 30,000 bucks! I'm still not sure that it's worth that much dough.

Jennifer: I have a quick way of checking that. It's another technique I learned in my management science course. It's called finding the **expected value of perfect information (EVPI).** The expected value of perfect information is the increase in the expected payoff you would get if the seismic survey could tell you for sure if there is oil there.

Max: But it can't tell you for sure.

Jennifer: Yes, I know. But finding out for sure if oil is there is what we refer to as perfect information. So the increase in the expected payoff if you find out for sure is the expected value of perfect information. We know that's better than you actually can do with a seismic survey.

Max: Right.

Jennifer: OK, suppose we find that the expected value of perfect information is less than $30,000. Since that is better than we can do with a seismic survey, that tells us right off the bat that it wouldn't pay to do the seismic survey.

Max: OK, I get it. But what if this expected value of perfect information is more than $30,000?

Jennifer: Then you don't know for sure whether the seismic survey is worth it until you do some more analysis. This analysis takes some time, whereas it is very quick to calculate the expected value of perfect information. So it is well worth simply checking whether the expected value of perfect information is less than $30,000 and, if so, saving a lot of additional work.

Max: OK. Let's do it.

Review Questions

1. Why might it be helpful to use sensitivity analysis with Bayes' decision rule?
2. When preparing to perform sensitivity analysis, what are a couple of advantages of consolidating the data and results on the spreadsheet that contains the decision tree?
3. What is shown by a data table when it is used to perform sensitivity analysis?
4. What conclusion was drawn for the first Goferbroke Co. problem regarding how the decision should depend on the prior probability of oil?

9.5 CHECKING WHETHER TO OBTAIN MORE INFORMATION

Definitely identifying the true state of nature is referred to as perfect information. This represents the best outcome of seeking more information.

Prior probabilities may provide somewhat inaccurate estimates of the true probabilities of the states of nature. Might it be worthwhile for Max to spend some money for a seismic survey to obtain better estimates? The quickest way to check this is to pretend that it is possible for the same amount of money to actually determine which state is the true state of nature ("perfect information") and then determine whether obtaining this information would make this expenditure worthwhile. If having perfect information would not be worthwhile, then it definitely would not be worthwhile to spend this money just to learn more about the probabilities of the states of nature.

The key quantities for performing this analysis are

EP (without more info) = Expected payoff from applying Bayes' decision rule with the original prior probabilities
= 100 (as given in Figure 9.6)

EP (with perfect info) = Expected payoff if the decision could be made after learning the true state of nature

EVPI = Expected value of perfect information

C = Cost of obtaining more information
= 30 (cost of the seismic survey in thousands of dollars)

The **expected value of perfect information** is calculated as

$$EVPI = EP \text{ (with perfect info)} - EP \text{ (without more info)}$$

After calculating EP (with perfect info) and then EVPI, the last step is to compare EVPI with C.

If $C >$ EVPI, then it is not worthwhile to obtain more information.

If $C \leq$ EVPI, then it might be worthwhile to obtain more information.

To calculate EP (with perfect info), we pretend that the decision can be made *after* learning the true state of nature. Given the true state of nature, we then would automatically choose the alternative with the maximum payoff for that state. Thus, we drill if we know there is oil, whereas we sell if we know the site is dry. Figure 9.10 finds the MaximumPayoff (C7:D7) for both possible states of nature. If the site contains oil, we drill with the maximum payoff of

FIGURE 9.10
Calculation of the
expected payoff with
perfect information in cell
D11 as the
SUMPRODUCT of
PriorProbability (C9:D9)
and MaximumPayoff
(C7:D7).

	A	B	C	D	E
1		**Expected Payoff with Perfect Information**			
2					
3		**Payoff Table**	**State of Nature**		
4		Alternative	Oil	Dry	
5		Drill	700	-100	
6		Sell	90	90	
7		Maximum Payoff	700	90	
8					
9		Prior Probability	0.25	0.75	
10					
11		EP (with perfect info)		242.5	

Range Name	Cells
DryPayoff	D5:D6
MaximumPayoff	C7:D7
OilPayoff	C5:C6
PriorProbability	C9:D9

	B	C	D
7	Maximum Payoff	=MAX(OilPayoff)	=MAX(DryPayoff)

	C	D
11	EP (with perfect info)	=SUMPRODUCT(PriorProbability,MaximumPayoff)

FIGURE 9.11
By starting with an event
node involving the states
of nature, TreePlan uses
this decision tree to obtain
the expected payoff with
perfect information for the
first Goferbroke Co.
problem.

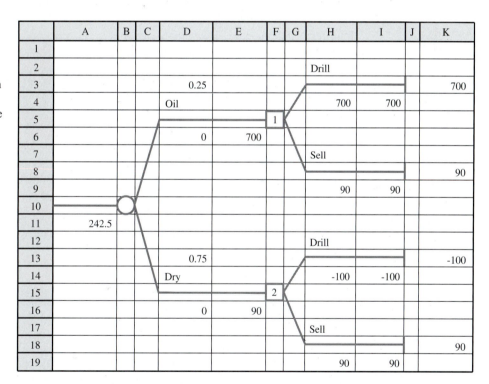

700. If the site is dry, we sell with the maximum payoff of 90. The prior probabilities still give the probability that each state of nature will turn out to be the true one. EP (with perfect info) is therefore the weighted average of the maximum payoff for each state, multiplying each maximum payoff by the prior probability of the corresponding state of nature. This calculation is performed in cell D11 on the spreadsheet in Figure 9.10, with the formula

$$\text{EP (with perfect info)} = \text{SUMPRODUCT (PriorProbability, MaximumPayoff)}$$
$$= (0.25)(700) + (0.75)(90)$$
$$= 242.5$$

TreePlan also can be used to calculate EP (with perfect info) by constructing and solving the decision tree shown in Figure 9.11. The clever idea here is to *start* the decision tree with

Starting the decision tree with an event node whose branches are the various states of nature corresponds to starting with perfect information about the true state of nature.

an event node whose branches are the various states of nature (oil and dry in this case). Since a decision node follows each of these branches, the decision is being made with perfect information about the true state of nature. Therefore, the expected payoff of 242.5 obtained by TreePlan in cell A11 is the expected payoff with perfect information.

Since EP(with perfect info) = 242½, we now can calculate the expected value of perfect information as

$$\text{EVPI} = \text{EP (with perfect info)} - \text{EP (without more info)}$$
$$= 242.5 - 100$$
$$= 142.5$$

Conclusion: EVPI > C, since 142.5 > 30. Therefore, it might be worthwhile to do the seismic survey.

Max's Reaction

Max: So you're telling me that if the seismic survey could really be definitive in determining whether oil is there, doing the survey would increase my average payoff by about $142,500?

Jennifer: That's right.

Max: So after subtracting the $30,000 cost of the survey, I would be ahead $112,500. Well, too bad the surveys aren't that good. In fact, they're not all that reliable.

Jennifer: Tell me more. How reliable are they?

Max: Well, they come back with seismic soundings. If the seismic soundings are favorable, then oil is fairly likely. If they are unfavorable, then oil is pretty unlikely. But you can't tell for sure.

Jennifer: OK. Suppose oil is there. How often would you get favorable seismic soundings?

Max: I can't give you an exact number. Maybe 60 percent.

Jennifer: OK, good. Now suppose that the land is dry. How often would you still get favorable seismic soundings?

Max: Too often! I've lost a lot of money drilling when the seismic survey said to and then nothing was there. That's why I don't like to spend the 30,000 bucks.

Jennifer: Sure. So it tells you to drill when you shouldn't close to half the time?

Max: No. It's not that bad. But fairly often.

Jennifer: Can you give me a percentage?

Max: OK. Maybe 20 percent.

Jennifer: Good. Thanks. Now I think we can do some analysis to determine whether it is really worthwhile to do the seismic survey.

Max: How do you do the analysis?

Jennifer: Well, I'll describe the process in detail pretty soon. But here is the general idea. We'll do some calculations to determine what the chances of oil would be if the seismic soundings turn out to be favorable. Then we'll calculate the chances if the soundings are unfavorable. We called the consulting geologist's numbers prior probabilities because they were prior to obtaining more information. The improved numbers are referred to as **posterior probabilities.**

Posterior probabilities are the revised probabilities of the states of nature after doing a test or survey to improve the prior probabilities.

Max: OK.

Jennifer: Then we'll use these posterior probabilities to determine the average payoff, after subtracting the $30,000 cost, if we do the seismic survey. If this payoff is better than we would do without the seismic survey, then we should do it. Otherwise, not.

Max: That makes sense.

Review Questions

1. What is meant by perfect information regarding the states of nature?
2. How can the expected payoff with perfect information be calculated from the payoff table?
3. How should a decision tree be constructed to obtain the expected payoff with perfect information by solving the tree?
4. What is the formula for calculating the expected value of perfect information?
5. What is the conclusion if the cost of obtaining more information is more than the expected value of perfect information?
6. What is the conclusion if the cost of obtaining more information is less than the expected value of perfect information?
7. Which of these two cases occurs in the Goferbroke Co. problem?

9.6 USING NEW INFORMATION TO UPDATE THE PROBABILITIES

The prior probabilities of the possible states of nature often are quite subjective in nature, so they may be only very rough estimates of the true probabilities. Fortunately, it frequently is possible to do some additional testing or surveying (at some expense) to improve these estimates. These improved estimates are called **posterior probabilities.**

In the case of the Goferbroke Co., these improved estimates can be obtained at a cost of $30,000 by conducting a detailed seismic survey of the land. The possible findings from such a survey are summarized below.

Possible Findings from a Seismic Survey

FSS: Favorable seismic soundings; oil is fairly likely.

USS: Unfavorable seismic soundings; oil is quite unlikely.

To use either finding to calculate the posterior probability of oil (or of being dry), it is necessary to estimate the probability of obtaining this finding for each state of nature. During the conversation at the end of the preceding section, Jennifer elicited these estimates from Max, as summarized in Table 9.7. (Max actually only estimated the probability of favorable seismic soundings, but subtracting this number from one gives the probability of unfavorable seismic soundings.) The symbol used in the table for each of these estimated probabilities is

$$P(\text{finding} \mid \text{state}) = \text{Probability that the indicated finding will occur, given that the state of nature is the indicated one}$$

This kind of probability is referred to as a *conditional probability,* because it is conditioned on being given the state of nature.

Recall that the prior probabilities are

$$P(\text{Oil}) = 0.25$$
$$P(\text{Dry}) = 0.75$$

The next step is to use these probabilities and the probabilities in Table 9.7 to obtain a combined probability called a *joint probability.* Each combination of a state of nature and a finding from the seismic survey will have a joint probability that is determined by the following formula.

$$P(\text{state and finding}) = P(\text{state}) \, P(\text{finding} \mid \text{state})$$

TABLE 9.7
Probabilities of the Possible Findings from the Seismic Survey, Given the State of Nature, for the Goferbroke Co. Problem

| State of Nature | *P* (finding | state) | |
	Favorable (FSS)	Unfavorable (USS)
Oil	$P(\text{FSS} \mid \text{Oil}) = 0.6$	$P(\text{USS} \mid \text{Oil}) = 0.4$
Dry	$P(\text{FSS} \mid \text{Dry}) = 0.2$	$P(\text{USS} \mid \text{Dry}) = 0.8$

For example, the joint probability that the state of nature is Oil *and* the finding from the seismic survey is favorable (FSS) is

$$P(\text{Oil and FSS}) = P(\text{Oil})\, P(\text{FSS} \mid \text{Oil})$$
$$= 0.25(0.6)$$
$$= 0.15$$

The calculation of all these joint probabilities is shown in the third column of the **probability tree diagram** given in Figure 9.12. The case involved is identified underneath each branch of the tree and the probability is given over the branch. The first column gives the prior probabilities and then the probabilities from Table 9.7 are shown in the second column. Multiplying each probability in the first column by a probability in the second column gives the corresponding joint probability in the third column.

Having found each joint probability of both a particular state of nature and a particular finding from the seismic survey, the next step is to use these probabilities to find each probability of just a particular finding without specifying the state of nature. Since any finding can be obtained with any state of nature, the formula for calculating the probability of just a particular finding is

$$P(\text{finding}) = P(\text{Oil and finding}) + P(\text{Dry and finding})$$

For example, the probability of a favorable finding (FSS) is

$$P(\text{FSS}) = P(\text{Oil and FSS}) + P(\text{Dry and FSS})$$
$$= 0.15 + 0.15 = 0.3$$

where the two joint probabilities on the right-hand side of this equation are found on the first and third branches of the third column of the probability tree diagram. The calculation of both

> Each joint probability in the third column of the probability tree diagram is the product of the probabilities in the first two columns.

> The probability of a finding is the sum of the corresponding joint probabilities in the third column of the probability tree diagram.

FIGURE 9.12

Probability tree diagram for the Goferbroke Co. problem showing all the probabilities leading to the calculation of each posterior probability of the state of nature given the finding of the seismic survey.

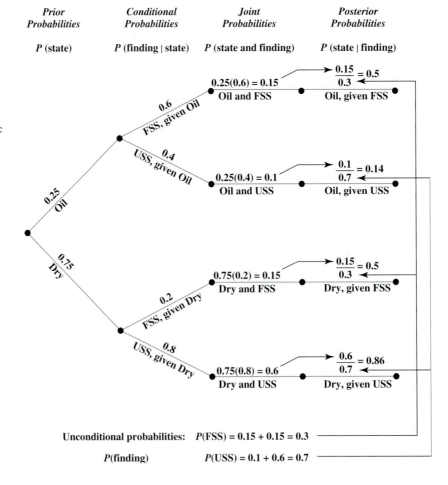

P(FSS) and P(USS) is shown underneath the diagram. (These are referred to as *unconditional* probabilities to differentiate them from the *conditional* probabilities of a finding given the state of nature, shown in the second column.)

Finally, we now are ready to calculate each *posterior probability* of a particular state of nature given a particular finding from the seismic survey. The formula involves combining the joint probabilities in the third column with the unconditional probabilities underneath the diagram as follows.

$$P(\text{state} \mid \text{finding}) = \frac{P(\text{state and finding})}{P(\text{finding})}$$

For example, the posterior probability that the true state of nature is oil, given a favorable finding (FSS) from the seismic survey, is

$$P(\text{Oil} \mid \text{FSS}) = \frac{P(\text{Oil and FSS})}{P(\text{FSS})}$$

$$= \frac{0.15}{0.3} = 0.5$$

The arrows in the probability tree diagram show where the numbers come from for calculating the posterior probabilities.

The fourth column of the probability tree diagram shows the calculation of all the posterior probabilities. The arrows indicate how each numerator comes from the corresponding joint probability in the third column and the denominator comes from the corresponding unconditional probability below the diagram.

By using the formulas given earlier for the joint probabilities and unconditional probabilities, each posterior probability also can be calculated directly from the prior probabilities (first column) and the conditional probabilities (second column) as follows.

$$P(\text{state} \mid \text{finding}) = \frac{P(\text{state})\, P(\text{finding} \mid \text{state})}{P(\text{Oil})\, P(\text{finding} \mid \text{Oil}) + P(\text{Dry})\, P(\text{finding} \mid \text{Dry})}$$

For example, the posterior probability of oil, given a favorable finding (FSS), is

$$P(\text{Oil} \mid \text{FSS}) = \frac{P(\text{Oil})\, P(\text{FSS} \mid \text{Oil})}{P(\text{Oil})\, P(\text{FSS} \mid \text{Oil}) + P(\text{Dry})\, P(\text{FSS} \mid \text{Dry})}$$

$$= \frac{0.25(0.6)}{0.25(0.6) + 0.75(0.2)}$$

$$= 0.5$$

This formula for a posterior probability is known as **Bayes' theorem,** in honor of its discovery by the Reverend Bayes. The clever Reverend Bayes found that any posterior probability can be found in this way for any decision analysis problem, regardless of how many states of nature it has. The denominator in the formula would contain one such term for each of the states of nature. Note that the probability tree diagram also is applying Bayes' theorem, but in smaller steps rather than a single long formula.

Table 9.8 summarizes all the posterior probabilities calculated in Figure 9.12.

After you learn the logic of calculating posterior probabilities, we suggest that you use the computer to perform these rather lengthy calculations. We have provided an Excel template (labeled Posterior Probabilities) for this purpose in this chapter's Excel files in your MS Courseware. Figure 9.13 illustrates the use of this template for the Goferbroke Co. problem.

TABLE 9.8
Posterior Probabilities of the States of Nature, Given the Finding from the Seismic Survey, for the Goferbroke Co. Problem

	P(state | finding)	
Finding	**Oil**	**Dry**
Favorable (FSS)	$P(\text{Oil} \mid \text{FSS}) = 1/2$	$P(\text{Dry} \mid \text{FSS}) = 1/2$
Unfavorable (USS)	$P(\text{Oil} \mid \text{USS}) = 1/7$	$P(\text{Dry} \mid \text{USS}) = 6/7$

FIGURE 9.13

The Posterior Probabilities template in your MS Courseware enables efficient calculation of posterior probabilities, as illustrated here for the Goferbroke Co. problem.

	A	B	C	D	E	F	G	H
1		**Template for Posterior Probabilities**						
2								
3		Data:			*P*(Finding I State)			
4		State of	Prior	Finding				
5		Nature	Probability	FSS	USS			
6		Oil	0.25	0.6	0.4			
7		Dry	0.75	0.2	0.8			
8								
9								
10								
11								
12		Posterior		*P*(State I Finding)				
13		Probabilities:		State of Nature				
14		Finding	*P*(Finding)	Oil	Dry			
15		FSS	0.3	0.5	0.5			
16		USS	0.7	0.14286	0.85714			
17								
18								
19								

	B	C	D
12	Posterior		*P*(State I Finding)
13	Probabilities:		State of Nature
14	Finding	*P*(Finding)	=B6
15	=D5	=SUMPRODUCT(C6:C10,D6:D10)	=C6*D6/SUMPRODUCT(C6:C10,D6:D10)
16	=E5	=SUMPRODUCT(C6:C10,E6:E10)	=C6*E6/SUMPRODUCT(C6:C10,E6:E10)
17	=F5	=SUMPRODUCT(C6:C10,F6:F10)	=C6*F6/SUMPRODUCT(C6:C10,F6:F10)
18	=G5	=SUMPRODUCT(C6:C10,G6:G10)	=C6*G6/SUMPRODUCT(C6:C10,G6:G10)
19	=H5	=SUMPRODUCT(C6:C10,H6:H10)	=C6*H6/SUMPRODUCT(C6:C10,H6:H10)

All you do is enter the prior probabilities and the conditional probabilities from the first two columns of Figure 9.12 into the top half of the template. The posterior probabilities then immediately appear in the bottom half. (The equations entered into the cells in columns E through H are similar to those for column D shown at the bottom of the figure.)

Max's Reaction

Max: So this is saying that even with favorable seismic soundings, I still only have one chance in two of finding oil. No wonder I've been disappointed so often in the past when I've drilled after receiving a favorable seismic survey. I thought those surveys were supposed to be more reliable than that. So now I'm even more unenthusiastic about paying 30,000 bucks to get a survey done.

Jennifer: But one chance in two of oil. Those are good odds.

Max: Yes, they are. But I'm likely to lay out 30,000 bucks and then just get an unfavorable survey back.

Jennifer: My calculations indicate that you have about a 70 percent chance of that happening.

Max: See what I mean?

Jennifer: But even an unfavorable survey tells you a lot. Just one chance in seven of oil then. That might rule out drilling. So a seismic survey really does pin down the odds of oil a lot better. Either one chance in two or one chance in seven instead of the ballpark estimate of one chance in four from the consulting geologist.

Max: Yes, I suppose that's right. I really would like to improve the consulting geologist's numbers. It sounds like you're recommending that we do the seismic survey.

Jennifer: Well, actually, I'm not quite sure yet. What we'll do is sketch out a decision tree, showing the decision on whether to do the seismic survey and then the decision on whether to drill or sell. Then we'll work out the average payoffs for these decisions on the decision tree.

Max: OK, let's do it. I want to make a decision soon.

Review *Questions*

1. What are posterior probabilities of the states of nature?
2. What are the possible findings from a seismic survey for the Goferbroke Co.?
3. What probabilities need to be estimated in addition to prior probabilities in order to begin calculating posterior probabilities?
4. What five kinds of probabilities are considered in a probability tree diagram?
5. What is the formula for calculating P(state and finding)?
6. What is the formula for calculating P(finding)?
7. What is the formula for calculating a posterior probability, P(state | finding), from P(state and finding) and P(finding)?
8. What is the name of the famous theorem for how to calculate posterior probabilities?

9.7   USING A DECISION TREE TO ANALYZE THE PROBLEM WITH A SEQUENCE OF DECISIONS

We now turn our attention to analyzing the *full* Goferbroke Co. problem with the help of a decision tree. For the full problem, there is a sequence of two decisions to be made. First, should a seismic survey be conducted? Second, after obtaining the results of the seismic survey (if it is conducted), should the company drill for oil or sell the land?

As described in Section 9.3, a **decision tree** provides a graphical display of the progression of decisions and random events for the problem. Figure 9.2 in that section shows the decision tree for the first Goferbroke problem where the only decision under consideration is whether to drill for oil or sell the land. Figure 9.5 then shows the same decision tree as it would be constructed and solved with TreePlan.

Constructing the Decision Tree

Now that a prior decision needs to be made on whether to conduct a seismic survey, this same decision tree needs to be expanded as shown in Figure 9.14 (before including any numbers). Recall that each *square* in the tree represents a *decision node,* where a decision needs to be made, and each *circle* represents an *event node,* where a random event will occur.

Thus, the first decision (should we have a seismic survey done?) is represented by decision node *a* in Figure 9.14. The two branches leading out of this node correspond to the two alternatives for this decision. Node *b* is an event node representing the random event of the outcome of the seismic survey. The two branches emanating from node *b* represent the two possible outcomes of the survey. Next comes the second decision (nodes *c, d,* and *e*) with its two possible choices. If the decision is to drill for oil, then we come to another event node (nodes *f, g,* and *h*), where its two branches correspond to the two possible states of nature.

The numbers in parentheses are probabilities.

The next step is to insert numbers into the decision tree as shown in Figure 9.15. The numbers under or over the branches that are *not* in parentheses are the cash flows (in thousands of dollars) that occur at those branches. For each path through the tree from node *a* to a final branch, these same numbers then are added to obtain the resulting total payoff shown in boldface to the right of that branch. The last set of numbers is the probabilities of random events. In particular, since each branch emanating from an event node represents a possible random event, the probability of this event occurring from this node has been inserted in parentheses along this branch. From event node *h,* the probabilities are the *prior probabilities* of these states of nature, since no seismic survey has been conducted to obtain more information in this case. However, event nodes *f* and *g* lead out of a decision

FIGURE 9.14

The decision tree for the full Goferbroke Co. problem (before including any numbers) when first deciding whether to conduct a seismic survey.

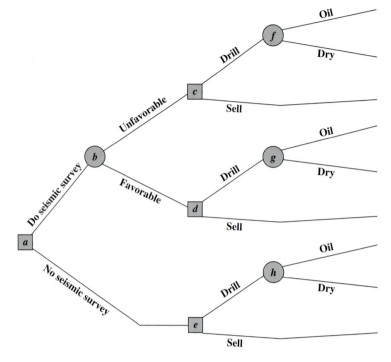

FIGURE 9.15

The decision tree in Figure 9.14 after adding both the probabilities of random events and the payoffs.

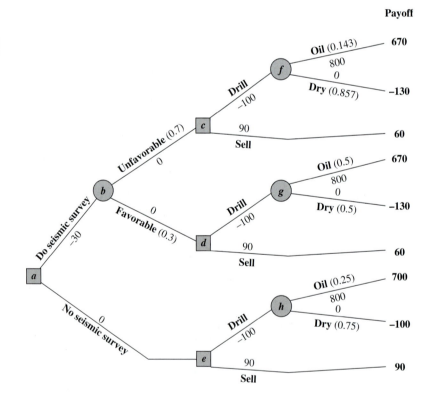

to do the seismic survey (and then to drill). Therefore, the probabilities from these event nodes are the *posterior probabilities* of the states of nature, given the outcome of the seismic survey, where these numbers are obtained from Table 9.8 or from cells D15:E16 in Figure 9.13. Finally, we have the two branches emanating from event node *b*. The numbers here are the probabilities of these findings from the seismic survey, Favorable (FSS) or Unfavorable (USS), as given underneath the probability tree diagram in Figure 9.12 or in cells C15:C16 of Figure 9.13.

The Westinghouse Science and Technology Center is the Westinghouse Electric Corporation's main research and development (R & D) arm to develop new technology. The process of evaluating R & D projects to decide which ones should be initiated and then which ones should be continued as progress is made (or not made) is particularly challenging for management because of the great uncertainties and very long time horizons involved. The actual launch date for an embryonic technology may be years, even decades, removed from its inception as a modest R & D proposal to investigate the technology's potential.

As the center came under increasing pressure to reduce costs and deliver high-impact technology quickly, the center's controller funded a management science project to improve this evaluation process. The management science team developed a decision tree approach to analyzing any R & D proposal while considering its complete sequence of

key decision points. The first decision point is whether to fund the proposed embryonic project for the first year or so. If its early technical milestones are reached, the next decision point is whether to continue funding the project for some period. This may then be repeated one or more times. If the late technical milestones are reached, the next decision point is whether to prelaunch because the innovation still meets strategic business objectives. If a strategic fit is achieved, the final decision point is whether to commercialize the innovation now or to delay its launch or to abandon it altogether. A decision tree with a progression of decision nodes and intervening event nodes provides a natural way of depicting and analyzing such an R & D project.

Source: R. K. Perdue, W. J. McAllister, P. V. King, and B. G. Berkey, "Valuation of R and D Projects Using Options Pricing and Decision Analysis Models," *Interfaces* 29, no. 6 (November–December 1999), pp. 57–74.

Performing the Analysis

Having constructed the decision tree, including its numbers, we now are ready to analyze the problem by using the following procedure.

1. Start at the right side of the decision tree and move left one column at a time. For each column, perform either step 2 or step 3 depending on whether the nodes in that column are event nodes or decision nodes.

The expected payoff needs to be calculated for each event node.

2. For each event node, calculate its *expected payoff* by multiplying the expected payoff of each branch (shown in boldface to the right of the branch) by the probability of that branch and then summing these products. Record this expected payoff for each event node in boldface next to the node, and designate this quantity as also being the expected payoff for the branch leading to this node.

3. For each decision node, compare the expected payoffs of its branches and choose the alternative whose branch has the largest expected payoff. In each case, record the choice on the decision tree.

To begin the procedure, consider the rightmost column of nodes, namely, event nodes f, g, and h. Applying step 2, their expected payoffs (EP) are calculated as

$$\text{EP} = \frac{1}{7}(670) + \frac{6}{7}(-130) = -15.7 \quad \text{for node } f$$

$$\text{EP} = \frac{1}{2}(670) + \frac{1}{2}(-130) = 270 \quad \text{for node } g$$

$$\text{EP} = \frac{1}{4}(700) + \frac{3}{4}(-100) = 100 \quad \text{for node } h$$

These expected payoffs then are placed above these nodes, as shown in Figure 9.16.

Next, we move one column to the left, which consists of decision nodes c, d, and e. The expected payoff for a branch that leads to an event node now is recorded in boldface over that event node. Therefore, step 3 can be applied as follows.

Node c: Drill alternative has EP $= -15.7$

Sell alternative has EP $= 60$

$60 > -15.7$, so choose the Sell alternative

Node d: Drill alternative has EP $= 270$

Sell alternative has EP $= 60$

$270 > 60$, so choose the Drill alternative

Node *e*:   Drill alternative has EP = 100

Sell alternative has EP = 90

100 > 90, so choose the Drill alternative

A double dash indicates a rejected decision.

The expected payoff for each chosen alternative now would be recorded in boldface over its decision node, as shown in Figure 9.16. The chosen alternative also is indicated by inserting a double dash as a barrier through each rejected branch.

Next, moving one more column to the left brings us to node *b*. Since this is an event node, step 2 of the procedure needs to be applied. The expected payoff for each of its branches is recorded over the following decision node. Therefore, the expected payoff is

$$EP = 0.7(60) + 0.3(270) = 123 \quad \text{for node } b$$

as recorded over this node in Figure 9.16.

Finally, we move left to node *a,* a decision node. Applying step 3 yields

Node *a*:   Do seismic survey has EP = 123

No seismic survey has EP = 100

123 > 100, so choose Do seismic survey.

This expected payoff of 123 now would be recorded over the node, and a double dash inserted to indicate the rejected branch, as already shown in Figure 9.16.

This procedure has moved from right to left for analysis purposes. However, having completed the decision tree in this way, the decision maker now can read the tree from left to right to see the actual progression of events. The double dashes have closed off the undesirable paths. Therefore, given the payoffs for the final outcomes shown on the right side, *Bayes' decision rule* says to follow only the open paths from left to right to achieve the largest possible expected payoff.

The open paths (no double dashes) provide the optimal decision at each decision node.

Following the open paths from left to right in Figure 9.16 yields the following optimal policy, according to Bayes' decision rule.

FIGURE 9.16

The final decision tree that records the analysis for the full Goferbroke Co. problem when using monetary payoffs.

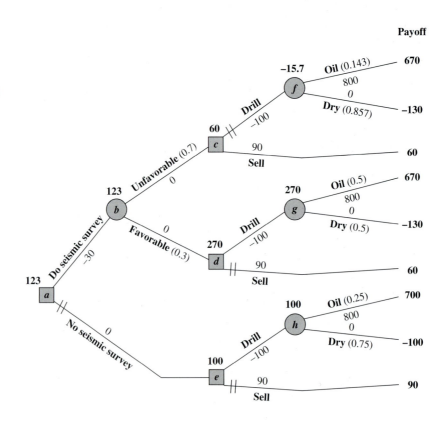

Optimal Policy

Do the seismic survey.

If the result is unfavorable, sell the land.

If the result is favorable, drill for oil.

The expected payoff (including the cost of the seismic survey) is 123 ($123,000).

Expected Value of Sample Information

We have assumed so far that the cost of the seismic survey for the full Goferbroke Co. problem is known in advance to be $30,000. However, suppose that there is uncertainty about this cost. How would this change the analysis described above?

In this case, the analysis would begin by identifying two key quantities,

EP (with more info)   = Expected payoff (excluding the cost of the survey) when the survey is done

EP (without more info) = Expected payoff when the survey is not done

where Bayes' decision rule is applied to find both quantities. EP (with more info) is obtained by using the top half of the decision tree in Figure 9.17 *except* that the (unknown) cost of the seismic survey is not included, so all the payoffs and expected payoffs would be 30 larger than shown there. Therefore, cell E19 indicates that

$$\text{EP (with more info)} = 123 + 30 = 153$$

EP (without more info) is described at the beginning of Section 9.5, and is obtained here from the bottom half of the decision tree in Figure 9.17 without any change, so cell E42 shows that

$$\text{EP (without more info)} = 100$$

Now we can calculate the **expected value of sample information (EVSI)** (where "sample information" refers to the information from the seismic survey in this case) as

$$\text{EVSI} = \text{EP (with more info)} - \text{EP (without more info)}$$
$$= 153 - 100$$
$$= 53$$

Let

$C =$ best available estimate of the cost of the seismic survey (in thousands of dollars)

The final step in the analysis is to compare C and EVSI.

If $C <$ EVSI, then perform the seismic survey.

If $C \geq$ EVSI, then do not perform the seismic survey.

Using TreePlan

Using the procedures described in Section 9.3, TreePlan can be used to construct and solve this same decision tree on a spreadsheet. Figure 9.17 shows the decision tree obtained with TreePlan. Although the form is somewhat different, note that this decision tree is completely equivalent to the one in Figure 9.16. Besides the convenience of constructing the tree directly on a spreadsheet, TreePlan also provides the key advantage of automatically solving the decision tree. Rather than relying on hand calculations as in Figure 9.16, TreePlan instantaneously calculates all the expected payoffs at each stage of the tree, as shown below and to the left of each node, as soon as the decision tree is constructed. Instead of using double dashes, TreePlan puts a number inside each decision node indicating which branch should be chosen (assuming the branches emanating from that node are numbered consecutively from top to bottom).

FIGURE 9.17

The decision tree constructed and solved by TreePlan for the full Goferbroke Co. problem that also considers whether to do a seismic survey.

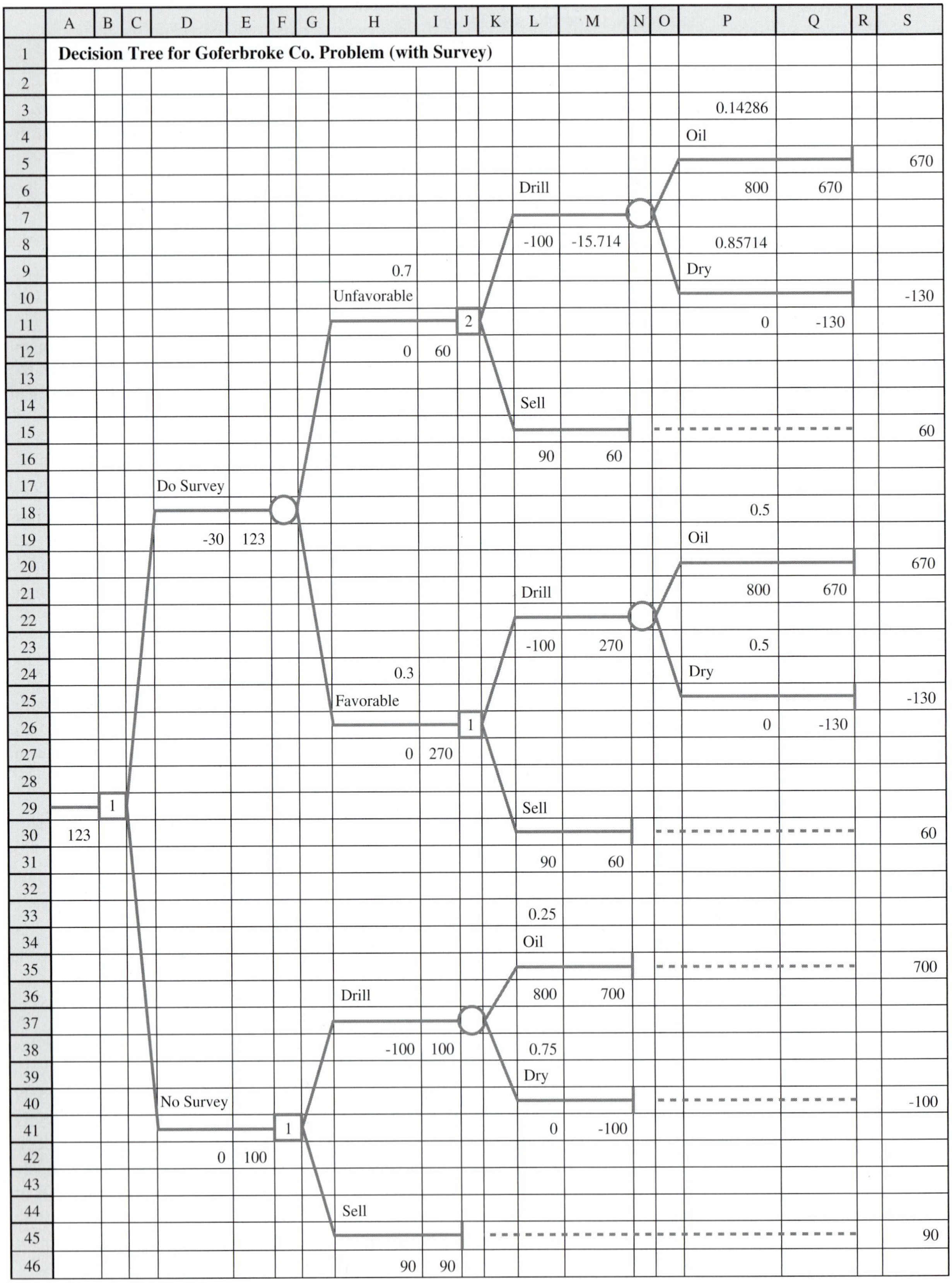

	A	B	C	D	E	F	G	H	I	J	K	L	M	N	O	P	Q	R	S
1	**Decision Tree for Goferbroke Co. Problem (with Survey)**																		
2																			
3																0.14286			
4															Oil				
5																			670
6												Drill				800	670		
7														○					
8												-100	-15.714			0.85714			
9															Dry				
10								0.7											-130
11								Unfavorable		2						0	-130		
12									0	60									
13																			
14												Sell							
15																			60
16												90	60						
17				Do Survey															
18							○										0.5		
19				-30	123										Oil				
20																			670
21												Drill				800	670		
22														○					
23												-100	270			0.5			
24								0.3							Dry				
25								Favorable											-130
26										1						0	-130		
27									0	270									
28																			
29		1										Sell							
30	123																		60
31												90	60						
32																			
33												0.25							
34												Oil							
35																			700
36							Drill					800	700						
37										○									
38							-100	100				0.75							
39												Dry							
40				No Survey															-100
41							1					0	-100						
42				0	100														
43																			
44							Sell												
45																			90
46							90	90											

Max's Reaction

Max: I see that this decision tree gives me some numbers to compare alternatives. But how reliable are those numbers?

Jennifer: Well, you have to remember that these average payoffs for the alternatives at the decision nodes are based on both the payoffs on the right and the probabilities at the event nodes. These probabilities are based in turn on the consulting geologist's numbers and the numbers you gave me on how frequently you get favorable seismic soundings when you have oil or when the land is dry.

Max: That doesn't sound so good. You know what I think about the consulting geologist's numbers. And the numbers I gave you were pretty rough estimates.

Jennifer: True. So the average payoffs shown in the decision tree are only approximations. This is when some sensitivity analysis can be helpful, like we did earlier before we considered doing the seismic survey.

Max: OK. So let's do it.

Review Questions

1. What does a decision tree display?
2. What is happening at a decision node?
3. What is happening at an event node?
4. What kinds of numbers need to be inserted into a decision tree before beginning the analysis?
5. When performing the analysis, where do you begin on the decision tree and in which direction do you move for dealing with the nodes?
6. What calculation needs to be performed at each event node?
7. What comparison needs to be made at each decision node?
8. What is meant by the expected value of sample information and how might it be used?

9.8   PERFORMING SENSITIVITY ANALYSIS ON THE PROBLEM WITH A SEQUENCE OF DECISIONS

Section 9.4 describes how the decision tree created with TreePlan (Figures 9.5 and 9.6) was used to perform sensitivity analysis for the first Goferbroke problem where the only decision being made was whether to drill for oil or sell the land (without conducting the seismic survey). The focus was on one particularly critical piece of data, the prior probability of oil, so the analysis involved checking whether the decision would change if the original value of this prior probability (0.25) were changed to various other trial values. New trial values first were considered in a trial-and-error manner (Figure 9.7) and then were investigated more systematically by constructing a data table (Figure 9.9).

Since Max Flyer wants to consider whether to have a seismic survey conducted before deciding whether to drill or sell, the relevant decision tree now is the one in Figure 9.17 instead of the one in Figure 9.5. With this sequence of decisions and the resulting need to obtain and apply posterior probabilities, conducting **sensitivity analysis** becomes somewhat more involved. Let's see how it is done.

Organizing the Spreadsheet

As was done in Section 9.4, it is helpful to begin by consolidating the data and results into one section of the spreadsheet, as shown in Figure 9.18. The data cells in the decision tree now make reference to the consolidated data cells to the right of the decision tree (cells V4:V11). Similarly, the summarized results to the right of the decision tree make reference to the output cells within the decision tree (the decision nodes in cells B29, F41, J11, and J26, as well as the expected payoff in cell A30).

The probability data in the decision tree are complicated by the fact that the posterior probabilities will need to be updated any time a change is made in any of the prior probability data. Fortunately, the template for calculating posterior probabilities (as shown in Figure 9.13) can be used to do these calculations. The relevant portion of this template (B3:H19) has been copied (using the Copy and Paste commands in the Edit menu) to the spreadsheet in Figure 9.18 (now

Consolidating the data and results on the spreadsheet is important for sensitivity analysis.

FIGURE 9.18

In preparation for performing sensitivity analysis on the full Goferbroke Co. problem, the data and results have been consolidated on the spreadsheet to the right of the decision tree.

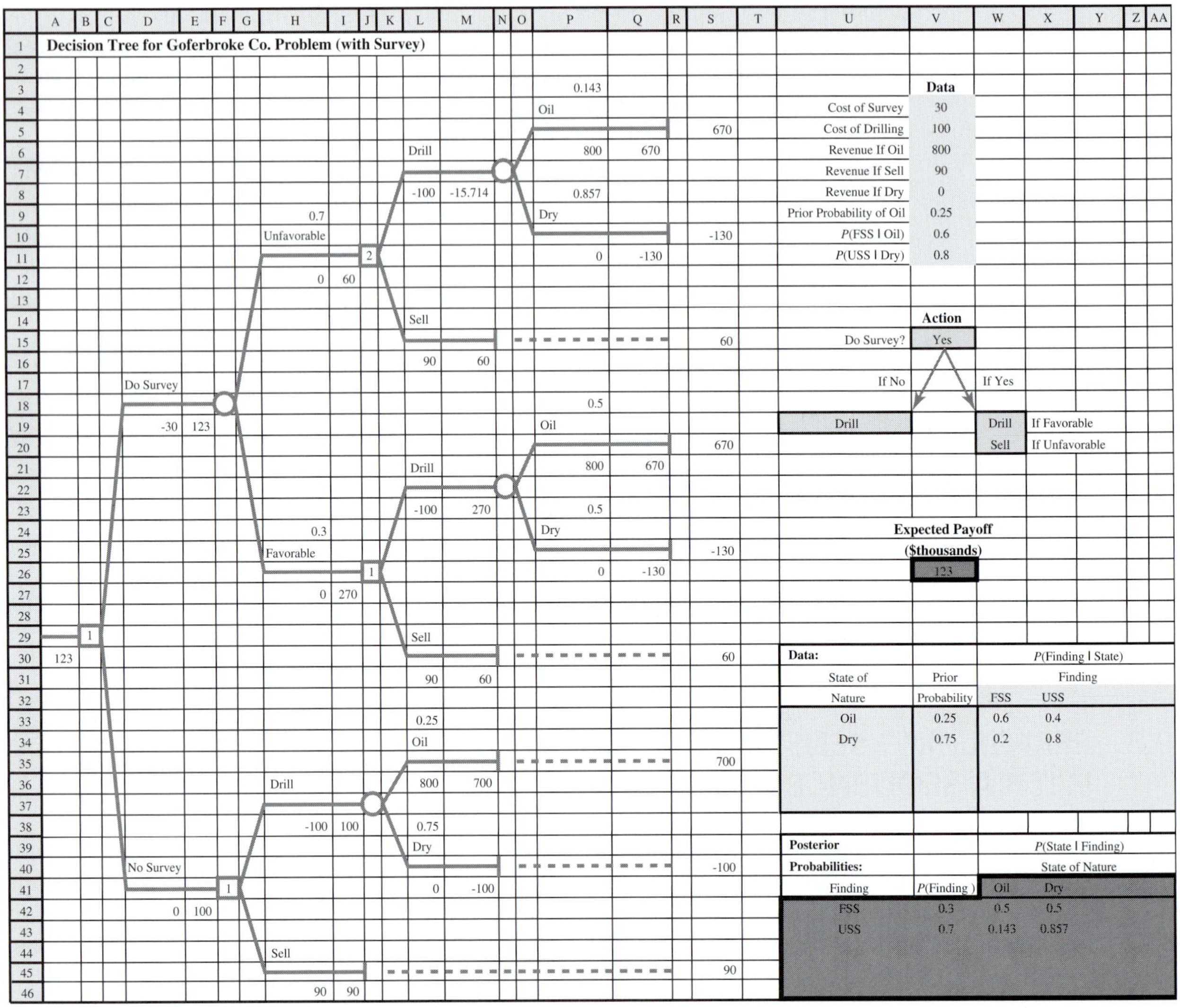

Decision Tree for Goferbroke Co. Problem (with Survey)

Data

Cost of Survey	30
Cost of Drilling	100
Revenue If Oil	800
Revenue If Sell	90
Revenue If Dry	0
Prior Probability of Oil	0.25
P(FSS I Oil)	0.6
P(USS I Dry)	0.8

Action

Do Survey?   Yes

If No | If Yes
Drill | Drill   If Favorable
| Sell   If Unfavorable

Expected Payoff ($thousands)   123

Data: P(Finding I State)

State of Nature	Prior Probability	FSS	USS
Oil	0.25	0.6	0.4
Dry	0.75	0.2	0.8

Posterior Probabilities: P(State I Finding)   State of Nature

Finding	P(Finding)	Oil	Dry
FSS	0.3	0.5	0.5
USS	0.7	0.143	0.857

Range Name	Cell
CostOfDrilling	V5
CostOfSurvey	V4
PriorProbabilityOfOil	V9
ProbDryGivenFSS	X42
ProbDryGivenUSS	X43
ProbFSS	V42
ProbFSSGivenOil	V10
ProbOilGivenFSS	W42
ProbOilGivenUSS	W43
ProbUSS	V43
ProbUSSGivenDry	V11
RevenueIfDry	V8
RevenueIfOil	V6
RevenueIfSell	V7

	U	V	W	X
14		Action		
15	Do Survey?	=IF(B29=1,"Yes","No")		
16				
17	If No		If Yes	
18				
19	=IF(F41=1,"Drill","Sell")		=IF(J26=1,"Drill","Sell")	If Favorable
20			=IF(J11=1,"Drill","Sell")	If Unfavorable

	P
3	=ProbOilGivenUSS
4	Oil
5	
6	=RevenueIfOil
7	
8	=ProbDryGivenUSS
9	Dry
10	
11	=RevenueIfDry

	V
23	Expected
24	Payoff
25	($thousands)
26	=A30

	U	V	W	X
30	Data:		P(Finding I State)	
31	State of	Prior	Finding	
32	Nature	Probability	FSS	USS
33	Oil	=PriorProbabilityOfOil	=ProbFSSGivenOil	=1–ProbFSSGivenOil
34	Dry	=1–PriorProbabilityOfOil	=1–ProbUSSGivenDry	=ProbUSSGivenDry

appearing in U30:AA46). The data for the template refer to the probability data in the data cells PriorProbabilityOfOil (V9), ProbFSSGivenOil (V10), and ProbUSSGivenDry (V11), as shown in the formulas for cells V33:X34 at the bottom of Figure 9.18. The template automatically calculates the probability of each finding and the posterior probabilities (in cells V42:X43) based on these data. The decision tree then refers to these calculated probabilities when they are needed, as shown in the formulas for cells P3:P11 in Figure 9.18.

While it takes some time and effort to consolidate the data and results, including all the necessary cross-referencing, this step is truly essential for performing sensitivity analysis. Many pieces of data are used in several places on the decision tree. For example, the revenue if Goferbroke finds oil appears in cells P6, P21, and L36. Performing sensitivity analysis on this piece of data now requires changing its value in only one place (cell V6) rather than three (cells P6, P21, and L36). The benefits of consolidation are even more important for the probability data. Changing any prior probability may cause *all* the posterior probabilities to change. By including the posterior probability template, the prior probability can be changed in one place and then all the other probabilities are calculated and updated appropriately.

After making any change in the cost data, revenue data, or probability data in Figure 9.18, the spreadsheet nicely summarizes the new results after the actual work to obtain these results is instantly done by the posterior probability template and the decision tree. Therefore, experimenting with alternative data values in a trial-and-error manner is one useful way of performing sensitivity analysis.

However, it would be desirable to have another method of performing this sensitivity analysis more systematically. Using a data table as described in Section 9.4 is one such method. However, data tables have their limitations, particularly when dealing with large problems. For example, one major limitation is that each data table can consider changes in only one or two data cells.

Fortunately, your MS Courseware includes an Excel add-in called *SensIt* that overcomes this limitation, providing an easy way to create informative sensitivity analysis graphs that display the effect of changing *any* number of data cells. SensIt was developed by Professor Michael Middleton, who also developed TreePlan, so it is designed to be integrated with TreePlan (although it also can perform other types of sensitivity analysis that don't require the use of TreePlan).

Using SensIt to Create Three Types of Sensitivity Analysis Graphs

Installing SensIt adds a Sensitivity Analysis menu item to the Add-Ins tab (for Excel 2007) or Tools menu (for earlier versions of Excel). This menu item has a submenu giving a choice of three different kinds of sensitivity analysis graphs: Plot, Spider, and Tornado (along with a Help option). Let's see how each of these types of graphs can be used to perform sensitivity analysis.

Plot is used to generate a graph that shows how an output cell varies for different values of a single data cell. Choosing this option brings up the Plot dialogue box shown in Figure 9.19. The left side of the SensIt-Plot dialogue box is used to specify the data cell that will be varied (the prior probability of oil in cell V9) and the output cell of interest (the expected payoff in cell V26). Optionally, the cells containing the labels for these cells may also be specified (cells U9 and V24, respectively). These labels are used to label the axes of the graph that is created. The right side of the SensIt-Plot dialogue box is used to specify the range of values to be considered for the single data cell (the prior probability of oil). In this case, all values between 0 and 1 (at intervals of 0.05) will be considered. Clicking OK then generates the graph shown in Figure 9.20 that reveals the relationship between the prior probability of oil and the expected payoff that results from using the optimal policy given this probability.

This graph indicates that the expected payoff starts increasing when the prior probability is a little over 0.15 and then starts increasing more rapidly when this probability is around 0.3. This suggests that the optimal policy changes at roughly these values of the prior probability. To check this out, the spreadsheet in Figure 9.18 can be used to see how the results change when the prior probability of oil is slowly increased in the vicinity of these values. This kind of trial-and-error analysis soon leads to the following conclusions about how the optimal policy depends on this probability.

FIGURE 9.19

The dialogue box used by the Plot option of SensIt.

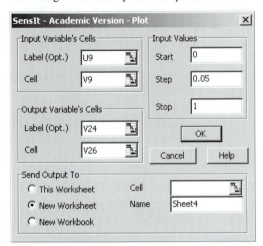

FIGURE 9.20

The graph generated by the Plot option of SensIt for the full Goferbroke Co. problem to show how the expected payoff (when using Bayes' decision rule) depends on the prior probability of oil.

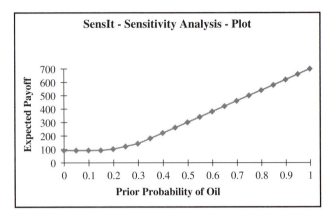

Optimal Policy

Let	p = Prior probability of oil.
If	$p \leq 0.168$, then sell the land (no seismic survey).
If	$0.169 \leq p \leq 0.308$, then do the survey: drill if favorable and sell if not.
If	$p \geq 0.309$, then drill for oil (no seismic survey).

This sensitivity analysis has focused so far on investigating the effect if the true probability of finding oil is different from the original prior probability of 0.25. Similar analysis could be done with respect to the probabilities in cells V10:V11 of Figure 9.18. However, since there is significant uncertainty about some of the cost and revenue data in cells V4:V8, we turn next to performing sensitivity analysis with respect to these data.

Suppose we want to investigate how the expected payoff would change if one of the costs or revenues in cells V4:V7 were to change by up to *plus or minus 10 percent.* The **spider graph** (the second item in the Sensitivity Analysis menu on the Add-Ins tab for Excel 2007 or under the Tools menu for earlier versions of Excel) is used for this sort of analysis. The left side of the SensIt-Spider dialogue box (shown in Figure 9.21) is used to specify a range of data cells to be varied (the cost and revenue data in the range V4:V7) and the output cell of interest (the expected payoff in cell V26). In the right side of the SensIt- Spider dialogue box, specify the range of values to consider for the data cells in percentage terms relative to their base value. To consider a change of plus or minus 10 percent for each data value, we consider values between 90 percent and 110 percent of the base value. Clicking OK then generates the graph shown in Figure 9.22.

SensIt Tip: The data cells to be varied in a spider chart need to be in contiguous cells before choosing Spider in the Sensitivity Analysis submenu. Also be sure that the data cells contain the base case values.

FIGURE 9.21

The dialogue box used by the Spider option of SensIt.

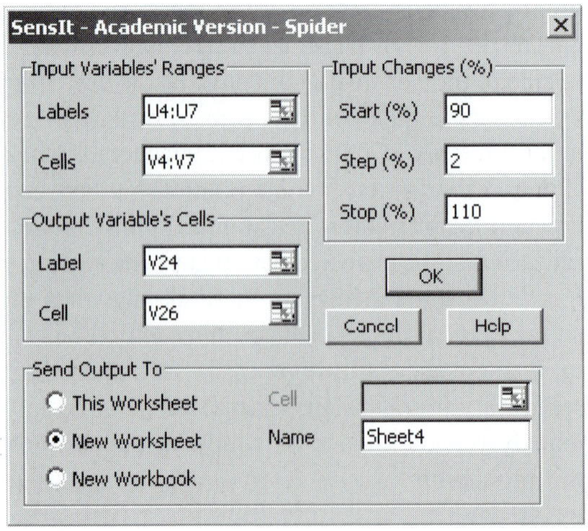

FIGURE 9.22

The spider graph generated by the Spider option of SensIt for the full Goferbroke Co. problem to show how the expected payoff (when using Bayes' decision rule) varies with changes in any one of the cost or revenue estimates.

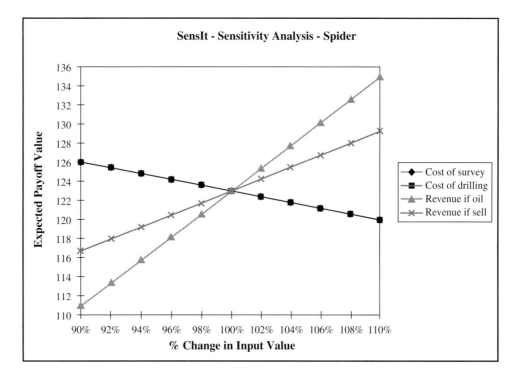

Each line in the spider graph in this figure plots the expected payoff as one of the selected data cells (V4:V7) is changed from its original value by being multiplied by the percentage indicated along the bottom of the graph. (The diamonds for the *cost of survey line* are hidden under the squares for the *cost of drilling line*.) The fact that the *revenue if oil line* is the steepest one reveals that the expected payoff is particularly sensitive to the estimate of the revenue if oil is found, so any additional work on refining the estimates should focus the most attention on this one.

A limitation of SensIt's Spider graph is that it assumes that each data value varies by the same amount. For example, we considered the case where any one piece of the cost or revenue data could change by up to plus or minus 10 percent. It may be the case that some of the data are more unknown (and hence more variable) than other data. The SensIt **tornado diagram** overcomes this limitation. However, it requires some additions to the original spreadsheet (Figure 9.18). As shown in Figure 9.23, three columns are added for each data cell that will be varied, indicating the lowest value, base value, and highest value. The cost of the survey and the revenue if Max sells the land are fairly predictable (thus varying over a small range of 28–32 and 85–95, respectively), while the cost of drilling and the revenue if oil is struck are more variable (thus varying over a large range of 75–140 and 600–1,000, respectively).

A tornado diagram allows different data cells to have different degrees of variability.

The SensIt-Tornado dialogue box (called up by choosing the third item in the Sensitivity Analysis menu on the Add-Ins tab for Excel 2007 or under the Tools menu for earlier versions of Excel) is shown in Figure 9.24. It is used to specify which data cells will be varied, which output cell will be examined, and the location of the cells specifying the range (low, base, and high) for the data cells. Clicking OK generates the chart shown in Figure 9.25. Each bar in the graph shows the range of change in the expected payoff as the corresponding cost or revenue is varied over the range of values indicated numerically at the ends of each bar. The width of each bar measures how sensitive the expected payoff is to changes in that bar's cost or revenue. Once again, *revenue if oil* stands out as causing much more sensitivity than the other costs or revenues.

SensIt Tip: The data cells to be varied in a tornado diagram should be in contiguous cells and additional columns need to be added to give the low, base, and high value for each data cell. Rearrange the spreadsheet in this way before choosing Tornado in the Sensitivity Analysis submenu.

Max's Reaction

Max: Very interesting. I especially liked the way we were able to use that sensitivity analysis spreadsheet to see immediately what would happen when we change some of the numbers. And there was one thing that I found particularly encouraging.

FIGURE 9.23

Expansion of the spreadsheet in Figure 9.18 to prepare for generating a tornado diagram with SensIt.

	U	V	W	X	Y
3		**Data**	Low	Base	High
4	Cost of Survey	30	28	30	32
5	Cost of Drilling	100	75	100	140
6	Revenue If Oil	800	600	800	1000
7	Revenue If Sell	90	85	90	95
8	Revenue If Dry	0			
9	Prior Probability of Oil	0.25			
10	P(FSS I Oil)	0.6			
11	P(USS I Dry)	0.8			

FIGURE 9.24

The dialogue box used by the Tornado option of SensIt.

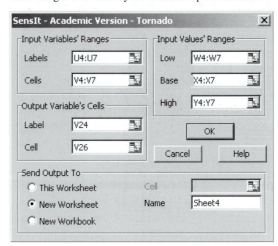

FIGURE 9.25

The tornado diagram generated by the Tornado option of SensIt for the full Goferbroke Co. problem to show how much the expected payoff (when using Bayes' decision rule) can vary over the entire range of likely values of any one of the cost or revenue estimates.

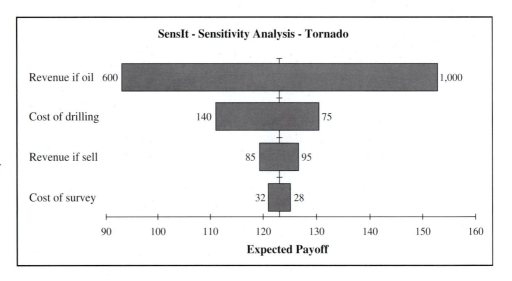

Jennifer: What was that?

Max: When we changed that prior probability of oil to nearly every other plausible value, it kept coming back with the same answer. Do the seismic survey and then drill only if the survey is favorable. Otherwise, sell. So the consulting geologist's numbers can be off by quite a bit and we still would be doing the right thing.

Jennifer: Yes, that was a key finding, wasn't it? What did you think of the sensitivity analysis involving the cost and revenue data?

Max: Those spider and tornado graph things were pretty clever. However, what they were saying didn't particularly surprise me. Sure, my payoff will depend much more on the revenue we get if we find oil than on anything else.

Jennifer: But what that is telling us is that it is especially important to try to better pin down what that revenue would be. Fortunately, based on both the decision tree and the sensitivity results we've already gotten, I can tell you right now that the sensitivity analysis spreadsheet will give us the same results for what to do even if we make fairly substantial changes in the estimate of the revenue if oil is found. The average payoff with and without the survey (shown in cell E19 and cell E42, respectively, in Figures 9.17 and 9.18) in the decision tree indicates that the suggested policy is far from a close call. If the revenue from oil were considerably less than $800,000, then the question would become whether to do the seismic survey or simply sell the land immediately. However, the tornado diagram tells me that the revenue if oil is found could be as much as 25 percent less than the estimate of $800,000 and our average payoff from the suggested policy still would exceed the $90,000 we could get from selling the land immediately.

Max: It's pretty unlikely that the revenue would be that much less than our estimate. So I am satisfied with going ahead with $800,000 as our estimate.

Jennifer: OK. Does this mean that you are comfortable now with a decision to proceed with the seismic survey and then either drill or sell depending on the outcome of the survey?

Max: Not quite. There is still one thing that bothers me.

Jennifer: What's that?

Max: Suppose the seismic survey gives us a favorable seismic sounding, so we drill. If the land turns out to be dry, then I'm out 130,000 bucks! As I said at the beginning, that would nearly put us out of business. That scares me. I currently am shorter of working capital than I normally am. Therefore, losing $130,000 now would hurt more than it normally does. It doesn't look like this approach is really taking that into account.

Jennifer: No, you're right. It really doesn't. This approach just looks at average *monetary* values. That isn't good enough when you're dealing with such large amounts. You wouldn't be willing to flip a coin to determine whether you win or lose $130,000, right?

Max: No, I sure wouldn't.

Jennifer: OK, that's the tipoff. As I mentioned the first time we talked about this problem, I think the circumstances here indicate that we need to go beyond dollars and cents to look at the consequences of the possible outcomes. Fortunately, decision analysis has a way of doing this by introducing utilities. The basic idea is that the utility of an outcome measures the true value to you of that outcome rather than just the monetary value. So by expressing payoffs in terms of utilities, the decision tree analysis would find the average utility at each node instead of the average monetary value. So now the decisions would be based on giving you the highest possible average utility.

Considering average *monetary* values isn't good enough when uncomfortably large losses can occur.

Review *Questions*

1. When preparing to perform sensitivity analysis, how should one begin organizing the spreadsheet that contains the decision tree?
2. Performing sensitivity analysis on a certain piece of data should require changing its value in how many places on the spreadsheet?
3. What is a major limitation of using a data table to perform sensitivity analysis on a large problem?
4. How many data cells can be varied at a time when using the Plot option of SensIt?
5. Can the Spider option of SensIt consider more data cells at a time than the Plot option?
6. What is a limitation of a spider graph that is overcome by a tornado diagram?

9.9 USING UTILITIES TO BETTER REFLECT THE VALUES OF PAYOFFS

Thus far, when applying Bayes' decision rule, we have assumed that the expected payoff in *monetary terms* is the appropriate measure of the consequences of taking an action. However, in many situations where very large amounts of money are involved, this assumption is inappropriate.

For example, suppose that an individual is offered the choice of (1) accepting a 50–50 chance of winning $100,000 or (2) receiving $40,000 with certainty. Many people would prefer the $40,000 even though the expected payoff on the 50–50 chance of winning $100,000 is $50,000. A company may be unwilling to invest a large sum of money in a new product, even when the expected profit is substantial, if there is a risk of losing its investment and thereby becoming bankrupt. People buy insurance even though it is a poor investment from the viewpoint of the expected payoff.

Do these examples invalidate Bayes' decision rule? Fortunately, the answer is no, because there is a way of transforming monetary values to an appropriate scale that reflects the decision maker's preferences. This scale is called the *utility function for money.*

Utility Functions for Money

Figure 9.26 shows a typical **utility function *U(M)* for money *M*.** The intuitive interpretation is that it indicates that an individual having this utility function would value obtaining $30,000 twice as much as $10,000 and would value obtaining $100,000 twice as much as $30,000. This reflects the fact that the person's highest-priority needs would be met by the first $10,000. Having this decreasing slope of the function as the amount of money increases is referred to as having a *decreasing marginal utility for money.* Such an individual is referred to as being **risk averse.**

Two different individuals can have very different utility functions for money.

However, not all individuals have a decreasing marginal utility for money. Some people are **risk seekers** instead of *risk averse,* and they go through life looking for the "big score." The slope of their utility function *increases* as the amount of money increases, so they have an *increasing marginal utility for money.*

Figure 9.27 compares the shape of the utility function for money for risk-averse and risk-seeking individuals. Also shown is the intermediate case of a **risk-neutral** individual, who prizes money at its face value. Such an individual's utility for money is simply proportional to

FIGURE 9.26

A typical utility function for money, where *U(M)* is the utility of obtaining an amount of money *M.*

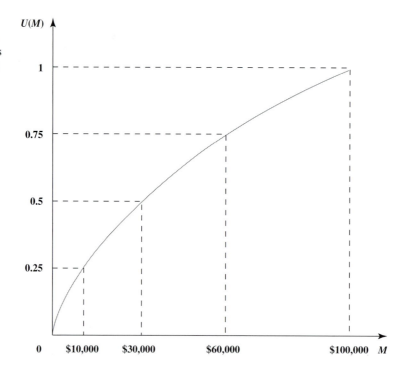

FIGURE 9.27

The shape of the utility function for money for (*a*) risk-averse, (*b*) risk-seeking, and (*c*) risk-neutral individuals.

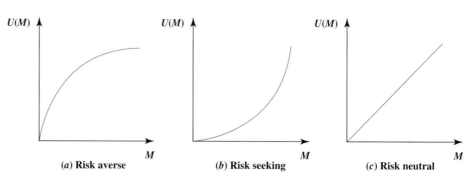

the amount of money involved. Although some people appear to be risk neutral when only small amounts of money are involved, it is unusual to be truly risk neutral with very large amounts.

It also is possible to exhibit a mixture of these kinds of behavior. For example, an individual might be essentially risk neutral with small amounts of money, then become a risk seeker with moderate amounts, and then turn risk averse with large amounts. In addition, one's attitude toward risk can shift over time depending on circumstances.

Managers of a business firm need to consider the company's circumstances and the collective philosophy of top management in determining the appropriate attitude toward risk when making managerial decisions.

The fact that different people have different utility functions for money has an important implication for decision making in the face of uncertainty.

> When a *utility function for money* is incorporated into a decision analysis approach to a problem, this utility function must be constructed to fit the current preferences and values of the decision maker involved. (The decision maker can be either a single individual or a group of people.)

The key to constructing the utility function for money to fit the decision maker is the following fundamental property of utility functions.

> **Fundamental Property:** Under the assumptions of utility theory, the decision maker's *utility function for money* has the property that the decision maker is *indifferent* between two alternative courses of action if the two alternatives have the *same expected utility.*

To illustrate, suppose that the decision maker has the utility function shown in Figure 9.26. Further suppose that the decision maker is offered the following opportunity.

> **Offer:** An opportunity to obtain either $100,000 (utility = 1) with probability p or nothing (utility = 0) with probability $(1 - p)$.

Thus, by weighting the two possible utilities (1 and 0) by their probabilities, the expected utility is

$$E(\text{utility}) = p + 0(1 - p)$$
$$= p \text{ for this offer}$$

Therefore, for *each* of the following three pairs of alternatives, the above fundamental property indicates that the decision maker is indifferent between the first and second alternatives.

In all three of these cases, a decision maker with the utility function in Figure 9.26 would be indifferent between the two alternatives because they have the same expected utility.

1. *First alternative:* The offer with $p = 0.25$, so $E(\text{utility}) = 0.25$.
   Second alternative: Definitely obtain $10,000, so utility = 0.25.

2. *First alternative:* The offer with $p = 0.5$, so $E(\text{utility}) = 0.5$.
   Second alternative: Definitely obtain $30,000, so utility = 0.5.

3. *First alternative:* The offer with $p = 0.75$, so $E(\text{utility}) = 0.75$.
   Second alternative: Definitely obtain $60,000, so utility = 0.75.

This example also illustrates one way in which the decision maker's utility function for money can be constructed in the first place. The decision maker would be made the same hypothetical offer to obtain a large amount of money (e.g., $100,000) with probability *p,* or nothing otherwise. Then, for each of a few smaller amounts of money (e.g., $10,000, $30,000, and $60,000), the decision maker would be asked to choose a value of *p* that would make him or her *indifferent* between the offer and definitely obtaining that amount of money. The utility of the smaller amount of money then is *p* times the utility of the large amount. When the utility of the large amount has been set equal to 1, as in Figure 9.26, this conveniently makes the utility of the smaller amount simply equal to *p.* The utility values in Figure 9.26 imply that the decision maker has chosen $p = 0.25$ when $M = \$10,000$, $p = 0.5$ when $M = \$30,000$, and $p = 0.75$ when $M = \$60,000$. (Constructing the utility function in this way is an example of the *lottery procedure* described later in this section.)

The *scale* of the utility function is irrelevant. In other words, it doesn't matter whether the values of $U(M)$ at the dashed lines in Figure 9.26 are 0.25, 0.5, 0.75, 1 (as shown) or 10,000, 20,000, 30,000, 40,000, or whatever. All the utilities can be multiplied by any positive constant without affecting which decision alternative will have the largest expected utility. It also is possible to add the same constant (positive or negative) to all the utilities without affecting which decision alternative will have the largest expected utility.

For these reasons, we have the liberty to set the value of $U(M)$ arbitrarily for two values of M, so long as the higher monetary value has the higher utility. It is particularly convenient to set $U(M) = 0$ for the smallest value of M under consideration and to set $U(M) = 1$ for the largest M. By assigning a utility of 0 to the worst outcome and a utility of 1 to the best outcome, and then determining the utilities of the other outcomes accordingly, it becomes easy to see the relative utility of each outcome along the scale from worst to best.

Now we are ready to summarize the basic role of utility functions in decision analysis.

> When the decision maker's utility function for money is used to measure the relative worth of the various possible monetary outcomes, *Bayes' decision rule* replaces monetary payoffs by the corresponding utilities. Therefore, the optimal decision (or series of decisions) is the one that *maximizes the expected utility.*

Only utility functions for *money* have been discussed here. However, we should mention that utility functions can sometimes still be constructed when some or all of the important consequences of the decision alternatives are *not* monetary in nature. (For example, the consequences of a doctor's decision alternatives in treating a patient involve the future health of the patient.) This is not necessarily easy, since it may require making value judgments about the relative desirability of rather intangible consequences. Nevertheless, under these circumstances, it is important to incorporate such value judgments into the decision process.

The objective now is to maximize the expected utility rather than the expected payoff in monetary terms.

Dealing with the Goferbroke Co. Problem

Recall that the Goferbroke Co. is operating without much capital, so a loss of $100,000 would be quite serious. As the owner of the company, Max already has gone heavily into debt to keep going. The worst-case scenario would be to come up with $30,000 for a seismic survey and then still lose $100,000 by drilling when there is no oil. This scenario would not bankrupt the company at this point but definitely would leave it in a precarious financial position.

On the other hand, striking oil is an exciting prospect, since earning $700,000 finally would put the company on fairly solid financial footing.

Max is the decision maker for this problem. Therefore, to prepare for using utilities to analyze the problem, it is necessary to construct Max's utility function for money, $U(M)$, where we will express the amount of money M in units of thousands of dollars.

We start by assigning utilities of 0 and 1, respectively, to the smallest and largest possible payoffs. Since the smallest possible payoff is $M = -130$ (a loss of $130,000) and the largest is $M = 700$ (a gain of $700,000), this gives $U(-130) = 0$ and $U(700) = 1$.

To determine the utilities for other possible monetary payoffs, it is necessary to probe Max's attitude toward risk. Especially important are his feelings about the consequences of the worst possible loss ($130,000) and the best possible gain ($700,000), as well as how he compares these consequences. Let us eavesdrop as Jennifer probes these feelings with Max.

Interviewing Max

Jennifer: Well now, these utilities are intended to reflect your feelings about the true value to you of these various possible payoffs. Therefore, to pin down what your utilities are, we need to talk some about how you feel about these payoffs and their consequences for the company.

Max: Fine.

Jennifer: A good place to begin would be the best and worst possible cases. The possibility of gaining $700,000 or losing $130,000.

Max: Those are the big ones all right.

Jennifer: OK, suppose you drill without paying for a seismic survey and then you find oil, so your profit is about $700,000. What would that do for the company?

Max: A lot. That would finally give me the capital I need to become more of a major player in this business. I then could take a shot at finding a big oil field. That big strike I've talked about.

Jennifer: OK, good. Now let's talk about the consequences if you were to get that biggest possible loss instead. Suppose you pay for a seismic survey, then you drill and the land is dry. So you're out about $130,000. How bad would that be? What kind of future would the company have?

Max: Well, let me put it this way. It would put the company in a pretty uncomfortable financial position. I would need to work hard on getting some more financing. Then we would need to cautiously work our way out of the hole by forming some partnerships for some low-risk, low-gain drilling. But I think we could do it. I've been in that position a couple times before and come out of it. We'd be OK.

Jennifer: It sounds like you wouldn't be overly worried about such a loss as long as you have reasonable odds for a big payoff to justify this risk.

Max: That's right.

Jennifer: OK, now let's talk about those odds. What I'm going to do is set up a simpler hypothetical situation. Suppose these are your alternatives. One is to drill. If you find oil, you clear $700,000. If the land is dry, you're out $130,000. The only other alternative is to sell the land for $90,000. I know this isn't your actual situation since $700,000 does not include the cost of a survey whereas the loss of $130,000 does, but let's pretend that these are your alternatives.

Max: I don't understand why you want to talk about a situation that is different from what we are facing.

Jennifer: Trust me. Considering these kinds of hypothetical situations are going to enable us to determine your utilities.

Max: OK.

Jennifer: Now presumably if you had a 50–50 chance of either clearing $700,000 or losing $130,000, you would drill.

Max: Sure.

Jennifer: If you had a smaller chance, say one-in-four of gaining $700,000, versus a three-in-four chance of losing $130,000, would you choose to drill or sell the land for $90,000?

Max: Well, that's almost the original decision we were trying to make, before we considered the seismic survey. However, there is one big difference. Now you're asking me to suppose that the loss if there is no oil is $130,000 rather than $100,000. The higher loss would be quite a bit more painful. I wouldn't be willing to take this risk with just a one-in-four chance of gaining $700,000.

Jennifer: OK, so now we know that the point at which you would be indifferent between going ahead or not is somewhere between having a one-in-four chance and a 50–50 chance of gaining $700,000 rather than losing $130,000. Let's see if we can pin down just where your **point of indifference** is within this range from one-in-four and 50–50. Let's try a one-in-three chance. Would you go ahead and drill with a one-in-three chance of gaining $700,000 versus a two-in-three chance of losing $130,000, or would you choose to sell the land for $90,000?

Max: Hmm. That's not so clear. What would be the average payoff in this case?

Jennifer: Almost $147,000.

Max: Not bad. Hmm, one chance in three of gaining $700,000. That's tempting. But two chances in three of losing $130,000 with all the problems involved with that. I don't know. $90,000 would be a sure thing. That's a tough one.

Jennifer: OK, let's try this. Suppose your chances of gaining $700,000 were a little better than one-in-three. Would you do it?

Max: Yes, I think so.

Jennifer: And if your chances were a little under one-in-three?

Max: Then I don't think I would do it.

Jennifer: OK. You've convinced me that your point of indifference is one-in-three. That's exactly what I needed to know.

The *point of indifference* is the point where the decision maker is indifferent between two hypothetical alternatives.

Finding $U(90)$

Max has indeed given Jennifer just the information she needs to determine $U(90)$, Max's utility for a payoff of 90 (a gain of \$90,000). Recall that $U(-130)$ already has been set at $U(-130) = 0$ and that $U(700)$ already has been set at $U(700) = 1$. Here is the procedure that Jennifer is using to find $U(90)$.

The decision maker (Max) is offered two alternatives, A_1 and A_2.

> A_1: Obtain a payoff of 700 with probability p.
>
> Obtain a payoff of -130 with probability $(1 - p)$.
>
> A_2: Definitely obtain a payoff of 90.

Question to the decision maker: What value of p makes you *indifferent* between these two alternatives? Recall that Max has chosen $p = 1/3$.

For a given choice of p, the expected utility for A_1 is

$$E(\text{utility for } A_1) = pU(700) + (1 - p)U(-130)$$
$$= p(1) + (1 - p)(0)$$
$$= p$$

If the decision maker is indifferent between the two alternatives, the fundamental property of utility functions says that the two alternatives must have the same expected utility. Therefore, the utility for A_2 must also be p. Since Max chose a point of indifference of $p = 1/3$, the utility for A_2 must be 1/3, so $U(90) = 1/3$.

The Equivalent Lottery Method for Determining Utilities

The above procedure for finding $U(90)$ illustrates that the key to finding the utility for any payoff M is having the decision maker select a *point of indifference* between two alternatives, where one of them (A_1) involves a *lottery* between the largest payoff and the smallest payoff and the other alternative (A_2) is to receive a sure payoff of M. At the point of indifference, the lottery is *equivalent* to the sure payoff in the sense that they have the same expected utility, so the procedure is referred to as the **equivalent lottery method.** Here is an outline of the procedure.

Equivalent Lottery Method

1. Determine the largest potential payoff, $M = $ maximum, and assign it a utility of 1:

$$U(\text{maximum}) = 1$$

2. Determine the smallest potential payoff, and assign it a utility of 0:

$$U(\text{minimum}) = 0$$

3. To determine the utility of another potential payoff M, the decision maker is offered the following two hypothetical alternatives:

> A_1: Obtain a payoff of *maximum* with probability p.
>
> Obtain a payoff of *minimum* with probability $1 - p$.
>
> A_2: Definitely obtain a payoff of M.

Question to the decision maker: What value of p makes you *indifferent* between these two alternatives? Then $U(M) = p$.

Constructing Max's Utility Function for Money

We now have found utilities for three possible payoffs (-130, 90, and 700) for Goferbroke. Plotting these values on a graph of the utility function $U(M)$ versus the monetary payoff M and then drawing a smooth curve through these points gives the curve shown in Figure 9.28

This curve is an estimate of Max's utility function for money. To find the utility values for the other possible payoffs (-100, 60, and 670), Max could repeat step 3 of the equivalent lottery method for $M = -100$, $M = 60$, and $M = 670$. However, since -100 is so close to -130, 60 is so close to 90, and 670 is so close to 700, an alternative is to estimate these utilities as

FIGURE 9.28

Max's utility function for money as the owner of Goferbroke Co.

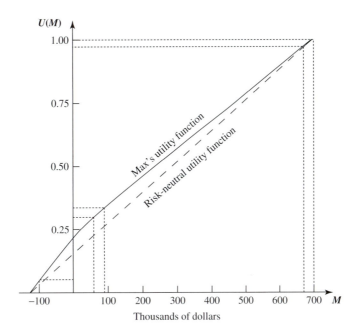

the values on the curve in Figure 9.28 at $M = -100$, $M = 60$, and $M = 670$. Following the corresponding dotted lines in the figure leads to $U(-100) = 0.05$, $U(60) = 0.30$, and $U(670) = 0.97$. Table 9.9 gives the complete list of possible payoffs and their utilities.

For comparative purposes, the dashed line in Figure 9.28 shows the utility function that would result if Max were completely *risk neutral*. By nature, Max is inclined to be a risk seeker. However, the difficult financial circumstances of his company that he badly wants to keep solvent has forced him to adopt a moderately risk-averse stance in addressing his current decisions.

Using a Decision Tree to Analyze the Problem with Utilities

Now that Max's utility function for money has been constructed in Table 9.9 (and Figure 9.28), this information can be used with a decision tree as summarized below.

> The procedure for using a decision tree to analyze the problem now is *identical* to that described in Section 9.7 *except* for substituting utilities for monetary payoffs. Therefore, the value obtained to evaluate each node of the tree now is the *expected utility* there rather than the expected (monetary) payoff. Consequently, the optimal decision selected by Bayes' decision rule maximizes the expected utility for the overall problem.

Thus, using TreePlan once again, our final decision tree with utilities shown in Figure 9.29 closely resembles the one in Figure 9.17 given in Section 9.7. The nodes and branches are exactly the same, as are the probabilities for the branches emanating from the event nodes. However, the key difference from Figure 9.17 is that the monetary payoff at each terminal node now has been replaced by the corresponding utility from Table 9.9. (This was accomplished with TreePlan by entering this same utility as the "cash flow" at the terminal branch and then entering "cash flows" of 0 at all the preceding branches.) It is these utilities that have been used by TreePlan to compute the *expected utilities* given next to all the nodes.

At each terminal branch, enter the utility of that outcome as the "cash flow" there and then do not change the default value of 0 for the "cash flow" at the preceding branches.

TABLE 9.9

Utilities for the Goferbroke Co. Problem

Monetary Payoff, *M*	Utility, *U(M)*
−130	0
−100	0.05
60	0.30
90	0.333
670	0.97
700	1

FIGURE 9.29

The final decision tree constructed and solved by TreePlan for the full Goferbroke Co. problem when using Max's utility function for money to maximize expected utility.

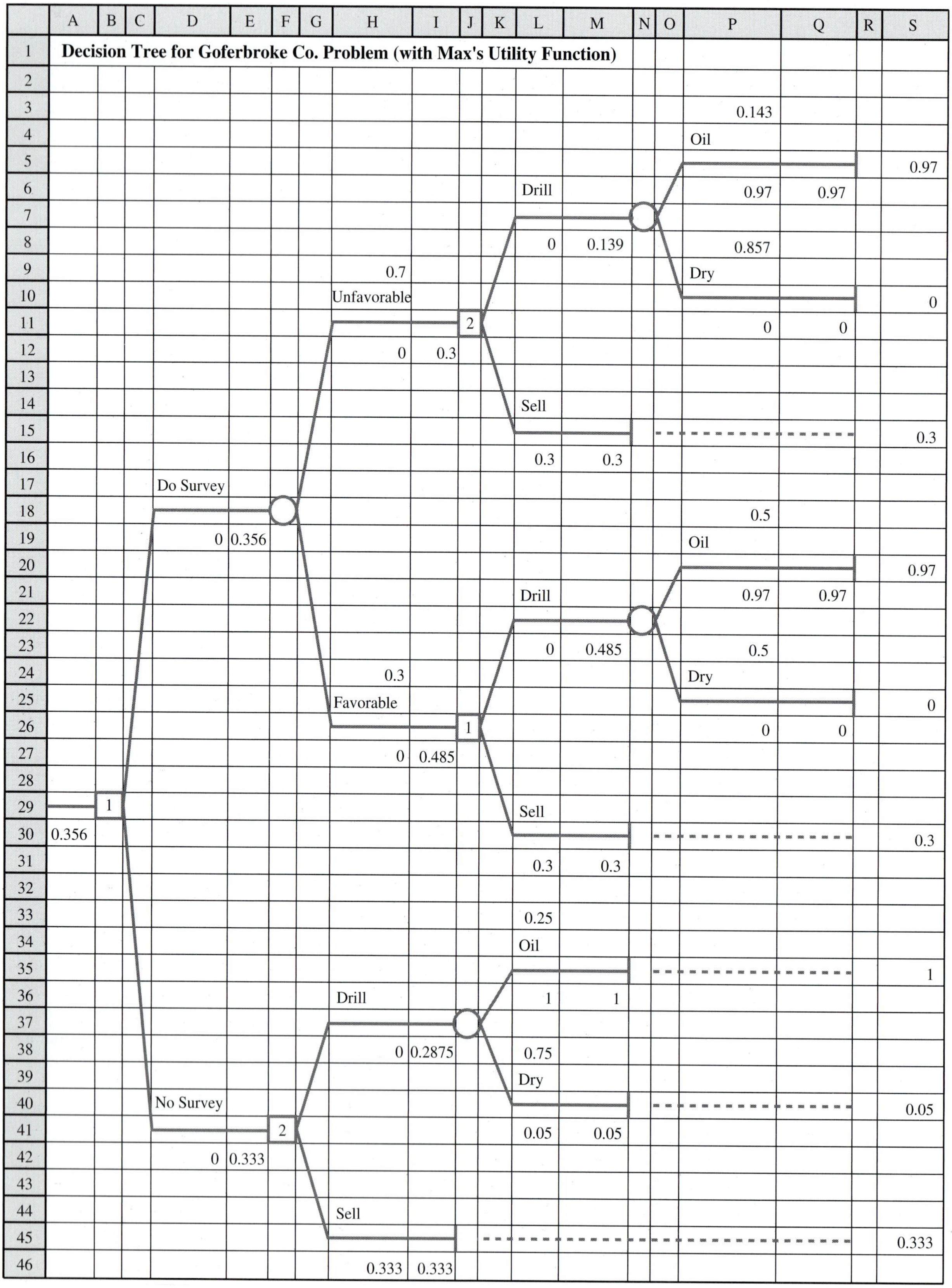

	A	B	C	D	E	F	G	H	I	J	K	L	M	N	O	P	Q	R	S
1	**Decision Tree for Goferbroke Co. Problem (with Max's Utility Function)**																		
2																			
3																0.143			
4																Oil			
5																			0.97
6												Drill				0.97	0.97		
7														◯					
8										0	0.139					0.857			
9								0.7								Dry			
10								Unfavorable											0
11											2						0	0	
12								0	0.3										
13																			
14												Sell							
15																			0.3
16												0.3	0.3						
17				Do Survey															
18																0.5			
19					0	0.356		◯								Oil			
20																			0.97
21												Drill				0.97	0.97		
22														◯					
23										0	0.485					0.5			
24								0.3								Dry			
25								Favorable											0
26											1						0	0	
27								0	0.485										
28																			
29			1									Sell							
30	0.356																		0.3
31												0.3	0.3						
32																			
33												0.25							
34												Oil							
35																			1
36							Drill					1	1						
37														◯					
38								0	0.2875										
39												0.75							
40				No Survey								Dry							
41							2												0.05
42					0	0.333						0.05	0.05						
43																			
44								Sell											
45																			0.333
46								0.333	0.333										

These expected utilities lead to the same decisions as in Figure 9.17 at all decision nodes except the bottom one in cell F41. The decision at this node now switches to *sell* instead of *drill.* However, the solution procedure still leaves this node on a *closed* path, as indicated by the 1 in cell B29. Therefore, the overall optimal policy remains the same as that obtained in Figure 9.17 (do the seismic survey; sell if the result is unfavorable; drill if the result is favorable).

The previous approach of maximizing the expected monetary payoff assumes a risk-neutral decision maker.

The approach of maximizing the expected monetary payoff used in the preceding sections was equivalent to assuming that the decision maker is neutral toward risk. By using utility theory with an appropriate utility function, the optimal solution now reflects the decision maker's attitude about risk. Because Max adopted only a moderately risk-averse stance, the optimal policy did not change from before. For a somewhat more risk-averse decision maker, the optimal solution would switch to the more conservative approach of immediately selling the land (no seismic survey).

Jennifer and Max are to be commended for incorporating utilities into a decision analysis approach to his problem. Utilities help to provide a rational approach to decision making in the face of uncertainty. However, many managers are not sufficiently comfortable with the relatively abstract notion of utilities, or with working with probabilities to construct a utility function, to be willing to use this approach. Consequently, utilities are not used nearly as widely in practice as some of the other techniques of decision analysis described in this chapter, including Bayes' decision rule (with monetary payoffs) and decision trees.

Another Approach for Estimating $U(M)$

The procedure described earlier for constructing $U(M)$ asks the decision maker to repeatedly apply the equivalent lottery method, which requires him (or her) each time to make a difficult decision about which probability would make him indifferent between two alternatives. Many managers would be uncomfortable with making this kind of decision. Therefore, an alternative approach is sometimes used instead to estimate the utility function for money.

This approach assumes that the utility function has a certain mathematical form and then adjusts this form to fit the decision maker's attitude toward risk as closely as possible. For example, one particularly popular form to assume (because of its relative simplicity) is the **exponential utility function,**

$$U(M) = R\left(1 - e^{-\frac{M}{R}}\right)$$

where R is the decision maker's *risk tolerance.* This utility function has the kind of shape shown in Figure 9.27(*a*), so it is designed to fit a *risk-averse* individual. A great aversion to risk corresponds to a small value of R (which would cause the curve in this figure to bend sharply), whereas a small aversion to risk corresponds to a large value of R (which gives a much more gradual bend in the curve).

Since R measures the decision maker's *risk tolerance,* the *aversion* to risk decreases as R increases.

A drawback of the exponential utility function is that it assumes a constant aversion to risk (a fixed value of R), regardless of how much (or how little) money the decision maker currently has. This doesn't fit Max's situation well, since his current shortage of money makes him much more concerned about incurring a large loss than usual. This is why Jennifer never raised the possibility of using an exponential utility function.

In other situations where the consequences of the potential losses are not as severe, assuming an exponential utility function may provide a reasonable approximation. In such a case, here is an easy way of estimating the appropriate value of R. The decision maker would be asked to choose the number R that would make him indifferent between the following two alternatives.

A_1:   A 50–50 gamble where he would gain R dollars with probability 0.5 and lose $R/2$ dollars with probability 0.5.

A_2:   Neither gain nor lose anything.

For example, if the decision maker were indifferent between doing nothing or taking a 50–50 gamble where he would gain $1,000 with probability 0.5 and lose $500 with probability 0.5, then $R = 1,000$.

An Application Vignette

Following the merger of Conoco Inc. and the Phillips Petroleum Company in 2002, ConocoPhillips became the third-largest integrated energy company in the United States with $160 billion in assets and 38,000 employees. Like any company in this industry, the management of ConocoPhillips must grapple continually with decisions about the allocation of limited investment capital across a set of risky petroleum exploration projects. These decisions have a great impact on the profitability of the company.

In the early 1990s, the then Phillips Petroleum Company became an industry leader in the application of sophisticated management science methodology to aid these decisions by developing a decision analysis software package called DISCOVERY. The user interface allows a geologist or engineer to model the uncertainties associated with a project and then the software interprets the inputs and constructs a decision tree that shows all the decision nodes (including opportunities to obtain additional seismic information) and the intervening event nodes. A key feature of the software is the use of an exponential utility function to incorporate management's attitudes about financial risk. An intuitive questionnaire is used to measure corporate risk preferences in order to determine an appropriate value of the risk tolerance parameter for this utility function.

Management uses the software to (1) evaluate petroleum exploration projects with a consistent risk-taking policy across the company, (2) rank projects in terms of overall preference, (3) identify the firm's appropriate level of participation in these projects, and (4) stay within budget.

Source: M. R. Walls, G. T. Morahan, and J. S. Dyer, "Decision Analysis of Exploration Opportunities in the Onshore US at Phillips Petroleum Company," *Interfaces* 25, no. 6 (November–December 1995), pp. 39–56.

Using TreePlan with an Exponential Utility Function

TreePlan Tip: The Option dialogue box lets you specify whether to use expected monetary values or the exponential utility function for applying Bayes' decision rule. The dialogue box also lets you specify whether the objective is to maximize profit (as was used throughout this chapter) or to minimize cost.

TreePlan includes the option of using the exponential utility function. First, the value of R needs to be specified on the spreadsheet. The cell containing this value then needs to be given a range name of RT (TreePlan refers to this term as the risk tolerance). Then click on the Options button in the TreePlan dialogue box, which brings up the dialogue box shown in Figure 9.30. Select the "Use Exponential Utility Function" option. Clicking OK then revises the decision tree to incorporate the exponential utility function.

To illustrate, suppose that the exponential utility function with a risk tolerance of $R = 1,000$ were to be used as a rough approximation for analyzing the full Goferbroke Co. problem. (Since this problem expresses payoffs in units of thousands of dollars, $R = 1,000$ here is equivalent to using $R = 1,000,000$ when payoffs are in units of dollars.) The resulting decision tree is shown in Figure 9.31. There are now two expected payoffs calculated below and to the left of each node. The lower number represents the expected utility value at that stage in the decision tree. The upper number represents the certain payoff that is equivalent to this expected utility value. For example, cell A31 indicates that the expected value of the exponential utility function for this decision would be 0.0932. This is equivalent to a certain payoff of $98,000, as indicated in cell A30.

The exponential utility function leads to the same decisions as in Figure 9.29. The overall optimal policy remains to do the seismic survey; sell if the result is unfavorable; drill if the result is favorable. However, the optimal policy changes when the value of R is decreased. For

FIGURE 9.30

Clicking on the Option button of the TreePlan dialogue box brings up this dialogue box, which provides the option of using an exponential utility function.

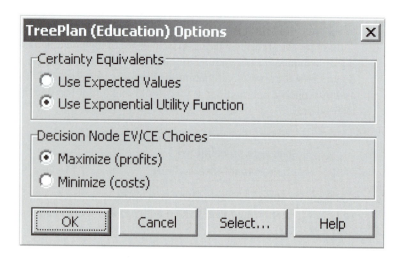

FIGURE 9.31

The final decision tree constructed and solved by TreePlan for the full Goferbroke Co. problem when using an exponential utility function with R = 1,000.

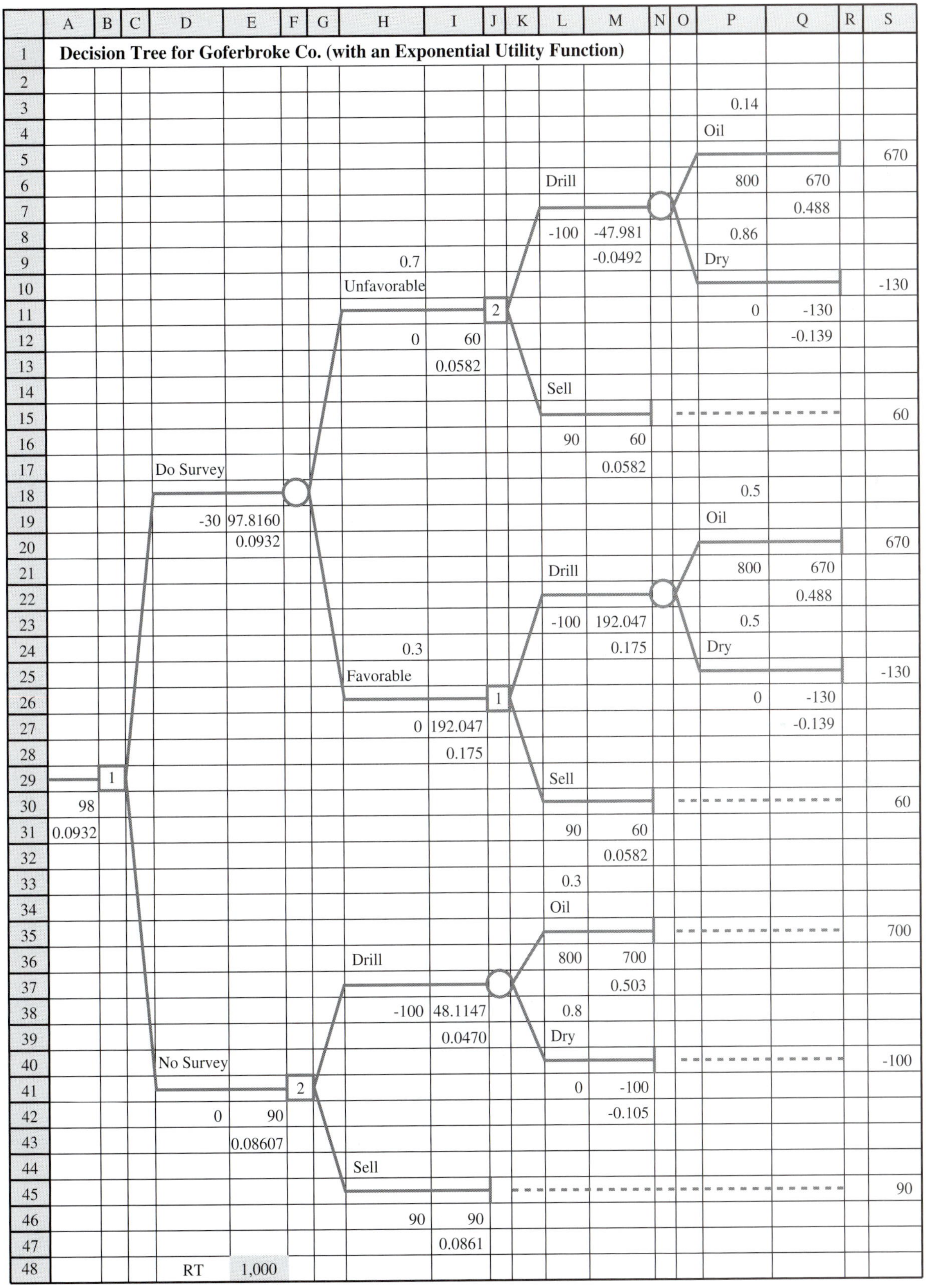

	A	B	C	D	E	F	G	H	I	J	K	L	M	N	O	P	Q	R	S
1	**Decision Tree for Goferbroke Co. (with an Exponential Utility Function)**																		
2																			
3																0.14			
4																Oil			
5																			670
6									Drill							800	670		
7																	0.488		
8												-100	-47.981			0.86			
9								0.7					-0.0492			Dry			
10								Unfavorable											-130
11										2						0	-130		
12								0	60								-0.139		
13									0.0582										
14												Sell							
15																- - - - - - - - - -			60
16												90	60						
17				Do Survey									0.0582						
18																0.5			
19					-30	97.8160										Oil			
20						0.0932													670
21									Drill							800	670		
22																	0.488		
23												-100	192.047			0.5			
24								0.3					0.175			Dry			
25								Favorable											-130
26										1						0	-130		
27								0	192.047								-0.139		
28									0.175										
29			1									Sell							
30		98														- - - - - - - - - -			60
31		0.0932										90	60						
32													0.0582						
33												0.3							
34												Oil							
35																- - - - - - - - - -			700
36								Drill					800	700					
37														0.503					
38								-100	48.1147				0.8						
39									0.0470				Dry						
40				No Survey												- - - - - - - - - -			-100
41							2						0	-100					
42					0	90								-0.105					
43						0.08607													
44								Sell											
45																- - - - - - - - - -			90
46								90	90										
47									0.0861										
48				RT	1,000														

Range Name	Cells
RT	E48

values of R less than 728, the optimal policy switches to not doing the survey and selling the land. Thus, a more risk-averse decision maker would make the safer decision for Goferbroke—sell the land and receive $90,000 for sure.

Review
Questions

1. What are utilities intended to reflect?
2. What is the shape of the utility function for money for a risk-averse individual? A risk-seeking individual? A risk-neutral individual?
3. What is the fundamental property of utility functions?
4. What is the lottery when using the equivalent lottery method?
5. Given two hypothetical alternatives where one of them involves a probability p, what is meant by the point of indifference between these two alternatives?
6. When using utilities with a decision tree, what kind of value is obtained to evaluate each node of the tree?
7. What decisions did Max make regarding the full Goferbroke Co. problem?

9.10 THE PRACTICAL APPLICATION OF DECISION ANALYSIS

In one sense, the Goferbroke Co. problem is a very typical application of decision analysis. Like other applications, Max needed to make his decisions (Do a seismic survey? Drill for oil or sell the land?) in the face of great uncertainty. The decisions were difficult because their payoffs were so unpredictable. The outcome depended on factors that were outside Max's control (does the land contain oil or is it dry?). He needed a framework and methodology for rational decision making in this uncertain environment. These are the usual characteristics of applications of decision analysis.

However, in other ways, the Goferbroke problem is not such a typical application. It was oversimplified to include only two possible states of nature (oil and dry), whereas there actually would be a considerable number of distinct possibilities. For example, the actual state might be dry, a small amount of oil, a moderate amount, a large amount, and a huge amount, plus different possibilities concerning the depth of the oil and soil conditions that impact the cost of drilling to reach the oil. Max also was considering only two alternatives for each of two decisions. Real applications commonly involve more decisions, more alternatives to be considered for each one, and many possible states of nature.

The Goferbroke Co. problem could have included many more states of nature.

Problems as tiny as the Goferbroke problem can be readily analyzed and solved by hand. However, real applications typically involve large decision trees, whose construction and analysis require the use of a software package (such as TreePlan introduced in this chapter). In some cases, the decision tree can explode in size with many thousand terminal branches. Special algebraic techniques are being developed and incorporated into the solvers for dealing with such large problems.[2]

Sensitivity analysis also can become unwieldy on large problems. Although it normally is supported by the computer software, (as with SensIt), the amount of data generated can easily overwhelm an analyst or decision maker. Therefore, some graphical techniques, such as the spider graph and tornado diagram introduced in Figures 9.22 and 9.25, have been developed to organize the data in a readily understandable way.[3]

Other kinds of graphical techniques also are available to complement the decision tree in representing and solving decision analysis problems. One that has become quite popular is called the **influence diagram**, and researchers continue to develop others as well.[4]

[2] For example, see C. W. Kirkwood, "An Algebraic Approach to Formulating and Solving Large Models for Sequential Decisions under Uncertainty," *Management Science* 39 (July 1993), pp. 900–13.
[3] For further information, see T. G. Eschenbach, "Spiderplots versus Tornado Diagrams for Sensitivity Analysis," *Interfaces* 22 (November–December 1992), pp. 40–46.
[4] For example, see P. P. Schnoy, "A Comparison of Graphical Techniques for Decision Analysis," *European Journal of Operational Research* 78 (October 13, 1994), pp. 1–21. Also see Z. Covaliu and R. M. Oliver, "Representation and Solution of Decision Problems Using Sequential Decision Diagrams," *Management Science* 41 (December 1995), pp. 1860–81, as well as Chapters 4 and 9 in K. T. Marshall and R. M. Oliver, *Decision Making and Forecasting* (New York: McGraw-Hill, 1995).

Although the Goferbroke problem only involved a single decision maker (Max) assisted by a single analyst (Jennifer), many strategic business decisions are made collectively by management. One technique for group decision making is called **decision conferencing.** This is a process where the group comes together for discussions in a decision conference with the help of an analyst and a group facilitator. The facilitator works directly with the group to help it structure and focus discussions, think creatively about the problem, bring assumptions to the surface, and address the full range of issues involved. The analyst uses decision analysis to assist the group in exploring the implications of the various decision alternatives. With the assistance of a computerized *group decision support system,* the analyst builds and solves models on the spot, and then performs sensitivity analysis to respond to what-if questions from the group.[5]

Applications of decision analysis commonly involve a partnership between the managerial decision maker (whether an individual or a group) and an analyst (whether an individual or a team) with training in management science. Some managers are not as fortunate as Max in having a staff member (let alone a daughter) like Jennifer who is qualified to serve as the analyst. Therefore, a considerable number of management consulting firms specializing in decision analysis have been formed to fill this role.

If you would like to do more reading about the practical application of decision analysis, a good place to begin would be the November–December 1992 issue of *Interfaces.* This is a special issue devoted entirely to decision analysis and the related area of risk analysis. It includes many interesting articles, including descriptions of basic methods, sensitivity analysis, and decision conferencing. Also included are several articles on applications.

Review
Questions

1. How does the Goferbroke Co. problem compare with typical applications of decision analysis?
2. What is the purpose of an influence diagram?
3. Who are the typical participants in a decision-conferencing process?
4. Where can a manager go for expert help in applying decision analysis if a qualified analyst is not available on staff?

[5] For further information, see the two articles on decision conferencing in the November–December 1992 issue of *Interfaces,* where one describes an application in Australia and the other summarizes the experience of 26 decision conferences in Hungary.

9.11   Summary

Decision analysis is a valuable technique for decision making in the face of great uncertainty. It provides a framework and methodology for rational decision making when the outcomes are uncertain.

In a typical application, a decision maker needs to make either a single decision or a short sequence of decisions (with additional information perhaps becoming available between decisions). A number of alternatives are available for each decision. Uncontrollable random factors affect the payoff that would be obtained from a decision alternative. The possible outcomes of the random factors are referred to as the possible *states of nature.*

Which state of nature actually occurs will be learned only after making the decisions. However, prior to the decisions, it often is possible to estimate *prior probabilities* of the respective states of nature.

Various alternative decision criteria are available for making the decisions. A particularly popular one is *Bayes' decision rule,* which uses the prior probabilities to determine the expected payoff for each decision alternative and then chooses the one with the largest expected payoff. This is the criterion (accompanied by sensitivity analysis) that is mostly used in practice, so it is the focus of much of the chapter.

Sensitivity analysis is very helpful for evaluating the effect of having inaccurate estimates of the data for the problem, including the probabilities, revenues, and costs. Software such as SensIt is available to assist in performing sensitivity analysis.

It sometimes is possible to pay for a test or survey to obtain additional information about the probabilities of the various states of nature. Calculating the *expected value of perfect information* provides a quick way of checking whether doing this might be worthwhile.

When more information is obtained, the updated probabilities are referred to as *posterior probabilities*. A *probability tree diagram* is helpful for calculating these new probabilities.

For problems involving a sequence of decisions (including perhaps a decision on whether to obtain more information), a decision tree commonly is used to graphically display the progression of decisions and random events. The calculations for applying Bayes' decision rule then can be performed directly on the decision tree one event node or decision node at a time. Spreadsheet packages, such as TreePlan, are very helpful for constructing and solving decision trees.

When the problem involves the possibility of uncomfortably large losses, utilities provide a way of incorporating the decision maker's attitude toward risk into the analysis. Bayes' decision rule then is applied by expressing payoffs in terms of utilities rather than monetary values.

Decision analysis is widely used. Versatile software packages for personal computers have become an integral part of the practical application of decision analysis.

Glossary

alternatives The options available to the decision maker for the decision under consideration. (Section 9.1), 306

Bayes' decision rule A popular criterion for decision making that uses probabilities to calculate the expected payoff for each decision alternative and then chooses the one with the largest expected payoff. (Section 9.2), 310

Bayes' theorem A formula for calculating a posterior probability of a state of nature. (Section 9.6), 325

branch A line emanating from a node in a decision tree. (Section 9.3), 312

decision conferencing A process used for group decision making. (Section 9.10), 351

decision maker The individual or group responsible for making the decision under consideration. (Section 9.1), 306

decision node A point in a decision tree where a decision needs to be made. (Section 9.3), 312

decision tree A graphical display of the progression of decisions and random events to be considered. (Sections 9.3 and 9.7), 312, 327

equivalent lottery method The procedure for finding the decision maker's utility for a specific amount of money by comparing two hypothetical alternatives where one involves a gamble. (Section 9.9), 344

event node A point in a decision tree where a random event will occur. (Section 9.3), 312

expected payoff (EP) For a decision alternative, it is the weighted average of the payoffs, using the probabilities of the states of nature as the weights. (Section 9.2), 310

expected value of perfect information (EVPI) The increase in the expected payoff that could be obtained if it were possible to learn the true state of nature before making the decision. (Sections 9.4 and 9.5), 319, 320

expected value of sample information (EVSI) The increase in the expected payoff that could be obtained by performing a test to obtain more information, excluding the cost of the test. (Section 9.7), 331

exponential utility function A utility function designed to fit a risk-averse individual. (Section 9.9), 347

influence diagram A diagram that complements the decision tree for representing and analyzing decision analysis problems. (Section 9.10), 350

maximax criterion A very optimistic decision criterion that does not use prior probabilities and simply chooses the decision alternative that could give the largest possible payoff. (Section 9.2), 308

maximin criterion A very pessimistic decision criterion that does not use prior probabilities and simply chooses the decision alternative that provides the best guarantee for its minimum possible payoff. (Section 9.2), 308

maximum likelihood criterion A criterion for decision making with probabilities that focuses on the most likely state of nature. (Section 9.2), 309

node A junction point in a decision tree. (Section 9.3), 312

payoff A quantitative measure of the outcome from a decision alternative and a state of nature. (Section 9.1), 307

payoff table A table giving the payoff for each combination of a decision alternative and a state of nature. (Section 9.1), 307

Plot An option provided by SensIt for generating a graph that shows how an output cell varies for different values of a single data cell. (Section 9.8), 335

point of indifference The point where the decision maker is indifferent between the two hypothetical alternatives in the equivalent lottery method. (Section 9.9), 343

posterior probabilities Revised probabilities of the states of nature after doing a test or survey to improve the prior probabilities. (Sections 9.5 and 9.6), 322, 323

prior probabilities The estimated probabilities of the states of nature prior to obtaining additional information through a test or survey. (Section 9.1), 307

probability tree diagram A diagram that is helpful for calculating the posterior probabilities of the states of nature. (Section 9.6), 324

risk-averse individual An individual whose utility function for money has a decreasing slope as the amount of money increases. (Section 9.9), 340

risk-neutral individual An individual whose utility for money is proportional to the amount of money involved. (Section 9.9), 340

risk-seeking individual An individual whose utility function for money has an increasing slope as the amount of money increases. (Section 9.9), 340

sensitivity analysis The study of how other plausible values for the probabilities of the states of nature (or for the payoffs) would affect the recommended decision alternative. (Sections 9.4 and 9.8), 315, 333

spider graph A graph that provides helpful comparisons for sensitivity analysis. (Section 9.8), 336

states of nature The possible outcomes of the random factors that affect the payoff that would be obtained from a decision alternative. (Section 9.1) 306

tornado diagram A diagram that organizes the data from sensitivity analysis in a readily understandable way. (Section 9.8), 337

utility The utility of an outcome measures the true value to the decision maker of that outcome. (Sections 9.1 and 9.9), 306

utility function for money, *U(M)* A plot of utility versus the amount of money *M* being received. (Section 9.9), 340

Learning Aids for This Chapter in Your MS Courseware

Chapter 9 Excel Files:

Bayes' Decision Rule for First Goferbroke Problem

Decision Tree for First Goferbroke Problem

Data Table for First Goferbroke Problem

EP with Perfect Info for First Goferbroke Problem

Decision Tree for EVPI for First Goferbroke Problem

Template for Posterior Probabilities

Decision Tree for Full Goferbroke Problem (with SensIt Graphs)

Decision Tree for Full Goferbroke Problem with Max's Utility Function

Decision Tree for Full Goferbroke Problem with Exponential Utility Function

Excel Add-ins:

TreePlan (academic version)

SensIt (academic version)

Supplement to This Chapter on the CD-ROM:

Decision Criteria

"Ch. 9 Supplement" Excel Files:

Template for Maximax Criterion

Template for Maximin Criterion

Template for Realism Criterion

Template for Minimax Regret Criterion

Template for Maximum Likelihood Criterion

Template for Equally Likely Criterion

Solved Problems (See the CD-ROM for the Solutions)

9.S1. New Vehicle Introduction

The General Ford Motors Corporation (GFMC) is planning the introduction of a brand new SUV—the Vector. There are two options for production. One is to build the Vector at the company's existing plant in Indiana, sharing production time with its line of minivans that are currently being produced there. If sales of the Vector are just moderate, this will work out well as there is sufficient capacity to produce both types of vehicles at the same plant. However, if sales of the Vector are strong, this option would require the operation of a third shift, which would lead to significantly higher costs.

A second option is to open a new plant in Georgia. This plant would have sufficient capacity to meet even the largest projections for sales of the Vector. However, if sales are only moderate, the plant would be underutilized and therefore less efficient.

This is a new design, so sales are hard to predict. However, GFMC predicts that there would be about a 60 percent chance of strong sales (annual sales of 100,000), and a 40 percent chance of moderate sales (annual sales of 50,000). The average revenue

per Vector sold is $30,000. Production costs per vehicle for the two production options depend upon sales, as indicated in the table below.

Expected Production Cost per Vehicle for the Vector ($thousands)

	Moderate Sales	Strong Sales
Shared plant in Indiana	16	24
Dedicated plant in Georgia	22	20

The amortized annual cost of plant construction and other associated fixed costs for the Georgia plant would total $4 million per year (regardless of sales volume). The fixed costs for adding Vector production to the plant in Indiana would total $2 million per year (regardless of sales volume).

a. Construct a decision tree to determine which production option maximizes the expected annual profit, considering fixed costs, production costs, and sales revenues.

b. Because of the uncertainty in expected sales for the Vector, GFMC is considering conducting a marketing survey to determine customer attitudes toward the Vector to better predict the likelihood of strong sales. The marketing survey would give one of two results—a positive attitude or a negative attitude toward the design. GFMC has used this marketing survey for other vehicles. For vehicles that eventually had strong sales, the marketing survey indicated positive attitudes toward the design 70 percent of the time and negative attitudes 30 percent of the time. For vehicles that eventually had moderate sales, the marketing survey indicated positive attitudes toward the design 20 percent of the time and negative attitudes 80 percent of the time. Assuming GFMC conducts such a survey, construct a decision tree to to determine how the company should proceed and what the expected annual profit would be (ignoring the cost of the survey).

c. What is the expected value of sample information in part *b?* What does this say about how large the cost of the marketing survey can be before it would no longer be worthwhile to conduct the survey?

9.S2. Settle or Go to Trial

Meredith Delgado owns a small firm that has developed software for organizing and playing music on a computer. Her software contains a number of unique features that she has patented, so her company's future has looked bright.

However, there now has been an ominous development. It appears that a number of her patented features were copied in similar software developed by MusicMan Software, a huge software company with annual sales revenue in excess of $1 billion. Meredith is distressed. MusicMan Software has stolen her ideas and that company's marketing power is likely to enable it to capture the market and drive Meredith out of business.

In response, Meredith has sued MusicMan Software for patent infringement. With attorney fees and other expenses, the cost of going to trial (win or lose) is expected to be $1 million. She feels that she has a 60 percent chance of winning the case, in which case she would receive $5 million in damages. If she loses the case, she gets nothing. Moreover, if she loses the case, there is a 50 percent chance that the judge would also order Meredith to pay for court expenses and lawyer fees for MusicMan (an additional $1 million cost). MusicMan Software has offered Meredith $1.5 million to settle this case out of court.

a. Construct and use a decision tree to determine whether Meredith should go to court or accept the settlement offer, assuming she wants to maximize her expected payoff.

b. To implement the equivalent lottery method to determine appropriate utility values for all the possible payoffs in this problem, what questions would need to be asked of Meredith?

c. Suppose that Meredith's attitude toward risk is such that she would be indifferent between doing nothing and a gamble where she would win $1 million with 50 percent probability and lose $500 thousand with 50 percent probability. Use the exponential utility function to re-solve the decision tree from part *a.*

Problems

To the left of the following problems (or their parts), we have inserted the symbol A (for Add-in) whenever one of the Excel add-ins listed on page 353 can be used. The symbol T indicates that the Excel template for posterior probabilities can be helpful. Nearly all the problems can be conveniently formulated in a spreadsheet format, so no special symbol is used to designate this. An asterisk on the problem number indicates that at least a partial answer is given in the back of the book.

9.1 You are given the following payoff table (in units of thousands of dollars) for a decision analysis problem without probabilities.

Alternative	State of Nature		
	S_1	S_2	S_3
A_1	6	2	4
A_2	3	4	3
A_3	8	1	5

a. Which alternative should be chosen under the maximax criterion?

b. Which alternative should be chosen under the maximin criterion?

9.2 Follow the instructions of Problem 9.1 with the following payoff table.

Alternative	State of Nature			
	S_1	S_2	S_3	S_4
A_1	25	30	20	24
A_2	17	14	31	21
A_3	22	22	22	22
A_4	29	21	26	27

9.3 Jean Clark is the manager of the Midtown Saveway Grocery Store. She now needs to replenish her supply of strawberries. Her regular supplier can provide as many cases as she wants. However, because these strawberries already are very ripe, she will need to sell them tomorrow and then discard any that remain unsold. Jean estimates that she will be able to sell 10, 11, 12, or 13 cases tomorrow. She can purchase the strawberries for $3 per case and sell them for $8 per case. Jean now needs to decide how many cases to purchase.

Jean has checked the store's records on daily sales of strawberries. On this basis, she estimates that the prior probabilities are 0.2, 0.4, 0.3, and 0.1 for being able to sell 10, 11, 12, and 13 cases of strawberries tomorrow.

a. Develop a decision analysis formulation of this problem by identifying the decision alternatives, the states of nature, and the payoff table.

b. If Jean is dubious about the accuracy of these prior probabilities and so chooses to ignore them and use the maximax criterion, how many cases of strawberries should she purchase?

c. How many cases should be purchased if she uses the maximin criterion?

d. How many cases should be purchased if she uses the maximum likelihood criterion?

e. How many cases should be purchased according to Bayes' decision rule?

f. Jean thinks she has the prior probabilities just about right for selling 10 cases and selling 13 cases, but is uncertain about how to split the prior probabilities for 11 cases and 12 cases. Reapply Bayes' decision rule when the prior probabilities of 11 and 12 cases are (*i*) 0.2 and 0.5, (*ii*) 0.3 and 0.4, and (*iii*) 0.5 and 0.2.

9.4* Warren Buffy is an enormously wealthy investor who has built his fortune through his legendary investing acumen. He currently has been offered three major investments and he would like to choose one. The first one is a *conservative investment* that would perform very well in an improving economy and only suffer a small loss in a worsening economy. The second is a *speculative investment* that would perform extremely well in an improving economy but would do very badly in a worsening economy. The third is a *countercyclical investment* that would lose some money in an improving economy but would perform well in a worsening economy.

Warren believes that there are three possible scenarios over the lives of these potential investments: (1) an improving economy, (2) a stable economy, and (3) a worsening economy. He is pessimistic about where the economy is headed, and so has assigned prior probabilities of 0.1, 0.5, and 0.4, respectively, to these three scenarios. He also estimates that his profits under these respective scenarios are those given by the following table:

	Improving Economy	Stable Economy	Worsening Economy
Conservative investment	$ 30 million	$ 5 million	$−10 million
Speculative investment	40 million	10 million	−30 million
Countercyclical investment	−10 million	0	15 million
Prior probability	0.1	0.5	0.4

Which investment should Warren make under each of the following criteria?

a. Maximax criterion.

b. Maximin criterion.

c. Maximum likelihood criterion.

d. Bayes' decision rule.

9.5 Reconsider Problem 9.4. Warren Buffy decides that Bayes' decision rule is his most reliable decision criterion. He believes that 0.1 is just about right as the prior probability of an improving economy, but is quite uncertain about how to split the remaining probabilities between a stable economy and a worsening economy. Therefore, he now wishes to do sensitivity analysis with respect to these latter two prior probabilities.

a. Reapply Bayes' decision rule when the prior probability of a stable economy is 0.3 and the prior probability of a worsening economy is 0.6.

b. Reapply Bayes' decision rule when the prior probability of a stable economy is 0.7 and the prior probability of a worsening economy is 0.2.

c. Construct a decision tree by hand for this problem with the original prior probabilities.

A d. Use TreePlan to construct and solve a decision tree for this problem with the original prior probabilities.

A e. In preparation for performing sensitivity analysis, consolidate the data and results on the same spreadsheet as the decision tree constructed in part *d* (as was done in Figure 9.6 for the case study).

A f. Use the spreadsheet (including the decision tree) obtained in parts *d* and *e* to do parts *a* and *b*.

A g. Expanding the spreadsheet as needed, generate a data table that shows which investment Warren should make and the resulting expected profit for the following prior probabilities of a stable economy: 0, 0.1, 0.2, 0.3, 0.4, 0.5, 0.6, 0.7, 0.8, 0.9.

h. For each of the three investments, find the expected profit when the prior probability of a stable economy is 0 and then when it is 0.9 (with the prior probability of an improving economy fixed at 0.1). Plot these expected profits on a single graph that has expected profit as the vertical axis and the prior probability of a stable economy as the horizontal axis. For each of the three investments, draw a line segment connecting its two points on this graph to show how its expected profit would vary with the prior probability of a stable economy. Use this graph to describe how the choice of the investment depends on the prior probability of a stable economy.

9.6* Consider a decision analysis problem whose payoffs (in units of thousands of dollars) are given by the following payoff table:

Alternative	State of Nature	
	S_1	S_2
A_1	80	25
A_2	30	50
A_3	60	40
Prior probability	0.4	0.6

a. Which alternative should be chosen under the maximax criterion?

b. Which alternative should be chosen under the maximin criterion?

c. Which alternative should be chosen under the maximum likelihood criterion?

d. Which alternative should be chosen under Bayes' decision rule?

A e. Use TreePlan to construct and solve a decision tree for this problem.

A f. Expanding the spreadsheet containing this decision tree as needed, perform sensitivity analysis with the decision tree by re-solving when the prior probability of S_1 is 0.2 and again when it is 0.6.

A g. Now perform this sensitivity analysis systematically by generating a data table that shows the best alternative (according to Bayes' decision rule) and the resulting expected payoff as the prior probability of S_1 increases in increments of 0.04 from 0.2 to 0.6.

9.7 You are given the following payoff table (in units of thousands of dollars) for a decision analysis problem:

Alternative	State of Nature		
	S_1	S_2	S_3
A_1	220	170	110
A_2	200	180	150
Prior probability	0.6	0.3	0.1

a. Which alternative should be chosen under the maximax criterion?

b. Which alternative should be chosen under the maximin criterion?

c. Which alternative should be chosen under the maximum likelihood criterion?

d. Which alternative should be chosen under Bayes' decision rule?

e. Construct a decision tree by hand for this problem.

A f. Use TreePlan to construct and solve a decision tree for this problem.

A g. Perform sensitivity analysis with this decision tree by generating a data table that shows what happens when the prior probability of S_1 increases in increments of 0.05 from 0.3 to 0.7 while the prior probability of S_3 remains fixed at its original value. Then use trial and error to estimate the value of the prior probability of S_1 at which the best alternative changes as this prior probability increases.

A h. Repeat part g when it is the prior probability of S_2 that remains fixed at its original value.

A i. Repeat part g when it is the prior probability of S_1 that remains fixed at its original value while the prior probability of S_2 increases in increments of 0.05 from 0 to 0.4.

j. If you feel that the true probabilities of the states of nature should be within 10 percent of the given prior probabilities, which alternative would you choose?

9.8 Dwight Moody is the manager of a large farm with 1,000 acres of arable land. For greater efficiency, Dwight always devotes the farm to growing one crop at a time. He now needs to make a decision on which one of four crops to grow during the upcoming growing season. For each of these crops, Dwight has obtained the following estimates of crop yields and net incomes per bushel under various weather conditions.

Weather	Expected Yield, Bushels/Acre			
	Crop 1	Crop 2	Crop 3	Crop 4
Dry	20	15	30	40
Moderate	35	20	25	40
Damp	40	30	25	40
Net income per bushel	$1.00	$1.50	$1.00	$0.50

After referring to historical meteorological records, Dwight also has estimated the following prior probabilities for the weather during the growing season:

Dry	0.3
Moderate	0.5
Damp	0.2

a. Develop a decision analysis formulation of this problem by identifying the decision alternatives, the states of nature, and the payoff table.

A b. Construct a decision tree for this problem and use Bayes' decision rule to determine which crop to grow.

A   *c.* Using Bayes' decision rule, do sensitivity analysis with respect to the prior probabilities of moderate weather and damp weather (without changing the prior probability of dry weather) by re-solving when the prior probability of moderate weather is 0.2, 0.3, 0.4, and 0.6.

9.9   Barbara Miller makes decisions according to Bayes' decision rule. For her current problem, Barbara has constructed the following payoff table (in units of hundreds of dollars) and she now wishes to maximize the expected payoff.

| | State of Nature | | |
Alternative	S_1	S_2	S_3
A_1	$2x$	50	10
A_2	25	40	90
A_3	35	$3x$	30
Prior probability	0.4	0.2	0.4

The value of x currently is 50, but there is an opportunity to increase x by spending some money now.

What is the maximum amount Barbara should spend to increase x to 75?

9.10   You are given the following payoff table (in units of thousands of dollars) for a decision analysis problem:

| | State of Nature | | |
Alternative	S_1	S_2	S_3
A_1	4	0	0
A_2	0	2	0
A_3	3	0	1
Prior probability	0.2	0.5	0.3

a. According to Bayes' decision rule, which alternative should be chosen?

b. Find the expected value of perfect information.

A   *c.* Check your answer in part *b* by recalculating it with the help of a decision tree.

d. You are given the opportunity to spend $1,000 to obtain more information about which state of nature is likely to occur. Given your answer to part *b,* might it be worthwhile to spend this money?

9.11*   Betsy Pitzer makes decisions according to Bayes' decision rule. For her current problem, Betsy has constructed the following payoff table (in units of dollars):

| | State of Nature | | |
Alternative	S_1	S_2	S_3
A_1	50	100	-100
A_2	0	10	-10
A_3	20	40	-40
Prior probability	0.5	0.3	0.2

a. Which alternative should Betsy choose?

b. Find the expected value of perfect information.

A   *c.* Check your answer in part *b* by recalculating it with the help of a decision tree.

d. What is the most that Betsy should consider paying to obtain more information about which state of nature will occur?

9.12   Using Bayes' decision rule, consider the decision analysis problem having the following payoff table (in units of thousands of dollars):

| | State of Nature | | |
Alternative	S_1	S_2	S_3
A_1	-100	10	100
A_2	-10	20	50
A_3	10	10	60
Prior probability	0.2	0.3	0.5

a. Which alternative should be chosen? What is the resulting expected payoff?

b. You are offered the opportunity to obtain information that will tell you with certainty whether the first state of nature S_1 will occur. What is the maximum amount you should pay for the information? Assuming you will obtain the information, how should this information be used to choose an alternative? What is the resulting expected payoff (excluding the payment)?

c. Now repeat part *b* if the information offered concerns S_2 instead of S_1.

d. Now repeat part *b* if the information offered concerns S_3 instead of S_1.

A   *e.* Now suppose that the opportunity is offered to provide information that will tell you with certainty which state of nature will occur (perfect information). What is the maximum amount you should pay for the information? Assuming you will obtain the information, how should this information be used to choose an alternative? What is the resulting expected payoff (excluding the payment)?

f. If you have the opportunity to do some testing that will give you partial additional information (not perfect information) about the state of nature, what is the maximum amount you should consider paying for this information?

9.13   Reconsider the Goferbroke Co. case study, including its analysis in Sections 9.6 and 9.7. With the help of the consulting geologist, Jennifer Flyer now has obtained some historical data that provides more precise information than Max could supply on the likelihood of obtaining favorable seismic soundings on similar tracts of land. Specifically, when the land contains oil, favorable seismic soundings are obtained 80 percent of the time. This percentage changes to 40 percent when the land is dry.

a. Revise Figure 9.12 to find the new posterior probabilities.

T   b. Use the corresponding Excel template to check your answers in part *a*.

c. Revise Figure 9.16 to find the new decision tree. What is the resulting optimal policy?

A   d. Use TreePlan to construct and solve this new decision tree.

A9.14 Reconsider Problem 9.13. Max is skeptical that his estimates (60 percent and 20 percent) could be so far off the percentages (80 percent and 40 percent) obtained by Jennifer, so he requests that sensitivity analysis be conducted regarding these percentages.

a. Use the spreadsheet shown in Figure 9.18 (available in one of this chapter's Excel files) to obtain the results when Jennifer's probabilities are used.

b. Use SensIt to generate two graphs like Figure 9.20 where the horizontal axis for one is the probability in cell W33, P(FSS|Oil), and the horizontal axis for the other is the probability in cell W34, P(FSS|Dry).

c. Generate the spider graph and tornado diagram when Jennifer's probabilities are used instead of Max's estimates.

9.15* Vincent Cuomo is the credit manager for the Fine Fabrics Mill. He is currently faced with the question of whether to extend $100,000 of credit to a potential new customer, a dress manufacturer. Vincent has three categories for the creditworthiness of a company—poor risk, average risk, and good risk—but he does not know which category fits this potential customer. Experience indicates that 20 percent of companies similar to this dress manufacturer are poor risks, 50 percent are average risks, and 30 percent are good risks. If credit is extended, the expected profit for poor risks is −$15,000, for average risks $10,000, and for good risks $20,000. If credit is not extended, the dress manufacturer will turn to another mill. Vincent is able to consult a credit-rating organization for a fee of $5,000 per company evaluated. For companies whose actual credit records with the mill turn out to fall into each of the three categories, the following table shows the percentages that were given each of the three possible credit evaluations by the credit-rating organization.

	Actual Credit Record		
Credit Evaluation	**Poor**	**Average**	**Good**
Poor	50%	40%	20%
Average	40	50	40
Good	10	10	40

a. Develop a decision analysis formulation of this problem by identifying the decision alternatives, the states of nature, and the payoff table when the credit-rating organization is not used.

b. Assuming the credit-rating organization is not used, use Bayes' decision rule to determine which decision alternative should be chosen.

A   c. Find the expected value of perfect information. Does this answer indicate that consideration should be given to using the credit-rating organization?

d. Assume now that the credit-rating organization is used. Develop a probability tree diagram to find the posterior probabilities of the respective states of nature for each of the three possible credit evaluations of this potential customer.

T   e. Use the corresponding Excel template to obtain the answers for part *d*.

f. Draw the decision tree for this entire problem by hand. Use this decision tree to determine Vincent's optimal policy.

A   g. Use TreePlan to construct and solve this decision tree.

A   h. Find the expected value of sample information. If the fee for using the credit-rating organization is open to negotiation, how large can the fee be and use of this organization still be worthwhile?

9.16 You are given the following payoff table (in units of dollars):

	State of Nature	
Alternative	S_1	S_2
A_1	400	−100
A_1	0	100
Prior probability	0.4	0.6

You have the option of paying $100 to have research done to better predict which state of nature will occur. When the true state of nature is S_1, the research will accurately predict S_1 60 percent of the time (but will inaccurately predict S_2 40 percent of the time). When the true state of nature is S_2, the research will accurately predict S_2 80 percent of the time (but will inaccurately predict S_1 20 percent of the time).

a. Given that the research is not done, use Bayes' decision rule to determine which decision alternative should be chosen.

A   b. Use a decision tree to help find the expected value of perfect information. Does this answer indicate that it might be worthwhile to do the research?

c. Given that the research is done, find the joint probability of each of the following pairs of outcomes: (*i*) the state of nature is S_1 and the research predicts S_1, (*ii*) the state of nature is S_1 and the research predicts S_2, (*iii*) the state of nature is S_2 and the research predicts S_1, and (*iv*) the state of nature is S_2 and the research predicts S_2.

d. Find the unconditional probability that the research predicts S_1. Also find the unconditional probability that the research predicts S_2.

e. Given that the research is done, use your answers in parts *c* and *d* to determine the posterior probabilities of the states of nature for each of the two possible predictions of the research.

T *f.* Use the corresponding Excel template to obtain the answers for part *e*.

g. Given that the research predicts S_1, use Bayes' decision rule to determine which decision alternative should be chosen and the resulting expected payoff.

h. Repeat part *g* when the research predicts S_2.

i. Given that research is done, what is the expected payoff when using Bayes' decision rule?

j. Use the preceding results to determine the optimal policy regarding whether to do the research and the choice of the decision alternative.

A *k.* Construct and solve the decision tree to show the analysis for the entire problem. (Using TreePlan is optional.)

9.17 An athletic league does drug testing of its athletes, 10 percent of whom use drugs. The test, however, is only 95 percent reliable. That is, a drug user will test positive with probability 0.95 and negative with probability 0.05, and a nonuser will test negative with probability 0.95 and positive with probability 0.05.

Develop a probability tree diagram to determine the posterior probability of each of the following outcomes of testing an athlete.

a. The athlete is a drug user, given that the test is positive.

b. The athlete is not a drug user, given that the test is positive.

c. The athlete is a drug user, given that the test is negative.

d. The athlete is not a drug user, given that the test is negative.

T *e.* Use the corresponding Excel template to check your answers in the preceding parts.

9.18 Management of the Telemore Company is considering developing and marketing a new product. It is estimated to be twice as likely that the product would prove to be successful as unsuccessful. If it were successful, the expected profit would be $1,500,000. If unsuccessful, the expected loss would be $1,800,000. A marketing survey can be conducted at a cost of $100,000 to predict whether the product would be successful. Past experience with such surveys indicates that successful products have been predicted to be successful 80 percent of the time, whereas unsuccessful products have been predicted to be unsuccessful 70 percent of the time.

a. Develop a decision analysis formulation of this problem by identifying the decision alternatives, the states of nature, and the payoff table when the market survey is not conducted.

b. Assuming the market survey is not conducted, use Bayes' decision rule to determine which decision alternative should be chosen.

c. Find the expected value of perfect information. Does this answer indicate that consideration should be given to conducting the market survey?

T *d.* Assume now that the market survey is conducted. Find the posterior probabilities of the respective states of nature for each of the two possible predictions from the market survey.

A *e.* Use TreePlan to construct and solve the decision tree for this entire problem.

A *f.* Use SensIt to generate a spider graph and tornado diagram with respect to the profit, loss, and cost data when each can vary as much as 25 percent in either direction from its base value.

9.19 The Hit-and-Miss Manufacturing Company produces items that have a probability p of being defective. These items are produced in lots of 150. Past experience indicates that p for an entire lot is either 0.05 or 0.25. Furthermore, in 80 percent of the lots produced, p equals 0.05 (so p equals 0.25 in 20 percent of the lots). These items are then used in an assembly, and ultimately their quality is determined before the final assembly leaves the plant. Initially the company can *either* screen each item in a lot at a cost of $10 per item and replace defective items *or* use the items directly without screening. If the latter action is chosen, the cost of rework is ultimately $100 per defective item. Because screening requires scheduling of inspectors and equipment, the decision to screen or not screen must be made two days before the screening is to take place. However, one item can be taken from the lot and sent to a laboratory for inspection, and its quality (defective or nondefective) can be reported before the screen/no-screen decision must be made. The cost of this initial inspection is $125.

a. Develop a decision analysis formulation of this problem by identifying the decision alternatives, the states of nature, and the payoff table if the single item is not inspected in advance.

b. Assuming the single item is not inspected in advance, use Bayes' decision rule to determine which decision alternative should be chosen.

c. Find the expected value of perfect information. Does this answer indicate that consideration should be given to inspecting the single item in advance?

T *d.* Assume now that the single item is inspected in advance. Find the posterior probabilities of the respective states of nature for each of the two possible outcomes of this inspection.

A *e.* Construct and solve the decision tree for this entire problem.

A *f.* Find the expected value of sample information. If the cost of using the laboratory to inspect the single item in advance is open to negotiation, how large can the cost of using the laboratory be and still be worthwhile?

9.20* Silicon Dynamics has developed a new computer chip that will enable it to begin producing and marketing a personal computer if it so desires. Alternatively, it can sell the rights to the computer chip for $15 million. If the company chooses to build computers, the profitability of the venture depends on the company's ability to market the computer during the first year. It has sufficient access to retail outlets that it can guarantee sales of 10,000 computers. On the other hand, if this computer catches on, the company can sell 100,000 machines. For analysis purposes, these two levels of sales are taken to be the two possible outcomes of marketing the computer, but it is unclear what their prior probabilities are.

The cost of setting up the assembly line is $6 million. The difference between the selling price and the variable cost of each computer is $600.

a. Develop a decision analysis formulation of this problem by identifying the decision alternatives, the states of nature, and the payoff table.

b. Construct a decision tree for this problem by hand.

A c. Assuming the prior probabilities of the two levels of sales are both 0.5, use TreePlan to construct and solve this decision tree. According to this analysis, which decision alternative should be chosen?

A d. Use SensIt to develop a graph that plots the expected payoff (when using Bayes' decision rule) versus the prior probability of selling 10,000 computers.

e. Draw a graph that plots the expected payoff for each of the decision alternatives versus the prior probability of selling 10,000 computers.

f. Referring to this graph, use algebra to solve for the value of the prior probability of selling 10,000 computers at the point where the two lines in the graph intersect. Explain the significance of this point.

9.21* Reconsider Problem 9.20. Management of Silicon Dynamics now is considering doing full-fledged market research at an estimated cost of $1 million to predict which of the two levels of demand is likely to occur. Previous experience indicates that such market research is correct two-thirds of the time.

a. Find the expected value of perfect information for this problem.

b. Does the answer in part a indicate that it might be worthwhile to perform this market research?

c. Develop a probability tree diagram to obtain the posterior probabilities of the two levels of demand for each of the two possible outcomes of the market research.

T d. Use the corresponding Excel template to check your answers in part c.

A9.22* Reconsider Problem 9.21. The management of Silicon Dynamics now wants to see a decision tree displaying the entire problem.

a. Use TreePlan to construct and solve this decision tree.

b. Find the expected value of sample information. How large can the cost of doing full-fledged market research be and still be worthwhile?

c. Assume now that the estimate of $1 million for the cost of doing full-fledged market research is correct but that there is some uncertainty in the financial data ($15 million, $6 million, and $600) stated in Problem 9.20. Each could vary from its base value by as much as 10 percent. For each one, perform sensitivity analysis to find what would happen if its value were at either end of this range of variability (without any change in the other two pieces of data). Then do the same for the

eight cases where all these pieces of data are at one end or the other of their ranges of variability.

d. Because of the uncertainty described in part c, use SensIt to generate a graph that plots the expected profit over the range of variability for each piece of financial data (without any change in the other two pieces of data).

e. Generate the corresponding spider graph and tornado diagram.

9.23 You are given the following decision tree, where the numbers in parentheses are probabilities and the numbers on the right are payoffs at these terminal points.

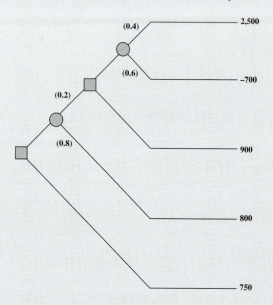

a. Analyze this decision tree to obtain the optimal policy.

A b. Use TreePlan to construct and solve the same decision tree.

9.24 You are given the following decision tree, with the probabilities at event nodes shown in parentheses and with the payoffs at terminal points shown on the right. Analyze this decision tree to obtain the optimal policy.

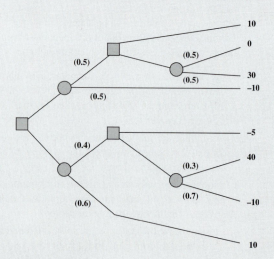

9.25* The Athletic Department of Leland University is considering whether to hold an extensive campaign next year to raise funds for a new athletic field. The response to the campaign depends heavily on the success of the football team this fall. In the past, the football team has had winning seasons 60 percent of the time. If the football team has a winning season (W) this fall, then many of the alumni will contribute and the campaign will raise $3 million. If the team has a losing season (L), few will contribute and the campaign will lose $2 million. If no campaign is undertaken, no costs are incurred. On September 1, just before the football season begins, the Athletic Department needs to make its decision about whether to hold the campaign next year.

a. Develop a decision analysis formulation of this problem by identifying the decision alternatives, the states of nature, and the payoff table.

b. According to Bayes' decision rule, should the campaign be undertaken?

c. What is the expected value of perfect information?

d. A famous football guru, William Walsh, has offered his services to help evaluate whether the team will have a winning season. For $100,000, he will carefully evaluate the team throughout spring practice and then throughout preseason workouts. William then will provide his prediction on September 1 regarding what kind of season, W or L, the team will have. In similar situations in the past when evaluating teams that have winning seasons 50 percent of the time, his predictions have been correct 75 percent of the time. Considering that this team has more of a winning tradition, if William predicts a winning season, what is the posterior probability that the team actually will have a winning season? What is the posterior probability of a losing season? If William predicts a losing season instead, what is the posterior probability of a winning season? Of a losing season? Show how these answers are obtained from a probability tree diagram.

T   *e.* Use the corresponding Excel template to obtain the answers requested in part *d.*

f. Draw the decision tree for this entire problem by hand. Analyze this decision tree to determine the optimal policy regarding whether to hire William and whether to undertake the campaign.

A   *g.* Use TreePlan to construct and solve this decision tree.

A   *h.* Find the expected value of sample information. If the fee for hiring William Walsh is open to negotiation, how large can William's fee be and still be worthwhile?

9.26 The comptroller of the Macrosoft Corporation has $100 million of excess funds to invest. She has been instructed to invest the entire amount for one year in either stocks or bonds (but not both) and then to reinvest the entire fund in either stocks or bonds (but not both) for one year more. The objective is to maximize the expected monetary value of the fund at the end of the second year.

The annual rates of return on these investments depend on the economic environment, as shown in the following table:

Economic Environment	Rate of Return	
	Stocks	Bonds
Growth	20%	5%
Recession	−10	10
Depression	−50	20

The probabilities of growth, recession, and depression for the first year are 0.7, 0.3, and 0, respectively. If growth occurs in the first year, these probabilities remain the same for the second year. However, if a recession occurs in the first year, these probabilities change to 0.2, 0.7, and 0.1, respectively, for the second year.

a. Construct by hand the decision tree for this problem and then analyze the decision tree to identify the optimal policy.

A   *b.* Use TreePlan to construct and solve the decision tree.

9.27 On Monday, a certain stock closed at $10 per share. On Tuesday, you expect the stock to close at $9, $10, or $11 per share, with respective probabilities 0.3, 0.3, and 0.4. On Wednesday, you expect the stock to close 10 percent lower, unchanged, or 10 percent higher than Tuesday's close, with the following probabilities:

Today's Close	10 Percent Lower	Unchanged	10 Percent Higher
$ 9	0.4	0.3	0.3
10	0.2	0.2	0.6
11	0.1	0.2	0.7

On Tuesday, you are directed to buy 100 shares of the stock before Thursday. All purchases are made at the end of the day, at the known closing price for that day, so your only options are to buy at the end of Tuesday or at the end of Wednesday. You wish to determine the optimal strategy for whether to buy on Tuesday or defer the purchase until Wednesday, given the Tuesday closing price, to minimize the expected purchase price.

a. Develop and evaluate a decision tree by hand for determining the optimal strategy.

A   *b.* Use TreePlan to construct and solve the decision tree.

A9.28 Jose Morales manages a large outdoor fruit stand in one of the less affluent neighborhoods of San Jose, California. To replenish his supply, Jose buys boxes of fruit early each morning from a grower south of San Jose. About 90 percent of the boxes of fruit turn out to be of satisfactory quality, but the other 10 percent are unsatisfactory.

A satisfactory box contains 80 percent excellent fruit and will earn $200 profit for Jose. An unsatisfactory box contains 30 percent excellent fruit and will produce a loss of $1,000. Before Jose decides to accept a box, he is given the opportunity to sample one piece of fruit to test whether it is excellent. Based on that sample, he then has the option of rejecting the box without paying for it. Jose wonders (1) whether he should continue buying from this grower, (2) if so, whether it is worthwhile sampling just one piece of fruit from a box, and (3) if so, whether he should be accepting or rejecting the box based on the outcome of this sampling.

Use TreePlan (and the Excel template for posterior probabilities) to construct and solve the decision tree for this problem.

9.29* The Morton Ward Company is considering the introduction of a new product that is believed to have a 50–50 chance of being successful. One option is to try out the product in a test market, at an estimated cost of $2 million, before making the introduction decision. Past experience shows that ultimately successful products are approved in the test market 80 percent of the time, whereas ultimately unsuccessful products are approved in the test market only 25 percent of the time. If the product is successful, the net profit to the company will be $40 million; if unsuccessful, the net loss will be $15 million.

a. Discarding the test market option, develop a decision analysis formulation of the problem by identifying the decision alternatives, states of nature, and payoff table. Then apply Bayes' decision rule to determine the optimal decision alternative.

b. Find the expected value of perfect information.

A   c. Now including the option of trying out the product in a test market, use TreePlan (and the Excel template for posterior probabilities) to construct and solve the decision tree for this problem.

A   d. Find the expected value of sample information. How large can the cost of trying out the product in a test market be and still be worthwhile to do?

A   e. Assume now that the estimate of $2 million for the cost of trying out the product in a test market is correct. However, there is some uncertainty in the stated profit and loss figures ($40 million and $15 million). Either could vary from its base by as much as 25 percent in either direction. For each of these two financial figures, perform sensitivity analysis to check how the results in part c would change if the value of the financial figure were at either end of this range of variability (without any change in the value of the other financial figure). Then do the same for the four cases where both financial figures are at one end or the other of their ranges of variability.

A   f. Because of the uncertainty described in part e, use SensIt to generate a graph that plots the expected profit over the range of variability for each of the two financial figures (without any change in the other figure).

A   g. Generate the corresponding spider graph and tornado diagram. Interpret each one.

A9.30 Chelsea Bush is an emerging candidate for her party's nomination for president of the United States. She now is considering whether to run in the high-stakes Super Tuesday primaries. If she enters the Super Tuesday (S.T.) primaries, she and her advisers believe that she will either do well (finish first or second) or do poorly (finish third or worse) with probabilities 0.4 and 0.6, respectively. Doing well on Super Tuesday will net the candidate's campaign approximately $16 million in new contributions, whereas a poor showing will mean a loss of $10 million after numerous TV ads are paid for. Alternatively, she may choose not to run at all on Super Tuesday and incur no costs.

Chelsea's advisers realize that her chances of success on Super Tuesday may be affected by the outcome of the smaller New Hampshire (N.H.) primary occurring three weeks before Super Tuesday. Political analysts feel that the results of New Hampshire's primary are correct two-thirds of the time in predicting the results of the Super Tuesday primaries. Among Chelsea's advisers is a decision analysis expert who uses this information to calculate the following probabilities:

P(Chelsea does well in S.T. primaries, given she does well in N.H.) = $\frac{4}{7}$

P(Chelsea does well in S.T. primaries, given she does poorly in N.H.) = $\frac{1}{4}$

P(Chelsea does well in N.H. primary) = $\frac{7}{15}$

The cost of entering and campaigning in the New Hampshire primary is estimated to be $1.6 million.

Chelsea feels that her chance of winning the nomination depends largely on having substantial funds available after the Super Tuesday primaries to carry on a vigorous campaign the rest of the way. Therefore, she wants to choose the strategy (whether to run in the New Hampshire primary and then whether to run in the Super Tuesday primaries) that will maximize her expected funds after these primaries.

a. Construct and solve the decision tree for this problem.

b. There is some uncertainty in the estimates of a gain of $16 million or a loss of $10 million depending on the showing on Super Tuesday. Either amount could differ from this estimate by as much as 25 percent in either direction. For each of these two financial figures, perform sensitivity analysis to check how the results in part a would change if the value of the financial figure were at either end of this range of variability (without any change in the value of the other financial figure). Then do the same for the four cases where both financial figures are at one end or the other of their ranges of variability.

A   c. Because of the uncertainty described in part b, use SensIt to generate a graph that plots Chelsea's expected funds after these primaries over the range of variability for each of the two financial figures (without any change in the other figure).

d. Generate the corresponding spider graph and tornado diagram. Interpret each one.

A9.31   The executive search being conducted for Western Bank by Headhunters Inc. may finally be bearing fruit. The position to be filled is a key one—vice president for Information Processing—because this person will have responsibility for developing a state-of-the-art management information system that will link together Western's many branch banks. However, Headhunters feels it has found just the right person, Matthew Fenton, who has an excellent record in a similar position for a midsized bank in New York.

After a round of interviews, Western's president believes that Matthew has a probability of 0.7 of designing the management information system successfully. If Matthew is successful, the company will realize a profit of $2 million (net of Matthew's salary, training, recruiting costs, and expenses). If he is not successful, the company will realize a net loss of $600,000.

For an additional fee of $40,000, Headhunters will provide a detailed investigative process (including an extensive background check, a battery of academic and psychological tests, etc.) that will further pinpoint Matthew's potential for success. This process has been found to be 90 percent reliable, that is, a candidate who would successfully design the management information system will pass the test with probability 0.9, and a candidate who would not successfully design the system will fail the test with probability 0.9.

Western's top management needs to decide whether to hire Matthew and whether to have Headhunters conduct the detailed investigative process before making this decision.

a. Construct and solve the decision tree for this problem to identify the optimal policy.

b. Now suppose that Headhunters's fee for administering its detailed investigative process is negotiable. What is the maximum amount that Western Bank should pay?

9.32   Reconsider the Goferbroke Co. case study, including the application of utilities in Section 9.9. Max Flyer now has decided that, given the company's precarious financial situation, he needs to take a much more risk-averse approach to the problem. Therefore, he has revised the utilities given in Table 9.9 as follows: $U(-130) = 0$, $U(-100) = 0.07$, $U(60) = 0.40$, $U(90) = 0.45$, $U(670) = 0.99$, and $U(700) = 1$.

a. Analyze the revised decision tree corresponding to Figure 9.29 by hand to obtain the new optimal policy.

A   *b.* Use TreePlan to construct and solve this revised decision tree.

9.33*   You live in an area that has a possibility of incurring a massive earthquake, so you are considering buying earthquake insurance on your home at an annual cost of $180. The probability of an earthquake damaging your home during one year is 0.001. If this happens, you estimate that the cost of the damage (fully covered by earthquake insurance) will be $160,000. Your total assets (including your home) are worth $250,000.

a. Apply Bayes' decision rule to determine which alternative (take the insurance or not) maximizes your expected assets after one year.

b. You now have constructed a utility function that measures how much you value having total assets worth x dollars ($x \geq 0$). This utility function is $U(x) = \sqrt{x}$. Compare the utility of reducing your total assets next year by the cost of the earthquake insurance with the expected utility next year of not taking the earthquake insurance. Should you take the insurance?

9.34.   For your graduation present from college, your parents are offering you your choice of two alternatives. The first alternative is to give you a money gift of $19,000. The second alternative is to make an investment in your name. This investment will quickly have the following two possible outcomes:

Outcome	Probability
Receive $10,000	0.3
Receive $30,000	0.7

Your utility for receiving M thousand dollars is given by the utility function $U(M) = \sqrt{M + 6}$. Which choice should you make to maximize expected utility?

9.35   Reconsider Problem 9.34. You now are uncertain about what your true utility function for receiving money is, so you are in the process of constructing this utility function by using the equivalent lottery method and units of thousands of dollars. You have concluded that you are indifferent between the two alternatives offered to you by your parents. Use this information to find $U(19)$ after setting $U(10) = 0$ and $U(30) = 1$.

9.36   You wish to construct your personal utility function $U(M)$ for receiving M thousand dollars. After setting $U(0) = 0$, you next set $U(10) = 1$ as your utility for receiving $10,000. You next want to find $U(1)$ and then $U(5)$.

a. You offer yourself the following two hypothetical alternatives:

A_1: Obtain $10,000 with probability p.
   Obtain 0 with probability $(1 - p)$.

A_2: Definitely obtain $1,000.

You then ask yourself the question: What value of p makes you indifferent between these two alternatives? Your answer is $p = 0.125$. Find $U(1)$ by using the equivalent lottery method.

b. You next repeat part *a* except for changing the second alternative to definitely receiving $5,000. The value of p that makes you indifferent between these two alternatives now is $p = 0.5625$. Find $U(5)$.

c. Repeat parts *a* and *b*, but now use *your* personal choices for p.

9.37 You are given the following payoff table:

Alternative	State of Nature	
	S_1	S_2
A_1	25	36
A_2	100	0
A_3	0	49
Prior probability	p	$1 - p$

a. Assume that your utility function for the payoffs is $U(x) = \sqrt{x}$. Plot the expected utility of each decision alternative versus the value of p on the same graph. For each decision alternative, find the range of values of p over which this alternative maximizes the expected utility.

A b. Now assume that your utility function is the exponential utility function with a risk tolerance of $R = 50$. Use TreePlan to construct and solve the resulting decision tree in turn for $p = 0.25$, $p = 0.5$, and $p = 0.75$.

A9.38 Dr. Switzer has a seriously ill patient but has had trouble diagnosing the specific cause of the illness. The doctor now has narrowed the cause down to two alternatives: disease A or disease B. Based on the evidence so far, she feels that the two alternatives are equally likely.

Beyond the testing already done, there is no test available to determine if the cause is disease B. One test is available for disease A, but it has two major problems. First, it is very expensive. Second, it is somewhat unreliable, giving an accurate result only 80 percent of the time. Thus, it will give a positive result (indicating disease A) for only 80 percent of patients who have disease A, whereas it will give a positive result for 20 percent of patients who actually have disease B instead.

Disease B is a very serious disease with no known treatment. It is sometimes fatal, and those who survive remain in poor health with a poor quality of life thereafter. The prognosis is similar for victims of disease A if it is left untreated. However, there is a fairly expensive treatment available that eliminates the danger for those with disease A, and it may return them to good health. Unfortunately, it is a relatively radical treatment that always leads to death if the patient actually has disease B instead.

The probability distribution for the prognosis for this patient is given for each case in the following table, where the column headings (after the first one) indicate the disease for the patient.

	Outcome Probabilities			
	No Treatment		Receive Treatment for Disease A	
Outcome	A	B	A	B
Die	0.2	0.5	0	1.0
Survive with poor health	0.8	0.5	0.5	0
Return to good health	0	0	0.5	0

The patient has assigned the following utilities to the possible outcomes:

Outcome	Utility
Die	0
Survive with poor health	10
Return to good health	30

In addition, these utilities should be incremented by -2 if the patient incurs the cost of the test for disease A and by -1 if the patient (or the patient's estate) incurs the cost of the treatment for disease A.

Use decision analysis with a complete decision tree to determine if the patient should undergo the test for disease A and then how to proceed (receive the treatment for disease A?) to maximize the patient's expected utility.

9.39 Consider the following decision tree, where the probabilities for each event node are shown in parentheses.

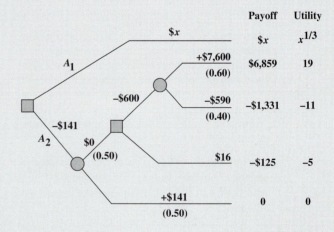

	Payoff	Utility
	$x	$x^{1/3}$
	+$7,600 (0.60) → $6,859	19
	−$590 (0.40) → −$1,331	−11
	$16 → −$125	−5
	+$141 (0.50) → 0	0

The dollar amount given next to each branch is the cash flow generated along that branch, where these intermediate cash flows add up to the total net cash flow shown to the right of each terminal branch. (The unknown amount for the top branch is represented by the variable *x*.) The decision maker has a utility function $U(y) = y^{1/3}$ where *y* is the total net cash flow after a terminal branch. The resulting utilities for the various terminal branches are shown to the right of the decision tree.

Use these utilities to analyze the decision tree. Then determine the value of *x* for which the decision maker is indifferent between decision alternatives A_1 and A_2.

A9.40 Reconsider the Goferbroke Co. case study when using utilities, as presented in Section 9.9.

a. Beginning with the decision tree shown in Figure 9.29 (available in one of this chapter's Excel files), prepare to perform sensitivity analysis by expanding and organizing the spreadsheet to (1) consolidate the data and results in one section and (2) incorporate the Excel template for posterior probabilities in another section (similar to what was done in Figure 9.18).

b. Perform sensitivity analysis by re-solving the decision tree (after using the Excel template for posterior probabilities to revise these probabilities) when the prior probability of oil is changed in turn to 0.15, 0.2, 0.3, and 0.35.

Case 9-1

Who Wants to be a Millionaire?

You are a contestant on "Who Wants to be a Millionaire?" You already have answered the $250,000 question correctly and now must decide if you would like to answer the $500,000 question. You can choose to walk away at this point with $250,000 in winnings or you may decide to answer the $500,000 question. If you answer the $500,000 question correctly, you can then choose to walk away with $500,000 in winnings or go on and try to answer the $1,000,000 question. If you answer the $1,000,000 question correctly, the game is over and you win $1,000,000. If you answer either the $500,000 or the $1,000,000 question incorrectly, the game is over immediately and you take home "only" $32,000.

A feature of the game "Who Wants to be a Millionaire?" is that you have three "lifelines"—namely "50–50," "ask the audience," and "phone a friend." At this point (after answering the $250,000 question), you already have used two of these lifelines, but you have the "phone a friend" lifeline remaining. With this option, you may phone a friend to obtain advice on the correct answer to a question before giving your answer. You may use this option only once (i.e., you can use it on either the $500,000 question or the $1,000,000 question, but not both).

Since some of your friends are smarter than you are, "phone a friend" significantly improves your odds for answering a question correctly. Without "phone a friend," if you choose to answer the $500,000 question you have a 65 percent chance of answering correctly, and if you choose to answer the $1,000,000 question you have a 50 percent chance of answering correctly (the questions get progressively more difficult). With "phone a friend," you have an 80 percent chance of answering the $500,000 question correctly and a 65 percent chance of answering the $1,000,000 question correctly.

a. Use TreePlan to construct and solve a decision tree to decide what to do. What is the best course of action, assuming your goal is to maximize your *expected* winnings?

b. Use the equivalent lottery method to determine your personal utility function (in particular, your utility values for all of the possible payoffs in the game).

c. Re-solve the decision tree, replacing the payoffs with your utility values, to maximize your expected utility. Does the best course of action change?

Case 9-2

University Toys and the Business Professor Action Figures

University Toys has developed a brand new product line—a series of Business Professor Action Figures (BPAFs) featuring likenesses of popular professors at the local business school. Management needs to decide how to market the dolls.

One option is to immediately ramp up production and simultaneously launch an ad campaign in the university newspaper. This option would cost $1,000. Based on past experience, new action figures either take off and do well or fail miserably. Hence, the prediction is for one of two possible outcomes—total sales of 2,500 units or total sales of only 250 units. University Toys receives revenue of $2 per unit sold. Management currently thinks that there is about a 50 percent chance that the product will do well (sell 2,500 units) and a 50 percent chance that it will do poorly (sell 250 units).

Another option is to test-market the product. The company could build a few units, put up a display in the campus bookstore, and see how they sell without any further advertising. This would require less capital for the production run and no money for advertising. Again, the prediction is for one of two possible outcomes for this test market, namely, the product will either do well (sell 200 units) or do poorly (sell 20 units). The cost for this option is estimated to be $100. University Toys receives revenue of $2 per unit sold for the test market as well. The company has often test marketed toys in this manner. Products that sell well when fully marketed have also sold well in the test market 80 percent of the time. Products that sell poorly when fully marketed also sell poorly in the test market 60 percent of the time.

There is a complication with the test market option, however. A rival toy manufacturer is rumored to be considering the development of Law School Professor Action Figures (LSPAF). After doing the test marketing, if University Toys decides to go ahead and ramp up production and fully market the BPAF, the cost of doing so would still be $1,000. However, the sales prospects depend upon whether LSPAF has been introduced into the market or not. If LSPAF has not entered the market, then the sales prospects will be the same as described above (i.e., 2,500 units if BPAF does well, or 250 units if BPAF does poorly, on top of any units sold in the test market). However, if LSPAF has been introduced, the increased competition will diminish sales of BPAF. In particular, management expects in this case to sell 1,000 if BPAF does well or 100 units if it does poorly (on top of any units sold in the test market). Note that the probability of BPAF doing well or doing poorly is not affected by LSPAF, just the final sales totals of each possibility. The probability that LSPAF will enter the market *before the end* of the test market is 20 percent. On the other hand, if University Toys markets BPAF immediately, they are guaranteed to beat the LSPAF to market (thus making LSPAF a nonfactor).

a. Suppose that the test marketing is done. Use the Posterior Probabilities template to determine the likelihood that the BPAF would sell well if fully marketed, given that it sells well in the test market and then given that it sells poorly in the test market.

b. Use TreePlan to develop and solve a decision tree to help University Toys decide the best course of action and the expected payoff.

c. Now suppose that University Toys is uncertain of the probability that the LSPAFs will enter the market before the test marketing would be completed (if it were done). How would you expect the expected payoff to vary as the probability that the LSPAFs will enter the market changes?

d. Generate a data table that shows how the expected payoff and the test marketing decision changes as the probability that the LSPAFs will enter the market varies from 0 percent to 100 percent (at 10 percent increments).

e. At what probability does the test marketing decision change?

Case 9-3

Brainy Business

While El Niño is pouring its rain on northern California, Charlotte Rothstein, CEO, major shareholder, and founder of Cerebrosoft, sits in her office, contemplating the decision she faces regarding her company's newest proposed product, Brainet. This has been a particularly difficult decision. Brainet might catch on and sell very well. However, Charlotte is concerned about the risk involved. In this competitive market, marketing Brainet also could lead to substantial losses. Should she go ahead anyway and start the marketing campaign? Or just abandon the product? Or perhaps buy additional marketing research information from a local market research company before deciding whether to launch the product? She has to make a decision very soon and so, as she slowly drinks from her glass of high-protein-power multivitamin juice, she reflects on the events of the past few years.

Cerebrosoft was founded by Charlotte and two friends after they had graduated from business school. The company is located in the heart of Silicon Valley. Charlotte and her friends managed to make money in their second year in business and have continued to do so every year since. Cerebrosoft was one of the first companies to sell software over the World Wide Web and to develop PC-based software tools for the multimedia sector. Two of the products generate 80 percent of the company's revenues: Audiatur and Videatur. Each product has sold more than 100,000 units during the past year. Business is done over the Web: Customers can download a trial version of the software, test it, and if they are satisfied with what they see, they can purchase the product (by using a password that enables them to disable the time counter in the trial version). Both products are priced at $75.95 and are sold exclusively over the Web.

Although the World Wide Web is a network of computers of different types, running different kinds of software, a standardized protocol between the computers enables them to communicate. Users can surf the Web and visit computers many thousands of miles away, accessing information available at the site. Users also can make files available on the Web, and this is how Cerebrosoft generates its sales. Selling software over the Web eliminates many of the traditional cost factors of consumer products: packaging, storage, distribution, sales force, and so on. Instead, potential customers can download a trial version, take a look at it (that is, use the product) before its trial period expires, and then decide whether to buy it. Furthermore, Cerebrosoft can always make the most recent files available to the customer, avoiding the problem of having outdated software in the distribution pipeline.

Charlotte is interrupted in her thoughts by the arrival of Jeannie Korn. Jeannie is in charge of marketing for online products and Brainet has had her particular attention from the beginning. She is more than ready to provide the advice that Charlotte has requested. "Charlotte, I think we should really go ahead with Brainet. The software engineers have convinced me that the current version is robust and we want to be on the market with this as soon as possible! From the data for our product launches during the past two years, we can get a rather reliable estimate of how the market will respond to the new product, don't you think? And look!" She pulls out some presentation slides. "During that time period we launched 12 new products altogether and 4 of them sold more than 30,000 units during the first six months alone! Even better: The last two we launched even sold more than 40,000 copies during the first two quarters!" Charlotte knows these numbers as well as Jeannie does. After all, two of these launches have been products she herself helped to develop. But she feels uneasy about this particular product launch. The company has grown rapidly during the past three years and its financial capabilities are already rather stretched. A poor product launch for Brainet would cost the company a lot of money, something that isn't available right now due to the investments Cerebrosoft has recently made.

Later in the afternoon, Charlotte meets with Reggie Ruffin, a jack of all trades and the production manager. Reggie has a solid track record in his field and Charlotte wants his opinion on the Brainet project.

"Well, Charlotte, quite frankly, I think that there are three main factors that are relevant to the success of this project: competition, units sold, and cost—ah, and, of course, our pricing. Have you decided on the price yet?"

"I am still considering which of the three strategies would be most beneficial to us. Selling for $50.00 and trying to maximize revenues—or selling for $30.00 and trying to maximize market share. Of course, there is still your third alternative; we could sell for $40.00 and try to do both."

At this point, Reggie focuses on the sheet of paper in front of him. "And I still believe that the $40.00 alternative is the best one. Concerning the costs, I checked the records; basically we

have to amortize the development costs we incurred for Brainet. So far we have spent $800,000 and we expect to spend another $50,000 per year for support and shipping the CDs to those who want a hardcopy on top of their downloaded software." Reggie next hands a report to Charlotte. "Here we have some data on the industry. I just received that yesterday, hot off the press. Let's see what we can learn about the industry here." He shows Charlotte some of the highlights. Reggie then agrees to compile the most relevant information contained in the report and have it ready for Charlotte the following morning. It takes him long into the night to gather the data from the pages of the report, but in the end he produces three tables, one for each of the three alternative pricing strategies. Each table shows the corresponding probability of various amounts of sales given the level of competition (severe, moderate, or weak) that develops from other companies.

TABLE 1
Probability Distribution of Unit Sales, Given a High Price ($50)

	Level of Competition		
Sales	Severe	Moderate	Weak
50,000 units	0.2	0.25	0.3
30,000 units	0.25	0.3	0.35
20,000 units	0.55	0.45	0.35

TABLE 2
Probability Distribution of Unit Sales, Given a Medium Price ($40)

	Level of Competition		
Sales	Severe	Moderate	Weak
50,000 units	0.25	0.30	0.40
30,000 units	0.35	0.40	0.50
20,000 units	0.40	0.30	0.10

TABLE 3
Probability Distribution of Unit Sales, Given a Low Price ($30)

	Level of Competition		
Sales	Severe	Moderate	Weak
50,000 units	0.35	0.40	0.50
30,000 units	0.40	0.50	0.45
20,000 units	0.25	0.10	0.05

The next morning, Charlotte is sipping from another power drink. Jeannie and Reggie will be in her office any moment now and, with their help, she will have to decide what to do with Brainet. Should they launch the product? If so, at what price?

When Jeannie and Reggie enter the office, Jeannie immediately bursts out: "Guys, I just spoke to our marketing research company. They say that they could do a study for us about the competitive situation for the introduction of Brainet and deliver the results within a week."

"How much do they want for the study?"

"I knew you'd ask that, Reggie. They want $10,000, and I think it's a fair deal."

At this point, Charlotte steps into the conversation. "Do we have any data on the quality of the work of this marketing research company?"

"Yes, I do have some reports here. After analyzing them, I have come to the conclusion that the predictions of the marketing research company are pretty good: Given that the competition

turned out to be severe, they predicted it correctly 80 percent of the time, while 15 percent of the time they predicted moderate competition in that setting. Given that the competition turned out to be moderate, they predicted severe competition 15 percent of the time and moderate competition 80 percent of the time. Finally, for the case of weak competition, the numbers were 90 percent of the time a correct prediction, 7 percent of the time a 'moderate' prediction and 3 percent of the time a 'severe' prediction."

Charlotte feels that all these numbers are too much for her. "Don't we have a simple estimate of how the market will react?"

"Some prior probabilities, you mean? Sure, from our past experience, the likelihood of facing severe competition is 20 percent, whereas it is 70 percent for moderate competition and 10 percent for weak competition," says Jeannie, her numbers always ready when needed.

All that is left to do now is to sit down and make sense of all this . . .

a. For the initial analysis, ignore the opportunity of obtaining more information by hiring the marketing research company. Identify the decision alternatives and the states of nature. Construct the payoff table. Then formulate the decision problem in a decision tree. Clearly distinguish between decision and event nodes and include all the relevant data.

b. What is Charlotte's decision if she uses the maximum likelihood criterion?

c. What is Charlotte's decision if she uses Bayes' decision rule?

d. Now consider the possibility of doing the market research. Develop the corresponding decision tree. Calculate the relevant probabilities and analyze the decision tree. Should Cerebrosoft pay the $10,000 for the marketing research? What is the overall optimal policy?

Case 9-4

Smart Steering Support

On a sunny May morning, Marc Binton, CEO of Bay Area Automobile Gadgets (BAAG), enters the conference room on the 40th floor of the Gates building in San Francisco, where BAAG's offices are located. The other executive officers of the company have already gathered. The meeting has only one item on its agenda: planning a research and development project to develop a new driver support system (DSS). Brian Huang, manager of Research and Development, is walking around nervously. He has to inform the group about the R&D strategy he has developed for the DSS. Marc has identified DSS as the strategic new product for the company. Julie Aker, vice president of Marketing, will speak after Brian. She will give detailed information about the target segment, expected sales, and marketing costs associated with the introduction of the DSS.

BAAG builds electronic nonaudio equipment for luxury cars. Founded by a group of Stanford graduates, the company sold its first product—a car routing system relying on a technology called Global Positioning Satellites (GPS)—a few years ago. Such routing systems help drivers to find directions to their desired destinations using satellites to determine the exact position of the car. To keep up with technology and to meet the wishes of its customers, the company has added a number of new features to its router during the last few years. The DSS will be a completely new product, incorporating recent developments in GPS as well as voice recognition and display technologies. Marc strongly supports this product, as it will give BAAG a competitive advantage over its Asian and European competitors.

Driver support systems have been a field of intense research for more than a decade. These systems provide the driver with a wide range of information, such as directions, road conditions, traffic updates, and so forth. The information exchange can take place verbally or via projection of text onto the windscreen. Other features help the driver avoid obstacles that have been identified by cars ahead on the road (these cars transmit the information to the following vehicles). Marc wants to incorporate all these features and other technologies into one support system that would then be sold to BAAG's customers in the automobile industry.

After all the attendees have taken their seats, Brian starts his presentation: "Marc asked me to inform you about our efforts with the driver support system, particularly the road scanning device. We have reached a stage where we basically have to make a go or no-go decision concerning the research for this device, which, as you all know by now, is a key feature in the DSS. We have already integrated the other devices, such as the

GPS-based positioning and direction system. The question with which we have to deal is whether to fund basic research into the road scanning device. If this research is successful, we then will have to decide if we want to develop a product based on these results—or if we just want to sell the technology without developing a product. If we do decide to develop the product ourselves, there is a chance that the product development process might not be successful. In that case, we could still sell the technology. In the case of successful product development, we would have to decide whether to market the product. If we decide not to market the developed product, we could at least sell the product concept that was the result of our successful research and development efforts. Doing so would earn more than just selling the technology prematurely. If, on the other hand, we decide to market the driver support system, then we are faced with the uncertainty of how the product will be received by our customers."

"You completely lost me," snipes Marc.

Max, Julie's assistant, just shakes his head and murmurs, "those techno-nerds. . . ."

Brian starts to explain: "Sorry for the confusion. Let's just go through it again, step by step."

"Good idea—and perhaps make smaller steps!" Julie obviously dislikes Brian's style of presentation.

"OK, the first decision we are facing is whether to invest in research for the road scanning device."

"How much would that cost us?" asks Marc.

"Our estimated budget for this is $300,000. Once we invest that money, the outcome of the research effort is somewhat uncertain. Our engineers assess the probability of successful research at 80 percent."

"That's a pretty optimistic success rate, don't you think?" Julie remarks sarcastically. She still remembers the disaster with Brian's last project, the fingerprint-based car-security-system. After spending half a million dollars, the development engineers concluded that it would be impossible to produce the security system at an attractive price.

Brian senses Julie's hostility and shoots back: "In engineering, we are quite accustomed to these success rates—something we can't say about marketing. . . ."

"What would be the next step?" intervenes Marc.

"Hm, sorry. If the research is not successful, then we can only sell the DSS in its current form."

"The profit estimate for that scenario is $2 million," Julie throws in.

"If, however, the research effort is successful, then we will have to make another decision, namely, whether to go on to the development stage."

"If we wouldn't want to develop a product at that point, would that mean that we would have to sell the DSS as it is now?" asks Max.

"Yes, Max. Except that additionally we would earn some $200,000 from selling our research results to GM. Their research division is very interested in our work and they have offered that money for our findings."

"Ah, now that's good news," remarks Julie.

Brian continues, "If, however, after successfully completing the research stage, we decide to develop a new product, then we'll have to spend another $800,000 for that task, at a 35 percent chance of not being successful."

"So you are telling us we'll have to spend $800,000 for a ticket in a lottery where we have a 35 percent chance of not winning anything?" asks Julie.

"Julie, don't focus on the losses but on the potential gains! The chance of winning in this lottery, as you call it, is 65 percent. I believe that that's much more than with a normal lottery ticket," says Marc.

"Thanks, Marc," says Brian. "Once we invest that money in development, we have two possible outcomes: either we will be successful in developing the road scanning device or we won't. If we fail, then once again we'll sell the DSS in its current form and cash in the $200,000 from GM for the research results. If the development process is successful, then we have to decide whether to market the new product."

"Why wouldn't we want to market it after successfully developing it?" asks Marc.

"That's a good question. Basically what I mean is that we could decide not to sell the product ourselves but instead give the right to sell it to somebody else, to GM for example. They would pay us $1 million for it."

"I like those numbers!" remarks Julie.

"Once we decide to build the product and market it, we will face the market uncertainties and I'm sure that Julie has those numbers ready for us. Thanks."

At this point, Brian sits down and Julie comes forward to give her presentation. Immediately some colorful slides are projected on the wall behind her as Max operates the computer.

"Thanks, Brian. Well, here's the data we have been able to gather from some marketing research. The acceptance of our new product in the market can be high, medium, or low." Julie is pointing to some figures projected on the wall behind her. "Our estimates indicate that high acceptance would result in profits of $8.0 million and that medium acceptance would give us $4.0 million. In the unfortunate case of a poor reception by our customers, we still expect $2.2 million in profit. I should mention that these profits do not include the additional costs of marketing or R&D expenses."

"So, you are saying that in the worst case we'll make barely more money than with the current product?" asks Brian.

"Yes, that's what I am saying."

"What budget would you need for the marketing of our DSS with the road scanner?" asks Marc.

"For that we would need an additional $200,000 on top of what has already been included in the profit estimates," Julie replies.

"What are the chances of ending up with a high, medium, or low acceptance of the new DSS?" asks Brian.

"We can see those numbers at the bottom of the slide," says Julie, while she is turning toward the projection behind her. There is a 30 percent chance of high market acceptance and a 20 percent chance of low market acceptance.

At this point, Marc moves in his seat and asks: "Given all these numbers and bits of information, what are you suggesting that we do?"

a. Organize the available data on cost and profit estimates in a table.

b. Formulate the problem in a decision tree. Clearly distinguish between decision and event nodes.

c. Calculate the expected payoffs for each node in the decision tree.

d. What is BAAG's optimal policy according to Bayes' decision rule?

e. What would be the expected value of perfect information on the outcome of the research effort?

f. What would be the expected value of perfect information on the outcome of the development effort?

g. Marc is a risk-averse decision maker. In a number of interviews, his utility function for money was assessed to be

$$U(M) = \frac{1 - e^{-\frac{M}{12}}}{1 - e^{-\frac{1}{12}}}$$

where M is the company's net profit in units of hundreds of thousands of dollars (e.g., $M = 8$ would imply a net profit of $800,000). Using Marc's utility function, calculate the utility for each terminal branch of the decision tree.

h. Determine the expected utilities for all nodes in the decision tree.

i. Based on Marc's utility function, what is BAAG's optimal policy?

j. Based on Marc's utility function, what would be the expected value of perfect information on the outcome of the research effort?

k. Based on Marc's utility function, what would be the expected value of perfect information on the outcome of the development effort?

Chapter Ten

Forecasting

Learning objectives

After completing this chapter, you should be able to

1. Describe some important types of forecasting applications.
2. Identify two common measures of the accuracy of forecasting methods.
3. Adjust forecasting data to consider seasonal patterns.
4. Describe several forecasting methods that use the pattern of historical data to forecast a future value.
5. Apply these methods either by hand or with the software provided.
6. Compare these methods to identify the conditions when each is particularly suitable.
7. Describe and apply an approach to forecasting that relates the quantity of interest to one or more other quantities.
8. Describe several forecasting methods that use expert judgment.

How much will the economy grow over the next year? Where is the stock market headed? What about interest rates? How will consumer tastes be changing? What will be the hot new products?

Forecasters have answers to all these questions. Unfortunately, these answers will more than likely be wrong. Nobody can accurately predict the future every time.

Nevertheless, the future success of any business depends heavily on how savvy its management is in spotting trends and developing appropriate strategies. The leaders of the best companies often seem to have a sixth sense for when to change direction to stay a step ahead of the competition, but this sixth sense actually is guided by frequent use of the best forecasting techniques. These companies seldom get into trouble by badly misestimating what the demand will be for their products. Many other companies do. The ability to forecast well makes the difference.

When historical sales data are available, some proven **statistical forecasting methods** have been developed for using these data to forecast future demand. Such methods assume that historical trends will continue, so management then needs to make adjustments to reflect current changes in the marketplace.

Several **judgmental forecasting methods** that solely use expert judgment also are available. These methods are especially valuable when little or no historical sales data are available or when major changes in the marketplace make these data unreliable for forecasting purposes.

Forecasting product demand is just one important application of these forecasting methods. For other applications, forecasts might be needed for such diverse quantities as the need for spare parts, production yields, and staffing needs. Forecasting techniques also are heavily used for forecasting economic trends on a regional, national, or even international level.

We begin the chapter with an overview of forecasting techniques. Section 10.2 then introduces a case study that will be carried through much of the chapter. Sections 10.3–10.5 focus on statistical forecasting methods and Section 10.6 on judgmental forecasting methods. A supplement to this chapter on the CD-ROM describes an Excel add-in called CB Predictor that is designed to perform statistical forecasting within a spreadsheet environment. CB Predictor, Excel templates for various forecasting methods, and a forecasting module that is part of your Interactive Management Science Modules are included in your MS Courseware.

10.1 AN OVERVIEW OF FORECASTING TECHNIQUES

To illustrate various forecasting techniques, consider the following problem.

A Forecasting Problem

Fastchips is a leading producer of microprocessors. Six months ago, it launched the sales of its latest microprocessor. The month-by-month sales (in thousands) of the microprocessor over the initial six months have been

$$17 \quad 25 \quad 24 \quad 26 \quad 30 \quad 28$$

In this highly competitive market, sales can shift rather quickly, depending largely on when competitors launch the latest version of their microprocessors. Therefore, it always is important to have a forecast of the next month's sales to guide what the production level should be.

Let us look at some alternative ways of obtaining this forecast.

Some Forecasting Techniques

The most straightforward technique is the **last-value forecasting method** (sometimes also called the *naive method*), which says simply to use the last month's sales as the forecast for the next month. For Fastchips, this yields

$$\text{Forecast} = 28$$

This is a reasonable forecasting method when conditions tend to change so quickly that sales before the last month's are not a reliable indicator of future sales.

The **averaging forecasting method** says to use the average of *all* the monthly sales to date as the forecast for the next month. This gives

$$\text{Forecast} = \frac{17 + 25 + 24 + 26 + 30 + 28}{6} = 25$$

for Fastchips. This is a reasonable forecasting method when conditions tend to remain so stable that even the earliest sales are a reliable indicator of future sales (a dubious assumption for Fastchips).

The **moving-average forecasting method** provides a middle ground between the last-value and averaging method by using the average of the monthly sales for only the most recent months as the forecast for the next month. The number of months being used must be specified. For example, a three-month moving average forecast for Fastchips is

$$\text{Forecast} = \frac{26 + 30 + 28}{3} = 28$$

This is a reasonable forecasting method when conditions tend to change occasionally but not extremely rapidly.

The **exponential smoothing forecasting method** provides a more sophisticated version of the moving-average method in the way that it gives primary consideration to sales in only the most recent months. In particular, rather than giving equal weight to the sales in the most recent months, the exponential smoothing method gives the greatest weight to the last month and then progressively smaller weights to the older months. (The formula for this method will be given in Section 10.3.) This forecasting method is a reasonable one under the same conditions as described for the moving-average method.

Additional sophistication is added to the exponential smoothing forecasting method by using **exponential smoothing with trend.** This latter method adjusts exponential smoothing by also directly considering any current upward or downward trend in the sales. (Formulas are given in Section 10.3.)

If the sales data show a relatively constant trend in some direction, then **linear regression** provides a reasonable forecasting method. This method uses a two-dimensional graph with sales measured along the vertical axis and time measured along the horizontal axis. After plotting the sales data month by month, this method finds a line passing through the midst of the data as closely as possible. The extension of the line into future months provides the forecast of sales in these future months.

Section 10.5 fully presents the linear regression method. The other forecasting methods mentioned above are described in detail in Section 10.3. The discussion in both sections is in the context of the case study introduced in Section 10.2.

Which of these forecasting techniques should Fastchips use? On the basis of the sales data so far, it appears that either the moving-average forecasting method or the exponential smoothing forecasting method would be a reasonable choice. However, as time goes on, further analysis should be done to see which of the forecasting methods provides the smallest **forecasting errors** (the difference between the actual sales and forecasted sales). After determining the forecasting error in each of a number of months for any forecasting method, one common measure of the accuracy of that method is the *average* of these forecasting errors. (This average is referred to as the **mean absolute deviation,** which is abbreviated as **MAD.**) Because large forecasting errors are far more serious than small ones, another popular measure of the accuracy of a forecasting method is the average of the *square* of its forecasting errors. (This measure is referred to as the **mean square error,** which is abbreviated as **MSE.**) Throughout this chapter, MAD and MSE values are used to help analyze which forecasting method should be used in the case study.

For some types of products, the sales to be anticipated in a particular month are influenced by the time of the year. For example, a product which is popular for Christmas presents could well have December sales that are twice as large as January sales. For any product influenced by seasonal factors, it is important to incorporate these seasonal factors into the forecasts. This plays a fundamental role in the analysis of the case study throughout the chapter.

Although we have described the various forecasting techniques in terms of forecasts of sales month by month for the Fastchips problem, other forecasting applications can be somewhat different. The quantity being forecasted might be something other than sales and the periods involved might be something like quarters or years instead of months. For example, this chapter's case study involves forecasts of the number of calls to a call center on a quarterly basis.

When using any of these forecasting techniques, it is also important to look behind the numbers to try to understand what is driving the quantity being forecasted in order to adjust the forecast provided by the forecasting technique in an appropriate way. This is a key lesson provided by the analysis of the case study. When there are factors that are driving changes in the quantity being forecasted, the judgmental forecasting methods described in Section 10.6 also can play a useful role.

Review
Questions

1. What is the last-value forecasting method and when might it be a reasonable method to use?
2. What is the averaging forecasting method and when might it be a reasonable method to use?
3. What is the moving-average forecasting method and when might it be a reasonable method to use?
4. How does the exponential smoothing forecasting method differ from the moving-average forecasting method?
5. How does exponential smoothing with trend differ from the exponential smoothing forecasting method?
6. How does the linear regression forecasting method obtain forecasts?
7. What are the two main measures of the accuracy of a forecasting method?

10.2 A CASE STUDY: THE COMPUTER CLUB WAREHOUSE (CCW) PROBLEM

The Computer Club Warehouse (commonly referred to as CCW) sells various computer products at bargain prices by taking telephone orders (as well as website and fax orders) directly from customers. Its products include desktop and laptop computers, peripherals, hardware accessories, supplies, software (including games), and computer-related furniture. The company mails catalogs to its customers and numerous prospective customers several times per year, as well as publishing minicatalogs in computer magazines. These catalogs prominently display the 800 toll-free telephone number to call to place an order. These calls come into the company's call center.

The CCW Call Center

The call center is never closed. During busy hours, it is staffed by dozens of agents. Their sole job is to take and process customer orders over the telephone. (A second, much smaller call center uses another 800 number for callers making inquiries or reporting problems. This case study focuses on just the main call center.)

New agents receive a week's training before beginning work. This training emphasizes how to efficiently and courteously process an order. An agent is expected not to average more than five minutes per call. Records are kept and an agent who does not meet this target by the end of the probationary period will not be retained. Although the agents are well-paid, the tedium and time pressure associated with the job leads to a fairly high turnover rate.

A large number of telephone trunks are provided for incoming calls. If an agent is not free when the call arrives, it is placed on hold with a recorded message and background music. If all the trunks are in use (referred to as *saturation*), an incoming call receives a busy signal instead.

Although some customers who receive a busy signal, or who hang up after being on hold too long, will try again later until they get through, many do not. Therefore, it is very important to have enough agents on duty to minimize these problems. On the other hand, because of the high labor costs for the agents, CCW tries to avoid having so many agents on duty that they have significant idle time.

Consequently, obtaining forecasts of the demand for the agents is crucial to the company.

The Call Center Manager, Lydia Weigelt

The current manager of the call center is Lydia Weigelt. As the top student in her graduating class from business school, she was wooed by several top companies before choosing CCW. Extremely bright and hard driving, she is being groomed to enter top management at CCW in the coming years.

When Lydia was hired a little over three years ago, she was assigned to her current position in order to learn the business from the ground up. The call center is considered to be the nerve center of the entire CCW operation.

Before Lydia's arrival, the company had suffered from serious management problems with the call center. Orders were not being processed efficiently. A few were even misdirected. Staffing levels never seemed to be right. Management directives to adjust the levels kept over-compensating in the opposite direction. Data needed to get a handle on the staffing level problem hadn't been kept. Morale was low.

All that changed when Lydia arrived. One of her first moves was to install procedures for gathering the data needed to make decisions on staffing levels. The key data included a detailed record of call volume and how much of the volume was being handled by each agent. Efficiency improved substantially. Despite running a tight ship, Lydia took great pains to praise and reward good work. Morale increased dramatically.

Although gratified by the great improvement in the operation of the call center, Lydia still has one major frustration. At the end of each quarter, when she knows how many agents are not being retained at the end of their probationary period, she makes a decision on how many new agents to hire to go through the next training session (held at the beginning of each quarter). She has developed an excellent procedure for estimating the staffing level needed to cover any particular call volume. However, each time she has used this procedure to set the staffing level for the upcoming quarter, based on her forecast of the call volume, the forecast usually has turned out to be considerably off. Therefore, she still isn't getting the right staffing levels.

Better forecasts of call volume are needed.

Lydia has concluded that her next project should be to develop a better forecasting method to replace the current one.

Lydia's Current Forecasting Method

Thanks to Lydia's data-gathering procedures installed shortly after her arrival, reliable data on call volume now are available for the past three years. Figure 10.1 shows the average number of calls received per day in each of the four quarters of these years. The right side also displays these same data to show the pattern graphically. (This graph was generated from the data by choosing "Chart" under the Insert menu, selecting the Line chart type, and following the directions of the Chart Wizard.)

L. L. Bean, Inc., is a widely known retailer of high-quality outdoor goods and apparel, with an annual sales volume of over $1.4 billion. The company markets its products primarily through the mailing of millions of copies of various catalogs each year. Thus, most of its sales volume is generated through orders taken at the company's call center, which is open seven days per week. The sales volume is seasonal, with an especially large spike during the Christmas season. The sales within each week tend to slowly decrease from Monday through Sunday, except for a sharp drop on the day of a holiday and a sharp rise immediately after the arrival of a catalog.

Staffing the call center at an appropriate level day by day is critical for the company. Understaffing results in lost sales from customers who don't get through to the call center and then give up. Overstaffing results in excessive labor costs. Therefore, accurate forecasts of daily call volumes are needed.

Because previous subjective forecasting methods had proven to be unsatisfactory, L. L. Bean management hired a team of management science consultants to improve the forecasting procedures. After L. L. Bean call-center managers compiled an exhaustive list of 35 possible factors that could logically affect call volumes, this team developed and helped implement a highly sophisticated time-series forecasting method (the Box and Jenkins autoregressive/integrated/moving-average method). This methodology incorporates all the important factors, including seasonal patterns, the effect of holidays, and the effect of the arrival of catalogs. Each week, forecasts are obtained for the daily call volumes for the next three weeks. The forecasts for the last of the three weeks are then used to determine the Monday-to-Sunday work schedule at the call center two weeks in advance.

The improved precision of this forecasting methodology is estimated to have saved L. L. Bean $300,000 annually through enhanced scheduling efficiency. The computerization of the methodology also greatly reduced the labor costs required to prepare the forecast every week.

Source: B. H. Andrews and S. M. Cunningham, "L. L. Bean Improves Call-Center Forecasting," *Interfaces* 25, no. 6 (November–December 1995), pp. 1–13.

Forecasts need to take into account the seasonal pattern of increased sales in Quarter 4 due to Christmas purchases.

Note that the sales in Quarter 4 jump up each year due to Christmas purchases. When Lydia first joined CCW, the president told her about the "25 percent rule" that the company had traditionally used to forecast call volume (and sales).

The 25 Percent Rule: Since sales are relatively stable through the year except for a substantial increase during the Christmas season, assume that each quarter's call volume will be the same as for the preceding quarter, except for adding 25 percent for Quarter 4. Thus,

Forecast for Quarter 2 = Call volume for Quarter 1
Forecast for Quarter 3 = Call volume for Quarter 2
Forecast for Quarter 4 = 1.25(Call volume for Quarter 3)

The forecast for the next year's Quarter 1 then would be obtained from the current year's Quarter 4 by

FIGURE 10.1

The average number of calls received per day at the CCW call center in each of the four quarters of the past three years.

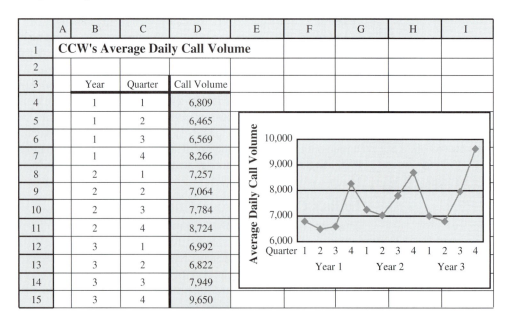

	A	B	C	D	E	F	G	H	I
1	CCW's Average Daily Call Volume								
2									
3		Year	Quarter	Call Volume					
4		1	1	6,809					
5		1	2	6,465					
6		1	3	6,569					
7		1	4	8,266					
8		2	1	7,257					
9		2	2	7,064					
10		2	3	7,784					
11		2	4	8,724					
12		3	1	6,992					
13		3	2	6,822					
14		3	3	7,949					
15		3	4	9,650					

FIGURE 10.2

This spreadsheet records the results of applying the 25 percent rule over the past three years to forecast the average daily call volume for the upcoming quarter.

	A	B	C	D	E	F	G	H	I	J	K	L
1		**Lydia's Current Forecasting Method for CCW's Average Daily Call Volume**										
2												
3						**Forecasting**						
4		**Year**	**Quarter**	**Data**	**Forecast**	**Error**		**Mean Absolute Deviation**				
5		1	1	6,809				MAD =	424			
6		1	2	6,465	6,809	344						
7		1	3	6,569	6,465	104		**Mean Square Error**				
8		1	4	8,266	8,211	55		MSE =	317,815			
9		2	1	7,257	6,613	644						
10		2	2	7,064	7,257	193						
11		2	3	7,784	7,064	720						
12		2	4	8,724	9,730	1,006						
13		3	1	6,992	6,979	13						
14		3	2	6,822	6,992	170						
15		3	3	7,949	6,822	1,127						
16		3	4	9,650	9,936	286						
17		4	1		7,720							
18		4	2									
19		4	3									
20		4	4									

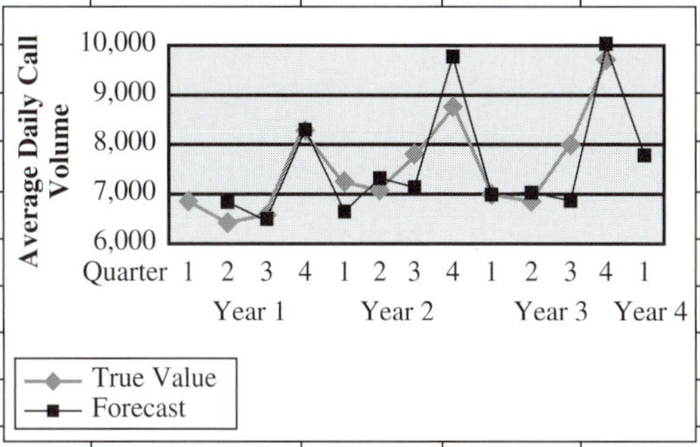

Range Name	Cells
Data	D5:D20
Forecast	E5:E20
ForecastingError	F5:F20

	E	F
3		**Forecasting**
4	**Forecast**	**Error**
5		
6	=D5	=ABS(D6-E6)
7	=D6	=ABS(D7-E7)
8	=1.25*D7	=ABS(D8-E8)
9	=D8/1.25	=ABS(D9-E9)
10	=D9	=ABS(D10-E10)
11	:	:
12	:	:

	H	I
5	MAD =	=AVERAGE(ForecastingError)

	H	I
8	MSE =	=SUMSQ(ForecastingError)/ COUNT(ForecastingError)

$$\text{Forecast for next Quarter 1} = \frac{\text{Call volume for Quarter 4}}{1.25}$$

This is the forecasting method that Lydia has been using.

Figure 10.2 shows the forecasts that Lydia obtained with this method. Column F gives the **forecasting error** (the deviation of the forecast from what then turned out to be the true value of the call volume) in each case. Since the total of the 11 forecasting errors is 4,662, the average is

$$\text{Average forecasting error} = \frac{4{,}662}{11}$$

$$= 424$$

As mentioned in section 10.1, the average forecasting error is commonly called **MAD,** which stands for **mean absolute deviation.** Its formula is

MAD is simply the average of the forecasting errors.

$$\text{MAD} = \frac{\text{Sum of forecasting errors}}{\text{Number of forecasts}}$$

Thus, in this case, cell I5 gives

$$\text{MAD} = 424$$

To put this value of MAD = 424 into perspective, note that 424 is over 5 percent of the average daily call volume in most quarters. With forecasting errors ranging as high as 1,127, two of the errors are well over 10 percent. Although errors of this size are common in typical applications of forecasting, greater accuracy is needed for this particular application. Errors of 5 and 10 percent make it impossible to properly set the staffing level for a quarter. No wonder Lydia is *mad* about the poor job that the 25 percent rule is doing. A better forecasting method is needed.

Another popular measure of the accuracy of forecasting methods is called the **mean square error** and is abbreviated as **MSE.** Its formula is

> MSE is the average of the *square* of the forecasting errors.

$$\text{MSE} = \frac{\text{Sum of square of forecasting errors}}{\text{Number of forecasts}}$$

Thus, in Figure 10.2,

$$\text{MSE} = \frac{(344)^2 + (104)^2 + \cdots + (286)^2}{11}$$

$$= 317{,}815$$

> A bad forecasting error greatly increases the value of the MSE.

as given in cell I8. The advantage of squaring the forecasting errors is that it increases the weight of the large errors relative to the weight given to the small errors. Small errors are only to be expected with even the best forecasting methods and, since such errors have no serious consequences, decreasing their weight is desirable. It is the large forecasting errors that have serious consequences. Therefore, it is good to give a relatively large penalty to a forecasting method that occasionally allows large forecasting errors while rewarding a forecasting method that consistently keeps the errors reasonably small. When comparing two such methods, this can result in the former kind of method receiving the larger value of MSE even though it has the smaller MAD value. Thus, MSE provides a useful complement to MAD by providing additional information about how consistently a forecasting method avoids seriously large errors. However, the disadvantage of MSE compared to MAD is a greater difficulty in interpreting the significance of its value for an individual forecasting method. Consequently, Lydia (who is familiar with both measures) will focus most of her attention on MAD values while keeping her eye on MSE values as well.

The Plan to Find a Better Forecasting Method

Lydia remembers taking a management science course in college. She recalls that one of the topics in the course was *forecasting,* so she decides to review her textbook and class notes on this topic.

This review reminds her that she is dealing with what is called a *time series.*

A **time series** is a series of observations over time of some quantity of interest. For example, the series of observations of average daily call volume for the most recent 12 quarters, as given in Figure 10.1, constitute a time series.

She also is reminded that a variety of statistical methods are available for using the historical data from a time series to forecast a future observation in the series. Her task now is to review these methods and assess which one is best suited for her particular forecasting problem.

To assist her in this task for a few weeks, Lydia gains approval from the CCW president to contract for the services of a consultant (a former classmate) from a management science consulting firm that specializes largely in forecasting.

The next section describes their approach to the problem.

Review Questions

1. How does the Computer Club Warehouse (CCW) operate?
2. What are the consequences of not having enough agents on duty in the CCW call center? Of having too many?
3. Who is the call center manager? What is her current major frustration?

4. What is CCW's 25 percent rule?
5. What is MAD?
6. What is MSE?
7. What is a time series?

10.3   APPLYING TIME-SERIES FORECASTING METHODS TO THE CASE STUDY

Figure 10.1 in the preceding section highlights the seasonal pattern of CCW's call volumes, with a large jump up each fourth quarter due to Christmas shopping. Therefore, before considering specific forecasting methods, Lydia and the consultant begin by addressing how to deal with this seasonal pattern.

Considering Seasonal Effects

For many years, the folklore at CCW has been that the call volume (and sales) will be pretty stable over the first three quarters of a year and then will jump up by about 25 percent in Quarter 4. This has been the basis for the 25 percent rule.

To check how close this folklore still is to reality, the consultant uses the data previously given in Figure 10.1 to calculate the average daily call volume for each quarter over the past three years. For example, the average for Quarter 1 is

$$\text{Average (Quarter 1)} = \frac{6{,}809 + 7{,}257 + 6{,}992}{3}$$

$$= 7{,}019$$

These averages for all four quarters are shown in the second column of Table 10.1. Underneath this column, the *overall average* over all four quarters is calculated to be 7,529. Dividing the average for each quarter by this overall average gives the *seasonal factor* shown in the third column.

> In general, the **seasonal factor** for any period of a year (a quarter, a month, etc.) measures how that period compares to the overall average for an entire year. Specifically, using historical data, the seasonal factor is calculated to be

$$\text{Seasonal factor} = \frac{\text{Average for the period}}{\text{Overall average}}$$

Your MS Courseware includes an Excel template for calculating these seasonal factors. Figure 10.3 shows this template applied to the CCW problem.

This Excel template calculates seasonal factors on either a monthly or quarterly basis.

TABLE 10.1
Calculation of the Seasonal Factors for the CCW Problem

Quarter	Three-Year Average	Seasonal Factor
1	7,019	$\frac{7{,}019}{7{,}529} = 0.93$
2	6,784	$\frac{6{,}784}{7{,}529} = 0.90$
3	7,434	$\frac{7{,}434}{7{,}529} = 0.99$
4	8,880	$\frac{8{,}880}{7{,}529} = 1.18$
	Total = 30,117	
	Average = $\frac{30{,}117}{4} = 7{,}529$	

FIGURE 10.3

The Excel template in your MS Courseware for calculating seasonal factors is applied here to the CCW problem.

	A	B	C	D	E	F	G
1	**Estimating Seasonal Factors for CCW**						
2							
3				**True**			
4		**Year**	**Quarter**	**Value**		**Type of Seasonality**	
5		1	1	6,809		Quarterly	
6		1	2	6,465			
7		1	3	6,569			
8		1	4	8,266			**Estimate for**
9		2	1	7,257		**Quarter**	**Seasonal Factor**
10		2	2	7,064		1	0.9323
11		2	3	7,784		2	0.9010
12		2	4	8,724		3	0.9873
13		3	1	6,992		4	1.1794
14		3	2	6,822			
15		3	3	7,949			
16		3	4	9,650			

Range Name	Cells
SeasonalFactor	G10:G21
TrueValue	D5:D41
TypeOfSeasonality	F5

	G
8	**Estimate for**
9	**Seasonal Factor**
10	=AVERAGE(D5,D9,D13)/AVERAGE(TrueValue)
11	=AVERAGE(D6,D10,D14)/AVERAGE(TrueValue)
12	=AVERAGE(D7,D11,D15)/AVERAGE(TrueValue)
13	=AVERAGE(D8,D12,D16)/AVERAGE(TrueValue)

Note the significant differences in the seasonal factors for the first three quarters, with Quarter 3 considerably above the other two. This makes sense to Lydia, who has long suspected that back-to-school buying should give a small boost to sales in Quarter 3.

In contrast to the 25 percent rule, the seasonal factor for Quarter 4 is only 19 percent higher than that for Quarter 3. (However, the Quarter 4 factor *is* about 25 percent above 0.94, which is the *average* of the seasonal factors for the first three quarters.)

Although data on call volumes are not available prior to the most recent three years, reliable sales data have been kept. Upon checking these data several years back, Lydia finds the same seasonal patterns occurring.

Conclusion: The seasonal factors given in Table 10.1 appear to accurately reflect subtle but important differences in all the seasons. Therefore, these factors now will be used, instead of the 25 percent rule, to indicate seasonal patterns until such time as future data indicate a shift in these patterns.

The Seasonally Adjusted Time Series

It is much easier to analyze sales data and detect new trends if the data are first adjusted to remove the effect of seasonal patterns. To remove the seasonal effects from the time series shown in Figure 10.1, each of these average daily call volumes needs to be divided by the corresponding seasonal factor given in Table 10.1 and Figure 10.3. Thus, the formula is

$$\text{Seasonally adjusted call volume} = \frac{\text{Actual call volume}}{\text{Seasonal factor}}$$

Applying this formula to all 12 call volumes in Figure 10.1 gives the seasonally adjusted call volumes shown in column F of the Excel template in Figure 10.4.

FIGURE 10.4

The seasonally adjusted time series for the CCW problem obtained by dividing each actual average daily call volume in Figure 10.1 by the corresponding seasonal factor obtained in Figure 10.3.

	A	B	C	D	E	F	G	H	I	J
1		**Seasonally Adjusted Time Series for CCW**								
2										
3				**Seasonal**	**Actual**	**Seasonally Adjusted**				
4		**Year**	**Quarter**	**Factor**	**Call Volume**	**Call Volume**				
5		1	1	0.93	6,809	7,322				
6		1	2	0.90	6,465	7,183				
7		1	3	0.99	6,569	6,635				
8		1	4	1.18	8,266	7,005				
9		2	1	0.93	7,257	7,803				
10		2	2	0.90	7,064	7,849				
11		2	3	0.99	7,784	7,863				
12		2	4	1.18	8,724	7,393				
13		3	1	0.93	6,992	7,518				
14		3	2	0.90	6,822	7,580				
15		3	3	0.99	7,949	8,029				
16		3	4	1.18	9,650	8,178				

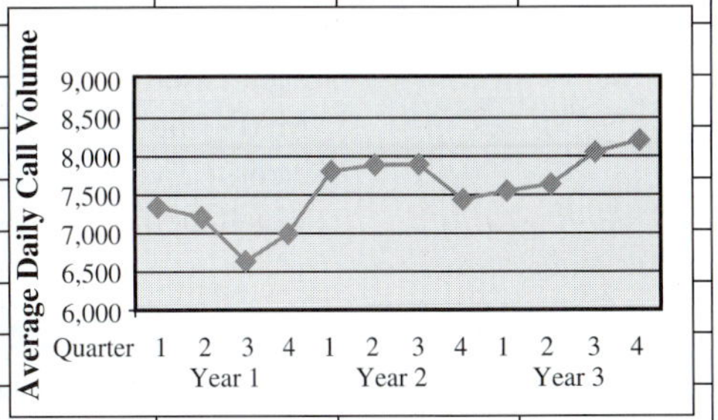

	F
3	**Seasonally Adjusted**
4	**Call Volume**
5	=E5/D5
6	=E6/D6
7	=E7/D7
8	=E8/D8
9	:
10	:

In effect, these seasonally adjusted call volumes show what the call volumes would have been if the calls that occur because of the time of the year (Christmas shopping, back-to-school shopping, etc.) had been spread evenly throughout the year instead. Compare the plots in Figures 10.4 and 10.1. After considering the smaller vertical scale in Figure 10.4, note how much less fluctuation this figure has than Figure 10.1 because of removing seasonal effects. However, this figure still is far from completely flat because fluctuations in call volume occur for other reasons besides just seasonal effects. For example, hot new products attract a flurry of calls. A jump also occurs just after the mailing of a catalog. Some random fluctuations occur without any apparent explanation. Figure 10.4 enables seeing and analyzing these fluctuations in sales volumes that are not caused by seasonal effects.

Removing seasonal effects provides a much clearer picture of trends.

The pattern in these remaining fluctuations in the **seasonally adjusted time series** (especially the pattern for the most recent data points) is particularly helpful for forecasting where the next data point will fall. Thus, in Figure 10.4, the data points fall in the range between 6,635 and 8,178, with an average of 7,529. However, the last few data points are trending upward above this average, and the last point is the highest in the entire time series. This suggests that the next data point for the upcoming quarter probably will be above the 7,529 average and may well be near or even above the last data point of 8,178.

The various **time-series forecasting methods** use different approaches to projecting forward the pattern in the seasonally adjusted time series to forecast the next data point. The main methods will be presented in this section.

After obtaining a forecast for the seasonally adjusted time series, all these methods then convert this forecast to a forecast of the actual call volume (without seasonal adjustments), as outlined below.

Outline for Forecasting Call Volume

If seasonal adjustments are not needed, you can obtain your forecast directly from the original time series and then skip step 3.

1. Select a time-series forecasting method.
2. Apply this method to the seasonally adjusted time series to obtain a forecast of the seasonally adjusted call volume for the next quarter.[1]
3. Multiply this forecast by the corresponding seasonal factor in Table 10.1 to obtain a forecast of the actual call volume (without seasonal adjustment).

The following descriptions of forecasting methods focus on how to perform step 2, that is, how to forecast the next data point for a given time series. We also include a spreadsheet in each case that applies steps 2 and 3 throughout the past three years and then calculates both MAD (the average forecasting error) and MSE (the average of the square of the forecasting errors). Lydia and the consultant are paying particular attention to the MAD values to assess which method seems best suited for forecasting CCW call volumes.

The Last-Value Forecasting Method

The **last-value forecasting method** ignores all the data points in a time series except the last one. It then uses this last value as the forecast of what the next data point will turn out to be, so the formula is simply

$$\text{Forecast} = \text{Last value}$$

Figure 10.5 shows what would have happened if this method had been applied to the CCW problem over the past three years. (We are supposing that the seasonal factors given in Table 10.1 already were being used then.) Column E gives the true values of the seasonally adjusted call volumes from column F of Figure 10.4. Each of these values then becomes the seasonally adjusted forecast for the *next* quarter, as shown in column F.

Rows 22–33 show separate plots of these values in columns E and F. Note how the plot of the seasonally adjusted forecasts follows exactly the same path as the plot of the seasonally adjusted call volumes but shifted to the right by one quarter. Therefore, each time there is a large shift up or down in the call volume, the forecasts are one quarter late in catching up with the shift.

Multiplying each seasonally adjusted forecast in column F by the corresponding seasonal factor in column K gives the forecast of the actual call volume (without seasonal adjustment) presented in column G. The difference between this forecast and the actual call volume in column D gives the forecasting error in column H.

Thus, column G is using the following formula:

$$\text{Actual forecast} = \text{Seasonal factor} \times \text{Seasonally adjusted forecast}$$

as indicated by the equations at the bottom of the figure. For example, since cell K9 gives 0.93 as the seasonal factor for Quarter 1, the forecast of the actual call volume for Year 2, Quarter 1 given in cell G10 is

$$\text{Actual forecast} = (0.93)(7,005) = 6,515$$

Since the true value of this call volume turned out to be 7,257, the forecasting error calculated in cell H10 for this quarter is

$$\text{Forecasting error} = 7,257 - 6,515 = 742$$

Summing these forecasting errors over all 11 quarters of forecasts gives a total of 3,246, so the average forecasting error given in cell K23 is

$$\text{MAD} = \frac{3,246}{11} = 295$$

---

[1] This forecast also can be projected ahead to subsequent quarters, but we are focusing on just the next quarter.

FIGURE 10.5
The Excel template in your MS Courseware for the last-value method with seasonal adjustments is applied here to the CCW problem.

	A	B	C	D	E	F	G	H	I	J	K
1		**Last-Value Forecasting Method with Seasonality for CCW**									
2											
3					**Seasonally**	**Seasonally**					
4				**True**	**Adjusted**	**Adjusted**	**Actual**	**Forecasting**			
5		**Year**	**Quarter**	**Value**	**Value**	**Forecast**	**Forecast**	**Error**			**Type of Seasonality**
6		1	1	6,809	7,322						Quarterly
7		1	2	6,465	7,183	7,322	6,589	124			
8		1	3	6,569	6,635	7,183	7,112	543		**Quarter**	**Seasonal Factor**
9		1	4	8,266	7,005	6,635	7,830	436		1	0.93
10		2	1	7,257	7,803	7,005	6,515	742		2	0.90
11		2	2	7,064	7,849	7,803	7,023	41		3	0.99
12		2	3	7,784	7,863	7,849	7,770	14		4	1.18
13		2	4	8,724	7,393	7,863	9,278	554			
14		3	1	6,992	7,518	7,393	6,876	116			
15		3	2	6,822	7,580	7,518	6,766	56			
16		3	3	7,949	8,029	7,580	7,504	445			
17		3	4	9,650	8,178	8,029	9,475	175			
18		4	1			8,178	7,606				
19		4	2								
20											
21											
22											**Mean Absolute Deviation**
23											MAD = 295
24											
25											**Mean Square Error**
26											MSE = 145.909
27											
28											
29											
30											
31											
32											
33											
34											
35											

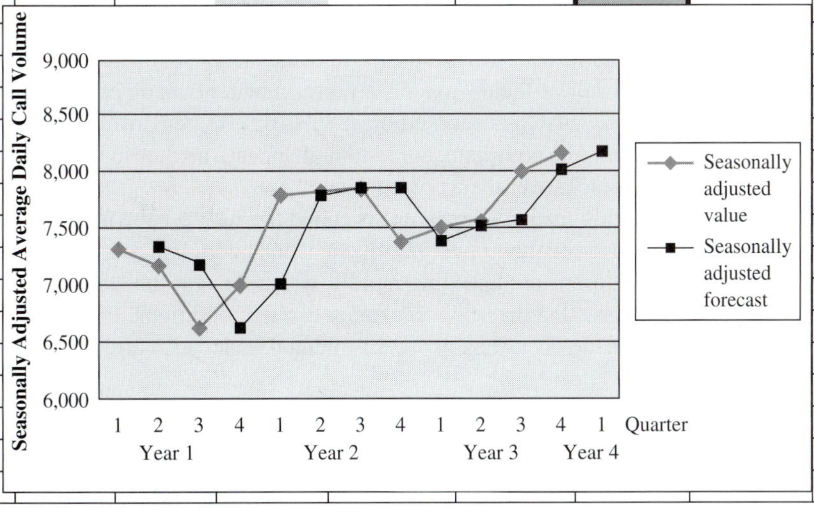

Range Name	Cells
ActualForecast	G6:G30
ForecastingError	H6:H30
MAD	K23
MSE	K26
SeasonalFactor	K9:K20
SeasonallyAdjustedForecast	F6:F30
SeasonallyAdjustedValue	E6:E30
TrueValue	D6:D30
TypeOfSeasonality	K6

	E	F	G	H
3	**Seasonally**	**Seasonally**		
4	**Adjusted**	**Adjusted**	**Actual**	**Forecasting**
5	**Value**	**Forecast**	**Forecast**	**Error**
6	=D6/K9			
7	=D7/K10	=E6	=K10*F7	=ABS(D7-G7)
8	=D8/K11	=E7	=K11*F8	=ABS(D8-G8)
9	=D9/K12	=E8	=K12*F9	=ABS(D9-G9)
10	=D10/K9	=E9	=K9*F10	=ABS(D10-G10)
11	=D11/K10	=E10	=K10*F11	=ABS(D11-G11)
12	:	:	:	:
13	:	:	:	:

	J	K
23	MAD =	=AVERAGE(ForecastingError)

	J	K
26	MSE =	=SUMSQ(ForecastingError)/COUNT(ForecastingError)

This compares with MAD = 424 for the 25 percent rule that Lydia has been using (as described in the preceding section).

Similarly, the average of the *square* of these forecasting errors is calculated in cell K26 as

$$\text{MSE} = \frac{(124)^2 + (543)^2 + \cdots + (175)^2}{11}$$

$$= 145{,}909$$

This value also is considerably less than the corresponding value, MSE = 317,815, shown in Figure 10.2 for the 25 percent rule.

Except for its graph, Figure 10.5 displays one of the templates in this chapter's Excel file. In fact, your MS Courseware includes two Excel templates for each of the forecasting methods presented in this section. One template performs all the calculations for you for the case where no seasonal adjustments are needed. The second template does the same when seasonal adjustments are included, as illustrated by this figure. With all templates of the second type, you have complete flexibility for what to enter as the seasonal factors. One option is to *calculate* these factors based on historical data (as was done with another Excel template in Figure 10.3). Another is to *estimate* them based on historical experience, as with the 25 percent rule.

The 25 percent rule actually is a *last-value forecasting method* as well, but with different seasonal factors. Since this rule holds that the call volume in the fourth quarter will average 25 percent more than *each* of the first three quarters, its seasonal factors are essentially 0.94 for Quarters 1, 2, and 3 and 1.18 (25 percent more than 0.94) for Quarter 4. Thus, the lower value of MAD in Figure 10.5 is entirely due to refining the seasonal factors in Table 10.1.

Lydia is enthusiastic to see the substantial improvement obtained by simply refining the seasonal factors. However, the consultant quickly adds a note of caution. The forecasts obtained in Figure 10.5 are using the same data that were used to calculate these refined seasonal factors, which creates some bias for these factors to tend to perform better than on new data (future call volumes). Fortunately, Lydia also has checked older sales data to confirm that these seasonal factors seem quite accurate. The consultant agrees that it appears that these factors should provide a significant improvement over the 25 percent rule.

The last-value forecasting method sometimes is called the **naive method,** because statisticians consider it naive to use just a *sample size of one* when additional relevant data are available. However, when conditions are changing rapidly, it may be that the last value is the only relevant data point for forecasting the next value under current conditions. Therefore, managers who are anything but naive do occasionally use this method under such circumstances.

> This method is a good one to use when conditions are changing rapidly.

The Averaging Forecasting Method

The **averaging forecasting method** goes to the other extreme. Rather than using just a sample size of one, this method uses *all* the data points in the time series and simply *averages* these points. Thus, the forecast of what the next data point will turn out to be is

Forecast = Average of all data to date

Using the corresponding Excel template to apply this method to the CCW problem over the past three years gives the seasonally adjusted forecasts shown in column F of Figure 10.6. At the bottom of the figure, the equation entered into each of the column F cells is just the average of the column E cells in the preceding rows. The middle of the figure shows a plot of these seasonally adjusted forecasts for all three years next to the true values of the seasonally adjusted call volumes. Note how each forecast lies at the average of the preceding call volumes. Therefore, each time there is a large shift in the call volume, the subsequent forecasts are very slow in catching up with the shift.

Multiplying all the seasonally adjusted forecasts in column F by the corresponding seasonal factors in column K then gives the *forecasts of the actual call volumes* shown in column G. Based on the resulting forecasting errors given in column H, the average forecasting error in this case (cell K23) is

MAD = 400

FIGURE 10.6

The Excel template in your MS Courseware for the averaging method with seasonal adjustments is applied here to the CCW problem.

	A	B	C	D	E	F	G	H	I	J	K
1		**Averaging Forecasting Method with Seasonality for CCW**									
2											
3					**Seasonally**	**Seasonally**					
4				**True**	**Adjusted**	**Adjusted**	**Actual**	**Forecasting**			
5		**Year**	**Quarter**	**Value**	**Value**	**Forecast**	**Forecast**	**Error**			**Type of Seasonality**
6		1	1	6,809	7,322						Quarterly
7		1	2	6,465	7,183	7,322	6,589	124			
8		1	3	6,569	6,635	7,252	7,180	611		**Quarter**	**Seasonal Factor**
9		1	4	8,266	7,005	7,047	8,315	49		1	0.93
10		2	1	7,257	7,803	7,036	6,544	713		2	0.90
11		2	2	7,064	7,849	7,190	6,471	593		3	0.99
12		2	3	7,784	7,863	7,300	7,227	557		4	1.18
13		2	4	8,724	7,393	7,380	8,708	16			
14		3	1	6,992	7,518	7,382	6,865	127			
15		3	2	6,822	7,580	7,397	6,657	165			
16		3	3	7,949	8,029	7,415	7,341	608			
17		3	4	9,650	8,178	7,471	8,816	834			
18		4	1			7,530	7,003				
19		4	2								
20											
21											
22											**Mean Absolute Deviation**
23											MAD = 400
24											
25											**Mean Square Error**
26											MSE = 242.876

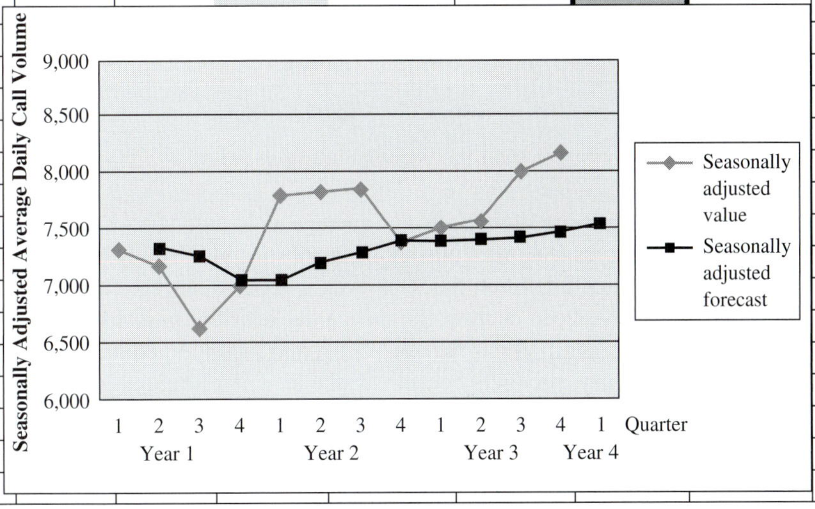

Range Name	Cells
ActualForecast	G6:G30
ForecastingError	H6:H30
MAD	K23
MSE	K26
SeasonalFactor	K9:K20
SeasonallyAdjustedForecast	F6:F30
SeasonallyAdjustedValue	E6:E30
TrueValue	D6:D30
TypeOfSeasonality	K6

	E	F	G	H
3	**Seasonally**	**Seasonally**		
4	**Adjusted**	**Adjusted**	**Actual**	**Forecasting**
5	**Value**	**Forecast**	**Forecast**	**Error**
6	=D6/K9			
7	=D7/K10	=AVERAGE(E$6:E6)	=K10*F7	=ABS(D7-G7)
8	=D8/K11	=AVERAGE(E$6:E7)	=K11*F8	=ABS(D8-G8)
9	=D9/K12	=AVERAGE(E$6:E8)	=K12*F9	=ABS(D9-G9)
10	=D10/K9	=AVERAGE(E$6:E9)	=K9*F10	=ABS(D10-G10)
11	=D11/K10	=AVERAGE(E$6:E10)	=K10*F11	=ABS(D11-G11)
12	:	:	:	:
13	:	:	:	:

	J	K
23	MAD =	=AVERAGE(ForecastingError)

	J	K
26	MSE =	=SUMSQ(ForecastingError)/COUNT(ForecastingError)

An Application Vignette

Taco Bell Corporation has over 6,500 quick-service restaurants in the United States and a growing international market. It serves approximately 2 billion meals per year, generating about $5.4 billion in annual sales income.

At each Taco Bell restaurant, the amount of business is highly variable throughout the day (and from day to day), with a heavy concentration during the normal meal times. Therefore, determining how many employees should be scheduled to perform what functions in the restaurant at any given time is a complex and vexing problem.

To attack this problem, Taco Bell management instructed a team of management scientists (including several consultants) to develop a new labor–management system. The team concluded that the system needed three major components: (1) a forecasting model for predicting customer transactions at any time, (2) a simulation model (such as those described in Chapters 12 and 13) to translate customer transactions to labor requirements, and (3) an integer programming model to schedule employees to satisfy labor requirements and minimize payroll.

To enable application of a forecasting model in each restaurant, a procedure is needed to continually gather data on the number of customer transactions during each 15-minute interval throughout the day, each day of the week. Therefore, the management science team developed and implemented a rolling database containing six weeks of in-store and drive-through transaction data to be stored on each restaurant's computer. After some testing of alternative forecasting methods, the team concluded that a six-week moving average is best. In other words, the forecast of the number of transactions in a particular 15-minute period on a particular day of the week should be the average of the number of transactions during the corresponding period in the preceding six weeks. However, the restaurant manager has the authority to modify the forecast if unusual events distorted the data being used.

The implementation of this forecasting procedure along with the other components of the labor–management system has provided Taco Bell with documented savings of $13 million per year in labor costs.

Source: J. Hueter and W. Swart, "An Integrated Labor–Management System for Taco Bell," *Interfaces* 28, no. 1 (January–February 1998), pp. 75–91.

---

which is considerably larger than the 295 obtained for the last-value forecasting method. Similarly, the average of the square of the forecasting errors given in cell K26 is

$$\text{MSE} = 242{,}876$$

which also is considerably larger than the corresponding value of 145,909 for the last-value forecasting method.

Lydia is quite surprised, since she expected an average to do much better than a sample size of one. The consultant agrees that averaging should perform considerably better if conditions remain the same throughout the time series. However, it appears that the conditions affecting the CCW call volume have been changing significantly over the past three years. The call volume was quite a bit higher in year 2 than in year 1, and then jumped up again late in year 3, apparently as popular new products became available. Therefore, the Year 1 values were not very relevant for forecasting under the changed conditions of years 2 and 3. Including the year 1 call volumes in the overall average caused *every* forecast for years 2 and 3 to be too low, sometimes by large amounts.

The averaging forecasting method is a good one to use when conditions are very stable, which is not the case for CCW.

The Moving-Average Forecasting Method

Rather than using old data that may no longer be relevant, the **moving-average forecasting method** averages the data for only the most recent time periods. Let

n = Number of most recent periods considered particularly relevant for forecasting the next period

Then the forecast for the next period is

$$\text{Forecast} = \text{Average of last } n \text{ values}$$

Lydia and the consultant decide to use $n = 4$, since conditions appear to be relatively stable for only about four quarters (one year) at a time.

With $n = 4$, the first forecast becomes available after four quarters of call volumes have been observed. Thus, the initial seasonally adjusted forecasts in cells F10:F12 of Figure 10.7 are

$$\text{Y2, Q1:} \quad \text{Seas. adj. forecast} = \frac{7{,}322 + 7{,}183 + 6{,}635 + 7{,}005}{4} = 7{,}036$$

FIGURE 10.7

The Excel template in your MS Courseware for the moving-average method with seasonal adjustments is applied here to the CCW problem.

	A	B	C	D	E	F	G	H	I	J	K
1		**Moving-Average Forecasting Method with Seasonality for CCW**									
2											
3					Seasonally	Seasonally					
4				**True**	**Adjusted**	**Adjusted**	**Actual**	**Forecasting**		**Number of previous**	
5		**Year**	**Quarter**	**Value**	**Value**	**Forecast**	**Forecast**	**Error**		**periods to consider**	
6		1	1	6,809	7,322					*n =*	4
7		1	2	6,465	7,183						
8		1	3	6,569	6,635					**Type of Seasonality**	
9		1	4	8,266	7,005					Quarterly	
10		2	1	7,257	7,803	7,036	6,544	713			
11		2	2	7,064	7,849	7,157	6,441	623		**Quarter**	**Seasonal Factor**
12		2	3	7,784	7,863	7,323	7,250	534		1	0.93
13		2	4	8,724	7,393	7,630	9,003	279		2	0.90
14		3	1	6,992	7,518	7,727	7,186	194		3	0.99
15		3	2	6,822	7,580	7,656	6,890	68		4	1.18
16		3	3	7,949	8,029	7,589	7,513	436			
17		3	4	9,650	8,178	7,630	9,004	646			
18		4	1			7,826	7,279				
19		4	2								

	Mean Absolute Deviation	
	MAD =	437
	Mean Square Error	
	MSE =	238,816

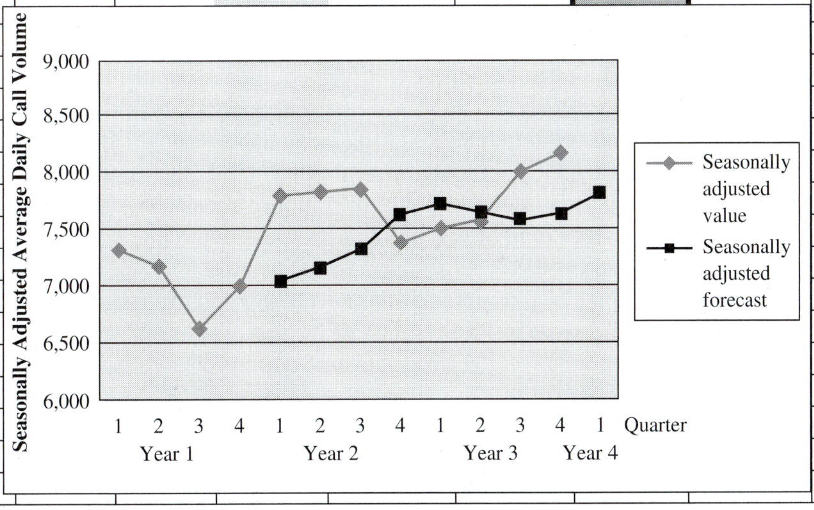

Range Name	Cells
ActualForecast	G6:G30
ForecastingError	H6:H30
MAD	K26
MSE	K29
NumberOfPeriods	K6
SeasonalFactor	K12:K23
SeasonallyAdjustedForecast	F6:F30
SeasonallyAdjustedValue	E6:E30
TrueValue	D6:D30
TypeOfSeasonality	K9

	E	F	G	H
3	**Seasonally**	**Seasonally**		
4	**Adjusted**	**Adjusted**	**Actual**	**Forecasting**
5	**Value**	**Forecast**	**Forecast**	**Error**
6	=D6/K12			
7	=D7/K13			
8	=D8/K14			
9	=D9/K15			
10	=D10/K12	=AVERAGE(E6:E9)	=K12*F10	=ABS(D10-G10)
11	=D11/K13	=AVERAGE(E7:E10)	=K13*F11	=ABS(D11-G11)
12	=D12/K14	=AVERAGE(E8:E11)	=K14*F12	=ABS(D12-G12)
13	=D13/K15	=AVERAGE(E9:E12)	=K15*F13	=ABS(D13-G13)
14	=D14/K12	=AVERAGE(E10:E13)	=K12*F14	=ABS(D14-G14)
15	=D15/K13	=AVERAGE(E11:E14)	=K13*F15	=ABS(D15-G15)
16	:	:	:	:
17	:	:	:	:

	J	K
26	MAD =	=AVERAGE(ForecastingError)

	J	K
29	MSE =	=SUMSQ(ForecastingError)/COUNT(ForecastingError)

Y2, Q2: Seas. adj. forecast $= \dfrac{7{,}183 + 6{,}635 + 7{,}005 + 7{,}803}{4} = 7{,}157$

Y2, Q3: Seas. adj. forecast $= \dfrac{6{,}635 + 7{,}005 + 7{,}803 + 7{,}849}{4} = 7{,}323$

Note how each forecast is updated from the preceding one by lopping off one observation (the oldest one) and adding one new one (the most recent observation).

Column F of Figure 10.7 shows all the seasonally adjusted forecasts obtained in this way with the equations at the bottom. For each of these forecasts, note in the plot how it lies at the average of the four preceding (seasonally adjusted) call volumes. Consequently, each time there is a large shift in the call volume, it takes four quarters for the forecasts to fully catch up with this shift (by which time another shift may already have occurred). Consequently, the average of the eight forecasting errors in column H is

$$\text{MAD} = 437$$

the highest of any of the methods so far, including even the 25 percent rule. The average of the square of the forecasting errors is somewhat better at

$$\text{MSE} = 238{,}816$$

since this is slightly lower than for the averaging method and considerably below the value for the 25 percent rule, but it is still substantially higher than for the last-value method.

Lydia is very puzzled about this surprisingly high MAD value. The moving-average method seemed like a very sensible approach to forecasting, with more rationale behind it than any of the previous methods. (It uses only recent history *and* it uses multiple observations.) So why should it do so poorly?

The moving-averaging forecasting method is a good one to use when conditions don't change much over the number of time periods included in the average.

The consultant explains that this is indeed a very good forecasting method when conditions remain pretty much the same over *n* time periods (or four quarters in this case). For example, the seasonally adjusted call volumes remained reasonably stable throughout year 2 and the first half of year 3. Consequently, the forecasting error dropped all the way down to 68 (cell H15) for the last of these six quarters. However, when conditions shift sharply, as with the big jump up in call volumes at the beginning of year 2, and then again in the middle of year 3, the next few forecasting errors tend to be very large.

Thus, the moving-average method is somewhat slow to respond to changing conditions. One reason is that it places the *same* weight on each of the last *n* values in the time series even though the older values may be less representative of current conditions than the last value observed.

The next method corrects this weighting defect.

The Exponential Smoothing Forecasting Method

The **exponential smoothing forecasting method** modifies the moving-average method by placing the greatest weight on the last value in the time series and then progressively smaller weights on the older values. However, rather than needing to calculate a *weighted average* each time, it uses a simpler formula to obtain the same result.

This formula for forecasting the next value in the time series combines the *last value* and the *last forecast* (the one used one time period ago to forecast this last value) as follows:

$$\text{Forecast} = \alpha(\text{Last value}) + (1 - \alpha)(\text{Last forecast})$$

where α (the Greek letter alpha) is a constant between 0 and 1 called the **smoothing constant.** For example, if the last value in a time series (not the CCW time series) is 24, the last forecast is 20, and $\alpha = 0.25$, then

$$\text{Forecast} = 0.25(24) + 0.75(20)$$

$$= 21$$

Two Excel templates (one without seasonal adjustments and one with) are available in your MS Courseware for applying this formula to generate a series of forecasts (period by period) for a time series when you specify the value of α.

The more unstable the conditions, the larger the smoothing constant α needs to be (but never bigger than 1).

The choice of the value for the smoothing constant α has a substantial effect on the forecast, so the choice should be made with care. A small value (say, $\alpha = 0.1$) is appropriate if conditions are remaining relatively stable. However, a larger value (say, $\alpha = 0.3$) is needed if significant changes in the conditions are occurring relatively frequently. Because of the frequent shifts in the CCW seasonally adjusted time series, Lydia and the consultant conclude that $\alpha = 0.5$ would be an appropriate value. (The values selected for most applications are between 0.1 and 0.3, but a larger value can be used in this kind of situation.)

When making the first forecast, there is no *last forecast* available to plug into the right-hand side of the above formula. Therefore, to get started, a reasonable approach is to make an *initial estimate* of the average value anticipated for the time series. This initial estimate is used as the forecast for the first value, and then the formula is used to forecast the second value onward.

CCW call volumes have averaged just over 7,500 for the past three years, and the level of business just prior to Year 1 was comparable. Consequently, Lydia and the consultant decide to use

$$\text{Initial estimate} = 7,500$$

to begin retrospectively generating the forecasts over the past three years. Recall that the first few seasonally adjusted call volumes are 7,322, 7,183, and 6,635. Thus, using the above formula with $\alpha = 0.5$ for the second quarter onward, the first few seasonally adjusted forecasts are

Y1, Q1:   Seas. adj. forecast $= 7,500$

Y1, Q2:   Seas. adj. forecast $= 0.5(7,322) + 0.5(7,500) = 7,411$

Y1, Q3:   Seas. adj. forecast $= 0.5(7,183) + 0.5(7,411) = 7,297$

Y1, Q4:   Seas. adj. forecast $= 0.5(6,635) + 0.5(7,297) = 6,966$

To see why these forecasts are weighted averages of the time series values to date, look at the calculations for Quarters 2 and 3. Since

$$0.5(7,322) + 0.5(7,500) = 7,411$$

the forecast for Quarter 3 can be written as

$$\begin{aligned}\text{Seas. adj. forecast} &= 0.5(7,183) + 0.5(7,411)\\ &= 0.5(7,183) + 0.5[0.5(7,322) + 0.5(7,500)]\\ &= 0.5(7,183) + 0.25(7,322) + 0.25(7,500)\\ &= 7,297\end{aligned}$$

Similarly, the forecast for Quarter 4 is

$$\begin{aligned}\text{Seas. adj. forecast} &= 0.5(6,635) + 0.5(7,297)\\ &= 0.5(6,635) + 0.5[0.5(7,183) + 0.25(7,322) + 0.25(7,500)]\\ &= 0.5(6,635) + 0.25(7,183) + 0.125(7,322) + 0.125(7,500)\\ &= 6,966\end{aligned}$$

The exponential smoothing forecasting method places the greatest weight on the last value and then decreases the weights as the values get older.

Thus, this latter forecast places a weight of 0.5 on the last value, 0.25 on the next-to-last value, and 0.125 on the next prior value (the first one), with the remaining weight on the initial estimate. With other values of α, these weights would be α, $\alpha(1 - \alpha)$, $\alpha(1 - \alpha)^2$, and so forth.

Therefore, choosing the value of α amounts to using this pattern to choose the desired progression of weights on the time series values. With frequent shifts in the time series, a large weight needs to be placed on the most recent value, with rapidly decreasing weights on older values. However, with a relatively stable time series, it is desirable to place a significant weight on many values in order to have a large sample size.

Further insight into the choice of α is provided by an alternative form of the forecasting formula.

$$\begin{aligned}\text{Forecast} &= \alpha(\text{Last value}) + (1 - \alpha)(\text{Last forecast})\\ &= \alpha(\text{Last value}) + \text{Last forecast} - \alpha(\text{Last forecast})\\ &= \text{Last forecast} + \alpha(\text{Last value} - \text{Last forecast})\end{aligned}$$

where the absolute value of (Last value − Last forecast) is just the last forecasting error. Therefore, the bottom form of this formula indicates that each new forecast is adjusting the last forecast by adding or subtracting the quantity α *times* the last forecasting error. If the forecasting error usually is mainly due to random fluctuations in the time-series values, then only a small value of α should be used for this adjustment. However, if the forecasting error often is largely due to a shift in the time series, then a large value of α is needed to make a substantial adjustment quickly.

Using $\alpha = 0.5$, the Excel template in Figure 10.8 provides all the results for CCW with this forecasting method. Rows 22–32 show a plot of all the seasonally adjusted forecasts next to the true values of the seasonally adjusted call volumes. Note how each forecast lies midway between the preceding call volume and the preceding forecast. Therefore, each time there is a large shift in the call volume, the forecasts largely catch up with the shift rather quickly. The resulting average of the forecasting errors in column H is given in cell K28 as

$$MAD = 324$$

This is significantly smaller than for the previous forecasting methods, except for the value of MAD = 295 for the last-value forecasting method. The same comparison also holds for the average of the square of the forecasting errors, which is calculated in cell K31 as

$$MSE = 157,836$$

Lydia is somewhat frustrated at this point. She feels that she needs a method with average forecasting errors well below 295. Realizing that the last-value forecasting method is considered the *naive* method, she had expected that such a popular and sophisticated method as exponential smoothing would beat it easily.

The consultant is somewhat surprised also. However, he points out that the difference between MAD = 324 for exponential smoothing and MAD = 295 for last-value forecasting is really too small to be statistically significant. If the same two methods were to be applied the *next* three years, exponential smoothing might come out ahead. Lydia is not impressed.

Although he isn't ready to mention it to Lydia yet, the consultant is beginning to develop an idea for a whole new approach that might give her the forecasting precision she needs. But first he has one more time-series forecasting method to present.

To lay the groundwork for this method, the consultant explains a major reason why exponential smoothing did not fare well in this case. Look at the plot of seasonally adjusted call volumes in Figure 10.8. Note the distinct trend downward in the first three quarters, then a sharp trend upward for the next two, and finally a major trend upward for the last five quarters. Also note the large gap between the two plots (meaning large forecasting errors) by the end of each of these trends. The reason for these large errors is that exponential smoothing forecasts lag well behind such a trend because they place significant weight on values near the beginning of the trend. Although a large value of $\alpha = 0.5$ helps, exponential smoothing forecasts tend to lag further behind such a trend than last-value forecasts.

The next method adjusts exponential smoothing by also estimating the current trend and then projects this trend forward to help forecast the next value in the time series.

Exponential Smoothing with Trend

Exponential smoothing with trend uses the recent values in the time series to estimate any current upward or downward **trend** in these values. It is especially designed for the kind of time series depicted in Figure 10.9 where an upward (or downward) trend tends to continue for a considerable number of periods (but not necessarily indefinitely). This particular figure shows the estimated population of a certain state at midyear over a series of years. The line in the figure (commonly referred to as a *trend line*) shows the basic trend that the time series is following, but with fluctuations on both sides of the line. Because the basic trend is upward in this case, forecasts based on any of the preceding forecasting methods would tend to be considerably too low. However, by developing an estimate of the current slope of this trend line, and then adjusting the forecast to consider this slope, considerably more accurate forecasts should be obtained. This is the basic idea behind exponential smoothing with trend.

FIGURE 10.8

The Excel template in your MS Courseware for the exponential smoothing method with seasonal adjustments is applied here to the CCW problem.

	A	B	C	D	E	F	G	H	I	J	K
1		**Exponential Smoothing Forecasting Method with Seasonality for CCW**									
2											
3					Seasonally	Seasonally					
4				True	Adjusted	Adjusted	Actual	Forecasting		**Smoothing Constant**	
5		Year	Quarter	Value	Value	Forecast	Forecast	Error		α =	0.5
6		1	1	6,809	7,322	7,500	6,975	166			
7		1	2	6,465	7,183	7,411	6,670	205		**Initial Estimate**	
8		1	3	6,569	6,635	7,297	7,224	655		Average =	7,500
9		1	4	8,266	7,005	6,966	8,220	46			
10		2	1	7,257	7,803	6,986	6,497	760		**Type of Seasonality**	
11		2	2	7,064	7,849	7,394	6,655	409		Quarterly	
12		2	3	7,784	7,863	7,622	7,545	239			
13		2	4	8,724	7,393	7,742	9,136	412		Quarter	Seasonal Factor
14		3	1	6,992	7,518	7,568	7,038	46		1	0.93
15		3	2	6,822	7,580	7,543	6,789	33		2	0.90
16		3	3	7,949	8,029	7,561	7,486	463		3	0.99
17		3	4	9,650	8,178	7,795	9,199	451		4	1.18
18		4	1			7,987	7,428				
19		4	2								

Mean Absolute Deviation MAD = 324

Mean Square Error MSE = 157,836

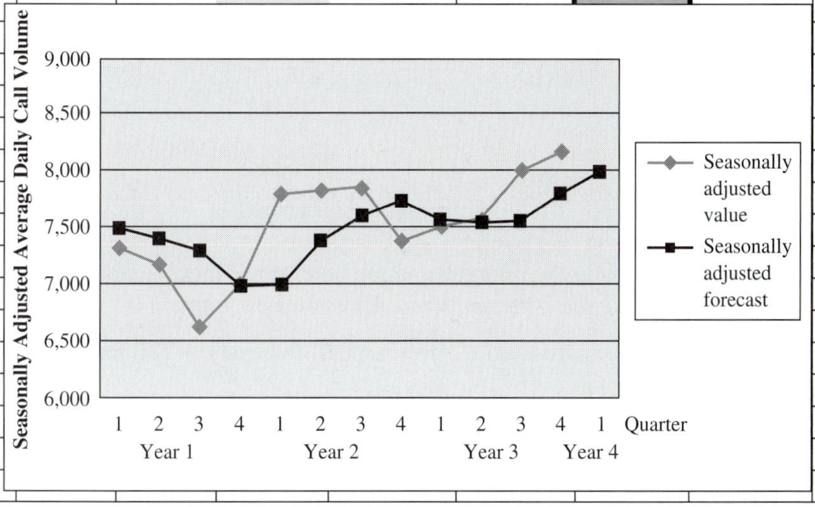

Range Name	Cells
ActualForecast	G6:G30
Alpha	K5
ForecastingError	H6:H30
InitialEstimate	K8
MAD	K28
MSE	K31
SeasonalFactor	K14:K25
SeasonallyAdjustedForecast	F6:F30
SeasonallyAdjustedValue	E6:E30
TrueValue	D6:D30
TypeOfSeasonality	K11

	E	F	G	H
3	Seasonally	Seasonally		
4	Adjusted	Adjusted	Actual	Forecasting
5	Value	Forecast	Forecast	Error
6	=D6/K14	=InitialEstimate	=K14*F6	=ABS(D6-G6)
7	=D7/K15	=Alpha*E6+(1-Alpha)*F6	=K15*F7	=ABS(D7-G7)
8	=D8/K16	=Alpha*E7+(1-Alpha)*F7	=K16*F8	=ABS(D8-G8)
9	=D9/K17	=Alpha*E8+(1-Alpha)*F8	=K17*F9	=ABS(D9-G9)
10	=D10/K14	=Alpha*E9+(1-Alpha)*F9	=K14*F10	=ABS(D10-G10)
11	=D11/K15	=Alpha*E10+(1-Alpha)*F10	=K15*F11	=ABS(D11-G11)
12	:	:	:	:
13	:	:	:	:

	J	K
28	MAD =	=AVERAGE(ForecastingError)

	J	K
31	MSE =	=SUMSQ(ForecastingError)/COUNT(ForecastingError)

FIGURE 10.9

A time series that gives the estimated population of a certain state over a series of years. The trend line shows the basic upward trend of the population.

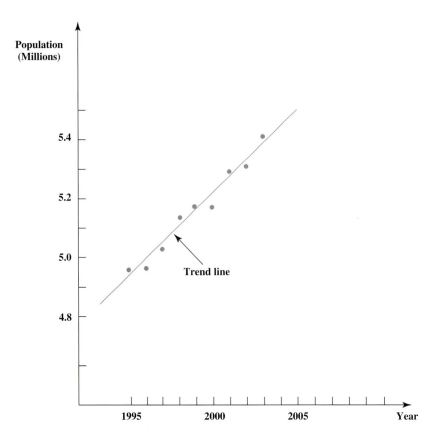

Trend is defined as

Trend = Average change from one time-series value to the next if the current pattern continues

The formula for forecasting the next value in the time series, then, is modified from the preceding method by *adding the estimated trend.* Thus, the new formula is

Forecast = α(Last value) + (1 − α)(Last forecast) + Estimated trend

Adding the estimated trend enables the forecast to keep up with the current trend in the data.

(A separate box describes how this formula can be easily modified to forecast *beyond* the next value in the time series as well.)

FORECASTING MORE THAN ONE TIME PERIOD AHEAD

We have focused thus far on forecasting what will happen in the *next* time period (the next quarter in the case of CCW). However, managers sometimes need to forecast further into the future. How can the various time-series forecasting methods be adapted to do this?

In the case of the last-value, averaging, moving-average, and exponential smoothing methods, the forecast for the next period also is the best available forecast for subsequent periods as well. However, when there is a *trend* in the data, it is important to take this trend into account for long-range forecasts. *Exponential smoothing with trend* provides a way of doing this. In particular, after determining the *estimated trend,* this method's forecast for *n* time periods into the future is

Forecast for *n* periods from now = α(Last value) + (1 − α)(Last forecast) + n × (Estimated trend)

Exponential smoothing also is used to obtain and update the *estimated trend* each time. The formula is

Estimated trend = β(Latest trend) + (1 − β)(Last estimate of trend)

The trend smoothing constant β is used to apply exponential smoothing to estimating the trend.

where β (the Greek letter beta) is the **trend smoothing constant,** which, like α, must be between 0 and 1. *Latest trend* refers to the trend based on just the last two values in the time series and the last two forecasts. Its formula is

$$\text{Latest trend} = \alpha(\text{Last value} - \text{Next-to-last value}) \\ + (1 - \alpha)(\text{Last forecast} - \text{Next-to-last forecast})$$

Getting started with this forecasting method requires making two initial estimates about the status of the time series just prior to beginning forecasting. These initial estimates are

1. Initial estimate of the *average value* of the time series if the conditions just prior to beginning forecasting were to remain unchanged without any trend.
2. Initial estimate of the *trend* of the time series just prior to beginning forecasting.

The forecast for the first period being forecasted then is

$$\text{First forecast} = \text{Initial estimate of average value} + \text{Initial estimate of trend}$$

The second forecast is obtained from the above formulas, where the *initial estimate of trend* is used as the last estimate of trend in the formula for estimated trend and the *initial estimate of average value* is used as both the next-to-last value and the next-to-last forecast in the formula for latest trend. The above formulas then are used directly to obtain subsequent forecasts.

The Excel templates for this method perform the calculations for you.

Since the calculations involved with this method are relatively involved, a computer commonly is used to implement the method. Your MS Courseware includes two Excel templates (one without seasonal adjustments and one with) for this method.

The considerations involved in choosing the trend smoothing constant β are similar to those for α. A large value of β (say, β = 0.3) is more responsive to recent changes in the trend, whereas a relatively small value (say, β = 0.1) uses more data in a significant way to estimate trend.

After trying various combinations of α and β on the CCW problem, the consultant concludes that α = 0.3 and β = 0.3 perform about as well as any. Both values are on the high end of the typically used range (0.1 to 0.3), but the frequent changes in the CCW time series call for large values. However, lowering α from the 0.5 value used with the preceding method seems justified since incorporating trend into the analysis would help respond more quickly to changes.

When applying exponential smoothing *without* trend earlier, Lydia and the consultant chose 7,500 as the initial estimate of the average value of the seasonally adjusted call volumes. They now note that there was no noticeable trend in these call volumes just prior to the retrospective generation of forecasts three years ago. Therefore, to apply exponential smoothing with trend, they decide to use

$$\text{Initial estimate of average value} = 7{,}500$$

$$\text{Initial estimate of trend} = 0$$

Working with the seasonally adjusted call volumes given in several recent figures, these initial estimates lead to the following seasonally adjusted forecasts.

Y1, Q1:   Seas. adj. forecast = 7,500 + 0 = 7,500

Y1, Q2:   Latest trend = 0.3(7,322 − 7,500) + 0.7(7,500 − 7,500) = −53.4

Estimated trend = 0.3(−53.4) + 0.7(0) = −16

Seas. adj. forecast = 0.3(7,322) + 0.7(7,500) − 16 = 7,431

Y1, Q3:   Latest trend = 0.3(7,183 − 7,322) + 0.7(7,431 − 7,500) = −90

Estimated trend = 0.3(−90) + 0.7(−16) = −38.2

Seas. adj. forecast = 0.3(7,183) + 0.7(7,431) − 38.2 = 7,318

The Excel template in Figure 10.10 shows the results from these calculations for all 12 quarters over the past three years, as well as for the upcoming quarter. The middle of the figure shows the plots of all the seasonally adjusted call volumes and seasonally adjusted forecasts. Note how each trend up or down in the call volumes causes the forecasts to gradually trend in

FIGURE 10.10

The Excel template in your MS Courseware for the exponential smoothing with trend method with seasonal adjustments is applied here to the CCW problem.

Exponential Smoothing with Trend Forecasting Method with Seasonality for CCW

	Year	Quarter	True Value	Seasonally Adjusted Value	Latest Trend	Estimated Trend	Seasonally Adjusted Value (Forecast)	Actual Forecast	Forecasting Error		Smoothing Constant	
6	1	1	6,809	7,322		0	7,500	6,975	166		α =	0.3
7	1	2	6,465	7,183	-54	-16	7,430	6,687	222		β =	0.3
8	1	3	6,569	6,635	-90	-38	7,318	7,245	676		**Initial Estimate**	
9	1	4	8,266	7,005	-243	-100	7,013	8,276	10		Average =	7,500
10	2	1	7,257	7,803	-102	-100	6,910	6,427	830		Trend =	0
11	2	2	7,064	7,849	167	-20	7,158	6,442	622			
12	2	3	7,784	7,863	187	42	7,407	7,333	451		**Type of Seasonality**	
13	2	4	8,724	7,393	179	83	7,627	9,000	276		Quarterly	
14	3	1	6,992	7,518	13	62	7,619	7,085	93			
15	3	2	6,822	7,580	32	53	7,642	6,877	55		**Quarter**	**Seasonal Factor**
16	3	3	7,949	8,029	34	47	7,670	7,594	355		1	0.93
17	3	4	9,650	8,178	155	80	7,858	9,272	378		2	0.90
18	4	1			176	108	8,062	7,498			3	0.99
19	4	2									4	1.18

Mean Absolute Deviation
MAD = 345

Mean Square Error
MSE = 180,796

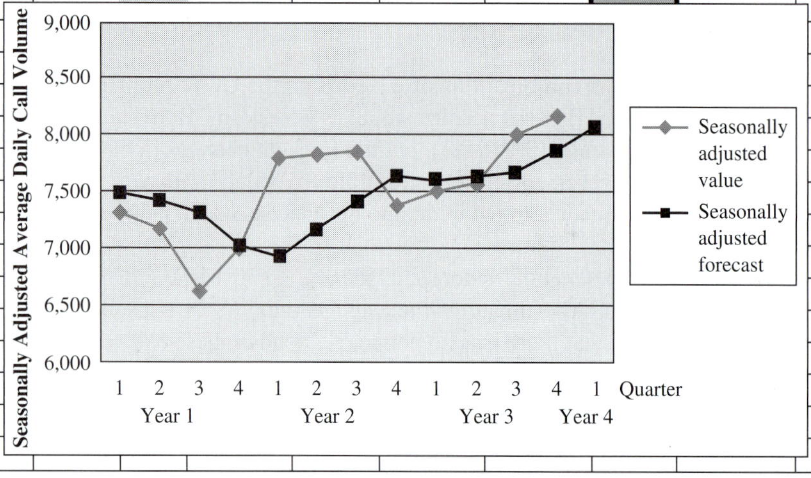

	E	F	G	H	I	J
3	Seasonally			Seasonally		
4	Adjusted	Latest	Estimated	Adjusted	Actual	Forecasting
5	Value	Trend	Trend	Forecast	Forecast	Error
6	=D6/M16		=InitialEstimateTrend	=InitialEstimateAverage+InitialEstimateTrend	=M16*H6	=ABS(D6-I6)
7	=D7/M17	=Alpha*(E6-InitialEstimateAverage)+(1-Alpha)*(H6-InitialEstimateAverage)	=Beta*F7+(1-Beta)*G6	=Alpha*E6+(1-Alpha)*H6+G7	=M17*H7	=ABS(D7-I7)
8	=D8/M18	=Alpha*(E7-E6)+(1-Alpha)*(H7-H6)	=Beta*F8+(1-Beta)*G7	=Alpha*E7+(1-Alpha)*H7+G8	=M18*H8	=ABS(D8-I8)
9	=D9/M19	=Alpha*(E8-E7)+(1-Alpha)*(H8-H7)	=Beta*F9+(1-Beta)*G8	=Alpha*E8+(1-Alpha)*H8+G9	=M19*H9	=ABS(D9-I9)
10	=D10/M16	=Alpha*(E9-E8)+(1-Alpha)*(H9-H8)	=Beta*F10+(1-Beta)*G9	=Alpha*E9+(1-Alpha)*H9+G10	=M16*H10	=ABS(D10-I10)
11	=D11/M17	=Alpha*(E10-E9)+(1-Alpha)*(H10-H9)	=Beta*F11+(1-Beta)*G10	=Alpha*E10+(1-Alpha)*H10+G11	=M17*H11	=ABS(D11-I11)
12	⋮	⋮	⋮	⋮	⋮	⋮

Range Name	Cells
ActualForecast	I6:I30
Alpha	M5
Beta	M6
ForecastingError	J6:J30
InitialEstimateAverage	M9
InitialEstimateTrend	M10
MAD	M30
MSE	M33
SeasonalFactor	M16:M27
SeasonallyAdjustedForecast	H6:H30
SeasonallyAdjustedValue	E6:E30
TrueValue	D6:D30
TypeOfSeasonality	M13

	L	M
30	MAD =	=AVERAGE(ForecastingError)

	L	M
33	MSE =	=SUMSQ(ForecastingError)/COUNT(ForecastingError)

TABLE 10.2

The Average Forecasting Error (MAD) and Mean Square Error (MSE) for the Various Time-Series Forecasting Methods When Forecasting CCW Call Volumes

Forecasting Method	MAD	MSE
CCW's 25 percent rule	424	317,815
Last-value method	295	145,909
Averaging method	400	242,876
Moving-average method	437	238,816
Exponential smoothing	324	157,836
Exponential smoothing with trend	345	180,796

When the trend in the data suddenly reverses direction, it takes a little while for the estimated trend to turn around.

the same direction, but then the trend in the forecasts takes a couple quarters to turn around when the trend in call volumes suddenly reverses direction. The resulting forecasting errors in column J then give an average forecasting error (cell M30) of

$$MAD = 345$$

a little above the 324 value for regular exponential smoothing and 295 for last-value forecasting. A similar result is obtained when using the square of the forecasting errors since the mean square error given in cell M33,

$$MSE = 180,796$$

also is a little above the MSE values for these other two forecasting methods.

Table 10.2 summarizes the values of MAD and MSE for all the forecasting methods so far. Here is Lydia's reaction to the large MAD value for exponential smoothing with trend.

Lydia: I'm very discouraged. These time-series forecasting methods just aren't doing the job I need. I thought this one would. It sounded like an excellent method that also would deal with the trends we keep encountering.

Consultant: Yes, it is a very good method under the right circumstances. When you have trends that may occasionally shift some over time, it should do a great job.

Lydia: So what went wrong here?

Consultant: Well, look at the trends you have here in the seasonally adjusted time series. You have a fairly sharp downward trend the first three quarters and then suddenly a very sharp upward trend for a couple quarters. Then it flattens out before a big drop in the eighth quarter. Then suddenly it is going up again. It is really tough to keep up with such abrupt big shifts in the trends. This method is better suited for much more gradual shifts in the trends.

Lydia: OK. But aren't there any other methods? None of these will do.

Consultant: There is one other main time-series forecasting method. It is called the **ARIMA** method, which is an acronym for AutoRegressive Integrated Moving Average. It also is sometimes called the Box-Jenkins method, in honor of its founders. It is a very sophisticated method, but some excellent software is available for implementing it. Another nice feature is that it is well-suited for dealing with strong seasonal patterns.

Lydia: Sounds good. So shouldn't we be trying this ARIMA method?

The ARIMA method is another good forecasting method, but it requires much more data than CCW currently has available.

Consultant: Not at this point. It is such a sophisticated method that it requires a great amount of past data, say, a minimum of 50 time periods. We don't have nearly enough data.

Lydia: A pity. So what are we going to do? I haven't seen anything that will do the job.

Consultant: Cheer up. I have an idea for how we can use one of these time-series forecasting methods in a different way that may do the job you want.

Lydia: Really? Tell me more.

Consultant: Well, let me hold off on the details until we can check out whether this is going to work. What I would like you to do is contact CCW's marketing manager and set up a meeting between the three of us. Also, send him your data on call volumes for the past three years. Ask him to dig out his sales data for the same period and compare it to your data.

Lydia: OK. What should I tell him is the purpose of the meeting?

Consultant: Explain what we're trying to accomplish here about forecasting call volumes. Then tell him that we're trying to understand better what has been causing these sudden shifts in call volumes. He knows more about what has been driving sales up or down than anybody. We just want to pick his brain about this.

Lydia: OK. Will do.

The Meeting with the Marketing Manager

This meeting takes place a few days later. As you eavesdrop (after the preliminaries), you will find it helpful to refer to the call volume data in one of the recent spreadsheets, such as Figure 10.10.

Lydia: Did you receive the call volume data I mailed to you?

Marketing manager: Yes, I did.

Consultant: How does it compare with your own sales data for these three years?

Marketing manager: Your data track mine pretty closely. I see the same ups and downs in both sets of data.

Lydia: That makes sense, since it's the calls to my call center that generate those sales.

Marketing manager: Right.

Consultant: Now, let me check on what caused the ups and downs. Three years ago, what we labeled as Year 1 in our data, there was a definite trend down for most of the year. What caused that?

Marketing manager: Yes, I remember that year all too well. It wasn't a very good year. The new Klugman operating system had been scheduled to come out early that year. Then they kept pushing the release date back. People kept waiting. They didn't manage to get it out until the beginning of the next year, so we even missed the Christmas sales.

Lydia: But our call volume did jump up a little more than usual during that holiday season.

Marketing manager: Yes. So did sales. I remember that we came out with a new networking tool, one with faster data transfer, in time for the holiday season. It turned out to be very popular for a few months. It really bailed us out during that slow period.

Consultant: Then the Klugman operating system was released and sales jumped the next year.

Marketing manager: Right.

Lydia: What happened late in the year? We weren't as busy as we expected to be.

Marketing manager: I assume that most people already had updated to the new operating system by then. There wasn't any major change in our product mix during that period.

Consultant: Then sales moved back up the next year. Last year.

Marketing manager: Yes, last year was a rather good year. We had a couple new products that did very well. One was a new data storage device that came out early in the year. Very inexpensive. The other was a color plain-paper printer that was released in July. We were able to offer it at a very competitive price and our customers gobbled it up.

Consultant: Thanks. That really clarifies what lies behind those call volume numbers we've been working with. Now I have another key question for you. When you look at your sales data and do your own forecasting, what do you see as the key factors that drive total sales up or down?

Marketing manager: There really is just one big factor: Do we have any hot new products out there? We have well over a hundred products. But most of them just fill a small niche in the market. Many of them are old standbys that, with updates, just keep going indefinitely. All these small-niche products together provide most of our total sales. A nice stable market base. Then, in addition, we should have three or four major new products out there. Maybe a couple that have been out for a few months but still have some life left in them. Then one or two just coming out that we hope will do very well.

> The one big factor that drives total sales up or down is whether the company has just released any hot new products.

Consultant: I see. A large market base and then three or four major new products.

Marketing manager: That's what we shoot for.

Consultant: Are you able to predict how well a major new product will do?

Marketing manager: I try. I've gotten better at it. I'm usually fairly close on what the initial response will be, but it is difficult to predict how long the product will hold up. I would like to have a better handle on it.

Consultant: Thanks very much for all your information. It has verified what I've been suspecting for awhile now.

Lydia: What's that?

Forecasting call volumes better requires coordinating directly with what is driving sales.

Consultant: That we really need to coordinate directly with what is driving sales in order to do a better job of forecasting call volumes.

Lydia: Good thought!

Consultant: How would the two of you feel about coordinating in developing better procedures for forecasting both sales and call volumes?

Lydia: You bet.

Marketing manager: Sounds good.

We will return to this story in Section 13.4 after introducing some useful forecasting software below.

Helpful Educational Software

A helpful forecasting module is included in your Interactive Management Science Modules at **www.mhhe.com/hillier3e.** An offline version also is included in your MS Courseware on the CD-ROM.

This module includes all the time-series forecasting methods presented in this section (as well as in Section 10.5). All you need to do is select a forecasting method, enter the time-series data from which you want to obtain a forecast, and then press the Forecast button. (It does not explicitly make seasonal adjustments, so you will need to enter seasonally adjusted data if such adjustments are necessary.) In addition to listing the forecasts and forecasting errors period by period, the module also plots a graph that shows both the time-series data (in blue dots) and the resulting forecasts (in red dots).

What is unique about this software is its interactive graphing feature that immediately shows you graphically how the forecasts will change as you change any piece of data. You move your mouse onto the blue dot that corresponds to the piece of data and then drag the dot vertically to change its value. As you drag the blue dot, the red dots corresponding to the forecasts instantaneously change accordingly. The purpose is to allow you to play with the data and gain a better feeling for how the forecasts perform with various configurations of data for each of the forecasting methods. Thus, this module is designed primarily to be an educational tool rather than professional forecasting software. It is limited to dealing with small, textbook-sized problems.

Review *Questions*

1. What does a seasonal factor measure?
2. What is the formula for calculating the seasonally adjusted call volume from the actual call volume and the seasonal factor?
3. What is the formula for calculating the forecast of the actual call volume from the seasonal factor and the seasonally adjusted forecast?
4. Why is the last-value forecasting method sometimes called the *naive method?*
5. Why did the averaging forecasting method not perform very well on the case study?
6. What is the rationale for replacing the averaging forecasting method by the moving-average forecasting method?
7. How does the exponential smoothing forecasting method modify the moving-average forecasting method?
8. With exponential smoothing, when is a small value of the smoothing constant appropriate? A larger value?
9. What is the formula for obtaining the next forecast with exponential smoothing? What is added to this formula when using exponential smoothing with trend?
10. What does the marketing manager say is the one big factor that drives CCW's total sales up or down?

10.4 THE TIME-SERIES FORECASTING METHODS IN PERSPECTIVE

Section 10.3 presented several methods for forecasting the next value of a time series in the context of the CCW case study. We now will take a step back to place into perspective just what these methods are trying to accomplish. After providing this perspective, CCW's consultant then will give his recommendation for setting up a forecasting system.

The Goal of the Forecasting Methods

It actually is something of a misnomer to talk about forecasting *the* value of the next observation in a time series (such as CCW's call volume in the next quarter). It is impossible to predict *the value* precisely, because this next value can turn out to be anything over some range. What it will be depends upon future circumstances that are beyond our control.

In other words, the next value that will occur in a time series is a *random variable.* It has some *probability distribution.* For example, Figure 10.11 shows a typical probability distribution for the CCW call volume in a future quarter in which the mean of this distribution happens to be 7,500. This distribution indicates the relative likelihood of the various possible values of the call volume. Nobody can say in advance which value actually will occur.

So what is the meaning of the single number that is selected as the "forecast" of the next value in the time series? If possible, we would like this number to be the *mean* of the distribution. The reason is that random observations from the distribution tend to cluster around the mean of the distribution. Therefore, using the mean as the forecast would tend to minimize the average forecasting error.

Unfortunately, we don't actually know what this probability distribution is, let alone its mean. The best we can do is use all the available data (past values from the time series) to estimate the mean as closely as possible.

> The goal of time-series forecasting methods is to estimate the *mean* of the underlying probability distribution of the next value of the time series as closely as possible.

Given some random observations from a single probability distribution, the best estimate of its mean is the *sample average* (the average of all these observations). Therefore, if a time series has exactly the same distribution for each and every time period, then the *averaging forecasting method* provides the best estimate of the mean.

However, other forecasting methods commonly are used instead because the distribution may be changing over time.

Problems Caused by Shifting Distributions

Section 10.3 began by considering seasonal effects. This then led to estimating CCW's seasonal factors as 0.93, 0.90, 0.99, and 1.18 for Quarters 1, 2, 3, and 4, respectively.

If the overall average daily call volume for a year is 7,500, these seasonal factors imply that the probability distributions for the four quarters of that year fall roughly as shown in Figure 10.12. Since these distributions have different means, we should no longer simply average the random

The next value in a time series cannot be forecasted with certainty because it has a probability distribution rather than a fixed value that definitely will occur.

FIGURE 10.11

A typical probability distribution of what the average daily call volume will be for CCW in a quarter when the mean is 7,500.

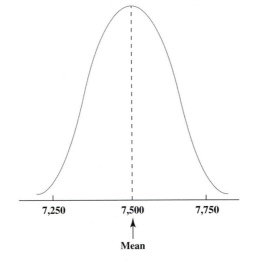

| 7,250 | 7,500 | 7,750 |

↑
Mean

FIGURE 10.12

Typical probability distributions of CCW's average daily call volumes in the four quarters of a year in which the overall average is 7,500.

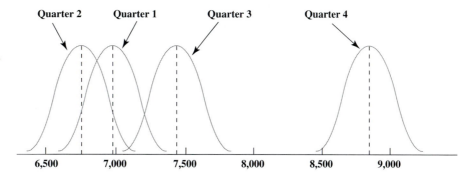

FIGURE 10.13

Comparison of typical probability distributions of CCW's average daily call volumes (seasonally adjusted) in years 1 and 2.

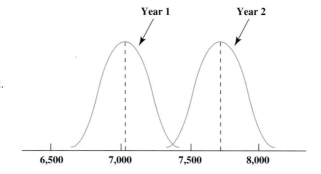

observations (observed call volumes) from all four quarters to estimate the mean for any one of these distributions.

This complication is why the preceding section seasonally adjusted the time series. Dividing each quarter's call volume by its seasonal factor shifts the distribution of this seasonally adjusted call volume over to basically the distribution shown in Figure 10.11 with a mean of 7,500. This allows averaging the seasonally adjusted values to estimate this mean.

Unfortunately, even after seasonally adjusting the time series, the probability distribution may not remain the same from one year to the next (or even from one quarter to the next). For example, as CCW's marketing manager explained, total sales jumped substantially at the beginning of Year 2 when the new Klugman operating system became available. This also caused the average daily call volume to increase by about 10 percent, from just over 7,000 in Year 1 to over 7,700 in Year 2. Figure 10.13 compares the resulting distributions for typical quarters (seasonally adjusted) in the two years.

Random observations from the Year 1 distribution in this figure provide a poor basis for estimating the mean of the Year 2 distribution. Yet, except for the last-value method, *each* of the forecasting methods presented in the preceding section placed at least some weight on these observations from Year 1 to estimate the mean for *each* quarter in Year 2. This was a major part of the reason why both the average forecasting errors (MAD) and the mean square errors (MSE) were higher for these methods than for the last-value method.

When the probability distribution for a time series shifts frequently, recent data quickly become outdated for forecasting purposes.

Judging from the marketing manager's information, it appears that some shift in the distribution also occurred several times from just one quarter to the next. This further added to the forecasting errors.

Comparison of the Forecasting Methods

Section 10.3 presented five methods for forecasting the next value in a time series. Which of these methods is particularly suitable for a given application depends greatly on how *stable* the time series is.

A time series is said to be **stable** if its underlying probability distribution usually remains the same from one time period to the next. (Any shifts that do occur in the distribution are both infrequent and small.) A time series is **unstable** if both frequent and sizable shifts in the distribution tend to occur.

CCW's seasonally adjusted time series shown in Figure 10.4 (and many subsequent figures) appears to have had several shifts in the distribution, including the sizable one depicted in Figure 10.13. Therefore, this time series is an example of a relatively *unstable* one.

Here is a summary of which type of time series fits each of the forecasting methods.

> The key factor in choosing a forecasting method is how stable the time series is.

Last-value method: Suitable for a time series that is so unstable that even the next-to-last value is not considered relevant for forecasting the next value.

Averaging method: Suitable for a very stable time series where even its first few values are considered relevant for forecasting the next value.

Moving-average method: Suitable for a moderately stable time series where the last few values are considered relevant for forecasting the next value. The number of values included in the moving average reflects the anticipated degree of stability in the time series.

Exponential smoothing method: Suitable for a time series in the range from somewhat unstable to rather stable, where the value of the smoothing constant needs to be adjusted to fit the anticipated degree of stability. Refines the moving-average method by placing the greatest weight on the most recent values, but is not as readily understood by managers as the moving-average method.

Exponential smoothing with trend: Suitable for a time series where the mean of the distribution tends to follow a trend either up or down, provided that changes in the trend occur only occasionally and gradually.

Unfortunately for CCW, its seasonally adjusted time series proved to be a little too unstable for any of these methods except the last-value method, which is considered to be the least powerful of these forecasting methods. Even when using exponential smoothing with trend, the changes in the trend occurred too frequently and sharply.

In light of these considerations, the consultant now is ready to present his recommendations to Lydia for a new forecasting procedure.

The Consultant's Recommendations

1. Forecasting should be done monthly rather than quarterly in order to respond more quickly to changing conditions.

2. Hiring and training of new agents also should be done monthly instead of quarterly in order to fine-tune staffing levels to meet changing needs.

3. Recently retired agents should be offered the opportunity to work part-time on an on-call basis to help meet current staffing needs more closely.

4. Since sales drive call volume, the forecasting process should begin by forecasting sales.

> Forecasting call volume should begin by separately forecasting the major components of total sales.

5. For forecasting purposes, total sales should be broken down into the major components described by the marketing manager, namely, (1) the relatively stable market base of numerous small-niche products and (2) *each* of the few (perhaps three or four) major new products whose success or failure can significantly drive total sales up or down. These major new products would be identified by the marketing manager on an ongoing basis.

6. Exponential smoothing with a relatively small smoothing constant is suggested for forecasting sales of the marketing base of numerous small-niche products. However, before making a final decision on the forecasting method, retrospective testing should be conducted to check how well this particular method would have performed over the past three years. This testing also should guide selection of the value of the smoothing constant.

7. Exponential smoothing with trend, with relatively large smoothing constants, is suggested for forecasting sales of *each* of the major new products. Once again, retrospective testing should be conducted to check this decision and to guide choosing values for the smoothing constants. The marketing manager should be asked to provide the initial estimate of anticipated sales in the first month for a new product. He also should be asked

to check the subsequent exponential smoothing forecasts and make any adjustments he feels are appropriate based on his knowledge of what is happening in the marketplace.

8. Because of the strong seasonal sales pattern, seasonally adjusted time series should be used for each application of these forecasting methods.

9. After separately obtaining forecasts of actual sales for each of the major components of total sales identified in recommendation 5, these forecasts should be summed to obtain a forecast of total sales.

10. *Causal forecasting with linear regression* (as described in the next section) should be used to obtain a forecast of *call volume* from this forecast of total sales.

The next section describes how to obtain a forecast of call volume from a forecast of total sales.

Lydia accepts these recommendations with considerable enthusiasm. She also agrees to work with the marketing manager to gain his cooperation.

Read on to see how the last recommendation is implemented.

Review
Questions

1. What kind of variable is the next value that will occur in a time series?
2. What is the goal of time-series forecasting methods?
3. Is the probability distribution of CCW's average daily call volume the same for every quarter?
4. What is the explanation for why the average forecasting errors were higher for the other time-series forecasting methods than for the supposedly less powerful last-value method?
5. What is the distinction between a *stable* time series and an *unstable* time series?
6. What is the consultant's recommendation regarding what should be forecasted instead of call volumes to begin the forecasting process?
7. What are the major components of CCW's total sales?

10.5   CAUSAL FORECASTING WITH LINEAR REGRESSION

We have focused so far on *time-series forecasting methods,* that is, methods that forecast the next value in a time series based on its previous values. These methods have been used retrospectively in Section 10.3 to forecast CCW's call volume in the next quarter based on its previous call volumes.

Causal Forecasting

However, the consultant's last recommendation suggests another approach to forecasting. It is really sales that drive call volume, and sales can be forecasted considerably more precisely than call volume. Therefore, it should be possible to obtain a better forecast of call volume by relating it directly to forecasted sales. This kind of approach is called *causal forecasting.*

For the CCW problem, call volume is the dependent variable and total sales is the independent variable.

> **Causal forecasting** obtains a forecast of the quantity of interest (the **dependent variable**) by relating it directly to one or more other quantities (the **independent variables**) that drive the quantity of interest.

Table 10.3 shows some examples of the kinds of situations where causal forecasting sometimes is used. In each of the first four cases, the indicated dependent variable can be expected

TABLE 10.3
Possible Examples of Causal Forecasting

Type of Forecasting	Possible Dependent Variable	Possible Independent Variables
Sales	Sales of a product	Amount of advertising
Spare parts	Demand for spare parts	Usage of equipment
Economic trends	Gross domestic product	Various economic factors
CCW call volume	Call volume	Total sales
Any quantity	This same quantity	Time

FIGURE 10.14

The data needed to do causal forecasting for the CCW problem by relating call volume to sales.

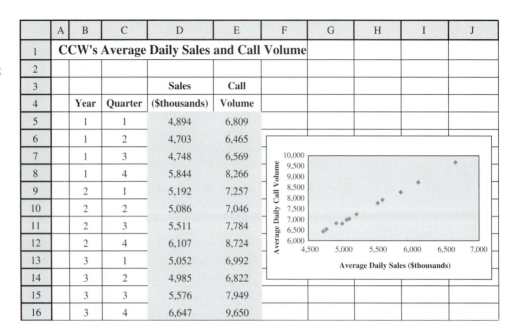

	A	B	C	D	E	F	G	H	I	J
1		**CCW's Average Daily Sales and Call Volume**								
2										
3				**Sales**	**Call**					
4		**Year**	**Quarter**	**($thousands)**	**Volume**					
5		1	1	4,894	6,809					
6		1	2	4,703	6,465					
7		1	3	4,748	6,569					
8		1	4	5,844	8,266					
9		2	1	5,192	7,257					
10		2	2	5,086	7,046					
11		2	3	5,511	7,784					
12		2	4	6,107	8,724					
13		3	1	5,052	6,992					
14		3	2	4,985	6,822					
15		3	3	5,576	7,949					
16		3	4	6,647	9,650					

to go up or down rather directly with the independent variable(s) listed in the rightmost column. The last case also applies when some quantity of interest (e.g., sales of a product) tends to follow a steady trend upward (or downward) with the passage of time (the independent variable that drives the quantity of interest).

Linear Regression

At Lydia's request, the marketing manager brought sales data for the past three years to their recent meeting. These data are summarized in Figure 10.14. In particular, column D gives the average daily sales (in units of thousands of dollars) for each of the 12 past quarters. Column E repeats the data given previously on average daily call volumes. None of the data have been seasonally adjusted.

The right side of the figure was generated by choosing Chart under the Insert menu, selecting an XY (Scatter) chart type, and following the directions of the Chart Wizard. This graph shows a plot of the data in columns D and E on a two-dimensional graph. Thus, each of the 12 points in the graph shows the combination of sales and call volume for one of the 12 quarters (without identifying which quarter).

This graph shows a close relationship between call volume and sales. Each increase or decrease in sales is accompanied by a roughly proportional increase or decrease in call volume. This is not surprising since the sales are being made through the calls to the call center.

It appears from this graph that the relationship between call volume and sales can be approximated by a straight line. Figure 10.15 shows such a line. (This line was generated by clicking on the graph in Figure 10.14, selecting Add Trendline under the Chart menu, and then selecting Linear Trend under the Options tab. The equation above the line was added by choosing Display Equation on Chart under the Options tab.) This line is referred to as a *linear regression line.*

A linear regression line estimates what the value of the dependent variable should be for any particular value of the independent variable.

When doing causal forecasting with a single independent variable, **linear regression** involves approximating the relationship between the dependent variable (call volume for CCW) and the independent variable (sales for CCW) by a straight line. This **linear regression line** is drawn on a graph with the independent variable on the horizontal axis and the dependent variable on the vertical axis. The line is constructed after plotting a number of points showing each observed value of the independent variable and the corresponding value of the dependent variable.

Thus, the linear regression line in Figure 10.15 can be used to estimate what the call volume should be for a particular value of sales. In general, the equation for the linear regression line has the form

$$y = a + bx$$

FIGURE 10.15
Figure 10.14 has been modified here by adding a trend line to the graph.

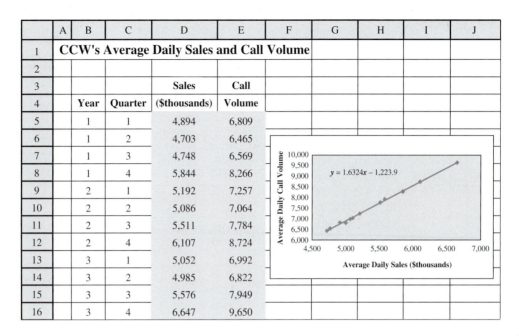

	A	B	C	D	E	F	G	H	I	J
1										
3				Sales	Call					
4		Year	Quarter	($thousands)	Volume					
5		1	1	4,894	6,809					
6		1	2	4,703	6,465					
7		1	3	4,748	6,569					
8		1	4	5,844	8,266					
9		2	1	5,192	7,257					
10		2	2	5,086	7,064					
11		2	3	5,511	7,784					
12		2	4	6,107	8,724					
13		3	1	5,052	6,992					
14		3	2	4,985	6,822					
15		3	3	5,576	7,949					
16		3	4	6,647	9,650					

CCW's Average Daily Sales and Call Volume

where

y = Estimated value of the dependent variable, as given by the linear regression line

a = Intercept of the linear regression line with the y-axis

b = Slope of the linear regression line

x = Value of the independent variable

The equation for a linear regression line is called the regression equation.

(If there is more than one independent variable, then this **regression equation** has a term, a constant times the variable, added on the right-hand side for *each* of these variables.) For the linear regression line in this figure, the exact values of a and b happen to be

$$a = -1,223.9 \qquad b = 1.6324$$

Figure 10.16 shows the Excel template in your MS Courseware that can be used to find these values of a and b, and so on. You need to input all the observed values of the independent variable (sales) and of the dependent variable (call volume) in columns C and D, and then the template performs all the calculations. On the right, note that you have the option of inserting a value for x (sales) in cell J10 and then the template calculates the corresponding value of y (call volume) that lies on the linear regression line. This calculation can be repeated for as many values of x as desired. In addition, column E already shows these calculations for each value of x in column C, so each cell in column E gives the estimate of call volume provided by the linear regression line for the corresponding sales level in column C. The difference between this estimate and the actual call volume in column D gives the estimation error in column F. The *square* of this error is shown in column G.

The procedure used to obtain a and b is called the **method of least squares.** This method chooses the values of a and b that *minimize* the sum of the *square of the estimation errors* given in column G of Figure 10.16. Thus, the sum of the numbers in column G (22,051) is the minimum possible. Any significantly different values of *a and b* would give different estimation errors that would cause this sum to be larger.

The method of least squares chooses the values of a and b that make the sum of the resulting numbers in column G as small as possible.

The *average* of the square of the estimation errors in column G (1,838) has an interesting interpretation. Suppose that the sales for a quarter could be known in advance (either because of advance orders or an exact prediction). In this case, using the linear regression line to forecast call volume would give a mean square error (MSE) of 1,838. What the method of least squares has done is place the linear regression line exactly where it would minimize MSE in this situation. Note that this minimum value of MSE = 1,838 is roughly 1 percent of the MSE values given earlier in Table 10.2 for the time-series forecasting methods presented in Section 10.3.

FIGURE 10.16

The Excel template in your MS Courseware for doing causal forecasting with linear regression, as illustrated here for the CCW problem.

	A	B	C	D	E	F	G	H	I	J
1		**Linear Regression of Call Volume vs. Sales Volume for CCW**								
2										
3		**Time**	**Independent**	**Dependent**		**Estimation**	**Square**		**Linear Regression Line**	
4		**Period**	**Variable**	**Variable**	**Estimate**	**Error**	**of Error**		*y = a + bx*	
5		1	4,894	6,809	6,765	43.85	1,923		*a* =	-1,223.86
6		2	4,703	6,465	6,453	11.64	136		*b* =	1.63
7		3	4,748	6,569	6,527	42.18	1,780			
8		4	5,844	8,266	8,316	49.93	2,493			
9		5	5,192	7,257	7,252	5.40	29		**Estimator**	
10		6	5,086	7,064	7,079	14.57	212		if *x* =	5,000
11		7	5,511	7,784	7,772	11.66	136			
12		8	6,107	8,724	8,745	21.26	452		then *y* =	6,938.18
13		9	5,052	6,992	7,023	31.07	965			
14		10	4,985	6,822	6,914	91.70	8,408			
15		11	5,576	7,949	7,878	70.55	4,977			
16		12	6,647	9,650	9,627	23.24	540			
17		13								
18		14								
19		15								
20		16								
21		17								
22		18								
23		19								
24		20								
25		21								
26		22								
27		23								
28		24								
29		25								
30		26								
31		27								
32		28								
33		29								
34		30								

Range Name	Cells
a	J5
b	J6
DependentVariable	D5:D34
Estimate	E5:E34
EstimationError	F5:F34
IndependentVariable	C5:C34
SquareOfError	G5:G34
x	J10
y	J12

	E	F	G
3		**Estimation**	**Square**
4	**Estimate**	**Error**	**of Error**
5	=*a+b**C5	=ABS(D5-E5)	=F5^2
6	=*a+b**C6	=ABS(D6-E6)	=F6^2
7	=*a+b**C7	=ABS(D7-E7)	=F7^2
8	=*a+b**C8	=ABS(D8-E8)	=F8^2
9	=*a+b**C9	=ABS(D9-E9)	=F9^2
10	:	:	:
11	:	:	:

	I	J
5	*a* =	=INTERCEPT(DependentVariable,IndependentVariable)
6	*b* =	=SLOPE(DependentVariable,IndependentVariable)

	I	J
12	then *y* =	=*a+b**x

The numbers in column F also are interesting. Averaging these numbers reveals that the *average estimation error* for the 12 quarters is only 35. This indicates that if the sales for a quarter were known in advance (or could be predicted exactly), then using the linear regression line to forecast call volume would give an average forecasting error (MAD) of only 35. This is only about 10 percent of the values of MAD obtained for the various time-series forecasting methods in Section 10.3.

For some applications of causal forecasting, the value of the independent variable will be known in advance. This is not the case here, where the independent variable is the total sales for the upcoming time period. However, the consultant is confident that a very good forecast of total sales can be obtained by following his recommendations. This forecast can then be used as the value of the independent variable for obtaining a good forecast of call volume from the linear regression line.

CCW's New Forecasting Procedure

1. Obtain a forecast of total (average daily) sales for the upcoming month by implementing the consultant's recommendations.

2. Use this forecast as the value of total sales in forecasting the average daily call volume for the upcoming month from the linear regression line identified in Figures 10.15 and 10.16.

Seasonal adjustments play a role in step 1 of this procedure, but not in step 2. Based on the consultant's recommendations presented at the end of the preceding section (see recommendation no. 8), seasonal adjustments should be incorporated into whatever forecasting method is used in step 1. However, a forecast of seasonally adjusted sales would then be converted back into a forecast of actual sales for use in step 2. By using a forecast of actual sales, the forecast of call volume obtained from the linear regression line in step 2 will be the desired forecast of actual call volume rather than seasonally adjusted call volume.

Linear regression with multiple independent variables is sometimes referred to as *multiple linear regression.*

This application of linear regression to the CCW problem involves only one independent variable (total sales) that drives the dependent variable (call volume). As mentioned at the beginning of this section, some applications of causal forecasting with linear regression involve multiple independent variables that together drive the dependent variable. For example, when using linear regression to forecast the nation's gross domestic product (the dependent variable) for the next quarter, the independent variables might include such leading indicators of future economic performance as the current level of the stock market, the current index of consumer confidence, the current index of business activity (measuring orders placed), and so forth. If there are, say, two independent variables, the regression equation would have the form

$$y = a + b_1x_1 + b_2x_2$$

where x_1 and x_2 are the independent variables with b_1 and b_2 as their respective coefficients. The corresponding linear regression line now would lie in a three-dimensional graph with y (the dependent variable) as the vertical axis and both x_1 and x_2 as horizontal axes in the other two dimensions. Regardless of the number of independent variables, the *method of least squares* still can be used to choose the value of a, b_1, b_2, etc., that minimizes the sum of the square of the estimation errors when comparing the values of the dependent variable at the various data points with the corresponding estimates given by the regression equation. However, we will not delve further into this more advanced topic.

The CCW Case Study a Year Later

A year after implementing the consultant's recommendations, Lydia gives him a call.

Lydia: I just wanted to let you know how things are going. And to congratulate you on the great job you did for us. Remember that the 25 percent rule was giving us MAD values over 400? And then the various time-series forecasting methods were doing almost as badly?

Consultant: Yes, I do remember. You were pretty discouraged there for awhile.

Lydia: I sure was! But I'm feeling a lot better now. I just calculated MAD for the first year under your new procedure. 120. Only 120!

Consultant: Great. That's the kind of improvement we like to see. What do you think has made the biggest difference?

Lydia: I think the biggest factor was tying our forecasting into forecasting sales. We never had much feeling for where call volumes were headed. But we have a much better handle on what sales will be because, with the marketing manager's help, we can see what is causing the shifts.

A key to successful forecasting is to understand what is causing shifts so that they can be caught as soon as they occur.

A good forecasting procedure combines a well-constructed statistical forecasting procedure and a savvy manager who understands what is driving the numbers and so is able to make appropriate adjustments in the forecasts.

Consultant: Yes. I think that is a real key to successful forecasting. You saw that we can get a lot of garbage by simply applying a time-series forecasting method to historical data without understanding what is causing the shifts. You have to get behind the numbers and see what is really going on, then design the forecasting procedure to catch the shifts as they occur, like we did by having the marketing manager identify the major new products that impact total sales and then separately forecasting sales for each of them.

Lydia: Right. Bringing the marketing manager in on this was a great move. He's a real supporter of the new procedure now, by the way. He says it is giving him valuable information as well.

Consultant: Good. Is he making adjustments in the statistical forecasts, based on his knowledge of what is going on in the marketplace, like I recommended?

Lydia: Yes, he is. You have a couple fans here. We really appreciate the great job you did for us.

Review
Questions

1. What is causal forecasting?
2. When applying causal forecasting to the CCW problem, what is the dependent variable and what is the independent variable?
3. When doing causal forecasting with a single independent variable, what does linear regression involve?
4. What is the form of the equation for a linear regression line with a single independent variable? With more than one independent variable?
5. What is the name of the method for obtaining the value of the constants, *a* and *b,* for a linear regression line?
6. How does the MAD value for CCW's new forecasting procedure compare with that for the old procedure that used the 25 percent rule?

10.6 JUDGMENTAL FORECASTING METHODS

We have focused so far on **statistical forecasting methods** that base the forecast on historical data. However, such methods cannot be used if no data are available, or if the data are not representative of current conditions. In such cases, **judgmental forecasting methods** can be used instead.

Judgmental forecasting methods use expert opinion to make forecasts.

Even when good data are available, some managers prefer a judgmental method instead of a formal statistical method. In many other cases, a combination of the two may be used. For example, in the CCW case study, the marketing manager uses his judgment, based on his long experience and his knowledge of what is happening in the marketplace, to adjust the sales forecasts obtained from time-series forecasting methods.

Here is a brief overview of the main judgmental forecasting methods.

1. **Manager's opinion:** This is the most informal of the methods, because it simply involves a single manager using his or her best judgment to make the forecast. In some cases, some data may be available to help make this judgment. In others, the manager may be drawing solely on experience and an intimate knowledge of the current conditions that drive the forecasted quantity.
2. **Jury of executive opinion:** This method is similar to the first one, except now it involves a small group of high-level managers who pool their best judgments to collectively make the forecast. This method may be used for more critical forecasts for which several executives share responsibility and can provide different types of expertise.
3. **Salesforce composite:** This method is often used for sales forecasting when a company employs a salesforce to help generate sales. It is a *bottom-up approach* whereby each salesperson provides an estimate of what sales will be in his or her region. These estimates then are sent up through the corporate chain of command, with managerial review at each level, to be aggregated into a corporate sales forecast.

The salesforce composite method uses a bottom-up approach.

4. **Consumer market survey:** This method goes even further than the preceding one in adopting a *grass-roots approach* to sales forecasting. It involves surveying customers and

potential customers regarding their future purchasing plans and how they would respond to various new features in products. This input is particularly helpful for designing new products and then in developing the initial forecasts of their sales. It also is helpful for planning a marketing campaign.

5. **Delphi method:** This method employs a panel of experts in different locations who independently fill out a series of questionnaires. However, the results from each questionnaire are provided with the next one, so each expert then can evaluate this group information in adjusting his or her responses next time. The goal is to reach a relatively narrow spread of conclusions from most of the experts. The decision makers then assess this input from the panel of experts to develop the forecast. This involved process normally is used only at the highest levels of a corporation or government to develop long-range forecasts of broad trends.

Review *Questions*

1. Statistical forecasting methods cannot be used under what circumstances?
2. Are judgmental forecasting methods only used when statistical forecasting methods cannot be used?
3. How does the jury of executive opinion method differ from the manager's opinion method?
4. How does the salesforce composite method begin?
5. When is a consumer market survey particularly helpful?
6. When might the Delphi method be used?

10.7 Summary

The future success of any business depends heavily on the ability of its management to forecast well. Forecasting may be needed in several areas, including sales, the need for spare parts, production yields, economic trends, and staffing needs.

The Computer Club Warehouse (CCW) case study illustrates a variety of approaches to forecasting, some of which prove unsatisfactory for this particular application. Ultimately, it becomes necessary to get behind the CCW data to understand just what is driving the call volumes at its call center in order to develop a good forecasting system.

A time series is a series of observations over time of some quantity of interest. Several statistical forecasting methods use these observations in some way to forecast what the next value will be. These methods include the last-value method, the averaging method, the moving-average method, the exponential smoothing method, and exponential smoothing with trend.

The goal of all these methods is to estimate the mean of the underlying probability distribution of the next value of the time series as closely as possible. This may require using seasonal factors to seasonally adjust the time series, as well as identifying other factors that may cause this underlying probability distribution to shift from one time period to the next.

Another statistical forecasting approach is called causal forecasting. This approach obtains a forecast of the quantity of interest (the dependent variable) by relating it directly to one or more other quantities (the independent variables) that drive the quantity of interest. Frequently, this involves using linear regression to approximate the relationship between the dependent variable and each independent variable by a straight line.

The software accompanying this book includes Excel templates for the various statistical forecasting methods, a forecasting module in the Interactive Management Science Modules, and a commercial Excel add-in called CB Predictor for performing time-series forecasting within a spreadsheet environment.

Still another key category of forecasting methods is judgmental methods. This category involves basing the forecast on a manager's opinion, a jury of executive opinion, a salesforce composite, a consumer market survey, or the Delphi method.

Glossary

ARIMA   An acronym for the AutoRegressive Integrated Moving Average method, a sophisticated time-series forecasting method commonly referred to as the Box-Jenkins method. (Section 10.3), 393

averaging forecasting method   A method that uses the average of the past observations from a time series as a forecast of the next value. (Sections 10.1 and 10.3), 371, 382

causal forecasting   Obtaining a forecast of the dependent variable by relating it directly to one or more independent variables. (Section 10.5), 399

consumer market survey   A judgmental forecasting method that uses surveys of customers and potential customers. (Section 10.6), 404

Delphi method   A judgmental forecasting method that uses input from a panel of experts in different locations. (Section 10.6), 405

dependent variable   The quantity of interest when doing causal forecasting. (Section 10.5), 399

exponential smoothing forecasting method   A method that uses a weighted average of the last value from a time series and the last forecast to obtain the forecast of the next value. (Sections 10.1 and 10.3), 371, 386

exponential smoothing with trend   An adjustment of the exponential smoothing forecasting method that projects the current trend forward to help forecast the next value of a time series (and perhaps subsequent values as well). (Sections 10.1 and 10.3), 371, 388

forecasting error   The deviation of the forecast from the realized quantity. (Sections 10.1 and 10.2), 372, 375

independent variable   A quantity that drives the value of the dependent variable in causal forecasting. (Section 10.5), 399

judgmental forecasting methods   Methods that use expert judgment to make forecasts. (Introduction and Section 10.6), 370, 404

jury of executive opinion   A judgmental forecasting method that involves a small group of high-level managers pooling their best judgment to collectively make the forecast. (Section 10.6), 404

last-value forecasting method   A method that uses the last value of a time series as the forecast of the next value. (Sections 10.1 and 10.3), 371, 380

linear regression   Approximating the relationship between the dependent variable and each independent variable by a straight line. (Sections 10.1 and 10.5), 371, 400

linear regression line   The line that approximates the relationship between the dependent variable and each independent variable when using causal forecasting. (Section 10.5), 400

MAD   An acronym for mean absolute deviation, the average forecasting error. (Sections 10.1 and 10.2), 372, 375

manager's opinion   A judgmental forecasting method that involves using a single manager's best judgment to make the forecast. (Section 10.6), 404

mean absolute deviation (MAD)   The average forecasting error. (Sections 10.1 and 10.2), 372, 375

mean square error (MSE)   The average of the square of the forecasting errors. (Sections 10.1 and 10.2), 372, 376

method of least squares   The procedure used to obtain the constants in the equation for a linear regression line. (Section 10.5), 401

moving-average forecasting method   A method that uses the average of the last n observations from a time series as a forecast of the next value. (Sections 10.1 and 10.3), 371, 384

MSE   An acronym for mean square error, the average of the square of the forecasting errors. (Sections 10.1 and 10.2), 372, 376

naive method   Another name for the last-value forecasting method. (Section 10.3), 382

regression equation   The equation for a linear regression line. (Section 10.5), 401

salesforce composite   A judgmental forecasting method that aggregates the sales forecasts of the salesforce from their various regions. (Section 10.6), 404

seasonal factor   A factor for any period of a year that measures how that period compares to the overall average for an entire year. (Section 10.3), 377

seasonally adjusted time series   An adjustment of the original time series that removes seasonal effects. (Section 10.3), 379

smoothing constant   A parameter of the exponential smoothing forecasting method that gives the weight to be placed on the last value in the time series. (Section 10.3), 386

stable time series   A time series whose underlying probability distribution usually remains the same from one time period to the next. (Section 10.4), 397

statistical forecasting methods   Methods that use historical data to forecast future quantities. (Introduction and Sections 10.1–10.5), 370, 404

time series   A series of observations over time of some quantity of interest. (Section 10.2), 376

time-series forecasting methods   Methods that use the past observations in a time series to forecast what the next value will be. (Sections 10.3 and 10.4), 379

trend   The average change from one time series value to the next if the current pattern continues. (Section 10.3), 388

trend smoothing constant   A smoothing constant for estimating the trend when using exponential smoothing with trend. (Section 10.3), 391

unstable time series   A time series that has frequent and sizable shifts in its underlying probability distribution. (Section 10.4), 397

Summary of Key Formulas

Forecasting error = Difference between a forecasted value and the true value then obtained   (Section 10.2)

$$\text{MAD} = \frac{\text{Sum of forecasting errors}}{\text{Number of forecasts}} \quad \text{(Section 10.2)}$$

$$\text{MSE} = \frac{\text{Sum of square of forecasting errors}}{\text{Number of forecasts}} \quad \text{(Section 10.2)}$$

$$\text{Seasonal factor} = \frac{\text{Average for the period}}{\text{Overall average}} \quad \text{(Section 10.3)}$$

$$\text{Seasonally adjusted value} = \frac{\text{Actual value}}{\text{Seasonal factor}} \quad \text{(Section 10.3)}$$

Last-Value Method: (Section 10.3)

$$\text{Forecast} = \text{Last value}$$

Averaging Method: (Section 10.3)

$$\text{Forecast} = \text{Average of all data to date}$$

Moving-Average Method: (Section 10.3)

$$\text{Forecast} = \text{Average of last } n \text{ values}$$

Exponential Smoothing Method: (Section 10.3)

$$\text{Forecast} = \alpha(\text{Last value}) + (1 - \alpha)(\text{Last forecast})$$

Exponential Smoothing with Trend: (Section 10.3)

$$\text{Forecast} = \alpha\,(\text{Last value}) + (1 - \alpha)(\text{Last forecast}) + \text{Estimated trend}$$

$$\text{Estimated trend} = \beta(\text{Latest trend}) + (1 - \beta)(\text{Last estimate of trend})$$

$$\text{Latest trend} = \alpha(\text{Last value} - \text{Next-to-last value}) + (1 - \alpha)(\text{Last forecast} - \text{Next-to-last forecast})$$

Linear Regression Line: (Section 10.5)

$$y = a + bx$$

Learning Aids for This Chapter in Your MS Courseware

Chapter 10 Excel Files:

Template for *Seasonal Factors*

Templates for *Last-Value Method* (with and without Seasonality)

Templates for *Averaging Method* (with and without Seasonality)

Templates for *Moving-Average Method* (with and without Seasonality)

Templates for *Exponential Smoothing Method* (with and without Seasonality)

Templates for *Exponential Smoothing with Trend* (with and without Seasonality)

Template for *Linear Regression*

An Excel Add-in:

CB Predictor (part of Crystal Ball, Professional Edition)

Interactive Management Science Modules:

Module for forecasting

Supplement to This Chapter on the CD-ROM:

Time-Series Forecasting with CB Predictor

Solved Problem (See the CD-ROM for the Solution)

10.S1. Forecasting Charitable Donations at the Union Mission

Cash donations (in thousands of dollars) at the Union Mission for 2004–2006 were as shown below.

Quarter	Donations	Quarter	Donations	Quarter	Donations
Q1 2004	242	Q1 2005	253	Q1 2006	270
Q2 2004	282	Q2 2005	290	Q2 2006	286
Q3 2004	254	Q3 2005	262	Q3 2006	271
Q4 2004	345	Q4 2005	352	Q4 2006	378

a. Ignoring seasonal effects, compare both the MAD and MSE values for the last-value method, the averaging method, the moving-average method (based on the most recent 4 quarters), the exponential smoothing method (with an initial estimate of 275 and a smoothing constant of $\alpha = 0.2$), and the exponential smoothing method with trend (with initial estimates of 275 for the average value, 2 for the trend, along with smoothing constants of $\alpha = 0.2$ and $\beta = 0.2$) when they are applied retrospectively to the years 2004–2006.

b. Determine the seasonal factors for the four quarters.

c. Repeat part *a*, but now consider the seasonal effects.

d. Using the forecasting method from part *a* or *c* with the lowest MAD value, make long-range forecasts for charitable donations in each of the quarters of 2007.

Problems

The first 16 problems should be done by hand without using the templates on page 407. To the left of the subsequent problems (or their parts), we have inserted the symbol E (for Excel) to indicate that one of the templates on page 407 can be helpful. (The forecasting module in your Interactive Management Science Modules should be used for certain problems, but this will be specified in the statement of the problem whenever needed.) An asterisk on the problem number indicates that at least a partial answer is given in the back of the book.

10.1.* The Hammaker Company's newest product has had the following sales during its first five months: 5, 17, 29, 41, 39. The sales manager now wants a forecast of sales in the next month.

 a. Use the last-value method.

 b. Use the averaging method.

 c. Use the moving-average method with the three most recent months.

 d. Given the sales pattern so far, do any of these methods seem inappropriate for obtaining the forecast? Why?

10.2. Sales of stoves have been going well for the Good-Value Department Store. These sales for the past five months have been 15, 18, 12, 17, 13. Use the following methods to obtain a forecast of sales for the next month.

 a. The last-value method.

 b. The averaging method.

 c. The moving-average method with three months.

 d. If you feel that the conditions affecting sales next month will be the same as in the last five months, which of these methods do you prefer for obtaining the forecast? Why?

10.3.* You have been forecasting sales the last four quarters. These forecasts and the true values that subsequently were obtained are shown below.

Quarter	Forecast	True Value
1	327	345
2	332	317
3	328	336
4	330	311

Calculate the forecasting error for each quarter. Then calculate MAD and MSE.

10.4. Sharon Johnson, sales manager for the Alvarez-Baines Company, is trying to choose between two methods for forecasting sales that she has been using during the past five months. During these months, the two methods obtained the forecasts shown next for the company's most important product, where the subsequent actual sales are shown on the right.

	Forecast		
Month	Method 1	Method 2	Actual Sales
1	5,324	5,208	5,582
2	5,405	5,377	4,906
3	5,195	5,462	5,755
4	5,511	5,414	6,320
5	5,762	5,549	5,153

 a. Calculate and compare MAD for these two forecasting methods. Then do the same with MSE.

 b. Sharon is uncomfortable with choosing between these two methods based on such limited data, but she also does not want to delay further before making her choice. She does have similar sales data for the three years prior to using these forecasting methods the past five months. How can these older data be used to further help her evaluate the two methods and choose one?

10.5. Figure 10.1 shows CCW's average daily call volume for each quarter of the past three years and Figure 10.4 gives the seasonally adjusted call volumes. Lydia Weigelt now wonders what these seasonally adjusted call volumes would have been had she started using seasonal factors two years ago rather than applying them retrospectively now.

 a. Use only the call volumes in year 1 to determine the seasonal factors for year 2 (so that the "average" call volume for each quarter is just the actual call volume for that quarter in year 1).

 b. Use these seasonal factors to determine the seasonally adjusted call volumes for year 2.

 c. Use the call volumes in years 1 and 2 to determine the seasonal factors for year 3.

 d. Use the seasonal factors obtained in part c to determine the seasonally adjusted call volumes for year 3.

10.6. Even when the economy is holding steady, the unemployment rate tends to fluctuate because of seasonal effects. For example, unemployment generally goes up in Quarter 3 (summer) as students (including new graduates) enter the labor market. The unemployment rate then tends to go down in Quarter 4 (fall) as students return to school and temporary help is hired for the Christmas season. Therefore, using seasonal factors to obtain a seasonally adjusted unemployment rate is helpful for painting a truer picture of economic trends.

Over the past 10 years, one state's average unemployment rates (not seasonally adjusted) in Quarters 1, 2, 3, and 4 have been 6.2 percent, 6.0 percent, 7.5 percent, and 5.5 percent, respectively. The overall average has been 6.3 percent.

a. Determine the seasonal factors for the four quarters.

b. Over the next year, the unemployment rates (not seasonally adjusted) for the four quarters turn out to be 7.8 percent, 7.4 percent, 8.7 percent, and 6.1 percent. Determine the seasonally adjusted unemployment rates for the four quarters. What does this progression of rates suggest about whether the state's economy is improving?

10.7. Ralph Billett is the manager of a real estate agency. He now wishes to develop a forecast of the number of houses that will be sold by the agency over the next year.

The agency's quarter-by-quarter sales figures over the last three years are shown below.

Quarter	Year 1	Year 2	Year 3
1	23	19	21
2	22	21	26
3	31	27	32
4	26	24	28

a. Determine the seasonal factors for the four quarters.

b. After considering seasonal effects, use the last-value method to forecast sales in Quarter 1 of next year.

c. Assuming that each of the quarterly forecasts is correct, what would the last-value method forecast as the sales in each of the four quarters next year?

d. Based on his assessment of the current state of the housing market, Ralph's best judgment is that the agency will sell 100 houses next year. Given this forecast for the year, what is the quarter-by-quarter forecast according to the seasonal factors?

10.8.* You are using the moving-average forecasting method based on the last four observations. When making the forecast for the last period, the oldest of the four observations was 1,945 and the forecast was 2,083. The true value for the last period then turned out to be 1,977. What is your new forecast for the next period?

10.9. You are using the moving-average forecasting method based on sales in the last three months to forecast sales for the next month. When making the forecast for last month, sales for the third month before were 805. The forecast for last month was 782 and then the actual sales turned out to be 793. What is your new forecast for next month?

10.10. After graduating from college with a degree in mathematical statistics, Ann Preston has been hired by the Monty Ward Company to apply statistical methods for forecasting the company's sales. For one of the company's products, the moving-average method based on sales in the 10 most recent months already is being used. Ann's first task is to update last month's forecast to obtain the forecast for next month. She learns that the forecast for last month was 1,551 and that the actual sales then turned out to be 1,532. She also learns that the sales for the 10th month before last month were 1,632. What is Ann's forecast for next month?

10.11. The J. J. Bone Company uses exponential smoothing to forecast the average daily call volume at its call center. The forecast for last month was 782, and then the actual value turned out to be 792. Obtain the forecast for next month for each of the following values of the smoothing constant: $\alpha = 0.1, 0.3, 0.5$.

10.12.* You are using exponential smoothing to obtain monthly forecasts of the sales of a certain product. The forecast for last month was 2,083, and then the actual sales turned out to be 1,973. Obtain the forecast for next month for each of the following values of the smoothing constant: $\alpha = 0.1, 0.3, 0.5$.

10.13. Three years ago, the Admissions Office for Ivy College began using exponential smoothing with a smoothing constant of 0.25 to forecast the number of applications for admission each year. Based on previous experience, this process was begun with an initial estimate of 5,000 applications. The actual number of applications then turned out to be 4,600 in the first year. Thanks to new favorable ratings in national surveys, this number grew to 5,300 in the second year and 6,000 last year.

a. Determine the forecasts that were made for each of the past three years.

b. Calculate MAD and MSE for these three years.

c. Determine the forecast for next year.

10.14. Reconsider Problem 10.13. Notice the steady trend upward in the number of applications over the past three years—from 4,600 to 5,300 to 6,000. Suppose now that the Admissions Office of Ivy College had been able to foresee this kind of trend and so had decided to use exponential smoothing with trend to do the forecasting. Suppose also that the initial estimates just over three years ago had been *average value* = 3,900 and *trend* = 700. Then, with any values of the smoothing constants, the forecasts obtained by this forecasting method would have been exactly correct for all three years.

Illustrate this fact by doing the calculations to obtain these forecasts when the smoothing constant is $\alpha = 0.25$ and the trend smoothing constant is $\beta = 0.25$.

10.15.* Exponential smoothing with trend, with a smoothing constant of $\alpha = 0.2$ and a trend smoothing constant of $\beta = 0.3$, is being used to forecast values in a time series. At this point, the last two values have been 535 and then 550. The last two forecasts have been 530 and then 540. The last estimate of trend has been 10. Use this information to forecast the next value in the time series.

10.16. The Healthwise Company produces a variety of exercise equipment. Healthwise management is very pleased with the increasing sales of its newest model of exercise bicycle. The sales during the last two months have been 4,655 and then 4,935.

Management has been using exponential smoothing with trend, with a smoothing constant of $\alpha = 0.1$ and a trend smoothing constant of $\beta = 0.2$, to forecast sales for the next month each time. The forecasts for the last two months were 4,720 and then 4,975. The last estimate of trend was 240.

Calculate the forecast of sales for next month.

10.17.* Ben Swanson, owner and manager of Swanson's Department Store, has decided to use statistical forecasting to

get a better handle on the demand for his major products. However, Ben now needs to decide which forecasting method is most appropriate for each category of product. One category is major household appliances, such as washing machines, which have a relatively stable sales level. Monthly sales of washing machines last year are shown below.

Month	Sales	Month	Sales	Month	Sales
January	23	May	22	September	21
February	24	June	27	October	29
March	22	July	20	November	23
April	28	August	26	December	28

a. Considering that the sales level is relatively stable, which of the most basic forecasting methods—the last-value method, the averaging method, or the moving-average method—do you feel would be most appropriate for forecasting future sales? Why?

E b. Use the last-value method retrospectively to determine what the forecasts would have been for the last 11 months of last year. What are MAD and MSE?

E c. Use the averaging method retrospectively to determine what the forecasts would have been for the last 11 months of last year. What are MAD and MSE?

E d. Use the moving-average method with $n = 3$ retrospectively to determine what the forecasts would have been for the last nine months of last year. What are MAD and MSE?

e. Use their MAD values to compare the three methods.

f. Use their MSE values to compare the three methods.

g. Do you feel comfortable in drawing a definitive conclusion about which of the three forecasting methods should be the most accurate in the future based on these 12 months of data?

E10.18. Reconsider Problem 10.17. Ben Swanson now has decided to use the exponential smoothing method to forecast future sales of washing machines, but he needs to decide on which smoothing constant to use. Using an initial estimate of 24, apply this method retrospectively to the 12 months of last year with $\alpha = 0.1, 0.2, 0.3, 0.4,$ and 0.5. Compare MAD for these five values of the smoothing constant α. Then do the same with MSE.

10.19. Reconsider Problem 10.17. For each of the forecasting methods specified in parts b, c, and d, use the forecasting module in your Interactive Management Science Modules to obtain the requested forecasts. Then use the accompanying graph that plots both the sales data and forecasts to answer the following questions for these forecasting methods.

a. Based on your examination of the graphs for the three forecasting methods, which method do you feel is doing the best job of forecasting with the given data? Why?

b. Ben Swanson now has found that an error was made in determining the sales for April, but he has not yet obtained the corrected sales figure. For each of the three forecasting methods, Ben wants to know which of the original monthly forecasts would change now because of changing the sales figure for April. Answer this question by dragging vertically the blue dot that corresponds to April sales and observing which of the red dots (corresponding to monthly forecasts) move.

c. Repeat part a if the sales for April change from 28 to 16.

d. Repeat part a if the sales for April change from 28 to 40.

10.20. Management of the Jackson Manufacturing Corporation wishes to choose a statistical forecasting method for forecasting total sales for the corporation. Total sales (in millions of dollars) for each month of last year are shown below.

Month	Sales	Month	Sales	Month	Sales
January	126	May	153	September	147
February	137	June	154	October	151
March	142	July	148	November	159
April	150	August	145	December	166

a. Note how the sales level is shifting significantly from month to month—first trending upward and

then dipping down before resuming an upward trend. Assuming that similar patterns would continue in the future, evaluate how well you feel each of the five forecasting methods introduced in Section 10.3 would perform in forecasting future sales.

E *b.* Apply the last-value method, the averaging method, and the moving-average method (with $n = 3$) retrospectively to last year's sales and compare their MAD values. Then compare their MSE values.

E *c.* Using an initial estimate of 120, apply the exponential smoothing method retrospectively to last year's sales with $\alpha = 0.1, 0.2, 0.3, 0.4$, and 0.5. Compare both MAD and MSE for these five values of the smoothing constant α.

E *d.* Using initial estimates of 120 for the average value and 10 for the trend, apply exponential smoothing with trend retrospectively to last year's sales. Use all combinations of the smoothing constants where $\alpha = 0.1, 0.3$, or 0.5 and $\beta = 0.1, 0.3$, or 0.5. Compare both MAD and MSE for these nine combinations.

e. Which one of the above forecasting methods would you recommend that management use? Using this method, what is the forecast of total sales for January of the new year?

10.21. Reconsider Problem 10.20. Use the lessons learned from the CCW case study to address the following questions.

a. What might be causing the significant shifts in total sales from month to month that were observed last year?

b. Given your answer to part *a*, how might the basic statistical approach to forecasting total sales be improved?

c. Describe the role of managerial judgment in applying the statistical approach developed in part *b*.

10.22. Reconsider Problem 10.20. For each of the forecasting methods specified in parts *b, c,* and *d* (with smoothing constants $\alpha = 0.5$ and $\beta = 0.5$ as needed), use the forecasting module in your Interactive Management Science Modules to obtain the requested forecasts. Then use the accompanying graph that plots both the sales data and forecasts to answer the following questions for these forecasting methods.

a. Based on your examination of the graphs for the five forecasting methods, which method do you feel is doing the best job of forecasting with the given data? Why?

b. Management now has been informed that an error was made in calculating the sales for April, but a corrected sales figure has not yet been obtained. Therefore, for each of the five forecasting methods, management wants to know which of the original monthly forecasts would change now because of changing the sales figure for April. Answer this question by dragging vertically the blue dot that corresponds to April sales and observing which of the red dots (corresponding to monthly forecasts) move.

c. Repeat part *a* if the sales for April change from 150 to 125.

d. Repeat part *a* if the sales for April change from 150 to 175.

E10.23. Choosing an appropriate value of the smoothing constant α is a key decision when applying the exponential smoothing method. When relevant historical data exist, one approach to making this decision is to apply the method retrospectively to these data with different values of α and then choose the value of α that gives the smallest MAD. Use this approach for choosing α with each of the following time series representing monthly sales. In each case, use an initial estimate of 50 and compare $\alpha = 0.1, 0.2, 0.3, 0.4$, and 0.5.

a. 51, 48, 52, 49, 53, 49, 48, 51, 50, 49

b. 52, 50, 53, 51, 52, 48, 52, 53, 49, 52

c. 50, 52, 51, 55, 53, 56, 52, 55, 54, 53

E10.24. The choice of the smoothing constants, α and β, has a considerable effect on the accuracy of the forecasts obtained by using exponential smoothing with trend. For each of the following time series, set $\alpha = 0.2$ and then compare MAD obtained with $\beta = 0.1, 0.2, 0.3, 0.4$, and 0.5. Begin with initial estimates of 50 for the average value and 2 for the trend.

a. 52, 55, 55, 58, 59, 63, 64, 66, 67, 72, 73, 74

b. 52, 55, 59, 61, 66, 69, 71, 72, 73, 74, 73, 74

c. 52, 53, 51, 50, 48, 47, 49, 52, 57, 62, 69, 74

10.25. The Andes Mining Company mines and ships copper ore. The company's sales manager, Juanita Valdes, has been using the moving-average method based on the last three years of sales to forecast the demand for the next year. However, she has become dissatisfied with the inaccurate forecasts being provided by this method.

The annual demands (in tons of copper ore) over the past 10 years are 382, 405, 398, 421, 426, 415, 443, 451, 446, 464.

a. Explain why this pattern of demands inevitably led to significant inaccuracies in the moving-average forecasts.

E *b.* Determine the moving-average forecasts for the past seven years. What are MAD and MSE? What is the forecast for next year?

E *c.* Determine what the forecasts would have been for the past 10 years if the exponential smoothing method had been used instead with an initial estimate of 380 and a smoothing constant of $\alpha = 0.5$. What are MAD and MSE? What is the forecast for next year?

E *d.* Determine what the forecasts would have been for the past 10 years if exponential smoothing with trend had been used instead. Use initial estimates of 370 for the average value and 10 for the trend, with smoothing constants $\alpha = 0.25$ and $\beta = 0.25$.

e. Based on the MAD and MSE values, which of these three methods do you recommend using hereafter?

10.26. Reconsider Problem 10.25. For each of the forecasting methods specified in parts *b, c,* and *d,* use the forecasting module in your Interactive Management Science

Modules to obtain the requested forecasts. After examining the accompanying graph that plots both the demand data and forecasts, write a one-sentence description for each method regarding whether its plot of forecasts tends to lie below or above or at about the same level as the demands being forecasted. Then use these conclusions to select one of the methods to recommend using hereafter.

E10.27.*The Pentel Microchip Company has started production of its new microchip. The first phase in this production is the wafer fabrication process. Because of the great difficulty in fabricating acceptable wafers, many of these tiny wafers must be rejected because they are defective. Therefore, management places great emphasis on continually improving the wafer fabrication process to increase its *production yield* (the percentage of wafers fabricated in the current lot that are of acceptable quality for producing microchips).

So far, the production yields of the respective lots have been 15 percent, 21 percent, 24 percent, 32 percent, 37 percent, 41 percent, 40 percent, 47 percent, 51 percent, and 53 percent. Use exponential smoothing with trend to forecast the production yield of the next lot. Begin with initial estimates of 10 percent for the average value and 5 percent for the trend. Use smoothing constants of $\alpha = 0.2$ and $\beta = 0.2$.

10.28. The Centerville Water Department provides water for the entire town and outlying areas. The number of acre-feet of water consumed in each of the four seasons of the three preceding years is shown below.

Season	Year 1	Year 2	Year 3
Winter	25	27	24
Spring	47	46	49
Summer	68	72	70
Fall	42	39	44

E   a. Determine the seasonal factors for the four seasons.

E   b. After considering seasonal effects, use the last-value method to forecast water consumption next winter.

   c. Assuming that each of the forecasts for the next three seasons is correct, what would the last-value method forecast as the water consumption in each of the four seasons next year?

E   d. After considering seasonal effects, use the averaging method to forecast water consumption next winter.

E   e. After considering seasonal effects, use the moving-average method based on four seasons to forecast water consumption next winter.

E   f. After considering seasonal effects, use the exponential smoothing method with an initial estimate of 46 and a smoothing constant of $\alpha = 0.1$ to forecast water consumption next winter.

E   g. Compare both the MAD and MSE values of these four forecasting methods when they are applied retrospectively to the last three years.

10.29. Reconsider Problem 10.7. Ralph Billett realizes that the last-value method is considered to be the naive forecasting method, so he wonders whether he should be using another method. Therefore, he has decided to use the available Excel templates that consider seasonal effects to apply various statistical forecasting methods retrospectively to the past three years of data and compare both their MAD and MSE values.

E   a. Determine the seasonal factors for the four quarters.

E   b. Apply the last-value method.

E   c. Apply the averaging method.

E   d. Apply the moving-average method based on the four most recent quarters of data.

E   e. Apply the exponential smoothing method with an initial estimate of 25 and a smoothing constant of $\alpha = 0.25$.

E   f. Apply exponential smoothing with trend with smoothing constants of $\alpha = 0.25$ and $\beta = 0.25$. Use initial estimates of 25 for the average value and 0 for the trend.

E   g. Compare both the MAD and MSE values for these methods. Use the one with the smallest MAD to forecast sales in Quarter 1 of next year.

   h. Use the forecast in part g and the seasonal factors to make long-range forecasts now of the sales in the remaining quarters of next year.

E10.30. Transcontinental Airlines maintains a computerized forecasting system to forecast the number of customers in each fare class who will fly on each flight in order to allocate the available reservations to fare classes properly. For example, consider *economy-class customers* flying in midweek on the noon flight from New York to Los Angeles. The following table shows the average number of such passengers during each month of the year just completed. The table also shows the seasonal factor that has been assigned to each month based on historical data.

Month	Average Number	Seasonal Factor	Month	Average Number	Seasonal Factor
January	68	0.90	July	94	1.17
February	71	0.88	August	96	1.15
March	66	0.91	September	80	0.97
April	72	0.93	October	73	0.91
May	77	0.96	November	84	1.05
June	85	1.09	December	89	1.08

a. After considering seasonal effects, compare both the MAD and MSE values for the last-value method, the averaging method, the moving-average method (based on the most recent three months), and the exponential smoothing method (with an initial estimate of 80 and a smoothing constant of $\alpha = 0.2$) when they are applied retrospectively to the past year.

b. Use the forecasting method with the smallest MAD value to forecast the average number of these passengers flying in January of the new year.

10.31. Reconsider Problem 10.30. The economy is beginning to boom so the management of Transcontinental

Airlines is predicting that the number of people flying will steadily increase this year over the relatively flat (seasonally adjusted) level of last year. Since the forecasting methods considered in Problem 10.30 are relatively slow in adjusting to such a trend, consideration is being given to switching to exponential smoothing with trend.

Subsequently, as the year goes on, management's prediction proves to be true. The following table shows the corresponding average number of passengers in each month of the new year.

Month	Average Number	Month	Average Number	Month	Average Number
January	75	May	85	September	94
February	76	June	99	October	90
March	81	July	107	November	106
April	84	August	108	December	110

E *a.* Repeat part *a* of Problem 10.30 for the two years of data.

E *b.* After considering seasonal effects, apply exponential smoothing with trend to just the new year. Use initial estimates of 80 for the average value and 2 for the trend, along with smoothing constants of $\alpha = 0.2$ and $\beta = 0.2$. Compare MAD for this method to the MAD values obtained in part *a*. Then do the same with MSE.

E *c.* Repeat part *b* when exponential smoothing with trend is begun at the beginning of the first year and then applied to both years, just like the other forecasting methods in part *a*. Use the same initial estimates and smoothing constants except change the initial estimate of trend to 0.

d. Based on these results, which forecasting method would you recommend that Transcontinental Airlines use hereafter?

10.32. Quality Bikes is a wholesale firm that specializes in the distribution of bicycles. In the past, the company has

maintained ample inventories of bicycles to enable filling orders immediately, so informal rough forecasts of demand were sufficient to make the decisions on when to replenish inventory. However, the company's new president, Marcia Salgo, intends to run a tighter ship. Scientific inventory management is to be used to reduce inventory levels and minimize total variable inventory costs. At the same time, Marcia has ordered the development of a computerized forecasting system based on statistical forecasting that considers seasonal effects. The system is to generate three sets of forecasts—one based on the moving-average method, a second based on the exponential smoothing method, and a third based on exponential smoothing with trend. The average of these three forecasts for each month is to be used for inventory management purposes.

The following table gives the available data on monthly sales of 10-speed bicycles over the past three years. The last column also shows monthly sales this year, which is the first year of operation of the new forecasting system.

	Past Sales			
Month	Year 1	Year 2	Year 3	Current Sales This Year
January	352	317	338	364
February	329	331	346	343
March	365	344	383	391
April	358	386	404	437
May	412	423	431	458
June	446	472	459	494
July	420	415	433	468
August	471	492	518	555
September	355	340	309	387
October	312	301	335	364
November	567	629	594	662
December	533	505	527	581

E   *a.* Determine the seasonal factors for the 12 months based on past sales.

E   *b.* After considering seasonal effects, apply the moving-average method based on the most recent three months to forecast monthly sales for each month of this year.

E   *c.* After considering seasonal effects, apply the exponential smoothing method to forecast monthly sales this year. Use an initial estimate of 420 and a smoothing constant of $\alpha = 0.2$.

E   *d.* After considering seasonal effects, apply exponential smoothing with trend to forecast monthly sales this year. Use initial estimates of 420 for the average value and 0 for the trend, along with smoothing constants of $\alpha = 0.2$ and $\beta = 0.2$.

   e. Compare both the MAD and MSE values obtained in parts *b, c,* and *d.*

   f. Calculate the combined forecast for each month by averaging the forecasts for that month obtained in parts *b, c,* and *d.* Then calculate MAD for these combined forecasts.

   g. Based on these results, what is your recommendation for how to do the forecasts next year?

10.33.* Long a market leader in the production of heavy machinery, the Spellman Corporation recently has been enjoying a steady increase in the sales of its new lathe. The sales over the past 10 months are shown below.

Month	Sales	Month	Sales
1	430	6	514
2	446	7	532
3	464	8	548
4	480	9	570
5	498	10	591

Because of this steady increase, management has decided to use *causal forecasting,* with the month as the independent variable and sales as the dependent variable, to forecast sales in the coming months.

   a. Plot these data on a two-dimensional graph with the month on the horizontal axis and sales on the vertical axis.

E   *b.* Find the formula for the linear regression line that fits these data.

   c. Plot this line on the graph constructed in part *a.*

   d. Use this line to forecast sales in month 11.

   e. Use this line to forecast sales in month 20.

   f. What does the formula for the linear regression line indicate is roughly the average growth in sales per month?

10.34.   Reconsider Problems 10.13 and 10.14. Since the number of applications for admission submitted to Ivy College has been increasing at a steady rate, causal forecasting can be used to forecast the number of applications in future years by letting the year be the independent variable and the number of applications be the dependent variable.

   a. Plot the data for years 1, 2, and 3 on a two-dimensional graph with the year on the horizontal axis and the number of applications on the vertical axis.

   b. Since the three points in this graph line up in a straight line, this straight line is the linear regression line. Draw this line.

E   *c.* Find the formula for this linear regression line.

   d. Use this line to forecast the number of applications for each of the next five years (years 4 through 8).

   e. As these next years go on, conditions change for the worse at Ivy College. The favorable ratings in the national surveys that had propelled the growth in applications turn unfavorable. Consequently, the number of applications turn out to be 6,300 in year 4 and 6,200 in year 5, followed by sizable drops to 5,600 in year 6 and 5,200 in year 7. Does it still make sense to use the forecast for year 8 obtained in part *d?* Explain.

E   *f.* Plot the data for all seven years. Find the formula for the linear regression line based on all these data and plot this line. Use this formula to forecast the number of applications for year 8. Does the linear regression line provide a close fit to the data? Given this answer, do you have much confidence in the forecast it provides for year 8? Does it make sense to continue to use a linear regression line when changing conditions cause a large shift in the underlying trend in the data?

E   *g.* Apply exponential smoothing with trend to all seven years of data to forecast the number of applications in year 8. Use initial estimates of 3,900 for the average and 700 for the trend, along with smoothing constants of $\alpha = 0.5$ and $\beta = 0.5$. When the underlying trend in the data stays the same, causal forecasting provides the best possible linear regression line (according to the method of least squares) for making forecasts. However, when changing conditions cause a shift in the underlying trend, what advantage does exponential smoothing with trend have over causal forecasting?

10.35.   Reconsider Problem 10.25. Despite some fluctuations from year to year, note that there has been a basic trend upward in the annual demand for copper ore over the past 10 years. Therefore, by projecting this trend forward, causal forecasting can be used to forecast demands in future years by letting the year be the independent variable and the demand be the dependent variable.

   a. Plot the data for the past 10 years (years 1 through 10) on a two-dimensional graph with the year on the horizontal axis and the demand on the vertical axis.

E   *b.* Find the formula for the linear regression line that fits these data.

   c. Plot this line on the graph constructed in part *a.*

   d. Use this line to forecast demand next year (year 11).

   e. Use this line to forecast demand in year 15.

   f. What does the formula for the linear regression line indicate is roughly the average growth in demand per year?

g. Use the forecasting module in your Interactive Management Science Modules to generate a graph of the data and the linear regression line. Then experiment with the data to see how the linear regression line shifts as you drag any of the data points up or down.

10.36. Luxury Cruise Lines has a fleet of ships that travel to Alaska repeatedly every summer (and elsewhere during other times of the year). A considerable amount of advertising is done each winter to help generate enough passenger business for that summer. With the coming of a new winter, a decision needs to be made about how much advertising to do this year.

The following table shows the amount of advertising (in thousands of dollars) and the resulting sales (in thousands of passengers booked for a cruise) for each of the past five years.

Amount of advertising ($1,000s)	225	400	350	275	450
Sales (thousands of passengers)	16	21	20	17	23

a. To use causal forecasting to forecast sales for a given amount of advertising, which need to be the dependent variable and the independent variable?

b. Plot the data on a graph.

E c. Find the formula for the linear regression line that fits these data. Then plot this line on the graph constructed in part *b*.

d. Forecast the sales that would be attained by expending $300,000 on advertising.

e. Estimate the amount of advertising that would need to be done to attain a booking of 22,000 passengers.

f. According to the linear regression line, about how much increase in sales can be attained on the average per $1,000 increase in the amount of advertising?

10.37. Reconsider Problem 10.36. Use the forecasting module in your Interactive Management Science Modules to generate the linear regression line. On the resulting graph that shows this line and the five data points (as blue dots), note that the leftmost data point, the middle data point, and the rightmost data point all lie very close to the line. You can see how the linear regression line shifts as any one of these data points moves up or down by moving your mouse onto the blue dot at this point and dragging it vertically.

For each of these three data points, determine whether the linear regression line shifts above or below this point or whether it still passes essentially through it when the following change is made in one of these data points (but none of the others).

a. Change the sales from 16 to 19 when the amount of advertising is 225.

b. Change the sales from 23 to 26 when the amount of advertising is 450.

c. Change the sales from 20 to 23 when the amount of advertising is 350.

10.38. To support its large fleet, North American Airlines maintains an extensive inventory of spare parts, including wing flaps. The number of wing flaps needed in inventory to replace damaged wing flaps each month depends partially on the number of flying hours for the fleet that month, since increased usage increases the chances of damage.

The following table shows both the number of replacement wing flaps needed and the number of thousands of flying hours for the entire fleet for each of several recent months.

Thousands of flying hours	162	149	185	171	138	154
Number of wing flaps needed	12	9	13	14	10	11

a. Identify the dependent variable and the independent variable for doing causal forecasting of the number of wing flaps needed for a given number of flying hours.

b. Plot the data on a graph.

E c. Find the formula for the linear regression line.

d. Plot this line on the graph constructed in part *b*.

e. Forecast the average number of wing flaps needed in a month in which 150,000 flying hours are planned.

f. Repeat part *e* for 200,000 flying hours.

g. Use the forecasting module in your Interactive Management Science Modules to generate a graph of the data and the linear regression line. Then experiment with the data to see how the linear regression line shifts as you drag any of the data points up or down.

E10.39. Joe Barnes is the owner of Standing Tall, one of the major roofing companies in town. Much of the company's business comes from building roofs on new houses. Joe has learned that general contractors constructing new houses typically will subcontract the roofing work about two months after construction begins. Therefore, to help him develop long-range schedules for his work crews, Joe has decided to use county records on the number of housing construction permits issued each month to forecast the number of roofing jobs on new houses he will have two months later.

Joe has now gathered the following data for each month over the past year, where the second column gives the number of housing construction permits issued in that month and the third column shows the number of roofing jobs on new houses that were subcontracted out to Standing Tall in that month.

Month	Permits	Jobs	Month	Permits	Jobs
January	323	19	July	446	34
February	359	17	August	407	37
March	396	24	September	374	33
April	421	23	October	343	30
May	457	28	November	311	27
June	472	32	December	277	22

Use a causal forecasting approach to develop a forecasting procedure for Joe to use hereafter.

Case 10-1

Finagling the Forecasts

Mark Lawrence has been pursuing a vision for more than two years. This pursuit began when he became frustrated in his role as director of Human Resources at Cutting Edge, a large company manufacturing computers and computer peripherals. At that time, the Human Resources Department under his direction provided records and benefits administration to the 60,000 Cutting Edge employees throughout the United States, and 35 separate records and benefits administration centers existed across the country. Employees contacted these records and benefits centers to obtain information about dental plans and stock options, change tax forms and personal information, and process leaves of absence and retirements. The decentralization of these administration centers caused numerous headaches for Mark. He had to deal with employee complaints often since each center interpreted company policies differently—communicating inconsistent and sometimes inaccurate answers to employees. His department also suffered high operating costs since operating 35 separate centers created inefficiency.

His vision? To centralize records and benefits administration by establishing one administration center. This centralized records and benefits administration center would perform two distinct functions: data management and customer service. The data management function would include updating employee records after performance reviews and maintaining the human resource management system. The customer service function would include establishing a call center to answer employee questions concerning records and benefits and to process records and benefits changes over the phone.

One year after proposing his vision to management, Mark received the go-ahead from Cutting Edge corporate headquarters. He prepared his "to do" list—specifying computer and phone systems requirements, installing hardware and software, integrating data from the 35 separate administration centers, standardizing record-keeping and response procedures, and staffing the administration center. Mark delegated the systems requirements, installation, and integration jobs to a competent group of technology specialists. He took on the responsibility of standardizing procedures and staffing the administration center.

Mark had spent many years in human resources and therefore had little problem with standardizing record-keeping and response procedures. He encountered trouble in determining the number of representatives needed to staff the center, however. He was particularly worried about staffing the call center since the representatives answering phones interact directly with customers—the 60,000 Cutting Edge employees. The customer service representatives would receive extensive training so that they would know the records and benefits policies backwards and forwards—enabling them to answer questions accurately and process changes efficiently. Overstaffing would cause Mark to suffer the high costs of training unneeded representatives and paying the surplus representatives the high salaries that go along with such an intense job. Understaffing would cause Mark to continue to suffer the headaches from customer complaints—something he definitely wanted to avoid.

The number of customer service representatives Mark needed to hire depended on the number of calls that the records and benefits call center would receive. Mark therefore needed to forecast the number of calls that the new centralized center would receive. He approached the forecasting problem by using judgmental forecasting. He studied data from one of the 35 decentralized administration centers and learned that the decentralized center had serviced 15,000 customers and had received 2,000 calls per month. He concluded that since the new centralized center would service four times the number of customers—60,000 customers—it would receive four times the number of calls—8,000 calls per month.

Mark slowly checked off the items on his "to do" list, and the centralized records and benefits administration center opened one year after Mark had received the go-ahead from corporate headquarters.

Now, after operating the new center for 13 weeks, Mark's call center forecasts are proving to be terribly inaccurate. The number of calls the center receives is roughly three times as large as the 8,000 calls per month that Mark had forecasted. Because of demand overload, the call center is slowly going to hell in a handbasket. Customers calling the center must wait an average of five minutes before speaking to a representative, and Mark is receiving numerous complaints. At the same time, the customer service representatives are unhappy and on the verge of quitting because of the stress created by the demand overload. Even corporate headquarters has become aware of the staff and service inadequacies, and executives have been breathing down Mark's neck demanding improvements.

Mark needs help, and he approaches you to forecast demand for the call center more accurately.

Luckily, when Mark first established the call center, he realized the importance of keeping operational data, and he provides you with the number of calls received on each day of the week over the last 13 weeks. The data (shown next) begins in week 44 of the last year and continues to week 5 of the current year.

	Monday	Tuesday	Wednesday	Thursday	Friday
Week 44	1,130	851	859	828	726
Week 45	1,085	1,042	892	840	799
Week 46	1,303	1,121	1,003	1,113	1,005
Week 47	2,652	2,825	1,841	0	0
Week 48	1,949	1,507	989	990	1,084
Week 49	1,260	1,134	941	847	714
Week 50	1,002	847	922	842	784
Week 51	823	0	0	401	429
Week 52/1	1,209	830	0	1,082	841
Week 2	1,362	1,174	967	930	853
Week 3	924	954	1,346	904	758
Week 4	886	878	802	945	610
Week 5	910	754	705	729	772

Mark indicates that the days where no calls were received were holidays.

a. Mark first asks you to forecast daily demand for the next week using the data from the past 13 weeks. You should make the forecasts for all the days of the next week now (at the end of week 5), but you should provide a different forecast for each day of the week by treating the forecast for a single day as being the actual call volume on that day.

1. From working at the records and benefits administration center, you know that demand follows "seasonal" patterns within the week. For example, more employees call at the beginning of the week when they are fresh and productive than at the end of the week when they are planning for the weekend. You therefore realize that you must account for the seasonal patterns and adjust the data that Mark gave you accordingly. What is the seasonally adjusted call volume for the past 13 weeks?

2. Using the seasonally adjusted call volume, forecast the daily demand for the next week using the last-value forecasting method.

3. Using the seasonally adjusted call volume, forecast the daily demand for the next week using the averaging forecasting method.

4. Using the seasonally adjusted call volume, forecast the daily demand for the next week using the moving-average forecasting method. You decide to use the five most recent days in this analysis.

5. Using the seasonally adjusted call volume, forecast the daily demand for the next week using the exponential smoothing forecasting method. You decide to use a smoothing constant of 0.1 because you believe that demand without seasonal effects remains relatively stable. Use the daily call volume average over the past 13 weeks for the initial estimate.

b. After one week, the period you have forecasted passes. You realize that you are able to determine the accuracy of your forecasts because you now have the actual call volumes from the week you had forecasted. The actual call volumes are shown below.

	Monday	Tuesday	Wednesday	Thursday	Friday
Week 6	723	677	521	571	498

For each of the forecasting methods, calculate the mean absolute deviation for the method and evaluate the performance of the method. When calculating the mean absolute deviation, you should use the actual forecasts you found in part *a* above. You should not recalculate the forecasts based on the actual values. In your evaluation, provide an explanation for the effectiveness or ineffectiveness of the method.

You realize that the forecasting methods that you have investigated do not provide a great degree of accuracy, and you decide to use a creative approach to forecasting that combines the statistical and judgmental approaches. You know that Mark had used data from one of the 35 decentralized records and benefits administration centers to perform his original forecasting. You

therefore suspect that call volume data exists for this decentralized center. Because the decentralized centers performed the same functions as the new centralized center currently performs, you decide that the call volumes from the decentralized center will help you forecast the call volumes for the new centralized center. You simply need to understand how the decentralized volumes relate to the new centralized volumes. Once you understand this relationship, you can use the call volumes from the decentralized center to forecast the call volumes for the centralized center.

You approach Mark and ask him whether call center data exist for the decentralized center. He tells you that data exist, but data do not exist in the format that you need. Case volume data—not call volume data—exist. You do not understand the distinction, so Mark continues his explanation. There are two types of demand data—case volume data and call volume data. Case volume data count the actions taken by the representatives at the call center. Call volume data count the number of calls answered by the representatives at the call center. A case may require one call or multiple calls to resolve it. Thus, the number of cases is always less than or equal to the number of calls.

You know you only have case volume data for the decentralized center, and you certainly do not want to compare apples and oranges. You therefore ask if case volume data exist for the new centralized center. Mark gives you a wicked grin

and nods his head. He sees where you are going with your forecasts, and he tells you that he will have the data for you within the hour.

c. At the end of the hour, Mark arrives at your desk with two data sets: weekly case volumes for the decentralized center and weekly case volumes for the centralized center. You ask Mark if he has data for daily case volumes, and he tells you that he does not. You therefore first have to forecast the weekly demand for the next week and then break this weekly demand into daily demand.

	Decentralized Case Volume	Centralized Case Volume
Week 44	612	2,052
Week 45	721	2,170
Week 46	693	2,779
Week 47	540	2,334
Week 48	1,386	2,514
Week 49	577	1,713
Week 50	405	1,927
Week 51	441	1,167
Week 52/1	655	1,549
Week 2	572	2,126
Week 3	475	2,337
Week 4	530	1,916
Week 5	595	2,098

The decentralized center was shut down last year when the new centralized center opened, so you have the decentralized case data spanning from week 44 of two years ago to week 5 of last year. You compare this decentralized data to the centralized data spanning from week 44 of last year to week 5 of this year. The weekly case volumes are shown in the above table.

1. Find a mathematical relationship between the decentralized case volume data and the centralized case volume data.

2. Now that you have a relationship between the weekly decentralized case volume and the weekly centralized case volume, you are able to forecast the weekly case volume for the new center. Unfortunately, you do not need the weekly case volume; you need the daily call volume. To calculate call volume from case volume, you perform further analysis and determine that each case generates an average of 1.5 calls. To calculate daily call volume from weekly call volume, you decide to use the seasonal factors

as conversion factors. Given the following case volume data from the decentralized center for week 6 of last year, forecast the daily call volume for the new center for week 6 of this year.

	Week 6
Decentralized case volume	613

3. Using the actual call volumes given in part *b*, calculate the mean absolute deviation and evaluate the effectiveness of this forecasting method.

d. Which forecasting method would you recommend Mark use and why? As the call center continues its operation, how would you recommend improving the forecasting procedure?

Chapter **Eleven**

Queueing Models

Learning objectives

After completing this chapter, you should be able to

1. Describe the elements of a queueing model.
2. Identify the characteristics of the probability distributions that are commonly used in queueing models.
3. Give many examples of various types of queueing systems that are commonly encountered.
4. Identify the key measures of performance for queueing systems and the relationships between these measures.
5. Describe the main types of basic queueing models.
6. Determine which queueing model is most appropriate from a description of the queueing system being considered.
7. Apply a queueing model to determine the key measures of performance for a queueing system.
8. Describe how differences in the importance of customers can be incorporated into priority queueing models.
9. Describe some key insights that queueing models provide about how queueing systems should be designed.
10. Apply economic analysis to determine how many servers should be provided in a queueing system.

In Great Britain, waiting lines are referred to as *queues,* so this term has been adopted by management scientists.

Queues (waiting lines) are a part of everyday life. We all wait in queues to buy a movie ticket, make a bank deposit, pay for groceries, mail a package, obtain food in a cafeteria, start a ride in an amusement park, and so on. We have become accustomed to considerable amounts of waiting, but still we get annoyed by unusually long waits.

However, having to wait is not just a petty personal annoyance. The amount of time that a nation's populace wastes by waiting in queues is a major factor in both the quality of life there and the efficiency of the nation's economy. For example, before its dissolution, the USSR was notorious for the tremendously long queues that its citizens frequently had to endure just to purchase basic necessities. Even in the United States today, it has been estimated that Americans spend 37,000,000,000 hours per year waiting in queues. If this time could be spent productively instead, it would amount to nearly 20 million person-years of useful work each year!

Even this staggering figure does not tell the whole story of the impact of causing excessive waiting. Great inefficiencies also occur because of other kinds of waiting than people standing in line. For example, making machines wait to be repaired may result in lost production. Vehicles (including ships and trucks) that need to wait to be unloaded may delay subsequent shipments. Airplanes waiting to take off or land may disrupt later travel schedules. Delays in telecommunication transmissions due to saturated lines may cause data glitches. Causing manufacturing jobs to wait to be performed may disrupt subsequent production. Delaying service jobs beyond their due dates may result in lost future business.

Making customers, employees, or jobs wait very long in a queue can have serious consequences for any business.

Queueing theory is the study of waiting in all these various guises. It uses *queueing models* to represent the various types of *queueing systems* (systems that involve queues of some kind) that arise in practice. Formulas for each model indicate how the corresponding queueing system should perform, including the average amount of waiting that will occur, under a variety of circumstances.

Queueing models often are used to determine how much service capacity should be provided to a queue to avoid excessive waiting.

Therefore, these queueing models are very helpful for determining how to operate a queueing system in the most effective way. Providing too much service capacity to operate the system involves excessive costs. But not providing enough service results in excessive waiting and all its unfortunate consequences. The models enable finding an appropriate balance between the cost of service and the amount of waiting.

The first three sections of this chapter describe the elements of queueing models, give various examples of important queueing systems to which these models can be applied, and present measures of performance for these queueing systems. Section 11.4 then introduces a case study that will be carried through most of the chapter. Three subsequent sections present the most important queueing models in the context of analyzing the case study. Section 11.8 summarizes some key insights from the case study for designing queueing systems and Section 11.9 describes how economic analysis can be used to determine the number of servers to provide in a queueing system. Additional queueing models are described in the supplement to this chapter on the CD-ROM.

11.1 ELEMENTS OF A QUEUEING MODEL

We begin by describing the basic type of queueing system assumed by the queueing models in this chapter.

A Basic Queueing System

Figure 11.1 depicts a typical **queueing system. Customers** arrive individually to receive some kind of service. If an arrival cannot be served immediately, that customer joins a **queue** (waiting line) to await service. (The queue does not include the customers who are currently being served.) One or more **servers** at the service facility provide the service. Each customer is individually served by one of the servers and then departs. You can see a demonstration of a queueing system in action by viewing the Waiting Line module in your Interactive Management Science Modules at **www.mhhe.com/hillier3e** or on the CD-ROM.

The customers coming to some queueing systems are vehicles or machines or jobs instead of people.

For some queueing systems, the customers are *people.* However, in other cases, the customers might be *vehicles* (e.g., airplanes waiting to take off on a runway), *machines* (e.g., machines waiting to be repaired), or other *items* (e.g., jobs waiting for a manufacturing operation).

A server commonly is an individual person. However, it might instead be a crew of people working together to serve each customer. The server can also be a machine, a vehicle, an electronic device, and so forth.

In most cases, the queue is just an ordinary waiting line. However, it is not necessary for the customers to be standing in line in front of a physical structure that constitutes the service

FIGURE 11.1

A basic queueing system, where each customer is indicated by *C* and each server by *S*. Although this figure shows four servers, some queueing systems (including the example in this section) have only a single server.

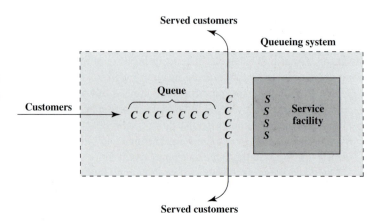

TABLE 11.1
The Data for Herr Cutter's First Five Customers

Customer	Time of Arrival	Haircut Begins	Duration of Haircut	Haircut Ends
1	8:03	8:03	17 minutes	8:20
2	8:15	8:20	21 minutes	8:41
3	8:25	8:41	19 minutes	9:00
4	8:30	9:00	15 minutes	9:15
5	9:05	9:15	20 minutes	9:35
6	9:43	—	—	—

facility. They might be sitting in a waiting room. They might even be scattered throughout an area waiting for a server to come to them (e.g., stationary machines needing repair).

The next section presents many more examples of important queueing systems that fit Figure 11.1 and the above description. All the queueing models in this chapter also are based on this figure.

However, we also should mention that more complicated kinds of queueing systems sometimes do arise in practice. For example, a server might serve a group of customers simultaneously. Customers also might arrive in a group rather than individually. Impatient customers might leave before receiving service. The queueing system might include multiple queues, one for each server, with customers occasionally switching queues. It might include multiple service facilities, where some customers need to go to more than one of the facilities to obtain all the required service. (This last type of queueing system is referred to as a *queueing network.*) Such queueing systems also are quite important, but we will not delve into the more complicated queueing models that have been developed to deal with them. The next two chapters will describe another technique (computer simulation) that often is used to analyze complex queueing systems.

An Example

Herr Cutter is a German barber who runs a one-man barber shop. Thus, his shop is a basic queueing system for which he is the only server.

Herr Cutter opens his shop at 8:00 A.M. each weekday morning. Table 11.1 shows his queueing system in action over the beginning of a typical morning. For each of his first five customers, the table indicates when the customer arrived, when his haircut began, how long the haircut took, and when the haircut was finished.

Figure 11.2 plots the number of customers in this queueing system over the first 100 minutes. This number includes both the customers waiting to begin a haircut and the one already

FIGURE 11.2
The evolution of the number of customers in Herr Cutter's barber shop over the first 100 minutes (from 8:00 to 9:40), given the data in Table 11.1.

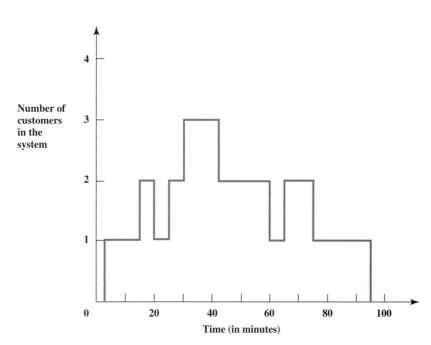

under way. Thus, the number of customers in the queue (only those waiting to begin) is one less (except that this number is zero when the number of customers in the queueing system is zero).

Referring to this example, let us now look at the kinds of assumptions that the queueing models make about the different parts of a basic queueing system.

Arrivals

The times between consecutive arrivals to a queueing system are called the **interarrival times.** For Herr Cutter's barber shop, the second column of Table 11.1 indicates that the interarrival times on this particular morning are 12 minutes, 10 minutes, 5 minutes, 35 minutes, and 38 minutes.

This high variability in the interarrival times is common for queueing systems. As with Herr Cutter, it usually is impossible to predict just how long until the next customer will arrive.

However, after gathering a lot more data such as in the second column of Table 11.1, it does become possible to do two things:

1. Estimate the *expected number* of arrivals per unit time. This quantity is normally referred to as the **mean arrival rate.** (The symbol for this quantity is λ, which is the Greek letter lambda.)
2. Estimate the *form* of the probability distribution of interarrival times.

The mean of this distribution actually comes directly from item 1. Since

$$\lambda = \text{Mean arrival rate for customers coming to the queueing system}$$

the mean of the probability distribution of interarrival times is

$$\frac{1}{\lambda} = \text{Expected interarrival time}$$

For example, after gathering more data, Herr Cutter finds that 300 customers have arrived over a period of 100 hours.[1] Therefore, the estimate of λ is

$$\lambda = \frac{300 \text{ customers}}{100 \text{ hours}} = 3 \text{ customers per hour on the average}$$

The corresponding estimate of the expected interarrival time is

$$\frac{1}{\lambda} = \frac{1}{3} \text{hour between customers on the average}$$

Most queueing models assume that the *form* of the probability distribution of interarrival times is an *exponential distribution,* as explained below.

The Exponential Distribution for Interarrival Times

Figure 11.3 shows the shape of an exponential distribution, where the height of the curve at various times represents the relative likelihood of those times occurring. Note in the figure how the highest points on the curve are at very small times and then the curve drops down "exponentially" as time increases. This indicates a high likelihood of small interarrival times, well under the mean. However, the long tail of the distribution also indicates a small chance of a very large interarrival time, much larger than the mean. All this is characteristic of interarrival times observed in practice. Several customers may arrive quickly. Then there may be a long pause until the next arrival.

This variability in interarrival times makes it impossible to predict just when future arrivals will occur. When the variability is as large as for the exponential distribution, this is referred to as having *random arrivals.*

---

[1] The count of 300 arrivals includes those customers who enter the barber shop but decide not to stay because the wait would be too long. The effect of these immediate departures is analyzed in the supplement to this chapter on the CD-ROM.

FIGURE 11.3

The shape of an exponential distribution, commonly used in queueing models as the distribution of interarrival times (and sometimes as the distribution of service times as well).

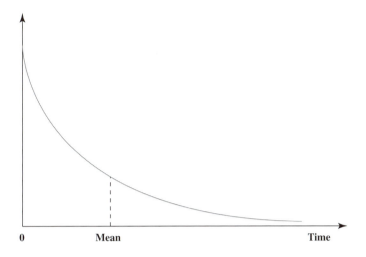

0   Mean   **Time**

For most queueing systems, the servers have no control over when customers will arrive. In this case, the customers generally arrive *randomly*. Having *random arrivals* means that arrival times are completely unpredictable in the sense that the chance of an arrival in the next minute always is just the same (no more and no less) as for any other minute. It does not matter how long it has been since the last arrival occurred. The only distribution of interarrival times that fits having random arrivals is the exponential distribution.

Interarrival times have an exponential distribution when the customers arrive randomly. In this case, the time of the next arrival always is completely uninfluenced by when the last arrival occurred (called the lack-of-memory property).

The fact that the probability of an arrival in the next minute is completely uninfluenced by when the last arrival occurred is called the **lack-of-memory property** (or the *Markovian property*). This is a strange property, because it implies that the probability distribution of the *remaining time from now* until the next arrival occurs always is the same, regardless of whether the last arrival occurred just now or a long time ago. Therefore, this distribution of the remaining time from now is the same as the distribution of the *total interarrival time* given in Figure 11.3. (This is what causes the probability of an arrival in the next minute to always be the same.) Although this concept of a lack-of-memory property takes some getting used to, it is an integral part of what is meant by having random arrivals.

The Queue

The queue is where customers wait before being served. For Herr Cutter's barber shop, the customers in the queue sit in chairs (other than the barber's chair) while waiting to begin a haircut.

Because there are two ways of counting the customers, queueing models distinguish between them with the following terminology.

The queue does not include the customers who are already being served.

The **number of customers in the queue** (or *queue size* for short) is the number of customers waiting for service to begin. The **number of customers in the system** is the number in the queue *plus* the number currently being served.

For example, Figure 11.1 shows 7 customers in the queue plus 4 more being served by the 4 servers, so a total of 11 customers are in the system. Since Herr Cutter is the only server for his queueing system, the number of customers in his queue is one less than the number of customers in the system shown in Figure 11.2 (except that the number in the queue is zero when the number in the system is zero).

The **queue capacity** is the maximum number of customers that can be held in the queue. An **infinite queue** is one in which, for all practical purposes, an unlimited number of customers can be held there. When the capacity is small enough that it needs to be taken into account, then the queue is called a **finite queue.** During those times when a finite queue is full, any arriving customers will immediately leave.

Herr Cutter's queue actually is a finite queue. The queue capacity is three since he provides only three chairs (other than the barber's chair) for waiting. (He has found that his customers

All the queueing models in this chapter assume an infinite queue, so no limit is placed on the number of customers that can be held in the queue.

typically are unwilling to wait for a haircut when there already are three customers waiting in front of them.)

Unless specified otherwise, queueing models conventionally assume that the queue is an *infinite* queue. (All the models in this chapter make this assumption, but the chapter supplement on the CD-ROM introduces a model that assumes a finite queue. This model is used to analyze Herr Cutter's barber shop.)

The **queue discipline** refers to the order in which members of the queue are selected to begin service. The most common is *first-come, first-served* (FCFS). However, other possibilities include *random selection,* some *priority procedure,* or even *last-come, first-served.* (This last possibility occurs, for example, when jobs brought to a machine are piled on top of the preceding jobs and then the machine operator takes the next job to be performed off the top of the pile.)

Section 11.7 will focus on priority queueing models. Otherwise, the queueing models throughout the chapter make the conventional assumption that the queue discipline is first-come, first-served.

Service

For a basic queueing system, each customer is served individually by one of the servers. A system with more than one server is called a *multiple-server system,* whereas a *single-server system* has just one server (as for Herr Cutter's barber shop).

When a customer enters service, the elapsed time from the beginning to the end of the service is referred to as the **service time.** Service times generally vary from one customer to the next. However, basic queueing models assume that the service time has a particular probability distribution, independent of which server is providing the service.

The symbol used for the *mean* of the service-time distribution is

$$\frac{1}{\mu} = \text{Expected service time}$$

where μ is the Greek letter mu. The interpretation of μ itself is

$$\mu = \text{Expected number of service completions per unit time for a single continuously busy server}$$

where this quantity is called the **mean service rate.** For example, Herr Cutter's expected time to give a haircut is

$$\frac{1}{\mu} = 20 \text{ minutes} = \frac{1}{3} \text{ hour per customer}$$

so his mean service rate is

$$\mu = 3 \text{ customers per hour}$$

Different queueing models provide a choice of service-time distributions, as described next.

Some Service-Time Distributions

The most popular choice for the probability distribution of service times is the **exponential distribution,** which has the shape already shown in Figure 11.3. The main reason for this choice is that this distribution is *much* easier to analyze than any other. Although this distribution provides an excellent fit for *interarrival times* for most situations, this is much less true for *service times.* Depending on the nature of the queueing system, the exponential distribution can provide either a reasonable approximation or a gross distortion of the true service-time distribution. Caution is needed.

As suggested by Figure 11.3, the exponential distribution implies that many of the service times are quite short (considerably less than the mean) but occasional service times are very long (far more than the mean). This accurately describes the kind of queueing system where many customers have just a small amount of business to transact with the server but occasional customers have a lot of business. For example, if the server is a bank teller, many

For some queueing systems, the service times have much less variability than implied by the exponential distribution, so queueing models that use other distributions should be considered.

customers have just a single check to deposit or cash, but occasional customers have many transactions.

However, the exponential distribution is a poor fit for the kind of queueing system where service consists basically of a fixed sequence of operations that require approximately the same time for every customer. For example, this describes the situation where the server is an ATM machine. Although there may be small variations in service times from one customer to the next, these times generally are just about the same.

For the latter kind of queueing system, a much better approximation would be to assume **constant service times,** that is, the same service time for every customer. (This also is referred to as having a *degenerate distribution* for service times.)

Other probability distributions also can be used to represent service times. For example, the *Erlang distribution* allows the amount of variability in the service times to fall somewhere between those for the exponential and degenerate distributions. The Erlang distribution is described further in the chapter supplement on the CD-ROM. Unfortunately, these other possibilities for service-time distributions such as the Erlang distribution are not nearly as convenient to work with as the exponential and degenerate distributions.

Labels for Queueing Models

To identify which probability distribution is being assumed for service times (and for interarrival times), a queueing model for a basic queueing system conventionally is labeled as follows:

$$\text{Distribution of service times}$$
$$\underline{\quad} / \underset{\uparrow}{\overset{\downarrow}{\underline{\quad}}} / \underline{\quad} \leftarrow \text{Number of servers}$$
$$\text{Distribution of interarrival times}$$

The symbols used for the possible distributions (for either service times or interarrival times) are

M = Exponential distribution (Markovian)

D = Degenerate distribution (constant times)

The first symbol identifies the distribution of interarrival times and the second symbol identifies the distribution of service times.

For example, the *M/M/*1 model is the single-server model that assumes that both interarrival times and service times have an exponential distribution. The *M/M/*2 model is the corresponding model with two servers. Letting *s* be the symbol that represents the number of servers, the *M/M/s* model is the corresponding model that permits any number of servers. Similarly, the *M/D/s* model has exponential interarrival times, constant service times, and any desired number of servers.

Interarrival times also can have a degenerate distribution instead of an exponential distribution. The *D/M/s* model has constant interarrival times, exponential service times, and any desired number of servers.

All the queueing models mentioned above will be considered at least briefly later in the chapter, along with results on how well such queueing systems perform.

There even are queueing models (with limited results) that permit choosing *any* probability distribution for the interarrival times or for the service times. The symbols used in these cases are

GI = General independent interarrival-time distribution (any arbitrary distribution allowed)

G = General service-time distribution (any arbitrary distribution allowed)

Thus, the *GI/M/s* model allows any interarrival-time distribution (with independent interarrival times), exponential service times, and any desired number of servers. The *M/G/*1 model has exponential interarrival times and one server but allows any service-time distribution. (We will touch later on just the latter model.)

Summary of Model Assumptions

To summarize, we list below the assumptions generally made by queueing models of a basic queueing system. Each of these assumptions should be taken for granted unless a model explicitly states otherwise.

1. Interarrival times are independent and identically distributed according to a specified probability distribution.
2. All arriving customers enter the queueing system and remain there until service has been completed.
3. The queueing system has a single *infinite queue,* so that the queue will hold an unlimited number of customers (for all practical purposes).
4. The queue discipline is first-come, first-served.
5. The queueing system has a specified number of servers, where each server is capable of serving any of the customers.
6. Each customer is served individually by any one of the servers.
7. Service times are independent and identically distributed according to a specified probability distribution.

Review
Questions

1. What might the customers of a queueing system be other than people?
2. What might the server of a queueing system be other than an individual person?
3. What is the relationship between the mean arrival rate and the mean of the probability distribution of interarrival times?
4. What is the shape of the exponential distribution?
5. How would you characterize the amount of variability in the times given by the exponential distribution?
6. What is meant by customers arriving *randomly?* Which distribution of interarrival times corresponds to random arrivals?
7. What is the distinction between the number of customers in the queue and the number in the system?
8. What is the conventional assumption made by most queueing models about the queue capacity? About the queue discipline?
9. What is the relationship between the mean of the service-time distribution and the mean service rate for a single continuously busy server?
10. What are the two most important service-time distributions?
11. What information is provided by the three parts of the label for queueing models?

11.2   SOME EXAMPLES OF QUEUEING SYSTEMS

Our description of queueing systems in the preceding section may appear relatively abstract and applicable to only rather special practical situations. On the contrary, queueing systems are surprisingly prevalent in a wide variety of contexts. To broaden your horizons on the applicability of queueing models, let us take a brief look at a variety of examples of real queueing systems.

A commercial service system is a queueing system where a commercial organization provides a service to customers from outside the organization.

One important class of queueing systems that we all encounter in our daily lives is **commercial service systems,** where outside customers receive service from commercial organizations. The first column of Table 11.2 lists a sampling of typical commercial service systems. Each of these is a queueing system whose customers and servers are identified in the second and third columns.

Most of these examples involve the customers coming to the server at a fixed location, where a physical queue forms if customers need to wait to begin service. However, for the plumbing services and roofing services examples, the server comes to the customers, so the customers in the queue are geographically dispersed. In several other cases, the service

TABLE 11.2
Examples of Commercial Service Systems That Are Queueing Systems

Type of System	Customers	Server(s)
Barber shop	People	Barber
Bank teller service	People	Teller
ATM service	People	ATM
Checkout at a store	People	Checkout clerk
Plumbing services	Clogged pipes	Plumber
Ticket window at a movie theater	People	Cashier
Check-in counter at an airport	People	Airline agent
Brokerage service	People	Stockbroker
Gas station	Cars	Pump
Call center for ordering goods	People	Telephone agent
Call center for technical assistance	People	Technical representative
Travel agency	People	Travel agent
Automobile repair shop	Car owners	Mechanic
Vending services	People	Vending machine
Dental services	People	Dentist
Roofing services	Roofs	Roofer

TABLE 11.3
Examples of Internal Service Systems That Are Queueing Systems

Type of System	Customers	Server(s)
Secretarial services	Employees	Secretary
Copying services	Employees	Copy machine
Computer programming services	Employees	Programmer
Mainframe computer	Employees	Computer
First-aid center	Employees	Nurse
Faxing services	Employees	Fax machine
Materials-handling system	Loads	Materials-handling unit
Maintenance system	Machines	Repair crew
Inspection station	Items	Inspector
Production system	Jobs	Machine
Semiautomatic machines	Machines	Operator
Tool crib	Machine operators	Clerk

An internal service system is a queueing system where the customers receiving service are internal to the organization providing the service.

is performed over the telephone, perhaps after some customers have been placed on hold (the queue).

Organizations also have their own **internal service systems,** where the customers receiving service are internal to the organization. As the examples in Table 11.3 indicate, these too are queueing systems. In some cases, the customers are employees of the organizations. In other examples, the customers are loads to be moved, machines to be repaired, items to be inspected, jobs to be performed, and so forth.

Transportation service systems provide another important category of queueing systems. Table 11.4 gives some examples. For several of the cases, the vehicles involved are the customers. For others, each vehicle is a server. A few of the examples go beyond the basic kind of queueing system described in the preceding section. In particular, the airline service

TABLE 11.4
Examples of Transportation Service Stations That Are Queueing Systems

Type of System	Customers	Server(s)
Highway tollbooth	Cars	Cashier
Truck loading dock	Trucks	Loading crew
Port unloading area	Ships	Unloading crew
Airplanes waiting to take off	Airplanes	Runway
Airplanes waiting to land	Airplanes	Runway
Airline service	People	Airplane
Taxicab service	People	Taxicab
Elevator service	People	Elevator
Fire department	Fires	Fire truck
Parking lot	Cars	Parking space
Ambulance service	People	Ambulance

A transportation service system is a queueing system involving transportation so that either the customers or the server(s) are vehicles.

and elevator service examples involve a server that serves a group of customers simultaneously rather than just one at a time. The queue in the parking lot example has zero capacity because arriving cars (customers) go elsewhere to park if all the parking spaces are occupied (all the servers are busy).

There are many additional examples of important queueing systems that may not fit nicely into any of the above categories. For example, a judicial system is a queueing network, where the courts are service facilities, the judges (or panels of judges) are the servers, and the cases waiting to be tried are the customers. Various health care systems, such as hospital emergency rooms, also are queueing systems. For example, x-ray machines and hospital beds can be viewed as servers in their own queueing systems. The initial applications of queueing theory were to telephone engineering, and the general area of telecommunications continues to be a very important area of application. Furthermore, we all have our own personal queues—homework assignments, books to be read, and so forth. Queueing systems do indeed pervade many areas of society.

Review Questions

1. What are commercial service systems? Also give a new example (not included in Table 11.2) of such a system, including identifying the customers and server.
2. What are internal service systems? Also give a new example (not included in Table 11.3) of such a system, including identifying the customers and server.
3. What are transportation service systems? Also give a new example (not included in Table 11.4) of such a system, including identifying the customers and server.

11.3   MEASURES OF PERFORMANCE FOR QUEUEING SYSTEMS

Managers who oversee queueing systems are mainly concerned with two types of measures of performance:

1. How many customers typically are waiting in the queueing system?
2. How long do these customers typically have to wait?

These measures are somewhat related, since how long a customer has to wait is partially determined by how many customers are already there when this customer arrives. Which measure is of greater concern depends on the situation.

Choosing a Measure of Performance

When the customers are internal to the organization providing the service (internal service systems), the first measure tends to be more important. In this situation, forcing customers to wait causes them to be unproductive members of the organization during the wait. For example, this is the case for machine operators waiting at a tool crib or for machines that are down waiting to be repaired. Having such customers wait causes *lost productivity,* where the amount of lost productivity is directly related to the number of waiting customers. The active members of the organization may be able to fill in for one or two idle members, but not for more.

Having customers wait in an internal service system causes lost productivity.

Commercial service systems (where outside customers receive service from commercial organizations) tend to place greater importance on the second measure. For such queueing systems, an important goal is to keep customers happy so they will return again. Customers are more concerned with how long they have to wait than with how many other customers are there. The consequence of making customers wait too long may be *lost profit from lost future business.*

Making customers wait too long in a commercial service system may result in lost profit from lost future business.

Defining the Measures of Performance

The two measures of performance commonly are expressed in terms of their *expected values* (in the statistical sense). To do this, it is necessary to clarify whether we are counting customers only while they are in the queue (i.e., before service begins) or while they are anywhere in the queueing system (i.e., either in the queue or being served). These two ways of defining the two types of measures thereby give us four measures of performance. These four measures and their symbols are shown below.

L = Expected **number of customers in the system,** including those being served (the symbol L comes from *Line Length*)

L_q = Expected **number of customers in the queue,** which excludes customers being served

W = Expected **waiting time in the system** (includes service time) for an individual customer (the symbol W comes from *Waiting time*)

W_q = Expected **waiting time in the queue** (excludes service time) for an individual customer

These definitions assume that the queueing system is in a **steady-state condition,** that is, the system is in its normal condition after operating for some time. During the initial *startup period* after a queueing system opens up with no customers there, it takes awhile for the expected number of customers to reach its normal level. After essentially reaching this level, the system is said to be in a steady-state condition. (This condition also rules out such abnormal operating conditions as a temporary "rush hour" jump in the mean arrival rate.)

The choice of whether to focus on the entire queueing system (L or W) or just on the queue (L_q or W_q) depends on the nature of the queueing system. For a hospital emergency room or a fire department, the queue (the time until service can begin) probably is more important. For an internal service system, the entire queueing system (the total number of members of the organization that are idle there) may be more important.

Relationships between *L, W, L_q,* and *W_q*

The only difference between W and W_q is that W includes the expected service time and W_q does not. Therefore, since $1/\mu$ is the symbol for the expected service time (where μ is called the *mean service rate*),

$$W = W_q + \frac{1}{\mu}$$

For example, if

W_q = ¾ hour waiting in the queue on the average

$\dfrac{1}{\mu}$ = ¼ hour service time on the average

then

W = ¾ hour + ¼ hour

= 1 hour waiting in the queueing system on the average

Perhaps the most important formula in queueing theory provides a direct relationship between L and W. This formula is

$$L = \lambda W$$

where

λ = Mean arrival rate for customers coming to the queueing system

This is called **Little's formula,** in honor of the eminent management scientist John D. C. Little (a long-time faculty member at MIT), who provided the first rigorous proof of the formula in 1961.

To illustrate the formula, suppose that

W = 1 hour waiting in the queueing system on the average

λ = 3 customers per hour arrive on the average

These are four key measures of performance for any queueing system.

This is a very handy formula for immediately obtaining either L or W from the other one.

It then follows that

$$L = (3 \text{ customers/hour})(1 \text{ hour})$$

$$= 3 \text{ customers in the queueing system on the average}$$

Here is an intuitive way to view Little's formula. Since L is the expected number of customers in the queueing system at any time, a customer looking back at the system after completing service should see L customers there on the average. With a first-come, first-served queue discipline, all L customers there normally would have arrived during this customer's waiting time in the queueing system. This waiting time is W on the average. Since λ is the expected number of arrivals per unit time, λW is the expected number of arrivals during this customer's waiting time in the system. Therefore, $L = \lambda W$.

Professor Little's proof that $L = \lambda W$ also applies to the relationship between L_q and W_q. Therefore, another version of Little's formula is

$$L_q = \lambda W_q$$

For example, if

$W_q = \frac{3}{4}$ hour waiting in the queue on the average

$\lambda = 3$ customers per hour arrive on the average

then

$$L_q = (3 \text{ customers/hour})(\tfrac{3}{4} \text{ hour})$$

$$= 2\tfrac{1}{4} \text{ customers in the queue on the average}$$

Combining the above relationships also gives the following direct relationship between L and L_q.

$$L = \lambda W = \lambda \left(W_q + \frac{1}{\mu} \right)$$

$$= L_q + \frac{\lambda}{\mu}$$

For example, if $L_q = 2\tfrac{1}{4}$, $\lambda = 3$, and $\mu = 4$, then

$$L = 2\tfrac{1}{4} + \tfrac{3}{4} = 3 \text{ customers in the system on the average}$$

These relationships are extremely important because they enable all four of the fundamental quantities—L, W, L_q, and W_q—to be immediately determined as soon as one is found analytically. This situation is fortunate because some of these quantities often are much easier to find than others when a queueing model is solved from basic principles.

Using Probabilities as Measures of Performance

Managers frequently are interested in more than what happens *on the average* in a queueing system. In addition to wanting L, L_q, W, and W_q not to exceed target values, they also may be concerned with *worst-case scenarios*. What will be the *maximum* number of customers in the system (or in the queue) that will only be exceeded a small fraction of the time (that is, with a small probability)? What will be the *maximum* waiting time of customers in the system (or in the queue) that will only be exceeded a small fraction of the time? A manager might specify that the queueing system should be designed in such a way that these maximum numbers do not exceed certain values.

Meeting such a goal requires using the steady-state *probability distribution* of these quantities (the number of customers and the waiting time). For example, suppose that the goal is to have no more than three customers in the system at least 95 percent of the time. Using the notation

(margin note) These expressions show the relationships between all four measures of performance.

$$P_n = \text{Steady-state probability of having exactly } n \text{ customers in the system}$$
$$(\text{for } n = 0, 1, 2, \ldots)$$

meeting this goal requires that

$$P_0 + P_1 + P_2 + P_3 \geq 0.95$$

Since waiting times vary from customer to customer, $\mathcal{W}$ has a probability distribution, whereas W is the mean of this distribution.

Similarly, suppose that another goal is that the waiting time in the system should not exceed two hours for at least 95 percent of the customers. Let the *random variable* $\mathcal{W}$ be the waiting time in the system for an individual customer while the system is in a steady-state condition. (Thus, W is the expected value of this random variable.) Using the probability distribution for this random variable, meeting the goal requires that

$$P(\mathcal{W} \leq 2 \text{ hours}) \geq 0.95$$

If the goal is stated in terms of the waiting time in the *queue* instead, then a different random variable $\mathcal{W}_q$ representing this waiting time would be used in the same way.

Formulas are available for calculating at least some of these probabilities for several of the queueing models considered later in the chapter. Excel templates in your MS Courseware will perform these calculations for you.

Review Questions

1. Which type of measure of performance of queueing systems tends to be more important when the customers are internal to the organization?
2. Which type of measure of performance tends to be more important for commercial service systems?
3. What are the four basic measures of performance based on expected values? What are their symbols?
4. What is meant by a queueing system being in a steady-state condition?
5. What is the formula that relates W and W_q?
6. What is Little's formula that relates L and W? That relates L_q and W_q?
7. What is the formula that relates L and L_q?
8. What kinds of probabilities can also be used as measures of performance of queueing systems?

11.4   A CASE STUDY: THE DUPIT CORP. PROBLEM

The Dupit Corporation is a long-time leader in the office photocopier marketplace. One reason for this leadership position is the service the company provides its customers. Dupit has enjoyed a reputation of excellent service and intends to maintain that reputation.

Some Background

Dupit has a service division that is responsible for providing high-quality support to the company's customers by promptly repairing the Dupit machines when needed. This work is done on the customer's site by the company's *service technical representatives,* more commonly known as **tech reps.**

Each tech rep currently is assigned his or her own territory for servicing the machines.

Each tech rep is given responsibility for a specified territory. This enables providing personalized service, since a customer sees the same tech rep on each service call. The tech rep generally feels like a one-person territory manager and takes pride in this role.

John Phixitt is the Dupit senior vice president in charge of the service division. He has spent his entire career with the company and actually began as a tech rep. While in this initial position, John took classes in the evening for several years to earn his business degree. Since then, he has moved steadily up the corporate ladder. He is well respected for his sound judgment and his thorough understanding of the company's business from the ground up.

John's years as a tech rep impressed upon him the importance of the tech rep's role as an ambassador of the company to its customers. He continues to preach this message regularly. He has established high personnel standards for becoming and remaining a tech rep and has built up the salaries accordingly. The morale in the division is quite high, largely through his efforts.

John also emphasizes obtaining regular feedback from a random sample of the company's customers on the quality of the service being provided. He likes to refer to this as keeping his ear to the ground. The customer feedback is channeled to both the tech reps and management for their information.

Another of John's themes is the importance of not overloading the tech reps. When he was a tech rep himself, the company policy had been to assign each tech rep enough machines in his or her territory that the tech rep would be active repairing machines 90 percent of the time (during an eight-hour working day). The intent was to maintain a high utilization of expensive personnel while providing some slack so that customers would not have to wait very long for repairs. John's own experience was that this did not work very well. He did have his idle periods about 10 percent of the time, which was helpful for catching up on his paperwork and maintaining his equipment. However, he also had frequent busy periods with many repair requests, including some long ones, and a large backlog of unhappy customers waiting for repairs would build up.

Therefore, when he was appointed to his current position, one of his first moves was to make the case to Dupit top management that tech reps needed to have more slack time to ensure providing prompt service to customers. A major part of his argument was that customer feedback indicated that the company was failing to deliver on the second and third parts of the company slogan given below.

Tech reps need considerable slack time to ensure providing prompt service to customers.

1. High-quality products.
2. High-quality service.
3. All delivered efficiently.

The company president had been promoting this slogan for years and so found this argument persuasive. Despite continuing pressure to hold costs down, John won approval for changing company policy regarding tech reps as summarized below.

Each tech rep's territory currently has approximately 150 machines, which requires a tech rep to be busy on service calls approximately 75 percent of the time.

Current Policy: Each tech rep's territory should be assigned enough machines so that the tech rep will be active repairing machines (or traveling to the repair site) approximately 75 percent of the time. When working continuously, each tech rep should be able to repair an average of four machines per day (an average of two hours per machine, including travel time). Therefore, to minimize customer waiting times, the goal is to have an average of three repair calls per working day. Since the company's machines now are averaging 50 work days between needing repairs, the target is to assign approximately 150 machines to each tech rep's territory.

Under this policy, the company now has nearly 10,000 tech reps, with a total payroll (including benefits) of approximately $600 million per year.

The Issue Facing Top Management

A long succession of very successful products has helped Dupit maintain its position as a market leader for many years. Furthermore, its latest product has been a particularly big winner. It is a color printer-copier that collates, staples, and so on, as well as having faxing capabilities. Thus, it is a state-of-the-art, all-in-one copier for the modern office. Sales have even exceeded the optimistic predictions made by the vice president for marketing.

The company's new color printer-copier is such a vital part of each purchaser's office that a much higher level of service is required to reduce downtime.

However, the success of this product also has brought problems. The fact that the machine performs so many key functions makes it a vital part of the purchaser's office. The owner has great difficulty in getting along without it for even a few hours when it is down requiring repair. Consequently, even though the tech reps are giving the same level of service as they have in the past, complaints about intolerable waits for repairs have skyrocketed.

This crisis has led to an emergency meeting of top management, with John Phixitt the man on the spot. He assures his colleagues that service has not deteriorated in the least. There is agreement that the company is a victim of its own success. The new machine is so valuable that a much higher level of service is required.

After considerable discussion about how to achieve the needed service, Dupit's president suggests the following four-step approach to dealing with the problem.

1. Agree on a tentative new standard for the level of service that needs to be provided.
2. Develop some proposals for alternative approaches that might achieve this standard.
3. Have a management science team work with John Phixitt to analyze these alternative approaches in detail to evaluate the effectiveness and cost of each one.
4. Reconvene this group of top management to make a final decision on what to do.

The group agrees.

Discussion then turns to what the new standard should be for the level of service. John proposes that this standard should specify that a customer's average waiting time before the tech rep can respond to the request for a repair should not exceed some maximum quantity. The customer relations manager agrees and argues that this average waiting time should not exceed two hours (versus about six hours now). The group agrees to adopt two hours as the tentative standard, pending further analysis by the management science team.

> **Proposed New Service Standard:** The average waiting time of customers before the tech rep begins the trip to the customer site to repair the machine should not exceed two hours.

The proposal is to reduce average waiting times before the repair process begins from six hours to two hours.

Alternative Approaches to the Problem

After further discussion of various ideas about how to meet this service standard, the meeting concludes. The president asks the participants who had proposed some approach to think further about their idea. If they conclude that their idea should be a particularly sound approach to the problem, they are to send him a memorandum supporting that approach.

The president subsequently receives four memoranda supporting the approaches summarized below.

> **Approach Suggested by John Phixitt:** Modify the current policy by decreasing the percentage of time that tech reps are expected to be active repairing machines. This involves simply decreasing the number of machines assigned to each tech rep and adding more tech reps. This approach would enable continuing the mode of operation for the service division that has served the company so well in the past while increasing the level of service to meet the new demands of the marketplace.

> **Approach Suggested by the Vice President for Engineering:** Provide new state-of-the-art equipment to the tech reps that would substantially reduce the time required for the longer repairs. Although expensive, this would significantly reduce the average repair time. Perhaps more importantly, it would greatly reduce the variability of repair times, which might decrease average waiting times for repairs.

> **Approach Suggested by the Chief Financial Officer:** Replace the current one-person tech rep territories by larger territories that would be served by multiple tech reps. Having teams of tech reps to back each other up during busy periods might decrease average waiting times for repairs enough that the company would not need to hire additional tech reps.

> **Approach Suggested by the Vice President for Marketing:** Give owners of the new printer-copier priority for receiving repairs over the company's other customers. Since the complaints about slow service are coming mainly from these owners, this approach might give them the service they require while still giving adequate service to other customers.

The president is pleased to have four promising approaches to consider. As previously agreed, his next step is to set up a team of management scientists (three from the company plus an outside consultant) to work with John Phixitt in analyzing these approaches in detail. They are to report back to top management with their results and recommendations in six weeks.

Before reading further, we suggest that you think about these four alternative approaches and decide which one seems most promising. You then will be able to compare your conclusions with the results from the management science study.

Queueing models will be used to analyze each of the four proposed approaches.

The Management Science Team's View of the Problem

The management science team quickly recognizes that *queueing theory* will be a key technique for analyzing this problem. In particular, each tech rep's territory can be viewed as including the basic queueing system described below.

The Queueing System for Each Tech Rep

1. **The customers:** The machines needing repair.
2. **Customer arrivals:** The calls to the tech rep on his or her cellular telephone requesting repairs.
3. **The queue:** The machines waiting for repair to begin at their sites.
4. **The server:** The tech rep.
5. **Service time:** The total time the tech rep is tied up with a machine, either traveling to the machine site or repairing the machine. (Thus, a machine is viewed as leaving the queue and entering service when the tech rep begins the trip to the machine site.)

With the approach suggested by the chief financial officer (enlarge the territories with multiple tech reps for each territory), this single-server queueing system would be changed to a multiple-server queueing system.

The management science team now needs to decide which specific queueing model is most appropriate for analyzing each of the four approaches. You will see this story unfold in the next few sections while we are presenting various important queueing models.

Review Questions

1. What is the company's current policy regarding the workload for tech reps?
2. What is the issue currently facing top management?
3. What is the proposed new service standard?
4. How many alternative approaches have been suggested for dealing with the issue facing top management?
5. Who now will be analyzing these approaches?
6. In the queueing system interpretation of this problem, what are the customers? The server?

11.5 SOME SINGLE-SERVER QUEUEING MODELS

Using the background on the elements of queueing models presented in Section 11.1, this section focuses on models of basic queueing systems having just one server. Key symbols introduced in Section 11.1 that will continue to be used here (and throughout the remainder of the chapter) are

λ = Mean arrival rate for customers coming to the queueing system

= Expected number of arrivals per unit time

μ = Mean service rate (for a continuously busy server)

= Expected number of service completions per unit time

Also recall that $1/\lambda$ is the *expected interarrival time* (the average time between the arrival of consecutive customers) and $1/\mu$ is the *expected service time* for each customer.

A new symbol for this section is

$$\rho = \frac{\lambda}{\mu}$$

The utilization factor plays a key role in the efficiency of a queueing system.

where ρ is the Greek letter rho. This quantity ρ is referred to as the **utilization factor,** because it represents the average fraction of time that the server is being utilized serving customers.

An Application Vignette

For many decades, General Motors Corporation (GM) has enjoyed its position as the world's largest automotive manufacturer. It has manufacturing operations in 32 countries, employs over 300,000 people worldwide, and generates annual revenues of close to $200 billion. However, ever since the late 1980s, when the productivity of GM's plants ranked near the bottom in the industry, the company's market position has been steadily eroding because of ever-increasing foreign competition.

To counter this foreign competition, GM management initiated a long-term management science project many years ago to predict and improve the throughput performance of the company's several hundred production lines throughout the world. The goal was to greatly increase the company's productivity throughout its manufacturing operations and thereby provide GM with a strategic competitive advantage.

The most important analytical tool used in this project has been a complicated queueing model that uses a simple single-server model as a building block. The overall model begins by considering a two-station production line where each station is modeled as a single-server queueing system with constant interarrival times and constant service times with the following exceptions. The server (commonly a machine) at each station occasionally breaks down and does not resume serving until a repair is completed. The server at the first station also shuts down when it completes a service and the buffer between the stations is full. The server at the second station shuts down when it completes a service and has not yet received a job from the first station.

The next step in the analysis is to extend this queueing model for a two-station production line to one for a production line with any number of stations. This larger queueing model then is used to analyze how production lines should be designed to maximize their throughput. (The technique of computer simulation described in the next two chapters also is used for this purpose for relatively complex production lines.)

This application of queueing theory (and computer simulation), along with supporting data-collection systems, has reaped remarkable benefits for GM. According to impartial industry sources, its plants, which once were among the least productive in the industry, now rank among the very best. The resulting improvements in production throughput in over 30 vehicle plants and 10 countries has yielded over $2.1 billion in documented savings and increased revenue.

Source: J. M. Alden, L. D. Burns, T. Costy, R. D. Hutton, C. A. Jackson, D. S. Kim, K. A. Kohls, J. H. Owen, M. A. Turnquist, and D. J. VamderVeen, "General Motors Increases Its Production Throughput," *Interfaces* 36, no. 1 (January–February 2006), pp. 6–25.

In the Dupit Corp. case study, under the company's current policy, a typical tech rep experiences

λ = 3 customers (machines needing repair) arriving per day on the average

μ = 4 service completions (repair completions) per day on the average when the tech rep is continuously busy

Since

$$\rho = \frac{3}{4} = 0.75$$

the tech rep is active repairing machines 75 percent of the time.

For each of the queueing models, we will consider the measures of performance introduced in Section 11.3. Because of the relationships between the four basic measures—L, L_q, W, and W_q—including Little's formula given in that section, recall that all four quantities can be calculated easily as soon as one of their values has been determined. Therefore, we sometimes will be focusing on just one of these measures of performance for the following models.

The *M/M/*1 Model

Using the labels for queueing models given near the end of Section 11.1, recall that the first symbol (*M*) in the *M/M/*1 label identifies the probability distribution of *interarrival times*, the second symbol (*M*) indicates the distribution of *service times*, and the third symbol (1) gives the number of servers. Since *M* is the symbol used for the *exponential distribution*, the *M/M/*1 model makes the following assumptions.

Assumptions

1. *Interarrival times* have an exponential distribution with a mean of $1/\lambda$. (See Figure 11.3 and the description of this distribution in Section 11.1.)
2. *Service times* have an exponential distribution with a mean of $1/\mu$.
3. The queueing system has 1 server.

As discussed in Section 11.1, the first assumption corresponds to having customers arrive *randomly.* Consequently, this assumption commonly is a valid one for real queueing systems.

The second assumption also is a reasonable one for those queueing systems where many service times are quite short (well under the mean) but occasional service times are very long. Some queueing systems fit this description, but some others do not even come close.

Along with its multiple-server counterpart (considered in Section 11.6), the *M/M/1* model is the most widely used queueing model. (It is even sometimes used for queueing systems that don't fit the second assumption very well.) A key reason is that this model has the most results readily available. Because the formulas are relatively simple, we give them for all the measures of performance below. (All these measures assume that the queueing system is in a *steady-state condition.*)

Although the second assumption is sometimes questionable, this model is widely used because it provides so many useful results.

Using $\rho = \lambda/\mu$, two equivalent formulas for the *expected number of customers in the system* are

$$L = \frac{\rho}{1 - \rho} = \frac{\lambda}{\mu - \lambda}$$

Because of Little's formula ($L = \lambda W$), the *expected waiting time in the system* is

$$W = \frac{1}{\lambda}L = \frac{1}{\mu - \lambda}$$

Therefore, the *expected waiting time in the queue* (excludes service time) is

$$W_q = W - \frac{1}{\mu} = \frac{1}{\mu - \lambda} - \frac{1}{\mu} = \frac{\mu - (\mu - \lambda)}{\mu(\mu - \lambda)}$$

$$= \frac{\lambda}{\mu(\mu - \lambda)}$$

Applying the other version of Little's formula again ($L_q = \lambda W_q$), the *expected number of customers in the queue* (excludes customers being served) is

$$L_q = \lambda W_q = \frac{\lambda^2}{\mu(\mu - \lambda)} = \frac{\rho^2}{1 - \rho}$$

Even the formulas for the various probabilities are relatively simple. The probability of having exactly *n* customers in the system is

$$P_n = (1 - \rho)\rho^n \quad \text{for } n = 0, 1, 2, \ldots$$

Thus,

$$P_0 = 1 - \rho$$
$$P_1 = (1 - \rho)\rho$$
$$P_2 = (1 - \rho)\rho^2$$

$$\cdot$$
$$\cdot$$
$$\cdot$$

The probability that the *waiting time in the system* exceeds some amount of time *t* is

$$P(\mathcal{W} > t) = e^{-\mu(1 - \rho)t} \quad \text{for } t \geq 0$$

The corresponding probability that the *waiting time in the queue* exceeds *t* is

$$P(\mathcal{W}_q > t) = \rho e^{-\mu(1 - \rho)t} \quad \text{for } t \geq 0$$

Since this waiting time in the queue is 0 if there are no customers in the system when an arrival occurs,

$$P(\mathcal{W}_q = 0) = P_0 = 1 - \rho$$

on) well over half the time. However, he or she also will have *much* larger backlogs with some frequency. For example, $P_0 + P_1 + P_2 + \ldots + P_7 = 0.9$, which indicates that the tech rep will have *at least* eight machines needing repair (about two days' work or more) 10 percent of the time. With all the randomness inherent in such a queueing system (the great variability in both interarrival times and service times), these very big backlogs (and many unhappy customers) will occur occasionally despite the tech rep only having a utilization factor of 0.75.

Finally, look at the results in cells C8:C12. By setting $t = 1$, the probability that a customer has to wait more than one day (eight work hours) before a failed machine is operational again is given as $P(W > 1 \text{ day}) = 0.368$. The probability of waiting more than one day before the repair begins is $P(W_q > 1 \text{ day}) = 0.276$.

Upon being shown all these results, John Phixitt comments that he understands better now why the complaints have been pouring in. No owner of such a vital machine as the new printer-copier should be expected to go more than a day (or even most of a day) before it is repaired.

Applying the *M/M*/1 Model to John Phixitt's Suggested Approach

The management science team now is ready to begin analyzing each of the suggested approaches for lowering to two hours (¼ workday) the average waiting time before service begins. Thus, the new constraint is that

$$W_q \leq \text{¼ day}$$

The first approach, suggested by John Phixitt, is to modify the current policy by lowering a tech rep's utilization factor sufficiently to meet this new service requirement. This involves decreasing the number of machines assigned to each tech rep from about 150 to some smaller number. Since each machine needs repair about once every 50 work days on the average, decreasing the number of machines in a tech rep's territory results in decreasing the mean arrival rate λ from 3 to

$$\lambda = \frac{\text{Number of machines assigned to tech rep}}{50}$$

With μ fixed at four, this decrease in λ will decrease the utilization factor, $\rho = \lambda/\mu$.

Since decreasing λ decreases W_q, the largest value of λ that has $W_q \leq$ ¼ day is the one that makes W_q equal to ¼ day. The easiest way to find this λ is by trial and error with the Excel template, trying various values of λ until one is found where $W_q = 0.25$. Figure 11.5 shows

---

All the results from the *M/M*/1 model indicate that unacceptably long delays in repairing failed machines will occur too frequently under the current policy.

To meet the proposed new service standard that $W_q \leq \dfrac{1}{4}$ day, John Phixitt suggests reducing the number of machines assigned to each tech rep from 150 to some smaller number.

FIGURE 11.5

This application of the spreadsheet in Figure 11.4 shows that, when $\mu = 4$, the *M/M*/1 model gives an expected waiting time to begin service of $W_q = 0.25$ day (the largest value that satisfies Dupit's proposed new service standard) when λ is changed from $\lambda = 3$ to $\lambda = 2$.

	A	B	C	D	E	F	G
1		M/M/1 Queueing Model for John Phixitt's Approach (Reduce Machines/Rep)					
2							
3			Data				Results
4		$\lambda =$	2	(mean arrival rate)		$L =$	1
5		$\mu =$	4	(mean service rate)		$L_q =$	0.5
6		$s =$	1	(# servers)			
7						$W =$	0.5
8		$Pr(W > t) =$	0.135			$W_q =$	0.25
9		when $t =$	1				
10						$\rho =$	0.5
11		$Prob(W_q > t) =$	0.0677				
12		when $t =$	1			n	P_n
13						0	0.5
14						1	0.25
15						2	0.125
16						3	0.0625
17						4	0.0313
18						5	0.0156
19						6	0.00781
20						7	0.00391
21						8	0.00195
22						9	0.00098
23						10	0.00049

the template that gives this value of W_q by setting $\lambda = 2$. (By using the formula for W_q, it also is possible to solve algebraically to find $\lambda = 2$.)

Decreasing λ from three to two would require decreasing the target for the number of machines assigned to each tech rep from 150 to 100. This 100 is the *maximum* number that would satisfy the requirement that $W_q \leq \frac{1}{4}$ day. With $\lambda = 2$ and $\mu = 4$, the utilization factor for each tech rep would be only

> The *M/M/1* model indicates that the number of machines assigned to each tech rep would need to be reduced to 100 with John Phixitt's approach.

$$\rho = \frac{\lambda}{\mu} = \frac{2}{4} = 0.5$$

Recall that the company's payroll (including benefits) for its nearly 10,000 tech reps currently is about $600 million annually. Decreasing the number of machines assigned to each tech rep from 150 to 100 would require hiring nearly 5,000 more tech reps to cover all the machines. The additional payroll cost would be about $270 million annually. (It is a little less than half the current payroll cost because the new tech reps would have less seniority than the current ones.) However, the management science team estimates that the additional costs of hiring and training the new tech reps, covering their work expenses, providing them with equipment, and adding more field service managers to administer them would be equivalent to about $30 million annually.

> **Total Additional Cost of the Approach Suggested by John Phixitt:** Approximately $300 million annually.

The *M/G/1* Model

This queueing model differs from the *M/M/1* model only in the second of its assumptions summarized below.

Assumptions

1. *Interarrival times* have an exponential distribution with a mean of $1/\lambda$.
2. *Service times* can have *any* probability distribution. It is not even necessary to determine the form of this distribution. You just need to estimate the mean ($1/\mu$) and standard deviation (σ) of the distribution.
3. The queueing system has one server.

> You now need to also estimate σ, the standard deviation of the service-time distribution.

Thus, this is an extremely flexible model that only requires the common situation of *random arrivals* (equivalent to the first assumption) and a single server, plus estimates of λ, μ, and σ.

Using $\rho = \lambda/\mu$, here are the available formulas for this model.

$$P_0 = 1 - \rho$$

$$L_q = \frac{\lambda^2\sigma^2 + \rho^2}{2(1 - \rho)}$$

$$L = L_q + \rho$$

$$W_q = \frac{L_q}{\lambda}$$

$$W = W_q + \frac{1}{\mu}$$

These steady-state measures of performance require only that $\rho < 1$, which allows the queueing system to reach a steady-state condition.

To illustrate the formulas, suppose that the service-time distribution is the exponential distribution with mean $1/\mu$. Then, since the standard deviation σ is

$$\sigma = \text{mean} = \frac{1}{\mu} \quad \text{for the exponential distribution}$$

the formula for L_q indicates that

$$L_q = \frac{\lambda^2\left(\frac{1}{\mu^2}\right) + \rho^2}{2(1 - \rho)} = \frac{\rho^2 + \rho^2}{2(1 - \rho)}$$

$$= \frac{\rho^2}{(1 - \rho)}$$

just as for the *M/M/*1 model. Having $\sigma = 1/\mu$ also causes the formulas for L, W_q, and W to reduce algebraically to those given earlier for the *M/M/*1 model. In fact, the *M/M/*1 model is just the special case of the *M/G/*1 model where $\sigma = 1/\mu$. (However, the *M/M/*1 model yields some results that are not available from the *M/G/*1 model.)

Another important special case of the *M/G/*1 model is the *M/D/*1 model, which assumes that the service-time distribution is the degenerate distribution (constant service times). Since

$$\sigma = 0 \quad \text{for the degenerate distribution}$$

the formula for L_q yields

$$L_q = \frac{\lambda^2(0) + \rho^2}{2(1 - \rho)} = \frac{1}{2}\frac{\rho^2}{1 - \rho}$$

which is just half that for the *M/M/*1 model. Thus, going from a service-time distribution that has high variability (the exponential distribution) to one that has no variability (the degenerate distribution) has a dramatic effect on reducing L_q.

As this illustrates, the L_q formula for the *M/G/*1 model is an enlightening one, because it reveals what effect the variability of the service-time distribution has on this measure of performance. With fixed values of λ, μ, and ρ, decreasing this variability (i.e., decreasing σ) definitely decreases L_q. The same thing happens with L, W, and W_q. Thus, the consistency of the server has a major bearing on the performance of the queueing system. Given the choice between two servers with the same average speed (the same value of $1/\mu$), the one with less variability (smaller σ) definitely should be preferred over the other one. (We will discuss this further in Section 11.8.)

Considering the complexity involved in analyzing a model that permits *any* service-time distribution, it is remarkable that such a simple formula can be obtained for L_q. This formula is one of the most important results in queueing theory because of its ease of use and the prevalence of *M/G/*1 queueing systems in practice. This equation for L_q (or its counterpart for W_q) commonly is referred to as the Pollaczek-Khintchine formula, named after two pioneers in the development of queueing theory who derived the formula independently in the early 1930s.

> Decreasing the variability of the service-time distribution has the beneficial effect of decreasing L_q, L, W, and W_q.

Applying the *M/G/*1 Model to the Approach Suggested by the Vice President for Engineering

Dupit's vice president for engineering has suggested providing the tech reps with new state-of-the-art equipment that would substantially reduce the time required for the longer repairs. This would decrease the average repair time a little, and also would substantially decrease the variability of the repair times.

> The new state-of-the-art equipment suggested by the vice president for engineering would substantially reduce both the mean and the standard deviation of the service-time distribution.

After gathering more information from this vice president and analyzing it further, the management science team makes the following estimates about the effect of this approach on the service-time distribution.

The mean would decrease from ¼ day to ⅕ day.

The standard deviation would decrease from ¼ day to ⅒ day.

Thus, the standard deviation would decrease from equaling the previous mean (as for the exponential distribution) to being just half the new mean. Since $\mu = 1/\text{mean}$, we now have $\mu = 5$ instead of $\mu = 4$.

FIGURE 11.6

This Excel template for the *M/G/*1 model shows the results from applying this model to the approach suggested by Dupit's vice president for engineering to use new state-of-the-art equipment.

	A	B	C	D	E	F	G
1				**M/G/1 Model for VP of Engineering's Approach (New Equipment)**			
2							
3			**Data**				**Results**
4		$\lambda =$	3	(mean arrival rate)		$L =$	1.163
5		$1/\mu =$	0.2	(expected service time)		$L_q=$	0.563
6		$\sigma =$	0.1	(standard deviation)			
7		$s =$	1	(# servers)		$W =$	0.388
8						$W_q=$	0.188
9							
10						$\rho =$	0.6
11							
12						$P_0 =$	0.4

Range Name	Cell
L	G4
Lambda	C4
L_q	G5
OneOverMu	C5
Rho	G10
s	C7
Sigma	C6
W	G7
W_q	G8

	F	G
4	$L =$	=L_q+Rho
5	$L_q=$	=((Lambda)^2)*(Sigma^2)+(Rho^2))/(2*(1-Rho))
6		
7	$W =$	=W_q+OneOverMu
8	$W_q=$	=L_q/Lambda
9		
10	$\rho =$	=Lambda*OneOverMu
11		
12	$P_0 =$	=1-Rho

With $\sigma = 0.1$, the Excel template for the *M/G/*1 model in your MS Courseware yields the results shown in Figure 11.6. Note that $W_q = 0.188$ day. This big reduction from $W_q = 0.75$ day under the current policy (as given in Figure 11.4) is largely due to the big decrease in σ. If the service-time distribution continued to be an exponential distribution, then increasing μ from 4 to 5 would decrease W_q from 0.75 day to 0.3 day. The additional reduction from 0.3 day to 0.188 day is because of the large reduction in the variability of service times.

The *M/G/*1 model indicates that the proposed new service standard would be met easily by this approach.

Recall that the proposed new service standard is $W_q \leq 0.25$ day. Therefore, the approach suggested by the vice president for engineering would satisfy this standard.

Unfortunately, the management science team also determines that this approach would be expensive, as summarized below.

Total Additional Cost of the Approach Suggested by the Vice President for Engineering: A one-time cost of approximately $500 million (about $50,000 for new equipment per tech rep).

Review Questions

1. What are represented by the symbols λ and μ? By $1/\lambda$ and $1/\mu$? By ρ?
2. What are the assumptions of the *M/M/*1 model?
3. For which measures of performance (both expected values and probabilities) are formulas available for the *M/M/*1 model?
4. Which values of ρ correspond to the server in a single-server queueing system having a manageable utilization factor that allows the system to reach a steady-state condition?
5. Under Dupit's current policy, what is the average waiting time of customers until service begins on their failed machines?
6. How much more would it cost Dupit to reduce this average waiting time to ¼ workday by decreasing the number of machines assigned to each tech rep?
7. How does the *M/G/*1 model differ from the *M/M/*1 model?
8. Which service-time distribution is assumed by the *M/D/*1 model?
9. For the *M/G/*1 model, what is the effect on L_q, L, W, and W_q of decreasing the standard deviation of the service-time distribution?
10. What is the total additional cost of the approach suggested by Dupit's vice president for engineering?

11.6   SOME MULTIPLE-SERVER QUEUEING MODELS

Many queueing systems have more than one server, so we now turn our attention to multiple-server queueing models. In particular, we will discuss what results are available for the multiple-server counterparts of the single-server models introduced in the preceding section.

Recall that the third symbol in the label for a queueing model indicates the number of servers. For example, the *M/M/2* model has two servers. The *M/M/s* model allows the choice of any number of servers, where *s* is the symbol for this number.

Also recall that ρ ($=\lambda/\mu$) was the symbol used for the *utilization factor* for the server in a single-server queueing system. With multiple servers, the formula for this symbol changes to

$$\rho = \frac{\lambda}{s\mu} \qquad \text{(utilization factor)}$$

where λ continues to be the mean arrival rate (so $1/\lambda$ still is the expected interarrival time) and μ continues to be the mean service rate for a single continuously busy server (so $1/\mu$ still is the expected service time). The models assume that all the servers have the same service-time distribution, so μ is the same for every server. Since

λ = Expected number of arrivals per unit time

$s\mu$ = Expected number of service completions per unit time when all *s* servers are continuously busy

As with single-server queueing models, the utilization factor ρ still is the average fraction of time that the individual servers are being utilized serving customers.

it follows that $\rho = \lambda/s\mu$ is indeed the average fraction of time that individual servers are being utilized serving customers.

In order for the servers to have a manageable utilization factor, it is again necessary that

$$\rho < 1$$

All the models make this assumption to enable the queueing system to reach a steady-state condition.

Of the three previously considered single-server models (*M/M/1*, *M/G/1*, and *M/D/1*), the *M/G/1* model is the only one whose multiple-server counterpart yields no useful analytical results. Combining the complication of multiple servers with the complication of allowing the choice of any service-time distribution is too much to handle.

We begin with the *M/M/s* model, including its application to the Dupit case study. We then mention the limited results available for the *M/D/s* model.

The *M/M/s* Model

Except for the last one, the assumptions are the same as for the *M/M/1* model.

Assumptions

1. Interarrival times have an exponential distribution with a mean of $1/\lambda$.
2. Service times have an exponential distribution with a mean of $1/\mu$.
3. Any number of servers (denoted by *s*) can be chosen for the queueing system.

Explicit formulas are available for all the measures of performance (including the probabilities) considered for the *M/M/1* model. However, when $s > 1$, the formulas are too tedious to want to do by hand. Therefore, you should use the Excel template for the *M/M/s* model (as demonstrated earlier in Figures 11.4 and 11.5) to generate all these results. (You also can see a demonstration of the *M/M/s* queueing system in action by viewing the Waiting Line module in your Interactive Management Science Modules at **www.mhhe.com/hillier3e** or on the CD-ROM.)

The Excel template for the *M/M/s* model provides all the measures of performance that were described in Section 11.5 for the *M/M/1* model.

Another alternative is to use Figure 11.7, which shows the values of *L* versus the utilization factor for various values of *s*. (Be aware that the vertical axis uses a logarithmic scale, so you need to refer to the notches to determine the value along this axis.) By estimating *L* from this graph, you then can use Little's formula ($L = \lambda W$ and $L_q = \lambda W_q$), plus $W = W_q + 1/\mu$, to calculate *W*, W_q, and L_q.

KeyCorp is a Fortune 500 company headquartered in Cleveland, Ohio. It is the 13th largest bank holding company in the United States with 19,000 employees, assets of $93 billion, and annual revenues of $6.7 billion. The company emphasizes consumer banking and has 2.4 million customers across more than 1,300 branch banks and many additional affiliate offices.

To help grow its business, KeyCorp management initiated an extensive management science study to determine how to improve customer service (defined primarily as reducing customer waiting time before beginning service) while also providing cost-effective staffing. A service-quality goal was set that at least 90 percent of the customers should have waiting times of less than five minutes.

The key tool in analyzing this problem was the *M/M/s* queueing model, which proved to fit this application very well. To apply this model, data were gathered that revealed that the average service time required to process a customer was a distressingly high 246 seconds. With this average service time and typical mean arrival rates, the model indicated that a 30 percent increase in the number of tellers would be

needed to meet the service-quality goal. This prohibitively expensive option led management to conclude that an extensive campaign needed to be undertaken to drastically reduce the average service time by both reengineering the customer session and providing better management of staff. Over a period of three years, this campaign led to a reduction in the average service time all the way down to 115 seconds. Frequent reapplication of the *M/M/s* model then revealed how the service-quality goal can be substantially surpassed while actually reducing personnel levels through improved scheduling of the personnel in the various branch banks.

The net result has been savings of nearly $20 million per year with vastly improved service that enables 96 percent of the customers to wait less than five minutes. This improvement extended throughout the company as the percentage of branch banks that met the service-quality goal increased from 42 percent to 94 percent. Surveys also confirm a great increase in customer satisfaction.

Source: S. K. Kotha, M. P. Barnum, and D. A. Bowen, "KeyCorp Service Excellence Management System," *Interfaces* 26, no. 1 (January–February 1996), pp. 54–74.

Applying These Models to the Approach Suggested by the Chief Financial Officer

Dupit's chief financial officer has suggested combining the current one-person tech rep territories into larger territories that would be served jointly by multiple tech reps. The hope is that, without changing the total number of tech reps, this reorganization might decrease W_q

FIGURE 11.7

Values of L for the *M/M/s* model for various values of s, the number of servers.

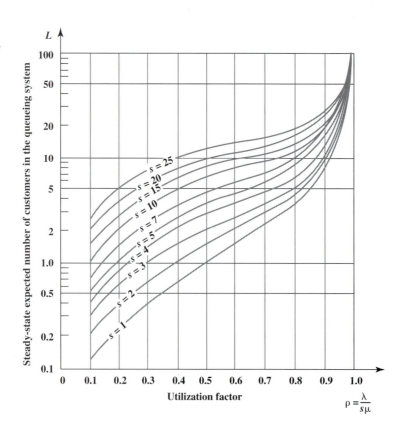

FIGURE 11.8

This Excel template for the *M/M/s* model shows the results from applying this model to the approach suggested by Dupit's chief financial officer with two tech reps assigned to each territory.

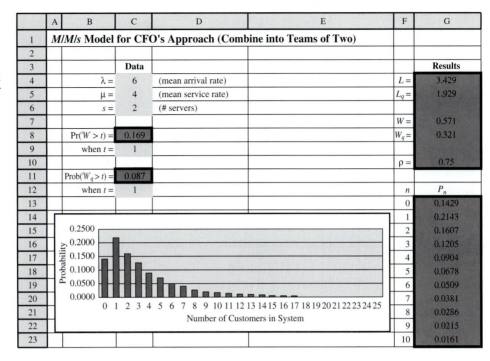

	A	B	C	D	E	F	G
1		\multicolumn{3}{l}{*M/M/s* **Model for CFO's Approach (Combine into Teams of Two)**}				
2							
3			**Data**				**Results**
4		$\lambda =$	6	(mean arrival rate)		$L =$	3.429
5		$\mu =$	4	(mean service rate)		$L_q =$	1.929
6		$s =$	2	(# servers)			
7						$W =$	0.571
8		$\Pr(W > t) =$	0.169			$W_q =$	0.321
9		when $t =$	1				
10						$\rho =$	0.75
11		$\text{Prob}(W_q > t) =$	0.087				
12		when $t =$	1			n	P_n
13						0	0.1429
14						1	0.2143
15						2	0.1607
16						3	0.1205
17						4	0.0904
18						5	0.0678
19						6	0.0509
20						7	0.0381
21						8	0.0286
22						9	0.0215
23						10	0.0161

sufficiently from its current value ($W_q = 0.75$ day) to satisfy the proposed new service standard ($W_q \leq 0.25$ day).

Let us first try it with *two* tech reps assigned to each territory.

A Territory with Two Tech Reps

Number of machines:	300	(versus 150 before)
Mean arrival rate:	$\lambda = 6$	(versus $\lambda = 3$ before)
Mean service rate:	$\mu = 4$	(same as before)
Number of servers:	$s = 2$	(versus $s = 1$ before)
Utilization factor:	$\rho = \dfrac{\lambda}{s\mu} = 0.75$	(same as before)

Applying the Excel template for the *M/M/s* model with these data yields the results shown in Figure 11.8, including $W_q = 0.321$ day. (The equations entered into the output cells are not given in this figure because they are very complicated, but they can be viewed in this chapter's Excel file that contains this template.)

This is a very big improvement over the current value of $W_q = 0.75$ day, but it does not quite satisfy the service standard of $W_q \leq 0.25$ day. So let us next see what would happen if *three* tech reps were assigned to each territory.

A Territory with Three Tech Reps

Number of machines:	450	(versus 150 before)
Mean arrival rate:	$\lambda = 9$	(versus $\lambda = 3$ before)
Mean service rate:	$\mu = 4$	(same as before)
Number of servers:	$s = 3$	(versus $s = 1$ before)
Utilization factor:	$\rho = \dfrac{\lambda}{s\mu} = 0.75$	(same as before)

With this utilization factor, Figure 11.7 indicates that L is very close to 4. Using 4 as the approximate value, and applying the relationships given in Section 11.3 (Little's formula, etc.),

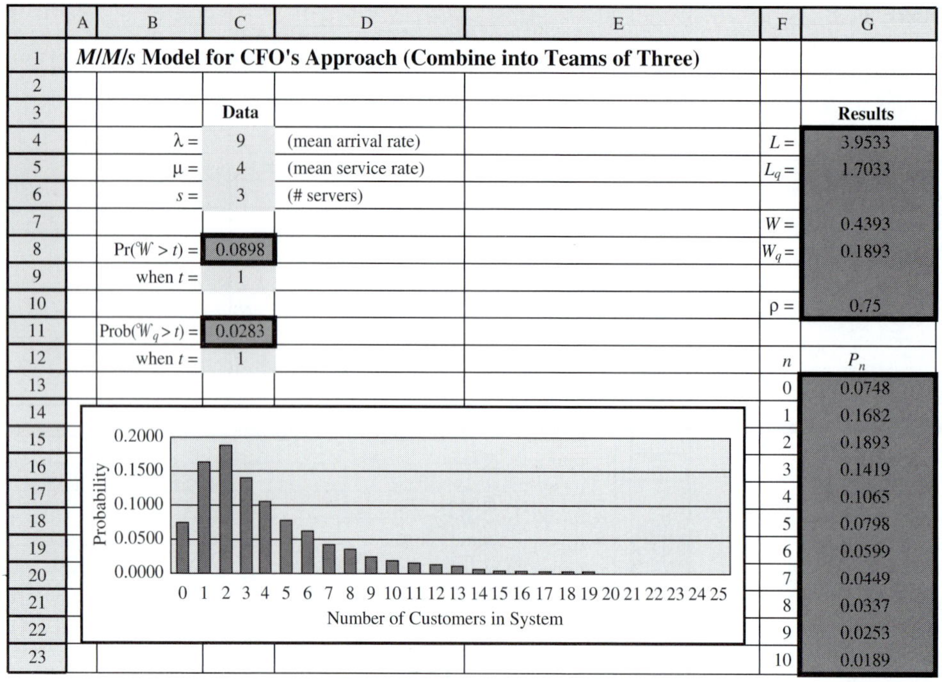

FIGURE 11.9
This Excel template modifies the results in Figure 11.8 by assigning three tech reps to each territory.

	A	B	C	D	E	F	G
1		*M/M/s* Model for CFO's Approach (Combine into Teams of Three)					
2							
3			Data				Results
4		$\lambda =$	9	(mean arrival rate)		$L =$	3.9533
5		$\mu =$	4	(mean service rate)		$L_q =$	1.7033
6		$s =$	3	(# servers)			
7						$W =$	0.4393
8		$\Pr(W > t) =$	0.0898			$W_q =$	0.1893
9		when $t =$	1				
10						$\rho =$	0.75
11		$\text{Prob}(W_q > t) =$	0.0283				
12		when $t =$	1			n	P_n
13						0	0.0748
14						1	0.1682
15						2	0.1893
16						3	0.1419
17						4	0.1065
18						5	0.0798
19						6	0.0599
20						7	0.0449
21						8	0.0337
22						9	0.0253
23						10	0.0189

TABLE 11.5
Comparison of W_q Values with Territories of Different Sizes for the Dupit Problem

Number of Tech Reps	Number of Machines	λ	μ	s	ρ	W_q
1	150	3	4	1	0.75	0.75 workday (6 hours)
2	300	6	4	2	0.75	0.321 workday (2.57 hours)
3	450	9	4	3	0.75	0.189 workday (1.51 hours)

The *M/M/s* model indicates that the proposed new service standard would be comfortably satisfied by combining three one-person tech rep territories into a single larger territory that would be served jointly by all three tech reps.

$$W = \frac{L}{\lambda} = \frac{4}{9} = 0.44 \text{ day}$$

$$W_q = W - \frac{1}{\mu} = 0.44 - 0.25 = 0.19 \text{ day}$$

More precisely, the Excel template in Figure 11.9 gives $L = 3.953$ and $W_q = 0.189$ day. Since a workday is eight hours, this expected waiting time converts to just over one hour and 30 minutes.

Consequently, three-person territories would easily satisfy the proposed new service standard of $W_q \leq 0.25$ workday (two hours). Even considering that these larger territories would modestly increase the travel times for the tech reps, they still would comfortably satisfy the service standard.

Table 11.5 summarizes the data and values of W_q for territories with one, two, and three tech reps. Note how sharply W_q decreases as the number of tech reps (servers) increases without changing the utilization factor. In fact, W_q for $s = 2$ is well under *half* that for $s = 1$, and W_q for $s = 3$ is about a *fourth* of that for $s = 1$.

These results suggest that further enlarging the territories by assigning four or more tech reps to each one would decrease W_q even further. However, there also are disadvantages to enlarging the territories. One is the possibility of a significant increase in the average time required for a tech rep to travel to the site of a failed machine. When combining only two or three one-person tech rep territories into a single joint territory, the average travel times should not increase much since the tech reps can effectively coordinate in dividing up the repair jobs based on the proximity of the jobs to the current locations of the tech reps. However, this becomes more difficult with even more tech reps in an even larger territory, so occasional travel times might become excessive. Since time traveling to a repair site is part of the total time a tech rep must devote to a repair, the *mean service rate* μ may decrease slightly

Combining too many tech reps into a very large territory can cause excessive travel times, among other problems.

from the four repairs per day assumed in Table 11.5 when the number of tech reps is more than three. For any given number of tech reps, decreasing μ increases W_q. Therefore, it is unclear how much further W_q can be decreased, if at all, by increasing the number of tech reps per territory beyond three.

Assigning a large number of tech reps to each territory has a number of practical drawbacks as well. Coordination between tech reps becomes more difficult. Customers lose the feeling of receiving personalized service when they are visited by so many different tech reps. Furthermore, tech reps lose the pride of ownership in managing their own territory and dealing with "their" customers. Personal or professional conflicts between tech reps also can arise when they share the same territory, and the opportunities for such conflicts increase with larger teams.

For all these reasons, John Phixitt concludes that normally assigning three tech reps to each territory would provide the best trade-off between minimizing these disadvantages of large territories and reducing W_q to a satisfactory level.

> **Conclusion:** The approach suggested by the chief financial officer would indeed satisfy the proposed new service standard ($W_q \leq 0.25$ day) if each three contiguous one-person tech rep territories are combined into a larger territory served jointly by the same three tech reps. Since the total number of tech reps does not change, there would be no significant additional cost from implementing this approach other than the disadvantages of larger territories just cited. To minimize these disadvantages, the territories should not be enlarged any further than having three tech reps per territory.

The *M/D/s* Model

The service times in many queueing systems have much less variability than is assumed by the *M/M/s* model. In some cases, there may be no variability (or almost no variability) at all in the service times. The *M/D/s* model is designed for these cases.

> **Assumptions:** Same as for the *M/M/s* model, except now all the service times are the *same*. This *constant service time* is denoted by $1/\mu$. (This is referred to as having a *degenerate* service-time distribution, which provides the symbol *D* for the model label.)

Constant service times arise when exactly the same work is being performed to serve each customer. When the servers are *machines,* there may literally be no variability at all in the service times. The assumption of constant service times also can be a reasonable approximation with *human servers* if they are performing the same routine task for all customers.

Just as for single-server queueing systems, eliminating the variability of service times substantially increases the efficiency of multiple-server queueing systems.

We found in the preceding section that, when $s = 1$, the value of L_q for the *M/D/1* model is only *half* that for the *M/M/1* model. Similar differences in L_q between the two models also occur when $s > 1$ (especially with larger values of the utilization factor ρ). Substantial differences between the models also occur for W_q, W, and L.

These large differences emphasize the importance of using the model that best fits the queueing system under study. Because the *M/M/s* model is the most convenient one, it is common practice to routinely use this model for most applications. However, doing so when there is little or no variability in the service times causes a large error in some measures of performance.

The procedures for calculating the various measures of performance for the *M/D/s* model are far more complicated than for the *M/M/s* model, so no Excel template is available in the case when $s > 1$. However, special projects have been conducted to calculate the measures. Figure 11.10 shows the values of L versus ρ for many values of s. The other main measures (W, W_q, and L_q) then can be obtained from L by using Little's formula, and so forth (as described in Section 11.3).

Review Questions

1. For multiple-server queueing models, what is the formula for the utilization factor ρ? What is the interpretation of ρ in terms of how servers use their time?
2. Which values of ρ correspond to the servers having a manageable utilization factor that allows the system to reach a steady-state condition?

FIGURE 11.10
Values of L for the *M/D/s* model for various values of s, the number of servers.

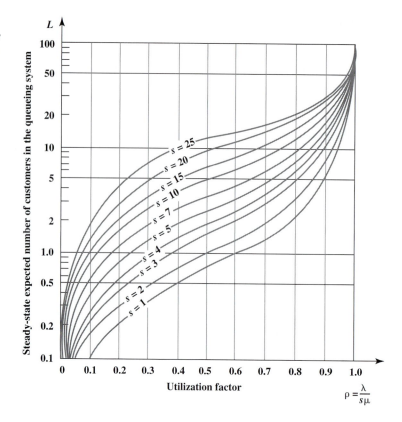

3. Are there any measures of performance that can be calculated for the *M/M/1* model but not the *M/M/s* model?

4. How many one-person tech rep territories need to be combined into a larger territory in order to satisfy Dupit's proposed new service standard?

5. Compare the *M/M/s* and *M/D/s* models in terms of the amount of variability in the service times.

11.7 PRIORITY QUEUEING MODELS

Priority queueing models are used when high-priority customers are served ahead of others who have waited longer.

All the queueing models presented so far assume that the customers are served on a first-come, first-served basis. Not all queueing systems operate that way. In some systems, the more important customers are served ahead of others who have waited longer. Management may want certain special customers to be given priority over others. In some cases, the customers in the queueing system are jobs to be performed, and the different deadlines for the jobs dictate the order in which these customers are served. Rush jobs need to be done before routine jobs.

A *hospital emergency room* is an example of a queueing system where priorities automatically are used. An arriving patient who is in critical condition naturally will be treated ahead of a routine patient who was already there waiting.

The models for such queueing systems generally make the following general assumptions.

General Assumptions

1. There are two or more categories of customers. Each category is assigned to a **priority class.** Customers in priority class 1 are given priority for receiving service over customers in priority class 2. If there are more than two priority classes, customers in priority class 2 then are given priority over customers in priority class 3, and so on.

2. After deferring to higher priority customers, the customers within each priority class are served on a first-come, first-served basis. Thus, within a priority class, priority for receiving service is based on the time already spent waiting in the queueing system.

There actually are two types of priorities, as described below.

Nonpreemptive priorities: Once a server has begun serving a customer, the service must be completed without interruption even if a higher priority customer arrives while this service is in process. However, once service is completed, if there are customers in the queue, priorities are applied to select the one to begin service. In particular, the one selected is that member of the *highest* priority class represented in the queue who has waited longest.

Preemptive priorities: The lowest priority customer being served is *preempted* (ejected back into the queue) whenever a higher priority customer enters the queueing system. A server is thereby freed to begin serving the new arrival immediately. Whenever a server does succeed in *finishing* a service, the next customer to begin receiving service is selected just as described above for nonpreemptive priorities. (The preempted customer becomes the member of its priority class in the queue who has waited longest, so it hopefully will get back into service soon and, perhaps after additional preemptions, will eventually finish.)

This section includes a basic queueing model for each of these two types of priorities.

A Preemptive Priorities Queueing Model

Along with the general assumptions about priorities given above, this model makes the following assumptions.

Additional Assumptions

1. Preemptive priorities are used as just described. (Let n denote the number of priority classes.)
2. For priority class i $(i = 1, 2, \ldots, n)$, the *interarrival times* of customers in that class have an *exponential* distribution with a mean of $1/\lambda_i$.
3. All *service times* have an *exponential* distribution with a mean of $1/\mu$, regardless of the priority class involved.
4. The queueing system has a single server.

This model fits the *M/M*/1 model except for also having preemptive priorities.

Thus, except for the complication of using preemptive priorities, the assumptions are the same as for the *M/M*/1 model.

Since λ_i is the mean arrival rate for customers in priority class i $(i = 1, 2, \ldots, n)$, $\lambda = (\lambda_1 + \lambda_2 + \ldots + \lambda_n)$ is the overall mean arrival rate for all customers. Therefore, the *utilization factor* for the server is

$$\rho = \frac{\lambda_1 + \lambda_2 + \cdots + \lambda_n}{\mu}$$

As with the previous models, $\rho < 1$ is required to enable the queueing system to reach a steady-state condition for all priority classes.

The reason for using priorities is to *decrease* the waiting times for high-priority customers. This is accomplished at the expense of *increasing* the waiting times for low-priority customers.

Assuming $\rho < 1$, formulas are available for calculating the main measures of performance $(L, W, L_q,$ and $W_q)$ for *each* of the priority classes. An Excel template in your MS Courseware quickly performs all these calculations for you.

A Nonpreemptive Priorities Queueing Model

Along with the general assumptions given earlier, this model makes the following assumptions.

Additional Assumptions

1. Nonpreemptive priorities are used as described earlier in the section. (Again, let n be the number of priority classes.)
2. and 3. Same as for the preemptive priorities queueing model.
4. The queueing system can have any number of servers.

This model fits the M/M/s model except for also having nonpreemptive priorities.

Except for using nonpreemptive priorities, these assumptions are the same as for the *M/M/s* model.

The utilization factor for the servers is

$$\rho = \frac{\lambda_1 + \lambda_2 + \cdots + \lambda_n}{s\mu}$$

Again, $\rho < 1$ is needed to enable the queueing system to reach a steady-state condition for all the priority classes.

As before, an Excel template is available in your MS Courseware to calculate all the main measures of performance for *each* of the priority classes.

Applying the Nonpreemptive Priorities Queueing Model to the Approach Suggested by the Vice President for Marketing

Now we come to the last of the four approaches being investigated by Dupit's management science team. The vice president for marketing has proposed giving the printer-copiers priority over other machines for receiving service. In other words, whenever a tech rep finishes a repair, if there are *both* printer-copiers and other machines still waiting to be repaired, the tech rep *always* should choose a printer-copier (the one that has waited longest) to be repaired next, even if other machines have waited longer.

The suggestion of the vice president for marketing is to apply the proposed new service standard to the printer-copiers only and then to give them nonpreemptive priority over the other machines.

The rationale for this proposal is that the printer-copier performs so many vital functions that its owners cannot tolerate being without it as long as other machines. Indeed, nearly all the complaints about excessive waiting for repairs have come from these owners even though other machines wait just as long. Therefore, the vice president for marketing feels that the proposed new service standard ($W_q \leq 2$ hours) only needs to be applied to the printer-copiers. Giving them priority for service hopefully will result in meeting this standard while still providing satisfactory service to other machines.

To investigate this, the management science team is applying the nonpreemptive priorities queueing model. There are two priority classes.

Priority class 1:   Printer-copiers.
Priority class 2:   Other machines.

Therefore, a distinction is made between these two types of arriving customers (machines needing repairs) for the queueing system in each tech rep territory. To determine the *mean arrival rate* for each of these two priority classes (denoted by λ_1 and λ_2, respectively), the team has ascertained that about a third of the machines assigned to tech reps currently are printer-copiers. Each printer-copier requires service with about the same frequency (approximately once every 50 workdays) as other machines. Consequently, since the *total* mean arrival rate for all the machines in a one-person tech rep territory typically is three machines per day,

$\lambda_1 = 1$ customer (printer-copier) per workday   (now)

$\lambda_2 = 2$ customers (other machines) per workday   (now)

However, the proportion of the machines that are printer-copiers is expected to gradually increase until it peaks at about *half* in a couple of years. At that point, the mean arrival rates will have changed to

$\lambda_1 = 1.5$ customers (printer-copiers) per workday   (later)

$\lambda_2 = 1.5$ customers (other machines) per workday   (later)

The *mean service rate* for each tech rep is unchanged by applying priorities, so its best estimate continues to be $\mu = 4$ customers per workday. Under the company's current policy of one-person tech rep territories, the queueing system for each territory has a single server ($s = 1$). Since $(\lambda_1 + \lambda_2) = 3$ both now and later, the value of the utilization factor will continue to be

$$\rho = \frac{\lambda_1 + \lambda_2}{s\mu} = \frac{3}{4}$$

FIGURE 11.11

This Excel template applies the nonpreemptive priorities queueing model to the Dupit problem *now* under the approach suggested by the vice president for marketing to give priority to the printer-copiers.

	A	B	C	D	E	F	G
1		**Nonpreemptive Priorities Model for VP of Marketing's Approach**					
2		**(Current Arrival Rates)**					
3							
4		$n =$	2	(# of priority classes)			
5		$\mu =$	4	(mean service rate)			
6		$s =$	1	(# servers)			
7							
8							
9			λ_i	L	L_q	W	W_q
10		Priority Class 1	1	0.5	0.25	0.5	0.25
11		Priority Class 2	2	2.5	2	1.25	1
12							
13							
14							
15							
16		$\lambda =$	3				
17		$\rho =$	0.75				

FIGURE 11.12

The modification of Figure 11.11 that applies the same model to the *later* version of the Dupit problem.

	A	B	C	D	E	F	G
1		**Nonpreemptive Priorities Model for VP of Marketing's Approach**					
2		**(Future Arrival Rates)**					
3							
4		$n =$	2	(# of priority classes)			
5		$\mu =$	4	(mean service rate)			
6		$s =$	1	(# servers)			
7							
8							
9			λ_i	L	L_q	W	W_q
10		Priority Class 1	1.5	0.825	0.45	0.55	0.3
11		Priority Class 2	1.5	2.175	1.8	1.45	1.2
12							
13							
14							
15							
16		$\lambda =$	3				
17		$\rho =$	0.75				

Figure 11.11 shows the results obtained by applying the Excel template for the nonpreemptive priorities model to this queueing system *now* ($\lambda_1 = 1$ and $\lambda_2 = 2$). Figure 11.12 does the same under the conditions expected *later* ($\lambda_1 = 1.5$ and $\lambda_2 = 1.5$).

The management science team is particularly interested in the values of W_q, the expected waiting time in the queue, given in the last column of these two figures. These values are summarized in Table 11.6, where the first row comes from Figure 11.11 and the second comes from Figure 11.12.

For the printer-copiers, note that $W_q = 0.25$ workday now, which barely meets the proposed new service standard of $W_q \leq 0.25$ workday, but this expected waiting time would deteriorate later to 0.3 workday. Thus, this approach falls a little short. Furthermore, the expected waiting time before service begins for the other machines would go from $W_q = 1$ workday now to $W_q = 1.2$ workdays later. This large increase from the average waiting times being experienced under the current policy of $W_q = 0.75$ workday (as given in Figure 11.4) is likely to alienate a considerable number of customers.

TABLE 11.6 Expected Waiting Times* when Nonpreemptive Priorities Are Applied to the Dupit Problem

s	When	λ_1	λ_2	μ	ρ	W_q for Printer-Copiers	W_q for Other Machines
1	Now	1	2	4	0.75	0.25 workday (2 hrs.)	1 workday (8 hrs.)
1	Later	1.5	1.5	4	0.75	0.3 workday (2.4 hrs.)	1.2 workdays (9.6 hrs.)
2	Now	2	4	4	0.75	0.107 workday (0.86 hr.)	0.429 workday (3.43 hrs.)
2	Later	3	3	4	0.75	0.129 workday (1.03 hrs.)	0.514 workday (4.11 hrs.)
3	Now	3	6	4	0.75	0.063 workday (0.50 hr.)	0.252 workday (2.02 hrs.)
3	Later	4.5	4.5	4	0.75	0.076 workday (0.61 hr.)	0.303 workday (2.42 hrs.)

*These times are obtained in units of *workdays*, consisting of eight hours each, and then converted to hours.

Since assigning nonpreemptive priorities doesn't help enough (especially later), let's also try combining one-person tech rep territories into larger joint territories.

Table 11.5 in the preceding section demonstrated what a great impact combining one-person tech rep territories into larger territories has on decreasing expected waiting times. Therefore, the management science team decides to investigate combining this approach with applying nonpreemptive priorities.

Combining pairs of one-person tech rep territories into single two-person tech rep territories doubles the mean arrival rates for both priority classes (λ_1 and λ_2) for each new territory. Since the number of servers also doubles (from $s = 1$ to $s = 2$) without any change in μ (the mean service rate for each server), the utilization factor ρ remains the same. These values now and later are shown in the third and fourth rows of Table 11.6. Applying the nonpreemptive priorities queueing model then yields the expected waiting times given in the last two columns.

These large reductions in the W_q values from the $s = 1$ case result in rather reasonable waiting times. Both now and later, W_q for printer-copiers is only about *half* of the maximum under the proposed new service standard ($W_q \leq 2$ hours). Although W_q for the other machines is somewhat over this maximum both now and later, these waiting times also are somewhat under the average waiting times currently being experienced (6 hours) without many complaints from members of this priority class. John Phixitt's reaction is favorable. He feels that the service standard of $W_q \leq 2$ hours really was proposed with the printer-copiers in mind and that the other members of top management probably will also be satisfied with the values of W_q shown in the third and fourth rows of Table 11.6.

Two-person tech rep territories with priorities reduce waiting times to satisfactory levels.

Since the analytical results reported in Table 11.5 were so favorable for three-person tech rep territories without priorities, the management science team decides to investigate this option *with priorities* as well. The last two rows of Table 11.6 show the results for this case. Note that these W_q values for $s = 3$ are even smaller than for $s = 2$. In fact, even the W_q values for other machines nearly satisfy the proposed new service standard at this point. However, John Phixitt points out that three-person territories have substantial disadvantages compared to two-person territories. One is longer travel times to machine sites. Another is that customers would feel that service is considerably less personalized when they are seeing three different tech reps coming for repairs instead of just two. Another perhaps more important disadvantage is that three tech reps would have considerably more difficulty coordinating their work than two. John does not feel that the decreases in W_q values for $s = 3$ are worth these (and related) disadvantages.

Three-person tech rep territories with priorities reduce waiting times even further but have substantial disadvantages compared to two-person territories.

Conclusion: Since the high-priority need is to improve service for the printer-copiers, strong consideration should be given to giving these machines priority over others for receiving repairs. However, the waiting times for both printer-copiers and other machines will remain unsatisfactory if the current one-person tech rep territories continue to be used. Enlarging to two-person territories would reduce these waiting times to levels that appear to be satisfactory, without any significant additional (monetary) costs. Enlarging the territories even further probably would not be worthwhile in light of the disadvantages of large territories.

Management's Conclusions

Having been assigned by Dupit's president to study the four suggested approaches to the company's problem, the management science team and John Phixitt were asked to report back to the top management group dealing with the problem in six weeks. They now do so by sending

TABLE 11.7
The Four Approaches Being Considered by Dupit Management

Proposer	Proposal	Additional Cost
John Phixitt	Maintain one-person territories, but reduce number of machines assigned to each from 150 to 100	$300 million per year
Vice president for engineering	Keep current one-person territories, but provide new state-of-the-art equipment to the tech reps	One-time cost of $500 million
Chief financial officer	Change to three-person territories	None, except disadvantages of larger territories
Vice president for marketing	Change to two-person territories, with priority given to the printer-copiers for repairs	None, except disadvantages of larger territories

their report to each member of the group. The report presents their conclusions (as stated above and in the preceding sections) on each of the four approaches they were asked to investigate. Also included are the projected measures of performance (such as in Tables 11.5 and 11.6) for these approaches.

Table 11.7 summarizes the four approaches as they now have been refined by the management science team.

At this point, the president reconvenes his top management group (including John Phixitt). The meeting begins with a brief (and well-rehearsed) presentation by the head of the management science team summarizing the analysis and conclusions of the team. The presentation is interrupted frequently by comments and questions from the group. The president next asks John Phixitt to present his recommendations.

John begins by emphasizing the many advantages of the current system of one-person territories. The first two proposals in Table 11.7 would enable continuing this system, but at a very high cost. He then concedes that he has concluded that the cost would be too high and that the time has come to modify the system in order to efficiently deliver the service that the marketplace now is demanding. (A brief discussion reveals strong agreement from the group on this point.)

This leaves the third and fourth proposals in Table 11.7 under consideration. John repeats the arguments he had given earlier to the management science team about the important advantages of two-person territories over three-person territories. He then points out that the fourth proposal not only would provide two-person territories but also would result in the printer-copiers having smaller average waiting times for repairs than under the third proposal. When the customer relations manager objects that the average waiting times of *other machines* would not meet the proposed new service standard (a maximum of two hours), John emphasizes that these waiting times still would decrease substantially from current levels and that the owners of these machines aren't even complaining now. In conclusion, John recommends adoption of the fourth proposal.

Some minor concerns are raised in the subsequent discussion, including the possibility that owners of other machines might feel that they are being treated as second-class customers. However, John indicates that the new policy would not be publicized, but, if discovered, could be easily justified to a customer. The group soon concurs with John's recommendation.

Decision: Adopt the fourth proposal in Table 11.7.

Finally, John points out that there currently are a relatively few one-person territories that are so sparsely populated that combining them into two-person territories would cause excessive travel times for the tech reps. Since this would defeat the purpose of the new policy, he suggests adopting the second proposal for these territories and then using the experience with the new equipment to make future decisions on which equipment to provide to all tech reps as service demands further increase. The group agrees.

Decision: As an exception to the new policy, the second proposal in Table 11.7 is adopted just for current one-person territories that are particularly sparsely populated. The experience with the new equipment will be closely monitored to help guide future equipment purchase decisions for all tech reps.

Although the first two proposals retain the many advantages of one-person territories, both proposals are too costly, so the choice is between the third and fourth proposals.

The president thanks John Phixitt and the management science team for their outstanding work in pointing the way toward what appears to be an excellent resolution of a critical problem for the company. John graciously states that the real key was the insights obtained by the management science team by making effective use of the appropriate queueing models. The president smiles and makes a mental note to seek John's advice more often.

Review
Questions

1. How does using priorities differ from serving customers on a first-come, first-served basis?
2. What is the difference between nonpreemptive priorities and preemptive priorities?
3. Except for using preemptive priorities, the assumptions of the preemptive priorities model are the same as for which basic queueing model?
4. Except for using nonpreemptive priorities, the assumptions of the nonpreemptive priorities model are the same as for which basic queueing model?
5. For these models, which values of the utilization factor ρ enable the queueing system to reach a steady-state condition for all priority classes?
6. When applying the nonpreemptive priorities queueing model to the Dupit case study, what are the two priority classes?
7. For this application, what is the conclusion about the minimum number of tech reps per territory needed to reduce waiting times for repairs to levels that appear to be satisfactory?
8. What is the decision of Dupit's top management regarding which of the four proposed approaches will be adopted (except for particularly sparsely populated territories)?

11.8 SOME INSIGHTS ABOUT DESIGNING QUEUEING SYSTEMS

The Dupit case study illustrates some key insights that queueing models provide about how queueing systems should be designed. This section highlights these insights in a broader context.

There are four insights presented here. Each one was first seen when analyzing one of the four approaches proposed for the Dupit problem. After summarizing each insight, we will briefly review its application to the case study and then describe the insight in general terms.

> **Insight 1:** When designing a single-server queueing system, beware that giving a relatively high utilization factor (workload) to the server provides surprisingly poor measures of performance for the system.[2]

This insight arose in Section 11.5 when analyzing John Phixitt's suggested approach of decreasing the utilization factor ρ for each tech rep sufficiently to meet the proposed new service standard (a maximum average waiting time for repairs of two hours). The current ρ = 0.75 gave average waiting times of six hours, which falls far short of this standard. It was necessary to decrease ρ all the way down to ρ = 0.5 to meet this standard.

To further demonstrate this insight, we have used the Excel template for the *M/M/s* model (previously shown in Figures 11.8 and 11.9), with $s = 1$ and $\mu = 1$ (so the utilization factor ρ equals λ), to generate the data table in Figure 11.13. Here are the steps to follow to do this. First make a table with the column headings shown in columns I, J, and K in Figure 11.13. In the first column of the table (I5:I16), list the trial values for the data cell (the mean arrival rate, or equivalently, the utilization factor), except leave the first row blank. The headings of the next columns specify which output will be evaluated. For each of these columns, use the first row of the table (cells J4:K4) to write an equation that refers to the relevant output cell. In this case, the cells of interest are the expected number of customers in the system (L) and in the queue (L_q), so the equations for J4:K4 are those shown below the spreadsheet in Figure 11.13.

Next, select the entire table (I4:K16) and then choose Data Table from the What-If Analysis menu of the Data tab (for Excel 2007) or Table from the Data menu (for earlier versions of Excel). In the Data Table dialogue box (as shown at the bottom left-hand side of Figure 11.13), indicate the column input cell (Lambda or C4), which refers to the data cell that is

---

[2] The one exception is a queueing system that has *constant* (or nearly constant) interarrival times and service times. Such a system will perform very well with a high utilization factor.

FIGURE 11.13

This data table demonstrates Insight 1 in Section 11.8.

	A	B	C	D	E	F	G
1				**Template for *M/M/s* Queueing Model**			
2							
3			**Data**				**Results**
4		$\lambda =$	0.5	(mean arrival rate)		$L =$	1.0000
5		$\mu =$	1	(mean service rate)		$L_q=$	0.5000

	H	I	J	K	L	M	N	O
1		**Data Table Demonstrating the Effect of Increasing** ρ **on** L_q **and** L **for** *M/M/1*						
2								
3		$\lambda = \rho$	L	L_q				
4			1	0.5				
5		0.01	0.010	0.000				
6		0.25	0.333	0.083				
7		0.5	1	0.5				
8		0.6	1.5	0.9				
9		0.7	2.333	1.633				
10		0.75	3	2.25				
11		0.8	4	3.2				
12		0.85	5.667	4.817				
13		0.9	9	8.1				
14		0.95	19	18.05				
15		0.99	99	98.01				
16		0.999	999	998.001				
17								
18								
19								
20								

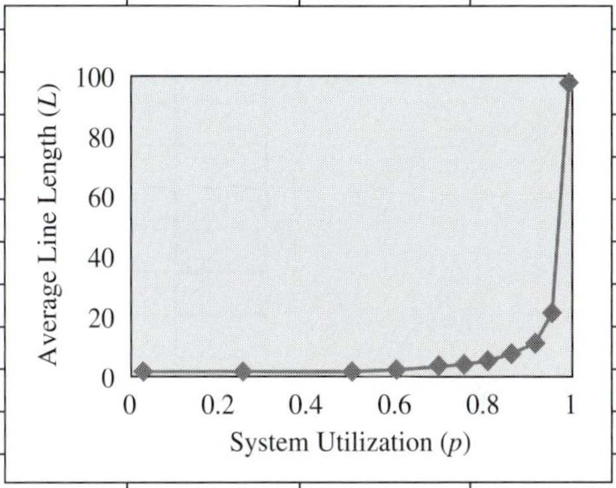

Select entire table (I4:K16), before choosing Table from the Data menu.

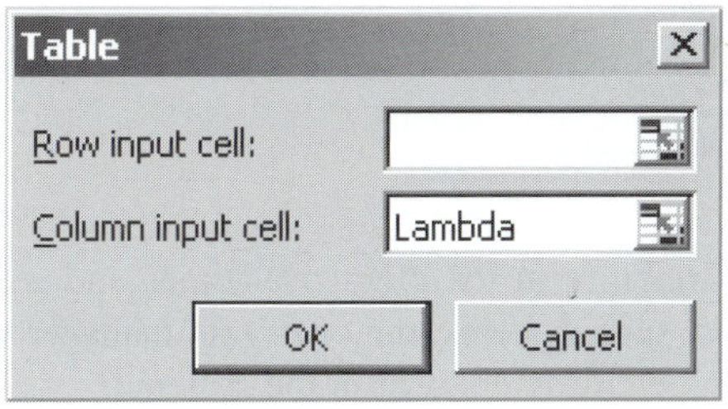

Table

Row input cell:

Column input cell: Lambda

OK   Cancel

	J	K
3	L	L_q
4	=L	=L_q

Range Name	Cell
L	G4
Lambda	C4
L_q	G5

The average number of customers waiting in a queueing system (L) increases rapidly with even small increases in the utilization factor ρ, so ρ should be kept well under 1.

being changed in the first column of the table. Nothing is entered for the row input cell because no row is being used to list the trial values of a data cell in this case.

Clicking OK then generates the data table shown in Figure 11.13. For each trial value for the data cell listed in the first column of the table, the corresponding output cell values are calculated and displayed in the other columns of the table. (The numbers in the first row of the table come from the original solution in the spreadsheet.)

Note in this data table how rapidly L_q and L increase with even small increases in ρ. For example, L triples when ρ is increased from 0.5 to 0.75, and then triples again when increasing ρ from 0.75 to 0.9. As ρ is increased above 0.9, L_q and L grow astronomically. (Although this data table has been generated with $\mu = 1$, the same values of L_q and L would be obtained with any other value of μ as well when the numbers in the first column are the utilization factor $\rho = \lambda/\mu$.)

Managers normally strive for a high utilization factor for their employees, machines, equipment, and so on. This is an important part of running an efficient business. A utilization factor of 0.9 or higher would be considered desirable. However, all this should change when the employee or machine or piece of equipment is the server in a single-server queueing system

FIGURE 11.14
This data table demonstrates Insight 2 in Section 11.8.

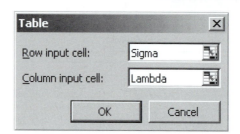

	A	B	C	D	E	F	G	H	I
1		**Template for the *M/G/*1 Queueing Model**							
2									
3			**Data**				**Results**		
4		$\lambda =$	0.5	(mean arrival rate)		$L =$	0.8125		
5		$1/\mu =$	1	(expected service time)		$L_q =$	0.3125		
6		$\sigma =$	0.5	(standard deviation)					
7		$s =$	1	(# servers)		$W =$	1.625		
8						$W_q =$	0.625		
9									
10						$\rho =$	0.5		
11									
12						$P_0 =$	0.5		
13									
14		**Data Table Demonstrating the Effect of Decreasing σ on L_q for *M/G/*1**							
15									
16				Body of Table Shows L_q Values					
17									
18					σ				
19			0.3125	1	0.5	0			
20			0.5	0.500	0.313	0.250	Select entire table		
21		$\rho\ (=\lambda)$	0.75	2.250	1.406	1.125	(C19:F23), before		
22			0.9	8.100	5.063	4.050	choosing Table from		
23			0.99	98.010	61.256	49.005	the Data menu.		

Table ✕

Row input cell: Sigma

Column input cell: Lambda

OK   Cancel

	C
19	$=L_q$

Range Name	Cell
Lambda	C4
L_q	G5
Sigma	C6

that has considerable variability in its interarrival times and service times (such as for an *M/M/*1 system). For most such systems, the cognizant manager would consider it unacceptable to *average* having nine customers wait in the system ($L = 9$ with $\rho = 0.9$). If so, a utilization factor somewhat less (perhaps much less) than 0.9 would be needed. For example, we just mentioned that meeting Dupit's proposed service standard with John Phixitt's original suggested approach required reducing the utilization factor all the way down to $\rho = 0.5$.

> **Insight 2:** Decreasing the *variability* of service times (without any change in the mean) improves the performance of a single-server queueing system substantially. (This also tends to be true for multiple-server queueing systems, especially with higher utilization factors.)

This insight was found in the Dupit study while analyzing the proposal by the vice president for engineering to provide new state-of-the-art equipment to all the tech reps. As described at the end of Section 11.5, this approach would decrease both the *mean* and *standard deviation* of the service-time distribution. Decreasing the mean also decreased the utilization factor, which decreased the expected waiting time W_q. Decreasing the standard deviation σ (which measures the amount of variability) then provided an *additional* 37.5 percent reduction in W_q. Insight 2 refers to this latter substantial improvement in W_q (and in the other measures of performance).

The two-way data table in Figure 11.14 demonstrates the effect on L_q of decreasing the standard deviation σ of the service-time distribution for any *M/G/*1 queueing system. (This table was generated from the Excel template introduced in Figure 11.6 for the *M/G/*1 model.)

To create this two-way data table, make a table with column and row headings as shown in rows 19–23 of the spreadsheet in Figure 11.14. In the upper left-hand corner of the table (C19), write an equation that refers to the output cell for which you are interested in seeing the results ($= L_q$ or G5). In the first column of the table (column C, below the equation in cell C19), insert all the different values for the first changing data cell (λ). In the first row of the table (row 19, to the right of the equation in cell C19), insert all the different values for the second changing data cell (σ).

Next, select the entire table (C19:F23) and then choose Data Table from the What-If Analysis menu of the Data tab (for Excel 2007) or Table from the Data menu (for earlier versions of Excel). In the Data Table dialogue box (shown at the bottom left-hand side of Figure 11.14), indicate which data cells are being changed simultaneously. The column input cell refers to the data cell whose various values are indicated in the first column of the table (Lambda, or cell C4), while the row input cell refers to the data cell whose various values are indicated in the first row of the table (Sigma, or cell C6).

The data table shown in Figure 11.14 is then generated automatically by clicking OK. For each pair of values of the input cell indicated in the first row and column of the table, Excel determines the corresponding value of the output cell referred to in the upper left-hand corner of the table. These values are then filled into the body of the table.

Before generating this data table, the mean of the service-time distribution has been set in cell C5 at $1/\mu = 1$ (which makes $\rho = \lambda$), so the column headings of $\sigma = 1$, $\sigma = 0.5$, and $\sigma = 0$ correspond to $\sigma =$ mean, $\sigma = 0.5$ mean, and $\sigma = 0$, respectively. Therefore, as you read the values of L_q in the table from left to right, σ decreases from equaling the mean of the distribution (as for the *M/M/*1 model) to being *half* the mean and then to $\sigma = 0$ (as for the *M/D/*1 model). If the mean were to be changed to some value different from 1, the same values of L_q still would be obtained for each value of the utilization factor $\rho = \lambda/\mu$ listed in cells C20:C23 as long as the values of σ for the respective columns are $\sigma =$ mean, $\sigma = 0.5$ mean, and $\sigma = 0$.

If service times are highly variable, eliminating this variability can reduce L_q by about half.

In each row of this table, the value in the $\sigma = 0$ column is only *half* that in the $\sigma = 1$ column, so completely eliminating the variability of the service times gives a large improvement. However, the value in the $\sigma = 0.5$ column is only 62.5 percent of that in the $\sigma = 1$ column, so even cutting the variability in half provides most of the improvement from completely eliminating the variability. Therefore, whatever can be done to reduce the variability even modestly is going to improve the performance of the system significantly.

> **Insight 3:** *Multiple-server* queueing systems can perform satisfactorily with somewhat higher utilization factors than can single-server queueing systems. For example, *pooling servers* by combining separate single-server queueing systems into one multiple-server queueing system (without changing the utilization factor) greatly improves the measures of performance.

This insight was gained during the Dupit study while investigating the proposal by the chief financial officer to combine one-person territories into larger territories served jointly by multiple tech reps. Table 11.5 in Section 11.6 summarizes the great impact that this approach would have on improving average waiting times to begin repairs (W_q). In particular, W_q for two-person territories is well under *half* that for one-person territories, and W_q for three-person territories is about a *fourth* of that for one-person territories, even though the utilization factor is the same for all these cases.

These dramatic improvements are not unusual. In fact, it has been found that pooling servers as described below *always* provides similar improvements.

Here is a way to reduce waiting times dramatically.

The Impact of Pooling Servers: Suppose you have a number (denoted by *n*) of identical single-server queueing systems that fit the *M/M/*1 model. Suppose you then combine these *n* systems (without changing the utilization factor) into a single queueing system that fits the *M/M/s* model, where the number of servers is $s = n$. This change *always* improves the value of W_q by *more* than dividing by *n*, that is,

$$W_q(\text{for combined system}) < \frac{W_q(\text{for each single-server system})}{n}$$

Although this inequality is not guaranteed to hold if these queueing systems do not fit the *M/M/*1 and *M/M/s* models, the improvement in W_q by combining systems still will be very substantial for other models as well.

> **Insight 4:** Applying *priorities* when selecting customers to begin service can greatly improve the measures of performance for high-priority customers.

Applying priorities can reduce waiting times dramatically for high-priority customers but will increase waiting times for low-priority customers.

This insight became evident during the Dupit study while investigating the proposal by the vice president for marketing to give higher (nonpreemptive) priority to repairing the printer-copiers than to repairing other machines. Table 11.6 in the preceding section gives the values of W_q for the printer-copiers and for the other machines under this proposal. Comparing these values to those in Table 11.5 without priorities shows that giving priority to the printer-copiers would reduce their waiting times now dramatically (but would also increase the waiting times for the other machines). Later, as printer-copiers become a larger proportion of the machines being serviced (half instead of a third), the reduction in their waiting times would not be quite as large.

For other queueing systems as well, the impact of applying priorities depends somewhat on the proportion of the customers in the respective priority classes. If the proportion in the top priority class is small, the measures of performance for these customers will improve tremendously. If the proportion is large, the improvement will be more modest.

Preemptive priorities give an even stronger preference to high-priority customers than do the *nonpreemptive* priorities used for the Dupit problem. Therefore, applying preemptive priorities improves the measures of performance for customers in the top priority class even more than applying nonpreemptive priorities.

Review Questions

1. What is the effect of giving a relatively large utilization factor (workload) to the server in a single-server queueing system?
2. What happens to the values of L_q and L for the *M/M/*1 model when ρ is increased well above 0.9?
3. What is the effect of decreasing the variability of service times (without any change in the mean) on the performance of a single-server queueing system?
4. For an *M/G/*1 queueing system, does cutting the variability (standard deviation) of service times in half provide most of the improvement that would be achieved by completely eliminating the variability?
5. What is the effect of combining separate single-server queueing systems into one multiple-server queueing system (without changing the utilization factor)?
6. What is the effect of applying priorities when selecting customers to begin service?
7. Do preemptive priorities or nonpreemptive priorities give the greater improvement in the measures of performance for customers in the top priority class?

11.9 ECONOMIC ANALYSIS OF THE NUMBER OF SERVERS TO PROVIDE

When designing a queueing system, a key question often is how many servers to provide. Providing too many causes excessive costs. Providing too few causes excessive waiting by the customers. Therefore, choosing the number of servers involves finding an appropriate trade-off between the cost of the servers and the amount of waiting.

In many cases, the consequences to an organization of making its customers wait can be expressed as a **waiting cost.** This is especially true when the customers are *internal* to the organization, such as the employees of a company. Making one's own employees wait causes *lost productivity,* which results in *lost profit.* This lost profit is the waiting cost.

A manager is interested in minimizing the total cost. Let

TC = Expected total cost per unit time

SC = Expected service cost per unit time

WC = Expected waiting cost per unit time

Then the objective is to choose the number of servers so as to

$$\text{Minimize} \quad \text{TC} = \text{SC} + \text{WC}$$

When each server costs the same, the **service cost** is

$$\text{SC} = C_s s$$

where

C_s = Cost of a server per unit time

s = Number of servers

When the waiting cost is proportional to the amount of waiting, this cost can be expressed as

$$WC = C_w L$$

where

C_w = Waiting cost per unit time for each customer in the queueing system

L = Expected number of customers in the queueing system

Therefore, after estimating the constants C_s and C_w, the goal is to choose the value of s so as to

$$\text{Minimize} \quad TC = C_s s + C_w L$$

By choosing the queueing model that fits the queueing system, the value of L can be obtained for various values of s. Increasing s decreases L, at first rapidly and then gradually more slowly.

Figure 11.15 shows the general shape of the SC, WC, and TC curves versus the number of servers s. (For better conceptualization, we have drawn these as smooth curves even though the only feasible values of s are $s = 1, 2, \ldots$). By calculating TC for consecutive values of s until TC stops decreasing and starts increasing instead, it is straightforward to find the number of servers that minimizes total cost. The following example illustrates this process.

Calculate TC for consecutive values of s until TC stops decreasing to find the optimal number of servers.

An Example

The Acme Machine Shop has a tool crib for storing tools required by the shop mechanics. Two clerks run the tool crib. The tools are handed out by the clerks as the mechanics arrive and request them and are returned to the clerks when they are no longer needed. There have been complaints from supervisors that their mechanics have had to waste too much time waiting to be served at the tool crib, so it appears that there should be *more* clerks. On the other hand, management is exerting pressure to reduce overhead in the plant, and this reduction would lead to *fewer* clerks. To resolve these conflicting pressures, a management science study is being conducted to determine just how many clerks the tool crib should have.

The tool crib constitutes a queueing system, with the clerks as its servers and the mechanics as its customers. After gathering some data on interarrival times and service times, the

FIGURE 11.15

The shape of the cost curves for determining the number of servers to provide.

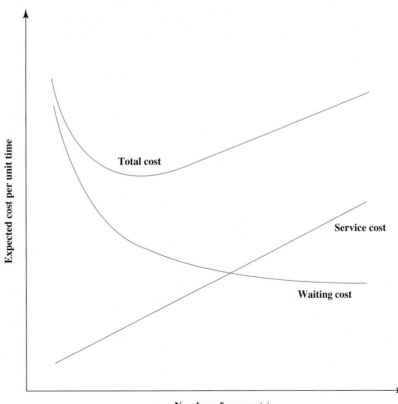

management science team has concluded that the queueing model that fits this queueing system best is the *M/M/s* model. The estimates of the mean arrival rate λ and the mean service rate (per server) μ are

$$\lambda = 120 \text{ customers per hour}$$

$$\mu = 80 \text{ customers per hour}$$

so the utilization factor for the two clerks is

$$\rho = \frac{\lambda}{s\mu} = \frac{120}{2(80)} = 0.75$$

The total cost to the company of each tool crib clerk is about \$20 per hour, so $C_s = \$20$. While a mechanic is busy, the value to the company of his or her output averages about \$48 per hour, so $C_w = \$48$. Therefore, the management science team now needs to find the number of servers (tool crib clerks) s that will

$$\text{Minimize} \quad TC = \$20\,s + \$48\,L$$

An Excel template has been provided in your MS Courseware for calculating these costs with the *M/M/s* model. All you need to do is enter the data for the model along with the unit service cost C_s, the unit waiting cost C_w, and the number of servers s you want to try. The template then calculates SC, WC, and TC. This is illustrated in Figure 11.16 with $s = 3$ for this example. By repeatedly entering alternative values of s, the template then can reveal which value minimizes TC in a matter of seconds.

Your MS Courseware includes an Excel template that will calculate TC for you.

FIGURE 11.16

This Excel template for using economic analysis to choose the number of servers with the *M/M/s* model is applied here to the Acme Machine Shop example with $s = 3$.

	A	B	C	D	E	F	G
1		**Economic Analysis of Acme Machine Shop Example**					
2							
3			**Data**				**Results**
4		$\lambda =$	120	(mean arrival rate)		$L =$	1.736842105
5		$\mu =$	80	(mean service rate)		$L_q =$	0.236842105
6		$s =$	3	(# servers)			
7						$W =$	0.014473684
8		$Pr(W > t) =$	0.02581732			$W_q =$	0.001973684
9		when $t =$	0.05				
10						$\rho =$	0.5
11		$Prob(W_q > t) =$	0.00058707				
12		when $t =$	0.05			n	P_n
13						0	0.210526316
14		**Economic Analysis:**				1	0.315789474
15		$C_s =$	\$20.00	(cost/server/unit time)		2	0.236842105
16		$C_w =$	\$48.00	(waiting cost/unit time)		3	0.118421053
17						4	0.059210526
18		Cost of Service	\$60.00			5	0.029605263
19		Cost of Waiting	\$83.37			6	0.014802632
20		Total Cost	\$143.37			7	0.007401316

	B	C
18	Cost of Service	$= C_s * s$
19	Cost of Waiting	$= C_w * L$
20	Total Cost	= CostOfService+CostOfWaiting

Range Name	Cell
CostOfService	C18
CostOfWaiting	C19
C_s	C15
C_w	C16
L	G4
s	C6
TotalCost	C20

FIGURE 11.17

This data table compares the expected hourly costs with various alternative numbers of clerks assigned to the Acme Machine Shop tool crib.

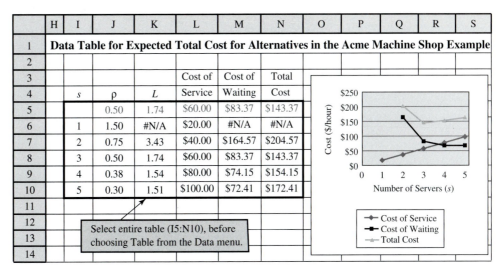

	H	I	J	K	L	M	N	O	P	Q	R	S
1				Data Table for Expected Total Cost for Alternatives in the Acme Machine Shop Example								
2												
3					Cost of	Cost of	Total					
4		s	ρ	L	Service	Waiting	Cost					
5			0.50	1.74	$60.00	$83.37	$143.37					
6		1	1.50	#N/A	$20.00	#N/A	#N/A					
7		2	0.75	3.43	$40.00	$164.57	$204.57					
8		3	0.50	1.74	$60.00	$83.37	$143.37					
9		4	0.38	1.54	$80.00	$74.15	$154.15					
10		5	0.30	1.51	$100.00	$72.41	$172.41					
11												
12												
13												
14												

Select entire table (I5:N10), before choosing Table from the Data menu.

	J	K	L	M	N
3			Cost of	Cost of	Total
4	ρ	L	Service	Waiting	Cost
5	=Rho	=L	=CostOfService	=CostOfWaiting	=TotalCost

Range Name	Cell
CostOfService	C18
CostOfWaiting	C19
L	G4
Rho	G10
s	C6
TotalCost	C20

Figure 11.17 shows a data table that has been generated from this template by repeating these calculations for $s = 1, 2, 3, 4,$ and 5. (See Section 11.8 for more information about generating data tables.) Since the utilization factor for $s = 1$ is $\rho = 1.5$, a single clerk would be unable to keep up with the customers (as indicated by #N/A in cells K6 and M6:N6), so this option is ruled out. All larger values of s are feasible, but $s = 3$ has the smallest total cost. Furthermore, $s = 3$ would decrease the current total cost for $s = 2$ by $62 per hour. Therefore, despite management's current drive to reduce overhead (which includes the cost of tool crib clerks), the management science team recommends that a third clerk be added to the tool crib. Note that this recommendation would decrease the utilization factor for the clerks from an already modest 0.75 all the way down to 0.5. However, because of the large improvement in the productivity of the mechanics (who are much more expensive than the clerks) through decreasing their time wasted waiting at the tool crib, management adopts the recommendation.

A low utilization factor of 0.5 is best for the tool crib clerks because this greatly reduces the time wasted by expensive mechanics waiting at the tool crib.

Review Questions

1. What is the trade-off involved in choosing the number of servers for a queueing system?
2. What is the nature of the waiting cost when the customers for the queueing system are the company's own employees?
3. When the waiting cost is proportional to the amount of waiting, what is an expression for the waiting cost?
4. What does the Acme Machine Shop example demonstrate about the advisability of always maintaining a relatively high utilization factor for the servers in a queueing system?

11.10 Summary

Queueing systems are prevalent throughout society. The adequacy of these systems can have an important effect on the quality of life and the productivity of the economy.

Key components of a queueing system are the *arriving customers,* the *queue* in which they wait for service, and the *servers* that provide the service. A queueing model representing a queueing system needs to specify the number of servers, the distribution of interarrival times, and the distribution of service times. An *exponential* distribution usually is chosen for the distribution of interarrival times because this corresponds to the common phenomenon of arrivals occurring randomly. An exponential distribution sometimes provides a reasonable fit to the service-time distribution as well, and is a particularly convenient choice in terms of ease of analysis. Other probability distributions sometimes used for the service-time distribution include the *degenerate* distribution (constant service times).

Key measures of the performance of queueing systems are the expected values of the number of customers in the queue or in the system (the latter adds on customers currently being served) and of the waiting time of a customer in the queue or in the system. General relationships between these expected values, including Little's formula, enable all four values to be determined immediately as soon as one has been found. In addition to the expected values, the probability distributions of these quantities are sometimes used as measures of performance as well.

This chapter's case study has the top management of the Dupit Corporation grappling with a difficult issue. The company's customers now are demanding a much higher level of service in promptly repairing the photocopiers (and particularly a new printer-copier) purchased from the company. Dupit already is spending $600 million per year servicing these machines. Each tech rep territory includes a queueing system with the tech rep as the server and the machines needing repairs as the customers. A management science team finds that the $M/M/1$ model, the $M/G/1$ model, the $M/M/s$ model, and a nonpreemptive priorities model enable analyzing the alternative approaches to redesigning this queueing system. This analysis leads to top management adopting a policy of combining pairs of one-person tech rep territories into two-person territories that give priority to repairing the new printer-copiers. This provides the needed level of service without a significant increase in cost.

Other queueing models discussed in the chapter include the $M/D/1$ and $M/D/s$ models, as well as a preemptive priorities model. A supplement to this chapter on the CD-ROM also introduces the finite queue variation and the finite calling population variation of the $M/M/s$ model, as well as models that use another service-time distribution (the Erlang distribution) that allow the amount of variability in the service times to fall somewhere between that for the exponential and degenerate distributions.

Section 11.8 presents four key insights that queueing models provide about how queueing systems should be designed. Each of these insights also is illustrated by the Dupit case study.

A key question when designing queueing systems frequently is how many servers to provide. Section 11.9 describes how to determine the number of servers that will minimize the expected total cost of the queueing system, including the cost of providing the servers and the cost associated with making customers wait.

Glossary

commercial service system A queueing system where a commercial organization provides a service to customers from outside the organization. (Section 11.2), 426

constant service times Every customer has the same service time. (Section 11.1), 425

customers A generic term that refers to whichever kind of entity (people, vehicles, machines, items, etc.) is coming to the queueing system to receive service. (Section 11.1), 420

exponential distribution The most popular choice for the probability distribution of both interarrival times and service times. Its shape is shown in Figure 11.3. (Section 11.1), 424

finite queue A queue that can hold only a limited number of customers. (Section 11.1), 423

infinite queue A queue that can hold an essentially unlimited number of customers. (Section 11.1), 423

interarrival time The elapsed time between consecutive arrivals to a queueing system. (Section 11.1), 422

internal service system A queueing system where the customers receiving service are internal to the organization providing the service. (Section 11.2), 427

lack-of-memory property When referring to arrivals, this property is that the time of the next arrival is completely uninfluenced by when the last arrival occurred. Also called the Markovian property. (Section 11.1), 423

Little's formula The formula $L = \lambda W$, or $L_q = \lambda W_q$. (Section 11.3), 429

mean arrival rate The expected number of arrivals to a queueing system per unit time. (Section 11.1), 422

mean service rate The expected number of service completions per unit time for a single continuously busy server. (Section 11.1), 424

nonpreemptive priorities Priorities for selecting the next customer to begin service when a server becomes free. However, these priorities do not affect customers who already have begun service. (Section 11.7), 449

number of customers in the queue The number of customers who are waiting for service to begin. (Sections 11.1, 11.3), 423, 429

number of customers in the system The total number of customers in the queueing system, either waiting for service to begin or currently being served. (Sections 11.1, 11.3), 423, 429

preemptive priorities Priorities for serving customers that include ejecting the lowest priority customer being served back into the queue in order to serve a higher priority customer that has just entered the queueing system. (Section 11.7), 449

priority classes Categories of customers that are given different priorities for receiving service. (Section 11.7), 448

queue The waiting line in a queueing system. The queue does not include customers who are already being served. (Section 11.1), 420

Key Symbols

λ = Mean arrival rate	(Section 11.1)	L_q = Expected number of customers in the queue	(Section 11.3)
μ = Mean service rate	(Section 11.1)	W = Expected waiting time in the system	(Section 11.3)
s = Number of servers	(Section 11.1)	W_q = Expected waiting time in the queue	(Section 11.3)
L = Expected number of customers in the system		ρ = Utilization factor for the servers	
	(Section 11.3)		(Sections 11.5 and 11.6)

Learning Aids for This Chapter in Your MS Courseware

Chapter 11 Excel Files:

Template for M/M/s Model

Template for M/G/1 Model

Template for M/D/1 Model

Template for Nonpreemptive Priorities Model

Template for Preemptive Priorities Model

Template for M/M/s Economic Analysis of Number of Servers

Interactive Management Science Modules:

Waiting Line Module

Supplement to This Chapter on the CD-ROM:

Additional Queueing Models

Supplement to Chapter 11 Excel Files:

Template for Finite Queue Variation of M/M/s Model

Template for Finite Calling Population Variation of M/M/s Model

Template for M/E_k/1 Model

Solved Problem (See the CD-ROM for the Solution)

11.S1. Managing Waiting Lines at First Bank of Seattle

Sally Gordon has just completed her MBA degree and is proud to have earned a promotion to vice president for Customer Services at the First Bank of Seattle. One of her responsibilities is to manage how tellers provide services to customers, so she is taking a hard look at this area of the bank's operations. Customers needing teller service arrive randomly at a mean rate of 30 per hour. Customers wait in a single line and are served by the next available teller when they reach the front of the line. Each service takes a variable amount of time (assume an exponential distribution), but on average can be completed in three minutes. The tellers earn an average wage of $18 per hour.

a. If two tellers are used, what will be the average waiting time for a customer before reaching a teller? On average, how many customers will be in the bank, including those currently being served?

b. Company policy is to have no more than a 10 percent chance that a customer will need to wait more than five minutes before reaching a teller. How many tellers need to be used in order to meet this standard?

c. Sally feels that a significant cost is incurred by making a customer wait because of potential lost future business. Sally estimates the cost to be $0.50 for each minute a customer spends in the bank, counting both waiting time and service time. Given this cost, how many tellers should Sally employ?

d. First Bank has two types of customers: merchant customers and regular customers. The mean arrival rate for each type of customer is 15 per hour. Both types of customers currently

wait in the same line and are served by the same tellers with the same average service time. However, Sally is considering changing this. The new system she is considering would have two lines—one for merchant customers and one for regular customers. There would be a single teller serving each line. What would be the average waiting time for each type of customer before reaching a teller? On average, how many total customers would be in the bank, including those currently being served? How do these results compare to those from part *a*?

e. Sally feels that if the tellers are specialized into merchant tellers and regular tellers, they would be more efficient and could serve customers in an average of 2.5 minutes instead of 3 minutes. Answer the questions for part *d* again with this new average service time.

Problems

To the left of the following problems (or their parts), we have inserted the symbol E (for Excel) whenever one of the above templates can be helpful. An asterisk on the problem number indicates that at least a partial answer is given in the back of the book.

11.1.   Consider a typical hospital emergency room.

   a. Describe why it is a queueing system.
   b. What is the *queue* in this case? Describe how you would expect the queue discipline to operate.
   c. Would you expect *random arrivals?*
   d. What are *service times* in this context? Would you expect much variability in the service times?

11.2.   Identify the customers and the servers in the queueing system in each of the following situations.

   a. The checkout stand in a grocery store.
   b. A fire station.
   c. The toll booth for a bridge.
   d. A bicycle repair shop.
   e. A shipping dock.
   f. A group of semiautomatic machines assigned to one operator.
   g. The materials-handling equipment in a factory area.
   h. A plumbing shop.
   i. A job shop producing custom orders.
   j. A secretarial word processing pool.

11.3.* For each of the following statements about using the exponential distribution as the probability distribution of interarrival times, label the statement as true or false and then justify your answer by referring to a specific statement in the chapter.

   a. It is the only distribution of interarrival times that fits having random arrivals.
   b. It has the lack-of-memory property because it cannot remember when the next arrival will occur.
   c. It provides an excellent fit for interarrival times for most situations.

11.4.   For each of the following statements about using the exponential distribution as the probability distribution of service times, label the statement as true or false and then justify your answer by referring to a specific statement in the chapter.

   a. It generally provides an excellent approximation of the true service-time distribution.
   b. Its mean and variance are always equal.
   c. It represents a rather extreme case regarding the amount of variability in the service times.

11.5.   For each of the following statements about the queue in a queueing system, label the statement as true or false and then justify your answer by referring to a specific statement in the chapter.

   a. The queue is where customers wait in the queueing system until their service is completed.
   b. Queueing models conventionally assume that the queue can hold only a limited number of customers.
   c. The most common queue discipline is first-come, first-served.

11.6.   Midtown Bank always has two tellers on duty. Customers arrive to receive service from a teller at a mean rate of 40 per hour. A teller requires an average of two minutes to serve a customer. When both tellers are busy, an arriving customer joins a single line to wait for service. Experience has shown that customers wait in line an average of one minute before service begins.

   a. Describe why this is a queueing system.
   b. Determine the basic measures of performance—W_q, W, L_q, and L—for this queueing system. (*Hint:* We don't know the probability distributions of interarrival times and service times for this queueing system, so you will need to use the relationships between these measures of performance to help answer the question.)

11.7.   Mom-and-Pop's Grocery Store has a small adjacent parking lot with three parking spaces reserved for the store's customers. During store hours, when the lot is not full, cars enter the lot and use one of the spaces at a mean rate of two per hour. When the lot is full, arriving cars leave and do not return. For $n = 0, 1, 2, 3$, the probability P_n that exactly n spaces currently are being used is $P_0 = 0.2, P_1 = 0.3, P_2 = 0.3, P_3 = 0.2$.

a. Describe how this parking lot can be interpreted as being a queueing system. In particular, identify the customers and the servers. What is the service being provided? What constitutes a service time? What is the queue capacity? (*Hint:* See Table 11.4.)

b. Determine the basic measures of performance—L, L_q, W, and W_q—for this queueing system. (*Hint:* You can use the given probabilities to determine the average number of parking spaces that are being used.)

c. Use the results from part b to determine the average length of time that a car remains in a parking space.

11.8.* Newell and Jeff are the two barbers in a barber shop they own and operate. They provide two chairs for customers who are waiting to begin a haircut, so the number of customers in the shop varies between 0 and 4. For $n = 0, 1, 2, 3, 4$, the probability P_n that exactly n customers are in the shop is $P_0 = \frac{1}{16}, P_1 = \frac{4}{16}, P_2 = \frac{6}{16}, P_3 = \frac{4}{16}, P_4 = \frac{1}{16}$.

a. Use the formula $L = 0P_0 + 1P_1 + 2P_2 + 3P_3 + 4P_4$ to calculate L. How would you describe the meaning of L to Newell and Jeff?

b. For each of the possible values of the number of customers in the queueing system, specify how many customers are in the queue. For each of the possible numbers in the queue, multiply by its probability, and then add these products to calculate L_q. How would you describe the meaning of L_q to Newell and Jeff?

c. Given that an average of four customers per hour arrive and stay to receive a haircut, determine W and W_q. Describe these two quantities in terms meaningful to Newell and Jeff.

d. Given that Newell and Jeff are equally fast in giving haircuts, what is the average duration of a haircut?

11.9. Explain why the utilization factor ρ for the server in a single-server queueing system must equal $1 - P_0$, where P_0 is the probability of having 0 customers in the system.

11.10. The Friendly Neighbor Grocery Store has a single checkout stand with a full-time cashier. Customers arrive randomly at the stand at a mean rate of 30 per hour. The service-time distribution is exponential, with a mean of 1.5 minutes. This situation has resulted in occasional long lines and complaints from customers. Therefore, because there is no room for a second checkout stand, the manager is considering the alternative of hiring another person to help the cashier by bagging the groceries. This help would reduce the expected time required to process a customer to 1 minute, but the distribution still would be exponential.

The manager would like to have the percentage of time that there are more than two customers at the checkout stand down below 25 percent. She also

would like to have no more than 5 percent of the customers needing to wait at least five minutes before beginning service, or at least seven minutes before finishing service.

a. Use the formulas for the $M/M/1$ model to calculate L, W, W_q, L_q, P_0, P_1, and P_2 for the current mode of operation. What is the probability of having more than two customers at the checkout stand?

E b. Use the Excel template for this model to check your answers in part a. Also, find the probability that the waiting time before beginning service exceeds five minutes, and the probability that the waiting time before finishing service exceeds seven minutes.

c. Repeat part a for the alternative being considered by the manager.

E d. Repeat part b for this alternative.

e. Which approach should the manager use to satisfy her criteria as closely as possible?

11.11.* The 4M Company has a single turret lathe as a key work center on its factory floor. Jobs arrive randomly at this work center at a mean rate of two per day. The processing time to perform each job has an exponential distribution with a mean of $\frac{1}{4}$ day. Because the jobs are bulky, those not being worked on are currently being stored in a room some distance from the machine. However, to save time in fetching the jobs, the production manager is proposing to add enough in-process storage space next to the turret lathe to accommodate three jobs in addition to the one being processed. (Excess jobs will continue to be stored temporarily in the distant room.) Under this proposal, what proportion of the time will this storage space next to the turret lathe be adequate to accommodate all waiting jobs?

a. Use available formulas to calculate your answer.

E b. Use an Excel template to obtain the information needed to answer the question.

11.12. Jerry Jansen, materials handling manager at the Casper-Edison Corporation's new factory, needs to decide whether to purchase a small tractor-trailer train or a heavy-duty forklift truck for transporting heavy goods between certain producing centers in the factory. Calls for the materials-handling unit to move a load would come essentially at random at a mean rate of four per hour. The total time required to move a load has an exponential distribution, where the expected time would be 12 minutes for the tractor-trailer train and 9 minutes for the forklift truck. The total equivalent uniform hourly cost (capital recovery cost plus operating cost) would be $50 for the tractor-trailer train and $150 for the forklift truck. The estimated cost of idle goods (waiting to be moved or in transit) because of increased in-process inventory is $20 per load per hour.

Jerry also has established certain criteria that he would like the materials-handling unit to satisfy in order to keep production flowing on schedule as much as possible. He would like to average no more than half an hour for completing the move of a load after receiving the call requesting the move. He also would like the time for completing the move to be no more than one hour 80 percent of the time. Finally, he would like to have no more than three loads waiting to start their move at least 80 percent of the time.

E   *a.* Obtain the various measures of performance if the tractor-trailer train were to be chosen. Evaluate how well these measures meet the above criteria.

E   *b.* Repeat part *a* if the forklift truck were to be chosen.

c. Compare the two alternatives in terms of their expected total cost per hour (including the cost of idle goods).

d. Which alternative do you think Jerry should choose?

E11.13. Suppose a queueing system fitting the $M/M/1$ model has $W = 120$ minutes and $L = 8$ customers. Use these facts (and the formula for W) to find λ and μ. Then find the various other measures of performance for this queueing system.

11.14.* The Seabuck and Roper Company has a large warehouse in southern California to store its inventory of goods until they are needed by the company's many furniture stores in that area. A single crew with four members is used to unload and/or load each truck that arrives at the loading dock of the warehouse. Management currently is downsizing to cut costs, so a decision needs to be made about the future size of this crew.

Trucks arrive randomly at the loading dock at a mean rate of one per hour. The time required by a crew to unload and/or load a truck has an exponential distribution (regardless of crew size). The mean of this distribution with the four-member crew is 15 minutes. If the size of the crew were to be changed, it is estimated that the mean service rate of the crew (now $\mu = 4$ customers per hour) would be *proportional* to its size.

The cost of providing each member of the crew is $20 per hour. The cost that is attributable to having a truck not in use (i.e., a truck standing at the loading dock) is estimated to be $30 per hour.

a. Identify the customers and servers for this queueing system. How many servers does it currently have?

E   *b.* Find the various measures of performance of this queueing system with four members on the crew. (Set $t = 1$ hour in the Excel template for the waiting-time probabilities.)

E   *c.* Repeat *b* with three members.

E   *d.* Repeat part *b* with two members.

e. Should a one-member crew also be considered? Explain.

f. Given the previous results, which crew size do you think management should choose?

g. Use the cost figures to determine which crew size would minimize the expected total cost per hour.

11.15. Jake's Machine Shop contains a grinder for sharpening the machine cutting tools. A decision must now be made on the speed at which to set the grinder.

The grinding time required by a machine operator to sharpen the cutting tool has an exponential distribution, where the mean $1/\mu$ can be set at 1 minute, 1.5 minutes, or 2 minutes, depending upon the speed of the grinder. The running and maintenance costs go up rapidly with the speed of the grinder, so the estimated cost per

minute is $1.60 for providing a mean of 1 minute, $0.90 for a mean of 1.5 minutes, and $0.40 for a mean of 2 minutes.

The machine operators arrive randomly to sharpen their tools at a mean rate of one every two minutes. The estimated cost of an operator being away from his or her machine to the grinder is $0.80 per minute.

E   *a.* Obtain the various measures of performance for this queueing system for each of the three alternative speeds for the grinder. (Set $t = 5$ minutes in the Excel template for the waiting-time probabilities.)

b. Use the cost figures to determine which grinder speed minimizes the expected total cost per minute.

E11.16. The Centerville International Airport has two runways, one used exclusively for takeoffs and the other exclusively for landings. Airplanes arrive randomly in the Centerville air space to request landing instructions at a mean rate of 10 per hour. The time required for an airplane to land after receiving clearance to land has an exponential distribution with a mean of three minutes, and this process must be completed before giving clearance to land to another airplane. Airplanes awaiting clearance must circle the airport.

The Federal Aviation Administration has a number of criteria regarding the safe level of congestion of airplanes waiting to land. These criteria depend on a number of factors regarding the airport involved, such as the number of runways available for landing. For Centerville, the criteria are (1) the average number of airplanes waiting to receive clearance to land should not exceed one, (2) 95 percent of the time, the actual number of airplanes waiting to receive clearance to land should not exceed four, (3) for 99 percent of the airplanes, the amount of time spent circling the airport before receiving clearance to land should not exceed 30 minutes (since exceeding this amount of time often would require rerouting the plane to another airport for an emergency landing before its fuel runs out).

a. Evaluate how well these criteria are currently being satisfied.

b. A major airline is considering adding this airport as one of its hubs. This would increase the mean arrival rate to 15 airplanes per hour. Evaluate how well the above criteria would be satisfied if this happens.

c. To attract additional business (including the major airline mentioned in part *b*), airport management is considering adding a second runway for landings. It is estimated that this eventually would increase the mean arrival rate to 25 airplanes per hour. Evaluate how well the above criteria would be satisfied if this happens.

11.17.* Consider the $M/G/1$ model. What is the effect on L_q and W_q if $1/\lambda$, $1/\mu$, and σ are all reduced by half? Explain.

11.18. Consider the $M/G/1$ model with $\lambda = 0.2$ and $\mu = 0.25$.

E   *a.* Use the Excel template for this model to generate a data table that gives the main measures of performance—L, L_q, W, W_q—for each of the following values of σ: 4, 3, 2, 1, 0.

b. What is the ratio of L_q with $\sigma = 4$ to L_q with $\sigma = 0$? What does this say about the importance of reducing the variability of the service times?

c. Calculate the reduction in L_q when σ is reduced from 4 to 3, from 3 to 2, from 2 to 1, and from 1 to 0. Which is the largest reduction? Which is the smallest?

E   d. Use trial and error with the template to see approximately how much μ would need to be increased with $\sigma = 4$ to achieve the same L_q as with $\mu = 0.25$ and $\sigma = 0$.

E   e. Use the template to generate a data table that gives the value of L_q with $\sigma = 4$ when μ increases in increments of 0.01 from 0.25 to 0.35.

E   f. Use the template to generate a two-way data table that gives the value of L_q for the various combinations of values of μ and σ where $\mu = 0.22, 0.24, 0.26, 0.28, 0.3$ and $\sigma = 4, 3, 2, 1, 0$.

11.19. Consider the following statements about the $M/G/1$ queueing model, where σ^2 is the variance of service times. Label each statement as true or false, and then justify your answer.

a. Increasing σ^2 (with fixed λ and μ) will increase L_q and L, but will not change W_q and W.

b. When the choice is between a tortoise (small μ and σ^2) and a hare (large μ and σ^2) to be the server, the tortoise always wins by providing a smaller L_q.

c. With λ and μ fixed, the value of L_q with an exponential service-time distribution is twice as large as with constant service times.

11.20. Marsha operates an espresso stand. Customers arrive randomly at a mean rate of 30 per hour. The time needed by Marsha to serve a customer has an exponential distribution with a mean of 75 seconds.

E   a. Use the Excel template for the $M/G/1$ model to find L, L_q, W, and W_q.

E   b. Suppose Marsha is replaced by an espresso vending machine that requires exactly 75 seconds to operate for each customer. Find L, L_q, W, and W_q.

c. What is the ratio of L_q in part b to L_q in part a?

E   d. Use trial and error with the template to see approximately how much Marsha would need to reduce her expected service time to achieve the same L_q as with the espresso vending machine.

E   e. Use the template to generate a data table that gives the value of L_q when Marsha is serving with the following values (in seconds) for her expected service time: 75, 70, 65, 64, 63, 62, 61, 60.

11.21.* The production of tractors at the Jim Buck Company involves producing several subassemblies and then using an assembly line to assemble the subassemblies and other parts into finished tractors. Approximately three tractors per day are produced in this way. An in-process inspection station is used to inspect the subassemblies before they enter the assembly line. At present, there are two inspectors at the station, and they work together to inspect each subassembly. The

inspection time has an exponential distribution, with a mean of 15 minutes. The cost of providing this inspection system is $40 per hour.

A proposal has been made to streamline the inspection procedure so that it can be handled by only one inspector. This inspector would begin by visually inspecting the exterior of the subassembly, and she would then use new efficient equipment to complete the inspection. Although this process with just one inspector would slightly increase the mean of the distribution of inspection times from 15 minutes to 16 minutes, it also would reduce the variance of this distribution to only 40 percent of its current value. The cost would be $30 per hour.

The subassemblies arrive randomly at the inspection station at a mean rate of three per hour. The cost of having the subassemblies wait at the inspection station (thereby increasing in-process inventory and possibly disrupting subsequent production) is estimated to be $20 per hour for each subassembly.

Management now needs to make a decision about whether to continue the status quo or adopt the proposal.

E   a. Find the main measures of performance—L, L_q, W, W_q—for the current queueing system.

E   b. Repeat part a for the proposed queueing system.

c. What conclusions can you draw about what management should do from the results in parts a and b?

d. Determine and compare the expected total cost per hour for the status quo and the proposal.

E11.22. The Security & Trust Bank employs four tellers to serve its customers. Customers arrive randomly at a mean rate of two per minute. However, business is growing and management projects that the mean arrival rate will be three per minute a year from now. The transaction time between the teller and customer has an exponential distribution with a mean of one minute.

Management has established the following guidelines for a satisfactory level of service to customers. The average number of customers waiting in line to begin service should not exceed one. At least 95 percent of the time, the number of customers waiting in line should not exceed five. For at least 95 percent of the customers, the time spent in line waiting to begin service should not exceed five minutes.

a. Use the $M/M/s$ model to determine how well these guidelines are currently being satisfied.

b. Evaluate how well the guidelines will be satisfied a year from now if no change is made in the number of tellers.

c. Determine how many tellers will be needed a year from now to completely satisfy these guidelines.

E11.23. Consider the $M/M/s$ model. For each of the following two cases, generate a data table that gives the values of L, L_q, W, W_q, and $P\{W > 5\}$ for the following mean arrival rates: 0.5, 0.9, and 0.99 customers per minute.

a. Suppose there is one server and the expected service time is one minute. Compare L for the cases where the mean arrival rate is 0.5, 0.9, and 0.99 customers per minute, respectively. Do the same for L_q, W, W_q, and $P\{W > 5\}$. What conclusions do you draw about the impact of increasing the utilization factor ρ from small values (e.g., $\rho = 0.5$) to fairly large values (e.g., $\rho = 0.9$) and then to even larger values very close to 1 (e.g., $\rho = 0.99$)?

b. Now suppose there are two servers and the expected service time is two minutes. Follow the instructions for part *a*.

E11.24. Consider the *M/M/s* model with a mean arrival rate of 10 customers per hour and an expected service time of five minutes. Use the Excel template for this model to print out the various measures of performance (with $t = 10$ and $t = 0$, respectively, for the two waiting-time probabilities) when the number of servers is one, two, three, four, and five. Then, for each of the following possible criteria for a satisfactory level of service (where the unit of time is one minute), use the printed results to determine how many servers are needed to satisfy this criterion.

a. $L_q \leq 0.25$

b. $L \leq 0.9$

c. $W_q \leq 0.1$

d. $W \leq 6$

e. $P\{W_q > 0\} \leq 0.01$

f. $P\{W > 10\} \leq 0.2$

g. $\sum_{n=0}^{s} P_n \geq 0.95$

11.25. Greg is making plans to open a new fast-food restaurant soon. He is estimating that customers will arrive randomly at a mean rate of 150 per hour during the busiest times of the day. He is planning to have three employees directly serving the customers. He now needs to make a decision about how to organize these employees.

Option 1 is to have three cash registers with one employee at each to take the orders and get the food and drinks. In this case, it is estimated that the average time to serve each customer would be one minute, and the distribution of service times is assumed to be exponential.

Option 2 is to have one cash register with the three employees working together to serve each customer. One would take the order, a second would get the food, and the third would get the drinks. Greg estimates that this would reduce the average time to serve each customer down to 20 seconds, with the same assumption of exponential service times.

Greg wants to choose the option that would provide the best service to his customers. However, since Option 1 has three cash registers, both options would serve the customers at a mean rate of three per minute when everybody is busy serving customers, so it is not clear which option is better.

E   a. Use the main measures of performance—L, L_q, W, W_q—to compare the two options.

b. Explain why these comparisons make sense intuitively.

c. Which measure do you think would be most important to Greg's customers? Why? Which option is better with respect to this measure?

E*11.26. In the Blue Chip Life Insurance Company, the deposit and withdrawal functions associated with a certain investment product are separated between two clerks. Deposit slips arrive randomly at Clerk Clara's desk at a mean rate of 16 per hour. Withdrawal slips arrive randomly at Clerk Clarence's desk at a mean rate of 14 per hour. The time required to process either transaction has an exponential distribution with a mean of three minutes. In order to reduce the expected waiting time in the system for both deposit slips and withdrawal slips, the Actuarial Department has made the following recommendations: (1) Train each clerk to handle both deposits and withdrawals; (2) put both deposit and withdrawal slips into a single queue that is accessed by both clerks.

a. Determine the expected waiting time in the system under current procedures for each type of slip. Then combine these results (multiply W for deposit slips by $\frac{16}{30}$, multiply W for withdrawal slips by $\frac{14}{30}$, and add these two products) to calculate the expected waiting time in the system for a random arrival of either type of slip.

b. If the recommendations are adopted, determine the expected waiting time in the system for arriving slips.

c. Now suppose that adopting the recommendations would result in a slight increase in the expected processing time. Use the Excel template for this model to determine by trial and error the expected processing time (within 0.01 minute) that would cause the expected waiting time in the system for a random arrival to be essentially the same under current procedures and under the recommendations.

E11.27. People's Software Company has just set up a call center to provide technical assistance on its new software package. Two technical representatives are taking the calls, where the time required by either representative to answer a customer's questions has an exponential distribution with a mean of eight minutes. Calls are arriving randomly at a mean rate of 10 per hour.

By next year, the mean arrival rate of calls is expected to decline to five per hour, so the plan is to reduce the number of technical representatives to one then. Determine L, L_q, W, and W_q for both the current queueing system and next year's system. For each of these four measures of performance, which system yields the smaller value?

11.28. The Southern Railroad Company has been subcontracting for the painting of its railroad cars as needed. However, management has decided that the company can save money by doing this work itself. A decision now needs to be made to choose between two alternative ways of doing this.

Alternative 1 is to provide two paint shops, where painting is done by hand (one car at a time in each shop), for a total hourly cost of $70. The painting time for a car would be six hours. Alternative 2 is to provide one spray shop involving an hourly cost of $100. In this case, the painting time for a car (again done one at a time) would be three hours. For both alternatives, the cars arrive randomly with a mean rate of 1 every 5 hours. The cost of idle time per car is $100 per hour.

    a. Use Figure 11.10 to estimate L, L_q, W, and W_q for Alternative 1.

E   *b.* Find these same measures of performance for Alternative 2.

    c. Determine and compare the expected total cost per hour for these alternatives.

11.29.* Southeast Airlines is a small commuter airline serving primarily the state of Florida. Its ticket counter at the Orlando airport is staffed by a single ticket agent. There are two separate lines—one for first-class passengers and one for coach-class passengers. When the ticket agent is ready for another customer, the next first-class passenger is served if there are any in line. If not, the next coach-class passenger is served. Service times have an exponential distribution with a mean of three minutes for both types of customers. During the 12 hours per day that the ticket counter is open, passengers arrive randomly at a mean rate of 2 per hour for first-class passengers and 10 per hour for coach-class passengers.

    a. What kind of queueing model fits this queueing system?

E   *b.* Find the main measures of performance—L, L_q, W, and W_q—for both first-class passengers and coach-class passengers.

    c. What is the expected waiting time before service begins for first-class customers as a fraction of this waiting time for coach-class customers?

    d. Determine the average number of hours per day that the ticket agent is busy.

11.30. The County Hospital emergency room always has one doctor on duty. In the past, having just a single doctor there has been sufficient. However, because of a growing tendency for emergency cases to use these facilities rather than go to a private doctor, the number of emergency room visits has been steadily increasing. By next year, it is estimated that patients will arrive randomly at a mean rate of two per hour during peak usage hours (the early evening). Therefore, a proposal has been made to assign a second doctor to the emergency room next year during those hours. Hospital management (an HMO) is resisting this proposal, but has asked a management scientist (you) to analyze whether a single doctor will continue to be sufficient next year.

    The patients are not treated on a first-come, first-served basis. Rather, the admitting nurse divides the patients into three categories: (1) *critical* cases, where prompt treatment is vital for survival; (2) *serious* cases, where early treatment is important to prevent further deterioration; and (3) *stable* cases, where treatment can be delayed without adverse medical consequences. Patients are then treated in this order of priority, where those in the same category are normally taken on a first-come, first-served basis. A doctor will interrupt treatment of a patient if a new case in a higher priority category arrives. Approximately 10 percent of the

patients fall into the first category, 30 percent into the second, and 60 percent into the third. Because the more serious cases will be sent to the hospital for further care after receiving emergency treatment, the average treatment time by a doctor in the emergency room actually does not differ greatly among these categories. For all of them, the treatment time can be approximated by an exponential distribution with a mean of 20 minutes.

    Hospital management has established the following guidelines. The average waiting time in the emergency room before treatment begins should not exceed 2 minutes for critical cases, 15 minutes for serious cases, and 2 hours for stable cases.

    a. What kind of queueing model fits this queueing system?

E   *b.* Use this model to determine if the management guidelines would be satisfied next year by continuing to have just a single doctor on duty.

    c. Use the formula for W_q for the $M/M/1$ model to determine if these guidelines would be satisfied if treatment were given on a first-come, first-served basis instead.

E   *d.* The mean arrival rate of two patients per hour during peak usage hours next year is only an estimate. Perform sensitivity analysis by repeating part *b* if this mean arrival rate were to turn out to be 2.25 patients per hour instead.

E11.31. The Becker Company factory has been experiencing long delays in jobs going through the turret lathe department because of inadequate capacity. The head of this department contends that five machines are required, as opposed to the three machines he now has. However, because of pressure from management to hold down capital expenditures, only one additional machine will be authorized unless there is solid evidence that a second one is necessary.

    This shop does three kinds of jobs, namely, government jobs, commercial jobs, and standard products. Whenever a turret lathe operator finishes a job, he starts a government job if one is waiting; if not, he starts a commercial job if any are waiting; if not, he starts on a standard product if any are waiting. Jobs of the same type are taken on a first-come, first-served basis.

    Although much overtime work is required currently, management wants the turret lathe department to operate on an eight-hour, five-day-per-week basis. The probability distribution of the time required by a turret lathe operator for a job appears to be approximately exponential, with a mean of 10 hours. Jobs come into the shop randomly at a mean rate of six per week for government jobs, four per week for commercial jobs, and two per week for standard products. (These figures are expected to remain the same for the indefinite future.)

    Management feels that the average waiting time before work begins in the turret lathe department should not exceed 0.25 (working) days for government jobs, 0.5 days for commercial jobs, and 2 days for standard products.

a. Determine how many additional turret lathes need to be obtained to satisfy these management guidelines.

b. It is worth about $750, $450, and $150 to avoid a delay of one additional (working) day in a government, commercial, and standard job, respectively. The incremental capitalized cost of providing each turret lathe (including the operator and so on) is estimated to be $250 per working day. Determine the number of additional turret lathes that should be obtained to minimize the expected total cost.

E11.32. When describing economic analysis of the number of servers to provide in a queueing system, Section 11.9 introduces a cost model where the objective is to minimize $TC = C_s s + C_w L$. The purpose of this problem is to enable you to explore the effect that the relative sizes of C_s and C_w have on the optimal number of servers.

Suppose that the queueing system under consideration fits the *M/M/s* model with $\lambda = 8$ customers per hour and $\mu = 10$ customers per hour. Use the Excel template for economic analysis with the *M/M/s* model to find the optimal number of servers for each of the following cases.

a. $C_s = \$100$ and $C_w = \$10$.

b. $C_s = \$100$ and $C_w = \$100$.

c. $C_s = \$10$ and $C_w = \$100$.

d. For each of these three cases, generate a data table that compares the expected hourly costs with various alternative numbers of servers.

E11.33.*Jim McDonald, manager of the fast-food hamburger restaurant McBurger, realizes that providing fast service is a key to the success of the restaurant. Customers who have to wait very long are likely to go to one of the other fast-food restaurants in town next time. He estimates that each minute a customer has to wait in line before completing service costs him an average of 30¢ in lost future business. Therefore, he wants to be sure that enough cash registers always are open to keep waiting to a minimum. Each cash register is operated by a part-time employee who obtains the food ordered by each customer and collects the payment. The total cost for each such employee is $9 per hour.

During lunchtime, customers arrive randomly at a mean rate of 66 per hour. The time needed to serve a customer is estimated to have an exponential distribution with a mean of two minutes.

Determine how many cash registers Jim should have open during lunchtime to minimize his expected total cost per hour.

E11.34. The Garrett-Tompkins Company provides three copy machines in its copying room for the use of its employees. However, due to recent complaints about considerable time being wasted waiting for a copier to become free, management is considering adding one or more additional copy machines.

During the 2,000 working hours per year, employees arrive randomly at the copying room at a mean rate of 30 per hour. The time each employee needs with a copy machine is believed to have an exponential distribution with a mean of five minutes. The lost productivity due to an employee spending time in the copying room is estimated to cost the company an average of $25 per hour. Each copy machine is leased for $3,000 per year.

Determine how many copy machines the company should have to minimize its expected total cost per hour.

Case 11-1

Queueing Quandary

A SEQUEL TO CASE 10.1

Never dull. That is how you would describe your job at the centralized records and benefits administration center for Cutting Edge, a large company manufacturing computers and computer peripherals. Since opening the facility six months ago, you and Mark Lawrence, the director of Human Resources, have endured one long roller-coaster ride. Receiving the go-ahead from corporate headquarters to establish the centralized records and benefits administration center was definitely an up. Getting caught in the crossfire of angry customers (all employees of Cutting Edge) because of demand overload for the records and benefits call center was definitely a down. Accurately forecasting the demand for the call center provided another up.

And today you are faced with another down. Mark approaches your desk with a not altogether attractive frown on his face.

He begins complaining immediately, "I just don't understand. The forecasting job you did for us two months ago really allowed us to understand the weekly demand for the center, but we still have not been able to get a grasp on the staffing problem. We used both historical data and your forecasts to calculate the average weekly demand for the call center. We transformed this average weekly demand into average hourly demand by dividing the weekly demand by the number of hours in the workweek. We then staffed the center to meet this average hourly demand by taking into account the average number of calls a representative is able to handle per hour.

But something is horribly wrong. Operational data records show that over 35 percent of the customers wait over four minutes for a representative to answer the call! Customers are still sending me numerous complaints, and executives from corporate headquarters are still breathing down my neck! I need help!"

You calm Mark down and explain to him that you think you know the problem: The number of calls received in a certain hour can be much greater (or much less) than the average because of the stochastic nature of the demand. In addition, the number of calls a representative is able to handle per hour can be much less (or much greater) than the average depending upon the types of calls received.

You then tell him to have no fear; you have the problem under control. You have been reading about the successful application of queueing theory to the operation of call centers, and you decide that the queueing models you learned about in school will help you determine the appropriate staffing level.

a. You ask Mark to describe the demand and service rate. He tells you that calls are randomly received by the call center and that the center receives an average of 70 calls per hour. The computer system installed to answer and hold the calls is so advanced that its capacity far exceeds the demand. Because the nature of a call is random, the time required to process a call is random, where the time frequently is small but occasionally can be much longer. On average, however, representatives can handle six calls per hour. Which queueing model seems appropriate for this situation? Given that slightly more than 35 percent of customers wait over four minutes before a representative answers the call, use this model to estimate how many representatives Mark currently employs.

b. Mark tells you that he will not be satisfied unless 95 percent of the customers wait only one minute or less for a representative to answer the call. Given this customer service level and the average arrival rates and service rates from part a, how many representatives should Mark employ?

c. Each representative receives an annual salary of $30,000, and Mark tells you that he simply does not have the resources available to hire the number of representatives required to achieve the customer service level desired in part b. He asks you to perform sensitivity analysis. How many representatives would he need to employ to ensure that 80 percent of customers wait one minute or less? How many would he need to employ to ensure that 95 percent of customers wait 90 seconds or less? How would you recommend Mark choose a customer service level? Would the decision criteria be different if Mark's call center were to serve external customers (not connected to the company) instead of internal customers (employees)?

d. Mark tells you that he is not happy with the number of representatives required to achieve a high customer service level. He therefore wants to explore alternatives to simply hiring additional representatives. The alternative he considers is instituting a training program that will teach representatives to more efficiently use computer tools to answer calls. He believes that this alternative will increase the average number of calls a representative is able to handle per hour from six calls to eight calls. The training program will cost $2,500 per employee per year since employees' knowledge will have to be updated yearly. How many representatives will Mark have to employ and train to achieve the customer service level desired in part b? Do you prefer this alternative to simply hiring additional representatives? Why or why not?

e. Mark realizes that queueing theory helps him only so much in determining the number of representatives needed. He realizes that the queueing models will not provide accurate answers if the inputs used in the models are inaccurate. What inputs do you think need reevaluation? How would you go about estimating these inputs?

Case 11-2
Reducing In-Process Inventory

Jim Wells, vice president for manufacturing of the Northern Airplane Company, is exasperated. His walk through the company's most important plant this morning has left him in a foul mood. However, he now can vent his temper at Jerry Carstairs, the plant's production manager, who has just been summoned to Jim's office.

"Jerry, I just got back from walking through the plant, and I am very upset."

"What is the problem, Jim?"

"Well, you know how much I have been emphasizing the need to cut down on our in-process inventory."

"Yes, we've been working hard on that," responds Jerry.

"Well, not hard enough!" Jim raises his voice even higher. "Do you know what I found by the presses?"

"No."

"Five metal sheets still waiting to be formed into wing sections. And then, right next door at the inspection station, 13 wing sections! The inspector was inspecting one of them, but the other 12 were just sitting there. You know we have a couple hundred thousand dollars tied up in each of those wing sections. So between the presses and the inspection station, we have a few million bucks' worth of terribly expensive metal just sitting there. We can't have that!"

The chagrined Jerry Carstairs tries to respond. "Yes, Jim, I am well aware that that inspection station is a bottleneck. It usually isn't nearly as bad as you found it this morning, but it is a bottleneck. Much less so for the presses. You really caught us on a bad morning."

"I sure hope so," retorts Jim, "but you need to prevent anything nearly this bad happening even occasionally. What do you propose to do about it?"

Jerry now brightens noticeably in his response. "Well, actually, I've already been working on this problem. I have a couple proposals on the table and I have asked a management scientist on my staff to analyze these proposals and report back with recommendations."

"Great," responds Jim, "glad to see you are on top of the problem. Give this your highest priority and report back to me as soon as possible."

"Will do," promises Jerry.

Here is the problem that Jerry and his management scientist are addressing. Each of 10 identical presses is being used to form wing sections out of large sheets of specially processed metal. The sheets arrive randomly at a mean rate of seven per hour. The time required by a press to form a wing section out of a sheet has an exponential distribution with a mean of one hour. When finished, the wing sections arrive randomly at an inspection station at the same mean rate as the metal sheets arrived at the presses (seven per hour). A single inspector has the full-time job of inspecting these wing sections to make sure they meet specifications. Each inspection takes her 7½ minutes, so she can inspect eight wing sections per hour. This inspection rate has resulted in a substantial average amount of in-process inventory at the inspection station (i.e., the average number of wing sheets waiting to complete inspection is fairly large), in addition to that already found at the group of machines.

The cost of this in-process inventory is estimated to be $8 per hour for each metal sheet at the presses or each wing section at the inspection station. Therefore, Jerry Carstairs has made two alternative proposals to reduce the average level of in-process inventory.

Proposal 1 is to use slightly less power for the presses (which would increase their average time to form a wing section to 1.2 hours), so that the inspector can keep up with their output better. This also would reduce the cost for each machine (operating cost plus capital recovery cost) from $7.00 to $6.50 per hour. (By contrast, increasing to maximum power would increase this cost to $7.50 per hour while decreasing the average time to form a wing section to 0.8 hours.)

Proposal 2 is to substitute a certain younger inspector for this task. He is somewhat faster (albeit with some variability in his inspection times because of less experience), so he should keep up better. (His inspection time would have a probability distribution with a mean of 7.2 minutes and a standard deviation of 5 minutes.)

This inspector is in a job classification that calls for a total compensation (including benefits) of $19 per hour, whereas the current inspector is in a lower job classification where the compensation is $17 per hour. (The inspection times for each of these inspectors are typical of those in the same job classifications.)

You are the management scientist on Jerry Carstair's staff who has been asked to analyze this problem. He wants you to "use the latest management science techniques to see how much each proposal would cut down on in-process inventory and then make your recommendations."

a. To provide a basis of comparison, begin by evaluating the status quo. Determine the expected amount of in-process inventory at the presses and at the inspection station. Then calculate the expected total cost per hour of the in-process inventory, the presses, and the inspector.

b. What would be the effect of proposal 1? Why? Make specific comparisons to the results from part a. Explain this outcome to Jerry Carstairs.

c. Determine the effect of proposal 2. Make specific comparisons to the results from part a. Explain this outcome to Jerry Carstairs.

d. Make your recommendations for reducing the average level of in-process inventory at the inspection station and at the group of machines. Be specific in your recommendations, and support them with quantitative analysis like that done in part a. Make specific comparisons to the results from part a, and cite the improvements that your recommendations would yield.

Chapter **Twelve**

Computer Simulation: Basic Concepts

Learning objectives

After completing this chapter, you should be able to

1. Describe the basic concept of computer simulation.
2. Describe the role computer simulation plays in many management science studies.
3. Use random numbers to generate random events that have a simple discrete distribution.
4. Use Excel to perform basic computer simulations on a spreadsheet.
5. Use the Queueing Simulator to perform computer simulations of basic queueing systems and interpret the results.
6. Describe and use the building blocks of a simulation model for a stochastic system.
7. Outline the steps of a major computer simulation study.

In this chapter, we now are ready to focus on the last of the key techniques of management science. *Computer simulation* ranks very high among the most widely used of these techniques. Furthermore, because it is such a flexible, powerful, and intuitive tool, it is continuing to rapidly grow in popularity. Many managers consider it one of their most valuable decision-making aids.

> By imitating the operation of a proposed system, a computer can simulate years of operation in a matter of seconds and then record the performance.

This technique involves using a computer to *imitate* (simulate) the operation of an entire process or system. For example, computer simulation is frequently used to perform risk analysis on financial processes by repeatedly imitating the evolution of the transactions involved to generate a profile of the possible outcomes. Computer simulation also is widely used to analyze systems that will continue operating indefinitely. For such systems, the computer randomly generates and records the occurrences of the various events that drive the system just as if it were physically operating. Because of its speed, the computer can simulate even years of operation in a matter of seconds. Recording the performance of the simulated operation of the system for a number of alternative designs or operating procedures then enables evaluating and comparing these alternatives before choosing one. For many processes and systems, all this now can be done with spreadsheet software.

The range of applications of computer simulation has been quite remarkable. The case study in this chapter will illustrate how it is used for the design and operation of queueing systems. A variety of applications have involved the design and operation of manufacturing systems, as well as the design and operation of distribution systems. Some more specific areas of application include managing inventory systems and estimating the probability of completing a project by the deadline. Financial risk analysis is a particularly active area of application. Health care applications also abound. The list goes on and on.

The first section of this chapter describes and illustrates the essence of computer simulation. The case study for this chapter (a revisit of Herr Cutter's barber shop from the preceding chapter) is discussed and analyzed in Sections 12.2 and 12.3. The following section then outlines the overall procedure for applying computer simulation. Chapter 13 will expand further on the application of computer simulation by describing how to apply Crystal Ball, a prominent Excel add-in for efficiently performing fairly complicated computer simulations on spreadsheets.

12.1 THE ESSENCE OF COMPUTER SIMULATION

The technique of *simulation* has long been an important tool of the designer. For example, simulating airplane flight in a wind tunnel is standard practice when a new airplane is designed. Theoretically, the laws of physics could be used to obtain the same information about how the performance of the airplane changes as design parameters are altered, but, as a practical matter, the analysis would be too complicated to do it all. Another alternative would be to build real airplanes with alternative designs and test them in actual flight to choose the final design, but this would be far too expensive (as well as unsafe). Therefore, after some preliminary theoretical analysis is performed to develop a rough design, simulating flight in a wind tunnel is a vital tool for experimenting with specific designs. This simulation amounts to imitating the performance of a real airplane in a controlled environment in order to estimate what its actual performance will be. After a detailed design is developed in this way, a prototype model can be built and tested in actual flight to fine-tune the final design.

The Role of Computer Simulation

Computer simulation plays essentially this same role in many management science studies. However, rather than designing an airplane, the management science team is concerned with developing a design or operating procedure for some system. In many cases, the system is a *stochastic system,* as defined below.

> A **stochastic system** is a system that evolves over time according to one or more probability distributions. For example, the queueing systems described in the preceding chapter are stochastic systems because both the interarrival times and service times occur according to probability distributions.

Computer simulation uses probability distributions to randomly generate the various events that occur in a system.

Computer simulation imitates the operation of such a system by using the corresponding probability distributions to *randomly generate* the various events that occur in the system (e.g., the arrivals and service completions in a queueing system). However, rather than literally operating a physical system, the computer is just recording the occurrences of the *simulated* events and the resulting performance of this simulated system.

When computer simulation is used as part of a management science study, commonly it is preceded and followed by the same steps described earlier for the design of an airplane. In particular, some preliminary analysis is done first (perhaps with approximate mathematical models) to develop a rough design of the system (including its operating procedures). Then computer simulation is used to experiment with specific designs to estimate how well each will perform. After a detailed design is developed and selected in this way, the system probably is tested in actual use to fine-tune the final design.

When dealing with relatively complex systems, computer simulation tends to be a relatively expensive procedure. To get started, a detailed model must be formulated to describe the operation of the system of interest and how it is to be simulated. Then considerable time often is required to develop and debug the computer programs needed to run the simulation. Next, many long computer runs may be needed to obtain good estimates of how well all the alternative designs of the system would perform. Finally, all these data should be carefully analyzed before drawing any final conclusions. This entire process typically takes a lot of time and effort. Therefore, computer simulation should not be used when a less-expensive procedure is available that can provide the same information.

Computer simulation typically is used when the stochastic system involved is too complex to be analyzed satisfactorily by the kinds of mathematical models (e.g., queueing models) described in the preceding chapters. One of the main strengths of a mathematical model is that

Computer simulation can predict the performance of proposed systems that are too complex to be analyzed by other mathematical models.

it abstracts the essence of the problem and reveals its underlying structure, thereby providing insight into the cause-and-effect relationships within the system. Therefore, if the modeler is able to construct a mathematical model that is both a reasonable approximation of the problem and amenable to solution, this approach usually is superior to computer simulation. However, many problems are too complex to permit this approach. Thus, computer simulation often provides the only practical approach to a problem.

Now let us look at a few examples to illustrate the basic ideas of computer simulation. These examples have been kept considerably simpler than the usual application of this technique in order to highlight the main ideas more readily. This also will enable us to obtain analytical solutions for the performance of the systems involved to compare with the estimates of the performance provided by computer simulation.

Example 1: A Coin-Flipping Game

You are the lucky winner of a sweepstakes contest. Your prize is an all-expense-paid vacation at a major hotel in Las Vegas, including some chips for gambling in the hotel casino.

Upon entering the casino, you find that, in addition to the usual games (blackjack, roulette, etc.), they are offering an interesting new game with the following rules.

Rules of the Game

1. Each play of the game involves repeatedly flipping an unbiased coin until the *difference* between the number of heads tossed and the number of tails is three.
2. If you decide to play the game, you are required to pay $1 for each flip of the coin. You are not allowed to quit during a play of the game.
3. You receive $8 at the end of each play of the game.

Thus, you win money if the number of flips required is fewer than eight, but you lose money if more than eight flips are required. Here are some examples (where H denotes a head and T a tail).

HHH	3 flips	You win $5
THTTT	5 flips	You win $3
THHTHTHTTTT	11 flips	You lose $3

How would you decide whether to play this game?

Many people would base this decision on *simulation,* although they probably would not call it by that name. In this case, simulation amounts to nothing more than playing the game alone many times until it becomes clear whether it is worthwhile to play for money. Half an hour spent in repeatedly flipping a coin and recording the earnings or losses that would have resulted might be sufficient. This is a true simulation because you are *imitating* the actual play of the game without actually winning or losing any money.

Since the topic of this chapter is *computer* simulation, let us see now how a computer can be used to perform this same *simulated experiment.* Although a computer cannot flip coins, it can *simulate* doing so. It accomplishes this by generating a sequence of *random numbers,* as defined below.

A number is a **random number** between 0 and 1 if it has been generated in such a way that *every* possible number within this interval has an equal chance of occurring. For example, if numbers with four decimal places are being used, every one of the 10,000 numbers between 0.0000 and 0.9999 has an equal chance of occurring. Thus, a random number between 0 and 1 is a *random observation* from a *uniform* distribution between 0 and 1. (Hereafter, we will delete the phrase *between 0 and 1* when referring to these random numbers.)

Random numbers play a key role in performing computer simulations, so Excel uses the RAND() function to generate them.

An easy way to generate random numbers is to use the RAND() function in Excel. For example, the lower left-hand corner of Figure 12.1 indicates that = RAND() has been entered into cell C13 and then copied into the range C14:C62. (The parentheses need to be included with this function, but nothing is inserted between them.) This causes Excel to generate the random numbers shown in cells C13:C62 of the spreadsheet. (Rows 27–56 have been hidden to save space in the figure.)

FIGURE 12.1

A spreadsheet model for a computer simulation of the coin-flipping game (Example 1).

	A	B	C	D	E	F	G
1		**Coin-Flipping Game**					
2							
3			Required Difference	3			
4			Cash at End of Game	$8			
5							
6				**Summary of Game**			
7			Number of Flips	11			
8			Winnings	–$3			
9							
10							
11			Random		Total	Total	
12		Flip	Number	Result	Heads	Tails	Stop?
13		1	0.3039	Heads	1	0	
14		2	0.7914	Tails	1	1	
15		3	0.8543	Tails	1	2	
16		4	0.6902	Tails	1	3	
17		5	0.3004	Heads	2	3	
18		6	0.0383	Heads	3	3	
19		7	0.3883	Heads	4	3	
20		8	0.6052	Tails	4	4	
21		9	0.2231	Heads	5	4	
22		10	0.4250	Heads	6	4	
23		11	0.3729	Heads	7	4	Stop
24		12	0.7983	Tails	7	5	NA
25		13	0.2340	Heads	8	5	NA
26		14	0.0082	Heads	9	5	NA
57		45	0.7539	Tails	26	19	NA
58		46	0.2989	Heads	27	19	NA
59		47	0.6427	Tails	27	20	NA
60		48	0.2824	Heads	28	20	NA
61		49	0.2124	Heads	29	20	NA
62		50	0.6420	Tails	29	21	NA

Range Name	Cells
CashAtEndOfGame	D4
Flip	B13:B62
NumberOfFlips	D7
RandomNumber	C13:C62
RequiredDifference	D3
Result	D13:D62
Stop?	G13:G62
TotalHeads	E13:E62
TotalTails	F13:F62
Winnings	D8

	C	D
6		**Summary of Game**
7	Number of Flips	=COUNTBLANK(Stop?)+1
8	Winnings	=CashAtEndOfGame–NumberOfFlips

	C	D	E	F
11	Random		Total	Total
12	Number	Result	Heads	Tails
13	=RAND()	=IF(RandomNumber<0.5,"Heads","Tails")	=IF(Results="Heads",1,0)	=Flip-TotalHeads
14	=RAND()	=IF(RandomNumber<0.5,"Heads","Tails")	=E13+IF(Results="Heads",1,0)	=Flip-TotalHeads
15	=RAND()	=IF(RandomNumber<0.5,"Heads","Tails")	=E14+IF(Results="Heads",1,0)	=Flip-TotalHeads
16	:	:	:	:
17	:	:	:	:

	G
12	Stop?
13	
14	
15	=IF(ABS(TotalHeads-TotalTails)>=RequiredDifference,"Stop","")
16	=IF(G15="",IF(ABS(TotalHeads-TotalTails)>=RequiredDifference,"Stop",""),"NA")
17	=IF(G16="",IF(ABS(TotalHeads-TotalTails)>=RequiredDifference,"Stop",""),"NA")
18	:
19	:

Although these numbers in cells C13:C62 have all the important properties of random numbers, Excel actually uses a fixed formula to calculate each random number from the preceding one, starting with a *seed value* to initialize the process. Since the sequence of random numbers is predictable in the sense that it can be reproduced by using the same seed value again (which sometimes is advantageous), these numbers sometimes are referred to as *pseudorandom numbers*.

The probabilities for the outcome of flipping a coin are

$$P(\text{heads}) = \tfrac{1}{2} \qquad P(\text{tails}) = \tfrac{1}{2}$$

Therefore, to simulate the flipping of a coin, the computer can just let any half of the possible random numbers correspond to heads and the other half correspond to tails. To be specific, we will use the following correspondence.

0.0000 to 0.4999	correspond to	heads
0.5000 to 0.9999	correspond to	tails

By using the formula

$$= \text{IF(RandomNumber} < 0.5, \text{"Heads", "Tails")}$$

in each of the column D cells in Figure 12.1, Excel inserts Heads if the random number is less than 0.5 and inserts Tails otherwise. Consequently, the first 11 random numbers generated in column C yield the following sequence of heads (H) and tails (T):

HTTTHHHTHHH

at which point the game stops because the number of heads (seven) exceeds the number of tails (four) by three. Cells D7 and D8 record the total number of flips (11) and resulting winnings ($8 − $11 = −$3).

Thus, Figure 12.1 records the computer simulation of one complete play of the game. To virtually ensure that the game will be completed, 50 flips of the coin have been simulated. Columns E and F record the cumulative number of heads and tails after each flip. The equations entered into the column G cells leave each cell blank until the difference in the numbers of heads and tails reaches 3, at which point Stop is inserted into the cell. Thereafter, NA (for Not Applicable) is inserted instead.

Such simulations of plays of the game can be repeated as often as desired with this spreadsheet. Each time, Excel will generate a new sequence of random numbers and so a new sequence of heads and tails. (Excel will repeat a sequence of random numbers only if you select the range of numbers you want to repeat, copy this range with the Copy command, select Paste Special from the Edit menu, choose the Values option, and click on OK.)

Computer simulations normally are repeated many times to obtain a more reliable estimate of an average outcome. Figure 12.2 shows how a data table can be used to trick Excel into repeating the simulation 14 times. You first make a table with the column headings shown in columns J, K, and L. The first column of the table (J7:J20) is used to label the 14 plays of the game, leaving the first row blank. The headings of the next two columns specify which output will be evaluated. For each of these two columns, use the first row of the table (cells K6:L6) to write an equation that refers to the relevant output cell. In this case, the cells of interest are the number of flips and the winnings, so the equations for K6:L6 are those shown to the right of the spreadsheet in Figure 12.2.

The next step is to select the entire table (J6:L20) and then choose Data Table from the What-If Analysis menu of the Data tab (for Excel 2007) or Table from the Data menu (for earlier versions of Excel). In the Data Table dialogue box (as shown on the right-hand side of Figure 12.2), choose any blank cell for the column input cell (for example, E4) but do not enter anything for the row input cell. Clicking OK then generates the data table shown in Figure 12.2.

The first thing Excel does while generating the data table is to enter the numbers in the first column of the table (J7:J20), one at a time, into the column input cell (E4), which has no direct impact on the simulation. However, each time a new number is entered into the column input cell, Excel recalculates the entire original spreadsheet (Figure 12.1) in cells C13:G62

FIGURE 12.2

A data table that records the results of performing 14 replications of a computer simulation with the spreadsheet in Figure 12.1.

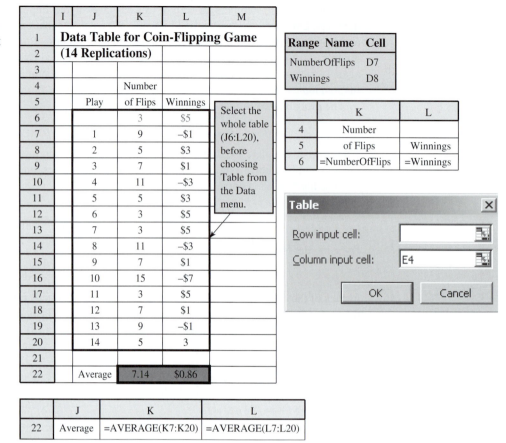

	I	J	K	L	M
1		**Data Table for Coin-Flipping Game**			
2		**(14 Replications)**			
3					
4			Number		
5		Play	of Flips	Winnings	
6			3	$5	
7		1	9	–$1	
8		2	5	$3	
9		3	7	$1	
10		4	11	–$3	
11		5	5	$3	
12		6	3	$5	
13		7	3	$5	
14		8	11	–$3	
15		9	7	$1	
16		10	15	–$7	
17		11	3	$5	
18		12	7	$1	
19		13	9	–$1	
20		14	5	3	
21					
22		Average	7.14	$0.86	

Select the whole table (J6:L20), before choosing Table from the Data menu.

Range Name	Cell
NumberOfFlips	D7
Winnings	D8

	K	L
4	Number	
5	of Flips	Winnings
6	=NumberOfFlips	=Winnings

Table   ✕

Row input cell: [   ]

Column input cell: [E4]

OK   Cancel

	J	K	L
22	Average	=AVERAGE(K7:K20)	=AVERAGE(L7:L20)

and then enters the resulting numbers in the output cells, NumberOfFlips (D7) and Winnings (D8), into the corresponding row of the data table. In essence, we have tricked Excel into repeating the simulation 14 times, each time generating new random numbers in column C to perform a completely new simulation.

Cell K22 shows that this sample of 14 plays of the game gives a sample average of 7.14 flips. The sample average provides an *estimate* of the true *mean* of the underlying probability distribution of the number of flips required for a play of the game. Hence, this sample average of 7.14 would seem to indicate that, on the average, you should win about $0.86 (cell L22) each time you play the game. Therefore, if you do not have a relatively high aversion to risk, it appears that you should choose to play this game, preferably a large number of times.

However, *beware!* One common error in the use of computer simulation is that conclusions are based on overly small samples, because statistical analysis was inadequate or totally lacking. It is very important to use a qualified statistician to help design the experiments to be performed with computer simulation. In this case, careful statistical analysis (using confidence intervals, etc.) would indicate that hundreds of simulated plays of the game would be needed before any conclusions should be drawn about whether you are likely to win or lose by playing this game numerous times.

It so happens that the true mean of the number of flips required for a play of this game is nine. (This mean can be found analytically, but not easily.) Thus, in the long run, you actually would average losing about $1 each time you played the game. Part of the reason that the above simulated experiment failed to draw this conclusion is that you have a small chance of a very large loss on any play of the game, but you can never win more than $5 each time. However, 14 simulated plays of the game were not enough to obtain any observations far out in the tail of the probability distribution of the amount won or lost on one play of the game. Only one simulated play gave a loss of more than $3, and that was only $7.

Figure 12.3 gives the results of running the simulation for 1,000 plays of the game (with rows 17–1,000 not shown). Cell K1008 records the average number of flips as 8.97, very

At least hundreds of simulated plays of this game are needed to obtain a reasonably reliable estimate of an average outcome.

FIGURE 12.3

This data table improves the reliability of the computer simulation recorded in Figure 12.2 by performing 1,000 replications instead of only 14.

	I	J	K	L	M
1		**Data Table for Coin-Flipping Game**			
2		**(1,000 Replications)**			
3					
4			Number		
5		Play	of Flips	Winnings	
6			5	$3	
7		1	3	$5	
8		2	3	$5	
9		3	7	$1	
10		4	11	−$3	
11		5	13	−$5	
12		6	7	$1	
13		7	3	$5	
14		8	7	$1	
15		9	3	$5	
16		10	9	−$1	
1001		995	5	$3	
1002		996	27	−$19	
1003		997	7	$1	
1004		998	3	$5	
1005		999	9	−$1	
1006		1,000	17	−$9	
1007					
1008		Average	8.97	−$0.97	

close to the true mean of 9. With this number of replications, the average winnings of −$0.97 in cell L1008 now provide a reliable basis for concluding that this game will not win you money in the long run. (You can bet that the casino already has used computer simulation to verify this fact in advance.)

Example 2: Corrective Maintenance versus Preventive Maintenance

The Heavy Duty Company has just purchased a large machine for a new production process. The machine is powered by a motor that occasionally breaks down and requires a major overhaul. Therefore, the manufacturer of the machine also provides a second standby motor. The two motors are rotated in use, with each one remaining in the machine until it is removed for an overhaul and replaced by the other one.

Given the planned usage of the machine, its manufacturer has provided the company with information about the *durability* of the motors (the number of days of usage until a breakdown occurs). This information is shown in the first two columns of Table 12.1. The first column lists the number of days the current machine has been in use. For each of these days, the second column then gives the probability that the breakdown will occur on that day. Since these probabilities are 0 except for days 4, 5, and 6, the breakdown always occurs on the fourth, fifth, or sixth day.

TABLE 12.1

The Probability Distribution of Breakdowns for Heavy Duty's Motors, and the Corresponding Random Numbers

Day	Probability of a Breakdown	Corresponding Random Numbers
1, 2, 3	0	
4	0.25	0.0000 to 0.2499
5	0.5	0.2500 to 0.7499
6	0.25	0.7500 to 0.9999
7 or more	0	

Fortunately, the time required to overhaul a motor never exceeds three days, so a replacement motor always is ready when a breakdown occurs. When this happens, the remainder of the day (plus overtime if needed) is used to remove the failed motor and install the replacement motor, so the machine then is ready to begin operation again at the beginning of the next day. The average costs incurred during each *replacement cycle* (the time from when a replacement of a motor begins until just before another replacement is needed) are summarized below.

Cost of a Replacement Cycle That Begins with a Breakdown

Replace a motor	$ 2,000
Lost production during replacement	5,000
Overhaul a motor	4,000
Total	$11,000

Using Computer Simulation

Computer simulation can be used to estimate what the *average daily cost* will be for replacing the motors as needed. This requires using random numbers to determine when breakdowns occur in the *simulated* process. Using the probabilities in the second column of Table 12.1, 25 percent of the possible random numbers need to correspond to a breakdown on day 4, 50 percent to a breakdown on day 5, and the remaining 25 percent to a breakdown on day 6. The rightmost column of Table 12.1 shows the natural way of doing this.

Excel provides a convenient VLOOKUP function for implementing this correspondence between a random number and the associated event. Figure 12.4 illustrates how it works. One step is to create the table shown in columns I, J, and K, where columns K and I come directly from the first two columns of Table 12.1. Column J gives the cumulative probability *prior* to the number of days in column K, so J8 = I7 and J9 = I7 + I8. Cells J7:K9 then constitute the lookup table for the VLOOKUP function. The bottom of the figure displays how the VLOOKUP command has been entered into the column D cells. The first argument of this function indicates that the cell in the same row of RandomNumber (C5:C34) provides the random number being used. The second argument gives the range for the lookup table. The third argument (2) indicates that column 2 of the lookup table is providing the number being entered into this cell in column D. The choice of the number in column 2 of the lookup table is based on where the random number falls within the ranges between rows in column 1 of this

The lookup table in cells J7:K9 provides this correspondence between a random number and the time until a breakdown occurs.

table. In particular, the three possible choices are

$$\text{if} \quad 0 \leq \text{RAND}() < 0.25 \quad \text{choose 4 days}$$
$$\text{if} \quad 0.25 \leq \text{RAND}() < 0.75 \quad \text{choose 5 days}$$
$$\text{if} \quad 0.75 \leq \text{RAND}() < 1 \quad \text{choose 6 days}$$

which is precisely the correspondence indicated in Table 12.1.

By generating 30 simulated breakdowns in this way in column D of Figure 12.4, columns E, F, and G then show the resulting cumulative number of days, the estimated cost for each replacement cycle, and the cumulative cost for the corresponding replacement cycles. (In a more detailed computer simulation, random numbers also could be used to generate the exact costs with each simulated breakdown.) Since the total number of days in this simulation (cell E34) is 153 and the cumulative cost (cell G34) is $330,000, the average daily cost is calculated in cell J34 as

$$\text{Average cost per day} = \frac{\$330,000}{153} = \$2,157$$

Comparisons with Example 1

Comparing this computer simulation with the ones run for the coin-flipping game reveal a couple of interesting differences. One is that the IF function was used to generate each simulated coin flip from a random number (see the equations entered into the column D cells in Figure 12.1), whereas the VLOOKUP function has just been used here to generate

FIGURE 12.4

A spreadsheet model for a computer simulation of performing corrective maintenance on the Heavy Duty Co. motors.

	A	B	C	D	E	F	G	H	I	J	K
1		**Heavy Duty Company Corrective Maintenance Simulation**									
2											
3			Random	Time Since Last	Cumulative		Cumulative		**Distribution of**		
4		Breakdown	Number	Breakdown	Day	Cost	Cost		**Time between Breakdowns**		
5		1	0.7142	5	5	$11,000	$11,000				Number
6		2	0.4546	5	10	$11,000	$22,000		Probability	Cumulative	of Days
7		3	0.3142	5	15	$11,000	$33,000		0.25	0	4
8		4	0.1722	4	19	$11,000	$44,000		0.5	0.25	5
9		5	0.0932	4	23	$11,000	$55,000		0.25	0.75	6
10		6	0.3645	5	28	$11,000	$66,000				
11		7	0.1636	4	32	$11,000	$77,000		Breakdown Cost	$11,000	
12		8	0.7572	6	38	$11,000	$88,000				
13		9	0.3067	5	43	$11,000	$99,000				
14		10	0.9520	6	49	$11,000	$110,000				
30		26	0.8548	6	131	$11,000	$286,000				
31		27	0.7464	5	136	$11,000	$297,000				
32		28	0.9781	6	142	$11,000	$308,000				
33		29	0.6584	5	147	$11,000	$319,000		Average Cost per Day		
34		30	0.8829	6	153	$11,000	$330,000			$2,157	

	C	D	E	F	G
3	Random	Time Since Last	Cumulative		Cumulative
4	Number	Breakdown	Day	Cost	Cost
5	=RAND()	=VLOOKUP(RandomNumber,$J$7:$K$9,2)	=TimeSinceLastBreakdown	=BreakdownCost	=Cost
6	=RAND()	=VLOOKUP(RandomNumber,$J$7:$K$9,2)	=E5+TimeSinceLastBreakdown	=BreakdownCost	=G5+Cost
7	=RAND()	=VLOOKUP(RandomNumber,$J$7:$K$9,2)	=E6+TimeSinceLastBreakdown	=BreakdownCost	=G6+Cost
8	:	:	:	:	:
9	:	:	:	:	:

Range Name	Cells
AverageCostPerDay	J34
Breakdown	B5:B34
BreakdownCost	J11
Cost	F5:F34
CumulativeCost	G5:G34
CumulativeDay	E5:E34
RandomNumber	C5:C34
TimeSinceLastBreakdown	D5:D34

	J
33	Average Cost per Day
34	=CumulativeCost/CumulativeDay

the simulated results. Actually, the VLOOKUP function could have been used instead for the coin flips, but the IF function was more convenient. Conversely, a nested IF function could have been used instead for the current example, but the VLOOKUP function was more convenient. In general, we prefer using the IF function to generate a random observation from a probability distribution that has only two possible values, whereas we prefer the VLOOKUP function when the distribution has more than two possible values.

A second difference arose in the way the replications of the two computer simulations were recorded. For the coin-flipping game, simulating a single play of the game involved using the spreadsheet with 62 rows shown in Figure 12.1. Therefore, to record many replications, this same spreadsheet was used to generate the data table in Figure 12.2, which summarized the results of each replication in a single row. For the current example, no separate data table was needed because each replication could be executed and displayed in a single row of the original spreadsheet in Figure 12.4.

However, one similarity between the two examples is that we purposely kept each one sufficiently simple that an analytical solution is available to compare with the simulation results. In fact, it is quite straightforward to obtain the analytical solution for the current version of the Heavy Duty Co. problem. Using the probabilities in Table 12.1, the *expected* number of days until a breakdown occurs is

$$E(\text{time until a breakdown}) = 0.25(4 \text{ days}) + 0.5(5 \text{ days}) + 0.25(6 \text{ days})$$
$$= 5 \text{ days}$$

Therefore, the *expected value* (in the statistical sense) of the cost per day is

$$E(\text{cost per day}) = \frac{\$11,000}{5 \text{ days}} = \$2,200 \text{ per day}$$

The average cost of $2,157 per day obtained by computer simulation (cell J34 of Figure 12.4) is an estimate of this true expected value.

The fact that computer simulation actually was not needed to analyze this version of the Heavy Duty Co. problem illustrates a possible pitfall with this technique. Computer simulation is easy enough to use that there occasionally is a tendency to rush into using this technique when a bit of careful thought and analysis first could provide all the needed information more precisely (and perhaps more quickly) than computer simulation. In other cases, starting with a simple analytical model sometimes can provide important insights as a prelude to using computer simulation to refine the analysis with a more precise formulation of the problem.

Some Preventive Maintenance Options

So far, we have assumed that the company will use a *corrective maintenance* policy. This means that the motor in the machine will be removed and overhauled only after it has broken down. However, many companies use a *preventive maintenance* policy instead. Such a policy in this case would involve *scheduling* the motor to be removed (and replaced) for an overhaul at a certain time even if a breakdown has not occurred. The goal is to provide maintenance early enough to prevent a breakdown. Scheduling the overhaul also enables removing and replacing the motor at a convenient time when the machine would not be in use otherwise, so that no production is lost. For example, by paying overtime wages for the removal and replacement, this work can be done after the normal workday ends so that the machine will be ready by the beginning of the next day. One possibility is to do this at the end of day 3, which would definitely be in time to prevent a breakdown. Other options are to do it at the end of day 4 or day 5 (if a breakdown has not yet occurred) in order to prevent disrupting production with a breakdown in the very near future. Computer simulation can be used to evaluate and compare each of these options (along with a corrective maintenance policy) when analytical solutions are not available.

The goal of preventive maintenance is to provide maintenance early enough to prevent a breakdown.

Consider the option of removing (and replacing) the motor for an overhaul at the end of day 3. The average cost each time this is done happens to be the following.

Cost of a Replacement Cycle That Begins without a Breakdown	
Replace a motor on overtime	$3,000
Lost production during replacement	0
Overhaul a motor before a breakdown	3,000
Total	$6,000

Since this total cost of $6,000 occurs every three days, the expected cost per day of this option would be

$$E(\text{cost per day}) = \frac{\$6,000}{3 \text{ days}} = \$2,000 \text{ per day}$$

Since this cost has been obtained analytically, computer simulation is not needed in this case.

Now consider the remaining two options of removing (and replacing) the motor after day 4 or after day 5 if a breakdown has not yet occurred. Since it is somewhat more difficult to find the expected cost per day analytically for these options, we now will use computer simulation. For either case, the average cost during a replacement cycle depends on whether the replacement began before or after a breakdown occurred. As outlined earlier, these average costs are

Cost of a replacement cycle that begins with a breakdown   = $11,000

Cost of a replacement cycle that begins without a breakdown = $ 6,000

Figure 12.5 shows the use of computer simulation for the option of scheduling the replacement of each motor after four days. The times until 30 consecutive motors would have broken down without the replacements are obtained from column D (except rows 15–29 are hidden). The cases where this time is four (indicating a breakdown *during* day 4) correspond to a motor breaking down before it is replaced. (This occurs in rows 6, 9, 13–14 and in five of the hidden rows.) The first cycle concludes with the replacement of the first motor after four days, as shown in row 5. Column G gives the cumulative number of days at the end of each cycle. Column F indicates whether each cycle ends with a breakdown or with a replacement that is soon enough to avoid a breakdown, and column H gives the resulting cost. Column I then cumulates these costs. Since the 30 cycles last 120 days (cell G34) and have a total cost of $225,000 (cell I34), this simulation yields

$$\text{Average cost per day} = \frac{\$225,000}{120} = \$1,875$$

as the *estimate* of the expected cost per day (which actually is $1,812 per day) for this option.

Figure 12.6 shows the corresponding simulation for the option of scheduling the replacement of each motor after five days. Thus, if the time until a breakdown would be on the sixth day (as indicated in column D), the replacement is made in time to avoid the breakdown (as indicated in column F). Since most of the times in column D are four or five instead, most of the cycles conclude with a breakdown. This leads to a much higher total cost for the 30 cycles of $300,000, along with a somewhat longer total time of 141 days. Therefore, the *estimate* of the expected cost per day for this option is

$$\text{Average cost per day} = \frac{\$300,000}{141} = \$2,128$$

(The true expected cost per day is $2,053.)

Based on all the above results, the clear choice for the least expensive option is the one that schedules the replacement of each motor after four days, since its estimated expected cost per day is only $1,875. Although this estimate based on the simulation in Figure 12.5 overestimates the true expected cost per day by $63, this option still is the least expensive one by a wide margin.

Longer and more detailed simulation runs are commonly conducted.

In practice, the simulation runs usually would be considerably longer than those shown in Figures 12.4, 12.5, and 12.6 in order to obtain more precise estimates of the true costs for the alternative options. The simulations typically also would include more details, such as when during a day a breakdown occurs and the resulting cost of lost production that day.

Both Examples 1 and 2 used random numbers to generate random observations from *discrete* probability distributions. Many computer simulations require generating random observations from *continuous* distributions instead. We next describe a general method for doing this with *either* continuous or discrete distributions.

Generating Random Observations from a Probability Distribution

Both Examples 1 and 2 generate random observations from a *discrete* probability distribution. As illustrated in Example 2, Excel's LOOKUP function can be useful for doing this for any discrete distribution.

However, many computer simulations require generating random observations from *continuous* distributions instead. A general mathematical procedure called the **inverse transformation method** is available for generating random observations from *either* discrete or continuous distributions. This procedure is described in the supplement to this chapter on the CD-ROM.

FIGURE 12.5

A spreadsheet model for a computer simulation of performing preventive maintenance (replace after four days) on the Heavy Duty Co. motors.

Heavy Duty Company Preventive Maintenance Simulation (Replace After 4 Days)

Main simulation table (columns B–I):

Cycle	Random Number	Time Until Breakdown	Scheduled Time Until Replacement	Event That Concludes Cycle	Cumulative Day	Cost	Cumulative Cost
1	0.7861	6	4	Replacement	4	$6,000	$6,000
2	0.0679	4	4	Breakdown	8	$11,000	$17,000
3	0.9296	6	4	Replacement	12	$6,000	$23,000
4	0.4430	5	4	Replacement	16	$6,000	$29,000
5	0.1223	4	4	Breakdown	20	$11,000	$40,000
6	0.4530	5	4	Replacement	24	$6,000	$46,000
7	0.3972	5	4	Replacement	28	$6,000	$52,000
8	0.9289	6	4	Replacement	32	$6,000	$58,000
9	0.2195	4	4	Breakdown	36	$11,000	$69,000
10	0.0706	4	4	Breakdown	40	$11,000	$80,000
⋮							
26	0.8720	6	4	Replacement	104	$6,000	$201,000
27	0.8902	6	4	Replacement	108	$6,000	$207,000
28	0.3839	5	4	Replacement	112	$6,000	$213,000
29	0.7404	5	4	Replacement	116	$6,000	$219,000
30	0.7264	5	4	Replacement	120	$6,000	$225,000

Distribution and cost table (columns K–M):

Distribution of Time between Breakdowns		
Probability	Cumulative	Number of Days
0.25	0	4
0.5	0.25	5
0.25	0.75	6

Breakdown Cost	$11,000	
Replacement Cost	$6,000	
Replace After	4	days
Average Cost per Day	$1,875	

Formula listing (columns C–E):

	Random Number	Time Until Breakdown	Scheduled Time Until Replacement
5	=RAND()	=VLOOKUP(RandomNumber,$L$7:$M$9,2)	=ReplaceAfter
6	=RAND()	=VLOOKUP(RandomNumber,$L$7:$M$9,2)	=ReplaceAfter
7	=RAND()	=VLOOKUP(RandomNumber,$L$7:$M$9,2)	=ReplaceAfter
8	⋮	⋮	⋮
9	⋮	⋮	⋮

Formula listing (column F):

	Event That Concludes Cycle
5	=IF(TimeUntilBreakdown<=ScheduledTimeUntilReplacement,"Breakdown","Replacement")
6	=IF(TimeUntilBreakdown<=ScheduledTimeUntilReplacement,"Breakdown","Replacement")
7	=IF(TimeUntilBreakdown<=ScheduledTimeUntilReplacement,"Breakdown","Replacement")
8	⋮
9	⋮

Formula listing (columns G–H):

	Cumulative Day	Cost
3	Cumulative	
4	Day	Cost
5	=MIN(D5,E5)	=IF(Event="Breakdown",BreakdownCost,ReplacementCost)
6	=G5+MIN(D6,E6)	=IF(Event="Breakdown",BreakdownCost,ReplacementCost)
7	=G6+MIN(D7,E7)	=IF(Event="Breakdown",BreakdownCost,ReplacementCost)
8	⋮	⋮
9	⋮	⋮

Formula listing (column I):

	Cumulative Cost
5	=Cost
6	=I5+Cost
7	=I6+Cost
⋮	⋮

Formula listing (column L):

33	Average Cost per Day
34	=CumulativeCost/CumulativeDay

Range Name	Cells
AverageCostPerDay	L34
BreakdownCost	L11
Cost	H5:H34
CumulativeCost	I5:I34
CumulativeDay	G5:G34
Cycle	B5:B34
Event	F5:F34
RandomNumber	C5:C34
ReplaceAfter	L14
ReplacementCost	L12
ScheduledTimeUntilReplacement	E5:E34
TimeUntilBreakdown	D5:D34

FIGURE 12.6

A revision of Figure 12.5 to schedule the replacement of the motors after five days instead of four.

	A	B	C	D	E	F	G	H	I	J	K	L	M
1		**Heavy Duty Company Preventive Maintenance Simulation (Replace After 5 Days)**											
2													
3			Random	Time Until	Scheduled Time	Event That	Cumulative		Cumulative		**Distribution of**		
4		Cycle	Number	Breakdown	Until Replacement	Concludes Cycle	Day	Cost	Cost		**Time between Breakdowns**		
5		1	0.0558	4	5	Breakdown	4	$11,000	$11,000				Number
6		2	0.0690	4	5	Breakdown	8	$11,000	$22,000		Probability	Cumulative	of Days
7		3	0.1889	4	5	Breakdown	12	$11,000	$33,000		0.25	0	4
8		4	0.9471	6	5	Replacement	17	$6,000	$39,000		0.5	0.25	5
9		5	0.9173	6	5	Replacement	22	$6,000	$45,000		0.25	0.75	6
10		6	0.3541	5	5	Breakdown	27	$11,000	$56,000				
11		7	0.7035	5	5	Breakdown	32	$11,000	$67,000		Breakdown Cost	$11,000	
12		8	0.0350	4	5	Breakdown	36	$11,000	$78,000		Replacement Cost	$6,000	
13		9	0.5755	5	5	Breakdown	41	$11,000	$89,000				
14		10	0.8910	6	5	Replacement	46	$6,000	$95,000		Replace After	5	days
30		26	0.7386	5	5	Breakdown	122	$11,000	$261,000				
31		27	0.2648	5	5	Breakdown	127	$11,000	$272,000				
32		28	0.6239	5	5	Breakdown	132	$11,000	$283,000				
33		29	0.9988	6	5	Replacement	137	$6,000	$289,000		Average Cost per Day		
34		30	0.0061	4	5	Breakdown	141	$11,000	$300,000			$2,128	

However, for relatively complicated continuous distributions, even the inverse transformation method becomes difficult to apply. One example is the *normal distribution*. This distribution is such an important one that more convenient special methods have been developed to generate random observations from this distribution. In particular, Excel uses the function

This is a very handy Excel function to generate a random observation from a normal distribution.

$$\text{NORMINV(RAND(), } \mu, \sigma)$$

to do this after you substitute the numerical values for the mean μ and standard deviation σ of the distribution. The next section describes how to generate random observations from two other important continuous distributions—the uniform distribution and the exponential distribution.

Several Excel add-ins have been developed to extend the simulation capabilities of the standard Excel package, including providing special functions to immediately generate random observations from a wide variety of probability distributions. Two of these (Crystal Ball and RiskSim) are included in your MS Courseware. Crystal Ball will be featured in the next chapter. RiskSim is shareware developed by Professor Michael Middleton. Although not as elaborate or powerful as Crystal Ball, RiskSim is easy to use and is well documented on the CD-ROM. (If you want to continue to use it after this course, you should register and pay the shareware fee.) Like any Excel add-ins, these add-ins need to be installed before they will show up in Excel.

Review Questions

1. How does computer simulation imitate the operation of a stochastic system?
2. Why does computer simulation tend to be a relatively expensive procedure?
3. When is computer simulation typically used despite being relatively expensive?
4. What is a random number? For what purpose is it used?

12.2   A CASE STUDY: HERR CUTTER'S BARBER SHOP (REVISITED)

If you have already studied the preceding chapter, you hopefully recall the brief description in Section 11.1 of Herr Cutter's barber shop as an example of a basic kind of queueing system. (A queueing system is a place where customers receive some kind of service from a server, perhaps after waiting in a line called a queue.) As indicated there, Herr Cutter is a German barber who runs a one-man barber shop. He opens his shop at 8:00 A.M. each weekday morning. His customers arrive randomly at an average rate of two customers per hour. He requires an average of 20 minutes for each haircut.

The case study concerns the problem described below.

The Decision Facing Herr Cutter

Herr Cutter has run his barber shop in the same location for nearly 25 years. Although his parents had wanted him to follow in his father's footsteps as a medical doctor, he has never regretted his decision to follow this more modest career path. He enjoys the relaxed working environment, the regular hours, and the opportunity to visit with his customers.

Over the years, he has built up a loyal clientele. He is a fine barber who takes pride in his work. As his business has increased, his customers now often need to wait awhile (sometimes over half an hour) to begin a haircut. However, his long-time customers are willing to do so.

The shop is in a growing city. As the pace of life has increased, Herr Cutter has noticed that new customers are much less likely to return than in the early years, especially if they have had to wait very long. He attributes this to a decreasing tolerance for waiting. However, since he is not gaining many new regular customers, his volume of business has leveled off at a steady average of two customers per hour.

The decision facing Herr Cutter is whether to add an associate to share the workload in the barber shop.

As he has grown older, Herr Cutter has wondered increasingly about whether he should add an associate to share the workload. He also would enjoy the company, as well as the additional flexibility. A second barber should reduce the waiting times of the customers considerably, so an additional benefit would be that the total volume of business for the shop should increase somewhat.

However, what has always held him back from adding an associate is the fear of decreasing his personal income from the business. He needs to be putting away considerable money toward retirement and really can't afford a significant decrease in his already modest income. Given the salary and commission he would need to pay an associate, business would need to almost double just to maintain his current level of income. (We will spell out the financial details in the next section when the analysis takes place.) He is doubtful that business would increase nearly this much.

But now opportunity has come knocking on the door. A fellow barber (and friend) in the city has decided to retire and close his shop. This friend has had the same associate for several years, and he now has invited Herr Cutter to hire this fine young man. The friend highly recommends him, and also points out that the associate would bring considerable business with him.

So now Herr Cutter is in a quandary as to whether he should take the plunge in hiring this associate.

Fortunately, help is at hand for making this decision. This friend has shown Herr Cutter an interesting recent article in *The Barber's Journal.* The article describes a study that has been done of barber shops and how long customers now are willing to wait for haircuts to begin. The article concludes with two rules of thumb.

> **First Rule of Thumb:** In a well-run barber shop with a long-established clientele, these loyal customers are willing to tolerate an average waiting time of about 20 minutes until the haircut begins.

Herr Cutter feels that this description fits his situation. He has never tried to estimate the waiting times of his customers, but guesses that an average of 20 minutes sounds about right.

> **Second Rule of Thumb:** In a well-run barber shop, new customers are willing to tolerate an average waiting time of about 10 minutes before the haircut begins. (With longer waits, they tend to take their business elsewhere in the future.)

Again, Herr Cutter feels that this rule of thumb agrees with his own experience.

This second rule of thumb has given Herr Cutter a good idea about how to view his decision. With his current clientele, adding an associate probably would reduce their average waiting time to less than 10 minutes. This prompt service then should help to gradually attract and retain new customers (including some of the associate's customers from the barber shop that is closing). According to the rule of thumb, the level of business should increase until it reaches the point where the average waiting time before the haircut begins has increased to about 10 minutes. Estimating the level of business at that point would indicate the new level of income to the shop and his share of that income. The dilemma is that he does not see how to estimate this level of business in advance.

Herr Cutter asks for advice from his nephew Fritz (a university student majoring in business) about how to resolve this dilemma. Fritz excitedly responds that he thinks he knows just the right approach to use. Computer simulation.

Fritz recently took a course in management science. In fact, he has a copy of MS Courseware, including its Queueing Simulator for simulating queueing systems like his uncle's barber shop. Although not as sophisticated as expensive commercial software packages for performing computer simulations, Fritz explains to his uncle how this routine can indeed provide a good estimate in advance of what the level of business would be with an associate.

Fritz proposes spending a little time with his uncle to gather some data and develop a *simulation model* in preparation for performing the computer simulations. His first simulation will be of the barber shop under its current mode of operation (without an associate) to estimate the current average waiting time. Comparing the results from this simulation with what is actually happening in the barber shop also will help to test the validity of the simulation model. If necessary, the model will be adjusted to better represent the real system. The subsequent simulations will be run of the barber shop *with* an associate. These simulations will assume that the associate's speed in giving a haircut is the same as Herr Cutter's. Different means of the interarrival-time distribution will be tried to determine which mean (i.e., which level of business) would lead to an average waiting time of 10 minutes before the haircut begins.

With an associate, the level of business should reach the point where the average waiting time to begin a haircut is about 10 minutes.

Here is the plan for using computer simulation to estimate what the new level of business would be with an associate.

Fritz asks his uncle if he should proceed with this plan. Herr Cutter urges him to do so.

The remainder of this section describes the execution of this plan, including the mechanics of how these simulations are performed. The next section then presents the results of the actual computer simulations and the analysis of what Herr Cutter should do.

Gathering Data

As with other basic queueing systems, the key events for this barber shop are *service (haircut) completions* and *customer arrivals*. Table 11.1 (in Section 11.1) records the times at which these events occurred over a typical early morning. Figure 11.2 displays these data in a different form by plotting the number of customers in the system (a basic measure of performance) over this same early morning.

By observing the barber shop over an extended period of time, extensive data of the same kind could be gathered to estimate various measures of performance for the barber shop under its current mode of operation. However, it is not necessary to spend months or years gathering such data. Once it has been set up on a computer, computer simulation can accomplish the same thing in a matter of seconds by *simulating* the operation of the barber shop over a lengthy period (even years if desired). However, performing this simulation does require gathering a bit of other data first.

In particular, it is necessary to estimate the *probability distributions* involving the random events (service completions and customer arrivals) in the system. These probability distributions are the distribution of *service times* (the times required to give a haircut) and the distribution of *interarrival times* (the times between consecutive arrivals).

Herr Cutter has found that the time required to give a haircut varies between 15 and 25 minutes, depending on the customer's amount of hair, the desired hair style, and so forth. Furthermore, his best estimate is that the times between 15 and 25 minutes are *equally likely*, which indicates the following distribution.

> **Estimated distribution of service times:** The *uniform distribution* over the interval from 15 minutes to 25 minutes.

Since the barber shop has *random arrivals* of customers, Section 11.1 points out that the distribution of interarrival times must be an exponential distribution.

> **Estimated distribution of interarrival times:** An *exponential distribution* (described in Section 11.1) with a mean of 30 minutes.

The shape of an exponential distribution is shown in Figure 11.3 (Section 11.1).

Generating Random Observations from These Probability Distributions

A computer simulation of the operation of the barber shop requires generating a series of *random observations* from the distributions identified above. As usual, *random numbers* will be used to do this. However, since these probability distributions are *continuous* distributions, it is not very convenient to use random numbers in the ways described for the *discrete* distributions in Examples 1 and 2 (which employed Excel's IF and VLOOKUP functions, respectively).

Fortunately, it is relatively straightforward to generate a random observation from any uniform distribution, including this one over the interval from 15 minutes to 25 minutes. The key is that a random number between 0 and 1 is, in fact, a random observation from a uniform distribution between 0 and 1. Thus, the Excel function RAND() generates such a random observation. Similarly, 10 RAND() generates a random observation from a uniform distribution between 0 and 10. Adding 15 to such a random observation thereby provides a random observation from a uniform distribution between 15 and 25.

Therefore, when developing a simulation model for the operation of Herr Cutter's barber shop, the equation to be entered into each cell receiving a random observation from this uniform distribution is

$$= 15 + 10*RAND()$$

(margin note) Estimates are needed of the probability distributions of both the time required to give a haircut (the "service time") and the time between consecutive arrivals of customers (the "interarrival time").

The Excel equation for a random observation from a uniform distribution over the interval from a to b is $= a + (b - a)$ RAND().

For a uniform distribution with lower and upper bounds different from 15 and 25, the lower bound would be substituted for 15 in this equation and the difference between the two bounds would be substituted for 10.

Although the exponential distribution is more complicated than the uniform distribution, an Excel equation also is available for generating a random observation from an exponential distribution with a mean of 30 minutes (the distribution of interarrival times for Herr Cutter's barber shop). The supplement to this chapter on the CD-ROM describes how the inverse transformation method is used to derive this equation by using the Excel function LN(), which calculates the *natural logarithm* of whatever quantity is inside the parentheses.

In particular, for each cell in a spreadsheet model that receives a random observation from this exponential distribution, the Excel equation to be entered into this cell is

$$= -30*\text{LN}(\text{RAND}())$$

After replacing 30 by the mean, this is the Excel equation for generating a random observation from any exponential distribution.

For an exponential distribution with a different mean, this mean would be substituted for 30 in this equation.

The Building Blocks of a Simulation Model for a Stochastic System

With its multiple probability distributions, the case study has some of the complications that are typical of the stochastic systems for which many computer simulations are performed. When preparing for a relatively complex simulation of this type, it is sometimes helpful to develop a formal *simulation model.*

A **simulation model** is a representation of the system to be simulated that also describes how the simulation will be performed.

Here are the basic building blocks of a typical simulation model for a stochastic system.

1. A description of the components of the system, including how they are assumed to operate and interrelate.
2. A simulation clock.
3. A definition of the state of the system.
4. A method for randomly generating the (simulated) events that occur over time.
5. A method for changing the state of the system when an event occurs.
6. A procedure for advancing the time on the simulation clock.

We will use the case study to illustrate each of these building blocks.

As first described in Section 11.1, Herr Cutter's barber shop is a basic kind of single-server queueing system. The *components* of this system are the customers, the queue, and Herr Cutter as the server. (The queue is the waiting line of customers waiting to begin a haircut.) The assumed distributions of service times and interarrival times were described earlier in this section.

Once a computer simulation is under way, it is necessary to keep track of the passage of time in the system being simulated. Starting at time 0, let

$$t = \text{Amount of } simulated \text{ time that has elapsed so far}$$

The variable t in the computer program is referred to as the **simulation clock.** The program continually updates the current value of this variable as the simulation proceeds. With today's powerful computers, simulated time typically proceeds millions of times faster than running time on the computer.

For Herr Cutter's barber shop, the simulation clock records the amount of simulated time (in minutes) that has elapsed so far since the shop opened at 8:00 A.M. A precise simulation then would start anew for each successive day of simulated operation of the shop. (The next section describes a simplifying assumption that Fritz makes at this point.) A small amount of running time can simulate years of operation.

The key information that defines the current status of the system is called the **state of the system.** For Herr Cutter's barber shop (the system in this case), the state of the system is

$$N(t) = \text{Number of customers in the barber shop at time } t$$

The computer program for the simulation typically records the cumulative amount of time that the system spends in each state, as well as other measures of performance (e.g., the waiting times of the customers).

For queueing systems such as this barber shop, the key events are the arrivals of customers and the completions of service (haircuts). The preceding subsection describes how these events are randomly generated in a computer simulation by generating random observations from the distributions of interarrival times and service times.

Both of these types of events change the state of the system. The method used to adjust the state accordingly is to

$$\text{Reset} \quad N(t) = \begin{cases} N(t) + 1 & \text{if an arrival occurs at time } t \\ N(t) - 1 & \text{if a service completion occurs at time } t \end{cases}$$

Whenever a customer arrives or a haircut is completed, the computer program adjusts the number of customers in the barber shop in this way.

The main procedure for advancing the time on the simulation clock is called **next-event time advance.** Here is how it works.

The Next-Event Time-Advance Procedure

1. Observe the current time t on the simulation clock and the randomly generated times of the next occurrence of each event type that can occur next. Determine which event will occur first.
2. Advance the time on the simulation clock to the time of this next event.
3. Update the system by determining its new state as a result of this event and by randomly generating the time until the next occurrence of any event type that can occur from this state (if not previously generated). Also record desired information about the performance of the system. Then return to step 1.

This process continues until the computer simulation has run as long as desired.

Illustrating the Computer Simulation Process

The Excel spreadsheet in Figure 12.7 shows a computer simulation of the operation of Herr Cutter's barber shop (without an associate) over a period when 100 customers arrive. The pertinent data regarding each customer is recorded on a single row of the spreadsheet (where the rows for customers 11–95 are hidden). All the times are in minutes. As indicated by the equations at the bottom of the figure, the inverse transformation method is being used to generate random observations for the interarrival times and service times in columns C and F. These two times then enable calculating the other pertinent times for each customer in order. Column H records the waiting time *before* the haircut begins for each customer and column I gives the total waiting time in the barber shop (including the haircut) for the customer.

The next-event time-advance procedure is used to carry out this simulation. The procedure focuses on the two key types of events—arrivals and service completions—being recorded in columns D and G, and then moves chronologically through these events. To start, $t = 0$ and $N(t) = 0$ (no customers are in the shop at the instant it opens). Since no service completions can occur without any customers there, the only type of event that can occur next is a customer arrival, so the time on the simulation clock is advanced next to $t = 0.5$ minute (cell D16), the time when the first customer arrives. Subsequently, the clock is moved ahead to $t = 22.3$ minutes (cell G16 indicates a service completion for this customer), then to $t = 46.0$ (arrival of customer 2 according to cell D17), then to $t = 48.6$ and then to $t = 50.1$ (arrival of customers 3 and 4 according to cells D18 and D19, respectively), then to $t = 67.9$ (service completion for customer 2 according to cell G17), and so forth.

The next-event time-advance procedure moves chronologically through the arrivals and service completions as they occur.

Figure 12.8 shows the evolution of the state of this system (the number of customers in the barber shop) throughout the first 100 minutes of simulated operation. Thus, the number of customers in the barber shop fluctuates between 0 and 3 during this period.

Estimating Measures of Performance

The purpose of performing a computer simulation of a system is to estimate the measures of performance of the system. The most important measure of performance for Herr Cutter's barber shop (the system of interest here) is the expected waiting time of his customers before

FIGURE 12.7

A computer simulation of Herr Cutter's barber shop (as currently operated) over a period of 100 customer arrivals.

	A	B	C	D	E	F	G	H	I
1		**Herr Cutter's Barber Shop**							
2									
3				(exponential)					
4		Mean Interarrival Time		30	minutes				
5									
6				(uniform)					
7		Min Service Time		15	minutes				
8		Max Service Time		25	minutes				
9									
10		Average Time in Line (W_q)		12.8	minutes				
11		Average Time in System (W)		33.0	minutes				
12									
13				Time	Time		Time	Time	Time
14		Customer	Interarrival	of	Service	Service	Service	in	in
15		Arrival	Time	Arrival	Begins	Time	Ends	Line	System
16		1	0.5	0.5	0.5	21.9	22.3	0.0	21.9
17		2	45.6	46.0	46.0	21.9	67.9	0.0	21.9
18		3	2.6	48.6	67.9	20.8	88.8	19.4	40.2
19		4	1.5	50.1	88.8	18.9	107.7	38.7	57.6
20		5	27.6	77.7	107.7	17.2	124.9	30.0	47.2
21		6	29.2	106.9	124.9	16.3	141.2	18.0	34.3
22		7	18.6	125.5	141.2	24.6	165.8	15.7	40.3
23		8	21.8	147.4	165.8	22.7	188.6	18.5	41.2
24		9	7.4	154.8	188.6	24.3	212.9	33.8	58.1
25		10	12.1	166.9	212.9	18.4	231.3	46.0	64.4
111		96	48.8	3,132.8	3,132.8	22.2	3,155.0	0.0	22.2
112		97	12.3	3,145.1	3,155.0	25.0	3,180.0	9.9	34.9
113		98	82.7	3,227.7	3,227.7	19.0	3,246.7	0.0	19.0
114		99	4.0	3,231.8	3,246.7	20.1	3,266.8	14.9	35.0
115		100	85.2	3,317.0	3,317.0	19.5	3,336.5	0.0	19.5

Range Name	Cells
AverageTimeInLine	D10
AverageTimeInSystem	D11
InterarrivalTime	C16:C115
MaxServiceTime	D8
MeanInterarrivalTime	D4
MinServiceTime	D7
ServiceTime	F16:F115
TimeInLine	H16:H115
TimeInSystem	I16:I115
TimeOfArrival	D16:D115
TimeServiceBegins	E16:E115
TimeServiceEnds	G16:G115

	C	D
10	Average Time in Line (W_q)	=AVERAGE(TimeInLine)
11	Average Time in System (W)	=AVERAGE(TimeInSystem)

	C	D	E	F
13		Time	Time	
14	Interarrival	of	Service	Service
15	Time	Arrival	Begins	Time
16	=-MeanInterarrivalTime*LN(RAND())	=InterarrivalTime	=TimeOfArrival	=MinServiceTime+(MaxServiceTime-MinServiceTime)*RAND()
17	=-MeanInterarrivalTime*LN(RAND())	=D16+InterarrivalTime	=MAX(G16,D17)	=MinServiceTime+(MaxServiceTime-MinServiceTime)*RAND()
18	=-MeanInterarrivalTime*LN(RAND())	=D17+InterarrivalTime	=MAX(G17,D18)	=MinServiceTime+(MaxServiceTime-MinServiceTime)*RAND()
19	:	:	:	:
20	:	:	:	:

	G	H	I
13	Time	Time	Time
14	Service	in	in
15	Ends	Line	System
16	=TimeServiceBegins+ServiceTime	=TimeServiceBegins-TimeOfArrival	=TimeServiceEnds-TimeOfArrival
17	=TimeServiceBegins+ServiceTime	=TimeServiceBegins-TimeOfArrival	=TimeServiceEnds-TimeOfArrival
18	=TimeServiceBegins+ServiceTime	=TimeServiceBegins-TimeOfArrival	=TimeServiceEnds-TimeOfArrival
19	:	:	:
20	:	:	:

FIGURE 12.8

This graph shows the evolution of the number of customers in Herr Cutter's barber shop over the first 100 minutes of the computer simulation in Figure 12.7.

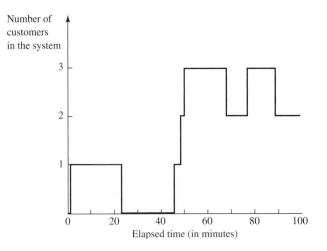

beginning a haircut. By averaging the waiting times in column H, cell D10 in Figure 12.7 provides an estimate of 12.8 minutes for this quantity. Similarly, cell D11 averages the times in column I to give an estimate of 33.0 minutes for the expected total waiting time in the shop, including the haircut. (In the notation introduced for queueing models in the preceding chapter, these expected waiting times are W_q and W, respectively.)

Various other measures of performance also could be estimated from this simulation. For example, the probability that a customer has to wait more than 20 minutes to begin a haircut is estimated by the fraction of the customers with a time greater than 20 in column H. An

The numbers in columns H and I provide estimates of various other measures of performance as well.

estimate of the expected number of customers in the system (including receiving a haircut) is estimated by summing the numbers in column I and dividing by the total simulated time. The expected number of customers waiting to begin a haircut is estimated from column H in the same way.

The probability distribution of the number of customers in the system also might be of interest. As suggested by Figure 12.8, the probability of any particular number of customers in the system can be estimated by the fraction of time that the simulated system spends in that state.

The computer simulation displayed in Figure 12.7 is a rather short one, so it only provides fairly rough estimates of the desired measures of performance. To obtain relatively precise estimates, a computer simulation might run for some years of simulated operation (as we will demonstrate in the next section).

Simulating the Barber Shop with an Associate

Figures 12.7 and 12.8 have illustrated the simulation of the barber shop under its current mode of operation (*without* an associate). In most respects, the procedure for the shop *with* an associate is the same. Each time an arrival occurs (or the shop opens), the next interarrival time needs to be randomly generated. Similarly, each time a customer enters service (begins a haircut), this service time needs to be randomly generated.

When adding a second server, the simulation procedure remains the same except for needing to also keep track of service completions by the second server.

The only difference comes when the next-event time-advance procedure is determining which event occurs next. Instead of just two possibilities for this next event, there now are the following three:

1. A departure because Herr Cutter completes a haircut.
2. A departure because the associate completes a haircut.
3. An arrival.

However, other than needing to separately keep track of the time until the next departure of each of these two kinds, the simulation proceeds in basically the same way.

The next section presents the results of several lengthy computer simulations of the barber shop, both with and without an associate.

Review
Questions

1. What is the decision facing Herr Cutter?
2. What are the two rules of thumb that will help guide this decision?
3. Which probability distributions need to be estimated in order to apply computer simulation to this case study?
4. What is a simulation clock?
5. What is the name of the main procedure used to advance the time on the simulation clock?
6. What is the state of the system for Herr Cutter's barber shop?
7. What is the basic difference in the procedure between simulating Herr Cutter's barber shop without an associate and with an associate?

12.3 ANALYSIS OF THE CASE STUDY

Recall that the decision facing Herr Cutter is whether to add an associate to work with him as a second barber in his shop. The basic issue is whether he would still be able to at least maintain his current income level if he were to add the associate.

The Financial Factors

Here are the main financial factors (converted from German currency to American dollars) for addressing this decision.

$$\text{Revenue} = \$15 \text{ per haircut}$$

$$\text{Average tip} = \$2 \text{ per haircut}$$

$$\text{Cost of maintaining the shop} = \$50 \text{ per working day}$$
(with or without an associate)

$$\text{Salary of an associate} = \$120 \text{ per working day}$$

$$\text{Commission for an associate} = \$5 \text{ per haircut given by the associate}$$

In addition to his salary and commission, the associate would keep his own tips. Otherwise, the revenue would go to Herr Cutter.

The shop opens at 8:00 A.M. and closes its door to new customers at 5:00 P.M., so it admits customers for nine hours. Herr Cutter and any associate eat their sack lunches and take other breaks only during times when no customers are waiting. Thus, any customer who wants to enter the shop at any time during the nine hours is welcomed by a barber on duty.

Analysis of Continuing without an Associate

As indicated in the preceding section, the current distribution of interarrival times has a mean of 30 minutes. Thus, Herr Cutter is averaging two customers per hour, or an average of 18 customers per working day. Therefore, after subtracting the cost of maintaining the shop, his average net income per working day is

$$\text{Net daily income} = (\$15 + \$2)(18 \text{ customers}) - \$50$$
$$= \$306 - \$50$$
$$= \$256$$

Herr Cutter's nephew Fritz is helping his uncle analyze his decision by using the Queueing Simulator in your MS Courseware to run computer simulations of the barber shop. This routine is specifically designed to efficiently run long simulations for a variety of queueing systems. It operates basically as illustrated in Figure 12.7, but with more flexibility as to the type of system and with far more output, as outlined below.

The Queueing Simulator is available in one of this chapter's Excel files.

Features of the Queueing Simulator

1. Can run computer simulations of various kinds of basic queueing systems described in Section 11.1.
2. Can have any number of servers up to a maximum of 25.

3. Can use any of the following probability distributions for either interarrival times or service times:
   a. Constant time (also called the degenerate distribution).
   b. Exponential distribution (described in Section 11.1).
   c. Translated exponential distribution (the sum of a constant time and a time from an exponential distribution).
   d. Uniform distribution.
   e. Erlang distribution (described in the supplement to Chapter 11).

4. Provides estimates of various key measures of performance described in Section 11.3 for queueing systems, namely,

L = Expected number of customers in the system, including those being served

L_q = Expected number of customers in the queue, which excludes customers being served

W = Expected waiting time in the system (includes service time) for an individual customer

W_q = Expected waiting time in the queue (excludes service time) for an individual customer

P_n = Probability of exactly n customers in the system (for $n = 0, 1, 2, \ldots, 10$)

(If you have not previously studied Chapter 11 to learn about queueing systems, you might find it helpful to see the live demonstration of a queueing system in action that is provided by the Waiting Line module in your Interactive Management Science Modules at **www.mhhe.com/hillier3e.** An offline version also is included in your MS Courseware on the CD-ROM.)

Largely to help test the validity of his simulation model (described in the preceding section), Fritz is beginning by simulating the current operation of the shop. Although Figure 12.7 already did this for roughly a week of simulated operation (100 customer arrivals), he now wishes to simulate several years of operation (100,000 arrivals).

Figure 12.9 shows the output that Fritz obtains from this computer simulation. If you wish, you can duplicate this simulation run by using the Queueing Simulator yourself. You should

FIGURE 12.9

The output obtained by using the Queueing Simulator in one of this chapter's Excel files to perform a computer simulation of Herr Cutter's barber shop (without an associate) over a period of 100,000 customer arrivals.

	A	B	C	D	E	F	G	H
1		**Queueing Simulator for Herr Cutter's Barber Shop**						
2								
3		Number of Servers	1			Point	95% Confidence Interval	
4						Estimate	Low	High
5		**Interarrival Times**			$L =$	1.358	1.332	1.385
6		Distribution	Exponential		$L_q =$	0.689	0.666	0.712
7		Mean	30		$W =$	40.582	39.983	41.180
8					$W_q =$	20.577	19.980	21.174
9								
10		**Service Times**			$P_0 =$	0.330	0.326	0.335
11		Distribution	Uniform		$P_1 =$	0.310	0.307	0.313
12		Minimum	15		$P_2 =$	0.183	0.180	0.185
13		Maximum	25		$P_3 =$	0.0942	0.0920	0.0963
14					$P_4 =$	0.0451	0.0433	0.0469
15		**Length of Simulation Run**			$P_5 =$	0.0206	0.0192	0.0220
16		Number of Arrivals	100,000		$P_6 =$	0.00950	0.00849	0.0105
17					$P_7 =$	0.00432	0.00360	0.00503
18					$P_8 =$	0.00219	0.00163	0.00274
19					$P_9 =$	0.000876	0.000540	0.00121
20		**Run Simulation**			$P_{10} =$	0.000372	0.000165	0.000579

obtain very similar results, although they will be slightly different because different random numbers are used each time.

The measures of performance in column E are the same as those described for any queueing system in Section 11.3. Column F gives the **point estimate,** the single number that is the best estimate of the measure from this simulation run. Using statistical theory, columns G and H then provide a 95 percent **confidence interval** for each measure. Thus, there is a 95 percent chance that the *true* value of the measure lies within this interval. Because the simulation run was so long (100,000 arrivals), each of these confidence intervals is quite narrow.

A confidence interval is an interval within which the true value of a measure of performance is likely to lie.

Testing the Validity of the Simulation Model

When starting a management science study that will use computer simulation, it is a good idea to first run the simulation model on a simple version of the system for which analytical results are available (if such a version exists). Comparing the results from this simulation run with the analytical results then provides a good test of the validity of the simulation model.

Since a queueing model is available for the single-server version of the system, Fritz will use its results to test the validity of his simulation model.

Fritz recalls that the $M/G/1$ queueing model presented in Section 11.5 provides some exact analytical results for the same queueing system that has been assumed for the simulation run in Figure 12.9. This queueing model uses four parameters:

λ = Mean arrival rate

$\quad$ = $\frac{1}{30}$ customer per minute

μ = Mean service rate

$\quad$ = $\frac{1}{20}$ customer per minute

$\rho = \dfrac{\lambda}{\mu} = \dfrac{1/30}{1/20} = \dfrac{2}{3}$

σ = Standard deviation of the distribution of service times

Because the standard deviation of the uniform distribution from 0 to 1 is $1/\sqrt{12}$, the standard deviation of the service-time distribution (the uniform distribution between 15 and 25) is

$$\sigma = \frac{10}{\sqrt{12}} = 2.887$$

After entering these values of λ, $1/\mu$, and σ, the Excel template for the $M/G/1$ model in the Chapter 11 portion of your MS Courseware yields the results shown in Figure 12.10. Note how each of these exact results for the measures of performance fall well within the corresponding 95 percent confidence interval in Figure 12.9. This provides some reassurance that the simulation model and the computer simulation are operating as intended.

To make sure that no big mistake has been made when constructing a simulation model, its results should be checked for reasonableness by someone familiar with the system being simulated.

To further test the validity of the simulation model, Fritz shows the results in column F of Figure 12.9 to Herr Cutter and asks whether these numbers seem consistent with what he has been experiencing in the barber shop. Although Herr Cutter has not been keeping such data, his impression is that the numbers seem about right. He also points out that the average waiting time of about 20 minutes before beginning a haircut is consistent with the first rule of thumb in the article in *The Barber's Journal* (described at the beginning of the preceding section).

Unfortunately, no queueing model yielding useful analytical results is available for the *two-server* queueing system that corresponds to Herr Cutter's barber shop *with* an associate. (None of the multiple-server queueing models presented in Chapter 11 allows a service-time distribution even close to the one in this barber shop.) Therefore, it will be necessary to use computer simulation to obtain good estimates of how the barber shop would perform with an associate. However, after the above testing of the validity of his simulation model, Fritz now is confident that this model will indeed provide good estimates.

Fritz does recognize that his simulation model (just like the $M/G/1$ queueing model) makes two simplifying assumptions that are only approximations of how the barber shop actually operates. (These assumptions are incorporated into the Queueing Simulator.)

FIGURE 12.10

This Excel template for the *M/G/*1 model shows the basic measures of performance for Herr Cutter's barber shop without an associate.

	A	B	C	D	E	F	G
1		**Analytical *M/G/*1 Queueing Results for Herr Cutter**					
2							
3			**Data**				**Results**
4		$\lambda =$	0.0333	(Mean arrival rate)		$L =$	1.344
5		$1/\mu =$	20	(Expected service time)		$L_q=$	0.678
6		$\sigma =$	2.887	(Standard deviation)			
7		$s =$	1	(# servers)		$W =$	40.356
8						$W_q=$	20.356
9							
10						$\rho =$	0.666
11							
12						$P_0 =$	0.334

Range Name	Cell
L	G4
Lambda	C4
L_q	G5
OneOverMu	C5
Rho	G10
s	C7
Sigma	C6
W	G7
W_q	G8

	F	G
4	$L =$	=L_q+Rho
5	$L_q=$	=((Lambda^2)*(Sigma^2)+(Rho^2))/(2*(1-Rho))
6		
7	$W =$	=W_q+OneOverMu
8	$W_q=$	=L_q/Lambda
9		
10	$\rho =$	=Lambda*OneOverMu
11		
12	$P_0=$	=1-Rho

Simplifying Assumptions

1. The system (barber shop) has an *infinite queue,* so arriving customers always enter the system regardless of how many customers already are there. (In reality, Herr Cutter has found that arriving customers normally do not stay if three customers already are there waiting to begin a haircut, so he now only provides three chairs for waiting customers.)

2. Once started, the system operates continually without ever closing and reopening. (In reality, the barber shop closes its door at 5:00 P.M. each working day and reopens at 8:00 A.M. the next day.)

To evaluate the effect of the first assumption, Fritz notes that the results in Figure 12.9 estimate that

$$P_0 + P_1 + P_2 + P_3 + P_4 = 0.330 + 0.310 + 0.183 + 0.094 + 0.045$$
$$= 0.962$$

Thus, the simulation run exceeds the actual maximum of four customers in the barber shop (one receiving a haircut and three waiting to begin) less than 4 percent of the time. The effect of exceeding the actual maximum so infrequently is to slightly inflate the estimates of L, L_q, W, and W_q above their true values for the barber shop. Thus, the numbers in Figure 12.9 provide conservative estimates (which are preferable to overly optimistic estimates). If Herr Cutter does add an associate, he would provide three additional chairs for waiting customers. There also would be less waiting to begin a haircut, so having arriving customers not stay would become very unusual. Therefore, the first simplifying assumption seems very reasonable for simulating the barber shop with an associate.

The effect of the second simplifying assumption also is to slightly inflate the estimates of L, L_q, W, and W_q above their true values. The reason is that the barber shop begins empty each morning and then gradually builds up to a steady-state condition, whereas the simulation model has the shop operating in a steady-state condition for all but the very beginning of the simulation run. Fortunately, adding an associate would tend to keep the number of customers in the shop down to minimal levels, even in a steady-state condition (which would be nearly

Simplifying assumptions that provide conservative estimates are preferable to those that lead to overly optimistic estimates.

reached early in the day). Therefore, the estimation errors from using this assumption to simulate the shop with an associate should be reasonably small.

By obtaining a more expensive computer simulation package and devoting additional preparation time, Fritz would be able to closely simulate the actual operation of the barber shop without making these two approximations. A key advantage of computer simulation is the ability to incorporate as many realistic features into the model as desired.

However, just as with the mathematical model for any other management science technique, there always is a trade-off between the amount of realism incorporated into a model and the ease with which the model can be used. A simulation model does not need to be a completely realistic representation of the real system. Many simulation models err on the side of being overly realistic rather than overly idealistic. An overly realistic model includes unimportant details that do not significantly affect the estimates obtained from the simulation runs. Such a model often is very difficult to debug, and may never be completely debugged. It also is likely to require a great deal of programming and computer time to obtain a small amount of information. The goal should be to incorporate only the important features of the system into the model in order to generate reasonably accurate information that will enable management to make well-informed decisions in a timely fashion.

Fritz feels that his current simulation model meets this goal.

Although some software packages enable adding many realistic features into a simulation model, unimportant details that make the model overly complex should be avoided.

Analysis of the Option of Adding an Associate

As described near the beginning of Section 12.2, Herr Cutter and his nephew Fritz have agreed on a plan for analyzing the option of adding an associate. They assume that the probability distribution of service times (the times required to give a haircut) for the associate would be the same as for Herr Cutter. Based on the second rule of thumb given in Section 12.2, they also are assuming that adding the associate would (1) reduce the average waiting time before a haircut begins to less than 10 minutes and (2) then gradually attract new business until this average waiting time reaches about 10 minutes. The level of business (say, the average number of customers per day) determines the mean of the probability distribution of interarrival times. Therefore, a number of computer simulations will be run with different means of this distribution to determine which mean would result in an average waiting time of about 10 minutes. Given the corresponding level of business, a financial analysis can then be conducted.

The level of business is expected to increase to the point where the average waiting time to begin a haircut is 10 minutes, so computer simulations will be run to estimate this level of business.

The current mean (without an associate) of the distribution of interarrival times is 30 minutes. Therefore, proceeding by trial and error, Fritz tries the series of means shown in the first column of Table 12.2. To quickly hone in on the neighborhood for the right mean, he uses the Queueing Simulator to run computer simulations of only moderate length, namely, 10,000 arrivals each (roughly half a year of simulated operation). The point estimates of W_q (the average waiting time until a haircut begins) in the second column indicate that the mean that gives a true value of W_q of 10 minutes should be somewhere close to 14.3 minutes. The 95 percent confidence intervals for W_q in the rightmost column further suggest that this mean should be within about half a minute of 14.3 minutes.

To check this further, Fritz next does a long simulation run (100,000 arrivals) with a mean of 14.3 minutes for the interarrival-time distribution. The complete results for all the measures of performance are shown in Figure 12.11. The point estimate of W_q (and most of the 95 percent confidence interval for W_q) now is slightly over 10. However, Fritz also recalls that the

TABLE 12.2
The Estimates of W_q Obtained by Using the Queueing Simulator to Simulate Herr Cutter's Barber Shop with an Associate for 10,000 Arrivals for Different Means of the Distribution of Interarrival Times

Mean of Interarrival Times	Point Estimate of W_q	95 Percent Confidence Interval for W_q
20 minutes	3.33 minutes	3.05 to 3.61 minutes
15 minutes	8.10 minutes	6.98 to 9.22 minutes
14 minutes	10.80 minutes	9.51 to 12.08 minutes
14.2 minutes	9.83 minutes	8.83 to 10.84 minutes
14.3 minutes	9.91 minutes	8.76 to 11.05 minutes

FIGURE 12.11

The results obtained by using the Queueing Simulator to perform a computer simulation of Herr Cutter's barber shop with an associate over a period of 100,000 customer arrivals.

	A	B	C	D	E	F	G	H
1		**Queueing Simulator for Herr Cutter's Barber Shop with an Associate**						
2								
3		Number of Servers	2			Point	95% Confidence Interval	
4						Estimate	Low	High
5		**Interarrival Times**			$L =$	2.126	2.090	2.163
6		Distribution	Exponential		$L_q =$	0.719	0.689	0.748
7		Mean	14.3		$W =$	30.212	29.833	30.591
8					$W_q =$	10.211	9.834	10.588
9								
10		**Service Times**			$P_0 =$	0.163	0.160	0.166
11		Distribution	Uniform		$P_1 =$	0.266	0.262	0.270
12		Minimum	15		$P_2 =$	0.233	0.230	0.235
13		Maximum	25		$P_3 =$	0.1541	0.1518	0.1564
14					$P_4 =$	0.0877	0.0855	0.0898
15		**Length of Simulation Run**			$P_5 =$	0.0467	0.0448	0.0487
16		Number of Arrivals	100,000		$P_6 =$	0.02417	0.02264	0.0257
17					$P_7 =$	0.01282	0.01162	0.01401
18					$P_8 =$	0.00634	0.00546	0.00722
19		**Run Simulation**			$P_9 =$	0.003208	0.002530	0.00389
20					$P_{10} =$	0.001546	0.001076	0.002017

two simplifying assumptions discussed in the preceding subsection cause this estimate to slightly overstate the true value of W_q for the barber shop. Therefore, he concludes that 14.3 minutes is the best available estimate of the mean that would result in an average waiting time of about 10 minutes.

Fritz realizes that he could spend more time running long computer simulations with means slightly different from 14.3 minutes in order to pin down this estimate even better. However, he already knows from the confidence intervals in Table 12.2 that 14.3 minutes is at least very close. Furthermore, given the slight inaccuracies known to be in the simulation model due to the two simplifying assumptions, there is no point in trying to obtain an estimate of the mean that is more precise than the model is. This would only give a false sense of accuracy. He is content that 14.3 minutes provide a very adequate and conservative estimate of the mean for purposes of analysis.

A conservative estimate is that the level of business will increase to the point where customers are arriving at an average of one every 14.3 minutes.

Based on this estimate, Fritz concludes that having his uncle add an associate should gradually increase the level of business to around the point where

$$\text{Average interarrival time} = 14.3 \text{ minutes}$$

which would yield

$$\text{Mean arrival rate} = \frac{60}{14.3} \text{ customers per hour}$$

$$= 4.2 \text{ customers per hour}$$

$$= 4.2(9) \text{ customers per day}$$

$$= 37.8 \text{ customers per day}$$

This level of business would be more than double the current average of 18 customers per day for the shop. Herr Cutter would plan to divide the customers equally with the associate, so each would average 18.9 customers per day.

Therefore, using the cost factors given at the beginning of this section, Herr Cutter's average net income per working day would become

$$\text{Net daily income} = 37.8(\$15) \quad \text{(shop revenue)}$$

$$+ 18.9(\$2) \quad \text{(his tips)}$$

$$-\$50 \qquad \text{(shop maintenance)}$$

$$-\$120 \qquad \text{(associate's salary)}$$

$$-18.9(\$5) \qquad \text{(associate's commission)}$$

$$= \$567 + \$37.80 - \$50 - \$120 - \$94.50$$

$$= \$340.30$$

This compares with Herr Cutter's current net daily income of $256. Thus, it is estimated that the change in his net daily income from adding an associate would eventually become

$$\text{Change in net daily income} = \$340.30 - \$256$$

$$= \$84.30$$

Thus, he actually would increase his income significantly.

When presenting this analysis to his uncle, Fritz emphasizes that this $84.30 figure is just an *estimate* of what will happen *after* the level of business gradually increases to its new level. It may take awhile, even a year or two, to reach this new level. Meanwhile, Herr Cutter's income may start off less than it has been before gradually increasing. Furthermore, the optimistic conclusion of a substantial increase in income eventually is based largely on the rather shaky premise that the second rule of thumb in the article in *The Barber's Journal* will prove to be valid and applicable to his shop. This premise leads to an estimate that his level of business would more than double eventually. Achieving this big increase in business would seem realistic only if the associate is able to bring a considerable number of customers with him from his current shop and then the two of them are able to attract many additional new customers.

> This estimate of increased income needs to be interpreted carefully.

Herr Cutter feels confident that they can accomplish this. This associate was highly recommended by his friend. Furthermore, he feels that his own skill as a barber already would have attracted many new customers if he didn't already have as much business as he could handle alone. In this growing city, the opportunity is there. He also likes the fact that adding an associate would enable him to improve the level of service for his current loyal clientele by substantially decreasing their average waiting time before beginning a haircut. Finally, he also sees many personal advantages to having a good associate that cannot be measured in monetary terms. Therefore, he wouldn't mind a temporary decrease in income as long as he probably would at least equal his current income level in a year or two. Actually increasing his income would be a pleasant bonus.

> Herr Cutter decides to hire the associate.

On these grounds, Herr Cutter decides to hire the associate. He also thanks his nephew for the invaluable help that Fritz's computer simulations provided him in making his decision.

Review Questions

1. What did Fritz simulate in his first simulation run? For what purpose?
2. What are the two types of estimates of a measure of performance obtained by the Queueing Simulator?
3. What were the two ways with which Fritz tested the validity of his simulation model?
4. Does Fritz's simulation model make any simplifying assumptions? Is it necessary for a simulation model to be a completely realistic representation of the real system?
5. Does Fritz's analysis estimate that Herr Cutter's income will eventually increase or decrease (compared to its current level) if he adds an associate?

12.4 OUTLINE OF A MAJOR COMPUTER SIMULATION STUDY

Thus far, this chapter has focused mainly on the *process* of performing a computer simulation and its illustration by a case study. We now place this material into broader perspective by briefly outlining all the typical steps involved when a management science team performs a

Call centers have been one of the fastest-growing industries worldwide for many years. In the United States alone, many hundreds of thousands of businesses use call centers located around the world to enable customers to place an order simply by placing a free telephone call to an 800 number.

The 800-network market is a lucrative one for telecommunication companies, so they are happy to sell the needed technology to their business customers and then to help these customers design efficient call centers. AT&T was the pioneer in developing and marketing this service to its customers. Its approach was to develop a highly flexible and sophisticated computer simulation model, called the *Call Processing Simulator (CAPS)*, that enables its customers to study various scenarios for how to design and operate their call centers.

CAPS contains four modules. The *call generation module* generates incoming calls arriving randomly, with mean arrival rates varying over the course of the day. The *network module* simulates how an incoming call can be answered immediately or placed on hold or receive a busy signal, where the latter cases can result in either the caller persevering until getting through or giving up and taking his or her business elsewhere. The *automatic call distribution module* simulates how AT&T's automatic call distribution system equitably distributes calls to available agents. The *call service module* simulates agents serving calls and then doing any necessary follow-up work.

The development and refinement of CAPS over a period of many years carefully followed the steps of a major computer simulation study described in this section. This meticulous approach has paid off big time for AT&T. The company has completed as many as 2,000 CAPS studies per year for its business customers, helping it increase, protect, and regain more than $1 billion in an $8 billion 800-network market. This also has generated more than $750 million in annual profit for AT&T's business customers who received CAPS studies.

Source: A. J. Brigandi, D. R. Dargon, M. J. Sheehan, and T. Spencer III, "AT&T's Call Processing Simulator (CAPS) Operational Design for Inbound Call Centers," *Interfaces* 24, no. 1 (January–February 1994), pp.6–28.

major study that is based on applying computer simulation. (Nearly the same steps also apply when the study is applying other management science techniques instead.)

Step 1: Formulate the Problem and Plan the Study

The management science team needs to begin by meeting with management to address the following kinds of questions.

These are key questions that management should answer to initiate any management science study.

1. What is the problem that management wants studied?
2. What are the overall objectives for the study?
3. What specific issues should be addressed?
4. What kinds of alternative system configurations should be considered?
5. What measures of performance of the system are of interest to management?
6. What are the time constraints for performing the study?

In addition, the team needs to meet with engineers and operational personnel to learn the details of just how the system would operate. (The team generally will also include one or more members with a firsthand knowledge of the system.)

Step 2: Collect the Data and Formulate the Simulation Model

The types of data needed depend on the nature of the system to be simulated. For Herr Cutter's barber shop, the key pieces of data were the distribution of *interarrival times* and the distribution of *service times* (times needed to give a haircut). For most other cases as well, it is the *probability distributions* of the relevant quantities that are needed. Generally, it will only be possible to *estimate* these distributions, but it is important to do so. In order to generate representative scenarios of how a system will perform, it is essential for a computer simulation to generate *random observations* from these distributions rather than simply using averages.

Computer simulations should use probability distributions of the relevant quantities rather than averages.

Step 3: Check the Accuracy of the Simulation Model

Before constructing a computer program, the management science team should engage the people most intimately familiar with how the system will operate in checking the accuracy of the simulation model. This often is done by performing a structured walk-through of the conceptual model, using an overhead projector, before an audience of all the key people. Typically at such meetings, several erroneous model assumptions will be discovered and corrected, a few new assumptions will be added, and some issues will be resolved about how much detail is needed in the various parts of the model.

Step 4: Select the Software and Construct a Computer Program

There are four major classes of software used for computer simulations. One is *spreadsheet software.* Section 12.1 described how Excel is able to perform some basic computer simulations on a spreadsheet. In addition, some excellent Excel add-ins now are available to enhance this kind of spreadsheet modeling. Chapter 13 focuses on the use of one of these add-ins in your MS Courseware.

The other three classes of software for computer simulations are intended for more extensive applications where it is no longer convenient to use spreadsheet software. One such class is a *general-purpose programming language,* such as C, FORTRAN, PASCAL, BASIC, and so on. Such languages (and their predecessors) often were used in the early history of the field because of their great flexibility for programming any sort of simulation. However, because of the considerable programming time required, they are not used nearly as much now.

The third class is a **general-purpose simulation language.** These languages provide many of the features needed to program a simulation model, and so may reduce the required programming time substantially. They also provide a natural framework for simulation modeling. Although less flexible than a general-purpose programming language, they are capable of programming almost any kind of simulation model. However, some degree of expertise in the language is needed.

The fourth class consists of **applications-oriented simulators** (or just **simulators** for short). Each of these simulators is designed for simulating fairly specific types of systems, such as certain types of manufacturing, computer, and communications systems. Their *goal* is to be able to construct a simulation "program" by the use of menus and graphics, without the need for programming. They are relatively easy to learn and have modeling constructs closely related to the system of interest.

Some simulation software includes **animation** capabilities for displaying computer simulations in action. In an animation, key elements of a system are represented in a computer display by icons that change shape, color, or position when there is a change in the state of the simulation system. (One example of an animation of a computer simulation of a queueing system is provided by the Waiting Line module in your Interactive Management Science Modules at **www.mhhe.com/hillier3e** or on the CD-ROM.) The major reason for the popularity of animation is its ability to communicate the essence of a simulation model (or of a computer simulation run) to managers and other key personnel.

Step 5: Test the Validity of the Simulation Model

After the computer program has been constructed and debugged, the next key step is to test whether the simulation model incorporated into the program is providing valid results for the system it is representing. Specifically, will the measures of performance for the real system be closely approximated by the values of these measures generated by the simulation model?

In some cases, a mathematical model may be available to provide results for a simple version of the system. If so, these results also should be compared with the simulation results.

For example, in the case study, the barber shop currently is in operation with Herr Cutter as the only barber. Therefore, as described in Section 12.3 (see the subsection entitled "Testing the Validity of the Simulation Model"), Fritz compared the results from an applicable queueing model with a simulation of this current version of the barber shop.

When no real data are available to compare with simulation results, one possibility is to conduct a *field test* to collect such data. This would involve constructing a small prototype of some version of the proposed system and placing it into operation.

General-purpose simulation languages often are used for large computer simulation studies.

Animation capabilities for displaying computer simulations in action are very useful for communicating the essence of a simulation model to managers and other key personnel.

A field test of a small prototype of the proposed system is sometimes used to collect real data to compare with the simulation results and to fine-tune the design.

Another useful validation test is to have knowledgeable operational personnel check the credibility of how the simulation results change as the configuration of the simulated system is changed. Watching animations of simulation runs also is a useful way of checking the validity of the simulation model.

Step 6: Plan the Simulations to Be Performed

At this point, you need to begin making decisions as to which system configurations to simulate. This often is an evolutionary process, where the initial results for a range of configurations help you to hone in on which specific configurations warrant detailed investigation.

Decisions also need to be made now on such issues as the lengths of simulation runs. Keep in mind that computer simulation does not produce *exact* values for the measures of performance of a system. Instead, each simulation run can be viewed as a *statistical experiment* that is generating *statistical observations* of the performance of the simulated system. These observations are used to produce *statistical estimates* of the measures of performance. Increasing the length of a run increases the precision of these estimates.

The statistical theory for designing statistical experiments conducted through computer simulation is little different than for experiments conducted by directly observing the performance of a physical system. Therefore, the services of a professional statistician (or at least an experienced simulation analyst with a strong statistical background) can be invaluable at this step.

Each simulation run generates statistical observations of the performance of the simulated system, so statistical theory should guide the planning of the runs.

Step 7: Conduct the Simulation Runs and Analyze the Results

The output from the simulation runs now provides statistical estimates of the desired measures of performance for each system configuration of interest. In addition to a *point estimate* of each measure, a *confidence interval* normally should be obtained to indicate the range of likely values of the measure (just as was done for the case study).

These results might immediately indicate that one system configuration is clearly superior to the others. More often, they will identify the few strong candidates to be the best one. In the latter case, some longer simulation runs would be conducted to better compare these candidates. Additional runs also might be used to fine-tune the details of what appears to be the best configuration.

After identifying the few best system configurations, longer simulation runs should be used to select the single best one and to fine-tune its design.

Step 8: Present Recommendations to Management

After completing its analysis, the management science team needs to present its recommendations to management. This usually would be done through both a written report and a formal oral presentation to the managers responsible for making the decisions regarding the system under study.

The report and presentation should summarize how the study was conducted, including documentation of the validation of the simulation model. A demonstration of the *animation* of a simulation run might be included to better convey the simulation process and add credibility. Numerical results that provide the rationale for the recommendations need to be included.

Management usually involves the management science team further in the initial implementation of the new system, including the indoctrination of the affected personnel.

Both the written report and the oral presentation should highlight the recommendations and the rationale for those recommendations.

Review Questions

1. When beginning a computer simulation study, with whom should a management science team meet to address some key questions and then to learn the details of how the system would operate?
2. Who should the team engage to help check the accuracy of the simulation model?
3. What is the difference between a general-purpose simulation language and an applications-oriented simulator?
4. When using animation to display a computer simulation in action, how are the key elements of the system represented?
5. What is the specific question being addressed when testing the validity of a simulation model?
6. A simulation run can be viewed as what kind of statistical experiment?
7. What kinds of estimates are obtained from simulation runs?
8. What are the two ways in which a management science team usually presents its recommendations to management?

12.5 Summary

Computer simulation is one of the most popular management science techniques because it is such a flexible, powerful, and intuitive tool. It involves using a computer to *imitate* (simulate) the operation of an entire process or system. For a system that evolves over time according to one or more probability distributions, random observations are generated from these distributions to generate the various events that occur in the simulated system over time. This provides a relatively quick way of investigating how well a proposed system configuration would perform without incurring the great expense of actually constructing and operating the system. Therefore, many alternative system configurations can be investigated and compared in advance before choosing the one to use.

Herr Cutter's barber shop provides a case study of how computer simulation was able to provide the needed information to decide whether to change this stochastic system by adding a second barber. Like so many others, this stochastic system is a *queueing system,* but one that is too complicated to be analyzed solely by using queueing models.

This case study also illustrates the building blocks of a *simulation model* that represents the system to be simulated and describes how the simulation will be performed. One key building block is a *simulation clock,* which is the variable in the computer program that records the amount of simulated time that has elapsed so far. The *next-event time-advance procedure* advances the time on the simulation clock by repeatedly moving from the current event to the next event that will occur in the simulated system.

In a matter of seconds or minutes, a computer simulation can simulate even years of operation of a typical system. Each simulation run generates a series of statistical observations about the performance of the system over the period of time simulated. These observations then are used to estimate the interesting measures of performance of the system. Both a *point estimate* and a *confidence interval* can be obtained for each measure.

Some computer simulation studies can be done relatively quickly by a single individual, who might be the manager concerned with the problem. For a more extensive study, however, the manager might want to assign a staff member, or even a full-fledged management science team, to the project. A major management science study based on computer simulation requires a series of important steps before the team is ready to obtain results from simulation runs. A series of questions must be addressed to management to properly define the problem from their viewpoint. Collecting good data generally is a difficult and time-consuming process. Another big task is formulating the simulation model, checking its accuracy, and then testing the validity of the model for closely approximating the system being simulated. One of the team's most important decisions is the choice of the software to be used. Several excellent *general-purpose simulation languages* are available. *Simulators* designed for simulating rather specific types of systems also have come on the market. Most simulation software vendors also now offer a version of their software with *animation* capabilities. Animation is very useful for illustrating the results of computer simulation for managers and other key personnel, which can add much credibility to the study.

Even after the computer program is ready to go, the management science team needs to design the statistical experiments to be conducted through computer simulation. Then the simulation runs can be conducted and the results analyzed. Finally, the team usually needs to both prepare a written report and make a formal oral presentation to present its recommendations to management.

Glossary

animation A computer display with icons that shows what is happening in a computer simulation. (Section 12.4), 501

applications-oriented simulator A software package designed for simulating a fairly specific type of stochastic system. (Section 12.4), 501

confidence interval An interval within which the true value of a measure of performance is likely to lie. (Section 12.3), 495

general-purpose simulation language A general-purpose language for programming almost any kind of simulation model. (Section 12.4), 501

inverse transformation method A method for generating random observations from a probability distribution. (Section 12.1), 483

next-event time advance A procedure for advancing the time on the simulation clock by repeatedly moving from the current event to the next event that will occur in the simulated system. (Section 12.2), 490

point estimate The single number that provides the best estimate of a measure of performance. (Section 12.3), 495

random number A random observation from the uniform distribution over the interval from 0 to 1. (Section 12.1), 475

simulation clock A variable in the computer program that records how much simulated time has elapsed so far. (Section 12.2), 489

simulation model A representation of the system to be simulated that also describes how the simulation will be performed. (Section 12.2), 489

simulator The common short name for *applications-oriented simulator* (defined on page 503). (Section 12.4), 501

state of the system The key information that defines the current status of the system. (Section 12.2), 489

stochastic system A system that evolves over time according to one or more probability distributions. (Section 12.1), 474

Learning Aids for This Chapter in Your MS Courseware

Chapter 12 Excel Files:

Coin-Flipping Game Example

Heavy Duty Co. Examples (3)

Herr Cutter's Barber Shop Case Study

Queueing Simulator

Template for M/G/1 Queueing Model

Excel Add-ins:

Crystal Ball (to be featured in the next chapter)

RiskSim

Routine:

Queueing Simulator (in an Excel file)

Interactive Management Science Modules:

Waiting Line Module

Supplement to This Chapter on the CD-ROM:

The Inverse Transformation Method for Generating Random Observations

Solved Problem (See the CD-ROM for the Solution)

12.S1. Estimating the Cost of Insurance Claims

The employees of General Manufacturing Corp. receive health insurance through a group plan issued by Wellnet. During the past year, 40 percent of the employees did not file any health insurance claims, 40 percent filed only a small claim, and 20 percent filed a large claim. The small claims were spread uniformly between 0 and $2,000, whereas the large claims were spread uniformly between $2,000 and $20,000.

On the basis of this experience, Wellnet now is negotiating the corporation's premium payment per employee for the upcoming year. You are a management science analyst for the insurance carrier, and you have been assigned the task of estimating the average cost of insurance coverage for the corporation's employees.

a. Use the random numbers 0.4071, 0.5228, 0.8185, 0.5802, and 0.0193 to simulate whether each of five employees files no claim, a small claim, or a large claim. Then use the random numbers 0.9823, 0.0188, 0.8771, 0.9872, and 0.4129 to simulate the size of the claim (including zero if no claim was filed). Calculate the average of these claims to estimate the mean of the overall distribution of the size of employees' health insurance claims.

b. Formulate and apply a spreadsheet model to simulate the cost for 300 employees' health insurance claims. Calculate the average of these random observations.

c. The true mean of the overall probability distribution of the size of an employee's health insurance claim is $2,600. Compare the estimates of this mean obtained in parts *a* and *b* with the true mean of the distribution.

Problems

The symbols to the left of some of the problems (or their parts) have the following meaning:

E*: Use Excel.
Q*: Use the Queueing Simulator.

An asterisk on the problem number indicates that at least a partial answer is given in the back of the book.

12.1.* Use the random numbers in cells C13:C18 of Figure 12.1 to generate six random observations for each of the following situations.

a. Throwing an unbiased coin.

b. A baseball pitcher who throws a strike 60 percent of the time and a ball 40 percent of the time.

c. The color of a traffic light found by a randomly arriving car when it is green 40 percent of the time, yellow 10 percent of the time, and red 50 percent of the time.

12.2. Reconsider the coin-flipping game introduced in Section 12.1 and analyzed with computer simulation in Figures 12.1, 12.2, and 12.3.

     a. Simulate one play of this game by repeatedly flipping your own coin until the game ends. Record your results in the format shown in columns B, D, E, F, and G of Figure 12.1. How much would you have won or lost if this had been a real play of the game?

E*   *b.* Revise the spreadsheet model in Figure 12.1 by using Excel's VLOOKUP function instead of the IF function to generate each simulated flip of the coin. Then perform a computer simulation of one play of the game.

E*   *c.* Use this revised spreadsheet model to generate a data table with 14 replications like Figure 12.2.

E*   *d.* Repeat part *c* with 1,000 replications (like Figure 12.3).

12.3. Each time an unbiased coin is flipped three times, the probability of getting 0, 1, 2, and 3 heads is ⅛, ⅜, ⅜, and ⅛, respectively. Therefore, with eight groups of three flips each, *on the average,* one group will yield no heads, three groups will yield one head, three groups will yield two heads, and one group will yield three heads.

     a. Using your own coin, flip it 24 times divided into eight groups of three flips each, and record the number of groups with no head, with one head, with two heads, and with three heads.

     b. Use random numbers in the order in which they are given in column C of Figure 12.4 and then in cells C5:C13 of Figure 12.5 to simulate the flips specified in part *a* and record the information indicated in part *a*.

E*   *c.* Formulate a spreadsheet model for performing a computer simulation of three flips of the coin and recording the number of heads. Perform one replication of this simulation.

E*   *d.* Use this spreadsheet to generate a data table with eight replications of the simulation. Compare this frequency distribution of the number of heads with the probability distribution of the number of heads with three flips.

E*   *e.* Repeat part *d* with 800 replications.

12.4. The weather can be considered a stochastic system, because it evolves in a probabilistic manner from one day to the next. Suppose for a certain location that this probabilistic evolution satisfies the following description:

     The probability of rain tomorrow is 0.6 if it is raining today. The probability of its being clear (no rain) tomorrow is 0.8 if it is clear today.

     a. Use the random numbers in cells C17:C26 of Figure 12.1 to simulate the evolution of the weather for 10 days, beginning the day after a clear day.

E*   *b.* Now use a computer with the random numbers generated by Excel to perform the simulation requested in part *a* on a spreadsheet.

12.5.* The game of craps requires the player to throw two dice one or more times until a decision has been reached as to whether he (or she) wins or loses. He wins if the first throw results in a sum of seven or 11 or, alternatively, if the first sum is 4, 5, 6, 8, 9, or 10 and the same sum reappears before a sum of seven has appeared. Conversely, he loses if the first throw results in a sum of 2, 3, or 12 or, alternatively, if the first sum is 4, 5, 6, 8, 9, or 10 and a sum of 7 appears before the first sum reappears.

E*   *a.* Formulate a spreadsheet model for performing a computer simulation of the throw of two dice. Perform one replication.

E*   *b.* Perform 25 replications of this simulation.

     c. Trace through these 25 replications to determine the number of times the simulated player would have won the game of craps when each play starts with the next throw after the previous play ends.

12.6. Jessica Williams, manager of kitchen appliances for the Midtown Department Store, feels that her inventory levels of stoves have been running higher than necessary. Before revising the inventory policy for stoves, she records the number sold each day over a period of 25 days, as summarized below.

Number sold	2	3	4	5	6
Number of days	4	7	8	5	1

     a. Use these data to estimate the probability distribution of daily sales.

     b. Calculate the mean of the distribution obtained in part *a*.

     c. Describe how random numbers can be used to simulate daily sales.

     d. Use the random numbers 0.4476, 0.9713, and 0.0629 to simulate daily sales over three days. Compare the average with the mean obtained in part *b*.

E*   *e.* Formulate a spreadsheet model for performing a computer simulation of the daily sales. Perform 300 replications and obtain the average of the sales over the 300 simulated days.

12.7. Generate three random observations from the uniform distribution between −10 and 40 by using the following random numbers: 0.0965, 0.5692, 0.6658.

12.8. Eddie's Bicycle Shop has a thriving business repairing bicycles. Trisha runs the reception area where customers check in their bicycles to be repaired and then later pick up their bicycles and pay their bills. She estimates that the time required to serve a customer on each visit has a uniform distribution between three minutes and eight minutes.

a. Simulate the service times for five customers by using the following five random numbers: 0.6505, 0.0740, 0.8443, 0.4975, 0.8178.

b. Calculate the average of the five service times and compare it to the mean of the service-time distribution.

E*   c. Use Excel to generate 500 random observations and calculate the average. Compare this average to the mean of the service-time distribution.

12.9.*   Reconsider Eddie's Bicycle Shop described in the preceding problem. Forty percent of the bicycles require only a minor repair. The repair time for these bicycles has a uniform distribution between zero and one hour. Sixty percent of the bicycles require a major repair. The repair time for these bicycles has a uniform distribution between one hour and two hours. You now need to estimate the mean of the overall probability distribution of the repair times for all bicycles by using the following alternative methods.

a. Use the random numbers 0.7256, 0.0817, and 0.4392 to simulate whether each of three bicycles requires minor repair or major repair. Then use the random numbers 0.2243, 0.9503, and 0.6104 to simulate the repair times of these bicycles. Calculate the average of these repair times to estimate the mean of the overall distribution of repair times.

b. Repeat part *a* with the complements of the random numbers used there, so the new random numbers are 0.2744, 0.9183, 0.5608, and then 0.7757, 0.0497, and 0.3896.

c. Combine the random observations from parts *a* and *b* and calculate the average of these six observations to estimate the mean of the overall distribution of repair times. (This is referred to as the *method of complementary random numbers.*)

d. The true mean of the overall probability distribution of repair times is 1.1. Compare the estimates of this mean obtained in parts *a, b,* and *c.* For the method that provides the closest estimate, give an intuitive explanation for why it performed so well.

E*   e. Formulate a spreadsheet model to apply the method of complementary random numbers described in part *c.* Use 600 random numbers and their complements, to generate 600 random observations of the repair times and calculate the average of these random observations. Compare this average with the true mean of the distribution.

12.10.   The William Graham Entertainment Company will be opening a new box office where customers can come to make ticket purchases in advance for the many entertainment events being held in the area. Computer simulation is being used to analyze whether to have one or two clerks on duty at the box office.

While simulating the beginning of a day at the box office, the first customer arrives five minutes after it opens and then the interarrival times for the next four customers (in order) are three minutes, nine minutes, one minute, and four minutes, after which there is a long delay until the next customer arrives. The service times for these first five customers (in order) are eight minutes, six minutes, two minutes, four minutes, and seven minutes.

a. For the alternative of a single clerk, draw a figure like Figure 12.8 that shows the evolution of the number of customers at the box office over this period.

b. Use this figure to estimate the usual measures of performance—L, L_q, W, W_q, and the P_n (as defined in Section 11.3)—for this queueing system.

c. Repeat part *a* for the alternative of two clerks.

d. Repeat part *b* for the alternative of two clerks.

12.11.   The Rustbelt Manufacturing Company employs a maintenance crew to repair its machines as needed. Management now wants a computer simulation study done to analyze what the size of the crew should be, where the crew sizes under consideration are two, three, and four. The time required by the crew to repair a machine has a uniform distribution over the interval from zero to twice the mean, where the mean depends on the crew size. The mean is four hours with two crew members, three hours with three crew members, and two hours with four crew members. The time between breakdowns of some machine has an exponential distribution with a mean of five hours. When a machine breaks down and so requires repair, management wants its average waiting time before repair begins to be no more than three hours. Management also wants the crew size to be no larger than necessary to achieve this.

a. Develop a simulation model for this problem by describing its six basic building blocks listed in Section 12.2 as they would be applied to this situation.

E*   b. Formulate a spreadsheet model to perform a computer simulation to estimate the average waiting time before repair begins. Perform this simulation over a period of 100 breakdowns for each of the three crew sizes under consideration. What do these results suggest the crew size should be?

Q*   c. Use the Queueing Simulator to perform this computer simulation over 10,000 breakdowns for each of the three crew sizes.

E*   d. Use the Excel template for the *M/G/*1 queueing model in this chapter's Excel file to obtain the expected waiting time analytically for each of the three crew sizes. Which crew size should be used?

12.12.   Refer to the first 100 minutes of the computer simulation of the current operation of Herr Cutter's barber shop presented in Figure 12.7 and summarized in Figure 12.8. Now consider the alternative of adding an associate. Perform a simulation of this alternative by hand by using exactly the same interarrival times (in the same order) and exactly the same service times (in the same order) as in Figure 12.7.

a. Determine the new waiting time before beginning a haircut for each of the 5 customers who arrive in the first 100 minutes. Use these results to estimate W_q, the expected waiting time before the haircut.

b. Plot the new version of Figure 12.8 to show the evolution of the number of customers in the barber shop over these 100 minutes.

12.13. While performing a computer simulation of a single-server queueing system, the number of customers in the system is zero for the first 10 minutes, one for the next 17 minutes, two for the next 24 minutes, one for the next 15 minutes, two for the next 16 minutes, and one for the next 18 minutes. After this total of 100 minutes, the number becomes 0 again. Based on these results for the first 100 minutes, perform the following analysis (using the notation for queueing models introduced in Section 11.3).

a. Draw a figure like Figure 12.8 showing the evolution of the number of customers in the system.

b. Develop estimates of P_0, P_1, P_2, P_3.

c. Develop estimates of L and L_q.

d. Develop estimates of W and W_q.

12.14. A major banking institution, Best Bank, plans to open a new branch office in Littletown. Preliminary estimates suggest that two tellers (and teller windows) should be provided, but this decision now awaits further analysis.

Marketing surveys indicate that the new Littletown bank will attract enough business that customers requiring teller service will enter the bank at the rate of about one per minute on the average. Thus, the average time between consecutive customer arrivals is estimated to be one minute.

No parking is available near the bank, so a special parking lot for bank customers only will be provided. A parking lot attendant will be on duty to validate each customer's parking before he or she leaves the car to enter the bank. This validation process takes at least 0.5 minutes, so the *minimum* time between consecutive arrivals of customers into the bank is 0.5 minutes. The amount by which the interarrival time exceeds 0.5 minutes is estimated to have an *exponential* distribution with a mean of 0.5 minutes. Therefore, the total interarrival time has a *translated exponential* distribution with a mean of $(0.5 + 0.5) = 1.0$ minute. (A translated exponential distribution is just an exponential distribution with a constant added.)

Based on past experience in other branch offices, it is known that the time required by a teller to serve a customer will vary widely from customer to customer, but the average time is about 1.5 minutes. This experience also indicates that service time has approximately an *Erlang* distribution with a mean of 1.5 minutes and a shape parameter of $k = 4$, which provides a standard deviation of 0.75 minute (half that for an exponential distribution with the same mean).

These data suggest that two tellers should be able to keep up with the customers quite well. However, management wants to be sure that customers will not frequently encounter a long waiting line and an excessive wait before receiving service. Therefore, computer simulation will be used to study these measures of performance.

Q* a. Use the Queueing Simulator with 5,000 customer arrivals to estimate the usual measures of performance for this queueing system if two tellers are provided.

Q* b. Repeat part *a* if three tellers are provided.

Q* c. Now perform some sensitivity analysis by checking the effect if the level of business turns out to be even higher than projected. In particular, assume that the average time between customer arrivals turns out to be only 0.9 minutes (0.5 minutes plus a mean of only 0.4 minutes). Evaluate the alternatives of two tellers and three tellers under this assumption.

d. Suppose *you* were the manager of this bank. Use your computer simulation results as the basis for a managerial decision on how many tellers to provide. Justify your answer.

12.15.* Hugh's Repair Shop specializes in repairing German and Japanese cars. The shop has two mechanics. One mechanic works on only German cars and the other mechanic works on only Japanese cars. In either case, the time required to repair a car has an exponential distribution with a mean of 0.2 days. The shop's business has been steadily increasing, especially for German cars. Hugh projects that, by next year, German cars will arrive randomly to be repaired at a mean rate of four per day, so the time between arrivals will have an exponential distribution with a mean of 0.25 days. The mean arrival rate for Japanese cars is projected to be two per day, so the distribution of interarrival times will be exponential with a mean of 0.5 days.

For either kind of car, Hugh would like the average waiting time in the shop before the repair is completed to be no more than 0.5 days.

E* a. Formulate a spreadsheet model to perform a computer simulation to estimate what the average waiting time until repair is completed will be next year for either kind of car.

E* b. Perform this simulation for German cars over a period of 100 car arrivals.

E* c. Repeat part *b* for Japanese cars.

Q* d. Use the Queueing Simulator to do parts *b* and *c* with 10,000 car arrivals in each case.

Q* e. Hugh is considering hiring a second mechanic who specializes in German cars so that two such cars can be repaired simultaneously. (Only one mechanic works on any one car.) Use the Queueing Simulator with 10,000 arrivals of German cars to evaluate this option.

Q* f. Another option is to train the two current mechanics to work on either kind of car. This would increase the mean repair time by 10 percent, from 0.2 days to 0.22 days. Use the Queueing Simulator with 20,000 arrivals of cars of either kind to evaluate this option.

E* g. Because both the interarrival-time and service-time distributions are exponential, the *M/M/*1 and *M/M/s* queueing models introduced in Sections 11.5 and 11.6 can be used to evaluate all the above options analytically. Use the template for the *M/M/s* queueing model (with *s* = 1 or 2) in an Excel file for Chapter 11 to determine *W,* the expected waiting time until repair is completed for each of the cases considered in parts *b* through *f.* For each case, compare the estimate of *W* obtained by computer simulation with the analytical value. What does this say about the number of car arrivals that should be included in the computer simulation?

h. Based on the above results, which option would you select if you were Hugh? Why?

12.16. Vistaprint produces monitors and printers for computers. In the past, only some of them were inspected on a sampling basis. However, the new plan is that they all will be inspected before they are released. Under this plan, the monitors and printers will be brought to the inspection station one at a time as they are completed. For monitors, the interarrival time will have a uniform distribution between 10 and 20 minutes. For printers, the interarrival time will be a constant 15 minutes.

The inspection station has two inspectors. One inspector works on only monitors and the other one inspects only computers. In either case, the inspection time has an exponential distribution with a mean of 10 minutes.

Before beginning the new plan, management wants an evaluation made of how long the monitors and printers will be held up waiting at the inspection station.

E* a. Formulate a spreadsheet model to perform a computer simulation to estimate the average waiting times (both before beginning inspection and after completing inspection) for either the monitors or the printers.

E* b. Perform this simulation for the monitors over a period of 100 arrivals.

E* c. Repeat part *b* for the printers.

Q* d. Use the Queueing Simulator to repeat parts *b* and *c* with 10,000 arrivals in each case.

Q* e. Management is considering the option of providing new inspection equipment to the inspectors. This equipment would not change the mean time to perform an inspection but it would decrease the variability of the times. In particular, for either product, the inspection time would have an Erlang distribution with a mean of 10 minutes and shape parameter *k* = 4. Use the Queueing Simulator to repeat part *d* under this option. Compare the results with those obtained in part *d.*

12.17. Consider the case study introduced in Section 12.2. After observing the operation of the barber shop, Herr Cutter's nephew Fritz is concerned that his uncle's estimate that the time required to give a haircut has a uniform distribution between 15 and 25 minutes appears to

be a poor approximation of the actual probability distribution of haircut times. Based on the data he has gathered, Fritz's best estimate is that the actual distribution is an Erlang distribution with a mean of 20 minutes and a shape parameter of *k* = 8.

a. Repeat the simulation run that Fritz previously used to obtain Figure 12.9 (with a mean of 30 minutes for the interarrival-time distribution) except substitute this new distribution of haircut times.

b. Repeat the simulation run that Fritz previously used to obtain Figure 12.11 (with a mean of 14.3 minutes for the interarrival-time distribution) except substitute this new distribution of haircut times.

12.18. For the Dupit Corp. case study introduced in Section 11.4, the management science team was able to apply a variety of queueing models by making the following simplifying approximation. Except for the approach suggested by the vice president for engineering, the team assumed that the total time required to repair a machine (including travel time to the machine site) has an exponential distribution with a mean of two hours (¼ workday). However, the team was somewhat uncomfortable in making this assumption because the total repair times are never extremely short, as allowed by the exponential distribution. There always is some travel time and then some setup time to start the actual repair, so the total time generally is at least 40 minutes (⅟₁₂ workday).

A key advantage of computer simulation over mathematical models is that it is not necessary to make simplifying approximations like this one. For example, one of the options available in the Queueing Simulator is to use a *translated* exponential distribution, which has a certain *minimum* time and then the *additional* time has an exponential distribution with some mean. (Commercial packages for computer simulation have an even greater variety of options.)

Use computer simulation to refine the results obtained by queueing models as given by the Excel templates in the figures indicated below. Use a translated exponential distribution for the repair times where the *minimum* time is ⅟₁₂ workday and the *additional* time has an exponential distribution with a mean of ⅙ workday (80 minutes). In each case, use a run size of 25,000 arrivals and compare the point estimate obtained for W_q (the key measure of performance for this case study) with the value of W_q obtained by the queueing model.

Q* a. Figure 11.4.

Q* b. Figure 11.5.

Q* c. Figure 11.8.

Q* d. Figure 11.9.

e. What conclusion do you draw about how sensitive the results from a computer simulation of a queueing system can be to the assumption made about the probability distribution of service times?

Case 12-1

Planning Planers

This was the first time that Carl Schilling had been summoned to meet with the bigwigs in the fancy executive offices upstairs. And he hopes it will be the last time. Carl doesn't like the pressure. He has had enough pressure just dealing with all the problems he has been encountering as the foreman of the planer department on the factory floor. What a nightmare this last month has been!

Fortunately, the meeting had gone better than Carl had feared. The bigwigs actually had been quite nice. They explained that they needed to get Carl's advice on how to deal with a problem that was affecting the entire factory. The origin of the problem is that the planer department has had a difficult time keeping up with its workload. Frequently there are a number of workpieces waiting for a free planer. This waiting has seriously disrupted the production schedule for subsequent operations, thereby greatly increasing the cost of in-process inventory as well as the cost of idle equipment and resulting lost production. They understood that this problem was not Carl's fault. However, they needed to get his ideas on what changes were needed in the planer department to relieve this bottleneck. Imagine that! All these bigwigs with graduate degrees from the fanciest business schools in the country asking advice from a poor working slob like him who had barely made it through high school. He could hardly wait to tell his wife that night.

The meeting had given Carl an opportunity to get two pet peeves off his chest. One peeve is that he has been telling his boss for months that he really needs another planer, but nothing ever gets done about this. His boss just keeps telling him that the planers he already has aren't being used 100 percent of the time, so how can adding even more capacity be justified? Doesn't his boss understand about the big backlogs that build up during busy times?

Then there is the other peeve—all those peaks and valleys of work coming to his department. At times, the work just pours in and a big backlog builds up. Then there might be a long pause when not much comes in so the planers stand idle part of the time. If only those departments that are feeding castings to his department could get their act together and even out the work flow, many of his backlog problems would disappear.

Carl was pleased that the bigwigs were nodding their heads in seeming agreement as he described these problems. They really appeared to understand. And they seemed very sincere in thanking him for his good advice. Maybe something is actually going to get done this time.

Here are the details of the situation that Carl and his "bigwigs" are addressing. The company has two planers for cutting flat smooth surfaces in large castings. The planers currently are being used for two purposes. One is to form the top surface of the *platen* for large hydraulic lifts. The other is to form the mating surface of the final drive *housing* for a large piece of earth-moving equipment. The time required to perform each type of job varies somewhat, depending largely upon the number of passes that must be made. In particular, for each platen or each housing, the time required by a planer has a translated exponential distribution, where the minimum time is 10 minutes and the additional time beyond 10 minutes has an exponential distribution with a mean of 10 minutes. (A distribution of this type is one of the options in the Queueing Simulator in this chapter's Excel file.)

Castings of both types arrive one at a time to the planer department. For the castings for forming platens, the arrivals occur randomly with a mean rate of two per hour. For the castings for forming housings, the arrivals again occur randomly with a mean rate of two per hour.

Based on Carl Schilling's advice, management has asked a management scientist (you) to analyze the following two proposals for relieving the bottleneck in the planer department:

Proposal 1: Obtain one additional planer. The total incremental cost (including capital recovery cost) is estimated to be $30 per hour. (This estimate takes into account the fact that, even with an additional planer, the total running time for all the planers will remain the same.)

Proposal 2: Eliminate the variability in the interarrival times of the castings, so that the castings would arrive regularly, one every 15 minutes, alternating between platen castings and housing castings. This would require making some changes in the preceding production processes, with an incremental cost of $60 per hour.

These proposals are not mutually exclusive, so any combination can be adopted.

It is estimated that the total cost associated with castings having to wait to be processed (including processing time) is $200 per hour for each platen casting and $100 per hour for each housing casting, provided the waits are not excessive. To avoid excessive waits for either kind of casting, all the castings are processed as soon as possible on a first-come, first-served basis.

Management's objective is to minimize the expected total cost per hour.

Use computer simulation to evaluate and compare all the alternatives, including the status quo and the various combinations of proposals. Then make your recommendation to management.

Are there any other alternatives you would recommend considering?

Case 12-2

Reducing In-Process Inventory (Revisited)

Reconsider Case 11-2. The current and proposed queueing systems in this case were to be analyzed with the help of queueing models to determine how to reduce in-process inventory as much as possible. However, these same queueing systems also can be effectively analyzed by applying computer simulation with the help of the Queueing Simulator in your MS Courseware.

Use computer simulation to perform all the analysis requested in this case.

Chapter **Thirteen**

Computer Simulation with Crystal Ball

Learning objectives

After completing this chapter, you should be able to

1. Describe the role of Crystal Ball in performing computer simulations.
2. Use Crystal Ball to perform various basic computer simulations that cannot be readily performed with the standard Excel package.
3. Interpret the results generated by Crystal Ball when performing a computer simulation.
4. Use a Crystal Ball feature that enables stopping a simulation run after achieving the desired level of precision.
5. Describe the characteristics of many of the probability distributions that can be incorporated into a computer simulation when using Crystal Ball.
6. Use a Crystal Ball procedure that identifies the continuous distribution that best fits historical data.
7. Use a Crystal Ball feature that generates both a decision table and a trend chart as an aid to decision making.

The preceding chapter presented the basic concepts of computer simulation. Its emphasis throughout was on the use of spreadsheet modeling to perform basic computer simulations. Except for the use of the Queueing Simulator to deal with queueing systems, all of the computer simulations in Chapter 12 were executed using nothing more than the standard Excel package.

Although the standard Excel package has some basic simulation capabilities, an exciting development in recent years has been the development of powerful Excel add-ins that greatly extend these capabilities. An especially popular one is *Crystal Ball,* developed by Decisioneering, Inc. Decisioneering has generously provided a license to download and use the latest version of Crystal Ball (Professional Edition) on a 140-day trial basis. (The license code and download instructions are on a card included at the back of this book.) In addition to its strong functionality for performing computer simulations, this advanced version of Crystal Ball also includes two other modules. One is CB Predictor, which is used for generating forecasts from time-series data, as described and illustrated in Section 10.4. The other is OptQuest, which enhances Crystal Ball by using its output from a series of simulation runs to automatically search for an optimal solution for a simulation model.

This chapter focuses on describing and illustrating the advances in spreadsheet simulation modeling that are made possible by Crystal Ball. (Other Excel add-ins for spreadsheet simulation modeling provide some of the same functionality.) Section 13.1 begins with a case study that will be revisited in Sections 13.7–13.8. Sections 13.2–13.6 present several other examples of important business problems that can be effectively addressed by using computer simulations with Crystal Ball. Section 13.7 focuses on how to choose the right probability distributions as inputs for a computer simulation. Section 13.8 then describes how decision tables (which work much like data tables or like Solver Table in your MS Courseware) can be constructed and applied to make a decision about the problem being simulated. The supplement to this chapter on the CD-ROM discusses and illustrates the powerful optimization tool provided by OptQuest.

13.1 A CASE STUDY: FREDDIE THE NEWSBOY'S PROBLEM

This case study concerns a newsstand in a prominent downtown location of a major city. The newsstand has been there longer than most people can remember. It has always been run by a well-known character named Freddie. (Nobody seems to know his last name.) His many customers refer to him affectionately as Freddie the newsboy, even though he is considerably older than most of them.

Freddie sells a wide variety of newspapers and magazines. The most expensive of the newspapers is a large national daily called the *Financial Journal.* Our case study involves this newspaper.

Freddie's Problem

The day's copies of the *Financial Journal* are brought to the newsstand early each morning by a distributor. Any copies unsold at the end of the day are returned to the distributor the next morning. However, to encourage ordering a large number of copies, the distributor does give a small refund for unsold copies.

Here are Freddie's cost figures.

Freddie pays $1.50 per copy delivered.
Freddie charges $2.50 per copy.
Freddie's refund is $0.50 per unsold copy.

Partially because of the refund, Freddie always has taken a plentiful supply. However, he has become concerned about paying so much for copies that then have to be returned unsold, particularly since this has been occurring nearly every day. He now thinks he might be better off ordering only a minimal number of copies and saving this extra cost.

To investigate this further, Freddie has been keeping a record of his daily sales. This is what he has found.

- Freddie sells anywhere between 40 and 70 copies on any given day.
- The frequency of the numbers between 40 and 70 are roughly equal.

Freddie's problem involves determining the order quantity that will maximize his average daily profit.

Freddie needs to determine how many copies to order per day from the distributor. His objective is to maximize his average daily profit.

If you have previously studied inventory management in an operations management course, you might recognize this problem as being an example of what is now called either the *newsboy problem* or the *newsvendor problem.* In fact, we use a basic inventory model to analyze a simplified version of this same case study in Chapter 19 (one of the supplementary chapters on the CD-ROM). However, we will use computer simulation to analyze this problem in this chapter.

A Spreadsheet Model for This Problem

Figure 13.1 shows a spreadsheet model for this problem. Given the data cells C4:C6, the decision variable is the order quantity to be entered in cell C9. (The number 60 has been entered arbitrarily in this figure as a first guess of a reasonable value.) The bottom of the figure shows the equations used to calculate the output cells C14:C16. These output cells are then used to calculate the output cell Profit (C18).

A day's demand for the Financial Journal appears to have a uniform distribution between 40 and 70.

The only uncertain input quantity in this spreadsheet is the day's demand in cell C12. This quantity can be anywhere between 40 and 70. Since the frequency of the numbers between 40 and 70 are about the same, the probability distribution of the day's demand can be reasonably assumed to be a *uniform distribution* between 40 and 70, as indicated in cells D12:F12. Rather

FIGURE 13.1

A spreadsheet model for applying computer simulation to the case study that involves Freddie the newsboy. The assumption cell is Demand (C12), the forecast cell is Profit (C18), and the decision variable is OrderQuantity (C9).

	A	B	C	D	E	F
1		**Freddie the Newsboy**				
2						
3			**Data**			
4		Unit Sale Price	$2.50			
5		Unit Purchase Cost	$1.50			
6		Unit Salvage Value	$0.50			
7						
8			**Decision Variable**			
9		Order Quantity	60			
10						
11			**Simulation**		Minimum	Maximum
12		Demand	55	*Discrete Uniform*	40	70
13						
14		Sales Revenue	$137.50			
15		Purchasing Cost	$90.00			
16		Salvage Value	$2.50			
17						
18		Profit	$50.00			

	B	C
14	Sales Revenue	=UnitSalePrice*MIN(OrderQuantity,Demand)
15	Purchasing Cost	=UnitPurchaseCost*OrderQuantity
16	Salvage Value	=UnitSalvageValue*MAX(OrderQuantity-Demand,0)
17		
18	Profit	=SalesRevenue-PurchasingCost+SalvageValue

Range Name	Cell
Demand	C12
OrderQuantity	C9
Profit	C18
PurchasingCost	C15
SalesRevenue	C14
SalvageValue	C16
UnitPurchaseCost	C5
UnitSalePrice	C4
UnitSalvageValue	C6

than enter a single number permanently into Demand (C12), what Crystal Ball does is enter this probability distribution into this cell. (Before turning to Crystal Ball, an arbitrary number 55 has been entered temporarily into this cell in Figure 13.1.) By using Crystal Ball to generate a *random observation* from this probability distribution, the spreadsheet can calculate the output cells in the usual way. Each time this is done is referred to as a **trial** by Crystal Ball. By running the number of trials specified by the user (typically hundreds or thousands), the computer simulation thereby generates the same number of random observations of the values in the output cells. Crystal Ball records this information for the output cell(s) of particular interest (Freddie's daily profit) and then, at the end, displays it in a variety of convenient forms that reveal an estimate of the underlying probability distribution of Freddie's daily profit. (More about this later.)

The Application of Crystal Ball

Four steps must be taken to use the spreadsheet in Figure 13.1 to perform the computer simulation with Crystal Ball. They are:

1. Define the random input cells.
2. Define the output cells to forecast.
3. Set the run preferences.
4. Run the simulation.

We now describe each of these four steps in turn.

Crystal Ball Tip: Before defining an assumption cell, the cell must contain a value. Any number can be entered, since it will not be used during the actual simulation. When a simulation run is completed, Crystal Ball restores the same value.

Define the Random Input Cells

A random input cell is an input cell that has a random value (such as the daily demand for the *Financial Journal*). Therefore, an assumed probability distribution must be entered into the cell instead of permanently entering a single number. The only random input cell in Figure 13.1 is Demand (C12). Crystal Ball refers to each such random input cell as an **assumption cell.**

The following procedure is used to define an assumption cell.

Procedure for Defining an Assumption Cell

1. Select the cell by clicking on it.
2. If the cell does not already contain a value, enter *any* number into the cell.
3. Click on the Define Assumption button (🔺) in the Crystal Ball tab (for Excel 2007) or toolbar (for earlier versions of Excel).
4. Select a probability distribution to enter into the cell by clicking on this distribution in the Distribution Gallery shown in Figure 13.2.
5. Click on OK (or double click on the distribution) to bring up a dialogue box for the selected distribution.
6. Use this dialogue box to enter the parameters for the distribution, preferably by referring to the cells in the spreadsheet that contain the values of these parameters. If desired, a name also can be entered for the assumption cell. (If the cell already has a name next to it or above it on the spreadsheet, that name will appear in the dialogue box.)

The Distribution Gallery includes 21 probability distributions.

7. Click on OK.

The **Distribution Gallery** mentioned in step 4 provides a wide variety of 21 probability distributions from which to choose. Figure 13.2 displays six basic distributions, but 15 more also are available by clicking on the All button. (Section 13.7 will focus on the question of how to choose the right distribution.)

Which distribution is appropriate in Freddie's case? Since the frequency of sales between 40 and 70 are all roughly equal, the two uniform distributions are possibilities. The uniform distribution assumes *all* values (including fractional values) between some minimum and maximum value are equally likely. The discrete uniform distribution assumes just the *integer* values are possible. Since newspaper sales are always integer, the discrete uniform distribution is the appropriate distribution for Freddie.

FIGURE 13.2

The Crystal Ball Distribution Gallery dialogue box showing the basic distributions. In addition to the 6 distributions displayed here, 15 more distributions can be accessed by clicking on the All button.

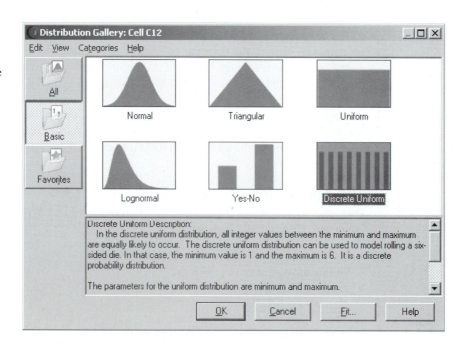

FIGURE 13.3

The Crystal Ball Discrete Uniform Distribution dialogue box. It is being used here to enter a discrete uniform distribution with the parameters 40(=E12) and 70(=F12) into the assumption cell Demand (C12) in the spreadsheet model in Figure 13.1.

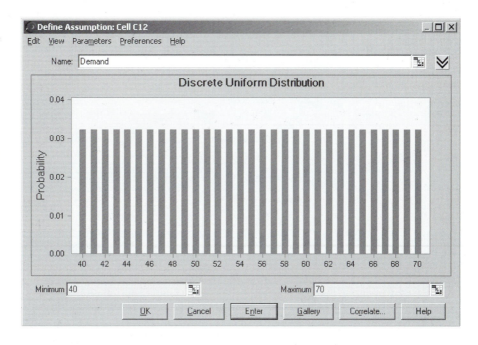

Crystal Ball Tip: Rather than entering raw numbers, use cell references for the distribution parameters (e.g., type =E12 and =F12). This allows changes to be made directly on the spreadsheet rather than having to dig into Crystal Ball dialogue boxes.

Double-clicking on the discrete uniform distribution in the Distribution Gallery brings up the Discrete Uniform Distribution dialogue box shown in Figure 13.3, which is used to enter the parameters of the distribution. For each of the parameters (Minimum and Maximum), we refer to the data cells in E12 and F12 on the spreadsheet by typing the formulas =E12 and =F12 for Minimum and Maximum, respectively. After entering the cell references, the dialogue box will show the actual value of the parameter based on the cell reference (40 and 70 as shown in Figure 13.3). To see or make a change to a cell reference, clicking on the parameter will show the underlying cell reference.

Define the Output Cells to Forecast

Crystal Ball refers to the output of a computer simulation as a *forecast,* since it is forecasting the underlying probability distribution for the performance of the system (now being simulated) when it actually is in operation. Thus, each output cell that is being used by a computer simulation to forecast a measure of performance is referred to as a **forecast cell.** The spreadsheet model for a computer simulation does not include a target cell, but a forecast cell plays roughly the same role.

The measure of performance of interest to Freddie the newsboy is his daily profit from selling the *Financial Journal,* so the only forecast cell in Figure 13.1 is Profit (C18). The following procedure is used to define such an output cell as a forecast cell.

Procedure for Defining a Forecast Cell

1. Select the cell by clicking on it.
2. Click on the Define Forecast button ( ) in the Crystal Ball tab (Excel 2007) or toolbar (earlier versions of Excel), which brings up the Define Forecast dialogue box (as shown in Figure 13.4 for Freddie's problem).

FIGURE 13.4

The Crystal Ball Define Forecast dialogue box. It is being used here to define the forecast cell Profit (C18) in the spreadsheet model in Figure 13.1.

FIGURE 13.5
The Crystal Ball Run
Preferences dialogue box
after selecting the
Trials tab.

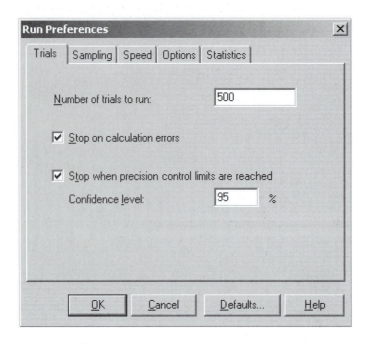

3. This dialogue box can be used to define a name and (optionally) units for the forecast cell.
   (If a range name already has been assigned to the cell, that name will appear in the dialogue box.)
4. Click on OK.

Set the Run Preferences

The third step—setting run preferences—refers to such things as choosing the number of trials to run and deciding on other options regarding how to perform the computer simulation. This step begins by clicking on Run Preferences in the Crystal Ball tab (Excel 2007) or toolbar (earlier versions of Excel). The Run Preferences dialogue box has the five tabs shown on the top of Figure 13.5. By clicking on these tabs, you can enter or change any of the specifications controlled by that tab for how to run the computer simulation. For example, Figure 13.5 shows the version of the dialogue box that is obtained by selecting the Trials tab. This figure indicates that 500 has been chosen as the maximum number of trials for the computer simulation. (The other option in the Run Preferences Trials dialogue box—Stop If Specified Precision Is Reached—will be described later.)

Run the Simulation

At this point, the stage is set to begin running the computer simulation. To start, you only need to click on the Start Simulation button (▷). However, if a computer simulation has been run previously, you should first click on the Reset Simulation button (◁◁) to reset the simulation before starting a new one.

Once started, a forecast window displays the results of the computer simulation as it runs. Figure 13.6 shows the forecast for Profit (Freddie's daily profit from selling the *Financial Journal*) after all 500 trials have been completed. The default view of the forecast is the frequency chart shown on the left side of the figure. The height of the vertical lines in the frequency chart indicates the relative frequency of the various profit values that were obtained during the simulation run. For example, consider the tall vertical line at $60. The right-hand side of the chart indicates a frequency of about 175 there, which means that about 175 of the 500 trials led to a profit of $60. Thus, the left-hand side of the chart indicates that the estimated probability of a profit of $60 is 175/500 = 0.350. This is the profit that results whenever the demand equals or exceeds the order quantity of 60. The remainder of the time, the profit was scattered fairly evenly between $20 and $60. These profit values correspond to trials where the demand was between 40 and 60 units, with lower profit values corresponding to

FIGURE 13.6

The frequency chart and statistics table provided by Crystal Ball to summarize the results of running the simulation model in Figure 13.1 for the case study that involves Freddie the newsboy.

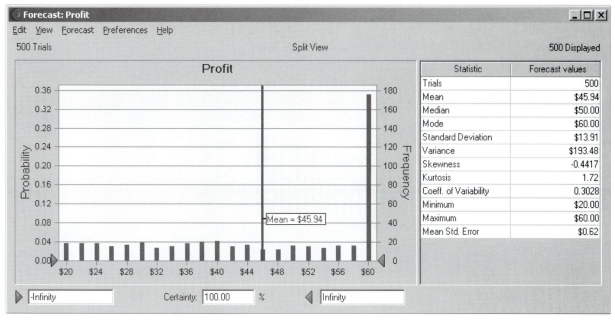

Crystal Ball Tip: To display the mean line on the frequency chart, as in Figure 13.6, choose this option in "Chart . . ." under the Preferences menu on the Chart Type tab.

Crystal Ball Tip: To view more than one chart or table in the same window (e.g., a frequency chart and statistics, as shown in Figure 13.6), choose Split View from the View menu of the forecast window. Any combination of charts and tables can then be selected in the View menu to appear in the split view.

In general, the *x* percent percentile is the dividing line between the smallest *x* percent of the values and the rest of the values.

demands closer to 40 and higher profit values corresponding to demands closer to 60. The mean of the 500 profit values is $45.94, as indicated by the *mean line* at this point.

The statistics table in Figure 13.6 is obtained by choosing Statistics from the View menu. These statistics summarize the outcome of the 500 trials of the computer simulation. These 500 trials provide a sample of 500 random observations from the underlying probability distribution of Freddie's daily profit. The most interesting statistics about this sample provided by the table include the *mean* of $45.94, the *median* of $50.00 (indicating that $50 was the middle profit value from the 500 trials when listing the profits from smallest to largest), the *mode* of $60 (meaning that this was the profit value that occurred most frequently), and the *standard deviation* of $13.91. The information near the bottom of the table regarding the *minimum* and *maximum* profit values also is particularly useful.

In addition to the frequency chart and statistics table presented in Figure 13.6, the View menu provides some other useful ways of displaying the results of a simulation run, including a percentiles table, a cumulative chart, and a reverse cumulative chart. These alternative displays are shown in a split view in Figure 13.7. The percentiles table is based on listing the profit values generated by the 500 trials from smallest to largest, dividing this list into 10 equal parts (50 values in each), and then recording the value at the end of each part. Thus, the value 10 percent through the list is $24, the value 20 percent through the list is $30, and so forth. (For example, the intuitive interpretation of the 10 percent percentile of $24 is that 10 percent of the trials have profit values less than or equal to $24 and the other 90 percent of the trials have profit values greater than or equal to $24, so $24 is the dividing line between the smallest 10 percent of the values and the largest 90 percent.) The cumulative chart on the top left of Figure 13.7 provides similar (but more detailed) information about this same list of the smallest-to-largest profit values. The horizontal axis shows the entire range of values from the smallest possible profit value ($20) to the largest possible profit value ($60). For each value in this range, the chart cumulates the number of actual profits generated by the 500 trials that are less than or equal to that value. This number equals the frequency shown on the right or, when divided by the number of trials, the probability shown on the left. The reverse cumulative chart on the bottom left of Figure 13.7 is constructed in the same way as the cumulative chart except for the following crucial difference. For each value in the range from $20 to $60, the reverse cumulative chart cumulates the number of actual profits generated by the 500 trials that are *greater* than or equal to that value.

FIGURE 13.7

Three more forms in which Crystal Ball displays the results of running the simulation model in Figure 13.1 for the case study that involves Freddie the newsboy.

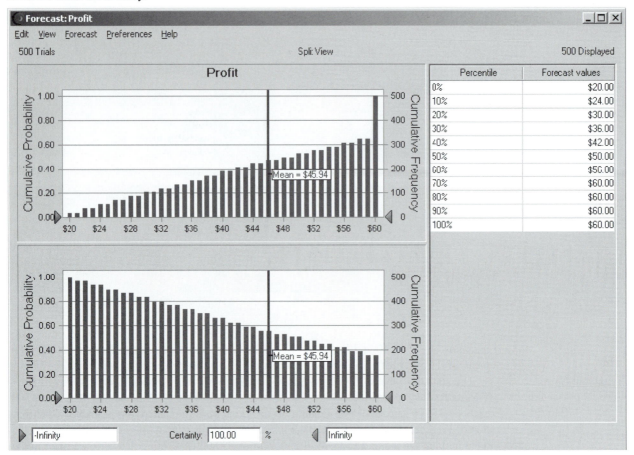

FIGURE 13.8

After setting a lower bound of $40 for desirable profit values, the Certainty box below this frequency chart reveals that 65.80 percent of the trials in Freddie's simulation run provided a profit at least this high.

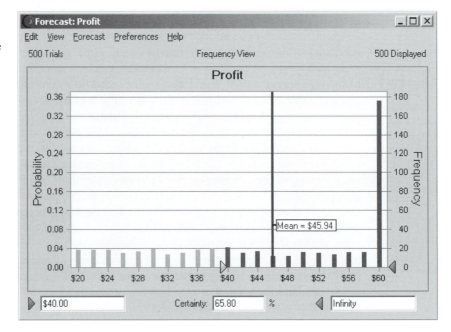

Figure 13.8 illustrates another of the many helpful ways provided by Crystal Ball for extracting helpful information from the results of a simulation run. Freddie the newsboy feels that he has had a reasonably successful day if he obtains a profit of at least $40 from selling the *Financial Journal.* Therefore, he would like to know the percentage of days that he could

expect to achieve this much profit if he were to adopt the order quantity currently being analyzed (60). An estimate of this percentage (65.80 percent) is shown in the Certainty box below the frequency chart in Figure 13.8. Crystal Ball can provide this percentage in two ways. First, the user can drag the triangle on the left just under the chart (originally at $20 in Figure 13.6) to the right until it is at $40 (as in Figure 13.8). Alternatively, $40 can be typed directly into the box in the lower left-hand corner. If desired, the probability of obtaining a profit between any two values also could be estimated immediately by dragging the two triangles to those values.

How Accurate Are the Simulation Results?

An important number provided by Figure 13.6 is the mean of $45.94. This number was calculated as the *average* of the 500 random observations from the underlying probability distribution of Freddie's daily profit that were generated by the 500 trials. This *sample average* of $45.94 thereby provides an *estimate* of the *true mean* of this distribution. The true mean might deviate somewhat from $45.94. How accurate can we expect this estimate to be?

The answer to this key question is provided by the *mean standard error* of $0.62 given at the bottom of the statistics table in Figure 13.6. In particular, the true mean can readily deviate from the sample mean by any amount up to the mean standard error, but most of the time (approximately 68 percent of the time), it will not deviate by more than that. Thus, the interval from $45.94 − $0.62 = $45.32 to $45.94 + $0.62 = $46.56 is a 68 percent *confidence interval* for the true mean. Similarly, a larger confidence interval can be obtained by using an appropriate multiple of the mean standard error to subtract from the sample mean and then to add to the sample mean. For example, the appropriate multiple for a 95 percent confidence interval is 1.965, so such a confidence interval ranges from $45.94 − 1.965($0.62) = $44.72 to $45.94 + 1.965($0.62) = $47.16. (This multiple of 1.965 will change slightly if the number of trials is different from 500.) Therefore, it is very likely that the true mean is somewhere between $44.72 and $47.16.

If greater precision is required, the mean standard error normally can be reduced by increasing the number of trials in the simulation run. However, the reduction tends to be small unless the number of trials is increased substantially. For example, cutting the mean standard error in half requires approximately quadrupling the number of trials. Thus, a surprisingly large number of trials may be required to obtain the desired degree of precision.

Since the number of trials required to obtain the desired degree of accuracy cannot be predicted very well in advance of the simulation run, the temptation is to specify an extremely large number of trials. This specified number may turn out to be many times as large as necessary and thereby cause an excessively long computer run. Fortunately, Crystal Ball has a special method of precision control for stopping the simulation run early as soon as the desired precision has been reached. This method is triggered by choosing the option "Stop If Specified Precision Is Reached" in the Run Preferences Trials dialogue box shown in Figure 13.5. The specified precision is entered in the Expanded Define Forecast dialogue box displayed in Figure 13.9. (This dialogue box is brought up by clicking on the More button (⌄) in the Define Forecast dialogue box shown in Figure 13.4.) Figure 13.9 indicates that the precision control is being applied to the mean (but not to the standard deviation or to a specified percentile). The run preferences in Figure 13.5 indicate that a 95 percent confidence interval is being used. The width of half of the confidence interval, measured from its midpoint to either end, is considered to be the precision that has been achieved. The desired precision can be specified in either absolute terms (using the same units as for the confidence interval) or in relative terms (expressed as a percentage of the midpoint of the confidence interval).

Figure 13.9 indicates that the decision was made to specify the desired precision in absolute terms as $1. The 95 percent confidence interval for the mean after 500 trials was found to be $45.94 plus-or-minus $1.22, so $1.22 is the precision that was achieved after all these trials. Crystal Ball also calculates the confidence interval (and so the current precision) periodically to check whether the current precision is under $1, in which case the run would be stopped. However, this never happened, so Crystal Ball allowed the simulation to run until the maximum number of trials (500) was reached.

The Certainty box gives the percentage of the trials that generated values between the values in the adjacent boxes.

The *mean standard error* specifies how close the mean obtained in a simulation run is likely to be to the true mean.

FIGURE 13.9
This Expanded Define Forecast dialogue box is being used to specify how much precision is desired in Freddie's simulation run.

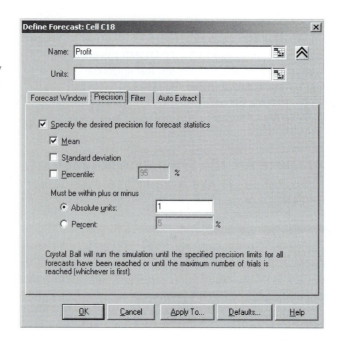

FIGURE 13.10
The results obtained after continuing Freddie's simulation run until the precision specified in Figure 13.9 is achieved.

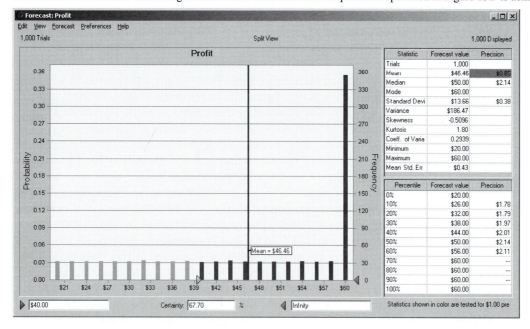

To obtain the desired precision, the simulation would need to be restarted to generate additional trials. This is done by entering a larger number (such as 5,000) for the maximum number of trials (including the 500 already obtained) in the Run Preferences dialogue box (shown in Figure 13.5) and then clicking on the Start Simulation button (▷). Figure 13.10 shows the results of doing this. The first row indicates that the desired precision was obtained after only 500 additional trials, for a total of 1,000 trials. (The default value for the frequency of checking the precision is every 500 trials, so the precision of $1 actually was reached somewhere between 500 and 1,000 trials.) Because of the additional trials, some of the statistics have

1,000 trials were needed to have 95 percent confidence that the true value of the mean is within $1 of the mean obtained in the simulation run.

changed slightly from those given in Figure 13.6. For example, the best estimate of the mean now is $46.46, with a precision of $0.85. Thus, it is very likely (95 percent confidence) that the true value of the mean is within $0.85 of $46.46.

$$95\% \text{ confidence interval: } \$45.61 \leq \text{Mean} \leq \$47.31$$

The precision also is given for the current estimates of the median and the standard deviation, as well as for the estimates of the percentiles given in the percentiles table. Therefore, a 95 percent confidence interval also can be calculated for each of these quantities by adding and subtracting its precision from its estimate.

Freddie's Conclusions

The results presented in Figures 13.6 and 13.10 were from a simulation run that fixed Freddie's daily order quantity at 60 copies of the *Financial Journal* (as indicated in cell C9 of the spreadsheet in Figure 13.1). Freddie wanted this order quantity tried first because it seems to provide a reasonable compromise between being able to fully meet the demand on many days (about two-thirds of them) while often not having many unsold copies on those days. However, the results obtained do not reveal whether 60 is the *optimal* order quantity that would maximize his average daily profit. Many more simulation runs with other order quantities will be needed to determine (or at least estimate) the optimal order quantity. Section 13.8 will describe how this search for the optimal order quantity can be done for Freddie with the help of a decision table and a trend chart. The supplement to this chapter on the CD-ROM then describes how the OptQuest module in your Crystal Ball software package uses a powerful optimization technique to search systematically for the optimal order quantity. That presentation will bring the case study to a close.

Freddie now has 95 percent confidence that an order quantity of 60 would provide an average daily profit between $45.61 and $47.31 in the long run.

Although there is still much more to come, Freddie already has learned from Figure 13.10 that an order quantity of 60 would provide a nice average daily profit of approximately $46.46. This is only an estimate, but Freddie also has learned from the 95 percent confidence interval that the average daily profit probably would turn out to be somewhere between $45.61 and $47.31.

However, these profit figures provided by computer simulation are based on the assumption in the spreadsheet model (see cells D12:F12 in Figure 13.1) that demand has a discrete uniform distribution between 40 and 70. Therefore, these profit figures will be correct only if this assumption is a valid one. More work is needed to either verify that this assumed distribution is the appropriate one or to identify another probability distribution that provides a better fit to the data of daily demands that Freddie actually has been experiencing. This issue will be explored further in Section 13.7.

Computer simulation with Crystal Ball is an extremely versatile tool that can address a myriad of managerial issues. Therefore, before continuing the case study in Sections 13.7–13.8, we turn in the intervening sections to presenting five additional examples of the application of computer simulation with Crystal Ball.

Review Questions

1. What is the decision that Freddie the newsboy needs to make?
2. What is an *assumption cell* when using Crystal Ball?
3. What is entered into the assumption cell in Freddie's spreadsheet model?
4. What is a *forecast cell* when using Crystal Ball?
5. What is entered into the forecast cell in Freddie's spreadsheet model?
6. What kind of information is provided by a frequency chart when using Crystal Ball?
7. What are the key statistics provided by the statistics table when using Crystal Ball?
8. What is the significance of the *mean standard error* of the results from a computer simulation?
9. What provision does Crystal Ball provide for perhaps stopping a simulation run before the specified number of trials have been completed?
10. What has Freddie the newsboy learned so far about what his order quantity should be?

13.2 BIDDING FOR A CONSTRUCTION PROJECT: A PRELUDE TO THE RELIABLE CONSTRUCTION CO. CASE STUDY

Managers frequently must make decisions whose outcomes will be greatly affected by the corresponding decisions being made by the management of competitor firms. For example, marketing decisions often fall into this category. To illustrate, consider the case in which a manager must determine the price for a new product being brought to market. How well this decision works out will depend greatly on the pricing decisions being made nearly simultaneously by other firms marketing competitive new products. Similarly, the success of a decision on how soon to market a product under development will be determined largely by whether this product reaches the market before competitive products are released by other firms.

When a decision must be made before learning the corresponding decisions being made by competitors, the analysis needs to take into account the uncertainty surrounding what competitors' decisions will be. Computer simulation provides a natural way of doing this by using assumption cells to represent competitors' decisions.

The following example illustrates this process by considering a situation where the decision being made is the bid to submit on a construction project while three other companies are simultaneously preparing their own bids.

The Reliable Construction Co. Bidding Problem

The case study carried throughout Chapter 16 on the CD-ROM involves the Reliable Construction Co. and its project to construct a new plant for a major manufacturer. That chapter describes how the project manager (David Perty) made extensive use of PERT/CPM models to help guide his management of the project.

As the opening sentence of Section 16.1 indicates, this case study begins as the company has just made the winning bid of $5.4 million to do this project. We now will back up in time to describe how the company's management used computer simulation with Crystal Ball to guide its choice of $5.4 million as its bid for the project. You will not need to review the case study in Chapter 16 to follow this example.

This section reveals how the company chose the bid of $5.4 million, which won the contract.

Reliable's first step in this process was to estimate what the company's total cost would be if it were to undertake the project. This was determined to be $4.55 million. (This amount excludes the penalty for missing the deadline for completion of the project, as well as the bonus for completion well before the deadline, since management considers either event to be relatively unlikely.) There also is an additional cost of approximately $50,000 for preparing the bid, including estimating the project cost and analyzing the bidding strategies of the competition.

Three other construction companies also were invited to submit bids for this project. All three have been long-standing competitors of the Reliable Construction Co., so the company has had a great deal of experience in observing their bidding strategies. A veteran analyst in the bid preparation office has taken on the task of estimating what bid each of these competitors will submit. Since there is so much uncertainty in this process, the analyst has determined that each of these estimates needs to be in the form of a probability distribution. Competitor 1 is known to use a 30 percent profit margin above the total (direct) cost of a project in setting its bid. However, competitor 1 also is a particularly unpredictable bidder because of an inability to estimate the true costs of a project with much accuracy. Its actual profit margin on past bids has ranged from as low as minus 5 percent to as high as 60 percent. Competitor 2 uses a 25 percent profit margin and is somewhat more accurate than competitor 1 in estimating project costs, but it still has set bids in the past that have missed this profit margin by as much as 15 percent in either direction. On the other hand, competitor 3 is unusually accurate in estimating project costs (as is the Reliable Construction Co.). Competitor 3 also is adept at adjusting its bidding strategy, so it is equally likely to set its profit margin anywhere between 20 and 30 percent, depending on its assessment of the competition, its current backlog of work, and various other factors. Therefore, the estimated probability distributions of the bids that the three competitors will submit, expressed as a percentage of Reliable's assessment of the total project cost, are as follows.

Competitor 1: A triangular distribution with a minimum value of 95 percent, a most likely value of 130 percent, and a maximum value of 160 percent.

Competitor 2: A triangular distribution with a minimum value of 110 percent, a most likely value of 125 percent, and a maximum value of 140 percent.

Competitor 3: A uniform distribution between 120 percent and 130 percent.

A Spreadsheet Model for Applying Computer Simulation

Figure 13.11 shows the spreadsheet model that has been formulated to evaluate any possible bid that Reliable might submit. Since there is uncertainty about what the competitors' bids will be, this model needs CompetitorBids (C8:E8) to be *assumption cells,* so the above probability

FIGURE 13.11

A spreadsheet model for applying computer simulation to the Reliable Construction Co.'s contract bidding problem. The assumption cells are CompetitorBids (C8:E8), the forecast cell is Profit (C29), and the decision variable is OurBid (C25).

	A	B	C	D	E
1		**Reliable Construction Co. Contract Bidding**			
2					
3		**Data**			
4		Our Project Cost ($million)	4.550		
5		Our Bid Cost ($million)	0.050		
6					
7		**Competitor Bids**	Competitor 1	Competitor 2	Competitor 3
8		Bid ($million)	5.839	5.688	5.688
9					
10		Distribution	*Triangular*	*Triangular*	*Uniform*
11					
12		Competitor Distribution Parameters (Proportion of Our Project Cost)			
13		Minimum	95%	110%	120%
14		Most Likely	130%	125%	
15		Maximum	160%	140%	130%
16					
17		Competitor Distribution Parameters ($million)			
18		Minimum	4.323	5.005	5.460
19		Most Likely	5.915	5.688	
20		Maximum	7.280	6.370	5.915
21					
22		**Minimum Competitor**			
23		**Bid ($million)**	5.688		
24					
25		**Our Bid ($million)**	5.400		
26					
27		**Win Bid?**	1	(1=yes, 0=no)	
28					
29		**Profit ($million)**	0.800		

Range Name	Cells
CompetitorBids	C8:E8
MinimumCompetitorBid	C23
OurBid	C25
OurBidCost	C5
OurProjectCost	C4
Profit	C29
WinBid?	C27

	B	C	D	E
18	Minimum	=OurProjectCost*C13	=OurProjectCost*D13	=OurProjectCost*E13
19	Most Likely	=OurProjectCost*C14	=OurProjectCost*D14	
20	Maximum	=OurProjectCost*C15	=OurProjectCost*D15	=OurProjectCost*E15

	B	C
22	**Minimum Competitor**	
23	**Bid ($million)**	=MIN(C8:E8)
24		
25	**Our Bid ($million)**	5.4
26		
27	**Win Bid?**	=IF(OurBid<MinimumCompetitorBid,1,0)
28		
29	**Profit ($million)**	=WinBid?*(OurBid-OurProjectCost)-OurBidCost

FIGURE 13.12

The Triangular Distribution dialogue box. It is being used here to enter a triangular distribution with the parameters 4.323 (=C18), 5.915 (=C19), and 7.280 (=C20) into the assumption cell C8 in the spreadsheet model in Figure 13.11.

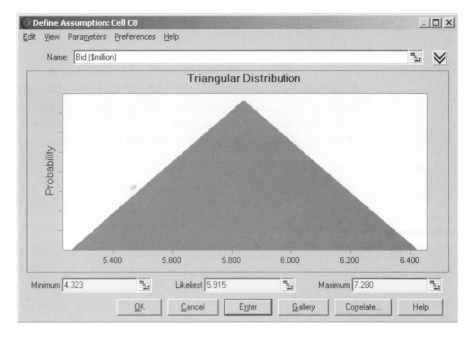

The bids that other companies will submit are uncertain, so they need to be assumption cells.

distributions are entered into these cells. As described in the preceding section, this is done by selecting each cell in turn, entering any number into the cell, and then clicking on the appropriate distribution in the Distribution Gallery, which brings up the dialogue box for that distribution. Figure 13.12 shows the Triangular Distribution dialogue box that has been used to set the parameter values (Minimum, Likeliest, and Maximum) for competitor 1, and competitor 2 would be handled similarly. These parameter values for competitor 1 come from cells C18:C20, where the parameters in percentage terms (cells C13:C15) have been converted to dollars by multiplying them by OurProjectCost (C4). The Uniform Distribution dialogue box is used instead to set the parameter values for cell E8.

MinimumCompetitorBid (C23) records the smallest of the competitors' bids for each trial of the computer simulation. The company wins the bid on a given trial only if the quantity entered into OurBid (C25) is less than the smallest of the competitors' bids. The IF function entered into WinBid? (C27) then returns a 1 if this occurs and a 0 otherwise.

Since management wants to maximize the expected profit from the entire process of determining a bid (if the bid wins) and then doing the project, the forecast cell in this model is Profit (C29). The profit achieved on a given trial depends on whether the company wins the bid. If not, the profit actually is a loss of $50,000 (the bid cost). However, if the bid wins, the profit is the amount by which the bid exceeds the sum of the project cost and the bid cost. The equation entered into Profit (C29) performs this calculation for whichever case applies.

The objective is to determine the bid that would maximize the resulting expected profit.

Here is a summary of the key cells in this model.

Assumption cells:	CompetitorBids (C8:E8)
Decision variable:	OurBid (C25)
Forecast cell:	Profit (C29)

The Simulation Results

To evaluate a possible bid of $5.4 million entered into OurBid (C25), a computer simulation of this model ran for 1,000 trials. Figure 13.13 shows the results in the form of a frequency chart and a statistics table, while Figure 13.14 displays the corresponding percentiles table and cumulative chart. Using units of millions of dollars, the profit on each trial has only two possible values, namely, a loss shown as −0.050 in these figures (if the bid loses) or a profit of 0.800 (if the bid wins). The frequency chart indicates that this loss of $50,000 occurred on about 380 of the 1,000 trials whereas the profit of $800,000 occurred on the other 620 trials.

FIGURE 13.13

The frequency chart and statistics table that summarize the results of running the simulation model in Figure 13.11 for the Reliable Construction Co. contract bidding problem.

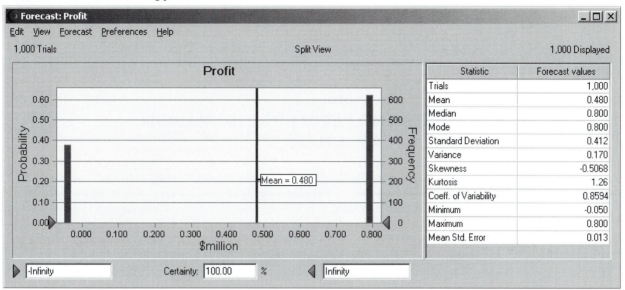

FIGURE 13.14

Further results for the Reliable Construction Co. contract bidding problem.

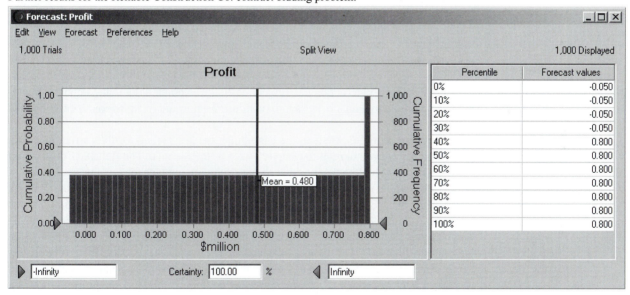

This resulted in a mean profit of 0.480 ($480,000) from all 1,000 trials, as well as the other statistics recorded in the statistics table. In Figure 13.14, note how the possibility of only two profit values results in only these values appearing in the percentiles table and also results in having a flat cumulative chart until the upper value is reached.

By themselves, these results do not show that $5.4 million is the best bid to submit. We still need to estimate with additional simulation runs whether a larger expected profit could be obtained with another bid value. Section 13.8 will describe how doing this with a decision table leads to choosing $5.4 million as the bid. This turned out to be the winning bid for the Reliable Construction Co., which then led into the case study for Chapter 16.

This story will continue in Section 13.8.

1. What is the project for which the Reliable Construction Co. is submitting a bid?
2. The bids of the competitors are being estimated in what form?
3. What are the quantities in the assumption cells in this example's spreadsheet model for applying computer simulation?
4. What quantity appears in the forecast cell for this spreadsheet model?
5. What are the possible outcomes on each trial of this computer simulation?

13.3 PROJECT MANAGEMENT: REVISITING THE RELIABLE CONSTRUCTION CO. CASE STUDY

Computer simulation improves upon a PERT/CPM method for estimating the probability of completing a project by the deadline.

One of the most important responsibilities of a project manager is to meet the deadline that has been set for the project. Therefore, a skillful project manager will revise the plan for conducting the project as needed to ensure a strong likelihood of meeting the deadline. But how does the project manager estimate the probability of meeting the deadline with any particular plan? Section 16.4 describes one method provided by PERT/CPM. We now will illustrate how computer simulation provides a better method.

This example illustrates a common role for computer simulation—refining the results from a preliminary analysis conducted with approximate mathematical models. You also will get a first look at assumption cells where the random inputs are *times*. Another interesting feature of this example is its use of a special kind of Crystal Ball chart called the *sensitivity chart*. This chart will provide a key insight into how the project plan should be revised.

The Problem Being Addressed

Like the example in the preceding section, this one also revolves around the Reliable Construction Co. case study introduced in Section 16.1 and continued throughout Chapter 16. However, rather than preceding the part of the story described in Chapter 16, this example arises in the middle of the case study. In particular, Section 16.4 discusses how a PERT/CPM procedure was used to obtain a rough approximation of the probability of meeting the deadline for the Reliable Construction Co. project. It then was pointed out that computer simulation could be used to obtain a better approximation. We now are in a position to describe how this is done.

The deadline for completing the project is 47 weeks from now.

Here are the essential facts about the case study that are needed for the current example. (There is no need for you to refer to Chapter 16 for further details.) The Reliable Construction Company has just made the winning bid to construct a new plant for a major manufacturer. However, the contract includes a large penalty if construction is not completed by the deadline 47 weeks from now. Therefore, a key element in evaluating alternative construction plans is the *probability of meeting this deadline* under each plan. There are 14 major activities involved in carrying out this construction project, as listed on the right-hand side of Figure 13.15 (which repeats Figure 16.1 for your convenience). The project network in this figure depicts the precedence relationships between the activities. Thus, there are six sequences of activities (paths through the network), all of which must be completed to finish the project. These six sequences are listed below.

Path 1:	Start → A → B → C → D → G → H → M → Finish
Path 2:	Start → A → B → C → E → H → M → Finish
Path 3:	Start → A → B → C → E → F → J → K → N → Finish
Path 4:	Start → A → B → C → E → F → J → L → N → Finish
Path 5:	Start → A → B → C → I → J → K → N → Finish
Path 6:	Start → A → B → C → I → J → L → N → Finish

The numbers next to the activities in the project network represent the *estimates* of the number of weeks the activities will take if they are carried out in the normal manner with the usual

FIGURE 13.15

The project network for
the Reliable Construction
Co. project.

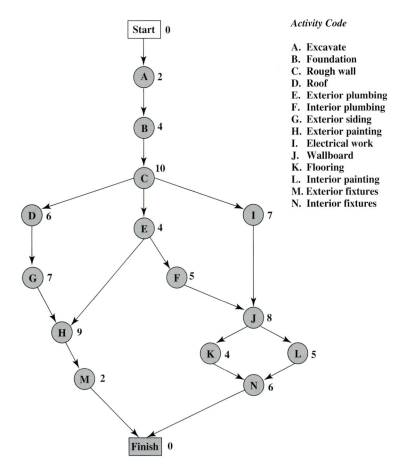

Activity Code

A. Excavate
B. Foundation
C. Rough wall
D. Roof
E. Exterior plumbing
F. Interior plumbing
G. Exterior siding
H. Exterior painting
I. Electrical work
J. Wallboard
K. Flooring
L. Interior painting
M. Exterior fixtures
N. Interior fixtures

crew sizes, and so forth. Adding these times over each of the paths (as was done in Table 16.2)
reveals that path 4 is the *longest path,* requiring a total of 44 weeks. Since the project is finished as soon as its longest path is completed, this indicates that the project can be completed
in 44 weeks, 3 weeks before the deadline.

Now we come to the crux of the problem. The times for the activities in Figure 13.15 are
only estimates, and there actually is considerable uncertainty about what the duration of each
activity will be. Therefore, the duration of the entire project could well differ substantially
from the estimate of 44 weeks, so there is a distinct possibility of missing the deadline of 47
weeks. What is the *probability* of missing this deadline? To estimate this probability, we need
to learn more about the probability distribution of the duration of the project.

This is the reason for the PERT three-estimate approach described in Section 16.4. This
approach involves obtaining three estimates—a *most likely estimate,* an *optimistic estimate,*
and a *pessimistic estimate*—of the duration of each activity. (Table 16.4 lists these estimates
for all 14 activities for the project under consideration.) These three quantities are intended to
estimate the most likely duration, the minimum duration, and the maximum duration, respectively. Using these three quantities, PERT assumes (somewhat arbitrarily) that the form of the
probability distribution of the duration of an activity is a *beta distribution.* By also making
three simplifying approximations (described in Section 16.4), this leads to an analytical
method for roughly approximating the probability of meeting the project deadline.

One key advantage of computer simulation is that it does not need to make most of the
simplifying approximations that may be required by analytical methods. Another is that there
is great flexibility about which probability distributions to use. It is not necessary to choose an
analytically convenient one.

When dealing with the duration of an activity, computer simulations commonly use a
triangular distribution as the distribution of this duration. A triangular distribution for the

*Computer simulation has
two key advantages over
analytical methods like
PERT/CPM.*

FIGURE 13.16
The shape of a triangular distribution for the duration of an activity, where the minimum lies at the optimistic estimate *o,* the most likely value lies at the most likely estimate *m,* and the maximum lies at the pessimistic estimate *p.*

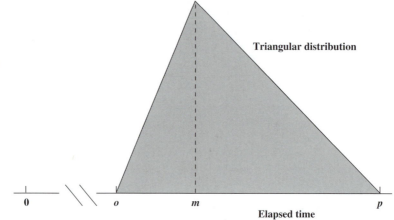

Triangular distribution

0   *o*   *m*   *p*

Elapsed time

duration of an activity has the shape shown in Figure 13.16, where *o, m,* and *p* are the labels for the optimistic estimate, the most likely estimate, and the pessimistic estimate, respectively. For each *assumption cell* containing this distribution, a Triangular Distribution dialogue box (such as the one shown in Figure 13.12) is used to enter the values of *o, m,* and *p* by entering their respective cell references into the Minimum, Likeliest, and Maximum boxes.

A Spreadsheet Model for Applying Computer Simulation

Figure 13.17 shows a spreadsheet model for simulating the duration of the Reliable Construction Co. project. The values of *o, m,* and *p* in columns D, E, and F are obtained directly from Table 16.4. The equations entered into the cells in columns G and I give the start times and finish times for the respective activities. For each trial of the simulation, the maximum of the finish times for the last two activities (M and N) gives the duration of the project (in weeks), which goes into the forecast cell ProjectCompletion (I21).

Variable activity times need to be assumption cells.

Since the activity times generally are variable, the cells H6:H19 all need to be *assumption cells* with the one exception of cell H16. Since *o* = *m* = *p* = 4 for activity K, its activity time actually is a constant 4, so this constant is entered into cell H16. (Crystal Ball would give an error message if cell H16 were specified to be an assumption cell with a triangular distribution where Minimum = Likeliest = Maximum.) Figure 13.18 shows the Triangular Distribution dialogue box after it has been used to specify the parameters for the first assumption cell H6. Rather than repeating this process for all the other assumption cells, it is quicker to simply copy and paste the parameters for the other assumption cells. This is begun by selecting cell H6 and clicking on the Copy Data button on the Crystal Ball tab or toolbar. Then select the cells in which to paste the data (H7:H15 and H17:H19) and choose Paste Data by clicking this button on the Crystal Ball tab or toolbar. The cell references for the parameters in Figure 13.18 are entered as =D6, =E6, and =F6 (relative references without $ signs). Therefore, the row numbers will update appropriately to refer to the data cells in the correct row during this copy-and-paste process. For example, the cell references for the parameters of the triangular distribution in cell H7 will update to =D7, =E7, and =F7.

Here is a summary of the key cells in this model.

Assumption cells: Cells H6:H15 and H17:H19

Forecast cell: ProjectCompletion (I21)

The Simulation Results

We now are ready to undertake a computer simulation of the spreadsheet model in Figure 13.17. Using the Run Preferences dialogue box to specify 1,000 trials, Figure 13.19 shows the results in the form of a frequency chart, a statistics table, and a percentiles table. These results show a very wide range of possible project durations. Out of the 1,000 trials, both the statistics table and percentiles table indicate that one trial had a duration as short as 35.98 weeks

FIGURE 13.17

A spreadsheet model for applying computer simulation to the Reliable Construction Co. project scheduling problem. The assumption cells are cells H6:H15 and H17:H19. The forecast cell is ProjectCompletion (I21).

	A	B	C	D	E	F	G	H	I
1		**Simulation of Reliable Construction Co. Project**							
2									
3								Activity	
4			Immediate	Time Estimates			Start	Time	Finish
5		Activity	Predecessor	o	m	p	Time	(triangular)	Time
6		A	—	1	2	3	0	2	2
7		B	A	2	3.5	8	2	4.5	6.5
8		C	B	6	9	18	6.5	11	17.5
9		D	C	4	5.5	10	17.5	6.5	24
10		E	C	1	4.5	5	17.5	3.5	21
11		F	E	4	4	10	21	6	27
12		G	D	5	6.5	11	24	7.5	31.5
13		H	E, G	5	8	17	31.5	10	41.5
14		I	C	3	7.5	9	17.5	6.5	24
15		J	F, I	3	9	9	27	7	34
16		K	J	4	4	4	34	4	38
17		L	J	1	5.5	7	34	4.5	38.5
18		M	H	1	2	3	41.5	2	43.5
19		N	K, L	5	5.5	9	38.5	6.5	45
20									
21								Project Completion	45

	G	H	I
3		Activity	
4	Start	Time	Finish
5	Time	(triangular)	Time
6	0	2	=AStart+ATime
7	=AFinish	4.5	=BStart+BTime
8	=BFinish	11	=CStart+CTime
9	=CFinish	6.5	=DStart+DTime
10	=CFinish	3.5	=EStart+ETime
11	=EFinish	6	=FStart+FTime
12	=DFinish	7.5	=GStart+GTime
13	=MAX(EFinish,GFinish)	10	=HStart+HTime
14	=CFinish	6.5	=IStart+ITime
15	=MAX(FFinish,IFinish)	7	=JStart+JTime
16	=JFinish	4	=KStart+KTime
17	=JFinish	4.5	=LStart+LTime
18	=HFinish	2	=MStart+MTime
19	=MAX(KFinish,LFinish)	6.5	=NStart+NTime
20			
21		Project Completion	=MAX(MFinish,NFinish)

Range Name	Cell
AFinish	I6
AStart	G6
ATime	H6
BFinish	I7
BStart	G7
BTime	H7
CFinish	I8
CStart	G8
CTime	H8
DFinish	I9
DStart	G9
DTime	H9
EFinish	I10
EStart	G10
ETime	H10
FFinish	I11
FStart	G11
FTime	H11
GFinish	I12
GStart	G12
GTime	H12
HFinish	I13
HStart	G13
HTime	H13
IFinish	I14
IStart	G14
ITime	H14
JFinish	I15
JStart	G15
JTime	H15
KFinish	I16
KStart	G16
KTime	H16
LFinish	I17
LStart	G17
LTime	H17
MFinish	I18
MStart	G18
MTime	H18
NFinish	I19
NStart	G19
NTime	H19
ProjectCompletion	I21

while another was as long as 58.81 weeks. The frequency chart indicates that the duration that occurred most frequently during the 1,000 trials is close to 47 weeks (the project deadline), but that many other durations up to a few weeks either shorter or longer than this also occurred with considerable frequency. The mean is 46.20 weeks, which is much too close to the deadline of 47 weeks to leave much margin for slippage in the project schedule. (The small mean standard error of 0.12 weeks reported at the bottom of the statistics table shows that the sample average of 46.20 weeks from the 1,000 trials probably is extremely close to the true mean of the underlying probability distribution of project duration.) The 70 percent percentile of 48.05 weeks in the percentiles table reveals that 30 percent of the trials missed the deadline by at least a week.

FIGURE 13.18

A triangular distribution with parameters 1 (=D6), 2 (=E6), and 3 (=F6) is being entered into the first assumption cell H6 in the spreadsheet model in Figure 13.17.

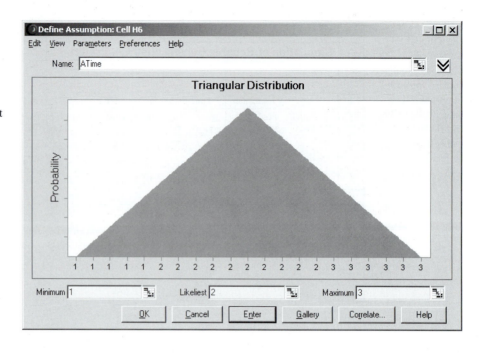

FIGURE 13.19

The frequency chart, statistics table, and percentiles table that summarize the results of running the simulation model in Figure 13.17 for the Reliable Construction Co. project scheduling problem.

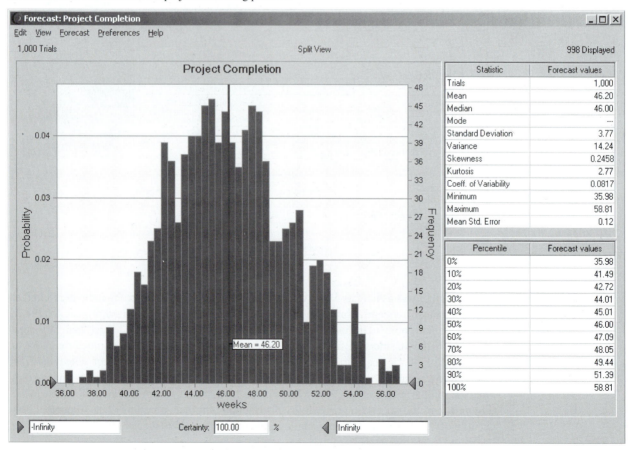

FIGURE 13.20

After entering the project deadline of 47 weeks into the box in the lower right-hand corner, the Certainty box reveals that about 58.88 percent of the trials resulted in the project being completed by the deadline.

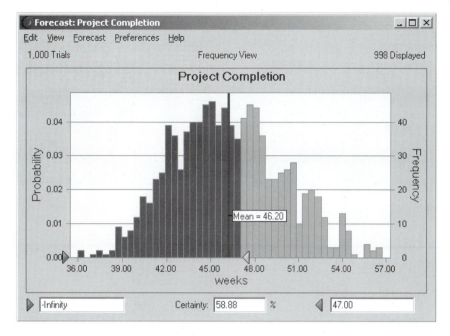

A statistic of special interest to Reliable's management is the probability of meeting the deadline of 47 weeks under the current project plan. (Remember that the contract includes a severe penalty of $300,000 for missing this deadline.) The 60 percent percentile of 47.09 weeks in the percentiles table suggests that slightly under 60 percent of the trials made the deadline, but nothing else in Figure 13.19 pins down this percentage any closer. Figure 13.20 shows that all you need to do to identify the exact percentage is to type the deadline of 47.00 in the box in the lower right-hand corner of the frequency chart. The Certainty box then reveals that about 58.88 percent of the trials met the deadline.[1]

If the simulation run were to be repeated with another 1,000 trials, this percentage probably would change a little. However, with such a large number of trials, the difference in the percentages should be slight. Therefore, the probability of 0.588 provided by the Certainty box in Figure 13.20 is a close estimate of the true probability of meeting the deadline under the assumptions of the spreadsheet model in Figure 13.17. Note how much smaller this relatively precise estimate is than the rough estimate of 0.84 obtained by the PERT three-estimate approach in Section 16.4. Thus, the simulation estimate provides much better guidance to management in deciding whether the project plan should be changed to improve the chances of meeting the deadline. This illustrates how useful computer simulation can be in refining the results obtained by approximate analytical results.

Computer simulation provides a close estimate of the probability of meeting the project deadline (0.588) that is much smaller than the rough PERT/CPM estimate (0.84).

A Key Insight Provided by the Sensitivity Chart

Given such a low probability (0.588) of meeting the project deadline, Reliable's project manager (David Perty) will want to revise the project plan to improve the probability substantially. Crystal Ball has another tool, called the *sensitivity chart,* that provides strong guidance in identifying which revisions in the project plan would be most beneficial.

To open a sensitivity chart after running a simulation, click on the Open Sensitivity Chart button on the Crystal Ball tab or toolbar. Both a contribution to variance chart and a rank correlation chart are then available under the View menu, as shown in Figure 13.21. Using range names, the left side of both charts identify various assumption cells (activity times) in column H of the spreadsheet model in Figure 13.17. The other key cell in the spreadsheet model that is considered in the sensitivity charts (as indicated at the top of both charts) is the forecast cell

---

[1] Actually 588 of the 1,000 trials met the deadline. The certainty is shown as 58.88 rather than 58.8 because Crystal Ball further refines the certainty estimate based on where the 47-week deadline falls relative to the 588th longest trial (which just barely met the deadline) and the 589th longest (which just barely did not).

FIGURE 13.21

This sensitivity chart shows how strongly various activity times in the Reliable Construction Co. project are influencing the project completion time.

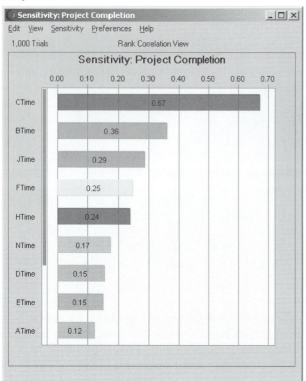 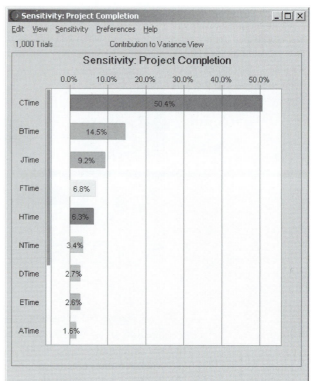

Project Completion (I21) that gives the duration of the project. The contribution to variance chart indicates what percentage of the variability that exists in the forecast cell is due to the variability of each assumption cell. The rows in the chart are listed in descending order. For example, roughly half the variability in project completion time is due to variability in CTime (the time to complete Activity C: Rough Wall).

The rank correlation chart gives the correlation coefficient (based on rank values) between each assumption cell and the forecast cell. A correlation coefficient between two variables measures the strength of the relationship between those variables. Thus, each correlation coefficient in Figure 13.21 measures how strongly that activity time is influencing the project completion time. The higher the correlation coefficient, the stronger is this influence. Therefore, the activities with the highest correlation coefficients are those where the greatest effort should be made to reduce their activity times.

Figure 13.21 indicates that CTime has a far higher contribution to variance and correlation coefficient than the times for any of the other activities. An examination of Figures 13.15 and 13.17 suggests why. Figure 13.15 shows that activity C precedes *all* the other activities except activities A and B, so any delay in completing activity C would delay the start time for all these other activities. Furthermore, cells D8:F8 in Figure 13.17 indicate that CTime is highly variable, with an unusually large spread of 9 weeks between its most likely estimate and its pessimistic estimate, so long delays beyond the most likely estimate may well occur.

This very high contribution to variance and correlation coefficient for CTime suggest that the best way to reduce the project completion time (and its variability) is to focus on reducing this activity time (and its variability). This can be accomplished by revising the project plan to assign activity C more personnel, better equipment, stronger supervision, and so forth. Crystal Ball's sensitivity chart clearly highlights this insight into where the project plan needs to be revised.

The sensitivity chart reveals that reducing the time for activity C would most improve the chances of completing the project before the deadline.

Review
Questions

1. What is the project that is being considered in this section's example?
2. A PERT/CPM procedure can obtain only a rough approximation of a certain key quantity, so computer simulation is used to obtain a much closer estimate of the quantity. What is this quantity?
3. Computer simulations commonly use which kind of probability distribution as the distribution of the duration of an activity?
4. What are the three estimates provided by the PERT three-estimate approach that give the parameters of this distribution of the duration of an activity?
5. What can be done to quickly enter these parameters into all the assumption cells after using the dialogue box for the distribution of the duration of only the first activity?
6. What quantity appears in the forecast cell of the spreadsheet model for this example?
7. What needs to be done to identify the exact percentage of trials of a computer simulation of this spreadsheet model that will result in meeting the project completion deadline?
8. What kind of chart is used to highlight where a project plan needs to be revised to best improve the chances of meeting the project deadline?

13.4 CASH FLOW MANAGEMENT: REVISITING THE EVERGLADE GOLDEN YEARS COMPANY CASE STUDY

Many applications of computer simulation involve scenarios that evolve far into the future. Since nobody can predict the future with certainty, computer simulation is needed to take future uncertainties into account. For example, businesses typically have great uncertainty about what their future cash flows will be. An attempt often is made to predict these future cash flows as a first step toward making decisions about what should be done (e.g., arranging for loans) to meet cash flow needs. However, effective cash management requires going a step further to consider the effect of the uncertainty in the future cash flows. This is where computer simulation comes in, with assumption cells being used for the cash flows in various future periods. This process is illustrated by the following example.

The Everglade Cash Flow Management Problem

The case study analyzed in Chapter 4 involves the Everglade Golden Years Company (which operates upscale retirement communities) and its efforts to manage its cash flow problems. In particular, because of both a temporary decline in business and some current or future construction costs, the company is facing some negative cash flows in the next few years as well as in some more distant years. As first provided in Table 4.1, Table 13.1 shows the projected net cash flows over the next 10 years (2007 to 2016). The company has some new retirement communities opening within the 10 years, so it is anticipated (or at least hoped) that a large positive cash flow will occur in 2016. Therefore, the problem confronting Everglade management is how to best arrange Everglade's financing to tide the company over until its investments in new retirement communities can start to pay off.

TABLE 13.1
Projected Net Cash
Flows for the Everglade
Golden Years Company
over the Next 10 Years

Year	Projected Net Cash Flow (millions of dollars)
2007	−8
2008	−2
2009	−4
2010	3
2011	6
2012	3
2013	−4
2014	7
2015	−2
2016	10

Chapter 4 describes how a decision was made to combine taking a long-term (10-year) loan now (the beginning of 2007) and a series of short-term (1-year) loans as needed to maintain a positive cash balance of at least $500,000 (as dictated by company policy) throughout the 10 years. Assuming no deviation from the projected cash flows shown in Table 13.1, linear programming was used to optimize the size of both the long-term loan and the short-term loans so as to maximize the company's cash balance at the beginning of 2017 when all of the loans have been paid off. Figure 4.5 in Chapter 4 shows the complete spreadsheet model after using the Excel Solver to obtain the optimal solution. For your convenience, Figure 4.5 is repeated here as Figure 13.22. The changing cells, LTLoan (D11) and STLoan (E11:E20), give the sizes of the long-term loan and the short-term loans at the beginning of the various years. The target cell EndBalance (J21) indicates that the resulting cash balance at the end of the 10 years (the beginning of 2017) would be $2.92 million. Since this is the cell that is being maximized, any other plan for the sizes of the loans would result in a smaller cash balance at the end of the 10 years.

The drawback of the linear programming solution in Figure 13.22 is that it does not assess the effect of the great uncertainty regarding future cash flows, so computer simulation is needed to do this.

Obtaining the "optimal" financing plan presented in Figure 13.22 is an excellent first step in developing a final plan. However, the drawback of the spreadsheet model in Figure 13.22 is that it makes no allowance for the inevitable deviations from the projected cash flows shown in Table 13.1. The actual cash flow for the first year (2007) probably will turn out to be quite close to the projection. However, it is difficult to predict the cash flows in even the second and third years with much accuracy, let alone up to 10 years into the future. Computer simulation is needed to assess the effect of these uncertainties.

A Spreadsheet Model for Applying Computer Simulation

Figure 13.23 shows the modification of the spreadsheet model in Figure 13.22 that is needed to apply computer simulation. One key difference is that the constants in CashFlow (C11:C20) in Figure 13.22 have turned into random inputs in CashFlow (F12:F21) in Figure 13.23. Thus, the latter cells, CashFlow (F12:F21), are *assumption cells*. (The numbers appearing in these cells have been entered arbitrarily as a first step in defining these assumption cells.) As indicated in cells D9:E9, the assumption has been made that each of the cash flows has a triangular distribution. Estimates have been made of the three parameters of this distribution (minimum, most likely, and maximum) for each of the years, as presented in cells C12:E21.

The uncertain future cash flows need to be assumption cells.

The number 6.65 entered into LTLoan (G12) is the size of the long-term loan (in millions of dollars) that was obtained in Figure 13.22. However, because of the variability in the cash flows, it no longer makes sense to lock in the sizes of the short-term loans that were obtained in STLoan (E11:E20) in Figure 13.22. It is better to be flexible and adjust these sizes based on the actual cash flows that occur in the preceding years. If the balance at the beginning of a year (as calculated in BalanceBeforeSTLoan [L12:L22]) already exceeds the required minimum balance of $0.50 million, then there is no need to take any short-term loan at that point. However, if the balance is not this large, then a sufficiently large short-term loan should be taken to bring the balance up to $0.50 million. This is what is done by the equations entered into STLoan (M12:M22) that are shown at the bottom of Figure 13.23.

The target cell EndBalance (J21) in Figure 13.22 becomes the forecast cell EndBalance (N22) in Figure 13.23. On any trial of the computer simulation, if the simulated cash flows in CashFlow (F12:F21) in Figure 13.23 are more favorable than the projected cash flows given in Table 13.1 (as is the case for the current numbers in Figure 13.23), then EndBalance (N22) in Figure 13.23 would be larger than EndBalance (J21) in Figure 13.22. However, if the simulated cash flows are less favorable than the projections, then EndBalance (N22) in Figure 13.23 might even be a negative number. For example, if all the simulated cash flows are close to the corresponding minimum values given in cells C12:C21, then the required short-term loans will become so large that paying off the last one at the beginning of 2017 (along with paying off the long-term loan then) will result in a very large negative number in EndBalance (N22). This would spell serious trouble for the company. Computer simulation will reveal the relative likelihood of this occurring versus a favorable outcome.

A key question is the likelihood of achieving a positive cash balance at the end of the 10 years.

Here is a summary of the key cells in this model.

FIGURE 13.22

The spreadsheet model that used linear programming in Chapter 4 (Figure 4.5) to analyze the Everglade Golden Years Company cash flow management problem without taking the uncertainty in future cash flows into account.

Everglade Cash Flow Management Problem When Applying Linear Programming

	A	B	C	D	E	F	G	H	I	J	K	L
3		LT Rate	7%									
4		ST Rate	10%									
6		Start Balance	1									
7		Minimum Cash	0.5									
5						(all cash figures in millions of dollars)						
9			Cash	LT	ST	LT	ST	LT	ST	Ending		Minimum
10		Year	Flow	Loan	Loan	Interest	Interest	Payback	Payback	Balance		Balance
11		2007	-8	6.65	0.85					0.50	≥	0.5
12		2008	-2		3.40	-0.47	-0.09		-0.85	0.50	≥	0.5
13		2009	-4		8.21	-0.47	-0.34		-3.40	0.50	≥	0.5
14		2010	3		6.49	-0.47	-0.82		-8.21	0.50	≥	0.5
15		2011	6		1.61	-0.47	-0.65		-6.49	0.50	≥	0.5
16		2012	3		0	-0.47	-0.16		-1.61	1.27	≥	0.5
17		2013	-4		3.70	-0.47	0		0	0.50	≥	0.5
18		2014	7		0	-0.47	-0.37		-3.70	2.97	≥	0.5
19		2015	-2		0	-0.47	0		0	0.50	≥	0.5
20		2016	10		0	-0.47	0		0	10.03	≥	0.5
21		2017	10			-0.47	0	-6.65	0	2.92	≥	0.5

Range Name	Cells
CashFlow	C11:C20
EndBalance	J21
EndingBalance	J11:J21
LTLoan	D11
LTRate	C3
MinimumBalance	L11:L21
MinimumCash	C7
StartBalance	C6
STLoan	E11:E20
STRate	C4

	F	G	H	I	J	K	L
9	LT	ST	LT	ST	Ending		Minimum
10	Interest	Interest	Payback	Payback	Balance		Balance
11					=StartBalance+SUM(C11:I11)	≥	=MinimumCash
12	=-LTRate*LTLoan	=-STRate*E11		=-E11	=J11+SUM(C12:I12)	≥	=MinimumCash
13	=-LTRate*LTLoan	=-STRate*E12		=-E12	=J12+SUM(C13:I13)	≥	=MinimumCash
14	=-LTRate*LTLoan	=-STRate*E13		=-E13	=J13+SUM(C14:I14)	≥	=MinimumCash
15	=-LTRate*LTLoan	=-STRate*E14		=-E14	=J14+SUM(C15:I15)	≥	=MinimumCash
16	=-LTRate*LTLoan	=-STRate*E15		=-E15	=J15+SUM(C16:I16)	≥	=MinimumCash
17	=-LTRate*LTLoan	=-STRate*E16		=-E16	=J16+SUM(C17:I17)	≥	=MinimumCash
18	=-LTRate*LTLoan	=-STRate*E17		=-E17	=J17+SUM(C18:I18)	≥	=MinimumCash
19	=-LTRate*LTLoan	=-STRate*E18		=-E18	=J18+SUM(C19:I19)	≥	=MinimumCash
20	=-LTRate*LTLoan	=-STRate*E19		=-E19	=J19+SUM(C20:I20)	≥	=MinimumCash
21	=-LTRate*LTLoan	=-STRate*E20	=-LTLoan	=-E20	=J20+SUM(C21:I21)	≥	=MinimumCash

Solver Parameters

Set Target Cell: EndBalance

Equal To: ● Max ○ Min

By Changing Cells: LTLoan,STLoan

Subject to the Constraints:

EndingBalance >= MinimumBalance

Solver Options

☑ Assume Linear Model
☑ Assume Non-Negative

FIGURE 13.23

A spreadsheet model for applying computer simulation to the Everglade Golden Years Company cash flow management problem. The assumption cells are CashFlow (F12:F21) and the forecast cell is EndBalance (N22).

Everglade Cash Flow Management Problem When Applying Simulation

LT Rate	7%									
ST Rate	10%									
Start Balance	1									
Minimum Cash	0.5									

(all cash figures in millions of dollars)

		Cash Flow (Triangular Distribution)			Simulated								Balance				
	Year	Minimum	Most Likely	Maximum	Cash Flow	LT Loan	LT Interest	ST Interest	LT Payback	ST Payback	Before ST Loan	ST Loan	Ending Balance			Minimum Balance
2007	-9	-8	-7	-8.00	6.65					-0.35	0.85	0.50	≥	0.50
2008	-4	-2	1	-1.67		-0.47	-0.09		-0.85	-2.57	3.07	0.50	≥	0.50
2009	-7	-4	0	-3.67		-0.47	-0.31		-3.07	-7.01	7.51	0.50	≥	0.50
2010	0	3	7	1.33		-0.47	-0.75		-7.51	-4.89	5.39	0.50	≥	0.50
2011	3	6	9	6.00		-0.47	-0.54		-5.39	0.11	0.39	0.50	≥	0.50
2012	1	3	5	3.00		-0.47	-0.04		-0.39	2.60	0.00	2.60	≥	0.50
2013	-6	-4	-2	-4.00		-0.47	0		0	-1.86	2.36	0.50	≥	0.50
2014	4	7	12	7.67		-0.47	-0.24		-2.36	5.10	0.00	5.10	≥	0.50
2015	-5	-2	4	-1.00		-0.47	0		0	3.64	0.00	3.64	≥	0.50
2016	5	10	18	11.00		-0.47	0		0	14.17	0.00	14.17	≥	0.50
2017						-0.47	0	-6.65	0	7.05	0.00	7.05	≥	0.50

Range Name	Cells
BalanceBeforeSTLoan	L12:L22
CashFlow	F12:F21
EndBalance	N22
EndingBalance	N12:N22
LTLoan	G12
LTRate	C3
MinimumBalance	P12:P22
MinimumCash	C7
StartBalance	C6
STLoan	M12:M22
STRate	C4

	H	I	J	K	L
10	LT	ST	LT	ST	Before
11	Interest	Interest	Payback	Payback	ST Loan
12					=StartBalance+SUM(F12:K12)
13	=-LTRate*LTLoan	=-STRate*M12		=-M12	=N12+SUM(F13:K13)
14	=-LTRate*LTLoan	=-STRate*M13		=-M13	=N13+SUM(F14:K14)
15	=-LTRate*LTLoan	=-STRate*M14		=-M14	=N14+SUM(F15:K15)
16	=-LTRate*LTLoan	=-STRate*M15		=-M15	=N15+SUM(F16:K16)
17	=-LTRate*LTLoan	=-STRate*M16		=-M16	=N16+SUM(F17:K17)
18	=-LTRate*LTLoan	=-STRate*M17		=-M17	=N17+SUM(F18:K18)
19	=-LTRate*LTLoan	=-STRate*M18		=-M18	=N18+SUM(F19:K19)
20	=-LTRate*LTLoan	=-STRate*M19		=-M19	=N19+SUM(F20:K20)
21	=-LTRate*LTLoan	=-STRate*M20		=-M20	=N20+SUM(F21:K21)
22	=-LTRate*LTLoan	=-STRate*M21	=-LTLoan	=-M21	=N21+SUM(F22:K22)

	M	N	P
10	ST	Ending	Minimum
11	Loan	Balance	Balance
12	=MAX(MinimumBalance−BalanceBeforeSTLoan,0)	=BalanceBeforeSTLoan+STLoan	=MinimumCash
13	=MAX(MinimumBalance−BalanceBeforeSTLoan,0)	=BalanceBeforeSTLoan+STLoan	=MinimumCash
14	=MAX(MinimumBalance−BalanceBeforeSTLoan,0)	=BalanceBeforeSTLoan+STLoan	=MinimumCash
15	=MAX(MinimumBalance−BalanceBeforeSTLoan,0)	=BalanceBeforeSTLoan+STLoan	=MinimumCash
16	=MAX(MinimumBalance−BalanceBeforeSTLoan,0)	=BalanceBeforeSTLoan+STLoan	=MinimumCash
17	=MAX(MinimumBalance−BalanceBeforeSTLoan,0)	=BalanceBeforeSTLoan+STLoan	=MinimumCash
18	=MAX(MinimumBalance−BalanceBeforeSTLoan,0)	=BalanceBeforeSTLoan+STLoan	=MinimumCash
19	=MAX(MinimumBalance−BalanceBeforeSTLoan,0)	=BalanceBeforeSTLoan+STLoan	=MinimumCash
20	=MAX(MinimumBalance−BalanceBeforeSTLoan,0)	=BalanceBeforeSTLoan+STLoan	=MinimumCash
21	=MAX(MinimumBalance−BalanceBeforeSTLoan,0)	=BalanceBeforeSTLoan+STLoan	=MinimumCash
22	=MAX(MinimumBalance−BalanceBeforeSTLoan,0)	=BalanceBeforeSTLoan+STLoan	=MinimumCash

FIGURE 13.24

The frequency chart and cumulative chart that summarize the results of running the simulation model in Figure 13.23 for the Everglade Golden Years cash flow management problem.

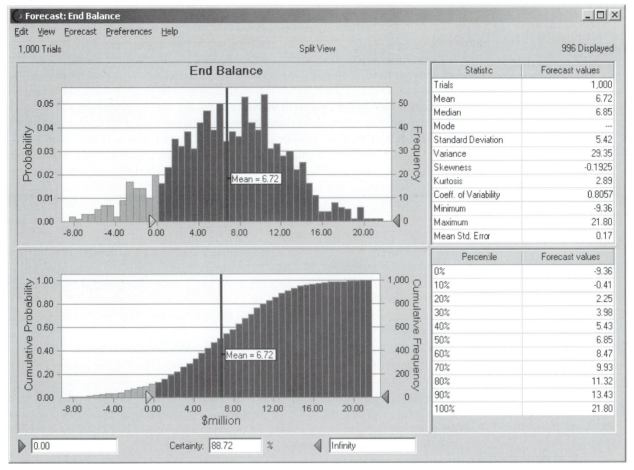

Assumption cells: CashFlow (F12:F21)

Forecast cell: EndBalance (N22)

The Simulation Results

The Certainty box in the frequency chart reveals that nearly 89 percent of the trials resulted in a positive cash balance at the end of the 10 years.

Figure 13.24 shows the results from applying computer simulation with 1,000 trials. Because Everglade management is particularly interested in learning how likely it is that the current financing plan would result in a positive cash balance at the end of the 10 years, the number 0 has been entered into the lower left-hand box in the frequency chart. The Certainty box in the lower middle box then indicates that nearly 89 percent of the trials resulted in a positive cash balance at the end. Furthermore, both the frequency chart and the cumulative chart show that many of these positive cash balances are reasonably large, with some exceeding $10 million. The overall mean is $6.72 million.

On the other hand, it is worrisome that more than 11 percent of the trials resulted in a negative cash balance at the end. Although huge losses were rare, most of these negative cash balances were quite significant, ranging from $1 million to $3 million.

Conclusions

Everglade management is pleased that the simulation results indicate that the proposed financing plan is likely to lead to a favorable outcome at the end of the 10 years. At the same time, management feels that it would be prudent to take steps to reduce the 11 percent chance of an unfavorable outcome.

One possibility would be to increase the size of the long-term loan, since this would reduce the sizes of the higher interest short-term loans that would be needed in the later years if the cash flows are not as good as currently projected. This possibility is investigated in Problem 13.19.

The scenarios that would lead to a negative cash balance at the end of the 10 years are those where the company's retirement communities fail to achieve full occupancy because of overestimating the demand for this service. Therefore, Everglade management concludes that it should take a more cautious approach in moving forward with its current plans to build more retirement communities over the next 10 years. In each case, the final decisions regarding the start date for construction and the size of the retirement community should be made only after obtaining and carefully assessing a detailed forecast of the trends in the demand for this service.

After adopting this policy, Everglade management approves the financing plan that is incorporated into the spreadsheet model in Figure 13.23. In particular, a 10-year loan of $6.65 million will be taken now (the beginning of 2007). In addition, a one-year loan will be taken at the beginning of each year from 2007 to 2016 if it is needed to bring the cash balance for that year up to the level of $500,000 required by company policy.

A more cautious expansion plan is needed to improve the chances of ending with a positive cash balance.

Review Questions

1. What is the cash flow management problem that is currently confronting the management of the Everglade Golden Years Company?
2. Which management science technique was previously used to address this cash flow management problem before applying computer simulation?
3. What aspect of the problem does computer simulation take into account that this prior management science technique could not?
4. What are the quantities in the assumption cells in this example's spreadsheet model for applying computer simulation?
5. How are the sizes of the short-term loans determined in this spreadsheet model?
6. What can happen in a trial of the computer simulation that would result in a negative cash balance at the end of 10 years?
7. What percentage of the trials actually resulted in a negative cash balance at the end of 10 years?
8. What policy did Everglade management adopt to reduce the possibility of having a negative cash balance at the end of 10 years?

13.5 FINANCIAL RISK ANALYSIS: REVISITING THE THINK-BIG DEVELOPMENT CO. PROBLEM

One of the earliest areas of application of computer simulation, dating back to the 1960s, was *financial risk analysis*. This continues today to be one of the most important areas of application.

When assessing any financial investment (or a portfolio of investments), the key trade-off is between the *return* from the investment and the *risk* associated with the investment. Of these two quantities, the less difficult one to determine is the return that would be obtained if everything evolves as currently projected. However, assessing the risk is relatively difficult. Fortunately, computer simulation is ideally suited to perform this risk analysis by obtaining a **risk profile,** namely, a *frequency distribution* of the return from the investment. The portion of the frequency distribution that reflects an unfavorable return clearly describes the risk associated with the investment.

The following example illustrates this approach in the context of real estate investments. Like the Everglade example in the preceding section, you will see computer simulation being used to refine prior analysis done by linear programming because this prior analysis was unable to take the uncertainty in future cash flows into account.

The Think-Big Financial Risk Analysis Problem

As introduced in Section 3.2, the Think-Big Development Co. is a major investor in commercial real estate development projects. It has been considering taking a share in three large construction projects—a high-rise office building, a hotel, and a shopping center. In each case,

An Application Vignette

Since its founding in 1914, Merrill Lynch has been a leading full-service financial service firm that strives to bring Wall Street to Main Street by making financial markets accessible to everyone. It employs a highly trained salesforce of over 15,000 financial advisors throughout the United States as well as operating in 36 countries. A Fortune 100 company with net revenues of $26 billion in 2005, it manages client assets that total over $1.7 trillion.

Faced with increasing competition from discount brokerage firms and electronic brokerage firms, a task force was formed in late 1998 to recommend a product or service response to the marketplace challenge. Merrill Lynch's strong management science group was charged with doing the detailed analysis of two potential new pricing options for clients. One option would replace charging for trades individually by charging a fixed percentage of a client's assets at Merrill Lynch and then allowing an unlimited number of free trades and complete access to a financial advisor. The other option would allow self-directed investors to invest online directly for a fixed low fee per trade without consulting a financial advisor.

The great challenge facing the management science group was to determine a "sweet spot" for the prices for these options that would be likely to grow the firm's business and increase its revenues while minimizing the risk of losing revenue instead. A key tool in attacking this problem proved to be computer simulation. To undertake a major computer simulation study, the group assembled and evaluated an extensive volume of data on the assets and trading activity of the firm's 5 million clients. For each segment of the client base, a careful analysis was done of its offer-adoption behavior by using managerial judgment, market research, and experience with clients. With this input, the group then formulated and ran a simulation model with various pricing scenarios to identify the pricing sweet spot.

The implementation of these results had a profound impact on Merrill Lynch's competitive position, restoring it to a leadership role in the industry. Instead of continuing to lose ground to the fierce new competition, client assets managed by the company had increased by $22 billion and its incremental revenue reached $80 million within 18 months. The CEO of Merrill Lynch called the new strategy "the most important decision we as a firm have made (in the last 20 years)."

Source: S. Altschuler, D. Batavia, J. Bennett, R. Labe, B. Liao, R. Nigam, and J. Oh, "Pricing Analysis for Merrill Lynch Integrated Choice," *Interfaces* 32, no. 1 (January–February 2002), pp. 5–19.

---

the partners in the project would spend three years with the construction, then retain ownership for three years while establishing the property, and then sell the property in the seventh year. By using estimates of expected cash flows, Section 3.2 describes how linear programming has been applied to obtain the following proposal for how big a share Think-Big should take in each of these projects.

Proposal

Do not take any share of the high-rise building project.

Take a 16.50 percent share of the hotel project.

Take a 13.11 percent share of the shopping center project.

This proposal is estimated to return a *net present value* (NPV) of $18.11 million to Think-Big.

However, Think-Big management understands very well that such decisions should not be made without taking risk into account. These are very risky projects since it is unclear how well these properties will compete in the marketplace when they go into operation in a few years. Although the construction costs during the first three years can be estimated fairly roughly, the net incomes during the following three years of operation are very uncertain. Consequently, there is an extremely wide range of possible values for each sale price in year 7. Therefore, management wants *risk analysis* to be performed in the usual way (with computer simulation) to obtain a *risk profile* of what the total NPV might actually turn out to be with this proposal.

Management needs a risk profile of the proposal to assess whether the likelihood of a sizable profit justifies the risk of possible large losses.

To perform this risk analysis, Think-Big staff now has devoted considerable time to estimating the amount of uncertainty in the cash flows for each project over the next seven years. These data are summarized in Table 13.2 (in units of millions of dollars) for a 100 percent share of each project. Thus, when taking a smaller percentage share of a project, the numbers in the table should be reduced proportionally to obtain the relevant numbers for Think-Big. In years 1 through 6 for each project, the probability distribution of cash flow is assumed to be a

TABLE 13.2
The Estimated Cash
Flows for 100 Percent of
the Hotel and Shopping
Center Projects

	Hotel Project		Shopping Center Project	
Year	**Cash Flow ($1,000,000s)**		**Year**	**Cash Flow ($1,000,000s)**
0	−80		0	−90
1	Normal (−80, 5)		1	Normal (−50, 5)
2	Normal (−80, 10)		2	Normal (−20, 5)
3	Normal (−70, 15)		3	Normal (−60, 10)
4	Normal (+30, 20)		4	Normal (+15, 15)
5	Normal (+40, 20)		5	Normal (+25, 15)
6	Normal (+50, 20)		6	Normal (+40, 15)
7	Uniform (+200, 844)		7	Uniform (160, 600)

normal distribution, where the first number shown is the estimated *mean* and the second number is the estimated *standard deviation* of the distribution. In year 7, the income from the sale of the property is assumed to have a *uniform distribution* over the range from the first number shown to the second number shown.

To compute NPV, a cost of capital of 10 percent per annum is being used. Thus, the cash flow in year n is divided by 1.1^n before adding these discounted cash flows to obtain NPV.

A Spreadsheet Model for Applying Computer Simulation

A spreadsheet model has been formulated for this problem in Figure 13.25. There is no uncertainty about the immediate (Year 0) cash flows appearing in cells D6 and D16, so these are data cells. However, because of the uncertainty for Years 1–7, cells D7:D13 and D17:D23 containing the simulated cash flows for these years need to be assumption cells. (The numbers in these cells in Figure 13.25 happen to be mean values that were entered merely to start the process of defining these assumption cells.) Table 13.2 specifies the probability distributions and their parameters that have been estimated for these cash flows, so the form of the distributions has been recorded in cells E7:E13 and E17:E23 while entering the corresponding parameters in cells F7:G13 and F17:G23. Figure 13.26 shows the Normal Distribution dialogue box that is used to enter the parameters (mean and standard deviation) for the normal distribution into the first assumption cell D7 by referencing cells F7 and G7. The parameters for the other normal distributions are then copied and pasted into the corresponding assumption cells. The Uniform Distribution dialogue box (like the similar one displayed earlier in Figure 13.3 for a discrete uniform distribution) is used in a similar way to enter the parameters (minimum and maximum) for this kind of distribution into the assumption cells D13 and D23.

The simulated cash flows in cells D6:D13 and D16:D23 are for 100 percent of the hotel project and the shopping center project, respectively, so Think-Big's share of these cash flows needs to be reduced proportionally based on its shares in these projects. The proposal being analyzed is to take the shares shown in cells H28:H29. The equations entered into cells D28:D35 (see the bottom of Figure 13.25) then gives Think-Big's total cash flow in the respective years for its share of the two projects.

Think-Big's management wants to obtain a risk profile of what the total net present value (NPV) might be with this proposal. Therefore, the forecast cell is NetPresent Value (D37).

Here is a summary of the key cells in this model.

Assumption cells: Cells D7:D13 and D17:D23
Decision variables: HotelShare (H28) and ShoppingCenterShare (H29)
Forecast cell: NetPresentValue (D37)

The Simulation Results

Using the Run Preferences dialogue box to specify 1,000 trials, Figure 13.27 shows the results of applying computer simulation to the spreadsheet model in Figure 13.25. The frequency chart in Figure 13.27 provides the risk profile for the proposal since it shows the relative likelihood of the various values of NPV, including those where NPV is negative. The mean is $18.117 million, which is very attractive. However, the 1,000 trials generated an extremely wide range of

Excel Tip: The NPV (*discount rate, cash flows*) function calculates the net present value of a stream of *future* cash flows at regular intervals (e.g., annually) in a range of cells (*cash flows*) using the specified *discount rate* per interval.

The frequency chart provides the risk profile for the proposal.

FIGURE 13.25

A spreadsheet model for applying computer simulation to the Think-Big Development Co. financial risk analysis problem. The assumption cells are cells D7:D13 and D17:D23, the forecast cell is NetPresentValue (D37), and the decision variables are HotelShare (H28) and ShoppingCenterShare (H29).

	A	B	C	D	E	F	G	H
1		**Simulation of Think-Big Development Co. Problem**						
2								
3				**Project Simulated**				
4				**Cash Flow**				
5		**Hotel Project:**		**($millions)**				
6		Construction Costs:	Year 0	-80				
7			Year 1	-80	*Normal*	-80	5	(mean, st. dev.)
8			Year 2	-80	*Normal*	-80	10	(mean, st. dev.)
9			Year 3	-70	*Normal*	-70	15	(mean, st. dev.)
10		Revenue per Share	Year 4	30	*Normal*	30	20	(mean, st. dev.)
11			Year 5	40	*Normal*	40	20	(mean, st. dev.)
12			Year 6	50	*Normal*	50	20	(mean, st. dev.)
13		Selling Price per Share	Year 7	522	*Uniform*	200	844	(min,max)
14								
15		**Shopping Center Project**						
16		Construction Costs:	Year 0	-90				
17			Year 1	-50	*Normal*	-50	5	(mean, st. dev.)
18			Year 2	-20	*Normal*	-20	5	(mean, st. dev.)
19			Year 3	-60	*Normal*	-60	10	(mean, st. dev.)
20		Revenue per Share	Year 4	15	*Normal*	15	15	(mean, st. dev.)
21			Year 5	25	*Normal*	25	15	(mean, st. dev.)
22			Year 6	40	*Normal*	40	15	(mean, st. dev.)
23		Selling Price per Share	Year 7	387.5	*Uniform*	160	615	(min,max)
24								
25				**Think-Big's**				
26				**Simulated Cash Flow**				
27				**($millions)**				**Share**
28			Year 0	-24.999			Hotel	16.50%
29			Year 1	-19.755		Shopping Center		13.11%
30			Year 2	-15.822				
31			Year 3	-19.416		Cost of Capital		10%
32			Year 4	6.917				
33			Year 5	9.878				
34			Year 6	13.494				
35			Year 7	136.931				
36								
37		Net present Value ($millions)		18.120				

	C	D
25		**Total Simulated**
26		**Cash Flow**
27		**($millions)**
28	Year 0	=HotelShare*D6+ShoppingCenterShare*D16
29	Year 1	=HotelShare*D7+ShoppingCenterShare*D17
30	Year 2	=HotelShare*D8+ShoppingCenterShare*D18
31	Year 3	=HotelShare*D9+ShoppingCenterShare*D19
32	Year 4	=HotelShare*D10+ShoppingCenterShare*D20
33	Year 5	=HotelShare*D11+ShoppingCenterShare*D21
34	Year 6	=HotelShare*D12+ShoppingCenterShare*D22
35	Year 7	=HotelShare*D13+ShoppingCenterShare*D23
36		
37	Net Present Value ($millions)	=CashFlowYear0+NPV(CostOfCapital,CashFlowYear1To7)

Range Name	Cells
CashFlowYear0	D28
CashFlowYear1To7	D29:D35
CostOfCapital	H31
HotelShare	H28
NetPresentValue	D37
ShoppingCenterShare	H29

FIGURE 13.26

A normal distribution with parameters −80 (=F7) and 5 (=G7) is being entered into the first assumption cell D7 in the spreadsheet model in Figure 13.25.

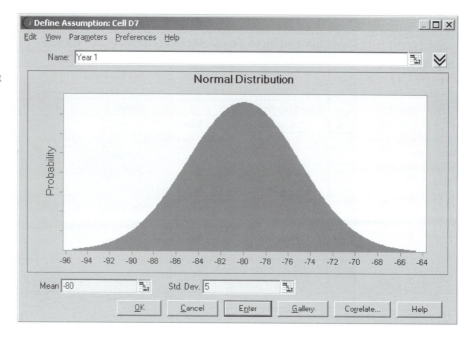

FIGURE 13.27

The frequency chart and percentiles table that summarize the results of running the simulation model in Figure 13.25 for the Think-Big Development Co. financial risk analysis problem. The Certainty box under the frequency chart reveals that 81.39 percent of the trials resulted in a positive value of the net present value.

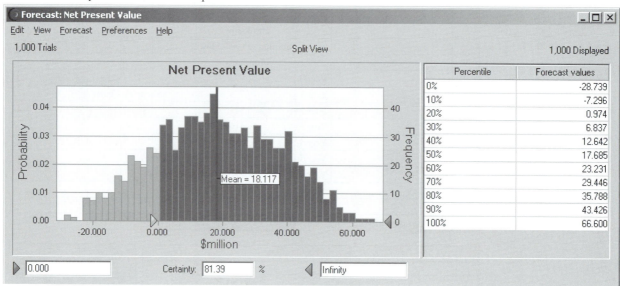

NPV values, all the way from about −$29 million to over $66 million. Thus, there is a significant chance of incurring a huge loss. By entering 0 into the box in the lower left-hand corner of the frequency chart, the Certainty box indicates that 81.39 percent of the trials resulted in a profit (a positive value of NPV). This also gives the bad news that there is nearly a 19 percent chance of incurring a loss of some size. The lightly shaded portion of the chart to the left of 0 shows that most of the trials with losses involved losses up to about $10 million, but that quite a few trials had losses that ranged from $10 million to nearly $30 million.

The percentiles table in Figure 13.27 also provides management with some specific numbers for better assessing the risk. The 10 percent percentile of −7.296 indicates a 10 percent chance of incurring a loss greater than about $7.3 million. On the other hand, the 90 percent percentile of 43.426 indicates a 10 percent chance of achieving a huge profit (NPV) exceeding $43.4 million.

Armed with all this information, a managerial decision now can be made about whether the likelihood of a sizable profit justifies the significant risk of incurring a loss and perhaps even a very substantial loss. Thus, the role of computer simulation is to provide the information needed for making a sound decision, but it is management that uses its best judgment to make the decision.

Review **Questions**

1. What is a *risk profile* for an investment (or a portfolio of investments)?
2. What is the investment proposal that the management of the Think-Big Development Co. needs to evaluate?
3. What are the estimates that need to be made to prepare for applying computer simulation to this example?
4. What quantities appear in the assumption cells of the spreadsheet model for this example?
5. What quantity appears in the forecast cell for this example?
6. Does computer simulation indicate a significant chance of incurring a loss if Think-Big management approves the investment proposal?

13.6   REVENUE MANAGEMENT IN THE TRAVEL INDUSTRY

One of the most prominent areas for the application of management science in recent years has been in improving *revenue management* in the travel industry. Revenue management refers to the various ways of increasing the flow of revenues through such devices as setting up different fare classes for different categories of customers. The objective is to maximize total income by setting fares that are at the upper edge of what the different market segments are willing to pay and then allocating seats appropriately to the various fare classes.

As the example in this section will illustrate, one key area of revenue management is *overbooking,* that is, accepting a slightly larger number of reservations than the number of seats available. There usually are a small number of no-shows, so overbooking will increase revenue by essentially filling the available seating. However, there also are costs incurred if the number of arriving customers exceeds the number of available seats. Therefore, the amount of overbooking needs to be set carefully so as to achieve an appropriate trade-off between filling seats and avoiding the need to turn away customers who have a reservation.

A new overbooking model increased annual revenues for American Airlines by about $225 million.

American Airlines was the pioneer in making extensive use of management science for improving its revenue management. The guiding motto was "selling the right seats to the right customers at the right time." This work won the 1991 Franz Edelman Award as that year's best application of management science anywhere throughout the world. As described in an article in the January–February 1992 issue of *Interfaces,* this application was credited with increasing annual revenues for American Airlines by over $500 million. Nearly half of these increased revenues came from the use of a new overbooking model.

Following this breakthrough at American Airlines, other airlines quickly stepped up their use of management science in similar ways. These applications to revenue management then spread to other segments of the travel industry (train travel, cruise lines, rental cars, hotels, etc.) around the world. Our example below involves overbooking by an airline company.

The Transcontinental Airlines Overbooking Problem

Transcontinental Airlines has a daily flight (excluding weekends) from San Francisco to Chicago that is mainly used by business travelers. There are 150 seats available in the single cabin. The average fare per seat is $300. This is a nonrefundable fare, so no-shows forfeit the entire fare. The fixed cost for operating the flight is $30,000, so more than 100 reservations are needed to make a profit on any particular day.

For most of these flights, the number of requests for reservations considerably exceeds the number of seats available. The company's management science group has been compiling data on the number of reservation requests per flight for the past several months. The average number has been 195, but with considerable variation from flight to flight on both sides of this average. Plotting a frequency chart for these data suggests that they roughly follow a bell-shaped curve. Therefore, the group estimates that the number of reservation requests per flight has a *normal distribution* with a mean of 195. A calculation from the data estimates that the standard deviation is 30.

The company's policy is to accept 10 percent more reservations than the number of seats available on nearly all its flights, since roughly 10 percent of all its customers making reservations end up being no-shows. However, if its experience with a particular flight is much different from this, then an exception is made and the management science group is called in to analyze what the overbooking policy should be for that particular flight. This is what has just happened regarding the daily flight from San Francisco to Chicago. Even when the full quota of 165 reservations has been reached (which happens for most of the flights), there usually are a significant number of empty seats. While gathering its data, the management science group has discovered the reason why. Only 80 percent of the customers who make reservations for this flight actually show up to take the flight. The other 20 percent forfeit the fare (or, in most cases, allow their company to do so) because their plans have changed.

An unusually high 20 percent no-show rate requires developing a special overbooking policy for this particular flight.

Now that the data have been gathered, the management science group decides to begin its analysis by investigating the option of increasing the number of reservations to accept for this flight to 190. If the number of reservation requests for a particular day actually reaches this level, then this number should be large enough to avoid many, if any, empty seats. Furthermore, this number should be small enough that there will not be many occasions when a significant number of customers need to be bumped from the flight because the number of arrivals exceeds the number of seats available (150). Thus, 190 appears to be a good first guess for an appropriate trade-off between avoiding many empty seats and avoiding bumping many customers.

When a customer is bumped from this flight, Transcontinental Airlines arranges to put the customer on the next available flight to Chicago on another airline. The company's average cost for doing this is $150. In addition, the company gives the customer a voucher worth $200 for use on a future flight. The company also feels that an additional $100 should be assessed for the intangible cost of a loss of goodwill on the part of the bumped customer. Therefore, the total cost of bumping a customer is estimated to be $450.

The management science group now wants to investigate the option of accepting 190 reservations by using computer simulation to generate frequency charts for the following three measures of performance for each day's flight:

1. The profit.
2. The number of filled seats.
3. The number of customers denied boarding.

A Spreadsheet Model for Applying Computer Simulation

Figure 13.28 shows a spreadsheet model for this problem. Because there are three measures of interest here, the spreadsheet model needs three forecast cells. These forecast cells are Profit (F23), NumberOfFilledSeats (C20), and NumberDeniedBoarding (C21). The decision variable ReservationsToAccept (C13) has been set at 190 for investigating this current option. Some basic data have been entered near the top of the spreadsheet in cells C4:C7.

Having three measures of performance means that the simulation model needs three forecast cells.

Each trial of the computer simulation will correspond to one day's flight. There are two random inputs associated with each flight, namely, the number of customers requesting reservations (abbreviated as Ticket Demand in cell B10) and the number of customers who actually arrive to take the flight (abbreviated as Number That Show in cell B17). Thus, the two assumption cells in this model are SimulatedTicketDemand (C10) and NumberThatShow (C17).

Since the management science group has estimated that the number of customers requesting reservations has a normal distribution with a mean of 195 and a standard deviation of 30, this information has been entered into cells D10:F10. The Normal Distribution dialogue box (shown earlier in Figure 13.26) then has been used to enter this distribution with these parameters into SimulatedTicketDemand (C10). Because the normal distribution is a continuous distribution, whereas the number of reservations must have an integer value, Demand (C11) uses Excel's ROUND function to round the number in SimulatedTicketDemand (C10) to the nearest integer.

Excel Tip: The Excel function ROUND(x, 0) rounds the value x to the nearest integer. The zero specifies that 0 digits after the decimal point should be included when rounding.

FIGURE 13.28

A spreadsheet model for applying computer simulation to the Transcontinental Airlines overbooking problem. The assumption cells are SimulatedTicketDemand (C10) and NumberThatShow (C17). The forecast cells are Profit (F23), NumberOfFilledSeats (C20), and NumberDeniedBoarding (C21). The decision variable is ReservationsToAccept (C13).

	A	B	C	D	E	F
1		**Airline Overbooking**				
2						
3			**Data**			
4		Available Seats	150			
5		Fixed Cost	$30,000			
6		Avg. Fare / Seat	$300			
7		Cost of Bumping	$450			
8						
9					Mean	Standard Dev.
10		Ticket Demand	195	*Normal*	195	30
11		Demand (rounded)	195			
12						
13		Reservations to Accept	190			
14						
15					Tickets	Probability
16					Purchased	to Show Up
17		Number That Show	152	*Binomial*	190	80%
18						
19						
20		Number of Filled Seats	150		Ticket Revenue	$45,000
21		Number Denied Boarding	2		Bumping Cost	$900
22					Fixed Cost	$30,000
23					Profit	$14,100

	B	C
11	Demand (rounded)	=ROUND(SimulatedTicketDemand,0)

	E
15	Tickets
16	Purchased
17	=MIN(Demand,ReservationsToAccept)

Range Name	Cell
AvailableSeats	C4
AverageFare	C6
BumpingCost	F21
CostOfBumping	C7
Demand	C11
FixedCost	C5
NumberDeniedBoarding	C21
NumberOfFilledSeats	C20
NumberThatShow	C17
Profit	F23
ReservationsToAccept	C13
SimulatedTicketDemand	C10
TicketRevenue	F20
TicketsPurchased	E17

	B	C
20	Number of Filled Seats	=MIN(AvailableSeats,NumberThatShow)
21	Number Denied Boarding	=MAX(0,NumberThatShow–AvailableSeats)

	E	F
20	Ticket Revenue	=AverageFare*NumberOfFilledSeats
21	Bumping Cost	=CostOfBumping*NumberDeniedBoarding
22	Fixed Cost	=FixedCost
23	Profit	=TicketRevenue–BumpingCost–FixedCost

The random input for the second assumption cell NumberThatShow (C17) depends on two key quantities. One is TicketsPurchased (E17), which is the minimum of Demand (C11) and ReservationsToAccept (C13). The other key quantity is the probability that an individual making a reservation actually will show up to take the flight. This probability has been set at 80 percent in cell F17 since this is the *average* percentage of those who have shown up for the flight in recent months.

However, the *actual* percentage of those who show up on any particular day may vary somewhat on either side of this average percentage. Therefore, even though NumberThat-Show (C17)

FIGURE 13.29

A binomial distribution with parameters 0.8 (=F17) and 190 (=E17) is being entered into the assumption cell NumberThatShow (C17).

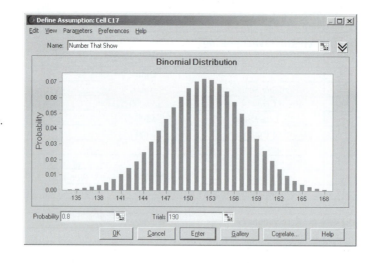

These characteristics of the binomial distribution are just what is needed for the assumption cell NumberThatShow (C17).

would be expected to be fairly close to the product of cells E17 and F17, there will be some variation according to some probability distribution. What is the appropriate distribution for this assumption cell? Section 13.7 will describe the characteristics of various distributions. The one that has the characteristics to fit this assumption cell turns out to be the *binomial distribution.*

As indicated in Section 13.7, the binomial distribution gives the distribution of the number of times a particular event occurs out of a certain number of opportunities. In this case, the *event* of interest is a passenger showing up to take the flight. The *opportunity* for this event to occur arises when a customer makes a reservation for the flight. These opportunities are conventionally referred to as *trials* (not to be confused with a trial of a computer simulation). The binomial distribution assumes that the trials are statistically independent and that, on each trial, there is a fixed probability (80 percent in this case) that the event will occur. The parameters of the distribution are this fixed probability and the number of trials.

Figure 13.29 displays the Binomial Distribution dialogue box that enters this distribution into NumberThatShow (C17) by referencing the parameters in cells F17 and E17. The actual value in Trials for the binomial distribution will vary from simulation trial to simulation trial because it depends on the number of tickets purchased which in turn depends on the ticket demand which is random. Crystal Ball therefore must determine the value for TicketsPurchased (E17) *before* it can randomly generate NumberThatShow (C17). Fortunately, Crystal Ball automatically takes care of the order in which to generate the various assumption cells so that this is not a problem.

The equations entered into all the output cells and forecast cells are given at the bottom of Figure 13.28.

Here is a summary of the key cells in this model.

Assumption cells:	SimulatedTicketDemand (C10) and NumberThatShow (C17)
Decision variable:	ReservationsToAccept (C13)
Forecast cells:	Profit (F23), NumberOfFilledSeats (C20), and NumberDeniedBoarding (C21)

The Simulation Results

Figure 13.30 shows the frequency chart obtained for each of the three forecast cells after applying computer simulation for 1,000 trials to the spreadsheet model in Figure 13.28, with ReservationsToAccept (C13) set at 190.

The profit results estimate that the mean profit per flight would be $11,693. However, this mean is a little less than the profits that had the highest frequencies. The reason is that a small number of trials had profits far below the mean, including even a few that incurred losses, which dragged the mean down somewhat. By entering 0 into the lower left-hand box, the Certainty box reports that 98.87 percent of the trials resulted in a profit for that day's flight.

FIGURE 13.30

The frequency charts that summarize the results for the respective forecast cells—Profit (F23), NumberOfFilledSeats (C20), and NumberDeniedBoarding (C21)—from running the simulation model in Figure 13.28 for the Transcontinental Airlines overbooking problem. The Certainty box below the first frequency chart reveals that 98.87 percent of the trials resulted in a positive profit.

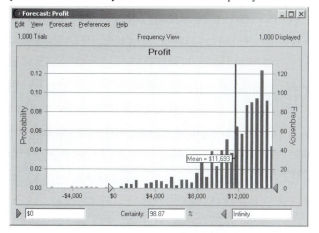
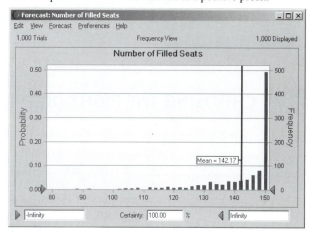

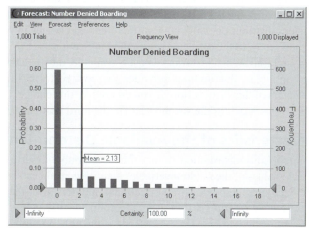

The frequency chart for NumberOfFilledSeats (C20) indicates that almost half of the 1,000 trials resulted in all 150 seats being filled. Furthermore, most of the remaining trials had at least 130 seats filled. The fact that the mean of 142.17 is so close to 150 shows that a policy of accepting 190 reservations would do an excellent job of filling seats.

The price that would be paid for filling seats so well is that a few customers would need to be bumped from some of the flights. The frequency chart for NumberDeniedBoarding (C21) indicates that this occurred over 40 percent of the time. On nearly all of these trials, the number ranged between 1 and 10. Considering that no customers were denied boarding for 60 percent of the trials, the mean number is only 2.13.

We will return to this example in Section 13.8 to further evaluate how many reservations to accept.

Although these results suggest that a policy of accepting 190 reservations would be an attractive option for the most part, they do not demonstrate that this is necessarily the best option. Additional simulation runs are needed with other numbers entered in ReservationsTo Accept (C13) to pin down the optimal value of this decision variable. We will demonstrate how to do this efficiently with the help of a decision table in Section 13.8.

Review Questions

1. What is meant by *revenue management* in the travel industry?
2. In the pioneering application of management science to revenue management at American Airlines, what increase in annual revenues was achieved?
3. What problem is being addressed by the management science group at Transcontinental Airlines in this section's example?
4. What trade-off must be considered in addressing this problem?

5. What is the decision variable for this problem?
6. What quantities appear in the forecast cells of the spreadsheet model for this problem?
7. What quantities appear in the assumption cells of the spreadsheet model?
8. What are the parameters of a binomial distribution?
9. Did the simulation results obtained in this section determine how many reservations should be accepted for the flight under consideration?

13.7 CHOOSING THE RIGHT DISTRIBUTION

As mentioned in Section 13.1, Crystal Ball's **Distribution Gallery** provides a wealth of choices. Any of 21 probability distributions can be selected as the one to be entered into any assumption cell. In the preceding sections, we have illustrated the use of five of these distributions (the discrete uniform, uniform, triangular, normal, and binomial distributions). However, not much was said about *why* any particular distribution was chosen.

In this section, we focus on the issue of how to choose the right distribution. We begin by surveying the characteristics of many of the 21 distributions and how these characteristics help to identify the best choice. We next describe a special feature of Crystal Ball for creating a custom distribution when none of the other 20 choices in the Distribution Gallery will do. We then return to the case study presented in Section 13.1 to illustrate another special feature of Crystal Ball. When historical data are available, this feature will identify which of the available continuous distributions provides the best fit to these data while also estimating the parameters of this distribution. If you do not like this choice, it will even identify which of the distributions provides the second best fit, the third best fit, and so on.

Characteristics of the Available Distributions

The probability distribution of any random variable describes the relative likelihood of the possible values of the random variable. A *continuous* distribution is used if *any* values are possible, including both integer and fractional numbers, over the entire range of possible values. A *discrete* distribution is used if only certain specific values (e.g., only the integer numbers over some range) are possible. However, if the only possible values are integer numbers over a relatively broad range, a continuous distribution may be used as an approximation by rounding any fractional value to the nearest integer. (This approximation was used in cells C10:C11 of the spreadsheet model in Figure 13.28.) Crystal Ball's Distribution Gallery includes both continuous and discrete distributions. We will begin by looking at the continuous distributions.

The right-hand side of Figure 13.31 shows the dialogue box for three popular continuous distributions from the Distribution Gallery. The dark figure in each dialogue box displays a typical *probability density function* for that distribution. The height of the probability density function at the various points shows the relative likelihood of the corresponding values along the horizontal axis. Each of these distributions has a most likely value where the probability density function reaches a peak. Furthermore, all the other relatively high points are near the peak. This indicates that there is a tendency for one of the central values located near the most likely value to be the one that occurs. Therefore, these distributions are referred as *central-tendency distributions*. The characteristics of each of these distributions are listed on the left-hand side of Figure 13.31.

The Normal Distribution

The normal distribution is widely used by both management scientists and others because it describes so many natural phenomena. One reason that it arises so frequently is that the sum of many random variables tends to have a normal distribution (approximately) even when the individual random variables do not. Using this distribution requires estimating the mean and the standard deviation. The mean coincides with the most likely value because this is a symmetric distribution. Thus, the mean is a very intuitive quantity that can be readily estimated,

FIGURE 13.31

The characteristics and dialogue boxes for three popular central-tendency distributions in Crystal Ball's Distribution Gallery: (1) the normal distribution, (2) the triangular distribution, and (3) the lognormal distribution.

Popular Central-Tendency Distributions

Normal Distribution:
- Some value most likely (the mean)
- Values close to mean more likely
- Symmetric (as likely above as below mean)
- Extreme values possible, but rare

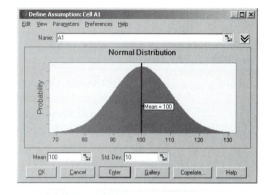

Triangular Distribution:
- Some value most likely
- Values close to most likely value more common
- Can be asymmetric
- Fixed upper and lower bound

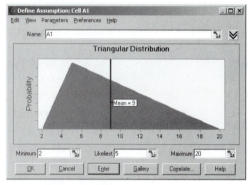

Lognormal Distribution:
- Some value most likely
- Positively skewed (below mean more likely)
- Values cannot fall below zero
- Extreme values (high end only) possible, but rare

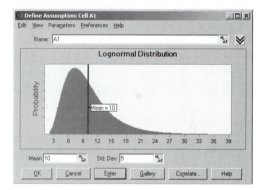

but the standard deviation is not. About two-thirds of the distribution lies within one standard deviation of the mean. Therefore, if historical data are not available for calculating an estimate of the standard deviation, a rough estimate can be elicited from a knowledgeable individual by asking for an amount such that the random value will be within that amount of the mean about two-thirds of the time.

One danger with using the normal distribution for some applications is that it can give negative values even when such values actually are impossible. Fortunately, it can give negative values with significant frequency only if the mean is less than three standard deviations. For example, consider the situation where a normal distribution was entered into an assumption cell in Figure 13.28 to represent the number of customers requesting a reservation. A negative number would make no sense in this case, but this was no problem since the mean (195) was much larger than three standard deviations ($3 \times 30 = 90$) so a negative value essentially could never occur. (When normal distributions were entered into assumption cells in Figure 13.25 to represent cash flows, the means were small or even negative, but this also was no problem since cash flows can be either negative or positive.)

The normal distribution allows negative values, which is not appropriate for some applications.

The Triangular Distribution

A comparison of the shapes of the triangular and normal distributions in Figure 13.31 reveals some key differences. One is that the triangular distribution has a fixed minimum value and a fixed maximum value, whereas the normal distribution allows rare extreme values far into the tails. Another is that the triangular distribution can be asymmetric (as shown in the figure), because the most likely value does not need to be midway between the bounds, whereas the normal distribution always is symmetric. This provides additional flexibility to the triangular distribution. Another key difference is that all its parameters (the minimum value, most likely value, and maximum value) are intuitive ones, so they are relatively easy to estimate.

The parameters of a triangular distribution are relatively easy to estimate because they are so intuitive.

These advantages have made the triangular distribution a popular choice for computer simulations. They are the reason why this distribution was used in previous examples to represent competitors' bids for a construction contract (in Figure 13.11), activity times (in Figure 13.17), and cash flows (in Figure 13.23).

However, the triangular distribution also has certain disadvantages. One is that, in many situations, rare extreme values far into the tails are possible, so it is quite artificial to have fixed minimum and maximum values. This also makes it difficult to develop meaningful estimates of the bounds. Still another disadvantage is that a curve with a gradually changing slope, such as the bell-shaped curve for the normal distribution, should describe the true distribution more accurately than the straight line segments in the triangular distribution.

The Lognormal Distribution

The lognormal distribution shown at the bottom of Figure 13.31 combines some of the advantages of the normal and triangular distributions. It has a curve with a gradually changing slope. It also allows rare extreme values on the high side. At the same time, it does not allow negative values, so it automatically fits situations where this is needed. This is particularly advantageous when the mean is less than three standard deviations and the normal distribution should not be used.

The lognormal distribution has a long tail to the right but does not allow negative values to the left.

This distribution always is "positively skewed," meaning that the long tail always is to the right. This forces the most likely value to be toward the left side (so the mean is on its right), so this distribution is less flexible than the triangular distribution. Another disadvantage is that it has the same parameters as the normal distribution (the mean and the standard deviation), so the less intuitive one (the standard deviation) is difficult to estimate unless historical data are available.

When a positively skewed distribution that does not allow negative values is needed, the lognormal distribution provides an attractive option. That is why this distribution frequently is used to represent stock prices or real estate prices.

The Uniform and Discrete Uniform Distributions

Although the preceding three distributions are all central-tendency distributions, the uniform distributions shown in Figure 13.32 definitely are not. They have a fixed minimum value and a fixed maximum value. Otherwise, they say that no value between these bounds is any more likely than any other possible value. Therefore, these distributions have more variability than the central-tendency distributions with the same range of possible values (excluding rare extreme values).

The choice between these two distributions depends on which values between the minimum and maximum values are possible. If *any* values in this range are possible, including even *fractional* values, then the uniform distribution would be preferred over the discrete uniform distribution. If only integer values are possible, then the discrete uniform distribution would be the preferable one.

Either of these distributions is a particularly convenient one because it has only two parameters (the minimum value and the maximum value) and both are very intuitive. These distributions receive considerable use for this reason. Earlier in this chapter, the discrete uniform distribution was used to represent the demand for a newspaper (in Figure 13.1), whereas the uniform distribution was used to generate the bid for a construction

FIGURE 13.32

The characteristics and dialogue box for the uniform distribution in Crystal Ball's Distribution Gallery.

Uniform and Discrete Uniform Distribution

Uniform Distribution:

• Fixed minimum and maximum value

• All values equally likely

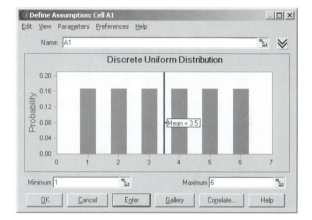

Discrete Uniform Distribution:

• Fixed minimum and maximum value

• All integer values equally likely

The uniform distribution is easy to use but usually is only a rough approximation of the true distribution.

project by one competitor (in Figure 13.11), and the future sale price for real estate property (in Figure 13.25).

The disadvantage of this distribution is that it usually is only a rough approximation of the true distribution. It is uncommon for either the minimum value or the maximum value to be just as likely as any other value between these bounds while any value barely outside these bounds is impossible.

The Weibull and Beta Distributions

We will describe the Weibull and beta distributions together because, as suggested by their similar shapes in Figure 13.33, these two distributions have similar characteristics. In contrast to the uniform distribution, both are central-tendency distributions. In contrast to the normal, lognormal, and uniform distributions, both have more than two parameters. The three (for the Weibull) or four (for the beta) parameters provide great flexibility in adjusting the shape of the curve to fit the situation. This enables making the distribution positively skewed, symmetric, or negatively skewed as desired. This flexibility is the key advantage of these distributions. Another advantage is that they have a minimum value, so negative values can be avoided. The location parameter sets the minimum value for the Weibull distribution. The Weibull distribution allows rare extreme values to the right, whereas the beta distribution has a fixed maximum value.

Certain parameters, such as the location parameter mentioned above for the Weibull distribution, or the minimum and maximum parameter for the beta distribution, have an intuitive interpretation. The scale parameter for the Weibull distribution simply sets the width of the distribution (excluding rare extreme values). However, neither the shape parameter for

FIGURE 13.33

The characteristics and dialogue boxes for three- and four-parameter distributions in Crystal Ball's Distribution Gallery: (1) the Weibull distribution and (2) the beta distribution.

Three- and Four-Parameter Distributions

Weibull Distribution:

- Random value above some number (location)
- Shape > 0 (usually ≤10)
- Shape < 3 becomes more positively skewed (below mean more likely) until it resembles exponential distribution (equivalent at Shape = 1)
- Symmetrical at Shape = 3.25, becomes more negatively skewed above that
- Scale defines width

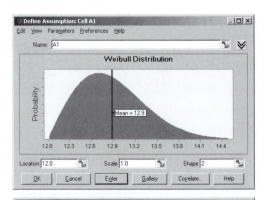

Beta Distribution:

- Random value between some minimum and maximum
- Shape specified using two positive values (alpha, beta)
- Alpha < beta: positively skewed (below mean more likely)
- Beta < alpha: negatively skewed

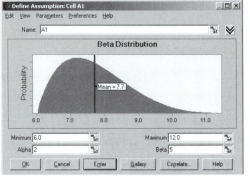

The Weibull and beta distributions are flexible enough to fit many situations, but they usually require historical data in order to calculate good estimates of their parameters.

the Weibull distribution nor the alpha and beta parameters for the beta distribution are particularly intuitive. Therefore, these distributions are mainly used only when historical data are available for calculating estimates of these parameters. (One exception is the innovative use of the beta distribution by the PERT three-estimate approach described in Section 16.4, which uses the minimum, most likely, and maximum values to calculate approximate values of the mean and standard deviation.) With historical data available, the choice between these two distributions (and other options as well) then can be based on which one provides the best fit with the data after obtaining statistical estimates of its parameters. We will describe a little later how Crystal Ball can do all of this for you.

The Exponential Distribution

If you have studied Chapter 11 on queueing models, you hopefully will recall that the most commonly used queueing models assume that the time between consecutive arrivals of customers to receive a particular service has an exponential distribution. The reason for this assumption is that, in most such situations, the arrivals of customers are random events and the exponential distribution is the probability distribution of the time between random events. Section 11.1 describes this property of the exponential distribution in some detail.

As first depicted in Figure 11.3, this distribution has the unusual shape shown in Figure 13.34. In particular, the peak is at 0 but there is a long tail to the right. This indicates that the most likely times are short ones well below the mean but that very long times also are possible. This is the nature of the time between random events.

Since the only parameter is the rate at which the random events occur on the average, this distribution is a relatively easy one to use.

The Poisson Distribution

Although the exponential distribution (like most of the preceding ones) is a continuous distribution, the Poisson distribution is a discrete distribution. The only possible values are nonnegative integers: 0, 1, 2, ... However, it is natural to pair this distribution with the exponential

FIGURE 13.34

The characteristics and dialogue boxes for two distributions that involve random events. These distributions in Crystal Ball's Distribution Gallery are (1) the exponential distribution and (2) the Poisson distribution.

Distributions for Random Events

Exponential Distribution:

- Widely used to describe time between random events (e.g., time between arrivals)
- Events are independent
- Rate = average number of events per unit time (e.g., arrivals per hour)

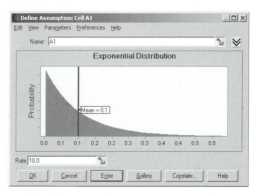

Poisson Distribution:

- Describes the number of times an event occurs during a given period of time or space
- Occurrences are independent
- Any number of events is possible
- Rate = average number of events during period of time (e.g., arrivals per hour), assumed constant over time

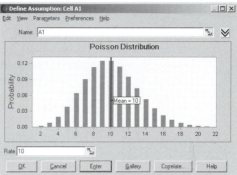

distribution for the following reason. If the time between consecutive events has an exponential distribution (i.e., the events are occurring at random), then the number of events that occur within a certain period of time has a Poisson distribution. This distribution has some other applications as well.

When considering the number of events that occur within a certain period of time, the "Rate" to be entered into the one parameter field in the dialogue box should be the average number of events that occur within that period of time.

The Yes–No and Binomial Distributions

The yes–no distribution is a very simple discrete distribution with only two possible values (1 or 0) as shown in Figure 13.35. It is used to simulate whether a particular event occurs or not. The only parameter of the distribution is the probability that the event occurs. The yes–no distribution gives a value of 1 (representing yes) with this probability; otherwise, it gives a value of 0 (representing no).

The binomial distribution is an extension of the yes–no distribution for when an event might occur a number of times. The binomial distribution gives the probability distribution of the number of *times* a particular event occurs, given the number of independent opportunities (called trials) for the event to occur, where the probability of the event occurring remains the same from trial to trial. For example, if the event of interest is getting heads on the flip of a coin, the binomial distribution (with Prob. = 0.5) gives the distribution of the number of heads in a given number of flips of the coin. Each flip constitutes a trial where there is an opportunity for the event (heads) to occur with a fixed probability (0.5). The binomial distribution is equivalent to the yes–no distribution when the number of trials is equal to 1.

You have seen another example in the preceding section when the binomial distribution was entered into the assumption cell NumberThatShow (C17) in Figure 13.28. In this airline overbooking example, the events are customers showing up for the flight and the trials are customers making reservations, where there is a fixed probability that a customer making a reservation actually will arrive to take the flight.

FIGURE 13.35

The characteristics and dialogue box for the yes–no and binomial distributions in Crystal Ball's Distribution Gallery.

Distributions for Number of Times an Event Occurs

Yes–No Distribution:

- Describes whether an event occurs or not
- Two possible outcomes: 1 (Yes) or 0 (No)

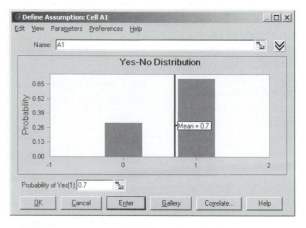

Binomial Distribution:

- Describes number of times an event occurs in a fixed number of trials (e.g., number of heads in 10 flips of a coin)
- For each trial, only two outcomes possible
- Trials independent
- Probability remains same for each trial

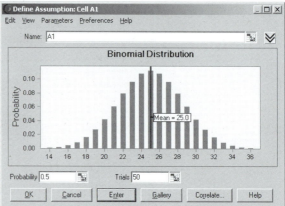

The only parameters for this distribution are the number of trials and the probability of the event occurring on a trial.

The Geometric and Negative Binomial Distributions

These two distributions displayed in Figure 13.36 are related to the binomial distribution because they again involve trials where there is a fixed probability on each trial that the event will occur. The *geometric distribution* gives the distribution of the number of trials until the event occurs for the first time. After entering a positive integer into the Shape field in its dialogue box, the *negative binomial distribution* gives the distribution of the number of trials until the event occurs the number of times specified in the Shape field. Thus, shape is a parameter for this distribution and the fixed probability of the event occurring on a trial is a parameter for both distributions.

To illustrate these distributions, suppose you are again interested in the event of getting heads on a flip of a coin (a trial). The geometric distribution (with Prob. = 0.5) gives the distribution of the number of flips until the first head occurs. If you want five heads, the negative binomial distribution (with Prob. = 0.5 and Shape = 5) gives the distribution of the number of flips until heads have occurred five times.

Similarly, consider a production process with a 50 percent yield, so each unit produced has an 0.5 probability of being acceptable. The geometric distribution (with Prob. = 0.5) gives the distribution of the number of units that need to be produced to obtain one acceptable unit. If a customer has ordered five units, the negative binomial distribution (with Prob. = 0.5 and Shape = 5) gives the distribution of the production run size that is needed to fulfill this order.

Other Distributions

The Distribution Gallery includes 10 additional distributions: gamma, max extreme, min extreme, logistic, student's-t, Pareto, hypergeometric, negative binomial, and custom.

FIGURE 13.36

The characteristics and dialogue boxes for two distributions that involve the number of trials until events occur. These distributions in Crystal Ball's Distribution Gallery are (1) the geometric distribution and (2) the negative binomial distribution.

Distributions for Number of Trials Until Event Occurs

Geometric Distribution:

- Describes number of trials until an event occurs (e.g., number of times to spin roulette wheel until you win)
- Probability same for each trial
- Continue until succeed
- Number of trials unlimited

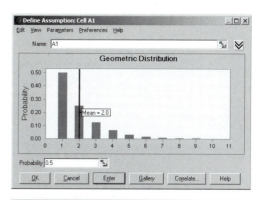

Negative Binomial Distribution:

- Describes number of trials until an event occurs n times
- Same as geometric when Shape = n = 1
- Probability same for each trial
- Continue until n^{th} success
- Number of trials unlimited

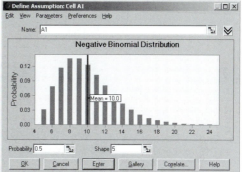

The custom distribution is an especially useful one because it enables you to design your own distribution when none of the other 20 distributions in the Distribution Gallery will do. The next subsection will focus on how this is done.

The remaining nine distributions are not widely used in computer simulations, so they will not be discussed further.

The Custom Distribution

Of the 21 probability distributions included in the Distribution Gallery, 20 of them are standard types that might be discussed in a course on probability and statistics. In most cases, one of these standard distributions will be just what is needed for an assumption cell. However, unique circumstances occasionally arise where none of the standard distributions fit the situation. This is where the 21st member of the Distribution Gallery, called the "custom distribution," enters the picture.

Choosing the custom distribution from the Distribution Gallery enables you to custom-design your own distribution to fit a special situation.

The custom distribution actually is not a probability distribution until you make it one. Rather, choosing this member of the Distribution Gallery triggers a process that enables you to custom-design your own probability distribution to fit almost any unique situation you might encounter. In designing your distribution, you are given five choices under the Parameters menu: unweighted values, weighted values, continuous ranges, discrete ranges, and sloping ranges. The choice determines how many parameters are available. For unweighted values, there is just one parameter (*Value*). A list of values are entered and each of these values are assumed to be equally likely. For weighted values, there are two parameters (*Value* and *Probability*) allowing each value to have a different probability. Continuous ranges have three parameters (*Minimum, Maximum,* and *Probability*) to specify the range (or ranges) of the distribution and the total probability of each range. Discrete ranges add a fourth parameter (*Step*) to specify the distance between the possible discrete values in the range. Finally, sloping ranges have two parameters (*Height of Minimum* and *Height of Maximum*) to allow the distribution to slope from the minimum to the maximum. Furthermore, these values or ranges can be combined in any possible way, such as combining a set of discrete values with a continuous range. We will show two examples.

FIGURE 13.37

Following the instructions on the left, this dialogue box illustrates how Crystal Ball's custom distribution can enable you to custom-design your own distribution to enter a set of discrete values and their probabilities.

- Enter set of values with varying probabilities

- For each discrete value, enter *Value* and *Probability*

Custom Distribution (Weighted Values)

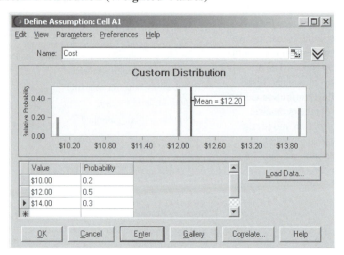

In the first example, a company is developing a new product but it is unclear which of three production processes will be needed to produce the product. The unit production cost will be $10, $12, or $14, depending on which process is needed. The probabilities for these individual discrete values of the cost are the following.

20 percent chance of $10

50 percent chance of $12

30 percent chance of $14

To enter this distribution, first choose weighted values under the Parameters menu in the Custom Distribution dialogue box. Each discrete value and probability (expressed as a decimal number) is then entered in the Value and Probability columns as shown in Figure 13.37.

The other distribution types (unweighted values, continuous ranges, discrete ranges, and sloping ranges) are entered in a similar fashion by choosing the appropriate option under the Parameter menu. We next illustrate how to enter a combination of a weighted value and a continuous range.

The example in this case is a variation of the probability distribution of the revenue from drilling for oil in the Goferbroke Company case study introduced in Section 9.1. In that case study, there was a probability of 0.75 of not finding oil (so a revenue of $0) and a probability of 0.25 of finding oil, in which case the revenue would be $800,000. However, there actually is some uncertainty about how much revenue would be received if oil were found, so the following distribution would be more realistic.

Revenue of $0 has probability 0.75

A range of revenue values: $600,000 to $1,000,000

The values over this range are equally likely

Probability of a value in this range: 0.25

This distribution combines a single discrete value at $0 with a continuous portion between $600,000 and $1,000,000. To enter such a combination distribution, choose the member of the combination under the Parameters menu with the most parameters needed. The weighted value requires two parameters (*Value* and *Probability*) while the continuous range requires three (*Minimum, Maximum,* and *Probability*), so choose Continuous Range under the Parameters menu. This leads to the Custom Distribution dialogue box with three columns for data (*Minimum, Maximum,* and *Probability*), as shown in Figure 13.38.

FIGURE 13.38

Following the instructions on the left, this dialogue box for the custom distribution demonstrates combining two of the options in Figure 13.37: (1) enter a discrete value at $0 and (2) enter a uniform distribution between $600,000 and $1,000,000.

Combinations with the Custom Distribution

- For discrete values, enter *Value* and *Probability*

- For continuous range, enter *Minimum*, *Maximum*, and *Probability*

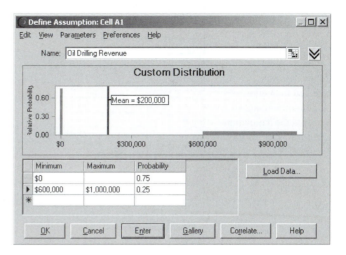

For a discrete value, only two parameters are needed (*Value* = $0 and *Probability* = 0.75), so the middle column is left blank in the middle of Figure 13.38. For the continuous range, we enter the *Minimum* ($600,000), *Maximum* ($1,000,000), and *Probability* (0.25) in the bottom of Figure 13.38.

Identifying the Continuous Distribution That Best Fits Historical Data

If you don't know which continuous distribution should be chosen for an assumption cell, Crystal Ball can do it for you if historical data are available.

We now have at least mentioned all 21 types of probability distributions in the Distribution Gallery and have described the characteristics of many of them. This brings us to the question of how to identify which distribution is best for a particular assumption cell. When historical data are available, Crystal Ball provides a powerful feature for doing this with the continuous distributions by using the Fit button on the Distribution Gallery dialogue box. We will illustrate this feature next by returning to the case study presented in Section 13.1.

Recall that one of the most popular newspapers that Freddie the newsboy sells from his newsstand is the daily *Financial Journal*. Freddie purchases copies from his distributor early each morning. Since excess copies left over at the end of the day represent a loss for Freddie, he is trying to decide what his order quantity should be in the future. This led to the spreadsheet model in Figure 13.1 that was shown earlier in Section 13.1. This model includes the assumption cell Demand (C12). To get started, a discrete uniform distribution between 40 and 70 has been entered into this assumption cell.

To better guide his decision on what the order quantity should be, Freddie has been keeping a record of the *demand* (the number of customers requesting a copy) for this newspaper each day. Figure 13.39 shows a portion of the data he has gathered over the last 60 days in cells F4:F63, along with part of the original spreadsheet model from Figure 13.1. These data indicate a lot of variation in sales from day to day—ranging from about 40 copies to 70 copies. However, it is difficult to tell from these numbers which distribution in the Distribution Gallery best fits these data.

Crystal Ball provides the following procedure for addressing this issue.

Procedure for Fitting the Best Continuous Distribution to Data

1. Gather the data needed to identify the best distribution to enter into an assumption cell.

2. Enter the data into the spreadsheet containing your simulation model.

3. Select the cell that you want to define as an assumption cell that contains the distribution that best fits the data.

FIGURE 13.39

Cells F4:F63 contain the historical demand data that have been collected for the case study involving Freddie the newsboy that was introduced in Section 13.1. Columns B and C come from the simulation model for this case study in Figure 13.1.

	A	B	C	D	E	F
1		**Freddie the Newsboy**				Historical
2						Demand
3			**Data**		Day	Data
4		Unit Sale Price	$2.50		1	62
5		Unit Purchase Cost	$1.50		2	45
6		Unit Salvage Value	$0.50		3	59
7					4	65
8			**Decision Variable**		5	50
9		Order Quantity	60		6	64
10					7	56
11			**Simulation**		8	51
12		Simulated Demand	55		9	55
13		Demand (rounded)	55		10	61
14					11	40
15		Sales Revenue	$137.50		12	47
16		Purchasing Cost	$90.00		13	63
17		Salvage Value	$2.50		14	68
18					15	67
19		Profit	$50.00		16	67
20					17	68
58					55	41
59					56	42
60					57	64
61					58	45
62					59	59
63					60	70

4. Choose Define Assumption from the Crystal Ball tab or toolbar, which brings up the Distribution Gallery dialogue box.

5. Click the Fit button on this dialogue box, which brings up the Fit Distribution dialogue box.

6. Use the Range box in this dialogue box to enter the range of the historical data in your worksheet.

7. Specify which continuous distributions are being considered for fitting. (Discrete distributions are not considered in this procedure.)

8. Also use this dialogue box to select which ranking method should be used to evaluate how well a distribution fits the data. (The default is the chi-square test, since this is the most popular choice.)

9. Click OK, which brings up the comparison chart that identifies the distribution (including its parameter values) that best fits the data.

10. If desired, the Next button can be clicked repeatedly for identifying the other types of distributions (including their parameter values) that are next in line for fitting the data well.

11. After choosing the distribution (from steps 9 and 10) that you want to use, click the Accept button while that distribution is showing. This will enter the appropriate parameters into the dialogue box for this distribution. Clicking OK then enters this distribution into the assumption cell.

Since Figure 13.39 already includes the needed data in cells F4:F63, applying this procedure to Freddie's problem begins by selecting SimulatedDemand (C12) as the cell we want to

FIGURE 13.40

The Fit Distribution dialogue box specifies the range of the data in Figure 13.39 for the case study, which continuous distributions will be considered (all) and which ranking method will be used (the chi-square test) to evaluate how well each of the distributions fit the data.

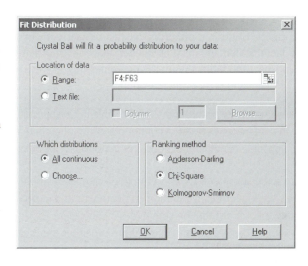

FIGURE 13.41

On the right, this comparison chart identifies the continuous distribution that provides the best fit with the historical demand data in Figure 13.39. This distribution then is plotted (the horizontal line) so that it can be compared with the frequency distribution of the historical demand data.

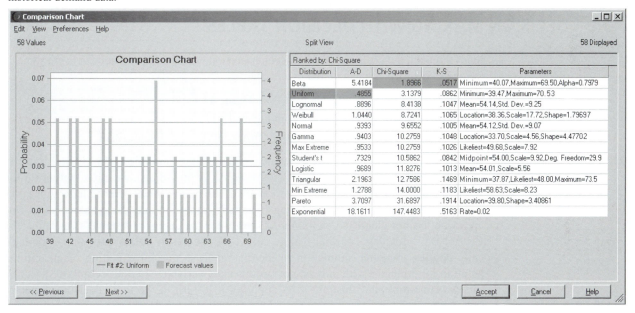

define as an assumption cell that contains the distribution that best fits the data. Then applying steps 4 and 5 brings up the Fit Distribution dialogue box displayed in Figure 13.40. The range F4:F63 of the data in Figure 13.39 is entered into the Range box of this dialogue box. When deciding which continuous distributions should be considered for fitting, the default option of considering all the continuous distributions in the Distribution Gallery has been selected here. The default choice of the chi-square test also has been selected for the ranking method. Clicking OK then brings up the comparison chart displayed in Figure 13.41. The vertical lines show the frequency chart for the data in Figure 13.39. The right side of the comparison chart identifies the best-fitting distribution according to the Anderson-Darling, Chi-Square, and Kolmogorov-Smirnov tests. Lower numbers in these columns indicate a better fit. The Anderson-Darling test indicates that the uniform distribution is the best fit, while the Chi-Square and Kolmogorov-Smirnov tests indicate that the beta distribution is a slightly better fit.

This procedure only compares the continuous distributions. Of these distributions, the continuous uniform distribution is either the best fit or nearly the best fit to the data. In combination with the fact that demand must be integer, this confirms that the choice made in Freddie's original spreadsheet model in Figure 13.1 to enter the discrete uniform distribution into the assumption cell Demand (C12) was reasonable.

Review Questions

1. How many probability distributions are available in Crystal Ball's Distribution Gallery?
2. What is the difference between a continuous distribution and a discrete distribution?
3. What is a possible danger with choosing the normal distribution to enter into an assumption cell?
4. What are some advantages of choosing the triangular distribution instead?
5. How does the lognormal distribution compare with the normal and triangular distributions?
6. Why is the uniform distribution sometimes a convenient choice for an assumption cell?
7. What would be the key advantage of choosing either the Weibull distribution or a beta distribution for an assumption cell?
8. The binomial distribution gives the probability distribution of what?
9. What does choosing the custom distribution from the Distribution Gallery enable you to do?
10. What procedure does Crystal Ball provide for helping to identify the best distribution to enter into an assumption cell?

13.8 DECISION MAKING WITH DECISION TABLES

Many simulation models include at least one decision variable. For example, here are some of the decision variables encountered in this chapter.

The case study: OrderQuantity (C9) in Figure 13.1
Bidding example: OurBid (C25) in Figure 13.11
Overbooking example: ReservationsToAccept (C13) in Figure 13.28

In each of these cases, you have seen how well computer simulation with Crystal Ball can *evaluate* a particular value of the decision variable by providing a wealth of output for the forecast cell(s). However, in contrast to many of the management science techniques presented in previous chapters (including linear programming and decision analysis), this approach has not identified an *optimal solution* for the decision variable(s). Fortunately, Crystal Ball provides a special feature called the **Decision Table tool** that systematically applies computer simulation to identify at least an approximation of an optimal solution for problems with only one or two decision variables. In this section, we describe this valuable tool and illustrate it by applying it in turn to the three decision variables listed above.

An intuitive approach for doing this would be to use trial and error. Try different values of the decision variable(s), run a simulation for each, and see which one provides the best estimate of the chosen measure of performance. This is what the Decision Table tool does, but it does it in a systematic way. Its dialogue boxes enable you to quickly specify what you want to do. Then, after you click one button, all the desired simulations are run and the results soon are displayed nicely in the Decision Table. If desired, you also can view some charts, including an enlightening *trend chart,* which provide additional details about the results.

The Decision Table tool systematically applies computer simulation over a range of values of one or two decision variables and then displays the results in a table.

If you have previously used either an Excel data table or the Solver Table that is included in your MS Courseware for performing sensitivity analysis systematically, the Decision Table works in much the same way. In particular, the layout for a Decision Table with either one or two decision variables is similar to that for either a one-dimensional or two-dimensional Solver Table (described in Appendix A). Two is the maximum number of decision variables that can be varied simultaneously in a Decision Table.

Let us begin by returning to this chapter's case study to apply the Decision Table tool.

Application of the Decision Table Tool to the Case Study

Recall that Freddie the newsboy wants to determine what his daily order quantity should be for copies of the *Financial Journal.* Figures 13.1–13.10 in Section 13.1 show the application of computer simulation for evaluating the option of using an order quantity of 60. The final estimate of the average daily profit that would be obtained with this order quantity is $46.46. As indicated in Figure 13.39, the number of copies that Freddie's customers want to purchase varies widely from day to day. The chi-square test comparison chart in Figure 13.41 suggests that the probability distribution that best describes this variability is the discrete uniform distribution between 40 and 70. Given such a high degree of variability, it is unclear where the order quantity should be set within the range between 40 and 70. Could an average daily profit larger than $46.46 be obtained by choosing an order quantity different from 60? Which order quantity between 40 and 70 would maximize the average daily profit?

To address these questions, it would seem sensible to begin by trying a sampling of possible order quantities, say, 40, 45, 50, 55, 60, 65, and 70. To do this with the Decision Table tool, the first step is to define the decision variable being investigated, namely, OrderQuantity (C9) in Figure 13.1, by using the following procedure.

Before applying the Decision Table to any problem, the one or two decision variables being investigated must be defined.

Procedure for Defining a Decision Variable

1. Select the cell containing the decision variable by clicking on it.
2. If the cell does not already contain a value, enter *any* number into the cell.
3. Click on the Define Decision button (⊛) on the Crystal Ball tab or toolbar which brings up the Define Decision Variable dialogue box (as shown in Figure 13.42 for Freddie's problem).
4. Enter the lower limit and the upper limit of the range of values to be simulated for the decision variable.
5. Click on either Continuous or Discrete to define whether the decision variable is continuous or discrete.
6. If Discrete is selected in step 5, use the Step box to specify the difference between the successive possible values (not just those to be simulated) of the decision variable. (The default value is 1.)
7. Click on OK.

Figure 13.42 shows the application of this procedure to Freddie's problem. Since simulations will be run for order quantities ranging from 40 to 70, these limits for the range have been entered on the left. The order quantity can have any integer value within this range, so this is indicated on the right.

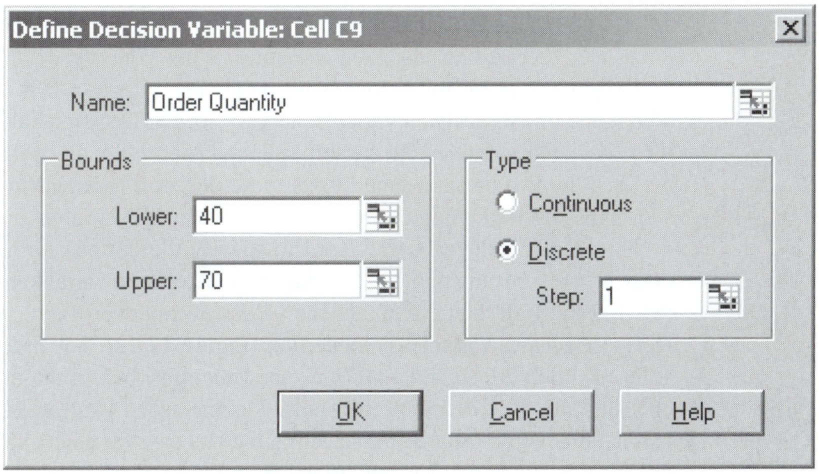

FIGURE 13.42
This Define Decision Variable dialogue box specifies the characteristics of the decision variable OrderQuantity (C9) in the simulation model in Figure 13.1 for the case study that involves Freddie the newsboy.

FIGURE 13.43

To prepare for generating a Decision Table, these three dialogue boxes specify (1) which forecast cell will be the target cell, (2) which one or two decision variables will be varied, and (3) the running options. The choices made here are for the case study that involves Freddie the newsboy.

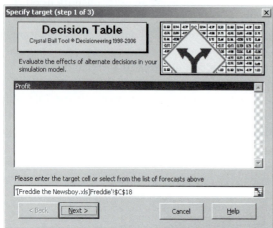

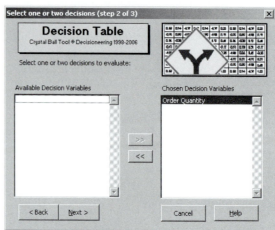

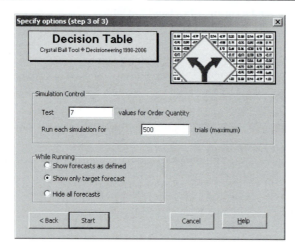

Now we are ready to choose Decision Table from the Crystal Ball Tools menu. This brings up the sequence of three dialogue boxes shown in Figure 13.43.

The Step 1 dialogue box is used to choose one of the forecast cells listed there to be the target cell for the Decision Table. Freddie's spreadsheet model in Figure 13.1 has only one forecast cell, Profit (C19), so select it and then click on the Next button.

Initially, the left-hand side of the Step 2 dialogue box includes a list of all the cells that have been defined as decision variables. This consists of the single decision variable, OrderQuantity (C9), for Freddie's problem. The purpose of this dialogue box is to choose which one or two decision variables to vary for the Decision Table. This is done by selecting these decision variables on the left side and then clicking on the double right arrows (>>) between the two boxes, which brings these decision variables to the right side. Figure 13.43 shows the result of doing this with Freddie's decision variable.

The Step 3 dialogue box is used to specify the options for the Decision Table. The first entry box records the number of values of the decision variable for which simulations will be run. Crystal Ball then distributes the values evenly over the range of values specified in the Define Decision Variable dialogue box (Figure 13.42). For Freddie's problem, the range of values is 40 to 70, so entering 7 into the first entry box in the Step 3 dialogue box results in choosing 40, 45, 50, 55, 60, 65, and 70 as the seven values of the order quantity for which simulations will be run. After selecting the run size for each simulation and specifying what you want to see while the simulations are running, the last step is to click the Start button.

After specifying the number of values of a decision variable to consider, Crystal Ball distributes the values evenly over the range of values specified in the Define Decision Variable dialogue box.

FIGURE 13.44

The Decision Table for the case study introduced in Section 13.1.

	A	B	C	D	E	F	G	H
1	Trend Chart / Overlay Chart / Forecast Charts	Order Quantity (40)	Order Quantity (45)	Order Quantity (50)	Order Quantity (55)	Order Quantity (60)	Order Quantity (65)	Order Quantity (70)
2		$40.00	$44.04	$46.46	$47.27	$46.46	$44.04	$40.01
3		1	2	3	4	5	6	7

FIGURE 13.45

The overlay chart that compares the frequency distributions for order quantities of 55 and 60 for Freddie's problem.

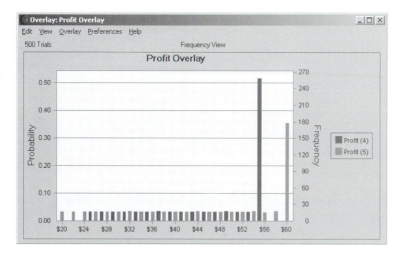

This is a one-dimensional Decision Table because the problem has only one decision variable. For problems where two decision variables have been defined and selected, the resulting Decision Table will be a two-dimensional table, with one variable changing in the rows and the other in the columns.

After Crystal Ball runs the simulations, the Decision Table is created in a new spreadsheet as shown in Figure 13.44. For each of the order quantities shown at the top, row 2 gives the mean of the values of the target cell, Profit (C19), obtained in all the trials of that simulation run. Cells D2:F2 reveal that an order quantity of 55 achieved the largest mean profit of $47.27, while order quantities of 50 and 60 essentially tied for the second largest mean profit.

The sharp drop off in mean profits on both sides of these order quantities virtually guarantees that the optimal order quantity lies between 50 and 60 (and probably close to 55). To pin this down better, the logical next step would be to generate another Decision Table that considers all integer order quantities between 50 and 60. You are asked to do this in Problem 13.14.

The upper left-hand corner of the Decision Table provides three options for obtaining more detailed information about the results of the simulation runs for the cells that you select. One option is to view the forecast chart of interest, such as a frequency chart or cumulative chart, by choosing a forecast cell in row 2 and then clicking on the Forecast Charts button. Another option is to see the results of two or more simulation runs together. This is done by selecting a set of forecast cells, say, cells E2:F2 in Figure 13.44, and then clicking on the Overlay Chart button. The resulting overlay chart is shown in Figure 13.45. The dark lines show the frequency chart for cell E2 (an order quantity of 55) while the light lines do the same for cell F2 (an order quantity of 60), so the results for these two cases can be compared side by side. (On a color monitor, you will see different colors being used to distinguish between the different cases.)

The third option is to select all the forecast cells of interest (cells B2:H2 in Figure 13.44) and then click on the Trend Chart button. This generates an interesting chart, called the *trend chart,* shown in Figure 13.46. The key points along the horizontal axis are the seven vertical grid lines that correspond to the seven cases (order quantities of 40, 45, . . . 70) for which the simulations were run. The vertical axis gives the profit values obtained in the trials of these simulation runs. The bands in the chart summarize information about the frequency distribution of the profit values from each simulation run. (On a color monitor, the bands appear in

FIGURE 13.46
The trend chart that shows the trend in the range of various portions of the frequency distribution as the order quantity increases for Freddie's problem.

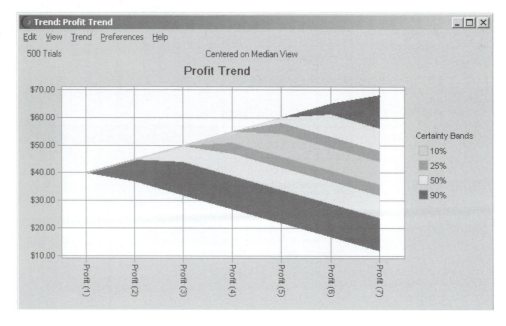

color—light blue for the center band, red for the adjacent pair of bands, green for the next pair, and dark blue for the outer pair of bands.) These bands are centered on the *medians* of the frequency distributions. In other words, the center of the middle band (the lightest one) gives the profit value such that half of the trials gave a larger value and half gave a smaller value. This middle band contains the middle 10 percent of the profit values (so 45 percent are on each side of the band). Similarly, the middle three bands contain the middle 25 percent of the profit values, the middle five bands contain the middle 50 percent of the profit values, and all seven bands contain the middle 90 percent of the profit values. (These percentages are listed to the right of the trend chart.) Thus, 5 percent of the profit values generated in the trials of each simulation run lie above the top band and 5 percent lie below the bottom band.

The trend chart received its name because it shows the trends graphically as the value of the decision variable (the order quantity in this case) increases. In Figure 13.46, for example, consider the middle band (which gets hidden in the narrow part of the chart on the left). In going from the third order quantity (50) to the fourth one (55), the middle band is trending upward, but then it is trending downward thereafter. Thus, the median value of the profit values generated in the respective simulation runs increases as the order quantity increases until the median reaches its peak at an order quantity of 55, after which the median trends downward. Similarly, most of the other bands also are trending downward as the order quantity increases above 55. This suggests that an order quantity of 55 is a particularly attractive one in terms of its entire frequency distribution and not just its mean value. The fact that the trend chart is spreading out as it moves to the right provides the further insight that the variability of the profit values increases as the order quantity is increased. Although the largest order quantities provide some chance of particularly high profits on occasional days, they also give some likelihood to obtaining an unusually low profit on any given day. This risk profile may be relevant to Freddie if he is concerned about the variability of his daily profits.

A trend chart shows the trends graphically as the value of a decision variable increases.

Application of the Decision Table Tool to the Reliable Construction Co. Bidding Problem

We turn now to the application of the Decision Table tool to the Reliable Construction Co. bidding problem presented in Section 13.2. Since the procedure for how to generate a Decision Table already has been presented in the preceding subsection, our focus here is on summarizing the results.

FIGURE 13.47

This dialogue box specifies the characteristics of the decision variable OurBid (C25) in Figure 13.11 for the Reliable Construction Co. contract bidding problem.

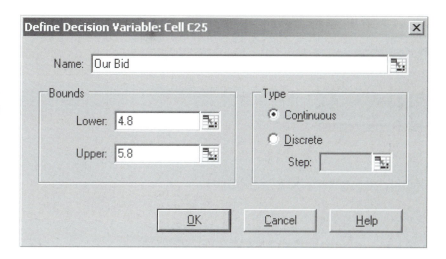

Recall that the management of the company is concerned with determining what bid it should submit for a project that involves constructing a new plant for a major manufacturer. Therefore, the decision variable in the spreadsheet model in Figure 13.11 is OurBid (C25). The Define Decision Variable dialogue box in Figure 13.47 is used to further describe this decision variable. Management feels that the bid should be in the range between $4.8 million and $5.8 million, so these are the numbers (in units of millions of dollars) that are entered into the entry boxes for Variable Bounds in this dialogue box. Because the bid can be *any* amount (down to the cent) within this range, the variable has been classified as a continuous variable on the right-hand side of the dialogue box.

Management wants to choose the bid that would maximize its expected profit. Consequently, the forecast cell in the spreadsheet model is Profit (C29). In the Decision Table dialogue box for Step 1 shown in Figure 13.48, this forecast cell has been selected to be the target cell. In the Step 2 dialogue box, the decision variable OurBid (C25) already has been brought over to the right-hand side as the variable to be considered. The decision has been made in the Step 3 dialogue box to test six values for this decision variable. The six values automatically are distributed evenly over the range specified in Figure 13.47, so simulations will be run for bids of 4.8, 5.0, 5.2, 5.4, 5.6, and 5.8 (in millions of dollars). The Step 3 dialogue box also has been used to specify that each simulation will run for 1,000 trials.

Figure 13.49 shows the resulting Decision Table. A bid of $5.4 million gives the largest mean value of the profits obtained on the 1,000 trials of the simulation run. This mean value of $480,000 in cell E2 should be a close estimate of the expected profit from using this bid. The case study in Chapter 16 begins with the company having just won the contract by submitting this bid.

Problem 13.17 asks you to refine this analysis by generating a Decision Table that considers all bids between $5.2 million and $5.6 million in multiples of $0.05 million.

A bid of $5.4 million was the winning bid for the Reliable Construction Co. in the case study for Chapter 16.

Application of the Decision Table Tool to the Transcontinental Airlines Overbooking Problem

As described in Section 13.6, Transcontinental Airlines has a popular daily flight from San Francisco to Chicago with 150 seats available. The number of requests for reservations usually exceeds the number of seats by a considerable amount. However, even though the fare is nonrefundable, an average of only 80 percent of the customers who make reservations actually show up to take the flight, so it seems appropriate to accept more reservations than can be flown. At the same time, significant costs are incurred if customers with reservations are not allowed to take the flight. Therefore, the company's management science group is analyzing what number of reservations should be accepted to maximize the expected profit from the flight.

The decision variable in Figure 13.28 is ReservationsToAccept (C13).

In the spreadsheet model in Figure 13.28, the decision variable is ReservationsToAccept (C13) and the forecast cell is Profit (F23). The management science group wants to consider

FIGURE 13.48

The three Decision Table dialogue boxes for the Reliable Construction Co. contract bidding problem.

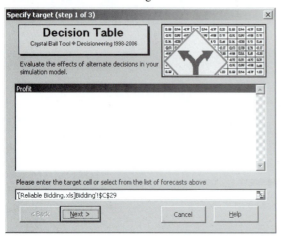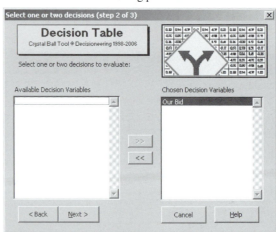

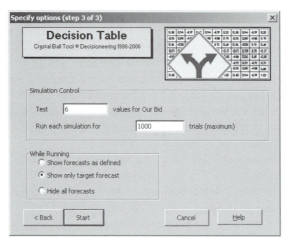

FIGURE 13.49

The Decision Table for the Reliable Construction Co. contract bidding problem described in Section 13.2.

	A	B	C	D	E	F	G
	Trend Chart	OurBid (4.800)	OurBid (5.000)	OurBid (5.200)	OurBid (5.400)	OurBid (5.600)	OurBid (5.800)
	Overlay Chart						
1	Forecast Charts						
2		0.188	0.356	0.473	0.480	0.241	0.025
3		1	2	3	4	5	6

integer values of the decision variable over the range between 150 and 200, so the Define Decision Variable dialogue box is used in the usual way to specify these bounds on the variable and to define the variable as being discrete. The three Decision Table dialogue boxes also are used in the usual way. In the Step 3 dialogue box, the decision is made to test 11 values of ReservationsToAccept (C13), so simulations will be run for values in intervals of five between 150 and 200. The number of trials for each simulation run also is set at 1,000 in this dialogue box.

The results are shown in Figure 13.50. The Decision Table in the figure reveals that the mean of the profit values obtained in the respective simulation runs climbs rapidly as ReservationsToAccept (C13) increases until the mean reaches a peak of $11,926 at 185 reservations, after which it starts to drop. Only the means at 180 and 190 reservations are close to this peak, so it seems clear that the most profitable number of reservations lies somewhere between 180 and 190. (Now that the range of numbers that need to be considered has been narrowed down this far, Problem 13.20 asks you to continue that analysis by generating a Decision Table that considers all integer values over this range.)

FIGURE 13.50

The Decision Table and trend chart for the Transcontinental Airlines overbooking problem described in Section 13.6.

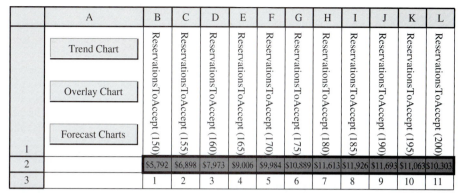

	A	B	C	D	E	F	G	H	I	J	K	L
	Trend Chart / Overlay Chart / Forecast Charts	ReservationsToAccept (150)	ReservationsToAccept (155)	ReservationsToAccept (160)	ReservationsToAccept (165)	ReservationsToAccept (170)	ReservationsToAccept (175)	ReservationsToAccept (180)	ReservationsToAccept (185)	ReservationsToAccept (190)	ReservationsToAccept (195)	ReservationsToAccept (200)
1												
2		$5,792	$6,898	$7,973	$9,006	$9,984	$10,889	$11,613	$11,926	$11,693	$11,063	$10,303
3		1	2	3	4	5	6	7	8	9	10	11

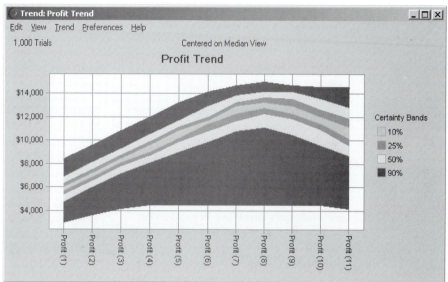

The trend chart in Figure 13.50 provides additional insight. All seven bands in this chart trend upward until the number of reservations to accept reaches approximately 185; then they start trending slowly downward. This indicates that the *entire* frequency distribution from the respective simulation runs keeps shifting upward until the eighth run (the one for 185 reservations) and then starts shifting downward. Also note that the width of the entire set of seven bands increases until about the eighth simulation run and then remains about the same thereafter. This indicates that the amount of variability in the profit values also increases until about the eighth simulation run and then remains about the same thereafter.

Review Questions

1. What does the Decision Table tool enable you to do that a single simulation run with one value of the decision variable(s) does not?
2. What are the advantages of using the Decision Table tool instead of simply using trial and error to try different values of the decision variable(s) and running a simulation for each?
3. What is the maximum number of decision variables that can be varied simultaneously in a Decision Table?
4. What procedure needs to be used before choosing Decision Table from the Crystal Ball Tools menu?
5. After choosing Decision Table from this menu, what is the purpose of the Step 1 dialogue box?
6. What is the purpose of the Step 2 dialogue box?
7. What is the purpose of the Step 3 dialogue box?
8. What does an overlay chart show?
9. What kind of information is summarized by the bands in a trend chart?
10. After a Decision Table has been used to narrow down the range of values of a decision variable that need to be considered, how can another Decision Table be used to better approximate the optimal value of the decision variable?

13.9 Summary

Increasingly, spreadsheet software is being used to perform computer simulations. As described in the preceding chapter, the standard Excel package sometimes is sufficient to do this. In addition, some Excel add-ins now are available that greatly extend these capabilities. Crystal Ball is an especially powerful add-in of this kind.

When using Crystal Ball, each input cell that has a random value is referred to as an *assumption cell.* The procedure for defining an assumption cell includes selecting one of 21 types of probability distributions from a Distribution Gallery to enter into the cell. When historical data are available, Crystal Ball also has a procedure for identifying which continuous distribution fits the data best.

An output cell that is used to forecast a measure of performance is called a *forecast cell.* Each trial of a simulation run generates a value in each forecast cell. When the simulation run is completed, Crystal Ball provides the results in a variety of useful forms, including a frequency distribution, a statistics table, a percentiles table, and a cumulative chart.

When a simulation model has one or two decision variables, Crystal Ball provides a *Decision Table tool* that systematically applies computer simulation to identify at least an approximation of an optimal solution. A *trend chart* also provides additional insights to aid in decision making.

The availability of such powerful software now enables managers to add computer simulation to their personal tool kit of management science techniques for analyzing some key managerial problems. A variety of examples in this chapter illustrate some of the many possibilities for important applications of computer simulation.

Glossary

assumption cell   An input cell that has a random value so that an assumed probability distribution must be entered into the cell instead of permanently entering a single number. (Section 13.1), 514

Decision Table tool   A Crystal Ball module that systematically applies computer simulation over a range of values of one or two decision variables and then displays the results in a table. (Section 13.8), 560

Distribution Gallery   Crystal Ball's gallery of 21 probability distributions from which one is chosen to enter into any assumption cell. (Sections 13.1 and 13.7), 514, 548

forecast cell   An output cell that is being used by a computer simulation to forecast a measure of performance. (Section 13.1), 515

risk profile   A frequency distribution of the return from an investment. (Section 13.5), 538

trial   A single application of the process of generating a random observation from each probability distribution entered into the spreadsheet and then calculating the output cells in the usual way and recording the results of interest. (Section 13.1), 513

Learning Aids for This Chapter in Your MS Courseware

Chapter 13 Excel Files:

Freddie the Newsboy Case Study
Reliable Co. Bidding Example
Reliable Co. Project Scheduling Example
Everglade Co. Cash Flow Linear Programming
Everglade Co. Cash Flow Management Example
Think-Big Co. Financial Risk Analysis Example
Transcontinental Airlines Overbooking Example

Sales Data 1
Sales Data 2

An Excel Add-in:
Crystal Ball Professional Edition

Supplement to Chapter 13 on the CD-ROM
Optimizing with OptQuest

Solved Problem (See the CD-ROM for the Solution)

13.S1. Saving for Retirement

Patrick Gordon is 10 years away from retirement. He has accumulated a $100,000 nest egg that he would like to invest for his golden years. Furthermore, he is confident that he can invest $10,000 more each year until retirement. He is curious about what kind of nest egg he can expect to have accumulated at retirement 10 years from now.

Patrick plans to split his investments evenly among four investments: a money market fund, a domestic stock fund, a global stock fund, and an aggressive growth fund. On the basis of past performance, Patrick expects each of these funds to earn a return in each of the upcoming 10 years according to the distributions shown in the following table.

Fund	Distribution
Money market	Uniform (minimum = 2%, maximum = 5%)
Domestic stock	Normal (mean = 6%, standard deviation = 5%)
Global stock	Normal (mean = 8%, standard deviation = 10%)
Aggressive growth	Normal (mean = 11%, standard deviation = 16%)

Assume that the initial nest egg ($100,000) and the first year's investment ($10,000) are made right now (year 0) and are split evenly among the four funds (i.e., $27,500 in each fund). The returns of each fund are allowed to accumulate (i.e., are reinvested) in the same fund and no redistribution will be done before retirement. Furthermore, nine additional investments of $10,000 will be made and split evenly among the four funds ($2,500 each) at year 1, year 2, . . . , year 9.

A financial advisor told Patrick that he can retire comfortably if he can accumulate $300,000 by year 10 to supplement his other sources of retirement income. Use a 2000-trial Crystal Ball simulation to estimate each of the following.

a. What will be the expected value (mean) of Patrick's nest egg at year 10?

b. What will be the standard deviation of Patrick's nest egg at year 10?

c. What is the probability that the total nest egg at year 10 will be at least $300,000?

Problems

Crystal Ball should be used for all of the following problems. An asterisk on the problem number indicates that a partial answer is given in the back of the book.

13.1.   The results from a simulation run are inherently random. This problem will demonstrate this fact and investigate the impact of the number of trials on this randomness. Consider the case study involving Freddie the newsboy that was introduced in Section 13.1. The spreadsheet model is available on your MS Courseware CD-ROM. Make sure that the "Use Same Sequence of Random Numbers" option is *not* checked and that the Monte-Carlo Sampling Method is selected in the Sampling tab of Run Preferences. Use an order quantity of 60.

a. Set the number of trials to 100 in Run Preferences and run the simulation of Freddie's problem five times. Note the mean profit for each simulation run.

b. Repeat part *a* except set the number of trials to 1,000 in Run Preferences.

c. Compare the results from part *a* and part *b* and comment on any differences.

13.2.   Consider the Reliable Construction Co. project scheduling example presented in Section 13.3. Recall that computer simulation was used to estimate the probability of meeting the deadline and that Figure 13.20 revealed that the deadline was met on 58.88 percent of the trials from one simulation run. As discussed while interpreting this result, the percentage of trials on which the project is completed by the deadline will vary from simulation run to simulation run. This problem will demonstrate this fact and investigate the impact of the number of trials on this randomness. The spreadsheet model is available on your MS Courseware CD-ROM. Make sure that the "Use Same Sequence of Random Numbers" option is *not* checked and that the Monte-Carlo Sampling Method is selected in the Sampling tab of Run Preferences.

a. Set the number of trials to 100 in Run Preferences and run the simulation of the project five times. Note the mean completion time and the percentage of trials on which the project is completed within the deadline of 47 weeks for each simulation run.

b. Repeat part *a* except set the number of trials to 1,000 in Run Preferences.

c. Compare the results from part *a* and part *b* and comment on any differences.

13.3.*   Consider the historical data contained in the Excel File "Sales Data 1" on your MS Courseware CD-ROM. Use Crystal Ball to fit all continuous distributions to these data.

a. Which distribution provides the closest fit to the data? What are the parameters of the distribution?

b. Which distribution provides the second-closest fit to the data? What are the parameters of the distribution?

13.4.   Consider the historical data contained in the Excel File "Sales Data 2" on your MS Courseware CD-ROM. Use Crystal Ball to fit all continuous distributions to these data.

a. Which distribution provides the closest fit to the data? What are the parameters of the distribution?

b. Which distribution provides the second-closest fit to the data? What are the parameters of the distribution?

13.5.   The Aberdeen Development Corporation (ADC) is reconsidering the Aberdeen Resort Hotel project. It would be located on the picturesque banks of Grays Harbor and have its own championship-level golf course.

The cost to purchase the land would be $1 million, payable now. Construction costs would be approximately $2 million, payable at the end of year 1. However, the construction costs are uncertain. These costs could be up to 20 percent higher or lower than the estimate of $2 million. Assume that the construction costs would follow a triangular distribution.

ADC is very uncertain about the annual operating profits (or losses) that would be generated once the hotel is constructed. Its best estimate for the annual operating profit that would be generated in years 2, 3, 4, and 5 is $700,000. Due to the great uncertainty, the estimate of the standard deviation of the annual operating profit in each year also is $700,000. Assume that the yearly profits are statistically independent and follow the normal distribution.

After year 5, ADC plans to sell the hotel. The selling price is likely to be somewhere between $4 and $8 million (assume a uniform distribution). ADC uses a 10 percent discount rate for calculating net present value. (For purposes of this calculation, assume that each year's profits are received at year-end.) Use Crystal Ball to perform 1,000 trials of a computer simulation of this project on a spreadsheet.

a. What is the mean net present value (NPV) of the project? (*Hint:* The NPV (rate, cash stream) function in Excel returns the NPV of a stream of cash flows assumed to start one year from now. For example, NPV(10%, C5:F5) returns the NPV at a 10% discount rate when C5 is a cash flow at the end of year 1, D5 at the end of year 2, E5 at the end of year 3, and F5 at the end of year 4.)

b. What is the estimated probability that the project will yield an NPV greater than $2 million?

c. ADC also is concerned about cash flow in years 2, 3, 4, and 5. Use Crystal Ball to generate a forecast of the distribution of the *minimum* annual operating profit (undiscounted) earned in any of the four years. What is the mean value of the minimum annual operating profit over the four years?

d. What is the probability that the annual operating profit will be at least $0 in all four years of operation?

13.6. Ivy University is planning to construct a new building for its business school. This project will require completing all of the activities in the table to the right. For most of these activities, a set of predecessor activities must be completed before the activity begins. For example, the foundation cannot be laid until the building is designed and the site prepared.

Activity	Predecessors
A. Secure funding	—
B. Design building	A
C. Site preparation	A
D. Foundation	B, C
E. Framing	D
F. Electrical	E
G. Plumbing	E
H. Walls and roof	F, G
I. Finish construction	H
J. Landscaping	H

Obtaining funding likely will take approximately six months (with a standard deviation of one month). Assume that this time has a normal distribution. The architect has estimated that the time required to design the building could be anywhere between 6 and 10 months. Assume that this time has a uniform distribution. The general contractor has provided three estimates for each of the construction tasks—an optimistic scenario (minimum time required if the weather is good and all goes well), a most likely scenario, and a pessimistic scenario (maximum time required if there are weather and other problems). These estimates are provided in the table that follows. Assume that each of these construction times has a triangular distribution. Finally, the landscaper has guaranteed that his work will be completed in five months.

Construction Time Estimates (months)

Activity	Optimistic Scenario	Most Likely Scenario	Pessimistic Scenario
C. Site preparation	1.5	2	2.5
D. Foundation	1.5	2	3
E. Framing	3	4	6
F. Electrical	2	3	5
G. Plumbing	3	4	5
H. Walls and roof	4	5	7
I. Do the finish work	5	6	7

Use Crystal Ball to generate 1,000 trials of a computer simulation for this project. Use the results to answer the following questions.

a. What is the mean project completion time?

b. What is the probability that the project will be completed in 36 months or less?

c. Generate a sensitivity chart. Based on this chart, which activities have the largest impact on the variability in the project completion time?

13.7.* Consider Problem 16.12, which involves estimating both the duration of a project and the probability that it will be completed by the deadline. Assume now that the duration of each activity has a triangular distribution that is based on the three estimates shown in Problem 16.12. Use Crystal Ball to perform 1,000 trials of a computer simulation of the project on a spreadsheet.

a. What is the mean project completion time?

b. What is the probability that the project can be completed within 22 months?

c. Generate a sensitivity chart. Based on this chart, which two activities have the largest impact on the variability in the project completion time?

13.8. The employees of General Manufacturing Corp. receive health insurance through a group plan issued by Wellnet. During the past year, 40 percent of the employees did not file any health insurance claims, 30 percent filed only a small claim, and 20 percent filed a large claim. The small claims were spread uniformly between 0 and $2,000, whereas the large claims were spread uniformly between $2,000 and $20,000.

Based on this experience, Wellnet now is negotiating the corporation's premium payment per employee for the upcoming year. To obtain a close estimate of the average cost of insurance coverage for the corporation's employees, use Crystal Ball with a spreadsheet to perform 500 trials of a computer simulation of an employee's health insurance experience. Generate a frequency chart and a statistics table.

13.9. Reconsider the Heavy Duty Co. problem that was presented as Example 2 in Section 12.1. For each of the following three options in parts *a* through *c,* obtain an estimate of the expected cost per day by using Crystal Ball to perform 1,000 trials of a computer simulation of the problem on a spreadsheet. Generate a frequency chart and a statistics table.

 a. The option of not replacing a motor until a breakdown occurs.

 b. The option of scheduling the replacement of a motor after four days (but replacing it sooner if a breakdown occurs).

 c. The option of scheduling the replacement of a motor after five days (but replacing it sooner if a breakdown occurs).

 d. An analytical result of $2,000 per day is available for the expected cost per day if a motor is replaced every three days. Comparing this option and the above three, which one appears to minimize the expected cost per day?

13.10. The Avery Co. factory has been having a maintenance problem with the control panel for one of its production processes. This control panel contains four identical electromechanical relays that have been the cause of the trouble. The problem is that the relays fail fairly frequently, thereby forcing the control panel (and the production process it controls) to be shut down while a replacement is made. The current practice is to replace the relays only when they fail. The average total cost of doing this has been $3.19 per hour. To attempt to reduce this cost, a proposal has been made to replace all four relays whenever any one of them fails to reduce the frequency with which the control panel must be shut down. Would this actually reduce the cost?

 The pertinent data are the following. For each relay, the operating time until failure has approximately a uniform distribution from 1,000 to 2,000 hours. The control panel must be shut down for one hour to replace one relay or for two hours to replace all four relays. The total cost associated with shutting down the control panel and replacing relays is $1,000 per hour plus $200 for each new relay.

 Use computer simulation on a spreadsheet to evaluate the cost of the proposal and compare it to the current practice. Use Crystal Ball to perform 1,000 trials (where the end of each trial coincides with the end of a shutdown of the control panel) and determine the average cost per hour.

13.11. For one new product produced by the Aplus Company, bushings need to be drilled into a metal block and cylindrical shafts need to be inserted into the bushings. The shafts are required to have a radius of at least 1.0000 inch, but the radius should be as little larger than this as possible. With the proposed production process for producing the shafts, the probability distribution of the radius of a shaft has a triangular distribution with a minimum of 1.0000 inch, a most likely value of 1.0010 inches, and a maximum value of 1.0020 inches. With the proposed method of drilling the bushings, the probability distribution of the radius of a bushing has a normal distribution with a mean of 1.0020 inches and a standard deviation of 0.0010 inches. The clearance between a bushing and a shaft is the difference in their radii. Because they are selected at random, there occasionally is interference (i.e., negative clearance) between a bushing and a shaft to be mated.

 Management is concerned about the disruption in the production of the new product that would be caused by this occasional interference. Perhaps the production processes for the shafts and bushings should be improved (at considerable cost) to lessen the chance of interference. To evaluate the need for such improvements, management has asked you to determine how frequently interference is likely to occur with the currently proposed production processes.

 Estimate the probability of interference by using Crystal Ball to perform 500 trials of a computer simulation on a spreadsheet.

13.12. Refer to the financial risk analysis example presented in Section 13.5, including its results shown in Figure 13.27. Think-Big management is quite concerned about the risk profile for the proposal. Two statistics are causing particular concern. One is that there is nearly a 20 percent chance of losing money (a negative NPV). Second, there is a 10 percent chance of losing more than a third ($7 million) as much as the mean gain ($18 million). Therefore, management is wondering whether it would be more prudent to go ahead with just one of the two projects. Thus, in addition to option 1 (the proposal), option 2 is to take a 16.50 percent share of the hotel project only (so no participation in the shopping center project) and option 3 is to take a 13.11 percent share of the shopping center only (so no participation in the hotel project). Management wants to choose one of the three options. Risk profiles now are needed to evaluate the latter two.

 a. Generate a frequency chart and a percentiles table for option 2 after performing a computer simulation with 1,000 trials for this option.

 b. Repeat part *a* for option 3.

 c. Suppose *you* were the CEO of the Think-Big Development Co. Use the results in Figure 13.27 for option 1 along with the corresponding results obtained for the other two options as the basis for a managerial decision on which of the three options to choose. Justify your answer.

13.13. Reconsider Problem 12.5 involving the game of craps. Now the objective is to estimate the probability of winning a play of this game. If the probability is greater than 0.5, you will want to go to Las Vegas to play the game numerous times until you eventually win a considerable amount of money. However, if the probability is less than 0.5, you will stay home.

 You have decided to perform computer simulation on a spreadsheet to estimate this probability. Use Crystal Ball to perform the number of trials (plays of the game) indicated below.

 a. 100 trials.

 b. 1,000 trials.

c. 10,000 trials.

d. The true probability is 0.493. Based upon the above simulation runs, what number of trials appears to be needed to give reasonable assurance of obtaining an estimate that is within 0.007 of the true probability?

13.14. Consider the case study involving Freddie the newsboy that was introduced in Section 13.1. The spreadsheet model is available on your MS Courseware CD-ROM. The Decision Table generated in Section 13.8 (see Figure 13.44) for Freddie's problem suggests that 55 is the best order quantity, but this table only considered order quantities that were a multiple of 5. Refine the search by generating a Decision Table for Freddie's problem that considers all integer order quantities between 50 and 60.

13.15.* Michael Wise operates a newsstand at a busy intersection downtown. Demand for the Sunday *Times* averages 300 copies with a standard deviation of 50 copies (assume a normal distribution). Michael purchases the papers for $0.75 and sells them for $1.25. Any papers left over at the end of the day are recycled with no monetary return.

a. Suppose that Michael buys 350 copies for his newsstand each Sunday morning. Use Crystal Ball to perform 500 trials of a computer simulation on a spreadsheet. What will be Michael's mean profit from selling the Sunday *Times?* What is the probability that Michael will make at least $0 profit?

b. Generate a Decision Table to consider five possible order quantities between 250 and 350. Which order quantity maximizes Michael's mean profit?

c. Generate a trend chart for the five order quantities considered in part *b.*

13.16. Susan is a ticket scalper. She buys tickets for Los Angeles Lakers games before the beginning of the season for $100 each. Since the games all sell out, Susan is able to sell the tickets for $150 on game day. Tickets that Susan is unable to sell on game day have no value. Based on past experience, Susan has predicted the probability distribution for how many tickets she will be able to sell, as shown in the following table.

Tickets	Probability
10	0.05
11	0.10
12	0.10
13	0.15
14	0.20
15	0.15
16	0.10
17	0.10
18	0.05

a. Suppose that Susan buys 14 tickets for each game. Use Crystal Ball to perform 500 trials of a computer simulation on a spreadsheet. What will be Susan's mean profit from selling the tickets? What is the probability that Susan will make at least $0 profit?

(*Hint:* Use the Custom Distribution to simulate the demand for tickets.)

b. Generate a Decision Table to consider all nine possible quantities of tickets to purchase between 10 and 18. Which purchase quantity maximizes Susan's mean profit?

c. Generate a trend chart for the nine purchase quantities considered in part *b.*

13.17. Consider the Reliable Construction Co. bidding problem discussed in Section 13.2. The spreadsheet Model is available on your MS Courseware CD-ROM. The Decision Table generated in Section 13.8 (see Figure 13.49) for this problem suggests that $5.4 million is the best bid, but this table only considered bids that were a multiple of $0.2 million. Refine the search by generating a Decision Table for this bidding problem that considers all bids between $5.2 million and $5.6 million in multiples of $0.05 million.

13.18. Road Pavers, Inc., (RPI) is considering bidding on a county road construction project. RPI has estimated that the cost of this particular job would be $5 million. The cost of putting together a bid is estimated to be $50,000. The county also will receive four other bids on the project from competitors of RPI. Past experience with these competitors suggests that each competitor's bid is most likely to be 20 percent over cost, but could be as low as 5 percent over or as much as 40 percent over cost. Assume a triangular distribution for each of these bids.

a. Suppose that RPI bids $5.7 million on the project. Use Crystal Ball to perform 500 trials of a computer simulation on a spreadsheet. What is the probability that RPI will win the bid? What is RPI's mean profit?

b. Generate a Decision Table to consider eight possible bids between $5.3 million and $6 million and forecast RPI's mean profit. Which bid maximizes RPI's mean profit?

c. Generate a trend chart for the eight bids considered in part *b.*

13.19. Consider the Everglade cash flow problem analyzed in Section 13.4. The spreadsheet model is available on your MS Courseware CD-ROM.

a. Generate a Decision Table to consider five possible long-term loan amounts between $0 million and $20 million and forecast Everglade's mean ending balance. Which long-term loan amount maximizes Everglade's mean ending balance?

b. Generate a trend chart for the five long-term loan amounts considered in part *a.*

13.20. Consider the airline overbooking problem discussed in Section 13.6. The spreadsheet model is available on the MS Courseware CD-ROM packaged with the textbook. The Decision Table generated in Section 13.8 (see Figure 13.50) for this problem suggests that 185 is the best number of reservations to accept in order to maximize profit, but the only numbers considered were a multiple of five.

a. Refine the search by generating a Decision Table for this overbooking problem that considers all integer values for the number of reservations to accept between 180 and 190.

b. Generate a trend chart for the 11 forecasts considered in part *a*.

13.21. Flight 120 between Seattle and San Francisco is a popular flight among both leisure and business travelers. The airplane holds 112 passengers in a single cabin. Both a discount 7-day advance fare and a full-price fare are offered. The airline's management is trying to decide (1) how many seats to allocate to its discount 7-day advance fare and (2) how many tickets to issue in total.

The discount ticket sells for $150 and is nonrefundable. Demand for the 7-day advance fares is typically between 50 and 150, but is most likely to be near 90. (Assume a triangular distribution.) The full-price fare (no advance purchase requirement and fully refundable prior to check-in time) is $400. Excluding customers who purchase this ticket and then cancel prior to check-in time, demand is equally likely to be anywhere between 30 and 70 for these tickets (with essentially all of the demand occurring within one week of the flight). The average no-show rate is 5 percent for the nonrefundable discount tickets and 15 percent for the refundable full-price tickets. If more ticketed passengers show up than there are seats available, the extra passengers must be bumped. A bumped passenger is rebooked on another flight and given a voucher for a free ticket on a future flight. The total cost to the airline for bumping a passenger is $600. There is a fixed cost of $10,000 to operate the flight.

There are two decisions to be made. First, prior to one week before flight time, how many tickets should be made available at the discount fare? Too many and the airline risks losing out on potential full-fare passengers. Too few and the airline may have a less-than-full flight. Second, how many tickets should be issued in total? Too many and the airline risks needing to bump passengers. Too few and the airline risks having a less-than-full flight.

a. Suppose that the airline makes available a maximum of 75 tickets for the discount fare and a maximum of

120 tickets in total. Use Crystal Ball to generate a 1,000 trial forecast of the distribution of the profit, the number of seats filled, and the number of passengers bumped.

b. Generate a two-dimensional Decision Table that gives the mean profit for all combinations of the following values of the two decision variables: (1) the maximum number of tickets made available at the discount fare is a multiple of 10 between 50 and 90 and (2) the maximum number of tickets made available for either fare is 112, 117, 122, 127, or 132.

13.22. Now that Jennifer is in middle school, her parents have decided that they really must start saving for her college education. They have $6,000 to invest right now. Furthermore, they plan to save another $4,000 each year until Jennifer starts college in five years. They plan to split their investment evenly between a stock fund and a bond fund. Historically, the stock fund has had an average annual return of 8 percent with a standard deviation of 6 percent. The bond fund has had an average annual return of 4 percent with a standard deviation of 3 percent. (Assume a normal distribution for both.)

Assume that the initial investment ($6,000) and the first year's investment ($4,000) are made right now (year 0) and are split evenly between the two funds (i.e., $5,000 in each fund). The returns of each fund are allowed to accumulate (i.e., are reinvested) in the same fund and no redistribution will be done before Jennifer starts college. Furthermore, four additional investments of $4,000 will be made and split evenly between both funds ($2,000 each) at year 1, year 2, year 3, and year 4. Use a 1000-trial Crystal Ball simulation to estimate each of the following.

a. What will be the expected value (mean) of the college fund at year 5?

b. What will be the standard deviation of the college fund at year 5?

c. What is the probability that the college fund at year 5 will be at least $30,000?

d. What is the probability that the college fund at year 5 will be at least $35,000?

Case 13-1

Action Adventures

The Adventure Toys Company manufactures a popular line of action figures and distributes them to toy stores at the wholesale price of $10 per unit. Demand for the action figures is seasonal, with the highest sales occurring before Christmas and during the spring. The lowest sales occur during the summer and winter months.

Each month the monthly "base" sales follow a normal distribution with a mean equal to the previous month's actual "base"

sales and with a standard deviation of 500 units. The actual sales in any month are the monthly base sales multiplied by the seasonality factor for the month, as shown in the table on page 574. Base sales in December 2006 were 6,000, with actual sales equal to (1.18)(6,000) = 7,080. It is now January 1, 2007.

Month	Seasonality Factor	Month	Seasonality Factor
January	0.79	July	0.74
February	0.88	August	0.98
March	0.95	September	1.06
April	1.05	October	1.10
May	1.09	November	1.16
June	0.84	December	1.18

Cash sales typically account for about 40 percent of monthly sales, but this figure has been as low as 28 percent and as high as 48 percent in some months. The remainder of the sales are made on a 30-day interest-free credit basis, with full payment received one month after delivery. In December 2006, 42 percent of sales were cash sales and 58 percent were on credit.

The production costs depend upon the labor and material costs. The plastics required to manufacture the action figures fluctuate in price from month to month, depending on market conditions. Because of these fluctuations, production costs can be anywhere from $6 to $8 per unit. In addition to these variable production costs, the company incurs a fixed cost of $15,000 per month for manufacturing the action figures. The company assembles the products to order. When a batch of a particular action figure is ordered, it is immediately manufactured and shipped within a couple of days.

The company utilizes eight molding machines to mold the action figures. These machines occasionally break down and require a $5,000 replacement part. Each machine requires a replacement part with a 10 percent probability each month.

The company has a policy of maintaining a minimum cash balance of at least $20,000 at the end of each month. The balance at the end of December 2006 (or equivalently, at the beginning of January 2007) is $25,000. If required, the company will take out a short-term (one-month) loan to cover expenses and maintain the minimum balance. The loans must be paid back the following month with interest (using the current month's loan interest rate). For example, if March's annual interest rate is 6 percent (so 0.5 percent per month) and a $1,000 loan is taken out in March, then $1,005 is due in April. However, a new loan can be taken out each month.

Any balance remaining at the end of a month (including the minimum balance) is carried forward to the following month and also earns savings interest. For example, if the ending balance in March is $20,000 and March's savings interest is 3 percent per annum (so 0.25 percent per month), then $50 of savings interest is earned in April.

Both the loan interest rate and the savings interest rate are set monthly based upon the prime rate. The loan interest rate is set at prime + 2%, while the savings interest rate is set at prime − 2%. However, the loan interest rate is capped at (can't exceed) 9 percent and the savings interest rate will never drop below 2 percent.

The prime rate in December 2006 was 5 percent per annum. This rate depends upon the whims of the Federal Reserve Board. In particular, for each month there is a 70 percent chance it will stay unchanged, a 10 percent chance it will increase by 25 basis points (0.25 percent), a 10 percent chance it will decrease by 25 basis points, a 5 percent chance it will increase by 50 basis points, and a 5 percent chance it will decrease by 50 basis points.

a. Formulate a simulation model on a spreadsheet to track the company's cash flows from month to month. Indicate the probability distributions (both the type and the parameters) for the assumption cells directly on the spreadsheet. Use Crystal Ball to simulate 1,000 trials for the year 2007 and paste your results in the spreadsheet.

b. Adventure Toys management wants information about what the company's net worth might be at the end of 2007, including the likelihood that the net worth will exceed $0. (The net worth is defined here as the ending cash balance *plus* savings interest and account receivables *minus* any loans and interest due.) Display the results of your simulation run from part *a* in the various forms that you think would be helpful to management in analyzing this issue.

c. Arrangements need to be made to obtain a specific credit limit from the bank for the short-term loans that might be needed during 2007. Therefore, Adventure Toys management also would like information regarding the size of the maximum short-term loan that might be needed during 2007. Display the results of your simulation run from part *a* in the various forms that you think would be helpful to management in analyzing this issue.

Case 13-2

Pricing under Pressure

Elise Sullivan moved to New York City in September to begin her first job as an analyst working in the Client Services Division of FirstBank, a large investment bank providing brokerage services to clients across the United States. The moment she arrived in the Big Apple after receiving her undergraduate business degree, she hit the ground running—or, more appropriately, working. She spent her first six weeks in training, where she met new FirstBank analysts like herself and learned the basics of

FirstBank's approach to accounting, cash flow analysis, customer service, and federal regulations.

After completing training, Elise moved into her bullpen on the 40th floor of the Manhattan FirstBank building to begin work. Her first few assignments have allowed her to learn the ropes by placing her under the direction of senior staff members who delegate specific tasks to her.

Today, she has an opportunity to distinguish herself in her career, however. Her boss, Michael Steadman, has given her an assignment that is under her complete direction and control. A very eccentric, wealthy client and avid investor by the name of Emery Bowlander is interested in purchasing a European call option that provides him with the right to purchase shares of Fellare stock for $44.00 on the first of February—12 weeks from today. Fellare is an aerospace manufacturing company operating in France, and Mr. Bowlander has a strong feeling that the European Space Agency will award Fellare with a contract to build a portion of the International Space Station some time in January. In the event that the European Space Agency awards the contract to Fellare, Mr. Bowlander believes the stock will skyrocket, reflecting investor confidence in the capabilities and growth of the company. If Fellare does not win the contract, however, Mr. Bowlander believes the stock will continue its current slow downward trend. To guard against this latter outcome, Mr. Bowlander does not want to make an outright purchase of Fellare stock now.

Michael has asked Elise to price the option. He expects a figure before the stock market closes so that if Mr. Bowlander decides to purchase the option, the transaction can take place today.

Unfortunately, the investment science course Elise took to complete her undergraduate business degree did not cover options theory; it only covered valuation, risk, capital budgeting, and market efficiency. She remembers from her valuation studies that she should discount the value of the option on February 1 by the appropriate interest rate to obtain the value of the option today. Because she is discounting over a 12-week period, the formula she should use to discount the option is (Value of the Option/ [1 + Weekly Interest Rate]^{12}). As a starting point for her calculations, she decides to use an annual interest rate of 8 percent. But she now needs to decide how to calculate the value of the option on February 1.

Elise knows that on February 1, Mr. Bowlander will take one of two actions: either he will exercise the option and purchase shares of Fellare stock or he will not exercise the option. Mr. Bowlander will exercise the option if the price of Fellare stock on February 1 is above his exercise price of $44.00. In this case, he purchases Fellare stock for $44.00 and then immediately sells it for the market price on February 1. Under this scenario, the value of the option would be the difference between the stock price and the exercise price. Mr. Bowlander will not exercise the option if the price of Fellare stock is below his exercise price of $44.00. In this case, he does nothing, and the value of the option would be $0.

The value of the option is therefore determined by the value of Fellare stock on February 1. Elise knows that the value of the stock on February 1 is uncertain and is therefore represented by a probability distribution of values. Elise recalls from a management science course in college that she can use computer simulation to estimate the mean of this distribution of stock values. Before she builds the simulation model, however, she needs to know the price movement of the stock. Elise recalls from a probability and statistics course that the price of a stock can be modeled as following a random walk and either growing or decaying according to a lognormal distribution. Therefore, according to this model, the stock price at the end of the next week is the stock price at the end of the current week multiplied by a growth factor. This growth factor is expressed as the number e raised to

a power that is equal to a normally distributed random variable. In other words:

$$s_n = e^N s_c$$

where

s_n = The stock price at the end of next week

s_c = The stock price at the end of the current week

N = A random variable that has a normal distribution

To begin her analysis, Elise looks in the newspaper to find that the Fellare stock price for the current week is $42.00. She decides to use this price to begin her 12-week analysis. Thus, the price of the stock at the end of the first week is this current price multiplied by the growth factor. She next estimates the mean and standard deviation of the normally distributed random variable used in the calculation of the growth factor. This random variable determines the degree of change (volatility) of the stock, so Elise decides to use the current annual interest rate and the historical annual volatility of the stock as a basis for estimating the mean and standard deviation.

The current annual interest rate is $r = 8$ percent, and the historical annual volatility of the aerospace stock is 30 percent. But Elise remembers that she is calculating the *weekly* change in stock—*not* the *annual* change. She therefore needs to calculate the weekly interest rate and weekly historical stock volatility to obtain estimates for the mean and standard deviation of the weekly growth factor. To obtain the weekly interest rate w, Elise must make the following calculation:

$$w = (1 + r)^{(1/52)} - 1$$

The historical weekly stock volatility equals the historical annual volatility divided by the square root of 52. She calculates the mean of the normally distributed random variable by subtracting one-half of the square of the weekly stock volatility from the weekly interest rate w. In other words:

$$\text{Mean} = w - 0.5(\text{Weekly Stock Volatility})^2$$

The standard deviation of the normally distributed random variable is simply equal to the weekly stock volatility.

Elise is now ready to build her simulation model.

a. Build a simulation model in a spreadsheet to calculate the value of the option in today's dollars. Use Crystal Ball to run three separate simulations to estimate the value of the call option and hence the price of the option in today's dollars. For the first simulation, run 100 trials of the simulation. For the second simulation, run 500 trials of the simulation. For the third simulation, run 1,000 trials of the simulation. For each simulation, record the price of the option in today's dollars.

b. Elise takes her calculations and recommended price to Michael. He is very impressed, but he chuckles and indicates that a simple, closed-form approach exists for calculating the value of an option: the Black-Scholes formula. Michael grabs an investment science book from the shelf above his desk and reveals the very powerful and very complicated Black-Scholes formula:

$$V = N[d_1]P - N[d_2]\text{PV}[K]$$

where

$$d_1 = \frac{\ln[P/PV[K]]}{\sigma\sqrt{t}} + \frac{\sigma\sqrt{t}}{2}$$

$$d_2 = d_1 - \sigma\sqrt{t}$$

$N[x]$ = The Excel function NORMSDIST (x) where $x = d_1$
   or $x = d_2$

P = Current price of the stock

K = Exercise price

$PV[K]$ = Present value of exercise price = $\dfrac{K}{(1 + w)^t}$

t = Number of weeks to exercise date

σ = Weekly volatility of stock

Use the Black-Scholes formula to calculate the value of the call option and hence the price of the option. Compare this value to the value obtained in part *a*.

c. In the specific case of Fellare stock, do you think that a random walk as described above completely describes the price movement of the stock? Why or why not?

Appendix **A**

Using the Solver Table

Solver Table is an add-in developed by the authors that is useful for doing sensitivity analysis on any spreadsheet model that has been solved using the Solver. In particular, it will allow you to vary one or two data cells in a model and see the impact on the optimal values of the changing cells, the target cell, and/or any other output cells of interest. The Solver Table add-in and installation instructions are contained on the CD-ROM that is packaged with this textbook. This appendix gives instructions for using the Solver Table add-in.

USING SOLVER TABLE TO DO ONE-WAY SENSITIVITY ANALYSIS

Solver Table is used to show the results in the changing cells and/or certain output cells for various trial values in a data cell. For each trial value in the data cell, Solver is called on to re-solve the problem.

Before using Solver Table, the model must first be developed in the spreadsheet in the usual way, including entering all of the appropriate parameters into the Solver (e.g., the location of the target cell, changing cells, constraints, etc.). Figure A.1 shows the spreadsheet solution for the Wyndor Glass Co. problem from Chapters 2 and 5. Although this particular example is a linear programming model, Solver Table also can be used on integer and nonlinear programming models, as well as on any other model that can be solved using Solver.

After formulating the model in a spreadsheet, Solver Table can then be used to determine how the optimal solution will change for various trial values of a data cell (for example, the unit profit from producing doors in the Wyndor problem). To use Solver Table, make a table on the spreadsheet, with column headings for the data cell that will be changing, followed by any output cells of interest, such as the changing cells and/or the target cell. For the Wyndor example, the table might appear as in Figure A.2.

In the first column of the table (cells B19:B28 in Figure A.2), list the trial values for the data cell (the unit profit for doors in this example), except leave the first row blank. The headings of the next columns specify which output will be evaluated. For each of these columns, use the first row of the table (cells C18:E18 in Figure A.2) to write an equation that refers to the relevant changing cell or output cells of interest. In this example, the cells of interest are

FIGURE A.1.

The spreadsheet model for the Wyndor Glass Co. product-mix problem.

	A	B	C	D	E	F	G
1		**Wyndor Glass Co. Product-Mix Problem**					
2							
3			Doors	Windows			
4		Unit Profit	$300	$500			
5					Hours		Hours
6			Hours Used per Unit Produced		Used		Available
7		Plant 1	1	0	2	<=	4
8		Plant 2	0	2	12	<=	12
9		Plant 3	3	2	18	<=	18
10							
11			Doors	Windows			Total Profit
12		Units Produced	2	6			$3,600

FIGURE A.2.

A table in a spreadsheet set up for Solver Table to determine the optimal solution for various trial values of a data cell.

	B	C	D	E
16	Unit Profit	Optimal Units Produced		Total
17	for Doors	Doors	Windows	Profit
18		=C12	=D12	=G12
19	$100			
20	$200			
21	$300			
22	$400			
23	$500			
24	$600			
25	$700			
26	$800			
27	$900			
28	$1,000			

FIGURE A.3.

The Solver Table dialogue box.

Solver Table

Row input cell: [ ]

Column input cell: [C4]

Cancel   OK

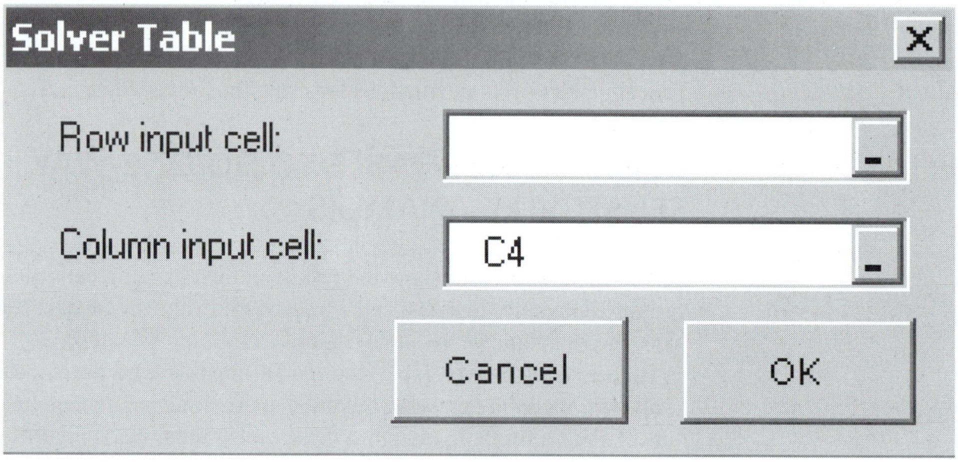

FIGURE A.4.

The completed Solver Table showing the optimal solution for the Wyndor Glass Co. product-mix problem for various trial values of a data cell.

	B	C	D	E
16	Unit Profit	Optimal Units Produced		Total
17	for Doors	Doors	Windows	Profit
18		2	6	$3,600
19	$100	2	6	$3,200
20	$200	2	6	$3,400
21	$300	2	6	$3,600
22	$400	2	6	$3,800
23	$500	2	6	$4,000
24	$600	2	6	$4,200
25	$700	2	6	$4,400
26	$800	4	3	$4,700
27	$900	4	3	$5,100
28	$1,000	4	3	$5,500

the doors produced (C12), windows produced (D12), and total profit (G12), so the equations for C18:E18 are those shown in Figure A.2.

Next, select the entire table (not including the text headings). For this example, you would click and drag from cell B18 through E28. Then choose Solver Table from the Add-Ins tab (for Excel 2007) or the Tools menu (for earlier versions of Excel). In the Solver Table dialogue box (shown in Figure A.3), indicate the column input cell (C4 for this example), which refers to the data cell that is being changed in the first column of the table. Nothing is entered for the row input cell because no row is being used to list the trial values of a data cell in this case.

The Solver Table is then generated automatically by clicking on the OK button. For each trial value listed in the first column of the table for the data cell of interest, Excel re-solves the problem using Solver and then fills in the corresponding values in the other columns of the table. (The numbers in the first row of the table come from the original solution in the spreadsheet before the original value in the data cell was changed.) For this example, the results would appear as shown in Figure A.4.

SUMMARY OF STEPS TO CREATE A ONE-WAY SOLVER TABLE

1. Create a column heading for both the data cell to be changed and the output cells of interest.
2. In the first column of the table (skipping the first row), list the trial values for the data cell to be changed.
3. In the first row of the table, write equations referring to the output cells of interest.
4. Select the entire table (not including the headings).
5. Choose Solver Table from the Add-Ins tab (for Excel 2007) or Tools menu (for earlier versions of Excel).
6. Enter the location of the data cell to be changed in the Column Input Cell box, and press OK.

USING SOLVER TABLE TO DO TWO-WAY SENSITIVITY ANALYSIS

A *two-way* Solver Table provides a way of systematically investigating the effect of simultaneously changing two different data cells (for example, the unit profit for *both* doors and windows in the Wyndor Glass Co. problem). This kind of Solver Table shows the results in a single output cell for various trial values in two data cells. For example, it can be used to show how the total profit (G12 in Figure A.1) varies over a range of trial values in the two data cells, such as the unit profits. For each pair of trial values in the data cells, Solver is called on to re-solve the problem.

To create a two-way Solver Table for the problem, expand the original spreadsheet to make a table with column and row headings like those shown in Figure A.5. In the upper left-hand corner of the table (C17 in Figure A.5), write an equation that refers to the output cell of interest. In this Wyndor example, =G12 is entered in cell C17 to show the results of the target cell. In the first column of the table (column C, below the equation in cell C17 in Figure A.5), insert various trial values for the first data cell of interest (the unit profit for doors for this example). In the first row of the table (row 17, to the right of the equation in cell C17 in Figure A.5), insert various trial values for the second data cell of interest (the unit profit for windows for this example).

Next, select the entire table (not including the text headings). For this example, you would click and drag from cell C17 through H21. Then choose Solver Table from the Add-Ins tab (for Excel 2007) or the Tools menu (for earlier versions of Excel). In the Solver Table dialogue box (shown in Figure A.6), indicate which data cells are being changed simultaneously. The column input cell C4 refers to the data cell whose various trial values are listed in the first column of the table (C18:C21), while the row input cell refers to the data cell whose various trial values are listed in the first row of the table (D17:H17).

The Solver Table is then generated automatically by clicking on the OK button. For each pair of trial values for the two data cells, Excel re-solves the problem using Solver and then fills in the output cell of interest in the corresponding spot in the table. For this example, the results are shown in Figure A.7. (The number in C17 comes from the target cell in the original spreadsheet before the original values in the two data cells are changed.)

FIGURE A.5.

A table in a spreadsheet set up for Solver Table to determine the optimal total profit for the Wyndor Glass Co. product-mix problem for various trial values of two data cells.

	B	C	D	E	F	G	H
16	**Total Profit**			Unit Profit for Windows			
17		=G12	$100	$200	$300	$400	$500
18		$300					
19	Unit Profit	$400					
20	for Doors	$500					
21		$600					

SUMMARY OF STEPS TO CREATE A TWO-WAY SOLVER TABLE

1. In the first row of the table, list the trial values for the first data cell to be changed.
2. In the first column of the table, list the trial values for the second data cell to be changed.
3. In the upper left corner of the table, write an equation referring to the output cell of interest.
4. Select the entire table (not including the headings).
5. Choose Solver Table from the Add-Ins tab (for Excel 2007) or Tools menu (for earlier versions of Excel).
6. Enter the cell location of the first data cell to be changed in the Row Input Cell box.
7. Enter the cell location of the second data cell to be changed in the Column Input Cell box and press OK.

FIGURE A.6.

The Solver Table dialogue box.

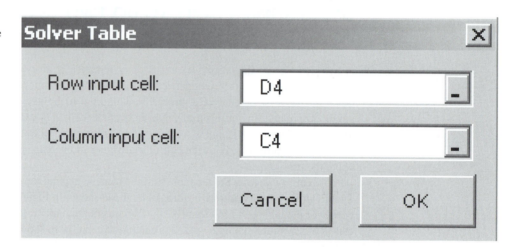

FIGURE A.7.

The completed two-way Solver Table showing the optimal total profit for the Wyndor Glass Co. product-mix problem for various trial values of two data cells.

	B	C	D	E	F	G	H
16	**Total Profit**			Unit Profit for Windows			
17		$3,600	$100	$200	$300	$400	$500
18		$300	$1,500	$1,800	$2,400	$3,000	$3,600
19	Unit Profit	$400	$1,900	$2,200	$2,600	$3,200	$3,800
20	for Doors	$500	$2,300	$2,600	$2,900	$3,400	$4,000
21		$600	$2,700	$3,000	$3,300	$3,600	$4,200

Appendix **B**

Tips for Using Microsoft Excel for Modeling

Microsoft Excel is a powerful and flexible tool with a myriad of features. It is certainly not necessary to master all the features of Excel in order to successfully build models in spreadsheets. However, there are some features of Excel that are particularly useful for modeling that we will highlight here. This appendix is not designed to be a basic tutorial for Excel. It is designed instead for someone with a working knowledge of Excel (at least at a basic level) who wants to take advantage of some of the more advanced features of Excel that are useful for building models more efficiently.

B.1 ANATOMY OF THE MICROSOFT EXCEL WINDOW

When Microsoft Excel is first opened (e.g., by choosing Microsoft Excel from the Start menu), a blank spreadsheet appears in an Excel window. The various components of the Excel window are labeled in Figure B.1.

The Excel file is called a *workbook.* A workbook consists of a number of *worksheets* or *spreadsheets,* identified in the sheet tabs at the bottom of the screen (Sheet1, Sheet2, and Sheet3 in Figure B.1). Only one spreadsheet at a time is shown in the window, with the currently displayed spreadsheet highlighted in the sheet tab (Sheet1 in Figure B.1). To show a different spreadsheet (e.g., Sheet2 or Sheet3), click on the appropriate sheet tab.

Each spreadsheet consists of a huge grid, with many rows and columns. The rows are labeled on the left of the grid by numbers (1, 2, 3, . . .). The columns are labeled on the top of the grid by letters (A, B, C, . . .). Each element of the grid is referred to as a *cell,* and is referred to by its row and column label (e.g., cell C7). The currently selected cell is highlighted by the cell cursor (a dark or colored border). A different cell can be selected either by clicking on it or by moving the cell cursor with the arrow keys.

Only a portion of the spreadsheet is shown at any one time. For example, in Figure B.1 only the first 9 columns and first 17 rows are shown. The scroll bars can be used to show a different portion of the spreadsheet.

B.2 WORKING WITH WORKBOOKS

When Microsoft Excel is first opened (e.g., by choosing Microsoft Excel from the Start menu), a new workbook is created and given a default name that is visible in the Title Bar (e.g., Book1 in Figure B.1). To give the workbook a different name, save it under whatever name you desire by choosing Save As under the Office Button (for Excel 2007) or File menu (for earlier versions of Excel).

To open an existing workbook that has been saved previously, choose Open from the Office Button (Excel 2007) or Edit menu (earlier versions). It is possible to have more than one workbook open at a time within Excel. This may be desirable if you want to copy worksheets from

FIGURE B.1.
The Microsoft Excel
window for Excel 2007
(top) and for earlier
versions of Excel
(bottom).

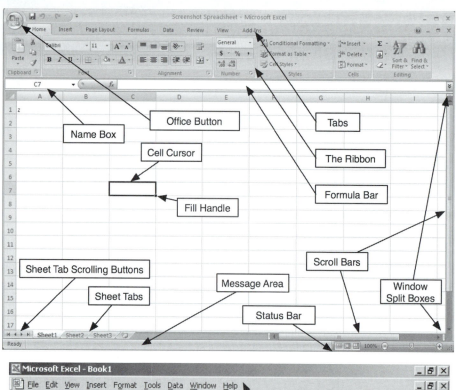

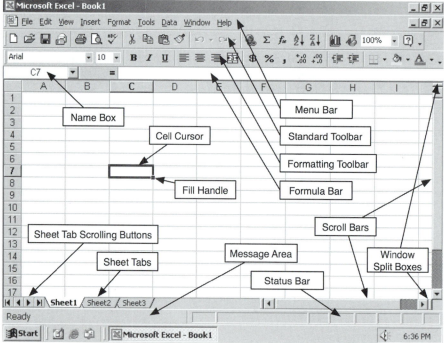

one workbook to another or if you want to see the contents of another workbook while you are
working on an existing workbook. When multiple workbooks are open, some of the workbooks
can become hidden behind another workbook that is being displayed. To bring any workbook to
the front, select it under the Switch Windows menu on the View tab (Excel 2007) or the Window menu (earlier versions). The workbooks also can be arranged on the screen (e.g., one over
the other, or one next to the other) by choosing Arrange All on the View tab (Excel 2007) or
Arrrange under the Window menu (earlier versions).

B.3 WORKING WITH WORKSHEETS

By default, a new Excel workbook consists of a few worksheets titled Sheet1, Sheet2, Sheet3, and so on. The currently displayed sheet is highlighted in the sheet tabs. To display a different sheet, click on the appropriate tab. If the desired tab is not visible because there are more tabs than can be displayed, the list of tabs can be scrolled using the sheet tab scroll buttons.

The sheets can be given descriptive names by double-clicking on the sheet tab and typing a new name. A new sheet can be added to the workbook by choosing Sheet from the Insert menu of the Cells group on the Home tab (for Excel 2007) or choosing Worksheet from the Insert menu (for earlier versions of Excel). The sheet tabs can be reordered by clicking and dragging a tab to a new location. To make a copy of a sheet, control-click (option-click on a Mac) and drag the tab. If multiple workbooks are open, you can also click (or control-click) and drag a sheet tab to a different workbook to move (or copy) a sheet to a different workbook.

Using Worksheets with Solver

A model must be confined to a single sheet. When using the standard Excel Solver, all cell references (e.g., the target cell, changing cells, etc.) must be on the currently displayed sheet. Thus, the different components of the Solver model cannot be spread among different sheets. (The Premium Solver for Education included on the CD-ROM with this textbook allows the cell references to be on different sheets.)

The Solver information is saved with the sheet. When data are entered in the Solver dialogue box (e.g., the target cell, changing cells, etc.), all of that information is saved with the sheet when the workbook is saved.

Separate sheets can contain separate models. Separate Solver dialogue box information (e.g., the target cell, changing cells, etc.) is kept for each sheet in the workbook. Thus, each sheet in a workbook can contain a separate and independent model. When the Solve button is clicked in Solver, only the model on the currently displayed sheet is solved.

Copy the whole sheet rather than just the relevant cells to copy models. To copy a model to another workbook or within the current workbook, it is important to control-click and drag the worksheet tab rather than simply selecting the cells containing the model and using copy and paste. Copying the sheet (by control-clicking and dragging the sheet tab) will copy *all* the contents of the sheet (formulas, data, *and* the Solver dialog box information). Using copy and paste copies only the formulas and data, but does *not* include the Solver dialogue box information.

Using Worksheets with TreePlan

Separate sheets can contain separate TreePlan decision trees. If the currently displayed sheet does not contain an existing TreePlan decision tree, then choosing Decision Tree under the Add-Ins tab (for Excel 2007) or Tools menu (for earlier versions of Excel) will present the option of adding a new tree to the existing sheet. However, if a decision tree already exists on the sheet, then choosing Decision Tree instead presents options for modifying the existing tree. To create a new decision tree, first switch to (or add) a new sheet. A workbook can contain separate decision trees so long as they are on separate sheets.

Using Worksheets with Crystal Ball

The entire workbook is treated as a single model for Crystal Ball. In contrast with the Solver and TreePlan, Crystal Ball treats the entire workbook as part of a single model. Assumption cells, decision variables, and forecast cells can be defined on any or all of the different sheets of the workbook. When a simulation is run, all assumption cells are randomly generated and a forecast window is shown for all forecast cells regardless of whether they are on the currently displayed sheet. This can be an advantage with complicated simulation models, since it allows splitting the model into separate manageable components on different sheets.

Although it is possible to create separate models on different sheets for applying Crystal Ball in the same workbook, it would be confusing to do so. When you start running a simulation in a workbook containing separate models on different sheets, *all* the models on *all* the sheets will be run. To avoid this confusion, it is best to keep separate simulation models for applying Crystal Ball in separate workbooks and only keep a single workbook open at a time.

B.4 WORKING WITH CELLS

Selecting Cells

To make any changes to a cell or range of cells, such as entering or editing data or changing the formatting, the cell or cells involved first need to be selected. The cell cursor shows the currently selected cell (or range of cells). To select a different single cell, either click on it or use the arrow keys to move the cell cursor to that location. To select an entire row or an entire column, click the row or column heading (i.e., the A, B, C along the top of the spreadsheet, or the 1, 2, 3 along the left of the spreadsheet). To select the entire spreadsheet, click in the blank box at the upper left corner of the worksheet.

There are three ways to select a range of cells within a spreadsheet, which we will illustrate by considering the 3-by-3 range of cells from A1 to C3:

1. Click on one corner of the range (A1) and, without releasing the mouse button, drag to the other corner of the range (C3).
2. Click on one corner of the range (A1) and then hold down the SHIFT key and click on the other corner of the range (C3).
3. Click on one corner of the range (A1), hold down SHIFT or press F8 to turn on the extend mode, use the arrow keys to extend the range to the other corner (C3), and then either release the SHIFT key or press F8 again to turn the extend mode off.

Entering or Editing Data, Text, and Formulas into Cells

There are a number of ways to enter and edit the contents of a cell:

1. **Use the Formula Bar:** The contents of the currently selected cell appear in the formula bar (see Figure B.1). To enter data, text, or a formula into a cell, click on the cell and type or edit the contents in the formula bar. Press Enter when you are done.
2. **Double-click:** Double-clicking on a cell (or pressing F2) will display the contents of the cell and allow typing or editing directly within the cell on the spreadsheet. If the cell contains a formula, the cells referred to in the formula will be highlighted in different colors on the spreadsheet. The formula can be modified either by clicking and typing within the cell or by dragging the highlighted cell markers to new locations.
3. **Insert Function:** In an empty cell, pressing the f_x button next to the formula bar (for Excel 2007) or on the standard toolbar (for earlier versions of Excel) will bring up a dialogue box showing all of the functions available in Excel sorted by type. After choosing a function from the list, the function is inserted into the cell and all the parameters of the function are shown in a small window.

Moving or Copying Cells

To move a cell or range of cells on the spreadsheet, first select the cell(s). To move the cell(s) a short distance on the spreadsheet (e.g., down a few rows), it is usually most convenient to use the dragging method. Click on an edge of the cell cursor and, without releasing the mouse button, drag the cell(s) to the new location. To move the cell(s) a large distance (e.g., down 100 rows, or to a different worksheet), it is usually more convenient to use Cut and Paste from the Home tab (for Excel 2007) or Edit menu (for earlier versions of Excel).

Similar methods can be used to make a copy of a cell or range of cells. To copy a cell (or range of cells), press ctrl (option on a Mac) while clicking on the edge of the cell cursor and dragging, or use Copy and Paste from the Home tab (Excel 2007) or Edit menu (earlier versions).

Filling Cells

When building a spreadsheet, it is common to need a series of numbers or dates in a row or column. For example, Figure B.2 shows a spreadsheet that calculates the projected annual

FIGURE B.2.

A simple spreadsheet to calculate projected annual cash flow and tax due.

	A	B	C	D	E	F	G	H	I	J	K	L	M	N	O
1						Cash Flow ($000)								Annual	Tax
2		Jan	Feb	Mar	Apr	May	Jun	Jul	Aug	Sep	Oct	Nov	Dec	Cash Flow	Due
3	2007	10	−2	4	5	4	6	8	10	12	3	−4	8	64	16.0
4	2008	15	3	−4	3	10	4	6	10	3	6	−2	12	66	16.5
5	2009	8	4	2	−3	−5	7	4	8	8	11	−3	11	52	13.0
6	2010	7	5	5	3	2	6	10	12	14	8	2	8	82	20.5
7	2011	5	2	2	−4	9	7	12	14	3	−4	6	10	62	15.5
8															
9														Tax Rate	25%

	N	O
1	Annual	Tax
2	Cash Flow	Due
3	=SUM(B3:M3)	=N3*$O$9
4	=SUM(B4:M4)	=N4*$O$9
5	=SUM(B5:M5)	=N5*$O$9
6	=SUM(B6:M6)	=N6*$O$9
7	=SUM(B7:M7)	=N7*$O$9
8		
9	Tax Rate	0.25

cash flow and taxes due for 2007 through 2011, based upon monthly cash flows. Rather than typing all 12 column labels for the months in cells B2:M2, the fill handle (the small box on the lower right corner of the cell cursor) can be used to fill in the series. After entering the first couple of elements of the series, for example Jan in cell B2 and Feb in cell C2, select cells B2:C2 and then click and drag the fill handle to cell M2. The remainder of the series (Mar, Apr, May, etc.) will be filled in automatically. The year labels in cells A3:A7 can be filled in a similar fashion. After entering the first couple of years, 2007 in A3 and 2008 in A4, select cells A3:A4 and then click and drag the fill handle down to A7. On the basis of the data in the cells selected, the fill handle will try to guess the remainder of the series.

The fill handle is also useful for copying similar formulas into adjacent cells in a row or a column. For example, the formula to calculate the annual cash flows in N3:N7 is basically the same formula for every year. After entering the formula for 2007 in cell N3, select cell N3 and then click and drag the fill handle to copy the formula down through cell N7. Similarly, the taxes due formula in cell O3 can be copied down to cells O4:O7. In fact, both the annual cash flow and tax due formulas can be copied at once by selecting both cells N3 and O3 (the range N3:O3) and then dragging the fill handle down to cell O7. This will fill both formulas down into the cells N4:O7.

Relative and Absolute References

When using the fill handle, it is important to understand the difference between relative and absolute references. Consider the formula in cell N3 (=SUM(B3:M3)). The references to cells in the formula (B3:M3) are based upon their relative position to the cell containing the formula. Thus, B3:M3 are treated as the 12 cells immediately to the left. This is known as a **relative reference.** When this formula is copied to new cells using the fill handle, the references are automatically adjusted to refer to the new cell(s) at the same relative location (the 12 cells immediately to the left). For example, the formula in N4 becomes =SUM(B4:M4), the formula in N5 becomes =SUM(B5:M5), and so on.

In contrast, the reference to the tax rate ($O$9) in the formula in cell O3 is called an **absolute reference.** These references do not change when they are filled into other cells. Thus, when the formula in cell O3 is copied into cells O4:O7, the reference still refers to cell O9.

To make an absolute reference, put $ signs in front of the letter and number of the cell reference (e.g., $O$9). Similarly, you can make the column absolute and the row relative (or vice versa) by putting a $ sign in front of only the letter (or number) of the cell reference. After entering a cell reference, repeatedly pressing the F4 key (or command-T on a Mac) will rotate among the four possibilities of relative and absolute references (e.g., O9, $O$9, O$9, $O9).

Using Range Names

A block of related cells can be given a range name. Then, rather than referring to the cells by their cell addresses (e.g., L11:L21 or C3), a more descriptive name can be used (e.g., Total-Profit). To give a cell or range of cells a range name, first select the cell(s). Then click in the Name Box (see Figure B.1) and type a name. For example, for the spreadsheet in Figure B.2 we could define a range name for the tax rate by selecting cell O9 and typing TaxRate into the name box. Spaces are not allowed in range names, so use capital letters or underscore characters to separate words in a name.

Once a range name is defined, rather than typing the cell reference (e.g., O9) when it is used in a formula, the range name can be used instead (e.g., TaxRate). If you click on a cell (or cells) to use it in a formula, the range name is automatically used rather than the cell reference. This can make the formula easier to interpret (e.g., =SUM(B3:M3)*TaxRate, rather than =SUM(B3:M3)*$O$9). When using a range name in a formula, it is treated as an absolute reference. To make a relative reference to a cell that has a range name, type the cell address (e.g., O9) rather than either typing the range name or clicking on the cell (which then automatically uses the range name).

Formatting Cells

To make formatting changes to a cell or range of cells, first select the cell(s). If a range of cells is selected, any formatting changes will apply to every cell in the range. Most common types of formatting of cells, for example, changing the font, making text bold or italic, or changing the borders or shading of a cell, can be done by using the Home tab (for Excel 2007) or the formatting toolbar (for earlier versions of Excel).

Clicking on the .0→.00 or .00→.0 buttons changes the number of decimal places shown in a cell. Note that this only changes how the number is displayed, since Excel always uses the full precision when this cell is used in other formulas.

For more advanced types of formatting, choose Format Cells under the Format menu of the Cells group on the Home tab (Excel 2007) or Cells under the Format menu (earlier versions). A shortcut is to press ctrl-1 on a PC or command-1 on a Mac. This brings up the Format cells dialogue box, as shown in Figure B.3. Under the Numbers tab you can choose to display the contents in a cell as a number with any number of decimal places (e.g., 123.4 or 123.486), as currency (e.g., $1,234.10), as a date (e.g., 12/10/2009 or Dec 2009), and so on. The other tabs

FIGURE B.3.

The Format Cells dialogue box.

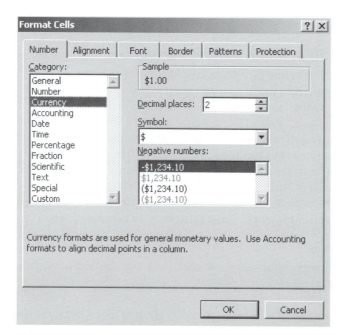

are used to change the alignment of the text (e.g., left or right justified, printed vertically or horizontally, etc.), the font, the borders, the patterns, and the protection.

If a cell displays ####, this means that the column width is not wide enough to show the contents of the cell. To change column widths or row heights, click and drag the vertical or horizontal lines between the column or row labels. Double-clicking on the vertical line between column labels will make the column just wide enough to show the entire contents of every cell in the column.

Appendix C

Partial Answers to Selected Problems

CHAPTER 2

2.5. *d.* Fraction of 1st = 0.667, fraction of 2nd = 0.667. Profit = $6,000.

2.12. *b.* x_1 = 13, x_2 = 5. Profit = $31.

CHAPTER 3

3.2. *c.* 3.333 of Activity 1, 3.333 of Activity 2. Profit = $166.67.

3.5. *d.* 26 of Product 1, 54.76 of Product 2, 20 of Product 3. Profit = $2,904.76.

3.10. *d.* 1.14 kg of corn, 2.43 kg of alfalfa. Cost = $2.42.

3.15. *b.* Cost = $410,000.

Shipment Quantities	Customer 1	Customer 2	Customer 3
Factory 1	300	0	100
Factory 2	0	200	300

3.17. *c.* $60,000 in Investment A (year 1), $84,000 in Investment A (year 3), $117,600 in Investment D (year 5). Total accumulation in year 6 = $152,880.

3.20. *a.* Profit = $13,330.

Cargo Placement	Front	Center	Back
Cargo 1	0	5	10
Cargo 2	7.333	4.167	0
Cargo 3	0	0	0
Cargo 4	4.667	8.333	0

CHAPTER 4

4.2. *d.* 0 end tables, 40 coffee tables, 30 dining room tables. Profit = $10,600.

4.4. *e.* 19% participation in Project A, 0% participation in Project B, and 100% participation in Project C. Ending Balance = $59.5 million.

4.6. *d.* 4 FT (8AM–4PM), 4 FT (12PM–8PM), 4 FT (4PM–midnight), 2 PT (8AM–12PM), 0 PT (12PM–4PM), 4 PT (4PM–8PM), 2 PT (8PM–midnight). Total cost per day = $1,728.

CHAPTER 5

5.1. *e.* Allowable range for unit profit from producing toys: $2.50 to $5.00.
Allowable range for unit profit from producing subassemblies: $-$3.00 to $-$1.50.

5.4. *f.* (*Part a*)

Optimal solution does not change (within allowable increase of $10).

(*Part b*)

Optimal solution does change (outside of allowable decrease of $5).

(*Part c*)

By the 100% rule for simultaneous changes in the objective function, the optimal solution may or may not change.

$$C_{8AM}: \ \$160 \rightarrow \$165 \quad \% \text{ of allowable increase} = 100\left(\frac{165 - 160}{10}\right) = 50\%$$

$$C_{4PM}: \ \$180 \rightarrow \$170 \quad \% \text{ of allowable decrease} = 100\left(\frac{180 - 170}{5}\right) = \underline{200\%}$$

$$\text{Sum} = 250\%$$

5.8. *a.* Produce 2,000 toys and 1,000 sets of subassemblies. Profit = $3,500.
b. The shadow price for subassembly A is $0.50, which is the maximum premium that the company should be willing to pay.

5.12. *a.* The total expected number of exposures could be increased by 3,000 for each additional $1,000 added to the advertising budget.
b. This remains valid for increases of up to $250,000.
e. By the 100% rule for simultaneous changes in right-hand sides, the shadow prices are still valid. Using units of thousands of dollars,

$$C_A: \ \$4,000 \rightarrow \$4,100 \quad \% \text{ of allowable increase} = 100\left(\frac{4,100 - 4,000}{250}\right) = 40\%$$

$$C_P: \ \$1,000 \rightarrow \$1,100 \quad \% \text{ of allowable increase} = 100\left(\frac{1,100 - 1,000}{450}\right) = \underline{22\%}$$

$$\text{Sum} = 62\%$$

CHAPTER 6

6.1. *b.* 0 S1-D1, 10 S1-D2, 30 S1-D3, 30 S2-D1, 30 S2-D2, 0 S2-D3. Total cost = $580.
6.4. *c.* $2,187,000.
6.7. Maximum flow = 15.
6.12. *b.* Replace after year 1. Total cost = $29,000.

CHAPTER 7

7.2. *b.* Marketing and dishwashing by Eve, cooking and laundry by Steven. Total time = 18.4 hours.
7.6. Optimal path = OADT. Total distance = 10 miles.

CHAPTER 8

8.6. *c.* Invest $46,667 in Stock 1 and $3,333 in Stock 2 for $13,000 expected profit.
    Invest $33,333 in Stock 1 and $16,667 in Stock 2 for $15,000 expected profit.

8.10. *d.* Dorwyn should produce 1 window and 1 door.

CHAPTER 9

9.4. *a.* Speculative investment.
  d. Counter-cyclical investment.

9.6. *b.* A_3
  c. A_2

9.11. *a.* A_1
  b. $18.

9.15. *c.* EVPI = $3,000. The credit-rating organization should not be used.

9.20. *c.* Choose to build computers (expected payoff is $27 million).
  f. They should build when $p \leq 0.722$ and sell when $p > 0.722$.

9.21. *a.* EVPI = $7.5 million.
  c. P(Sell 10,000 | Predict Sell 10,000) = 0.667.
    P(Sell 100,000 | Predict Sell 100,000) = 0.667.

9.22. *a.* The optimal policy is to do no market research and build the computers.

9.25. *c.* $800,000.
  f, g. Leland University should hire William. If he predicts a winning season, then they should hold the campaign. If he predicts a losing season, then they should not hold the campaign.

9.29. *a.* Choose to introduce the new product (expected payoff is $12.5 million).
  b. $7.5 million.
  c. The optimal policy is not to test but to introduce the new product.
  g. Both charts indicate that the expected profit is sensitive to both parameters, but is somewhat more sensitive to changes in the profit if successful than to changes in the loss if unsuccessful.

9.33. *a.* Choose not to buy insurance (expected payoff is $249,840).
  b. Choose to buy insurance (expected utility is 499.82).

CHAPTER 10

10.1. *a.* 39.
  b. 26.
  c. 36.

10.3. MAD = 15.

10.8. 2,091.

10.12. When $\alpha = 0.1$, forecast = 2,072.

10.15. 552.

10.17. *b.* MAD = 5.18.
  c. MAD = 3.
  d. MAD = 3.93.

10.27. 62 percent.

10.33. *b.* $y = 410 + 17.6x$.
  d. 604.

CHAPTER 11

11.3. *a.* True.

    b. False.

    c. True.

11.8. *a.* $L = 2$

    b. $L_q = 0.375$

    c. $W = 30$ minutes, $W_q = 5.625$ minutes.

11.11. *a.* 96.9% of the time.

11.14. *b.* $L = 0.333$

    g. Two members.

11.17. L_q is unchanged and W_q is reduced by half.

11.21. *a.* $L = 3$

    d. TC (status quo) = $85/hour.

        TC (proposal) = $73/hour.

11.26. *a.* 0.211 hours.

    c. Approximately 3.43 minutes.

11.29. *c.* 0.4.

    d. 7.2 hours.

11.33. Jim should operate 4 cash registers. Expected cost per hour = $80.59.

CHAPTER 12

12.1. *b.* Let the numbers 0.0000 to 0.5999 correspond to strikes and the numbers 0.6000 to 0.9999 correspond to balls. The random observations for pitches are 0.3039 = strike, 0.7914 = ball, 0.8543 = ball, 0.6902 = ball, 0.3004 = strike, 0.0383 = strike.

12.5. *a.* Here is a sample replication.

Summary of Results:

Win? (1 = Yes, 0 = No)	0
Number of Tosses =	3

Simulated Tosses

Toss	Die 1	Die 2	Sum
1	4	2	6
2	3	2	5
3	6	1	7
4	5	2	7
5	4	4	8
6	1	4	5
7	2	6	8

Results

Win?	Lose?	Continue?
0	0	Yes
0	0	Yes
0	1	No
NA	NA	No
NA	NA	No
NA	NA	No
NA	NA	No

12.9. *a.* Let the numbers 0.0000 to 0.3999 correspond to a minor repair and 0.4000 to 0.9999 correspond to a major repair. The average repair time is then $(1.224 + 0.950 + 1.610)/3 = 1.26$ hours.

12.15. *b.* The average waiting time should be approximately 1 day.

    c. The average waiting time should be approximately 0.33 days.

CHAPTER 13

13.3. *a.* Triangular distribution (Min = 293.51, Likeliest = 501.00, Max = 599.72).

13.7. *a.* The mean project completion time should be approximately 33 months.

    c. Activities B and J have the greatest impact on the variability in the project completion time.

13.15. *a.* Mean profit should be around $107, with about a 96.5% chance of making at least $0.

Index

Page numbers followed by n indicate notes.

Student CD Content

- Quizzes
- Spreadsheets
- PowerPoint Slides
- Solver Table
- Solved Problem Solutions
- Chapter Supplements
- Software
  - Premium Solver
  - Interactive Management Science Modules
  - Decision ToolKit Academic:
    - TreePlan
    - Sensit
    - RiskSim
- Link to OMC Website

*Each text comes with a unique access code to Crystal Ball Software, found as an insert in this book. Visit their site http://textbook.crystalball.com and enter your Textbook Code to use the software.